PUBLIC PAPERS OF THE PRESIDENTS
OF THE
UNITED STATES

PUBLIC PAPERS OF THE PRESIDENTS
OF THE
UNITED STATES

Barack Obama

2010
(IN TWO BOOKS)

BOOK II—JULY 1 TO DECEMBER 31, 2010

UNITED STATES GOVERNMENT PRINTING OFFICE
WASHINGTON : 2013

Published by the
Office of the Federal Register
National Archives and Records Administration

For sale by the Superintendent of Documents, U.S. Government Printing Office
• Internet: bookstore.gpo.gov • Phone: (202) 512–1800 • Fax: (202) 512–1204
• Mail: Stop IDCC, Washington, DC 20401

Foreword

The second half of 2010 found us in the middle of a tough battle to accelerate private sector job creation. Many challenges lay ahead, but there were reasons for hope and signs of progress on the road to recovery.

One of the most important economic success stories of the year was the rebirth of the American auto industry. Once teetering on the brink of collapse, with about one million jobs hanging in the balance, the auto industry was healthier than it had been in years. Taxpayer money used to save some of America's proudest companies from liquidation had been paid back with interest. Workers who had been laid off were back on the job. And a symbol of American drive and ingenuity was once again leading the world.

The recovery of the auto industry represented a huge step forward for workers, suppliers, and entire towns that depended on it for survival. But we wanted to do more to give the middle class some much-needed help. That is why we extended a tax cut that put more money into the pockets of working families. And we extended unemployment insurance to avoid putting further strain on an already-fragile economy.

In 2010, we also took steps to address the underlying causes of the recession. I signed the Dodd-Frank Wall Street Reform and Consumer Protection Act, the most sweeping overhaul of the financial industry since the New Deal. This law will ensure that the actions of an irresponsible few will never again bring our economy to the brink of collapse. And we created the Bureau of Consumer Financial Protection to protect the American people from misleading and predatory practices while guaranteeing they have the clear and concise information they need to make the best financial decisions.

As we finally brought our combat mission in Iraq to an end and turned over responsibility to the Iraqi people, we continued to take the fight to the Taliban in Afghanistan and train Afghan forces to take responsibility for their own security. We paid tribute to our men and women in uniform, including Staff Sergeant Salvatore Giunta, who became the first living recipient of the Medal of Honor from a current conflict since Vietnam.

I was proud to sign legislation repealing the discriminatory policy known as "Don't Ask, Don't Tell." Particularly at a time of war, when Americans make incredible sacrifices in some of the most dangerous places on earth, no one should be forced to hide who they are in order to serve the country they love.

The last 6 months have not been easy. But I believe the progress we've made has brought us closer to the ideals that this country was founded on. And as I've traveled across the country and met Americans of every background and walk of life, I remain more hopeful than ever.

Preface

This book contains the papers and speeches of the President of the United States that were issued by the Office of the Press Secretary during the period July 1–December 31, 2010. The material has been compiled and published by the Office of the Federal Register, National Archives and Records Administration.

The material is presented in chronological order, and the dates shown in the headings are the dates of the documents or events. In instances when the release date differs from the date of the document itself, that fact is shown in the textnote. Every effort has been made to ensure accuracy: Remarks are checked against an audio recording, and signed documents are checked against the original. Textnotes and cross references have been provided by the editors for purposes of identification or clarity. Speeches were delivered in Washington, DC, unless otherwise indicated. The times noted are local times. All materials that are printed in full text in the book have been indexed in the subject and name indexes and listed in the document categories list.

The Public Papers of the Presidents series was begun in 1957 in response to a recommendation of the National Historical Publications Commission. An extensive compilation of messages and papers of the Presidents covering the period 1789 to 1897 was assembled by James D. Richardson and published under congressional authority between 1896 and 1899. Since then, various private compilations have been issued, but there was no uniform publication comparable to the Congressional Record or the United States Supreme Court Reports. Many Presidential papers could be found only in the form of mimeographed White House releases or as reported in the press. The Commission therefore recommended the establishment of an official series in which Presidential writings, addresses, and remarks of a public nature could be made available.

The Commission's recommendation was incorporated in regulations of the Administrative Committee of the Federal Register, issued under section 6 of the Federal Register Act (44 U.S.C. 1506), which may be found in title 1, part 10, of the Code of Federal Regulations.

A companion publication to the Public Papers series, the Weekly Compilation of Presidential Documents, was begun in 1965 to provide a broader range of Presidential materials on a more timely basis to meet the needs of the contemporary reader. Beginning with the administration of Jimmy Carter, the Public Papers series expanded its coverage to include additional material as printed in the Weekly Compilation. On January 20, 2009, the printed Weekly Compilation of Presidential Documents was superseded by the online Daily Compilation of Presidential Documents. The Daily Compilation provides a listing of the President's daily schedule and meetings, when announced, and other items of general interest issued by the Office of the Press Secretary. In 2012, the Government Printing Office and the Office of the Federal Register released a mobile web application (http://m.gpo.gov/dcpd) that catalogues the daily public activities of the President of the United States and enhances features of the online Daily Compilation with user-friendly search capability, allowing users to access Presidential content by date, category, subject, or location.

Also included in the printed edition are lists of the President's nominations submitted to the Senate, materials released by the Office of the Press Secretary that are not printed in full text in the book, and proclamations, Executive orders, and other Presidential documents released by the Office of the Press Secretary and published in the Federal Register. This information appears in the appendixes at the end of the book.

Volumes covering the administrations of Presidents Herbert Hoover, Harry S. Truman, Dwight D. Eisenhower, John F. Kennedy, Lyndon B. Johnson, Richard Nixon, Gerald R. Ford, Jimmy Carter, Ronald Reagan, George H.W. Bush, William J. Clinton, and George W. Bush are also included in the Public Papers series.

The Public Papers of the Presidents publication program is under the direction of Michael L. White, Managing Editor, Office of the Federal Register. The series is produced by the Presidential and

Legislative Publications Unit. The Chief Editor of this book was Laurice A. Clark, assisted by Lead Editors Joshua H. Liberatore, Amelia E. Otovo, and Joseph K. Vetter and unit editors Lois M. Davis, Michael J. Forcina, Joseph G. Frankovic, Martin V. Franks, Heather N. McDaniel, Stacey A. Mulligan, and Matthew R. Regan.

The frontispiece and photographs used in the portfolio were supplied by the White House Photo Office. The typography and design of the book were developed by the Government Printing Office under the direction of Davita E. Vance-Cooks, Public Printer.

Charles A. Barth
Director of the Federal Register

David S. Ferriero
Archivist of the United States

Contents

Cabinet

Vice President	Joseph R. Biden, Jr.
Secretary of State	Hillary Rodham Clinton
Secretary of the Treasury	Timothy F. Geithner
Secretary of Defense	Robert M. Gates
Attorney General	Eric H. Holder, Jr.
Secretary of the Interior	Kenneth L. Salazar
Secretary of Agriculture	Thomas J. Vilsack
Secretary of Commerce	Gary F. Locke
Secretary of Labor	Hilda L. Solis
Secretary of Health and Human Services	Kathleen Sebelius
Secretary of Housing and Urban Development	Shaun L.S. Donovan
Secretary of Transportation	Raymond H. LaHood
Secretary of Energy	Steven Chu
Secretary of Education	Arne Duncan
Secretary of Veterans Affairs	Eric K. Shinseki
Secretary of Homeland Security	Janet A. Napolitano
Chief of Staff	Rahm I. Emanuel (resigned October 1) Peter M. Rouse (appointed October 1)
Administrator of the Environmental Protection Agency	Lisa P. Jackson
United States Trade Representative	Ronald Kirk

Director of the Office of Management and Budget	Peter R. Orszag (resigned July 30) Jacob J. "Jack" Lew (confirmed November 18)
Chair of the Council of Economic Advisers	Christina D. Romer (resigned September 7) Austan D. Goolsbee (designated September 10)
United States Permanent Representative to the United Nations	Susan E. Rice

Administration of Barack Obama

2010

Remarks at American University
July 1, 2010

Thank you. Everyone, please have a seat. Thank you very much. Let me thank Pastor Hybels from near my hometown in Chicago, who took time off his vacation to be here today. And we are blessed to have him.

I want to thank President Neil Kerwin and our hosts here at American University; acknowledge my outstanding Secretary of Labor, Hilda Solis, and members of my administration; all the Members of Congress—[*applause*]. Hilda deserves applause. To all the Members of Congress, the elected officials, faith and law enforcement, labor, business leaders, and immigration advocates who are here today, thank you for your presence.

I want to thank American University for welcoming me to the campus once again. Some may recall that the last time I was here I was joined by a dear friend and a giant of American politics, Senator Edward Kennedy. Teddy's not here right now, but his legacy of civil rights and health care and worker protections is still with us.

I was a candidate for President that day, and some may recall I argued that our country had reached a tipping point, that after years in which we had deferred our most pressing problems and too often yielded to the politics of the moment, we now faced a choice: We could squarely confront our challenges with honesty and determination, or we could consign ourselves and our children to a future less prosperous and less secure.

I believed that then, and I believe it now. And that's why, even as we've tackled the most severe economic crisis since the Great Depression, even as we've wound down the war in Iraq and refocused our efforts in Afghanistan, my administration has refused to ignore some of the fundamental challenges facing this generation.

We launched the most aggressive education reforms in decades so that our children can gain the knowledge and skills they need to compete in a 21st-century global economy.

We have finally delivered on the promise of health reform, reform that will bring greater security to every American and that will rein in the skyrocketing costs that threaten families, businesses, and the prosperity of our Nation.

We're on the verge of reforming an outdated and ineffective set of rules governing Wall Street to give greater power to consumers and prevent the reckless financial speculation that led to this severe recession.

And we're accelerating the transition to a clean energy economy by significantly raising the fuel efficiency standards of cars and trucks and by doubling our use of renewable energies like wind and solar power, steps that have the potential to create whole new industries and hundreds of thousands of new jobs in America.

So despite the forces of the status quo, despite the polarization and the frequent pettiness of our politics, we are confronting the great challenges of our times. And while this work isn't easy and the changes we seek won't always happen overnight, what we've made clear is that this administration will not just kick the can down the road.

Immigration reform is no exception. In recent days, the issue of immigration has become once more a sense—a source of fresh contention in our country, with the passage of a controversial law in Arizona and the heated reactions we've seen across America. Some have rallied behind this new policy. Others have protested and launched boycotts of the State. And everywhere, people have expressed frustration with a system that seems fundamentally broken.

Of course, the tensions around immigration are not new. On the one hand, we've always defined ourselves as a nation of immigrants, a nation that welcomes those willing to embrace America's precepts. Indeed, it is this constant flow of immigrants that helped to make America what it is. The scientific breakthroughs of Albert Einstein, the inventions of Nikola Tesla, the great ventures of Andrew Carnegie's U.S. Steel and Sergey Brin's Google Inc., all this was possible because of immigrants.

And then there are the countless names and the quiet acts that never made the history books but were no less consequential in building this country, the generations who braved hardship and great risk to reach our shores in search of a better life for themselves and their families; the millions of people, ancestors to most of us, who believed that there was a place where they could be, at long last, free to work and worship and live their lives in peace.

So this steady stream of hard-working and talented people has made America the engine of the global economy and a beacon of hope around the world. And it's allowed us to adapt and thrive in the face of technological and societal change. To this day, America reaps incredible economic rewards because we remain a magnet for the best and brightest from across the globe. Folks travel here in the hopes of being a part of a culture of entrepreneurship and ingenuity, and by doing so, they strengthen and enrich that culture. Immigration also means we have a younger workforce and a faster growing economy than many of our competitors. And in an increasingly interconnected world, the diversity of our country is a powerful advantage in global competition.

Just a few weeks ago, we had an event of small-business owners at the White House. And one business owner was a woman named Prachee Devadas who came to this country, became a citizen, and opened up a successful technology services company. When she started, she had just one employee. Today, she employs more than a hundred people.

This past April, we held a naturalization ceremony at the White House for members of our Armed Forces. Even though they were not yet citizens, they had enlisted. One of them was a woman named Perla Ramos, born and raised in Mexico, came to the United States shortly after 9/11, and she eventually joined the Navy. And she said, "I take pride in our flag and the history that forged this great nation and the history we write day by day."

These women, and men and women across this country like them, remind us that immigrants have always helped to build and defend this country and that being an American is not a matter of blood or birth, it's a matter of faith. It's a matter of fidelity to the shared values that we all hold so dear. That's what makes us unique. That's what makes us strong. Anybody can help us write the next great chapter in our history.

Now, we can't forget that this process of immigration and eventual inclusion has often been painful. Each new wave of immigrants has generated fear and resentments towards newcomers, particularly in times of economic upheaval. Our founding was rooted in the notion that America was unique as a place of refuge and freedom for, in Thomas Jefferson's words, "oppressed humanity." But the ink on our Constitution was barely dry when, amidst conflict, Congress passed the Alien and Sedition Acts, which placed harsh restrictions of those suspected of having foreign allegiances. A century ago, immigrants from Ireland, Italy, Poland, other European countries were routinely subjected to rank discrimination and ugly stereotypes. Chinese immigrants were held in detention and deported from Angel Island in the San Francisco Bay. They didn't even get to come in.

So the politics of who is and who is not allowed to enter this country and on what terms has always been contentious. And that remains true today. And it's made worse by a failure of those of us in Washington to fix a broken immigration system.

To begin with, our borders have been porous for decades. Obviously, the problem is greatest along our southern border, but it's not restricted to that part of the country. In fact, because we don't do a very good job of tracking who comes in and out of the country as visitors, large numbers avoid immigration laws simply by overstaying their visas.

The result is an estimated 11 million undocumented immigrants in the United States. The overwhelming majority of these men and women are simply seeking a better life for themselves and their children. Many settle in low-wage sectors of the economy; they work hard, they save, they stay out of trouble. But because they live in the shadows, they're vulnerable to unscrupulous businesses who pay them less than the minimum wage or violate worker safety rules, thereby putting companies who follow those rules and Americans who rightly demand the minimum wage or overtime at an unfair advantage [disadvantage].° Crimes go unreported as victims and witnesses fear coming forward. And this makes it harder for the police to catch violent criminals and keep neighborhoods safe. And billions in tax revenue are lost each year because many undocumented workers are paid under the table.

More fundamentally, the presence of so many illegal immigrants makes a mockery of all those who are going through the process of immigrating legally. Indeed, after years of patchwork fixes and ill-conceived revisions, the legal immigration system is as broken as the borders. Backlogs and bureaucracy means the process can take years. While an applicant waits for approval, he or she is often forbidden from visiting the United States, which means even husbands and wives may be forced to spend many years apart. High fees and the need for lawyers may exclude worthy applicants. And while we provide students from around the world visas to get engineering and computer science degrees at our top universities, our laws discourage them from using those skills to start a business or power a new industry right here in the United States. Instead of training entrepreneurs to create jobs on our shores, we train our competition.

In sum, the system is broken. And everybody knows it. Unfortunately, reform has been held hostage to political posturing and special-interest wrangling and to the pervasive sentiment in Washington that tackling such a thorny and emotional issue is inherently bad politics.

Now, just a few years ago, when I was a Senator, we forged a bipartisan coalition in favor of comprehensive reform. Under the leadership of Senator Kennedy, who had been a longtime champion of immigration reform, and Senator John McCain, we worked across the aisle to help pass a bipartisan bill through the Senate. But that effort eventually came apart. And now, under the pressures of partisanship and election-year politics, many of the 11 Republican Senators who voted for reform in the past have now backed away from their previous support.

Into this breach, States like Arizona have decided to take matters into their own hands. Now, given the levels of frustration across the country, this is understandable. But it is also ill conceived. And it's not just that the law Arizona passed is divisive—although it has fanned the flames of an already contentious debate—laws like Arizona's put huge pressures on local law enforcement to enforce rules that ultimately are unenforceable. It puts pressure on already hard-strapped State and local budgets. It makes it difficult for people here illegally to report crimes, driving a wedge between communities and law enforcement, making our streets more dangerous and the jobs of our police officers more difficult. And you don't have to take my word for this. You can speak to the police chiefs and others from law enforcement here today who will tell you the same thing.

These laws also have the potential of violating the rights of innocent American citizens and legal residents, making them subject to possible stops or questioning because of what they look like or how they sound. And as other States and localities go their own ways, we face the prospect that different rules for immigration will apply in different parts of the country, a patchwork of local immigration rules where we all know one, clear national standard is needed.

Our task then is to make our national laws actually work, to shape a system that reflects our values as a nation of laws and a nation of immigrants. And that means being honest about the problem and getting past the false debates that divide the country rather than bring it together.

° White House correction.

For example, there are those in the immigrants' rights community who have argued passionately that we should simply provide those who are [here]° illegally with legal status or at least ignore the laws on the books and put an end to deportation until we have better laws. And often this argument is framed in moral terms: Why should we punish people who are just trying to earn a living?

I recognize the sense of compassion that drives this argument, but I believe such an indiscriminate approach would be both unwise and unfair. It would suggest to those thinking about coming here illegally that there will be no repercussions for such a decision. And this could lead to a surge in more illegal immigration. And it would also ignore the millions of people around the world who are waiting in line to come here legally. Ultimately, our Nation, like all nations, has the right and obligation to control its borders and set laws for residency and citizenship. And no matter how decent they are, no matter their reasons, the 11 million who broke these laws should be held accountable.

Now, if the majority of Americans are skeptical of a blanket amnesty, they are also skeptical that it is possible to round up and deport 11 million people. They know it's not possible. Such an effort would be logistically impossible and wildly expensive. Moreover, it would tear at the very fabric of this Nation, because immigrants who are here illegally are now intricately woven into that fabric. Many have children who are American citizens. Some are children themselves, brought here by their parents at a very young age, growing up as American kids, only to discover their illegal status when they apply for college or a job. Migrant workers—mostly here illegally—have been the labor force of our farmers and agricultural producers for generations. So even if it was possible, a program of mass deportations would disrupt our economy and communities in ways that most Americans would find intolerable.

Now, once we get past the two poles of this debate, it becomes possible to shape a practical, commonsense approach that reflects our heritage and our values. Such an approach demands

accountability from everybody: from government, from businesses, and from individuals.

Government has a threshold responsibility to secure our borders. That's why I directed my Secretary of Homeland Security, Janet Napolitano—a former border Governor—to improve our enforcement policy without having to wait for a new law.

Today, we have more boots on the ground near the Southwest border than at any time in our history. Let me repeat that: We have more boots on the ground on the Southwest border than at any time in our history. We doubled the personnel assigned to Border Enforcement Security Task Forces. We tripled the number of intelligence analysts along the border. For the first time, we've begun screening 100 percent of southbound rail shipments. And as a result, we're seizing more illegal guns, cash, and drugs than in years past. Contrary to some of the reports that you see, crime along the border is down. And statistics collected by Customs and Border Protection reflect a significant reduction in the number of people trying to cross the border illegally.

So the bottom line is this: The southern border is more secure today than at any time in the past 20 years. That doesn't mean we don't have more work to do. We have to do that work, but it's important that we acknowledge the facts. Now, even as we are committed to doing what's necessary to secure our borders, even without passage of the new law, there are those who argue that we should not move forward with any other elements of reform until we have fully sealed our borders. But our borders are just too vast for us to be able to solve the problem only with fences and border patrols. It won't work. Our borders will not be secure as long as our limited resources are devoted to not only stopping gangs and potential terrorists, but also the hundreds of thousands who attempt to cross each year simply to find work.

That's why businesses must be held accountable if they break the law by deliberately hiring and exploiting undocumented workers. We've already begun to step up enforcement against the worst workplace offenders. And we're implementing and improving a system to give em-

---

° White House correction.

ployers a reliable way to verify that their employees are here legally. But we need to do more. We cannot continue just to look the other way as a significant portion of our economy operates outside the law. It breeds abuse and bad practices. It punishes employers who act responsibly and undercuts American workers. And ultimately, if the demand for undocumented workers falls, the incentive for people to come here illegally will decline as well.

Finally, we have to demand responsibility from people living here illegally. They must be required to admit that they broke the law. They should be required to register, pay their taxes, pay a fine, and learn English. They must get right with the law before they can get in line and earn their citizenship, not just because it is fair, not just because it will make clear to those who might wish to come to America they must do so inside the bounds of the law, but because this is how we demonstrate that being an—what being an American means. Being a citizen of this country comes not only with rights, but also with certain fundamental responsibilities. We can create a pathway for legal status that is fair, reflective of our values, and works.

Now, stopping illegal immigration must go hand in hand with reforming our creaky system of legal immigration. We've begun to do that by eliminating a backlog in background checks that at one point stretched back almost a year. That's just for the background check. People can now track the status of their immigration applications by e-mail or text message. We've improved accountability and safety in the detention system. And we've stemmed the increases in naturalization fees. But here too we need to do more. We should make it easier for the best and the brightest to come to start businesses and develop products and create jobs.

Our laws should respect families following the rules, instead of splitting them apart. We need to provide farms a legal way to hire the workers they rely on and a path for those workers to earn legal status. And we should stop punishing innocent young people for the actions of their parents by denying them the chance to stay here and earn an education and contribute their talents to build the country

where they've grown up. The "DREAM Act" would do this, and that's why I supported this bill as a State legislator and as a U.S. Senator and why I continue to support it as President.

So these are the essential elements of comprehensive immigration reform. The question now is whether we will have the courage and the political will to pass a bill through Congress, to finally get it done. Last summer, I held a meeting with leaders of both parties, including many of the Republicans who had supported reform in the past and some who hadn't. I was pleased to see a bipartisan framework proposed in the Senate by Senators Lindsey Graham and Chuck Schumer, with whom I met to discuss this issue. I've spoken with the Congressional Hispanic Caucus to plot the way forward and meet—and I met with them again earlier this week.

And I've spoken with representatives from a growing coalition of labor unions and business groups, immigrant advocates and community organizations, law enforcement, local government, all who recognize the importance of immigration reform. And I've met with leaders from America's religious communities, like Pastor Hybels, people of different faiths and beliefs, some liberal, some conservative, who nonetheless share a sense of urgency, who understand that fixing our broken immigration system is not only a political issue, not just an economic issue, but a moral imperative as well.

So we've made progress. I'm ready to move forward, the majority of Democrats are ready to move forward, and I believe the majority of Americans are ready to move forward. But the fact is, without bipartisan support, as we had just a few years ago, we cannot solve this problem. Reform that brings accountability to our immigration system cannot pass without Republican votes. That is the political and mathematical reality. The only way to reduce the risk that this effort will again falter because of politics is if members of both parties are willing to take responsibility for solving this problem once and for all.

And yes, this is an emotional question and one that lends itself to demagoguery. Time and again, this issue has been used to divide and inflame and to demonize people. And so the understandable, the natural impulse among those who run for office is to turn away and defer this question for another day or another year or another administration. Despite the courageous leadership in the past shown by many Democrats and some Republicans—including, by the way, my predecessor, President Bush—this has been the custom. That is why a broken and dangerous system that offends our most basic American values is still in place.

But I believe we can put politics aside and finally have an immigration system that's accountable. I believe we can appeal not to people's fears, but to their hopes, to their highest ideals, because that's who we are as Americans. It's been inscribed on our Nation's seal since we declared our independence: *E pluribus unum.* Out of many, one. That is what has drawn the persecuted and impoverished to our shores. That's what led the innovators and risk takers from around the world to take a chance here in the land of opportunity. That's what has led people to endure untold hardships to reach this place called America.

One of the largest waves of immigration in our history took place little more than a century ago. At the time, Jewish people were being driven out of Eastern Europe, often escaping to the sounds of gunfire and the light from their villages burning to the ground. The journey could take months, as families crossed rivers in the dead of night, traveled miles by foot, endured a rough and dangerous passage over the North Atlantic. And once here, many made their homes in a teeming and bustling Lower Manhattan.

And it was at this time that a young woman named Emma Lazarus, whose own family fled persecution from Europe generations earlier, took up the cause of these new immigrants. Although she was a poet, she spent much of her time advocating for better health care and housing for the newcomers. And inspired by what she saw and heard, she wrote down her thoughts and donated a piece of work to help pay for the construction of a new statue—the Statue of Liberty—which actually was funded in part by small donations from people across America.

Years before the statue was built, years before it would be seen by throngs of immigrants craning their necks skyward at the end of a long and brutal voyage, years before it would come to symbolize everything that we cherish, she imagined what it could mean. She imagined the sight of a giant statue at the entry point of a great nation, but unlike the great monuments of the past, this would not signal an empire. Instead, it would signal one's arrival to a place of opportunity and refuge and freedom.

"Here at our sea-washed, sunset gates shall stand," she wrote,

A mighty woman with a torch . . .
From her beacon-hand
Glows world-wide welcome . . .
"Keep, ancient lands, your storied pomp!" . . .
"Give me your tired, and your poor,
Your huddled masses yearning to be free . . .
Send these, the homeless, tempest-tossed to me,
I lift my lamp beside the golden door!"

Let us remember these words. For it falls on each generation to ensure that that lamp, that beacon continues to shine as a source of hope around the world and a source of our prosperity here at home.

Thank you. God bless you, and may God bless the United States of America. Thank you.

NOTE: The President spoke at 11:12 a.m. at the School of International Service. In his remarks, he referred to Bill Hybels, founding and senior pastor, Willow Creek Community Church in South Barrington, IL; Cornelius M. Kerwin, president, American University; Sergey Brin, cofounder and president, Google Inc.; Prachee J. Devadas, founder, chief executive officer, and president, Synergy Enterprises, Inc.; and former President George W. Bush. The Office of the Press Secretary also released a Spanish language transcript of these remarks.

Remarks Honoring the Women's Professional Soccer Champion Sky Blue FC
July 1, 2010

The President. Well, hello. Welcome to the White House. Congratulations to Sky Blue on winning your first Women's Professional Soccer championship. Congratulations. Give them a big round of applause.

I want to recognize the mayor of Piscataway, Brian Wahler, who's with us here today. Where's Brian? Hey, he's got the video camera going on.

I want to thank the six players who took part in the WPS All-Star Game yesterday and rearranged their travel plans so they could be in Washington here today. We're glad you could make it. Thank you.

This is a pretty exciting time for soccer in America. We've all been glued to our TVs over the last couple of weeks as the men's team made their run at the World Cup. I know my staff, by the way, was watching when the U.S. beat Algeria, because I could hear them whooping it up as I was having important meetings in the Oval Office. [*Laughter*] Malia's team did very well this summer, which I think is also important to know. [*Laughter*] And today it's an honor to welcome the first-ever champions of the Women's Professional Soccer league to the White House.

Now, I know there were some bumps in the road for this team last season. They dealt with multiple coaching changes. They squeaked into the playoffs at the last minute. And then they had to play three games on the road in 8 days to win it all.

But this team came together when it counted. No matter what obstacles they faced, no matter what disappointments and distractions they had to deal with, they had each other's backs, and they stayed focused on their ultimate goal. That's what teams do. They work hard. This team loves being an underdog, and in the end, that made all the difference.

I know she's probably sick of hearing that story, but I have to single out your captain, Christie Rampone. Where's Christie? This is very impressive. This impresses me. After Sky Blue won the championship last season, Christie's teammates tried to get her to take a celebratory drink with them in the locker room and she had to turn it down because she was almost 3 months pregnant. That's really impressive. [*Laughter*]

Christie didn't want it to be a distraction, and so she had been waiting until the season was over to tell her teammates. After all, she said, "We can't have the trophy taken away for having 11½ women on the field." [*Laughter*] Is it going to be a girl? Do we know?

Sky Blue FC Team Captain Christie Rampone. Yes.

The President. Okay, well, there you go.

Today, Christie is the mother of two beautiful daughters, including—so Reece already came, she showed up.

Ms. Rampone. Yes. She's here.

The President. Where is she? Where is she?

Ms. Rampone. She's right there.

The President. Hey, oh, she's precious. [*Laughter*] Yes. She looks a little hungry, though. [*Laughter*] So Reece is going to be 4 months old next week. And in the meantime, Christie is already back in the lineup helping her teammates chase another title.

Now, even though Christie's story is unique, her dedication is not. The women on this team aren't playing for fame or fortune. They are spending countless hours in the gym and on the practice field because they recognize a rare opportunity to do the thing that they love. They believe in using their God-given talent to inspire the next generation to reach a little higher and work a little harder.

And that sense of responsibility also extends off the pitch. I'm pleased that the WPS is creating a program called "Get Active!" that will sponsor three-on-three soccer tournaments and help young people learn about the importance of living healthy, active lives. Obviously, this is an issue that the First Lady, Michelle, is talking about all across the country, and so I want to thank this league for joining the cause.

Today, nearly 14 million children in America play soccer; 40 percent of them are girls. And as the father of one of them, I want to say a special thanks to this group, and to all the women who came before them, for serving as such outstanding role models. Together, you've changed the way our young women look at themselves, you've expanded the realm of what they believe is possible, and for that, we all owe you a great debt of gratitude.

So congratulations on your championship, and best of luck this season.

All right, I think they're going to pull this out and then we're going to take some pictures, okay? Oh, but I've got my jersey—yes, okay. [*Laughter*] I've got to have my jersey.

Ms. Rampone. First, before we take a photo, we would like to present this to you on behalf of Sky Blue FC professional soccer.

The President. And it is sky blue, by the way. [*Laughter*] That's very nice.

Ms. Rampone. A perfect color for you. It matches your tie. Looking good. [*Laughter*]

The President. I might have to get in the weight room a little bit before I wear this. [*Laughter*] Thank you very—come on, and I'll hold it while we're taking our picture.

NOTE: The President spoke at 5:01 p.m. in the East Room at the White House.

Remarks on Signing the Comprehensive Iran Sanctions, Accountability, and Divestment Act of 2010
July 1, 2010

Thank you. Please have a seat, everybody. Good evening, everybody. As President, one of my highest national security priorities is to prevent the spread of nuclear weapons. That's why my administration has aggressively pursued a comprehensive agenda of nonproliferation and nuclear security.

Leading by example, we agreed with Russia to reduce our nuclear arsenals through the new START Treaty, and I've urged the Senate to move forward with ratification this year. And with allies and partners, we've strengthened the global nonproliferation regime, including the cornerstone of our efforts, the Nuclear Non-Proliferation Treaty.

Now, in the entire world, there is only one signatory to the NPT—only one—that has been unable to convince the International Atomic Energy Agency that its nuclear program is for peaceful purposes—one nation—and that nation is Iran. For years, the Iranian Government has violated its commitments, defied United Nations Security Council resolutions, and forged ahead with its nuclear program, all while supporting terrorist groups and suppressing the aspirations of the Iranian people.

Since taking office, I've made it clear that the United States was prepared to begin a new chapter of engagement with the Islamic Republic of Iran. We offered the Iranian Government a clear choice: It could fulfill its international obligations and realize greater security, deeper economic and political integration with the world, and a better future for all Iranians, or it could continue to flout its responsibilities and face even more pressure and isolation.

To date, Iran has chosen the path of defiance. That's why we have steadily built a broader and deeper coalition of nations to pressure the Iranian Government. Last month, we joined with our partners at the U.N. Security Council to pass the toughest and most comprehensive multilateral sanctions that the Iranian Government has ever faced. And I want to specifically single out our tireless—and I mean tireless—Ambassador to the United Nations, Susan Rice, for all—for her terrific accomplishment.

As I said last month, we are going to make sure that these sanctions are vigorously enforced. At the same time, we'll work with our allies and friends to refine and enforce our own sanctions on Iran. And that's exactly what we've been doing. Here in the United States, thanks to the efforts of my Treasury Secretary, Tim Geithner, and Under Secretary Stuart Levey—[*applause*]—they have been terrific on this effort; Stuart's been just outstanding—we have imposed sanctions against more institutions, more individuals involved with Iran's nuclear and missile programs.

Other nations are now acting alongside us, nations like Australia, which announced new sanctions, including those against a major Iranian bank and Iran's shipping company. The European Union is moving ahead with additional strong measures against Iran's financial, banking, insurance, transportation, and energy sectors, as well as Iran's Revolutionary Guard. Other countries, like Canada, have indicated they will also be taking action. In other words, we are ratcheting up the pressure on the Iranian Government for its failure to meet its obligations.

And today we're taking another step, a step that demonstrates the broad and bipartisan support for holding Iran accountable. I'm pleased to sign into law the toughest sanctions against Iran ever passed by the United States Congress: the Comprehensive Iran Sanctions, Accountability, and Divestment Act.

I want to thank all the Members of Congress who worked on behalf of this legislation, including another tireless person, but who never seems to break a sweat, the Speaker of the House, Nancy Pelosi. I want to thank Representatives Steny Hoyer and Eric Cantor for doing outstanding work. Although they weren't able to join us, I want to acknowledge Senators Harry Reid, Jon Kyl, and Richard Shelby. And I want to thank those who led the effort to forge a final bill that received overwhelming bipartisan support: Senator Chris Dodd and Representative Howard Berman. Thank you for your good work.

Consistent with the Security Council mandate, this legislation strengthens existing sanctions, authorizes new ones, and supports our multilateral diplomatic strategy to address Iran's nuclear program. It makes it harder for the Iranian Government to purchase refined petroleum and the goods, services, and materials to modernize Iran's oil and natural gas sector. It makes it harder for the Revolutionary Guards and banks that support Iran's nuclear programs and terrorism to engage in international finance. It says to companies seeking procurement contracts with the United States Government, if you want to do business with us, you first have to certify that you're not doing prohibited business with Iran.

In short, with these sanctions, along with others, we are striking at the heart of the Iranian Government's ability to fund and develop its nuclear program. We're showing the Iranian Government that its actions have consequences. And if it persists, the pressure will continue to mount and its isolation will continue to deepen. There should be no doubt, the United States and the international community are determined to prevent Iran from acquiring nuclear weapons.

Now, finally, even as we increase pressure on the Iranian Government, we're sending an unmistakable message that the United States stands with the Iranian people as they seek to exercise their universal rights. This legislation imposes sanctions on individuals who commit serious human rights abuses. And it exempts from our trade embargo technologies that allow the Iranian people to access information and communicate freely. In Iran and around the world, the United States of America will continue to stand with those who seek justice and progress and the human rights and dignity of all people.

So again, this is not a day that we sought, but it is an outcome that was chosen by the Iranian Government when it repeatedly failed to meet its responsibilities. And the Government of Iran still has a choice. The door to diplomacy remains open. Iran can prove that its intentions are peaceful. It can meet its obligations under the NPT and achieve the security and prosperity worthy of a great nation.

It can have confidence in the Iranian people and allow their rights to flourish, for Iranians are heirs to a remarkable history. They are renowned for their talents and their contributions to humanity. Here in the United States, Iranian Americans have thrived. And within Iran, there's a great potential for the Iranian people to forge greater prosperity through deeper integration with the international community, including with the United States.

That's the future we do seek, one where Iran's leaders do not hold their own people back by failing to live up to Iran's international obligations and where Iran can reclaim its place in the community of nations and find greater peace and prosperity.

That is the Iranian Government's choice. And it remains our hope that they choose this path, even as we are clear-eyed and vigilant about the difficult challenges ahead.

So with that, I will sign this legislation into law.

NOTE: The President spoke at 6:30 p.m. in the East Room at the White House. H.R. 2194, approved July 1, was assigned Public Law No. 111–195.

Statement on Signing the Comprehensive Iran Sanctions, Accountability, and Divestment Act of 2010
July 1, 2010

Today, I have signed into law H.R. 2194, the "Comprehensive Iran Sanctions, Accountability, and Divestment Act of 2010". This Act builds upon the recently passed United Nations Security Council Resolution and its strong foundation for new multilateral sanctions. It is designed to pressure Iran by requiring sanctions on those persons investing in Iran's development of petroleum resources and exporting to Iran refined petroleum and items needed to strengthen Iran's refined petroleum production capability. Further, it requires sanctions on financial institutions facilitating certain activities involving Iran, the Islamic Revolutionary Guard Corps, or other sanctioned persons. The Act also puts in place new authorities to demonstrate the strong and sustained commitment of the United States to advancing the universal rights of all Iranians, and to sanction those who have abused their rights.

The Act provides a powerful tool against Iran's development of nuclear weapons and support of terrorism, while at the same time preserving flexibility to time and calibrate sanctions. In particular, it provides new authority for addressing the situation of those countries that are closely cooperating in multilateral efforts to constrain Iran. The Act appropriately provides this special authority to waive the application of petroleum-related sanctions provisions to a person from such a closely cooperating country, out of recognition for the key role such a country plays in ongoing multilateral efforts to constrain Iran. The Act permits the President to exercise this authority flexibly, as warranted, and when vital to the national security interests of the United States.

BARACK OBAMA

The White House,
July 1, 2010.

NOTE: H.R. 2194, approved July 1, was assigned Public Law No. 111–195.

Remarks at Joint Base Andrews, Maryland
July 2, 2010

Good morning, everybody. Before I depart, I'd like to say a quick word about the state of our economy.

This morning we received the June employment report. It reflected the planned phaseout of 225,000 temporary census jobs. But it also showed the sixth straight month of job growth in the private sector. All told, our economy has created nearly 600,000 private sector jobs this year. That's a stark turnaround from the first 6 months of last year, when we lost 3.7 million jobs at the height of the recession.

Now, make no mistake: We are headed in the right direction. But as I was reminded on a trip to Racine, Wisconsin, earlier this week, we're not headed there fast enough for a lot of Americans. We're not headed there fast enough for me either. The recession dug us a hole of about

8 million jobs deep, and we continue to fight headwinds from volatile global markets. So we still have a great deal of work to do to repair the economy and get the American people back to work.

That's why we're continuing a relentless effort across multiple fronts to keep this recovery moving. And today I'd like to make a quick announcement regarding new infrastructure investments under the Recovery Act, investments that will create private sector jobs and make America more competitive.

Secretary Locke and Secretary Vilsack have joined me here today to announce that the Departments of Commerce and Agriculture will invest in 66 new projects across America that will finally bring reliable broadband Internet service to communities that currently have little or no access.

In the short term, we expect these projects to create about 5,000 construction and installation jobs around the country. And once we emerge from the immediate crisis, the long-term economic gains to communities that have been left behind in the digital age will be immeasurable.

All told, these investments will benefit tens of millions of Americans, more than 685,000 businesses, 900 health care facilities, and 2,400 schools around the—across the country. And studies have shown that when communities adopt broadband access, it can lead to hundreds of thousands of new jobs. Broadband can remove geographic barriers between patients and their doctors. It can connect our kids to the dig-

ital skills and 21st-century education required for the jobs of the future. And it can prepare America to run on clean energy by helping us upgrade to a smarter, stronger, more secure electrical grid.

So we're investing in our people and we're investing in their future. We're competing aggressively to make sure that jobs and industries and the markets of tomorrow take root right here in the United States. We're moving forward. And to every American who is looking for work, I promise you we are going to keep on doing everything that we can. I will do everything in my power to help our economy create jobs and opportunity for all people.

Sunday is the Fourth of July. And if that date reminds us of anything, it's that America has never backed down from a challenge. We've faced our share of tough times before. But in such moments, we don't flinch. We dig deeper, we innovate, we compete, and we win. That's in our DNA, and it's going to be what brings us through these tough times towards a brighter day.

So I want to say happy Fourth of July to everybody. I want our troops overseas to know that we are thinking of your bravery and grateful for your service.

Thank you very much, everybody.

NOTE: The President spoke at 9:38 a.m. The Office of the Press Secretary also released a Spanish language transcript of these remarks.

Eulogy at the Funeral Service for Senator Robert C. Byrd in Charleston, West Virginia
July 2, 2010

Thank you. To Mona and Marjorie and to Senator Byrd's entire family, including those adorable great-granddaughters that I had a chance to meet, Michelle and I offer you our deepest sympathies.

To Senator Byrd's friends, including the Speaker of the House, the majority leader, the Republican leader, President Clinton, Vice President Biden, Vicki Kennedy, Nick Rahall,

and all the previous speakers; Senator Rockefeller for the outstanding work that you've done for the State of West Virginia; to his larger family, the people of West Virginia: I want you all to know that all America shares your loss. May we all find comfort in a verse of Scripture that reminds me of our dear friend: "The time of my departure has come. I have fought the good fight, I have finished the race, I have kept the faith."

It's interesting that you've heard that passage from several speakers now, because it embodies somebody who knew how to run a good and long race and somebody who knew how to keep the faith, with his State, with his family, with his country, and his Constitution.

Years from now, when I think of the man we memorialize today, I'll remember him as he was when I came to know him, his white hair full like a mane, his gait steadied with a cane. Determined to make the most of every last breath, the distinguished gentleman from West Virginia could be found at his desk until the very end, doing the people's business, delivering soul-stirring speeches, a hint of the Appalachians in his voice, stabbing the air with his finger, fiery as ever, years into his tenth decade.

He was a Senate icon. He was a party leader. He was an elder statesman. And he was my friend. That's how I'll remember him.

Today we remember the path he climbed to such extraordinary peaks. Born Cornelius Calvin Sale, Jr.—Corny, he joked, for short—his mother lost her life in the great influenza pandemic of 1918. From the aunt and uncle who raised him, amid West Virginia's coal camps, he gained not only his Byrd name but a reverence for God Almighty, a love of learning that was nurtured at Mark Twain School. And there he met Erma, his sweetheart for over 70 years, by whose side he will now rest for eternity.

Unable to afford college, he did what he could to get by, finding work as a gas station attendant, a produce salesman, a meat cutter, and a welder in the shipyards of Baltimore and Tampa during World War II. Returning home to West Virginia after the war, he ran for the State House of Delegates, using his fiddle case as a briefcase, the better to stand out on the stump.

Before long, he ran for Congress, serving in the House before jumping over to the Senate, where he was elected nine times, held almost every leadership role imaginable, and proved as capable of swaying others as standing alone, marking a row of milestones along the way: longest serving Member of Congress; nearly 19,000 votes cast; not a single loss at the polls, a record that speaks to the bond that he had with you, the people of his State.

Transplanted to Washington, his heart remained here, in West Virginia, in the place that shaped him, with the people he loved. His heart belonged to you. Making life better here was his only agenda. Giving you hope, he said, was his greatest achievement. Hope in the form of new jobs and industries. Hope in the form of black lung benefits and union protections. Hope through roads and research centers, schools and scholarships, health clinics and industrial parks that bear his name.

His early rival and late friend, Ted Kennedy, used to joke about campaigning in West Virginia. When his bus broke down, Ted got hold of the highway patrol, who asked where he was. And he said, "I'm on Robert Byrd Highway." And the dispatcher said, "Which one?" [*Laughter*]

It's a life that immeasurably improved the lives of West Virginians. Of course, Robert Byrd was a deeply religious man, a Christian. And so he understood that our lives are marked by sins as well as virtues, failures as well as successes, weakness as well as strength. We know there are things he said and things he did that he came to regret. I remember talking about that the first time I visited with him. He said: "There are things I regretted in my youth. You may know that." And I said, "None of us are absent some regrets, Senator. That's why we enjoy and seek the grace of God."

And as I reflect on the full sweep of his 92 years, it seems to me that his life bent towards justice. Like the Constitution he tucked in his pocket, like our Nation itself, Robert Byrd possessed that quintessential American quality, and that is a capacity to change, a capacity to learn, a capacity to listen, a capacity to be made more perfect.

Over his nearly six decades in our Capitol, he came to be seen as the very embodiment of the Senate, chronicling its history in four volumes that he gave to me just as he gave to President Clinton. I too read it. I was scared he was going to quiz me. [*Laughter*]

But as I soon discovered, his passion for the Senate's past, his mastery of even its most arcane procedures, it wasn't an obsession with the trivial or the obscure; it reflected a profoundly noble impulse, a recognition of a basic truth about this country that we are not a nation of men, we are a nation of laws. Our way of life rests on our democratic institutions. Precisely because we are fallible, it falls to each of us to safeguard these institutions, even when it's inconvenient, and pass on our Republic more perfect than before.

Considering the vast learning of this self-taught Senator—his speeches sprinkled with the likes of Cicero and Shakespeare and Jefferson—it seems fitting to close with one of his favorite passages in literature, a passage from "Moby Dick":

And there is a Catskill eagle in some souls that can alike dive down into the blackest gorges, and soar out of them again and become invisible in the sunny spaces. And even if he forever flies within the gorge, that gorge is in the mountains; so that even in his lowest swoop the mountain eagle is still higher than any other bird upon the plain, even though they soar.

Robert Byrd was a mountain eagle, and his lowest swoop was still higher than the other birds upon the plain.

May God bless Robert C. Byrd. May he be welcomed kindly by the Righteous Judge, and may his spirit soar forever like a Catskill eagle, high above the Heavens. Thank you very much.

NOTE: The President spoke at approximately 1:09 p.m. at the West Virginia State Capitol. In his remarks, he referred to Mona Byrd Fatemi and Marjorie Byrd Moore, daughters of Sen. Byrd; Victoria R. Kennedy, wife of former Sen. Edward M. Kennedy; and Rep. Nick J. Rahall II. The transcript released by the Office of the Press Secretary also included the remarks of Vice President Joe Biden.

Message on the Observance of Independence Day, 2010
July 2, 2010

Today we celebrate the 234th anniversary of the signing of the Declaration of Independence and the beginning of a great experiment, American democracy. In every corner of our country, we recall the valor and vision of patriots from Thirteen Colonies who declared independence from a powerful empire and gave birth to a new Nation. We gather in town centers and wave flags in parades not only to recall this history we share, but also to honor the vibrant and enduring spirit of America established on this day.

For those gallant first Americans, such a Nation as ours may have seemed like an unattainable dream. Their concept was revolutionary: a government of, by, and for the people. Yet our Founders' tenacity, resolve, and courage in the face of seemingly impossible odds became the bedrock of our country. That essence has permeated our land and inspired generations of Americans to explore, discover, and redefine the outer reaches of our infinite potential. It has become the foundation of the American dream.

This dream has not come without tremendous cost. From the farmers and tradesmen who served in militias during our American Revolution to the present day women and men protecting our Nation around the world, the sacrifices of our Armed Forces have been extraordinary. Today we pay tribute to our servicemembers, many of whom have paid the ultimate sacrifice. We also acknowledge the contributions and sacrifices of their loving families. It is their heroism that has paved the remarkable path of freedom's march.

Just as this day serves as a reminder of the immeasurable bravery of those who have made America what it is today, it also renews in us the solemn duty we share to ensure our Nation lives up to its promise. We must not simply commemorate the work begun over two and a quarter centuries ago; we are called to join together, hoist their mantle upon our shoulders, and carry that spirit of service into tomorrow.

America again faces a daunting set of challenges, yet our history shows these are not insurmountable. We need only to draw upon the perseverance of those before us—our Founders who declared and fought for their ideals; our ancestors who emigrated here and struggled to build a better future for their children; and our pioneers and entrepreneurs who blazed trails that have continually expanded our horizons. Their spirit—our spirit—will guide our Nation now and in our bright future.

On our Nation's birthday, may we come together in the enduring spirit of America to begin that work anew. I wish you all the best for a happy Fourth of July. May God Bless all those who serve, and may God Bless the United States of America.

BARACK OBAMA

NOTE: An original was not available for verification of the content of this message.

The President's Weekly Address
July 3, 2010

This week, I spent some time in Racine, Wisconsin, talking with folks who are doing their best to cope with the aftermath of a brutal recession. And while I was there, a young woman asked me a question I hear all the time: "What are we doing as a nation to bring jobs back to this country?"

Well, on Friday we learned that after 22 straight months of job loss, our economy has now created jobs in the private sector for 6 months in a row. That's a positive sign. But the truth is, the recession from which we're emerging has left us in a hole that's about 8 million jobs deep. And as I've said from the day I took office, it's going to take months, even years, to dig our way out, and it's going to require an all-hands-on-deck effort.

In the short term, we're fighting to speed up this recovery and keep the economy growing by all means possible. That means extending unemployment insurance for workers who lost their job. That means getting small businesses the loans they need to keep their doors open and hire new workers. And that means sending relief to States so they don't have to lay off thousands of teachers and firefighters and police officers.

Still, at a time when millions of Americans feel a deep sense of urgency in their own lives, Republican leaders in Washington just don't get it. While a majority of Senators support taking these steps to help the American people, some are playing the same old Washington games and using their power to hold this relief hostage, a move that only ends up holding back our recovery. It doesn't make sense.

But I promised those folks in Wisconsin, and I promise all of you, that we won't back down. We're going to keep fighting to advance our recovery. And we're going to keep competing aggressively to make sure the jobs and industries of the future are taking root right here in America.

That's one of the reasons why we're accelerating the transition to a clean energy economy and doubling our use of renewable energy sources like wind and solar power, steps that have the potential to create whole new industries and hundreds of thousands of new jobs in America. In fact, today I'm announcing that the Department of Energy is awarding nearly $2 billion in conditional commitments to two solar companies.

The first is Abengoa Solar, a company that has agreed to build one of the largest solar plants in the world right here in the United States. After years of watching companies build things and create jobs overseas, it's good news that we've attracted a company to our shores to build a plant and create jobs right here in America. In the short term, construction will create approximately 1,600 jobs in Arizona. What's more, over 70 percent of the components and products used in construction will be manufactured in the U.S.A., boosting jobs and communities in States up and down the supply chain. Once completed, this plant will be the first large-scale solar plant in the U.S. to actually store the energy it generates for later use, even at night, and it will generate enough clean, renewable energy to power 70,000 homes.

The second company is Abound Solar manufacturing, which will manufacture advanced solar panels at two new plants, creating more than 2,000 construction jobs and 1,500 permanent jobs. A Colorado plant is already underway, and an Indiana plant will be built in what's now an empty Chrysler factory. When fully operational, these plants will produce millions of state-of-the-art solar panels each year.

These are just two of the many clean energy investments in the Recovery Act. Already, I've seen the payoff from these investments. I've seen once-shuttered factories humming with new workers who are building solar panels and wind turbines, rolling up their sleeves to help America win the race for the clean energy economy.

So that's some of what we're doing. But the truth is, steps like these won't replace all the jobs we've lost overnight. I know folks are struggling. I know this Fourth of July weekend finds many Americans wishing things were a bit easier right now. I do too.

But what this weekend reminds us, more than any other, is that we are a nation that has always risen to the challenges before it. We're a nation that, 234 years ago, declared our independence from one of the greatest empires the world had ever known. We're a nation that mustered a sense of common purpose to overcome depression and fear itself. We're a nation that embraced a call to greatness and saved the world from tyranny. That is who we are, a nation that turns times of trial into times of triumph, and I know America will write our own destiny once more.

I wish every American a safe and happy Fourth of July. And to all our troops serving in harm's way, I want you to know you have the support of a grateful nation and a proud Commander in Chief. Thank you, God bless you, and God bless the United States of America.

NOTE: The address was recorded at approximately 8:45 a.m. on July 2 in the Roosevelt Room at the White House for broadcast on July 3. The transcript was made available by the Office of the Press Secretary on July 2, but was embargoed for release until 6 a.m. on July 3. The Office of the Press Secretary also released a Spanish language transcript of this address.

Statement on the 10th Anniversary of the Community of Democracies
July 3, 2010

Today Foreign Ministers from around the world gather in Krakow to mark the 10th anniversary of the Community of Democracies. The United States was a leader in the formation of the Community of Democracies and remains firmly committed to supporting its efforts to advance democratic values and institutions.

Its founding document, the Warsaw Declaration, stands as a powerful expression of our shared commitment to universal values and democratic principles. Ten years ago, 106 nations affirmed their dedication to respecting and upholding core democratic values including the right of citizens to choose their representatives through regular, free, and fair elections with universal and equal suffrage; to equal protection under the law; and to freedom of opinion and expression, peaceful assembly and association, and freedom of thought, conscience, and religion. The Warsaw Declaration also recognizes a core lesson that the United States draws from our own democratic journey: Transparent, participatory, and accountable democratic institutions are essential for protecting and upholding these universal values.

The Community of Democracies reflects our determination to work together to promote and strengthen democracy around the world. This means focusing on what each of our countries can do to strengthen our own democratic practices and institutions. As I have said many times, there is no more powerful tool for advancing democracy and human rights than our own example. We promote our values by living our values at home.

This forum also challenges us to act collectively, as a community of democratic nations, to support countries undergoing democratic transitions and to push back against threats to democratic progress. For instance, the United States is particularly concerned about the spread of restrictions on civil society, the growing use of law to curb rather than enhance freedom, and widespread corruption that is undermining the faith of citizens in their governments. As people around the world confront these challenges, they have tools that could not have been imagined 10 years ago, including new technologies that provide unique and powerful opportunities for advancing human rights and democracy.

I commend Lithuania for its leadership of the Community and its efforts to focus the group's work on today's pressing challenges including growing threats to civil society, the empowerment of women, and the linkages between poverty, democracy, and development.

I welcome this celebration of the Community's first 10 years and believe that its role in fostering strong and effective cooperation among the world's democracies is essential for confronting the challenges ahead. Working together in partnership, we can advance the dignity of all human beings and the rights that are universal.

Remarks at an Independence Day Celebration
July 4, 2010

The President. Good evening, everybody. On behalf of Michelle and myself and the girls and Bo—[*laughter*]—welcome to the White House, and happy Fourth of July.

All across our great country today, folks are coming together, decked out in their red and white and blue, firing up the grill, having a good time with family, just like here today. Now, of course, I'll admit that the backyard is a little bigger here. [*Laughter*] But it's the same spirit. And Michelle and I couldn't imagine a better way to celebrate America's birthday than with America's extraordinary men and women in uniform and your families.

Now, we decided to let you leave your uniforms at home for today. Although, I have to say, I met a young corporal here who was wearing a black suit. And I said, "Man, it's hot here." He said, "I'm sorry, sir. I know you're my Commander in Chief, but my grandma told me I had to wear a suit." [*Laughter*] I can't—you can't argue with grandma. [*Laughter*]

But we do want all of you to relax and have some fun today. And that also goes for the leaders who are joining us here today, including Deputy Secretary of Defense Bill Lynn, the vice chairman of the Joint Chiefs of Staff, General Jim "Hoss" Cartwright, Navy Secretary Ray Mabus, Air Force Secretary Mike Donley, Coast Guard Commandant Admiral Robert Papp, and the many outstanding senior enlisted officers who are here today.

I want to acknowledge that my Vice President, Joe Biden, and his wonderful wife Dr. Jill Biden aren't with us because they're spending the Fourth of July with our troops in Iraq. And I would add that because of the honor and heroism of our troops, we are poised to end our combat mission in Iraq this summer, on schedule. That's thanks to so many of you.

Now, this is the day when we celebrate the very essence of America and the spirit——

Audience member. [*Inaudible*]—bring the boys home!

The President. They're coming. [*Laughter*] This is the day when we celebrate the very essence of America and the spirit that has defined us as a people and as a nation for more than two centuries. Even now, all these years later, we still look in awe at the small band of patriots who stood up and risked everything and defied an empire to declare "that these united Colonies are, and of right ought to be free and independent States."

We're amazed at the debt to a founding generation that gave their blood to give meaning to those words, pledging to each other their lives, their fortunes, and their sacred honor. And we celebrate the principles that are timeless, tenets first declared by men of property and wealth, but which gave rise to what Lincoln called a "new birth of freedom" in America: civil rights and voting rights, workers' rights and women's rights, and the rights of every American.

And on this day that is uniquely American, we're reminded that our Declaration, our example, made us a beacon to the world, not only inspiring people to demand their own freedom, from Latin American to Africa, from Europe to Asia, but even now, in this time, these ideals still light the world.

Two hundred and thirty-four years later, the words are just as bold, just as revolutionary, as they were when they were first pronounced: "We hold these truths to be self-evident, that all men are created equal, that they are endowed by their Creator with certain inalienable rights, that among these are life, liberty, and the pursuit of happiness."

These are not simply words on aging parchment. They are the principles that define us as a nation, the values we cherish as a people, and the ideals we strive for as a society, even as we know that we constantly have to work in order to perfect our Union, and that work is never truly done.

The Founders understood this. There in that hall in Philadelphia, as they debated the Declaration, John Adams wrote to his beloved Abigail. He predicted that independence would be celebrated "from one end of the continent to the other, from this time forward forever." But he added, "I am well aware of the toil and blood and treasure that it will cost us to maintain this declaration and support and defend these states."

So today we also celebrate all of you, the men and women of our Armed Forces who defend this country we love.

We salute the United States Army, including a soldier who served on more than 150 combat missions in Afghanistan, and after losing most of his arm in an IED attack, recently completed a grueling 26-mile run, inspiring all who know him and all of us; that's Staff Sergeant Gabriel Garcia. Gabriel.

We salute the United States Navy, and a sailor who excels in a job few can imagine but for which all are grateful, a commander of an explosive ordnance disposal team in Iraq, his nerve and steady hand has diffused countless bombs and saved countless lives; that's Lieutenant Erich Frandrup. Where's Erich?

We salute the United States Air Force, and an airman who during an attack on her vehicle in Iraq that left her seriously wounded, directed medics to help another wounded American first and offered her own bandages to help save his life; that's Captain Wendy Kosek.

We salute the United States Marine Corps, and a marine who for his heroic actions in Afghanistan, exposing himself to enemy machine gunfire to help rescue his fellow marines, was recognized with the Bronze Star for valor, Staff Sergeant Jonathan Piel.

And we salute the United States Coast Guard, including a coastguardsman who commanded the first U.S. vessel to arrive in Haiti after the earthquake, helping to pave the way for the one of the most complex humanitarian efforts ever attempted, Commander Diane Durham.

This is the spirit of which Adams spoke so long ago. You are the men and women who toil to defend these States. You are patriots, and you have earned your place among the greatest of generations.

Yet on this day, we know that America's journey is not sustained by those in uniform alone. It must be the calling and cause of every American. So let us ensure that our troops always have the support that they need to succeed in the missions we ask of them, and that includes public support here at home.

Let us forge a national commitment to support our extraordinary military families, not just now, during war, but at every stage of your lives. And thanks to Michelle and Jill Biden for challenging us to do that.

Let us resolve, as citizens, to carry on the improbable experiment that began more than 200 years ago; not simply declaring our principles, but living them here at home; not simply celebrating our Union, but always working to perfect it.

And here in a still young century, let us renew our commitment to stand with those around the world who, like us, still believe in that simple yet revolutionary notion that we are all endowed by our Creator "with certain inalienable rights."

So happy Fourth of July, everybody. God bless all of you and all our men and women in uniform and your families, and God bless the United States of America.

And with that, let me turn it over to our outstanding United States Marine Band.

NOTE: The President spoke at 7 p.m. from the Blue Room Balcony at the White House. The transcript was released by the Office of the Press Secretary on July 6.

Remarks Following a Meeting With Prime Minister Benjamin Netanyahu of Israel and an Exchange With Reporters
July 6, 2010

President Obama. Well, I just completed an excellent one-on-one discussion with Prime Minister Netanyahu, and I want to welcome him back to the White House.

I want to, first of all, thank him for the wonderful statement that he made in honor of the Fourth of July, our Independence Day, when he was still in Israel. And it marked just one more chapter in the extraordinary friendship between our two countries.

As Prime Minister Netanyahu indicated in his speech, the bond between the United States and Israel is unbreakable. It encompasses our national security interests, our strategic interests, but most importantly, the bond of two democracies who share a common set of values and whose people have grown closer and closer as time goes on.

During our discussions in our private meeting, we covered a wide range of issues. We discussed the issue of Gaza, and I commended Prime Minister Netanyahu on the progress that's been made in allowing more goods into Gaza. We've seen real progress on the ground. I think it's been acknowledged that it has moved more quickly and more effectively than many people anticipated.

Obviously, there's still tensions and issues there that have to be resolved, but our two countries are working cooperatively together to deal with these issues. The Quartet has been, I think, very helpful as well. And we believe that there is a way to make sure that the people of Gaza are able to prosper economically, while Israel is able to maintain its legitimate security needs in not allowing missiles and weapons to get to Hamas.

We discussed the issue of Iran, and we pointed out that as a consequence of some hard work internationally, we have instituted through the U.N. Security Council the toughest sanctions ever directed at an Iranian Government. In addition, last week, I signed our own set of sanctions, coming out of the United States Congress, as robust as any that we've ever seen. Other countries are following suit. And so we intend to continue to put pressure on Iran to meet its international obligations and to cease the kinds of provocative behavior that has made it a threat to its neighbors and the international community.

We had a extensive discussion about the prospects for Middle East peace. I believe that Prime Minister Netanyahu wants peace. I think he's willing to take risks for peace. And during our conversation, he once again reaffirmed his willingness to engage in serious negotiations with the Palestinians around what I think should be the goal not just of the two principals involved, but the entire world, and that is two states living side by side in peace and security.

Israel's security needs met, the Palestinians having a sovereign state that they call their own, those are goals that have obviously escaped our grasp for decades now. But now more than ever, I think, is the time for us to seize on that vision. And I think that Prime Minister Netanyahu is prepared to do so. It's going to be difficult; it's going to be hard work. But we've seen already proximity talks taking place. My envoy,

George Mitchell, has helped to organize five of them so far. We expect those proximity talks to lead to direct talks, and I believe that the Government of Israel is prepared to engage in such direct talks, and I commend the Prime Minister for that.

There are going to need to be a whole set of confidence-building measures to make sure that people are serious and that we're sending a signal to the region that this isn't just more talk and more process without action. I think it is also important to recognize that the Arab States have to be supportive of peace, because, although ultimately this is going to be determined by the Israeli and Palestinian peoples, they can't succeed unless you have the surrounding states having as—a greater investment in the process than we've seen so far.

Finally, we discussed issues that arose out of the nuclear nonproliferation conference. And I reiterated to the Prime Minister that there is no change in U.S. policy when it comes to these issues. We strongly believe that, given its size, its history, the region that it's in, and the threats that are leveled against us—against it, that Israel has unique security requirements. It's got to be able to respond to threats or any combination of threats in the region. And that's why we remain unwavering in our commitment to Israel's security. And the United States will never ask Israel to take any steps that would undermine their security interests.

So I just want to say once again that I thought the discussion that we had was excellent. We've seen over the last year how our relationship has broadened. Sometimes it doesn't get publicized, but on a whole range of issues—economic, military to military, issues related to Israel maintaining its qualitative military edge, intelligence sharing, how we are able to work together effectively on the international front—that in fact our relationship is continuing to improve. And I think a lot of that has to do with the excellent work that the Prime Minister has done. So I'm grateful.

And welcome, once again, to the White House. Thank you.

Prime Minister Netanyahu. Thank you, Mr. President.

The President and I had an extensive, excellent discussion in which we discussed a broad range of issues. These include of course our own cooperation in the fields of intelligence and security. And exactly as the President said, it is extensive. Not everything is seen by the public, but it is seen and appreciated by us.

We understand fully that we will work together in the coming months and years to protect our common interests, our countries, our peoples against new threats. And at the same time, we want to explore the possibilities of peace.

The greatest new threat on the horizon, the single most dominant issue for many of us, is the prospect that Iran would acquire nuclear weapons. Iran is brutally terrorizing its people, spreading terrorism far and wide. And I very much appreciate the President's statements that he is determined to prevent Iran from acquiring nuclear weapons.

That has been translated by the President into his leadership at the Security Council, which passed sanctions against Iran, by the U.S. bill that the President signed just a few days ago. And I urge other leaders to follow the President's lead and other countries to follow the U.S. lead, to adopt much tougher sanctions against Iran, primarily those directed against its energy sector.

As the President said, we discussed a great deal about activating, moving forward the quest for peace between Israel and the Palestinians. We're committed to that peace. I'm committed to that peace. And this peace, I think, will better the lives of Israelis, of Palestinians, and it certainly would change our region.

Israelis are prepared to do a lot to get that peace in place, but they want to make sure that after all the steps they take, that what we get is a secure peace. We don't want a repeat of the situation where we vacate territories and those are overtaken by Iran's proxies and used as a launching ground for terrorist attacks or rocket attacks.

I think there are solutions that we can adopt. But in order to proceed to the solutions, we need to begin negotiations in order to end them. We've begun proximity talks, and I think it's high time to begin direct talks. I think with the help of President Obama, President Abbas and myself should engage in direct talks to reach a political settlement of peace, coupled with security and prosperity.

This requires that the Palestinian Authority prepare its people for peace: schools, textbooks, and so on. But I think at the end of the day, peace is the best option for all of us, and I think we have a unique opportunity and a unique time to do it.

The President says that he has a habit of confounding all the cynics and all the naysayers and all those who preclude possibility, and he's shown it time and time again. I think I've had my opportunity to confound some cynics myself, and I think if we work together with President Abbas, then we can bring a great message of hope to our peoples, to the region, and to the world.

One final point, Mr. President: I want to thank you for reaffirming to me in private and now in public as you did the longstanding U.S. commitments to Israel on matters of vital strategic importance. I want to thank you too for the great hospitality you and the First Lady have shown Sara and me and our entire delegation. And I think we have to redress the balance. You know, I've been coming here a lot. It's about time you——

President Obama. I'm ready.

Prime Minister Netanyahu. ——and the First Lady came to Israel, sir.

President Obama. We're looking forward to it. Thank you.

Prime Minister Netanyahu. Any time.

President Obama. Thank you very much. Thank you.

All right, we've got time for one question each. I'm going to call on Stephen Collinson, AFP [Agence France-Presse].

Middle East Peace Process

Q. Thank you, Mr. President. As part of the steps which need to be taken to move proximity talks on to direct talks, do you think it would be helpful for Israel to extend the partial settlement moratorium, which is set to expire in September?

And if I could just briefly ask the Prime Minister, with regards to the sanctions you mentioned, do you think that these measures will contain or halt Iran's nuclear program where others have failed?

President Obama. Well, let me first of all say that I think the Israeli Government, working through layers of various governmental entities and jurisdictions, have shown restraint over the last several months that I think has been conducive to the prospects of us getting into direct talks.

And my hope is, is that once direct talks have begun, well before the moratorium has expired, that that will create a climate in which everybody feels a greater investment in success. Not every action by one party or the other is taken as a reason for not engaging in talks. So there ends up being more room created by more trust. And so I want to just make sure that we sustain that over the next several weeks.

I do think that there are a range of confidence-building measures that can be taken by all sides that improve the prospects of a successful negotiation. And I've discussed some of those privately with the Prime Minister. When President Abbas was here, I discussed some of those same issues with him.

I think it's very important that the Palestinians not look for excuses for incitement, that they are not engaging in provocative language, that at the international level, they are maintaining a constructive tone, as opposed to looking for opportunities to embarrass Israel.

At the same time, I've said to Prime Minister Netanyahu—I don't think he minds me sharing it publicly—that Abu Mazen, working with Fayyad, have done some very significant things when it comes to the security front. And so us being able to widen the scope of their responsibilities in the West Bank is something that I think would be very meaningful to the Palestinian people.

I think that some of the steps that have already been taken in Gaza help to build confidence. And if we continue to make progress on that front, then Palestinians can see in very concrete terms what peace can bring that rhetoric and violence cannot bring, and that is people actually having an opportunity to raise their children and make a living and buy and sell goods and build a life for themselves, which is ultimately what people in both Israel and the Palestinian Territories want.

Prime Minister Netanyahu. I think the latest sanctions adopted by the U.N. create illegitimacy or create delegitimization for Iran's nuclear program, and that is important. I think the sanctions the President signed the other day actually have teeth. They bite.

The question is, how much do you need to bite is something I cannot answer now. But if other nations adopted similar sanctions, that would increase the effect. The more like-minded countries join in the American-led effort that President Obama has signed into act, into law, I think the better we'll be able to give you an answer to your question.

President Obama. Is there somebody you want to call on here?

Israel-U.S. Relations

Q. Mr. President, in the past year, you distanced yourself from Israel and gave a cold shoulder to the Prime Minister. Do you think this policy was a mistake? Do you think it contributes to the bashing of Israel by others? And is that a—you change it now, and do you trust now Prime Minister Netanyahu?

And if I may, Mr. Prime Minister, specifically, did you discuss with the President the continuing of the freezing of settlements after September? And did you tell him that you're going to keep on building after this period is over?

President Obama. Well, let me first of all say that the premise of your question was wrong, and I entirely disagree with it. If you look at every public statement that I've made over the last year and a half, it has been a constant reaffirmation of the special relationship between the United States and Israel, that our commitment to Israel's security has been unwavering. And in fact, there aren't any concrete policies that you could point to that would contradict that.

And in terms of my relationship with Prime Minister Netanyahu, I know the press, both in Israel and stateside, enjoys seeing if there's news there. But the fact of the matter is, is that

I've trusted Prime Minister Netanyahu since I met him before I was elected President, and have said so both publicly and privately.

I think that he is dealing with a very complex situation in a very tough neighborhood. And what I have consistently shared with him is my interest in working with him—not at cross-purposes—so that we can achieve the kind of peace that will ensure Israel's security for decades to come.

And that's going to mean some tough choices. And there are going to be times where he and I are having robust discussions about what kind of choices need to be made. But the underlying approach never changes, and that is, the United States is committed to Israel's security, we are committed to that special bond, and we are going to do what's required to back that up, not just with words but with actions.

We are going to continually work with the Prime Minister and the entire Israeli Government, as well as the Israeli people, so that we can achieve what I think has to be everybody's goal, which is, is that people feel secure. They don't feel like a rocket is going to be landing on their head sometime. They don't feel as if there's a growing population that wants to direct violence against Israel.

That requires work and that requires some difficult choices, both at the strategic level and the tactical level. And this is something that the Prime Minister understands, and why I think that we're going to be able to work together not just over the next few months, but hopefully, over the next several years.

Prime Minister Netanyahu. The President and I discussed concrete steps that could be done now, in the coming days and the coming weeks, to move the peace process further along in a very robust way. This is what we focused our conversation on. And when I say the next few weeks, that's what I mean. The President means that too.

Let me make a general observation about the question you forwarded to the President. And here I'll have to paraphrase Mark Twain, that the reports about the demise of the special U.S.-Israel relations—relationship aren't just premature, they're just flat wrong. There's a depth and richness of this relationship that is expressed every day. Our teams talk. We don't make it public. The only thing that's public is that you can have differences on occasion in the best of families and the closest of families; that comes out public, and sometimes in a twisted way too.

What is not told is the fact that we have an enduring bond of values, interests, beginning with security and the way that we share both information and other things to help the common defense of our common interests, and many others in the region who don't often admit to the beneficial effect of this cooperation.

So I think there's—the President said it best in his speech in Cairo. He said in front of the entire Islamic world, he said, the bond between Israel and the United States is unbreakable. And I can affirm that to you today.

President Obama. Thank you very much, everybody.

NOTE: The President spoke at 12:38 p.m. in the Oval Office at the White House. In his remarks, he referred to U.S. Special Envoy for Middle East Peace George J. Mitchell; and President Mahmoud Abbas and Prime Minister Salam Fayyad of the Palestinian Authority.

Remarks Announcing the President's Export Council
July 7, 2010

Thank you very much. Everybody, please be seated. Well, good morning. Thank you, Jim McNerney, for being here. And thank you to members of my Cabinet and my administration for coming. Thank you, Gary Locke, for the introduction and the outstanding work that you've been doing at Commerce to move America's economy forward.

Now, that work has been my driving focus since we walked through these doors a year and a half ago. And at that time, our economy was shrinking at an alarming rate. Nearly 3 million jobs were lost in the last half of 2008. In January 2009 alone, more than 750,000 jobs had been lost here in the United States. So every alarm bell was ringing at the prospect of a second Great Depression.

So our imperative was to stop that freefall and reverse direction to get our economy moving and get jobs growing again, which meant we took a series of dramatic and frankly sometimes unpopular actions. But as a result of those actions, we broke the recession's momentum, and we're in a much different place today.

Our economy has now grown for three consecutive quarters and created nearly 600,000 private sector jobs in the first half of this year, a stark contrast to the 3.7 [million]° we lost over

the first half of last year. And despite uncertain world events and the resulting ups and downs in the market, we are moving America forward again.

But the progress we've made to date isn't nearly enough to undo the damage that the recession visited on people and communities across our country. Our businesses are hiring again, but there are still five unemployed workers for each job opening. The economy is growing, but empty storefronts still haunt too many Main Streets. And the truth is the middle class families that are the backbone of our economy have felt their economic security eroding since long before this recession hit.

So we've got much more work to do to spur stronger job growth and to keep the larger recovery moving. The question is, over the months and years to come, how do we encourage the strong and lasting economic growth required for America to lead in this new century? Where are we going to find the growth necessary to help us address all of our priorities, from creating jobs and prosperity to boosting our businesses and our workers, to improving our fiscal health and reducing our long-term deficits?

Now, one thing we know is this growth won't come from an economy where prosperity is based on fleeting bubbles of consumption, of debt; it can't rely on paper gains. We've seen

---

° White House correction.

where that led us, and we're not going back. The truth is we've had to face over the past year and a half the truth that if we want to once again approach full employment and fuel real economic growth, then we need to put an end to the policies that got us here, tackle the challenges we've put off for decades, and move this economy forward. We need to lay a new and stronger foundation on which businesses can thrive and create jobs and rising incomes, on which innovators and entrepreneurs can lead the world in generating new technologies and products and services. We have to rely on a new foundation on which America can harness what has made our economy the engine and the envy of the world: the talent and drive and creativity of our people.

So as business leaders and labor leaders representing some of America's largest corporations and America's workers, that's what I want to talk to you about all today, because America's success ultimately depends on your success. It's the private sector that has always been the source of our job creation, our economic growth, and our prosperity. And it's our businesses and workers who will take the reins of this recovery and lead us forward.

Same time, some might argue that Government has no role to play at all in our economy. But everybody in this room understands that the free market depends on a government that sets clear rules that ensure fair and honest competition, that lives within its means, that invests in certain things that the private sector can't invest on its own. In the absence of this kind of responsible government, whenever government is dragged too far to one end or the other of the spectrum, we see negative consequences for our economy.

So too much regulation or too much spending can stifle innovation, can hamper confidence and growth, and hurt business and families. A government that does too little can be just as irresponsible as a government that does too much, because, for example, in the absence of sound oversight, responsible businesses are forced to compete against unscrupulous and underhanded businesses, who are unencumbered by any restrictions on activities that might harm the environment, or take advantage of middle class families, or threaten to bring down the entire financial system. That's bad for everybody. That's the reason we pursued Wall Street reforms. And when the Senate takes up its business again, I hope it moves as quickly as possible to finish this chapter and settle this issue.

In the absence of sensible policies that invest in long-term public goods like education or basic research, roads, railways, broadband, a smart electric grid, an absence of those investments can be equally disastrous. Over time, failure to make such investments slowly degrades our competitiveness, leaving us without the skilled workforce or the technologies or the basic infrastructure that a 21st-century economy requires.

So to make sure our workers can outcompete anybody, anywhere in the world, we've invested in the skills and education of our people. Through the Race to the Top, we're challenging our schools to raise their standards. And I've pledged that by 2020, America will once again lead the world in the percentage of students graduating from college, and by making higher education more affordable, we're on our way to achieving that goal.

To strengthen our standing in a 21st-century economy, we've invested in upgrading our critical infrastructure, from high-speed rail to high-speed Internet. We've enacted reforms that will reduce the drag of health care costs on businesses and consumers alike. And we are committed to bringing down the unsustainable debt that has ballooned over the past 10 years.

To spur lasting growth, we've invested in science and technology, research and development, and clean energy projects that will strengthen our global leadership. Eighteen months ago, for example, American companies commanded just 2 percent of the global capacity for advanced battery technology. Today the seed money we provided has helped leverage substantial private investment, and by 2012, we expect America's capacity to reach 20 percent of the global market—and as high as 40 percent in 2015.

But Government has another responsibility, and that is to remove barriers that stand in the way of opportunity and prosperity so that our people, all of our people—our workers, our entrepreneurs, our CEOs—can build the future that we seek. And that's what I want to focus on now.

In my State of the Union Address, I set a goal for America: Over the next 5 years, we will double our exports of goods and services around the world, an increase that will boost economic growth and support millions of American jobs in a manner that is deficit friendly.

Export growth leads to job growth and economic growth. In 2008, American exports accounted for nearly 7 percent of our total employment, one in three manufacturing jobs, and supported 10.3 million jobs in all, jobs that pay 15 percent more than average. So at a time when jobs are in short supply, building exports is an imperative.

But this isn't just about where jobs are today; this is where American jobs will be tomorrow. Ninety-five percent of the world's customers and fastest growing markets are beyond our borders. So if we want to find new growth streams, if we want to find new markets and new opportunity, we've got to compete for those new customers, because other nations are competing for those new customers.

As I've said many times, the United States of America should not, cannot, will not play for second place. We mean to compete for those jobs and we mean to win. But we're going to have to change how we do business.

To meet this goal, we launched the National Export Initiative, an ambitious effort to team up with America's businesses, large and small, and help them unleash their energy and innovation, grow their markets, support new jobs selling their goods and services all across the globe. And we're bringing to bear the full resources of the United States Government.

One of the first things we did was establish an Export Promotion Cabinet made up of Cabinet members and senior administration officials whose work affects exports. Yesterday I assembled this cabinet for an update on our efforts so far. We're going to hold these meetings every few months, and I've asked for a progress report at our next meeting in September.

But this is about more than what Government can do; this is about what our businesses can do. And that's why we are relaunching the President's Export Council, a group that includes business and labor leaders who will offer their unfiltered advice and expertise on how best to promote exports. We've also included congressional leaders and senior representatives of my administration.

And earlier today, members of my Cabinet and I met with this council to begin soliciting advice. And I want to again thank Jim, president and CEO of Boeing, as well as Ursula Burns, CEO of Xerox, for agreeing to serve as the chair and vice chair.

Our efforts are off to a solid start. American exports grew almost 17 percent over the first 4 months of this year compared to the same period last year. Part of this, of course, is due to the global recovery. But we're also moving forward on improving conditions for America's exporters. And since we launched the National Export Initiative, we've made progress across its five objectives.

First, we said that America would be a strong partner and better advocate in the international marketplace for its businesses and workers. And we're going to go to bat for everyone from the largest corporations to the smallest business owner with an idea that she wants to market and sell to the world.

So, for example, already this year, the Commerce Department has coordinated 18 trade missions with over 160 companies that compete in 24 countries, and we've got 8 more planned over the next 3 months. Their Advocacy Center has assisted American companies competing for export opportunities, supporting $11.4 billion in exports and an estimated 70,000 jobs.

Secretary Clinton recently held a roundtable with businesses in Shanghai, and next week, she'll host another one with Secretary Locke to discuss removing barriers that stand in the way of their success.

Meanwhile, we're moving forward with strengthening our business assistance centers across the country and in our embassies and consulates abroad so that they can provide a comprehensive toolkit of services to help potential exporters gain a foothold in new markets and expand, especially small businesses that might not know how to sell their products abroad.

Second, we're increasing access to export financing for small and medium-sized businesses that want to export their goods and services, but just need a boost. So the Export-Import Bank has more than doubled its loans in support of American exporters since last year, and that step alone has helped support nearly 110,000 jobs.

Third, we're upping our efforts to remove barriers to trade and open new markets and new opportunities for American business. On a global level, this begins with pushing hard in the Doha round to improve those negotiations so that they have a higher level of ambition in the way that will translate directly into more opportunities for American exporters. Regionally, we're working on the Trans-Pacific Partnership free trade agreement to expand our commercial presence in some of the most dynamic markets in Asia. And where our businesses run up against barriers in individual markets, we are acting.

In March, for example, we reached an agreement with China to reopen their market to American pork and pork products. And last month, during President Medvedev's visit, we reached an agreement with Russia to reopen their market to American poultry. And these steps are worth more than $1 billion to American businesses.

We're also reforming our own restrictions on exports, consistent with our national security interests. And we hope to move forward on new agreements with some of our key partners. I've instructed U.S. Trade Representative Ron Kirk to begin discussions to help resolve outstanding issues with the pending Korean Free Trade Agreement before my visit to Korea in November. It's an agreement that will create new jobs and opportunity for people in both of our countries.

We also want to deepen and broaden our relations with Panama and Colombia. So we're working to resolve outstanding issues with the free trade agreements with those key partners,

and we're focused on submitting them as soon as possible for congressional consideration. And we'll make sure each agreement we pursue doesn't just advance the interests of our businesses, workers, and farmers, but also upholds our most cherished values.

Fourth, as we help American businesses access new markets, we're making sure that the access is free and fair. The United States offers some of the world's lowest barriers to trade, and when we give other countries the privilege of that free and fair access, we expect it in return. Where American producers face unfair trade practices, we'll use every tool at our disposal to enforce trade agreements. Last week, for example, the WTO ruled in favor of the United States on a case that found European governments were subsidizing planes that Airbus manufactures. That practice was unfair and hurt American workers. This ruling will help keep the playing field level and boost American jobs.

And finally, we continue to coordinate with other nations around the world to promote strong, sustainable, and balanced growth. At last month's G–20 summit, we built on the actions we took last year, actions that have replaced global contraction with global growth, and trade that was plummeting with trade that's bounced back.

Sustaining that recovery, however, also involves rebalancing our economies. As I told other leaders at the G–20, after years of taking on too much debt, Americans will no longer borrow and buy the world's way to lasting prosperity. We alone cannot be the engines of economic growth. Furthermore, a strong and durable recovery requires that countries not have an undue advantage.

So we discussed the need for market-driven currencies. And I welcome China's decision to allow its currency to appreciate in response to market forces. Our discussion with China has also addressed the important challenge of how to create a more level playing field for American companies seeking to expand their access to the growing Chinese market. And I made it clear to all that the United States of America is prepared to compete aggressively for the jobs and industries and markets of the future.

The bottom line is this: For a long time we were trapped, I think, in a false political debate in this country where business was on one side, labor was on the other. There were partisan divides. The argument was either you were pro-trade or you were antitrade. What we now have an opportunity to do is to refocus our attention where we're all in it together. Businesses, workers, Government—everybody is focused on the same goal.

We live in a interconnected world. There are global challenges and global opportunities. This Nation has never shied away from the prospect of competition. We thrive on competition. And we are better positioned than anybody—as uniquely positioned as ever—to compete with anyone in the world. We've got the most respected brands, the best products, the most vibrant companies in the world. We've got the most productive workers in the world. We've got the finest universities in the world. We've got the most open, dynamic, and competitive market in the world. When the playing field is even, nobody can beat us. And we are upping our game for the playing field of the 21st century.

But we've got to do it together. We've got to all row in the same direction. There's no doubt that these are challenging times. But I am absolutely convinced that we will rise to meet them, to grow our economy, to put our people back to work, to forge our own future once more. We are Americans, and that is what we do.

I appreciate all your participation, and I'm looking forward to getting busy working with you. Thank you.

NOTE: The President spoke at 11:50 a.m. in the East Room at the White House.

Statement on Food Safety Modernization Legislation
July 7, 2010

A year ago today, the Food Safety Working Group, chaired by Health and Human Service Secretary Kathleen Sebelius and Secretary of Agriculture Tom Vilsack, announced key findings on how to upgrade the food safety system. Since then, my administration has taken steps to reduce the prevalence of E. coli, implemented new standards to reduce exposure to Campylobacter, and issued a rule to control Salmonella contamination. Among other accomplishments, the FDA has conducted a pilot study on a tracing system, and HHS, in collaboration with USDA, has rolled out an enhanced and updated www.foodsafety.gov site to provide consumers rapid access to information on food recalls.

But there is more to be done. Today I thank the House for its work and support efforts in the Senate to pass S. 510, the FDA Food Safety Modernization Act. This bipartisan bill would complement the work already undertaken by the Food Safety Working Group. The bill addresses longstanding challenges in the food safety and defense system by promoting a prevention-oriented approach to the safety of our food supply and provides the Federal Government with the appropriate tools to accomplish its core food safety goals.

Statement on the Elections in Guinea
July 7, 2010

On behalf of the American people, I extend my congratulations to the people of Guinea, who peacefully and successfully conducted an initial round of voting in the country's first free elections since becoming an independent state in 1958. Just months ago, the world was shocked by the September 28 massacre and rape of prodemocracy demonstrators in Conakry. Many feared that brutality and instability would consume Guinea and even spread across its borders to threaten the recovery of a war-weary region. The Guinean people, however, demonstrated extraordinary courage and determination to pull their country out of crisis and to chart a new course toward a democratic future. They were supported by the leadership of Interim President General Sekouba Konate, who has focused intensely and urgently on transitioning the country to civilian rule. The United States joined other members of the international community, including the African Union and ECOWAS, in supporting these elections, but it was the Guinean Government, the electoral commission, civil society, the political party leadership, and the people of Guinea who

made it succeed. Indeed, the character and resilience of the Guinean people in claiming their democratic rights sends a powerful message around the world.

The people of Guinea now have an opportunity to build on this historic achievement as they move toward a second round of voting. I urge all parties in Guinea to continue to choose the rule of law and peaceful political participation over ethnic division and violence. They can continue to count on the support of the United States as they move forward.

Interview With Yonit Levi of Israel's Channel 2 News
July 7, 2010

Ms. Levi. President Barack Obama, shalom, and thank you so much for talking with us today.

The President. Thank you. Thank you very much.

Outlook for Middle East Peace

Ms. Levi. I'd like to actually open up by asking you about hope, which was such a prominent notion in your campaign and in your Presidency. And how can you convey that concept of hope to Israelis, who've seen so many failed attempts at a peace process?

The President. Well, look, it's always a challenge. And one of the things I used to say during the campaign, but also at the beginning of my Presidency, is, being hopeful is not the same as being blindly optimistic. I think you have to be clear eyed about the situation. And Israelis rightly look at the past and have skepticism about what's possible. They see the enmity of neighbors that surround them in a very tough neighborhood. They see a track record of attempts at peace where, even when concessions were made, a deal could not be consummated. They see rockets fired from Gaza or from areas in Lebanon and say to themselves that the hatreds or history are so deep-seated that change is not possible.

And yet if you think back to the founding of Israel, there were a lot of people who thought

that that wasn't possible either. And if Herzl or Ben-Gurion were looking at Israel today, they would be astonished at what they saw: a country that's vibrant, that is growing economically at a extraordinary pace, that has overcome not just security challenges, but also has been able to overcome challenges related to geography. And so that should be a great source of hope.

Middle East Peace Process

Ms. Levi. Is a peace agreement, in your opinion—can—it can be reached in the first term of your Presidency?

The President. I think so. I had an excellent meeting with Prime Minister Netanyahu. And I think that he is somebody who understands that we've got a fairly narrow window of opportunity. On the Palestinian side, moderates like Abu Mazen and Fayyad are, I think, willing to make the concessions and engage in negotiations that can result in peace. But their timeframe in power may be limited if they aren't able to deliver for their people.

There's a constant contest between moderates and rejectionists within the Arab world. And then there's the demographic challenges that Israel is going to be facing if it wants to remain not only a Jewish state but a democratic state. So you look at all these pressures and you say to yourself, we probably won't have a better opportunity than we have right now. And that

1027

has to be seized. Now, it's going to be wrenching. It's going to be difficult.

Prime Minister Benjamin Netanyahu of Israel

Ms. Levi. Do you believe Benjamin Netanyahu is the right man? You believe that he can bring peace?

The President. I think that not only is Prime Minister Netanyahu a smart and savvy politician, but the fact that he is not perceived as a dove in some ways can be helpful in the sense that any successful peace will have to include the hawks and the doves on both sides. And in the same way that Richard Nixon here in the United States was able to go to China because he had very strong anti-Communist credentials, I think Prime Minister Netanyahu may be very well positioned to bring this about. And in our conversations yesterday, I had the impression that Prime Minister Netanyahu isn't interested in just occupying a space, a position, but he's interested in being a statesman and putting his country on a more secure track.

So I hope that opportunity is seized. But ultimately, one of the things you learn very quickly, whether you're President or a Prime Minister, is that your power derives from the people. And it goes back to your first question: The Israeli people are going to have to overcome legitimate skepticism, more-than-legitimate fears, in order to get a change that I think will secure Israel for another 60 years.

Israel-U.S. Relations

Ms. Levi. You know, you met with him on Tuesday, and you both said that the meeting was excellent. And you know, perfect photo— an idyllic photo notwithstanding, it wasn't exactly—hasn't exactly been smooth sailing in your relationship so far.

The President. Well, some of this has been greatly overstated. I mean, the last time that the Prime Minister came here, we had a terrific meeting. It was so good that it spilled over. And the reports then came out that somehow I had snubbed the Prime Minister, when in fact what had happened was the Prime Minister was interested and eager enough in working out some issues that he wanted to convene with his team, and then I came back and we had this meeting. That——

Ms. Levi. And the fact that there was no— there were no briefings, no photo ops in that meeting, it doesn't——

The President. Well, I mean, all of that fed this impression that somehow there were more strains than there were.

Now, I don't want to be disingenuous. There have been differences. I think that our view on settlements, for example, is consistent with all previous U.S. administrations. But the fact of the matter is, is that that view was always voiced not in the spirit of trying to undermine Israel's security, but to strengthen it. Because we believe strongly that if we can achieve calm on the ground that will help in the negotiations that lead to peace. And in fact, the moratorium that's been in place, I think, has been conducive to us rebuilding trust on all sides. And as a consequence, I'm more optimistic about the ability to get into direct talks.

Middle East Peace Process

Ms. Levi. Will you, by the way, extend—request that Israel extends that settlement freeze after September?

The President. You know, what I want is for us to get into direct talks. Now, as I said yesterday, I think that if you have direct talks between Abu Mazen, Netanyahu, their teams, that builds trust. And trust then allows for both sides to not be so jumpy or paranoid about every single move that's being made, whether it's related to Jerusalem or any of the other issues that have to be dealt with, because people feel as if there's a forum in which conflicts can get resolved. And the problem, what we've had over the last several years is just a constant erosion of trust that has been counterproductive.

Israel-U.S. Relations

Ms. Levi. Now, I must ask you this, Mr. President. There are people in Israel who are anxious about you——

The President. Right.

Ms. Levi. ——and who—you know, I'm quoting their sentiments—feel like you don't have a special connection to Israel. How do you respond to that?

The President. Well, it's interesting, this is the thing that actually surfaced even before I was elected President, in some of the talk that was circulating within the Jewish American community. Ironically, I've got a Chief of Staff named Rahm Israel Emanuel. My top political adviser is somebody who's a descendent of Holocaust survivors. My closeness to the Jewish American community was probably what propelled me to the U.S. Senate.

And my not just knowledge but sympathy and identification with the Jewish experience is rooted in part because of the historic connection between the African American freedom movement here in the United States and the civil rights efforts of Jewish Americans and some of the same impulses that led to the creation of Israel.

And so I think what this arises from—some of it may just be the fact that my middle name is Hussein, and that creates suspicion. Some of it may have to do with the fact that I have actively reached out to the Muslim community, and I think that sometimes, particularly in the Middle East, there's the feeling of the friend of my enemy must be my enemy. And the truth of the matter is, is that my outreach to the Muslim community is designed precisely to reduce the antagonism and the dangers posed by a hostile Muslim world to Israel and to the West.

Ms. Levi. So that fear, the tangible fear that some Israelis have that their best ally in the world might abandon them is——

The President. Yes, well, it's pretty hard to square with the fact that not only have I, in every speech that I've ever given, talked about the unbreakable bond to Israel, not only did I describe that special relationship and condemn those who would try to drive a rift between us in Cairo in front of a Muslim audience, but if you look at our actions—and Prime Minister Netanyahu will confirm this, and even critics, I think, will have to confirm that the United States, under my administration, has provided more security assistance to Israel than any administration in history. And we've got greater security cooperation between our two countries than at any time in our history. And the single most important threat to Israel, Iran and its potential possession of a nuclear weapon, has been my number-one foreign policy priority over the course of the last 18 months. So it's hard to, I think, look at that track record and look at my public statements and in any way think that my passions for Israel's survival, its security, and its people are in any way diminished.

Iran

Ms. Levi. You mentioned Iran, and obviously, you instituted tough sanctions against Iran. You said that with the meeting with Netanyahu. How long are you going to give the Iranian President, and what are you willing to do if he continues with his nuclear program?

The President. Well, what I've said consistently is, is that it is unacceptable for Iran to possess a nuclear weapon, that we're going to do everything we can to prevent that from happening. What I've also tried to do is build a international consensus so that Iran can't somehow play a victim, can't suggest somehow that they're being singled out by the West. They are the only country that has not been able to convince the International Atomic Energy Agency that they are pursuing nuclear power for peaceful means. It's not hard to do, but they haven't been able to do it because all indicators are that they are in fact pursuing a nuclear weapon.

So we just pursued the toughest sanctions that have ever been applied against the Iranian Government. We followed those up with U.S. sanctions that are going to be tough. Allies and partners are following up with those sanctions. We want to continually ratchet up the costs of them pursuing this nuclear program.

Now, will that work? We don't know. And we are going to continue to keep the door open for a diplomatic resolution of this challenge. But I assure you that I have not taken options off the table.

Israel-U.S. Relations

Ms. Levi. Are you concerned that Prime Minister Netanyahu might try unilaterally to attack Iran?

The President. You know what? I think that the relationship that—the U.S. and Israel is sufficiently strong that neither of us try to surprise each other, but we try to coordinate on issues of mutual concern. And that approach is one that I think Prime Minister Netanyahu is committed to.

The Presidency/President's Historical Significance

Ms. Levi. You know, I must ask you—I was—forgive me for getting nostalgic—I was here—well, not here—in Chicago the night of the election. And I remember seeing that great mass of people and looking at them and looking at you and thinking, there is no man on Earth that is capable of living up to those expectations. [*Laughter*] Do you feel that burden every day?

The President. Oh, absolutely. Look, our campaign, I think, became a repository for a lot of hopes and a lot of dreams, and I think that's a good thing. But we understood that governance is different from campaigning. It's hard. It's complicated. It involves making choices, some of them not very attractive choices, and that at any given stage, there are going to be some people who are disappointed.

But what keeps me hopeful is not any oversized view of my own capabilities; what keeps me hopeful is that the more I meet people here in this country, the more I meet people abroad, the more convinced I am that there is a common humanity, a common set of aspirations that people have for their children. I think there's a core decency to people that sometimes history, institutions, lack of opportunity prevent from being realized, and that the general trajectory of history is in a positive direction. But it takes time. And so my job is to do my small part to move the ball forward.

One of my favorite phrases is from Martin Luther King, who said, "The arc of the moral universe is long, but it bends towards justice." And I believe that. And I think that that's consummate with Jewish traditions, that sense that if we are working hard, if we apply the principles of *tikkun* and repairing the world, that it's possible for us not to create a perfect world, but one that's a little more just, a little more fair, a little better for our children. I continue to believe that.

Ms. Levi. My final question, Mr. President. Much has been made about, obviously, your historic victory and being the first African American President. Can I ask you to share with us that moment where the enormity of the historic significance sort of hit you?

The President. I don't think it still has hit me yet.

Ms. Levi. Really?

The President. We were just talking about how you broke some ground as a woman anchor, and I'm sure that's not what you think about every day. You think about, can I get this story done? Am I performing in a way that meets my standards?

And that's how you feel when you're in the Presidency. I think you have a lot of responsibilities and a lot of concerns, and each day you are just trying to make sure that you are, A, doing the best you can; B, making sure that you're making decisions for the right reason.

And I do think that there have been moments in the Presidency when I'm making a decision about deploying young men and women into the battlefield, or we're making very consequential decisions about the world economy, where the answers are not always a hundred-percent obvious, and you're making judgment calls, and it's during those moments where you are reminded that you can't behave like a politician. You can't put your finger out to the wind; you can't base your actions on polls. You have to make a decision on what you think is right, and then let history judge how you did.

Ms. Levi. Can you tell us what is the thing you miss most about your life before the Presidency?

The President. Taking walks. There is a value to anonymity in terms of just being able to wander around, sit on a park bench, take your kids to get ice cream without having Secret Service and helicopters over you. That part of this life I'll never get used to. In fact, I remember when

I first visited Jerusalem, I could wander through the Old City and haggle for some gifts to bring back to Michelle or stand at the Wailing Wall and people didn't know who I was. And that is a profound pleasure that is very hard to experience now. The last time—the second time I went to the Wailing Wall, I put my prayer, and somebody pulled it out, and the next thing I know it was printed in the newspaper.

Ms. Levi. Yes. [*Laughter*]

The President. And that, I think, was——

Ms. Levi. We have to do our job. [*Laughter*]

The President. ——that was a pretty good metaphor for the changes that you experience as time goes on.

Ms. Levi. Indeed a change. Thank you so much, Mr. President.

The President. Thank you. I enjoyed it.

Ms. Levi. Thank you.

The President. Take care.

NOTE: The President spoke at 5:23 p.m. in the Diplomatic Reception Room at the White House. In his remarks, he referred to President Mahmoud Abbas and Prime Minister Salam Fayyad of the Palestinian Authority. Ms. Levi referred to President Mahmud Ahmadi-nejad of Iran. The transcript was released by the Office of the Press Secretary on July 8.

Remarks at Smith Electric Vehicles in Kansas City, Missouri
July 8, 2010

Hello, everybody. Good to see you. [*Applause*] You don't need to do that. It's good to see you. Thank you very much. Thank you. Thank you so much. Everybody have a seat.

Usually they announce me with some fancy thing, and I think I messed up; I just walked out here. [*Laughter*] So I hope you didn't mind. But on the way out, if you want, we can play the ruffles and flourishes and all that.

I want to, before I start, acknowledge some people who have just done a wonderful job for this area, but also a wonderful job for the country: first of all, one of the best Governors that we've got in the United States of America, Governor Jay Nixon; one of my—not just my favorite Senators, but one of my favorite people and a great friend of mine who is fighting every day for the people of Missouri, Senator Claire McCaskill. We've got two outstanding Members of Congress, one from this side and one from that side, Congressman Emanuel Cleaver and Congressman Dennis Moore. And finally, I just want to acknowledge all the wonderful people at Smith Electric Vehicles and their energetic and outstanding staff.

It is outstanding to be here, and I'm not going to take a long time. I just want to spend some time shaking hands and thanking you for the great work that you've done. I just had a chance to get a tour and saw some of the battery-powered trucks that you're manufacturing. I had a chance to talk to some of the folks who build them. But the reason I'm here today is because at this plant you're doing more than just building new vehicles. You are helping to fight our way through a vicious recession and you are building the economy of America's future.

Now, it's not easy. We've gone through as bad a economic situation as we've had since the Great Depression. And this recession was a culmination of a decade of irresponsibility, a decade that felt like a sledgehammer hitting middle class families. For the better part of 10 years, people have faced stagnant incomes, skyrocketing health care costs, skyrocketing tuition costs, and declining economic security. And this all came to a head in a massive financial crisis that sent our economy into a freefall and cost 8 million American jobs, including many in this community.

So it was in the middle of this crisis that my administration walked through the door, and we had to make some difficult decisions at a moment of maximum peril, to avoid a Great Depression, to make sure that we didn't have a complete meltdown in our financial system. It was a moment when the markets were in turmoil and we were losing 750,000 jobs every month.

Some of the decisions we made weren't popular at the time, and some of them may still be unpopular today. But we made those decisions because we had to stop that freefall. And because we made those hard choices, our economy is in a different place today than it was just a year ago.

One of those decisions was to provide critical funding to promising, innovative businesses like Smith Electric Vehicles. And because we did, there is a thriving enterprise here instead of an empty, darkened warehouse. Because of the grant that went to this company, we can hear the sounds of machines humming and people doing their work, instead of just the ghostly silence of an emptied-out building and the memory of workers who were laid off a long time ago.

And we made that kind of decision all across America last year. And we were guided by a simple idea: Government doesn't have all the answers. Ultimately, government doesn't create all the jobs. Government can't guarantee growth by itself. But what government can do is lay the foundation for small businesses to expand and to thrive, for entrepreneurs to open up shop and test out new products, for workers to get the training that they need, and for families to achieve some measure of economic security. And that role is especially important in tough economic times.

And that's why, when my administration began, we immediately cut taxes. That's right. You wouldn't know it from listening to folks, but we cut taxes for working families and for small-business owners all across American to help them weather the storm. Through our small-business loans, and our focus on research and development, and our investment in high-tech, fast-growing sectors like clean energy, we're helping to speed our recovery by harnessing the talent and the drive and the innovative spirit of the American people. So our goal has never been to create another government program, our goal has been to spur growth in the private sector.

For example, right here at Smith, you've recently passed a milestone, hiring a 50th employee, and I know you're on the way to hire 50

more. And we're seeing similar things all across America, with incentives and investments that are creating wind turbines and solar panels. We're seeing investments in energy-efficient appliances and home-building materials and in advanced battery technologies and clean energy vehicles.

So just give you a couple examples, just last week, Abound manufacturing in Colorado received backing for two plants to produce solar panels. This is going to create 2,000 construction jobs and 1,500 permanent jobs. One of the plants is actually taking over what's now an empty Chrysler supplier factory. Another company, called Abengoa Solar, is now planning to build one of the world's largest solar plants right here in the United States. And when it's finished, this facility will be the first large-scale solar plant in the United States that can actually store energy that it creates for later use, even at night.

All told, we expect energy investments alone to generate 700,000 jobs over the next few years. And this is not just going to boost our economy in the short term; this is going to lay a platform for the future. It's going to create opportunities year after year after year, decade after decade after decade, as companies like Smith, that start small, begin to expand. And I was just talking to your CEO, and he says he wants to open up 20 of these all across the country so that in each region you're able to service—Smith is able to service its customers, and they're going to have a reliable sense that Smith is always going to be there for them, making sure that customer satisfaction and performance is high.

I'll give you another example. Just a few years ago, America had the capacity to build only about 2 percent of the world's advanced batteries for electric and hybrid vehicles like Smith's. Two percent, that was it. We account for 25 percent of the world's economy, and we were only making 2 percent of the world's advanced batteries.

But thanks to our new focus on clean energy and the work that's taking place in plants like this one, we could have as much as 40 percent of the world's market by 2015—5 years. That means jobs. But that also means we're going to have an expertise in a sector that's just going to keep on growing all around the world for years to come. So all these efforts taken together are making a difference.

A year and a half ago, our economy was shrinking at 6 percent a year; now it's growing. The economy was bleeding jobs. We've now created private sector jobs, added private sector jobs, for 6 consecutive months.

Now, obviously, the progress we've made isn't nearly enough to undo all the damage that was done as a consequence of the economic crisis. There's still five unemployed workers for every vacancy. There's still too many empty storefronts on Main Street all across America. And I've said since I took office that my administration will not rest until every American who is able and ready and willing to work can find a job, and a job that pays a decent wage and has decent benefits to support a family.

We're not there yet. We've got a long way to go. But what is absolutely clear is we're moving in the right direction. We are headed in the right direction. And that's—the surest way out of this storm is to go forward, not to go backwards. There are some people who argue that we should abandon some of these efforts, some people who make the political calculation that it's better to just say no to everything than to lend a hand to clean up the mess that we've been in.

But my answer to those who don't have confidence in our future, who want to stop, my answer is come right here to Kansas City. Come see what's going on at Smith Electric. I think they're going to be hard-pressed to tell you that you're not better off than you would be if we hadn't made the investments in this plant.

For the naysayers, they ought to travel all across America and meet the people that I've met at places like Navistar in Indiana where folks are being hired to build new electric trucks; or Siemens wind power in Iowa where they're making wind turbines in a factory that used to be empty just like this one; or Celgard, which is a battery technology company in North Carolina that hired more than 50 people because of the investments we made; or POET biorefinery here in Missouri that's putting people to work harvesting homegrown energy.

While they're at it, they ought to talk to all the small-business owners who've gotten tax breaks to pay for their health plans and new SBA loans to expand or keep their doors open, and that includes tens of millions of dollars in loans for companies right here in Kansas City.

Or they ought to talk to the crews that are rebuilding all the highways and laying tracks for new rail lines, including road projects that are putting hundreds of people to work in this area. They ought to talk to the scientists who are toiling day and night to develop the technologies and the cures with the potential to improve our economy and our health and our well-being.

And they might want to talk to the teachers who didn't get laid off because of the budget help that we gave the State of Missouri, who are then going to be teaching our kids, and they're being incentivized to reform how they do business so we've got the best education system in the world, and we've got the highest number of folks who are going to community colleges or 4-year colleges than anyplace in the world.

That's how we're going to take charge of our destiny. That's how we create jobs and create lasting growth. That's how we ensure that America doesn't just limp along, maybe recover to where we were before, but instead that we're prospering, that this Nation leads the industries of the future.

I mean, this has been a difficult time for America right now: 2 years of brutal recession, a decade of economic insecurity. And there are going to be some hard days ahead. That's the truth. It's going to take a while for us to dig ourselves out of this hole. But what you are proving here—each and every one of you who work here at Smith Electric—is the promise of a brighter future. What you're proving is that if we hold fast to that spirit of entrepreneurship and innovation that's always defined America, we're not just going to emerge from this period of turmoil; we're going to emerge stronger than we were before.

You're proving that as long as we keep on moving forward, nobody can stop us. And for that I want to thank you. You are setting a model for what we need to be doing all across the country.

So congratulations. Thank you very much.

NOTE: The President spoke at 12:13 p.m. In his remarks, he referred to Gov. Jeremiah W. "Jay"

Nixon of Missouri; and Bryan L. Hansel, president and chief executive officer, Smith Electric Vehicles U.S. Corp. The Office of the Press Secretary also released a Spanish language transcript of these remarks.

Remarks at a Fundraiser for Senatorial Candidate Robin Carnahan in Kansas City
July 8, 2010

The President. Thank you. Everybody, have a seat. Everybody, have a seat. Everybody enjoy themselves. The—how's lunch?

Audience members. It's good.

The President. All right, good.

Hello, Kansas City. It is good to be back in the Midwest, even better to be back in the Midwest with Robin Carnahan.

I—you all have had a long tradition of sending tough, independent, no-nonsense leaders to Washington, from Harry Truman to my great friend Claire McCaskill to some wonderful Missourians who go by the name of Carnahan.

Nobody fits this mold better than Robin. She's not going to Washington to represent the oil industry or the insurance industry or the banks on Wall Street. She's not even going there to represent every aspect of either party's agenda or my agenda. She's going to Washington to represent one constituency, and that's you, the people of Missouri. She's going to call them like she sees them, and she sees them the same way that most of you do, the same way that most of the people of Missouri do.

Robin's a small-business owner, still runs her family farm. That's why as your secretary of state, she cut redtape for small businesses and saved small-business owners millions of dollars so they can focus on growing their companies and creating jobs right here in this State. That's why she spent her time in office standing up for consumers, got $10 billion back for Missourians who were being taken advantage of by big institutions. That's worth applauding; $10 billion is real money. That's why she worked with Democrats and Republicans to pass one of the strictest laws in the Nation protecting seniors from fraud. That's why Missouri needs somebody like

Robin Carnahan in Washington, DC. She is a fighter, she is a survivor, and she will never forget where she comes from or who she represents. And that's why I'm glad to see that all of you are here today, because you know that about Robin.

Now, we need tough leaders like Robin in Washington because these are tough times for America; I don't need to tell you that. Eighteen months ago, I took office after almost a decade of economic policies that gave us sluggish growth and falling or flat incomes and record deficits. They were the policies that culminated in an economic crisis that was the worst since the Great Depression. Three million Americans lost their jobs in the last 6 months of 2008. The month I was sworn in, in January of 2009, more than 750,000 jobs were lost in that month alone. These aren't just numbers. Most of you in this room were either touched by this or know somebody who was.

And the policies that led to this economic disaster were pretty straightforward: You cut taxes for millionaires and billionaires who don't need the tax cuts, didn't even ask for them, you cut rules and regulations for the most powerful institutions, whether it's big banks on Wall Street or big oil companies in the Gulf, and you cut working people loose to fend for themselves. You tell them, you're on your own. You put a fancy name on it. You call it the "ownership society" or whatever the new slogan is. But it's the same policy over and over again.

And I think everybody here would agree, those policies were bad for the people of Missouri. They were bad for workers. They were bad for responsible business owners. They were bad for America. And that's why we took a different path when I got elected, so we could stop the freefall and rebuild our economy for the long run.

And our ideas have been pretty straightforward. We cut taxes—didn't raise them, we cut them—for 95 percent of working families and small-business owners, the people who needed it most and were most impacted by the recession. We're making sure that everybody—the Wall Street banks, other big corporations—are playing by the same rules as small-business owners and everybody else in America. We can't have two sets of rules. And we're investing in our people, investing in them and their future, in the skills and education of our workforce, in the research and clean energy technologies that will create thousands of new jobs and new industries and make our country competitive in the 21st century. That's our vision for America.

Now, we knew from the very beginning that some of the steps that we had to take would be difficult and unpopular. I love sometimes—the pundits will say, "Boy, Obama's doing this stuff; it's not very popular." I've got pollsters too. [*Laughter*] I know—[*applause*]—before we make decisions, we know initially how they're going to play. But our decision was not to worry about the next election. We decided to worry about the next generation.

We knew it took years to dig the hole that we were in and it would take some time to dig out, longer than anybody would like. But here's what I also knew: An economy that was shrinking, if we did what we needed to do, would be growing. And it has now been growing for the better part of a year. An economy that was once losing jobs has now been adding private sector jobs for 6 consecutive months. During that time we have created nearly 600,000 jobs in the private sector, not public sector jobs, private sector jobs—600,000.

Now, that's not enough. Not when there's still five folks out of work for every available job. Not when there are still storefronts on Main Streets all across the country that are sitting there empty. It's frustrating, and it's heartbreaking. And we've got plenty more work to do. But here's what you need to know: We are

headed in the right direction, and the last thing we should do is go back to the very ideas that got us into this mess in the first place.

That's the choice that you're going to be facing in November. It's a choice between the policies that led us into this mess and the policies that are leading us out of this mess. It's a choice between falling backwards or moving forward. Robin wants to move us forward. I want to move us forward. And I believe that you and the rest of America are ready to move forward, and that's why you're going to send Robin Carnahan to Washington, DC.

Some of the same folks in the other party whose policies gave us the economic crisis are now looking for another chance to lead. They spent nearly a decade driving the economy into the ditch, and now they're asking for the car keys back. [*Laughter*] They can't have them back. They don't know how to drive. Don't know how to drive, drive in the wrong direction, get us stuck. And by the way, Robin's opponent hasn't just been along for the ride. As one of the Republican leaders in the House of Representatives, he had his hands on the wheel. He was there giving those tax breaks to millionaires and billionaires and oil companies without paying for them, adding to our deficit, adding to our debt. He fought for fewer rules and less oversight for Wall Street—still fighting for them. That's how he makes his money.

So we already know how this story ends. We don't have to guess how the other party will govern because we're still living with the results from the last time they governed. And in the 18 months since I've been President, they have been singing from the same hymnal.

Right after I took office, we passed an economic plan that cut taxes for over 2 million Missouri families, a plan that provided more than 1,500 loans to Missouri small businesses, a plan that has extended unemployment benefits to 170,000 Missourians who lost their jobs through no fault of their own. Fifty-five thousand men and women in this State are working today because of this plan. I just met 50 of them at the Smith Electric Vehicles plant in Kansas City that I visited right before I came here.

So our plan was to provide grants to companies like Smith Electric Vehicles all across America, businesses that are investing in clean energy manufacturing and technology. Smith Electric is making the world's largest battery-electric-powered trucks. But there are also companies like Siemens Wind Power in Iowa that are making these wind turbines, delivering energy—clean energy—all across America, or Celgard in North Carolina, which is a battery technology company, or a biofuel refinery plant called POET right here in Missouri. That's how we create jobs and economic growth. That's how we ensure that America leads in the industries of the future.

I'll give you an example. Just a few years ago, America had the capacity to build only 2 percent of the world's advanced batteries for electric and hybrid cars and trucks. Today, thanks to our policies, thanks to a new focus on clean energy and the work taking place at plants like Smith Electric, in 5 years, we could have as much as 40 percent of the world's capacity to build these batteries—40 percent. That means jobs right here in Missouri. It also means we're developing the expertise in a sector that is going to keep building and growing and innovating far into the future.

That's what our economic plan is doing. Robin Carnahan supports that plan. Her opponent doesn't. Like almost every member of the other party in Congress, he said no. If he had his way, there would be a lot of Missouri families and small businesses paying higher taxes today. There would be a lot of small-business owners who wouldn't have received the loans they needed to keep their doors open and make payroll. Those jobs at Smith Electric, those clean energy jobs and businesses that our policies are supporting across America, a lot of them wouldn't be here today.

These folks in the other party in Washington want to take us backwards. But Robin and I and Claire McCaskill, Jay Nixon—we want to take America forward. And that's the choice in this election.

You'd think that after this devastating financial crisis, we'd all agree that we believe in the free market system, we want a dynamic financial sector, but it makes sense to have a little better oversight on Wall Street to prevent something like this from happening again. Right? That would be the sensible thing to do. You'd think that would be a nonpartisan issue. When we lost trillions of dollars of wealth, people's 401(k)s plunged, stock market plunged, the entire economy went into a tailspin, maybe we just want to make sure that doesn't happen again. That'd be the sensible approach.

Robin's opponent and almost all of our friends in the other party are against Wall Street reform. The Republican leader, Mr. Boehner, said this reform was like employing nuclear weapons to kill "an ant," he said. An ant—that's what he called what we just went through. You can imagine a movie: "The Ant That Ate Our Economy." It's just—[*laughter*]—that's a big ant.

So they continue to defend the status quo that got us into this mess, a system that allowed reckless speculators to gamble and left the rest of America to pay for their mistakes. That doesn't make sense to you; it doesn't make sense to me. It's not good for our country.

In the end, it's not good for all the hardworking, honest people in the financial industry who were put at a competitive disadvantage because of the recklessness of a few.

So let me tell you, when the Senate returns, we're going to pass reform that ends this era of irresponsibility, reform that protects consumers against unfair practices of credit card companies and mortgage lenders, reform that makes sure taxpayers are never again on the hook for Wall Street's mistakes.

It'd be a lot easier to get it passed—it would already have been done—if I had Robin Carnahan there. She doesn't want to move us backwards. She wants to move us forward, and that's the choice in this election. I need another vote. It'd be helpful. [*Laughter*]

Despite the growing burdens on middle class families struggling to send their kids to college, Robin's opponent and almost all of our friends in the other party voted against a law that provides billions of dollars that were going to financial institutions, senseless subsidies, and now will be going to young people for scholarships, billions of dollars for student loans paid for because we're eliminating subsidies that shouldn't have been there in the first place. Nearly a million more students from working families will have access to financial aid, access to college, because of what we did. The other side said no.

They said no to laws that we passed to stop insurance companies from denying coverage to people with preexisting conditions. They said no to requiring women to get equal pay for equal work. They said no to extended unemployment insurance for folks who desperately needed help. They said no to holding oil companies accountable when they bring on catastrophe.

You may have read the top Republican on the House Energy Committee, Mr. Barton, publicly apologizing to BP after we compelled them to set aside $20 billion to pay for the folks who have suffered as a consequence of the oil spill. Does anybody here think BP should get an apology?

Audience members. No!

The President. Mr. Barton did. He called this "a tragedy," this fund that we had set up to compensate fishermen and small-business owners throughout the Gulf. That's not the tragedy; the tragedy is if they didn't get compensated.

So this is the leadership that we've gotten from Barton and Boehner and Blunt. Sometimes I wonder if that "no" button is just stuck—[*laughter*]—in Congress, so they just—they can't do what's right for the American people.

And this isn't just about politics. But a awful lot of it has to do with politics, because I think they figure if they just keep on saying no to everything and nothing gets done, they're going to get more votes in November. The theory is, if I lose, then they win. But that's the old brand of politics. That just takes us backwards. Robin wants to move America forward. We want America to win, not just Democrats to win. That's the choice in this election. Are we all going to pull in a single direction to get this country moving?

Last point I'm going to make: Lot of our friends in the other party like to talk a big game about fiscal responsibility and out-of-control spending. Now, I'll be honest with you, it's one

of the things that keeps me up at night, thinking about all the debt and deficits that we inherited that have accumulated. Often I hear Claire McCaskill's voice in my head reminding me of that. [*Laughter*] Maybe it's just my voicemail. [*Laughter*] Robin feels the same way. She's a small-business owner. She knows about making sure that she stays on budget, that she's not spending more than she takes in. And families around the country have been tightening their belts for a few years now. So, rightly, they think it's time that their Government did the same thing.

So that's why we proposed a 3-year freeze on all Government spending outside of national security, something that was never enacted in the previous administration. That's why we've gone through the budget line by line, identified more than 120 programs for elimination. That's why we put forward a fiscal commission that's bringing both parties together to come up with a long-term solution for our deficit. And working with leaders like Claire and Robin, we're going to keep on taking the steps we need to in the months and years ahead, steps that don't just make Government leaner, but also smarter and more efficient and more accountable. That's what Harry Truman did when he fought to hold war profiteers accountable. That's what Claire and I are fighting for today.

So I got to say, when I hear the other party talking about fiscal responsibility, criticizing us for fiscal responsibility when I had a $1.3 trillion deficit wrapped in a big bow waiting for me when I got to the White House—[*laughter*]—I've got to scratch my head a little. You'd think that after turning a record Clinton surplus into a record deficit and record debt, they'd be a little shy about this. [*Laughter*] On their watch, they neglected to pay for two wars, neglected to pay for two tax cuts for the wealthiest Americans, didn't control spending, set up a worthy, but expensive prescription drug program. Didn't pay for any of it. So it's a little odd getting lectures on sobriety from folks who spent like drunken sailors for the better part of the last decade. [*Laughter*] They want to take us backwards. Robin and I and Claire, we want to take America forward. That's the choice in this election.

So here's the bottom line: These are incredibly challenging times, there's no doubt about it. And as I said every day during the campaign, change is hard. Change takes time. The problems we face have been building up for decades; they're not going to go away overnight. Not in 1 year, not in 4 years. No President, no politician has the power to snap their fingers and fix everything. A lot of folks will tell you that the closer you get to election day, that they can, but you can't believe them.

Here's what we can do, though. We can make choices about which direction we want to take this country. We can stop putting off the things that have been holding us back and going ahead and tackling them and fixing them. We can do what we've always done, whether it was on a farm or dealing with a crisis overseas: We shape our own destiny as a nation. We decide what we're going to bequeath to our children and our grandchildren.

The interests of the status quo, they'll always have the most influential and vocal defenders. There will always be lobbyists for the powerful industries that don't want more regulation or would rather see tax breaks instead of more investments in education and infrastructure. And let's face it: The prospect of change is scary, even when we know the status quo isn't working.

But there are no powerful interests to lobby for the clean energy company that may start for a few—hiring folks a few years from now or the research that may lead to a lifesaving medical breakthrough or the student who may not be able to afford a college education, but if they got that education, their dreams would not just carry them, but carry other people with them.

It's our job as a nation to advocate on behalf of the America that we hope for, even when it's not popular, even if we can't always see benefits in the short term, because we know it will pay off in the long term. It's our job to fight not just for the next election but for the next generation, for our children and our children's children.

And that's what I've tried to do every day as President. That's what Robin Carnahan will do when she is the next great Senator from the State of Missouri. I need all of you to join us on this journey. And if you're willing to make that investment, I guarantee you our better days are not behind us, they are in front of us.

Thank you very much, everybody. God bless you.

NOTE: The President spoke at 1:36 p.m. at the Kansas City Marriott Downtown hotel. In his remarks, he referred to former Sen. Jean Carnahan; Rep. J. Russell Carnahan; Missouri senatorial candidate Rep. Roy D. Blunt; and Gov. Jeremiah W. "Jay" Nixon of Missouri.

Remarks at a Rally for Senatorial Candidate Robin Carnahan in Kansas City
July 8, 2010

The President. Hello, Kansas City! Thank you. It's a nice-looking crowd. Thank you so much, everybody. Thank you, everybody. Everybody, have a seat. Everybody, have a seat. I'm going to take off my jacket; it's a little warm in here. Hello, everybody! It is good to be back in Kansas City. Good to be back.

I've got some wonderful friends here in Kansas City——

Audience member. Yes, we can!

The President. Yes, we can.

Some of you know, my mom was from Kansas. Just met a cousin I'd never met before. [*Laughter*] I did. Nice person, nice family. I've got some old friends who are here—not old in years, but have been just terrific working alongside me—Congressman and former mayor Emanuel Cleaver is in the house. Congressman Dennis Moore is here. Attorney General Chris Koster is here. One of my earliest supporters in Missouri, State Auditor Susan Montee is here. And Jackson County Executive Mike Sanders is here. And all of you are here.

And the next Senator from the great State of Missouri is here, Robin Carnahan. And the Royals have won a few games. [*Laughter*]

Now, Missouri is the "Show Me" State. It has a long tradition of no-nonsense, independent leaders going to Washington: Harry Truman, my great friend Claire McCaskill, and some wonderful Missourians who go by the name of Carnahan.

Robin is cut from this mold. She's not going to Washington to look good and—although she does look good—[*laughter*]—to be on a bunch of cable shows and represent the oil industry or the insurance industry or the big banks on Wall Street. That's not why she wants to go. She's not even going there to represent Democrats, although she's a strong Democrat. She's not going there to represent me, although she's a great friend. She's going to Washington for only one reason: to represent one constituency, and that is the people of Missouri. She will call them like she sees them, and she sees them the way you do and the way most Missourians do.

Think about her background: small-business owner, still runs the family farm just outside of Rolla. That's why, as your secretary of state, she has been looking out for you, because she knows what your lives are like—cut redtape for small businesses, saves small-business owners millions of dollars so they could focus on growing their companies and adding to their payroll, creating jobs. When she got elected, she decided, I'm going to stand up for consumers; got $10 billion back for the people of Missouri who were being taken advantage of by big institutions. That's real money. That's real money. She worked with Democrats and Republicans to pass one of the strictest laws to make sure that seniors weren't victimized by fraud.

She's got a track record of looking out for the people of Missouri, and that's why Missouri needs to send her to Washington so she can fight for you, so she doesn't forget you, so she's not wining and dining and going to the fancy cocktail parties and then coming back and acting like she's been here the whole time. [*Laughter*]

Robin's tough. And you've got to have tough leaders in Washington because, first of all, the other folks call you a lot of names. [*Laughter*] They'll just make up stuff about you. [*Laughter*] Make it up. But you got to be tough because these are also tough times for America.

Eighteen months ago when I took office, we had already gone through a decade of economic policies that had resulted in stagnant incomes, and the average wage of the average worker in America actually went down when you adjusted it for inflation during the previous 10 years before I had gotten elected. So falling or stagnant incomes, sluggish job growth, record deficits, that's what we had been going through. And they culminated—these policies culminated in the worst crisis we've had since the Great Depression.

Think about that. The Great Depression happened a long time ago, 1930s; haven't seen anything this bad as a consequence of economic policies that had been put in place. Three million Americans lost their jobs in the last 6 months of 2008. The month I got sworn in, in January, we lost 750,000 jobs that month. And these aren't just numbers. Those are real folks wondering if they can pay the mortgage, wondering if they can pay the bills, feeling desperate, some of them feeling embarrassed because maybe they can't look after their families the way they wanted to. Everybody in this room was touched by this crisis. You definitely know somebody who was.

Now, these policies were pretty straightforward. They were all spelled out. Sometimes they put fancy names on them like the "ownership society" or—you remember that? But we know what the policies were: You cut taxes for the richest people, who don't need tax cuts and weren't even asking for them—Warren Buffett got real big tax cuts that whole time—then you cut rules and regulations for the most powerful corporations, whether it's big banks on Wall Street or big oil companies who are operating in the Gulf, and then you basically say to everybody else, you're on your own.

Audience member. That's bull! [*Laughter*]

The President. But that was the philosophy, right? You don't have health insurance? Tough luck, you're on your own. Can't afford to send your kid to college? Tough luck, on your own.

Now, I think we all know these policies were bad for the people of Missouri. They were bad for workers. They were bad for responsible businesses because it put those responsible businesses at a disadvantage. If you're following rules and other folks aren't, if you're a local small-town banker and you're doing what you're supposed to be doing, lending for businesses, helping people create jobs, and the next thing you know somebody has gone off some cocka-mamie scheme with derivatives, that's not good for you. These policies were bad for America.

And that's why, when I was sworn in, we took a different path. The first thing we had to do was to stop the freefall right away. And then we had to rebuild the economy for the long run. And our policies have been pretty straightfor-ward. We didn't raise taxes; we cut taxes for 95 percent of working families and for small-busi-ness owners because that was the right thing to do, putting money in people's pockets, making sure business owners could make payroll.

We made sure that Wall Street banks and other big corporations played by the same rules as small businesses and small banks. Everybody plays by the same rules. That's not—that wasn't antibusiness; that's probusiness. It's pro–free market to make sure everybody is following the rules and there's transparency and accountabili-ty and responsibility.

And then we decided we're going to invest in America's people and in our future because we knew we couldn't go back to pretending like ev-erything was okay by maxing out our credit cards and taking out more and more home equi-ty loans and got a housing bubble that's keeping everything afloat. We knew we weren't going to be able to go back to that. So we had to invest in our long-term future: the skills and education of our workforce, research in clean energy tech-nologies that can create new jobs and industries and make us—make sure we can compete in the 21st century. That was our vision for Ameri-ca. That's what we talked about during the cam-paign, and that's what we started to deliver on.

And we knew from the very beginning that some of the steps we took would be difficult and unpopular. You know, sometimes these pundits, they can't figure me out. They say, well, why is he doing that? That doesn't poll well. Well, I've got my own pollsters, I know it doesn't poll well. [*Laughter*] But it's the right thing to do for America, and so we go ahead and do it.

That's why stuff in Washington doesn't get done. It's because people put their finger out to the wind, and they say, well, I don't know, which way is the wind blowing? [*Laughter*] So all these folks who were all getting a bunch of earmarks for everybody, spending all this mon-ey, suddenly, "Oh, no, I'm for deficit cutting," because the polls changed. Folks don't mean what they say, and they don't do what they say.

People get surprised when we follow through and keep our campaign promises. It's like, well, he went ahead and did health care. Why did he do that? [*Laughter*] I said I was going to do health care. It was the right thing to do. I made a commitment to you. We said we would do something; we did it.

Audience member. Yes, we did!

The President. Yes, we did. And we're still doing it.

We knew that it would take years to dig our-selves out of the hole that we found ourselves in. And that's longer than any of us would like. But here's what I also know: An economy that was shrinking, it's been growing for the better part of a year. An economy that was losing jobs, we've now had 6 consecutive months of private sector job growth; there's 600,000 private sector jobs.

It's not enough. There are still folks out of work. But we are moving in the right direction. And I know when Robin Carnahan gets there, she's going to help us keep on moving in the right direction. That's why I need you to elect Robin Carnahan.

You're going to face a choice in November, and I want everybody to be very clear about what that choice is. This is a choice between the policies that got us into this mess in the first place and the policies that are getting us out of this mess. And what the other side is counting on is people not having a very good memory. [*Laughter*] Think about it. I mean, they're not making any new arguments. They're not coming back and saying, you know what, we really screwed up, but we've learned our lesson, and now we've got this new approach, and this is how things are going to turn out really well. That's not their argument. They are trying to sell you the same stuff that they've been peddling——

Audience members. No!

The President. I'm just saying. [*Laughter*] They are peddling that same snake oil that they've been peddling now for years. And somehow they think you will have forgotten that it didn't work.

Audience member. Kick them out!

The President. Well, we did kick them out, because it wasn't working. You know, the—I don't have teenagers yet; Malia's just turned 12—[*laughter*].

Audience member. Good luck!

The President. Say, good luck, huh? [*Laughter*] She's my baby. She's going—[*laughter*]— even though she's 5′9″ now—[*laughter*]—she's still my baby. And she just got braces, which is good because, you know, she looks like a kid, and she was getting—I was—she's starting to look too old for me. [*Laughter*]

But I digress. What was my point? [*Laughter*] Here was my point: I don't have a teenager yet, but in a couple years, Malia is going to be able to drive, right? She gets—that's what happens with teenagers, right, they go get the learner's permit, they—now, if your teenager drives into a ditch, your car, bangs it up, you've got to pay a lot of money to get it out, what do you do? You take the keys away. [*Laughter*]

These folks drove the economy into a ditch, and they want the keys back. And you got to say the same thing to them that you say to your teenager: You can't have the keys back because you don't know how to drive yet. You can't have the keys. You can't have them. Maybe you take a remedial course. [*Laughter*] I'll take you out to the parking lot, and you can drive in circles. [*Laughter*] But we're not going to let you out on the open road. You can't drive. [*Laughter*]

And by the way, Robin's opponent, he wasn't just along for the ride. He was the guy—one of the guys with his hand on the wheel when it drove into the ditch. He's the guy who gave tax breaks to billionaires. He's the guy who gave tax breaks to oil companies. He's the guy who wanted to deregulate and eliminate oversight for Wall Street. And that's who he still works for, how he makes his money.

So we know how this movie ends, right? We don't want to see it again. [*Laughter*] We've seen this one. They're trying to run the okey-doke on you. [*Laughter*] Trying to bamboozle you. So that made you laugh, huh, okeydoke. You remember that? [*Laughter*]

But that's what they're trying to do. They run these ads thinking, well, we might be able to fool them one more time. [*Laughter*] This might work again. It's not going to work. We don't have to guess how the other party will govern because we're still living with the results from the last time. They are still singing from the same hymnbook.

Right after I took office, we passed an economic plan, cut taxes for 2 million families here in Missouri—didn't raise taxes, cut taxes for 2 million—because that's what was necessary to give the economy a boost. It provided 1,500 loans to Missouri's small businesses so they could keep their doors open, extended unemployment benefits for 170,000 Missourians who had lost their jobs through no fault of their own. Fifty-five thousand men and women in this State are working because of this plan. Jay Nixon didn't have to lay off as many teachers or police officers or firefighters because of this plan.

I was just over at Smith Electric Vehicles— very cool plant right out at the airport. They are making these electric trucks, cutting-edge stuff. And 50 new employees there, making these brand-spanking-new electric trucks that are being used by companies like Frito-Lay and Pepsi-Co. Those folks wouldn't have a job if it hadn't been for the fact that we decided we need to invest in clean energy all across America—all across America.

You know what? The other party, they said no to all this. Just said no, we're not going to do it. So those 50 workers at Smith Electric would not have a job making electric trucks that are going to lead us into the future, a whole bunch of teachers would be out of work, the economy would still be in the ditch.

They say no to everything. Don't they, though?

Audience members. Yes!

The President. Everything. And I go and I talk to them, and I say, come on, we can get something going here. No! [*Laughter*] Don't want to.

We decided, you know what, since this financial crisis wrecked havoc, cost the American people trillions of dollars of wealth, retirees see their 401(k)s plunge, businesses suddenly shuttered, you know it might be smart for us to try to prevent this from happening again. Right? That's some common sense.

So we craft this very carefully, this financial regulatory bill, to make sure that consumers are protected from predatory loans and credit card abuses, to make sure that we never have another taxpayer bailout because we can shut down one firm without—and quarantine it so it doesn't affect all the other firms. We put tons of work into this thing, consult with everybody. What does the other side say?

Audience members. No!

The President. No! The leader of the Republican Party in the House of Representatives, John Boehner, he says: "Well, we don't need all this. This is like using a nuclear weapon to kill an ant." The worst crisis since the Great Depression he calls an ant. You got to make a movie: "The Ant That Ate the Economy." [*Laughter*] An ant.

We just—we thought that it made sense for us to do something about Wall Street, but they don't. I think most Missourians want to see something done. So does Robin Carnahan. That's why you need to send her to the Senate instead of the other guy, because she gets it. She understands what you've been going through, and this is not a game to her. These are real lives at stake.

We said during the campaign, you know what, our future is going to depend on education. And we've got to get back to the point where we send more people to college than any other country. That's a goal I set for 2020: I want the most college graduates here in the United States than in any country in the world.

Now, some of that means making sure parents are parenting, turning off the TV set, instilling a sense of excellence in our kids. You know, Xbox, PlayStation, you just got to put those away for a while. Hit the books. Do your

math. Read. But even students who do well, a lot of them can't afford to go to college.

So what did we do? We decided, you know what, as part of our overall education reform—raising standards, initiating reforms—here's what we'll do. The Government student loan program was going through banks and financial intermediaries, middlemen, and they were siphoning off billions of dollars in subsidies. Now, the loans were guaranteed, so they weren't taking any risk. They were just taking the money.

So we said, you know what, we'll eliminate the subsidies. And that will give tens of billions of dollars in additional money to student loans. We passed that bill. One million more students are getting student loans now, financial aid, because of what we did. You know what the other side said?

Audience members. No!

The President. No! Said no. How do you say no to that? [*Laughter*] But they did. Got no support for it.

Robin Carnahan understands that young people need help getting to college. That's why you need to send her to the Senate, not the other guy, because she knows what your life is like, she knows what you're going through.

Most recently, obviously, we've had this oil spill, an environmental disaster. And it's going to take some time for us to clean it up. But the first thing that we could do was to say all those fishermen down there, all those small-business owners who've got maybe a little restaurant, they rely on tourist season, we've got to make them whole. BP has got to pay.

And so we—so I met with BP. I want BP to do well because obviously their ability to pay depends on them staying solvent. But I said to them, do right by these folks. And they agreed to put together a $20 billion fund to make sure that everybody was being compensated. Seems pretty sensible, doesn't it? I mean, I know you're a friendly crowd, but even if you weren't a friendly crowd, you'd kind of say, well, that makes sense, right? They caused this big disaster and they pay the people who've been hurt by it.

So I've got the House Republican chairman of the Energy Committee, who has jurisdiction over the oil companies—he, in a hearing, says to them, "I apologize that the President strong-armed you, Chicago-style." [*Laughter*] "I apologize. I think this is a tragedy that you are being made to compensate these folks." Really? [*Laughter*] I mean, when I heard that I was—I said, no, he didn't say that. [*Laughter*] No, he didn't say that. [*Laughter*] But he did. Because they don't think in terms of representing ordinary folks. That's not their orientation.

So that's the choice that we face in this election. You've got the Bartons, the Boehners, and the Blunts. They've got that "no" philosophy, that "you're on your own" philosophy, the status quo philosophy, a philosophy that says everything is politics and we're just going to gun for the next election, we don't care what it means for the next generation. And they figure if they just keep on saying no, it will work for them, they'll get more votes in November, because if Obama loses, they win; if we can stop him, then we'll look better.

But that's not what's going to lead our country out of this mess that we're in. That just takes us backwards. We need to move forward. Robin Carnahan wants to move forward. Missouri wants to move forward. America wants to move forward. That's the choice in this election: moving backward or moving forward.

And if you fight for Robin Carnahan and if you work for Robin Carnahan, then I guarantee you that she will make sure that America moves forward and Missouri moves forward and people are put back to work and we are building a clean energy future and we are making sure that small businesses are prospering. That's what we're fighting for. That's what you are fighting for. Let's make this happen, Missouri.

Thank you. God bless you, and God bless the United States of America.

NOTE: The President spoke at 2:23 p.m. at the Folly Theater. In his remarks, he referred to former Sen. Jean Carnahan; Rep. J. Russell Carnahan; Warren E. Buffett, chief executive officer and chairman, Berkshire Hathaway Inc.; Missouri senatorial candidate Rep. Roy D. Blunt; Gov. Jeremiah W. "Jay" Nixon of Missouri; and Rep. Joseph L. Barton. A portion of these remarks could not be verified because the audio was incomplete.

Statement on the European Union-United States Agreement on the Terrorist Finance Tracking Program
July 8, 2010

The United States welcomes today's decision by the European Parliament to join the Council and Commission of the European Union in approving a revised agreement between the United States and the European Union on the processing and transfer of financial messaging data for the Terrorist Finance Tracking Program (TFTP). We look forward to the Council's completion of the process, allowing the agreement to enter into force on August 1, 2010, thus fully restoring this important counterterrorism tool and resuming the sharing of investigative data that has been suspended since January 2010. The threat of terrorism faced by the United States and the European Union continues, and with this agreement all of our citizens will be safer.

The TFTP has provided critical investigative leads—more than 1,550 to EU member states—since its creation after the September 11, 2001, terrorist attacks. These leads have aided countries around the world in preventing or investigating many of the past decade's most visible and violent terrorist attacks and attempted attacks, including Bali (2002), Madrid (2004), London (2005), the liquids bomb plot against transatlantic aircraft (2006), New York's John F. Kennedy Airport (2007), Germany (2007), Mumbai (2008), and Jakarta (2009).

This new, legally binding agreement reflects significant additional data privacy safeguards, but still retains the effectiveness and integrity of this indispensable counterterrorism program.

Protecting privacy and civil liberties is a top priority of the Obama administration. We are determined to protect citizens of all nations while also upholding fundamental rights, using every legitimate tool available to combat terrorism that is consistent with our laws and principles.

The United States values the European Union's partnership in meeting the complex challenges of this era. Putting the TFTP on this cooperative course is another example of how we can work with our European partners to prevent terrorism and simultaneously respect the rule of law. This cooperation strengthens our transatlantic ties and makes all our people safer.

Remarks at a Fundraiser for Senator Harry M. Reid in Las Vegas, Nevada
July 8, 2010

The President. Hello, Nevada! Hello, Vegas! *Si se puede!* Oh, it is good to be back in Vegas. This is a pretty good crowd. I know you're disappointed, but I'm not singing tonight. [*Laughter*]

Listen, I love being in Vegas again, love being in Vegas. I love this town. Maybe not as much as my staff. [*Laughter*] For some reason, every time we come here, Air Force One is a little more crowded. [*Laughter*] It's like I'm seeing people in the couches and——

Audience member. We love you, Obama!

The President. I love you back. I love you back. A couple other people I love here. I want to make mention—Congresswoman Dina Titus is in the house. There she is right there. Love Dina. Secretary of State Ross Miller is in the house; give a big round of applause to Ross, right here. One of my earliest supporters, not just here in Nevada, but anywhere in the country, State Senate Majority Leader Steven Horsford is in the house. He's somewhere out here. Your wonderful speaker of the State assembly, Barbara Buckley, is here.

Give it up for Brandon, David, and Mark, The Killers. These guys, by the way, for the Fourth of July performed for military families in the South Lawn, and so have just been unbelievable for us. Really nice guys; they don't look like killers, let's face it. [*Laughter*] I mean, one of them is tall, but they don't look like you'd be scared of them. [*Laughter*] But they are wonderful people, and we are grateful to them. And then how about Sarah McLachlan? She was—I met her backstage—just delightful, and a couple of beautiful daughters. And I'm always partial to daughters. [*Laughter*]

Now, despite the entertainment, despite the nice digs, despite seeing all these old friends, the main reason I'm here is because there's a guy from Searchlight, Nevada, who has been fighting on behalf of Nevada for most of his life and is now fighting for working families all across America, and that's your Senate majority leader, Harry Reid.

I have known Harry since I arrived in the Senate 5 years ago, and we have become dear friends. He is a man of principle. He is a straight shooter. He is a man of his word. He comes across as soft-spoken—you know, how he's all like, "Well, you know." [*Laughter*] Even when he's in front of a big crowd, he's like, "Well, you know." [*Laughter*] "Okay, okay, we're trying here, trying hard." [*Laughter*] I mean, that's just how Harry is. But anybody who knows Harry knows he is made of strong stuff. This is one tough guy. A lot of people talk tough; Harry is tough.

A lot of people in Washington forget where they came from. Harry remembers every single day. A lot of people, instead of taking the tough votes, showing leadership, making difficult decisions, they do what's politically expedient. They're not making the choices that give them the best chance of staying in Washington. That's not Harry Reid. He doesn't always do what's easy. He doesn't always do what is popular. But he always does what's right for the people of Nevada. And that's why you've got to send him back there for one more term. As Senate majority leader, he has always done what's right. You've got to send him back.

You know, Harry used to be a boxer. He likes to brag about this. [*Laughter*] But it's—you know, he brags in his Harry way—he's all, "Well, I used to box." [*Laughter*] He'll say, "You know, I wasn't the most talented guy." [*Laughter*] "I wasn't very fast. I wasn't big, obviously." [*Laughter*] "But I could take a punch. I could take a punch."

He would outlast the other guy. And that's exactly how Harry Reid has been able to orchestrate one of the most productive legislative sessions in the history of America. And that's how he's going to win this race, so he can serve the people of Nevada one more time.

He's taken his lumps. We all have. But I have no doubt that the people of Nevada will realize the quality of public servant that they have in Harry Reid, partly because he knows no matter what kind of lumps he's taking, they're nothing compared to the lumps that folks back home have been taking.

Harry comes from humble beginnings. He knows what it's like not to have a lot. He knows what it's like to see your folks scraping by and have to tell you, no, I'm sorry, we can't afford this, we can't afford that. He's been there. And so when he hears the stories of Nevadans who are losing their homes, or he hears stories of Nevadans who have lost their jobs, when he hears stories about people who are feeling desperate, who, after doing the right thing, somehow have gotten the short end of the stick, that's who he identifies with. That's who he's fighting for.

I just came from the birthplace of another Harry, a guy named Harry Truman. Harry Truman was a lot like Harry Reid. You know, in 1948, Harry Truman campaigned across this country, making the case against the do-nothing Republicans in Congress. Right?

For the last 2 years, Harry has been dealing with the do-nothing Republican leadership in the Senate, just like Harry Truman. But despite all their tactics, despite all their political maneuvering, he's just been steady, and we keep on making progress. He does not give up; he does not give in. He keeps on fighting, and he outlasts them. And he's changed the landscape of America as a consequence.

We need Harry Reid because we've taken quite a few punches as a nation. About 17

months ago, I took office after almost a decade of economic policies that gave us sluggish job growth, falling incomes, a record deficit—I want everybody to remember this—a decade of economic policies that culminated in the worst crisis since the Great Depression.

Three million Americans had lost their jobs in the last 6 months of 2008. Another 750,000 Americans lost their jobs the month I was sworn in. The month I was sworn in—the next month, it was 600,000. And these weren't just numbers. Most of you have somebody in your family who was touched by this crisis, if you weren't yourself.

And the economic policies that led to this economic disaster were pretty straightforward. Harry mentioned it: You cut taxes for millionaires and billionaires, even if they don't need them and weren't even asking for them, you cut rules and regulations for the most powerful industries—big banks on Wall Street, big oil in the Gulf—and then you cut working families loose. You tell people, you're on your own. You don't have health care? Too bad, you're on your own. Young person born into poverty, can't afford college—tough luck, you're on your own. That was their reigning philosophy. They might call it different things, the "ownership society" or laissez-faire or whatever, but this was their philosophy.

Now, I want somebody to argue that somehow this was working well for the people in Nevada.

Audience members. No!

The President. It was bad for workers, it was bad for business owners, and it was bad for this country. And that's why, with Harry Reid's help, I took a different path as President. I had a different philosophy, one that's based on how do we help ordinary families seize opportunity and use their innovation and their drive to rebuild an America that's stronger than before. That was our job. That was our task.

So we've got a different philosophy. We said we'd cut taxes for the 95 percent of working families and small-business owners who really needed help in this recession. We believe in the free market, but we also think that everybody should be following basic rules of the road, so we made sure Wall Street banks and other big corporations have to play by the same rules that small banks and small-business owners have to play with. That just makes sense. There shouldn't be two sets of rules. There shouldn't be loopholes and special tax breaks and lack of oversight. And we decided that we were going to invest in our people and in our future, in the skills and education of our workforce, in the research and clean energy technologies that will create new jobs and new industries and make sure America is competitive in the 21st century. That's our vision for America.

Now, since we had a crisis on our hands, since the financial system was melting down, since we—people couldn't get auto loans, couldn't get home loans, people weren't traveling. You remember. You remember last year. So we had to make a bunch of decisions, and we had to make them fast. And they were tough decisions, difficult decisions. Some of them weren't popular.

Audience member. It's all right.

The President. And by the way—well, I know it's all right, because you know what? Let me tell you something. As we were making these decisions, sometimes the pundits would say, boy, you know, why is he doing that, why is Harry Reid doing that? That's not going to be popular. Well, we've got poll. You know, Harry Reid and I, we've got pollsters. They let us know when things aren't going to be popular. [*Laughter*] It's not like we were surprised. [*Laughter*] But my job isn't to put my finger up to the wind and see which way the wind is blowing. That's not Harry Reid's job. That's not leadership. Our job is to focus not on the next election but on the next generation, and that's why we made those decisions.

We knew it would take us months, years to dig ourselves out of the holes that we found ourselves in. That's longer than anybody would like, but here's what I also know: An economy that last year was shrinking by 6 percent is now growing; an economy that was shredding jobs at an unbelievable pace, we've now had 6 months in a row of private sector job growth. That's because of policies that Harry Reid helped bring

about. We have turned things around, and we are moving in the right direction.

Now, that's not enough. It hasn't moved as fast as I want. I'm not going to be satisfied and Harry won't be satisfied until everybody in Nevada who wants a job can find a job. We don't want to just survive; we want to thrive. We want Nevada to be on the move. We want the Las Vegas dream to be a reality for everybody. And so we understand we've got a lot of work to do.

Basically, the other party, their whole argument is based on the notion, well, it hasn't moved fast enough. Well, I agree. I'd like to see us get out of this hole sooner, but you have to understand we are heading in the right direction. And what the other side is offering is basically to go back to the same ideas that got us into this mess in the first place. That's all they're doing.

This is a choice between the policies that led us into the mess or the policies that are leading us out of the mess. This is the choice between falling backwards or moving forward. Now, I don't know about you, but Harry Reid wants to move forward. I want to move forward. I think most people in Nevada want to move forward. They don't want to go backwards. America doesn't go backwards, we go forward. That's who we are as Americans.

What the other party is counting on is that all of you don't have very good memories. [*Laughter*] I mean, think about it. They're not making new arguments. It's not like they're coming back and saying, you know what, we know we screwed up, and we learned from our mistakes, and we're going to do things differently this time. That's not what you're hearing. They are peddling the same stuff they've been peddling for years and years and years.

They basically—they spent a decade driving the economy into a ditch, and now they're asking for the keys back. [*Laughter*] And my answer is, no, you can't have the keys. You can't drive. You don't know how to drive. You drive in the wrong direction. You can't have them back. We're just getting the car out of the ditch. We can't have you drive it back in the ditch.

Harry Reid and I, we got mud on our shoes. We're—we've been pushing and shoving, car is just kind of getting out, almost on some pavement. [*Laughter*] Suddenly, they're all, "No, no, we want to pull into reverse." [*Laughter*] Run right over Harry and me. [*Laughter*] Get you back in the mud. That doesn't make sense.

I mean, look, Harry Reid's opponent doesn't just believe in these old, worn-out theories. On a lot of these issues, she favors an approach that's even more extreme than the Republicans we got in Washington. [*Laughter*] That's saying something. [*Laughter*] That is saying something. I mean, she wants to phase out and privatize Social Security and Medicare.

Audience members. Boo!

The President. Phase out and privatize them.

Audience member. Phase her out. [*Laughter*]

The President. Wants to eliminate our investment in clean energy. Wants to eliminate the Federal investment in our children's educations.

Audience members. Boo!

The President. Said the answer to the BP oil spill is to deregulate the oil industry.

Audience members. No!

The President. I'm not making this up. Harry, am I making this up? [*Laughter*] I know some of you are saying, no, she didn't really say that. [*Laughter*] She said it. She said that if only there were fewer rules and safeguards, then BP would have been more careful—[*laughter*]—about their drilling.

Some of you might have heard about the Republican Congressman who apologized to BP. I think you heard Harry mention him. This, by the way, is the guy who heads up the Energy Committee for the Republicans. We decided, let's get $20 billion to make sure fishermen and small-businesspeople and hotels are compensated for their loss. That makes sense. I mean, most people around the country, it doesn't matter whether you're Democrat, Republican, Independent, you'd say, well, yes, of course that makes sense. They shouldn't be punished for somebody else's carelessness.

Well, this Congressman, he, in a hearing, apologized to BP executives, said that the fund we'd set up was a "tragedy," a "shakedown." A tragedy? You think about all those people down there who—a lot of folks down there, just like

Vegas, rely on tourism. And it's much more seasonal than Vegas, so they've got basically 3, 4 months where they make money for the entire year. You talk to some fishermen—they had already—or guys who own boats who take fishermen out—they'd already bought all their supplies, bought all their gasoline, and suddenly, that's it, wiped out. That's the tragedy. It's not asking BP to do what's right and what's fair.

But Harry's opponent, she agreed with this guy. She called the compensation we're providing a "slush fund."

Audience members. Boo!

The President. To compensate fishermen and compensate shrimpers and compensate small-restaurant owners.

Now, a few hours later, her campaign puts out a memo saying, well, she didn't mean that. [*Laughter*] They said there was some, quote, "confusion." [*Laughter*] And I'm sure she meant "slush fund" in the nicest possible way. [*Laughter*]

Let me tell you, most of the Nevadans I meet—and I've spent a lot of time here; you know that. [*Laughter*] I've been seeing you. Most of the people I meet here in this State, they don't think like that. They don't subscribe to that kind of thinking. So why would you want somebody who has that philosophy representing the people of Nevada?

Audience members. No!

The President. You need somebody like Harry Reid representing you in Nevada.

My simple point is this: You have a choice in this election. And look, obviously, you're here, you guys are some diehards, you guys are supporters, and you need to be energized in this election. But when you're talking to your friends and your neighbors, and they're not following politics as closely, they're not sure how things should go, they're frustrated about what's happening, and they say, ah, it doesn't make any difference, you have to remind them, it makes a difference. There is a real choice here. We know how the movie ends if the other party is in charge. [*Laughter*] You don't have to guess how they'll govern because we're still living with the damage from the last time they were governing. And they're singing from the same hymnal.

They haven't changed. They want to do the same stuff.

Right after we took office, working with Harry, we passed tax cuts for over 1 million families here in Nevada, made over 400 loans to Nevada's small businesses, extended unemployment benefits to 300,000 Nevadans who'd lost their jobs. Twenty-seven thousand men and women in this State are working today because of what Harry Reid did. They're in clean energy companies, producing solar power and geothermal power and new jobs.

That's what Harry Reid fought for, but you know what, his opponent, she's got a different way of seeing things. And if we had had her way, there would be a lot of Nevada families and small businesses right now paying higher taxes. There would be a lot of small-business owners who wouldn't have received those loans to keep their doors open and make payroll. Those 27,000 jobs, they wouldn't be there today. All that clean energy work that those companies are doing wouldn't be here today. They want to take us backwards. We want to move forwards. That's the choice in this election.

You would have thought that after this financial crisis—bear with me here, because you might be scratching your head—you would think that everybody would agree that proper oversight over the financial sector would be the smart thing to do, just to prevent this from happening again. We want businesses to thrive. We want banks to thrive. But we want to make sure that they're doing sensible things. We don't want them selling crazy derivatives that nobody understands. We don't want them selling subprime mortgages with fine print that result in people losing their homes and entire communities collapsing. We don't want them overcharging people on their credit cards for hidden fees.

So we—so Harry and I and a bunch of people just tried to put together a sensible bit of reform. Now, the Republican leader in the House says, no, we can't do that; we're against that. He says having this big financial regulatory reform, that's "like killing an ant with a nuclear weapon." That's what he said. [*Laughter*] So he thinks the worst crisis since the worst—since the Great Depression, he analogized to an ant.

It's like it should be a movie: "The Ant That Ate the Economy." [*Laughter*]

So all the Republicans—a whole bunch of the Republican leadership fought against Wall Street reform. There are a handful of Republicans who are supporting it, and we appreciate that. And they're pretty much the same handful that have been supporting us on just about everything, and they're good people. But Harry's opponent said she'd leave everything exactly the way it is, the status quo.

Now, I don't believe in the status quo. Harry Reid doesn't believe in the status quo. You don't believe in the status quo.

Audience members. No!

The President. So thanks to Harry's leadership, we are about to pass this landmark legislation that will end this era of irresponsibility. That's the kind of leadership that you'll have in place. That's what he's fighting for. That's why you've got to send him back for one more term.

You go through the list. Health care—now, this is an interesting example. People in Washington, they were all surprised when I said, "Well, I said in the campaign I was going to do health care, so yes, we're going to do health care reform."

They said: "Well, no, this is hard. This is hard. You're going to use up a lot of political capital." They said the same thing to Harry: "Harry, you're going to have a tough race. You don't want to do this. This is hard." But we said we were going to do it because we had met too many families out there who, because of a preexisting condition, couldn't get insurance. We had met folks working two, three jobs, still couldn't get insurance. We'd met too many people who had hit lifetime limits, couldn't get insurance. So we said, we're going to do the right thing. And we did it, even though it was hard, because it was the right thing to do.

Now, not only do the folks in the other party say no to reform, now they say they want to repeal it, go back to the days when insurance companies could jack up your rates any time they felt like it or drop your coverage when you get sick. That's going backwards. What do you want to do?

Audience members. Forward!

The President. I want to go forward. But in order to go forward, you got to send Harry for another term as the senior Senator from Nevada.

Look, the bottom line is this: This is going to be a tough race. Harry reminds me, he's never been in an easy race. [*Laughter*] That's because he talks softly and he says, "Well, you know"—[*laughter*]. "I don't like to brag about myself." [*Laughter*] "I'm from Searchlight." [*Laughter*]

So Harry is always in a tough race. He's just not a flashy guy. I mean, considering we're in Vegas, you'd think somebody could give him some tips. [*Laughter*] You know, spruce up the wardrobe a little bit—[*laughter*]—take some voice lessons. [*Laughter*] So he's always in a tough race. But ultimately, what you want out of your elected officials is somebody who knows your life, who remembers what it's like to struggle so that when we're making a whole bunch of decisions that continue to face us over the next several months and the next several years, that person is going to advocate for you. He's going to have you in mind when he's deciding, are we going to have an energy future that is clean and bright and creating jobs and allowing us to compete? Are we going to make sure that young people continue to get the student loans and scholarships they need so we've got the best trained workforce in the world?

Are we finally going to get our budget and our debt under control in a way that doesn't do it on the backs of working families? Let me just talk about—let me talk about this whole debt and deficit thing. This keeps me up at night. We've got serious issues with debt and debt—deficits and debt.

Now, keep in mind that we had a surplus—you remember that?—with the last Democratic President. Do you remember that? But when I walked in—this is right in the middle of this huge crisis—what had been a record surplus was suddenly a $1.3 trillion deficit. That was when we walked in. All right?

So we said, even though we're doing all these other things, even though we're giving tax cuts, even though we have to make sure that small businesses get loans, even though we are making sure that the economy stays afloat, despite

all that, let's start taking some steps that over the long term can help control the budget.

So I proposed a 3-year freeze on all Government spending outside of national security, something that was never enacted by the previous administration. And then we identified 120 Government programs that weren't working that well. So we said, let's eliminate those and consolidate and streamline and make them work. And then I—then we said, well, let's form a bipartisan fiscal commission, an idea of a Republican Senator and a Democratic Senator, the two leading experts on the budget in the Senate. Let's go ahead and adopt this proposal to come up with a long-term solution on how we're going to deal with entitlements and all this stuff.

Now, here's what happens. Harry knows this; Harry remembers this. We had seven Republicans who were sponsors of this fiscal commission. They said, we've got to deal with the deficit, we've got to deal with the debt. So I say, okay, let's do it. I make an announcement. And in front of the entire country I said, I embrace this bipartisan fiscal commission idea. Let's get this legislation passed. I'll sign it into law. Next thing you know, the seven folks on the Republican side who had been cosponsors of it voted against it—[*laughter*]—their legislation.

Now, this is typical. So look, I don't want you guys to get bamboozled. I don't want—when these folks start running the okeydoke on you, I want you to be clear. [*Laughter*] When they start intoning about how "we care so much about the deficit and debt" and "we're tired of this out-of-control Government spending," look, these are the folks who delivered to you a structural debt—deficits that broke the record, turned record surpluses into record deficits. So this is like a lecture on sobriety from folks who had been spending money like drunken sailors. [*Laughter*] You don't want to put them in charge. You definitely don't want to put them behind the wheel. Given their track record, they've been weaving on the road when it comes to fiscal responsibility. That's part of the reason they drove us into the ditch. Don't give them the keys back.

You got to make sure that Harry Reid is in a position to look after you when we make these difficult debates. So here's my hope. This is going to be a close election. Everybody here, I expect, will vote for Harry. That's good. Everybody here will vote for Harry. And a couple of you who won't—he—you know, because you're scouting out what we're saying—[*laughter*]—that's okay. That's part of politics. And then the other two of you who thought this was how you got to the slots. [*Laughter*] But all the rest of you, you're going to all vote for Harry Reid.

But it's not enough for you just to vote for him. I need you to work for him. I need you to knock on doors for him. I need you to make phone calls for him. Don't do it for me. Do it for you. More importantly, do it for your children and do it for your grandchildren. And do it because despite the storm clouds we've been going through, you see out in the horizon a future that's bright.

You see a future where we're no longer relying just on dirty energy and expensive energy, but clean energy. And it's creating jobs all across Nevada. We're harnessing the sun and the wind. You see a future where every child in Nevada has a world-class education, and they're getting the jobs of the future. You see a future where health care is available for every Ameri-

can, and we're driving the costs of health care down for every American. And you see a future where we're respected around the world. And you see a future where you can retire with dignity and respect. And you see a future where our air and water is clean. And you see a future where the 21st century is just like the 20th century: It is the American century.

And you know in your heart of hearts the only way that's going to happen is if we make sure that leaders with the integrity and honesty and the willingness to take tough decisions like Harry Reid are sent back to Washington to fight for you. I need you to work for Harry Reid. And if you do, then our future is, indeed, bright and Nevada's future is bright and Las Vegas future is bright.

Thank you very much, everybody. God bless you. God bless the United States of America.

NOTE: The President spoke at 6:25 p.m. at the ARIA Resort & Casino. In his remarks, he referred to musicians Brandon Flowers, Mark Stoermer, David Keuning, and Ronnie Vannucci; India Ann and Taja Sood, daughters of musician Sarah McLachlan; Nevada senatorial candidate Sharron Angle; Rep. Joseph L. Barton; and Sens. Judd A. Gregg and G. Kent Conrad.

Remarks at the University of Nevada, Las Vegas, in Las Vegas
July 9, 2010

The President. Thank you, everybody. Good to see you. Thank you. Please have a seat. Have a seat. Well, thank you, Harry. Thanks for giving me a chance to get out of Washington. It's very hot there. [*Laughter*] It's hot here too, but there's a little more humidity there. And I just love coming to Vegas. I love being here. I mentioned last night, I'm not the only one who loves it, because I noticed that, for some reason, Air Force One is more crowded when we're coming to Vegas. [*Laughter*] Somehow I need more staff and logistical support and a couple extra Secret Service guys. [*Laughter*]

We've got some wonderful leaders here, and I just want to acknowledge them very quickly. U.S. Representative Dina Titus is here, doing a

great job. And Nevada's secretary of state, Ross Miller, is here. Dr. Neal Smatresk is here, and his family. And they're doing a great job on behalf of UNLV. And all of you are here. And I am thrilled to see you.

But I'm especially here to be with my friend and your Senator, Harry Reid. One of the first stories I heard about Harry was that he was a boxer back in the day here in Nevada. And I was mentioning last—she's laughing, she's, "Oh, I can't believe it." [*Laughter*] No, he was. [*Laughter*] You wouldn't know that because he's so soft-spoken. You know, he's all, "Well, I'm Harry Reid." [*Laughter*] But when he first told me he was a boxer, he said, "Barack, I wasn't the fastest, I wasn't the hardest hitting, but I knew how to take a punch." [*Laughter*] He knew how to take a punch. And Harry Reid became a pretty good boxer because he would simply outlast his opponents. He had a stronger will.

And I think that tells you something about the kind of person he is, the kind of Senator he is, the kind of Senate majority leader he is. He is a fighter, and you should never bet against him. And that's just what we need right now. That's what Nevada needs right now. That's what Nevada needs, is somebody who's going to fight for the people of Nevada and for the American people.

And you know that he wasn't born with a silver spoon in his mouth, in Searchlight, Nevada. So when you're going through tough times, Harry Reid has been there. He knows what it feels like to be scraping and scrimping, and struggle to make ends meet. And so when his home State is having a tough time, when the country is having a tough time, he knows that he's got to be fighting on behalf of not those who are powerful, but on behalf of those who need help the most.

Now, let me tell you, when we first took office, amidst the worst economy since the Great Depression, we needed Harry's fighting spirit, because we had lost nearly 3 million jobs during the last 6 months of 2008. The month I was sworn in, January 2009, we lost 750,000 jobs in that month alone. The following month we lost 600,000 jobs. And these were all the consequence of a decade of misguided economic policies, a decade of stagnant wages, a decade of declining incomes, a decade of spiraling deficits.

So our first mission was to break the momentum of the deepest and most vicious recession since the Great Depression. We had to stop the freefall and get the economy and jobs growing again. And digging out of this mess required us taking some tough decisions, and sometimes those decisions were not popular. And Harry knew they weren't popular. I knew they weren't popular. But they were the right thing to do.

And Harry was willing to lead those fights because he knew that we had to change course, that to do nothing, to simply continue with the policies that had gotten us into this mess in the first place would mean further disaster. And to fail to act on some of the great challenges facing the country that we had been putting off for decades would mean a lesser future for our children and our grandchildren.

Now, as a result of those tough steps that we took, we're in a different place today than we were a year ago. An economy that was shrinking is now growing. We've gained private sector jobs for each of the past 6 months instead of losing them, almost 600,000 new jobs.

But as Harry pointed out, that's not enough. I don't have to tell you that. The unemployment rate is still unacceptably high, particularly in some States like Nevada. And a lot of you have felt that pain personally or you've got somebody in your family who's felt the pain. Maybe you found yourself underwater on your mortgage and faced the terrible prospect of losing your home. Maybe you're out of work and worried about how you're going to provide for your family. Or maybe you're a student at UNLV, and you're wondering if you're going to be able to find a job when you graduate, or if you're going to be able to pay off your student loans, or if you're going to be able to start your career off on the right foot.

Now, the simple truth is it took years to dig this hole; it's going to take more time than any of us would like to climb out of it. But the question is, number one, are we on the right track? And the answer is, yes. And number two, how do we accelerate the process? How do we get the recovery to pick up more steam? How do we fill this hole faster?

There's a big debate in Washington right now about the role that Government should play in all this. As I said in the campaign, and as I've repeated many times as President, the greatest generator of jobs in America is our private sector. It's not Government. It's our entrepreneurs and innovators who are willing to take a chance on a good idea. It's our businesses, large and small, who are making payroll and working with suppliers and distributing goods and services across the country and now across the world.

The private sector, not Government, is, was, and always will be the source of America's economic success. That's our strength, the dynamism of our economy. And that's why one of the first things Harry Reid did, one of the first things we did, was cut dozens of taxes—not raise them, cut them—for middle class and small-businesspeople. And we extended loan programs to put capital in the hands of startups. And we worked to reduce the cost of health care for small businesses.

And right now Harry is fighting to pass additional tax breaks and loan authority to help small businesses grow and hire all across the country. But he has also tried to look out specifically for Nevada. He understands, for example, that tourism is so enormous an aspect of our economy, and so helped to move our trade promotion act that is going to be helping to do exactly what it says, promote tourism and bring folks here to enjoy the incredible hospitality.

The point is, our role in Government, especially in difficult times like these, is to break down barriers that are standing in the way of innovation, to unleash the ingenuity that springs from our people, to give an impetus to businesses to grow and expand. That's not some abstract theory. We've seen the results. We've seen what we can do to catalyze job growth in the private sector.

And one of the places we've seen it most is in the clean-energy sector, an industry that will not only produce jobs of the future, but help free America from our dependence on foreign oil in the process, clean up our environment in the process, improve our national security in the process.

So let me give you an example. Just yesterday I took a tour of Smith Electric Vehicles in Kansas City, Missouri, on the way here. This is a company that just hired its 50th worker, it's on the way to hiring 50 more, and is aiming to produce 500 electric vehicles at that plant alone. And these are spiffy-looking trucks. I mean, they are, and they're used by Fortune 500 companies for distribution: PepsiCo, Frito-Lay. They're also used for the United States military, electric trucks with a lot of—they're very strong, great horsepower.

And the reason for their success is their entrepreneurial drive. But it's also partly because

of a grant that we're offering companies that manufacture electric vehicles and the batteries that power them.

Because of these grants, we're going to be going from only having 2 percent of the global capacity to make advanced batteries that go in trucks and cars, run on electricity—we're going to go from 2 percent of advanced battery market share to 40 percent just in the next 5 years—just in the next 5 years. And that will create thousands of jobs across the country, not just this year, not just next year, but for decades to come. So it's a powerful example of how we can generate jobs and promote robust economic growth here in Nevada and all across the country by incentivizing private sector investments.

That's what we're working to do with the clean energy manufacturing tax credits that we enacted last year, thanks to Harry's leadership. Thanks to Harry's leadership.

Some people know these tax credits by the name 48c, which refers to their section in the Tax Code. But here's how these credits work. We said to clean energy companies, if you're willing to put up 70 percent of the capital for a worthy project, a clean energy project, we'll put up the remaining 30 percent. To put it another way, for every dollar we invest, we leverage two more private sector dollars. We're betting on the ingenuity and talent of American businesses.

Now, these manufacturing tax credits are already having an extraordinary impact. A solar panel company called Amonix received a roughly $6 million tax credit for a new facility they're building in the Las Vegas area, a tax credit they were able to match with roughly $12 million in private capital. That's happening right now. And that's just one of over 180 projects that received manufacturing tax credits in over 40 States.

Now, here's the—the only problem we have is these credits were working so well, there aren't enough tax credits to go around. There are more worthy projects than there are tax credits. When we announced the program last year, it was such a success we received 500 applications requesting over $8 billion in tax credits, but we only had $2.3 billion to invest. In other words, we had almost four times as many worthy requests as we had tax credits.

Now, my attitude, and Harry's attitude, is that if an American company wants to create jobs and grow, we should be there to help them do it. So that's why I'm urging Congress to invest $5 billion more in these kinds of clean energy manufacturing tax credits, more than doubling the amount that we made available last year. And this investment would generate nearly 40,000 jobs and $12 billion or more in private sector investment, which could trigger an additional 90,000 jobs.

Now, I'm gratified that this initiative is drawing support from Members of Congress from both sides of the aisle, including Republican Senators Richard Lugar and Orrin Hatch. Unfortunately, that kind of bipartisanship has been absent on a lot of efforts that Harry and I have taken up over the past year and a half.

We fought to keep Nevada teachers and firefighters and police officers on the job and to extend unemployment insurance and COBRA so folks have health insurance while they're looking for work. We fought to stop health insurance companies from dropping your coverage on the basis of preexisting conditions or right when you get sick or placing lifetime limits on the amount of care that you can receive.

We fought to eliminate wasteful subsidies that go to banks that were acting as unnecessary middlemen for guaranteed student loans from the Federal Government, and as a consequence, freed up tens of billions of dollars that are now going directly to students, which means more than a million students have access to financial aid that they didn't have before.

And we're now on the cusp of enacting Wall Street reforms that will empower consumers with clear and concise information that they need to make financial decisions that are best

for them and to help prevent another crisis like this from ever happening again and putting an end to some of the predatory lending and the subprime loans that had all kinds of fine print and hidden fees that have been such a burden for the economy of a State like Nevada and haven't been fair to individual consumers in the process.

So that's what Harry and I fought for. And frankly, at every turn we've met opposition and obstruction from a lot of leaders across the aisle. And that's why I'm glad I've got a boxer in the Senate who is not afraid to fight for what he believes in. And Harry and I are going to keep on fighting until wages and incomes are rising and businesses are hiring again right here in Nevada and Americans are headed back to work again and we've recovered from this recession and we're actually rebuilding this economy stronger than before. That's what we're committed to doing.

So, Nevada, I know we've been through tough times. And not all the difficult days are behind us. There are going to be some tough times to come. But I can promise you this: We are headed in the right direction. We are moving forward. We are not going to move backwards.

And I'm absolutely confident that if we keep on moving forward, if we refuse to turn backwards, if we're willing to show the same kind of fighting spirit as Harry Reid has shown throughout his career, then out of this storm brighter days are going to come.

Thank you very much, everybody. God bless you.

NOTE: The President spoke at 9:33 a.m. In his remarks, he referred to Neal J. Smatresk, president, University of Nevada, Las Vegas.

The President's Weekly Address
July 10, 2010

Last weekend, on the Fourth of July, Michelle and I welcomed some of our extraordinary military men and women and their families to the White House.

They were just like the thousands of Active Duty personnel and veterans that I've met across this country and around the globe: proud, strong, determined men and women with the courage to answer their country's call and the character to serve the United States of America.

Because of that service, because of the honor and heroism of our troops around the world, our people are safer, our Nation is more secure, and we are poised to end our combat mission in Iraq by the end of August, completing a drawdown of more than 90,000 troops since last January.

Still, we are a nation at war. For the better part of a decade, our men and women in uniform have endured tour after tour in distant and dangerous places. Many have risked their lives. Many have given their lives. And as a grateful nation, humbled by their service, we can never honor these American heroes or their families enough.

Just as we have a solemn responsibility to train and equip our troops before we send them into harm's way, we have a solemn responsibility to provide our veterans and wounded warriors with the care and benefits they've earned when they come home. That's our sacred trust with all who serve, and it doesn't end when their tour of duty does.

To keep that trust, we're building a 21st-century VA, increasing its budget and ensuring the steady stream of funding it needs to support medical care for our veterans. To help our veterans and their families pursue a college education, we're funding and implementing the post-9/11 GI bill. To deliver better care in more places, we're expanding and increasing VA health care, building new wounded warrior facilities, and adapting care to better meet the needs of female veterans. To stand with those who sacrifice, we've dedicated new support for wounded warriors and the caregivers who put their lives on hold for a loved one's long recovery. And to do right by our vets, we're working to prevent and end veteran homelessness. Because in the United States of America, no one who served in our uniform should sleep on our streets.

We also know that for many of today's troops and their families, the war doesn't end when they come home. Too many suffer from the signature injuries of today's wars: posttraumatic stress disorder and traumatic brain injury. And too few receive the screening and treatment they need.

Now, in past wars, this wasn't something America always talked about. And as a result, our troops and their families often felt stigmatized or embarrassed when it came to seeking help. Today, we've made it clear up and down the chain of command that folks should seek help if they need it. In fact, we've expanded mental health counseling and services for our vets.

But for years, many veterans with PTSD who have tried to seek benefits—veterans of today's wars and earlier wars—have often found themselves stymied. They've been required to produce evidence proving that a specific event caused their PTSD. And that practice has kept the vast majority of those with PTSD who served in noncombat roles, but who still waged war, from getting the care they need.

Well, I don't think our troops on the battlefield should have to keep notes just in case they need to apply for a claim. And I've met enough veterans to know that you don't have to engage in a firefight to endure the trauma of war. So we're changing the way things are done.

On Monday, the Department of Veterans Affairs, led by Secretary Ric Shinseki, will begin making it easier for a veteran with PTSD to get the benefits he or she needs. This is a long-overdue step that will help veterans not just of the Afghan and Iraq Wars, but generations of their brave predecessors who proudly served and sacrificed in all our wars.

It's a step that proves that America will always be there for our veterans, just as they've always been there for us. We won't let them down. We take care of our own. And as long as I'm Commander in Chief, that's what we're going to keep doing. Thanks.

NOTE: The address was recorded at approximately 5:40 p.m. on July 9 in the Library at the White House for broadcast on July 10. The transcript was made available by the Office of the Press Secretary on July 9, but was embargoed for release until 6 a.m. on July 10. The Office of the Press Secretary also released a Spanish language transcript of this address.

Statement on the 15th Anniversary of the Srebrenica Genocide
July 11, 2010

On the occasion of the 15th anniversary of the genocide at Srebrenica and on behalf of the United States, I join my voice with those who are gathered to mourn a great loss and to reflect on an unimaginable tragedy.

Fifteen years ago today, despite decades of pledges of "never again," 8,000 men and boys were murdered in these fields and hills. They were brothers, sons, husbands, and fathers, and they all became victims of genocide. I have said, and I believe, that the horror of Srebrenica was a stain on our collective conscience. We honor their memories and grieve with their families as many of them are laid to rest here today. They were people who sought to live in peace and had relied on the promise of international protection, but in their hour of greatest need, they were left to fend for themselves. Only those of you who suffered through those days, who lost loved ones, can comprehend the unspeakable horror. You have carried this burden and live with pain and loss every moment of your lives.

This atrocity galvanized the international community to act to end the slaughter of civilians, and the name Srebrenica has since served as a stark reminder of the need for the world to respond resolutely in the face of evil. For 15 years, the United States has joined with you to foster peace and reconciliation in this troubled land. We recognize that there can be no lasting peace without justice, and we know that we will all be judged by the efforts we make in pursuit of justice for Srebrenica's victims and those who mourn them. Justice must include a full accounting of the crimes that occurred, full identification and return of all those who were lost, and prosecution and punishment of those who carried out the genocide. This includes Ratko Mladic, who presided over the killings and remains at large. The United States calls on all governments to redouble their efforts to find those responsible, to arrest them, and to bring them to justice. In so doing, we will honor Srebrenica's victims and fulfill our moral and legal commitments to end impunity for crimes of such awful magnitude.

We have a sacred duty to remember the cruelty that occurred here and to prevent such atrocities from happening again. We have an obligation to victims and to their surviving family members. And we have a responsibility to future generations all over the globe to agree that we must refuse to be bystanders to evil; whenever and wherever it occurs, we must be prepared to stand up for human dignity.

May God bless you all, and may God bless the memory of all those who rest here.

NOTE: The statement referred to former Bosnian Serb army commander Ratko Mladic.

Remarks Following a Meeting With President Leonel Fernandez Reyna of the Dominican Republic
July 12, 2010

President Obama. Hello, everybody. Good afternoon. President Fernandez and I just had an excellent conversation. We first met and, I think, forged a good working relationship and friendship at the Summit of the Americas last year. And we have built on that relationship, as have our respective administrations, on a whole host of issues.

We had a wide-ranging discussion. One of the first messages I wanted to deliver was my appreciation for the role that the Dominican Republic played in helping the international community respond to the crisis in Haiti after the devastating earthquake there. And I think that the Dominican Republic's role, President Fernandez's role in particular, in helping to facilitate a rapid response was extraordinarily important. It saved lives, and it continues, as we look at how we can reconstruct and rebuild in Haiti in a way that is good not only for the people of Haiti, but also good for the region as a whole.

That was just one example of the leadership that President Fernandez has shown. He and his Government have been extremely helpful in resolving the political crisis that existed in Honduras. And we discussed ways that we can manage that process so that Honduras can once again be fully integrated into the regional groupings and organizations and—in a way that is respectful of democracy, and we coordinated closely between our two countries on that issue.

We discussed the critical issue of drug trafficking and crime and how that has the potential to be destabilizing throughout the region. And we have already seen great cooperation between our countries through the Caribbean Basin Security Initiative, but more needs to be done. And so President Fernandez and I discussed how we can do a better job coordinating through multinational groupings to address what is a scourge on so many countries. And that involves us dealing both with the supply side of the equation, but also the demand side. And as I've said before in conversations, for example, with President Calderon in Mexico, we here in the United States have an important obligation to make sure that we are dealing with the demand of drugs. There are also cross-border flows that involve guns and weapons and cash. So the problem involves all of us, and if we're going to solve it, we're going to have to work coordinating together.

And we also talked about how working together we can expand trade opportunities, commercial opportunities, business opportunities. One area that I expressed to the President that is of particular interest to me is clean energy. Last year, when I met with President Lula of Brazil, I noted that Brazil had made enormous progress around clean energy, sugarcane-based ethanol, the possibilities of real energy independence in the region. I think those same opportunities exist for the Dominican Republic. And President Fernandez and I discussed how we can work more closely together around energy security issues, something that my administration is very interested in partnering with

Central American and Latin American countries to work on.

So the main message I have to the people of the Dominican Republic is thank you for your friendship. I think the American people appreciate greatly the bonds between our two countries, bonds that express themselves obviously in our extraordinary Dominican population, Dominican American population, that we have here in this country. And obviously, I've got to note that we got some pretty good baseball players here from the Dominican Republic.

President Fernandez. Yes, sir.

President Obama. But for some reason I've got a lot of Red Sox fans here, so they keep on talking about Ortiz, but I'm a White Sox guy.

But, Mr. President, welcome. Thank you for your friendship. And we look forward to a long and constructive relationship between not only our countries but our two governments.

President Fernandez. Thank you, Mr. President. Well, first of all, I would like to thank President Obama for extending an invitation to come here to the White House and speak on issues that are of mutual interest for the U.S. Government and for the Dominican Republic. As the President has indicated, we have agreed on several issues, some bilateral issues between the U.S. and the Dominican Republic, and also on regional issues.

We do appreciate, Mr. President, that with all you have on your agenda, with all the international issues, with all the crises, with the economic situation that's affecting worldwide, you have put on your agenda the Caribbean, Latin America, and the Dominican Republic. I think this is evidence that you do have an interest for the region and the problems that affect not only the Dominican Republic, but the region as a whole.

As you have indicated, one of our major concerns has to do with drug trafficking, with transnational crime, with violence related to all these criminal activities. I think that the Caribbean Basin Security Initiative has been the right path forward. I commend you for that, Mr. President. And I think now we should move into a more collaborative environment with the other Caribbean nations, Central America, and Mexico. It is only by coordinating our efforts that we can really defeat this epidemic that has become overwhelming to all of our countries. And whatever we can do from the supply side, as you said, or the demand side, will be of great significance for the safety and security of our people.

Other issues, like you said, related to clean energy, we're working on that in the Dominican Republic with wind energy and with the potential production of ethanol in our country. We'll move on also with trade. We have a free trade agreement between both of our countries, of which we have not benefited fully because of the global financial crisis and how it has affected trade. But we can look into the future hopefully that we will increase our trade activities and

more investment coming from the U.S. into the Dominican Republic.

So once again, Mr. President, I thank you for your friendship, I thank you for your vision, for your leadership, and for your commitment to the region and the Dominican Republic.

President Obama. Thank you very much. Thank you, everybody.

NOTE: The President spoke at 2:50 p.m. in the Oval Office at the White House. In his remarks, he referred to David "Big Papi" Americo Ortiz, designated hitter, Boston Red Sox. The Office of the Press Secretary also released a Spanish language transcript of these remarks.

Letter to the Speaker of the House of Representatives Transmitting Fiscal Year 2011 Budget Amendments
July 12, 2010

Dear Madam Speaker:

I ask the Congress to consider the enclosed amendments to Fiscal Year (FY) 2010 proposals in my FY 2011 Budget for the Department of Commerce.

Included are amendments that would support efforts to reduce backlogs in processing patent applications—by spurring innovation and reforming U.S. Patent and Trademark Office operations to make them more effective—and assure the continuation of efforts to administer and oversee grants awarded under the Broadband Technology Opportunity Program.

The amounts requested for these amendments would be fully offset by a proposed cancellation of FY 2010 unobligated balances from within the Department of Commerce's Census Bureau. The proposed budget authority totals for FY 2010 in my FY 2011 Budget would not be affected by these amendments.

The details of this request are set forth in the enclosed letter from the Director of the Office of Management and Budget.

Sincerely,

BARACK OBAMA

Remarks on the Nomination of Jacob J. "Jack" Lew To Be Director of the Office of Management and Budget
July 13, 2010

Good afternoon. Before I begin, I just want to note a breakthrough that we've had on our efforts to pass the most comprehensive reform of Wall Street since the Great Depression. Three Republican Senators have put politics and partisanship aside to support this reform, and I'm grateful for their decision, as well as all the Democrats who've worked so hard to make

this reform a reality, particularly Chairman Dodd and Chairman Barney Frank.

What members of both parties realize is that we can't allow a financial crisis like this one that we just went through to happen again. This reform will prevent that from happening. It will prevent a financial crisis like this from happening again by protecting consumers against the unfair practices of credit card companies and mortgage lenders. It will ensure that taxpayers are never again on the hook for Wall Street's mistakes. And it will end an era of irresponsibility that led to the loss of 8 million jobs and trillions of dollars of wealth. This reform is good for families, it's good for businesses, it's good for the entire economy, and I urge the Senate to act quickly so that I can sign it into law next week.

Now, as we finish our work on Wall Street reform, we're also mindful that we've got significant work to do when it comes to reforming our Government and reducing our deficit. As part of that work, today I am proud to announce the nomination of Jack Lew to be our Nation's next Director of Office of Management and Budget, or OMB.

Before telling you a little bit about Jack, I just want to say a few words about the man that he will be replacing at the helm of OMB, and that's Mr. Peter Orszag. A few weeks ago, Peter told me that after more than a year and a half of tireless, around-the-clock service in what is one of the toughest jobs around, Peter was ready to move on to a job that offers a little more sanity and fewer line items.

Putting a budget together for the entire Federal Government is an enormously difficult task, no matter what the state of the economy, but Peter's job was even tougher. When we walked through the doors of the White House, we not only faced the worst economic crisis since the Great Depression, we also faced a $1.3 trillion deficit, a deficit that was caused both by the recession and nearly a decade of not paying for key policies and programs.

In light of these challenges, Peter's accomplishments as Director of OMB are even more impressive. He was instrumental in designing and helping us pass an economic plan that prevented a second depression, a plan that is slowly but surely moving us in the right direction again. Thanks to his innovative ideas and gritty determination, we passed a health insurance reform plan that is not only paid for but will significantly lower the cost of health care as well as our deficit over the next several decades. In fact, a recent report by independent experts say

this reform will cut the deficit even more than the Congressional Budget Office first estimated.

Peter has also helped us single out more than a hundred programs for elimination that have outlived their purposes and made hard decisions that will save tens of billions of dollars. And he helped draft a budget for next year that freezes all discretionary Government spending outside of national security for 3 years, something that was never enacted in the prior administration. It's a budget that would reduce the deficit by more than $1 trillion over the next decade, which is more than any other budget in a decade. And I expect that freeze to become a reality next year.

Now, Peter also shares my view that the long-running debate between big government and small government misses the point; it isn't relevant to today's challenges. The real debate is about how we make government smarter, more effective, and more efficient in the 21st century. It's easy for any institution to get in the habit of doing things the way they've always been done. We in Government can't afford that habit, not only because it wastes taxpayer dollars, but because it erodes people's belief that their Government can actually work for them.

Over the last year and a half, we've been able to employ new technology to make Government more responsive and customer friendly, the same way that so many businesses have used technology to make better products and provide better services.

As a result of these efforts, today we're creating a single electronic medical record for our men and women in uniform that will follow them from the day they enlist until the day they are laid to rest. We're cutting down the time that it takes to get a patent approved by cutting out unnecessary paperwork and modernizing the process. We're working to give people the chance to go online and book an appointment at the Social Security office or check the status of their citizenship application. We're cutting waste by getting rid of Federal office space that hasn't been used in years. We're closing the IT gap in the Federal Government and have created mobile apps that provide nutrition information for your favorite foods or wait times at the airport. And the examples go on and on.

Now, inertia is a powerful thing. Constituencies grow around every agency and department with a vested interest in doing things the same way. And that's why we have to keep on challenging every aspect of Government to rethink its core mission, to make sure we're pursuing that mission as effectively and efficiently as possible, and to ask if that mission is better achieved by partnering with the civic, faith, and private sector communities.

This is a mission that requires some special leadership. And Jack Lew is somebody who has proven himself already equal to this extraordinary task.

You know, if there was a hall of fame for Budget Directors, then Jack Lew surely would have earned a place for his service in that role under President Clinton, when he helped balance the Federal budget after years of deficits. When Jack left that post at the end of the Clinton administration, he handed the next administration a record $236 billion budget surplus. The day I took office, 8 years later, America faced a record $1.3 trillion deficit.

Jack's challenge over the next few years is to use his extraordinary skill and experience to cut down that deficit and put our Nation back on a fiscally responsible path. And I have the utmost faith in his ability to achieve this goal as a central member of our economic team.

Jack is the only Budget Director in history to preside over a budget surplus for three consecutive years. When Jack was Deputy Director at OMB, he was part of the team that reached a bipartisan agreement to balance the budget for the first time in decades. He was a principal domestic policy adviser to Tip O'Neill and worked with him on the bipartisan agreement to reform Social Security in the 1980s. He was executive vice president at New York University, where he oversaw budget and finances. And for the past year and a half, he's been successful in overseeing the State Department's extremely complex and challenging budget as Deputy Secretary of State for Management and Resources. I was actually worried that Hillary would not let him go. I had to trade a number of number-one draft picks—[*laughter*]—to get Jack back at OMB.

But I am grateful that Hillary agreed to have Jack leave, and I'm even more thrilled that Jack agreed to take on this challenge at this moment. Jack is going to be an outstanding OMB Director. We know it because he's been one before. At a time when so many families are tightening their belts, he's going to make sure that the Government continues to tighten its own. He's going to do this while making Government more efficient, more responsive to the people it serves.

And, Jack, I am looking forward to working with you on your critical mission. Thank you so much. And thanks to Jack's family, who has been putting up with him in multiple, very difficult jobs over and over again. We appreciate his service to our country and we appreciate yours as well.

Thank you, everybody.

NOTE: The President spoke at 12:18 p.m. in the Diplomatic Reception Room at the White House.

Remarks Announcing the National HIV/AIDS Strategy
July 13, 2010

The President. Hello, everybody! Well, good evening, everybody. This is a pretty feisty group here. [*Laughter*]

Audience member. We love you, President!

The President. Love you back. Thank you. Well, it is a privilege to speak with all of you. Welcome to the White House.

Audience members. Thank you.

The President. Let me begin by welcoming the Cabinet Secretaries who are here. I know I saw at least one of them, Kathleen Sebelius, our outstanding Secretary of Health and Human Services. I want to thank all the Members of Congress who are present and all the distinguished guests that are here—that includes all of you. [*Laughter*]

In particular, I want to recognize Ambassador Eric Goosby, our Global AIDS Coordinator. Eric's leadership of the President's Emergency Plan for AIDS Relief is doing so much to save so many lives around the world. He will be leading our delegation to the International AIDS Conference in Vienna next week. And so I'm grateful for his outstanding service.

And I want to also thank the Presidential Advisory Council on HIV/AIDS—thank you—and the Federal HIV Interagency Working Group for all the work that they are doing. So thank you very much.

Now, it's been nearly 30 years since a CDC publication called Morbidity and Mortality Weekly Report first documented five cases of an illness that would come to be known as HIV/AIDS. In the beginning, of course, it was known as the, quote, "gay disease," a disease surrounded by fear and misunderstanding, a disease we were too slow to confront and too slow to turn back.

In the decades since, as epidemics have emerged in countries throughout Africa and around the globe, we've grown better equipped, as individuals and as nations, to fight this disease. From activists, researchers, community leaders who've waged a battle against AIDS for so long, including many of you here in this room, we have learned what we can do to stop the spread of the disease. We've learned what we can do to extend the lives of people living with it. And we've been reminded of our obligations to one another, obligations that, like the virus itself, transcend barriers of race or station or sexual orientation or faith or nationality.

So the question is not whether we know what to do, but whether we will do it, whether we will fulfill those obligations, whether we will marshal our resources and the political will to confront a tragedy that is preventable.

All of us are here because we are committed to that cause. We're here because we believe that while HIV transmission rates in this country are not as high as they once were, every new case is one case too many. We're here because we believe in an America where those living with HIV/AIDS are not viewed with suspicion, but treated with respect, where they're provided the medications and health care they need, where they can live out their lives as fully as their health allows.

And we're here because of the extraordinary men and women whose stories compel us to stop this scourge. I'm going to call out a few people here, people like Benjamin Banks, who right now is completing a master's degree in public health, planning a family with his wife, and deciding whether to run another half marathon. [*Laughter*] Ben has also been HIV-positive for 29 years, a virus he contracted during cancer surgery as a child. So inspiring others to fight the disease has become his mission.

We're here because of people like Craig Washington, who after seeing what was happening in his community—friends passing away; life stories sanitized, as he put it, at funerals; homophobia, all the discrimination that surrounded the disease—Craig got tested, disclosed his status, with the support of his partner and his family, and took up the movement for prevention and awareness, in which he is a leader today.

We're here because of people like Linda Scruggs. Linda learned she was HIV-positive about two decades ago when she went in for prenatal care. Then and there, she decided to turn her life around, and she left a life of substance abuse behind. She became an advocate for women; she empowered them to break free from what she calls the bondage of secrecy. She inspired her son, who was born healthy, to become an AIDS activist himself.

So we're here because of Linda and Craig and Ben and because of the over 1 million Americans living with HIV/AIDS and the nearly 600,000 Americans who've lost their lives to the disease. It's on their behalf, and on the behalf of all Americans, that we began a national dialogue about combating AIDS at the beginning of this administration.

In recent months, we've held 14 community discussions. We've spoken with over 4,200 people. We've received over 1,000 recommendations on the White House web site, devising an approach not from the top down but from the bottom up.

And today we're releasing our national HIV/AIDS strategy, which is the product of these conversations and conversations with HIV-positive Americans and health care providers, with business leaders, with faith leaders, and the best policy and scientific minds in our country.

Now, I know that this strategy comes at a difficult time for Americans living with HIV/AIDS, because we've got cash-strapped States who are being forced to cut back on essentials, including assistance for AIDS drugs. I know the need is great. And that's why we've increased Federal assistance each year that I've been in office, providing an emergency supplement this year to help people get the drugs they need, even as we pursue a national strategy that focuses on three central goals.

First goal: prevention. We can't afford to rely on any single prevention method alone. So our strategy promotes a comprehensive approach to reducing the number of new HIV infections, from expanded testing so people can learn their status to education so people can curb risky behaviors to drugs that can prevent a mother from transmitting a virus to her child.

And to support our new direction, we're investing $30 million in new money, and I've committed to working with Congress to make sure these investments continue in the future.

The second——

Audience member. Mr. President——

The President. Let's—hold on—you can talk to me after—we'll be able to talk after I speak. That's why I invited you here, right? So you don't have to yell, right? Thank you.

Second is treatment. To extend lives and stem transmission, we need to make sure every HIV-positive American gets the medical care that they need. And by stopping health insurers from denying coverage because of a preexisting condition and by creating a marketplace where people with HIV/AIDS can buy affordable care, the health insurance reforms I signed into law this year are an important step forward. And we'll build on those reforms, while also understanding that when people have trouble putting food on the table or finding a place to live, it's

virtually impossible to keep them on lifesaving therapies.

Now, the third goal is reducing health disparities by combating the disease in communities where the need is greatest. Now, we all know the statistics. Gay and bisexual men make up a small percentage of the population, but over 50 percent of new infections. For African Americans, it's 13 percent of the population, nearly 50 percent of the people living with HIV/AIDS. HIV infection rates among Black women are almost 20 times what they are for White women. So such health disparities call on us to make a greater effort as a nation to offer testing and treatment to the people who need it the most.

So reducing new HIV infections, improving care for people living with HIV/AIDS, narrowing health disparities, these are the central goals of our national strategy. They must be pursued hand in hand with our global public health strategy to roll back the pandemic beyond our borders. And they must be pursued by a government that is acting as one. So we need to make sure all our efforts are coordinated within the Federal Government and across Federal, State, and local governments, because that's how we'll achieve results that let Americans live longer and healthier lives.

So yes, government has to do its part, but our ability to combat HIV/AIDS doesn't rest on government alone. It requires companies to contribute funding and expertise to the fight. It requires us to use every source of information, from TV to film to the Internet, to promote AIDS awareness. It requires community leaders to embrace all and not just some who are affected by the disease. It requires each of us to act responsibly in our own lives, and it requires all of us to look inward, to ask not only how we can end this scourge, but also how we can root out the inequities and the attitudes on which this scourge thrives.

When a person living with HIV/AIDS is treated as if she's done something wrong, when she's viewed as being somehow morally compromised, how can we expect her to get tested and disclose her diagnosis to others?

When we fail to offer a child a proper education, when we fail to provide him with accurate medical information and instill within him a sense of responsibility, then how can we expect him to take the precautions necessary to protect himself and others?

When we continue, as a community of nations, to tolerate poverty and inequality and injustice in our midst, we don't stand up for how women are treated in certain countries, how can we expect to end the disease, a pandemic that feeds on such conditions?

So fighting HIV/AIDS in America and around the world will require more than just fighting the virus. It will require a broader effort to make life more just and equitable for the people who inhabit this Earth. And that's a cause to which I'll be firmly committed so long as I have the privilege of serving as President.

So to all of you who have been out there in the field, working on this issue day in, day out, I know sometimes it's thankless work, but the truth is, you are representing what's best in all of us: our regard for one another, our willingness to care for one another. I thank you for that. I'm grateful for you. You're going to have a partner in me.

God bless you, and God bless the United States of America.

NOTE: The President spoke at 6:10 p.m. in the East Room at the White House. The related memorandum is listed in Appendix D at the end of this volume.

Interview With the South African Broadcasting Corporation
July 13, 2010

Terrorist Attacks in Uganda/Counterterrorism Efforts in Africa

Q. Mr. President, you reached out yesterday to President Yoweri Museveni of Uganda, pledging U.S. support after the twin bombings in Kampala.

The President. Right.

Q. Can you share some of the details of that conversation with us?

The President. Well, I expressed, obviously, most immediately, the condolences of the American people for this horrific crime that had been committed. And I told the President that the United States was going to be fully supportive of a thorough investigation of what had happened.

Al-Shabaab has now taken credit, taken responsibility for this atrocity, and we are going to redouble our efforts, working with Uganda, working with the African Union, to make sure that organizations like this are not able to kill Africans with impunity.

And it was so tragic and ironic to see an explosion like this take place when people in Africa were celebrating and watching the World Cup take place in South Africa. It—on the one hand, you have a vision of an Africa on the move, an Africa that is unified, an Africa that is modernizing and creating opportunities, and on the other hand, you've got a vision of Al Qaida and al-Shabaab that is about destruction and death. And I think it presents a pretty clear contrast in terms of the future that most Africans want for themselves and their children. And we need to make sure that we are doing everything we can to support those who want to build, as opposed to who want to destroy.

Counterterrorism Efforts in Somalia

Q. These attacks are very much about what is happening in Somalia today.

The President. Yes.

Q. How does that change, if at all, the game plan of the United States with regard to the transitional Government that is in power there?

The President. Well, look, obviously Somalia has gone through a generation now of war, of conflict. The transitional Government there is still getting its footing. But what we know is that if al-Shabaab takes more and more control within Somalia, that it is going to be exporting violence the way it just did in Uganda. And so we've got to have a multinational effort. This is not something that the United States should do alone, that Uganda or others should do alone, but rather, the African Union, in its mission in Somalia, working with the transitional Government to try to stabilize the situation and start putting that country on a pathway that provides opportunity for people, as opposed to creating a breeding ground for terrorism.

Radicalism in Africa/Africa's Development

Q. Former U.S. Ambassador to Tanzania—you might know him—Charles Stith has just written a piece about radical Islam in Africa specifically, and I'd like to quote something from it. He says, "It became clear to me that the dirty little secret that no one wanted to discuss openly was political Islam's corrosive effect and adverse impact on development and stability on the African Continent. It is inarguable that Islam is a factor in Africa," end quote.

In your view, are there strategies in place to deal with this?

The President. Well, I think—look, Islam is a great religion. It is one that has prospered side by side with other religions within Africa. And one of the great strengths of Africa is its diversity not only of faith, but of races and ethnicities. But what you have seen in terms of radical Islam is an approach that says that any efforts to modernize, any efforts to provide basic human rights, any efforts to democratize are somehow anti-Islam. And I think that is absolutely wrong. I think the vast majority of people of the Islamic faith reject that. I think the people of Africa reject it.

And what you've seen in some of the statements that have been made by these terrorist organizations is that they do not regard African life as valuable in and of itself. They see it as a potential place where you can carry out ideological battles that kill innocents without regard to long-term consequences for their short-term tactical gains.

And that's why it's so important, even as we deal with organizations like al-Shabaab militarily, that, more importantly, we also are dealing with the development agenda and building on models of countries like South Africa that are trying to move in the right direction, that have successful entrepreneurs, that have democracy

and have basic human freedoms; that we highlight those as an example whereby Africans can seize their own destiny, and hopefully, the United States can be an effective partner in that.

Q. So this is linked to poverty, that's what you're saying.

The President. Well, it's not just linked to poverty. I mean, I think there's an ideological component to it that also has to be rejected. There's—obviously, young people, if they don't have opportunity, are more vulnerable to these misguided ideologies, but we also have to directly confront the fact that issues like a anti-democratic, anti-free-speech, anti-freedom-of-religion agenda, which is what an organization like al-Shabaab promotes, also often goes hand in hand with violence.

Sudan

Q. Sudan.

The President. Yes.

Q. The International Criminal Court has added the charges of genocide to the arrest warrant of Sudan's President, Umar al-Bashir. There's a view in Africa, certainly with the African Union, that the pursuit of President Bashir will be undermining or detrimental to the Doha peace process. What's your view?

The President. Well, my view is that the ICC has put forward an arrest warrant. We think that it is important for the Government of Sudan to cooperate with the ICC. We think that it is also important that people are held accountable for the actions that took place in Darfur that resulted in, at minimum, hundreds of thousands of lives being lost.

And so there has to be accountability, there has to be transparency. Obviously, we are active in trying to make sure that Sudan is stabilized, that humanitarian aid continues to go in there, that efforts with respect to a referendum and the possibility of Southern Sudan gaining independence under the agreement that was brokered, that that moves forward.

So it is a balance that has to be struck. We want to move forward in a constructive fashion in Sudan, but we also think that there has to be accountability, and so we are fully supportive of the ICC.

Q. Is peace not at risk if he were to present himself to the ICC?

The President. Well, I think that peace is at risk if there's no transparency and accountability of the actions that are taking place, whether it's in Sudan or anywhere else in the world.

FIFA World Cup in South Africa/Africa's Development

Q. The World Cup, Mr. President, you mentioned that. To a certain extent, I imagine, around the world, it was overshadowed by what happened in Uganda. But South Africa was basking in the glory of having successfully hosted this World Cup. But let's acknowledge the skeptics, and there were a few—quite a few of them, and they were quite loud. I wonder if you were one of them.

The President. No, I wasn't. I, having visited South Africa and seen the extraordinary vitality of the people there, having gotten to know President Zuma and understanding the extraordinary pride that his administration expressed, which I think was a pride that was shared by all South Africans, I had confidence that this was going to be a success.

Obviously, it was an—just a terrific showcase, not just for South Africa, but for Africa as a whole, because what it lifted up was the fact that Africa—all the stereotypes that it suffers under, all the false perspectives about African capacity—that when given an opportunity, Africa is a continent full of leaders, entrepreneurs, governments that can operate effectively. What it—what we now have to do is build on that positive image that comes out of the World Cup.

And when I was in Ghana last year, I was very clear on what I think the agenda has to be: Africa for Africans. That means that we can be partners with Africans, but ultimately, on whether it's issues of eliminating corruption, ensuring smooth transitions of democratic governments, making sure that businesses are able to thrive and prosper and that markets are working for the smallest farmer and not just the most well connected person, those are issues that Africans can work on together.

And in terms of my orientation working to help in Africa's development, we want to provide resources, but we want to partner with those who are interested in growing their own capacity over time and not having a long-term dependency on foreign aid.

Government Corruption in Africa/Africa's Development

Q. You also spoke in Ghana about the need to stop the blame game.

The President. Absolutely. Well, I—look, the—I feel very strongly that—you talk to the average person in Kenya, South Africa, Nigeria, they will acknowledge a tragic history in terms of colonialism and negative Western influences. But I think what they'll also acknowledge is their biggest problem right now is the policeman who's shaking them down or the inability for them to be able to get a telephone in a timely fashion in their office or having to pay a bribe. Those are the impediments to development right now. And those are things that Africans can solve if there is a determination and there's strong leadership.

And Nelson Mandela set us on a path in understanding the standards of leadership that are needed, and I think those standards can be met. And you're seeing countries around the continent who are starting to meet those high standards that are so necessary to ultimately help the people.

U.S. FIFA World Cup Bid/Popularity of Soccer in the U.S.

Q. I want to talk about President—former President Nelson Mandela in a second, but before that, let's just touch on this bid, the U.S. bid for the World Cup in 2018 or '22. How serious are Americans about soccer? My sense is that they're fairly partial to it.

The President. Oh, listen, I think that you saw a quantum leap this year because of the excellence of the U.S. team. It's absolutely true that they call baseball the national pastime here in the United States, that basketball is obviously a homegrown invention, and we dominate American football. Those are all sports that developed here and that the United States is obsessed with.

Soccer is a late entry. But what you saw with the U.S. team was huge enthusiasm of the sort that I haven't seen about soccer before. And the younger generation is much more focused on soccer than the older generation. I mean, my daughters, they play soccer; they paid attention to who was doing what in the World Cup. And so I think what you're going to continue to see is a growing enthusiasm, and I think people are very serious about the World Cup being hosted here in the United States.

President's Emergency Plan for AIDS Relief

Q. I want to touch on AIDS, Mr. President. There's been a great deal of appreciation and good will towards——

The President. Right.

Q. ——the United States for the Global Health Initiative——

The President. Right.

Q. ——of which PEPFAR is the cornerstone. Some criticism, though, from AIDS groups in South Africa that there's a de facto decrease in funding, even though there's a 2.3-percent increase. How do you respond to that?

The President. Yes.

Q. It's based on inflation. Inflation in developing countries tends to be higher than it is in the United States. It's a 2.3-percent increase, and they're saying it's a de facto decrease.

The President. Well, I have to say that we are seeing not a decrease, but an increase in PEPFAR, an increase in the Global Health Initiative. And I promise you when I'm fighting for that budget here in the United States, people don't see it as a decrease. They see it as an increase. They understand we're putting more money into it, and it's the right thing to do.

What we do want to make sure of is that as successful as PEPFAR has been, as important as it is for us to, for example, get antiviral drugs in there, that we're also helping to build up capacity, consistent with what I said earlier.

So, for example, what are we doing in terms of creating public health systems and infrastructure in a place like South Africa so that the inci-

dents of infection are reduced? We're not just treating the disease itself, but we're also doing a much better job in terms of general public health so that fewer people are getting infected in the first place.

I think that kind of reorientation you're going to start seeing in some areas. We'll continue to provide increases in antiviral drugs, continue to provide millions of rand, millions of—billions of U.S. dollars to basic assistance, but we also want to build capacity at the same time.

Former President Nelson R. Mandela of South Africa

Q. Final question, Mr. President. Nelson Mandela will be 92 on Sunday. Your thoughts?

The President. Well, he looked terrific, first of all.

Q. Didn't he?

The President. And when I spoke to him on the phone after the tragic loss of his granddaughter [great-granddaughter],° he sounded as clear and charming as he always has been.

And he continues to be a model of leadership not just for South Africa, but for the world. So we celebrate him here in the United States, as you do in South Africa. We wish him all the best. And we are constantly reminded that his legacy of seeing every person as important and not making distinctions based on race or class, but the degree to which they are people of character, that's a good guidepost for how all of us should operate as leaders.

And so I wish him all the best. And South Africa continues, I think, to be blessed by a—not just a national treasure, but a world treasure.

Q. Well, South Africans wish you the best. Thank you very much.

The President. Thank you.

Q. Very good to meet you.

The President. I enjoyed it.

Q. Thank you, sir.

The President. Thank you.

NOTE: The interview began at 3:45 p.m. in the Diplomatic Reception Room at the White

---

° White House correction.

House. In his remarks, the President referred to President Jacob Zuma of South Africa. The transcript was released by the Office of the Press Secretary on July 14.

Letter to Congressional Leaders on Review of Title III of the Cuban Liberty and Democratic Solidarity (LIBERTAD) Act of 1996
July 14, 2010

Dear _____:

Consistent with section 306(c)(2) of the Cuban Liberty and Democratic Solidarity (LIBERTAD) Act of 1996 (Public Law 104–114)(the "Act"), I hereby determine and report to the Congress that suspension, for 6 months beyond August 1, 2010, of the right to bring an action under title III of the Act is necessary to the national interests of the United States and will expedite a transition to democracy in Cuba.

Sincerely,

BARACK OBAMA

NOTE: Identical letters were sent to Daniel K. Inouye, chairman, and W. Thad Cochran, vice chairman, Senate Committee on Appropriations; John F. Kerry, chairman, and Richard G. Lugar, ranking member, Senate Committee on Foreign Relations; David R. Obey, chairman, and Jerry Lewis, ranking member, House Committee on Appropriations; and Howard L. Berman, chairman, and Ileana Ros-Lehtinen, ranking member, House Committee on Foreign Affairs.

Remarks at Compact Power, Inc., in Holland, Michigan
July 15, 2010

Hello, everybody. Thank you so much. Thank you. Everybody, please have a seat. Have a seat.

Before I get started, first of all, let me thank your fine, young mayor. Mr. Mayor, it is wonderful to see you, and I am partial to daughters, as I know you are, and I hope at some point I get a chance to meet yours. But thank you for the great work that you've done.

To somebody who I think is one of the best Governors in the country, Jennifer Granholm, please give her another round of applause. Jennifer has been relentless about bringing manufacturing—21st-century manufacturing—here to Michigan. And this is just an example of the kinds of projects she's been working on for so long.

I'm very grateful for the presence of the chairman of LG Chem, Bon Moo Koo. Thank you very much for your presence here today, as well as the CEO and vice chairman, Peter Bahnsuk Kim. Thank you very much. Please give them a big round of applause.

And I want to acknowledge your Congressman, Pete Hoekstra is here in the audience. Please give him a round of applause.

Now, it is wonderful to be here in Holland, and I am—especially to be here as Compact Power breaks ground on this site. This is about more than just building a new factory; it's about building a better future for this city, for this State, and for this country.

Now, I want to say what everyone here in Holland and everybody here in Michigan knows too well, which is that these have been some pretty tough times. A brutal recession came on top of what was already a lost decade for the middle class, especially for manufacturing towns here in the Midwest. Even before this recession cost so many jobs, incomes had been flat, jobs were moving overseas, while the price of everything from health care to college tuitions were skyrocketing.

It was a decade in which it seemed like the values that built this country were turned upside down. Folks who were working hard and honestly every day to meet their responsibilities were running in place or falling behind, while high-flying financial speculators who were cutting corners were rewarded with lavish bonuses and benefits.

It got even worse when the financial crisis sent our economy into a freefall and cost 8 million Americans their jobs. Michigan was hit harder than anywhere else. And on top of this recession, you were also rocked by the near collapse of the domestic auto industry.

It was in the middle of this crisis that my administration walked through the door. And we had a number of difficult decisions that we had to make and make quickly. Some, including shoring up U.S. automakers, weren't real popular, as you will recall. But with millions of jobs at stake, with the future of so many families and businesses on the line, we acted to prevent the country from slipping into an even deeper crisis.

And that's why when my administration began, we cut taxes for small-business owners and for 95 percent of working families here in Michigan and across the country. We extended unemployment insurance to help folks get through these storms. And through small-business loans, a focus on research and development, and investments in high-tech, fast-growing sectors like clean energy, we've aimed to grow our economy by harnessing the innovative spirit of the American people.

Because we did, shovels will soon be moving earth and trucks will soon be pouring concrete where we are standing. Because of a grant to this company, a grant that's leveraging more than 150 million private dollars, as many as 300 people will be put to work doing construction and another 300 will eventually be hired to operate this plant when it's fully up and running. And this is going to lead to growth at local businesses like parts suppliers and restaurants. It will be a boost to the economy of the entire region.

Now, this is the ninth advanced battery plant to begin construction because of our economic plan. And these plants will put thousands of people to work. This includes folks who were working at a couple of facilities being built in Michigan by another battery technology company called A123. And in every case, we've been guided by a simple idea: Government can't generate the jobs or growth we need by itself, but what Government can do is lay the foundation for small businesses to expand and to hire, for entrepreneurs to open shop and test new products, for workers to get the training they need for the jobs of the 21st century, and for families to achieve some semblance of economic security.

So our goal has never been to create a Government program, but rather to unleash private sector growth. And we are seeing results. There are 4.5 million unemployed workers already hired whose employers are eligible for a payroll tax exemption, a tax break that I signed into law earlier this year.

Just yesterday the Council of Economic Advisers put out a detailed report, and it showed that for things like tax credits that go to advanced energy manufacturing or loan guarantees for small businesses or financing for infrastructure projects, we're leveraging nearly three private dollars for every public dollar that's spent. That's an incredible bang for our buck. By making critical seed money available, we've attracted more than $280 billion in investment from private companies and others, which will mean new jobs and brighter futures for families in Holland and in communities across the country.

And by the way, these aren't just any jobs; these are jobs in the industries of the future. Just a few years ago, American businesses manufactured only 2 percent of the world's advanced batteries for electric and hybrid vehicles—2 percent. But because of what's happening in places like this, in just 5 years, we'll have up to 40 percent of the world's capacity—40 percent. So for years, you've been hearing about manufacturing jobs disappearing overseas. You are leading the way in showing how manufacturing jobs are coming right back here to the United States of America.

For example, the workers at this plant, already slated to produce batteries for the new Chevy Volt, learned the other day that they're also going to be supplying batteries for the new electric Ford Focus as soon as this operation gears up. And that means that by 2012, the batteries will be manufactured here in Holland, Michigan. So when you buy one of these vehicles, the battery could be stamped "Made in America," just like the car.

And here's another benefit: Because of advances in the manufacture of these batteries, their costs are expected to come down by nearly 70 percent in the next few years. That's going to make electric and hybrid cars and trucks more affordable for more Americans. And that not only means more jobs, but it also means we're going to be less dependent on foreign oil.

So taken together, these are the efforts that are going to create jobs and help build a stronger economy in the long run. And I want to express my appreciation to the Michigan leaders, not only here but in Congress, who supported the economic plan that made this possible.

As a result of the steps that we took, an economy that was shrinking is now growing. We were bleeding jobs at a rate of 750,000 per month the January that I was sworn in. Now the economy is adding private sector jobs and has been for 6 straight months.

Now, this doesn't mean that we're out of the woods, not by a long shot. But it does mean that there are small-business owners who've been able to get the loans they need to hire a few more people. It means there are salespeople with a few more dollars in their pockets because customers are buying again. It means there are innovators and entrepreneurs finally able to take a chance on a new idea. And it means there are construction workers heading to the jobsite each day—just like some of the folks who are here today—because our country is slowly coming back from this vicious recession.

The progress we've made so far is not nearly enough to do—undo the enormous damage that this recession caused. And I've said since the first day I took office, it's going to take time to reverse the toll of the deepest downturn in a generation. I won't be satisfied as long as even one person who needs a job and wants to work can't find one.

But what I'm absolutely clear about and what this plant will prove is that we are headed in the right direction and that the surest way out of the storms we've been in is to keep moving forward and not go backwards.

There are some folks who want to go back, who think that we should return to the policies that helped to lead to this recession. Some of them made the political calculation that it's better to obstruct than to lend a hand. They said no to tax cuts; they said no to small-business loans; they said no to clean energy projects. Now, it doesn't stop them from being at ribbon cuttings, but—[*laughter*]—but that's okay. I just want to make sure that everybody understands that this country would not be better off if this plant hadn't gotten built and if the clean energy package that made it possible wasn't in place.

And when you head out to any of the two dozen battery technology plants coming on line that are going to be able to be stamped "Made in America" on their products, I want folks who have been pushing against these economic policies to explain to these workers why it'd be better for these things to be manufactured in other countries, or why the solar plants and wind turbines and biodiesel refineries that are being built shouldn't have happened.

Most workers and most entrepreneurs understand we're not in the clear yet. But they understand we're headed in the right direction. There's something about America that no matter what the trials are, what the tribulations are, we stay optimistic and we keep going forward. And we know if we work hard enough and we're determined enough, if we try as hard as we can and if we're willing to experiment, and if things don't work, we put them aside, but we keep on going, that sooner or later, we're going to see a brighter day, and we're going to pass on a better America to our children and our grandchildren.

That's been our history. That's the legacy that we inherit. So to everybody in Holland, I want you to understand these have been a tough few years, but we have been through tough times before. And at our best, we've risen to the challenges we face by tapping the drive and the talent and the ingenuity that has always been at the heart of America's success.

And that's what's happening all across America as we speak. That's not only how we're going to emerge from this period of turmoil, that's how we're going to actually come out stronger than we were before.

So to all of you who have been part of this project, thank you. This is a symbol of where Michigan's going, this is a symbol of where Holland's going, this is a symbol of where America is going.

God bless you, and God bless the United States of America.

NOTE: The President spoke at 1:36 p.m. In his remarks, he referred to Mayor Kurt D. Dykstra of Holland, MI, and his daughters Juliana and Emma-Elisabeth; and Bon Moo Koo, chairman of the board of directors and chief executive officer, LG Corp.

Remarks on Congressional Passage of Financial Regulatory Reform Legislation and an Exchange With Reporters
July 15, 2010

The President. Good afternoon, everybody. With today's vote in the Senate, the United States Congress has now passed a Wall Street reform bill that will bring greater economic security to families and businesses across the country.

It was clear from the moment it began that this recession was not the result of your typical economic downturn. It was the result of recklessness and irresponsibility in certain corners of Wall Street that infected the entire economy, irresponsibility that cost millions of Americans their jobs and millions more their hard-earned savings. It's why businesses can't get credit and why families haven't been able to see appreciation in their home values; in fact, the values of their homes have plummeted.

Even before the financial crisis that led to this recession, I spoke on Wall Street about the need for commonsense reforms to protect consumers and our economy as a whole. But the crisis came and only underscored the need for the kind of reform the Senate passed today: reform that will protect consumers when they take out a mortgage or sign up for a credit card, reform that will prevent the kind of shadowy deals that led to this crisis, reform that would never again put taxpayers on the hook for Wall Street's mistakes.

The reform that Congress passed today will accomplish these goals. It is a bill that was made possible first and foremost by the tireless efforts of Chairman Chris Dodd and Congressman and Chairman Barney Frank, as well as the leadership of Harry Reid and Nancy Pelosi. I am ex-

traordinarily grateful for their determination in the face of a massive lobbying effort from the financial industry, and I'm also grateful for all of the Members of Congress who stood on the side of reform, including three Republican Senators who put politics and partisanship aside today to vote for this bill.

The financial industry is central to our Nation's ability to grow, to prosper, to compete, and to innovate. This reform will foster that innovation, not hamper it. It's designed to make sure that everyone follows the same set of rules so that firms compete on price and quality, not on tricks and traps. It demands accountability and responsibility from everybody. It provides certainty to everyone from bankers to farmers to business owners to consumers. And unless your business model depends on cutting corners or bilking your customers, you have nothing to fear from this reform.

For all those Americans who are wondering what Wall Street reform means for you, here's what you should expect. If you've ever applied for a credit card, a student loan, a mortgage, you know the feeling of signing your name to pages of barely understandable fine print. It's a big step for most families and one that's often filled with unnecessary confusion and apprehension. As a result, many Americans are simply duped into hidden fees and loans they just can't afford by companies who know exactly what they're doing. Those days will soon end. From now on, every American will be empowered with the clear and concise information you need to make financial decisions that are best for you.

This bill will crack down on abusive practices and unscrupulous mortgage lenders. It will reinforce the new credit card law we passed banning unfair rate hikes and ensure that folks aren't unwittingly caught by overdraft fees when they sign up for a checking account. It will give students who take out college loans clear information and make sure lenders don't cheat the system. And it will ensure that every American receives a free credit score if they are denied a loan or insurance because of that score. All told, this reform puts in place the strongest consumer financial protections in history, and it creates a new consumer watchdog to enforce those protections.

Because of this reform, the American people will never again be asked to foot the bill for Wall Street's mistakes. There will be no more taxpayer-funded bailouts, period. If a large financial institution should ever fail, this reform gives us the ability to wind it down without endangering the broader economy. And there will be new rules to end the perception that any firm is too big to fail so that we don't have another Lehman Brothers or AIG.

Because of reform, the kind of complex, backroom deals that helped trigger this financial crisis will finally be brought into the light of day. And from now on, shareholders and other executives can know that the shareholders will have greater say on the pay of CEOs so that they can reward success instead of failure and help change the perverse incentives that encouraged so much reckless risk-taking in the past.

In short, Wall Street reform will bring greater security to folks on Main Street, to families who are looking to buy their first home or send their kids to college, to taxpayers who shouldn't have to pay for somebody else's mistakes or irresponsibility, to small businesses, community banks, and credit unions who play by the rules, to shareholders and investors who want to see their companies grow and thrive.

Now, already, the Republican leader in the House has called for repeal of this reform. I would suggest that America can't afford to go backwards, and I think that's how most Americans feel as well. We can't afford another financial crisis just as we're digging out from the last one.

Now, I said when I took office, we can't simply rebuild this economy on the same pile of sand, on maxed-out credit cards, houses used like ATM machines, or overleveraged firms on Wall Street. We need to rebuild on a firmer, stronger foundation for economic growth. That's why we invested in renewable energy that's currently creating new jobs all across America. That's why we're reforming our education system so that our workers can compete in the global economy. That's why we passed health reform that will lower costs for families and businesses. And that's why I'm about to sign Wall Street reform into law to protect consumers and lay the foundation for a stronger and safer financial system, one that is innovative, creative, competitive, and far less prone to panic and collapse. Along with the steps we're taking to spur innovation, encourage hiring, and rein in our deficits, this is how we're ultimately going to build an economy that is stronger and more prosperous than it was before and one that provides opportunity for all Americans.

Thanks very much.

Status of Oil Spill in the Gulf of Mexico

Q. Sir, are you encouraged that the oil has stopped flowing in the Gulf?

The President. I think it is a positive sign. We're still in the testing phase. I'll have more to say about it tomorrow.

NOTE: The President spoke at 4:43 p.m. on the South Driveway at the White House. In his remarks, he referred to H.R. 4173. The Office of the Press Secretary also released a Spanish language transcript of these remarks.

Statement on the Resignation of Dennis F. Hightower as Deputy Secretary of Commerce
July 15, 2010

I thank Dennis for his service to the country and to my administration. I appreciate his guidance and hard work on various important priorities, from expanding broadband Internet access across the country to reforming our export control system in a way that enhances our competitiveness and our security. I wish him the best in his future endeavors.

Remarks on the Oil Spill in the Gulf of Mexico and an Exchange With Reporters
July 16, 2010

The President. Good morning, everybody. I want to give everyone a quick update on the situation in the Gulf. As we all know, a new cap was fitted over the BP oil well earlier this week. And this larger, more sophisticated cap was designed to give us greater control over the oil flow as we complete the relief wells that are necessary to stop the leak.

Now, our scientists and outside experts have met through the night and continue this morning to analyze the data from the well integrity test. What they're working to determine is whether we can safely shut in the well using the new cap without creating new problems, including possibly countless new oil leaks in the sea floor.

Now, even if a shut-in is not possible, this new cap and the additional equipment being placed in the Gulf will be able to contain up to 80,000 barrels a day, which should allow us to capture nearly all the oil until the well is killed. It's important to remember that prior to the installation of this new cap, we were collecting on average about 25,000 barrels a day.

For almost 90 days of this environmental disaster, all of us have taken hope in the image of clean water instead of oil spewing in the Gulf. But it is our responsibility to make sure that we're taking a prudent course of action and not simply looking for a short-term solution that could lead to even greater problems down the road.

So to summarize, the new cap is good news. Either we will be able to use it to stop the flow, or we will be able to use it to capture almost all of the oil until the relief well is done. But we're not going to know for certain which approach makes sense until additional data is in. And all the American people should rest assured that all of these decisions will be based on the science and what's best for the people of the Gulf.

All right? I'll take just one or two questions. Go ahead.

Minor Earthquake in the Washington, DC, Metropolitan Area

Q. Did you feel the earthquake, Mr. President?

The President. I didn't.

Status of Oil Spill in the Gulf of Mexico

Q. Sir, do you think this means that basically we're turning the corner, at least, in the Gulf? Tell the American people what you anticipate in the next few weeks ahead, because they're still very anxious about this.

The President. Well, I think it's important that we don't get ahead of ourselves here. One of the problems with having this camera down there is, is that when the oil stops gushing, everybody feels like we're done, and we're not. The new cap is containing the oil right now, but scientists are doing a number of tests. What they want to make sure of is, is that by putting this cap on, the oil isn't seeping out elsewhere in ways that could be even more catastrophic. And that involves measuring pressures while this cap is on. The data is not all still in, and it has to be interpreted by the scientists.

But here's the good news that I think everybody needs to understand: Even if it turns out that we can't maintain this cap and completely shut off the flow of oil, what the new cap allows us to do is to essentially attach many more containment mechanisms so that we're able to take more oil up to the surface, put it on ships; it won't be spilling into the Gulf.

The final solution to this whole problem is going to be the relief wells and getting that completed, but there's no doubt that we have made progress as a consequence of this new cap fitting on, and that even if it turns out that we can't keep the containment cap on to completely stop the oil, it's going to allow us to capture much more oil and we'll see less oil flowing into the Gulf.

Now, in the meantime, obviously we've still got a big job to do. There's still a lot of oil out there, and that's why we've got more skimmers out there, there's better coordination on the ground along the shorelines. There's still going to be an enormous cleanup job to do, and there's still going to be the whole set of issues of—surrounding making sure people are compensated properly, that the $20 billion fund is set up and is acting expeditiously.

So we've got an enormous amount of work to do, and people down in the Gulf, particularly businesses, are still suffering as a consequence of this disaster. But we are making steady progress, and I think the American people should take some heart in the fact that we're making progress on this front.

Drilling of Relief Wells

Q. Are the relief wells still on target, sir?

The President. So far, it's actually slightly ahead of target, but the problem on the relief well is not simply drilling all the way down, it's also connecting it up, and that's a delicate operation that could take some time.

BP p.l.c. Cleanup Costs/Compensation for Gulf Coast Communities Affected by the Oil Spill

Q. Ahead of target—what does ahead of target mean, sir?

Q. Mr. President, when does BP begin paying fines according to the amount of oil spilled?

The President. Well, we are obviously going to be taking measures about how much oil has spilled, and those are calculations that are going to be continually refined. BP is going to be paying for the damage that it has caused, and that's going to involve not only paying for the environmental disaster and cleanup, but also compensating people who've been affected.

Yes, go ahead.

Q. On a per-barrel basis?

The President. That's going to be a component of the calculations that are made.

Go ahead.

President's Travel to the Gulf Coast/Oil Spill Relief Efforts/Status of Oil Spill in the Gulf of Mexico

Q. What do you want to say to the people there? When do you expect to go down next?

The President. Well, I would expect that sometime in the next several weeks I'll be back down. What we're trying to do right now is to make sure that the technical folks on the ground are making the best possible decisions to shut this well down as quickly as possible, that we're standing up the fund so that people are compensated quickly. I'm staying in touch each and every day, monitoring the progress and getting briefed by the scientists.

The key here right now is for us to make decisions based on science, based on what's best for the people of the Gulf, not based on PR, not based on politics. And that's part of the reason why I wanted to speak this morning, because I know that there were a lot of reports coming out in the media that seemed to indicate, well, maybe this thing is done. We won't be done until we actually know that we've killed the well and that we have a permanent solution in place. We're moving in that direction, but I don't want us to get too far ahead of ourselves.

All right? Thank you very much, everybody.

NOTE: The President spoke at 10:11 a.m. in the Rose Garden at the White House. The Office of the Press Secretary also released a Spanish language transcript of these remarks.

Statement on the Terrorist Attack in Zahedan, Iran
July 16, 2010

I strongly condemn the outrageous terrorist attacks on a mosque in southeast Iran. The murder of innocent civilians in their place of worship is an intolerable offense, and those who carried it out must be held accountable. The United States stands with the families and loved ones of those killed and injured, and with the Iranian people, in the face of this injustice. Together, the people of the world must condemn and oppose all forms of terrorism and support the universal right of human beings to live free from fear and senseless violence.

The President's Weekly Address
July 17, 2010

This week, many of our largest corporations reported robust earnings, a positive sign of growth. But too many of our small-business owners and those who aspire to start their own small businesses continue to struggle, in part because they can't get the credit they need to start up, grow, and hire. And too many Americans whose livelihoods have fallen prey to the worst recession in our lifetimes, a recession that cost our economy 8 million jobs, still wonder how they'll make ends meet. That's why we need to take new, commonsense steps to help small businesses, grow our economy, and create jobs. And we need to take them now.

For months, that's what we've been trying to do. But too often, the Republican leadership in the United States Senate chooses to filibuster our recovery and obstruct our progress. And that has very real consequences.

Consider what this obstruction means for our small businesses, the growth engines that create two of every three new jobs in this country. A lot of small businesses still have trouble getting the loans and capital they need to keep their doors open and hire new workers. So we proposed steps to get them that help: eliminating capital gains taxes on investments, establishing a fund for small lenders to help small businesses, enhancing successful SBA programs that help them access the capital they need. But again and again, a partisan minority in the Senate said no and used procedural tactics to block a simple up-or-down vote.

Think about what these stalling tactics mean for the millions of Americans who've lost their jobs since the recession began. Over the past several weeks, more than 2 million of them have seen their unemployment insurance expire. For many, it was the only way to make ends meet while searching for work, the only way to cover rent, utilities, even food.

Three times, the Senate has tried to temporarily extend that emergency assistance. And three times, a minority of Senators—basically the same crowd who said no to small businesses—said no to folks looking for work and blocked a straight up-or-down vote.

Some Republican leaders actually treat this unemployment insurance as if it's a form of welfare. They say it discourages folks from looking for work. Well, I've met a lot of folks looking for work these past few years, and I can tell you, I haven't met any American who would rather have an unemployment check than a meaningful job that lets you provide for your family. And we all have friends or neighbors or family members who already know how hard it is to land a job when five workers are competing for every opening.

Now, in the past, Presidents and Congresses of both parties have treated unemployment insurance for what it is, an emergency expenditure. That's because an economic disaster can devastate families and communities just as surely as a flood or tornado.

But suddenly, Republican leaders want to change that. They say we shouldn't provide unemployment insurance because it costs money. So after years of championing policies that turned a record surplus into a massive deficit, including a tax cut for the wealthiest Americans, they've finally decided to make their stand on the backs of the unemployed. They've got no problem spending money on tax breaks for folks at the top who don't need them and didn't even ask for them, but they object to helping folks laid off in this recession who really do need help. And every day this goes on, another 50,000 Americans lose that badly needed lifeline.

Well, I think these Senators are wrong. We can't afford to go back to the same misguided policies that led us into this mess. We need to move forward with the policies that are leading us out of this mess.

The fact is, most economists agree that extending unemployment insurance is one of the single most cost-effective ways to help jumpstart the economy. It puts money into the pockets of folks who not only need it most but who are also most likely to spend it quickly. That boosts local economies, and that means jobs.

Increasing loans to small businesses, renewing unemployment insurance, these steps aren't just the right thing to do for those hardest hit by the recession, they're the right thing to do for all of us. And I'm calling on Congress once more to take these steps on behalf of America's workers and their families and small-business owners, the people we were sent here to serve.

Because when storms strike Main Street, we don't play politics with emergency aid. We don't desert our fellow Americans when they fall on hard times. We come together. We do what we can to help. We rebuild stronger, and we move forward. That's what we're doing today. And I'm absolutely convinced that's how we're going to come through this storm to better days ahead.

Thanks.

NOTE: The address was recorded at approximately 5:20 p.m. on July 15 in the Diplomatic Reception Room at the White House for broadcast on July 17. The transcript was made available by the Office of the Press Secretary on July 16, but was embargoed for release until 6 a.m. on July 17. The Office of the Press Secretary also released a Spanish language transcript of this address.

Statement on Nelson Mandela International Day
July 18, 2010

On behalf of the United States, I wish Nelson Mandela a very happy 92d birthday. We are grateful to continue to be blessed with his extraordinary vision, leadership, and spirit. And we strive to build upon his example of tolerance, compassion, and reconciliation. I also join the American people, the South African people, the United Nations, and the world in celebrating the first annual Nelson Mandela International Day. I encourage us all to heed the call to engage in some form of service to others, in honor of the 67 years of sacrifice and service Madiba gave to us. We strive to follow his example of what it means to truly give back to our communities, our nations, and our world.

NOTE: The statement referred to former President Nelson R. Mandela of South Africa.

Remarks on Legislation Extending Unemployment Insurance Benefits
July 19, 2010

Good morning, everybody. Right now, across this country, many Americans are sitting at the kitchen table, they're scanning the classifieds, they're updating their resumes or sending out another job application, hoping that this time, they'll hear back from a potential employer. And they're filled with a sense of uncertainty about where their next paycheck will come from. And I know the only thing that will entirely free them of those worries, the only thing that will fully lift that sense of uncertainty is the security of a new job.

To that end, we all have to continue our efforts to do everything in our power to spur growth and hiring. And I hope the Senate acts this week on a package of tax cuts and expanded lending for small businesses, where most of America's jobs are created.

So we've got a lot of work to do to make sure that we are digging ourselves out of this tough economic hole that we've been in. But even as we work to jump-start job growth in the private sector, even as we work to get businesses hiring again, we also have another responsibility: to offer emergency assistance to people who desperately need it, to Americans who've been laid off in this recession. We've got a responsibility to help them make ends meet and support their families, even as they're looking for another job. And that's why it's so essential to pass the unemployment insurance extension that comes up for a vote tomorrow.

We need to pass it for men like Jim Chukalas, who's with me here today. Jim worked as a parts manager at a Honda dealership until about 2 years ago. He's posted resumes everywhere. He's gone door to door looking for jobs. But he hasn't gotten a single interview. Now, he's trying to be strong for his two young kids, but now that he's exhausted his unemployment benefits, that's getting harder to do.

We need to pass it for women like Leslie Macko, who lost her job at a fitness center last year and has been looking for work ever since. Because she's eligible for only a few more weeks of unemployment, she's doing what she never thought she'd have to do, not at this point anyway. She's turning to her father for financial support.

And we need to pass it for Americans like Denise Gibson, who was laid off from a real estate agency earlier this year. Denise has been interviewing for jobs, but so far, nothing's turned up. Meanwhile, she's fallen further and further behind on her rent. And with her unemployment benefits set to expire, she's worried about what the future holds.

And we need to pass it for all the Americans who haven't been able to find work in an economy where there are five applicants for every opening, who need emergency relief to help them pay the rent and cover their utilities and put food on the table while they're looking for another job.

And for a long time, there's been a tradition—under both Democratic and Republican Presidents—to offer relief to the unemployed. That was certainly the case under my predecessor, when Republican Senators voted several times to extend emergency unemployment benefits. But right now these benefits, benefits that are often the person's sole source of income while they are looking for work, are in jeopardy.

And I have to say, after years of championing policies that turned a record surplus into a massive deficit, the same people who didn't have any problem spending hundreds of billions of dollars on tax breaks for the wealthiest Americans are now saying we shouldn't offer relief to middle class Americans like Jim or Leslie or Denise who really need help.

Over the past few weeks, a majority of Senators have tried—not once, not twice, but three times—to extend emergency relief on a temporary basis. Each time, a partisan minority in the Senate has used parliamentary maneuvers to block a vote, denying millions of people who are out of work much needed relief. These leaders in the Senate who are advancing a misguided notion that emergency relief somehow discourages people from looking for a job should talk to these folks.

That attitude, I think, reflects a lack of faith in the American people, because the Americans I hear from in letters and meet in town hall meetings—Americans like Leslie and Jim and Denise—they're not looking for a handout. They desperately want to work. It's just right now they can't find a job. These are honest, decent, hard-working folks who've fallen on hard times through no fault of their own and who have nowhere else to turn except unemployment benefits and who need emergency relief to help them weather this economic storm.

Now, tomorrow we will have another chance to offer them that relief, to do right by not just Jim and Leslie and Denise, but all the Americans who need a helping hand right now. And I hope we seize it. It's time to stop holding workers laid off in this recession hostage to Washington politics. It's time to do what's right, not for the next election, but for the middle class. We've got to stop blocking emergency relief for Americans who are out of work. We've got to extend unemployment insurance. We need to pass those tax cuts for small businesses and the lending for small businesses.

Times are hard right now. We are moving in the right direction. I know it's getting close to an election, but there are times where you put elections aside. This is one of those times. And that's what I hope Members of Congress on both sides of the aisle will do tomorrow.

Thanks very much.

NOTE: The President spoke at 10:55 a.m. in the Rose Garden at the White House.

Remarks Honoring the 2009 Women's National Basketball Association Champion Phoenix Mercury
July 19, 2010

All right, everybody, have a seat now, have a seat. Well, it is just wonderful to welcome all of you here to the White House. And congratulations to the Phoenix Mercury on winning your second WNBA title in the last 3 years.

Now, I noticed my Department of Homeland Security Secretary—[*laughter*]—is kind of horning in on our event here. [*Laughter*] She has been a huge fan of Mercury ever since her days as Governor of Arizona. She's—I didn't know you'd been a guest coach. That is cool. Did you guys win that game? Nice, nice, nice. So I'm impressed.

I want to congratulate Head Coach Corey Gaines. He won a ring as assistant coach, now he's got a ring as head coach. So congratulations.

I know how much hard work goes into a championship——

[*At this point, there was a minor disruption in the audience.*]

——you guys all right back there? [*Laughter*] I know how much hard work goes into a championship season. But I hear that one of the real keys to the Mercury's title is sitting in the audience. For those of you who don't know, Assistant Coach Julie Hairgrove and her kids are the lucky charms of this team. Where are they? Julie? Sleeping? Not that excited to see the President. [*Laughter*]

My understanding, when the Mercury won their first title in 2007, Julie was pregnant with her second child. Wait, where's Julie by the way? Nice. When they won their second title,

Julie was pregnant with her third child, Grace, who's now 3 months old. And I understand the team is trying to talk Julie and her husband into their fourth. [*Laughter*] One more? [*Laughter*]

But beyond your lucky charms, the sacrifice, the dedication, and the heart that all of you have put into this sport is obvious. Team captain Diana Taurasi was named regular season and WNBA Finals MVP this year. That's pretty good. Last week, she won the ESPY Award for Best WNBA Player of 2010. Congratulations.

Tangela Smith became only the fourth player in WNBA history to score 4,500 career points and rack up 2,000 rebounds. Congratulations, Tangela. Nice! Nice!

But this is a true team. When Diana was named finals MVP, she turned around and gave the trophy to her teammates. She said, "It's not one player that makes an MVP. It never has been, and it never will be."

And this team set a new WNBA scoring record with 92.8 points per game. They made their way onto a box of Wheaties, I understand. [*Laughter*] But they have managed to keep themselves pretty grounded. I hear that rookies Taylor Lilley and Sequoia Holmes are still doing luggage duty—is that true? [*Laughter*] You guys didn't even—[*laughter*]—rooks, huh? That's rough. That's rough. [*Laughter*]

This team also goes above and beyond in serving the Phoenix community, from putting on basketball camps for children of veterans to collecting clothes for the homeless. And today they're bringing that commitment here to the White House. After we're done here, they'll be holding a clinic as part of Michelle's "Let's Move!" initiative to help our young people live healthy and active lives.

So I want to thank all of you guys for your extraordinary service as well as your championship spirit. And I want to thank you for setting a wonderful example, because I live with three tall, good-looking women—[*laughter*]—who are quite competitive and push me around under the boards all the time. [*Laughter*] But I want Malia and Sasha to know that there is absolutely no contradiction between women who are beautiful and healthy and contributing, and good athletes and competitive. And when they see you guys every day, that helps them in a way that—I think if you heard from Michelle, sometimes she feels like when she was coming up she didn't always have that. And I think that is just so important to everybody.

So, as a basketball fan, I congratulate you on your second championship. As a father, I thank you for being great role models. And good luck with the rest of the season. All right.

NOTE: The President spoke at 1:43 p.m. in the State Dining Room at the White House.

Statement on United Nations Accreditation of the International Lesbian and Gay Human Rights Commission
July 19, 2010

I welcome this important step forward for human rights as the International Lesbian and Gay Human Rights Commission (ILGHRC) will take its rightful seat at the table of the United Nations. The U.N. was founded on the premise that only through mutual respect, diversity, and dialogue can the international community effectively pursue justice and equality. Today, with the more full inclusion of the International Lesbian and Gay Human Rights Commission, the United Nations is closer to the ideals on which it was founded and to values of inclusion and equality to which the United States is deeply committed.

Message to the Congress on Continuation of the National Emergency With Respect to the Former Liberian Regime of Charles Taylor
July 19, 2010

To the Congress of the United States:

Section 202(d) of the National Emergencies Act (50 U.S.C. 1622(d)) provides for the automatic termination of a national emergency unless, prior to the anniversary date of its declaration, the President publishes in the *Federal Register* and transmits to the Congress a notice stating that the emergency is to continue in effect beyond the anniversary date. In accordance with this provision, I have sent the enclosed notice to the *Federal Register* for publication stating that the national emergency and related measures dealing with the former Liberian regime of Charles Taylor are to continue in effect beyond July 22, 2010.

The actions and policies of former Liberian President Charles Taylor and other persons, in particular their unlawful depletion of Liberian resources and their removal from Liberia and secreting of Liberian funds and property, continue to undermine Liberia's transition to democracy and the orderly development of its political, administrative, and economic institutions and resources. These actions and policies continue to pose an unusual and extraordinary threat to the foreign policy of the United States. For this reason, I have determined that it is necessary to continue the national emergency with respect to the former Liberian regime of Charles Taylor.

BARACK OBAMA

The White House,
July 19, 2010.

NOTE: The notice is listed in Appendix D at the end of this volume.

Remarks at PBS's "A Broadway Celebration: In Performance at the White House"
July 19, 2010

Well, welcome to the White House. I am just thrilled, and I know Michelle is thrilled, to host the sixth in a series of evenings celebrating the music that helped to shape America.

Now, so far we have heard from some of the biggest names in jazz, in country, in Latin, classical, and the music of the civil rights movement. And tonight we are honored to be joined by some of the biggest and brightest stars on Broadway.

And I notice—I should just point out that I see a lot of members of the New York delegation here. [*Laughter*] They take great pride in Broadway. I want to start by thanking George C. Wolfe and Margo Lion for making this event possible. So please give them a big round of applause. And I want to thank all of tonight's performers for sharing their gifts with us. They are just so generous with their time, and this will be a wonderful evening.

I also want to recognize my outstanding Secretary of Labor, Hilda Solis, who is in the house. Here she is right here. As well as the other members of the administration—thank you guys for the hard work you do each and every day. Thank you to the National Endowment for the Arts and the President's council on the arts and the humanities for their continued support. And I finally want to recognize Jerry Mitchell and everybody who participated in the dance workshop earlier this afternoon and helped inspire the next generation of performers—as well as my wife—to do a few dances. [*Laughter*] She was showing off backstage.

Now, as we're about to see this evening, there's nothing quite like the power and the passion of Broadway music. At its heart, it's the power of a story: of love and of heartbreak, of joy and sorrow, singing witches, dancing ogres. Musicals carry us to a different time and place, but in the end, they also teach us a little bit of something about ourselves. It's one of the few genres of music that can inspire the same pas-

sion in an 8-year-old that it can an 80-year-old, and make them both want to get up and dance. It transcends musical tastes, from opera and classical to rock and hip-hop. And whether we want to admit it or not, we all have the lyrics to a few Broadway songs stuck in our heads. [*Laughter*]

In many ways, the story of Broadway is also intertwined with the story if America. Some of the greatest singers and songwriters Broadway has ever known came to this country on a boat with nothing more than an idea in their head and a song in their heart. And they succeeded the same way that so many immigrants have succeeded, through talent and hard work and sheer determination.

Over the years, musicals have also been at the forefront of our social consciousness, challenging stereotypes, shaping our opinions about race and religion, death and disease, power and politics.

But perhaps the most American part of this truly American art form is its optimism. Broadway music calls us to see the best in ourselves and in the world around us, to believe that no matter how hopeless things may seem, the nice guy can still get the girl, the hero can still triumph over evil, and a brighter day can be waiting just around the bend.

As the great Mel Brooks once said, musicals "blow the dust off your soul." So to everyone watching, both here and at home, here's a taste of Broadway to help us do just that.

Thank you very much, everybody.

NOTE: The President spoke at 7:15 p.m. in the East Room at the White House. In his remarks, he referred to George C. Wolfe, private member, and Margo Lion, cochair, President's Committee on the Arts and the Humanities; Broadway theater director and choreographer Jerry Mitchell; and entertainer Mel Brooks.

The President's News Conference With Prime Minister David Cameron of the United Kingdom
July 20, 2010

President Obama. Good afternoon, everybody. Please have a seat. It is my great pleasure to welcome Prime Minister Cameron on his first visit to the White House as Prime Minister.

We have just concluded some excellent discussions, including whether the beers from our hometowns that we exchanged are best served warm or cold. My understanding is, is that the Prime Minister enjoyed our 312 beer, and we may send him some more. I thought the beer we got was excellent, but I did drink it cold. [*Laughter*]

Mr. Prime Minister, we can never say it enough: The United States and the United Kingdom enjoy a truly special relationship. We celebrate a common heritage. We cherish common values. And we speak a common language, most of the time. We honor the sacrifices of our brave men and women in uniform who have served together, bled together, and even lay at rest together.

Above all, our alliance thrives because it advances our common interests. Whether it's preventing the spread of nuclear weapons or securing vulnerable nuclear materials, thwarting terrorist attacks or confronting climate change or promoting global economic growth and development, when the United States and the United Kingdom stand together, our people, and people around the world, are more secure and they are more prosperous.

In short, the United States has no closer ally and no stronger partner than Great Britain. And I appreciate the opportunity to renew our relationship with my partner, Prime Minister Cameron.

In his campaign, David was known for his extensive town hall discussions with voters: "Cameron Direct." And that's the same spirit that we had here today. I appreciate David's steady leadership and his pragmatic approach. And just as he's off to an energetic start at home, I think we've had a brilliant start as partners who see eye to eye on virtually every challenge before us.

Great Britain is one of our largest trading partners, and we're committed to long-term, sustainable growth that keeps the global economy growing and puts our people to work. I told David that my administration's working hard with the Senate to move forward as soon as possible with our defense trade treaty with the U.K., which will be good for our workers and our troops in both our countries.

We reaffirmed our commitment to fiscal responsibility and reform. David's government is making some courageous decisions, and I've set a goal of cutting our deficit in half by 2013. Tomorrow I'll sign into law the toughest financial reforms since the aftermath of the Great Depression. And I commend David for his leadership in Europe to rebuild confidence in the financial sector. Together, we're determined to make sure the financial catastrophe that we are emerging from never happens again.

We discussed the Middle East, where both our governments are working to encourage Israelis and Palestinians to move to direct talks as soon as possible.

We discussed the continuing threat posed by Iran's nuclear program. On this we are united: The Iranian Government must fulfill its international obligations. The new sanctions imposed by the U.N. Security Council, the United States, and other countries are putting unprecedented pressure on the Iranian Government. And I thanked David for Great Britain's efforts to ensure strong European Union sanctions in the coming days.

Along with our P–5-plus-1 partners, we remain committed to a diplomatic solution. But the Iranian Government must understand that the path of defiance will only bring more pressure and more isolation.

Finally, much of our discussion focused on Afghanistan. After the United States, Great Britain is the largest contributor of combat forces in Afghanistan, and British troops and civilians have served and sacrificed in some of the most dangerous parts of the country.

This is not an easy fight, but it is a necessary one. Terrorists trained in Afghanistan and the tribal regions along the Pakistani border have killed innocent civilians in both of our countries. And an even wider insurgency in Afghanistan would mean an even larger safe haven for Al Qaida and its terrorist affiliates to plan their next attack. And we are not going to let that happen.

We have the right strategy. We're going to break the Taliban's momentum. We're going to build Afghan capacity so Afghans can take responsibility for their future. And we're going to deepen regional cooperation, including with Pakistan.

Now, today's historic Kabul conference is another major step forward. The Afghan Government presented, and its international partners unanimously endorsed, concrete plans to implement President Karzai's commitments to improve security, economic growth, governance, and the delivery of basic services. The Afghan Government presented its peace and reconciliation plan, which the United States firmly supports. Agreement was reached on a plan in which responsibility for security in Afghan Provinces will transition to Afghan security forces. In addition, Afghanistan and Pakistan reached a historic agreement to increase economic opportunity for people on both sides of the border.

So these are all important achievements, and they go a long way toward helping create the conditions needed for Afghans to assume greater responsibility for their country. Indeed, over the coming year, Afghans will begin to take the lead in security, and in July of next year will begin to transfer—we will begin to transfer some of our forces out of Afghanistan. And the Kabul conference shows that the Afghan—that Afghanistan has the support of the international community, including the United States, which will remain a long-term partner for the security and progress of the Afghan people.

As we go forward, we want to honor our fallen warriors with the respect and gratitude that they deserve, whether it's here at Dover or in the small British town of Wootton Bassett, where people line the streets in a solemn tribute that represents the best of the British character. With pride in their service and determination to carry on their work for a safer world, I am confident that we can be worthy of their sacrifice.

And I am confident that with my partner and friend, David Cameron, the special relationship between our countries will only grow stronger in the years to come.

Mr. Prime Minister.

Prime Minister Cameron. Well, first of all, can I thank you, Mr. President, for welcoming me so warmly to the White House today? Thank you for the meeting, for the lunch that we had, and also for the tour of part of your home. I have to say, I was most impressed by how tidy your children's bedrooms were. [*Laughter*] And I think if the President of the United States can get his children to tidy their bedrooms, then the British Prime Minister, it's about time——

President Obama. You can do it.

Prime Minister Cameron. ——he did exactly the same thing. [*Laughter*]

President Obama. You have to give them some notice, that's the only thing. [*Laughter*]

Prime Minister Cameron. Right. Well, they've got notice.

President Obama. Tell them the Prime Minister is coming. [*Laughter*]

Prime Minister Cameron. They should be in bed by now, but if they're not, they have notice. [*Laughter*]

I think we did have a very valuable opportunity today to discuss in real depth a strong and a shared agenda on Afghanistan, on global economic recovery, and on the Middle East. And this relationship isn't just, as you put it, an extraordinary special relationship. To me, it is also an absolutely essential relationship if we are going to deliver the security and the prosperity that our people need. And I thought again today in our discussions just how closely aligned our interests are on all of the issues that we discussed.

First, on Afghanistan, there is no clearer, no more tangible illustration of Britain and America standing shoulder to shoulder in our national interest than this mission that we are engaged in together. We have British troops working to an

American commander in Helmand, and we have American troops working to a British commander in Kandahar.

Today President Obama and I took stock of progress in this vital year. We reaffirmed our commitment to the overall strategy. A key part of that is training the Afghan National Army and police so they can provide security for their country and our troops can come home.

We also agreed on the need to reinvigorate the political strategy for Afghanistan. Insurgencies tend not to be defeated by military means alone. There must also be political settlement. And to those people currently fighting, if they give up violence, if they cut themselves off from Al Qaida, if they accept the basic tenets of the Afghan Constitution, they can have a future in a peaceful Afghanistan.

There is real progress. Last weekend, the first Afghan-led military operation took place successfully in Helmand, Afghans defending themselves. And today, as Barack has just said, for the first time in decades, the Government of Afghanistan has hosted an international conference on its own soil. Over 40 foreign ministers and 80 delegations assembled in Kabul to monitor progress and drive forward the international strategy. That is a real achievement, and we should congratulate President Karzai on it.

President Obama and I also discussed the economy. We're both taking action that our countries need. Our destination is a strong and stable growth, a sustained economic recovery, and a reformed financial system that will never again be open to the abuses of the past. We are confident that the right steps were taken at the Toronto G–20 summit to help achieve that.

The Middle East was the third area that we focused on today. We both want a secure, peaceful, and stable Middle East. And that means two things. First, as Barack has just said, Iran must give up its pursuit of a nuclear weapon. We urge the Iranian regime to resume negotiations with the international community without delay. It's not too late for it to do so. America and Britain, with our partners, stand ready to negotiate, and to do so in good faith. But in the absence of a willing partner, we will implement with vigor the sanctions package

agreed by the United Nations Security Council, and in Europe, we will be taking further steps as well.

Second, we desperately need a two-state solution between Israel and the Palestinians that provides security, justice, and hope. As we were discussing over lunch, it is time for direct talks, not least because it is time for each, Israel and Palestine, to test the seriousness of the other.

On BP, which we discussed at some length, I completely understand the anger that exists right across America. The oil spill in the Gulf of Mexico is a catastrophe for the environment, for the fishing industry, for tourism. I've been absolutely clear about that. And like President Obama, I've also been clear that it is BP's role to cap the leak, to clean up the mess, and to pay appropriate compensation. I'm in regular touch with senior management at BP, and the President is too, to make sure that happens. And the progress that's been made to cap the leak is a step in the right direction.

Equally, of course, BP is an important company to both the British and the American economies. Thousands of jobs on both sides of the Atlantic depend on it. So it's in the interest of both our countries, as we agreed, that it remains a strong and stable company for the future. And that's something we discussed today.

And let us not confuse the oil spill with the Libyan bomber. I've been absolutely clear about this right from the start, and in our meeting, we had what we call a violent agreement, which is that releasing the Lockerbie bomber, a mass murderer of 270 people, the largest act of terrorism ever committed in the United Kingdom, was completely wrong.

He showed his victims no compassion. They were not allowed to die in their beds at home, surrounded by their families. So in my view, neither should that callous killer have been given that luxury. That wasn't a decision taken by BP; it was a decision taken by the Scottish Government. We have to accept that under the laws of my country, where power on certain issues is devolved to Scotland, this was a decision for the Scottish Executive, a decision that they took.

I know that Senator Kerry's committee is looking into these issues. My Government will engage constructively with those hearings. And, indeed, my Foreign Secretary has already set out the Government's position.

So let me thank you again, Barack, for hosting me today. While at the World Cup, our teams could only manage a score draw. I believe our relationship can be a win-win. And, yes, I did enjoy drinking the 312 beer—cold—during the World Cup. [*Laughter*] I enjoyed it so much that when I watched Germany beat Argentina, I actually cheered for Germany. That's something that's a big admission for a British person to make, so the beer is obviously very effective. [*Laughter*]

But what you said, Barack, though, about British and American soldiers fighting together, sometimes dying together, serving together, is absolutely right. And we should never forget that, whether it's on the beaches of Normandy, whether it's in Korea, whether in Iraq, or whether now in Afghanistan.

Our relationship is one that has an incredibly rich history. It is based on ties of culture and history and, yes, emotion too. But for all those things, I think it has also an incredibly strong future that is based on results—results of a positive partnership of working together, agreeing where we agree; when we have disagreements, working through them and coming to a fair conclusion. It's a partnership that I profoundly want to make work as well as it possibly can in the years that I'm Prime Minister of Britain and with you as President of the United States.

So thank you again for welcoming me here today.

President Obama. Thank you, David.

With that, we're going to take a few questions. And I'm going to start with Mimi Hall of USA Today.

Release of Convicted Terrorist Abdelbaset Ali Mohmed Al-Megrahi/United Kingdom-U.S. Relations

Q. Thank you, Mr. President and Mr. Prime Minister. I wanted to ask you a little bit more about BP. You mentioned, Mr. Prime Minister, your decision to cooperate, et cetera, but you said we shouldn't confuse the two. Have you flatly ruled out opening a Government investi-

gation into the events around the release of the bomber?

And, President Obama, how do you feel about a congressional investigation into this? Would you like to see that happen, or do you think that confuses the two events?

President Obama. Well, why don't I start off, and I'll throw it over to David. I think all of us here in the United States were surprised, disappointed, and angry about the release of the Lockerbie bomber. And my administration expressed very clearly our objections prior to the decision being made and subsequent to the decision being made. So we welcome any additional information that will give us insights and a better understanding of why the decision was made.

But I think that the key thing to understand here is that we've got a British Prime Minister who shares our anger over the decision, who also objects to how it played out. And so I'm fully supportive of Prime Minister Cameron's efforts to gain a better understanding of it, to clarify it. But the bottom line is, is that we all disagreed with it. It was a bad decision. And going forward, that has to inform how we approach our relationship with respect to counterterrorism generally.

Now, one of the things that I want to emphasize that I think may get lost in this current debate is the extraordinarily strong ties between our two countries when it comes to fighting terrorism. We probably have the best coordination and cooperation of any two countries in the world. And those relationships are vital, and they keep people safe on both sides of the Atlantic.

And I want to make sure that even as we may express concern about what happened with respect to the release of this particular individual, that we stay focused on the cooperation that currently exists and build on that cooperation to make sure that there is no diminution of our joint efforts to make sure that the kinds of attacks that happened over Lockerbie do not happen again.

Prime Minister Cameron. Well, I agree with actually what's been said about the importance of the security cooperation, something we discussed today. On Megrahi, look, I'm not standing here today and saying it was a bad decision to release Megrahi because I'm here. I said this a year ago, at the time, that it was a bad decision. It shouldn't have been made. The British Government, as well, should have been clear that it was a bad decision, rather than going along with it. I took that very clear view. This was the biggest mass murderer in British history, and there was no business in letting him out of prison.

In terms of an inquiry, there has been an inquiry by the Scottish Parliament into the way the decision was made. The British Government—the last British Government released a whole heap of information about this decision. But I've asked the Cabinet Secretary today to go back through all of the paperwork and see if more needs to be published about the background to this decision.

But in terms of an inquiry, I'm not currently minded that we need to have a U.K.-based inquiry on this, partly for this reason: I don't need an inquiry to tell me what was a bad decision. It was a bad decision. And if you like, the big fact that's changed over the year that makes it an even worse decision is the fact that, of course, Megrahi is still free, at liberty, in Libya, rather than serving the prison sentence in Scotland, as he should be doing.

So that's what we're going to do, is go back over this information, see if more needs to be published, and of course, in terms of the congressional hearing, make sure that proper cooperation is extended to it.

President Obama. Somebody you want to call?

Prime Minister Cameron. Right. I think James Landale [BBC News].

U.S. Inquiry Into the Release of Convicted Terrorist Abdelbaset Ali Mohmed Al-Megrahi

Q. Just to stay on that subject, if we may. Mr. Prime Minister, first of all, would you be prepared to talk to your predecessors, Tony Blair and Gordon Brown, to get their agreements to release any documents if they are relevant to the paper search that the Cabinet Secretary will undergo?

And, Mr. President, can I ask you—the Prime Minister says he opposes an inquiry. Hillary Clinton has demanded an inquiry. Where do you stand?

President Obama. Well, go ahead, David.

Prime Minister Cameron. Well, first of all, on the documents, the proper process here is that the Cabinet Secretary should look back over this decision and the circumstances surrounding it, should identify those documents that should be published. It should be right that Ministers in the previous Government should be consulted about the publication of those documents. And of course we will consult with them over that.

But in my view, there is absolutely no harm to be done in giving the fullest possible explanation of the circumstances surrounding this decision. I think the key thing, though, to remember is that in the end, it was a decision by the Scottish Executive.

On the issue of an inquiry, as I said, I'm not currently minded to hold an inquiry because I think publishing this information, combined with the inquiry that has already been, will give people the certainty that they need about the circumstances surrounding this decision. But the key thing is to get the information out there so people can see. But I don't think there's any great mystery here. There was a decision taken by the Scottish Executive, in my view, a wholly wrong and misguided decision, a bad decision, but the decision nonetheless. That's what happened. And I don't think we need an extra inquiry to tell us that that's what happened. But the information, as I said, will be gone over and published, as appropriate. And of course I'll be consulting with previous Ministers and Prime Ministers, as you should do in the normal way.

President Obama. I think the simple answer is, we should have all the facts; they should be laid out there. And I have confidence that Prime Minister Cameron's government will be cooperative in making sure that the facts are there. That will not negate the fact that, as the Prime Minister indicated, it was a very poor decision and one that not only ran contrary to, I think, how we should be treating terrorists, but also didn't reflect the incredible pain that the families who were affected still suffer to this day. And my administration is in regular contact with these families, and this was a heartbreaking decision for them that reopened a whole host of new wounds.

So my expectation is, is that the facts will be out there, and, as David indicated, with all the facts out, I think we're going to be back to where we are right now, which it was—it's—it was a decision that should not have been made and one that we should learn from going forward.

Laura Meckler [Wall Street Journal].

Global Economy/Release of Convicted Terrorist Abdelbaset Ali Mohmed Al-Megrahi/Oil Spill in the Gulf of Mexico

Q. Thank you. Mr. President, in your opening statement, you referred to the fact that the British Government has been taking some very tough steps towards—to get their budget in order, and you said you had committed to cut the deficit in half. Could you talk about whether you think that those decisions are going to be— the decisions that they're making there are going to be needed to be made here on a similar level beyond pledges?

And, Mr. Prime Minister, specifically, could you address the matter of what role BP had in lobbying for the release of this man, and whether an inquiry or the review that you're planning is going to look at that specific question? Thank you.

President Obama. When I came into office in January of 2009, I was very clear at the time— even before we knew the severity of the recession that we would experience—that we have a structural deficit that is unsustainable, and that for our long-term growth and prosperity, we are going to have to get a handle on that. I talked about that during my campaign. I talked about it in the days after I was elected. I talked about it after I had been sworn in.

We had an emergency situation on our hands, and so the entire world, working through the G–20, coordinated in making sure that we filled this huge dropoff in demand. We got the economy growing again. And we had to take a number of steps, some of which were unpopu-

lar and that, yes, added to the short-term deficit.

What I also said at the time was we are then going to make sure, number one, that we pay down whatever additional deficit had been added as a consequence of the Recovery Act and other steps that we had to take last year, but then we're still going to have to go back and deal with these long-term structural deficits.

And, in fact, in the first G–20 visit that I made, in April to England, I was very clear to the rest of the world that what they cannot rely on is an economic model in which the United States borrows—consumers in the United States borrow, we take out home equity loans, we run up credit cards to purchase goods from all around the world. We cannot alone be the economic engine for the rest of the world's growth. So that rebalancing ended up being a central part of our long-term strategy working with the G–20.

Now, what we've done is we've initiated a freeze on our domestic discretionary budget. We are on the path to cutting our deficits in half. We have put forward a fiscal commission that is then going to examine how do we deal with these broader structural deficits. So this isn't just an empty promise. We've already started taking steps to deal with it, and we're going to be very aggressive in how we deal with it.

Now, our two countries are in slightly different situations. Their financial situation is slightly different; their levels of debt relative to GDP are somewhat higher. And as David and I discussed when we saw each other in Toronto, the goal here is the same, and we're all moving in the same direction. But there's going to be differentiation based on the different circumstances of different countries in terms of how they approach it tactically and at what pace.

But I can assure you this: that my administration is squarely committed not just to dealing with the short-term deficit and debt, which in some ways is the least troubling aspect of this problem, what we're going to have to tackle are some big structural reforms that are going to be tough. And they're going to be that much tougher because we're coming out of a recession as we do it. But I think that as we continue to see economic growth, as we continue to see the economy heal from last year, that the American people are going to want to approach this problem in a serious, realistic way. We owe it for the next generation.

And my hope is, is that we're going to end up getting a bipartisan solution to this thing that is realistic. And one concern that I have obviously is the politics of deficits and debt. When I announced that I was in favor of this fiscal commission, at the time, I had a number of Republicans who were cosponsors of the legislation who suddenly reversed themselves because, I suppose, I supported it.

And fortunately, what I've seen so far, all the reports from the fiscal commission, is that people are serious about this. Both Republicans and Democrats on the commission are taking their task seriously. I think it's going to be a good report, but is still going to require some tough choices, and we're committing to pursuing those tough choices after we get that report.

David.

Prime Minister Cameron. Thank you. You asked about the role of BP. I mean, the role of BP and any lobbying they might have done is an issue for BP and an issue that they should explain themselves. I mean, the decision to release Megrahi, though, was a decision made by the Scottish Government, and I haven't seen anything to suggest that the Scottish Government were in any way swayed by BP. They were swayed by their considerations about the need to release him on compassionate grounds, grounds that I think were completely wrong. I don't think it's right to show compassion to a mass murderer like that. I think it was wrong.

But it's a matter for BP to answer what activities they undertook. But the Scottish Government made its decision and has explained its decision on many occasions, and I'm sure will explain it again.

I'm very keen that we are clear here that BP should, rightly, be blamed for what has happened in the Gulf, and have real responsibilities to cap the well, to clean up the spill, to pay compensation—all of which they are getting on with, including putting aside the £20 billion in the escrow account. I think—$20 billion, sorry.

I think they've made good progress on that, and further progress needs to be made.

I think it's important to separate that from the decision to release Al-Megrahi, which, as I say, was a decision made by the Scottish Government and, as so far has been shown in investigations by the Scottish Parliament, was a decision which I wholly disagree with but, nonetheless, was taken in an appropriate way.

I think we have a question from Tom Bradby.

Cybersecurity/Extradition of Gary McKinnon to the U.S.

Q. Mr. President, Tom Bradby, ITV News. Quite a lot of people in the U.K. feel that your determination as a country to continue to push for the extradition of computer hacker and Asperger's sufferer Gary McKinnon is disproportionate and somewhat harsh. Do you think it is time now to consider some leniency in this case?

And, Prime Minister, you've expressed very strong views on this matter, suggesting that Mr. McKinnon shouldn't be extradited. Your Deputy Prime Minister has expressed even stronger views. Did you discuss that with the President today? And if not, would now be a good moment to share your views with us once again?

Prime Minister Cameron. Shall I go?

President Obama. Please, go ahead.

Prime Minister Cameron. It is something that we discussed in our meeting. I mean, clearly there's a discussion going on between the British and the Americans about this, and I don't want to prejudice those discussions. We completely understand that Gary McKinnon stands accused of a very important and significant crime in terms of hacking into vital databases. And nobody denies that that is an important crime that has to be considered. But I have had conversations with the U.S. Ambassador, as well as raising it today with the President, about this issue, and I hope a way through can be found.

President Obama. Well, one of the things that David and I discussed was the increasing challenge that we're going to face as a consequence of the Internet and the need for us to cooperate extensively on issues of cybersecurity.

We had a brief discussion about the fact that although there may still be efforts to send in spies and try to obtain state secrets through traditional cold war methods, the truth of the matter is, these days, where we're going to see enormous amounts of vulnerability when it comes to information is going to be through these kind of breaches in our information systems. So we take this very seriously. And I know that the British Government does as well.

Beyond that, one of the traditions we have is the President doesn't get involved in decisions around prosecutions, extradition matters. So what I expect is that my team will follow the law, but they will also coordinate closely with what we've just stated is an ally that is unparalleled in terms of our cooperative relationship. And I trust that this will get resolved in a way that underscores the seriousness of the issue, but also underscores the fact that we work together and we can find an appropriate solution.

All right? Thank you very much, everybody.

Prime Minister Cameron. Thank you very much.

NOTE: The President's news conference began at 1:58 p.m. in the East Room at the White House. In his remarks, the President referred to President Hamid Karzai of Afghanistan. Prime Minister Cameron referred to his daughter Nancy and son Arthur; Maj. Gen. Richard P. Mills, USMC, NATO International Security Assistance Force, Afghanistan, Regional Commander Southwest; Maj. Gen. Nick P. Carter, British Army, NATO International Security Assistance Force, Afghanistan, Regional Commander South; Secretary of State for Foreign and Commonwealth Affairs William J. Hague and Cabinet Secretary Gus O'Donnell of the United Kingdom; and U.S. Ambassador to the United Kingdom Louis B. Susman. A reporter referred to Deputy Prime Minister Nicholas Clegg of the United Kingdom.

Statement on Equal Pay Legislation
July 20, 2010

In America today, women make up half of the workforce and two-thirds of American families with children rely on a woman's wages as a significant portion of their families' income.

Yet, even in 2010, women make only 77 cents for every dollar that men earn. The gap is even more significant for working women of color, and it affects women across all education levels. As Vice President Biden and the Middle Class Task Force will discuss today, this is not just a question of fairness for hard-working women. Paycheck discrimination hurts families who lose out on badly needed income. And with so many families depending on women's wages, it hurts the American economy as a whole. In difficult economic times like these, we simply cannot afford this discriminatory burden.

My administration has already begun to address this problem. In my first week in office, I signed the Lilly Ledbetter Fair Pay Act, which helps women who face wage discrimination recover their lost wages, and in my State of the Union Address, I promised to crack down on violations of equal pay laws. Today the Equal Pay Enforcement Task Force will present its recommendations, which include ways to better coordinate among enforcement agencies and inform employees about their rights. These steps support women, and they also support businesses that are doing the right thing and paying their employees what they deserve.

We cannot do this work alone. So today I thank the House for its work on this issue and encourage the Senate to pass the "Paycheck Fairness Act," a commonsense bill that will help ensure that men and women who do equal work receive the equal pay that they and their families deserve. Passing this bill is one of the Task Force's key recommendations, and I hope Congress will act swiftly so that I can sign it into law.

Statement on the Senate Judiciary Committee Vote on Supreme Court Associate Justice-Designate Elena Kagan
July 20, 2010

Elena Kagan is one of this country's leading legal minds and has shown throughout this process that, if confirmed, she would be a fair and impartial Supreme Court Justice who understands how decisions made by the Court affect the lives of everyday Americans. Today's vote by the Senate Judiciary Committee is a bipartisan affirmation of her strong performance during her confirmation hearings. I want to thank the Judiciary Committee for giving her a thorough, timely, and respectful hearing, and I look forward to the full Senate taking up and voting on this nomination before the August recess.

Statement on the Senate Cloture Vote on Unemployment Insurance Extension Legislation
July 20, 2010

Today marks an important step toward passing the unemployment insurance extension which is critical to millions of Americans fighting to find a job, put food on the table, and make ends meet during this tough economic time. After a partisan minority blocked this critical aid to our Nation's families three separate times, the Senate has moved forward on restoring benefits to the 2.5 million Americans whose livelihood has been held hostage by obstruction and game playing over the past weeks.

I will continue to fight for economic policies that will lead us out of this mess and press Congress to act on more proposals to create new American jobs and strengthen our recovery, including a small-business jobs bill, aid for struggling States to prevent layoffs, and tax cuts for middle class families. Americans who are struggling to find a job and get back on their feet deserve more than the same political game-playing and failed policies that helped cause this recession. And I thank the Members of the Senate who stood on the side of these working families today.

Remarks on Signing the Dodd-Frank Wall Street Reform and Consumer Protection Act
July 21, 2010

The President. Thank you. Everybody, please have a seat. Have a seat. Well, good morning, everyone.

Audience members. Good morning.

The President. We are gathered in the heart of our Nation's Capital, surrounded by memorials to leaders and citizens who served our Nation in its earliest days and in its days of greatest trial. Now, today is such a time for America.

Over the past 2 years, we have faced the worst recession since the Great Depression. Eight million people lost their jobs. Tens of millions saw the value of their homes and retirement savings plummet. Countless businesses have been unable to get the loans they need, and many have been forced to shut their doors. And although the economy is growing again, too many people are still feeling the pain of the downturn.

Now, while a number of factors led to such a severe recession, the primary cause was a breakdown in our financial system. It was a crisis born of a failure of responsibility, from certain corners of Wall Street to the halls of power in Washington. For years, our financial sector was governed by antiquated and poorly enforced rules that allowed some to game the system and take risks that endangered the entire economy.

Unscrupulous lenders locked consumers into complex loans with hidden costs. Firms like AIG placed massive, risky bets with borrowed money. And while the rules left abuse and excess unchecked, they also left taxpayers on the hook if a big bank or financial institution ever failed.

Now, even before the crisis hit, I went to Wall Street and I called for commonsense reforms to protect consumers and our economy as a whole. And soon after taking office, I proposed a set of reforms to empower consumers and investors, to bring the shadowy deals that caused this crisis into the light of day, and to put a stop to taxpayer bailouts once and for all.

Today, thanks to a lot of people in this room, those reforms will become the law of the land. For the last year, Chairmen Barney Frank and Chris Dodd have worked day and night—[*applause*]—Barney and Chris have worked day and night to bring about this reform. And I am profoundly grateful to them. I would be remiss if I didn't also express my appreciation to Senator Harry Reid and Speaker Nancy Pelosi for their leadership. It wouldn't have happened without them.

Passing this bill was no easy task. To get there, we had to overcome the furious lobbying of an array of powerful interest groups and a partisan minority determined to block change. So the Members who are here today, both on the stage and in the audience, they have done a great service in devoting so much time and expertise to this effort, to looking out for the public interests and not the special interests. And I also want to thank the three Republican Senators who put partisanship aside, judged this bill on the merits, and voted for reform. We're grateful to them and the Republican House Members. Good to see you, Joe.

Now, let's put this in perspective. The fact is, the financial industry is central to our Nation's ability to grow, to prosper, to compete, and to innovate. There are a lot of banks that understand and fulfill this vital role, and there are a whole lot of bankers out there who want to do

right—and do right—by their customers. This reform will help foster innovation, not hamper it. It is designed to make sure that everybody follows the same set of rules so that firms compete on price and quality, not on tricks and not on traps. It demands accountability and responsibility from everyone. It provides certainty to everybody, from bankers to farmers to business owners to consumers. And unless your business model depends on cutting corners or bilking your customers, you've got nothing to fear from reform.

Now, for all those Americans who are wondering what Wall Street reform means for you, here's what you can expect. If you've ever applied for a credit card, a student loan, or a mortgage, you know the feeling of signing your name to pages of barely understandable fine print. What often happens as a result is that many Americans are caught by hidden fees and penalties or saddled with loans they can't afford. That's what happened to Robin Fox, hit with a massive rate increase on her credit card balance, even though she paid her bills on time. That's what happened to Andrew Giordano, who discovered hundreds of dollars in overdraft fees on his bank statement, fees he had no idea he might face. And both are here today. Well, with this law, unfair rate hikes, like the one that hit Robin, will end for good, and we'll ensure that people like Andrew aren't unwittingly caught by overdraft fees when they sign up for a checking account.

With this law, we'll crack down on abusive practices in the mortgage industry. We'll make sure that contracts are simpler, putting an end to many hidden penalties and fees in complex mortgages, so folks know what they're signing. With this law, students who take out college loans will be provided clear and concise information about their obligations. And with this law, ordinary investors, like seniors and folks saving for retirement, will be able to receive more information about the costs and risks of mutual funds and other investment products so that they can make better financial decisions as to what will work for them.

So all told, these reforms represent the strongest consumer financial protections in history—

in history. And these protections will be enforced by a new consumer watchdog with just one job: looking out for people—not big banks, not lenders, not investment houses—looking out for people as they interact with the financial system.

And that's not just good for consumers; that's good for the economy. Because reform will put a stop to a lot of the bad loans that fueled a debt-based bubble. And it will mean all companies will have to seek customers by offering better products instead of more deceptive ones.

Now, beyond the consumer protections I've outlined, reform will also rein in the abuse and excess that nearly brought down our financial system. It will finally bring transparency to the kinds of complex and risky transactions that helped trigger the financial crisis. Shareholders will also have a greater say on the pay of CEOs and other executives, so they can reward success instead of failure.

And finally, because of this law, the American people will never again be asked to foot the bill for Wall Street's mistakes. There will be no more tax-funded bailouts, period. If a large financial institution should ever fail, this reform gives us the ability to wind it down without endangering the broader economy. And there will be new rules to make clear that no firm is somehow protected because it is too big to fail, so we don't have another AIG.

That's what this reform will mean. Now, it doesn't mean our work is over. For these new rules to be effective, regulators will have to be vigilant. We may need to make adjustments along the way as our financial system adapts to these new changes and changes around the globe. No law can force anybody to be responsible; it's still incumbent on those on Wall Street to heed the lessons of this crisis in terms of how they conduct their businesses.

The fact is, every American, from Main Street to Wall Street, has a stake in our financial system. Wall Street banks and firms invest the capital that makes it possible for startups to sell new products. They provide loans to businesses to expand and to hire. They back mortgages for families purchasing a new home. That's why we'll all stand to gain from these reforms. We all win when investors around the world have confidence in our markets. We all win when shareholders have more power and more information. We all win when consumers are protected against abuse. And we all win when folks are rewarded based on how well they perform, not how well they evade accountability.

In the end, our financial system only works, our market is only free when there are clear rules and basic safeguards that prevent abuse, that check excess, that ensure that it is more profitable to play by the rules than to game the system. And that's what these reforms are designed to achieve, no more, no less. Because that's how we will ensure that our economy works for consumers, that it works for investors, that it works for financial institutions, that it works for all of us. This is the central lesson not only of this crisis but of our history.

Ultimately, there's no dividing line between Main Street and Wall Street. We rise or fall together as one Nation. So these reforms will help lift our economy and lead all of us to a stronger, more prosperous future.

And that's why I'm so honored to sign these reforms into law, and I'm so grateful to everybody who worked so hard to make this day possible. Thank you very much, everybody.

[At this point, the President signed the bill.]

It's done. Thank you.

NOTE: The President spoke at 11:34 a.m. at the Ronald Reagan Building and International Trade Center. In his remarks, he referred to Rep. Anh "Joseph" Quang Cao. H.R. 4173, approved July 21, was assigned Public Law No. 111–203. The Office of the Press Secretary also released a Spanish language transcript of these remarks.

Statement on Congressional Passage of Tribal Law and Order Legislation
July 21, 2010

Today's passage of the "Tribal Law and Order Act" is an important step to help the Federal Government better address the unique public safety challenges that confront tribal communities. The fact is, American Indians and Alaska Natives are victimized by violent crime at far higher rates than Americans as a whole. Native communities have seen increased gang and drug activity, with some tribes experiencing violent crime rates at more than 10 times the national average. And one in three Native women will be the victim of rape in her lifetime.

The Federal Government's relationship with tribal governments, its obligations under treaty and law, and our values as a nation require that we do more to improve public safety in tribal communities. And this act will help us achieve that. It will strengthen the relationship between the Federal Government and tribal governments. It will improve our ability to work with tribal communities in the investigation and prosecution of crime, and it authorizes resources for tribes to fight crime more effectively. While many Members helped pass this bill, I especially want to applaud Senators Dorgan, Barrasso, and Kyl and Representatives Herseth Sandlin, Kildee, Cole, Conyers, Scott, Rahall, Simpson, and Pastor for their leadership on this issue. I look forward to signing the act into law.

NOTE: The statement referred to H.R. 725.

Statement on Senate Passage of Unemployment Insurance Extension Legislation
July 21, 2010

Tonight the United States Senate finally overcame weeks of parliamentary roadblocks by a partisan minority and voted to restore desperately needed unemployment insurance assistance to 2½ million Americans who lost their jobs in the recession. Americans who are working day and night to get back on their feet and support their families in these tough economic times deserve more than obstruction and partisan game-playing that happens too often here in Washington. I thank the Members of the Senate who stood on the side of these working families today and urge Members of the House to pass this extension so I can quickly sign it into law. I also call on Congress to act on more proposals that support our economic recovery, including passing critical aid to our States and support to small businesses to create new private sector jobs.

NOTE: The statement referred to H.R. 4213.

Remarks on Signing the Improper Payments Elimination and Recovery Act of 2010
July 22, 2010

Morning, everybody. Thank you. Thank you. Everybody, please have a seat. Welcome to the White House. I am pleased that you could all join us today as I sign this bill, the Improper Payments Elimination and Recovery Act, which, translated into English, means cutting down on waste, fraud, and abuse and ensuring that our Government serves as a responsible steward for the tax dollars of the American people.

Now, this is a responsibility we've been working to fulfill from the very beginning of this administration. Back when I first started campaigning for office, I said I wanted to change the way Washington works so that it works for the American people. I meant making Government more open and more transparent and more responsive to the needs of the people. I meant getting rid of the waste and inefficiencies that squander the people's hard-earned money. And I meant finally revamping the systems that undermine our efficiency and threaten our security and fail to serve the interests of the American people.

Now, there are outstanding public servants doing essential work throughout our Government. But too often, their best efforts are thwarted by outdated technologies and outmoded ways of doing business. That needs to change. We have to challenge a status quo that accepts billions of dollars in waste as the cost of doing business and enables obsolete or underperforming programs to survive year after year simply because that's the way things have always been done.

This isn't just about lines on a spreadsheet or numbers in a budget, because when we fail to spend people's tax dollars wisely, that's money that we're not investing in better schools for our kids or tax relief for families or innovation to create new industries and new jobs. When Government doesn't work like it should, it has a real effect on people's lives, on small-business owners who need loans, on young people who want to go to college, on the men and women who've served this country and are trying to get the benefits that they've earned. And when we continue to spend as if deficits don't matter, that means our kids and our grandkids may wind up saddled with debts that they'll never be able to repay.

And the reality is that right now, in these difficult economic times, families across this country are cutting every frill and stretching every dollar as far as they can. And they should expect no less from their Government.

If folks can book a flight or buy a pair of shoes online with the click of a button, there's no reason they should have to fill out duplicative forms or endure endless redtape and delays when they deal with their Government. So that's why one of the first things we did when we arrived in Washington was to undertake an accountable Government initiative, an effort that spans every agency, department, and office in our Government.

We named our first ever Chief Performance Officer, Jeffrey Zients, and we're bringing to bear every tool at our disposal, a combination of 21st-century technology and old-fashioned common sense to ensure that our Government operates as efficiently as possible and provides the highest quality of service to its customers, the American people.

We began by combining—by going through the budget line by line and proposing $20 billion worth of cuts each year by targeting programs that are wasteful, duplicative, or, in some cases, just plain ridiculous, like the $35 million we're spending for a radio navigation system for ships. Since we now have this thing called GPS, we don't need it. Or the $3 million that was spent on consultants to create seals and logos for the Department of Homeland Security, their logos and seals are fine. [*Laughter*] Or the billions of dollars slated to be spent on a fancy, new Presidential helicopter fleet that I didn't want and didn't need because Marine One is also fine.

We've drafted a budget for next year that freezes all discretionary Government spending outside of national security for 3 years, a budget, by the way, that would reduce this spending—nondefense discretionary spending—to its lowest level as a share of the economy in 50 years. This isn't talked about a lot so I'm going to repeat it. Our budget would take nonsecurity defense—or nondefense spending to its lowest level since JFK—lowest level as a percentage of the economy since JFK.

We've gone after wasteful Government contracting with a vengeance, working to put an end to unnecessary no-bid contracts and dramatically reinforcing the way Government contracts are awarded. And we're now on track to reach our goal of saving $40 billion by the end of next—the next fiscal year. We're working to sell or lease out thousands of Federal buildings which we no longer need and aren't using, saving another $8 billion. We froze salaries for senior White House staff; hence, the glum faces. [*Laughter*]

And we've asked Congress for additional authority so that working together, we can move quickly to cut wasteful spending proposals before the money goes out the door. We've streamlined those college loan forms, eliminating nearly two dozen unnecessary questions. We're creating a single electronic medical record for our men and women in uniform that will follow them from the day they enlist until the day that they are laid to rest. We're revamping our Social Security and citizenship processes so that folks can book appointments and check the status of their applications online. We've created mobile apps that provide everything from disaster assistance to product safety information to the latest wait times for security lines at your local airport.

And we've begun an unprecedented effort to put an end to a problem known as improper payments, which is the purpose of the bill that I'm signing into law today. Now, these are payments sent by the Government to the wrong person or for the wrong reasons or in the wrong amount: payments to a defense contractor that's been disbarred for shoddy work, but somehow managed to get through the system, payments to companies that haven't paid their taxes or to folks who are incarcerated or who are dead.

Sometimes these payments are the result of innocent mistakes or reflect valid claims that were paid at the wrong time. But sometimes they result from abuses by scam artists and crooked companies. And all told, they added up to $110 billion. I want everybody to understand, just get some perspective on that: That is more than the budgets of the Departments of Education and the Small Business Administration combined. And that's unacceptable.

So that's why earlier this year, I directed our Federal agencies to launch rigorous audits conducted by auditors who are paid based on how many abuses or errors they uncover; the more they find, the more money they make. So they are highly incentivized. We're also creating a "do not pay" list, a consolidated database of every individual and company that's ineligible for Federal payments. Before checks are mailed, agencies will be required to check this list to make sure that the payment is to the right person, in the right amount, for the right reason.

Now, with these new tools, the challenge I'm making to my team today is to reduce improper payments by $50 billion between now and 2012. And this goal is fully achievable due in no small part to some of the great work of the Members of Congress standing with me today, particularly Senator Tom Carper and Representative Patrick Murphy, who sponsored the bill I'm about to sign and worked with all the other Members of Congress who are here today to get it passed.

And I think, by the way, it's worth noting that this bill passed unanimously in both the House and the Senate, a powerful reminder of what we can accomplish when we put partisanship aside and do what's best for the people we serve.

So this bill will dramatically expand and intensify our efforts to end improper payments. And going forward, every agency in our Government will be required to conduct annual assessments to determine which of their programs are at risk of making improper payments. Agencies will be required to audit more of their programs and recapture more taxpayer dollars. And we now have rigorous enforcement mechanisms to hold agencies accountable for how much money they save.

So in large part thanks to the great work of the people in this room, I think we're headed in the right direction. And today I'm pleased to announce that I will be charging Jack Lew, my choice for Director of Office of Management and Budget—once Peter Orszag, the current OMB Director, departs—with building on the good work that Peter began. I'm entrusting Jack with carrying forward our accountable Government initiative in the months ahead. I will be asking him and Jeff to give me regular updates on our progress in cutting waste and making our Government more efficient and effective.

And as the only OMB Director in history to preside over a budget surplus for 3 consecutive years, Jack Lew knows a thing or two about making Government work. I'm confident he's up to the challenge of building the kind of Government that the American people expect and deserve, one that spends their money wisely, serves their interests well, and is fully worthy of their trust and respect.

So I want to again thank these outstanding Members of Congress who are here today who have been on the case in both Chambers for quite some time. I want to thank all the people who worked on this bill, in this room for your outstanding efforts.

Thank you. God bless you. God bless America. And let me sign this bill.

NOTE: The President spoke at 11:28 a.m. in the State Dining Room at the White House. S. 1508, approved July 22, was assigned Public Law No. 111–204.

Statement on Signing the Unemployment Compensation Extension Act of 2010
July 22, 2010

Today I signed the unemployment insurance extension to restore desperately needed assistance to 2½ million Americans who lost their jobs in the recession. After a partisan minority used procedural tactics to block the authorization of this assistance three separate times over the past weeks, Americans who are fighting to find a good job and support their families will finally get the support they need to get back on their feet during these tough economic times. Now it's time for Congress to act on more pro-posals that support our economic recovery, including passing critical aid to our States and support to small businesses. Small businesses are the engine of job growth, and measures to cut their taxes and make lending available should not be held hostage to partisan tactics like those that unconscionably held up unemployment insurance.

NOTE: H.R. 4213, approved July 22, was assigned Public Law No. 111–205.

Remarks on the National Economy
July 23, 2010

Hello, everybody. Trying a little change of venue here, mix it up.

I want to talk about the progress that we made this week on three fronts, as we work to repair the damage to our economy from this recession and build a stronger foundation for the future.

First, I signed a Wall Street reform bill that will protect consumers and our entire economy from the recklessness and irresponsibility that led to the worst recession since the Great Depression. It's a reform that will help us put a stop to the abusive practices of mortgage lenders and credit card companies and ensure that people get the straight, unvarnished information that they need before they take out a loan or open a credit card. It will bring the shadowy deals that caused the financial crisis into the light of day. And it will end taxpayer bailouts of Wall Street firms and give shareholders a say on executive compensation.

The need for this reform, by the way, was underscored by the report issued by Ken Feinberg this morning, identifying a number of financial companies that continued to pay out lavish bonuses at the height of the financial crisis, even as they accepted billions of dollars in taxpayer assistance.

Second, I signed a law that will improve our ability to crack down on improper payments made by our Government. Every year, the Government wastes tens of billions of dollars—taxpayer dollars—on erroneous payments to companies that haven't paid their taxes or to prison inmates or even to people who died a long time ago. Today, we have the technology to block these payments, and the law I signed will give us new tools to do so. I've set a target to save at least $50 billion in—by 2012, savings that are more important today than ever because we simply don't have any money to waste.

Third, we finally overcame the procedural blockade of a partisan minority in the Senate to restore unemployment insurance for about 2.5 million Americans who are out of work and looking for a job.

So taken together, we made enormous progress this week on Wall Street reform, on making sure that we're eliminating waste and abuse in Government, and in providing immediate assistance to people who are out there looking for work.

But ultimately, our goal is to make sure the people who are looking for a job can find a job. And that's why it's so important for the Senate to pass the additional steps that I've asked for to cut taxes and expand lending for America's small businesses, our most important engine for hiring and for growth. And a small-business jobs bill that contains these measures may come up for a final vote in the Senate in the next few days.

With this small-business bill, we'll set up a new lending fund to help community banks offer small-business men and women the loans they need to grow and to hire. We'll help States encourage more private sector loans to small businesses in industries like manufacturing or construction that have been especially hard hit by this recession. We'll expand our most successful small-business initiatives and more than double the size of loans our small-business owners can take out.

And to unlock the growth of our entrepreneurs, we'll finally do what I've been advocating since I ran for President, which is to eliminate capital gains taxes entirely for key investments in small businesses.

Now, last night, after a series of partisan delays, the Senate took an important step forward by supporting a lending fund in the overall small-business jobs bill. I want to thank Senators Mary Landrieu and George LeMieux for their leadership and advocacy on behalf of the millions of small-businesspeople for whom this will make a meaningful difference. I was heartened that Senators LeMieux and Senator George Voinovich crossed party lines to help pass this lending provision last night, and I hope we can now finish the job and pass the small-business jobs plan without delay and without additional partisan wrangling.

You know, the small-business men and women who write to me every day and the folks who I've met with across this country, they can't afford any more political games. They need us to do what they sent us here to do. They didn't send us here to wage a never-ending campaign. They didn't send us here to do what's best for our political party. They sent us here to do what's best for the United States of America and all its citizens, whether Democrats or Republicans or Independents. In other words, they sent us here to govern. And that's what I hope we will do in the remaining days before the Congress takes its August recess.

Thank you very much, everybody.

NOTE: The President spoke at 12:10 p.m. in the Roosevelt Room at the White House. In his remarks, he referred to Special Master for TARP Executive Compensation Kenneth R. Feinberg. The Office of the Press Secretary also released a Spanish language transcript of these remarks.

The President's Weekly Address
July 24, 2010

This week, I signed into law a Wall Street reform bill that will protect consumers and our entire economy from the recklessness and irresponsibility that led to the worst recession of our lifetime. It's reform that will help put a stop to the abusive practices of mortgage lenders and credit card companies. It will end taxpayer bailouts of Wall Street firms, and it will finally bring the shadowy deals that caused the financial crisis into the light of day.

Wall Street reform is a key pillar of an overall economic plan we've put in place to dig ourselves out of this recession and build an economy for the long run, an economy that makes

America more competitive and our middle class more secure. It's a plan based on the Main Street values of hard work and responsibility, and one that demands new accountability from Wall Street to Washington.

Instead of giving tax breaks to corporations that ship jobs overseas, we want to give tax breaks to small-business owners who are creating jobs right here in America. Already, we've given small businesses eight new tax cuts and have expanded lending to more than 60,000 small-business owners.

We're also investing in a homegrown clean energy industry, because I don't want to see new solar panels and wind turbines and electric cars manufactured in some other country. I want to see them made in America, by American workers. So far, we've provided new tax credits, loan guarantees, and investments that will lead to more than 800,000 clean energy jobs by 2012. And throughout America, communities are being rebuilt by people working in hundreds of thousands of new private sector jobs repairing our roads, bridges, and railways.

Our economic plan is also aimed at strengthening the middle class. That's why we've cut taxes for 95 percent of working families. That's why we've offered tax credits that have made college more affordable for millions of students and why we're making a new commitment to our community colleges. And that's why we passed health insurance reform that will stop insurance companies from dropping or denying coverage based on an illness or preexisting condition.

This is our economic plan: smart investments in America's small businesses, America's clean energy industry, and America's middle class. Now, I can't tell you that this plan will bring back all the jobs we've lost and restore our economy to full strength overnight. The truth is, it took nearly a decade of failed economic policies to create this mess, and it will take years to fully repair the damage. But I am confident that we are finally headed in the right direction. We are moving forward. And what we can't afford right now is to go back to the same ideas that created this mess in the first place.

Unfortunately, those are the ideas we keep hearing from our friends in the other party. This week, the Republican leader in the House of Representatives offered his plan to create jobs. It's a plan that's surprisingly short and sadly familiar.

First, he would repeal health insurance reform, which would take away tax credits from millions of small-business owners and take us back to the days when insurance companies had free rein to drop coverage and jack up premiums. Second, he would say no to new investments in clean energy, after his party already voted against the clean energy tax credits and loans that are creating thousands of new jobs and hundreds of new businesses. And third, even though his party voted against tax cuts for middle class families, he would permanently keep in place the tax cuts for the very wealthiest Americans, the same tax cuts that have added hundreds of billions to our debt.

These aren't new ideas. They're the same policies that led us into this recession. They will not create jobs, they will kill them. They will not reduce our deficit, they will add $1 trillion to our deficit. They will take us backward at a time when we need to keep America moving forward.

I know times are tough. I know that the progress we've made isn't good enough for the millions of Americans who are still out of work or struggling to pay the bills. But I also know the character of this Nation. I know that in times of great challenge and difficulty, we don't fear the future, we shape the future. We harness the skills and ingenuity of the most dynamic country on Earth to reach a better day. We do it with optimism, and we do it with confidence. That's the spirit we need right now, and that's the future I know we can build together. Thanks.

NOTE: The address was recorded at approximately 3:15 p.m. on July 23 in the Map Room at the White House for broadcast on July 24. In the address, the President referred to House Republican Leader John A. Boehner. The transcript was made available by the Office of the Press Secretary on July 23, but was embargoed for release until 6 a.m. on July 24.

Remarks on Election Spending Disclosure Legislation
July 26, 2010

Good afternoon, everybody. Tomorrow there's going to be a very important vote in the Senate about how much influence special interests should have over our democracy. Because of the Supreme Court's decision earlier this year in the *Citizens United* case, big corporations, even foreign-controlled ones, are now allowed to spend unlimited amounts of money on American elections. They can buy millions of dollars' worth of TV ads, and worst of all, they don't even have to reveal who's actually paying for the ads. Instead, a group can hide behind a name like "Citizens for a Better Future," even if a more accurate name would be "Companies for Weaker Oversight." And these shadow groups are already forming and building war chests of tens of millions of dollars to influence the fall elections.

Now, imagine the power this will give special interests over politicians. Corporate lobbyists will be able to tell Members of Congress if they don't vote the right way, they will face an onslaught of negative ads in their next campaign. And all too often, no one will actually know who's behind those ads.

So the House has already passed a bipartisan bill that would change all this before the next election. The "DISCLOSE Act" would simply require corporate political advertisers to reveal who's funding their activities. So when special interests take to the airwaves, whoever is running and funding the ad would have to appear in the advertisement and claim responsibility for it, like a company's CEO or the organization's biggest contributor. And foreign-controlled corporations and entities would be restricted from spending money to influence American elections, just as they were in the past.

Now, you'd think that making these reforms would be a matter of common sense, particularly since they primarily involve just making sure that folks who are financing these ads are disclosed so that the American people can make up their own minds. Nobody is saying you can't run the ads; just make sure that people know

who in fact is behind financing these ads. And you'd think that reducing corporate and even foreign influence over our elections would not be a partisan issue, but of course, this is Washington in 2010. And the Republican leadership in the Senate is once again using every tactic and every maneuver they can to prevent the "DISCLOSE Act" from even coming up for an up-or-down vote, just like they did with unemployment insurance for Americans who'd lost their jobs in this recession, just like they're doing by blocking tax credits and lending assistance for small-business owners. On issue after issue, we are trying to move America forward, and they keep on trying to take us back.

Now, at a time of such challenge for America, we can't afford these political games. Millions of Americans are struggling to get by, and their voices shouldn't be drowned out by millions of dollars in secret, special interest advertising. The American people's voices should be heard.

A vote to oppose these reforms is nothing less than a vote to allow corporate and special interest takeovers of our elections. It is damaging to our democracy. It is precisely what led a Republican President named Theodore Roosevelt to tackle this issue a century ago.

Back then, President Roosevelt warned of the dangers of limitless corporate spending in our political system. He actually called it "one of the principal sources of corruption in our political affairs." And he proposed strict limits on corporate influence in elections, not because he was opposed to them expressing their views in the halls of democracy, but he didn't want everybody else being drowned out.

He said, "Every special interest is entitled to justice, but no one is entitled—not one is entitled to a vote in Congress or a voice on the bench or to representation in any public office," because he understood those weren't individual voters; these are amalgams of special interests. They have the right to hire their lobbyists. They have the right to put forward their view. They even have the right to advertise. But the least we should be able to do is know who they are.

So on Tuesday, we face the sort of challenge that Teddy Roosevelt talked about over a century ago. We've got a similar opportunity to prevent special interests from gaining even more clout in Washington. This should not be a Democratic issue or a Republican issue. This is an issue that goes to whether or not we're going to have a Government that works for ordinary Americans, a Government of, by, and for the people.

That's why these reforms are so important, and that's why I urge the Senate to pass the "DISCLOSE Act."

Thank you.

NOTE: The President spoke at 2:49 p.m. in the Rose Garden at the White House. In his remarks, he referred to H.R. 5175. The Office of the Press Secretary also released a Spanish language transcript of these remarks.

Remarks on the 20th Anniversary of the Americans with Disabilities Act
July 26, 2010

The President. Thank you. Good evening, everybody. Thank you so much. Well, we have a gorgeous day to celebrate an extraordinary event in the life of this Nation. Welcome, all of you, to our White House. And thank you, Robert, for the wonderful introduction. It is a pleasure and honor to be with all of you on the 20th anniversary of one of the most comprehensive civil rights bills in the history of this country, the Americans with Disabilities Act.

I see so many champions of this law here today. I wish I had time to acknowledge each and every one of you. I want to thank all of you. But I also want to thank our Cabinet Secretaries and the members of my administration here today who are working to advance the goals of the ADA so that it is not just the letter of the law, but the spirit of the law that's being applied all across this country.

I want to thank the Members of Congress in attendance who fought to make ADA possible and to keep improving it throughout the years. I want to acknowledge Dick Thornburgh, who worked hard to make this happen as Attorney General under President George H.W. Bush.

And by the way, I had a chance to speak to President Bush before I came out here, and he sends heartfelt regards to all of you. And it's—he's extraordinarily proud of the law that was passed. He was very humble about his own role, but I think it's worth acknowledging the great work that he did.

We also remember those we've lost who helped make this law possible, like our old friend Ted Kennedy—and I see Patrick here—

and Justin Dart, Jr., a man folks call the father of the ADA, whose wife Yoshiko is here. Yoshiko, so nice to see you.

I also notice that Elizabeth Dole is here, and I had a chance to speak to Bob Dole as well and thank him for the extraordinary role that he played in advancing this legislation.

Let me also say that Congressman Jim Langevin wanted to be here today, but he's currently presiding over the House Chamber, the first time in our history somebody using a wheelchair has done so.

Now, today, as we commemorate what the ADA accomplished, we celebrate who the ADA was all about. It was about the young girl in Washington State who just wanted to see a movie at her hometown theater, but was turned away because she had cerebral palsy; or the young man in Indiana who showed up at a worksite able to do the work, excited for the opportunity, but was turned away and called a cripple because of a minor disability he had already trained himself to work with; or the student in California who was eager and able to attend the college of his dreams and refused to let the iron grip of polio keep him from the classroom—each of whom became integral to this cause.

And it was about all of you. You understand these stories because you or someone you loved lived them. And that sparked a movement. It began when Americans no longer saw their own disabilities as a barrier to their success and set out to tear down the physical and social barriers that were. It grew when you realized you weren't alone. It became a massive wave of bottom-up change that swept across the country as you refused to accept the world as it was. And when you were told, "No, don't try, you can't," you responded with that age-old American creed: "Yes, we can."

Audience member. [*Inaudible*]

The President. Yes, we can!

Sit-ins in San Francisco, demonstrations in Denver, protests in Washington, DC, at Gallaudet, and before Congress, people marched and organized and testified, and laws changed and minds changed and progress was won.

Now, that's not to say it was easy. You didn't always have folks in Washington to fight on your behalf. And when you did, they weren't as powerful, as well connected, as well funded as the lobbyists who lined up to kill any attempt at change. And at first, you might have thought, what does anyone in Washington know or care about my battle? But what you knew from your own experience is that disability touches us all. If one in six Americans has a disability, then odds are the rest of us love somebody with a disability.

I was telling a story to a group that was in the Oval Office before I came out here about Michelle's father, who had MS. And by the time I met him, he had to use two canes just to walk. He was stricken with MS when he was 30 years old, but he never missed a day of work; had to wake up an hour early to get dressed——

Audience member. So what.

The President. ——to get to the job, but that was his attitude: So what. He could do it. Didn't miss a dance recital, did not miss a ball game of his son. Everybody's got a story like that somewhere in their family.

And that's how you rallied an unlikely assortment of leaders in Congress and in the White House to the cause, Congressmen like Steny Hoyer, who knew his wife Judy's battle with epilepsy; and Tony Coelho, who waged his own; and Jim Sensenbrenner, whose wife Cheryl is a tremendous leader and advocate for the community, and they're both here today.

Senators like Tom Harkin, who's here today and who signed part of a speech on the ADA so his deaf brother, Frank, would understand; and

Ted Kennedy, whose sister had a severe intellectual disability and whose son lost a leg to cancer; and Bob Dole, who was wounded serving heroically in World War II; senior officials in the White House; and even the President himself.

They understood this injustice from the depths of their own experience. They also understood that by allowing this injustice to stand, we were depriving of our Nation—we were depriving our Nation and our economy of the full talents and contributions of tens of millions of Americans with disabilities.

That is how the ADA came to be, when, to his enduring credit, President George H.W. Bush signed it into law, on this lawn, on this day, 20 years ago. That's how you changed America.

Equal access to the classroom, the workplace, and the transportation required to get there; equal opportunity to live full and independent lives the way we choose; not dependence, but independence, that's what the ADA was all about.

But while it was a historic milestone in the journey to equality, it wasn't the end. There was and is more to do. And that's why today I'm announcing one of the most important updates to the ADA since its original enactment in 1991.

Today the Department of Justice is publishing two new rules protecting disability-based discrimination—or prohibiting disability-based discrimination by more than 80,000 State and local government entities and 7 million private businesses. And beginning 18 months from now, all new buildings must be constructed in a way that's compliant with the new 2010 standards for the design of doors and windows and elevators and bathrooms, buildings like stores and restaurants and schools and stadiums and hospitals and hotels and theaters.

My predecessor's administration proposed these rules 6 years ago. And in those 6 years, they've been improved upon with more than 4,000 comments from the public. We've heard from all sides. And that's allowed us to do this in a way that makes sense economically and allows appropriate flexibility, while ensuring Americans with disabilities full participation in our society.

And for the very first time, these rules will cover recreational facilities like amusement parks and marinas and gyms and golf facilities and swimming pools and municipal facilities like courtrooms and prisons. From now on, businesses must follow practices that allow individuals with disabilities an equal chance to purchase tickets for accessible seating at sporting events and concerts.

And our work goes on. Even as we speak, Attorney General Eric Holder is preparing new rules to ensure accessibility of web sites.

Audience member. Yes, we can!

The President. Yes, we can. [*Laughter*]

We're also placing a new focus on hiring Americans with disabilities across the Federal Government. Today, only 5 percent of the Federal workforce is made up of Americans with disabilities, far below the proportion of Americans with disabilities in the general population. In a few moments, I'll sign an Executive order that will establish the Federal Government as a model employer of individuals with disabilities. So we're going to boost recruitment, we're going to boost training, we're going to boost retention. We'll better train hiring managers. Each agency will have a senior official who's accountable for achieving the goals we've set. And I expect regular reports. And we're going to post our progress online so that you can hold us accountable too. And these new steps build on the progress my administration has already made.

To see it that no one who signs up to fight for our country is ever excluded from its promise, we've made major investments in improving the care and treatment for our wounded warriors. To ensure full access to participation in our democracy and our economy, we're working to make all Government web sites accessible to persons with disabilities.

We're expanding broadband Internet access to Americans who are deaf and hard of hearing. We've followed through with a promise I made to create three new disability offices at the State Department and Department of Transportation and at FEMA.

And to promote equal rights across the globe, the United States of America joined 140 other nations in signing the U.N. Convention on the Rights of Persons with Disabilities, the first new human rights convention of the 21st century. America was the first nation on Earth to comprehensively declare equality for its citizens with disabilities; we should join the rest of the world to declare it again. And when I submit our ratification package to Congress, I expect passage to be swift.

And to advance the right to live independently, I launched the Year of Community Living on the 10th anniversary of the *Olmstead* decision, a decision that declared the involuntary institutional isolation of people with disabilities unlawful discrimination under the ADA.

So HHS Secretary Kathleen Sebelius and HUD Secretary Shaun Donovan have worked together to improve access to affordable housing and community supports and independent living arrangements for people with disabilities. And we continued a program that successfully helps people with disabilities transition to the community of their choice. And I'm proud of the work that the Department of Justice is doing to enforce *Olmstead* across the country.

And we've finally broken down one of the discriminatory barriers that the ADA left in place, because for too long, our health care system denied coverage to tens of millions of Americans with preexisting conditions, including Americans with disabilities. It was time to change that, and we did. Yes, we did.

So the Affordable Care Act I signed into law 4 months ago will give every American more control over their health care, and it will do more to give Americans with disabilities control over their own lives than any legislation since the ADA. I know many of you know the frustration of fighting with an insurance company. That's why this law finally shifts the balance of power from them to you and to other consumers.

No more denying coverage to children based on a preexisting condition or disability. No more lifetime limits on coverage. No more dropping your coverage when you get sick and need it the most because your insurance company found an unintentional error in your paperwork. And because Americans with disabilities are living longer and more independently, this law will establish better long-term care choices for Americans with disabilities as a consequence of the CLASS Act, an idea Ted Kennedy championed for years.

Equal access, equal opportunity, the freedom to make our lives what we will—these aren't principles that belong to any one group or any one political party. They are common principles. They are American principles. No matter who we are—young, old, rich, poor, Black, White, Latino, Asian, Native American, gay, straight, disabled, or not—these are the principles we cherish as citizens of the United States of America.

They were guaranteed to us in our founding documents. And one of the signers of those documents was a man named Stephen Hopkins. He was a patriot, a scholar, a nine-time Governor of Rhode Island. It's also said he had a form of palsy. And on July 4, 1776, as he grasped his pen to sign his name to the Declaration of Independence, he said, "My hand trembles, but my heart does not." My hand trembles, but my heart does not.

Life, liberty, the pursuit of happiness: words that began our never-ending journey to form a more perfect Union, to look out for one another, to advance opportunity and prosperity for all of our people, to constantly expand the meaning of life, liberty, the pursuit of happiness, to move America forward. That's what we did with the ADA, that is what we do today, and that's what we're going to do tomorrow, together.

So thank you. God bless you, and God bless the United States of America. Let me sign this order.

NOTE: The President spoke at 6:26 p.m. on the South Lawn at the White House. In his remarks, he referred to actor Robert D. Hall, who introduced the President; Rep. Patrick J. Kennedy and Edward M. Kennedy, Jr., sons of former Sen. Edward M. Kennedy; former Sen. Elizabeth H. Dole and her husband, former Sen. Robert J. Dole; and former Rep. Anthony L. Coelho. He also referred to his brother-in-law Craig M. Robinson. The related proclamation and Executive order are listed in Appendix D at the end of this volume.

Remarks Following a Meeting With Congressional Leaders
July 27, 2010

Good afternoon, everybody. I just concluded a productive discussion with the leaders of both parties in Congress. This was one of a series of regular meetings that I called for in the State of the Union because I think it's important for us to come together and speak frankly about the challenges we face and to work through areas where we don't agree; hopefully, find some areas where we do.

Our conversation today focused on an issue that's being discussed every day at kitchen tables across this country, and that's how do we create jobs that people need to support their families.

I believe that starts with doing everything we can to support small businesses. These are the stores, the restaurants, the startups, and other companies that create two out of every three new jobs in this country and that grow into the big businesses that transform industries here in America and around the world.

But we know that many of these businesses still can't get the loans and the capital they need to keep their doors open and hire new workers. That's why we've proposed steps to get them that help: eliminating capital gains taxes on investments, making it easier for small lenders to support small businesses, expanding successful SBA programs to help these businesses access the capital that they need.

This is how we create jobs, by investing in the innovators and entrepreneurs that have always driven our prosperity. These are the kind of commonsense steps that folks from both parties have supported in the past, steps to cut taxes and spur private sector growth and investment.

And I hope that in the coming days, we'll once again find common ground and get this legislation passed. We shouldn't let America's small businesses be held hostage to partisan politics and certainly not at this critical time.

We also talked about the need to move forward on energy reform. The Senate is now poised to act before the August recess, advancing legislation to respond to the BP oil spill and create new clean energy jobs.

That legislation is an important step in the right direction, but I want to emphasize it's only the first step. And I intend to keep pushing for broader reform, including climate legislation, because if we've learned anything from the tragedy in the Gulf, it's that our current energy policy is unsustainable.

And we can't afford to stand by as our dependence on foreign oil deepens, as we keep on pumping out the deadly pollutants that threaten our air and our water and the lives and livelihoods of our people. And we can't stand by as we let China race ahead to create the clean energy jobs and industries of the future. We should be developing those renewable energy resources and creating those high-wage, high-skill jobs right here in the United States of America. That's what comprehensive energy and climate reform would do. And that's why I intend to keep pushing this issue forward.

I also urged the House leaders to pass the necessary funding to support our efforts in Afghanistan and Pakistan. I know much has been written about this in recent days as a result of the substantial leak of documents from Afghanistan covering a period from 2004 to 2009.

While I'm concerned about the disclosure of sensitive information from the battlefield that could potentially jeopardize individuals or operations, the fact is, these documents don't reveal any issues that haven't already informed our public debate on Afghanistan. Indeed, they point to the same challenges that led me to conduct an extensive review of our policy last fall.

So let me underscore what I've said many times: For 7 years, we failed to implement a strategy adequate to the challenge in this region, the region from which the 9/11 attacks were waged and other attacks against the Unit-

ed States and our friends and allies have been planned.

That's why we've substantially increased our commitment there, insisted upon greater accountability from our partners in Afghanistan and Pakistan, developed a new strategy that can work, and put in place a team, including one of our finest generals, to execute that plan. Now we have to see that strategy through.

And as I told the leaders, I hope the House will act today to join the Senate, which voted unanimously in favor of this funding, to ensure that our troops have the resources they need and that we're able to do what's necessary for our national security.

Finally, during our meeting today, I urged Senator McConnell and others in the Senate to work with us to fill the vacancies that continue to plague our judiciary. Right now we've got nominees who've been waiting up to 8 months to be confirmed as judges. Most of these folks were voted out of committee unanimously or nearly unanimously by both Democrats and Republicans. Both Democrats and Republicans agreed that they were qualified to serve. Nevertheless, some in the minority have used parliamentary procedures time and again to deny them a vote in the full Senate.

Now, if we want our judicial system to work, if we want to deliver justice in our courts, then we need judges on our benches. And I hope that in the coming months, we'll be able to work together to ensure a timelier process in the Senate.

Now, we don't have many days left before Congress is out for the year. And everyone understands that we're less than 100 days from an election. It's during this time that the noise and the chatter about who's up in the polls and which party is ahead threatens to drown out just about everything else.

But the folks we serve—who sent us here to serve—they sent us here for a reason. They sent us here to listen to their voices. They sent us here to represent their interests, not our own. They sent us here to lead. And I hope that in the coming months, we'll do everything in our power to live up to that responsibility.

Thanks very much.

NOTE: The President spoke at 12:30 p.m. in the Rose Garden at the White House. In his remarks, he referred to Gen. David H. Petraeus, USA, commander, NATO International Security Assistance Force, Afghanistan. The Office of the Press Secretary also released a Spanish language transcript of these remarks.

Remarks in Edison, New Jersey
July 28, 2010

Well, I just had a terrific meeting with these small-business owners here at Tastee Sub Shop. And I want to thank Dave and Carl for hosting us here today. And I highly recommend everybody buy a sandwich while you're here. Although, as I said before, I can't eat a 12-inch these days, now that I'm 49—well, I will be in a week.

We talked about some of the difficulties that people have had making payroll and turning a profit during this recession. And we talked about what we can do to make it easier for small businesses to grow.

All of these folks here know why that's important. Small businesses create two out of every three jobs in this country, so our recovery depends on them. And if we want to keep America moving forward, we need to keep investing in our small businesses.

This is, by the way, more than—is more important than just our economy. It's also about who we are as a people, because America has always been a place where if you've had a good idea and you're willing to really work hard for it, you can see it through and you can succeed. That's what gives the worker the courage to leave her job to become her own boss. It's what propels people to risk their savings on an idea that they believe might just change the world. I was hearing from Tom, here, about how he was having trouble finding work 30, 40 years ago and decided that he would take over a business that only had two employees. And now he's an employer for a whole bunch of folks, and he's going to be passing on his business to his family. And that's the American story.

This town, Edison, is named after somebody who was not only one of history's greatest inventors, but also a pretty savvy small-business owner. And the small-businesspeople who are here with me today exemplify that same entrepreneurial spirit. And all these companies have seen their share of challenges. All of these small-business owners have had to improvise and adapt over the years, especially in tough times, and that includes over the last couple years.

So Tom and Catherine Horsburgh were telling me that they got through the downturn. In order to do so, they had to market their products to types of businesses that they hadn't sold to before. Brian Bovio's company had to let some people go when the recession hit. But in the 2 years since, he's transformed his business, and now he's making people's homes more energy efficient to save money on their utility bills, and he's been able to start hiring again. He is very interested in making sure that the Home Star proposal that we've put into Congress actually passes, because not only will that help to expand his business, but it's also going to help Americans save energy, not only in this part of the country but all across the country.

Now, all of this hasn't been easy. The recession hasn't—has meant that folks are spending less. It means that small businesses have had a tougher time getting credit and getting loans. And that's why when I took office, we put in place an economic plan specifically to help small businesses. And we were guided by a simple idea: Government can't guarantee success, but it can knock down barriers that keep entrepreneurs from opening or expanding. For example, the lack of affordable credit, that's something the Government can do something about. Government can't replace the millions of jobs that we lost in the recession, but it can create the conditions for small businesses to hire more people through steps like tax breaks.

That's why we've cut taxes for America's small businesses eight times—eight times have we cut taxes for small businesses all across the country. Because of a bill I signed into law a few months ago, businesses are now eligible for tax cuts when they hire unemployed workers, something that could benefit every business represented behind me. Companies are also able to write off more of their investments in new equipment, which Tom and Catherine have taken advantage of. As part of the health reform package, 4 million small-business owners recently received a postcard in their mailbox telling them that this year, they could be eligible for a health care tax credit that's worth perhaps tens of thousands of dollars.

And I was just talking to Dave, who does the right thing by his employees and is providing health insurance; they actually are not paying a significant share for that health insurance. Dave and Carl are doing the right thing by those workers. He's now going to be eligible to potentially get up to 35 percent tax relief on those— premium that he's paying, and that could make obviously an enormous difference in terms of his bottom line and may mean that he can hire some additional workers.

Our economic plan's also supported nearly 70,000 new loans to small businesses. One of these loans made it possible for Tom and Catherine to purchase new equipment. We've waived fees on new SBA loans to save folks money on payments. And that reduced Theo's costs when he opened his new restaurant. His family had a business, a family restaurant. He opened his own, and it saved him more than $20,000 in waived fees and—money that's now gone into that new restaurant and its 60 new employees.

So all told, these and other steps are making a difference. But when you listen to the struggles that small-business owners are still facing, it's clear that we need to do more. And that's why I'm urging the Senate to approve a jobs bill that will do two big things for small businesses: cut taxes and make more loans available. That's what Dave and Carl and Theo and Brian and Tom and Catherine tell me they can use. And that's what I've heard from small businesses all across America.

If this bill becomes law, small businesses and startups will see the positive benefits right away.

It eliminates capital gains taxes for key investments in small firms. It will increase the deductions that small businesses can take for new equipment and other expenses. I know Tom and Catherine are looking at expanding to a larger facility; this can help them do that.

This bill will also make more credit available. Everywhere I go, I hear from small-business owners who simply cannot get the credit they need to hire and expand. And we've been hearing from smaller community banks that they want to lend to these folks but need more capital to do it. So the initiatives in this bill will help them meet those challenges. And it will increase—allow them to increase loan sizes and make sure that we continue to waive fees for SBA loans that have helped a number of the people standing behind me.

Now, let me just make one last point. I know it's no secret that we've confronted a lot of partisan politics over the past year and a half. We've seen a fair amount of obstruction that's had more to do with gaining political advantage than helping the country. But surely, Democrats and Republicans ought to be able to agree on this bill. Now, when I had a conversation with Mitch McConnell and John Boehner yesterday, I told them that the provisions of this bill are things that the Republican Party has said it supported for years: helping small businesses, cutting taxes, making credit available. This is as American as apple pie. Small businesses are the backbone of our economy. They are central to our identity as a nation. They are going to lead this recovery. The folks standing beside me are going to lead this recovery.

So as I said yesterday at—in a meeting with congressional leaders at the White House, I expect us to get this done before they go on vacation, for the folks standing behind me and for small businesses and their employees all across the country.

All right? Thank you very much, everybody. Thank you, guys.

NOTE: The President spoke at 2:42 p.m. at Tastee Sub Shop. In his remarks, he referred to David Thornton and Carl Padovano, co-owners, Tastee Sub Shop; Thomas E. and

Catherine L. Horsburgh, co-owners, Ridgid Paper Tube Corporation, Wayne, NJ; Brian J. Bovio, operations manager, Bovio Advanced Comfort & Energy Solutions, Sicklerville, NJ; and Theo Mastorakos, owner, Mama Roxy's, Rochelle Park, NJ.

Statement on the Crash of Airblue Flight ED 202 in Pakistan
July 28, 2010

I extend my deepest condolences to the families and friends of all who died in today's tragic crash of Airblue flight ED 202 near Islamabad. Among those who were lost were two American citizens. Our thoughts and prayers go out to all of those touched by this horrible accident. The American people stand with the people of Pakistan in this moment of tragedy.

Remarks at the National Urban League Centennial Conference
July 29, 2010

The President. Thank you. Everybody, please have a seat. Have a seat. Take a load off. Thank you very much. Please, please, have a seat. Good morning, Urban Leaguers.

Audience members. Good morning.

The President. Well, it is wonderful to be here with all of you. It is wonderful to be here. And let me begin by congratulating Marc Morial for his outstanding leadership, his great friendship. I want to thank the entire National Urban League on your centennial. From your founding, amid the great migration, to the struggles of the civil rights movement, to the battles of today, the Urban League has been on the ground, in our communities, working quietly, day in, day out, without fanfare, opening up opportunity, rolling back inequality, making our Union just a little more perfect. So America is a better place because of the Urban League. And I'm grateful to all of you for the outstanding contributions that you've made.

Now, the last time I spoke with you was during your Orlando conference in August—[*applause*]—got Orlando in the house—[*laughter*]—Orlando conference back in August of 2008. I didn't have any gray hair back then. [*Laughter*]

Audience member. That's all right.

The President. Say, that's all right? [*Laughter*] Yes.

But I want to remind you what things were like in August of 2008. Our economy was in freefall. We had just seen 7 straight months of job loss. Foreclosures were sweeping the Nation. And we were on the verge of a financial crisis that threatened to plunge our economy into a second Great Depression.

So from the moment I took office, we had to act immediately to prevent an even greater catastrophe. And I knew that not everything we did would be popular. Sometimes when we do things, the scribes, the pundits here in Washington, they act surprised. They say, why would you do such a thing? It doesn't poll well. And I have to explain to them I've got my own pollsters. [*Laughter*] But I wasn't elected just to do what's popular, I was elected do what was right. That's what you supported me for.

And because of what we did, America, as a whole, is in a different place today. Our economy is growing instead of shrinking. Our private sector has been adding jobs for 6 straight months instead of losing them.

I was—[*applause*]—yesterday a report was put out by two prominent economists—one of them John McCain's old economist—that said if we hadn't taken the actions that we took, we would have had an additional 8 million people lose their jobs.

Now, that doesn't mean we're out of the woods yet. Every sector of our economy was shaking by the crisis, every demographic group felt its impact. And as has been true in the wake of other recent recessions, this one had an especially brutal impact on minority communities,

communities that were already struggling long before the financial crisis hit.

The African American unemployment rate was already much higher, the incomes and wealths of African American families already lower. There was less of a cushion. Many minority communities, whether in big cities or rural towns, had seen businesses and opportunities vanish for years, stores boarded up, young people hanging out on the street corners without prospects for the future.

So when we came in to office, we focused not just on rescuing our economy in the short run, but rebuilding our economy for the long run, creating an economy that lifts up all Americans, not just some, but all.

That's why we passed health insurance reform that will give every American more choices, more control over their health care, will narrow the cruel disparities between Americans of different backgrounds. That's why we passed Wall Street reform, not only to make sure that taxpayers aren't paying for somebody else's foolishness, but also to protect consumers from predatory credit cards and lending practices, regulating everything from mortgages to payday loans, making sure that we're protecting our economy from the recklessness and irresponsibility of a few.

Across agencies, we're taking on the structural inequalities that have held so many of our fellow citizens back, whether it's making more housing available and more affordable, making sure civil rights and antidiscrimination laws are enforced, making sure our crime policy is not only tough, but also smart. So yesterday we took an important step forward when Congress passed a fair sentencing bill that I look forward to signing into law, a bipartisan bill to help right a longstanding wrong by narrowing sentencing disparities between those convicted of crack cocaine and powder cocaine. It's the right thing to do. We've gotten that done.

So we've made progress. And yet for all of our progress—progress that's come through the efforts of groups like the Urban League, progress that makes it possible for me to stand here as President—we were reminded this past week that we've still got work to do when it comes to

promoting the values of fairness and equality and mutual understanding that must bind us together as a nation.

Now, last week, I had the chance to talk to Shirley Sherrod, an exemplary woman whose experiences mark both the challenges we have faced and the progress that we've made. She deserves better than what happened last week, when a bogus controversy based on selective and deceiving excerpts of a speech led her—led to her forced resignation.

Now, many are to blame for the reaction and overreaction that followed these comments, including my own administration. And what I said to Shirley was that the full story she was trying to tell—a story about overcoming our own biases and recognizing ourselves in folks who, on the surface, seem different—is exactly the kind of story we need to hear in America.

It's exactly what we need to hear because we've all got our biases. And rather than jump to conclusions and point fingers and play some of the games that are played on cable TV, we should all look inward and try to examine what's in our own hearts. We should all make more of an effort to discuss with one another, in a truthful and mature and responsible way, the divides that still exist—the discrimination that's still out there, the prejudices that still hold us back—a discussion that needs to take place not on cable TV, not just through a bunch of academic symposia or fancy commissions or panels, not through political posturing, but around kitchen tables and water coolers and church basements and in our schools and with our kids all across the country.

And if we can have that conversation in our own lives and if we can take an opportunity to learn from our imperfections and our mistakes, to grow as individuals and as a country, and if we engage in the hard work of translating words into deeds—because words are easy and deeds are hard—then I'm confident that we can move forward together and make this country a little more perfect than it was before.

Now, since we're on the topic of speaking honestly with one another, I want to devote the balance of my time, the balance of my remarks to an issue that I believe will largely determine not only African American success but the success of our Nation in the 21st century, and that is whether we are offering our children the very best education possible.

I know some argue that as we emerge from a recession, my administration should focus solely on economic issues. They said that during health care, as if health care had nothing to do with economics, said it during financial reform, as if financial reform had nothing to do with economics, and now they're saying it as we work on education issues. But education is an economic issue, if not *the* economic issue of our time.

It's an economic issue when the unemployment rate for folks who've never gone to college is almost double what it is for those who have gone to college. It's an economic issue when 8 in 10 new jobs will require workforce training or a higher education by the end of this decade. It's an economic issue when countries that outeducate us today are going to outcompete us tomorrow.

Now, for years, we've recognized that education is a prerequisite for prosperity. And yet we've tolerated a status quo where America lags behind other nations. Just last week, we learned that in a single generation, America went from number 1 to 12th in college completion rates for young adults—used to be number 1, now we're number 12.

At the same time, our eighth graders trail about 8—10 other nations, 10 other nations in science and math. Meanwhile, when it comes to Black students, African American students trail not only almost every other developed nation abroad, but they badly trail their White classmates here at home, an achievement gap that is widening the income gap between Black and White, between rich and poor.

We've talked about it, we know about it, but we haven't done enough about it. And this status quo is morally inexcusable, it is economically indefensible, and all of us are going to have to roll up our sleeves to change it.

And that's why—[*applause*]—that is why, from day one of this administration, we've made excellence in American education, excellence for all our students, a top priority. And no one

has shown more leadership on this issue than my Secretary of Education, Arne Duncan, who is here today.

I chose Arne not only because he's a great ballplayer—[*laughter*]—now, Arne and I play a little bit on the weekends—I chose Arne because I knew that for him, closing the achievement gap, unlocking the potential of every child, isn't just a job, it's been the cause of his life.

Now, because a higher education has never been more important or more expensive, it's absolutely essential that we put a college degree within reach for anyone who wants it. And that's why we're making higher education more affordable, so we can meet the goals I've set of producing a higher share of college graduates than any other nation by 2020. I want us to be back at number 1 instead of number 12.

And in pursuit of that goal, we eliminated taxpayer subsidies to big banks. We saved tens of billions of dollars, and we used those savings to open the door to additional financial aid, to open the door for college to millions more students. This is something that a lot of you may not be aware of, but we have added tens of billions of dollars that were going to bank middlemen so that that money is now going to students, millions more students who are getting scholarships to go to college. That's already been done. We're making loan repayment more manageable, so young people don't graduate like Michelle and me, with such big loan payments every month.

Audience member. Thank you!

The President. You're welcome. That right there. [*Laughter*] Yes, you can relate. [*Laughter*]

And we're reinvesting in our Historically Black Colleges and Universities, our HBCUs. We are reinvesting in them, while at the same time reforming and strengthening our community college, which are great, undervalued assets, great assets that are a lifeline to so many working families in every community across America.

But here's the thing: Even if we do all this good stuff for higher education, too many of our children see college as nothing but a distant dream because their education went off the rails long before they turned 18. These are young people who've been relegated to failing schools in struggling communities, where there are too many obstacles, too few role models, communities that I represented as a State senator, communities that I fought to lift up as a community organizer.

I remember going to a school back in my organizing days and seeing children, young children, maybe 5 or 6, eyes were brimming with hope, had such big dreams for the future. You'd ask them, what do you want to be when you grow up? They'd want to be a doctor; they'd want to be a lawyer. And then I remember the principal telling me that soon, all that would change. The hope would start fading from their eyes as they started to realize that maybe their dreams wouldn't come to pass, not because they weren't smart enough, not because they weren't talented enough, but because through a turn of fate, they happened to be born in the wrong neighborhood. They became victim of low expectations, a community that was not supporting educational excellence.

And it was heartbreaking. It is heartbreaking. And it reinforced in me a fundamental belief that we've got an obligation to lift up every child in every school in this country, especially those who are starting out furthest behind.

That's why I want to challenge our States to offer better early learning options to make sure our children aren't wasting their most formative years so that they can enter into kindergarten already ready to learn, knowing their colors, knowing their numbers, knowing their shapes, knowing how to sit still. [*Laughter*] Right? That's no joke. You got to learn that, especially when you're a boy. [*Laughter*] That's why we placed such heavy emphasis on the education our children are getting from kindergarten through 12th grade.

Now, over the past 18 months, the single most important thing we've done—and we've done a lot. I mean, we—the Recovery Act put a lot of money into schools, saved a lot of teacher jobs, made sure that schools didn't have to cut back even more drastically in every community across this country. But I think the single most

important thing we've done is to launch an initiative called Race to the Top. We said to States, if you are committed to outstanding teaching, to successful schools, to higher standards, to better assessments, if you're committed to excellence for all children, you will be eligible for a grant to help you attain that goal.

And so far, the results have been promising and they have been powerful. In an effort to compete for this extra money, 32 States reformed their education laws before we even spent a dime. The competition leveraged change at the State level. And because the standards we set were high, only a couple of States actually won the grant in the first round, which meant that the States that didn't get the money, they've now strengthened their applications, made additional reforms. Now 36 have applied in the second round, and 18 States plus the District of Columbia are in the running to get a second grant.

So understand what's happened. In each successive round, we've leveraged change across the country. And even students in those districts that haven't gotten a grant, they've still benefited from the reforms that were initiated. And this process has sown the seeds of achievement. It's forced teachers and principals and officials and parents to forge agreements on tough and often uncomfortable issues, to raise their sights and embrace education.

Now, for the most part, States, educators, reformers, they've responded with great enthusiasm around this promise of excellence. But I know there's also been some controversy about Race to the Top. Part of it, I believe, reflects a general resistance to change. We get comfortable with the status quo, even when the status quo isn't good. We make excuses for why things have to be the way they are. And when you try to shake things up, some people aren't happy.

There have been criticisms from some folks in the civil rights community about particular elements of Race to the Top. So I want to address some of those today. I told you we're going to have an honest conversation.

First, I know there's a concern that Race to the Top doesn't do enough for minority kids, because the argument is, well, if there's a competition, then somehow some States or some school districts will get more help than others. Let me tell you, what's not working for Black kids and Hispanic kids and Native American kids across this country is the status quo. That's what's not working. What's not working is what we've been doing for decades now.

So the charge that Race to the Top isn't targeted at those young people most in need is absolutely false because lifting up quality for all our children—Black, White, Hispanic—that is the central premise of Race to the Top. And you can't win one of these grants unless you've got a plan to deal with those schools that are failing and those young people who aren't doing well. Every State and every school district is directly incentivized to deal with schools that have been forgotten, been given up on.

I also want to directly speak to the issue of teachers. We may have some teachers here in the house. [*Applause*] I know Urban League has got some teachers. Nothing is more important than teachers. My sister is a teacher. I'm here because of great teachers. The whole premise of Race to the Top is that teachers are the single most important factor in a child's education from the moment they step into the classroom. And I know firsthand that the vast majority of teachers are working tirelessly, are passionate about their students, are often digging into their own pockets for basic supplies, are going above and beyond the call of duty.

So I want teachers to have higher salaries. I want them to have more support. I want them to be trained like the professionals they are, with rigorous residencies like the ones that doctors go through. I want to give them a career ladder so they've got opportunities to advance and earn real financial security. I don't want talented young people to say, I'd love to teach, but I can't afford it.

I want them to have a fulfilling and supportive workplace environment. I want them to have the resources, from basic supplies to reasonable class sizes, that help them succeed. And instead of a culture where we're always idolizing sports stars or celebrities, I want us to build a culture where we idolize the people who are shaping our children's future. I want some

teachers on the covers of some of those magazines, some teachers on MTV, featured.

I was on the "The View" yesterday, and somebody asked me who Snooki was. I said, I don't know who Snooki is. [*Laughter*] But I know some really good teachers that you guys should be talking about. [*Laughter*] I didn't say the teacher part, but I just—[*laughter*]. The question is, who are we lifting up? Who are we promoting? Who are we saying is important?

So I am 110 percent behind our teachers. But all I'm asking in return—as a President, as a parent, and as a citizen—is some measure of accountability. So even as we applaud teachers for their hard work, we've got to make sure that we're seeing results in the classroom. If we're not seeing results in the classroom, then let's work with teachers to help them become more effective. If that doesn't work, let's find the right teacher for that classroom.

Arne makes the point very simply: Our children get only one chance at an education, so we need to get it right.

Now, I want to commend some of the teachers unions across this country who are working with us to improve teaching, like the Delaware Education Association, which is working with State leaders as part of their Race to the Top efforts, not only to set aside 90 minutes of collaboration time a week to improve instruction, but to strengthen teacher development and evaluation. That's the right way to go.

So for anyone who wants to use Race to the Top to blame or punish teachers, you're missing the point. Our goal isn't to fire or admonish teachers; our goal is accountability. It's to provide teachers with the support they need to be as effective as they can be and to create a better environment for teachers and students alike.

Now, there's also the question of how hard our teachers should push students in the classroom. Nations in Asia and Europe have answered this question, in part by creating standards to make sure their teachers and students are performing at the same high levels throughout their nation. That's one of the reasons that their children are doing better than ours. But here at home, there's often a controversy about national standards, common standards; that violates the principle of local control. Now, there's a history to local control that we need to think about, but that's the argument.

So here's what Race to the Top says: Instead of Washington imposing standards from the top down, let's challenge States to adopt common standards voluntarily, from the bottom up. That doesn't mean more standards; it means higher standards, better standards, standards that clarify what our teachers are expected to teach and what our children are expected to learn, so high school graduates are actually prepared for college and a career. I do not want to see young people get a diploma, but they can't read that diploma.

Now, so far, about 30 States have come together to embrace and develop common standards, high standards. More States are expected to do so in the coming weeks. And by the way, this is different from No Child Left Behind, because what that did was it gave the States the wrong incentives. A bunch of States watered down their standards so that school districts wouldn't be penalized when their students fell short. And what's happened now is at least two States, Illinois and Oklahoma, that lowered standards in response to No Child Behind—No Child Left Behind are now raising those standards back up, partly in response to Race to the Top.

And part of making sure our young people meet these high standards is designing tests that accurately measure whether they are learning. Now, here too there's been some controversy. When we talk about testing, parents worry that it means more teaching to the test. Some worry that tests are culturally biased. Teachers worry that they'll be evaluated solely on the basis of a single standardized test. Everybody thinks that's unfair. It is unfair.

But that's not what Race to the Top is about. What Race to the Top says is there's nothing wrong with testing; we just need better tests applied in a way that helps teachers and students, instead of stifling what teachers and students do in the classroom; tests that don't dictate what's taught, but tell us what has been learned; tests that measure how well our children are mastering essential skills and answering complex ques-

tions; and tests that track how well our students are growing academically, so we can catch when they're falling behind and help them before they just get passed along.

Because of Race to the Top, States are also finding innovative ways to move beyond having just a snapshot of where students are and towards a real-time picture that shows how far they've come and how far they have to go. And armed with this information, teachers can get what amounts to a game tape that they can study to enhance their teaching and their focus on areas where students need help the most.

Now, sometimes a school's problems run so deep that you can do the better assessments and the higher standards and a more challenging curriculum, and that's not enough. If a school isn't producing graduates with even the most basic skills—year after year after year after year—something needs to be done differently. You know, the definition, somebody once said, of madness is you do the same thing over and over again and keep expecting a different result. If we want success for our country, we can't accept failure in our schools decade after decade.

And that's why we're challenging States to turn around our 5,000 lowest performing schools. And I don't think it's any secret that most of those are serving African American or Hispanic kids. We're investing over $4 billion to help them do that, to transform those schools—$4 billion, which even in Washington is real money. This isn't about—unlike No Child Left Behind, this isn't about labeling a troubled school a failure and then just throwing up your hands and saying, well, we're giving up on you. It's about investing in that school's future and recruiting the whole community to help turn it around and identifying viable options for how to move forward.

Now, in some cases, that's going to mean restarting the school under different management as a charter school, as an independent public school formed by parents, teachers, and civic leaders who've got broad leeway to innovate. And some people don't like charter schools. They say, well, that's going to take away money from other public schools that also need support. Charter schools aren't a magic bullet, but I want to give States and school districts the chance to try new things. If a charter school works, then let's apply those lessons elsewhere. And if a charter school doesn't work, we'll hold it accountable, we'll shut it down.

So no, I don't support all charter schools, but I do support good charter schools. I'll give you an example. There's a charter school called Mastery in Philadelphia. And in just 2 years, three of the schools that Mastery has taken over have seen reading and math levels nearly double, in some cases, triple. Chaka Fattah is here, so he knows what I'm talking about. One school called Pickett went from just 14 percent of students being proficient in math to almost 70 percent. Now—and here's the kicker: At the same time academic performance improved, violence dropped by 80 percent—80 percent. And that's no coincidence.

Now, if a school like Mastery can do it, if Pickett can do it, every troubled school can do it. But that means we're going to have to shake some things up: setting high standards, common standards, empowering students to meet them; partnering with our teachers to achieve excellence in the classroom; educating our children—all of them—to graduate ready for college, ready for a career, ready to make most of their lives. None of this should be controversial. There should be a fuss if we weren't doing these things. There should be a fuss if Arne Duncan wasn't trying to shake things up.

So Race to the Top isn't simply the name of an initiative. It sums up what's happening in our schools. It's the single most ambitious, meaningful education reform effort we've attempted in this country in generations.

And I know there are a number of other steps we need to take to lift up our education system—like saving teachers' jobs across this country from layoffs—and I'll continue fighting to take those steps and save those jobs. But I'll also continue to fight for Race to the Top with everything I've got, including using a veto to prevent some folks from watering it down.

Now, let me wrap up by saying this. I know there are some who say that Race to the Top won't work. There are cynics and naysayers who argue that the problems in our education sys-

tem are too entrenched, that think that we'll just fall back into the same old arguments and divides that have held us back for so long. And it is true, as I've said since I ran for President, and that everybody here knows firsthand, change is hard. I don't know if you've noticed. That's why I've got all this gray hair. [*Laughter*]

Fixing what was broken in our health care system is not easy. Fixing what was broken on Wall Street is not easy. Fixing what's broken in our education system is not easy. We won't see results overnight. It may take a decade for these changes to pay off. But that's not a reason not to make them. It's a reason to start making them right now, to feel a sense of urgency, the fierce urgency of now.

We also know that as significant as these reforms are, there's going to be one more ingredient to really make a difference: Parents are going to have to get more involved in their children's education. Now, in the past, even that statement has sparked controversy. Folks say, well, why are you talking about parents? [*Laughter*] Parents need help too. I know that. Parents need jobs. They need housing. They need, in some cases, social services. They may have substance abuse problems. We're working on all those fronts.

Then some people say, well, why are you always talking about parental responsibility in front of Black folks? [*Laughter*] And I say, I talk about parental responsibility wherever I talk about education. Michelle and I happen to be Black parents, so—[*laughter*]—I may add a little umph to it when I'm talking to Black parents. [*Laughter*]

But to paraphrase Dr. King, education isn't an either-or proposition, it's a both-and proposition. It will take both more focus from our parents and better schooling. It will take both more money and more reform. It will take both a collective commitment and a personal commitment.

So yes, our Federal Government has responsibilities that it has to meet, and I will keep on making sure the Federal Government meets those responsibilities. Our Governors, our superintendents, our States, our school districts have responsibilities to meet. And parents have responsibilities that they have to meet. And our children have responsibilities that they have to meet.

It's not just parents. It's the children too. Our kids need to understand nobody is going to hand them a future. An education is not something you just tip your head and they pour it in your ear. [*Laughter*] You've got to want it. You've got to reach out and claim that future for yourself. And you can't make excuses.

I know life is tough for a lot of young people in this country. The places where Urban League is working to make a difference, you see it every day. I'm coming from the South Side of Chicago, so I know—I see what young people are going through there. And at certain points in our lives, young Black men and women may feel the sting of discrimination. Too many of them may feel trapped in a community where drugs and violence and unemployment are pervasive, and they're forced to wrestle with things that no child should have to face.

There are all kinds of reasons for our children to say, "No, I can't." But our job is to say to them, "Yes, you can." Yes, you can overcome. Yes, you can persevere. Yes, you can make what you will out of your lives.

I know they can because I know the character of America's young people. I saw them volunteer on my campaign. They asked me questions in town hall meetings. They write me letters about their trials and aspirations.

I got a letter recently postmarked Covington, Kentucky. It was from Na'Dreya Lattimore, 10 years old, about the same age as Sasha. And she told me about how her school had closed, so she had enrolled in another. Then she had bumped up against other barriers to what she felt was her potential. So Na'Dreya was explaining to

me how we need to improve our education system. She closed by saying this: "One more thing," she said—[*laughter*]—this is a long letter—[*laughter*]—"You need to look at us differently. We are not Black, we're not White, biracial, Hispanic, Asian, or any other nationality." No, she wrote, "We are the future."

Na'Dreya, you are right. And that's why I will keep fighting to lead us out of this storm. But I'm also going to keep fighting alongside the Urban League to make America more perfect so that young people like Na'Dreya, people of every race, in every region, are going to be able to reach for that American Dream. They're going to know that there are brighter days ahead, that their future is full of boundless possibilities. I believe that, and I know the Urban League does too.

Thank you very much, everybody. God bless you. God bless the United States of America.

NOTE: The President spoke at 10:09 a.m. at the Walter E. Washington Convention Center. In his remarks, he referred to Marc H. Morial, president and chief executive officer, National Urban League; Alan S. Blinder, Gordon S. Rentschler Memorial Professor of Economics, Princeton University; Mark Zandi, chief economist and cofounder, Moody's Analytics, in his former capacity as chief economic adviser to 2008 Republican Presidential nominee Sen. John S. McCain III; Shirley Sherrod, former Georgia State Director for Rural Development, U.S. Department of Agriculture, who was fired after the release of an edited video of remarks she had made at a March 2010 NAACP event; his sister Maya Soetoro-Ng; and Nicole "Snooki" Polizzi, castmember, MTV's "The Jersey Shore" program. He also referred to S. 1789.

Remarks on Signing Legislation To Protect Indian Arts and Crafts Through the Improvement of Applicable Criminal Proceedings, and for Other Purposes
July 29, 2010

Thank you, everybody. Please have a seat.

I want to start obviously by thanking Lisa for her introduction and having the courage to

share her story with all of us today. It's for every survivor like Lisa who has never gotten their day in court and for every family that feels like justice is beyond reach and for every tribal community struggling to keep its people safe that I'll be signing the Tribal Law and Order Act into law today.

And in doing so, I intend to send a clear message that all of our people, whether they live in our biggest cities or our most remote reservations, have the right to feel safe in their own communities and to raise their children in peace and enjoy the fullest protection of our laws.

And as many of you know, I campaigned on this issue. And during our last—during our tribal conference last year, I pledged my administration's fullest support for this bill. And I told Senator Dorgan last week that I intended to sign it in a ceremony here at the White House with all of you. So today I am proud to make good on my word.

Now, I'm told there's a Seneca proverb that says, "He who would do great things should not attempt them all alone." [*Laughter*] And that's particularly true of this legislation, which is the product of tireless efforts by countless individuals across this country. Congressional leaders like Senator Dorgan, Representative Herseth Sandlin, and others who are here today, and tribal leaders like Chairman Marcus Levings, President Theresa Two Bulls, President Diane Enos, Chief Chad Smith, Vice Chairman Jonathan Windy Boy—we are grateful to all of them for their extraordinary support. And then we've got leaders in our administration like Attorney General Holder and Secretary Salazar, Kimberly Teehee, Jodi Gillette here at the White House who worked tirelessly on this legislation.

And that's nothing to say of all the dedicated judges and prosecutors and tribal and BIA law enforcement officers—some of whom are here today—who've supported these efforts, and the determined survivors most of all, like Lisa, who even when it's too late to undo what happened to them, still speak out to seek justice for others.

All of you come at this from different angles, but you're united in support of this bill because you believe, like I do, that it is unconscionable that crime rates in Indian Country are more than twice the national average and up to 20 times the national average on some reservations. And all of you believe, like I do, that when one in three Native American women will be raped in their lifetimes, that is an assault on our national conscience; it is an affront to our shared humanity; it is something that we cannot allow to continue.

So ultimately, it's not just the Federal Government's relationship with tribal governments that compels us to act, it's not just our obligations under treaty and under law, but it's also our values as a nation that are at stake. And that's why earlier this year, after extensive consultations with tribal leaders, Attorney General Holder announced significant reforms to increase prosecutions of crimes committed in Indian Country. He hired more assistant U.S. attorneys and more victim-witness specialists. And he even created a position for a National Indian Country Training Coordinator who will work with prosecutors and law enforcement officers throughout Indian Country.

And under Secretary Salazar's leadership, we're launching new community policing pilot programs. We've overhauled the recruitment process for BIA officers, resulting in a 500-percent jump in applications and the largest hiring increase in history. And we're working to deploy those officers to the field as quickly as possible.

The bill I'm signing into law today will build on these efforts, because it requires the Justice Department to disclose data on cases in Indian Country that it declines to prosecute, and it gives tribes greater authority to prosecute and punish criminals themselves. It expands recruitment and retention and training for BIA and tribal officers and gives them better access to criminal databases. It includes new provisions to prevent counterfeiting of Indian-produced crafts and new guidelines and training for domestic violence and sex crimes. And it strengthens tribal courts and police departments and enhances programs to combat drug and alcohol abuse and help at-risk youth.

So these are significant measures that will empower tribal nations and make a real difference in people's lives. Because as I said during our tribal conference, I have no interest in just paying lip service to the problems we face. I know that too often this community has heard grand promises from Washington that turned out to be little more than empty words. And I pledged to you then that if you gave me a chance, this time it would be different. I told you I was committed to moving forward and forging a new and better future together in every aspect of our government-to-government relationship.

And slowly but surely, that is exactly what we are doing. At this moment, agencies across our Government are implementing detailed plans to increase coordination and consultation with tribal governments, and I intend to hold them accountable for following through.

We've also included a permanent reauthorization of the Indian Health Care Improvement Act in the health care reform legislation we passed this spring. We're strengthening tribal education. We're working to spur economic development throughout Indian Country. And in consultation with Indian tribes, we're now formally reviewing the United Nations Declaration on the Rights of Indigenous Peoples. And after 14 long years, we've finally settled the *Cobell* case and we're working with Congress to get the settlement approved as quickly as possible.

So we're moving forward, and we're making progress. And as we celebrate today, I'm reminded of a visit I made a couple of years ago to the Crow Nation out in Montana. While I was there, I was adopted into the nation by a wonderful couple, Hartford and Mary Black Eagle—so I'm Barack Black Eagle. [*Laughter*] But I was also given a Crow name that means "One Who Helps People Throughout the Land." And it's a name that I view not as an honor that I deserve, but as a responsibility that I must work to fulfill.

And looking back, I can't help but think that only in America could a guy like me, named Barack Obama, adoptive son of the Crow Nation, go on to become President. [*Laughter*] So that was improbable when it happened 2 years ago—[*laughter*]—but it would have been in-

conceivable a generation or two before that. And I think the same could be said of this legislation.

And that should ultimately give us all hope. It should remind us that our Union has a way of, over time, becoming more, and not less, perfect, more inclusive, more fair, more free. And that's because of people like you and leaders and public servants and everyday folks who understand that we're more than just heirs to a difficult past. Here in America, we have a chance to choose a different future and to heed those better angels of our nature and cast our lot with something bigger than ourselves.

So it's in that spirit that I hope we define the relationship between our nations in the years ahead, and it is the goal of this legislation that I am proud to sign into law today.

Thank you very much, everybody. God bless you. God bless the United States of America.

[*At this point, the President signed the bill.*]

There you go. It's done.

NOTE: The President spoke at 4:58 p.m. in the East Room at the White House. In his remarks, he referred to Lisa M. Iyotte, education specialist, Sicangu Coalition Against Sexual & Domestic Violence; Marcus D. Levings, chairman, Three Affiliated Tribes; Theresa B. Two Bulls, president, Oglala Sioux Tribe; Diane Enos, president, Salt River Pima-Maricopa Indian Community; Chadwick "Corntassel" Smith, principal chief, Cherokee Nation; Jonathan Windy Boy, vice chairman, Chippewa Cree Tribal Council; Senior Policy Adviser for Native American Affairs Kimberly K. Teehee; and Jodi Archambault Gillette, Associate Director of the White House Office of Public Engagement and Deputy Associate Director of the Office of Intergovernmental Affairs. H.R. 725, approved July 29, was assigned Public Law No. 111–211.

Message to the Congress on the National Emergency With Respect to the Actions of Certain Persons To Undermine the Sovereignty of Lebanon or Its Democratic Processes and Institutions
July 29, 2010

To the Congress of the United States:

Section 202(d) of the National Emergencies Act (50 U.S.C.1622(d)) provides for the automatic termination of a national emergency unless, prior to the anniversary date of its declaration, the President publishes in the *Federal Register* and transmits to the Congress a notice stating that the emergency is to continue in effect beyond the anniversary date. In accordance with this provision, I have sent to the *Federal Register* for publication the enclosed notice stating that the national emergency declared with respect to the actions of certain persons to undermine the sovereignty of Lebanon or its democratic processes and institutions is to continue in effect beyond August 1, 2010.

While there have been some recent positive developments in the Syrian-Lebanese relationship, continuing arms transfers to Hizballah that include increasingly sophisticated weapons systems serve to undermine Lebanese sovereignty, contribute to political and economic instability in the region, and continue to pose an unusual and extraordinary threat to the national security and foreign policy of the United States. For these reasons, I have determined that it is necessary to continue the national emergency declared on August 1, 2007, to deal with that threat and the related measures adopted on that date to respond to the emergency.

BARACK OBAMA

The White House,
July 29, 2010.

NOTE: The notice is listed in Appendix D at the end of this volume.

Remarks at the Chrysler Jefferson North Assembly Plant in Detroit, Michigan
July 30, 2010

The President. Hello, Detroit! Well, it is good to be here. Everybody, if you have a seat, have a seat. [*Laughter*] It is good—it's good to be back.

Audience members. Yeah!

The President. Good to be back. First of all, give it up to Leah for that wonderful introduction.

We've got some special guests here that I want to acknowledge. First of all, your Secretary of Transportation, who has helped to make sure that we are guiding this process of rebuilding the American auto industry and is doing an outstanding job, from Peoria, Illinois, Secretary Ray LaHood. Give him a big round of applause.

Because of a funeral, she couldn't be here, but I want everybody to big—give a huge round of applause to one of the best Governors, in very tough times, that exists anywhere in the country, Jennifer Granholm. She's doing a great job. Your outstanding new mayor and close to my heart, NBA Hall of Famer, Dave Bing is in the house.

Two of the hardest working Senators anywhere—and they are always thinking about Michigan and Michigan manufacturing, making stuff right here in the United States of America—Carl Levin and Debbie Stabenow. Outstanding Member of Congress, Representative Carolyn Cheeks Kilpatrick; UAW President Bob King is in the house; and Chrysler CEO Sergio Marchionne. Sergio's modest. He doesn't stand up. [*Laughter*] But he's doing a great job.

So I just had a tour of this outstanding plant with Sergio and Pat Walsh, your plant manager, and General Holiefield—now, that's a name right there—[*laughter*]—General Holiefield, vice president of the UAW; Cynthia Holland, your local UAW president.

And it was great to see the work that you're doing and the cars that you're building, especially when you consider the fact that just over a year ago, the future here seemed very much in doubt.

Now, before I make my remarks, I've got to disclose, I'm a little biased here because the first new car that I ever bought was a Grand Cherokee—first new car. Up until that point, I had had some old, beat-up—[*laughter*]—used cars. They were not state of the art. And I still remember walking into that showroom and driving out with that new car. It had that new car smell, and everything worked. [*Laughter*] I wasn't used to that. Had all these—everything was electronic, and I had—all my—I'd had to roll up my windows up until that point. So I've got some good memories of that car. But I've got to tell you, when I sat in this car, this is a better car. This is a state-of-the-art car. This is a world-class car right here.

Now, I want everybody to think about where we were. We were in the midst, when I took office, of a deep and painful recession that cost our economy about 8 million jobs—8 million jobs—and took a terrible toll on communities like this one. Our economy was shrinking about 6 percent per quarter.

Now, this morning we learned that our economy grew by 2.4 percent in the second quarter of the year, so that means it's now been growing again for 1 full year. Our economy is growing again instead of shrinking. That's a welcome sign compared to where we were. But we've got to keep on increasing that rate of growth and keep adding jobs, so we can keep moving forward. And that's especially important for places like this.

In the 12 months before I took office, the American auto industry lost hundreds of thousands of jobs. Sales plunged 40 percent. Think about that. The industry looked like it was going over a cliff. As the financial crisis and the vicious recession collided with an industry that for too long had avoided hard choices and hadn't fully adapted to changing times, we finally reached the point where two of the Big Three, Chrysler and GM, were on the brink of liquidation.

And that left us with very few choices. One choice, one option was to keep the practice of giving billions of dollars of taxpayer money to the auto industry, but not really forcing any accountability or change, so you just keep on kicking the tough problems down the road year after year and, hopefully, seeing if you can get more and more money out of Washington.

A second option was to do nothing and risk allowing two of the Big Three to disintegrate. And that could have meant the end of an industry that, like no other industry, represents so much of what makes up the American spirit.

This industry's been the source of deep pride for generations of American workers whose imaginations led to some of the finest cars the world has ever known and whose sweat built a middle class that has held the dreams of millions of our people.

I just met one of your coworkers on a line. He's third generation working at Chrysler. His grandfather worked at Chrysler, his father worked at Chrysler, and now he's on the line at Chrysler. And that could have all vanished.

Now, the worse thing about it is that if we had done nothing, not only were your jobs gone, but supplier jobs were gone and dealership jobs were gone and the communities that depend on them would have been wiped out. And by the way, when you talk to the CEO of Ford, he'll tell you that wouldn't have been good for Ford either, because a lot of those suppliers that they depend on might have gone out of business.

Independent estimates suggest that more than 1 million jobs could have been lost if Chrysler and GM had liquidated. And in the middle of a deep recession, that would have been a brutal, irreversible shock not just to Detroit, not just to the Midwest, but to our entire economy. So I refused to let that happen.

And we came up with a third way. What we said was, if you're willing to take the tough and painful steps necessary to make yourselves more competitive, if you're willing to pull together—workers, management, suppliers, dealers, everybody—to remake yourself for changing times, then we'll stand by you and we'll invest in your future. Our strategy was to get this company and this industry back on its feet, taking a hands-off approach, saying, you guys know the business, we don't. We're going to give you a chance, but we do know you've got to change.

Now, not surprisingly, a lot of folks were skeptical. You remember last year. A lot of folks were saying: "Well, this is stupid. We shouldn't be helping them." And I understand that. Look, this was a hard decision. I didn't want Government to get into the auto business. I've got enough to do. [*Laughter*] And the politics of it weren't good. Your delegation was supportive, but Debbie and Carl and Carolyn and others, they'll tell you, there were a lot of folks in Washington who said it couldn't be done.

But I believed that if each of us were willing to work and sacrifice in the short term—workers, management, creditors, shareholders, retirees, communities—it could mark a new beginning for a great American industry. And if we could summon that sense of teamwork and common purpose, we could once again see the best cars in the world designed, engineered, forged, and built right here in Detroit, right here in the Midwest, right here in the United States of America.

So I placed that faith in you and all of America's autoworkers, and you've vindicated that belief. The fact that we're standing in this magnificent factory today is a testament to the decisions we made and the sacrifices that you and countless stakeholders across this industry and this country were willing to make. So today, this industry is growing stronger. It's creating new jobs. It's manufacturing the fuel-efficient cars and trucks that will carry us toward an energy-independent future. You are proving the naysayers wrong, all of you.

They thought it would be impossible for your company to make the kind of changes necessary to restore fiscal discipline and move towards viability. Today, for the first time since 2004, all three U.S. automakers are operating at a profit—first time in 6 years.

Last year, sales plummeted and manufacturers and suppliers across the country were forced to idle plants and furlough workers. Today, Chrysler is responding to more demand than anticipated by keeping this plant and others running through the usual summer shutdown. The same goes for GM's plants. Sales have rebounded. Across the supply chain, plants that wouldn't exist without the sacrifices made across this industry are running at nearly full capacity.

Last year, many thought this industry would keep losing jobs as it had for the better part of the past decade. Today, U.S. automakers have added 55,000 jobs since last June, the strongest job growth in more than 10 years in the auto industry. This plant just hired a new shift of 1,100 workers last week.

Met one of your coworkers on the line. He said: "Thank you, Mr. President. I needed to get out of the house." [*Laughter*] I said, "I know your wife really felt that way." [*Laughter*] "I'm sure you were driving her crazy."

The Dundee Chrysler plant will begin production of an American-made, advanced-technology, fuel-efficient engine this December. The Sterling Heights Chrysler plant that was scheduled to close after 2012 will stay open and add a second shift of 900 workers next year. And when a plant thrives, that doesn't just affect the new workers; that affects the entire community.

Now, it also helped that we took steps to stimulate demand, steps like Cash for Clunkers, which said, if you traded your old car in for a new, more fuel-efficient model, you'd get a rebate. That program was good for automakers. It was good for consumers. But you know what? It was also good for the environment. It was more successful than we ever imagined, and it saved at least 100,000 jobs, giving dealerships sales numbers they hadn't had in years and communities an economic boost they wouldn't have otherwise seen.

So there's no doubt that the auto industry is growing stronger. But look, the hard truth is, this industry lost a lot of jobs in recent years. Some of those jobs aren't coming back, partly because automakers have become so much more efficient than they used to be. This is a lean, mean operation. And so there are people who've still lost their jobs, haven't been hired back, and it wasn't their fault. Mistakes were made in managing the company that weren't theirs.

So that's why we've still also got to make targeted investments to encourage new private sector manufacturing growth. We've got to encourage clean energy. That's why we're taking steps to help communities revitalize and redevelop old, shuttered auto facilities, preparing them for new industries and new jobs and new opportunities.

I'll give you an example: Those investments that we're making are helping to create an entire new advanced battery industry take root right here in Michigan. That industry was producing only 2 percent of the world's advanced batteries last year, but by 2015, we expect to produce 40 percent of the advanced batteries that go into our cars. And we're going to do it right here in Michigan, all across the Midwest.

Investments like those mean jobs for American workers to do what they've always done: build great products and sell them around the world.

So the bottom line is this: We've got a long way to go, but we're beginning to see some of these tough decisions pay off. We are moving forward.

I want you to remember, though, if some folks had their way, none of this would have been happening. Just want to point that out. Right? I mean, this plant and your jobs might not exist. There were leaders of the "just say no" crowd in Washington—they were saying, oh, standing by the auto industry would guarantee failure. One of them called it "the worst investment you could possibly make."

Audience members. Boo!

The President. They said we should just walk way and let those jobs go.

Audience members. Boo!

The President. I wish they were standing here today. I wish they could see what I'm seeing in this plant and talk to the workers who are here taking pride in building a world-class vehicle. I don't think they'd be willing to look you in the eye and say that you were a bad investment. They might just come around if they were standing here and admit that by standing by a great American industry and the good people

who work for it, that we did the right thing. It's hard for them to say that. You know, they don't like admitting when I do the right thing. [*Laughter*] But they might have had to admit it. And I want all of you to know, I will bet on the American worker any day of the week.

You know, when World War II hit Pearl Harbor, we didn't throw up our arms and say: "Boy, this is tough. I don't know what we're going to do." We rolled up our sleeves. We got to work. And it was workers just like you, right here in Detroit, who built an arsenal of democracy that propelled America to victory. It was workers like you that built this country into the greatest economic power the world has ever known. It was workers like you that manufactured a miracle that was uniquely American.

We faced down impossible odds. We can rise to meet any challenge. As I was thinking about what to say today, an extraordinary story was brought to my attention.

I don't know if they're here, but I think some of you must know 14 of your fellow employees at the plant won the lottery. Where are they? That's one—a couple of them right there. You know—lunch is on them, by the way. [*Laughter*]

Now, the first assumption people might make is, you know, after you win the lottery, you just kick back and you retire. Nobody'd fault folks for that. This is tough work. But most of them, they just want to keep on working. And I—is William Shanteau here?

Audience member. No, he's not.

The President. He's not? Well, he was one of the guys who bought one of the—he bought the winning ticket, right? Turns out he used some of the winnings to buy his wife one of the Jeep Grand Cherokees that you build right here. He called it a sweet ride. [*Laughter*] And he's going to pay for new American flags for his hometown because he loves his country.

And he's going to keep coming to work because he loves this plant and he loves these workers. So don't bet against the American worker. Don't bet against the American people. We got more work to do. It's going to take some time to get back to where we need to be, but I have confidence in the American worker. I have confidence in you. I have confidence in this economy. We are coming back.

Thank you, everybody. Thank you. God bless you, and God bless the United States of America.

NOTE: The President spoke at 12:16 p.m. In his remarks, he referred to Chrysler employee Leah Soehartono; Alan Mulally, president and chief executive officer, Ford Motor Company; and Lisa Shanteau, wife of William Shanteau.

Remarks at the General Motors Detroit-Hamtramck Assembly Center in Hamtramck, Michigan
July 30, 2010

Hello, everybody! Hello, Detroit! Thank you. Listen, before I just make a few short remarks, I just want to acknowledge some people who are here who have been critical in helping make sure that we are putting the U.S. auto industry back on track. First of all, my Secretary of Transportation, Ray LaHood, from Peoria, Illinois, is here. The mayor of Hamtramck, Karen Majewski, is here. Give her a big round of applause. Detroit mayor and Hall of Famer Dave Bing is in the house. Two Senators who've been fighting for you each and every day, Carl Levin and Debbie Stabenow, are here. Wonderful Congresswoman Carolyn Cheeks Kilpatrick is here. UAW President Bob King is in the house. General Motors CEO Ed Whitacre is here. And I want to thank Teri Quigley and Frank Moultrie for the great tour that they gave me.

Now, I have to tell you, some of you saw me drive the Volt about 12 inches. They don't let me drive much these days. But the Cadillac that I drive in is made right here. I got to admit the Secret Service soups it up a little bit. But it's a nice ride. It's very smooth.

You know, it is great to be back here and to see this outstanding plant and to see all of you. And I want to take you down memory lane just a little bit to a year ago. At that point, we were coming out of the worst recession that we had seen since the Great Depression. The economy was shrinking. We had lost 8 million jobs. The day I was sworn in, we lost—that month, we lost 750,000 jobs, that month that I was sworn in. That's true.

The auto industry had lost hundreds of thousands of jobs. Sales had gone down by 40 percent. And two of the Big Three, GM and Chrysler, were on the brink of a liquidation bankrupt-

cy, which means they would have been wiped out. And if GM and Chrysler were wiped out, then suppliers would be wiped out and dealerships would have been wiped out and communities would have been even more devastated.

It's estimated that we would have lost another million jobs if we had not stepped in. Now, we basically had three options when I was confronting what was happening in the U.S. auto industry.

Option number one was to keep on doing what the previous administration had been doing, which is basically give about a billion dollars a month to the auto industry, but not really ask for any kind of change that would get it on the right track.

Option two was to do nothing, and as I said, we would have lost another million jobs. But more importantly, we would have lost what has been the heart and soul of American manufacturing, what has built a middle class not just here in Detroit, but all throughout the Midwest, what has made us proud and has been a symbol of our economic power.

So I didn't like either of those two options, and I went for a third option. The third option was, we are going to give you the help you need, but we are also going to insist that management, workers, creditors, suppliers, dealers, shareholders, everybody get together and come up with a plan so that we can start building for the future, so we're not looking backwards, but we're moving forward.

Now, that was a tough decision, and let's face it, a lot of people were skeptical. I don't know if you all remember, but I remember how last year, there were a whole bunch of folks who said, "Well, that makes no sense." There's the "just say no" crowd in Washington—they're still saying no—who basically said: "Well, this is a terrible investment. We should just let the market take its course, let GM, let Chrysler go bankrupt." So there was a lot of skepticism out there.

But we made the decision to step in. And the reason I did that was because I had confidence in you. I had faith in you, because I believe that the American worker is the best worker on Earth. We've got the best engineers, we've got the best technologies, and if we could just mobilize our strengths and our talents and feel confident about the future, nothing can stop us.

And now here we are a year later. And a year later, GM and Chrysler, along with Ford, are all posting a profit. The U.S. auto industry has hired 55,000 workers, the most job growth in a decade. And not only that, but you're producing the cars of the future right here at this plant, producing cars that are going to reduce our dependence on foreign oil. This car right here doesn't need a sip of gasoline for 40 miles and then keeps on going after that.

And along with creating these new products, we've also started to say, well, why don't we make the advanced batteries that go into the Volt right here in the United States of America? So we were making 2 percent of the advanced batteries right here in the United States. By 2015, in 5 years, we will have 40 percent of the market in advanced batteries right here in the United States of America being made by American workers.

Now, let's be clear: We're not out of the woods yet. The economy is now growing. It was shrinking at 6 percent. Now it's growing at 2.4 percent. We've added private sector jobs for 6 months in a row. But there's still too many folks unemployed. There are a lot of folks in the auto industry who haven't been hired back. We're still going to have to do a lot of work to put folks back to work.

But we are moving in the right direction. The trend lines are good. And as people get more confident, people are going to start saying, it's finally time for me to buy a new car. And they're not just going to look at some foreign-made car, they're going to say, you know what, GM is making the car of the future, and I'm going to take a look at what GM is making.

So we've got a lot of work to do. We've got some challenges out here. We're going to have to keep on being lean and mean. We're going to have to keep on marketing our products more effectively. We're going to have to make sure the Government, business, everybody is working in the same direction. We've got to export more. We can't just buy from other countries; we got to sell to other countries. And that means we've got to make sure that our trade deals are fair. But let me tell you, when I look out at this plant and I look out at all of you, it gives me hope. It confirms my conviction: Don't bet against the American worker; don't bet against the American people.

We are back on our feet. We are on the move. GM is on the move, the U.S. auto industry is on the move, and America is on the move. And I'm not going to rest until every single American worker who wants to get back to work is going to be back to work. You're helping lead the way, and I'm grateful to you.

God bless you, and God bless the United States of America. Thank you, everybody.

NOTE: The President spoke at 1:46 p.m. In his remarks, he referred to Teri Quigley, plant manager, Detroit-Hamtramck Assembly Center; and Frank Moultrie, chairman, UAW Local 22.

Statement on the Detention of American Citizens in Iran
July 30, 2010

Tomorrow marks 1 year since Sarah Shourd, Shane Bauer, and Josh Fattal were detained by the Islamic Republic of Iran. Sarah, Shane, and Josh committed absolutely no crime. When they were arrested and detained, they were hiking in the region along the border of Iran and Iraq. Yet for a full year, they have been held in prison, causing extraordinary grief and uncertainty for them, for their families, and for their loved ones.

I want to be perfectly clear: Sarah, Shane, and Josh have never worked for the United States Government. They are simply openminded and adventurous young people who represent the best of America and of the human spirit. They are teachers, artists, and advocates for social and environmental justice. They have never had any quarrel with the Government of Iran, and have great respect for the Iranian people.

I call on the Iranian Government to immediately release Sarah, Shane, and Josh. Their unjust detention has nothing to do with the issues that continue to divide the United States and the international community from the Iranian Government. This is a humanitarian imperative, as these three young people are innocent of any crime. As a signatory to multiple conventions on human rights, the Government of Iran should act in line with the principles of justice and allow Sarah, Shane, and Josh to be reunited with their families. This call has been echoed by people in many countries, and is shared by all who respect human freedom and decency.

I want to particularly acknowledge the suffering and advocacy of Sarah, Shane, and Josh's families. Earlier this week, I spoke with the mothers of these three young people, who have worked tirelessly for the release of their children. The Iranian Government's gesture of allowing these mothers to visit their children was welcome, but I cannot imagine how painful it was for these three courageous women to return home without their children. I told these three mothers that Sarah, Shane, and Josh are in my thoughts and prayers, and that the U.S. Government would continue to do all that it could to secure their release.

I also spoke earlier this week with the wife of Robert Levinson, who went missing in Iran over 3 years ago. We continue to have no information about his welfare and reiterate our call for the Government of Iran to provide any information that it has about his whereabouts. It is time to facilitate Robert Levinson's return to the family and friends who have suffered so greatly in his absence. We continue to have him in our thoughts and prayers and to do all that we can to reunite him with his family.

Each of these cases reminds us of the dignity that is shared by all human beings and the necessity of justice. All Americans stand together in support of our citizens who are suffering through unjust detention abroad, and we will not rest until they are home.

The President's Weekly Address
July 31, 2010

Hello, everybody. I'm speaking to you from the GM auto plant here in Detroit, Michigan, where a hopeful story is unfolding in a place that's been one of the hardest hit in America.

In the 12 months before I took office, American auto companies lost hundreds of thousands of jobs. Sales plunged 40 percent. Liquidation was a very real possibility. Years of papering over tough problems and a failing to adapt to changing times, combined with a vicious economic crisis, brought an industry that's been the symbol of our manufacturing might for a century to the brink of collapse.

We didn't have many good options. On the one hand, we could have continued the practice of handing out billions of taxpayer dollars to the auto industry with no real strings attached. On the other hand, we could have walked away and allowed two major auto companies to go out of business, which could have wiped out 1 million American jobs.

I refused to let that happen. So we came up with a third way. We said to the auto companies, if you're willing to make the hard decisions necessary to adapt and compete in the 21st century, we'll make a one-time investment in your future.

Of course, if some folks had their way, none of this would be happening at all. This plant might not exist because there were leaders of the "just say no" crowd in Washington who argued that standing by the auto industry would guarantee failure. One called it "the worst investment you could possibly make." They said we should just walk away and let these jobs go.

Today, the men and women in this plant are proving these cynics wrong. Since GM and Chrysler emerged from bankruptcy, our auto industry has added 55,000 jobs, the strongest period of job growth in more than 10 years. For the first time since 2004, all three American automakers are operating at a profit. Sales have begun to rebound. And plants like this that wouldn't have existed if all of us didn't act are now operating at maximum capacity.

What's more, thanks to our investments, a lot of these auto companies are reinventing themselves to meet the demands of a new age. At this plant, they're hard at work building the high-quality, fuel-efficient cars of tomorrow, cars like the plug-in hybrid Chevy Volt that can run 40 miles before taking a sip of gasoline. Throughout Michigan, an advanced battery industry is taking root that will power clean electric cars, an industry that produced only 2 percent of the world's advanced batteries last year, but will now be able to produce as much as 40 percent in a little over 5 years. That's real progress.

There's no doubt we have a long way to go and a lot of work to do before folks here and across America can feel whole again. But what's important is that we're finally beginning to see some of the tough decisions we made pay off. And if we had listened to the cynics and the naysayers, if we had simply done what the politics of the moment required, none of this progress would have happened.

Still, even as these icons of American industry are being reborn, we also need to stand shoulder to shoulder with America's small-business men and women, particularly since they're the ones who create most of the new jobs in this country.

As we work to rebuild our economy, I can't imagine anything more common sense than giving additional tax breaks and badly needed lending assistance to America's small-business owners so they can grow and hire. That's what we're trying to do with the "Small Business Jobs Act," a bill that has been praised as being good

for small businesses by groups like the Chamber of Commerce and the National Federation of Independent Business. It's a bill that includes provision after provision authored by both Democrats and Republicans. But yesterday the Republican leaders in the Senate once again used parliamentary procedures to block it. Understand, a majority of Senators support the plan. It's just that the Republican leaders in the Senate won't even allow it to come up for a vote.

That isn't right. And I'm calling on the Republican leaders in the Senate to stop holding America's small businesses hostage to politics and allow an up-or-down vote on this small-business jobs bill.

At a time when America is just starting to move forward again, we can't afford the do-nothing policies and partisan maneuvering that will only take us backward. I won't sit here and pretend everything's wonderful. I know that times are tough. But what I also know is that we've made it through tough times before. And we'll make it through again. The men and women hard at work in this auto plant makes me absolutely confident of that.

So to all the naysayers out there, I say this: Don't ever bet against the American people, don't bet against the American worker, because we don't take the easy way out. That's not how we deal with challenge. That's not how we built this country into the greatest economic power the world has ever known. We did it by summoning the courage to persevere and adapt and push this country forward, inch by inch. That's the spirit I see in this plant today, and as long as I have the privilege of being your President, I will keep fighting alongside you until we reach a better day.

Thanks.

NOTE: The address was recorded at approximately 2:20 p.m. on July 30 at the General Motors Detroit-Hamtramck Assembly Center in Hamtramck, MI. The transcript was made available by the Office of the Press Secretary on July 30, but was embargoed for release until 6 a.m. on July 31.

Remarks to the Disabled American Veterans National Convention in Atlanta, Georgia
August 2, 2010

The President. Thank you. Everyone, please have a seat. Thank you. Thank you very much.

Audience member. Happy birthday! [*Laughter*]

The President. Thank you so much. Thank you. It is——

Audience member. Happy birthday!

The President. Thank you. It is a great honor and—it is true, I will be 49 this week. [*Laughter*] I have a lot more gray hair than I did last year. [*Laughter*]

It is an extraordinary honor to be here. Thank you, Commander Barrera, for your kind introduction and for your lifetime of service in the Marines in Vietnam——

Audience members. Hooah!

The President. ——but also as a tireless advocate for your fellow disabled veterans. We are grateful to you. Thank you for everything that you've done.

I want to thank your great leadership team for welcoming me today: Chairman Ray Dempsey—[*applause*]—absolutely; incoming Commander Wally Tyson; National Adjutant Art Wilson; Judy Hezlep of the DAV Auxiliary; and your outstanding executive director in Washington, Dave Gorman.

And I am pleased to be joined by a decorated Vietnam veteran, wounded warrior, and a lifetime member of the DAV, my outstanding Secretary of Veterans Affairs, Ric Shinseki.

Disabled American Veterans, I valued your advice and counsel when I was a Senator and when I cosponsored the post-9/11 GI bill. You were one of the first veterans' organizations that I called upon when I began my Presidential campaign. And as President, it's been my pleasure to welcome you to the White House to make sure America is serving our veterans as well as you've served us and, most recently, to sign advanced appropriations into law so that veterans health care will never again be held hostage to the budget battles and the political games in Washington.

Now, there's another visit I won't forget. I was in the Oval Office expecting a visit from the DAV, and in comes Bobby carrying a baseball bat. [*Laughter*] Now, it's not every day that somebody gets past the Secret Service carrying a baseball bat. [*Laughter*] You may have heard about this. It turns out it was a genuine Louisville Slugger, a thank you for going to bat for our veterans on advanced appropriations.

So I'm grateful for that symbol of our partnership, and I'm proud of the progress we've achieved together. But as one of your outstanding DAV members from Illinois just reminded me, this is a promise I made during the campaign. It was a promise made, and it was a promise kept. And I intend to keep on keeping my promises to the veterans of America.

In the life of our Nation, not every generation has been summoned to defend our country in its hour of need. But every generation to answer that call has done so with honor and with courage.

Among you are members of that generation that saved the world from fascism. I was honored to stand with our World War II vets at Normandy last year for the anniversary of D-day. And this year, as we mark the 65th anniversary of our victory in that war, we once again salute our veterans of the Second World War.

Others among you faced a brutal foe on a cold Korean Peninsula. This year, as we mark the 60th anniversary of that conflict, I will be proud to travel to the Republic of Korea in November to pay tribute to our veterans of the Korean war.

Many of you served in the jungles of Vietnam. You also served with honor, exemplary dedication, and courage, but were often shunned when you came home. That was a national disgrace and it must never happen again. And that's why we're making sure our veterans from today's wars are shown the respect and the dignity they deserve.

And whether you served in the Gulf to free a captive Kuwait or fought in the streets of Mogadishu or stopped an ethnic slaughter in the Balkans, you too are part of an unbroken line of service stretching across two centuries.

For you, coming home was the beginning of another battle, the battle to recover. You fought to stand again and to walk again and to work again. You fought for each other and for the benefits and treatment you had earned. You became leaders in our communities, in our companies, and our country, including a former Vietnam vet and Senator, Max Cleland, who reminded us that America's disabled veterans are "strong at the broken places."

Today, your legacy of service is carried on by a new generation of Americans. Some stepped forward in a time of peace, not foreseeing years of combat. Others stepped forward in this time of war, knowing they could be sent into harm's way. For the past 9 years, in Afghanistan and Iraq, they have borne the burdens of war. They and their families have faced the greatest test in the history of our All-Volunteer Force, serving tour after tour, year after year. Through their extraordinary service, they have written their own chapter in the American story. And by any measure, they have earned their place among the greatest of generations.

Now one of those chapters is nearing an end. As a candidate for President, I pledged to bring the war in Iraq to a responsible end. Shortly after taking office, I announced our new strategy for Iraq and for a transition to full Iraqi responsibility. And I made it clear that by August 31, 2010, America's combat mission in Iraq would end. And that is exactly what we are doing, as promised and on schedule.

Already, we have closed or turned over to Iraq hundreds of bases. We're moving out millions of pieces of equipment in one of the largest logistics operations that we've seen in decades. By the end of this month, we'll have brought more than 90,000 of our troops home from Iraq since I took office—more than 90,000 have come home.

Today, even as terrorists try to derail Iraq's progress, because of the sacrifices of our troops and their Iraqi partners, violence in Iraq continues to be near the lowest it's been in years. And next month, we will change our military mission from combat to supporting and training Iraqi security forces. In fact, in many parts of the country, Iraqis have already taken the lead for security.

As agreed to with the Iraqi Government, we will maintain a transitional force until we remove all our troops from Iraq by the end of next year. And during this period, our forces will have a focused mission: supporting and training Iraqi forces, partnering with Iraqis in counterterrorism missions, and protecting our civilian and military efforts. Now, these are dangerous tasks. There are still those with bombs and bullets who will try to stop Iraq's progress. And the hard truth is, we have not seen the end of American sacrifice in Iraq.

But make no mistake: Our commitment in Iraq is changing from a military effort led by our troops to a civilian effort led by our diplomats. And as we mark the end of America's combat mission in Iraq, a grateful America must pay tribute to all who served there.

Remember, our Nation has had vigorous debates about the Iraq war. There are patriots who supported going to war and patriots who opposed it. But there has never been any daylight between us when it comes to supporting the more than 1 million Americans in uniform who have served in Iraq, far more than any conflict since Vietnam.

These men and women from across our country have done more than meet the challenges of this young century. Through their extraordinary courage and confidence and commitment, these troops and veterans have proven themselves as a new generation of American leaders. And while our country has sometimes been divided, they have fought together as one. While other individuals and institutions have shirked responsibility, they have welcomed responsibility. While it was easy to be daunted by overwhelming challenges, the generation that has served in Iraq has overcome every test before them.

They took to the skies and sped across deserts in the initial charge into Baghdad. And today we're joined by an infantryman who was there as part of the 101st Airborne Division: Sergeant Nicholas Bernardi is here.

When invasion gave way to insurgency, our troops persevered, block by block, city by city, from Baghdad to Fallujah. As a driver in a transportation company, this soldier endured constant attacks, but never waivered in his mission, and we thank Sergeant Dan Knabe. Thank you, Dan.

When terrorists and militias plunged Iraq into sectarian war, our troops adapted and adjusted, restoring order and effectively defeating Al Qaida in Iraq on the battlefield. And among those who served in those pivotal days was a scout with the 1st Cavalry Division, Specialist Matt Seidl. Matt.

For each of these men and women, there are countless others. And we honor them all: our young enlisted troops and noncommissioned officers who are the backbone of our military; the National Guardsmen and reservists who served in unprecedented deployments; more women tested by combat than in any war in American history, including a marine here today, Sergeant Patricia Ruiz. Patricia. I teased Patricia. I said she looks like she's still in high school. [*Laughter*] But she's a marine.

And we salute the families back home. They too have sacrificed in this war. That's why my wife Michelle and the Vice President's wife, Dr. Jill Biden, have made it their mission to make sure America takes care of our remarkable military families, including our veterans.

Now, this summer, tens of thousands of our troops in Iraq are coming home. Last week, Vice President Biden was at Fort Drum to help welcome back members of the legendary 10th Mountain Division. Families are being reunited at bases across the country, from Fort Bragg in North Carolina to Fort Riley in Kansas to Fort Lewis in Washington. And in this season of homecomings, every American can show their gratitude to our patriots who served in Iraq.

As we do, we are humbled by the profound sacrifice that has been rendered. Each of the veterans I have mentioned carried with them the wounds of this war. And as a nation, we will honor forever all who gave their lives—that last true measure of devotion—in service in Iraq: soldiers, sailors, airmen, marines, coastguardsmen, Active, Guard, Reserve.

Even as we end the war in Iraq, even as we welcome home so many of our troops, others are still deployed in Afghanistan. So I want to remind everyone, it was Afghanistan where Al Qaida plotted and trained to murder 3,000 innocent people on 9/11. It is Afghanistan and the tribal regions of Pakistan where terrorists have launched other attacks against us and our allies. And if Afghanistan were to be engulfed by an even wider insurgency, Al Qaida and its terrorist affiliates would have even more space to plan their next attack. And as President of the United States, I refuse to let that happen.

The effort in Afghanistan has been long and been difficult. And that's why after years in which the situation had deteriorated, I announced a new strategy last December: a military effort to break the Taliban's momentum and train Afghan forces so that they can take the lead for their security; and a civilian effort to promote good governance and development that improves the lives of the Afghan people; and deeper cooperation with Pakistan to root out terrorists on both sides of the border.

We will continue to face huge challenges in Afghanistan. But it's important that the American people know that we are making progress and we are focused on goals that are clear and achievable.

On the military front, nearly all the additional forces that I ordered to Afghanistan are now in place. Along with our Afghan and international partners, we are going on the offensive against the Taliban, targeting their leaders, challenging them in regions where they had free reign, and training Afghan National Security Forces. Our thoughts and prayers are with all our troops risking their lives for our safety in Afghanistan.

And on the civilian front, we're insisting on greater accountability. And the Afghan Government has taken concrete steps to foster development and combat corruption and to put forward a reintegration plan that allows Afghans to lay down their arms.

In Pakistan, we've seen the Government begin to take the fight to violent extremists within its borders, and major blows have been struck against Al Qaida and its leadership, because in this region and beyond, we will tolerate no safe haven for Al Qaida and their extremist allies. We will disrupt, we will dismantle, and we will ultimately defeat Al Qaida. And we will give our troops the resources and the equipment to get the job done and keep our country safe.

At the same time, every American who has ever worn the uniform must also know this: Your country is going to take care of you when you come home. Our Nation's commitment to our veterans, to you and your families, is a sacred trust, and to me and my administration, upholding that trust is a moral obligation; it's not just politics.

That's why I've charged Secretary Shinseki with building a 21st-century VA. And that includes one of the largest percentage increases to the VA budget in the past 30 years. We are going to cut this deficit that we've got, and I've proposed a freeze on discretionary domestic spending. But what I have not frozen is the spending we need to keep our military strong, our country safe, and our veterans secure. So we're going to keep on making historic commitments to our veterans.

For about 200,000 Vietnam vets who may have been exposed to agent orange and who now suffer from three chronic diseases, we're making it easier for you to get the health care and benefits you need.

For our Gulf war veterans, we've declared that nine infectious diseases are now presumed to be related to your service in Desert Storm.

For our disabled veterans, we've eliminated copays for those of you who are catastrophically disabled. We've kept our promise on concurrent receipt by proposing legislation that would allow severely disabled retirees to receive your military retired pay and your VA disability benefits. It's the right thing to do.

We've dramatically increased funding for veterans health care across the board, and that includes improving care for rural veterans and women veterans. For those half-million vets who had lost their eligibility, our Priority 8 veterans, we're restoring your access to VA health care.

And since the rumors continue to fly, even though they are wrong, let me say it as clearly as I can: The historic health care reform legislation that I signed into law does not—I repeat, does not—change your veterans benefits. The VA health care benefits that you know and trust are safe, and that includes prosthetics for our disabled veterans.

Thanks to advanced appropriations, the delays for funding of veterans medical care are over. And just as those delays were unacceptable, so too are long delays in the claims process. So Secretary Shinseki is working overtime to create a single, lifetime electronic record that our troops and veterans can keep for life.

And today I can announce that for the first time ever, veterans will be able to go to the VA web site, click a simple blue button, and download or print your personal health records so you have them when you need them and can share them with your doctors outside of the VA. That's happening this fall.

We're hiring thousands of new claims processors to break the backlog once and for all. And to make sure the backlog doesn't come back, we're reforming the claims process itself with new information technologies and a paperless system.

Audience member. Hallelujah! [*Laughter*]

The President. We got an amen over here. [*Laughter*]

As a result of the innovation competition that I announced last summer, our dedicated VA employees suggested more than 10,000 new ways to cut through the redtape and the bureaucracy. And we're already putting dozens of these innovative ideas into action. Additionally, we're enabling more veterans to check the status of their claims online and from their cell phone.

As a next step, we're opening this competition to entrepreneurs and academics, so the best minds in America can help us develop the technologies to serve our vets, including those of you with multiple traumatic injuries. And we're going to keep at this until we meet our commitment to cut those backlogs, slash those wait times, and deliver your benefits sooner. This is a priority and we are going to get it done.

We're making progress in ending homelessness among our veterans. Today, on any given night, there are about 20,000 fewer veterans on the streets than there were when we took office. But we're not going to be satisfied until every veteran who has fought for America has a home in America. We will not stop.

Finally, we're keeping faith with our newest veterans returning from Afghanistan and Iraq. We're offering more of the support and counseling they need to transition back to civilian life. That includes funding the post-9/11 GI bill, which is already helping more than 300,000 veterans and family members pursue their dream of a college education.

And for veterans trying to find work in a very tough economy, we're helping with job training and placement. And I've directed the Federal Government to make it a priority to hire more veterans, including disabled veterans. And every business in America needs to know our vets have the training, they've got the skills, they have the dedication: They are ready to work. And our country is stronger when we tap the incredible talents of our veterans.

For those coming home injured, we're continuing to direct unprecedented support to our wounded warriors in uniform—more treatment centers, more case managers—delivering the absolute best care available. For those who can, we want to help them get back to where they want to be, with their units. And that includes servicemembers with a disability, who still have so much to offer our military.

We're directing unprecedented resources to treating the signature wounds of today's wars: traumatic brain injury and posttraumatic stress disorder. And I recently signed into law the Caregivers and Veterans Omnibus Health Services Act. That's a long name, but let me tell you what it does. It not only improves treatment for traumatic brain injury and PTSD, it gives new support to many of the caregivers who put their own lives on hold to care for their loved one.

And as so many of you know, PTSD is a pain like no other: the nightmares that keep coming back, the rage that strikes suddenly, the hopelessness that's led too many of our troops and veterans to take their own lives. So today I want to say, in very personal terms, to anyone who is struggling: Don't suffer in silence. It's not a sign

of weakness to reach out for support, it's a sign of strength. Your country needs you. We are here for you. We are here to help you stand tall. Don't give up. Reach out.

We're making major investments in awareness, outreach, and suicide prevention, hiring more mental health professionals, improving care and treatment. For those of you suffering from PTSD, we're making it a whole lot easier to qualify for VA benefits. From now on, if a VA doctor confirms a diagnosis of posttraumatic stress disorder, that is enough, no matter what war you served in.

These are the commitments my administration has made. These are the promises we've worked to keep. This is the sacred trust we have pledged to uphold to you and all who serve.

I want to make special mention of a truly inspiring American, Staff Sergeant Cory Remsburg. He was at Bethesda during one of my periodic visits to see our wounded warriors. And as I walked into his room, I saw a picture on the wall, and it was a picture of the two of us together. See, I had met Cory before, back at the D-day anniversary in Normandy. A good-looking young man, a proud Army Ranger, he had joined in a reenactment of that historic paratroop jump.

Then soon after, Cory served on his 10th deployment since 9/11—that's right, his 10th deployment. And that's when an IED nearly took his life. The traumatic brain injury was severe. Cory was in a coma for months. It seemed possible that he would never wake up.

But then something happened. His doctors still can't explain it. His parents called it a miracle. Cory opened one of his eyes. Then a few weeks later, he moved a leg. Then he moved an arm.

And there at Bethesda, we were meeting again. And Cory still couldn't speak, but he looked me in the eye, he lifted his arm, and he shook my hand firmly. And when I asked how he was feeling, he held up his hand, pulled his fingers together and gave a thumbs up.

Today, Cory is at a VA hospital in Florida. And with the support of his family and VA staff, he's working hard every day to regain his strength. He's got to learn to speak all over again. He's grateful for the visits he's received from friends and supporters, including the Disabled American Veterans.

And Cory is only 27 years old. And he knows he's got a long and very hard road ahead. But he pushes on, and he's determined to get back to his fellow Rangers. And when someone at the hospital said, "Cory, you're going to walk out of here someday," he said, "No, I'm going to run out of here." [*Laughter*]

So to Staff Sergeant Cory Remsburg, to the Disabled American Veterans, I want to say to all of you: You are the very essence of America, the values that sustain us as a people, and the virtues our Nation needs most right now. And the resilience that, in the face of great loss, so many of you experienced, I know you, like Cory, know what it means to pick yourselves up and keep pushing on.

And that sense of purpose that tells us to carry on, not just when it's easy, but when it's hard, even when the odds seem overwhelming, that's what we're about. The confidence that our destiny is never written for us, it's written by us.

The faith, that fundamental American faith that there are always brighter days ahead and that we will not simply endure, but we will emerge from our tests and trials and tribulations stronger than before, that is your story. That is America's story. And I'm proud to stand with you as we write the next proud chapter in the life of the country we love.

God bless you, and God bless the United States of America.

NOTE: The President spoke at 11:23 a.m. at the Hyatt Regency Atlanta hotel. In his remarks, he referred to Roberto Barrera, national commander, Raymond E. Dempsey, chairman of the board of directors, Wallace E. Tyson, vice-chairman of the board of directors, Arthur H. Wilson, national adjutant and secretary of the board of directors, and David W. Gorman, Washington headquarters executive director, Disabled American Veterans; and Judy Hezlep, national adjutant, Disabled American Veterans Auxiliary.

Remarks at a Democratic National Committee Fundraiser in Atlanta
August 2, 2010

The President. Thank you. Everybody, please have a seat. Have a seat.

Well, we have some just extraordinary leaders here today. I want to acknowledge a few of them. First of all, please give another round of applause to your outstanding young mayor, Kasim Reed; three wonderful Members of Congress who are fighting day in, day out on behalf of the people of Georgia, but also on behalf of people all across this country, Congressman Sanford Bishop, Congressman David Scott, and one of the genuine heroes of this country, Congressman John Lewis.

Our labor commissioner and U.S. Senate candidate Michael Thurmond's in the house. Attorney General Thurbert Baker I think is here. If not, give him a round of applause anyway. [*Laughter*] AG Commissioner Tommy Irvin, State party chair Jane Kidd, and the DNC southern finance chair Daniel Halpern is in the house.

So, Atlanta, it is wonderful to be here, wonderful to be among so many good friends. A lot of people here worked hard on behalf of my campaign. I am reminded of the story President Lincoln told about one of his supporters who came to the White House seeking some patronage, seeking a job. And apparently, in the outdoor reception area, he said: "Look, I want to see Lincoln personally because I'm responsible for him getting that job. Nobody did more than me. It's payback time." So Lincoln lets him into his office. He says, "Sir, I understand that you take responsibility for me having this job." Guy says, "That's right." And Lincoln says, "You're forgiven." [*Laughter*]

Look, we all know that the last few years have been extraordinarily challenging for the United States. Now, 18 months ago, I took office after nearly a decade of economic policies that gave us sluggish growth, falling incomes, and a record deficit and policies that culminated in the worst financial crisis that we've seen since the Great Depression. In the last 6 months of 2008, 3 million Americans lost their jobs. The month I was sworn, January of 2009, 750,000 Americans lost their jobs; 600,000 were lost a month later. All told, 8 million jobs lost as a consequence of this crisis.

Now, we didn't get here by accident. We got here after 10 years of an economic agenda in Washington that was pretty straightforward: You cut taxes for millionaires, you cut rules for special interests, and you cut working folks loose to fend for themselves. That was the philosophy of the last administration and their friends in Congress. If you couldn't find a job or you couldn't go to college, tough luck, you're on your own. But if you're a Wall Street bank or an insurance company or an oil company, then you got to write your own ticket and play by your own rules. And we know how this turned out.

So when I took office, because of the help of some of the people in this room, we put forward a new economic plan, a plan that rewards hard work instead of greed, a plan that rewards responsibility instead of recklessness, a plan that's focused on making our middle class more secure and our country more competitive in the long run so that the jobs and industries of the future aren't all going to China and India, but are being created right here in the United States of America.

Instead of spending money on tax breaks for folks who don't need them and weren't even asking for them, we're making smart investments in innovation and clean energy and education that are going to benefit all of our people and our entire economy over the long run.

And instead of giving special interests free rein to do whatever they want, we're demanding new accountability from Wall Street to Washington so that big corporations have to play by the same rules that small businesses and entrepreneurs do.

Now, because the policies of the last decade got us in such a deep hole, it's going to take some time for us to dig ourselves out. We're certainly not there yet. But I want everybody to understand, after 18 months, I can say with confidence, we are on the right track.

When we were—[*applause*]—instead of losing millions of jobs, we have created jobs for 6 straight months in the private sector. Instead of an economy that is contracting, we've got an economy that is expanding. So the last thing we would want to do is go back to what we were doing before.

And I want everybody in this room to understand, that is the choice in this election. The choice is whether we want to go forward or we want to go backwards to the same policies that got us into this mess in the first place.

Now, understand, it'd be one thing if the Republicans had seen the error of their ways. [*Laughter*] All right? I mean, if after the rejections of 2006 and 2008 and realizing, gosh, look at this big disaster that we caused and taking record surpluses into record deficits and causing all this hardship, we're going to rethink our approach and go out in the wilderness for a while, come back with some new ideas. [*Laughter*]

But that's not what happened. It's not like they've engaged in some heavy reflection. They have not come up with a single, solitary, new idea to address the challenges of the American people. They don't have a single idea that's different from George Bush's ideas, not one.

Instead, they're betting on amnesia. [*Laughter*] That's what they're counting on. They're counting on that you all forgot. They think that they can run the okeydoke on you. [*Laughter*] Bamboozle you. [*Laughter*]

I mean, think about it. These are the folks who were behind the steering wheel and drove the car into the ditch. So we've had to put on our galoshes, we went down there in the mud, we've been pushing, we've been shoving. They've been standing back, watching—[*laughter*]—say: "You're not moving fast enough. You ain't doing it right." [*Laughter*] "Why are you doing it that way?" [*Laughter*] "You got some mud on the car." Right?

So we're—that's all right. We don't need help. We're just going to keep on pushing. We push, we push. Thing's slipping a little bit, but we stay with it. Every—finally—finally, we get this car out of the ditch, where we're just right there on the blacktop. We're about to start driving forward again. They say, "Hold on, we want the keys back." [*Laughter*] You can't have the keys back. You don't know how to drive. [*Laughter*] You don't know how to drive.

And I do want to point out, when you get in your car, when you go forward, what do you do? You put it in "D." [*Laughter*] When you want to go back, what do you do? [*Laughter*] You put it in "R." [*Laughter*] You don't want to go into reverse back in the ditch. We want to go forward. We got to put it in "D." Can't have the keys back. [*Laughter*]

The choice in this election is between policies that encourage job creation here in America or encourage jobs to go elsewhere. That's why I've said, instead of giving tax breaks to corporations that want to ship jobs overseas, we want to give tax breaks to companies that are investing right here in the United States of America. And by the way, we've already cut taxes for businesses eight times since I've been President—eight times. And we want to do more, because small-business owners are the lifeblood of this economy.

Right now, as we speak, there's a bill in the Senate that would cut taxes for small businesses, would help them get the loans they need to hire again. Members of Congress who are here, they already voted on this. They already passed this bill. And by the way, this is a bill that's based on Democratic and Republican ideas. It's been praised by groups like the Chamber of Commerce—they never praise me—[*laughter*]—National Federation of Independent Businesses. It's a bill that's fully paid for, doesn't add to our deficit.

So you would think—Republicans say they're the probusiness party. Isn't that what they say? You would think this is a bill that they would want to pass. And yet day after day, week after week, they keep on stalling this bill and stonewalling this bill and opposing this bill. Why? Pure politics.

They're more interested in the next election than the next generation. And that's why they can't have the keys back, because we need somebody who's driving with a vision to the future. That's what we've been doing over these last 20 months.

We're also jump-starting a homegrown clean energy industry, because I don't want to see the solar panels and the wind turbines and the biodiesel created in other countries. I don't want China and Germany and Brazil to get the jump on us in the industries of the future. I want to see all that stuff right here in the United States of America, with American workers. And the investments we've made so far are expected to create 800,000 jobs by 2012—800,000 jobs in an industry of the future.

We want to create the infrastructure for the future—not just roads and bridges, but also the broadband lines and the smart grid lines that will ensure we stay competitively on top for years to come, creating hundreds of thousands of new jobs all across the country in the process. So that's our plan to create jobs right here in America, not just short term, but long term.

But the fact is, most of the members of the other party voted no on each and every one of these initiatives: no on tax cuts to small businesses, no to clean energy jobs, no to the railroad and highway projects.

Now, I want to point out, that doesn't stop them from showing up at the ribbon cuttings. [*Laughter*] John, you notice that? They'll be voting no, no, this is Obama's—no, we don't believe in recovery, we don't believe in all this. And then you show up at that ribbon cutting, and they're all there right in the front—[*laughter*]—cheesing and grinning—[*laughter*]—sending out press releases. [*Laughter*]

So, a few weeks ago, the Republican leader of the House was asked, "What's your jobs plan if your party takes control of Congress next year?" He said, well, you know, our number-one priority—he was asked, "What's your jobs plan?" Your number-one priority is to repeal the health care bill.

Now, this is a bill that makes sure that insurance companies can't deny you coverage if you've got a preexisting condition, makes sure that young people can stay on their parents' insurance till they're 26, provides a 35-percent tax credit to small businesses that are doing the right thing, giving their employees health care, makes sure that companies can't drop you when you get sick.

Now, I have no idea why you would want to repeal that in the first place, but I sure don't understand how repealing it would create jobs—[*laughter*]—unless it's for some folks in the insurance company who are being hired to deny you your claims. But that can't be a real jobs plan.

Now, look, I may be wrong. Maybe they know something I don't or no other economist or expert understands. And if you think that's a good idea, then you should vote for them.

But I've got a different view. The health insurance reform we passed isn't just preventing insurance companies from denying you coverage; it's making the coverage that you've got more secure and is ultimately going to lower costs for all Americans. And one of the most important things we can do to reduce our budget deficit is to get control of health care costs.

These guys don't have a plan for that. They just have a plan to say no, because they're thinking about the next election instead of the next generation. And that's the choice that we're going to be making in this next election. The choice in this election is between policies that strengthen the hand of the special interests or strengthen America's middle class.

They want to repeal health care; we're not going to let it happen. We want to move forward. They pledged to repeal Wall Street reform. Here we've got the biggest financial crisis since the Great Depression. Everybody knows, having looked at it, that the incentives on Wall Street were skewed and people were doing crazy things with other people's money, making huge, risky bets and then expecting taxpayers to bail them out if it didn't work out. So after all the hardship we've gone through to repair this economy, you'd think it would be common sense to say, let's have some basic rules of the road in place to ensure that a crisis like this doesn't happen again.

But what did the other party say? No. They want to go back to the status quo that got us into this same situation. The reforms we passed protect consumers and responsible bankers and responsible business owners. That's what the free market's supposed to be about: setting some basic rules for the road so that everybody can compete, not on how to game the system, but how to provide good service and good products to customers.

Make sure that mortgage companies can't give you a mortgage that you don't understand; make sure that credit card companies can't jack up your rates without providing you some notification—commonsense stuff. But they want to repeal it because they're more interested in the next election than they are in the next generation. And that's the choice that we will face in this next election.

If the other party wants to keep on giving taxpayer subsidies to big banks, that's their prerogative. But that's not what America's about. That's not going to move us forward.

I'll give you another example. We had a law in place when I took office in which the Government was guaranteeing student loans, except they were going through financial middlemen who were taking out billions of dollars of profits issuing the loans. But the loans were guaranteed, so they weren't taking any risks. They were just making billions of dollars of money.

We said, well, that doesn't make sense at a time when young people are trying to get to college, so what we're going to do is we're going to cut out the middleman. We've added tens of billions of dollars to the student loans program. More than a million young people are going to get help that wouldn't otherwise get help because of the decision we've made. What side do you think they were on? The other party voted no.

We passed a law to prohibit pay discrimination. My attitude is, equal pay for equal work. Women should be paid just like men for doing the same job. They said no. They want to go backwards. We want to move forwards.

They want to extend the Bush tax cuts for millionaires and billionaires. Now, I believe in tax cuts for the right folks. I kept my campaign promise, cut taxes for 95 percent of working families. But I don't understand how do you get up here and talk about how you care so deeply about the deficit, and yet you want to perpetuate a tax cut that costs $700 billion, with a "b"—$700 billion—and would not provide the kind of economic growth or benefits for the vast majority of Americans. That's the choice that we face in this election.

They voted to make sure that oil companies continue to get protected from some liabilities with respect to oil spills. How do you do that? We just spent all this time and energy trying to cap this well in the Gulf. You'd think it would make just common sense to ensure that oil companies are fully accountable. They voted no against that.

When we forced BP to put $20 billion aside to make sure those fishermen and store owners and hotel owners were protected—[*applause*]—and what happened? The guy who would be the chairman of the Energy Committee in the House apologized to BP.

Audience member. Sure did.

The President. Sure did—[*laughter*]—apologized. Said we engaged in a shakedown to protect ordinary families from the devastation that had taken place.

So look, you go across the board, Atlanta, there's going to be a choice in this election. It's a choice between special interest policies that led us into this mess and policies that are finally leading us out, that are finally helping America grow again, policies that are making middle class Americans more secure and giving them greater opportunity.

Now, I know this Nation's been through incredibly difficult times. And I also know, by the way, that not all the steps we took have been popular. Folks in Washington, these pundits, sometimes they write—they're all surprised— "President Obama went ahead with some of these steps like health care reform and helping the auto companies, and those weren't popular."

Well, I knew they weren't popular. I've got pollsters too. [*Laughter*] You don't think I've got polls that tell me what's popular and what's not? [*Laughter*] But for the last 20 months, my job has been to govern.

So when I went to Detroit last week and I look out and I see plants producing clean energy cars that otherwise would have been shut down, a million jobs that would have been lost, cars no longer made in America because the entire industry had collapsed, and I say, we made the right decision. And now Ford and Chrysler and GM are all making a profit. They've all hired 55,000 workers back. They are on the move. They're about to pay the taxpayers back for every investment that we made. Then I say to myself, I'm not here just to do what's popular, I'm here to do what's right.

And that's the kind of leadership you need and you deserve. That's the choice we face in this election. And, Democrats, if you work hard, as hard as you worked for me in 2008, we're going to keep going forward. We are not going backwards.

Thank you very much, everybody. God bless you. God bless the United States of America.

NOTE: The President spoke at 12:50 p.m. at the Hyatt Regency Atlanta hotel. In his remarks, he referred to State Labor Commissioner Michael L. Thurmond, State Attorney General Thurbert E. Baker, and State Agriculture Commissioner Tommy Irvin of Georgia; House Republican Leader John A. Boehner; and Rep. Joseph L. Barton.

Remarks and a Question-and-Answer Session With Young African Leaders
August 3, 2010

The President. Thank you. Thank you, everybody, please have a seat. Have a seat.

Well, good afternoon, everybody.

Audience members. Good afternoon.

The President. Welcome to the White House, and welcome to the United States of America. And that includes even our friends from Ghana, who beat us in the World Cup. [*Laughter*] Where are you? There—over there? That's all right. It was close. We'll see you in 2014. [*Laughter*]

It's my great privilege to welcome all of you to this Young African Leaders Forum. You've joined us from nearly 50 countries. You reflect the extraordinary history and diversity of the continent. You've already distinguished yourselves as leaders in civil society and development and business and faith communities, and you've got an extraordinary future before you.

In fact, you represent the Africa that so often is overlooked: the great progress that many Africans have achieved and the unlimited potential that you've got going forward into the 21st century.

Now, I called this forum for a simple reason. As I said when I was in Accra last year, I don't see Africa as a world apart, I see Africa as a fundamental part of our interconnected world. Whether it's creating jobs in a global economy or delivering education and health care, combating climate change, standing up to violent extremists who offer nothing but destruction, or promoting successful models of democracy and development, for all this, we have to have a strong, self-reliant, and prosperous Africa. So the world needs your talents and your creativity. We need young Africans who are standing up and making things happen not only in their own countries, but around the world.

And the United States wants to be your partner. So I'm pleased that you've already heard from Secretary of State Clinton and that we're joined today by leaders from across my administration who are working to deepen that partnership every day.

I can't imagine a more fitting time for this gathering. This year, people in 17 nations across sub-Saharan Africa are proudly celebrating 50 years of independence. And by any measure, 1960 was an extraordinary year. From Senegal to Gabon, from Madagascar to Nigeria, Africans rejoiced in the streets as foreign flags were lowered and their own were hoisted up. So in 12 remarkable months, nearly one-third of the continent achieved independence, a burst of self-determination that came to be celebrated as "The Year of Africa." At long last, these Africans were free to chart their own course and to shape their own destiny.

Now, 1960, of course, was significant for another reason. Here in the United States of America, it was the year that a candidate for President first proposed an idea for young people in our own country to devote a year or two abroad in service to the world. And that candidate was John F. Kennedy, and that idea would become the Peace Corps, one of our great partnerships with the world, including with Africa.

Now, the great task of building a nation is never done. Here in America, more than two centuries since our independence, we're still working to perfect our Union. Across Africa today, there's no denying the daily hardships that are faced by so many, the struggle to feed their children, to find work, to survive another day. And too often, that's the Africa that the world sees.

But today you represent a different vision, a vision of Africa on the move. An Africa that's ending old conflicts, as in Liberia, where President Sirleaf told me, today's children have "not known a gun and not had to run." An Africa that's modernizing and creating opportunities: agribusiness in Tanzania, prosperity in Botswana, political progress in Ghana and Guinea. An Africa that's pursuing a broadband revolution that could transform the daily lives of future generations.

So it's an Africa that can do great things, such as hosting the world's largest sporting event. So we congratulate our South African friends. And while it may have been two European teams in the final match, it's been pointed out that it was really Africa that won the World Cup.

So once again, Africa finds itself at a moment of extraordinary promise. And as I said last year, while today's challenges may lack some of the drama of 20th-century liberation struggles, they ultimately may be even more meaningful, for it will be up to you, young people full of talent and imagination, to build the Africa for the next 50 years.

Africa's future belongs to entrepreneurs like the small-business owner from Djibouti who began selling ice cream and now runs his own accounting practice and advises other entrepreneurs; that's Miguil Hassan Farah. Is Miguil here? There he is right there. Don't be shy. There you go.

As you work to create jobs and opportunity, America will work with you, promoting the trade and investment on which growth depends. That's why we're proud to be hosting the AGOA Forum this week to expand trade between our countries. And today I'll also be meeting with trade, commerce, and agricultural ministers from across sub-Saharan Africa. It's also why our historic food security initiative isn't simply about delivering food, it's about sharing new technologies to increase African productivity and self-sufficiency.

Now, no one should have to pay a bribe to get a job or to get government to provide basic services. So as part of our development strategy, we're emphasizing transparency, accountability, and a strong civil society, the kind of reform that can help unleash transformational change. So Africa's future also belongs to those who take charge of that kind of transparency and are serious about anticorruption measures.

Africa's future belongs to those who take charge of their health, like the HIV/AIDS counselor from Malawi who helps others by bravely sharing her own experience of being HIV-positive; that's Tamara Banda. Where is Tamara? There she is right there. Thank you, Tamara. So our Global Health Initiative is not merely treating diseases, it's strengthening prevention and Africa's public health systems. And I want to be very clear: We've continued to increase funds to fight HIV/AIDS to record levels, and we'll continue to do whatever it takes to save lives and invest in healthier futures.

Africa's future also belongs to societies that protects the rights of all its people, especially its women, like the journalist in Ivory Coast who has championed the rights of Muslim women and girls, Aminata Kane Kone. Where is Aminata? There she is right there. To you and to people across Africa, know that the United States of America will stand with you as you seek justice and progress and human rights and dignity for all people.

So the bottom line is this: Africa's future belongs to its young people, including a woman who inspires young people across Botswana with her popular radio show called, "The Real Enchilada." And that's Tumie Ramsden. Where's Tumie? Right here—"The Real Enchilada."

As all of you go to—as all of you pursue your dreams—as you go to school, you find a job, you make your voices heard, you mobilize people—

America wants to support your aspirations. So we're going to keep helping empower African youth: supporting education, increasing educational exchanges, like the one that brought my father from Kenya in the days when Kenyans were throwing off colonial rule and reaching for a new future. And we're helping to strengthen grassroots networks of young people who believe, as they're saying in Kenya today: "Yes Youth Can! Yes Youth Can!" [*Laughter*]

Now, this is a forum, so we've devoted some time where I can answer some questions. I don't want to do all the talking. I want to hear from you about your goals and how we can partner more effectively to help you reach them. And we want this to be the beginning of a new partnership and create networks that will promote opportunities for years to come.

But I do want to leave you with this: You are the heirs of the independence generation that we celebrate this year. Because of their sacrifice, you were born in independent African States. And just as the achievements of the last 50 years inspire you, the work you do today will inspire future generations.

So I understand, Tumie, you like to tweet. [*Laughter*] And she shared words that have motivated so many. This is what Tumie said: "If your actions inspire others to dream more, to learn more, to do more, and become more, then you are a leader."

So each of you are here today because you are a leader. You've inspired other young people in your home countries; you've inspired us here in the United States. The future is what you make it. And so if you keep dreaming and keep working and keep learning and don't give up, then I'm confident that your countries and the entire continent and the entire world will be better for it.

So thank you very much, everybody.

All right, with that, I'm going to take questions. Now, here are the rules. [*Laughter*] People—everybody who has a question, they can raise their hand. In order to be fair, I'm going to call girl, boy, girl, boy. We're going to alternate. And try to keep your question relatively short; I'll try to keep my answer relatively short so I can answer as many questions as possible, because we have a limited amount of time, okay?

I'm going to start with this young lady right here. And please introduce yourself, and tell me where you're from also.

Young African Leaders Forum

Q. Okay. Thank you very much. I will express myself in French, if that is——

The President. That's fine. Somebody will translate for me? Yes? Go ahead. Just make sure that you stop after each sentence, because otherwise she will forget what you had to say.

Q. Thank you very much.

[At this point, the participant asked a question in French, which was translated as follows.]

Mr. President, hello. And hello, everybody. I'm Fatoumata Sangho of Mali. I do have a question for you, and I look forward to getting your answer. But before I do so, I'd like to begin by telling you, Mr. President, how truly honored and privileged we feel to be with you today and how privileged we are to express the voices of African youth, of African young leaders, and, of course, fully appreciate your recognizing us and giving us the opportunity to be here, and also recognizing our own responsibility to take your voice back home.

I'd like to say that I'm convinced this is an important watershed moment; this is the beginning of important change, the wonderful initiative you had to call us all here. I wonder when did you see that particular light? When did you imagine that bringing us here would be such a good idea? I'm wondering what your thought process was, Mr. President.

The President. Well, first of all, one of the things that happens when you're President is that other people have good ideas, and then you take credit for them. *[Laughter]* So I want to make sure that I don't take credit for my ideas—for these ideas, because the truth is, my staff works so hard in trying to find new ways that we can communicate not just to the heads of state, but also at the grassroots.

And the reason, I think, is because when you think about Africa, Africa is the youngest conti-

nent. Many of the countries that you represent, half of the people are under 30. And oftentimes, if all you're doing is talking to old men like me, then you're not reaching the people who are going to be providing the energy, the new initiatives, the new ideas. And so we thought that it would be very important for us to have an opportunity to bring the next generation of leaders together.

That's point number one. Point number two—and I'm going to be blunt occasionally during this forum, so I hope you don't mind—sometimes, the older leaders get into old habits, and those old habits are hard to break. And so part of what we wanted to do was to communicate directly to people who may not assume that the old ways of doing business are the ways that Africa has to do business.

So in some of your countries, freedom of the press is still restricted. There's no reason why that has to be the case; there's nothing inevitable about that. And young people are more prone to ask questions: Why shouldn't we have a free press? In some of your countries, it is—the problem of corruption is chronic. And so people who've been doing business in your country for 20, 30 years, they'll just throw up their hands, and they'll say, "Ah, that's the way it is."

But Robert Kennedy had a wonderful saying, where he said: "Some people see things and ask, 'Why?' And others see things that need changing and ask, 'Why not?'" And so I think that your generation is poised to ask those questions, "Why not?" Why shouldn't Africa be self-sustaining agriculturally? There's enough arable land that if we restructure how agriculture and markets work in Africa, not only could most countries in Africa feed themselves, but they could export those crops to help feed the world. Why not?

New infrastructure: It used to be that you had to have telephone lines and very capital intensive—in order to communicate. Now we have the Internet and broadband and cell phones, so you—the entire continent may be able to leapfrog some other places that were more highly developed and actually reach into the future of communications in ways that we can't even imagine yet. Why not?

So that's the purpose of this. I also want to make sure that all of you are having an opportunity to meet each other, because you can reinforce each other as you are struggling and fighting in your own countries for a better future. You will now have a network of people that help to reinforce what it is that you're trying to do. And you know that sometimes change makes you feel lonely; now you've got a group of people who can help reinforce what you're doing.

Okay. It's a gentleman's turn. This is why they're leaders—everybody has something to say. But you don't have to snap. No, no, no. It's a guy's turn. This gentleman right here.

Role of Young African Leaders in Africa's Development

Q. Mr. President, my name is Bai Best from Liberia. The late Dr. Solomon Carter Fuller was the first Black psychiatrist in America and probably in the world. In my country in Liberia, where there are a lot of great people who make landmark accomplishments in—both in their nation and in the world, many of them are not recognized for their accomplishments. Today, Dr. Fuller's name is etched where there's a medical—there is a psychiatric center named in his honor at a place in Boston. There are many other young African and young Liberian talented people who have great ideas and who want to come back home and contribute to their countries, to the development of their peoples. But many times, their efforts—their patriotic efforts—are stifled by corrupt or sometimes jealous officials in government and in other sectors. It's an age-old problem. Many times, they want to seek—that basically leads them to seek greener pastures and better appreciation abroad instead of coming back home. What are your thoughts on this?

The President. Well, look, this is a problem that's not unique to Africa. Given different stages of development around the world, one of the problems that poorer countries often have is that the best educated and the most talented have opportunities elsewhere. And so there's what's called the brain drain, people saying, "I

can make 10 times as much money if I'm a doctor in London as I can if I'm a doctor back home."

And so this is a historic problem. Here's the interesting moment that we're in, though: If you look at where the greatest opportunities are, they're actually now in emerging markets. There are countries in Africa that are growing 7, 8, 9 percent a year. So if you're an entrepreneur now with an idea, you may be able to grow faster and achieve more back home than you could here.

Now, it entails greater risk, so it may be safer to emigrate. But it may be that you can actually achieve more, more quickly back home. And so the question is for young leaders like yourselves, where do you want to have the most impact? And you're probably going to have more impact at home, whether you're a business man or woman or you are a doctor or you are an attorney or you are an organizer. That's probably going to be the place where you can make the biggest change.

Now, you're absolutely right, though, that the conditions back home have to be right, where you can achieve these things. So if you want to go back home and start a business, and it turns out that you have to pay too many bribes to just get the business started, at some point, you may just give up.

And that's why one of the things that we're trying to do—working with my team—when we emphasize development, good governance is at the center of development. It's not separate. Sometimes people think, well, that's a political issue, and then there's an economic issue. No. If you have a situation where you can't start a business or people don't want to invest because there's not a clear sense of rule of law, that is going to stifle development.

If farmers have so many middlemen to get their crops to market that they're making pennies when ultimately their crops are being sold for $10, over time, that stifles agricultural development in a country. So what we want to do is make sure that in our interactions with your Governments, we are constantly emphasizing this issue of good governance, because I have confidence that you'll be able to figure out what changes need to be made in your country.

I've always said the destiny of Africa is going to be determined by Africans. It's not going to be determined by me. It's not going to be determined by people outside of the continent. It's going to be determined by you. All we can do is make sure that your voices are heard and you're able to rise up and take hold of these opportunities. If you do that, I think that there are going to be a lot of people who, even if they're educated abroad, want to come home to make their mark.

All right. Let's see, I'm going to call on this young lady right here.

[The participant asked a question in Portuguese, which was translated as follows.]

Nonviolence/Development/Women's Rights/Fighting Government Corruption

Q. Good afternoon, everyone. And thank you, Mr. President, for this opportunity.

The President. That sounds like Portuguese. *[Laughter]*

Q. It is, indeed, from Mozambique, sir.

The President. Great.

Q. Knowing, Mr. President, that, of course, America is a reference point for democracy in the world, and that you, sir, are, indeed, a protagonist in that context today, I would love to hear from you, sir, what you would recommend to the young people in Africa and to civil society, in particular, in terms of following principles of nonviolence and good governance and democratic principles in our country, because, of course, our reality is very often quite starkly different. There are 80 percent abstentionism often in elections and elections that, indeed, lack transparency and that all too often lead, alas, to social conflict.

The President. Well——

Q. Thank you.

The President. ——let me say, first of all, that if you are—just as I said that you can't separate politics from economics, you can't separate conflict from development. So the constant conflict—often ethnically based conflict—that has

taken place in Africa is a profound detriment to development, and it's self-reinforcing.

If you have conflict and violence, that scares off investors. That makes it more difficult for businesspeople to create opportunities, which means that young people then don't have work, which means that they are more prone to be recruited in violent conflicts. And you can get a vicious cycle.

So I am a profound believer in not looking at violence as a solution to problems. And I think the moral and ethical power that comes with nonviolence when properly mobilized is profound.

Number two, I think the most important thing that maybe young people here can do is to promote the values of openness, transparency, honest debate, civil disagreements within your own groups and your own organizations, because that forms good habits. If you are part of an organization—and I'm going to speak to the men here, in particular—if you are part of an organization where you profess democracy, but women don't have an equal voice in your organization, then you're a hypocrite, right? And that is something that we have to be honest about. Oftentimes, women are not getting the same voice in African countries, despite the fact that they are carrying more than their fair share of burdens.

So within your own organizations, within your own networks, modeling good democratic practices, listening to people who you disagree with respectfully, making sure that everybody gets a seat at the table, all those things I think are very important.

Because part of what I'm going to—what I'm hoping for is, is that some of you will end up being leaders of your country some days. And if you think about it, back in the 1960s, when all these—your grandparents, great-grandparents were obtaining independence, fighting for independence, the first leaders, they all said they were for democracy. And then what ends up happening is, you've been in power for a while, and you say, well, I must be such a good ruler that it is for the benefit of the people that I need to stay here. And so then you start changing the laws or you start intimidating and jailing opponents. And pretty soon, young people just like yourself, full of hope and promise, end up becoming exactly what they fought against.

So one of the things that I think everybody here has to really internalize is the notion that you—I think it was Gandhi who once said, you have to be the change that you seek. You have to be the change that you seek. And one of the wonderful things about the United States is that in my position as President, there are often times where I get frustrated, I think I know more than some of my critics, and yet we have institutionalized the notion that those critics have every right to criticize me, no matter how unreasonable I think they may be. And I have to stand before the people for an election, and I'm limited to two terms—doesn't matter how good a job I do. And that's good, because what that means is, is that we've got a—we've instituted a culture where the institutions of democracy are more important than any one individual.

And now, it's not as if we're perfect. Obviously, we've got all kinds of problems as well. But what it does mean is, is that the peaceful transfer of power and the notion that people always have a voice, our trust in that democratic process is one that has to be embraced in all your countries as well.

Okay? All right, it's a gentleman's turn. I've got—let me try to get this side of the table here. The—this gentleman right here. I'm not going to get everybody, so——

Q. All right. Thank you——

The President. ——I apologize in advance.

President's Emergency Plan for AIDS Relief/Global Health Initiative

Q. Thank you very much, Mr. President. My name is Felix Limbani from Malawi. Mr. President, HIV/AIDS is greatly affecting development in Africa. And if this continues, I'm afraid I think Africa has no future. And I think it's young people like us that must bring change. And we really need a strong HIV prevention program. But, again, access to treatment must be there.

I attended the recent world AIDS conference in Vienna, and the critics were saying that the worst—the U.S. Government is not sup-

porting enough HIV/AIDS work in Africa through the PEPFAR and the Global Fund. But, again, on the other side, other HIV/AIDS activists are saying that Africa on its own has not mobilized enough resources to fight the HIV/AIDS pandemic, and they are largely depending on the West.

I think the challenge for us as African young leaders is to make sure that this comes to an end, and we really need to reduce the transmission. I don't know, from your perspective, what can we do to make sure that this comes to a stop? Otherwise, it's greatly affecting development in Africa.

The President. Good. Well, let me start by just talking about the United States and what we're doing. I had some disagreements with my predecessor, but one of the outstanding things that President Bush did was to initiate the PEPFAR program. It's a huge investment in battling HIV/AIDS, both with respect to prevention and also with respect to treatment. Billions of dollars were committed. We have built off of that.

So when you hear critics—what the critics are saying is that although I've increased the funding of the PEPFAR program, they would like to see it increased even more, which I'm sympathetic to, given the fact that the need is so great. But understand, I've increased it, I haven't decreased it, at a time when the United States is suffering from the worst economic—just coming out of the worst economic recession that we've seen since the 1930s. Nevertheless, because of our commitment to this issue, we've actually increased funding.

Now, we have couched it in a broader initiative we call the Global Health Initiative. Because even as we're battling HIV/AIDS, we want to make sure that we are thinking not only in terms of treatment, but also in terms of prevention and preventing transmission.

We're never going to have enough money to simply treat people who are constantly getting infected. We've got to have a mechanism to stop the transmission rate. And so one of the things we're trying to do is to build greater public health infrastructure, find what prevention programs are working, how can we institutionalize them, make them culturally specific, because not every program is going to be appropriate for every country.

I will say that in Africa, in particular, one thing we do know is that empowering women is going to be critical to reducing the transmission rate. We do know that. Because so often, women, not having any control over sexual practices and their own body, end up having extremely high transmission rates.

So the bottom line is, we're going to focus on prevention, building a public health infrastructure. We're still going to be funding, at very high levels, antiviral drugs. But keep in mind, we will never have enough money—it will be endless, an endless effort—if the transmission rates stay high and we're just trying to treat people after their sick.

It's the classic story of a group of people come upon all these bodies in a stream, and everybody jumps in and starts pulling bodies out, but one wise person goes downstream to see what's exactly happening that's causing all these people to drown or fall in the water. And that's, I think, what we have to do, is go downstream to see how can we reduce these transmission rates overall.

And obviously, when I visited Kenya, for example, just in terms of education, Michelle and I, we both got tested near the village where my father was born. We got publicly tested so that we would know what our status was. That was just one example of the kinds of educational mechanisms that we can use that hopefully can make some difference.

All right? Okay, it's a woman's turn. Okay, this one right here.

Africa-U.S. Relations

Q. Thank you very much, Mr. President, and greetings from Ghana. My name is Shamima. We are looking forward fervently to 2014—[*laughter*]—for a repeat. And I recollect that I was hosting a radio program the day of the match. And we have a football pundit in Ghana—he doesn't speak English quite well, but very passionate. And so I was interviewing him about what the psyche of our boys should be ahead of the match. And he said to me that: "Shamima, this is not war, it is football. If it

were to be war, then maybe we should be afraid because the might of America is more than us." [*Laughter*] "This is football. They should go out there and be the best that they could be." And they did. So that's by the way——

The President. Well, they did an excellent job. They were a great team.

Q. Mr. President, my question now is that I hear a lot of young African leaders wonder how committed America would be to a partnership. I hear those who are cynical about the notion of partnership. They ask—and always they ask, partnership? What kind of fair partnership can exist between a strong and a weak nation?

And so as we prepare ourselves for the future, we ask the same question of America: How committed is your country to ensuring that the difficult decisions that young people have to make about trade, about agriculture, about support are made, to the extent that they may not be in the interest of America? Because they tell me, also, that America will protect its interest over and above all else. Is America committed to ensuring a partnership that might not necessarily be beneficial to America, but truly beneficial to the sovereign interest of the countries that we represent?

The President. Well, let me say this. All countries look out for their interests. So—and I'm the President of the United States, so my job is to look out for the people of the United States. That's my job, all right? And that's—[*applause*].

Now, I actually think, though, that the interests of the United States and the interests of the continent of Africa greatly overlap. We have a huge interest in seeing development throughout Africa, because we are a more mature economy, Africa is a young and growing economy, and if you can buy more iPods and buy more products and buy more services and buy more tractors from us, that we can sell to a fast-growing continent, that creates jobs here in the United States of America.

We have a huge interest in your public health systems, because if we're reducing greatly HIV/AIDS transmissions in Africa, then that will have a positive effect on HIV rates internationally because of the transmigration of diseases back and forth in an international world. And not to mention, if I'm not spending all this money on PEPFAR, that's money I can spend somewhere else. So I'm going to be incentivized to see Africa do well. That's in our interest.

And the truth of the matter is, is that whereas with some regions of the world, we do have some genuine conflicts of interest—let's say on trade, for example—the truth is that the United States, we don't have huge conflicts when it comes to trade, because, frankly, the trade between the United States and Africa is so small, so modest, that very few U.S. companies, U.S. commercial interests are impacted.

That's why AGOA, our trade arrangement with Africa, is—we can eliminate tariffs and subsidies and allow all sorts of goods to come in, partly because you are not our primary competition.

Now, I don't want to pretend that there aren't ever going to be conflicts. There will be. There's going to be difference in world views. There are going to be some agricultural products where there are certain interests in the United States or there are certain interests in Europe that want to prevent those from coming in, even though in the aggregate it would not have a huge impact on the U.S. economy. And so there are going to be occasional areas of tension. But overall, the reason you should have confidence that we want a partnership is because your success will enhance our position rather than reduce it.

Also, Africa has some of our most loyal friends. I mean, every survey that's taken, when you ask what continent generally has the most positive views about America, it turns out Africa generally has a positive view of America and positive experiences. So I think that you should feel confident, even if I'm not President, that the American people genuinely want to see Africa succeed.

What the American people don't want is to feel like their efforts at helping are wasted. So if at a time of great constraint, we are coming up with aid, those aid dollars need to go to countries that are actually using them effectively. And if they're not using them effectively, then they should go to countries that are.

And one of the things that I've said to my development team is, I want us to have high standards in terms of performance and evaluation when we have these partnerships, because a partnership is a two-way street. It means that on the one hand, we're accountable to you and that we have to listen to you and make sure that any plans that we have, have developed indigenously. On the other hand, it also means you're accountable. So you can't just say, give me this, give me that, and then if it turns out that it's not working well, that's not your problem, right? It has to be a two-way street.

Okay, looks like this side has not gotten a question here. So how about this gentleman right here.

Zimbabwe/U.S. Foreign Policy

Q. Thank you, Mr. President. My name is Sydney Chisi from Zimbabwe. Currently, our Government is in a transition between the former ruling party ZANU-PF and the Movement for Democratic Change. And within this same context, Zimbabwe is currently under restrictive measures, especially for those who are party in line with Robert Mugabe under the ZIDERA Act. How has been the success of ZIDERA post the formation of the inclusive government? Because in Zimbabwe, Robert Mugabe is still using the rhetoric of sanctions, racist, property rights abuse, human rights abuse in violation to the rule of law. How has been the success of that towards the implementation, the success or the growth of young people?

The President. Well, you probably have a better answer than me. So you should be sharing with our team what you think would make the most sense. I'll be honest with you, I'm heartbroken when I see what's happened in Zimbabwe. I think Mugabe is an example of a leader who came in as a liberation fighter and—I'm just going to be very blunt—I do not see him serving his people well. And the abuses, the human rights abuses, the violence that's been perpetrated against opposition leaders, I think, is terrible.

Now, Tsvangirai has tried to work—he—despite the fact that he himself has been beaten and imprisoned, he has now tried to work to see

1139

if there is a gradual transition that might take place. But so far, the results have not been what we had hoped.

And this always poses a different—difficult question for U.S. foreign policy because on the one hand, we don't want to punish the people for the abuses of a leader. On the other hand, we have very little leverage other than saying, if there are just systematic abuses by a government, we are not going to deal with them commercially, we're not going to deal with them politically in ways that we would with countries that are observing basic human rights principles.

And so there have been discussions when I've traveled with leaders in the southern African region about whether or not sanctions against Zimbabwe are or are not counterproductive. I will tell you I would love nothing more than to be able to open up greater diplomatic relationships and economic and commercial relationships with Zimbabwe. But in order to do so, we've got to see some signal that it will not simply entrench the same past abuses, but rather, will move us in a new direction that actually helps the people.

And Zimbabwe is a classic example of a country that should be the breadbasket for an entire region. It's a spectacular country. Now, it had to undergo a transition from white minority rule that was very painful and very difficult. But they have chosen a path that's different than the path that South Africa chose.

South Africa has its problems, but from what everybody could see during the World Cup, the potential for moving that country forward in— as a multiracial, African democracy that can succeed on the world stage, that's a model that so far, at least, Zimbabwe has not followed. And that's where I'd like to see it go. All right?

How much more time do I have, guys? Last question? I'm sorry—last question. Last question. No, it's a young lady's turn. It's a—this one right here.

Somalia/Africa's Development

Q. Good afternoon, Mr. President, your excellencies. My name is Najma Ahmed Abdi. I'm from Somalia. I came all the way here with one question, and that is, living in conflict in a country that has confused the whole world, and being part of the diaspora that went back to risk our lives in order to make Somalia a better place, especially with what we're going through right now, how much support do we expect from the U.S.? And not support just in terms of financially or aid, but support as an ear, as a friend, as somebody who hears and listens to those of us who are putting our lives and our families at risk to defend humanity.

The President. Well, the—I think you will have enormous support from the people of the United States when it comes to trying to create a structure and framework in Somalia that works for the Somali people.

Now, the history of Somalia over the last 20 years has been equally heartbreaking, if not more so. You have not had a effective, functioning government that can provide basic services. It's been rife with conflict. And now the entire region is threatened because of radical extremists who have taken root in Somalia, taking advantage of what they perceive to be a failing state to use that as a base to launch attacks, most recently in Uganda.

And obviously, the United States expresses its deepest condolences to the lives that were lost in Kampala, at the very moment of the World Cup. And it offered two contrasting visions. You have this wonderful, joyous celebration in South Africa at the same time as you have a terrorist explosion in Kampala.

So we desperately want Somalia to succeed. And this is another example of where our interests intersect. If you have extremist organizations taking root in a Somalia, ultimately, that can threaten the United States, as well as Uganda, as well as Kenya, as well as the entire region.

So right now you've got a transitional Government that is making some efforts. I don't think anybody expects Somalia any time in the next few years to suddenly be transformed into a model democracy. Whatever governance structures take place in Somalia have to be aware of the tribal and traditional structures and clan structures that exist within Somalia. But certainly, what we can do is create a situation where people—young people—are not carrying around rifles, shooting each other on the streets. And we want to be a partner with Somalia in that effort, and we will continue to do so.

And some of it is financial, some of it is developmental, some of it is being able to help basic infrastructure. In some cases, we may try to find a portion of the country that is relatively stable and start work there to create a model that the rest of the country can then look at and say, this is a different path than the one that we're taking right now.

But in the end, I think that this metaphor of the success of the World Cup and the bombing shows that each of you are going to be confronted with two paths. There's going to be a path that takes us into a direction of more conflict, more bloodshed, less economic development, continued poverty, even as the rest of the world races ahead, or there's a vision in which people come together for the betterment and development of their own country.

And for all the great promise that's been fulfilled over the last 50 years, I want you to understand, because I think it's important for us to be honest with ourselves, Africa has also missed huge opportunities for too long. And I'll just give you one example.

When my father traveled to the United States and got his degree in the early sixties, the GDP of Kenya was actually on par—maybe actually higher than the GDP of South Korea. Think about that, all right? So when I was born, Kenya per capita might have been wealthier than South Korea. Now it's not even close. Well, that's 50 years that was lost in terms of opportunities. When it comes to natural resources, when it comes to the talent and potential of the people, there's no reason why Kenya shouldn't have been on that same trajectory.

And so 50 years from now, when you look back, you want to make sure that the continent hasn't missed those opportunities as well. We want to make sure of that as well. And the United States wants to listen to you and work with you. And so when you go back and you talk to your friends and you say, what was the main message the President had: We are rooting for your success, and we want to work with you to achieve that success, but ultimately, success is going to be in your hands. And being a partner means that we can be there by your side, but we can't do it for you. All right?

Okay, thank you very much, everybody. Thank you.

NOTE: The President spoke at 2:07 p.m. in the East Room at the White House. In his remarks, he referred to President Ellen Johnson Sirleaf of Liberia; and President Robert Mugabe and Prime Minister Morgan Tsvangirai of Zimbabwe.

Telephone Remarks to a Town Hall Meeting Hosted by Senator Michael F. Bennet
August 3, 2010

The President. Hello, everybody.

Senator Bennet. Mr. President.

The President. How are you?

Sen. Bennet. I'm not going to take any of your time. Thank you for—I'm doing great. How are you?

The President. I'm great.

Sen. Bennet. Good, thanks for joining us. And I'll turn it over to you.

The President. Well, look, everybody, it's great to talk to you. And by the way, I enjoyed Michael's answer on education. He was right on point. And I want to thank all of you for joining us on this call tonight.

You know, Michael arrived in Washington just as I took office as President, and this was one of the toughest times in our country's history. We'd just gone through nearly a decade of economic policies that weren't working for ordinary families. It culminated in the worst recession of our lifetimes. And so what we needed were leaders who were willing to stand up to the status quo and the special interests and start moving this country in a new direction.

And Michael has been that kind of leader. He's been a breath of fresh air in a town with a lot of hot air. And one of the things that I've discovered in Washington is there are basically two kinds of people who go into politics. There are folks who want to be something, and then there are folks who run because they want to do something, because they care about something bigger than themselves. And that's Michael.

He could have lived a comfortable life. Instead, he's devoted himself to every assignment he's undertaken to make a positive difference for his community and for the people of Colorado.

We saw that when he turned around Denver's public schools, fighting for change and reform, making sure that young people got the opportunity they deserve. All across this country, people who care about school reform admire and know what Michael did in Denver, so he's become the go-to guy for reforming America's public schools in Congress. And he stood up in the Senate again and again these past 18 months on a whole host of issues related to opening up opportunity.

So he stood up to the insurance lobbies to help pass reforms that finally make health insurance affordable and stop people from getting insurance because of preexisting conditions.

He stood up against big corporations that are getting tax breaks for offshoring, when we should actually be giving tax breaks to companies that create jobs here in the United States; stood up to credit card companies that were taking advantage of people with hidden fees and unfair rate hikes, and mortgage lenders who tricked families into buying homes they couldn't afford; and was one of the key people who I needed to make sure we passed Wall Street reform to prevent another financial crisis.

So Michael has been as good of a Senator as I expected him to be when I first met him and he was still head of the public schools out in Denver. And I know there have been a lot of negative ads running against Michael in the last few weeks, which is sort of politics as usual. But when he came to Washington, he came to get things done and not just play the usual political games. And he's running a campaign that we can be proud of. He's a public servant that we can be proud of. We need more folks like Michael in Washington.

And so the main reason I'm on this call is to make sure that everybody who's listening is thinking not just about the next election but about the next generation. That's how Michael approaches his job. And if you're already supporting Michael, we need you to help in these final weeks, this final week, to knock on doors and make phone calls to everyone you know to get out the vote. And if you're still trying to figure out what to do, I want you to support him, because Michael is somebody who has stood up on behalf of you, and we need to stand up on his behalf right now.

So I just want to say thank you to all of you for taking the time to join us. Thanks for staying engaged and interested. We need people who are involved in this process now more than ever. We've accomplished an incredible amount over the last 18 months, but we've got a lot more work to do. And Michael is the person that I want alongside me when we do it.

So make sure, guys, to go out there and cast your ballots for Michael. And I know that he's going to be one of the best Senators that Colorado's ever had. All right?

Sen. Bennet. Thank you, Mr. President. We deeply appreciate your taking the time to be on the call with everybody and everything you're doing. Let's see if we can't get Elena Kagan confirmed this week.

The President. Oh, I think we're going to get her confirmed. And after that we're just going to keep on going to make sure that we create the kind of economy that's working for all Americans.

So thanks for everything, Michael. Bye-bye.

Sen. Bennet. All right, thank you.

NOTE: The President spoke at 8:25 p.m. from the Residence at the White House to participants of the teleconference town hall meeting hosted by Sen. Bennet. Audio was not available for verification of the content of these remarks.

Remarks to the AFL–CIO Executive Council
August 4, 2010

The President. Thank you, everybody. Please have a seat. Thank you.

It is good to spend my birthday with some good friends. [*Laughter*] And as I look around the room, there are very few of you who I haven't, in some form or fashion, worked directly with on an issue, some of you dating back to when I was in the State legislature, some of you who I've worked with in the United States Senate, and all of you who I've had the opportunity to work with as President of the United States.

So I am grateful. And I want to first of all thank Rich, not only for inviting me here, not only for, I know, making clear my commitment to all of you during an earlier session today, but also for your outstanding leadership of the labor movement. And we very much appreciate everything that you do.

I want to thank Liz and Arlene for bucking up Rich all the time—[*laughter*]—and making him look good. This is a shared leadership, and we are very proud of them. I want to thank all the members of the executive council, all my brothers and sisters in the AFL–CIO.

Together, you are fighting for the hard-working men and women in this country after nearly 10 years of struggle. The middle class has been struggling now for about a decade, 10 years in which folks felt the sting of stagnant incomes and sluggish job growth and declining economic security, as well as at least 8 years in which there was a profound animosity towards the notion of unions.

It's going to take some time to reverse all that's been done, but we're on the right track. We're moving forward. And that's what I'm going to want to talk to you about briefly today.

I hope you don't mind me interjecting, though, a topic, because it's in the news right now and I want to make sure that all of you are aware of it.

One place in our country where people have faced particular struggles in the last few months is in the Gulf of Mexico, as a result of the BP oil spill. So it was very welcome news when we learned overnight that efforts to stop the well

through what's called a static kill appear to be working and that a report out today by our scientists show that the vast majority of the spilled oil has been dispersed or removed from the water. So the long battle to stop the leak and contain the oil is finally close to coming to an end. And we are very pleased with that.

Our recovery efforts, though, will continue. We have to reverse the damage that's been done. We will continue to work to hold polluters accountable for the destruction they've caused. We've got to make sure that folks who were harmed are reimbursed, and we're going to stand by the people of the region, however long it takes, until they're back on their feet.

Now, beyond the Gulf, many of those who've been hit hardest by the economic upheaval of recent years have been the people that you represent. For generations, manufacturing was the ticket to a better life for the American worker. But as the world became smaller, outsourcing, an easier way to increase profits, a lot of those jobs shifted to low-wage nations. So many who held those jobs went to work in the construction industry, as we had the housing boom. But when the subprime mortgage crisis hit, when those mortgages were called up on Wall Street, that bubble burst, leaving devastation everywhere.

So now we've got millions of our fellow Americans swept up in that disaster, hard-working people who've been left to sit idle for months and even years as their lives have been turned upside down.

And there's one last element to it, obviously. Having been plunged into a recession, it also means that teachers and firefighters and people who are providing public services each and every day are threatened because tax revenues at the State level and at the local levels have crashed. And so you have a perfect economic storm that's hit our middle class directly in every region, every segment of this country.

You know the stories; I don't need to tell you. You know what happens when a plant closes and hundreds of your members are suddenly without work and an entire community is devastated. You know how hard it is for somebody who's worked his whole life to be unable to find a job. And that pain goes beyond just the financial pain. It goes to who they are as a person. It hits them in their gut. Having a conversation with your spouse and saying, you know, maybe we can't afford this house anymore; maybe we're going to have to give up on being able to save for our kids' college education—that goes directly to people's identities, to their cores. And this is something that all of you know all too well.

But I'm here to tell you, we are not giving up and we are not giving in. We are going to keep fighting for an economy that works for everybody, not just for a privileged few. We want an economy that rewards, once again, people who work hard and fulfill their responsibilities, not just people who game the system. And that's been at the heart of the economic plan that we put in place over the past year and a half.

And I want to thank the AFL–CIO for all you've done to fight for jobs, to fight for tax cuts for the middle class, to fight for reforms that will rein in the special interests, and to fight for policies that aren't just going to rebuild this economy, but are actually going to put us on a long-term path of sustainable growth that is good for all Americans.

Because of you, we've been able to get a lot done over the last 20 months. Together, we're jump-starting a new American clean energy industry, an industry with the potential to generate perhaps millions of jobs building wind turbines and solar panels and manufacturing the batteries for the cars of the future, building nuclear plants, developing clean coal technology. There are other countries that are fighting for those jobs, in China and India and in Germany and other parts of Europe. But the United States doesn't play for second place. As long as I'm President, I'm going to keep fighting night and day to make sure that we win those jobs, that those are jobs that are created right here in the United States of America, and that your members are put to work.

So the message I want to deliver to our competitors and to those in Washington who've tried to block our progress at every step of the way is that we are going to rebuild this economy stronger than before, and at the heart of it are going to be three powerful words: Made in America. Made in America.

That's why we're finally enforcing our trade laws, in some cases for the very first time. That's why we're fighting for tax breaks for companies that invest here in the United States as opposed to companies that are investing overseas or that keep their profits offshore. Because it is my belief—and I know it's the belief of this room—that there are no better workers than U.S. workers. There are no better workers than your members. And they are absolutely committed to making sure that America is on the rise again. And we are going to keep moving forward with them, not moving backwards, but moving forward with them.

As we rebuild our economy, we're going to rebuild America as well. Over the last 20 months, bulldozers and backhoes have been whirring in communities across the country, as construction crews from local companies repair roads and bridges, railways, and ports. That was part of our plan, and it's put hundreds of thousands of folks to work. But there's a lot more to do to rebuild our infrastructure for the 21st century and a lot more Americans who are ready and willing to do that work. So that too is an area where we've got to keep moving forward.

We're going to have to cut taxes for middle class families, and after a tough fight, we finally extended emergency unemployment assistance for folks who had lost their jobs. We passed the Fair Pay Act to help put a stop to pay discrimination. We've reversed the Executive orders of the last administration that were designed to undermine organized labor. I've appointed folks who actually are fulfilling their responsibilities to make sure our workplaces are safe, whether in a mine or in an office, a factory, or anyplace else. And we are going to keep on fighting to pass the Employee Free Choice Act.

With your help, we passed health reform, enshrining the idea that everybody in America should be able to get decent health care and shouldn't go bankrupt when they get sick, health reform that is preventing insurers from denying and dropping people's coverage, that's lowering the price of prescription drugs for our seniors. It's going to make health care more affordable for everybody, including businesses, which means they can hire more workers.

Together, we passed Wall Street reform to protect consumers in our financial system and put an end to taxpayer bailouts and stop the abuses that almost dragged our economy into another Great Depression.

Now, the steps we're taking are making a difference, but the fact is—and Rich mentioned this—it took us nearly a decade to dig ourselves into the hole that we're in. It's going to take a lot longer than any of us would like to climb out of that hole. And I'd be lying to you if I thought that all these changes are going to be happening overnight. We've still got some tough times ahead. And your members obviously are bearing the brunt of a lot of those tough times.

But here's what we're not going to do: We're not going to go back to digging the hole. We're not going to go back to the policies that took Bill Clinton's surplus and in 8 years turned it into record deficits. We're not going back to policies that saw people working harder and harder, but falling further and further behind. We're not going back to policies that gave corporate special interests free rein to write their own rules and produced the greatest economic crisis in generations. We are not going back to those ideas.

Because as hard as it is out there right now for a lot of folks, as far as we've got to go, what's clear is that our Nation is headed in the right direction. Our economy is growing again instead of shrinking. We're adding jobs in the private sector instead of losing them. America is moving forward.

And we're moving forward largely without any help from the opposition party, a party that has voted no on just about every turn: no on making college more affordable, no on clean energy jobs, no on broadband, no on high-speed rail, no on water and highway projects. That doesn't stop them from showing up at the ribbon cuttings. It doesn't stop them from sending out press releases. They've even said no to tax cuts for small businesses and 95 percent of working families. They just said no to a small-business tax cut again just last week.

As we speak, they've been trying to block an emergency measure to save the jobs of police officers and firefighters and teachers and other critical public servants across the country who may be laid off because of State and local budget cuts.

And as if that was not enough, now they're talking about repealing this and repealing that. I guess they want to go back to hidden credit card fees and mortgage penalties buried in the fine print. They want to go back to a system that allowed for taxpayer bailouts. They want to go back to allowing insurance companies to discriminate against people based on preexisting conditions. They would repeal the tax cuts for small businesses that provide health care for their employees. They want to go backwards; we want to move America forward.

And that's what the choice is going to be in this upcoming election, and all your members need to understand it. I know if you're talking to a lot of your locals, I'm sure they're feeling like, boy, change is not happening fast enough; we are still hurting out here. They're frustrated. They've got every right to be frustrated. And I am happy, as President of the United States, to take responsibility for making decisions now that are going to put us in a stronger position down the road. And they need to know that, that we're going to be working with you to make sure that we're putting ourselves in a position where folks are working and working for a good wage and good benefits.

But you have to remind them for the next 3 months, this election is a choice. You've got these folks who drove America's economy into a ditch. And for the last 20 months, we put on our boots and we got into the mud and we've been shoving that car out of the ditch inch by inch. And they've been standing on the side the whole time watching, telling us, "No, you're not pushing hard enough; you're not doing it the right way," not lifting a finger to help. And now we've finally got that car up on the blacktop there, about to drive, and they say they want the keys back. Well, you can't have the keys, because you don't know how to drive. [*Laughter*] You don't know how to drive. You're not going to get the keys back. [*Laughter*] You're not going to get them back.

Somebody pointed out to me that when you're in a car and you want to go forward, you put it in "D." [*Laughter*] You want to go back in the ditch, you put it on "R." [*Laughter*] So I just want everybody to think about that.

All right, let me close by saying this. A few weeks ago, I had the opportunity to visit—not a few weeks ago, just a few days ago—I had the opportunity to visit a Chrysler plant in Detroit. This is a place obviously that's been harder hit than just about anywhere, not just during this financial crisis, but for a couple of decades now. The auto industry alone lost hundreds of thousands of jobs in the year before I took office. So we had to make a very difficult decision when I became President about whether to walk away from American automakers or help them get back on their feet.

And I decided we couldn't walk away from what could be a million middle class jobs. So we told the automakers that we would give them temporary assistance if they restructured to make themselves competitive for the 21st century. And most of the "just say no" crowd in Washington didn't agree with this decision. And let's face it: It was not popular in the polls. A lot of people weren't happy with that decision. But today, all three U.S. automakers are operating at a profit for the first time in more than 5 years. They've had the strongest job growth in more than 10 years; 55,000 workers have been hired. Instead of a planned shutdown, the plant that I was at is staying open this summer just to meet increased demand. They've even added another shift.

Now, just a few weeks before I visited that auto plant, 14 of its employees won the lottery. This is a true story. Now, you'd think they would have decided to retire, cash out, walk away. But most of them didn't. They're staying on their jobs. And the guy who bought the ticket was a guy named William Shanteau, took the money, and he bought his wife one of the Jeep Cherokees that they make at the plant. And then he bought a bunch of American flags for

his hometown because he loves his country, just like he loves the company that he works for and the workers that he works with and the union that represents him. And he's going to keep on showing up every day because he loves that plant, he loves his coworkers, and he loves the idea of making something right here in the United States that's worth something. He loves the idea of being productive and creating something of value for people.

That's the true character of our people. That's been the essence of the AFL–CIO. That's why even in these difficult times, I remain confident about our future, because of people like that, because of the workers that I meet all across this country, members of your unions who get up every morning and put in a hard day's work to build a company, build a future, support their families.

As Americans, they don't give up. They don't quit. I don't give up. I don't quit. The AFL–CIO does not give up. It does not quit. If we stand together, then I am absolutely confident that we are going to rebuild America, not just to where it was before this financial crisis, but stronger than it has ever been. That is a commitment that I am making to you. Thank you for the commitment that you've made to me. God bless you. Thank you, guys. [*Applause*] Thank you.

AFL–CIO President Richard L. Trumka. Mr. President, on behalf of our full executive council, first of all, let me thank you for sharing your special day with us, and let us wish you again a happy birthday.

Two, let us thank you for all that you've done for every working American out there. I know you're pressed for time——

The President. I'm a little disappointed there wasn't a cake, though. [*Laughter*] I'm going to have to talk to Secret Service about that.

Mr. Trumka. You've got to talk to those guys, because they nixed the cake.

The President. They're probably eating it right now. [*Laughter*]

Mr. Trumka. They are. They got it all over them. Do you see the guy back there——

The President. That's some good cake.

Mr. Trumka. He has a little bit on him——

The President. Had some frosting on his—I noticed that, all right. [*Laughter*]

Mr. Trumka. We know you only have time for one question. Mr. President, when I was a working coal miner, I understood from personal experience how my parents and my grandparents formed a union and changed coal mining from a life-threatening journey through poverty into reasonably safe and well-paid jobs. Now, so many Americans now work in bad jobs—jobs with no benefits, jobs with—that don't pay a living wage, jobs that aren't safe, jobs where they have no voice.

Now, we're going into a congressional election 3 months from today, and I think it's fair to say that workers' hopes for congressional action to protect workers' rights and to create jobs have been frustrated by a Republican minority that has filibustered every matter in front of them, every single thing that's been good for us.

I just want to ask you, what advice do you have for workers as the election approaches, particularly for workers who are trying to organize to have a voice on the job?

The President. Well, you guys don't need advice from me, but let me tell you what I see out there. We were hurt by this recession, badly hurt. This is going to take some time to recover. Unemployment is at unacceptably high levels.

But as I said before, we'd had challenges before the crisis hit. A lot of your membership had been hurting long before, partly because we just live in a more competitive world. There's nothing we can do about that; that's just the truth. But a lot of it also had to do with the fact that we put policies in place that were not good for working families. There's a reason why incomes, wages, were stagnant for average workers, even while the costs were going up. And part of it had to do with the fact that we had a philosophy that said that providing help to workers, allowing them to collectively bargain, allowing them to negotiate for better benefits, that that all was something of the past, instead of something we need for the future.

So on the one hand, I think everybody here understands we've got to be competitive in America. We've got to have competitive price structures. We've got to make the best products possible. Workers have to be invested in trying to help the companies they work for succeed. With respect to public employees, we've all got to work together to make sure that whatever we're doing, whether it's as firefighters or as teachers or postal workers, whatever it is, that we're providing the best possible service. I think everybody understands that there's no operation in the United States of America that shouldn't be efficient and effective in doing what it does.

But it is my profound belief that companies are stronger when their workers are getting paid well and have decent benefits and are treated with dignity and respect. It is my profound belief that our Government works best when it's not being run on behalf of special interests, but it's being run on behalf of the public interest, and that the dedication of public servants reflects that.

So FDR, I think, said—he was asked once what he thought about unions. He said, "If I was a worker in a factory and I wanted to improve my life, I would join a union." Well, I tell you what. I think that's true for workers generally. I think if I was a coal miner, I'd want a union representing me to make sure that I was safe and you did not have some of the tragedies that we've been seeing in the coal industry. If I was a teacher, I'd want a union to make sure that the teachers' perspective was represented as we think about shaping an education system for our future.

And that's why my administration has consistently implemented not just legislative strategies, but also where we have the power through Executive orders to make sure that those basic values are reflected.

I'm not telling anybody anything you don't know. Getting EFCA through a Senate is going to be tough. It's always been tough; it will continue to be tough. We'll keep on pushing. But our work doesn't stop there. I mean, there's a reason why we nominated people to the National Mediation Board that would ensure that folks in the rail industry and in the air industry were going to end up having a better deal.

We are going to make sure that the National Labor Relations Board is restored to have some balance so that if workers want to form a union, they can at least get a fair vote in a reasonable amount of time. And we don't want, by the way, Government dollars going in to pay for union busting. That's not something that we believe in. That's not right. That tilts the playing field in an unfair way.

So you're going to have an administration that's working alongside you. There are going to be times where we want to get something done and we can't get it done, at least not immediately, and we're going to just keep on at it. I think people have started to figure out I'm a persistent son of a gun. [*Laughter*] I just stay on things if I think they're the right thing to do. And we should be looking for opportunities, by the way, to make sure that the labor movement is, wherever possible, finding common ground with the business community, because I want America as a whole to be competitive.

One of the problems that we've had over the last decade is that so often the business community sees labor as the problem, and their basic attitude is, well, you know what, we'll just go to wherever we don't have any problems with labor and we can pay them the lowest wages and the fewest benefits, and then just ship the stuff back here, and our profits will be good. But over time, that hollows out America and hollows out our middle class. That makes us weaker, not stronger.

Now, on the other hand, when business and labor are working together, then we can compete against anybody and we can knock down trade barriers in other countries and we can start selling products around the world. And we make great products in this country. We've got the best workers in the world, the best universities in the world. We've got the most dynamic economy in the world. We have the freest market system in the world. And all those things

give us a huge competitive advantage if we're all working together.

So my bottom line is this: I'm going to continue to work with all of you on behalf of working families around the country, and I'm going to continue to reach out to businesses to try to make the argument that what's good for workers is going to be good for business. They're your customers as well as your workers. And if they've got a decent living standard, that's lifting the entire economy up. And they're going to be buying more products, and they're going to be buying more services. And all of us are going to be growing together. And the 21st century is going to end up being the American century, just like the 20th century was.

But we're not going to be able to do it when we're pitted against each other. And I'm actually confident that once we get through some of the political posturing and shenanigans that we've been seeing over the last several years, people are going to step back and say, you know what, the lesson we needed to learn out of hardship is: We're all in this thing together. We are all in this thing together.

That's what the union movement's always been about. We're stronger together than we are on our own. That is true within individual unions. That is true within industries; that is true for the country as a whole. And I hope that I will be your partner in trying to bring about that unity of purpose in the years to come.

All right. Thank you very much, everybody. God bless you. God bless America.

NOTE: The President spoke at 11:15 a.m. at the Walter E. Washington Convention Center. In his remarks, he referred to Elizabeth Shuler, secretary-treasurer, and Arlene Holt Baker, executive vice president, AFL–CIO.

Remarks on Presenting the Presidential Citizens Medals
August 4, 2010

Thank you. Please, have a seat.

Thank you very much, Senator Burris, and hello, everybody. Welcome to the White House, I want to start by recognizing the

very proud Members of Congress who are joining us to help celebrate a few of their outstanding constituents. So thank you all for coming.

We are here to recognize—and this is one of my favorite events that I do every year—we're here to recognize winners of the Citizens Medal. This is one of the highest honors a President can bestow. For 40 years, this medal has been given to men and women who have "performed exemplary deeds of service for their country or their fellow citizens." And their lives stand as shining examples of what it means to be an American. Today we've got an opportunity to tell their stories, to say thank you, and to offer them a small token of our appreciation.

Now, at first glance, the honorees behind me don't seem to have too much in common, although I did point out that the guys are outnumbered—[*laughter*]—which tells you something about who really gets stuff done in the neighborhoods. [*Laughter*] But they are mothers and fathers, nurses and bus drivers, veterans and immigrants. They come from different backgrounds, and they hail from every corner of our country. But what unites these citizens, what makes them special, is the determination they share, to right a wrong, to see a need and then meet it, to recognize when others are suffering and take it upon themselves to make a difference.

When they saw a veteran in need of proper care or a teenage mom who could use a helping hand, they didn't just shake their heads and keep on walking. They didn't write it off as another example of life not being fair. Instead, they saw it as a problem to solve, a challenge to meet, a call to action that they could not ignore.

So just to give a few examples here: When Jorge Munoz saw homeless men gathered on a street corner with nothing to eat, he could have rolled up his window and driven away. Instead, he came home from his job as a school bus driver and started cooking hot meals for anyone who was hungry. These days, the "Angel of Queens" feeds over 100 people every night, rain or shine. And Jorge says, "You have to see their smile. That's what I get paid."

Or, Susan Retik's husband was killed when his plane was flown into the World Trade Center on September 11th. And nobody would have blamed Susan if she had turned inward with grief or with anger. But that isn't who she is. So instead, she and another widow started Beyond the 11th, and this is a group that empowers Afghan widows affected by war and terrorism. And Susan says, "These women are not our enemy."

So for Jorge and Susan and the rest of today's honorees, the words "not my problem" don't exist. Instead, they ask themselves, "If I don't help this person, who will?" They recognize that no matter how difficult their lives may be, no matter how daunting their own challenges may seem, someone else will always have it harder than they do. There will always be a more important cause to fight for.

For these men and women, serving others isn't just the right thing to do, it's the obvious thing to do. They may not be rich or powerful in the traditional sense. But they believe that those of us with a roof over our heads, with loved ones to go home to, with food in our stomachs and strength in our limbs, have been blessed. And in return, it's our duty to use those gifts to reach out to those who aren't so lucky.

This humility and this selflessness has always been a part of the American story. From the patriots who have worn our Nation's uniform to everyday Americans who have marched and fought and raised their voices to help perfect our Union, it's no coincidence that our founding document begins with the words, "We the People." Ours is a nation founded on the power and freedom of individuals, but also on the belief that I am my brother's keeper and I am my sister's keeper, and that only if we look out for one another can we all move forward together.

As Lisa Nigro, another one of today's honorees, said, "Once you find a common bond in your humanity, you start to see the less fortunate as people—not 'them' or 'those' people, they are you and me." That was the idea behind the Edward M. Kennedy Serve America Act, the landmark piece of legislation that I signed into law last year. And together with the work of the Corporation of National and Community Service, as well as the Office of Social Innovation, it's giving more Americans the opportunity to serve others and help address our greatest challenges. And I want to thank Patrick Corvington and Melody Barnes for their leadership.

Because we know that real change does not come from Washington, it comes from the grassroots, from men and women in communities all across the country working together to make a difference.

In the end, that's what service is all about. It's not about the recognition or the awards—and it's obviously not about the money. [*Laughter*] To quote George Weiss, who's being honored here today: "We don't do it for the notoriety. We do it because we felt it has to be done." And that's why it is my hope that if this award serves a purpose, it will be to inspire more Americans to open their hearts, to strengthen their communities, and to follow the example of these amazing men and women who are here today.

So congratulations to all of the winners of the Citizens Medal. I've got some military aides here, and one of them is going to read the citations and I am going to get the medals to present to each of our honorees. With that, let's get started.

[*At this point, Maj. Barrett M. Bernard, USA, Army Aide to the President, read the citations, and the President presented the medals.*]

Well, you see why this is one of my favorite ceremonies? [*Laughter*] I want to thank all of you for joining us to honor these remarkable people. None of them asked for this award. They didn't apply for it. Instead they were nominated by the men and women all across the country whose lives they have touched. And even though their names may not be well-known—at least not until today—[*laughter*]—they are heroes to those who need it the most.

And together, they remind us that we all have a purpose on this Earth that goes beyond our own lives and our own individual needs. And they teach us that no matter what challenges we face, we each have the power to make the world a better place. So congratulations to all of you. We are better as a country as a consequence of your ordinary—extraordinary service. And you exemplify what it means to be a citizen of the United States of America. We're grateful.

Thank you all for coming.

NOTE: The President spoke at 2:26 p.m. in the East Room at the White House. In his remarks, he referred to Lisa Nigro, founder, Inspiration Corp.; Patrick A. Corvington, Chief Executive Officer, Corporation for National and Community Service; and George J. Weiss, Jr., founder, Fort Snelling National Cemetary Memorial Rifle Squad.

Statement on the Senate Cloture Vote on Federal Medical Assistance Percentage and Teacher Jobs Funding Legislation
August 4, 2010

Today Congress took an important step towards ensuring that teachers across the country can stay in the classroom and cash-strapped States can get the relief they need.

We know that economic prosperity and educational success go hand in hand. That's why I'm urging the Senate to pass this legislation that will prevent local budget cuts and save thousands of teacher jobs across the country.

I commend Senator Reid for his hard work and look forward to a final vote later this week.

Remarks at the Ford Motor Company Chicago Assembly Plant in Chicago, Illinois
August 5, 2010

The President. Hello, Chicago! Hello, hello, hello! What's going on? Thank you, everybody. And listen, it is good to see everybody. I appreciate everybody way back there. Hello, hello!

We—it is wonderful to be here. There are a couple of special guests I want to mention here before we get started. First of all, we got the Governor of the great State of Illinois, Pat Quinn. Give it up for Pat. Got one of the finest mayors in the country, Mayor Richard Daley is in the house. Our treasurer and soon-to-be United States Senator, Alexi Giannoulias, is here. A number of outstanding Members of Congress who've been very supportive of the auto industry: Congressman Jesse Jackson, Jr.; Congressman Bobby Rush; Congressman Danny Davis; Congresswoman Jan Schakowsky; Congressman Mike Quigley.

We've got Fred Hochberg of the—who's the chairman and President of the Export-Import Bank, which is going to help Ford sell all these outstanding cars overseas, not just here in the United States. And your own president, Mark Fields, is in the house. Give it up.

So it is good to be back in Chicago. It's good to see some friendly faces, be back in the old neighborhoods.

Audience members. Happy birthday!

The President. Thank you. I've gotten a little more gray hair since I was last down here. [*Laughter*] But it is wonderful to be back home.

Now, don't get me wrong, the White House is nice. And I've got a really short commute from my office to the house. I don't have to drive too far. And there's no greater honor than being your President. But let me tell you something: There's nothing like coming home, especially when your home is Chicago.

And I just had a chance to tour this extraordinary plant to see the great work that you're doing here. I notice that Mark and everybody, they put all the White Sox fans in front for me to meet. I didn't see a lot of Cubs guys on the line or Cardinals fans.

But this plant has a remarkable history. Henry Ford built it. Henry Ford built this plant in 1924 to manufacture the Model T. When the Great Depression struck and 25 Ford plants closed down, this one stayed open. When World War II was raging, this plant was churning out armored vehicles that helped make victory possible. In the 1990s, workers at this plant built the best-selling car in America 5 years in a row.

So this plant is part of American history. For nearly nine decades, this plant has been the backbone of this community. There are workers here whose fathers worked on this line—I just met one while I was on my way over here—whose fathers' fathers worked on this line. This plant, like the entire industry, has been a source of deep pride for generations of American workers whose imaginations and hard work led to some of the finest cars that the world has ever known and whose sweat helped build up the middle class that lifted up the dreams of millions of people all across America.

This plant has stood through the good times, when American auto industry ruled the world, and in the not-so-good times, when the future of the auto industry was very much in doubt.

And let's face it: We've seen some of those not-so-good times in recent years. The year before I took office, this industry lost hundreds of thousands of jobs. Sales plunged 40 percent—40 percent. When the financial crisis hit and this great recession hit, that collided with an industry that for a long time had put off some hard choices, had put off adapting to changing times. And we had to face a hard, unimaginable reality, which was two of the Big Three automakers, GM and Chrysler, were on the brink of liquidation. If that had happened, more than 1 million jobs could have been lost, and that would have been a devastating blow to the entire economy.

Now, Ford was in better financial shape and was able to weather the storm without Federal assistance. That's a testament to the hard work you all do and the choices this company made. But I don't have to tell you—and your CEO will—has said this publicly—if your competitors had gone down, they would have taken down a whole bunch of the suppliers you depend on. The brand of American autos would have diminished. That would have had severe consequences for Ford. And that's the challenge we faced when I took office: an industry that was on the brink.

Now, there were a lot of folks who were ready to write off the American auto industry, who thought we should just have walked away from you. Some still think that today. But you know what, that's not how you build a better future. That's not how you build a better America. We don't give up. The United States does not quit. We always compete. That's what we do. And that's what we're doing with the U.S. auto industry.

So I refused to walk away from this industry and American jobs. I put my faith in the American worker. I believe the American worker is the best worker in the world. And if we were willing to work hard together and rebuild and sacrifice in the short term, it would be a new beginning for a great American industry. If we could just get a sense of common purpose, we could once again see the best cars in the world designed, engineered, forged right here in Chicago, right here in the Midwest, right here in the United States of America.

So I tell you what. Last Friday, I stood with workers at a GM plant. I stood with workers at a Chrysler plant. Today I'm standing with workers at a Ford plant. I put my money on the American worker. I'd place my bets on the American worker any day of the week. And because of your efforts and the sacrifice that have been made across this industry over the past year, this industry is growing stronger. It's creating new jobs. It's manufacturing the fuel-efficient cars and trucks that will carry America towards an energy-independent future. Each and every one of you is proving the naysayers wrong.

All three automakers—all three U.S. automakers—are now operating at a profit. That's the first time it's happened in 6 years. America's automakers have added 55,000 jobs since last June. That's the best job growth in more than 10 years in this industry. Sales have rebounded. Automakers are keeping plants open through the usual summer shutdown to keep up with demand. Across the supply chain, plants that would not exist without the sacrifices made across industry are running at max or near-full capacity.

And this plant, right here, is shifting into higher gear. What I said last year was if American automakers were willing to make the tough choices necessary to make them more competitive in the future, America would stand by them. And one thing we did was put in place a new national fuel efficiency standard for all new cars and trucks sold in America. This was good for consumers, it was good for the environment, and it finally gave our automakers the certainty they needed to plan for the future, a future where American workers build 21st-century cars that the world wants to buy.

So Ford dedicated itself to increasing fuel efficiency of more than a dozen of its models. And the Department of Energy awarded Ford a 2-year loan commitment to help make that happen. And Ford used that loan to retool this factory to build the next-generation Explorer. That's a model that will be up to 30 percent more fuel efficient.

Now, I should add, by the way, my most recent car was a Ford. I had one of those Ford Escapes, and that was a spiffy car. [*Laughter*] Now, I have to admit that I bought it about 2 months before I got Secret Service—[*laughter*]—and they wouldn't let me drive anymore. [*Laughter*] So it only had like 2,000 miles after 5 years, but I really enjoyed those 2,000 miles. [*Laughter*]

But I just got in that Explorer and that's an outstanding car. And over the next 2 months, this plant will bring on a second shift of 1,200 workers to build that Explorer, nearly doubling your workforce. That's not just good for this plant, that's good for the stamping plant in Chicago Heights; it's good for the suppliers, who are investing in new facilities and adding shifts and hiring more than 600 workers in Illinois and Indiana and Michigan; it's good for the entire community; it's good for the city; it's good for the State.

And Ford's also committed to selling more of the cars you build around the world, including the Explorer that you manufacture right here. We're going to sell it in up to 90 countries.

So today, to support those efforts, my administration is announcing a new $250 million Export-Import Bank loan guarantee for Ford. And what this does is this helps Ford export—this will help Ford export more than 200,000 cars and trucks overseas, and that means more production and more manufacturing jobs right here in the United States of America.

And it's going to help us reach the goal that I set in my State of the Union Address, which is, we are going to double America's exports of goods and services over the next 5 years. We're tired of just buying from everybody else; we want to start selling to other people, because we know we can compete.

That's how we're going to grow our economy. That's how we're going to support millions of good jobs for American workers to do what they've always done: build great products and sell them around the world. Our workers can compete with anybody, and America is going to compete aggressively for every job out there and every industry out there and every market out there.

So, Chicago, here's the bottom line: We've still got a long way to go. We've gone through a very, very difficult time. The auto industry has gone through a difficult time. And it's not back to where it needs to be. Our economy is not yet where it needs to be. It's going to take more time to heal from all the damage that was done. But we're beginning to see our efforts pay off. We are headed in the right direction. We are moving forward. The industry isn't just on the way back; it's on the way to being number one again. And I am convinced we're going to rebuild not only the auto industry but the economy better and stronger than before. And at its heart is going to be three powerful words: Made in America. Made in America.

And to all those naysayers in Washington, what we call the "just say no" crowd—[*laughter*]—who said that investing in you would guarantee failure, who said we should just walk away from this industry, who said that standing by America's automakers was, quote, "the worst investment you could make," who tried to block us at every turn, I wish they were standing here today and saw what I see. I wish they could see

the pride you take in building these great cars, American-made cars.

And my message to them is, don't bet against the American worker, don't lose faith in the American people, don't lose faith in American industry. We are coming back.

Just a few weeks before I visited that Chrysler plant—this is a true story—I went to a Chrysler plant. A few weeks before, 14 employees had won the lottery. And when they won, everybody thought they were just going to cash in and kick back and retire. Nobody would have blamed them for that. This is tough work.

But here's the thing: Most of them aren't retiring. And the worker who bought the winning ticket, what he did was he went out and bought for his wife one of the new cars that was being made in that plant, and then he went out and he bought American flags for his hometown, because he's proud of his country. And he keeps on showing up to work every single day, because he's proud of his job.

And that's the character of America: proud of your job, proud of your community, proud of your country, proud of the company you work for. That's what Ford is about. That's what you are about. That's what Chicago's about. That's what Illinois's about. That's what the United States of America's about. We are coming back.

Thank you very much, everybody. God bless you, and God bless America.

NOTE: The President spoke at 10:25 a.m. In his remarks, he referred to Mark Fields, executive vice president and president of the Americas division, and Alan Mulally, president and chief executive officer, Ford Motor Company; and William Shanteau, a Chrysler Jefferson North Assembly Plant worker who purchased the winning June Powerball jackpot ticket in Curtice, OH, and his wife Lisa. The Office of the Press Secretary also released a Spanish language transcript of these remarks.

Remarks at a Fundraiser for Senatorial Candidate Alexi Giannoulias in Chicago
August 5, 2010

The President. Hello, everybody! Hello, Chicago! Thank you very much. Thank you. Everybody, have a seat. Have a seat, everybody.

It is good to be back home. It is good to be back home, and I am so proud to be standing here with the next Senator from the great State of Illinois, Alexi Giannoulias.

Now, we've got some other important personages here, so I want to make sure to make mention, because they have been great friends for many years to me and to so many of you. Now, first of all, our outstanding Governor, Pat Quinn, is here. Where's Pat? There he is. One of America's greatest mayors, Richard M. Daley, is in the house. Secretary of State Jesse White is here; a great friend of mine, Comptroller Dan Hynes. Senate President John Cullerton is here. Where's John? Over there. He's also a funny guy. [*Laughter*] Speaker Mike Madigan is here. Where's the speaker? Congressman Danny Davis from the West Side; Congresswoman Jan Schakowsky from the North Side; and Congresswoman Debbie Halvorson from the South Side.

It is wonderful to be here, and it is wonderful to be with Alexi. Alexi is my friend. I know his character. I know how much he loves this country. I know how committed he is to public service for all the right reasons.

I appreciate his strong sense of advocacy for ordinary Americans. He's not doing this to help the lobbyists; he's not doing it to help special interests. Alexi is not one of these politicians who puts his finger to the wind and who changes who he is or where he stands to suit the political moment. You can trust him. You can count on him.

On his very first day in office, Alexi enacted the most sweeping ethics reforms of any Illinois State treasurer and ensured that contractors and banks couldn't "pay to play" for State business.

And he's not funding this campaign with Federal PAC or lobbyist money—not a dime— because he wants to make a strong statement about who he will be fighting for in the United States Senate. And as State treasurer, Alexi has proven himself as someone who isn't afraid to stand up to special interests. He took on credit card companies and banned them from aggressively marketing on college campuses so that our kids don't graduate with credit card debt on top of tuition debt. He's reformed our State's college savings program so that it's now ranked one of the best in the country.

And I'm sure a lot of you have heard of what he did for Hartmarx. This is a clothing company that's employed people in this State for more than a century. And by the way, I'm a customer. [*Laughter*] And when they fell on hard times and a big bank threatened to pull their credit and destroy more than 600 jobs, Alexi stepped in, and he told the bank that if they did that, they would no longer be managing the money of Illinois taxpayers. And because of what he did, Alexi helped save that company and save those jobs. That's the kind of person you want in the United States Senate, somebody who's not going to forget where they came from, why they're in this, and who they're fighting for.

So we need fighters like Alexi in Washington because I don't know if you've noticed, but we've got a lot of work to do. [*Laughter*] The last few years have been incredibly challenging for the United States. Eighteen months ago, when I took office after nearly a decade of economic policies that gave us sluggish job growth, falling incomes, a record deficit—all culminating in the worst recession of our lifetimes, the worst recession since the Great Depression— that month that I was sworn in, in January of 2009, we lost 750,000 jobs, in that month alone. In total, we lost 8 million jobs during that recession.

Now, we didn't get to that point by accident. We got to that point after nearly 10 years of an economic agenda in Washington that was pretty straightforward. It basically said we're going to cut taxes for the wealthiest Americans, folks who don't need it and weren't even asking for it; we're going to cut rules for special interests; and then we're going to cut working folks loose to fend for themselves.

So if you were a kid in Chicago whose family had never gone to college and you aspire to go to college but you didn't have the money, tough luck, you're on your own. If you were a worker who was just barely hanging on, didn't have health insurance, even if you were working two jobs, those are the breaks, tough luck, you're on your own.

That was the philosophy of the last administration and their friends in Congress. They called it the "ownership society," but it really meant you were on your own. And if you were a Wall Street banker or an insurance company or an oil company like BP, you got to write your own rules. And we know how this turned out.

So when I took office, we decided not only were we going to have to heal the economy short term, we had to revamp how we thought about the American economy and put families and middle class workers at the center of it. We put in place a new economic plan, a plan that rewards hard work instead of greed, a plan that rewards responsibility instead of recklessness, a plan that's focused on making our middle class more secure and our country more competitive in the long run so that the jobs and industries of the future aren't just found in China or India or Brazil, but right here in the United States of America.

Instead of spending money on—that we don't have on tax breaks for those who don't need them, we're making smart investments in education and innovation and clean energy that will benefit all people and our entire economy. Instead of giving special interests free rein to do what they please, we're demanding new accountability from Wall Street to Washington so that big corporations play by the same rules that workers and small businesses do. It's only fair.

Now, because the policies of the last decade landed us in such a deep hole, it takes time to dig ourselves out. And we're not there yet. We've got a lot more work to do. There are a lot of people hurting all across this region and all across the country. But after 18 months, I can say unequivocally with confidence that our Nation is finally headed in the right direction. It is

headed in the right direction. Instead of shrinking, our economy is growing again. Instead of losing jobs, we're adding jobs. America is moving forward. And the last thing we can afford right now is to go back to the very same special interest-laden policies that created this mess in the first place.

And that's the choice in this election, that's the decision you'll have to make when you walk into the voting booth in November. And everybody here in Illinois and all across the country are going to have to make a choice: Do we go back to the policies of the past, or do we keep this country moving forward?

I believe we have to keep on moving forward. Alexi believes we've got to keep on moving forward. And I think the American people want to keep moving forward.

Now, if you doubt that that's the choice, if you're thinking, well, that's just some political rhetoric, I want you to think about what's transpired within the Republican Party. It would be one thing if after 2006 and 2008 and all the problems that have been taking place, that they went off into the wilderness and they meditated, and they thought, boy, we really screwed up, and we've got to think of some new ways of approaching things. If they were full of reflection and soul-searching, and then they finally came back and said, we've got some new ideas. We're going to do things differently. We may not agree with the President, but we have a vision for the future that might work. Then you could say, okay, maybe we should give them a shot.

But that's not what's happened. They haven't learned from all the mistakes that they made. They promise to do the exact same things that got us into this mess. They haven't come out with a single, solitary idea that is different from the policies that held sway for 8 years before Democrats took over. Not a single policy difference that's discernable from George W. Bush, not one.

So what they're really betting on is amnesia. [*Laughter*] They are betting that you just forgot about the 8 years that they were in charge of Washington. They're betting that you didn't notice that the recession started under their watch and the deficits started under their watch, and that instead of trying to work with us, they have been trying to oppose us every step of the way in solving these problems.

I mean, remember, these are the folks who spent almost a decade driving the economy into a ditch. And now they're asking for the keys back. So car went into the ditch, we had to put on our boots, we got in the mud, we're pushing, we're shoving, we're tired, sweaty. They're standing, watching. [*Laughter*] "You're not doing that fast enough." [*Laughter*] "Why don't you push a little harder? Why don't you—I think if you put your shoulder here, you'll get a better grip." [*Laughter*]

So after all our huffing and puffing, we finally get the car out of the ditch, finally back on blacktop, on level ground. And what do they say? "Give us the keys back." [*Laughter*] Well, you can't have the keys back; you don't know how to drive. [*Laughter*] You got us into the ditch in the first place. We can't give you these keys.

I also want to make a simple point—not to belabor this analogy—[*laughter*]—but when you want to go forward, what do you put the car in?

Audience members. "D"!

The President. "D." [*Laughter*] When you want to go backwards, what do you do? You put it in "R." We want to go forward. We don't want to go backwards. They can't have the keys because they want to take us back in the ditch. Don't want to do it. You thought that was just an accident? [*Laughter*] It's not. There was a sign there. [*Laughter*]

Look, the choice in this election is between policies that encourage job creation in America and policies that encourage job creation somewhere else. We've said repeatedly, instead of giving tax breaks to companies that ship jobs overseas, we want to give tax cuts to small-business owners who are creating jobs right here in the United States of America. These other folks talk about tax cuts; we've already cut taxes eight times for small businesses since I've been President. And we want to do more, because America's small-business owners are the backbone of America's economy.

We're also jump-starting a homegrown clean energy industry, because I don't want to see new solar panels and wind turbines and electric cars built in China. I want to see them built right here in Chicago, right here in the Midwest, right here in the United States. The investments we've made so far will lead to more than 800,000 clean energy jobs by 2012—800,000. And because our Nation has always been built to compete, from the transcontinental railroad to the Interstate Highway System, we're investing in a 21st-century infrastructure, not just new roads and bridges, but faster Internet access and high-speed railroads, projects that will lead to hundreds of thousands of new private sector jobs, but will also create the platform for us to compete in the future.

That's our plan to keep jobs in America not just short term, but over the long term. And yet most of the folks in the other party, they voted no on just about every one of these policies: no on tax cuts for small businesses, no on clean energy jobs, no on railroad and highway projects. Although, John, it doesn't stop them from showing up at ribbon cuttings, sending out press releases. They vote no for them, but they show up, try to get credit. They're pretty good at finding the cameras; they're waving and grinning. [*Laughter*]

The point is, their votes, their obstruction, that takes us backwards. We want businesses to create jobs in America. We want clean energy here in the United States. We want young people to be able to go to college in record numbers. We want it—the principle that everybody in America should be able to get affordable health care, we want that enshrined in this country. And that's the choice in this election. It's between policies that strengthen the hand of special interests and policies that strengthen America's middle class.

A few weeks ago, the Republican leader of the House was asked what was his jobs plan for the party. Let's say they took control of Congress next year. He said his number-one priority is repealing the law we passed to prevent health insurance companies from denying you coverage or dropping your coverage just because you got sick. Repealing the health care law, that's his jobs plan. Now, I'm not sure exactly how that creates jobs. It might create jobs for insurance executives or the folks who deny you claims, but it's not creating jobs for the American people.

But if they think that's a—look, if you think that's a good idea, if you think that's a good jobs plan, you should vote for the other party. We've got a different view. The health insurance reform we passed isn't just preventing insurers from denying you coverage. It's cutting taxes for small-business owners who cover their employees. It's allowing young adults to stay on their parents' coverage until they're 26. It's lowering the price of prescription drugs for our seniors. It will ultimately lower the cost of health care for every American. We just got a report today from the trust fund that manages Medicare saying we've extended the life of Medicare by 12 years because of the health insurance reform. It is going to be more secure for our seniors and it's going to be there for future generations because of the changes we made. They want to repeal that reform, take us back to the days when insurance companies could deny you care? We're not going to let that happen. We're moving forward.

The other party wants to repeal Wall Street reform. Most of them voted against it, including Alexi's opponent. Now they want to repeal it. Now, think about it: worst financial crisis since the Great Depression; almost put the entire economy over a cliff; 8 million people unemployed as a consequence of it. And their answer is, go back to the status quo that got us into this. This is reform that's finally going to stop credit card companies from charging you hidden fees and unfair rate hikes, that stops the abusive practices of mortgage lenders, that ends taxpayer bailouts of Wall Street banks, says we're going to be able to resolve problems in any single bank, quarantine them, isolate them without dragging the whole system with it. This is reform that protects consumers, responsible business owners, and our entire economy. We need this reform. We can't go back to the same rules, the same regulations that allowed this crisis to happen. And yet Alexi's opponent wants to get rid of that? That's the choice in this election.

On almost every issue that matters to middle class families, that's the choice. The other party voted to keep taxpayer subsidies for big banks that offer loans to college. I don't know if everybody understands, the Federal Government guaranteed these loans for young people so they can go to college. Banks were taking out tens of billions of dollars in profits, despite the fact that the loans were guaranteed. We said, let's cut out the middleman. We'll have an extra $40 billion that we can give to millions more college students so they can afford to go to college. Got no support on the other side.

For years, they did nothing about the fact that too many women aren't paid as much as men for doing the same work. I signed a law that helps end discrimination so that in the United States of America, an equal day of work means an equal day of pay. They didn't support it.

They want to extend the Bush tax cuts for millionaires and billionaires that have exploded our deficit. They talk a good game about deficit reduction, and then every time you ask them, "What's your plan?" they don't have one. I kept my campaign promise and gave a tax cut to the middle class, 95 percent of working Americans. They voted against it.

They voted against holding oil companies like BP accountable for every dime of the spills they cause. We forced BP to set aside $20 billion for the men and women of the Gulf Coast whose livelihoods depend on clean water and clean beaches. And then what happens? After we do that, the guy who, if they took over in the House of Representatives, would be the chairman of the Energy Committee apologizes to BP; says, I'm so sorry that the President is making you pay these fishermen and these hotel owners and others whose livelihoods have been wrecked by your carelessness. Apologized to them, called what we did a "shakedown." I think he might have added "Chicago shakedown" in there. [*Laughter*]

That's the choice in this election: a choice between folks who apologize to BP and folks who are looking out for small-business owners and fishermen; policies that are helping our economy grow again and policies that are going to make America more competitive and our middle class more secure, or more of the same.

I know this Nation has been through an incredibly difficult time. Not all the steps we took to dig us out of this recession have been popular. The pundits in Washington—I have befuddled them over the last 20 months. They keep on saying: "Well, why is he doing that? That doesn't poll well." And I keep on explaining to them, I have my own pollsters. I know how it polls. I know these things—some things we did were not popular, but they were right. I wasn't elected just to do what was popular. I was elected to do what was right.

My job is not to focus on the next election; it's to focus on the next generation. That's why I ran for office. That's what I try to do every day. That's why Alexi is running for the United States Senate. That's what he will do every day when he's in the United States Senate. We need your help. And if you're willing to invest in our future, we are going to keep on moving forward for years and decades to come.

Thank you, Chicago. God bless you. God bless the United States of America.

NOTE: The President spoke at 12:51 p.m. at the Palmer House Hilton hotel. In his remarks, he referred to Secretary of State Jesse White, State Comptroller Daniel W. Hynes, State Senate President John J. Cullerton, and State House of Representatives Speaker Michael J. Madigan of Illinois; House Republican Leader John A. Boehner; Sen. Mark S. Kirk; and Rep. Joseph L. Barton.

Remarks on Senate Confirmation of Elena Kagan as a Supreme Court Associate Justice in Chicago
August 5, 2010

Good afternoon. I am very pleased that the Senate has just voted to confirm Elena Kagan as our Nation's 112th Supreme Court Justice. And I want to thank the Senate Judiciary Committee, particularly its chairman, Senator Leahy, for giving her a full, fair, and timely hearing.

Over the past 2 months, the committee has scrutinized Elena's record as a scholar, as a law school dean, as a Presidential adviser, and as Solicitor General. And after 17 hours of testimony, during which she answered more than 540 questions, I'd say they got a pretty good look at Elena Kagan. They've gotten a sense of her formidable intelligence, her rich understanding of our Constitution, her commitment to the rule of law, and her excellent—and occasionally irreverent—sense of humor. And they have come to understand why, throughout her career, she has earned the respect and admiration of folks from across the political spectrum, an achievement reflected in today's bipartisan vote.

But today's vote wasn't just an affirmation of Elena's intellect and accomplishments. It was also an affirmation of her character and her temperament, her openmindedness and even-handedness, her determination to hear all sides of every story and consider all possible arguments. Because Elena understands that the law isn't just an abstraction or an intellectual exercise. She knows that the Supreme Court's decisions shape not just the character of our democracy, but the circumstances of our daily lives—or as she once put it, that "behind the law there are stories—stories of people's lives as shaped by the law, stories of people's lives as might be changed by law."

So I am confident that Elena Kagan will make an outstanding Supreme Court Justice. And I'm proud also of the history we're making with her appointment. For nearly two centuries, there wasn't a single woman on our Nation's highest court. When Elena takes her seat on that bench, for the first time in our history, there will be three women.

It is, as Ruth Bader Ginsburg recently stated, "one of the most exhilarating developments," a sign of progress that I relish not just as a father who wants limitless possibilities for my two daughters, but as an American proud that our Supreme Court will be more inclusive, more representative, and more reflective of us as a people than ever before.

Thanks very much, everybody.

NOTE: The President spoke at 3:56 p.m. at the Renaissance Chicago Downtown Hotel. The Office of the Press Secretary also released a Spanish language transcript of these remarks.

Remarks at a Democratic National Committee Fundraiser in Chicago
August 5, 2010

The President. Hello, hello, hello! Thank you. Thank you so much, everybody. Hello, hello! It is good to be back in Chicago. Somebody has got the "Obama 44" license plate.

Audience member. Happy birthday!

The President. Thank you, everybody. Thank you so much. What a wonderful birthday gift, to be back home with so many good friends.

There are a number of people I just want to make mention of. You probably have already heard from them, but I want you to know how much I appreciate what they are doing each and every day—outstanding leadership, leadership that's going to move this country forward. First of all, our wonderful Governor and the next Lieutenant Governor of Illinois, Pat Quinn and Sheila Simon. Give them both big rounds of applause.

Dear friend who fights each and every day on behalf of working families across her district, this State, and the country, Jan Schakowsky is in the house. Senate President John Cullerton is here, one of the smartest guys in the State legislature and one of the funniest as well—[*laughter*]—and did great work with me when I was in the State senate.

We've got the next Congressman from Illinois's 10th Congressional District, Dan Seals in the house. There's Dan. I want to thank the preprogram speakers, Sheena Patton from Organizing for America and Morgan McClelland, who is a first-time voter. I like that.

And I've got a few things to say about Alexi. [*Laughter*] Before I do that, though, one other person who actually wasn't on my sheet, but I see her right in front, so I have to say something—this was—this is, I guess, my—still my State representative almost—I'm right at the border—but also was a great friend for a very long time and is a wonderful leader in the

house of representatives, Barbara Flynn Currie. So I just wanted to acknowledge Barbara.

Now, I see so many good friends who've been with me since I was skinnier—[*laughter*]—less gray—[*laughter*]—and when nobody could pronounce my name. [*Laughter*] And I know that if it weren't for you, I might not be standing here tonight as President.

I am reminded of the story Abraham Lincoln told about a guy who comes to the White House, insists on seeing the President. He says, "I worked tirelessly on the President's behalf," and he was seeking a patronage job, and he insisted on an audience. And finally, Lincoln says, "Okay." The guy comes in, he says, "I am responsible—if it weren't for me, you would not be President." And Lincoln says, "I forgive you." [*Laughter*] It's a true story.

It is an extraordinary honor and privilege to be able to serve. And I'm able to serve because of you. I'm also proud to be here tonight with the next Senator from the State of Illinois, and that's Alexi Giannoulias.

Now, I want to say to everybody here, Alexi is my friend. I know his character. I know how much he loves this country. I know how committed he is to public service. I know he is in this race for the right reasons. I know he has been a great advocate on behalf of the people of Illinois.

He's not in this to help lobbyists or special interests. He's not one of those politicians who's going to put out his finger to the wind to see which way it's blowing. He is somebody who is committed to you. You can trust him. He is going to be an outstanding Senator, and I need you to fight for him so he can fight for you in Washington, because we've got a lot of work to do.

Now, look, the last few years have been incredibly challenging. Over almost 20 months ago, I stood in the Capitol and was sworn in as the President. And that month—some of you might have been there—it was cold, remember? [*Laughter*] It was cold, but a hopeful day.

But even as everybody was feeling that sense of hope and optimism, we had lost almost 800,000 jobs in that month alone. The economy was contracting at about 6 percent. Ultimately, we discovered that we lost 8 million jobs in this recession, the worst by far since the Great Depression. And had we not taken some steps immediately to address the crisis, we might have tipped into a second Great Depression.

Now, this would have caused enough hardship, but it was also compounded by the fact that we had had 10 years of sluggish growth, 10 years of inadequate job production, 10 years of incomes and wages that were flatlining, even as the costs for middle class families were going up on everything from health care to tuition. So the middle class, working families across America were already feeling under enormous pressure. A lot of them were just barely hanging on, and then suddenly, this storm sweeps in.

In the last 6 months of 2008 alone, 3 million Americans lost their jobs. And so these aren't just statistics. Behind each of these numbers is a story of heartache and frustration: a factory worker who might have just been a few years short of retiring, suddenly, he's lost his job, maybe he's lost his pension; a single mom who's sent out job applications to everywhere she can think of, she's still waiting for the phone to ring day after day after day; a college graduate who thought her degree would land her a good job with a decent paycheck, suddenly, all she's got is a mountain of debt.

I hear these stories every day. I read them in letters each night. I hear them when I'm on the road traveling. These struggles, but also the hope of these Americans, are why I ran for office in the first place. That's why we're going to work as hard as we can as long as it takes to turn this economy around and move this country forward. That's why I'm here. That is our goal.

But we're not going to be able to get to where we need to go unless we understand how, in fact, we got here. We spent nearly 10 years on an economic agenda that was pretty straightforward: You cut taxes for the wealthiest among us, folks who didn't need tax cuts and weren't even asking for them, you cut rules for special interests, and you cut working folks loose so they've got to fend for themselves.

That was the philosophy of the last administration and that was the philosophy of their friends in Congress. And basically, what they said is if you can't find a job, tough luck, you're on your own. If you don't have health insurance, too bad, tough luck, you're on your own. If you're a young person who's trying to get to college, tough luck, you're on your own. Now, if you're a Wall Street bank or an insurance company or an oil company like BP, then you can write your own rules. And we know how this turned out.

So when we came into office, we said, we are going to have a whole new approach. We want an economic plan that rewards hard work instead of greed, that rewards responsibility instead of recklessness, a plan that's more focused on securing the middle class and making our country more competitive for the global economy.

And we know there are other countries fighting for the jobs of the future, countries like China and India. And if we don't have the best education system in the country, if we don't have the most college graduates in the country, if we don't have the most productive research and development in the world, then we're not going to make it.

And I tell you this: The United States of America does not play for second place. We are going to rebuild this economy better and stronger than it was before. And at the heart of our economic plan is three powerful words: Made in America. We want to start making things here in the United States and selling things to other countries and creating good jobs and opportunity right here.

So instead of spending money for tax breaks that we can't afford, we're making smart investments in education and R&D and innovation and clean energy. So we're building wind turbines and solar panels and biodiesel plants that point us towards a clean energy future.

Instead of giving special interests free rein to do what they please, we're demanding new accountability from Wall Street to Washington so that everybody—big corporations have to play by the same rules as small businesses and as workers do. That's only fair.

Now, if you're unemployed or you can't pay the bills, I know the only plan you want to hear about is getting a job right now. And I wish I could stand here and tell you that there's a way to bring back all the jobs that were lost overnight, that the economy right away is going to get back to full strength.

And between now and November, you're going to hear a lot of promises from a lot of politicians. And they're going to be saying to you, you know what, if we just do this, or we just do that, all your problems will be solved. I can't do that because not only did I run for President promising that I wouldn't just tell you what you want to hear but tell you what you need to know, but now that I am President, and the sober realities of this job are ones that I've experienced over the last 2 years, I will tell you, I can't stand here and just tell you what you want to hear. We're going to have to work our way out of this hole that's been dug. It's going to take time.

But here's what I also know: Even though it's going to take years to repair all the damage caused by this recession, I am absolutely convinced that this Nation is finally headed in the right direction. Our economy is growing again. We are adding jobs again. America is moving forward again, and the last thing we can afford to do is go back to the policies that got us into this mess in the first place.

That's the choice in this election. You've got a pretty simple choice: Either you can support those policies that got us into this mess or you can support those policies that are getting us out of the mess.

Think about it. Think about it. This is not a situation in which the Republicans, after everything that they did to take record surpluses into record deficits, after all the failed policies that resulted ultimately in the worst recession since the 1930s, it's not as if they went back and they said, you know what, let's reflect on what we did wrong. [*Laughter*] You know, obviously, there

were some problems there; let's see if we've got a different set of theories about how we should approach the economy and how we should look after the middle class.

I mean, that would be one thing, if they had kind of gone off in the wilderness, they meditated—[*laughter*]—they came back, they said, we've learned from our mistakes; we've got a whole new set of approaches, a whole new set of policies. But they're not saying that.

They have not come up with a single, solitary idea that is any different from the policies of George W. Bush, the policies that they had in place for 8 years before we had a crisis. What they are betting on is amnesia. [*Laughter*] They are betting that you don't remember that they were in charge all this time.

I think Pat may have mentioned to you, they're trying to get you to forget that they drove the car into the ditch. [*Laughter*] And after we've pushed it out, now they're saying, "Give us the keys back." [*Laughter*] But we don't—we haven't forgotten, because we've got mud on our shoes, our back is sore from pushing that car out of the ditch. And I mean, if they want to get in the backseat, that's okay. [*Laughter*] But we're not going to put them behind the wheel. [*Laughter*]

I pointed out at lunch today—also just to carry this metaphor a little further—[*laughter*]—when you get in your car and you want to go forward, you put it in what?

Audience members. "D"!

The President. "D." [*Laughter*] When you want to go backwards, what do you do? You put it in "R."

So that's the choice. That's the choice we're facing. This is the choice we're facing. This is the choice we're facing. We want to take away tax breaks for companies that are shipping jobs overseas and give those tax breaks to companies that are investing here in the United States of America. They've got a different vision.

We've already cut taxes for small businesses eight times. Right now there's a debate in the Senate as we speak. We want to eliminate capital gains for small businesses and help them with getting more credit, and the Republicans are saying, "Just say no."

We believe in jump-starting a homegrown clean energy industry, because I don't want us to be second to China or Germany or anybody else when it comes to the clean energy technologies of the future putting Americans back to work. We have already made investments that will lead to 800,000 clean energy jobs by 2012. But you know what, the other side, they'll have none of it.

We want to invest in the 21st-century infrastructure of high-speed rail and broadband and a smart grid that can make our electric system more efficient. They don't want to see those investments made.

We've got plans to keep jobs in America not just for the short term, but over the long run. But on every single issue, just about, the other side has just said no: no to small-business tax cuts, no to clean energy jobs, no to railroad and highway projects. That doesn't mean they don't show up at the ribbon cuttings trying to take credit—[*laughter*]—even though they vote no. They'll show up, cheesing and grinning in front of the camera. They'll be waving. [*Laughter*]

But it's not just on these issues. It's not just on jobs issues. When we say that we want a country that's more equal, and so we're fighting for equal pay for equal work so that women are getting paid just the same as men, we don't get help. When we said that it makes sense to reform our health insurance system so that people aren't left without health insurance because of a preexisting condition and insurance companies can't drop you when you get sick or impose an arbitrary lifetime limit, they said no.

In fact, the leader in—of the Republicans in the House, when asked, "What's your jobs plan?" he said, "Repeal health care." I mean, now, other than giving jobs for folks who want to deny you coverage, I don't know what kind of jobs plan that is.

On Wall Street reform: Here we have the worst financial crisis since the Great Depression; we pass financial reform, have to eke it out with almost no help from the other side, except for a couple brave Republicans. And you're scratching your head saying: "Well, do they think that hidden fees in credit cards are good? Do they think that mortgage companies being

able to steer you to unaffordable mortgages are a smart thing to do?" Apparently so. [*Laughter*] They must think that's good stuff.

Look, on each of these items, they want to take us backwards. They basically think that the status quo before all that we've been through over the last 2½ years is perfectly fine. I think we can do better. I think we can do better than that.

I think we can have an America in which our health care system works for all Americans and we're driving down costs. I think we can have a financial sector that is fair and productive and won't require taxpayer bailouts. I think we can have an America in which women are being treated just like men in the workplace. I think we can have an America in which tobacco companies aren't marketing their products to kids.

I think we can have an America in which people who work hard, who take pride in their job, who are responsible to their families, who are responsible for their communities, that they've got opportunity; an America in which our young people have a chance to get a first-class education and can go to college and are able to go on and make a career for themselves; an America in which we are outcompeting every other country in the world and we are doubling exports, and in which the dynamism and innovation of this country continues throughout the 21st century, just like it existed in the 20th century.

All those things are possible. But this November is going to be a choice, and all of you are going to have to think about what kind of legacy are we going to leave for our kids. We are at a crossroads here. We are not through. We are not out of the woods, and we are going to need your help. So to all of you who worked so hard to help me get elected, you've got to work just as hard to get Alexi elected. You've got to work just as hard to get our congressional candidates like Dan elected. You've got to work just as hard to get our Governor and Lieutenant Governor elected.

You've got to go out there and knock on doors. You've got to go out there and make phone calls. You've got to understand what's at stake here, because the other side does. They are going to be well financed, and they are going to be working hard. They see this as their best opportunity to go back to the same system that they had in place all those years.

Now, ultimately, though, you know, when I ran for office, a lot of people were skeptical that I could win the Senate. Obviously, people were skeptical we could win the Presidency. There were times where I was skeptical, but the one thing I wasn't skeptical about was you, the American people.

I've always had confidence in you, that ultimately, despite all the special interest ads—and by the way, right now we've got a Supreme Court decision that's allowing uninhibited special interest spending on ads, and we've got legislation in the Senate and the House to try to fix this. But the other side, of course, is saying no. And we're going to keep on fighting to make sure that foreign corporations and big special interests can't just fund unlimited ads without even disclosing who they are. But despite all that, I always have confidence that the American people can cut through the nonsense and ultimately do what's best not just for the next election, but for the next generation.

I have confidence in you. And so if you will stand with me and if you will stand with all these outstanding candidates in the weeks to come, I promise you we will work as hard as we have ever worked for as long as it takes to create the kind of America that our children and our grandchildren deserve.

God bless you, Chicago. God bless you, Illinois. God bless the United States of America. Thank you, everybody. Thank you.

NOTE: The President spoke at 5:30 p.m. at the Chicago Cultural Center. In his remarks, he referred to Sheena Patton, regional field director, Organizing for America; and House Republican Leader John A. Boehner.

Statement on Kenya's Constitutional Referendum
August 5, 2010

The United States congratulates the Kenyan people and Government on the holding of a peaceful, transparent, and credible constitutional referendum. This was a significant step forward for Kenya's democracy, and the peaceful nature of the election was a testament to the character of the Kenyan people. My administration has been pleased to support Kenya's democratic development and the Kenyan people, including through the visit of Vice President Biden earlier this year.

The overwhelming approval of the proposed new constitution reflects the desire of the Kenyan people to put their country on a path toward improved governance, greater stability, and increased prosperity. As it is fully implemented, the new constitution can play a decisive role in achieving these objectives in a way which benefits all Kenyans.

Kenyans across the political, social, and ethnic spectrum now have a chance to come together to support implementation through an inclusive dialogue. Reaching out to one another, Kenyans will be able to take advantage of this historic opportunity to move their country forward. As Kenya's close friend and partner, the United States will work with the international community to support the implementation process and to stand with the Kenyan people as they reach for a better future.

Remarks Following a Tour of Gelberg Signs
August 6, 2010

Thank you, everybody. Thank you. Please, everybody, have a seat. It is wonderful to be here. I want to acknowledge a couple folks who are present. First of all, we've got Representative Eleanor Holmes Norton right here, doing great work. I want to thank Mayor Adrian Fenty for being here. We've got local city council members who are here with us today. And I want to finally make sure to acknowledge Luc, Guy, and Neil Brami, the owner of Gelberg Signs.

I just had a chance to tour Gelberg Signs and see the outstanding work that they're doing. This is the last sign-making company in Washington, DC, I just learned, and the Brami brothers, their father worked here when they were young and they came to buy the company. So it's a wonderful story of entrepreneurship. And I've been told that they don't argue as much now as they used to when they were kids. That's the story I've gotten.

But the work ethic, the craftsmanship, the entrepreneurialism of this company is an example of what makes our country so great. And I really commend them for the fine company that they've built. I'll be speaking about the challenges facing small businesses like Gelberg Signs in a moment, but first, I want to say a word about where we are in our economy more broadly.

We know from economic statistics what the stories of America's families have been telling us for quite some time, that the recession that we're still recovering from is the most serious downturn since the Great Depression. We also know, from studying the lessons of past recessions, that climbing out of any recession, much less a hole as deep as this one, takes some time. The road to recovery doesn't follow a straight line. Some sectors bounce back faster than others.

So what we need to do is keep pushing forward. We can't go backwards. This morning, the Department of Labor released its monthly jobs report, showing that July marked the seventh straight month of job creation in the private sector. So jobs have been growing in the private sector for seven straight months.

July's jobs numbers reflect, in part, expected losses related to the census winding down. But the fact is we've now added private sector jobs every month this year, instead of losing them, as we did for the first 7 months of last year. And that's a good sign.

Meanwhile, our manufacturing sector that's been hit hard for as long as folks can remember has actually added 183,000 jobs so far this year.

That's the most robust 7 months of manufacturing growth in over a decade. Just this morning there was a report about the growing trend of manufacturing plants returning to the United States from overseas, instead of the other way around.

Same time, each of the Big Three automakers—Ford, GM, and Chrysler, two of which were on the verge of bankruptcy a little over a year ago, a liquidation bankruptcy that would have destroyed those companies—all three U.S. automakers are now posting a profit for the first time since 2004. And since they emerged from bankruptcy, the auto industry as a whole has added 76,000 jobs. So there's some good trends out there.

That's the good news. But for America's workers, families, and small businesses, progress needs to come faster. Our job is to make sure that happens, not only to lay the foundation for private sector job creation, but also to accelerate hiring to fuel the small businesses that are the engines of economic growth, to speed our recovery so it reaches the people and places who need relief not a year from now, not 6 months from now, but now, right now.

And that's why I welcomed the news earlier this week that after a lot of partisan bickering and delay, the Senate passed a bill that will not only keep at least 160,000 teachers in the classroom this fall who would otherwise be out of a job, but will help States avoid making other painful layoffs of essential personnel, like police and firefighters.

One of the areas where we've been losing jobs even as we're gaining in manufacturing has actually been in State and local hiring, because their budgets have been plummeting. All the city council members are nodding here. And so this bill will help. Speaker Pelosi said she's going to bring the House back in session to pass this bill, and as soon as they do I'm ready to sign it into law.

We've also got to look at industries of the future. And that's why we're investing in a clean energy economy with the potential to create hundreds of thousands of jobs across the country by spurring two private sector dollars for every tax dollar we invest, strengthening our economy, at the same time cleaning up our planet and making all of us more secure in the process.

And that's why it's so important to pass a jobs bill for America's small businesses. Small businesses are where most jobs in this country are created, small businesses like the one I'm visiting today, Gelberg Signs. Now, our small businesses were especially hard hit by this recession and many are having a tough time getting back on their feet.

But Gelberg Signs actually is doing pretty well, and they're hopeful about the future. And that's mainly because of the people who work here, some of whom are standing with me today, but it's also because we've helped remove some of the obstacles that make it harder for small businesses like Gelberg Signs to grow and hire.

So, for example, they've taken advantage of a new hiring tax credit we created that says small businesses don't have to pay a dime of payroll tax when they hire a worker who's been out of a job for at least 60 days. So, in fact, almost half of the employees they've hired this year qualified for that tax credit, including one of the folks standing behind me today.

They've also taken out what's called 7(a) loans that are guaranteed by the Small Business Administration. And that's a lifeline for many small businesses that help them pay off old debts, buy new equipment, and bring on more workers. Last year, we took steps to cut fees and offer more robust guarantees on these loans. And partly as a result, the number of 7(a) loans offered to small businesses went up substantially. But since these enhancements expired, these loans have dried up, leaving many small-business owners in the lurch.

So the small-business jobs bill that's being debated in Congress right now would not only extend these successful policies, but the bill would also more than double the size of the loans that small businesses like Gelberg Signs can take out. It would create new small-business lending funds to unlock credit for entrepreneurs. It would provide new tax cuts to small-business men and women who want to accelerate investment in their companies and in our economy.

This is the right thing to do. We want Gelberg Signs not just to hang on, we want you guys to thrive and to grow and to hire more and more workers. And you know you create a great product. You know you provide great service. You stand behind what you do. But sometimes, it's hard to get financing, sometimes you need some help in terms of cutting your tax burden. That's what this bill does.

And yet a minority in the Senate is standing in the way of giving our small-businesspeople an up-or-down vote on this bill. And that's a shame. These kinds of delays mean contracts are being put off, debts are adding up, workers are going without a job, and we can't afford it. We need to do what's right, not what's political, and we need to do it right now.

We need to decide whether we're willing to do what's necessary to keep this economy moving in the right direction. Whether we're willing to rise above the election-time games and come together, all of us—Democrats and Republicans and Independents—all of us coming together not just to pass a jobs bill that is going to help small businesses like this one hire and grow, but also to secure a clean energy future and accelerate our recovery and rebuild our economy around three simple words: Made in America. That is what I'm committed to doing, and that's what I hope members of both parties will join me in doing in the days ahead and beyond.

So congratulations to this outstanding company for the great work you're doing. Congratulations to the workers, because ultimately, you are what makes this company. We want you to keep on growing and we want other companies like this one to keep on growing. And we want the next generation of young entrepreneurs, like these three brothers, who've got an idea to be able to buy a company and grow it just like they have.

That's our future. That's what I'm committed to doing. And I appreciate all of you being such great models for what America is all about. Thank you very much, everybody. Thank you.

NOTE: The President spoke at 11:57 a.m.

Remarks at a Reception Honoring Supreme Court Associate Justice Elena Kagan
August 6, 2010

Thank you. Everybody, please sit down. Have a seat. This is a good day. [*Laughter*] Good afternoon, everybody. Welcome to the White House. I am pleased that all of you could be here today as we celebrate the next member of our Nation's highest court. And while she may be feeling a twinge of sadness about giving up the title of "General"—[*laughter*]—a cool title—I think we can all agree that "Justice Elena Kagan" has a pretty nice ring to it.

We are very honored to be joined today by two of Elena's new colleagues, Justice Ruth Bader Ginsburg and Justice Anthony Kennedy, and we're thankful for their presence. Justice Kennedy assured me that he would keep Justice Kagan out of trouble, and Justice Ginsburg assured me that she would get Justice Kagan into trouble. [*Laughter*] So we'll see how that works out. [*Laughter*]

We're also pleased to have several Members of Congress, as well as our Cabinet, here today and of course members of Elena's family. And thanks to all of you for your service and for taking time to be here today.

I also want to express my gratitude to our Senate Judiciary Committee chairman, Senator Leahy; ranking member, Senator Sessions; Majority Leader Reid; and Republican Leader McConnell for seeing to it that Elena got a full, fair, and timely hearing.

After more than 80 one-on-one meetings and 17 hours of testimony, I'd say that the Senate got a pretty good look at Elena Kagan. They got a good sense of her judicial philosophy, her commitment to the rule of law, her rich understanding of our Constitution, and of course where she can be found on Christmas Day. [*Laughter*]

And the bipartisan support she received in yesterday's vote is yet another example of the high esteem in which she's held by folks across the political spectrum. There aren't many law school deans who receive standing ovations from both the Federalist Society and the American Constitution Society. And I don't know too many folks whose fans include President Clinton, Judge Abner Mikva, and Justice Ginsburg, as well as Ken Starr, Miguel Estrada, and Justice Scalia. In fact, I understand that Justice Scalia came to relish their spirited exchanges during Elena's appearances before the Court, even after Elena cheerfully informed him that he was, and I quote, "wrong" in his understanding of a recent case. [*Laughter*] I'm sure that was refreshing for him to hear. [*Laughter*]

These folks may not agree on much, but they've all been impressed, as I have, by Elena's formidable intellect and pathbreaking career as an acclaimed scholar and Presidential adviser, as the first woman to serve as dean of the Harvard Law School, and most recently as Solicitor General. They admire how, while she could easily have settled into a comfortable practice in corporate law, she chose instead to devote her life to public service. They appreciate her evenhandedness and openmindedness and her excellent and often irreverent sense of humor.

These are traits that she happens to share with the last Solicitor General who went on to become a Supreme Court Justice, one for whom Elena clerked and whom she considers one of her heroes, Justice Thurgood Marshall. And we are very proud to have Justice Marshall's widow here today joining us.

In a tribute she wrote after Justice Marshall's death, Elena recalled how she and her fellow clerks took turns standing guard when his casket lay in state at the Supreme Court and how 20,000 people stood in a line that stretched around the block to pay their respects. They were people from every background and every walk of life: Black, White, rich and poor, young and old. Many brought their children, hoping to impress upon them the lessons of Justice Marshall's extraordinary life. Some left notes; some left flowers. One mourner left a worn slip opinion of *Brown* v. *Board of Education*.

It is, to this day, a moving reminder that the work of our highest court shapes not just the character of our democracy, but the most fundamental aspects of our daily lives: how we work, how we worship, whether we can speak freely and live fully, whether those words put to paper more than two centuries ago will truly mean something for each of us in our time. Because as visionary as our Founders were, they did not presume to know exactly how the times would change and what new questions fate and history would set before us. Instead, they sought to articulate principles that would be timeless, ones that would accommodate the changing circumstances of our lives while preserving the rights and freedoms on which this country was founded.

Today is one of those moments when you can't help but appreciate the extraordinary success of their efforts. For nearly two centuries, there wasn't a single woman on the Supreme Court. When Elena was a clerk, there was just one. But when she takes her seat on that Bench, for the first time in history, there will be three women serving on our Nation's highest court. It is, as Justice Ginsburg recently put it, "one of the most exhilarating developments," a sign of progress that I relish not just as a father who wants limitless possibilities for my daughters, but as an American proud that our Supreme Court will be a little more inclusive, a little more representative, more reflective of us as a people than ever before.

And it is yet another example of how our Union has become more, not less, perfect over

time: more open, more fair, more free. That's not just a matter of accident or chance. While those founding truths about liberty and equality may have been self-evident, they were not self-perpetuating. And it is the members of our highest court who do the vital and constant work of ensuring that they endure. And that's work that I am confident Elena will carry out with integrity, with humanity, and an abiding commitment to the ideal inscribed above our courthouse doors: Equal justice under the law.

So it is now my great pleasure to introduce, as our next Supreme Court Justice, Elena Kagan.

[*At this point, Associate Justice Kagan made brief remarks.*]

I told Elena to go ahead and soak it in because I'm not sure they're allowed to clap in the Supreme Court. [*Laughter*] But thank you very much for joining us, and please enjoy the reception. Thank you.

NOTE: The President spoke at 2:25 p.m. in the East Room at the White House. In his remarks, he referred to former White House Counsel Abner J. Mikva; former Independent Counsel Kenneth W. Starr; Miguel A. Estrada, partner, Gibson, Dunn & Crutcher; and Cecilia "Cissy" Suyat Marshall, wife of former Justice Thurgood Marshall. The transcript released by the Office of the Press Secretary also included the remarks of Associate Justice Kagan.

Statement on the 45th Anniversary of the Voting Rights Act of 1965
August 6, 2010

Today we celebrate the 45th anniversary of the 1965 Voting Rights Act, one of the most historic and groundbreaking pieces of legislation in our Nation's history. For those who marched bravely, who worked tirelessly, who shed their blood and gave their lives in the pursuit of freedom for every American, the Act served as the culmination of decades of work to fulfill America's promise. And for the members of the Moses generation, including Dr. Martin Luther

King, Jr., and Rosa Parks, who stood alongside President Johnson when he signed the bill into law, it was an affirmation that although the arc of the moral universe may be long, it bends toward justice.

The Voting Rights Act guaranteed African Americans the right to vote at a time when thousands were being disenfranchised across the country. It extended the protection of our Constitution to every citizen regardless of race or religion, color or creed. And in the 45 years since it was passed, the Act has been reaffirmed four times, each one a reminder that we must remain vigilant in guaranteeing access to the ballot box.

As we pause to reflect on the anniversary of that historic moment, I encourage every Ameri-can to honor the legacy of the brave men and women who came before us, from the foot sol-diers to the Freedom Riders, by exercising the rights they fought so hard to guarantee. And to-gether let us recommit ourselves, in ways large and small, to continuing their journey to pro-mote equality and perfect our Union.

The President's Weekly Address
August 7, 2010

Forty-five years ago, we made a solemn com-pact as a nation that senior citizens would not go without the health care they need. This is the promise we made when Medicare was born. And it's the responsibility of each generation to keep that promise.

That's why a report issued this week by the trustees who oversee Medicare was such good news. According to this report, the steps we took this year to reform the health care system have put Medicare on a sounder financial foot-ing. Reform has actually added at least a dozen years to the solvency of Medicare, the single longest extension in history, while helping to preserve Medicare for generations to come.

We've made Medicare more solvent by going after waste, fraud, and abuse, not by changing seniors' guaranteed benefits. In fact, seniors are starting to see that because of health reform, their benefits are getting better all the time.

Seniors who fall into the doughnut hole, the gap in Medicare Part D drug coverage, are eli-gible right now for a $250 rebate to help cover the cost of their prescriptions. Now, I know for people facing drug costs far higher than that, they need more help. So starting next year, if you fall in the doughnut hole, you'll get a 50-percent discount on the brand-name medicine you need. And in the coming years, this law will close the doughnut hole completely once and for all.

Already, we've put insurance companies on notice that we have the authority to review and reject unreasonable rate increases for Medicare Advantage plans. And we've made it clear to the insurers that we won't hesitate to use this au-thority to protect seniors.

Beginning next year, preventive care, includ-ing annual physicals, wellness exams, and tests like mammograms, will be free for seniors as well. That will make it easier for folks to stay healthy. But it will also mean that doctors can catch things earlier, so treatment may be less in-vasive and less expensive.

And as reform ramps up in the coming years, we expect seniors to save an average of $200 per year in premiums and more than $200 each year in out of pocket costs too.

This is possible in part through reforms that target waste and abuse and redirect those re-sources to where they're supposed to go: our se-niors. We're already on track to cut improper payments in half, including money that goes to criminals who steal taxpayer dollars by setting up insurance scams and other frauds. And we won't stop there, because by preventing the loss of these tax dollars, we can both address the runaway costs of Medicare and improve the quality of care seniors receive, and we can crack down on those who prey on seniors and take ad-vantage of people.

So we are no longer accepting business as usual. We're making tough decisions to meet the challenges of our time. And as a result, Medicare is stronger and more secure. That's important, because Medicare isn't just a pro-gram. It's a commitment to America's seniors that after working your whole life, you've earned the security of quality health care you can afford. As long as I am President, that's a commitment this country is going to keep.

Thanks.

NOTE: The address was recorded at approxi-mately 4:45 p.m. on August 6 in the Map Room at the White House for broadcast on August 7. The transcript was made available by the Office of the Press Secretary on August 6, but was em-bargoed for release until 6 a.m. on August 7. The Office of the Press Secretary also released a Spanish language transcript of this address.

Remarks Honoring the 2010 Super Bowl Champion New Orleans Saints
August 9, 2010

Well, welcome, everybody. Please have a seat. Have a seat. It is wonderful to see all of you. Welcome, and congratulations to the 2009 [2010]° Super Bowl champions, the New Orleans Saints.

I want to start by recognizing some folks in my administration who are big fans of this team: Lisa Jackson from the EPA; Secretary Donovan from HUD; Craig Fugate from FEMA. We've got a few very proud Members of Congress with us: Senator Mary Landrieu and Representative Steve Scalise are in the house.

Congratulations to the owner, Tom Benson, who has led this team through times that would test anybody, and General Manager Mickey Loomis for building this extraordinary championship squad.

Congratulations to your outstanding head coach, Sean Payton, who's done just great work. I must point out, Sean is a Chicago guy—[laughter]—I'm just saying—[laughter]—by way of Naperville. You've got to be tough to be a Chicago guy. I make some tough decisions every day, but I never decided on an onside kick—[laughter]—in the second half of the Super Bowl. That I—that took some guts. Were you okay with that? Did he check off with you? [Laughter] Yes. I'm glad that thing went all right. [Laughter]

Coach Payton led this team to a remarkable season: 13–0 start, a franchise record for wins; a heck of an overtime win in the NFC Championship; and then, after falling behind in the Super Bowl, with the onside kick, huge second half, Tracy Porter's interception guaranteeing that the Lombardi Trophy would go to the city of New Orleans for the very first time. It was an unbelievable moment.

I want to congratulate the Super Bowl MVP, your quarterback, your captain, Drew Brees. Now, I have to say, all of us were very excited after the game. All my wife wanted to talk about was Baylen, that little boy sitting with Drew, and everybody going, "Aww"—[laughter]—which—I'm just saying, you made a lot of fans that day. [Laughter] Drew and his wife Brittany are expecting their second child in October. So congratulations to you both.

Drew threw six touchdowns in the opening weekend, making it pretty clear that the Saints were coming to play. And over the course of the season, he set a new NFL record for accuracy, completing more than 70 percent of his passes. I have a few staffers who were thrilled to have Drew on their fantasy team. [Laughter] So they are grateful for that.

And by the way, this is not Drew's first time to the White House. Last year, we filmed a PSA some of you may have seen, encouraging America's youth to get 60 minutes of physical activity every day. He tossed me a nice, tight spiral that I then lateraled to a kid on DeMarcus Ware's shoulders. Now, I also want to point out, I beat Troy Polamalu over the middle on that throw. [Laughter] You remember. [Laughter] Yes, yes. I mean, I'm not sure he was going top speed, but—[laughter].

Finally, Drew's agreed to serve as Cochair of the new President's Council on Fitness, Sports, and Nutrition. And I want to thank all the players who put on a clinic earlier this morning with children from the Boys and Girls Club as part of the "Let's Move!" and the NFL's Play 60 program. So thank you very much, guys, for participating in that.

° White House correction.

So look, this was a unbelievable season. After decades of frustration, the Saints finally won the big one. The "Ain'ts" and the "Sad Sacks" gave way to the "Who Dats." Local musicians even gave a jazz funeral to retire the "Ain'ts" nickname. But I think we all know that this season meant far more than that to the city of New Orleans, and to all Americans, really.

Look, I'm a Bears fan. I'm not going to lie. [*Laughter*] But this was a big win for the country, not just for New Orleans, because 5 years ago, this team played its entire season on the road. It didn't have a home field. The Superdome had been ruined by Hurricane Katrina. The heartbreaking tragedies that unfolded there when it was used as a shelter from that terrible storm lingered all too fresh in a lot of people's minds.

And back then, people didn't even know if the team was coming back. People didn't know if the city was coming back. Not only did the team come back, it took its city's hands and helped its city back on its feet. This team took the hopes and the dreams of a shattered city and placed them squarely on its shoulders.

And so these guys became more than leaders in the locker room, they became leaders of an entire region. And the victory parade that we saw earlier this year made one thing perfectly clear, that New Orleans and the New Orleans Saints are here to stay.

So plenty of cities carry their sports teams through a tough season. It's a rare thing when a sports team carries a city through tough times. And that's why there's such a deep bond between this organization and the city. I'm not sure there's any other city that feels that same way right now. And that's not just for what the Saints have done on the field, but what they've done off it to see that the city keeps rising. In fact, NFL Commissioner Roger Goodell recently said that every team in professional sports should use the Saints as a model for how to interact with their community.

This entire team has worked with Habitat for Humanity to rebuild neighborhoods in New Orleans. Many of these guys and the coaches and the players run foundations to help children in need. All of them are off to Walter Reed later this morning to spend some time with wounded warriors who served our country.

And obviously, the Gulf region has spent the last few months besieged by yet another crisis. But last week, we received the news that we had hoped for. Yesterday the—we learned that a procedure to prevent any more oil from spilling with a cement plug appears to have succeeded. And the final steps will be taken later in August, when the relief well is completed. But what is clear is that the battle to stop the oil from flowing into the Gulf is just about over.

Our work goes on, though. I made a commitment to the people of the Gulf Coast that I would stand by them not just until the well was closed, but until they recovered from the damage that's been done. And that's a commitment my administration is going to keep.

So with the ongoing reopening of Gulf fisheries, we're excited that fishermen can go back to work and Americans can confidently and safely enjoy Gulf seafood once again. We're certainly going to enjoy it here at the White House. In fact, we had some yesterday.

While they're here today, several Saints players are going to spend some time teaching our staff their favorite Gulf seafood recipes. So who's cooking? [*Laughter*] Which one—it's you back there? All right. [*Laughter*] And Sam Kass, the White House—he's very excited. He's very excited. And after weeks of hearing about food from our response teams down in the Gulf, I can tell you that our staff's excited about the 30-foot po'boy we're serving at lunch today. [*Laughter*]

But let me just say in closing, we are very proud of this team, and we are very proud of the owner of this team, because it required a great commitment on your part to help pull this team and this city along. And so there is a heartfelt congratulations not just from those of us here in the White House, but, I think, all across America. These are big guys with big hearts and shoulders big enough to carry the hopes and dreams of an entire city with them.

So with that, congratulations to all of you. New Orleans Saints, 2009 [2010]° Super Bowl champions. Congratulations.

NOTE: The President spoke at 9:20 a.m. in the East Room at the White House. In his remarks, he referred to Tracy Porter, cornerback, New Orleans Saints; DeMarcus Ware, linebacker, Dallas Cowboys; Troy Polamalu, strong safety, Pittsburgh Steelers; and White House Assistant Chef Sam Kass.

Remarks at a Democratic National Committee Fundraiser in Austin, Texas
August 9, 2010

Hello, everybody! Thank you. Hello, Austin! Thank you so much. Thank you very much. What's going on, Ronnie? Everybody, thank you. Please have a seat. Have a seat, have a seat. Well, first of all, thank you, Linda, for that terrific introduction. I would have heard it again. [*Laughter*] I would have been happy.

A few other great friends: Your own, somebody from Texas, but who is doing a great job internationally on behalf of all the American people as my Trade Representative, Ambassador Ron Kirk is here. More importantly, Ambassador Ron Kirk's mom is here. [*Laughter*]

A wonderful Congressman who is battling day in, day out on behalf of the people of Texas and the folks in his district, Lloyd Doggett is here. I want to thank Mayor Lee Leffingwell for his hospitality. Texas Democratic Party chair Boyd Richie and his lovely wife Betty are here. And our DNC deputy national finance chair Kirk Rudy is here.

It's good to be back in Texas. And it's really good to be back in Austin. I just love Austin, Texas. [*Laughter*] I do. Every time I come here, I like the people, I like the food, I like the music. I like that there are a bunch of Democrats here. [*Laughter*] I like that too. It is wonderful. And as I look out throughout this crowd, there's so many of you who did so much on behalf of our campaign, on behalf of my election. You were with us when we were up, you were with us when we were down, and you will recall we had some down days. And I know that if it weren't for you, I might not be standing here as President of the United States. So to all my good friends here in Texas, thank you very much for everything that you've done.

Of course, whenever I talk to my supporters, I am reminded of a story Abraham Lincoln liked to tell. A man comes to the White House demanding to see the President—and this is at a time when things were a little more relaxed in terms of security—so he insists that he was a big supporter of President Lincoln. Finally, he gets through reception, gets an audience with the President and says, "If it weren't for me, you would not be President of the United States." And President Lincoln says, "I forgive you." Now—[*laughter*].

Okay, I—it is an extraordinary honor, obviously, to be your President. But I will also say that the last few years have been incredibly challenging for so many people throughout America. You know that here; it's certainly true all across the country.

Eighteen months ago, when I took office, after nearly a decade of economic policies that has given us little more than sluggish job growth, sluggish economic growth, falling incomes, falling wages, a record deficit, all which culminated in the worst recession that we had experienced since the Great Depression, that's what we were walking into.

The month I was sworn in, we lost 750,000 jobs, just in that 1 month. We had lost 3 million jobs in the previous 6 months. The next month we lost 600,000. So we were facing what many economists thought might be a return not just to a recession, but a Great Depression.

Now, we didn't get to that point by accident. We got there after nearly 10 years of an

---

° White House correction.

economic theory in Washington that was pretty straightforward: You cut taxes for the wealthiest Americans, you cut back rules and enforcement when it comes to special interests, and then you cut the middle class loose to fend for themselves.

So if you're a young person who couldn't afford to go to college, tough luck, you're on your own. If you're a child here in Texas that doesn't have health insurance, them's the breaks, pull yourself up by your own bootstraps. If you're a worker who had been laid off, maybe short of retirement, and couldn't find anything that would allow you to pay the bills or pay the mortgage, that's too bad, you're on your own. Now, on the other hand, if you're a Wall Street bank or an insurance company or an oil company, then you got to write your own ticket.

And we know how this approach turned out. So when I took office, we put in place a new economic plan, a plan that rewards hard work instead of greed; a plan that rewards responsibility instead of recklessness; a plan that focused on our middle class, making them more secure, and making sure that our country was competitive over the long run, so the jobs and industries of the future weren't going to China or India or Germany, but were going to the United States of America, right here.

And instead of spending money on special interest tax loopholes that don't create American jobs, we said, we're going to make smart investments in education and innovation and clean energy that will benefit all people and our entire economy. Instead of giving special interests free rein to write their own regulations, we demanded new accountability from Washington to Wall Street so that big corporations had to play by the same rules as small companies and by individuals. That's only fair.

Now, it took us nearly a decade to dig ourselves into a very deep hole. And so I'm here to tell you that it's going to take us some more time to dig our way out of that hole. The devastation that has touched so many of our families, so many of our communities, that is going to take some time to heal. And I hear those stories firsthand wherever I travel. I hear about them in the letters that I receive every night that I

read from people who are doing their best to keep on striving towards that American Dream, but keep on hitting a bunch of roadblocks and are looking for help. So the road to recovery is long, and it's filled with challenges. And I'm under no illusion that we've gotten there yet. We've got a lot more work to do.

But here is the thing I want everybody here to understand, because you were part of that journey that we started 3 years ago: After 19 months in office, we are on the right track. An economy that was shrinking by up to 6 percent when I took office is now growing, not as fast as we want, but it is growing.

We were losing all those jobs, every month. We're now adding private sector jobs, 7 consecutive months now that we've seen private sector job growth. It's being offset some because State and local budgets are getting hammered so hard that they're laying off folks, even as the private sector is starting to pick up. But we're moving in the right direction.

And so the last thing we can afford to do at this critical juncture in our history is to go back to the same policies that got us into this mess in the first place. And that is what this November election is going to be all about. Are we going to move forward, or are we going to move backwards? Policies that crashed the economy, that undercut the middle class, that mortgaged our future, do we really want to go back to that? Or do we keep moving this country forward?

Now, when we talk about this going back thing, I notice some Republicans say, well, he just wants to bash the previous administration. He's looking backwards. He's trying to take the focus off the tough economic situation that a lot of people are feeling. No, no, no. The reason we're focused on it is because the other side isn't offering anything new. I mean, it would be one thing if having run the economy into the ground, having taken record surpluses and turned them into record deficits, if having presided over the meltdown of our financial system, that they had gone off into the desert for a while and reflected—[*laughter*]—and said, boy, we really screwed up. [*Laughter*] What we were selling didn't work. It badly damaged the American economy, and now we're going to come back with a whole new set of ideas. But that's not what's happening. Instead, they are trotting out the exact same ideas that got us into this mess in the first place. Their big economic plan is to renew the tax cuts that helped to turn surpluses into deficits, tax cuts for the wealthiest Americans. And once you get past that, they don't have another new idea. That's it.

In fact, when the leader of the Republicans in the House of Representatives was asked, what's your big jobs plan, he said, well, we should repeal health care. [*Laughter*] That was it. Now, I don't know how that would create jobs—[*laughter*]—other than maybe for folks who want to deny you coverage for health care. But it sure isn't a new plan.

And so we've got a choice between a forward-looking agenda that is rebuilding the structure of this economy so it's working for all Americans, or just going back to the same stuff that got us into this mess. In fact, I've been traveling around the country trying to use an analogy here, and it's as if these guys took the car, drove it into the ditch, then—so we put our boots on, we walked down into the ditch, into the mud. We pushed; we shoved. Meanwhile, they're standing back, they're watching us, drinking a Slurpee or something—[*laughter*]—and saying, "Well, you're not pushing fast enough," and, "You should push this way instead of that way." And they had a lot of commentary, but they sure weren't putting their shoulder behind pushing. And finally, we get this car up on level ground. Finally, we get it back on the road. And these guys turn to us and say, "Give us the keys back." [*Laughter*] Well, no, you can't have the keys back because you don't know how to drive. [*Laughter*] You do not know how to drive, and so you can't have the keys back.

Now, here's another interesting thing. I want you guys to think about this. If you have a car and you want to go forward, what do you do? You put it in "D." [*Laughter*] When you want to go backwards, what do you do? You put it in "R." I'm just saying. That's no coincidence. [*Laughter*] We are not going to give them the keys back.

What they're really counting on is amnesia. That's their basic theory in this election. They know they messed up, and they know that we pulled the country out of the problems that we were in. But they figure, well, you know what, he's been in office long enough, and this was a deep enough, tough enough recession, and things aren't where people know they should be, and so maybe they'll forget that actually this was the result of our economic policies, so we'll just offer the same policies.

But I think the American people are smarter than that. I think they understand that if we want the kind of America for our children and our grandchildren that we truly hope for, then we've got to move in a new direction, not only to solve some of these short-term economic problems, but to lay a foundation for long-term economic growth.

And what does that mean? That means that instead of giving tax breaks to companies that are shipping jobs overseas, we've got to give tax breaks to companies that are creating jobs right here in the United States of America. We have started to do that. We've given eight tax cuts to small businesses so far, and we are not done.

But you know what? The other side has resisted every attempt. We've got a bill right now that was pending in the Senate to provide assistance to small businesses. Now, this should be as American as apple pie. Small businesses create two out of every three jobs in America. So we put together a package, paid for—doesn't add to the deficit—that would help small businesses get loans, would eliminate the capital gains rate for small business startups. The Chamber of Commerce endorses it. Now, let me tell you, the Chamber of Commerce doesn't always go out of its way to say nice things about me.

And yet we still can't get it moving through the Senate, because these folks, their basic theory is, we don't want to do anything that helps the President move the country forward, because they're thinking about the next election instead of the next generation.

We've got a different approach. We've started to jump-start a homegrown clean energy economy. All across the country, you're seeing wind turbines and solar panels and biodiesel that is being built right here in the United States of America. We have singlehandedly started a advanced battery manufacturing industry right here. We used to have 2 percent of the batteries that go into electric cars. We're going to have 40 percent of that industry right here in the United States of America by 2015, thanks to some of the work that we've already done. Now, the other side, they don't want to do that. They've been saying no to a clean energy future.

We've said we needed 21st-century infrastructure that could put people back to work, particularly all those folks who've been laid off of the construction industry now that the housing bubble has burst, put them to work not just rebuilding roads and bridges, dams and sewer lines, all the traditional infrastructure, but building a smart grid that can carry energy efficiently all across America or creating broadband lines into rural areas so that they can compete in the global economy.

What did the others say—what did the other side say? They said no, because they're thinking about the next election instead of the next generation: no to small business tax cuts, no to clean energy jobs, no to infrastructure projects. I have to say, though, they do show up at the ribbon-cuttings for the infrastructure projects. [*Laughter*] Lloyd knows this. [*Laughter*] They will fulminate and say, it's going to be Armageddon if we pass all this stuff, but then they're cheesing and grinning right there—[*laughter*]—got the shovel all ready—[*laughter*]—sending out the press releases.

But the point is that there's been a fundamental lack of seriousness on the other side. We have spent the last 20 months governing. They spent the last 20 months politicking. Now we've got 3 months to go, and so we've decided, well, we can politick for 3 months. They've forgotten I know how to politick pretty good. [*Laughter*] And so I'm happy to make this argument. I am happy to have this debate over the next several months about what their vision of the future is, because they don't have one. They are trying to move us backwards, and we need to move us forward.

So I just want everybody here to understand—here in Texas, there's been some controversy around the issues of health care. No State stands to benefit more from our health care reform than the State of Texas, which has so many people who are uninsured in this State.

The health insurance reform we passed, it's not just preventing insurers from denying you coverage. It's cutting taxes for small-business owners that cover their employees, by up to 35 percent of the premiums they're paying for their employees. It's saying to young people, you can stay on your parents' health insurance until you're 26 so that there's not that gap in coverage just as they're starting their careers. It's providing assistance to seniors so that they can help to deal with that doughnut hole that was created by the prescription drug plan. And slowly, this plan is going to eliminate it.

And then there was just news last week that showed that because of our health reform plan, the life of Medicare is going to be extended for an additional 12 years. It has made Social Security—it has made Medicare stronger for the next generation, as well as this generation.

And in the meantime, it has enshrined a basic principle, which is, in a country as wealthy as ours, nobody should go bankrupt just because they get sick and no child should go without basic preventive care. Those are basic principles that we should all be able to agree on, unless you're thinking about the next election instead of the next generation.

The other party has pledged to repeal Wall Street reform. Now, this gives you some indication of what this election should be about. Here we have a situation in which the recklessness of a few on Wall Street—and I don't want to paint with a broad brush here. There are some people on Wall Street and in banks across America that do right by their customers. But a handful of folks took exorbitant bets with huge leverage and other people's money and almost brought this entire economy to a halt. Businesses large and small couldn't get credit. Everybody was panicked. The stock market plunged. People lost trillions of dollars' worth of wealth. And we are going to be digging ourselves out from that destructive force for years to come.

Now, you would think in the aftermath of that, that anybody sensible would say, you know what, we need to have some stronger rules of the road in place, not to stifle innovation, not to strangle the free market, but rather to make sure that everybody is playing by some basic rules, that financial institutions are making their money by providing good products and good services to their customers instead of trying to game the system.

And yet if you ask the Republican leaders in Washington, they all want to repeal the reforms that we just passed. Makes no sense, unless you're thinking about the next election, or you're thinking about the special interests that you've been working with hand in glove for the last 20 months or the last decade. It doesn't make sense, unless you're only thinking about the next election.

We're in a college town here. One of the things we did was we said, we've got to make college more affordable to all Americans. And yet a system where the Government was guaranteeing loans, but they were sending them through financial institutions who were skimming billions of dollars in profits. And so we said, you know what, let's just cut out the middleman, give that money directly to young people. We're now providing more than a million young people loans that they weren't getting before, because of this single measure that we took. But we got no help from the other side. We got no help from the other side.

For years, the other side did nothing about the fact that too many women aren't paid the same as men for doing the exact same work. We decided to pass a law that says we mean what we say, equal pay for equal work. We didn't get help on that.

They want to talk about tax cuts for the wealthiest Americans. We provided 95 percent of working families here in America a tax cut. We believe in trying to keep taxes low for folks who really need help, especially at a time when their incomes and their wages are flatlining. But for you to talk about being a deficit hawk, that want responsible governance, and then you're willing to argue for $700 billion worth of tax cuts for people who don't need them and

weren't even asking for them? That tells me you're thinking about the next election instead of the next generation.

And then most recently we've got the crisis in the Gulf. Now, thankfully, because of incredibly hard work by people from all across government, we are now finally able to say that the well is contained, and we could get a permanent kill of that well over the next couple of weeks. But the kind of damage that's been done, obviously, to the Gulf has been tremendous. And small-business owners and fishermen who've been impacted, when you talk to them directly, and they start tearing up because these are businesses and a way of life that has been in their families for generations they feel like may be lost, that prompted me to say to BP, we want you to be responsible, do the right thing, and put in place $20 billion to make sure that these folks get paid, because they were not at fault in this crisis.

And what does the ranking member, who would be the chairman of the Energy Committee if the Republicans took over the House next year, what did he have to say? He apologized to BP, said, I'm sorry; I'm sorry the President shook you down. I think he may have added in there "Chicago shakedown." [*Laughter*] I'm not sure. Maybe it was somebody else. Apologized to BP because we decided we needed to hold a company accountable for the environmental devastation and the economic devastation that had been caused in the Gulf.

I don't even think he was thinking about the next election. [*Laughter*] I don't know what he was thinking about. But it's consistent with a governing philosophy that says there shouldn't be any rules on the most powerful forces. They should be able to operate unconstrained.

Right now, all around this country, there are groups with harmless-sounding names, like Americans for Prosperity, who are running millions of dollars of ads against Democratic candidates all across the country. And they don't have to say who exactly the Americans for Prosperity are. You don't know if it's a foreign-controlled corporation. You don't know if it's a big oil company or a big bank. You don't know if it's a insurance company that wants to see some of the provisions in health reform repealed because it's good for their bottom line, even if it's not good for the American people.

A Supreme Court decision allowed this to happen. And we tried to fix it, just by saying, disclose what's going on and making sure that foreign companies can't influence our elections. Seemed pretty straightforward. The other side said no.

They don't want you to know who the Americans for Prosperity are, because they're thinking about the next election. But we've got to think about future generations. We've got to make sure that we're fighting for reform. We've got to make sure that we don't have a corporate takeover of our democracy.

So, Austin, the bottom line is this: We've traveled a long way over the last 19 months, in large part thanks to folks like you. We have had historic challenges, and we've had historic responses. But right now the choice is between whether we go back to those policies that got us into this mess, or we continue with the policies that are getting us out of this mess.

And I'm confident that the American people, when they're focused, as tough as these times are, they're going to say, you know what, we can't go back to policies that were eroding our middle class and leading jobs to move overseas and leaving our incomes and wages stagnant and vulnerable to forces that we don't have any control over. I'm confident that the American people want something different.

Yes, it's hard. In Washington, a lot of times during the course of these last 19 months, the pundits have written or they've talked to our press people and they say: "What's the President doing? Doesn't he know some of these steps that he's taking don't poll well?" Yes, I do. I have pollsters too. [*Laughter*] They tell me before any decision, boy, this is really unpopular. [*Laughter*]

Our decision on the autos was really unpopular, and we now have an auto industry that has posted profits in all three auto companies for the first time in a long time. And we're going to pretty soon get all our taxpayer dollars back that my administration put in, because of the steps that we took. And we've hired 50,000 new autoworkers and saved about a million jobs. But at the time, it was really unpopular. It polled really well.

But you did not elect me to just try to do what was politically expedient at the moment. You supported me to do what was right, and that's what we've been doing. You did not elect me to think about how I could get reelected; you hired me to make sure that I was thinking about how your children and your grandchildren are going to have an America that is strong and vibrant and competitive all around the world. That's why you put us in charge.

So, Austin, I am here to tell you, we are going to keep on moving this country forward, but we are going to need your help. We are going to need your help because this is a tough environment. People are frustrated. People have been traumatized by what's taken place over the last couple years. And Members of Congress, who've been taking tough votes, courageous votes, folks like Lloyd have time and again stood up against the prevailing political winds in order to do what's right. They are going to need your help.

So I need you to make phone calls. I need you to write—I need you to talk to your friends. I need you to talk to your neighbors. I need you to help them raise money. I need you to get information out. I need you to have the same kind of passion and the same kind of hope that helped elect me a couple of years ago.

And it's places like this and supporters like you that ultimately are going to make all the difference. If you are standing with us, I'm absolutely confident we're going to do well in November. But know—but understand this: More importantly, I'm absolutely confident that America is going to be back not just to as strong as we were before this crisis, but stronger than we've been before.

Thank you so much, everybody. God bless you. God bless the United States of America.

NOTE: The President spoke at 12:55 p.m. at the Four Seasons Hotel Austin. In his remarks, he referred to Linda Chavez-Thompson, candidate for Lieutenant Governor of Texas; Willie Mae Kirk, mother of U.S. Trade Representative Ronald Kirk; House Republican Leader John A. Boehner; and Rep. Joseph L. Barton.

Remarks at the University of Texas at Austin in Austin
August 9, 2010

The President. Thank you, everybody. Hello, Austin! Hello, Longhorns! It is good to be back. It is good to be back.

Audience member. I love you, Obama!

The President. I love you back. I love Austin. I love Austin. I remember—by the way, anybody who's got a seat, feel free to take a seat. [*Laughter*] I remember paying you a visit during the campaign. Mack Brown gave me a tour of the stadium, along with Colt and a couple other guys. And I got a photo with the Heisman. [*Laughter*] I rubbed the locker room's longhorns for good luck. And I'm just saying, it might have had something to do with how the election turned out. [*Laughter*] There might be a connection there.

I also remember the first time that I came to Austin on the campaign. And there are a number of friends who are here who have been great supporters; I want to make mention of them. Representative Lloyd Doggett is here, a great friend. Senator Kirk Watson is here. Congressman Sheila Jackson Lee is here. Mayor Leffingwell is here. And your own president, Bill Powers, is in the house.

But this is back in 2007, February 2007. It was just 2 weeks after I had announced my candidacy. I know it's hard to believe, but it's true—my hair was not gray back then. [*Laughter*] Not many people thought I had much of a shot at the White House. [*Applause*] All right, let me put it this way: A lot of folks in Washington didn't think I had a shot at the White House. [*Laughter*] A lot of people couldn't pronounce my name. [*Laughter*] They were still calling me "Alabama" or "Yo mama." That was—[*laughter*].

So then I come to Austin; this was back in February of 2007. And it was a drizzly day, and that's—usually tamps down turnout. But when I got to the rally over at Auditorium Shores, there was a crowd of over 20,000 people—20,000

people. It was people of all ages and all races and all walks of life.

And I said that day, all these people, they hadn't gathered just for me. You were there because you were hungry to see some fundamental change in America, because you believed in an America where all of us, not just some of us, but all of us, no matter what we look like, no matter where we come from, all of us can reach for our dreams, all of us can make of our lives what we will, that we can determine our own destiny. And that's what we've been fighting for over the past 18 months.

I said then that we'd end the Iraq war as swiftly and as responsibly as possible, and that is a promise that we are keeping. This month, we will end combat operations in Iraq.

I said we'd make health care more affordable and give you more control over your health care, and that's a promise we're keeping. And by the way, young people are going to be able to stay on their parents' health insurance until they're 26 because of the laws that we passed.

I said we'd build an economy that can compete in the 21st century, because the economy that we had even before the recession, even before the financial crisis, wasn't working for too many Americans. Too many Americans had seen their wages flatline, their incomes flatline. We were falling behind and unable to compete internationally. And I said, we need an economy that puts Americans back to work, an economy that is built around three simple words: Made in America. Because we are not playing for second place; we are the United States of America, and like the Texas Longhorns, you play for first, we play for first.

Now, when it comes to the economy, I said that in today's world, we're being pushed as never before. From Beijing to Bangalore, from Seoul to Sao Paolo, new industries and innovations are flourishing. Our competition is growing fiercer. And while our ultimate success has and always will depend on the incredible industriousness of the American worker and the ingenuity of American businesses and the power of our free market system, we also know that as a nation, we've got to pull together and do some fundamental shifts in how we've been operating to make sure America remains number one.

So that's why I've set some ambitious goals for this country. I've called for doubling our exports within the next 5 years so that we're not just buying from other countries. I want us to sell to other countries. We've talked about doubling our Nation's capacity to generate renewable energy by 2012, because I'm absolutely convinced that if we control the clean energy future, then our economic future will be bright, building solar panels and wind turbines and biodiesel and—[*applause*]. And I want us to produce 8 million more college graduates by 2020, because America has to have the highest share of graduates compared to every other nation.

But, Texas, I want you to know, we have been slipping. In a single generation, we've fallen from 1st place to 12th place in college graduation rates for young adults. Think about that. In one generation, we went from number 1 to number 12.

Now, that's unacceptable, but it's not irreversible. We can retake the lead. If we're serious about making sure America's workers, and America itself, succeeds in the 21st century, the single most important step we can take is make—is to make sure that every one of our young people, here in Austin, here in Texas, here in the United States of America, has the best education that the world has to offer. That's the number-one thing we can do.

Now, when I talk about education, people say, well, you know what, right now we're going through this tough time. We've emerged from the worst recession since the Great Depression. So, Mr. President, you should only focus on jobs, on economic issues. And what I've tried to explain to people—I said this at the National Urban League the other week—education is an economic issue. Education is the economic issue of our time.

It's an economic issue when the unemployment rate for folks who've never gone to college is almost double what it is for those who have gone to college. Education is an economic issue when nearly 8 in 10 new jobs will require workforce training or a higher education by the end of this decade. Education is an economic issue when we know beyond a shadow of a doubt that countries that outeducate us today, they will outcompete us tomorrow.

The single most important thing we can do is to make sure we've got a world-class education system for everybody. That is a prerequisite for prosperity. It is an obligation that we have for the next generation.

And here is the interesting thing, Austin. The fact is, we know what to do to offer our children the best education possible. We know what works. It's just we're not doing it. And so what I've said is, let's get busy. Let's get started. We can't wait another generation. We can't afford to let our young people waste their most formative years. That's why we need to set up an early learning fund to challenge our States and make sure our young people, our children, are entering kindergarten ready for success. That's something we've got to do.

We can't accept anything but the best in America's classrooms. And that's why we've launched an initiative called Race to the Top, where we are challenging States to strengthen their commitment to excellence and hire outstanding teachers and train wonderful principals and create superior schools with higher standards and better assessments. And we're already seeing powerful results across the country.

But we also know that in the coming decades, a high school diploma's not going to be enough. Folks need a college degree. They need workforce training. They need a higher education. And so today I want to talk about the higher education strategy that we're pursuing not only to lead the world once more in college graduation rates but to make sure our graduates are ready for a career, ready to meet the challenges of a 21st-century economy.

Now, part one of our strategy is to make college more affordable. I suspect that that's something you're all interested in. I don't have to tell you why this is so important. Many of you are living each day with worries about how you're going to pay off your student loans. And we all know why. Even as family incomes have been essentially flat over the past 30 years, college costs have grown higher and higher and higher and higher. They have gone up faster than housing, gone up faster than transportation. They've even gone up faster than health care costs, and that's saying something. [*Laughter*]

So it's no wonder that the amount student borrowers owe has risen almost 25 percent just over the last 5 years. Think about that. Just in the last 5 years, the debt of students has gone up 25 percent.

And this isn't some abstract policy for me. I understand this personally, because Michelle and I, we had big loans to pay off when we graduated. I remember what that felt like, especially early in your career where you don't make much money and you're sending all those checks to all those companies. And that's why I'm absolutely committed to making sure that here in America, nobody is denied a college education, nobody is denied a chance to pursue their dreams, nobody is denied a chance to make the most of their lives just because they can't afford it. We are a better country than that, and we need to act like we're a better country than that.

Now, there are a couple of components to this. Part of the responsibility for controlling these costs falls on our colleges and universities. Some of them are stepping up. Public institutions like the University of Maryland, University of North Carolina, some private institutions like Cornell, they're all finding ways to combat rising tuition without compromising on quality. And I know that your president is looking at some of these same approaches to make sure that the actual costs of college are going down. I want to challenge every university and college president to get a handle on spiraling costs.

So university administrators need to do more to make college more affordable, but we as a nation have to do more as well. So that's why we fought so hard to win a battle that had been going on in Washington for years, and it had to do with the Federal student loan program.

See, under the old system, we'd pay banks and financial companies billions of dollars in subsidies to act as middlemen. See, these loans were guaranteed by the Federal Government, but we'd still pass them through banks, and they'd take out billions of dollars in profits. So it was a good deal for them, but it wasn't a very good deal for you. And because these special interests were so powerful, this boondoggle survived year after year, Congress after Congress.

This year, we said, enough is enough. We said we could not afford to continue subsidizing special interests to the tunes of billions of dollars a year at the expense of taxpayers and of students. So we went to battle against the lobbyists and a minority party that was united in their support of this outrageous status quo. And, Texas, I am here to report that we won. We won.

So as a result, instead of handing over $60 billion in subsidies to big banks and financial institutions over the next decade, we're redirecting that money to you to make college more affordable for nearly 8 million students and families across this country. Eight million students will get more help from financial aid because of these changes.

We're tripling how much we're investing in the largest college tax credit for our middle class families. And thanks to Austin's own Lloyd Doggett, that tax credit is now worth $2,500 a year for 2 years of college. And we want to make it permanent, so it's worth $10,000 over 4 years of college—$10,000.

And because the value of Pell grants has fallen as the cost of college keeps going up, the cap on how much Pell grants are worth, we have decided to offer more support for the future, so the value of Pell grants don't erode with inflation, they keep up with inflation. And we're also making loan repayments more manageable for over 1 million more students in the coming years, so students at UT Austin and across this country don't graduate with massive loan payments each month. All right, that's—we're working on that right now.

Now, I should mention, by the way, we're also making information more widely available about college costs and completion rates so you can make good decisions. You can comparison shop. And we're simplifying financial aid forms by eliminating dozens of unnecessary questions. You should not have to take—you should not have to have a Ph.D. to apply for financial aid. [*Laughter*] You shouldn't have to do it. I want a bunch of you to get Ph.D.'s—[*laughter*]—don't get me wrong. I just don't want you to have to do it for your financial aid form. [*Laughter*]

So if you're married, for example, you don't need to answer questions anymore about how much money your parents have made. If you've lived in the same place for at least 5 years, you don't need to answer questions about your place of residency. Soon, you'll no longer need to submit information you've already provided on your taxes. And that's part of the reason why we've seen a 20-percent jump in financial aid applications, because we're going to make it easier and make the system more accessible.

So college affordability is the first part of the strategy that we're pursuing. The second part is making sure that the education being offered to our college students, especially, by the way, our students at community colleges, is—that it's preparing them to graduate ready for a career. See, institutions like UT are essential to our future, but community colleges are too. They are great, underappreciated assets that we have to value and we have to support.

So that's why we're upgrading our community colleges by tying the skills taught in our classrooms to the needs of local businesses in the growth sectors of our economy. And we're giving companies an assurance that the workers they hire will be up to the job. We're giving students the best chance to succeed. We're also that way giving America the best chance to thrive and to prosper. And that's why we're also reinvesting in our HBCUs and Hispanic-Serving Institutions, like Huston-Tillotson and St. Edward's.

The third part of our strategy is making sure every student completes their course of studies. I want everybody to think about this. Over a third of America's college students and over

half of our minority students don't earn a degree, even after 6 years. So we don't just need to open the doors of college to more Americans; we need to make sure they stick with it through graduation. That is critical.

And that means looking for some of the best models out there. There are community colleges like Tennessee's Cleveland State that are redesigning remedial math courses and boosting not only student achievement, but also graduation rates. And we ought to make a significant investment to help other States pick up on some of these models.

So we've got to lift graduation rates. We've got to prepare our graduates to succeed in this economy. We've got to make college more affordable. That's how we'll put a higher education within reach for anybody who's willing to work for it. That's how we'll reach our goal of once again leading the world in college graduation rates by the end of this decade. That's how we'll lead the global economy in this century, just like we did in the last century.

When I look out at all the young people here today, I think about the fact that you are entering into the workforce at a difficult time in this country's history. The economy took a body blow from this financial crisis and this great recession that we're going through. But I want everybody here to remember, at each and every juncture throughout our history, we've always recognized that essential truth that the way to move forward, in our own lives and as a nation, is to put education first.

It's what led Thomas Jefferson to leave as his legacy not just the Declaration of Independence, but a university in Virginia. It's what led a nation that was being torn apart by civil war to still set aside acreage, as a consequence of President Lincoln's vision, for the land-grant institutions to prepare farmers and factory workers to seize the promise of an industrial age. It's what led our parents and grandparents to put a generation of returning GIs through college and open the doors of our schools and universities to people of all races, which broadened opportunity and grew our middle class and produced a half a century of prosperity.

And that recognition that here in this great country of ours, education and opportunity, they always go hand in hand, that's what led the first president of the University of Texas to say, as he dedicated the cornerstone of the original Main Building, "Smite the rocks with the rod of knowledge and fountains of unstinted wealth will gush forth."

That's the promise at the heart of UT Austin. But that is also the promise at the heart of our colleges and of our universities, and it is the promise at the heart of our country, the promise of a better life, the promise that our children will climb higher than we did. That promise is why so many of you are seeking a college degree in the first place. That's why your families scrimped and saved to pay for your education.

And I know that as we make our way through this economic storm, some of you may be worried about what your college degree will be worth when you graduate and how you're going to fare in this economy and what the future holds. But I want you to know, when I look out at you, when I look into the faces of America's young men and women, I see America's future,

and it reaffirms my sense of hope. It reaffirms my sense of possibility. It reaffirms my belief that we will emerge from this storm and we will find brighter days ahead, because I am absolutely confident that if you keep pouring yourselves into your own education, and if we as a nation offer our children the best education possible, from cradle through career, not only will America—workers compete and succeed, America will compete and succeed.

And we will complete this improbable journey that so many of you took up over 3 years ago. And we're going to build an America where each of us, no matter what we look like or where we come from, can reach for our dreams and make of our lives what we will.

Thank you, Austin. Thank you, Texas. God bless you, and God bless the United States of America. Thank you. Good luck to the T.

NOTE: The President spoke at 2:05 p.m. In his remarks, he referred to Mack Brown, head coach, and D. Colt McCoy, former quarterback, University of Texas football team; and State Sen. Kirk Watson of Texas.

Statement on Secretary of Defense Robert M. Gates's Fiscal Reform Agenda
August 9, 2010

Today Secretary Gates advanced our effort to invest in the defense capabilities that we need in the 21st century, while being responsible and accountable in spending taxpayer dollars.

I have long said that we need to change the way that Washington works so that it works better for the American people. That's why we undertook the Accountable Government Initiative, to make Government more open and responsive to the American public and to cut waste and inefficiencies that squander the people's hard-earned money. This effort is particularly important when it comes to our national defense, since waste and inefficiency there detracts from our efforts to focus resources on

serving our men and women in uniform and to invest in the future capabilities we need.

Today's announcement by Secretary Gates is another step forward in the reform efforts he has undertaken to reduce excess overhead costs, cut waste, and reform the way the Pentagon does business. The funds saved will help us sustain the current force structure and make needed investments in modernization in a fiscally responsible way. Change is never easy, and I applaud Secretary Gates and his team for undertaking this critical effort to support our men and women in uniform and strengthen our national security. These reforms will ensure that our Nation is safer, stronger, and more fiscally responsible.

Remarks at a Democratic Senatorial Campaign Committee Fundraiser in Highland Park, Texas
August 9, 2010

Well, thank you very much, everybody. It is wonderful to be with you. And I just first of all want to thank Russell and Dori for the wonderful hospitality in a gorgeous home. So thank you very much. Give them a big round of applause.

And I want to also say thank you for doing such a great job training my Ambassador, Ron Kirk. [*Laughter*] He has been doing yeoman's work internationally, and I know it's because he has such good friends in Dallas who, along with Matrice, keep him straight. [*Laughter*] So we are pleased to have him in the administration. He is just a great friend as well as a great national leader.

And thanks to all of you who've done so much not only to help support my campaign in 2008, but to help Democrats here in Texas, here in Dallas County, and all across the United States of America.

I was down in Austin before we came here, and I mentioned that Austin was really the first big rally we had after I had just announced that I was running for President of the United States back in February of 2007. We had more than 20,000 people show up. And so I have a lot of friends in Texas, a lot of friends in Dallas, a lot of friends in Austin.

And I was reminded of a story Abraham Lincoln used to tell about a guy who came to see him looking for patronage work. He had really tried to get in to see the President, and back then, security was a little more lax than it is now. And eventually, he got an audience with the President. And he looked at Lincoln, and he said: "You know, I am responsible for you being in office. If it wasn't for me, you would not be here." And Lincoln said, "Is that true?" He said, "Yes." He said, "Well, I forgive you." [*Laughter*]

There are times, given all the gray hairs that I've been accumulating here over the last 2 years, that I understand Lincoln's joke. But obviously, being President is the most extraordinary privilege that anyone could have, and with it comes such sober responsibilities. That's particularly at a time of great national challenge.

All of you remember the wonderful spirit that existed in Washington on that very cold January day when I was sworn in, but I think we also have to remind ourselves that in the previous 6 months, we had already lost 3 million jobs, that the financial system had all but locked up and was on the verge of meltdown. The month that I was sworn in, we lost 750,000 jobs; subsequently, we lost 600,000 jobs in each month after that. The stock market plunged, the country had lost trillions of dollars' worth of wealth, and people were talking about us possibly tipping into a Great Depression.

And so we knew we had to act quickly, and we did. And as a consequence of the actions we took, not all of which were popular at the time, we were able to stabilize the financial system and get finance circulating again. We were able to stabilize the economy, stop just the complete bloodletting of jobs throughout the economy. And whereas we were losing 750,000 jobs every single month, we're now—we have now seen private sector job growth for 7 consecutive months. Where we were contracting at a rate of 6 percent per quarter, we're now growing once again.

And so there is a sense that we are now moving in the right direction, but understanding that we've got to move a little faster. We've got to keep on going. Because there are a lot of people here in Dallas, there are a lot of people all across America, who are struggling. I see it every single time I pick up a letter from a constituent who's working hard, has sent out resume after resume, and yet just haven't gotten hired yet; or the person who was laid off just on the verge of retirement, and they're trying to figure out, how can I ever possibly afford to retire? What are we going to do, because our—we had saved for our child's college education, but now we're on the verge of losing our house, and we're having to make that horrible choice between our child's future and the needs of the present?

So we've got some big challenges out there. And the question we're going to have in this election is whether we're going to continue down a path of creating greater opportunity, making that opportunity available to all people. Are we going to become more competitive in this 21st-century economy, or are we are going to go backwards to the exact same policies that got us into this mess in the first place?

And if you don't think that's what the choice is, you haven't been paying attention to what the other side is offering for November. I mean, this is not a situation where the Republicans, having run the economy into the ground, having taken record surpluses when Bill Clinton left office and turned them into record deficits, this is not a situation where they've done a bunch of reflection here. They didn't go off into the desert and say to themselves, "Boy, we really screwed up." [*Laughter*] "You know, I don't know exactly what we did wrong here, but gosh, things did not work out the way we expected. Let's come up with some new ideas for moving the country forward in how we're going to educate our kids and provide health care to all Americans and make sure that we've got the highest college graduation rates once again, that research and development and innovation here in this country is on the move."

That's not what's happened. They are not offering a single idea that is new. All they are offering is retreads of what they've offered before.

And so what they're counting on in this election is amnesia. [*Laughter*] They're counting on you not remembering the disastrous consequences of economic policies that, by the way, had caused problems for working class families, for middle class families before the recession hit, before the crisis hit. We had had almost a decade of sluggish growth, sluggish job growth, and incomes and wages that had flatlined, even as the cost of health care, the cost of college tuition, the cost of energy had all skyrocketed.

And so they are not offering a single new idea. They are counting on you forgetting that it was a consequence of these policies that got us into this mess in the first place.

You know, I've been using the analogy of the folks who drove the car into the ditch. And so

we decided, you know what, we're going to do the responsible thing. We put on our boots, we got into the mud, we got into the ditch. We pushed, we shoved, we're sweating. They're standing on the sidelines sipping a Slurpee— [*laughter*]—sort of watching us, saying, "Well, you're not pushing hard enough," or, "Your shoulder is not positioned the right way," giving us a whole bunch of advice on how to push, not lifting a finger to help.

And finally, we get this car up back on the road again, and finally, we're ready to move forward again. And these guys turn around and say, "Give us the keys." Well, no, you can't have the keys back; you don't know how to drive. You don't know how to drive.

They don't know how to drive. And I also want to point out, by the way, when you want to go forward in a car, what do you do? You put it in "D." [*Laughter*] When you want to go backwards, you put it in "R." [*Laughter*] We cannot go backwards; we've got to move forwards. That's what we're fighting for in this election: moving forwards.

Think about what we've done over the last 20 months to move the country forward. Not only did we prevent another Great Depression, not only did we stabilize the financial system, but we have finally enshrined the idea that every American should be able to get health care that's affordable and nobody should be bankrupt when they get sick.

We've done so, by the way, combining those reform efforts with the strongest patient bill of rights than we've ever seen so that insurance companies can't drop your coverage; can't deny you coverage because you've got a preexisting condition; making sure that young people are able to stay on their parents' health insurance until they're 26 years old; eliminating lifetime limits that were causing people great hardship; and reducing costs, so that the Medicare trustees just last week said that as a consequence of health reform, we have extended the life of Medicare for another 12 years, meaning this was one of the most important deficit-reduction steps that we could have taken.

We have instituted a financial regulatory reform package that makes sure that we're not going to have taxpayers bailouts again, at the same time making sure that you as consumers are not being taken advantage of, so that credit card companies can't just raise your rates arbitrarily on existing balances or mortgage companies can't have hidden fees or mortgage brokers can't steer you into more expensive interest rates on your mortgage.

We have instituted housing reform. We have instituted credit card reform. We have made sure that tobacco companies can't market to our kids. We have raised national mileage standards on cars and trucks—the first time in 30 years—so that we have the opportunity now to make sure that the clean energy cars of the future are made right here in the United States of America.

We have created wind turbine plants and solar plants all across America and are creating an advanced battery manufacturing industry in this country. Where we used to have 2 percent of that market, we're going to have 40 percent of that market by 2015, in 5 years. Oh, and by the way, we've also appointed two Supreme Court Justices.

So that's what we've got to offer, and we're just getting started. Because we've got more work to do. The problem we've got right now is we've got folks on the other side of the aisle who have spent 20 months politicking, while we've spent those 20 months governing. They've been thinking about the next election instead of the next generation.

I mean, think about it. When the leader of the Republicans on the House side was asked, "What's your idea for job creation?" he said, "Repeal health care reform." [*Laughter*] I don't know what jobs that would create, except maybe for the guys who are paid to deny you claims.

When they asked them about Wall Street reform, they said, no, we think actually the status quo is okay. Now, think about this. You have the worst financial crisis since the 1930s, and they said no to reforming the system.

When we had a crisis down in the Gulf—unprecedented oil spill—and I went down there and I met with fishermen and small-business owners who were being devastated economically and were seeing their way of life potentially

threatened, and we made sure that BP was going to be accountable to those folks and put together a $20 billion fund to make sure they were getting paid off, what happened? The guy who would be in line to chair the Energy Committee on behalf of the Republicans apologized to BP, said, "We are sorry about the President shaking you down." That's how he characterized our efforts to make sure that people were treated fairly after a big oil company wrecked their livelihood.

So across the board, what you see is a governing philosophy on their part that basically comes down to, we're going to extend tax cuts for the wealthiest among us, folks who don't need those tax cuts and weren't even asking for them, which would cost $700 billion. These are the folks who say they're concerned about the deficit, but are willing to spent $700 to those who are luckiest and least in need in our society.

Their agenda is, we're going to eliminate rules and regulations that rein in special interests, and then we're going to cut the middle class loose—say, you're on your own. You can't afford health care? Tough luck, you're on your own. You can't afford to send your kids to college? Tough luck, you're on your own. You can't afford to retire? Too bad, you're on your own.

That is the philosophy that held sway in Washington for 8 years before I came in, and that is what they want to go back to.

So I just want everybody here to understand very clearly, this is a sharp and clear choice. If you are interested in a clean energy future in which we continue to build our solar industry and wind power and biodiesel and natural gas and we are shaping a strategy to wean ourselves off our dependence on foreign oil, then you better go out there and support those Democratic members of Congress. Because the other side is just going to say no to that.

If you are interested in ending tax cuts for companies that ship jobs overseas, and instead want tax cuts to go to small businesses—like the bill that we've got right now in the Senate that would eliminate capital gains for small businesses, would be additional tax cuts on top of the eight tax cuts we've already given to small businesses so far—then you'd better go out there and help some Democratic candidates. Because the other side is not interested in helping folks who are starting things up; they're interested in the special interests who can afford to hire lobbyist in Washington.

If you're interested in things like equal pay for equal work—because I've got two daughters, and I want to make sure they're treated just like any boys as they're coming up—then you better make sure that you're working on behalf of these Democratic candidates out here, because we've got a big job ahead of us.

I was just down in Austin talking about education. We have gone in a single generation from ranking number 1 in college graduates to ranking number 12 in this country. We cannot compete if we lose our edge when it comes to having the best colleges and the best universities in the country, but also the best trained workers. Which is why one of the things that we did—didn't get a lot of notice over the last 20 months, but one of the most important thing we did was we eliminated the middleman on the Federal student loan program and obtained an additional $60 billion to provide student loans to millions of more young people all across America. By the way, the other side said no to that. The other side wouldn't have anything to do with it. They thought it was a bad idea.

So we're going to have choice after choice on every single issue that you care deeply about. If you care about education, if you care about health care, if you care about civil rights and equal pay for equal work, if you care about consumer protections, if you care about jobs and growth in this economy, if you care about building a new foundation so that we're not just going back to the same tired, wornout theories that didn't work for the last decade, but are instead instituting something that's going to work for the 21st century, then we're going to need you to really step up and work hard in this election.

Now, that's hard to do at a time when people are feeling like, boy, this is a polarized electorate. And it makes people dispirited—all the yelling and the shouting and the cable chatter and the punditry. And I'll be honest with you, sometimes Democrats, we're our own worst enemies, because we can do great stuff and somehow still feel depressed. [*Laughter*] You know, there's—sometimes we do a little too much handwringing—say, well, you know, I don't know; I wish we had gotten that public option. Well, that's great, but we got 31 million people health insurance, and we're reducing costs for people, and we are—[*applause*]—consumer protections when it comes to the health insurance industry.

We have had an extraordinary record of accomplishment over the last 20 months, and we can continue those efforts, but we're going to need you in this election season. We've got to have you talking to your friends; we've got to have you talking to your neighbors, your coworkers. We're going to need you to contribute to congressional candidates, who are going to have very tough races out there.

And part of what's happened in this landscape is the Supreme Court—those of you who don't think the Supreme Court matters, their ruling in *Citizens United*, which said that corporations, including potentially foreign corporations, can go ahead and spend unlimited amounts, without disclosing who they are, during election season, means that you're going to have a whole bunch of organizations like Americans for Prosperity—[*laughter*]—spending millions of dollars trying to roll back reforms that we've initiated. And you won't even know who they are, because right now the law says they don't have to disclose who they are.

Now, we're going to try to change that. We've got legislation in the Senate and the House that says, you know what, the least we can do is—on behalf of our democracy—is to make sure that if somebody is spending millions of dollars to try to influence an election, they've got to disclose who they are. That's the least we can do so the American people know who's out there making these arguments.

But the other side won't have any of that, because they want help and support from those special interests, and they don't want to face up to the consequences if the American people knew who was paying for these ads.

So we've got some tough work ahead of us. We've got some headwinds because we're still working our way out of this hole. We're going to have a lot of money on the other side. They think that the American people have forgotten how badly they mismanaged this economy. And the only way we are going to win is if all of you are engaged and informed and are out there engaging and informing other people.

But in the end, I'm confident you can do that. Remember when I started this fascinating journey, not a lot of people knew who I was. In fact, nobody could pronounce my name. But there were people all across America who had this basic sense that we had put off for too long some things that were holding this country back and who believed that there's nothing we can't accomplish when a group of citizens decide it's time to go out and about and bring about change.

That sense of fundamental optimism, that sense that this country still has its best days ahead of it, that belief that if we make sure that our young people get the educational opportunities they deserve, if we are spurring innovation, if we are making sure that we have a free market that works because it's got rules of the road that work for everybody and not just those who are well connected in Washington, that be-

lief that America works best when it's inclusive and everybody has a shot at the American Dream, that's what propelled me into office. That's what moved so many of you to get involved. That's what we're going to have to rekindle over the next several months.

I'm confident we can do it. And when we do—if you guys are working hard, if you're making those phone calls and sending out those e-mails and doing what needs to be done—I feel very optimistic not just about the next election, but more importantly, I feel optimistic about the next generation.

Thank you very much everybody. God bless you.

NOTE: The President spoke at 4:34 p.m. at the residence of Russell W. and Dorothy A. "Dori" Budd. In his remarks, he referred to Matrice Ellis-Kirk, wife of U.S. Trade Representative Ronald Kirk; Supreme Court Associate Justice Elena Kagan; House Republican Leader John A. Boehner; and Rep. Joseph L. Barton. The transcript was released by the Office of the Press Secretary on August 10. Audio was not available for verification of the content of these remarks.

Remarks on Legislation Creating the Education Jobs Fund
August 10, 2010

Good morning, everybody. One of the biggest challenges of this recession has been its impact on State and local communities. With so many Americans unemployed or struggling to get by, States have been forced to balance their budgets with fewer tax dollars, which means that they've got to cut critical services and lay off teachers and police officers and firefighters.

Now, it's one thing for States to get their fiscal houses in order and tighten their belts like families across America. Because families have been doing it, there's no reason that States can't do it too. That's a welcome thing. But we can't stand by and do nothing while pink slips are given to the men and women who educate our children or keep our communities safe. That doesn't make sense. And that's why a significant part of the economic plan that we passed last

year provided relief for struggling States, relief that has already prevented hundreds of thousands of layoffs.

And that's why today we're trying to pass a law that will save hundreds of thousands of additional jobs in the coming year. It will help States avoid laying off police officers, firefighters, nurses, and first-responders. And it will save the jobs of teachers like the ones who are standing with me today. If we do nothing, these educators won't be returning to the classroom this fall. And that won't just deprive them of a paycheck, it will deprive the children and parents who are counting on them to provide a decent education. It means that students in Illinois and West Virginia who count on Rachel and Shannon are going to be not getting the education that they deserve. It will deprive countless cities and towns of the law enforcement officials and first-responders who risk their lives to keep us out of harm's way. It will cost us jobs at a time when we need to be creating jobs. In other words, it will take us backwards at a time when we need to keep this country moving forward.

Now, this proposal is fully paid for, in part by closing tax loopholes that encourage corporations to ships American jobs overseas. So it will not add to our deficit. And the money will only go toward saving the jobs of teachers and other essential professionals.

It should not be a partisan issue. I heard the Republican leader in the House say the other day that this is a special interest bill. And I suppose if America's children and the safety of our communities are your special interests, then it is a special interest bill. But I think those interests are widely shared throughout this country. A challenge that affects parents, children, and citizens in almost every community in America should not be a Democratic problem or a Republican problem. It is an American problem.

I'm grateful that two Republicans joined Democrats to pass this proposal in the Senate last week. And I'm equally grateful that Speaker Pelosi has called back the House of Representatives to a special session so that they can vote as well.

I urge members of both parties to come together and get this done so that I can sign this bill into law. I urge Congress to pass this proposal so that the outstanding teachers who are here today can go back to educating our children. America's watching, and America's waiting for Washington to act. So let's show the Nation that we can.

I want to thank Rachel as well as Shannon not only for being here today but for the extraordinary work that they're doing each and every day with special education children, with kindergarteners so that they're getting off to a right start. And I also want to thank Arne Duncan, who has been doing as much as anybody all across the country to try to emphasize how important it is to make sure that we are providing a first-class education to every single one of our children.

This bill helps us do that. And so it's time for Democrats and Republicans to come together and get it done.

Thank you very much, everybody.

NOTE: The President spoke at 11:43 a.m. in the Rose Garden at the White House. In his remarks, he referred to Rachel Martin, kindergarten teacher, Park Forest, IL; Shannon Lewis, special education teacher, Romney, WV; House Republican Leader John A. Boehner; and Sens. Olympia J. Snowe and Susan M. Collins. He also referred to H.R. 1586.

Statement on the Death of Former Senator Theodore F. Stevens
August 10, 2010

A decorated World War II veteran, Senator Ted Stevens devoted his career to serving the people of Alaska and fighting for our men and women in uniform. Michelle and I extend our condolences to the entire Stevens family and to the families of those who perished alongside Senator Stevens in this terrible accident.

Remarks on Signing the United States Manufacturing Enhancement Act of 2010
August 11, 2010

Thank you very much. Everybody, please have a seat. Good afternoon, everybody. Welcome to the White House.

From the day I took office, my administration's highest priority has been to rescue our economy from crisis, rebuild it on a new foundation for lasting growth, and do everything we can, every single day, to help the American people whose lives have been upended by a brutal recession.

Now, we knew from the beginning that reversing the damage done by the worst financial crisis and the deepest recession in generations would take some time, more time than anyone would like. And we knew that it would require an ongoing effort across all fronts.

Now, the challenges we face have been confirmed not just by the economic data that we've seen since last spring, when events in Europe roiled the markets and created headwinds for our economic recovery. They're also confirmed every day in the conversations that I have with folks around the country and in the letters that I read at night, stories of Americans who are still looking for work and the men and women who are still struggling to grow their businesses and hire in these challenging times.

So while we have fought back from the worst of this recession, we've still got a lot of work to do. We've still got a long way to go. And I'm more determined than ever to do every single thing we can to hasten our economic recovery and get our people back to work. So that's why I'm pleased today to sign into law a bill that will strengthen American manufacturing and American jobs. And as I do, I'm joined by two members of my economic team, Secretary of Commerce Gary Locke, who's been a tireless advocate for America's manufacturers, and Ambassador Ron Kirk, who's been doing a great job and putting in a lot of miles as our U.S. Trade Representative.

A few areas of our economy have been as hard hit as manufacturing, not just in recent years, but in recent decades. Throughout the 20th century, manufacturing was the ticket to a better life for generations of American workers. It was the furnace that forged our middle class. But over time, the jobs dried up. Companies learned to do more with less and outsourced whatever they could. Other nations didn't always live up to trade agreements and we didn't always enforce them. And over the last decade, the manufacturing workforce shrank by 33 per-

cent, leaving millions of skilled, hard-working Americans sitting as idle as the plants that they once worked in. This was before the recent recession left them and millions more struggling in ways they never imagined.

Now, some suggest this decline is inevitable, that the only way for America to get ahead is to leave manufacturing communities and their workers behind. I do not see it that way. The answer isn't to stop building things, to stop making things; the answer is to build things better, make things better, right here in the United States. We will rebuild this economy stronger than before, and at its heart will be three powerful words: Made in America.

For too long, we've been buying too much from the rest of the world, when we should be selling more to the rest of the world. That's why in my State of the Union Address, I set an ambitious goal for this country. Over the next 5 years, we are going to double our exports of goods and services, an increase that will grow our economy and support millions of American jobs. We've got a lot of work to do to reach this goal. Our economy has fallen into the habit of buying from overseas and not selling the way it needs to. But it is vitally important that we reverse that trend. After all, 95 percent of the world's customers and the world's fastest growing markets are beyond our borders. And when the playing field is even, American workers can compete with anybody. And we're going to compete aggressively for every job, for every industry, and every market out there.

That's why we fought for and passed tax breaks for companies that are investing here in the United States rather than companies that are keeping profits offshore. That's why we closed loopholes that encourage corporations to ship American jobs overseas. That's why we're enforcing our trade laws, in some cases, for the very first time. That's why we told America's automakers that if they made the tough decisions required to compete in the future, that America would stand by them. And that's why we're investing in a clean energy industry and the jobs that come with it, jobs that pay well and carry

America to a cleaner, more secure, and more energy-independent future.

Now, already we're beginning to see some of these investments pay off. I've seen it myself in factories where American workers are now manufacturing wind turbines and solar panels, components for the advanced batteries of tomorrow.

I've seen it in retooled auto plants where American workers are building high-quality, fuel-efficient cars and trucks that can go toe to toe with any in the world. In fact, for the first time in more than 5 years, the Big Three are operating at a profit. And the auto industry has added 76,000 jobs since last June. That's the strongest period of job growth in more than 10 years.

So overall, the manufacturing sector has actually added 183,000 jobs so far this year. That's the strongest 7 months of manufacturing job growth in more than a decade. Instead of plants leaving America to set up shop overseas, we've actually begun to see the opposite: a growing number of firms setting up shop and hiring here at home.

So we're not yet where we need to be, but there are some good trends out there. And we can't let up. We've got to keep moving forward. And that's why today I'm signing a bill into law that will make it cheaper and easier for American manufacturers and American workers to do what they do best: build great products and sell them around the world.

The Manufacturing Enhancement Act of 2010 will create jobs, help American companies compete, and strengthen manufacturing as a key driver of our economic recovery. And here's how it works. To make their products, manufacturers—some of whom are represented here today—often have to import certain materials from other countries and pay tariffs on those materials. This legislation will reduce or eliminate some of those tariffs, which will significantly lower costs for American companies across the manufacturing landscape, from cars to chemicals, medical devices to sporting goods. And that will boost output, support good jobs here at home, and lower prices for American consumers.

This bill passed both Houses of Congress on an overwhelmingly bipartisan basis, and I want to thank Democrats and Republicans for coming together on behalf of America's businesses and workers. And before I sign it into law, I want to take this opportunity to encourage that same kind of bipartisan spirit on another step that will create jobs and move America forward.

The extraordinary growth we've seen in the clean energy sector is due first and foremost to the entrepreneurial drive of our businesses and our workers. But it's also due to the fact that we invested in them. One of these investments came in the form of clean energy manufacturing tax credits. What we said to clean energy firms was, if you're willing to put up 70 percent of the capital for a worthy endeavor, we'll put up the other 30 percent. That means that for every dollar we invest, we leverage more than two private sector dollars.

The only problem we have is these credits worked so well, there weren't enough to go around. More than 180 clean energy projects in over 40 States received $2.3 billion in tax credits, but the program was such a success that we received 500 qualified applications for $8 billion in tax credits.

So I believe that if an American company wants to innovate, grow, and create jobs right here in the United States, we should give them the support they need to do it. That's why I'm urging Congress, once again, to invest $5 billion in these clean energy manufacturing tax credits. It's an investment that will generate $12 billion or more in private sector investment and tens of thousands of new jobs.

And as I've said before, the nation that wins the race for the clean energy economy will lead the 21st-century economy. Other nations know this. They've been investing heavily in that future. They want those jobs. But the United States of America doesn't play for second place. We compete to win. And we will win this if we move forward free of politics and are focused on just what it takes to get the job done.

This is an idea that already has bipartisan support, but it's been delayed for months. So my simple message is, don't let politics get in the way of doing what's right for our economy and for our future, and don't bet against the American worker or lose faith in American industry. This is a nation that has always been proud of what it builds, and it is that spirit that's going to lead our recovery forward.

We've been through tough times before, and it is precisely in those times that we rebuilt, we retooled, we recaptured the ingenuity and resilience that makes this Nation so great. That's how our predecessors built the first American century. That's how we'll build the next. And it's in that spirit that I will now sign this bill into law. Thank you very much, everybody.

NOTE: The President spoke at 3:07 p.m. in the East Room at the White House. H.R. 4380, approved August 11, was assigned Public Law No. 111–227.

Statement on the Observance of Ramadan
August 11, 2010

On behalf of the American people, Michelle and I want to extend our best wishes to Muslims in America and around the world. *Ramadan Kareem.*

Ramadan is a time when Muslims around the world reflect upon the wisdom and guidance that comes with faith and the responsibility that human beings have to one another and to God. This is a time when families gather, friends host iftars, and meals are shared. But Ramadan is also a time of intense devotion and reflection, a time when Muslims fast during the day and pray during the night, when Muslims provide support to others to advance opportunity and prosperity for people everywhere. For all of us must remember that the world we want to build and the changes that we want to make must begin in our own hearts and our own communities.

These rituals remind us of the principles that we hold in common, and Islam's role in advancing justice, progress, tolerance, and the dignity of all human beings. Ramadan is a celebration of a faith known for great diversity and racial equality. And here in the United States, Ramadan is a reminder that Islam has always been part of America and that American Muslims have made extraordinary contributions to our country. And today I want to extend my best wishes to the 1.5 billion Muslims around the world—and your families and friends—as you welcome the beginning of Ramadan.

I look forward to hosting an iftar dinner celebrating Ramadan here at the White House later this week, and wish you a blessed month. May God's peace be upon you.

Statement on Congressional Passage of Southwest Border Security Legislation
August 12, 2010

I have made securing our Southwest border a top priority since I came to office. That is why my administration has dedicated unprecedented resources and personnel to combating the transnational criminal organizations that traffic in drugs, weapons, and money and smuggle people across the border with Mexico. Today's action by Congress answers my call to bolster the essential work of Federal law enforcement officials and improve their ability to partner with State, local, and tribal law enforcement. The resources made available through this legislation will build upon our successful efforts to protect communities along the Southwest border and across the country. And this new law will also strengthen our partnership with Mexico in targeting the gangs and criminal organizations that operate on both sides of our shared border. So these steps will make an important difference as my administration continues to work with Congress toward bipartisan comprehensive immigration reform to secure our borders and restore responsibility and accountability to our broken immigration system.

Letter to Congressional Leaders on Continuation of Emergency Regarding Export Control Regulations
August 12, 2010

Dear Madam Speaker: (Dear Mr. President:)

Section 202(d) of the National Emergencies Act (50 U.S.C. 1622(d)) provides for the automatic termination of a national emergency unless, prior to the anniversary date of its declaration, the President publishes in the *Federal Register* and transmits to the Congress a notice stating that the emergency is to continue in effect beyond the anniversary date. In accordance with this provision, I have sent to the *Federal Register* for publication the enclosed notice, stating that the emergency caused by the lapse of the Export Administration Act of 1979, as amended, is to continue in effect for 1 year beyond August 17, 2010.

Sincerely,

BARACK OBAMA

NOTE: Identical letters were sent to Nancy Pelosi, Speaker of the House of Representatives, and Joseph R. Biden, Jr., President of the Senate. This letter was released by the Office of the Press Secretary on August 13. The notice is listed in Appendix D at the end of this volume.

Statement on India's Independence Day
August 13, 2010

On behalf of my administration and the American people, I wish to congratulate all who will celebrate the 63d anniversary of India's independence. Indians around the world can not only look back on their history with pride, but can also look ahead to a future filled with hope and further progress. Ever since August 15, 1947, India's nonviolent struggle for freedom, its rejection of terrorism and extremism, and its belief in democracy, tolerance, and the rule of law have been an inspiration and beacon of hope for people around the world. India's example has had a profound effect on many countries, including the United States. Leaders of our civil rights movement, including Dr. Martin Luther King, Jr., spoke about the debt they owed to Mahatma Gandhi. Ties between our two peoples have never been stronger. The over 2 million members of the Indian American community are living examples of the bonds that bind our nations together and their accomplishments have become well known and admired in both countries. The strategic partnership between our countries will continue to grow, and I am looking forward to my November visit to India. Our goal is to make this one of the defining partnerships of the 21st century. Once again, congratulations and best wishes for a happy and safe independence day.

Statement on Pakistan's Independence Day
August 13, 2010

On behalf of the people of the United States of America, I send my congratulations and sincere best wishes to all who will celebrate the 63d anniversary of Pakistan's independence. Here at home, I am proud of the many contributions Pakistani Americans have made to our Nation and will continue to make in the years to come. Pakistan's independence day is a useful time to reflect on the friendships Pakistan has in the world and the expressions of true friendship that come in a time of need.

This independence day anniversary also comes at a time of great challenge for the people of Pakistan as they bravely respond to widespread and unprecedented flooding. In line with the deepening partnership between our two nations, I have directed my administration to continue to work closely with the Government of Pakistan and provide assistance in their response to this crisis. We have rushed financial assistance, life-saving and life-sustaining relief supplies, helicopters, rescue boats, and disaster management experts to assist the Pakistani authorities. The people of America stand with the people of Pakistan through this difficult time and will continue to urge the international community to increase their support and assistance. We will remain committed to helping Pakistan and will work side by side with you and the international community toward a recovery that brings back the dynamic vitality of your nation.

Statement on South Korea's Independence Day
August 13, 2010

On behalf of the American people, I congratulate the Republic of Korea and all those of Korean descent in the United States and around the world on the celebration of their independence day on August 15. In the 62 years since the founding of the Republic of Korea, our two nations have enjoyed a strong and enduring alliance. We are bound by a common belief in the values of democracy and freedom. Sixty years ago, Communist armies came across the 38th parallel and threatened the very survival of the Republic of Korea. Our alliance was as necessary then as it is now. As I said during my visit to Seoul last fall, our commitment to the security and defense of the Republic of Korea will never waver. Here in the United States, Korean Americans have contributed greatly to our Nation in all facets of life, from business and science to sports, the arts, and public service. I send my best wishes on this year's Korean independence day.

Remarks at the Iftar Dinner
August 13, 2010

Good evening, everybody. Welcome. Please, have a seat. Well, welcome to the White House. To you, to Muslim Americans across our country, and to more than 1 billion Muslims around the world, I extend my best wishes on this holy month. *Ramadan Kareem.*

I want to welcome members of the diplomatic corps, members of my administration, and Members of Congress, including Rush Holt, John Conyers, and Andre Carson, who is one of the two Muslim American Members of Congress, along with Keith Ellison. So welcome, all of you.

Here at the White House, we have a tradition of hosting iftars that goes back several years, just as we host Christmas parties and Seders and Diwali celebrations. And these events celebrate the role of faith in the lives of the American people. They remind us of the basic truth that we are all children of God and we all draw strength and a sense of purpose from our beliefs.

Now, these events are also an affirmation of who we are as Americans. Our Founders understood that the best way to honor the place of faith in the lives of our people was to protect their freedom to practice religion. In the Virginia Act of Establishing Religious Freedom, Thomas Jefferson wrote that "all men shall be free to profess, and by argument to maintain, their opinions in matters of religion." The First Amendment of our Constitution established the freedom of religion as the law of the land, and that right has been upheld ever since.

Indeed, over the course of our history, religion has flourished within our borders precisely because Americans have had the right to worship as they choose, including the right to believe in no religion at all. And it is a testament to the wisdom of our Founders that America remains deeply religious, a nation where the ability of peoples of different faiths to coexist peacefully and with mutual respect for one another stands in stark contrast to the religious conflict that persists elsewhere around the globe.

Now, that's not to say that religion is without controversy. Recently, attention's been focused on the construction of mosques in certain communities, particularly New York. Now, we must all recognize and respect the sensitivities surrounding the development of Lower Manhattan. The 9/11 attacks were a deeply traumatic event for our country. And the pain and the experience of suffering by those who lost loved ones is just unimaginable. So I understand the emotions that this issue engenders. And Ground Zero is, indeed, hallowed ground.

But let me be clear. As a citizen and as President, I believe that Muslims have the right to practice their religion as everyone else in this country. And that includes the right to build a place of worship and a community center on private property in Lower Manhattan, in accordance with local laws and ordinances. This is America. And our commitment to religious freedom must be unshakeable. The principle that people of all faiths are welcome in this country and that they will not be treated differently by their government is essential to who we are. The writ of the Founders must endure.

We must never forget those who we lost so tragically on 9/11, and we must always honor those who led the response to that attack, from the firefighters who charged up smoke-filled staircases to our troops who are serving in Afghanistan today. But let us also remember who we're fighting against and what we're fighting for. Our enemies respect no religious freedom. Al Qaida's cause is not Islam; it's a gross distortion of Islam. These are not religious leaders; they're terrorists who murder innocent men and women and children. In fact, Al Qaida has killed more Muslims than people of any other religion, and that list of victims includes innocent Muslims who were killed on 9/11.

So that's who we're fighting against. And the reason that we will win this fight is not simply the strength of our arms; it is the strength of our values, the democracy that we uphold, the freedoms that we cherish, the laws that we apply

without regard to race or religion or wealth or status. Our capacity to show not merely tolerance, but respect towards those who are different from us, and that way of life, that quintessentially American creed, stands in stark contrast to the nihilism of those who attacked us on that September morning and who continue to plot against us today.

In my Inaugural Address, I said that our patchwork heritage is a strength, not a weakness. We are a nation of Christians and Muslims, Jews and Hindus, and nonbelievers. We are shaped by every language and every culture, drawn from every end of this Earth. And that diversity can bring difficult debates. Our—this is not unique to our time. Past eras have seen controversies about the construction of synagogues or Catholic churches. But time and again, the American people have demonstrated that we can work through these issues and stay true to our core values and emerge stronger for it. So it must be—and will be—today.

And tonight we are reminded that Ramadan is a celebration of a faith known for great diversity. And Ramadan is a reminder that Islam has always been a part of America. The first Muslim Ambassador to the United States, from Tunisia, was hosted by President Jefferson, who arranged a sunset dinner for his guest because it was Ramadan, making it the first known iftar at the White House, more than 200 years ago.

Like so many other immigrants, generations of Muslims came to forge their future here. They became farmers and merchants, worked in mills and factories. They helped lay the railroads. They helped to build America. They founded the first Islamic center in New York City in the 19—in the 1890s. They built America's first mosque on the prairie of North Dakota. And perhaps the oldest surviving mosque in America, still in use today, is in Cedar Rapids, Iowa.

Today, our Nation is strengthened by millions of Muslim Americans. They excel in every walk of life. Muslim American communities, including mosques in all 50 States, also serve their neighbors. Muslim Americans protect our communities as police officers and firefighters and first-responders. Muslim American clerics have spoken out against terror and extremism, reaffirming that Islam teaches that one must save human life, not take it.

And Muslim Americans serve with honor in our military. At next week's iftar at the Pentagon, tribute will be paid to three soldiers who gave their lives in Iraq and now rest among the heroes of Arlington National Cemetery. These Muslim Americans died for the security that we depend on and the freedoms that we cherish. They're part of an unbroken line of Americans that stretches back to our founding, Americans of all faiths who have served and sacrificed to extend the promise of America to new generations and to ensure that what is exceptional about America is protected: our commitment to stay true to our core values and our ability, slowly but surely, to perfect our Union.

For in the end, we remain "one Nation, under God, indivisible." And we can only achieve "liberty and justice for all" if we live by that one rule at the heart of every great religion, including Islam, that we do unto others as we would have them do unto us.

So thank you all for being here. I wish you a blessed Ramadan. And with that, let us eat.

NOTE: The President spoke at 8:37 p.m. in the State Dining Room at the White House. The Office of the Press Secretary also released Arabic, Bengali, Dari, French, Hindi, Indonesian, Persian, Punjabi, Russian, Kurdish, and Urdu language transcripts of these remarks.

The President's Weekly Address
August 14, 2010

Seventy-five years ago today, in the midst of the Great Depression, Franklin Roosevelt signed Social Security into law, laying a cornerstone in the foundation of America's middle class and assuring generations of America's seniors that after a lifetime of hard work, they'd have a chance to retire with dignity. We have an obligation to keep that promise, to safeguard Social Security for our seniors, people with disabilities, and for all Americans, today, tomorrow, and forever.

Now, we've been talking for a long time about how to do that, about how to make sure Social Security is healthy enough to cover the higher costs that are kicking in now that baby boomers are retiring. And I'm committed to working with anyone, Democrat or Republican, who wants to strengthen Social Security. I'm also encouraged by the reports of serious bipartisan work being done on this and other issues in the fiscal commission that I set up several months ago.

One thing we can't afford to do though is privatize Social Security, an ill-conceived idea that would add trillions of dollars to our budget deficit while tying your benefits to the whims of Wall Street traders and the ups and downs of the stock market.

A few years ago, we had a debate about privatizing Social Security. And I'd have thought that debate would've been put to rest once and for all by the financial crisis we've just experienced. I'd have thought, after being reminded how quickly the stock market can tumble, after seeing the wealth people worked a lifetime to earn wiped out in a matter of days, that no one would want to place bets with Social Security on Wall Street, that everyone would understand why we need to be prudent about investing the retirement money of tens of millions of Americans.

But some Republican leaders in Congress don't seem to have learned any lessons from the past few years. They're pushing to make privatizing Social Security a key part of their legislative agenda if they win a majority in Congress this fall. It's right up there on their to-do list with repealing some of the Medicare benefits and reforms that are adding at least a dozen years to the fiscal health of Medicare, the single longest extension in history.

That agenda is wrong for seniors, it's wrong for America, and I won't let it happen, not while I'm President. I'll fight with everything I've got to stop those who would gamble your Social Security on Wall Street. Because you shouldn't be worried that a sudden downturn in the stock market will put all you've worked so hard for, all you've earned, at risk. You should have the peace of mind of knowing that after meeting your responsibilities and paying into the system all your lives, you'll get the benefits you deserve.

Seventy-five years ago today, Franklin Roosevelt made a promise. He promised that from that day forward, we'd offer, "some measure of protection to the average citizen and to his family against . . . poverty-stricken old age." That's a promise each generation of Americans has kept. And it's a promise America will continue to keep so long as I have the honor of serving as President.

Thanks for listening. Thanks for watching. And have a wonderful weekend.

NOTE: The address was recorded at approximately 4:05 p.m. on August 13 in the Library at the White House for broadcast on August 14. The transcript was made available by the Office of the Press Secretary on August 13, but was embargoed for release until 6 a.m. on August 14.

Remarks at the United States Coast Guard Station Panama City in Panama City Beach, Florida
August 14, 2010

Good afternoon, everybody. It is a privilege to be here in Panama City Beach with the men and women of the United States Coast Guard. I wanted to come here personally and express my gratitude to you for the effort that you've waged in response to the BP oil spill. And I know Michelle wanted to do the same, so we're looking forward to having a chance to shake hands with you and thank you personally for this great work that you've been doing day in, day out.

Michelle, just last month, was down in Mississippi, where she met folks from the Coast Guard about the spill, and she had the chance to christen the new cutter the *Stratton*.

The Coast Guard was the first on the scene, immediately launching a search-and-rescue operation for the missing. You were the first to recognize that we were potentially looking at a massive spill even before the rig collapsed and the oil began to leak from the seafloor. And a day and a half later, in a meeting with Thad Allen and others, I instructed the Coast Guard, the Department of Homeland Security, and other agencies to treat this response as their number-one priority. And that's exactly what all of you have done.

Under the leadership of Admiral Allen, the Coast Guard, along with other Federal agencies and State and local governments, has directed the largest response to an environmental disaster in American history. The response has included more than 7,000 vessels and more than 47,000 people on the ground. And I know that two cutters, the *Aspen* and the *Juniper*, are here in port this week, after tours skimming and performing other recovery work. As I said before, many of the folks here have toiled day and night, spending weeks, even months, away from their families to stop the leak, remove the oil, and protect waters and coastline. So I want to thank all those who continue to participate in this effort.

I also want to make mention and thank Dr. Steven Chu and our team of scientists assembled from across Federal agencies, around the country, and all over the world, who have been working nonstop to kill the well once and for all. This has not only been the biggest oil spill in our history; it's also been the most technologically complex. It pushed the boundaries of our scientific know-how, as engineers wrestled with a massive and unpredictable leak and faced setbacks, faced complications, all in pitch-black waters nearly a mile beneath the surface of the Gulf.

Well, today the well is capped. Oil is no longer flowing into the Gulf. It has not been flowing for a month. And I'm here to tell you that our job is not finished, and we are not going anywhere until it is. That's a message that I wanted to come here and deliver directly to the people along the Gulf Coast, because it's the men and women of this region who have felt the burden of this disaster. They've watched with anger and dismay as their livelihoods and their way of life was threatened these past few months. And that's why I made a commitment in my visits here that I was going to stand with you not just until the well was closed, not just until the oil was cleaned up, but until you have fully recovered from the damage that's been done. And that is a commitment that my administration is going to keep.

That also is why my Secretary of the Navy, Ray Mabus, is here. A former Governor of Mississippi, a son of the Gulf, he has been traveling all across this region, gathering up information and data to make sure that we are following through on our commitments for rebuilding.

I reiterated this just now when I met with a few small-business owners from the Panama City area, along with Governor Charlie Crist, and not only the mayors of this region, but also some of the business owners who are affected, folks like Captain Gary Jarvis, a charter boat operator from Destin. Gary started fishing as a deckhand back in 1978, and he's been captain for the past three decades, making his living on the water. He's lost fully half of his business because of the spill, though he's been able to use his boat as a vessel of opportunity to make some money in the past few months. And he's extraordinarily knowledgeable about these waters, being both a charter fisherman and a commercial fisherman. And he had some terrific suggestions about how, working with scientists from NOAA and other Federal agencies, we can do even more to make sure that we are monitoring and maintaining and improving the fishing off the coast of Florida and across the Gulf.

I also had a chance to speak to Lee Ann Leonard, general manager of By the Sea Resorts. She's seen a big decline in tourism. June wasn't too bad, but July was tough. And she's now hoping that August, September, and October can help them rebound from what have been significant losses.

I met with Carolyn Holman, who's got two commercial fishing boats and owns the Captain's Table Fish House in Panama City Beach with her husband. And I appreciated the chance to sit down with them to hear firsthand what they've been going through and to make clear that we're going to keep standing by them. Part of the concern that Carolyn expressed was the issue of seafood and our testing and making sure that it's safe. And we are all over that and monitoring that carefully each and every day, hopefully continuing to deliver good news as the days go on. And I mentioned to her that we already had some seafood in the White House. When the New Orleans Saints came up, we had a couple of po' boys. So right now we're feeling pretty good.

I also want to recognize that Mayor Gayle Oberst and Mayor Scott Clemons had some terrific suggestions about how we might help to diversify the economies down here so that they're in a better position to, if we ever had a crisis again, manage it, but more importantly, to provide more jobs and opportunity in this extraordinary and beautiful region.

Now, I want to go over a couple of the steps that we are going to be focused on over the next several weeks. First and foremost, we're going to continue to monitor and remove any oil that reaches the surface and clean up any oil that hits the shore. As I mentioned, Gary has been offering up his ship as a vessel of opportunity, and he confirms what you've been seeing in the news reports, which is there aren't a lot of patches out there that are visible right now. But we've got to constantly anticipate that at any given time you might see a patch of oil that starts coming in, and we've got to be able to capture that before it hits these beautiful beaches around here.

As a result of the massive cleanup operation that's already taken place, a recent report by our top scientists found that the majority of oil has now evaporated or dispersed or it's been burned, skimmed, or recovered from the wellhead. And the dispersed oil is in the process of degrading. But I will not be satisfied until the environment has been restored, no matter how long it takes.

I also want to point out that as a result of the cleanup effort, beaches all along the Gulf Coast are clean, they are safe, and they are open for business. That's one of the reasons Michelle, Sasha, and I are here. The Governor and the mayors and others invited us down to enjoy the beach and the water, to let our fellow Americans know that they should come on down here. It is spectacular. Not just to support the region; come down here because it's just a beautiful place to visit.

Next, we're going to continue testing fisheries, and we'll be reopening more areas for fishing as tests show that the waters are safe. Already, more than 26,000 square miles were reopened at the end of July and another 5,000 were reopened earlier this week. I know this takes some time, and it's been incredibly hard on the people who earn their living on the water. Carolyn's boats, for example, have had to find different areas to fish that are further away and require more fuel, so she's been having to make some decisions, maybe I don't send out my boat this time out. But their livelihoods, not to mention the health of the people across this country, obviously depends on making sure that folks can trust the seafood coming from the Gulf, trust that it's safe, as it always has been.

And as I told Carolyn, we've already been enjoying Gulf seafood, but we are going to keep on monitoring this to make sure that everybody's favorite seafood from the Gulf and favorite recipes are going to be treated—are going to be just fine.

The third thing we're focused on is claims. When I came down to the Gulf previously, I heard a lot of frustration about the way BP was handling claims. So in June I met with BP's executives, and in that meeting they agreed to put aside $20 billion in a special fund to pay damages. It's being run by an independent overseer so that people can trust that they'll get a fair shake. Now we need to make sure claims are processed quickly, because many who have lost their only source of income, they don't have a lot of leeway. They don't have months to wait to be compensated. The folks we just met with—Lee Ann, Gary, Carolyn—they've all got outstanding claims. So I want to be clear about this.

Any delay by BP or those managing the new funds are unacceptable. And I will keep pushing to get these claims expedited.

Finally, I have charged, as I mentioned earlier, Ray Mabus to develop a long-term Gulf Coast restoration plan as soon as possible. That plan needs to come from the people in the Gulf, which is why he's been meeting with folks from across the region to develop this plan of action. That's how we can ensure that we do everything in our power to restore the environment and reverse the economic damage caused by the spill.

So with the closure of the well, we mark an important milestone. But this is not the end of the journey. And in completing the work ahead I'm reminded of what I heard when I was in Louisiana back in June. I spent time with folks on Grand Isle, meeting with fishermen and small-business owners and the town's mayor, David Camardelle. And he told me what his friends and neighbors were going through. He talked about how hard things had been. But he also explained the way folks rallied to support one another, he said, the people in this community may not have a lot of money, but that didn't matter. "We help each other," he said. "That's what we do."

That's what folks do for one another in the Gulf. That's what the Coast Guard has been doing for folks in need. That's what we do as Americans. And my job is to make sure that we live up to this responsibility, that we keep up our efforts until the environment is clean, polluters are held accountable, businesses and communities are made whole, and the people of the Gulf Coast are back on their feet.

So, to the men and women of the Coast Guard, thank you again for your extraordinary service. To the people here in the Gulf, we are going to be standing by your side. And to Americans all across the country, come on down and visit.

Thank you.

NOTE: The President spoke at 12 p.m. In his remarks, he referred to Adm. Thad W. Allen, USCG (Ret.), in his capacity as national incident commander for the Deepwater Horizon oil spill; Gov. Charles J. Crist, Jr., of Florida;

Mayor Gayle Oberst of Panama City Beach, FL; Mayor Scott Clemons of Panama City, FL; and Special Master for TARP Executive Compensa- tion Kenneth R. Feinberg, in his capacity as ad- ministrator of the BP Deepwater Horizon oil spill compensation fund.

Remarks at ZBB Energy Corporation Manufacturing Facility in Menomonee Falls, Wisconsin
August 16, 2010

Thank you very much. Everybody, please have a seat. Thank you very much. It is wonder- ful to be at ZBB Energy. And thanks for your hospitality, and thanks for helping to build a fu- ture.

I've got a couple of people I want to acknowl- edge. First of all, your wonderful Governor and first lady, Jim and Jessica Doyle, are here. Please give them a big round of applause. We got somebody who is fighting on behalf of Wis- consin families each and every day, Russ Fein- gold, your wonderful U.S. Senator, a great friend and somebody who has been really doing great work over her first couple of years in Con- gress, Congresswoman Gwen Moore. Please give her a big round of applause. And thank you, Eric, for the wonderful tour that you pro- vided to us. Please give Eric Apfelbach a big round of applause, CEO of ZBB.

Now, it is great to be here. I just had a chance to see some of the batteries that you're manufacturing and talk to a few of the men and women who are building them. And the reason I'm here today is because at this plant, you're doing more than just making high-tech batter- ies; you're pointing the country towards a brighter economic future.

Now, that's not easy. We've been through a terrible recession, the worst that we've seen since the Great Depression. And this recession was the culmination of a decade that fell like a sledge hammer on middle class families. For the better part of 10 years, people were seeing stagnant incomes and sluggish growth and sky- rocketing health care costs and skyrocketing tu- ition bills, and people were feeling less secure economically.

And few parts of the economy were hit hard- er than manufacturing. Over the last 10 years, the number of people working in manufactur- ing shrank by a third. And that left millions of skilled, hard-working Americans sitting idle, just like their plants were sitting idle. That was before the recession hit. Obviously, once the re- cession took hold, millions more were strug- gling in ways that they never imagined. And there's nobody here who hasn't been touched in some way by this recession. And certainly a State like Wisconsin or my home State of Illi- nois can tell a lot of stories about how badly hit manufacturing was, particularly in the Midwest.

Now, there's some who suggest this decline is inevitable. But I don't see it that way, and I know neither do you. Yes, times are tough, but we've been through tough times before, and we've made it through because we are resilient. Americans are resilient. We don't give in to pes- simism. We don't give in to cynicism. We fight for our future. We work to shape our own desti- ny as a country.

And that's what we've been trying to do since I took office. We've been fighting on all fronts—inch by inch, foot by foot, mile by mile—to get this country moving forward again and going after every single job we can create right here in the United States of America.

So we're investing in 21st-century infrastruc- ture, roads and bridges, faster Internet access, high-speed railroads, projects that will lead to hundreds of thousands of private sector jobs but will also lay the groundwork so that our kids and our grandkids can keep prospering.

We've cut taxes for small businesses that hire unemployed workers. In fact, I've signed seven other small-business tax cuts so that entrepre- neurs can help expand and buy new equipment and add more employees. We've taken emer- gency steps to prevent layoffs of hundreds of thousands of teachers and firefighters and po- lice officers and other critical public servants in our communities. And I think that Governor Doyle will testify that we have made progress in part because everybody has pulled together. There was a great danger of even greater layoffs all across this State for vital services that would affect our kids and our families. These folks would have otherwise lost their jobs because of State and local budget cuts.

And at the same time, what we've been trying to do—and that's why I'm here at ZBB—is to jump-start a homegrown clean energy industry, building on the good work of your Governor and others in this State. That's why I'm here today. Because of the steps we've taken to strengthen the economy, ZBB received a loan that's helping to fund an expansion of your operations. Already it's allowed ZBB to retain nearly a dozen workers. And over time, the company expects to hire about 80 new workers. And this is leading to new business for your suppliers, including MGS Plastics and other manufacturers here in Wisconsin.

And ZBB is also planning to take advantage of a special tax credit to build another factory in southeastern Wisconsin, so we can create even more jobs and more opportunity. And Eric's confident that you can expand because you're seeing rising demand for advanced batteries. And all this is part of steps we've taken in clean energy, steps that have led to jobs manufacturing wind turbines and solar panels, building hybrid and electric vehicles, modernizing our electric grid so that we have more sources of renewable energy, but we can also use it more effectively.

We expect our commitment to clean energy to lead to more than 800,000 jobs by 2012. And that's not just creating work in the short term; that's going to help lay the foundation for lasting economic growth. I just want everybody to understand, just a few years ago, American businesses could only make 2 percent of the world's advanced batteries for hybrid and electric vehicles—2 percent. In just a few years, we'll have up to 40 percent of the world's capacity.

Here at ZBB, you're building batteries to store electricity from solar cells and wind turbines. And you've been able to export batteries

around the globe, and that's helping lead this new industry. For years, we've heard about manufacturing jobs disappearing overseas. Well, companies like this are showing us how manufacturing's—can come back right here in the United States of America, right back here to Wisconsin.

Now, obviously, we've got a lot more work to do. The damage that was done by this recession was enormous. Eight million people lost their job; 750,000 lost jobs the month I was sworn into office; 3 million had lost their jobs by the time we took office, and several more million in those first few months of 2009. So too many of our family members and our friends and our neighbors are still having a tough time finding work. And some of them have been out of work a long time.

And I've said before and I'll say it again: My administration will not rest till every American who is willing to work can find a job, and a job that pays decent wages and decent benefits to support a family.

But what's clear is that we're headed in the right direction. A year and a half ago, this economy was shrinking rapidly. The economy is now growing. A year and a half ago, we were losing jobs every month in the private sector. We've now added private sector jobs for 7 months in a row. And that means the worst mistake we could make is to go back to doing what we were doing that got us into the mess that we were in. We can't turn back. We've got to keep going forward. We've got to keep going forward.

Now, I'll be honest with you, there's going to be a big debate about where we go. There are folks in Washington right now who think we should abandon our efforts to support clean energy. They've made the political calculation that it's better to stand on the sidelines than work as a team to help American businesses and American workers.

So they said no to the small-business tax cuts I talked about. They said no to rebuilding infrastructure. And they said no to clean energy projects. They even voted against getting rid of tax breaks for shipping jobs overseas so we could give those tax breaks to companies that are investing right here in Wisconsin.

And my answer to people who've been playing politics the past year and a half is, they should come to this plant. They should go to any of the dozen new battery factories or the new electric vehicle manufacturers or the new wind turbine makers or to the solar plants that are popping up all over this country, and they should have to explain why they think these clean energy jobs are better off being made in Germany or China or Spain, instead of right here in the United States.

See, when folks lift up the hoods on the cars of the future, I want them to see engines stamped "Made in America." When new batteries to store solar power come off the line, I want to see printed on the side "Made in America." When new technologies are developed and new industries are formed, I want them made right here in America. That's what we're fighting for. That's what this is about.

So, ZBB, you're part of that process. You guys are at the cutting edge. You're how we're going to strengthen this economy.

These have been a couple of very hard years for America, and we're not completely out of the woods yet. There are going to be some more tough days ahead. It would be a mistake to pretend otherwise. But we are headed in the right direction. You're pointing us in the right direction. And I am confident about our future because of what I have seen at this plant and what I see when I talk to workers like all of you, what I've seen all across this country. When the chips are down, it's always a mistake to bet against the American worker; it's a mistake to bet against American businesses; it's a mistake to bet against the American people.

This is the home to the most skilled, hardworking people on Earth. There's nothing we cannot achieve when we set our minds to it. All we've got to do is harness the potential that's always been central to our success. That's not just how we're going to come through the storms we've been in recently; that's how we're going to emerge even stronger than before.

So I want to say thank you to Eric. I want to thank ZBB for hosting us. More importantly, I want to thank all of you for setting a model for how we're going to create the kind of lasting economy that's going to be good not just for this generation, but for the next generation.

Thank you very much, everybody. God bless you. God bless America. Thank you.

NOTE: The President spoke at 11:08 a.m.

Remarks at a Rally for Gubernatorial Candidate Thomas M. Barrett in Milwaukee, Wisconsin
August 16, 2010

Thank you. Hello, Milwaukee! Thank you very much. Everybody, please have a seat. Have a seat. It is good to be back in Milwaukee, good to be back in the Midwest. Good to be out of Washington once in a while. [*Laughter*] Good to be in the great State of Wisconsin.

And looking out at this crowd, I know that so many of you did so much on behalf of my campaign. You were with us when we were up; you were with us when we were down. So if it weren't for so many of you, I would not be standing here as President today. And I am grateful to all of you. So thank you very much.

We've got a few special guests that I want to acknowledge: Your outstanding Governor and wonderful first lady, Jim and Jessica Doyle, are in the house; one of the finest Senators we have and a pretty good owner—although he talks a lot of smack about the Bucks versus the Bulls—[*laughter*]—we're going to see this year—Senator Herb Kohl; and a wonderful Member of Congress, Congresswoman Gwen Moore is here.

Now, as your President, it is my honor to stand here—where I understand Al McGuire won the championship with Marquette a while back—[*applause*]—see, just the smattering of applause shows that I'm getting older—[*laughter*]—because I vividly remember that championship and about half of you don't. [*Laughter*]

But it's also a great honor to be here with Wisconsin's next Governor, Milwaukee's own Tom Barrett.

Now, Tom is the kind of leader this State needs right now. He's the kind of leader this country needs right now. This is a man of character. He hasn't forgotten where he came from. Grew up right here in Wisconsin, started off after college working on the assembly line at Harley-Davidson. And ever since then, he has been fighting to bring jobs and opportunity and hope to the people of this State.

And as this city's mayor, he's had success. He helped turn around the industrial wasteland into a thriving commercial center that supports nearly 3,000 jobs. He helped start a regional economic development group that helped bring another 2,000 jobs to Wisconsin in the past 10 months, a time when those jobs were desperately needed. No other candidate has this kind of record on jobs. No other candidate has put forth the kind of detailed plan that Tom's had—has been able to put forward to make sure that this State's economy is moving forward. And under his watch, this city has held the line on property taxes, it's expanded opportunity, it's put more cops on the street, and reduced crime as a result. But the most impressive thing about Tom goes beyond his accomplishments as an elected official. It goes to who he is as a human being. It goes to his character.

You know, I've heard stories about mayors who personally respond to calls about potholes and parking tickets and snowed-in driveways. But I've never heard about a mayor who risked his life to respond to an actual cry for help. That is some serious customer service from this mayor right here. Tom gets embarrassed when folks bring this up, but what he did for a local woman and her baby granddaughter when they were threatened by domestic violence, that's the kind of act you don't hear about every day. He stepped in, he tried to help, sustained serious injuries as a result. That's what counts in a leader—when the cameras aren't rolling, when nobody is watching—that's the mark of real character.

That means this is a person who is going to fight for you each and every day. And that's why I know Tom Barrett is going to win this race and lead Wisconsin to a better day. That's the kind of leader we need. It's the kind of leader we need for an incredibly challenging time for America.

Eighteen months ago, I took office after nearly a decade of economic policies that gave us sluggish job growth and falling incomes and falling wages and a record deficit, policies that culminated in the worst recession in our lifetimes. In the last 6 months of 2008, 3 million American jobs were lost—3 million. The month I swore—I was sworn in, we lost nearly 800,000 jobs that month, January 2009; 600,000 the next month; 600,000 the month after that.

And behind each of these stories is a story of heartache and frustration: a factory worker who was just a few years shy of retiring suddenly loses his job at the local plant; or a single mom who keeps sending out job applications everywhere she can, and still waiting for the phone to ring, day after day after day; a college graduate who thought her degree would land her a good job with a decent paycheck, instead just has a mountain of debt; or a college—somebody who was bound for college suddenly found out that they couldn't afford it, had to defer their dreams.

I hear these stories every day. Every night, I read letters from folks around the country, good, decent people who are having a tough time, middle class families who never thought they would see the kind of hardship that they're seeing right now. And those struggles and hopes are why I ran for office in the first place. That's why so many of you supported me. And that's why I intend to keep fighting as hard as I can, for as long as it takes, until we turn this economy around. That is why I'm here. That is our goal. That's why Tom Barrett is running for Governor, to get this economy moving so every single person in Wisconsin who wants to work can find a job. That's what we're fighting for.

Now, we're not there yet. We know that. It's going to take a few years to repair the damage that was caused by this recession. But I am confident—as confident as I've been about anything—that we are headed in the right direction. This Nation is moving in the right direction. We are moving forward. And the most important thing we can do right now is to keep moving forward.

We need to keep our economy growing. We need to keep adding private sector jobs. We need to keep making progress on all these fronts, and we've got to do it faster.

What we don't need, the worst thing we could do, is to go back to the very same policies that created this mess in the first place. That's the worst thing we could do. And in November, you're going to have that choice. The American people are going to walk into that voting booth and the question is going to be, are we going to move forward, or are we going to move backwards?

We didn't get to this point by accident. We got here after nearly 10 years of an economic agenda in Washington that was pretty easy to sum up: You cut taxes for millionaires and billionaires, you cut rules for special interests, you cut working folks loose to fend for themselves. If you're out of a job, tough luck, you're on your own. Don't have enough money for college? Tough luck, you're on your own. You don't have health insurance? Too bad, you're on your own. That was the philosophy of the last decade: You are on your own.

And now that we've actually begun to make progress, what we're seeing from the other side is just offering more of the same. I mean, think about it. This is not a situation where the Republicans, after having presided over these disastrous policies, said, you know what, we should go reflect for a while. We should go off into the desert and kind of think through, boy, we really messed up. [*Laughter*] Maybe we should come up with some new ideas to see if we can plot a new direction for the party. That's not what they're offering. They are offering the exact same policies that you rejected in 2006, that you rejected in 2008, because you knew they weren't working.

Think about it. I mean, they've said as much. People have asked them, "Well, what are you going to do different this time?" "Nothing. We want to go back to what we were doing." If you're a Wall Street banker or an insurance company or an oil company like BP, you get to play by your own rules. If you have special interests in Washington that don't like oversight, we're going to give you some breaks, maybe we'll give you some more tax cuts, all at the expense of middle class families and at the expense of the country as a whole.

That's why we've got a record deficit and the weakest economy since the Great Depression. And I bring this up not because I want to relitigate the past, I just don't want us to relive the past. I don't want us to relive the past.

And what the other side is basically counting on right now is amnesia. [*Laughter*] That's basically what they're counting on. It's as if they drove a car into the ditch and then we had to put on our boots and go down there in the mud, and we've been pushing and shoving. And they've been standing aside and watching us and saying, "You're not pushing right." [*Laughter*] "You're not pushing fast enough." You know, they're drinking on a Slurpee or something and—[*laughter*]—"No, no."

So we're huffing and puffing, and we finally get this car out of the ditch, finally have it on level ground. We're moving forward. And they turn to us and say, "We want the keys." [*Laughter*] Well, you can't have the keys back. You don't know how to drive. [*Laughter*] You got us into the ditch. You can get in the backseat if you want.

If you want to make your car go forward, what do you do? You put it in "D." [*Laughter*] If you want it going backwards, what do you do? You put it in "R." [*Laughter*] That's not an accident.

They can't have the keys back. We don't mind them hitching a ride. [*Laughter*] But we're not going to keep on doing the same things that got us into this mess. That's the choice in this election: Do we go back to the policies of the past, or do we keep moving forward—the policies that are getting us out of this mess?

And the America I believe in, it always moves forward. The America we believe in is a country that rewards hard work instead of greed, an America that rewards responsibility instead of recklessness. We did not become the most prosperous nation on Earth by letting special interests run wild. We did it by investing in people who've always built this country from the ground up: workers and middle class families and small-business owners and responsible entrepreneurs. We did it by outworking and outeducating and outcompeting the rest of the world. That's what we did, and that's what we need to do again.

Other countries are out there, they're competing, they're fighting for the jobs of the future: China, India, Germany, South Korea. And let me tell you, Milwaukee, the United States of America does not play for second place. We play for first place. We are going to rebuild this economy and we're going to rebuild it better and stronger than it was before. And at that heart of that strategy will be three powerful words: Made in America. We are going to make things right here in the United States of America and sell them all around the world.

Our choice in this election is between policies that encourage job creation in America and policies that encourage job creation someplace else. So instead of giving tax breaks to companies that ship jobs overseas, we want to cut taxes for small-business owners who create jobs right here in the United States of America.

We want to jump-start a homegrown clean energy industry. I don't want to see new solar panels and wind turbines and electric cars manufactured someplace else. I want to see them stamped with "Made in America," by American workers. We're investing in a 21st-century infrastructure, not just new roads and bridges, but faster Internet access and high-speed railroads, projects that can lead to hundreds of thousands of new private sector jobs.

And these ideas shouldn't be Democratic or Republican ideas. They are commonsense ideas. And yet most of the Republicans in Congress voted no on just about every one of these policies. Do you remember when I was running, we had a little slogan: "Yes, we can." These guys' slogan is, "No, we can't." [*Laughter*] No on closing loopholes for companies that ship jobs overseas; no on the tax cuts for small businesses; no on the clean energy jobs; no on the railroad and highway projects.

Just this weekend, the Republican leader in the Senate said—this is a quote from the Republican leader in the Senate—"I wish we had been able to obstruct more." Obstruct more? Is that even possible? [*Laughter*]

So apparently, that's their plan for the future: No, we can't. Clean energy? No, we can't. Health care? No, we can't. Wall Street reform? No, we can't.

Think about this. We had the worst financial crisis since the Great Depression, almost resulted in a complete meltdown, 8 million jobs lost. And when we try to repair the system to maintain innovation in the financial system, but to make sure that people have some idea what kind of mortgage they're buying or what kind of credit card interest is being charged, or making sure that if one bank goes down, taxpayers don't have to bail it out in order to ensure that the whole system goes down, they said no.

That kind of politicking they might think serves them for the next election. But that's not why Tom is running. That's not why I'm President. That's not why you're here. We're not here for the next election. We are here for the next generation. That is our priority, to think about the future, and that's the difference in this election. That's the choice in this election.

On issue after issue, the Republicans in Congress have sided with corporate special interests over middle class families. A few weeks ago, the Republican leader of the House was asked what his jobs plan was if he took control of Congress next year. You know what he said? "My number-one priority is repealing health care reform." That's his jobs plan—[*laughter*]—not his health care plan, his jobs plan.

Now, this is reform that finally prevents insurers from denying or dropping coverage because of an illness, reform that cuts taxes for small-business owners who cover their employees, so they're now getting a—35 percent of the premiums they're paying for their employees they're now getting a tax break for. It allows young adults to stay on their parents' coverage until they're 26. It lowers the price of prescription drugs for our seniors. It's going to lower the cost of health care for every American. The actuaries just reported 2 weeks ago that this is going to extend the life of Medicare, making it more secure for the next generation.

Now, I'm not sure how reform will create jobs, except for insurance executives who deny your claims. But I do know this. I got a letter a few weeks ago from a man in New Hampshire. In March, his wife was diagnosed with a serious form of cancer. They had no health insurance because her cancer was classified as a preexisting condition. Denied coverage by every insurance company they tried, they couldn't afford coverage on the individual market. But she desperately needed treatment. They had no idea what to do. And because reform finally passed, she now has health insurance. Because reform passed, she is now getting treatment. For the first time in history, a preexisting illness will not prevent you from getting covered.

That's the law you want to repeal? They're siding with the insurance companies who want to go back to the days when they could drop that woman from coverage or deny that woman coverage. But we can't afford to go backward. We need to move this country forward.

Same thing with the financial system: We can't go back to a status quo that almost brought this country to its knees. We've got to move forward so that, in fact, you now know what credit card companies are charging you for interest and mortgage companies can't steer you to the more expensive interest rate on your mortgage and there will not be taxpayer bailouts.

They say they want to repeal this. That can't be a strategy for the future. That's not what we're fighting for. That will not help middle class families across America. That's not going to help put people back to work. That should be something that we should get the parties to agree to.

The same thing is true on clean energy. And the same thing is true on equal pay for equal work. And the same thing is true for not having tobacco companies market to children. These are commonsense ideas. Democrats and Republicans across the country should be able to support it. But we've got folks in Washington who are more concerned with the next election than they are with the next generation.

So I know that Tom is going to have a tough race. Everybody is going to have a tough race across this country because we're going through tough times. But I just want everybody here, when you're talking to your friends, your neighbors, your coworkers, constantly ask the question, who do you think is fighting for you? Who is on your side?

When we had this disaster in the Gulf, thankfully, now we've capped the well, but a lot of people have been harmed. I just came back from there. You got folks who may have lost 50 percent of their revenues, if they're a small business; fishermen who put everything they had into the fishing season and suddenly they were without any customers. And we saw that happening, and we said, you know what, we're going to talk to BP, and we are going to make sure that BP meets their obligations and their claims. And we structured a $20 billion fund so that we could assure that all those fishermen and small-businesspeople and people who had lost their jobs that they would be taken care of. And the leading Republican on the Energy Committee, who would be in charge of energy if the Republicans took Congress, he apologized to BP— apologized to BP. He said, "You know what, this $20 billion fund is a shakedown." I think he called it a "Chicago-style shakedown." [*Laughter*] This is somebody who could be running our energy policy if the other party takes over. He wasn't apologizing to all those folks who had been affected because BP had caused this accident. He was apologizing to them.

That can't be the kind of leadership that we need going into the 21st century. We can't go backwards. We have to move forward. That's what's at stake in this election. If we give them the keys to this economy, they are going to drive it right back into the ditch. And riding shotgun will be the big banks and the insurance companies and the oil companies and every special interest under the Sun.

And I want to be very clear here: I want businesses in this country to succeed. And the vast majority of folks out here who are running a business, they are doing what's right by their communities and their workers. And I want to do everything we can to help you grow and to prosper and hire more employees. We just came back from a company that's building advanced batteries right here in this region, hiring more employees, and we are giving them all the help we can.

But I don't think it's antibusiness to say we should make sure an oil rig is safe before we start drilling. I don't think it's antibusiness to say that Wall Street banks should play the same—play by the same rules as everybody else. I don't think it's antibusiness to say that insurance companies shouldn't prevent that woman in New Hampshire from getting the care she needs because she's got cancer. We can't go back to an attitude that says, "What's good for me is good enough." We've got to start asking, what's good for America? What's best for all of our businesses? What's best for all of our people? That's what we do in this country. We move forward as one people and as one Nation, not just a few of us, but all of us.

A few weeks ago, I had the opportunity to visit a Chrysler plant in Detroit. Now, this is a place that's been hit harder by recession than almost anywhere else in the country. The auto industry alone lost hundreds of thousands of jobs in the year before I took office. Obviously, some of those jobs were lost here in Wisconsin. We had to make a very difficult decision when I was President about whether to walk away from U.S. automakers or help them get back on their feet. And we decided we could not walk away from up to a million jobs and an iconic industry that symbolizes the rise of American manufacturing. And so we told the automakers, we'll give you some temporary assistance, but you've got to restructure your plants so they can finally compete in the 21st century.

Now, most of the "No, we can't" crowd in Washington didn't agree with that decision. And let's face it: It wasn't that popular in the polls. But today, all three American automakers are operating a profit for the first time in over 5 years. They've had the strongest job growth in more than 10 years. All across the Midwest, folks are heading back to factories and building better cars, more energy-efficient cars.

And at the plant I visited, 14 of these workers at this Chrysler plant had just won the lottery.

[*Laughter*] Now, you'd think that most of them would just kick back and retire after that. They could have cashed out. They could have walked away. But it turns out most of them, they're going to work every day. The man who bought the winning ticket is a guy named William Shanteau. He decided to take the money and buy his wife one of the Jeep Grand Cherokees that he had helped to build. And then he went out and bought a bunch of American flags for his hometown, because he loves his country. And he keeps on showing up to work every day, because he loves the company he works for and he loves his coworkers.

And I—when I heard that story, I just wanted to say to all the naysayers in Washington, don't bet against the American worker. Don't lose faith in the American people, because the American people never lose faith in America. We do not give up. We do not quit. We do not fear the future. We shape the future. That's part of what this election is about.

The other side wants you to be afraid of the future. But in times of trial and hardship, we don't give in to fear. We don't give in to division. We move forward. We recapture the ingenuity and optimism of the most dynamic country on Earth. That's how we made the 20th century the American century. That's how we're going to make the 21st century the American century.

And as long as I have the privilege of being your President, I'm going to keep fighting alongside you to reach that better day. And if you give Tom Barrett a chance, he's going to make you proud as Governor, fighting for you to reach that better day.

But we're going to need you out there each and every day. Don't give in to fear. Let's reach for hope. Don't believe, "No, we can't." I believe, yes, we can.

Thank you, Milwaukee. God bless you.

NOTE: The President spoke at 1 p.m. at U.S. Cellular Arena. In his remarks, he referred to Senate Minority Leader A. Mitchell McConnell; House Republican Leader John A. Boehner; Rep. Joseph L. Barton; and Lisa Shanteau, wife of William Shanteau, a Chrysler Jefferson

North Assembly Plant worker who purchased the winning June Powerball jackpot ticket in Curtice, OH. The transcript was released by the Office of the Press Secretary on August 17.

Remarks at a Democratic Congressional Campaign Committee Fundraiser in Los Angeles, California
August 16, 2010

Hello, everybody. What a spectacular evening. Let's just hang out. [*Laughter*] We don't need to make speeches. [*Laughter*]

Well, it is wonderful to see all of you. There are a lot of friends here. There are a couple of people I've got to make special mention of. First of all, obviously, thanks to John and Marilyn for their incredible hospitality. Thank you very much. Please give them a big round of applause.

To the best Speaker of the House that I can imagine working with, she has just been a fighter day in and day out, I couldn't have a better partner in Washington than Nancy Pelosi. Please give her a big round of applause.

My Secretary of Labor is here, California's own Hilda Solis; Democratic Congressional Committee chairman, a thankless job, and he is handling it with grace, Chris Van Hollen; all of the members of California's congressional delegation who are here, I want to just say thank you for your outstanding work.

I'm going to make mention of one person who is not yet member of the congressional delegation, but is going to be soon, the former speaker of the house who is soon going to be the Congresswoman from this district, Karen Bass, is here. Give Karen a big round of applause.

The mayor of Los Angeles, Antonio Villaraigosa, is here. We're not going to let him on a bike any time soon. [*Laughter*] City Council President Eric Garcetti is here. Please give him a round of applause.

And there are at least—just at least two Members of Congress who are here that I just want to make special mention of: Barbara Lee, because she is the chairwoman of the Congressional Black Caucus and is doing outstanding work; and Howard Berman, who is helping to guide us through so many difficult foreign policy challenges, and I'm so grateful to him for his leadership. Please give Howard a big round of applause.

So it is wonderful to be back in Los Angeles. And I look out on this crowd and I see so many friends who helped me to get to the White House. I am reminded of Lincoln's story. He used to tell a story about a guy who showed up at the White House. Security was a little more lax at that time. [*Laughter*] He insists on seeing the President during his office hours, says, "I am the guy who got Lincoln elected." And he kept on badgering whoever was at the door. And finally, Lincoln lets him in. And Lincoln says, "So, sir, I understand you are responsible for me having this job." He says, "That's right." And Lincoln says, "I forgive you." [*Laughter*]

No, I—it is obviously an extraordinary honor to be the President, and an extraordinary privilege to be the President at this moment in history. A lot of people have said to me, "I just can't imagine all the things that you're juggling right now. We've got two wars, coming out of this extraordinary recession that we've gone through." And I say, "This is exactly when you want to be President." This is why I ran, because we have the opportunity to shape history for the better, to create an America that will serve our children and our grandchildren and our great-great-grandchildren well for—if we are taking the right steps, if we recognize this is an inflection point.

And that means it's difficult. That means it's contentious. And that means there's going to be passions that are stirred up that a quieter, more stable time might not. But it's also exactly when I'd want to be in Washington, because I think we have the opportunity to make such a difference for so many people who need that help right now. And I know Nancy feels the same way about being Speaker of the House.

Now, I want to make special mention of what Congress has done and the House of Representatives have done. When you're President, you've got the bully pulpit. And when you're President, you've got 4 years. And as a consequence, I think there are a lot of things I'm very proud of that we've done over the last 2 years. But the pressures on me are different than the pressures on some of these congressional Members.

Nancy has experienced the same thing that Harry Reid has experienced on the Senate side, which is just constant, nonstop opposition on everything. There hasn't been an item that has come up in which there has not been just uniform insistence on the other side that it was a bad idea, that it was going to wreck the country, and that we shouldn't be doing it.

And so for people like Nancy and Chris and all the Members here to have stood up again and again and again under just fierce, withering criticism and opposition, and to do so with a smile on Nancy's face and with the grace with which she's done it, and for the Members who've taken tough vote after tough vote over the course of the last 2 years because they knew it was the right thing to do even when it wasn't the popular thing to do, that's why we're here tonight.

That's my focus over the next several months, because when I ran for the Presidency, my firm belief was, if you did the right thing, then eventually that was going to be good politics. It might not be good politics in the short term, but it was going to be good politics in the long term. I believe that now, just like I believed it then. But we've got to make sure that all those Members in the House of Representatives who believed it and took a lot of big political risks over the last 2 years are rewarded for it.

So I hope you understand why we're here tonight. It's not to take a picture with the President. You know, those—you know, I'm a lot grayer now and—[*laughter*]. But we're here because we want to make sure that those folks who have taken the tough votes are supported.

I want to just remind everybody, because sometimes we've got short memories, of where we've been, the journey we've traveled over the last 20 months. When I was sworn in—a few of you were there; it was very cold that day—in January of 2009—you remember, it was cold—[*laughter*]—yes—that same month, we lost 750,000 jobs. In the 6 months leading up to my Inauguration, we had lost 3 million jobs. In subsequent months, we were losing 600,000, 500,000. Before any of the steps we could take were put into place, we had already seen 8 million jobs lost, the worst financial crisis since the Great Depression, the entire financial system on the verge of meltdown.

And I think it's a good thing that we tend not to remember how worried everybody was. But people were worried. In March, when the stock market was dropping 3, 400 points, people were not sure whether or not we were going to be dipping into a Great Depression.

And so we had to take action, and we had to take action quickly. And not everything we did was popular. But we knew that if we didn't act, if we were thinking about the next election instead of the next generation, then we were putting the country at risk.

So immediately, we took steps to shore up the economy, to lift up demand, to make sure that people who were vulnerable got support, to make sure that States like California were getting enough help that they didn't have to lay off teachers and firefighters and police officers across the board. And it worked. We were able to stabilize the economy.

But that still left all the damage that had already occurred. Eight million jobs had still been lost. And more than that, it still left undone the task that I had been running on as President, which was to create the kind of foundation for economic growth that had been missing for 10 years.

Part of what has made this recession so tough is middle class families were struggling before the crisis hit. They were hurting before the storm struck. They had seen a decade of sluggish growth. They had seen a decade of sluggish job growth. Incomes and wages had gone down for most families when you factored in inflation, at the same time that health care and tuition were all skyrocketing.

So people felt less secure than they'd ever felt. And they kept on seeing jobs moving overseas. And they had a sense that nobody was thinking about them. And you know what? They were right. They were right.

The previous administration and the Republican Congress that had been in charge, they had a simple philosophy. They put a fancy name on it. They called it the "ownership society." But when it came down to it, the philosophy was simple: We are going to cut taxes for millionaires and billionaires, folks who don't need it and weren't even asking for it, we're going to cut regulations and rules that provide some check on special interests, and then we're going to cut loose ordinary folks and tell them, you're on your own. You don't have health care, tough luck, you're on your own. You're a young person and you didn't choose your parents properly and so—[*laughter*]—you're poor, maybe can't afford college, too bad, you're on your own. You got laid off just short of retirement; you don't know what to do, too bad, you're on your own.

That was the reigning philosophy before this recession hit. And that's why I went to Washington, to change that. So our job wasn't just to make sure that we didn't go into a depression; our job was to figure out how are we going to put this economy back on track so it works for everybody, not just some, but for everybody. So every kid here in California is able to say to themselves, if I work hard, if I'm studying, I'm going to be able to afford to go to college. And if I go to college, then I'm going to be able to get a job that pays me a decent wage. And if I've got a job, I'm going to be able to get health care and protect my family. And if I do those right things during the course of my life, I'm going to be able to retire with some dignity and some respect.

That's why we went to Washington. That's why so many of you worked so hard to send me there. And so we had a tough task. We had to rescue the economy, but we also had to remind ourselves that we've got to put this country on a different trajectory than we've been on. And we went about the business of doing that, with the help of Nancy, with the help of Chris, with the help of every Member of Congress here, but

with no help from the other side. And as a consequence, we have been able to deliver the most progressive legislative agenda, one that helps working families in not just one generation, maybe two, maybe three.

So we were able to deliver on health care reform so that we enshrine the principle in this country, the wealthiest on Earth, that nobody should be bankrupt when they get sick. And we were able to make sure that we've got a financial system in which everybody follows the basic rules of the road and you don't make money by cheating people, you make money by offering them decent services.

And then we said, you know what, we're going to make sure that college is accessible to every young person in America. And so we transformed how our student loan program works so that millions more kids are able to get health—able to get help on their student loans and their tuition.

Item after item after item, when you look at what Nancy and the House have done, in combination with Harry Reid in the Senate, what we've delivered is a package of changes that are going to help bolster security for middle class families. And then we looked at the long term, and we said, look, what are we going to do about energy? And as a consequence, invested—made the biggest investments in clean energy in our history, building solar panels and wind turbines and advanced battery manufacturing plants and biodiesel all across the country. And we said, we're going to make the biggest investment in research and development in our history, and we did that. All designed to make sure that we are competitive in a 21st-century economy. And we did all this without any help from the other side.

Now, here's the challenge that we've got. We've got a long way to go. People are still hurting. All across America, I meet folks or I read letters that are sent to me every night: single moms who are sending out application after application and getting no response from potential employers; people who have been laid off their jobs and have been out of work for a year, year and a half, and now they've depleted all their savings and don't know where to turn.

And so in that environment, you can talk about saving the economy from a potential depression and you can talk about the long-term vision that makes me so optimistic about America, but right here, right now we've still got a lot of work to do. And that's what makes this election so challenging.

But having said that, I am absolutely confident that we will do well in this election as long as we understand what this election is about, and that is, we have a choice between the policies that got us into this mess and the policies that are getting us out of this mess. It's a very simple choice. It's pretty straightforward.

I've used this analogy before. You had a group of folks who drove the economy, drove the country, drove our car into the ditch. And so Nancy and Chris and Barbara and Howard and me, we put on our boots and walked down into the ditch. It's muddy and hot and dusty, and bugs everywhere, and—[laughter]—we're pushing and got our shoulders up, and we're slipping and sliding and sweating, and the other side, the Republicans, they're standing there with their Slurpees—[laughter]—watching us, "You're not pushing fast enough." [Laughter] "That's not how you do it. You do it this way." And so every once in a while, we'd offer, "Why don't you guys come down here"—[laughter]—"help us push?" "No, no, no."

Finally, we get this car to level ground. Finally, we're ready to move forward, go down that road once again of American prosperity, and what happens? They want the keys back. [Laughter] And what this election is about is saying to them, you cannot have the keys back. You do not know how to drive. You don't know how to drive. We're not going to let you go us—take us in the ditch again.

I would make this observation. When you are driving and you want to go forward, what do you do? You put your car in "D." [Laughter] You want to go backwards? You put your car in "R." We can't afford to reverse back into the ditch. We've got to go forward. That's what this election is about. That's what this election is about.

Now, the Republicans don't have an affirmative agenda. They're counting on two things: They're counting on fear, and they're counting

on amnesia. [Laughter] They understand the very legitimate fears that people have about the future. And so rather than offer solutions, practical solutions about how we are going to rework our energy policies so that we can deal not only with our national security challenges, not only with our economic challenges, but also create jobs right here in the United States of America—and by the way, maybe save the planet in the process—they don't have an answer for that, just more of the same, same policies. Drill more; that's, I think, basically all we've heard from them.

When it comes to education, we haven't heard new ideas out of them. When it comes to how we're going to spur on innovation in research and development, they're not talking about that. That's not what they are talking about.

When it comes to, supposedly, their signature issue—they want to do something about the big-spending Democrats, "We're going to do something about the deficit." And you keep on asking them, "Okay, well, what are you going to do?" "Well, we're going to cut waste, fraud, and abuse." "Okay, what exactly waste, fraud, and abuse are you going to cut?" "Well, we'll get to that later."

They're offering fear, and they're offering amnesia. They are counting on the notion that you won't remember what happened when they were in charge. I think the American people do remember. I think they understand exactly what happened when Republicans were in charge. And they've also been watching over the last several months, over the last 2 years.

My campaign, you'll recall, our slogan was, "Yes, we can." Their slogan is, "No, we can't," on every item. On health care, how many times, Nancy, did we reach out to them and say, you know what, we are willing to work with you to come up with some sort of cooperative way to make sure that people aren't prohibited from getting health care because of preexisting conditions and to take seriously how we're going to cut costs in our health care system and strengthen Medicare and make sure that people aren't having unnecessary tests when their results could just be e-mailed to doctors because of electronic medical records? All kinds of ideas that we kept on offering up, and, "No, we can't."

On energy, we're willing to compromise on a whole host of different issues, but we've got to have a strategy that starts reducing carbon, because we want those clean energy jobs built here in the United States, not in China, not in Germany. What did they say? "No, no, we can't."

When the auto crisis struck, and we said, we can't afford to lose a million jobs in the Midwest in the midst of this huge downturn, and rather than just write checks to the auto companies, which is what had been happening before our administration took over, what we said was, we're going to force the auto companies to restructure and hold them accountable and make sure management is producing the kinds of cars and trucks that speak to the future and not just the past. And we raised fuel efficiency standards on cars and trucks for the first time in 30 years. And we said to the Republicans, "This represents something iconic about America, the fact that we make things right here in the United States of America. Help us." "No, we can't."

On issue after issue, they've just said no. Mitch McConnell was quoted, I think, last week—maybe it was this week. He said, "If we could have obstructed even more, we would have." Is that even possible? [*Laughter*] How could you obstruct more?

And so that's what the choice in this election is going to be all about. Tax policy is going to be a major issue next year. The Democrats, Nancy, Chris, we want to stop giving tax breaks to companies that ship jobs overseas and give those tax breaks to companies that are creating jobs right here in the United States of America. That's common sense.

And we've got a track record. Right now we've got a bill pending to provide tax breaks, including the elimination of capital gains for small, startup businesses. We've been debating this thing how long now, 6 months, a year? And these guys still aren't going for it. The Chamber of Commerce is for it. [*Laughter*] You know, now, they usually don't side with me on a lot of things—[*laughter*]—although they sided with

me on the Recovery Act, and they've conveniently forgot about that.

So on issue after issue, the choice is going to be, are we moving forward or are we moving backwards? Now, I think that the American people want to move forward. I'm positive of it. And one of the things I've been saying as I travel around the country is, as tough as these times have been, we've been through tougher times. Our grandparents, our great-grandparents, the parents before them, they've gone through revolutionary war, civil wars, slavery and segregation, World War II, great depressions. This country has been through some tough stuff. There have been times where the naysayers and the cynics and the pessimists said, our better days are behind us. There have been times where the main currency of politics was making people afraid, trying to divide them, not offering up a way forward and a way to bring people together, but rather trying to point out who's to blame. We've seen that before.

But time after time, decade after decade, somehow we've always found it in ourselves to reach for what's best in us. We've always been able to set our sights on the future. And as tough and sometimes depressing as our politics can get, in opposition to this notion that we can't, somebody said, we can.

That's the choice in this election. And if all of you who 2 years ago or 4 years ago or 6 years ago, if all of you remember why we worked so hard and what's at stake and understand that our task is not yet done, but also recognize the enormous progress that we've made because of the leadership of these Members of Congress right here, then we're going to do just fine, and this country is going to be just fine.

While I was taking photos, a woman came up to me. She said, "Thank you for health care, because my child has type 1 diabetes, couldn't get health insurance once he graduated, and now I know that he's going to be covered."

Today I was in an advanced battery plant outside of Milwaukee where they are adding manufacturing jobs, stamping green technology "Made in America." Across the country, we're seeing States suddenly reforming their education systems to make sure that we're lifting up those who are underperforming, because we know that we've got to have the best possible workforce to compete in the 21st century. We are making progress. We are moving forward.

And so even as the other side wants to offer fear, we're going to offer hope. And I want to make sure everybody here understands, don't bet against the American worker. Don't bet against American businesses. Don't bet against Nancy Pelosi. [*Laughter*] We are going to move this country forward with your help. We're going to move this country forward with your help, but we are going to need your help. We're going to need your phone calls. We are going to need your knocking on doors. We need your en-

thusiasm. We need your spirit. We need your confidence that we can continue to make this country even better than it already is, all right? And if everybody here is able to marshal that spirit once again, I'm absolutely positive we're not just going to do well in this election, we're going to do right by the next generation.

Thank you very much, everybody. God bless you. God bless the United States of America. Thank you.

NOTE: The President spoke at 7:22 p.m. at the residence of John and Marilyn Wells. The transcript was released by the Office of the Press Secretary on August 17.

Remarks Following a Discussion With Small-Business Owners in Seattle, Washington
August 17, 2010

The President. All right. Hello, everybody. I just sat down here at Grand Central Bakery with the Secretary of Commerce and the former Governor of this great State, Gary Locke, the wonderful senior Senator from the great State of Washington, Patty Murray, as well as these three terrific small-business owners for a good discussion about the challenges that our small businesses face in this very tough economy.

And I have to say before we start, I also had a sandwich, a turkey sandwich here that was outstanding. So if you guys need to eat before we leave, try it out.

Gillian Allen-White and the founders of this bakery like to say that they built this business just like they bake everything, from scratch. What began as a little sandwich shop right here in this building nearly 40 years ago is today 8 cafes in Seattle and Portland that employ 250 people, and they are going to open their ninth cafe on Friday, which we're very excited about.

Tiffany Turner and her husband Brady gave up their careers in teaching and insurance to open their own inn on the coast. And despite the recession, business has been good. They're even looking to expand and hire new employees. For a time, their community bank couldn't

give them the loan they needed to grow, but recently that changed. In fact, many banks like theirs have begun to open the flow of credit to small businesses for the first time in 4 years, and that's good news.

Joe—I'm going to make sure I get this right—Fugere——

Joe Fugere. Fugere.

The President. Fugere—see, I thought I had it right—put everything on the line—his savings, his 401(k), even a second mortgage—to open his first pizzeria. With a little hard work, it succeeded. And he opened two more. After the crisis hit, he sought a loan to open a fourth because business was good. But at bank after bank, Joe heard no. The same big banks whose reckless actions nearly brought down the economy told Joe that loaning money to a restaurant, even one as successful as his, was too risky. Finally, a community bank invested in Joe, and his fourth restaurant has been his most successful opening yet. And recently, an SBA loan under the Recovery Act helped him to improve his cashflow.

So stories like this are at the core of the American experience. This has always been a country where anyone with a good idea and the guts to see it through can succeed. It's what gives a worker the courage to leave her job to become her own boss or somebody with a dream to risk it all on a great idea. But these are tough times for a lot of small-business owners. The financial crisis has made it particularly difficult for them to get the loans they need to grow. The recession has meant that folks are spending less. And across the country, many small businesses that were once the beating heart of the community are now empty storefronts haunting our Main Streets.

So we've all got a stake in helping our small businesses succeed. And because small businesses create two out of every three new jobs in this country, our economic recovery depends on it.

And that's why when I took office, we put in place an economic plan to help small businesses. And Patty Murray was there every step of the way in us putting forward these initiatives. At its heart was a simple idea: While Government can't guarantee their success, Government can knock down the barriers that stand in the way and help create the conditions to help small businesses grow and to hire.

And that's why we've passed eight tax cuts for America's small businesses: tax cuts for hiring unemployed workers, tax cuts for investing in new equipment. As part of health insurance reform, 4 million small-business owners recently received a postcard in their mailboxes telling them that they could be eligible for a health care tax credit worth perhaps tens of thousands of dollars. And I know that Tiffany and her husband are looking now about the possibilities, because of these incentives, to be able to maybe provide health insurance to their workers. Under the Recovery Act, we supported nearly 700—nearly 70,000 new loans to small businesses like Joe's, and we waived fees on new SBA loans so people like Joe save money, up to $20,000 with the SBA arrangement that Joe had.

These steps and others are making some difference. But when you listen to these three business owners and you talk to small-business owners across the country, it's clear that we've got to do more. And that's why I'm urging the Senate once again to approve a jobs bill that will do two big things for small businesses: cut more taxes and make available more loans. That's what folks like the three people standing behind me say would be helpful. That's what I've heard from small-business owners across America.

Joe and Tiffany could tell you firsthand just how critical community banks are to helping small businesses grow and create jobs. Well, this bill will help those banks access more capital so they can offer more small businesses the loans that they need. It will make sure we continue to waive some of the fees for SBA-backed loans. It will increase deductions small businesses can take for new equipment and other expenses. And it will finally do what I've championed since I ran for President, and that's eliminate capital gains taxes on investments in small businesses.

The bottom line is this: America's small businesses are the backbone of our economy and the cornerstones of our communities. The folks who own them work hard, meet their responsibilities. As Gillian pointed out, nobody here is getting too fat and happy; everybody here is operating on very lean margins, and they are constantly thinking about their employees and their obligations and responsibilities to them. So in the same way that they're looking out for their employees, we need to be looking out for these small businesses. They are who this bill is for. They will see the positive benefits right away.

Now, unfortunately, a partisan minority in the Senate has been standing in the way of giving our small-businesspeople a simple up-or-down vote on this bill. They won't even let it go to vote. And every day this obstruction goes on is another day a small business somewhere in the country can't get a loan or can't get the tax cuts that it needs to grow and to hire.

I think Patty would agree with me when I say there will be plenty of time between now and November to play politics, but the small-business owners beside me and around the country don't have time for political games. They're not interested in what's best for a political party; they're interested in what's best for their employees and their communities and for the country.

So when Congress reconvenes, this jobs bill will be the first business out of the gate, and I ask Senate Republicans to drop their efforts to block it. I believe we can work together to get this done for the folks standing beside me and for small businesses, their employees, and communities that depend on them all across the country.

Thank you very much, everybody.

NOTE: The President spoke at 12:20 p.m. at Grand Central Bakery. In his remarks, he referred to Gillian Allen-White, co-owner and general manager, Grand Central Bakery in Seattle, WA; Tiffany and Brady Turner, co-owners, Inn at Discovery Coast in Long Beach, WA; and Joe Fugere, owner, Tutta Bella Neapolitan Pizzeria in Seattle.

Remarks at a Luncheon for Senator Patricia L. Murray in Seattle
August 17, 2010

Thank you. It is good to be in Washington; it is good to be in Seattle. Seattle just looks terrific. I just want to go take a stroll, but Secret Service said no. [*Laughter*]

I am just thrilled to be here. I want to acknowledge some of the folks who are here who are so important to the life of this State, but also to what's taking place throughout the country. First of all, your wonderful Governor, Chris Gregoire, please give her a big round of applause. Your outstanding congressional delegation: Jim McDermott is in the house; Norm Dicks is here; Jay Inslee is here; Rick Larsen is here; Brian Baird is here.

To the mayor of Seattle, Mike McGinn, thank you so much. To the King County executive; Dow Constantine is here. And to somebody who I just adore, who I just think is terrific, your senior Senator from the great State of Washington, Patty Murray.

As I look out on the crowd, I see a lot of people who helped so much during the course of the campaign. You were with us when we were up, and you were with us when we were down. But you always were there, understanding that we were at a critical point in our history, and we needed to make some fundamental changes in order to deliver that promise to the next generation. And so to everybody here who supported me during my campaign and helped me become the President, thank you so much for your outstanding efforts.

Now, I am here to say thank you not only for my own election, but for having the wisdom to send Patty Murray to Washington. And when this State sent Patty to the Senate, she wasn't one of these lifelong politicians who wanted the job or the position for a fancy title or a nice office. She was a self-described "mom in tennis shoes" who was just looking to help a few people solve a few problems. And all these years later, Patty is that same person, except she's helped a whole lot of people solve a whole lot of big problems.

When I was in the Senate, I sat next to Patty on the Veterans Affairs Committee. And I can tell you there is no fiercer advocate for our veterans than Patty Murray—nobody. Whether it was keeping three VA hospitals open here in Washington or helping a World War II veteran break through the bureaucracy so he could receive his Purple Heart, no problem is too big, no problem is too small for Patty to fight for you.

And the same is true when it comes to fighting for jobs and opportunity for the people of this State. You've seen her go to bat to keep Boeing jobs and aerospace jobs right here in Washington. You've seen her fight for clean energy jobs and new infrastructure jobs right here in Washington. She's a Senator who still flies across the country every weekend to come home to listen, to listen to you and the cares and concerns of her constituents. So this is the kind of person you want representing you. Especially in a time like this, this is the kind of leader you need. The country needs Patty.

So I want everybody to understand, I'm asking you to cast a primary vote today. I know she's unopposed, but it doesn't hurt to practice. [*Laughter*] And then we need a whole bunch of votes in November, because we have to have a leader like Patty continuing to do battle on behalf of middle class families, working families all across this country.

She is rooted here in Washington, but her concerns, her vision, her passion for people, that's important for the country as a whole. And I am proud to call her a friend, and I can tell you we would not have been able to get some of the critical things we got done this year had it not been for her leadership. So make sure you send her back to Washington, please.

Now, look, this is obviously an incredibly challenging time for America. Eighteen months ago, I took office after nearly a decade of economic policies that had given us sluggish growth, sluggish job growth, falling incomes, falling wages, and a record deficit. And all those policies culminated in the worst recession in our lifetimes and, I think it's fair to say, the worst crisis that we've had economically since the Great Depression.

In the last 6 months of 2008, while I was still campaigning for the Presidency, 3 million American jobs were lost. The month I was sworn in, 800,000 jobs were lost; subsequent months, 600,000—600,000. Eight million jobs were lost, all told. And behind each of these numbers is a story of heartache and a story of frustration: the factory worker who gets laid off just a couple of years before retirement, the single mom who's sent out job application after job application and doesn't hear the phone ring day after day, a college graduate who thought that a degree would land her a good job with a decent paycheck and instead has just gotten her a mountain of debt, or somebody who aspires to college and then discovered that they just wouldn't be able to afford it because their family has fallen on tough times.

I hear these stories every day. I read them in letters each night. The struggles and the hopes of the American people are why I ran for this office in the first place. It's the reason that Patty ran for the Senate in the first place. And that's why we intend to keep fighting as hard as we can for as long as it takes to turn this economy around. That's why I'm here. That's why Patty's here. And we are going to succeed.

Now, we're not there yet. We've got a lot more work to do; we know that. The truth is, it's going to take a few years to fully dig ourselves out of this recession. It's going to take time to bring back 8 million jobs. Anybody who tells you otherwise is just looking for your vote. But here's what I can tell you: After 18 months, I have never been more confident that our Nation is headed in the right direction. We are doing what is needed to move forward. And we're doing what's necessary not just to rebuild the economy for the short term; we want to rebuild it for the long term, for our children, for our grandchildren.

We did not become the most prosperous nation on Earth by rewarding greed and recklessness of the sort that helped cause this financial crisis. We didn't come this far by just allowing a handful of banks and insurance companies and special interests to run wild. We did it by rewarding the values of hard work and responsibility. We did it by investing in the people who have built this country from the ground up, workers and families and small-business owners and responsible entrepreneurs. We did it because we outworked and we outeducated and outcompeted other nations.

That's who we are; that's who we need to be. Because right now countries like China and India and South Korea and Germany, they are fighting as hard as they can for the jobs of the future. They're trying to outcompete us when it comes to clean energy. They're trying to outcompete us when it comes to producing engineers and scientists. And frankly, in some cases, they've been catching up and even propelling forward ahead of us.

And I said this at the State of the Union a while back, and I will repeat it: The United States does not play for second place; we play for first. We are going to rebuild this economy stronger than it was before. And at the heart of this rebuilding effort are three simple words: Made in America. Made in America.

Instead of giving tax breaks to companies that are shipping jobs overseas, we want to cut taxes for companies that create jobs right here in the United States of America. We want to give tax cuts to small-business owners. We want to give tax breaks to clean energy companies. We also want to make sure that we keep taxes low for middle class families, and that's why we cut taxes for 95 percent of workers right at the beginning of my term, because they had been going through a tough time, and they needed to have a chance to deal with this economic crisis.

Instead of prolonging an addiction to oil that endangers everything from our security to our coastlines, we are jump-starting a homegrown energy industry in this country. I don't want to see solar panels and wind turbines and advanced batteries and electric cars manufactured in Europe or Asia. I want to see them made right here in the United States of America, by American workers.

We need a 21st-century infrastructure, not just roads and bridges, but faster Internet access and high-speed rail, projects that can lead to hundreds of thousands of new, private sector jobs.

And we're helping the U.S. auto industry get back on its feet and retool for the 21st century. This was an industry that lost hundreds of thousands of jobs in the year before I took office and were getting bailouts, but never asked to restructure to figure out how they could compete. So we had to make some tough decisions about whether to help them out or walk away from possibly a million jobs lost. And I decided we couldn't walk away. And by the way, this was not very popular. [*Laughter*]

You know, the—it's interesting in Washington, people keep asking me, "Gosh, why are you doing these things that don't poll well?" [*Laughter*] And I have to keep on explaining, I have pollsters. [*Laughter*] I know when things don't poll well. But I wasn't sent to Washington, you did not send me to the Oval Office to just do what was popular; you sent me there to do what was right. That's why you sent me. That's why you sent me to Washington, to stand up for things that were right.

So it turns out, lo and behold, all three U.S. automakers are now operating at a profit for the first time in years. They've got the strongest job growth in more than a decade. And when I visited—I went to a Chrysler plant in Detroit. This had been shut—it was on the verge of being shut down. And I had a chance to meet 14 workers who had just won the lottery. [*Laugh-*

ter] Now, you would think they might want to retire. But most of them had stayed on because they love their job, and they're proud of what they do.

In fact, one guy had used some of his winnings to buy a car, a Jeep Grand Cherokee, from the plant where he worked. He had helped build that car. He bought it for his wife, then bought a whole bunch of American flags for his hometown because he loves his country. He loves his company, and he loves his coworkers. And it captured the essence of who we are, coming out of tough times. Do not bet against the American worker. Do not bet against American businesses. Don't bet against American ingenuity.

That's the message that he was sending, and that's the message I want to send to you. We can compete. But we're going to have to take some steps to deal with longstanding problems, not ignore them, not pretend that they don't exist, to confront them.

We've got to make sure that our workers can compete on—with any other workers on Earth. And that's why we're reforming our education system based on what works for our children, not what works for the status quo. We've eliminated billions of dollars in taxpayer subsidies to the big banks that provide college loans so that all those billions of dollars can go to make a college education more affordable for millions of students. Patty was one of the people who took the lead in that critical change.

To lower costs for families and for businesses, we passed health insurance reform that will finally make coverage affordable and stop insurance companies from jacking up your premiums or refusing to cover you just because you're sick.

You just saw Marcelas Owens come up here. What a wonderful young man with a powerful story. And when he was standing next to me as we were signing that piece of legislation, I thought about his mom, and I thought about my mom, a single mom who didn't always have the kind of job that provided health insurance.

To ensure that a financial crisis like the one we just had doesn't happen again, we passed Wall Street reform that demands new accountability and tough oversight, reform that will stop credit card companies from charging you hidden fees and unfair rate hikes and that ends the era of Wall Street bailouts once and for all.

Patty was in the lead on all these measures. And all these reforms make America more competitive in the 21st century. They move us forward. And on each of these reforms, we reached out to Democrats and Republicans for ideas and support. But in just about every instance—I'm sure there's an exception that's escaping my mind—*[laughter]*—in almost every instance, Republicans in Congress said no: no on help for small businesses, no on middle class tax cuts, no on clean energy jobs, no on making college more affordable, no on Wall Street reform.

You remember our slogan during the campaign, "Yes, we can"? Their slogan is, "No, we can't." *[Laughter]* "No, we can't." That's really inspiring. *[Laughter]* This vision they have for the future—*[laughter]*—gives you a little pep in your step when you hear it, doesn't it? *[Laughter]* "No, we can't." *[Laughter]*

Now, what—let's unpack why they're doing this. I mean, part of it is, they refuse to give up on the economic philosophy that they've been peddling for much of the last decade. And their agenda was pretty straightforward. You remember it. You voted against it. *[Laughter]* That's why I'm President. *[Laughter]*

Their basic philosophy goes something like this: We're going to cut taxes for millionaires and billionaires, folks who don't need it, weren't even asking for it. And we're going to cut rules for special interests, gut regulations that protect clean air and clean water and things that most of us value. And then you're going to cut working folks loose to fend for themselves. So if you can't find a job or you can't afford college or you don't have health insurance, tough luck, you are on your own. Now, if you're a Wall Street bank or an insurance company or an oil company like BP, come on in, help us write the regulations.

Now, I think you may have noticed that their philosophy did not—didn't work out too well. It's not like we didn't test it, right? *[Laughter]* No, we—the American people tried it out. They said, all right, we'll go with that for 8 years. And it didn't work. It gave us record deficits and ulti-mately led to the worst economic crisis since the Great Depression. Remember that, it gave us record deficits. Remember, when they came in with this theory, we had record surpluses. You remember that, right? Yes. And at the end, wrapped up in a big bow for me when I arrived was a $1.3 trillion deficit. *[Laughter]*

So when these guys are going out talking about spending and deficits and debt, I'm thinking, well, what are you talking about? *[Laughter]*

Now, I bring all this stuff up not because I want to relitigate the past. I just don't want to relive the past. I don't want to go through that again. I mean, it would be one thing if the Republicans had gone through a period of soul-searching, right? If they had said, "Boy, we really messed up," and had kind of gone off into the wilderness and thought long and hard about their economic approach, and then came back and said, "You know what, we didn't know what we were doing, but now we've got some new ideas, we've got some new policies, we've learned from our mistakes, we're going to do something different this time," that would be a plausible argument. But that's not what they're doing.

One of their leaders in Congress was asked what his party would do if they took over Congress. He actually said they'd pursue "the exact same agenda" as before I took office. That's a quote, "the exact same agenda"—that didn't work.

So basically, what this campaign is coming down to is that between now and November, they're betting that you will all come down with a case of amnesia. *[Laughter]* They're basically—they're counting on the fact that you don't remember, that you're going to forget what happened when they were in charge for the—for 8 years.

They spent almost a decade driving the economy into a ditch. I mean, think about it if this—if the economy was a car and they drove it into the ditch. *[Laughter]* And so me and Patty and a bunch of others, we go down there and we put on our boots, and we're pushing and shoving. And it's muddy, and there are bugs, and we're sweating—*[laughter]*—and shoving, pushing hard. And they're all standing there sipping Slurpees—[*laughter*]—and watching and—"You're not pushing hard enough." "That's not the right way to push."

[*At this point, the President pretended to sip a Slurpee.*]

Right? So finally—finally—Patty and I and everybody, we finally get the car up on level ground, and we're about to go forward. And these guys come and tap us on the shoulder, and they say, "We want the keys back." [*Laughter*]

You can't have the keys back. You don't know how to drive. You don't know how to drive. You can't have them back. Can't have them back. You can't have them back. We are trying to go forward. We do not want to go backwards into the ditch again.

You notice, when you want to move forward in your car, what do you do? You put your car in "D." When you want to go backwards, you put it in "R," back into the ditch. Keep that in mind in November. That's not a coincidence. [*Laughter*]

So that's the choice in this election: Do we go back to the policies that got us into this mess, or do we keep moving forward? I believe we move forward. America always moves forward.

Do you want to know what will happen if the other party takes control of Congress in November? All you have to do is look what they've done over the last 18 months. I mean, they— one thing I will give them credit for, they have not been bashful, right? On issue after issue, they have sided with special interests over middle class families.

Name me an issue. They voted to keep giving tax breaks to corporations that ship jobs overseas. They voted to give insurance companies the power to keep denying coverage to people who are sick. The top Republican on the Energy Committee actually apologized to BP for us making sure the $20 billion was secured to help fishermen and small-businesspeople in the Gulf whose livelihoods were almost decimated. This guy called it a "shakedown." I think he said "Chicago shakedown," just to kind of underscore it. Apologized to BP.

They voted en masse against Wall Street reform. And now Patty Murray's opponent has earned the distinction of being the first candidate in the country to call for repeal of Wall Street reform. Think about this. He wants to go back to the old rules and the lack of oversight that caused the worst crisis since the Great Depression. That is—don't you think that's strange? [*Laughter*]

I mean, I could see him saying, well, here are certain provisions I might modify. But to just say we didn't need it, when we almost had a complete financial meltdown—he's counting on amnesia.

So this is what's at stake in this election: If we give them the keys back, they will drive us right back into the ditch. And riding shotgun will be every other special interest group under the Sun. And I want to be clear, because I just— Patty and I just had a wonderful meeting with three small-businesspeople, local folks right here, over at Grand Central—it was very good. They had this turkey sandwich—very tasty. [*Laughter*]

So I want businesses in this country to succeed. If you are a responsible business owner, I will do everything I can to help you grow and prosper and hire more employees—and Patty doing the same thing—helping to open up credit, help to keep your taxes low.

But I don't—it's not antibusiness to say that we should make sure an oil rig is safe before we start drilling. [*Laughter*] It's not antibusiness to say that Wall Street banks should play by the same rules as everybody else. It's not antibusiness to say insurance companies shouldn't be able to deny care to people just because they get sick. We can't go back to an attitude of what's good enough for me is just good enough. We've got to be asking, what's good for America? What's good for the people of Washington? What's good for Marcelas? What's good for the next generation? What's good for America?

That's what we do in this country. That's how we've always moved forward, as one people and as one Nation. So Washington, I want everybody to know, look, I know times are tough. And when times are tough, it can be easy to give in to cynicism and to fear, to set our sights lower, to settle for the status quo, to try to make us afraid of each other, drive wedges. That's— we've all seen that movie before. And that's what the other side is counting on in this election. They're not offering new plans. They're not offering new ideas. They're offering cynicism, and they're offering fear.

That's not who we are. That's not the country I know. We are Americans. We don't give in to fear. We do not give up. We do not quit. We don't shy away from the future. We don't look backwards. We shape the future. We seize our own destiny.

So I need you to join me, and I need you to join Patty, in building a future where our small businesses flourish on the power of their ideas and ingenuity; a future where clean energy powers not just America, but powers the world, produced in the fields and the factories of the United States; a future where our children get the education and training they need to compete with anyone and anywhere. I want to build a future where we recapture a sense of optimism and confidence, hope that's made America a beacon to the world.

That's how we built the last American century. That is how we are going to build the next American century. The American people don't believe in "No, we can't." In times of great challenge, we push forward with the unyielding faith that we can.

Thank you, everybody. God bless you, and God bless the United States of America.

NOTE: The President spoke at 1:03 p.m. at the Westin Seattle. In his remarks, he referred to Gov. Christine O. Gregoire of Washington; Chrysler employee William Shanteau and his wife Lisa; Marcelas Owens, whose mother died after losing her health insurance; Rep. Pete Sessions, in his capacity as chairman of the National Republican Congressional Committee; Rep. Joseph L. Barton; Washington senatorial candidate Dino Rossi; Gillian Allen-White, co-owner and general manager, Grand Central Bakery in Seattle, WA; Tiffany Turner, co-owner, Inn at Discovery Coast in Long Beach, WA; and Joe Fugere, owner, Tutta Bella Neapolitan Pizzeria in Seattle.

Remarks at a Fundraiser for Senator Patricia L. Murray in Seattle
August 17, 2010

Thank you, everybody. Thank you. This is a pretty good view. [*Laughter*] It's not bad. [*Laughter*]

I want to just say that Rob and Cori, they have been such great friends for so long. When we first met and they agreed to help on my Senate campaign, people could not pronounce my name. They were calling me "Alabama" and "Yo mama"—[*laughter*]—and yet they took a risk in supporting me, and I'm extraordinarily grateful.

I will also add, they did not have this huge brood that they now have—[*laughter*]—all these young ones running around. And so thank you, guys, for all the support, and congratulations on the beautiful family that you guys have.

To all of you who are here—I see some old friends and some new friends, people who were probably at that first fundraiser and people who have subsequently helped me in so many ways. I am reminded of the story that President Lincoln told, apparently at a time when security around the White House wasn't quite as strict. So a guy shows up at the door, and he says, "I want to see the President. I worked for him; I am responsible for him being in the White House." He was looking for a job of some sort. And finally, Lincoln says, "All right, let the guy in." He comes in, and he says, "Mr. President, I am responsible for you being here." "Is that right?" Lincoln says. He says, "Well, I forgive you." [*Laughter*]

I don't need to forgive you, obviously. It's an unbelievable privilege to be President. In fact, this is the time when you want to be President, because we are at one of these inflection points in our history where, after for decades putting off tough challenges, for decades not addressing problems that were structural in our economy, in how we are training our young people for the 21st-century economy, we now have the necessity to step up and do right not just for the next election, but for the next generation.

We also have—at a time when our leadership had been waning internationally, we've got an opportunity to step up and say that just as the 20th century was the American century, the 21st century will be the American century, but that our power is not just going to come from the might of our military, it's also going to come from the strength of our values and our ability to project core beliefs about democracy and equality and freedom around the world.

And so we've done a big job over the last 18 months. And I have to tell you, when I think about that month when we were first sworn in—some of you may have been at the Inauguration—it was cold that day. It was cold. [*Laughter*] But there was an incredibly warm spirit, and there was a sense of hopefulness.

But what we have to remind ourselves is, that same month that I was sworn in, we lost 800,000 jobs. We had lost 3 million jobs in the previous 6 months. And we would lose another several million jobs in the next 3 months before any of our economic policies had a chance to actually take root. So all together, we lost 8 million jobs. The financial system was on the verge of meltdown, and most economists thought that there were decent odds we might tip into the next Great Depression.

Because of the swift action that we took, we were able to stabilize the economy and stabilize the financial system. But that was not just because we drafted a whole bunch of clever plans on paper. We had to move all that stuff through Congress. And that brings me to your senior Senator, Patty Murray.

If I did not have a partner like Patty, we would not have been able to invest in clean energy like never before in our history. If I didn't have Patty Murray, we would not have been able to get small-business loans out at a time when most banks had completely contracted and a lot of folks were on the verge of going under. If it hadn't been for Patty, States like Washington would have had to lay off tens of thousands of teachers and firefighters and police officers. Because of Patty, we were able to get help that States and local governments needed.

So when I think about Patty, I think about one of the generals who helped to stave off what could have been a much worse crisis than we had. And partly because I served with her, I know how effective she is not just in coming home and listening to people, but how effective she is in fighting for them when she gets back into Washington.

I'm also always sympathetic to Patty because she was always trying to catch the plane back home, and when the votes went late, she'd be looking at her watch and thinking: Well, that one just left, and there's one more, and I've got 10 minutes, and Jim DeMint is talking. [*Laughter*]

And I know it's tough, but here's the thing, though. Our job was not just to rescue the economy. Our job, as I said, was to deal with a decade of putting off tough decisions. I'm not just interested in saving the economy in the short term. I'm interested in rebuilding the economy for the long term, for the next generation, for Rob and Cori's kids and for my kids and for your kids and for your grandkids.. And that means taking on some tough stuff and stuff that's not always popular.

If we did not deal with our health care system now, we were looking at the possibility that health care alone, Medicare and Medicaid, would consume all of our discretionary spending at the Federal level—all of it—because of the direction that health care cost was going. If we didn't tackle the education system now, then not only have we slipped already from 1st to 12th in college graduation rates, we might have slipped even further.

If we did not tackle energy now, then we don't know what this view will look like 50 years from now or 70 years from now or maybe even 20 years from now because of the impact it has on the environment. But we also don't know what kind of impact the next crisis in terms of oil supplies might have on our economy or our national security.

So we had to take on these tough problems now. And they weren't always popular. They didn't always poll well. And people in Washington would always get surprised. They'd say: "Well, why is the President doing this? It doesn't poll well." And I would have to explain to people, you know, I actually have pollsters, so I know when things aren't popular. I know when they don't poll well. But I was not sent to Washington just to do what was popular; I was sent to do what was right. That's why so many of you supported me in the election. And I know Patty feels the same way.

So as a consequence, if you take a look at what we've accomplished over the last 18 months—in addition to staving off a Great Depression—we can just tick it off: We finally have enshrined the basic core principle that everybody in America should have decent, affordable health care; that people should not be bankrupt just because they get sick; and that we should be able to get good bang for our health care dollars, and thereby slow the costs and the burdens on families and on businesses.

We revamped our student loan system so that, instead of sending tens of billions of dollars to the banks as middlemen for guaranteed loans, where they were taking no risk, we were able to cut out the middleman. And now millions more young people here in Washington State and all across the country are going to be able to get assistance to go to college, which means they're going to be able to go to work for Microsoft or all these other wonderful companies that are up here. And we'll be able to maintain our cutting edge—which reminds me, we also made the largest investment in research and development in our history, because the essence of America is innovation and entrepreneurship and technological leadership.

We decided that it was time for us to make sure that even as we're sending young men and women to fight in Iraq and Afghanistan, that we've got to make sure that we're doing right by our veterans. And nobody has been a fiercer advocate on behalf of veterans than Patty Murray. And with her help, we saw the largest increase in funding for veterans in at least 30 years. And we helped to pass a post-9/11 GI bill.

My grandfather, who actually lived here in Puget Sound when my mom was going to Mercer Island High School, well, he was a beneficiary of the original GI bill. And it was because of that GI bill that we built an entire middle class, educating folks, investing in people. Well, with Patty's help, we're doing the same thing with this next generation of veterans who are coming back home. And they're going to have opportunity.

On issue after issue—from making sure that tobacco companies can't market to kids to making sure that credit card companies can't arbitrarily raise your rates or impose hidden fees, to making sure that we're expanding national service for our young people, to making sure that housing programs and mortgages aren't taking advantage of people, to making sure that women are paid equally for doing the same work as men, to getting a couple of pretty smart women on the Supreme Court—on issue after issue, we've been able to make progress. And you know what, what's remarkable is we've done it without a single bit of help from the other side.

You remember, I campaigned on "Yes, we can." Their philosophy has been, "We can't." They said no to clean energy investment. They said no to health care. They want to go—in fact, they want to repeal it so that we can have a situation where people with preexisting conditions can't get health insurance.

They said no to Wall Street reform. Now, think about this. We had a complete utter meltdown of our financial system, and you would think that they would say, "Well, maybe we should at least cooperate on this one." They said no. Didn't get any help.

On issue after issue, their only response has been, let's go back to the same policies that got us into this mess in the first place. It's not like they, after presiding over 8 years of failed economic policies, they said, "You know what, we better reflect a little bit and see what we're doing wrong here," and they went off into the wilderness and meditated, and then they finally came back and said, "Well, we realize the error of our ways, but now we've got a whole new set of proposals to try." That's not what they're doing.

They're coming back and basically peddling the same old snake oil they were peddling before. They want to give tax breaks to folks who don't need them and weren't even asking for them. They want to keep on giving tax breaks to companies that are shipping jobs overseas. They want to deregulate so that oil companies, for example, could drill with minimum oversight. And they're basically saying to most middle class families, you're on your own.

And the excuse they give for these policies is, well, we can't afford any of these initiatives. And yet this is the same group of folks who took a record surplus from Bill Clinton and turned it into record deficits, so that I had a $1.3 trillion deficit wrapped in a big bow when I arrived in the White House. [*Laughter*]

So I was just talking to a group over at the Westin, and I used the analogy, imagine that our economy is a car. These guys drove it into a ditch. And so Patty and I have been down there in the ditch. We've been pushing and shoving. We've put our boots on and we're trying to get that car out of the ditch. And these Republicans have been standing, watching, drinking a Slurpee—[*laughter*]—and giving us advice. "You're not pushing hard enough. Push this way." And we finally get that car on level ground and we're about to move forward, and they say, "We want the keys back." [*Laughter*] And we say, "No, you can't have the keys back; you can't drive." [*Laughter*]

Now is not the time to reverse course and go back to the things that got us into this mess in the first place. We've got to move forward. And that's why your support is so important.

Now, we've still got a lot of work to do. The economy is stabilized, but it's stabilized at a very weak level. So Patty and I just had some lunch with some wonderful small-businesspeople who were talking about how it's still difficult for small businesses to access credit, which is why we've got initiatives in the Senate right now to make sure that small community banks are able to provide lending to small businesses. We want to cut taxes smartly—so, for example, eliminating capital gains taxes on investments in startup businesses.

We want to make sure that we are still pursuing a vision for clean energy, because I believe that whoever wins that race for clean energy in the 21st century, they are going to own the 21st-century economy. And so I want solar panels and wind turbines and biodiesel and hydroelec-

tric power; I want that here in the United States of America. And I want a smart grid that can transmit it all across the country.

And I want the cars of the future built here in the United States, which is why we made an investment in Detroit. A lot of people thought that was a bad idea, but we said, look, instead of giving bailouts year after year without asking anything in return, which is what the previous administration had been doing, we said, here's some help, but you're going to have to restructure so you can compete.

And we were able to mobilize the car companies, autoworkers, all the stakeholders involved, to actually negotiate the first increase in fuel efficiency standards in 30 years on both cars and trucks. And now we've got every U.S. automaker posting a profit, the best job growth in that industry in a decade. And they're building the cars of tomorrow, cars that people will want to drive, that get 40 miles a gallon or 50 miles a gallon or, ultimately, don't take any gallons in order to move.

So those are the kinds of things that we're going to have to work on. We've still got infrastructure that we've got to build. We're falling behind other countries not just in roads and bridges and ports and airports, all of which of important, but in broadband access and coverage, or in high-speed rail.

And in order for me to succeed over the next couple of years, I'm going to need Patty Murray. And there are a whole bunch of folks in Congress who are in tough races this year who stood up and did the right thing, without a lot of fanfare, knowing that they were going to be making themselves politically vulnerable. But they remembered why they went to Washington.

They remembered they didn't go to Washington to have a fancy office or to have a fancy title. They didn't go to Washington to take polls and put their finger out to the wind and figure out what's going to be the right thing to do at this particular moment because the cable chatter is moving in this direction or that direction.

They went to Washington because they believed that what makes this country special is our ability to provide every single person an opportunity to pursue their dreams. If they're willing to work hard enough and apply themselves, if they've got a big enough imagination and some pluck and some drive, whether it's starting a high-tech company or being a rock-and-roll star, that what makes this place special is that you can go as far as your dreams carry you.

And we've got to make sure that America is there not just for this generation, but for the next generation and the generation after that. And that means we've got to think not about the next election, but about the next generation. That's what Patty Murray does. That's what a whole bunch of folks who have helped us over the last 18 months do.

And that's why I'm so pleased that you are here to support them. If you stay with us, if you're willing to see this thing through, I'm confident that we're going to be able to look back, despite all the ups and all the downs, we're going to be able to look back and say that what we did mattered, that this was a moment that counted, and that you were standing there to be counted at that critical moment in this country's history.

Thanks so much, everybody. God bless you. Thank you.

NOTE: The President spoke at 2:34 p.m. at the residence of Robert D. and Cori Glaser. In his remarks, he referred to Cameron and Eva Glaser, children of Mr. and Mrs. Glaser. Audio was not available for verification of the content of these remarks.

Remarks and a Question-and-Answer Session in Columbus, Ohio
August 18, 2010

The President. Well, I'm just thrilled to be here. And I want to thank Joe and Rhonda and the entire family for being such great hosts. And I want to thank all of you for taking the time to be here.

I see that the mayor of Columbus is here, a great friend. Somebody who's going to be running—and I hope winning—for the U.S. Senate, Lee Fisher is here. And Mary Jo Kilroy is here. We've got one of the best Senators, I believe, in the United States Senate in Sherrod Brown—is here. And one of the finest Governors in the country, Ted Strickland is here. So give those folks a big round of applause.

Should we tell them to take off their jackets too? [*Laughter*] Take off your jackets, guys. Lighten up a little bit. [*Laughter*] Sheesh! [*Laughter*]

This is just a great opportunity for me to have a conversation with you. And I don't want this to be too formal. What I want to do is have a chance to listen to you and also answer your questions. What we've tried to do whenever we are in a setting like this is to talk about the things that folks are going through day to day, because, look, I'll be honest with you, sometimes when you're in Washington, you get caught up with the particular legislative battles or media spin on certain issues, and sometimes you lose touch in terms of what folks are talking about around the kitchen table.

One of the ways that I stay in touch is through events like this, as well as reading letters from constituents and voters all across the country every night. And obviously, what's on a lot of people's minds right now is the economy.

We went through the worst recession that we've had since the Great Depression. And when I was sworn in about 18 months ago, we had already lost several million jobs and we were about to lose several million more. We lost 800,000 jobs the month I was sworn in. And so we had to act fast and take some emergency steps to prevent the economy from going back into what could have been a Great Depression.

And we were successful in doing so. We stabilized the economy; we stabilized the financial system. We didn't have a complete meltdown. And whereas we were losing jobs in the private sector when I was first sworn in, we're now gaining jobs, and we've gained jobs 7 consecutive months in the private sector. The economy was shrinking about 6 percent; the economy is now growing. So we've made progress. But let's face it, the progress hasn't been fast enough.

And Joe and Rhonda and I were just talking about the challenges that they've had to go through when Rhonda got laid off—and by the way, also lost her health insurance in the process, at a time when her son was going through some significant medical needs. So in addition to trying to stop the crisis, what we also wanted to do was make sure that we were helping people get back on their feet. So something that I'm very pleased with is that Rhonda was able to use the provisions that we passed to help her get COBRA so that she had health insurance, could keep her health insurance, at a time when the family was very much in need. And millions of people across the country have been able to keep their health insurance.

We've also been trying to help our State and local governments so that they're not having to lay off as many teachers and firefighters and police officers. And I know that—I think the mayor and the Governor would acknowledge that the help that we provided them has really helped to plug some big budget holes.

And in addition, what we've been trying to do is to build infrastructure that puts people back to work, but also improves the quality of life in communities like Columbus. So Joe is an architect, and he's now working on a new police station that was funded in part with Recovery Act funds.

So all these things have made a difference, but we still got a long way to go. And so a couple of things that we're focused on right now is, number one, making sure that small businesses are getting help, because small businesses like Joe's architectural firm are really the key to our economy. They create two out of every three jobs. And so we want to make sure that they're getting financing. We want to make sure that we are cutting their taxes in certain key areas. One of the things that we've done, for example, is propose that we eliminate capital gains taxes on small businesses so that when they're starting up and they don't have a lot of cashflow, that's exactly the time when they should get a break and they should get some help.

We're focusing as well on trying to figure out can we build more infrastructure here in Ohio and all across the country that puts people back to work, not just building roads and bridges, but also building things like high-speed rail or building broadband lines that can connect communities and give people access to the Internet at a time when that's going to be critical in terms of long-term economic development.

We're also going to have to look at how do we, over the long term, get control of our deficit. And that's obviously something that a lot of people have on their minds. The key is to make sure that we do so in a way that doesn't impede recovery, but rather gives people confidence over the medium and the long term. And I'm going to be happy to talk about what we're doing in terms of spending.

But overall, what I—the main message that I want to deliver before I start taking questions—and I said this to Joe and Rhonda—is, slowly but surely, we are moving in the right direction. We're on the right track. The economy is getting stronger, but it really suffered a big trauma. And we're not going to get all 8 million jobs that were lost back overnight. It's going to take some time. And businesses are still trying to get more confident out there before they start hiring. And people—consumers are not going to start spending until they feel a little more confident that the economy is getting stronger. And so what we're trying to do is create sort of a virtuous cycle where people start feeling better and better about the economy. And a lot of it's sort of like recovering from an illness; you get a little bit stronger each day and you take a few more steps each day. And that's where our economy is at right now.

What we can't afford to do is to start going backwards and doing some of the same things that got us into trouble in the first place. This is why it's been so important for us to, for example, to pass something like Wall Street reform to make sure that we're not creating the same kinds of financial bubbles and the massive leverage and the reckless risks that helped to create this problem in the first place.

And I am very proud that we've got somebody like a Sherrod Brown or a Mary Jo, who worked really tirelessly with us in Congress to make sure that we don't have a situation where we've got to bail out banks that have taken reckless risks, that we are monitoring what's happening in the financial system a lot more carefully, that people—making sure people aren't cheated when it comes to their mortgages, or that there are a bunch of hidden fees in their credit cards that helped to create some of the problems that we've seen in the financial systems.

We can't go back to doing things the way we were doing them before. We've got to go forward. That's what we're trying to do. And hopefully, as we continue over the next several months and the next several years, we're going to see a Columbus and an Ohio and a United States of America that is going to be stronger than it was before this crisis struck. I am absolutely confident of that. But we've got more work to do.

All right. So with that, what I want to do is I just want to open it up and you guys can ask me questions about anything. And just ignore all these cameras who are here—[*laughter*]—pretend they're not there. The only thing I would ask is introduce yourselves so that I get a chance to know you. Or if you haven't met one of your neighbors, this is a good chance for you to do so.

But why don't we start with this gentleman right here. And we've got some mikes. The only reason—the main reason we're using mikes is so that these folks behind us can hear you. All right? This gentleman right here.

Health Care Reform

Q. Hi, President Obama. I hope I don't pass out while I'm asking this question. So my question is actually about health care. My brother is disabled. He—and is definitely what I would consider one of the working poor. He will not mature any more as far as mindset of a 12-year-old. Right now he works washing dishes at a local restaurant, and unfortunately, because the employer does not offer health care insurance, one whole check, which is 2 weeks worth of work, has to actually go towards him just paying for COBRA, which is obviously well out of his budget. But he has to simply because of various illnesses that he suffers from.

My question is, unfortunately, I'm not able to sit down and read a 2,000-page bill or law that—or with all the reform that happened with health care. With the present reforms that went into place, how will that help him? And if it doesn't, then how will—I know that you're not done with health care—how will your—the latest changes that you want to happen with health care, how will that help him?

And thank you for doing such a wonderful job.

The President. Well, thank you. Here's how specifically health reform should help your brother. Number one, it gives an incentive to his employer to provide health insurance, because one of the key components of health care reform was providing employers a 35-percent tax break on the premiums they pay for their employees, all right? So basically, it's cutting his potential costs—the employer's potential costs for providing your brother with health insurance; it's cutting it by a third. That's step number one.

And there are going to be companies out there that say, you know what, we want to provide health insurance, but we just couldn't afford to do it, but now that it's costing us up to a third less, saving us thousands of dollars, maybe we should go ahead and provide coverage for that. Okay, so that is step number one.

Step number two is if the employer still doesn't provide coverage, over the next couple of years, your brother is going to be able to join a pool, what we're calling an exchange, where he can basically buy the same kind of insurance that these Members of Congress are buying. And the advantage that he's going to have is that now he's part of a pool of millions of people who are buying it all at the same time, which means they've got leverage. The same way big companies are able to lower their costs per employee because the insurance company really wants their business, well, now your brother could be part of the same pool that these guys are. And that's going to give leverage, which will lower his rates.

And the final part of it is, if even with these lower rates, this better deal, he still can't afford it, then we're going to provide some subsidies to help him. So all those things combined should help make sure that your brother is getting health insurance.

Now, one of the things that I think people may not be aware of is that although this exchange isn't going to be set up until 2014—because it takes a while, we've got to set it up right—there's some immediate things that are helping right now.

If your child has a preexisting condition, insurance companies, starting this year, will not be able to deny those children coverage. And that's a big deal for a lot of folks whose children may have diabetes or some other illness and right now can't get insurance. Insurance companies are going to have to provide them insurance. That's number one.

Number two, how many people here have kids who are college age, about to go to college? All right. Well, one of the things you're going to be able to do is when those kids get out of college, if they don't get insurance right away, they're going to be able to stay on your insurance until they're 26 years old. That's a big deal because a lot of times that first job or those first couple of jobs out of college are the ones that don't provide health insurance.

So there are a number of changes that are being made right now that will make those of you who have health insurance more secure with the insurance they have. We're eliminating lifetime limits. There's a bunch of fine print on the insurance forms that sometimes have ended up creating real problems for people. Your insurance company decides to drop you right when you get sick, just when you need it most. Those kinds of practices are over now.

And the final aspect of health reform that's important is, is that by changing the incentives for how doctors get paid under Medicare and under Medicaid, we're actually encouraging doctors to become more efficient so that over time, health care costs actually start leveling out a little bit instead of skyrocketing each and every year. Because everybody here who's got health insurance, what's been happening? Your

premiums have been going up; copayments, deductibles, all that stuff's been going up. So we've got to actually try to control the costs of it, and part of it is just a matter of making sure that we get a better bang for our health care dollar.

So, for example, when you go to a doctor, we're still filling out forms in triplicate on paper. It's the only business there is where you still have a whole bunch of paperwork. And what we're trying to do is to encourage information technologies so that when you go into a doctor, they can already pull down your medical records electronically. If you take a test, then it's sent to all the specialists who are involved, so you don't end up having to take four or five tests and pay for four or five tests when all you needed was just one.

Those are the kinds of things that will take a little bit longer to actually take into effect, but hopefully, over time, they're actually going to lower costs.

All right. I'm going to go boy, girl here to make sure it's fair. [*Laughter*] Right here.

Q. [*Inaudible*]

The President. Absolutely. [*Laughter*]

Social Security

Q. Mr. President, I'm concerned about the furor lately that's been—it's similar to what's happened in the past, but it's reemerging, mostly from the Republican Party, but some Democrats—that Social Security needs to be privatized because it's losing money, and we're all going to—and it's going to go broke, and that sort of thing. How would you comment on that?

The President. I have been adamant in saying that Social Security should not be privatized, and it will not be privatized as long as I'm President. And here's the reason. I was opposed to it before the financial crisis. And what I said was that the purpose of Social Security is to have that floor, that solid, rock-solid security so that no matter what else happens, you've always got some income to support you in your retirement. And I've got no problem with people investing in their 401(k)s, and we want to encourage people to invest in private savings accounts. But Social Security has to be separate from that.

Now, imagine if Social Security, if a portion of that had been in the stock market back in 2006 and 2007. I mean, you saw what happened with your 401(k)s; you lost 20, 30, 40 percent of it. Now, we've recovered—in part because of the policies that we put into place to stabilize the situation—the stock market has recovered 60, 70 percent of its value from its peak. But if you were really in need last year or the year before, and suddenly you see your assets drop by 40 percent, and that's all you're relying on, it would have been a disaster.

So here's the thing: Social Security is not in crisis. What is happening is, is that the population is getting older, which means we've got more retirees per worker than we used to. We're going to have to make some modest adjustments in order to strengthen it. There are some fairly modest changes that could be made without resorting to any newfangled schemes that would continue Social Security for another 75 years, where everybody would get the benefits that they deserve. And what we've done is we've created a fiscal commission of Democrats and Republicans to come up with what would be the best combination to help stabilize Social Security for not just this generation, but the next generation.

I'm absolutely convinced it can be done. And as I said, I want to encourage people to save more on their own, but I don't want them taking money out of Social Security so that people are putting that into the stock market. There are other ways of doing this. For example, it turns out that if you set up a system with your employer where the employer automatically deducts some of your paycheck and puts it into your 401(k) account, unless you say you don't want it done, it turns out people save more just naturally. I mean, it's just kind of a psychological thing. If they take it out of your paycheck, and they automatically take it out, unless you affirmatively say don't take it out, you'll save more than if they ask you, do you want to save, and then you say, ah, nah, I'm going to keep the money. [*Laughter*] And then you save less.

So that's just a small change. It's voluntary, but that in and of itself could end up boosting savings rates significantly. So there are a bunch

of ways that we can do—make sure that retirement is more secure. But we've got to make sure that Social Security is there not just for this generation, but for the next one. Okay?

All right, gentleman's turn. And by the way, I know that some folks may be hot, and if they are, you guys can always move into the shade.

Job Growth/Alternative Energy Sources/Infrastructure Improvement/Employee Pensions

Q. Mr. President, sir, my name is Aaron McGreevy, I was born and raised in a good, blue-collar town in Toledo, Ohio. I grew up in a union family, and I work now for a significant number of pension assets in the labor union market with an investment firm. I think the question I have that most bothers me is what's important to my people out there that I talk to, and those two things are, the first, what's going to happen with their pensions, especially those, as you know, in the red and the yellow? The PPA has not exactly been that favorable to them. And the PBGC is not a very good option. My father had to take early retirement. He's not receiving the maximum amount—after decades of hard work and service—that he had anticipated.

The second part is, I'm not naive enough to think that just the pensions alone can help save workers. We've got 9.5 percent unemployment in this country, at least at last release, and I'm sure as you know, that's even more—it's larger than that for the manufacturing industry and us in the Rust Belt: Toledo, Detroit, Cleveland. Obviously, we need to put those guys back to work; they need to have man-hours out there. How can we create a sustainable, competitive product at an advantage to make us another leader in the manufacturing and labor force industry going forward, not just to get them back to work for a year or two, sir, but to get back to work for the long term, so they can grow the market on their own with their own product and their own work?

The President. Well, look, this is a great question, and it goes to the heart of what our economic strategy has to be. And Senator Brown and Congresswoman Kilroy and others, I know this is their number-one concern each and every day. And certainly, this is your Governor's number-one concern each and every day, is how do we make sure that we're creating a competitive America in which we aren't just buying things from other countries, we're selling things to other countries, that we're making things here in the United States of America?

Let me give you a couple of examples of areas that I think have enormous promise. Number one is the whole clean energy industry—and Toledo actually is becoming a leader in this—creating good jobs in areas like solar—building solar panels, wind turbines, advanced battery manufacturing. There is a whole series of huge potential manufacturing industries in which we end up being world leaders and as a bonus end up creating a more energy-efficient economy that is also good for the environment.

Now, we made, at the beginning of my term, the largest investment in clean energy in our history. And so there are plants that are opening up all across the country, creating products made in America that are now being shipped overseas. I'll give you one example, and that's the advanced battery manufacturing industry. These are the batteries that go into electric cars, or the batteries that are ending up helping to make sure that if you get solar power or wind power, that it can be transmitted in an efficient way.

We have 2 percent of the entire market—2 percent. By 2015, in 5 years, we're going to have 40 percent of that market because of the investments that we made. So one of the advanced battery manufacturing plants that we helped get going with some key loans and support and tax breaks, they're now putting those batteries into the Chevy Volt. And you combine it then with an entire new U.S. auto industry that is cleaner and smarter and has better designs and is making better products, those are potentially thousands, tens of thousands, hundreds of thousands of manufacturing jobs. And the Midwest is really poised to get a lot of those jobs. In a town like Toledo, where you've still got a lot of skilled workers, they are poised to be able to take off on that. But we've got to continue to support it.

The other area that I've already mentioned is infrastructure. I mean, we've got about $2 tril-lion worth of infrastructure improvements that need to be made all across the country: roads, bridges, sewer lines, water mains. It's crumbling. The previous generation made all these investments that not only put people to work right away, but also laid the foundation then for economic growth in the future.

And we used to always have the best infrastructure worldwide. Now, if it comes to rail, we certainly don't have the best rail system in the world. Our roads in a lot of places aren't the best. Our airports aren't the best. Somebody is laughing. They just got—obviously went through an airport. So we've got a lot of work to do on infrastructure. And this is an area where I hope we can get some bipartisan agreement.

It's hard to get bipartisan agreement these days. But I think that the notion that we can put people to work rebuilding America, investing in making stuff here in the United States that—by the way, every time you build a road, that's not just putting people to work on the actual construction; all those supplies that go into road building, all those supplies that go into a bridge, all those supplies that go into rail, that's creating a ripple effect all throughout the economy. So I think that's a second area of great potential.

Last point you made was—had to do with pensions. Look, the truth be told, the way we were handling pensions, both in private companies and among public employees, a lot of it wasn't that different from some of the stuff that was going on in Wall Street, because what happened was, is that these pensions weren't adequately funded. Some of these companies would underfund it and then say, well, we're going to get an 8-percent return or 10-percent return on our pension funds, to make it look like they were adequately funded when they weren't. That contributed to pension funds chasing a lot of risky investments that promised these high returns, but in fact were built on a house of cards. So you're going to see a number of pensions in a number of companies that are underfunded.

Now, we've got a mechanism at the Federal level that provides a certain percentage backup or guarantee for these pension funds if they fail. But we're going to have to, I think, work with these private sector companies so that—right now they've become very profitable; companies are making money right now. We were talking earlier about the economy and how it's moving slow. Well, corporate profits are doing just fine. They're holding onto a whole bunch of cash. They're kind of sitting on it, waiting to see if they can make more money and more opportunity, but they haven't started hiring yet. One of the things they need to be doing with some of this cash is shoring up their pension funds that are currently underfunded. Okay?

It's a girl's turn. Yes, right there.

Education Reform

Q. Mr. President, tied in with the jobs situation, I think, is the education system. And it seems to be in a crisis now, and people are not being educated to take these jobs that are going to be created. And I wondered what sort of plans you might have for that.

The President. That's a great question. Are you in education?

Q. No.

The President. No?

Q. I'm a nurse.

The President. Well, that's important too.

Q. Yes.

The President. Thanks for the care you give to people all day long. I'm a big fan of nurses.

The thing that will probably most determine our success in the 21st century is going to be our education system. I'll just give you a quick statistic. A generation ago, we ranked number one in the number of college graduates. We've now slipped to number 12 in the number of college graduates. That's just in one generation. That is putting us at a huge competitive disadvantage. Because, look, companies these days, they can locate anywhere. You've got an Internet line, you can set your company up in India, you can set up your company in the Czech Republic. It doesn't really matter where you are.

And so what that means is a lot of companies are going to look for where can they find the best workforce. And we have to make sure that that is in Columbus, Ohio. We've got to make sure that that's in Toledo. We've got to make sure that that's in the United States of America.

Now, we still have the best universities and the best colleges on Earth. But there are a couple of problems that have come up. First of all, our education starts at K–12. And we're not doing a good enough job at the K–12 level making sure that all our kids are proficient in math, in science, in reading and writing.

And what we've done is we've set up something called the Race to the Top, where, although a lot of Federal money still flows to schools just based on a formula and based on need, we've taken a certain amount of money and we've said, you know what, you've got to compete for this money. And you've got to show us that you've got a plan to improve the education system, to fix low-performing schools, to improve how you train teachers—because teachers are the single most important ingredient in the education system—to collect data to show that you're improving how these kids are learning.

And what's happened is, is that States all across the country have actually responded really well, and we've seen the majority of States change their laws to start doing this bottom-up, grassroots reform of the K–12 system. That's critical. That's number one.

Second thing that we've got to solve is that college became unaffordable for a lot of people. And Joe and Rhonda, we were just talking— we're about the same age, and we got married, I think, the same year. Our kids are about the same age. So we've kind of gone through the same stuff. And Michelle and I—I don't know about you guys; we didn't talk about this—but Michelle and I, we had a lot of debt when we finished school. It was really expensive. And neither of us came from wealthy families, so we just had to take out a bunch of student loans. It took us about 10 years to pay off our student loans. It was actually higher than our mortgage for most of the time.

And I don't want that burden to be placed on kids right now. Because a lot of them, as a consequence, maybe they decide not to go to college, or if they do, they end up getting off to a really tough start because their pay just is not going to support the amount of debt that they've got.

So here's what we did. Working with Sherrod, working with Mary Jo, Democrats in Congress, this didn't get a lot of attention, but we actually completely transformed how the Government student loan program works. Originally what was happening was all those loans were going through banks and financial intermediaries. And even though the loans were guaranteed by the Government, so the banks weren't taking any risks, they were skimming off billions of dollars in profits.

And we said, well, that doesn't make any sense. If we're guaranteeing it, why don't we just give the loans directly to the students? And we'll take all that extra billions of dollars that were going to the banks as profits, and we'll give more loans. And as a consequence, what we've been able to do is to provide millions more students additional loans and make college more affordable over time. That's the second thing.

Third thing we've got to do is we've got to focus on community colleges, which are a wonderful asset. Not everybody is going to go to a 4-year college. And even if you go to a 4-year college, you may need to go back and retrain 2 years, or for a year or two, even while you're working, to keep up, keep pace with new technologies and new developments in your industry. So what we've really tried to do is to partner with community colleges, figure out how we can strengthen them, put more resources into them, and link them up to businesses who are actually hiring so that they're training people for the jobs that exist, as opposed to the jobs that don't.

Now, one of the problems we've had for a lot of young people is they go to college, training for a job, thinking that their job—or thinking there's a job out there, and actually the economy has moved on. And what we need to do is tailor people's education so that they are linked up with businesses who say, we need this many engineers, or we need this kind of technical training. And we'll help design what that training is so that when that person goes to college and they're taking out some of those loans to go to college, they know at the end of the road there's actually going to be a job available to them.

Now, last thing: Math, science, we've really got to emphasize those. That's an area where we've really fallen far behind, and our technological competitiveness is going to depend on how well we do in math and science. All right?

Okay. Who we got? Yes, sir.

Support for State and Local First-Responders

Q. Mr. President, my name is Joe Richard. I am a proud firefighter for the great city of Columbus here in Ohio. [*Applause*] Thank you much.

The President. Joe, did you use to play for Ohio State, man? [*Laughter*]

Q. I must correct you. I was actually a part of the national championship team for Eastern Kentucky University.

The President. Oh, okay, all right. That's nice.

Q. For the national champion, no less. [*Laughter*]

The President. Well, there you go, okay. But you look like you could—we could put you on the line right now.

Q. Oh, that's what they all say. [*Laughter*]

The President. Anyway.

Q. But, Mr. President, I wanted to talk to you about a couple of things as it pertains to the safety and security of our firefighters. I want to share with you some good news as it pertains to the stimulus and the SAFER Act for which you championed and signed off on.

Locally and from the State standpoint, we had some firefighter jobs that were in jeopardy, up in the hundreds. The stimulus package—I know the State was strapped with its commitment and what it had to with those monies. Some of those areas we weren't able to be supported in. But because of your administration signing off on the SAFER Act, which is staffing adequate fire and emergency response, you provided over 300 million last year and upped that to over 400 million this year; that had allowed for the jobs in Ohio to come back—the firefighters, rather, who had jobs come back and get their jobs back.

In addition to that, the FIRE Act has provided safer equipment for us. We—don't want to sound cliche, but I'm just your average Joe. But what we do as firefighters, we want to make a significant difference to our citizens here in our community as well as our lives. That SAFER Act and that FIRE Act has provided us significant equipment—money, funding, rather, for significant equipment—face pieces, self-contained breathing apparatus, things of those nature. So we come to say how proud we are to be able to afford that opportunity to safely secure our firefighters.

The international president has sent a appreciative thank you, and we would hope that you would find—and I know your busy schedule—somewhere around this country—Cincinnati, Akron, Elyria, Niles—have brought back firefighters because of the SAFER Act. And if anywhere along your schedule you have the opportunity, as a symbolic gesture of support, to stop in to those stations, thank those firefighters, we would greatly appreciate that.

The President. Well, thank you. And as I said, you guys put your lives on the line each and every day. We wanted to make sure that public safety was not being threatened as a consequence of the recession. We've done that. We've helped to support not just firefighters, but also police officers, teachers, other vital services. We're going to continue to support you. And again, we're very grateful for everything you do.

And if this is your lovely wife here, we're grateful to her too, because she's got to put up with you—[*laughter*]—running off into fires and putting yourself in danger. And I'm sure that makes her a little bit stressed once in a while, but I'm sure she's very proud of you.

Q. Thank you.

The President. Okay. Anybody else? Yes, go ahead. Here, we've got a microphone over here.

Childcare

Q. Hi, Mr. President, my name is Pam Cohen, and I was actually recently laid off of a position working at our local community college, helping dislocated workers get back and get retrained. But the position was funded on workforce investment dollars, and the funding ended. As I look for a new position in social services, one of my concerns is I'm having trouble finding a position that pays enough so that I can pay my bills and also send my daughter to quality childcare. So I was wondering if there's anything that's been done to reduce childcare costs, in Washington.

The President. Well, we have a childcare credit in place. We'd like to make it stronger. This is one of those back-and-forths we've been having with the Republicans, because we actually think it is a good idea and they don't. [*Laughter*] But I think that giving families support who have to work each and every day is absolutely critical.

Now, there's some companies that are starting to get smart about providing childcare on site for their employees, which makes a huge difference. It's a huge relief. But those are usually bigger companies. And some of the smaller companies or small businesses don't have that capacity.

The bottom line is, we've just got to make sure that we're providing you more support, primarily through a tax credit mechanism. This is something that we have incorporated in the past in our budget; we haven't gotten everything that we'd like done on it. It will be something that we continue to try to work on a bipartisan basis to get the cost of childcare down.

There's another component of this, though, and that's also boosting the quality of childcare. Kids learn more from the age of zero to 3 than they do probably for the rest of their lives, and this goes to the earlier question about education. We want to get them off to a good start, knowing their colors and their numbers and their letters and just knowing how to sit still. And a high-quality childcare environment can help on that front. But that means that childcare workers, for example, have to be paid a decent wage and get decent training.

And we've been working—we set up actually a task force that is trying to lift up the best practices, who's really doing a great job in creating high-quality health care—or childcare at an affordable rate, and then trying to teach other States and other cities and other communities how to replicate some of that great progress that's been made. There are some terrific programs out there, but they're still too far and few between. Okay?

All right, I've got time for two more questions. Yes, sir, right here.

National Economy/Housing Market

Q. Hi. My name is Mike O'Reilly, and I work for a company who is just—is benefiting from some stimulus money here in Columbus, and it's keeping me and my crews afloat for a while. But what we really need is a stronger housing market here in Columbus. We need to be building new roads and making houses affordable for people. They need to get out there buying. They need to be able to get the loans. And what's up with that? [*Laughter*]

The President. Well, remember I told you that it's going to take some time for this economy to come back? One of the reasons it's going to take time for this economy to come back is the housing market is still a big drag on the economy as a whole. And the reason the housing market is still a big drag on the economy as a whole is we built a lot of homes over the previous 5, 7, 10 years. Every year, about 1.4 million families are formed that are ready to buy a new house or need some place to live.

And what happened over the previous 4, 5, 7 years during this housing bubble was we were building 2 million homes a year when only 1.4 were being absorbed. And then the bubble burst, and now we're only building 400,000. And all that inventory that's happened during the housing bubble, it's still out there. So some States are worse than others. You go to places like Nevada or Arizona or Florida, California, their inventory of unsold homes was so high that it is just going to take a whole bunch of years to absorb all that housing stock.

Now, what we can do is to help people who are currently in their homes stay in their homes. We can strengthen the economy overall so that that new family that just formed, they feel confident enough to say, you know what, it's time, honey, for us to go out and take the plunge and start looking. And right now they're kind of holding back, the way a lot of people are still holding back, because there's uncertainty in the market. And we've initiated, through the Treasury Department, a number of programs like that to help support the housing market generally.

But I want to be honest with you: It is going to take some time for us to absorb this over—this inventory that was just too high. And there's no really quick way to do it, because we're talking about a $5 trillion market. And we can't plug that big hole in terms of all the housing that needs to be absorbed. We're not going to be able subsidize all that overcapacity right now.

What we can do is just stabilize it and then improve the economy overall. What we're going to do is get back to the point where we're building 1.4 million homes a year, instead of 400,000, and that's a huge difference. So the industry is going to come back. The question is, can we just nudge it a little bit more? And the most important thing we can do now is to improve the economy overall so that people start feeling a little more confidence.

All right? I've got time for one more? You've got a question? Here, you can use mine.

Medicare/Health Care Reform

Q. Thank you. My name is Nadine Eggleston. I'm the practice manager at an ophthalmology practice at the Eye Center of Columbus, downtown. It is a great facility that the city of Columbus helped us get in place. There are over 30 ophthalmologists providing specialty care in separate practices, a state-of-the-art ambulatory surgery center. We see tens of thousands of patients a year. And I think we do a very efficient job of providing quality care, over 300 people employed. So I'm kind of on both sides of health care.

And when I started working for this practice 25 years ago, we are now getting reimbursed one-third of what we got paid for—I'm just going to pick cataract surgery—yet our operating costs continue to go up. My boss is kind enough to provide health care costs entirely for all of his employees. How does he continue to do that when Medicare continues to reduce what they're paying and there's the threat of more cuts coming and the private insurance companies follow suit?

The President. Well, it's a great question. And let me talk about Medicare generally.

Medicare, I think, is one of the cornerstones of our social safety net. The basic idea is, you've been working all your life, you retire; just like you've got Social Security that you can count on, you've also got health care that you can count on and you're not going to go bankrupt just because you get sick.

But in the same way that Social Security has to be tweaked because the population is getting older, we've got to refresh and renew Medicare to make sure that it's going to be there for the next generation as well. And the key problems are not just that more people, as they retire, are going to be part of Medicare. The big problem is just health care inflation generally. The costs of health care keep on skyrocketing.

Now, the way we've been dealing with it, which I think is the wrong way to deal with it, is basically underreimbursing our providers. The right way to deal with it is to work with the providers to figure out how can we make the system less wasteful, more efficient overall. And that way we're paying—your boss, if he's spending a dollar on care, he's getting reimbursed a dollar. But we're also making sure that the care he's providing is exactly what the person needs, and high quality for a better price.

And that's part of what health care reform was all about. I'll just give you a couple examples. One of the things that we were doing in Medicare was we were giving tens of billions of dollars of subsidies to insurance companies under the Medicare Advantage plan, even though that plan wasn't shown to make seniors any healthier than regular old Medicare.

So we said, all right, we're not going to end Medicare Advantage, but we are going to have some competitive bidding and we're going to force the insurance companies to show us, well, what exactly—what value are you adding? How are you helping to make these seniors healthier? And if you're not helping, then you shouldn't be getting paid. We should be giving that money to the doctor and the nurse and the other people who are actually providing care, not the insurance companies.

Well, there was a lot of hue and cry about this, but it was absolutely the right thing to do, because now we just found out—the actuaries for Medicare said the changes we've already made has extended the life of the Medicare trust fund for another 12 years, which is, by the way, the longest it's ever been extended as a consequence of a reform effort.

So we've made Medicare stronger just with some of the changes that we've already made. But you're absolutely right that we're going to have to keep on making these changes to continue to make it stronger. And that will affect not just Medicare; it will affect the entire health care system. Because there's no doctor out there who doesn't see Medicare as the 800-pound gorilla. If Medicare is saying you've got to improve your quality and efficiency, then they will, because they've got a lot of Medicare patients. But they also have a lot of regular patients. So hospitals, doctors, everybody starts getting more efficient as Medicare gets more efficient. The key is making sure that we're not just cutting benefits.

And frankly, this is an argument that I have with my friends in the Republican Party sometimes. One big change that some of them have advocated is to voucherize the Medicare system. You basically—instead of once you have Medicare, you knowing that you can take that and go get care anywhere you want, we would just give you—all right, here is whatever it is, $6,000 or $7,000 or whatever; you go shop and figure out what kind of best deal you can get.

The problem is, is that if Medicare costs keep—if health care costs keep on going up, but your voucher doesn't keep on going up, you're going to be in trouble. And suddenly, you've got seniors who find themselves way short of what they need in terms of providing care.

We've got to change how the health care system actually operates. And that means more prevention—more preventive care. It means better—that we reimburse people for checkups. It means we reimburse doctors when they're consulting with people on things like smoking cessation and weight control and exercise.

There are a whole bunch of things that can make us healthier, reduce our costs overall. But unfortunately, the system doesn't incentivize them right now. We need to change that. Okay? All right.

Anybody have any last burning question? That was technically the last question. But this has to be like one that you're just, man, I really need an answer for. [*Laughter*]

Q. [*Inaudible*]

The President. All right.

Financial Regulatory Reform

Q. I've got a very general question.

The President. Okay, go ahead.

Q. It's a very general question, here. My name is Colin O'Reilly. That's my dad Mike, my mom. I work on Wall Street. I was wondering what kind of changes we can expect to see in the reform in the next couple years.

The President. Well, here's the essential components of Wall Street reform that we set up. Number one is that we've got a—we had a system in which there was huge amounts of leverage that banks could take. And what leverage means is if they got a dollar in deposits, they were making a $40 bet using that $1, which when times are good, means you're making a lot of money, right? You're putting $1 down of your own money, and you got $40, and when the market is going up, you're making out like a bandit. But when the market goes down, when it starts deleveraging, you're in trouble. And that's basically what happened with Lehmans and a lot of these other companies.

So one thing that we've said is that we've got to have—for big firms that are what we call systemic, that if they go down, the whole system could go down with them—we've got to have a better check and say, you know what, you've got to control a little bit how you work in terms of leverage. You've got to have enough capital, actual money, to cover the bets that you're placing so that you're not putting the whole system at risk. That's number one.

Number two, there's a whole derivatives market out there, which, frankly, even the bankers don't completely understand. But you've got trillions of dollars—and if you work on Wall Street, you're familiar obviously with the derivatives market. I mean, you've got trillions of dollars that are basically outside of the regulated banking system, and people didn't know who's making bets on what. And what we

said was that derivatives market, it needs—it can continue, but it's got to be in an open, transparent marketplace so that everybody knows who is betting on what. And we're very clear about who the various parties are in these complex derivatives transactions, that means the regulators can follow it a little more closely. That's number two.

The third thing that we did is we made sure that we don't have taxpayer bailouts again. So we've set up a system whereby if a big firm gets in trouble, we're able to essentially quarantine it, separate it out from the rest of the pack, liquidate it without it spilling over into the system as a whole. That's the third thing.

And the fourth thing is having a consumer financial protection agency that is really going to do a good job making sure that consumers know what they're getting when it comes to financial products. I mean, when you buy a toaster, there has been some assurance provided that that toaster will not explode in your face, right? There are a whole bunch of laws in there; people have to do tests on the toasters to make sure that nothing happens. But if you buy a mortgage that explodes in your face because you didn't know what was going on, everybody acts like, well, that's your problem.

Well, no, it's actually all of our problems, because part of the reason we had this financial crisis was because people did not always understand the financial instruments that they were purchasing. A lot of these subprime loans that were being given out, a lot of these no-interest—you can buy your house and you don't put any money down and you don't pay any interest, you got this beautiful house—and naturally, people were thinking, well, this sounds great. But what they weren't looking at was, okay, all right, there's a balloon payment 5 years down. This is only going to work if your housing—the value of your house keeps on appreciating. And if it stops appreciating, suddenly it's not going to work anymore. People hadn't thought through all those ramifications. And that had an effect on the whole system.

So what we've said is we're going to have a strong consumer finance protection agency whose only job is to look after you when it comes to financial products. And Joe and Rhonda and I were just talking about how it was only 7, 8 years ago when Michelle and I were trying to figure out our student loans, how were we going to invest for the kids' college education. We had—at the end of the month, I'd be getting my credit card bills, and I'm a pretty smart guy, but you open up some of those credit card, you don't know what's going on. You don't read all that fine print. You just look at the statement.

Well, as an example of the kinds of things that this new agency are going to be enforcing, we've already passed a law—thanks, again, to Mary Jo and Sherrod—we've already passed a law that says a credit card company can't raise the interest rates on existing balances. So it can't attract you with a zero-percent interest, you run up a $3,000 balance, and then suddenly they send you your next statement and it says, oh, your interest went up to 29 percent. You can't do that. I mean, they'll still be able to say, we're going to raise your interest rate to 29 percent, but that can only be on the balances going forward. It can't be on the money that you borrowed where you thought it was at zero percent.

Well, that's an example of straightforward, honest dealing that we're going to be expecting. We think the financial markets will still make money, the banks can still make money, but they got to make money the old-fashioned way, which is loan money to small businesses who are providing services to the community. Loan money to Joe for his architectural firm, and he's going to make sure you pay him back. Loan people for mortgages, but make sure that you've done the due diligence so that you're not tricking them into something they can't afford. Make sure that it's something that you can afford, right?

They're just a bunch of basic, commonsense reforms that we're putting in place that will allow the market to function. Because the free market is the best system ever devised for creating wealth, but there have got to be some rules in the road so that you're making money not by gaming the system, but by providing a better product or a better service. All right?

Well, listen, I want to thank all of you for spending the time. I know it got a little warm, and you guys just hung in there like troopers. I want to make sure that I thank, once again, Ted Strickland, Sherrod Brown, Mayor Michael Coleman, your Lieutenant Governor—and I believe the next United States Senator—Lee Fisher, and Mary Jo Kilroy for being here. And obviously, I want to thank Joe and Rhonda Weithman and the whole Weithman family for sharing their backyard.

And we're going to have to make sure that we're helping their lawn here. [*Laughter*] It got trampled on a little bit. I hope you guys are not stepping in the corn. [*Laughter*] Michelle, by the way, would be very proud to see that you've got the vegetable garden working. All right? Give them a big round of applause, everybody.

Thank you very much. Thank you.

Oh, and by the way, I just wanted—is this still on? I just want you to know that the Weithmans made me the "O" in O–H–I–O. It's on tape. It's on tape somewhere.

NOTE: The President spoke at 10:47 a.m. at the residence of Joe and Rhonda Weithman. In his remarks, he referred to Josh and Rachel Weithman, children of Mr. and Mrs. Weithman. A participant referred to the Pension Protection Act of 2006 (PPA); and the Pension Benefit Guaranty Corporation (PBGC).

Remarks at a Fundraiser for Governor Theodore Strickland in Columbus
August 18, 2010

Thank you, everybody! Thank you, Ohio! Please, have a seat. Have a seat. Thank you so much. It is great to be here.

There are a couple of people I want to make sure to acknowledge. They may have already

been acknowledged, but not by me. So I'm going to acknowledge them because they are doing outstanding work: First of all, the mayor of the great city of Columbus, Michael Coleman; a champion of working families not just in Ohio, but all across the country, Senator Sherrod Brown; a wonderful Member of Congress who's fighting day in, day out, Mary Jo Kilroy is here; and although he is not on the list, he's down a little south from here but he's here, I saw him, so I want to acknowledge him because he is just an outstanding, outstanding young Member of Congress, Steve Driehaus is in the house. There he is.

Lieutenant Governor and soon to be Senator, Lee Fisher is here. Attorney General Rich Cordray is here. Treasurer Kevin Boyce is in the house. And candidate for Lieutenant Governor, Yvette McGee Brown is here.

It is good to be back in Ohio. And it is good to be among such good friends, because as I look out over the audience, I know so many of you worked so hard on behalf of our campaign. You were there when we were up; you were there when we were down. I might not be standing here if it weren't for the incredible efforts that all of you put in here in this State and around the country. So thank you so much for everything that you've done. It truly means a lot.

I have to say, by the way, that earlier today we had a wonderful little mini-town hall in the backyard of some folks, the Weithmans. And you will be pleased to know that for using their backyard, the price they charged was they made me be the "O" in O–H–I–O. [*Laughter*] The—this is true. This is true. This is on videotape—[*laughter*]—which I'm worried about when I go to Michigan. [*Laughter*] But I did their commencement, so hopefully things kind of will balance out.

Look, the main reason I'm here is to stand with somebody who I genuinely believe is one of the best public servants in the country, your Governor, Ted Strickland.

Ted took office during an enormously difficult time in Ohio's history. And this State had been hit harder than almost anyplace else by the loss of manufacturing. And when the recession hit in 2008, times got even tougher. But from the day he stepped in as Governor, Ted Strickland has not wasted a single, solitary minute fighting to turn this economy around. Not a minute has gone by that he hasn't thought about

how do we build an economy not just for the present, but for future generations.

And under Ted's watch, Ohio has invested in high-growth industries; he has invested in new infrastructure. He's provided new skills and job training to more than 150,000 workers. There are over 65,000 more students in college than when Ted took office. He's cut redtape. He's kept taxes low so this State can be a better place to do business.

And he hasn't just been concerned about the next election, he's been concerned about the next generation of Ohio families. And his work is not yet done. So I know I'm preaching to the choir in this room, but I want everybody who's going to be hearing me through the television, I want you guys to know Ted Strickland has done an outstanding job for Ohio, and he needs another term to finish what he has started here. You've got to turn out for Ted Strickland.

Now, we need leaders like Ted in this country—and like Sherrod and Mary Jo and Steve. We need them because we face an incredibly challenging time for America. Eighteen months ago, when I took office, after nearly a decade of economic policies that had given us sluggish growth and falling incomes and falling wages and a record deficit, we knew that it was going to be tough to rebuild this economy. But when I was sworn in, nobody fully, I think, appreciated at that point how bad this recession had become. It turned out this was the worst financial crisis and the worst recession since the Great Depression.

In the last 6 months of 2008, while I was still campaigning, 3 million Americans lost their jobs. In the month that I was sworn in, nearly 800,000 people lost their jobs, 600,000 a month after that, 600,000 a month after that. Before we had any opportunity to put in our economic policies, we had already seen millions of jobs lost, ultimately, 8 million jobs.

And these aren't just statistics. Behind each of these stories—behind these statistics is a story of heartache; it's a story of frustration. You got workers, midlife, who are suddenly laid off and don't know what they're going to do next; single moms sending out job application after job application, waiting for the phone to ring, trying to figure out how they're going to pay the bills; college graduates who thought, having worked hard in school, that a degree would land a good job and a decent paycheck, and instead just have a mountain of debt to show for it; and some young people who made the decision to forego college because their families couldn't afford it.

I hear these stories every single day. I read them in the letters that I get each night. The struggles and the hopes of these Americans are the reason I ran for office in the first place. They're the reason that Ted ran for office in the first place. That's why I intend to keep fighting as hard as I can, as long as it takes, to make sure that this economy is working for every single American. Anybody who wants a job got to be able to go out there and get one, and we're not going to be done until we get that result.

Now, we're not there yet. We know that. It will take a few years to fully dig ourselves out of this recession. It will take time to bring back 8 million jobs that have been lost. That's the hard truth. Anybody who's telling you otherwise, they're just running for office. [*Laughter*]

But here's what I can tell you: After 18 months, I have never been more confident that our Nation is headed in the right direction. We are doing what is needed to move the country forward. We're rebuilding this economy not just in the short term, but for the long term, for our children, for our grandchildren, for our great-grandchildren.

You see, we did not become the most prosperous country on Earth by rewarding greed and recklessness of the sort that helped cause this financial crisis. We didn't come this far by letting a handful of irresponsible folks on Wall Street or insurance companies or special interests run wild. We did it by rewarding the values of hard work and responsibility, by investing in people who've built this country from the ground up, middle class families and small-business owners. We did it by outworking and outeducating and outcompeting every nation on Earth. That's what we are going to do again.

But we've got to—but we're going to have to buckle down. We're going to have to buckle down because the competition is fierce out

there. Right now countries like China and India and South Korea and Germany, they are fighting as hard as they can for the jobs of the future. They are trying to outcompete us when it comes to clean energy. They're trying to outcompete us when it comes to how many engineers they're producing and how many entrepreneurs they're producing. And frankly, in some cases, they've pulled ahead. We used to be ranked number one in the number of college graduates. We have slipped to number 12 in a single generation. That's unacceptable.

The United States of America does not play for second place. We play for first place. We are going to rebuild this economy stronger than it was before. We're going to rebuild this economy stronger than it was before, and at its heart are going to be three powerful words: Made in America. Made in America.

We got to make stuff here and ship it over there, not the other way around. And that means instead of giving tax breaks to corporations that are shipping our jobs overseas, we need to cut taxes for companies that create jobs right here in the United States of America. It means giving smart tax breaks to small-business owners, tax cuts to clean energy companies. And yes, it means tax cuts, but for middle class families, the 95 percent of our workers that I pledged I would provide a tax cut to, and we delivered on that pledge.

And instead of prolonging an addiction to oil that endangers everything from our security to our coastlines, we're now jump-starting a homegrown clean energy industry in this country. I don't want to see solar panels and wind turbines and electric cars manufactured in Europe or in Asia. I want to see them made right here in the United States of America, by American workers. And that's starting to happen all across the Midwest.

Because of the clean energy investments we've made, you're seeing solar plants and wind turbine plants popping up, advanced battery manufacturing right here in the Midwest. But we've also got to not only spur on clean energy, we've got to build a 21st-century infrastructure. Yes, new roads, new bridges, but also faster Internet access, high-speed railroads, projects that will lead to hundreds of thousands of new private sector jobs.

And we're helping to get the American auto industry back on its feet and retool for the 21st century. Now, this is an industry that had lost hundreds of thousands of jobs in the year before I took office. We had to make a tough decision about whether to help them out or walk away from what could have potentially been another million jobs lost. And I decided we couldn't walk away.

And you'll recall that was not necessarily a popular decision. Folks in Washington are always puzzled by me doing things that don't poll well. [*Laughter*] But let's take the case of the automakers. They said, couldn't be done, it was better to just walk away. Instead of providing them bailouts with no obligations in return, like it had happened in the previous administration, we said, we'll help you out, but you got to restructure, because we want you to be able to compete in the 21st century.

And today all three U.S. automakers are operating at a profit for the first time in years. They've had the strongest job growth in more than 10 years. Folks are working across the Midwest because of the decision that we made.

I visited a Chrysler plant in Detroit a few weeks back. Turns out 14 workers had won the lottery. Now, you would have thought they might have decided to retire. But instead of quitting, most of them had stayed on their jobs because they love their work. They're proud of what they do. In fact, the guy who had bought the winning lottery ticket, not only is he staying on his job, but he used the money to buy a new Grand Cherokee that he had built for his wife.

So my message to the naysayers in Washington is this: Don't bet against the American worker. Don't bet against the American people. Don't bet against American businesses. Don't bet against American ingenuity. We are coming back, and we are coming back strong. We're moving forward, and Ohio is moving forward.

To ensure that our workers can compete with any workers on Earth, we are reforming our education system based on what works for our children, not on what works for the status quo. We've eliminated billions of dollars in taxpayer subsidies to the big banks that were providing college loans to take that money, the savings, and use it to make college more affordable for millions of students.

To lower the costs for families and businesses, we passed health insurance reform that is finally going to make coverage affordable and stop insurance companies from jacking up your premiums or refusing to cover you just because you're sick. To ensure that an equal day of work means an equal day of pay, I signed a law that will help end pay discrimination in the workforce. To keep faith with the brave men and women who risk their lives for ours, we are increasing access to health care and benefits and education for our veterans and their families.

And we are keeping the promise I made when I began my campaign for the Presidency: By the end of this month, we will have removed 100,000 troops from Iraq and our combat mission will be over in Iraq.

To ensure that a financial crisis like the one we just went through doesn't happen again, we passed financial reform that provides new accountability and tough oversight of Wall Street, reform that will stop credit card companies from charging you hidden fees or unfair rate hikes and that will end Wall Street bailouts once and for all.

All these reforms will make America more competitive in the 21st century. All these reforms are helping to move us forward. And on each of these reforms, we reached out to Democrats and Republicans for ideas and support. But in just about every instance, almost every Republican in Congress said no. They said no to help for small businesses. They're still saying no. They said no on middle class tax cuts. This is supposed to be the party of tax cuts—said no when it came to tax cuts for folks who needed them, no on clean energy jobs right here in Ohio and across the country, no on making college more affordable, no on Wall Street reform.

You remember our slogan during the campaign, "Yes, we can"? This year, their slogan is, "No, we can't." [*Laughter*] It's catchy. [*Laughter*] It's really inspiring. It puts a little pep in your step—"No, we can't." [*Laughter*] That's their philosophy.

And the reason they're saying no is because they won't give up on the economic policies, the philosophy that they've been peddling for most of this decade. And their agenda is pretty straightforward: You cut taxes for millionaires and billionaires, you cut rules for special interests, and then you cut working folks loose to fend for themselves. If you can't find a job or you can't afford college or you don't have health insurance or your child doesn't have health insurance, tough luck, you are on your own.

The thing is, we tried this philosophy, remember? For 8 years. And it didn't work out real well. All it gave us was record deficits and the worst economic crisis since the Great Depression.

Now, I bring this up not to relitigate the past. I bring it up because I don't want to relive the past. [*Laughter*] It would be one thing if Republicans, after y'all voted them out, had said, "You know what, maybe our philosophy doesn't work," they'd gone off into the desert and kind of meditated and came back: "We've learned from our mistakes; we promise to do things differently this time; we've got some new ideas we want you to try." I would have gladly said, "All right, come on, let's work together." But that's not what they're doing.

One of the leaders in Congress was asked what his party would do if he took over Congress. He said, we will pursue "the exact same agenda" as before President Obama took office—the exact same agenda. Now, think about that. Basically, they're betting on—between now and November—they're betting on you coming down with a case of amnesia. [*Laughter*] That's their strategy. They figure you're going to forget what their agenda did to this country over the last 8 years.

Now, I was using an analogy—I was talking out in California—it's—imagine our economy is a car. And these guys, I don't know what they were doing. I don't know whether they were on their BlackBerry while they were driving or they were doing something else irresponsible. They drive it into the ditch.

And so me and Sherrod and Mary Jo and Steve and Ted and a whole bunch of folks, we're all putting our boots on, and we go down into the ditch. And it's muddy down there, and it's hot, and there are bugs swirling around. And we're pushing on the car, trying to get it out of the ditch, putting our shoulder—shoving it, pushing it. And the Republicans are up there looking at us, sipping on their Slurpees. [*Laughter*] "You're not pushing hard enough. You're not pushing the right way. Push harder." And we invite them to come down and help us out, and they just sort of said: "No, we don't want to. No, we can't." [*Laughter*]

And then finally we get this car up on level ground, and it's ready to finally move forward. And we feel this tap on our shoulders, and we turn around, and it's those Republicans, and they're saying, "We want the keys back." [*Laughter*]

Well, no, you cannot have the keys to the car back. You drove it into the ditch. You don't know how to drive. We worked hard to get it out of the ditch. We now want to move forward; we don't want to move backwards. We don't want to move backwards. We don't want to move backwards. If you want, you can sit in the back. [*Laughter*] We're happy to have you along for the ride. But we're moving forward.

And I just want to point out, when you want your car to go forward, what do you do? You put it into "D." When you want it going backwards, what do you do? You put it into "R." [*Laughter*] We don't want to go into reverse. We don't want to go back into the ditch. That's not a coincidence. [*Laughter*] That's not a coincidence. That's not a coincidence. [*Laughter*]

Let me tell you what will happen if the other party takes over Congress in November. If you want to know what will happen if the other party takes over Congress, all you've got to do is look what they've done over the last 18 months on issue after issue. They've sided with special interests over the middle class families; voted to keep giving tax breaks to companies that ship jobs overseas, despite folks like Sherrod Brown, who fought hard on this issue; voted to give insurance companies the power to keep denying coverage to people who are sick.

The top Republican on the Energy Committee, you may recall—this is the guy who would be in charge of the Energy Committee in the

House of Representatives—apologized after the oil spill to BP. [*Laughter*] Remember this? He apologized because I had said to BP, you need to set aside $20 billion to make sure that we're making fishermen and small-business owners whole as a consequence of your mistakes. This guy, he apologized to BP. He said, "Oh, the President shook you down," a "Chicago-style shakedown." That's what he called it. [*Laughter*] That's what he called it. He had to throw in the Chicago thing in there. [*Laughter*]

Imagine that. That's what's at stake in this election. If we give them the keys back, they will drive right back into the ditch. And riding shotgun with them will be every other special interest under the Sun.

And by the way, let me make this point: I want business in this country to succeed. The free market is the greatest wealth producer in our history. We were built on entrepreneurship and private enterprise. And if you are a responsible business owner, I will do everything I can to help you grow and prosper and hire more employees. And Ted Strickland will do the same. But I don't think it's antibusiness to say we should make sure an oil rig is safe before we start drilling. I don't think it's antibusiness to say that Wall Street banks should play by the same rules as everybody else. I don't think it's antibusiness to say that insurance companies shouldn't deny people care just because they get sick.

We can't have an attitude that what's good enough for me is good enough. We've got to have an attitude that says, what's good for America? What's good for everybody? What's best for all of our businesses? What's best for all of our people? That's what we do in this country. That's how we move forward as one people, as one Nation. And that is what we've got to get back to, those core American values that moves everybody forward and builds a broad middle class where everybody can prosper.

Now, I know times are tough, Columbus. And when times are tough, it can be easy to give in to cynicism and it can be easy to give in to fear, to set our sights lower, to settle for the status quo, to pit people against each other, to find

wedge issues, to focus on those things that appear to give a tactical advantage, but have nothing to do with whether or not our country is going to be successful over the long term. That's—let's face it, that's how politics works too much.

That's what the other side is counting on in this election. They're not offering new plans. They're not offering new ideas. They're just offering cynicism, and they're offering fear.

But that's not who we are. That's not the country I know. We are Americans. We do not give up. We do not quit. We do not fear the future. We shape the future. We seize our own destiny.

That's what this election is about. And so I need all of you, every single one of you, to go out there and join me and Ted Strickland in building a future. Let's build a future where our small businesses flourish on the power of ideas and ingenuity and a future where clean energy powers the world, produced right here in factories and fields in America. Let's build a future where our children are getting the best education possible so they're competing with anybody. Let's build a future where we are bound by our sense of optimism and our confidence and our hopefulness, our fearlessness, all that's made America the most dynamic country on Earth.

That's how we built the last American century. That is how we are going to build the next American century. The American people do not believe in the words, "No, we can't." That's not how this country got built. In times of great challenge, we push forward with the unyielding faith that, yes, we can.

Thank you very much, Ohio. God bless you, and God bless the United States of America.

NOTE: The President spoke at 1:18 p.m. at the Columbus Athenaeum. In his remarks, he referred to Columbus, OH, residents Joe and Rhonda Weithman; Chrysler employee William Shanteau and his wife Lisa; Rep. Pete Sessions, in his capacity as chairman of the National Republican Congressional Committee; and Rep. Joseph L. Barton.

Remarks at a Florida Democratic Party Reception in Miami, Florida
August 18, 2010

The President. Hey! Hello, Florida! Hello, Miami! It is good to be back. It is good to be back in Miami. I was just in Florida, and it is true that Sasha outscored me on the first hole. [*Laughter*] I took her, I think, on the third. It was tight the whole way, though. [*Laughter*] But it is wonderful to see all of you. Looking out at this crowd, I know how many of you worked so hard on my campaign, have been—[*applause*]—worked hard on behalf of Democrats for years here in Florida, and are going to be working hard on behalf of the great ticket that we're going to be having this year.

There are a number of people that I want to acknowledge. Obviously, first of all, you have got a wonderful senior Senator right here in Florida, who's working hard every day, give Bill Nelson a big round of applause. An outstanding congressional delegation: Ron Klein is here; Alan Grayson is here; Ted Deutch is here; Debbie Wasserman Schultz is here; soon-to-be Member of Congress Joe Garcia, running in Florida's 25th. Running for Florida attorney general, Dan Gelber is here—State senator. Also running for Florida attorney general, Dave Aronberg—also State senator—is here. We've got Scott Maddox, who's running for agricultural commissioner for the State. And we've got Matti Bower, mayor of Miami Beach, in the house.

So as I said, it's just great to be with friends. And you were with me when we were up; you were with me when we were down. If it weren't for you, I would not be standing here as President of the United States. And as your President, it is my honor to stand in support of the next Governor of the great State of Florida, Alex Sink.

At a difficult time like this, you need somebody in Tallahassee like Alex. She combines the sensibility of a successful businesswoman with the tenacity of a consumer watchdog, which is what she's been for the last 4 years as Florida's CFO. She's cut waste; she's eliminated unnecessary contracts; she's saved the State tens of millions of dollars. She's protected countless seniors and homeowners from being taken advan-

tage of by predatory lenders. She's put this State's entire checkbook online so you know exactly how your tax dollars are being spent. And now she's running to be the economic ambassador for this State, with a plan to attract new companies and new jobs and new opportunities to the Sunshine State.

So Alex knows what it takes to change business as usual in Tallahassee. She's not afraid to take on the status quo. She's done it before; she's going to do it again. So I want all of you to do me a favor. I know everybody here, I'm preaching to the choir. [*Laughter*] But I need you to talk to your friends, I need you to talk to your neighbors, I need you to send out e-mail blasts, I need you to raise money, I need you to walk and knock on doors, whatever it takes to make sure that Alex Sink is the next Governor of Florida. We need to move forward in this State.

And let me also say something about the next Senator from the State of Florida, Kendrick Meek. Now, Kendrick has been a champion of middle class families and somebody who has not been afraid to stand up to the status quo and special interests. So we need that kind of fighter in the United States Senate. I need you to help him get there.

We need leaders like Alex and Kendrick in this country because we are facing an incredibly challenging time. Eighteen months ago, I took office after nearly a decade of economic policies that produced sluggish growth and falling incomes and falling wages and took a record surplus to a record deficit. And these policies culminated in the worst recession of our lifetimes. In the last 6 months of 2008, 3 million Americans lost their jobs. The month I was sworn in, 800,000 more Americans lost their jobs; the month after that, 600,000; the month after that, 600,000. Before we could even get our economic policies in place, we had already seen devastation across this country.

And behind these numbers, behind these statistics, there's a story of heartache and frustration: a factory worker who was just a few years shy of retirement suddenly seeing his plant closed and not knowing where to turn; or a single mom who sends out application after application, but doesn't get a call back and wonders how she's going to pay the bills; or a college graduate who worked hard, got a degree, and all they've got to show for it is a mountain of debt; and then some kids planning to go to college decided they couldn't afford it because their family needed their help.

I hear these stories every day. I read them in letters every night. The struggles and the hopes of these Americans are why I ran for office in the first place. That's why I am going to work as hard as I can for as long as it takes to turn this economy around. That's why I ran for office. That's why Alex is here. That's our goal.

Now, Florida, we're not there yet. We are not there yet. We know that. It took us close to a decade to dig ourselves into this hole; it's going to take some time to dig ourselves out of it.

Audience member. Eight years! [*Laughter*]

The President. It takes time to bring back 8 million jobs. That's the hard truth. Somebody tells you different, they're probably running for office. [*Laughter*]

But here's what I can tell you: After 18 months, I have never been more confident that we are headed in the right direction. We are doing what's needed to move forward. We are rebuilding this economy not just for the short term—we had to rescue the economy short term, but we're also building the economy for the long run, for our children and our grandchildren.

We did not become the most prosperous country in the world by rewarding greed and recklessness of the sort that helped cause this financial crisis. We did not come this far by letting special interests run wild in Washington, writing their own rules. We did not get here by just looking after ourselves and not looking after our neighbors. We got here by rewarding the values of hard work and responsibility and by investing in our people and making sure that economic growth happened from the bottom up—middle class families and small-business owners. We did it by outworking and outeducating and outcompeting every nation on Earth. That's who we are. That's who we need to be.

This is a serious time. Right now countries like China and India and South Korea, Germany, they are fighting as hard as they can for the jobs of the future. They are trying to outcompete us on things like clean energy. They're trying to outcompete us on education and how many engineers they produce. And frankly, in some cases, we've been slipping. We used to be number 1 in the number of college graduates; we now rank number 12.

Now, let me tell you, Florida, the United States of America, we do not play for second place. We play for first place. We've got to rebuild this economy stronger than it was before. And at the center of that agenda are three powerful words: Made in America. We've got to start making things here in the United States. Instead of giving tax breaks to companies that ship our jobs overseas, we've got to cut taxes for companies that create jobs right here in the United States of America. We've got to give tax cuts to small-business owners and tax cuts to clean energy companies and tax cuts to middle class families, which is what we did. Ninety-five percent of American workers got a tax cut under my administration. That was the right thing to do.

And we've got to have an energy strategy in this country. Instead of prolonging an addiction to oil that endangers everything from our security to our coastlines, we're jump-starting a homegrown clean energy industry in this country. I don't want to see solar panels and wind turbines and advanced batteries that go into electric cars—I don't want them manufactured elsewhere. I want them manufactured right here in the United States of America, by American workers.

We've got to invest in 21st-century infrastructure. That means new bridges and new roads, but it also means faster Internet, high-speed railroad, projects that will lay the foundation for long-term economic growth, but also produce hundreds of thousands of new private sector jobs. And we are helping old industries like the American auto industry get back on its feet and retool for the 21st century.

Now, you will remember, a while back, this was an industry—the auto industry—that had lost hundreds of thousands of jobs in the year before I took office. And we had to make a tough decision about whether to help them out or walk away, which might have cost another million jobs. And a lot of folks said we should walk away. We decided, no, we're going to take a different approach. Instead of continuing to give bailouts to the auto companies and asking nothing in return, we said, we are going to make sure you restructure so you can compete over the long haul. And we got all the stakeholders together and worked hard, helped GM through bankruptcy, helped Chrysler through bankruptcy. And today, all three automakers are operating at a profit for the first time in years. They've had the strongest job growth in more than 10 years. GM just announced it's going public again.

I visited a Chrysler plant in Detroit a few weeks back, and this was a plant that would have shut down had we not moved forward. And now they're producing these outstanding cars. And 14 workers had just won the lottery at this plant. [*Laughter*] Now, instead of cashing out, quitting their jobs, most of them stayed, because they love their work. They're proud of what they do. The guy who bought the winning ticket, he bought one of the cars that he helps assemble, for his wife. And then he bought flags for his hometown, because he loves his country and he loves his workers and he loves the company he works for. And that symbolizes something. It sends a message that sometimes the naysayers in Washington don't understand: Do not bet against the American worker. Do not bet against American businesses. Do not bet against the American people. Don't bet against American ingenuity. We are coming back, and we're coming back strong.

But to come back strong, to rebuild for the long run, we've got work. We've got to ensure that our workers can compete with any workers on Earth. And that's why we're reforming our education system based on what works for kids, not what works for the status quo. We eliminated billions of dollars in taxpayer subsidies to the big banks that were acting as middlemen on the college loan program. And as a consequence of this, we saved tens of billions of dollars that are now making college educations more affordable for millions of more students.

To lower the costs to families and businesses, we passed health insurance reform that will finally make coverage affordable and stop insurance companies from jacking up your premiums or refusing to cover you before you're sick—because you're sick.

To make sure that everybody is participating in our economy, I signed into law legislation that makes sure we've got equal pay for equal work, because we want our women getting paid just like men are getting paid on the workforce.

To keep faith with the brave men and women who risk their lives for ours and to help build the middle class like the greatest generation built itself up, we are increasing access to health care and benefits and education for our veterans and their families. And we're keeping the promise I made when I began campaigning for the Presidency. By the end of this month, we'll have removed 100,000 troops from Iraq and our combat mission will be over.

To ensure that a financial crisis like this one doesn't happen again, we passed financial reform that provides new accountability and tough oversight of Wall Street. It's going to stop credit card companies from charging hidden fees or unfair rate hikes. It's going to end the era of Wall Street bailouts once and for all.

And these reforms—all these reforms taken together are going to make America more competitive in the 21st century. They move us forward. And on each of these reforms, we reached out to Democrats and Republicans for ideas and for support. But I have to tell you, in just about every instance, almost every Republican in Congress said no: no on help for small businesses, no on middle class tax cuts, no on clean energy jobs, no on making college more affordable, no on Wall Street reform.

You remember our campaign slogan, "Yes, we can"? This year, their campaign slogan is, "No, we can't." [*Laughter*] It's pretty inspiring, huh? [*Laughter*] You know, you wake up in the morning and you hear "No!"—that just puts a little pep in your step. [*Laughter*]

Why do they keep on saying no? Well, part of it is, is that they just can't give up on the bankrupt economic policies that they have been peddling for much of the last decade. I mean, this agenda is pretty straightforward. And I give them credit, you know, they keep on coming back with it: You cut taxes for millionaires and billionaires, you cut rules for special interests, you cut working folks loose to fend for themselves. So if you don't have a job or you can't afford college or you don't have health insurance or you can't get health insurance for your kid, tough luck, you're on your own.

Now, the advantage of this economic philosophy is it's simple. [*Laughter*] The disadvantage of this philosophy is it doesn't work out real well. I mean, think about—we tried this for 8 years, and here's what it gave us: It gave us the worst economic crisis since the Great Depression, and it took us from record surpluses to record deficits.

These guys now, they're all running on, well, Democrats are the spending party. Think about this. We had record surpluses. When I arrived in the White House, I had a $1.3 trillion deficit wrapped in a bow waiting for me. [*Laughter*] So yes, we had to spend money to get us out of what could have been a depression. So we spent money on high-speed rail and we spent money on clean energy and we spent money making sure teachers and cops and firefighters weren't laid off. What did they have to show for the $1.3 trillion deficit that they delivered to us?

Audience members. War.

Audience members. Two wars.

Audience member. Bad President. [*Laughter*]

The President. All right, we've got a lot of options here. [*Laughter*] But it's not a real attractive list. [*Laughter*] So when these guys get on their high horse about spending, it's like, hold on a second.

Now, I'm bringing this up not to relitigate the past. I just don't want to relive the past. [*Laughter*] It was hard enough—it's been hard enough trying to rescue this economy the first time. I don't want to have to do it a second time. I mean, it would be one thing if Republicans, they all said to themselves, gosh, you know, what we did really didn't work out, so let's go off

and let's meditate a little bit—[*laughter*]—and see where we went wrong, come up with some new ideas, come up with a new philosophy, acknowledge the mistakes that we made, promise to do things differently. If that was their message, that would be plausible.

And I would embrace it. I would say, great, you've got new ideas? Come on, let's work together. Let's figure out how we can move the country forward. But that's not what they're saying. One of their leaders was asked what would he do if they took over Congress again, and he said—I'm quoting here—"We're going to pursue the exact same agenda as before Obama took office," the exact same agenda.

So basically, what they're really betting on—I mean, their whole campaign strategy is that all of you have come down with a case of amnesia. [*Laughter*] They are banking on the fact that you'll forget what their agenda did to this country over 8 years.

Imagine the economy is a car. And they're driving along, and I don't know what they're doing. They're not paying much attention to the road. Maybe they're on their BlackBerry. I don't know. [*Laughter*] They're talking on the phone—something. But they drive the economy into the ditch. And so now me and Bill Nelson and the congressional delegation here and all of us, we got to put on our boots, and we climb down into the ditch, and it's muddy down there and hot, bugs. [*Laughter*] We're pushing, we're shoving, trying to get this car out of the ditch. Republicans, they're standing there, watching us—[*laughter*]—sipping on a Slurpee or something. [*Laughter*] They're like—we say, "You guys want to come down and help push?" "No, no, that's okay. Push harder, though." [*Laughter*] "You're not pushing right." [*Laughter*] "If we were pushing, we'd be doing it differently." [*Laughter*]

Finally—finally—after all this work, we get the car back up on level ground. We're ready to move forward. Suddenly, these guys tap us on the shoulder. We turn around, they say, "We want the keys back." [*Laughter*] You can't have the keys back. You don't know how to drive. We don't want to go back into the ditch.

1243

I don't know if any of you have thought of this, but when you want your car going forward, what do you do?

Audience members. "D"!

The President. You put it into "D." When you want to go reverse, what do you do?

Audience members. "R"!

The President. Put it into "R." We don't want to go backwards, we want to go forwards. And that's why we're going to vote for Alex Sink. We need to go forward. That's what this election is about, moving forward. America always moves forward.

If you want to know what will happen if the other party takes over Congress, all you've got to do is take a look at what they've done the last 18 months. On issue after issue, they've sided with special interests over the middle class. They voted to give tax breaks to companies that ship jobs overseas. They voted to give insurance companies the power to deny you coverage if you've had a preexisting condition.

The top Republican on the Energy Committee, the guy who would be in charge of energy policy in this country if they take over—after the oil spill happened, he apologized, not to the people of Florida, he apologized to BP— [*laughter*]—said he was so sorry that the President forced them to put a $20 billion trust fund together so that fishermen and small-business owners and hotel owners would be compensated; called it a "shakedown," called it a "Chicago shakedown." That's—[*laughter*]. Are you serious? [*Laughter*]

On Wall Street reform, I mean, think about this: The worst financial crisis since the Great Depression, and they want to go back to doing the same things. How can that be? [*Laughter*] How can that be? The economy was almost brought to its knees. And we put together a very sensible, mainstream approach for making sure we wouldn't have taxpayer bailouts, making sure that consumers were protected. We kept on reaching out to them: Work with us. Wouldn't do it, because the special interests in Washington didn't want them to do it.

That's what's at stake in this election. If we give them the keys back, they will drive this economy right back into the ditch. And riding shotgun will be every special interest under the Sun.

And let me be clear about how we're going to move our economy forward. The key to moving this economy forward is going to be the private sector. Government is not going to be the primary driver of job creation in this country. We want businesses to succeed. The free market is the greatest instrument of wealth production in our history. But—[*applause*]—so if you're a responsible business owner, I want to do everything I can to help you grow and prosper and hire more employees. But I don't think it's antibusiness to say we should make sure an oil rig is safe before you start drilling. I don't think it's antibusiness to say Wall Street banks should play by the same rules as everybody else. I don't think it's antibusiness to say that insurance companies should deny people care just because they get sick, to make sure that we say to insurance companies, you got to treat people fairly. That's not being antibusiness; that's just being commonsense.

We can't go back to an attitude where whatever is good for me is good enough. We've got to start asking, what's good for America? What's best for all our businesses? What's best for all our people? What's best for the next generation, not just the next election? How do we move this country forward as one people and as one Nation?

So, Florida, I know times are tough. And when times are tough, it can be easy to give in to cynicism, it can be easy to give in to fear. Sometimes we set our sights lower, we settle for the status quo. And that's what the other side is counting on in this election. They're not offering new plans. They're not offering new ideas. They're offering cynicism, and they're offering fear. They're offering distractions and wedge issues.

You know, during the course of the last 18 months, there have been times where I've taken positions that surprise people in Washington. All the pundits, they say, boy, you know, what he's doing, it doesn't poll well. [*Laughter*] I know it doesn't poll well. I've got pollsters. [*Laughter*] But you didn't send me to Washington to do what was popular. You sent me to do what was right. That's who we are as a country. We are Americans. We do not give up. We do not quit. We do not fear the future, we shape the future.

And if you'll join Alex Sink and if you'll join Kendrick Meeks and you'll join me to build a future where all our kids are getting educated and small businesses are flourishing because of their ideas and their ingenuity and we're creating clean energy jobs all across America, if you'll join me in building a future that thinks about more than just politics, but thinks about how are we going to meet this solemn obligation we have to those who are coming after us, I'm ab-

solutely positive that the 21st century is going to be the American century, just like the 20th.

Thank you very much, everybody. God bless you. God bless the United States of America. Thank you.

NOTE: The President spoke at 5:35 p.m. at the Fontainebleau Hotel. In his remarks, he referred to William Shanteau, a Chrysler Jefferson North Assembly Plant worker who purchased the winning June Powerball jackpot ticket in Curtice, OH, and his wife Lisa; Rep. Pete Sessions, in his capacity as chairman of the National Republican Congressional Committee; and Rep. Joseph L. Barton.

Remarks on Job Promotion Legislation
August 19, 2010

Good morning, everybody. For the last several months, I have been urging Congress to pass a jobs bill that will do two big things for small businesses: cut their taxes and make loans more available.

I have been adamant about this because small businesses are the backbone of our economy. They create two out of every three new jobs in this country. And while a lot of big businesses and big banks have started recovering from this recession, small businesses and community banks that loan to small businesses have been lagging behind. They need help. And if we want this economy to create more jobs more quickly, we need to help them.

A report yesterday from the Labor Department underscores why this is so critical. In the final few months of last year, small businesses with fewer than 50 employees accounted for more than 60 percent of the job losses in America—more than 60 percent. These are the businesses that usually create most of the jobs in this country. And this report, combined with this morning's news that unemployment claims rose again, compels us to act. It compels us to stand with the small-business men and women who are trying to grow their companies and make payroll and hire new workers.

The jobs bill that is stalled in Congress would completely eliminate taxes on key investments

in small businesses. It would allow small-business owners to write off more expenses. And it would make it easier for community banks to do more lending to small businesses, while allowing small firms to take out larger SBA loans with fewer fees, which countless entrepreneurs have told me would make a big difference in their companies. I'd also like to point out this legislation is fully paid for and will not add one single dime to our deficit.

So this is a bill that makes sense, and normally we would expect Democrats and Republicans to join together. Unfortunately, a partisan minority in the Senate so far has refused to allow this jobs bill to come up for a vote.

Now, I recognize that there are times when Democrats and Republicans have legitimate differences rooted in different views about what's best for this country. There are times when good people disagree in good faith. But this is not one of those times. This small-business jobs bill is based on ideas both Democrat and Republican. In fact, many provisions in the bill were actually authored by Republican Senators. It has been praised as being good for small business by groups like the Chamber of Commerce and the National Federation of Independent Businesses.

A majority of Senators are in favor of the bill and yet the obstruction continues. It's obstruction that stands in the way of small-business owners getting the loans and the tax cuts that they need to prosper. It's obstruction that defies common sense.

So let me just make this simple point: There will be plenty of time between now and November to play politics. But the small-business owners I met with this week, the ones that I've met with across the country this year, they don't have time for political games. They're not interested in what's best for a political party. They're interested in what's best for the country.

When Congress reconvenes, this jobs bill will be the first business out of the gate. And the Senate Republican leadership needs to stop its efforts to block it. Let's put aside the partisanship for a while and work together for small businesses, for employees, and the communities that depend on them across this great country.

Thank you very much.

NOTE: The President spoke at 12:22 p.m. on the South Driveway at the White House.

Statement on World Humanitarian Day
August 19, 2010

Seven years ago today, terrorists heinously attacked the U.N. Headquarters in Baghdad, killing 22 innocent people who were in Iraq to support Iraqis in their quest to live with freedom, dignity, and security. That outrageous attack highlighted the increasing dangers faced by unarmed humanitarians from around the world who dedicate their lives to serving their fellow human beings, often in extremely difficult circumstances. It is our respect and gratitude for their contributions that has led the international community to designate August 19 as World Humanitarian Day.

These humanitarians live and work in the world's most dangerous and difficult places, often at great risk to their own lives. From Somalia to Sudan, Haiti to Iraq, Burma to the Democratic Republic of the Congo, and Pakistan to Afghanistan, these individuals, often unheralded, provide life-sustaining support to millions. Today we honor their selfless service and the humanitarian principles that they embody.

These local and international humanitarian aid workers have distinguished themselves again this year. In the aftermath of the deadly earthquake in Haiti, humanitarian aid workers from around the world mobilized immediately for emergency rescue efforts and remain in the country today to support ongoing relief and recovery efforts. Today, humanitarian aid workers are providing food, water, and other lifesaving assistance to millions of Pakistanis devastated by flooding. In Sudan, aid workers risk violent attacks and kidnaping to try to feed the displaced of Darfur and help the south prepare for its approaching referendum.

Today we also mourn the losses of those who have paid the ultimate sacrifice in pursuit of humanitarian ideals. This month, 10 American, Afghan, German, and British humanitarian workers in Afghanistan were brutally murdered. They died distributing medicine, eyeglasses, and other assistance urgently needed by the people of Afghanistan. And they are the victims of a dangerous trend. Armed groups are increasingly targeting the humanitarian workers whose simple goal is to help innocent civilians in times of danger and suffering. Over the past decade, over 700 humanitarian workers have lost their lives in service, and murders of humanitarian aid workers have more than tripled annually to 102 deaths in 2009.

On this World Humanitarian Day, the United States condemns the killing, kidnaping, and other attacks against humanitarian aid workers, and we reaffirm our enduring commitment to the goals to which they have dedicated their lives. Every humanitarian aid worker must be free to serve without fear for their safety, and every person in the world must be able to pursue their aspirations in peace and security.

Letter to the Speaker of the House of Representatives Transmitting Fiscal Year 2011 Budget Amendments
August 20, 2010

Dear Madam Speaker:

I ask the Congress to consider the enclosed Fiscal Year (FY) 2011 budget amendments for the Department of Health and Human Services. Overall, the discretionary budget authority proposed in my FY 2011 Budget would not be increased by these proposed requests.

Included are proposed increases for health-care workforce enhancement activities; HIV/AIDS treatment and prevention; State health insurance consumer assistance programs; and existing State high-risk health insurance pools. Also included are requests for necessary changes to appropriations language that support the Public Health Emergency Medical Countermeasure Enterprise Review described in the report issued by the Secretary of Health and Human Services on August 19, 2010.

The details of these amendments are set forth in the enclosed letter from the Acting Deputy Director of the Office of Management and Budget.

Sincerely,

BARACK OBAMA

The President's Weekly Address
August 21, 2010

As the political season heats up, Americans are already being inundated with the usual phone calls and mailings and TV ads from campaigns all across the country. But this summer, they're also seeing a flood of attack ads run by shadowy groups with harmless-sounding names. We don't know who's behind these ads, and we don't know who's paying for them.

The reason this is happening is because of a decision by the Supreme Court in the *Citizens United* case, a decision that now allows big corporations to spend unlimited amounts of money to influence our elections. They can buy millions of dollars' worth of TV ads, and worst of all, they don't even have to reveal who is actually paying for them. You don't know if it's a foreign-controlled corporation. You don't know if it's BP. You don't know if it's a big insurance company or a Wall Street bank. A group can hide behind a phony name like Citizens for a Better Future, even if a more accurate name would be "Corporations for Weaker Oversight."

We tried to fix this last month. There was a proposal supported by Democrats and Republicans that would have required corporate political advertisers to reveal who's funding their activities. When special interests take to the airwaves, whoever's running and funding the ad would have to appear in the advertisement and take responsibility for it, like a company's CEO or an organization's biggest contributor. And foreign-controlled corporations and entities would be restricted from spending money to influence American elections, just as they were in the past.

You would think that making these reforms would be a matter of common sense. You'd think that reducing corporate and even foreign influence over our elections wouldn't be a partisan issue. But the Republican leaders in Congress said no. In fact, they used their power to block the issue from even coming up for a vote.

This can only mean that the leaders of the other party want to keep the public in the dark. They don't want you to know which interests are paying for the ads. The only people who don't want to disclose the truth are people with something to hide.

Well, we cannot allow the corporate takeover of our democracy. So we're going to continue to fight for reform and transparency. And I urge all of you to take up the same fight. Let's challenge every elected official who benefits from these ads to defend this practice or join us in stopping it.

At a time of such challenge for America, we can't afford these political games. Millions of Americans are struggling to get by, and their voices shouldn't be drowned out by millions of dollars in secret, special interest advertising. Their voices should be heard.

Let's not forget that a century ago, it was a Republican President, Teddy Roosevelt, who first tried to tackle the issue of corporate influence on our elections. He actually called it "one of the principal sources of corruption in our political affairs." And he proposed strict limits on corporate influence in elections. "Every special interest is entitled to justice," he said, "but not one is entitled to a vote in Congress, to a voice on the bench, or to representation in any public office."

We now face a similar challenge and a similar opportunity to prevent special interests from gaining even more clout in Washington. This shouldn't be a Democratic issue or a Republican issue. This is an issue that goes to whether or not we have a democracy that works for ordinary Americans, a government of, by, and for the people. Let's show the cynics and the special interests that we still can.

NOTE: The address was recorded at approximately 4:05 p.m. on August 13 in the Library at the White House for broadcast on August 21. The transcript was made available by the Office of the Press Secretary on August 20, but was embargoed for release until 6 a.m. on August 21.

Statement on Consumer Financial Protection Legislation
August 23, 2010

Last year, I signed the Credit Card Accountability Responsibility and Disclosure Act into law to put a stop to deceptive credit card practices and hold credit card companies accountable to their customers. Yesterday the final reform provisions of the CARD Act took effect. As of today, consumers will be protected against unreasonable fees and penalties for late payments, as well as unfair practices involving gift cards. This law will also make the terms of credit cards more understandable and puts a stop to hidden over-the-limit fees and other practices designed to trap consumers. It restricts rate increases that apply retroactively to old balances. And the CARD Act prevents companies from increasing rates within the first year an account is opened.

In addition, the Wall Street Reform and Consumer Protection Act I signed into law last month will empower a new Consumer Financial Protection Bureau with just one job: looking out for consumers in our financial system. This includes making sure that credit card reforms are implemented forcefully and that big banks and lenders are living up to their responsibilities under the law. And in the wake of a terrible recession, these reforms and this independent consumer watchdog will not only protect consumers, they'll strengthen our economy as a whole, leveling the playing field for responsible lenders and ensuring that families and small-business owners are better able to make financial decisions that work for them.

Statement on Kenya's New Constitution
August 27, 2010

I congratulate Kenya on the promulgation of the new Constitution, which was approved by a majority of voters on August 4, 2010. This historic approval and signing of the Constitution is an important step forward and demonstrates the commitment of Kenya's leaders and people to a future of unity, democracy, and equal justice for all, even the powerful. With this Constitution, the people of Kenya have set a positive example for all of Africa and the world.

Today represents a moment of promise for Kenya similar to the early days of independence, a new moment of promise that must be seized to usher in an era of progress for the Kenyan people. The United States looks forward to partnering with Kenya as it moves through the multiyear process of implementing the new Constitution. We share the expectations of the Kenyan people that this process will usher in an era of deepened democracy and expanded economic opportunity for all Kenyans.

I am disappointed that Kenya hosted Sudanese President Umar al-Bashir in defiance of International Criminal Court arrest warrants for war crimes, crimes against humanity, and genocide. The Government of Kenya has committed itself to full cooperation with the ICC, and we consider it important that Kenya honor its commitments to the ICC and to international justice, along with all nations that share those responsibilities. In Kenya and beyond, justice is a critical ingredient for lasting peace.

The President's Weekly Address
August 28, 2010

On Tuesday, after more than 7 years, the United States of America will end its combat mission in Iraq and take an important step forward in responsibly ending the Iraq war.

As a candidate for this office, I pledged I would end this war. As President, that's what I'm doing. I've brought home more than 90,000 troops since I took office. We have closed or turned over to Iraq hundreds of bases. In many parts of the country, Iraqis have already taken the lead for security.

In the months ahead, our troops will continue to support and train Iraqi forces, partner with Iraqis in counterterrorism missions, and protect our civilians and military efforts. But the bottom line is this: The war is ending. Like any sovereign, independent nation, Iraq is free to chart its own course. And by the end of next year, all of our troops will be home.

As we mark the end of America's combat mission in Iraq, a grateful nation must pay tribute to all who have served there, because part of responsibly ending this war is meeting our responsibility to those who have fought it.

The wars in Iraq and Afghanistan now make up America's longest continuous combat engagement. For the better part of a decade, our troops and their families have served tour after tour with honor and heroism, risking and often giving their lives for the defense of our freedom and security. More than 1 million Americans in uniform have served in Iraq, far more than any conflict since Vietnam. And more than 1 million who have served in both wars have now finished their service and joined the proud ranks of America's veterans.

What this new generation of veterans must know is this: Our Nation's commitment to all who wear its uniform is a sacred trust that is as old as our Republic itself. It is one that, as President, I consider a moral obligation to uphold.

At the same time, these are new wars with new missions, new methods, and new perils. And what today's veterans have earned—what they have every right to expect—is new care, new opportunity, and a new commitment to their service when they come home.

That's why, from the earliest days of my administration, we've been strengthening that sacred trust with our veterans by making our veterans policy more responsive and ready for this new century.

We're building a 21st-century VA, modernizing and expanding VA hospitals and health care and adapting care to better meet the unique needs of female veterans. We're creating a single electronic health record that our troops and veterans can keep for life. We're breaking the claims backlog and reforming the process with new paperless systems. And we're building new wounded warrior facilities through the Department of Defense.

But for many of our troops and their families, the war doesn't end when they come home. Too many suffer from traumatic brain injury and posttraumatic stress disorder, the signature injuries of today's wars, and too few receive proper screening or care. Well, we're changing that. We're directing significant resources to treatment, hiring more mental health professionals, and making major investments in awareness, outreach, and suicide prevention. And we're making it easier for a vet with PTSD to get the benefits he or she needs.

To make sure our troops, veterans, and their families have full access to the American Dreams they've fought to defend, we're working to extend them new opportunity. Michelle and Jill Biden have forged a national commitment to support military families while a loved one is away. We've guaranteed new support to caregivers who put their lives on hold for a loved one's long recovery. We're funding and implementing the post-9/11 GI bill, which is already helping some 300,000 veterans and their family members pursue their dream of a college education.

And for veterans trying to find work in a very tough economy, we've devoted new resources to job training and placement. I've directed the Federal Government to hire more veterans, including disabled veterans, and I encourage every business in America to follow suit. This new generation of veterans has proven itself to be a new generation of leaders. They have unmatched training and skills, they're ready to work, and our country is stronger when we tap their extraordinary talents.

New care, new opportunity, a new commitment to our veterans.

If you'd like to send our troops and veterans a message of thanks and support, just visit whitehouse.gov. There, you'll find an easy way to upload your own text or video.

Let them know that they have the respect and support of a grateful nation, that when their tour ends, when they see our flag, when they touch our soil, they'll always be home in an America that is forever here for them, just as they've been there for us. That's the promise our Nation makes to those who serve. And as long as I'm Commander in Chief, it's a promise we will keep.

Thank you.

NOTE: The address was recorded at approximately 4:05 p.m. on August 13 in the Library at the White House for broadcast on August 28. The transcript was made available by the Office of the Press Secretary on August 27, but was embargoed for release until 6 a.m. on August 28.

Remarks at Xavier University in New Orleans, Louisiana
August 29, 2010

The President. Hello, everybody. It is good to be back. It is good to be back——

Audience member. It's good to have you back!

The President. I'm glad. [*Laughter*] And due to popular demand, I decided to bring the First Lady down here.

We have just an extraordinary number of dedicated public servants who are here. If you will be patient with me, I want to make sure that all of them are acknowledged. First of all, you've got the Governor of the great State of Louisiana, Bobby Jindal is here. We have the outstanding mayor of New Orleans, Mitch Landrieu. We have the better looking and younger Senator from Louisiana, Mary Landrieu.

I believe that Senator David Vitter is here. David, right here. We have—[*applause*]—hold on a second now. We've got—Congressman Joe Cao is here. Congressman Charlie Melancon is here. Congressman Steve Scalise is here.

Secretary of Housing and Urban Development, who has been working tirelessly down here in Louisiana, Shaun Donovan. We've got our EPA Administrator Lisa Jackson here—home girl. Administrator of FEMA Craig Fugate is here. The person who's heading up our community service efforts all across the country, Patrick Corvington is here. Louisiana's own Regina Benjamin, the Surgeon General, a Xavier grad, I might add. We are very proud to have all of these terrific public servants here.

It is wonderful to be back in New Orleans, and it is a great honor——

Audience member. We can't see you!

The President. It is a great honor—[*laughter*]—you can see me now? Okay. It is a great honor to be back at Xavier University. And I—it's just inspiring to spend time with people who've demonstrated what it means to persevere in the face of tragedy, to rebuild in the face of ruin.

I'm grateful to Jade for her introduction and congratulate you on being crowned Miss Xavier. I hope everybody heard during the introduction, she was a junior at Ben Franklin High School 5 years ago when the storm came. And after Katrina, Ben Franklin High was terribly damaged by wind and water. Millions of dollars were needed to rebuild the school. Many feared it would take years to reopen, if it could be reopened at all.

But something remarkable happened: Parents, teachers, students, volunteers, they all got to work making repairs. And donations came in from across New Orleans and around the world. And soon those silent and darkened corridors, they were bright, and they were filled with the sounds of young men and women, including Jade, who were going back to class. And then Jade committed to Xavier, a university that likewise refused to succumb to despair. So Jade, like so many students here at this university, embody hope. That sense of hope in difficult times, that's what I came to talk about today.

It's been 5 years since Katrina ravaged the Gulf Coast. There's no need to dwell on what you experienced and what the world witnessed. We all remember it keenly: water pouring through broken levees, mothers holding their children above the waterline, people stranded on rooftops begging for help, bodies lying in the streets of a great American city. It was a natural disaster, but also a manmade catastrophe, a shameful breakdown in government that left countless men and women and children abandoned and alone.

And shortly after the storm, I came down to Houston to spend time with some of the folks who had taken shelter there. And I'll never forget what one woman told me. She said, "We had nothing before the hurricane, and now we've got less than nothing."

In the years that followed, New Orleans could have remained a symbol of destruction and decay, of a storm that came and the inadequate response that followed. It was not hard to imagine a day when we'd tell our children that a once vibrant and wonderful city had been laid low by indifference and neglect. But that's not what happened. It's not what happened at Ben Franklin. It's not what happened here at Xavier. It's not what happened across New Orleans and across the Gulf Coast. Instead, this city has become a symbol of resilience and of community and of the fundamental responsibility that we have to one another.

And we see that here at Xavier. Less than a month after the storm struck, amidst debris and flood-damaged buildings, President Francis promised that this university would reopen in a matter of months. Some said he was crazy; some said it couldn't happen. But they didn't count on what happens when one force of nature meets another. And by January, 4 months later, class was in session. Less than a year after the storm, I had the privilege of delivering a commencement address to the largest graduating class in Xavier's history. That is a symbol of what New Orleans is all about.

We see New Orleans in the efforts of Joycelyn Heintz, who's here today. Katrina left her house 14 feet underwater. But after volunteers helped her rebuild, she joined AmeriCorps to serve the community herself, part of a wave of AmeriCorps members who've been critical to the rebirth of this city and the rebuilding of this region. So today, she manages a local center for mental health and wellness.

We see the symbol that this city has become in the St. Bernard Project, whose founder, Liz McCartney, is with us. This endeavor has drawn volunteers from across the country to rebuild hundreds of homes throughout St. Bernard Parish and the Lower Ninth Ward.

I've seen the sense of purpose people felt after the storm when I visited Musicians' Village in the Ninth Ward back in 2006. Volunteers were not only constructing houses, they were coming together to preserve the culture of music and art that's part of the soul of this city and the soul of this country. And today, more than 70 homes are complete, and construction's underway on the Ellis Marsalis Center for Music.

We see the dedication to the community in the efforts of Xavier grad Dr. Regina Benjamin, who mortgaged her home, maxed out her credit cards, so she could reopen her Bayou La Batre clinic to care for victims of the storm, and who is now our Nation's Surgeon General.

And we see resilience and hope exemplified by students at Carver High School, who have helped to raise more than a million dollars to build a new community track and football field—their Field of Dreams—for the Ninth Ward.

So because of all of you—all the advocates, all the organizers who are here today, folks standing behind me who've worked so hard, who never gave up hope—you are all leading the way toward a better future for this city with innovative approaches to fight poverty and improve health care, reduce crime, and create opportunities for young people. Because of you, New Orleans is coming back.

And I just came from Parkway Bakery and Tavern. And 5 years ago, the storm nearly destroyed that neighborhood institution. I saw the pictures. Now they're open, business is booming, and that's some good eats. I had the shrimp po'boy and some of the gumbo. But I skipped the bread pudding because I thought I might fall asleep while I was speaking. But I've got it saved for later. [*Laughter*]

Five years ago, many questioned whether people could ever return to this city. Today, New Orleans is one of the fastest growing cities in America, with a big new surge in small businesses. Five years ago, the Saints had to play every game on the road because of the damage to the Superdome. Two weeks ago, we welcomed the Saints to the White House as Super Bowl champions. There was also food associated with that. We marked the occasion with a 30-foot po'boy made with shrimps and oysters from the Gulf. And you'll be pleased to know there were no leftovers.

Now, I don't have to tell you that there's still too many vacant and overgrown lots. There's still too many students attending classes in trailers. There's still too many people unable to find work. And there's still too many New Orleans folks who haven't been able to come home. So while an incredible amount of progress has been made, on this fifth anniversary, I wanted to come here and tell the people of this city directly, my administration is going to stand with you and fight alongside you until the job is done, until New Orleans is all the way back—all the way.

When I took office, I directed my Cabinet to redouble our efforts to put an end to the turf wars between agencies, to cut the redtape, and cut the bureaucracy. I wanted to make sure that the Federal Government was a partner, not an obstacle, to recovery here in the Gulf Coast. And members of my Cabinet, including EPA Administrator Lisa Jackson, who grew up in Pontchartrain Park, they have come down here dozens of times. Shaun Donovan's come down here dozens of times. This is not just to make appearances; it's not just to get photo ops. They came down here to listen and to learn and make real the changes that were necessary, so that Government was actually working for you.

So, for example, efforts to rebuild schools and hospitals, to repair damaged roads and bridges, to get people back to their homes, they were tied up for years in a tangle of disagreements and byzantine rules. So when I took office, working with your outstanding delegation, particularly Senator Mary Landrieu, we put in place a new way of resolving disputes so that funds set aside for rebuilding efforts actually went toward rebuilding efforts. And as a result, more than 170 projects are getting underway: work on firehouses and police stations and roads and sewer systems and health clinics and libraries and universities.

We're tackling the corruption and inefficiency that has long plagued the New Orleans Housing Authority. We're helping homeowners rebuild and making it easier for renters to find affordable options. And we're helping people to move out of temporary homes. You know, when I took office, more than 3 years after the storm, tens of thousands of families were still stuck in disaster housing, many still living in small trailers that had been provided by FEMA. We were spending huge sums of money on temporary shelters when we knew it would be better for families and less costly for taxpayers to help people get into affordable, stable, and more permanent housing. So we've helped make it possible for people to find those homes, and we've dramatically reduced the number of families in emergency housing.

On the health care front, as a candidate for President, I pledged to make sure we were helping New Orleans recruit doctors and nurses and rebuild medical facilities, including a new veterans hospital. Well, we've resolved a longstanding dispute, one that had tied up hundreds of millions of dollars, to fund the replacement for Charity Hospital. And in June, Veterans Secretary Ric Shinseki came to New Orleans for the groundbreaking of that new VA hospital.

In education, we've made strides as well. As you know, schools in New Orleans were falling behind long before Katrina. But in the years since the storm, a lot of public schools opened themselves up to innovation and to reform. And as a result, we're actually seeing rising achievement, and New Orleans is becoming a model of innovation for the Nation. This is yet another sign that you're not just rebuilding, you're rebuilding stronger than before. Just this Friday, my administration announced a final agreement on $1.8 billion for Orleans Parish schools. This is money that had been locked up for years, but now it's freed up, so folks here can determine best how to restore the school system.

And in a city that's known too much violence, that's seen too many young people lost to drugs and criminal activity, we've got a Justice Department that's committed to working with New Orleans to fight the scourge of violent crime and to weed out corruption in the police force and to ensure the criminal justice system works for everyone in this city. And I want everybody to hear—to know and to hear me thank Mitch Landrieu, your new mayor, for his commitment to that partnership.

Now, even as we continue our recovery efforts, we're also focusing on preparing for future threats so that there's never another disaster like Katrina. The largest civil works project in American history is underway to build a fortified levee system. And as a—just as I pledged as a candidate, we're going to finish this system by next year so that this city is protected against a 100-year storm. We should not be playing Russian roulette every hurricane season. And we're also working to restore protective wetlands and natural barriers that were not only damaged by Katrina—were not just damaged by Katrina, but had been rapidly disappearing for decades.

In Washington, we are restoring competence and accountability. I am proud that my FEMA Director, Craig Fugate, has 25 years of experience in disaster management in Florida. He came from Florida, a State that has known its share of hurricanes. We've put together a group led by Secretary Donovan and Secretary Napolitano to look at disaster recovery across the country. We're improving coordination on the ground and modernizing emergency communications, helping families plan for a crisis. And we're putting in place reforms so that never again in America is somebody left behind in a disaster because they're living with a disability or because they're elderly or because they're infirm. That will not happen again.

Finally, even as you've been buffeted by Katrina and Rita, even as you've been impacted by the broader recession that has devastated communities across the country, in recent months the Gulf Coast has seen new hardship as a result of the BP Deepwater Horizon oil spill. And just as we've sought to ensure that we're doing what it takes to recover from Katrina, my administration has worked hard to match our efforts on the spill to what you need on the ground. And we've been in close consultation with your Governor, your mayors, your parish presidents, your local government officials.

And from the start, I promised you two things. One is that we would see to it that the leak was stopped, and it has been. The second promise I made was that we would stick with our efforts and stay on BP until the damage to the Gulf and to the lives of the people in this region was reversed. And this too is a promise that we will keep. We are not going to forget. We're going to stay on it until this area is fully recovered.

That's why we rapidly launched the largest response to an environmental disaster in American history—47,000 people on the ground, 5,700 vessels on the water—to contain and clean up the oil. When BP was not moving fast enough on claims, we told BP to set aside $20 billion in a fund, managed by an independent third party, to help all those whose lives have been turned upside down by the spill.

And we will continue to rely on sound science, carefully monitoring waters and coastlines, as well as the health of the people along the Gulf, to deal with any long-term effects of the oil spill. We are going to stand with you until the oil is cleaned up, until the environment is restored, until polluters are held accountable, until communities are made whole, and until this region is all the way back on its feet.

So that's how we're helping this city and this State and this region to recover from the worst natural disaster in our Nation's history. We're cutting through the redtape that has impeded rebuilding efforts for years. We're making government work better and smarter in coordination with one of the most expansive nonprofit efforts in American history. We're helping State and local leaders to address serious problems that had been neglected for decades, problems that existed before the storm came and have continued after the waters receded, from the levee system to the justice system, from the health care system to the education system.

And together, we are helping to make New Orleans a place that stands for what we can do in America, not just for what we can't do. Ultimately, that must be the legacy of Katrina: not one of neglect, but of action; not one of indifference, but of empathy; not of abandonment, but of a community working together to meet shared challenges.

The truth is, there are some wounds that have not yet healed. And there are some losses that can't be repaid. And for many who lived through those harrowing days 5 years ago, there's searing memories that time may not erase. But even amid so much tragedy, we saw stirrings of a brighter day. Five years ago, we saw men and women risking their own safety to save strangers. We saw nurses staying behind to care for the sick and the injured. We saw families coming home to clean up and rebuild not just their own homes, but their neighbors' homes as well. And we saw music and Mardi Gras and the vibrancy, the fun of this town undiminished. And we've seen many return to their beloved city with a newfound sense of appreciation and obligation to this community.

And when I came here 4 years ago, one thing I found striking was all the greenery that had begun to come back. And I was reminded of a passage from the Book of Job: "There is hope for a tree, if it be cut down, that it will sprout again and that its tender branch will not cease." The work ahead will not be easy, and there will be setbacks. There will be challenges along the way. But thanks to you, thanks to the great people of this great city, New Orleans is blossoming again.

Thank you, everybody. God bless you, and God bless the United States of America.

NOTE: The President spoke at 1:50 p.m. In his remarks, he referred to Patrick A. Corvington, Chief Executive Officer, Corporation for National and Community Service; Jade D. Young, student, and Norman C. Francis, president, Xavier University; and Special Master for TARP Executive Compensation Kenneth R. Feinberg, in his capacity as administrator of the BP Deepwater Horizon oil spill compensation fund.

Remarks on the National Economy
August 30, 2010

Good afternoon, everybody. I just finished a meeting with my economic team about the current state of our economy and some of the additional steps that we should take to move forward.

It's been nearly 2 years since that terrible September when our economy teetered on the brink of collapse. And at the time, no one knew just how deep the recession would go or the havoc that it would wreak on families and businesses across this country. What we did know was that it took nearly a decade——

[*At this point, the President experienced technical difficulties.*]

How are we doing on sound, guys? Is it still going in the press? Okay.

What we did know was that it was going to take nearly a decade in order for——

[*The President continued to experience technical difficulties.*]

Can you guys still hear us? Okay. Let me try this one more time.

What we did know was that it took nearly a decade to dig the hole that we're in and that it would take longer than any of us would like to climb our way out. And while we have taken a series of measures and come a long way since then, the fact is that too many businesses are still struggling, too many Americans are still looking for work, and too many communities are far from being whole again.

And that's why my administration remains focused every single day on pushing this economy forward, repairing the damage that's been done to the middle class over the past decade, and promoting the growth we need to get our people back to work.

So as Congress prepares to return to session, my economic team is hard at work in identifying additional measures that could make a difference in both promoting growth and hiring in the short term and increasing our economy's competitiveness in the long term, steps like extending the tax cuts for the middle class that are set to expire this year, redoubling our investment in clean energy and R&D, rebuilding more of our infrastructure for the future, further tax cuts to encourage businesses to put their capital to work creating jobs here in the United States. And I'll be addressing these pro-posals in further detail in the days and weeks to come.

In the meantime, there's one thing we know we should do, something that should be Congress's first order of business when it gets back, and that is making it easier for our small businesses to grow and hire.

We know that in the final few months of last year, small businesses accounted for more than 60 percent of the job losses in America. That's why we've passed eight different tax cuts for small businesses and worked to expand credit for them.

But we have to do more. And there's currently a jobs bill before Congress that would do two big things for small-business owners: cut more taxes and make available more loans. It would help them get the credit they need and eliminate capital gains taxes on key investments so they have more incentive to invest right now. And it would accelerate $55 billion of tax relief to encourage American businesses, small and large, to expand their investments over the next 14 months.

Unfortunately, this bill has been languishing in the Senate for months, held up by a partisan minority that won't even allow it to go to a vote. That makes no sense. This bill is fully paid for, it will not add to the deficit, and there is no reason to block it besides pure partisan politics.

The small-business owners and the communities that rely on them, they don't have time for political games. They shouldn't have to wait any longer. In fact, just this morning a story showed that small businesses have put hiring and expanding on hold while waiting for the Senate to act on this bill. Simply put, holding this bill hostage is directly detrimental to our economic growth.

So I ask Senate Republicans to drop the blockade. I know we're entering election season, but the people who sent us here expect us to work together to get things done and improve this economy.

Now, no single step is the silver bullet that will reverse the damage done by the bubble-and-bust cycles that caused our economy into this slide. It's going to take a full-scale effort, a full-scale attack that not only helps in the short term, but builds a firmer foundation that makes our Nation stronger for the long haul. But this step will benefit small-business owners and our economy right away. That's why it's got to get done.

There's no doubt we still face serious challenges. But if we rise above the politics of the moment to summon an equal seriousness of purpose, I'm absolutely confident that we will meet them. I've got confidence in the American economy, and most importantly, I've got confidence in the American people. We've just got to start working together to get this done.

Thank you very much.

NOTE: The President spoke at 1:17 p.m. in the Rose Garden at the White House. The Office of the Press Secretary also released a Spanish language transcript of these remarks.

Videotaped Remarks to the Department of Commerce Annual Update Conference on Export Controls and Policy
August 30, 2010

Hello, everyone. I'm sorry I'm not able to be with you in person today, but I'm pleased to have the chance to join you by video to talk about our export control reform initiative.

About a year ago, we launched a comprehensive review of our export controls and determined that we needed fundamental reform in all four areas of our current system: in what we control, how we control it, how we enforce those controls, and how we manage our controls. I want to thank Secretary Locke, Secretary Gates, Secretary Clinton, and many others for their work on this initiative. And today I want to highlight the key elements of our new approach and the first steps towards its implementation.

For too long, we've had two very different control lists, with agencies fighting over who has jurisdiction. Decisions were delayed, sometimes for years, and industries lost their edge or moved abroad. Going forward, we will have a single, tiered, positive list, one which will allow us to build higher walls around the export of our most sensitive items while allowing the export of less critical ones under less restrictive conditions.

In the past, there was a lot of confusion about when a license was required. It depended on which agency you asked. Now we will have a single set of licensing policies that will apply to each tier of control, bringing clarity and consistency across our system.

In addition, I plan to sign an Executive order that creates an Export Enforcement Coordination Center to coordinate and strengthen our enforcement efforts and eliminate gaps and duplication across all relevant departments and agencies.

Finally, right now export control licenses are managed by multiple, different IT systems or, in some cases, even on paper. Going forward, all agencies will transition to a single IT system, making it easier for exporters to seek licenses and ensuring that the Government has the full information needed to make informed decisions.

While there is still more work to be done, taken together, these reforms will focus our resources on the threats that matter most and help us work more effectively with our allies in the field. They'll bring transparency and coherence to a field of regulation which has long been lacking both. And by enhancing the competitiveness of our manufacturing and technology sectors, they'll help us not just increase exports and create jobs, but strengthen our national security as well.

All this represents significant progress. And as we implement these reforms and take further steps, including working to create a single licensing agency, I look forward to working with both Congress and the export control community to ensure their success.

Thanks so much.

NOTE: The President's remarks were video-taped at approximately 6:10 p.m. on August 13 in the Library at the White House for broadcast at the conference on August 31. The transcript was released by the Office of the Press Secretary on August 30. The Executive order of November 9 is listed in Appendix D at the end of this volume.

Letter to Congressional Leaders Reporting on the Executive Order Blocking Property of Certain Persons With Respect to North Korea
August 30, 2010

Dear Madam Speaker: (Dear Mr. President:)

Pursuant to the International Emergency Economic Powers Act (50 U.S.C. 1701 *et seq.*) (IEEPA), I hereby report that I have issued an Executive Order (the "order") that expands the scope of the national emergency declared in Executive Order 13466 of June 26, 2008, and takes additional steps with respect to that national emergency.

In 2008, the United States terminated the exercise of certain authorities under the Trading With the Enemy Act (TWEA) with respect to North Korea, and also declared a national emergency pursuant to IEEPA to deal with the unusual and extraordinary threat to the national security and foreign policy of the United States posed by the existence and risk of the proliferation of weapons-usable fissile material on the Korean Peninsula. Executive Order 13466 continued certain restrictions on North Korea and North Korean nationals that had been in place under TWEA.

I have determined that the Government of North Korea's continued provocative actions, such as its unprovoked attack on and sinking of the Republic of Korea Navy ship *Cheonan* in March 2010, which resulted in the deaths of 46 sailors; its announced test of a nuclear device and missile launches in 2009; its violations of United Nations Security Council Resolution (UNSCR) 1718 of October 14, 2006, and UNSCR 1874 of June 12, 2009, including the procurement of luxury goods; and the illicit and deceptive economic activities through which it obtains financial and other support, including money laundering, the counterfeiting of goods and currency, bulk cash smuggling, and narcotics trafficking, destabilize the Korean peninsula and imperil U.S. Armed Forces, allies, and trading partners in the region, and warrant the imposition of additional sanctions.

The United Nations Security Council, in Resolutions 1718 and 1874, requires Member States to take certain measures to prevent, among other activities, the transfer of most arms and related materiel to or from North Korea and the transfer of luxury goods to North Korea. The United States has implemented those two UNSCRs, and the order strengthens that implementation.

The order is not targeted at the people of North Korea, nor at those who provide legitimate humanitarian relief to those people, but rather is aimed at specific activities of the Government of North Korea and others undertaken in defiance of UNSCRs 1718 and 1874. The order targets the international network that supports the Government of North Korea through arms sales and illicit economic activities, including money laundering, the counterfeiting of goods and currency, bulk cash smuggling, and narcotics trafficking.

The order leaves in place all existing sanctions imposed under Executive Order 13466, and blocks the property and interests in property of persons listed in the Annex to the order. The order also provides criteria for designations of persons determined by the Secretary of the Treasury, in consultation with the Secretary of State:

- to have, directly or indirectly, imported, exported, or reexported to, into, or from North Korea any arms or related materiel;

- to have, directly or indirectly, provided training, advice, or other services or assistance, or engaged in financial transactions, related to the manufacture, maintenance, or use of any arms or related materiel to be imported, exported, or reexported to, into, or from North Korea, or following their importation, exportation, or reexportation to, into, or from North Korea;

- to have, directly or indirectly, imported, exported, or reexported luxury goods to or into North Korea;

- to have, directly or indirectly, engaged in money laundering, the counterfeiting of goods or currency, bulk cash smuggling, narcotics trafficking, or other illicit economic activity that involves or supports the Government of North Korea or any senior official thereof;

- to have materially assisted, sponsored, or provided financial, material, or technological support for, or goods or services to or in support of, the activities described in sections l(a)(ii)(A)–(D) of the order or any person whose property and interests in property are blocked pursuant to the order;

- to be owned or controlled by, or to have acted or purported to act for or on behalf of, directly or indirectly, any person whose property and interests in property are blocked pursuant to the order; or

- to have attempted to engage in any of the activities described in sections l(a)(ii)(A)–(F) of the order.

I have delegated to the Secretary of the Treasury the authority, in consultation with the Secretary of State, to take such actions, including the promulgation of rules and regulations, and to employ all powers granted to the President by IEEPA and the United Nations Participation Act, as may be necessary to carry out the purposes of the order. I have also delegated to the Secretary of the Treasury, in consultation with the Secretary of State, the authority to determine that circumstances no longer warrant the blocking of the property and interests in property of a person listed in the Annex to the order, and to take necessary action to give effect to that determination.

The order was effective at 12:01 p.m., eastern daylight time on August 30, 2010. All executive agencies of the United States Government are directed to take all appropriate measures within their authority to carry out the provisions of the order.

I am enclosing a copy of the Executive Order I have issued.

BARACK OBAMA

NOTE: Identical letters were sent to Nancy Pelosi, Speaker of the House of Representatives, and Joseph R. Biden, Jr., President of the Senate. The Executive order is listed in Appendix D at the end of this volume.

Remarks at Fort Bliss, Texas
August 31, 2010

Everybody, have a seat. Well, listen, I am extraordinarily honored to be with all of you today. And I want to thank General Pittard, I want to thank Command Sergeant Major Dave Davenport, who have shown such extraordinary leadership here.

I wanted to come down to Fort Bliss mainly to say thank you and to say welcome home.

I'm going to make a speech to the Nation tonight. It's not going to be a victory lap. It's not going to be self-congratulatory. There's still a lot of work that we've got to do to make sure that Iraq is an effective partner with us. But the fact of the matter is that because of the extraordinary service that all of you have done and so many people here at Fort Bliss have done, Iraq has an opportunity to create a better future for itself and America is more secure.

Now, I just met with some Gold Star families, and yesterday I was at Walter Reed. And there are no moments when I feel more keenly and more deeply my responsibilities as Commander in Chief than during those moments. And I know we've lost 51 fellow soldiers from here in Fort Bliss. A lot more than that were injured, some of them very severely. A million men and women in uniform have now served in Iraq, and this has been one of our longest wars.

But the fact of the matter is that there has not been a single mission that has been assigned to all of you in which you have not performed with gallantry, with courage, with excellence. And that is something that the entire country understands.

There are times where, in our country, we've got political disagreements. And appropriately, we have big debates about war and peace. But the one thing we don't argue about is the fact that we've got the finest fighting force in the history of the world. And the reason we have it is because of the men and women in uniform, in every branch of service, who make so many sacrifices, and their families make those sacrifices alongside them.

And so the main message I have tonight and the main message I have to you is, congratulations on a job well done. The country appreciates you. I appreciate you. And I—the most pride I take in my job is being your Commander in Chief.

It also means that as we transition in Iraq, that the one thing I will insist upon for however long I remain President of the United States is that we serve you and your families as well as you've served us.

So we've spent a lot of time over the last couple of years making sure that we're increasing our support of veterans: that we are making sure that our wounded warriors are cared for; that some of the signature injuries of our war, like posttraumatic stress disorder, traumatic brain injury, that we are devoting special services there; that we've got a post-9/11 GI bill that ensures that you and your family members are able to come back and fully contribute and participate in our economy; that our veterans are constantly getting the care and honor that they have earned.

So that's part of my message to the country. And one of the great things about the last several years has been to see how unified the country

is around support of our veterans and of our men and women who are currently serving.

Now, I know that, as I said at the beginning, our task in Iraq is not yet completed. Our combat phase is over, but we've worked too hard to neglect the continuing work that has to be done by our civilians and by those transitional forces, including some folks who are going to be deploying, I understand, today. And I'm going to be talking to them later.

The work that continues is absolutely critical: providing training and assistance to Iraqi security forces, because there's still violence in Iraq, and they're still learning how to secure their country the way they need to. And they've made enormous strides thanks to the training that they've already received, but there's still more work to do there.

We're going to have to protect our civilians— our aid workers and our diplomats—who are over there, who are still trying to expand and help what's going to be a long road ahead for the Iraqi people in terms of rebuilding their country.

We're still going to be going after terrorists in those areas. And so our counterterrorism operations are still going to be conducted jointly.

But the bottom line is, is that our combat phase is now over. We are in transition. And that could not have been accomplished had it not been for the men and women here at Fort Bliss and across the country.

The other thing that I'm going to talk about this evening is the fact that we obviously still have a very tough fight in Afghanistan. And a lot of families have been touched by the war in Iraq; a lot of families are now being touched in Afghanistan. We've seen casualties go up because we're taking the fight to Al Qaida and the Taliban and their allies.

It is going to be a tough slog, but what I know is that after 9/11, this country was unified in saying, we are not going to let something like that happen again, and we are going to go after those who perpetrated that crime, and we are going to make sure that they do not have safe haven.

And now, under the command of General Petraeus, we have the troops who are there in a position to start taking the fight to the terrorists.

And that's going to mean some casualties, and it's going to mean some heartbreak. But the one thing that I know from all of you is that when we put our minds to it, we get things done. And we're willing to make some sacrifices on behalf of our security here at home.

So to all of you and to your families, I want to express my deepest gratitude, the gratitude of Michelle, the First Lady, and our entire family. But also, I just want to say thank you on behalf of the country, because without you, we couldn't enjoy the freedoms and the security that are so precious. And all of you represent that long line of heroes that have served us so well generation after generation.

You know, when I was talking to the Gold Star families there, there were some widows dating back to World War II, and then there was a young woman who had just had a baby and had just lost her husband. And that de-scribes the arc of heroism and sacrifice that's been made by the men and women in uniform for so many generations. You're part of that line, part of that tradition, part of that heroism.

So what I'd like to do is just to come around and shake all of your hands personally, to say thank you to all of you, to say thank you for a job well done, and to know that you are welcome home with open arms from every corner of this country. People could not be prouder of you, and we are grateful.

Thank you very much, everybody.

NOTE: The President spoke at 10:54 a.m. In his remarks, he referred to Maj. Gen. Dana J.H. Pittard, USA, commanding general, Fort Bliss; and Gen. David H. Petraeus, USA, commander, NATO International Security Assistance Force, Afghanistan.

Address to the Nation on the End of Combat Operations in Iraq
August 31, 2010

Good evening. Tonight I'd like to talk to you about the end of our combat mission in Iraq, the ongoing security challenges we face, and the need to rebuild our Nation here at home.

I know this historic moment comes at a time of great uncertainty for many Americans. We've now been through nearly a decade of war. We've endured a long and painful recession. And sometimes in the midst of these storms, the future that we're trying to build for our Nation, a future of lasting peace and long-term prosperity, may seem beyond our reach.

But this milestone should serve as a reminder to all Americans that the future is ours to shape if we move forward with confidence and commitment. It should also serve as a message to the world that the United States of America intends to sustain and strengthen our leadership in this young century.

From this desk 7½ years ago, President Bush announced the beginning of military operations in Iraq. Much has changed since that night. A war to disarm a state became a fight against an insurgency. Terrorism and sectarian warfare threatened to tear Iraq apart. Thousands of Americans gave their lives; tens of thousands have been wounded. Our relations abroad were strained. Our unity at home was tested.

These are the rough waters encountered during the course of one of America's longest wars. Yet there has been one constant amidst these shifting tides. At every turn, America's men and women in uniform have served with courage and resolve. As Commander in Chief, I am incredibly proud of their service. And like all Americans, I'm awed by their sacrifice and by the sacrifices of their families.

The Americans who have served in Iraq completed every mission they were given. They defeated a regime that had terrorized its people. Together with Iraqis and coalition partners, who made huge sacrifices of their own, our troops fought block by block to help Iraq seize the chance for a better future. They shifted tactics to protect the Iraqi people, trained Iraqi security forces, and took out terrorist leaders. Because of our troops and civilians and because of the resilience of the Iraqi people, Iraq has the opportunity to embrace a new destiny, even though many challenges remain.

So tonight I am announcing that the American combat mission in Iraq has ended. Operation Iraqi Freedom is over, and the Iraqi people now have lead responsibility for the security of their country.

This was my pledge to the American people as a candidate for this office. Last February, I announced a plan that would bring our combat brigades out of Iraq, while redoubling our efforts to strengthen Iraq's security forces and support its Government and people.

That's what we've done. We've removed nearly 100,000 U.S. troops from Iraq. We've closed or transferred to the Iraqis hundreds of bases. And we have moved millions of pieces of equipment out of Iraq.

This completes a transition to Iraqi responsibility for their own security. U.S. troops pulled out of Iraq's cities last summer, and Iraqi forces have moved into the lead with considerable skill and commitment to their fellow citizens. Even as Iraq continues to suffer terrorist attacks, security incidents have been near the lowest on record since the war began. And Iraqi forces have taken the fight to Al Qaida, removing much of its leadership in Iraqi-led operations.

This year also saw Iraq hold credible elections that drew a strong turnout. A caretaker administration is in place as Iraqis form a Government based on the results of that election. Tonight I encourage Iraq's leaders to move forward with a sense of urgency to form an inclusive Government that is just, representative, and accountable to the Iraqi people. And when that Government is in place, there should be no doubt: The Iraqi people will have a strong partner in the United States. Our combat mission is ending, but our commitment to Iraq's future is not.

Going forward, a transitional force of U.S. troops will remain in Iraq with a different mission: advising and assisting Iraq's security forces, supporting Iraqi troops in targeted counterterrorism missions, and protecting our civilians. Consistent with our agreement with the Iraqi Government, all U.S. troops will leave by the end of next year. As our military draws down, our dedicated civilians—diplomats, aid workers, and advisers—are moving into the lead to support Iraq as it strengthens its Government, resolves political disputes, resettles those displaced by war, and builds ties with the region and the world. That's a message that Vice President Biden is delivering to the Iraqi people through his visit there today.

This new approach reflects our long-term partnership with Iraq, one based upon mutual interest and mutual respect. Of course, violence will not end with our combat mission. Extremists will continue to set off bombs, attack Iraqi civilians, and try to spark sectarian strife. But ultimately, these terrorists will fail to achieve their goals. Iraqis are a proud people. They have rejected sectarian war, and they have no interest in endless destruction. They understand that in the end, only Iraqis can resolve their differences and police their streets, only Iraqis can build a democracy within their borders. What America can do and will do is provide support for the Iraqi people as both a friend and a partner.

Ending this war is not only in Iraq's interest, it's in our own. The United States has paid a huge price to put the future of Iraq in the hands of its people. We have sent our young men and women to make enormous sacrifices in Iraq and spent vast resources abroad at a time of tight budgets at home. We've persevered because of a belief we share with the Iraqi people, a belief that out of the ashes of war, a new beginning could be born in this cradle of civilization.

Through this remarkable chapter in the history of the United States and Iraq, we have met our responsibilities. Now it's time to turn the page. As we do, I'm mindful that the Iraq war has been a contentious issue at home. Here too it's time to turn the page. This afternoon I spoke to former President George W. Bush. It's well known that he and I disagreed about the war from its outset. Yet no one can doubt President Bush's support for our troops or his love of country and commitment to our security. As I've said, there were patriots who supported this war and patriots who opposed it. And all of us are united in appreciation for our service men and women and our hopes for Iraqis' future.

The greatness of our democracy is grounded in our ability to move beyond our differences and to learn from our experience as we confront the many challenges ahead. And no challenge is more essential to our security than our fight against Al Qaida.

Americans across the political spectrum supported the use of force against those who attacked us on 9/11. Now, as we approach our 10th year of combat in Afghanistan, there are those who are understandably asking tough questions about our mission there. But we must never lose sight of what's at stake. As we speak, Al Qaida continues to plot against us, and its leadership remains anchored in the border regions of Afghanistan and Pakistan. We will disrupt, dismantle, and defeat Al Qaida, while preventing Afghanistan from again serving as a base for terrorists. And because of our drawdown in Iraq, we are now able to apply the resources necessary to go on offense. In fact, over the last 19 months, nearly a dozen Al Qaida leaders and hundreds of Al Qaida's extremist allies have been killed or captured around the world.

Within Afghanistan, I've ordered the deployment of additional troops, who, under the command of General David Petraeus, are fighting to break the Taliban's momentum. As with the surge in Iraq, these forces will be in place for a limited time to provide space for the Afghans to build their capacity and secure their own future. But as was the case in Iraq, we can't do for Afghans what they must ultimately do for themselves. That's why we're training Afghan security forces and supporting a political resolution to Afghanistan's problems. And next August, we will begin a transition to Afghan responsibility. The pace of our troop reductions will be determined by conditions on the ground, and our support for Afghanistan will endure. But make no mistake: This transition will begin, because open-ended war serves neither our interests nor the Afghan people's.

Indeed, one of the lessons of our effort in Iraq is that American influence around the world is not a function of military force alone. We must use all elements of our power, including our diplomacy, our economic strength, and the power of America's example, to secure our interests and stand by our allies. And we must project a vision of the future that's based not just on our fears, but also on our hopes, a vision that recognizes the real dangers that exist around the world, but also the limitless possibilities of our time.

Today, old adversaries are at peace and emerging democracies are potential partners. New markets for our goods stretch from Asia to the Americas. A new push for peace in the Middle East will begin here tomorrow. Billions of young people want to move beyond the shackles of poverty and conflict. As the leader of the free world, America will do more than just defeat on the battlefield those who offer hatred and destruction. We will also lead among those who are willing to work together to expand freedom and opportunity for all people.

Now, that effort must begin within our own borders. Throughout our history, America has been willing to bear the burden of promoting liberty and human dignity overseas, understanding its links to our own liberty and security. But we have also understood that our Nation's strength and influence abroad must be firmly anchored in our prosperity at home. And the bedrock of that prosperity must be a growing middle class.

Unfortunately, over the last decade, we've not done what's necessary to shore up the foundations of our own prosperity. We spent a trillion dollars at war, often financed by borrowing from overseas. This in turn has shortchanged investments in our own people and contributed to record deficits. For too long, we have put off tough decisions on everything from our manufacturing base to our energy policy to education reform. As a result, too many middle class families find themselves working harder for less, while our Nation's long-term competitiveness is put at risk.

And so at this moment, as we wind down the war in Iraq, we must tackle those challenges at home with as much energy and grit and sense of common purpose as our men and women in uniform who have served abroad. They have met every test that they faced. Now it's our turn. Now it's our responsibility to honor them by coming together, all of us, and working to secure the dream that so many generations have fought for, the dream that a better life awaits anyone who is willing to work for it and reach for it.

Our most urgent task is to restore our economy and put the millions of Americans who have lost their jobs back to work. To strengthen our middle class, we must give all our children the education they deserve and all our workers the skills that they need to compete in a global economy. We must jump-start industries that create jobs and end our dependence on foreign oil. We must unleash the innovation that allows new products to roll off our assembly lines and nurture the ideas that spring from our entrepreneurs. This will be difficult, but in the days to come, it must be our central mission as a people and my central responsibility as President.

Part of that responsibility is making sure that we honor our commitments to those who have served our country with such valor. As long as I am President, we will maintain the finest fighting force that the world has ever known and we will do whatever it takes to serve our veterans as well as they have served us. This is a sacred trust. That's why we've already made one of the largest increases in funding for veterans in decades. We're treating the signature wounds of today's wars, posttraumatic stress disorder and traumatic brain injury, while providing the health care and benefits that all of our veterans have earned. And we're funding a post-9/11 GI bill that helps our veterans and their families pursue the dream of a college education. Just as the GI bill helped those who fought World War II, including my grandfather, become the backbone of our middle class, so today's service men and women must have the chance to apply their gifts to expand the American economy, because part of ending a war responsibly is standing by those who have fought it.

Two weeks ago, America's final combat brigade in Iraq, the Army's 4th Stryker Brigade, journeyed home in the predawn darkness. Thousands of soldiers and hundreds of vehicles made the trip from Baghdad, the last of them passing into Kuwait in the early morning hours. Over 7 years before, American troops and coalition partners had fought their way across similar highways, but this time no shots were fired. It was just a convoy of brave Americans making their way home.

Of course, the soldiers left much behind. Some were teenagers when the war began. Many have served multiple tours of duty, far from families who bore a heroic burden of their own, enduring the absence of a husband's embrace or a mother's kiss. Most painfully, since the war began, 55 members of the 4th Stryker Brigade made the ultimate sacrifice, part of over 4,400 Americans who have given their lives in Iraq. As one staff sergeant said, "I know that to my brothers in arms who fought and died, this day would probably mean a lot."

Those Americans gave their lives for the values that have lived in the hearts of our people for over two centuries. Along with nearly 1.5 million Americans who have served in Iraq, they fought in a faraway place for people they never knew. They stared into the darkest of human creations—war—and helped the Iraqi people seek the light of peace.

In an age without surrender ceremonies, we must earn victory through the success of our partners and the strength of our own Nation. Every American who serves joins an unbroken line of heroes that stretches from Lexington to Gettysburg, from Iwo Jima to Inchon, from Khe Sanh to Kandahar, Americans who have fought to see that the lives of our children are better than our own. Our troops are the steel in our ship of state. And though our Nation may be traveling through rough waters, they give us confidence that our course is true and that beyond the predawn darkness, better days lie ahead.

Thank you. May God bless you, and may God bless the United States of America and all who serve her.

NOTE: The President spoke at 8 p.m. in the Oval Office at the White House. In his remarks, he referred to Gen. David H. Petraeus, USA, commander, NATO International Security Assistance Force, Afghanistan; and S. Sgt. Luke Dill, USA, 4th Battalion, 9th Infantry Regiment,

4th Stryker Brigade Combat Team, 2d Infantry Division. The Office of the Press Secretary also released a Spanish language transcript of this address.

Remarks Following a Meeting With Prime Minister Benjamin Netanyahu of Israel
September 1, 2010

President Obama. Hello, everybody. Prime Minister Netanyahu and I just had a very productive discussion about our shared efforts to advance the cause of peace between Israelis and Palestinians and throughout the Middle East. I'm going to have more to say about today's meetings not only with Prime Minister Netanyahu, but with the other participants of the talks here in the Rose Garden later this afternoon. But I did want to specifically take some time out to speak to the people of Israel and to the region about the senseless slaughter that took place near Hebron yesterday.

There are going to be extremists and rejectionists who, rather than seeking peace, are going to be seeking destruction. And the tragedy that we saw yesterday, where people were gunned down on the street by terrorists who are purposely trying to undermine these talks, is an example of what we're up against. But I want everybody to be very clear: The United States is going to be unwavering in its support of Israel's security, and we are going to push back against these kinds of terrorist activities.

And so the message should go out to Hamas and everybody else who is taking credit for these heinous crimes that this is not going to stop us from not only ensuring a secure Israel, but also securing a longer lasting peace in which people throughout the region can take a different course.

I also want to express the deepest condolences of the American people to the families of those who were gunned down. And I want to thank Prime Minister Netanyahu, during a very difficult time for his country, still being so committed to the cause of peace that he is here with us today.

Prime Minister.

Prime Minister Netanyahu. Well, thank you, Mr. President, for expressing what I think is the sentiment of decent people everywhere in the face of this savagery and brutality.

Four innocent people were gunned down and seven new orphans were added by people who have no respect for human life and trample human rights into the dust and butcher everything that they oppose.

I think that the President's statement is an expression of our desire to fight against this terror. And the talks that we had, which were, indeed, open, productive, serious in the quest for peace, also centered around the need to have security arrangements that are able to roll back this kind of terror and other threats to Israel's security. That is a fundamental element, an important foundation of the peace that we seek and work for.

And I appreciate, Mr. President, your efforts to advance this peace for us and for our neighbors, for our region, and I think we can say, for the world.

Thank you.

President Obama. Thank you.

And let me just say that I will be meeting with President Abbas this afternoon. He condemned this outrageous attack as well. I have the utmost confidence in him and his belief in a two-state solution in which the people of Israel and the Palestinians are living side by side in peace and security. And so I am also grateful to him for his presence here today.

We've got a lot of work to do. There are going to be those who are going to do everything they can to undermine these talks, but we are going to remain stalwart.

And so to Prime Minister Netanyahu and to Prime Minister—and to President Abbas, as well as to President Mubarak and King Abdullah of Jordan, I am very grateful for their partic-ipation. I will have a longer discussion about that this afternoon after my bilateral meetings.

Thank you.

NOTE: The President spoke at 12:24 p.m. on the Colonnade at the White House. In his re-marks, he referred to Yitzhak Ames, Tayla Ames, Kochava Even Chaim, and Avishai Shindler, Jewish settlers who were killed in He-bron on August 31; President Mahmoud Abbas of the Palestinian Authority; President Mo-hamed Hosni Mubarak of Egypt; and King Abdullah II of Jordan. The Office of the Press Secretary also released a Hebrew language transcript of these remarks.

Remarks on the Middle East Peace Process
September 1, 2010

Good afternoon, everybody. Upon taking of-fice, I declared that America is a friend of each nation and every person who seeks a future of peace and dignity and that the United States was ready to lead in pursuit of that future. At the beginning of my administration, I stated that it was our policy to actively and aggressively seek a lasting peace between Israel and the Pal-estinians, as well as a comprehensive peace be-tween Israel and all of its Arab neighbors. And to support my outstanding Secretary of State Hillary Clinton's leadership, I appointed a spe-cial envoy and one of our Nation's finest states-men, former Senator George Mitchell, to guide our efforts.

As I've said many times, our goal is a two-state solution that ends the conflict and ensures the rights and security of both Israelis and Pal-estinians. And despite the inevitable challenges, we have never wavered in pursuit of this goal. I've met with Israeli Prime Minister Benjamin Netanyahu and Palestinian Authority President Mahmoud Abbas on numerous occasions. Be-tween them, Secretary Clinton and Senator Mitchell have made countless trips to the re-gion.

Over the past year, both the Israeli Govern-ment and the Palestinian Authority have taken important steps to build confidence. And with Senator Mitchell's support, Israelis and Pales-tinians have engaged in several rounds of prox-imity talks, even in the face of difficult circum-stances. But we've always made it clear that the only path to lasting peace between Israelis and Palestinians is direct talks between Israelis and Palestinians. Tomorrow, after nearly 2 years, the parties will relaunch those direct talks.

Today I had a series of very productive meet-ings with key partners in this effort. I urged Prime Minister Netanyahu and President Abbas to recognize this as a moment of opportunity that must be seized. I thanked President Mubarak of Egypt and His Majesty King Abdul-lah of Jordan for their valuable leadership and for the support that will be necessary going for-ward. And I look forward to hosting these four leaders at a private working dinner at the White House tonight.

I also want to take this opportunity to express our gratitude to many friends and allies, espe-cially our Quartet partners. And former British Prime Minister Tony Blair will be joining us as representing the Quartet at the dinner this eve-ning.

The purpose of these talks is clear. These will be direct negotiations between Israelis and Pal-estinians. These negotiations are intended to re-solve all final status issues. The goal is a settle-ment, negotiated between the parties, that ends the occupation which began in 1967 and results in the emergence of an independent, democrat-ic, and viable Palestinian state, living side by side in peace and security with a Jewish State of Israel and its other neighbors. That's the vision we are pursuing.

Now, I know these talks have been greeted in some quarters with skepticism. We are under no illusions. Passions run deep. Each side has legitimate and enduring interests. Years of mis-trust will not disappear overnight. Building con-fidence will require painstaking diplomacy and trust by the parties. After all, there's a reason that the two-state solution has eluded previous generations. This is extraordinarily complex and extraordinarily difficult.

But we know that the status quo is unsustainable for Israelis, for Palestinians, for the region, and for the world. It is in the national interests of all involved, including the United States, that this conflict be brought to a peaceful conclusion.

So even as we are clear eyed about the challenges ahead, so too do we see the foundation for progress. The Israeli Government and the Palestinian Authority are already cooperating on a daily basis to increase security and reduce violence, to build institutions and improve conditions on the ground.

Among the Israeli and Palestinian publics, there is wide support for a two-state solution, the broad outlines of which are well known to both peoples. And even in the midst of discord, ordinary Israelis and Palestinians—faith leaders, civil society groups, doctors, scientists, businessmen, students—find ways to work together every day. Their heroic efforts at the grassroots show that cooperation and progress is possible and should inspire us all.

In addition, Prime Minister Netanyahu and President Abbas are two leaders who I believe want peace. Both sides have indicated that these negotiations can be completed within 1 year. And as I told each of them today, this moment of opportunity may not soon come again. They cannot afford to let it slip away. Now is the time for leaders of courage and vision to deliver the peace that their people deserve.

The United States will put our full weight behind this effort. We will be an active and sustained participant. We will support those who make difficult choices in pursuit of peace. But let me be very clear: Ultimately, the United States cannot impose a solution, and we cannot want it more than the parties themselves. There are enormous risks involved here for all the parties concerned, but we cannot do it for them. We can create the environment and the atmosphere for negotiations, but ultimately, it's going to require the leadership on both the Palestinian and the Israeli sides, as well as those in the region who say they want a Palestinian state.

A lot of times I hear from those who insist that this is a top priority and yet do very little to actually support efforts that could bring about a Palestinian state.

So only Israelis and Palestinians can make the difficult choices and build the consensus at home for progress. Only Israelis and Palestinians can prove to each other their readiness to end this conflict and make the compromises upon which lasting peace deserves. What the rest of us can do, including the United States, is to support those conversations, support those talks, support those efforts, not try to undermine them.

So the hard work is only beginning. Neither success nor failure is inevitable. But this much we know: If we do not make the attempt, then failure is guaranteed. If both sides do not commit to these talks in earnest, then the longstanding conflict will only continue to fester and consume another generation, and this we simply cannot allow.

We know that there will be moments that test our resolve. We know that extremists and enemies of peace will do everything in their power to destroy this effort, as we saw in the heinous attacks near Hebron, which we have strongly condemned. But we also know this: Too much blood has already been shed, too many lives have already been lost, too many hearts have already been broken.

And despite what the cynics say, history teaches us that there is a different path. It is the path of resolve and determination, where compromise is possible and old conflicts, at long last, can end. It is the path traveled by those who brought peace to their countries, from Northern Ireland—where Senator Mitchell was so deeply involved—to the Balkans, to Africa, Asia, to those who forged peace between Israel and Egypt and Israel and Jordan.

This path is open to Israelis and Palestinians. If all sides persevere in good faith and with a sense of purpose and possibility, we can build a just, lasting, and comprehensive peace in the Middle East.

Thank you very much.

NOTE: The President spoke at 5:27 p.m. in the Rose Garden at the White House. In his remarks, he referred to U.S. Special Envoy for Middle East Peace George J. Mitchell. The Office of the Press Secretary also released Arabic and Hebrew language transcripts of these remarks.

Remarks Prior to a Dinner With President Mohamed Hosni Mubarak of Egypt, King Abdullah II of Jordan, Prime Minister Benjamin Netanyahu of Israel, and President Mahmoud Abbas of the Palestinian Authority
September 1, 2010

President Obama. Good evening, everyone. Tomorrow, after nearly 2 years, Israelis and Palestinians will resume direct talks in pursuit of a goal that we all share: two states, Israel and Palestine, living side by side in peace and security. Tonight I am pleased to welcome to the White House key partners in this effort, along with Secretary of State Hillary Clinton and the representative of our Quartet partners, former Prime Minister Tony Blair.

President Abbas, Prime Minister Netanyahu, Your Majesty King Abdullah, and President Mubarak, we are but five men. Our dinner this evening will be a small gathering around a single table. Yet when we come together, we will not be alone. We'll be joined by the generations, those who have gone before and those who will follow.

Each of you are the heirs of peacemakers who dared greatly: Begin and Sadat, Rabin and King Hussein, statesmen who saw the world as it was, but also imagined the world as it should be. It is the shoulders of our predecessors upon which we stand. It is their work that we carry on. Now, like each of them, we must ask, do we have the wisdom and the courage to walk the path of peace?

Now, all of us are leaders of our people, who, no matter the language they speak or the faith they practice, all basically seek the same things: to live in security, free from fear; to live in dignity, free from want; to provide for their families and to realize a better tomorrow. Tonight they look to us, and each of us must decide, will we work diligently to fulfill their aspirations?

And though each of us holds a title of honor—President, Prime Minister, King—we are bound by the one title we share: We are fathers, blessed with sons and daughters. So we must ask ourselves, what kind of world do we want to bequeath to our children and our grandchildren?

Tonight and in the days and months ahead, these are the questions that we must answer. And this is a fitting moment to do so.

For Muslims, this is Ramadan. For Jews, this is Elul. It is rare for those two months to coincide. But this year, tonight, they do. Different faiths, different rituals, but a shared period of devotion and contemplation: a time to reflect on right and wrong; a time to ponder one's place in the world; a time when the people of two great religions remind the world of a truth that is both simple and profound, that each of us, all of us, in our hearts and in our lives, are capable of great and lasting change.

In this spirit, I welcome my partners. And I invite each to say a few words before we begin our meal, beginning with President Mubarak, on to His Majesty King Abdullah, Prime Minister Netanyahu, and President Abbas.

President Mubarak.

[*At this point, President Mubarak's remarks were joined in progress.*]

President Mubarak. ——in relaunching direct peace negotiations between Palestinians and Israelis. Like you and the millions of Palestinians, Israelis, Arabs, and the rest of the world—and the people of the Middle East and the world—look forward to have these negotiations as a final and decisive negotiations and that it will lead to a peace between the two parties within 1 year.

Our meeting today would not have taken place without the considerable effort exerted by the U.S. President and his administration under the leadership of President Obama. I pay tribute to you, Mr. President, for your personal, serious commitment and for your determination to work for a peaceful settlement of the question of Palestine since the early days of your Presidency. I appreciate your preservation throughout the past period to overcome the difficulties facing the relaunching of the negotiation. I consider this invitation a manifestation of your commitment and a significant message that the United States will shepherd these negotiations seriously and at the highest level.

No one realizes the value of peace more than those who have known wars and their havoc. It was my destiny to witness over many events in our region during the years of war and peace. I have gone through wars and hostilities and have participated in the quest for peace since the first day of my administration. I have never spared an effort to push it forward, and I still look forward to it—its success and completion.

The efforts to achieve peace between the Palestinians and the Israelis encountered many difficulties since the Madrid Conference in October 1999, and progress and regression, breakthroughs and setbacks, but the occupation of the Palestinian Territory remains an independent—an independent Palestinian state is yet—remains a dream in the conscious of the Palestinian people.

There is no doubt that this situation should raise great frustration and anger among our people, for it is no longer acceptable or conceivable, on the verge of the second decade of the third millennium, that we fail to achieve just and true peace, peace that would put an end to the century of conflict, fulfill the legitimate aspirations of the Palestinian people, lift the occupation, allow for the establishment of normal relations between the Palestinians and Israelis.

It is true that reaching a just and comprehensive peace treaty between both sides has been an elusive hope for almost two decades. Yet the accumulated experience of both parties, the extended rounds of negotiations, and the previous understandings, particularly during the Clinton parameters of 2000 and subsequent understandings in Taba and with the previous Israeli

Government, all contributed in setting the outline of the final settlement.

This outline has become well known to the international community and to both peoples, the Palestinian and Israeli people. Hence, it is expected that the current negotiations will not start from scratch or in void. No doubt, the position of the international community, as is stated in the consecutive statements of the Quartet—in particular, in its latest August 20 statement—paid due respect to relevant international resolutions and supported the outline of final settlements using different formulation without prejudice to the outcome of negotiations.

It has stressed that the aim of the soon-to-start direct negotiation is to reach a peaceful settlement that would end the Israeli occupation, which begins—began in 1967, allowing for the independent and sovereign state of Palestine to emerge and live side by side in peace and security with the State of Israel.

I met with Prime Minister Netanyahu many times since he took office last year. In our meetings, I listened to assertions on his willingness to achieve peace with the Palestinians and for history to record his name for such an achievement. I say to him today that I look forward to achieving those assertions in reality and his success in achieving the long-awaited peace, which I know the people of Israel yearn for, just like all other people in the region.

Reaching just peace with the Palestinians will require from Israel taking important and decisive decisions, decisions that are undoubtedly difficult, yet they will be necessary to achieve peace and stability, and in a different context than the one that prevailed before.

Settlement activities on the Palestinian Territory are contrary to international law. They will not create rights for Israel, nor they are going to achieve peace or security for Israel. It is therefore a priority to completely freeze all these activities until the entire negotiation process comes to a successful end.

I say to the Israelis, seize the current opportunity. Do not let it slip through your fingers. Make comprehensive peace your goal. Extend your hand to meet the hand already extended in the Arab Peace Initiative.

I say to President Mahmoud Abbas, Egypt will continue its faithful support to the patient Palestinian people and their just cause. We will continue our concerted efforts to help fulfill the aspirations of your people and retrieve the legitimate rights—their legitimate rights. We will stand by you until the independent state of Palestine on the land occupied since 1967, with East Jerusalem as its capital. We will also continue our efforts to achieve Palestinian reconciliation for the sake of the Palestinian national interest.

Once again, I'd like to express my thanks to President Obama, and I renew Egypt's commitment to continue exerting all efforts, sharing honest advice and a commitment to the principles on which Arab and regional policy rests upon.

Please accept my appreciation, and peace be upon you.

King Abdullah. Bismillah al Rahman al Raheem——

Interpreter. In the name of God most merciful, most compassionate——

King Abdullah. ——President Obama, Your Excellencies, *as-salaam alaikum.*

Interpreter. ——peace be upon you.

King Abdullah. The task at hand is not an easy one. For decades, a Palestinian-Israeli settlement has eluded us. Millions of men, women, and children have suffered. Too many people have lost faith in our ability to bring them the peace they want. Radicals and terrorists have exploited frustrations to feed hatred and ignite wars. The whole world has been dragged into regional conflicts that cannot be addressed effectively until Arabs and Israelis find peace.

This past record drives the importance of our efforts today. There are those on both sides who want us to fail, who will do everything in their power to disrupt our efforts today, because when the Palestinians and Israelis find peace, when young men and women can look to a future of promise and opportunity, radicals and extremists lose their most potent appeal. This is why we must prevail, for our failure would be their success in sinking the region into more instability and wars that will cause further suffering in our region and beyond.

President Obama, we value your commitment to the cause of peace in our region. We count on your continued engagement to help the parties move forward. You have said that Middle East peace is in the national security interests of your country, and we believe it is. And it is also a strategic European interest, and it is a necessary requirement for global security and stability. Peace is also a right for every citizen in our region.

A Palestinian-Israeli settlement on the basis of two states living side by side is a precondition for security and stability of all countries of the Middle East, with a regional peace that would lead to normal relations between Israel and 57 Arab and Muslim states that have endorsed the Arab Peace Initiative. That would be—or that would also be an essential step towards neutralizing forces of evil and war that threaten all peoples.

Mr. President, we need your support as a mediator, honest broker, and a partner as the parties move along the hard but inevitable path of settlements.

Your Excellencies, all eyes are upon us. The direct negotiations that will start tomorrow must show results, and sooner rather than later. Time is not on our side. That is why we must spare no effort in addressing all final status issues with a view to reaching the two-state solution, the only solution that can create a future worthy of our great region, a future of peace, in which fathers and mothers can raise their children without fear, young people can look forward to lives of achievement and hope, and 300 million people can cooperate for mutual benefit.

For too long, too many people of the region have been denied their most basic of human rights: the right to live in peace and security, respected in their human dignity, enjoying freedom and opportunity. If hopes are disappointed again, the price of failure will be too high for all.

Our peoples want us to rise to their expectations. And we can do so if we approach these negotiations with good will, sincerity, and courage.

Thank you.

Prime Minister Netanyahu. Mr. President, Excellencies, *shalom aleichem. Shalom al kulanu.* Peace unto you. Peace unto us all.

I am very pleased to be here today to begin our common effort to achieve a lasting peace between Israelis and Palestinians.

I want to thank you, President Obama, for your tireless efforts to renew this quest for peace. I want to thank Secretary of State Hillary Clinton, Senator Mitchell, the many members of the Obama administration, and Tony Blair, who've all worked so hard to bring Israelis and Palestinians together here today.

I also want to thank President Mubarak and King Abdullah for their dedicated and meaningful support to promote peace, security, and stability throughout our region. I deeply appreciate your presence here today.

I began with a Hebrew word for peace, "shalom." Our goal is shalom. Our goal is to forge a secure and durable peace between Israelis and Palestinians. We don't seek a brief interlude between two wars. We don't seek a temporary respite between outbursts of terror. We seek a peace that will end the conflict between us once and for all. We seek a peace that will last for generations: our generation, our children's generation, and the next.

This is the peace my people fervently want. This is the peace all our peoples fervently aspire to. This is the peace they deserve.

Now, a lasting peace is a peace between peoples, between Israelis and Palestinians. We must learn to live together, to live next to one another and with one another. But every peace begins with leaders.

President Abbas, you are my partner in peace. And it is up to us, with the help of our friends, to conclude the agonizing conflict between our peoples and to afford them a new beginning. The Jewish people are not strangers in our ancestral homeland, the land of our forefathers, but we recognize that another people shares this land with us.

I came here today to find an historic compromise that will enable both our peoples to live in peace and security and in dignity. I've been making the case for Israel all of my life. But I didn't come here today to make an argument. I came here today to make peace. I didn't come here today to play a blame game where even the winners lose. Everybody loses if there's no peace. I came here to achieve a peace that will bring a lasting benefit to us all.

I didn't come here to find excuses or to make them. I came here to find solutions. I know the history of our conflict and the sacrifices that have been made. I know the grief that has afflicted so many families who've lost their dearest loved ones. Only yesterday four Israelis, including a pregnant women—a pregnant woman and another woman, a mother of six children, were brutally murdered by savage terrorists. And 2 hours ago, there was another terror attack. And thank God no one died. I will not let the terrorists block our path to peace, but as these events underscore once again, that peace must be anchored in security.

I'm prepared to walk down the path of peace because I know what peace would mean for our children and for our grandchildren. I know it would herald a new beginning that could unleash unprecedented opportunities for Israelis, for Palestinians, and for the peoples—all the peoples of our region and well beyond our region. I think it would affect the world.

I see what a period of calm has created in the Palestinian cities of Ramallah, of Janin, throughout the West Bank: a great economic boom. And real peace can turn this boom into a permanent era of progress and hope.

If we work together, we could take advantage of the great benefits afforded by our unique place under the Sun. We're at the crossroads of three continents, at the crossroads of history, and at the crossroads of the future. Our geography, our history, our culture, our climate, the talents of our people can be unleashed to create extraordinary opportunities in tourism, in trade, in industry, in energy, in water, in so many areas.

But peace must also be defended against its enemies. We want the skyline of the West Bank to be dominated by apartment towers, not missiles. We want the roads of the West Bank to flow with commerce, not terrorists.

And this is not a theoretic request for our people. We left Lebanon, and we got terror. We left Gaza, and we got terror once again. We want to ensure that territory we'll concede will not be turned into a third Iranian-sponsored terror enclave armed at the heart of Israel and, may I add, also aimed at every one of us sitting on this stage.

This is why a defensible peace requires security arrangements that can withstand the test of time and the many challenges that are sure to confront us. And there will be many challenges, both great and small. And let us not get bogged down by every difference between us. Let us direct our courage, our thinking, and our decisions at those historic decisions that lie ahead.

Now, there are many skeptics. One thing there's no shortage of, Mr. President, are skeptics. This is something that you're so familiar with, that all of us in a position of leadership are familiar with. There are many skeptics. I suppose there are many reasons for skepticism. But I have no doubt that peace is possible.

President Abbas, we cannot erase the past, but it is within our power to change the future. Thousands of years ago, on these very hills where Israelis and Palestinians live today, the Jewish prophet Isaiah and the other prophets of my people envisioned a future of lasting peace for all mankind. Let today be an auspicious step in our joint effort to realize that ancient vision for a better future.

[President Abbas's remarks were joined in progress.]

President Abbas. ——most compassionate. His Excellency President Barack Obama, His Excellency President Hosni Mubarak, His Majesty King Abdullah II, His Excellency Prime Minister Benjamin Netanyahu, Mrs. Hillary Clinton, Mr. Tony Blair, ladies and gentlemen: I would like to start by thanking President Obama for his invitation to host us here today to relaunch the permanent status negotiations to reach a Palestinian-Israeli peace agreement covering all the permanent status issues within a year, in accordance with international law and relevant resolutions.

As we move towards the relaunch of these negotiations tomorrow, we recognize the difficulties, challenges, and obstacles that lie ahead.

Yet we assure you, in the name of the PLO, that we will draw on years of experience in negotiations and benefit from the lessons learned and—to make these negotiations successful.

We also reiterate our commitment to carry out all our obligations, and we call on the Israelis to carry out their obligations, including a freeze on all settlements activities, which is not setting a precondition, but a call to implement an agreed obligation and to end all the closure and blockades preventing freedom of movement, including the impose of siege.

We will spare no effort and will work diligently and tirelessly to ensure that these negotiations achieve their goals and objectives in dealing with all of the issues—Jerusalem, refugees, settlements, border security, water, as well as the release of all our prisoners—in order to achieve peace. That our—the people of our area are looking for peace that achieves freedom, independence, and justice to the Palestinian people in their country and in their homeland and in the diaspora—our people who have endured decades of lost—longstanding suffering.

We want a peace that will correct the historical injustice caused by the Nakba of 1948 and one that brings security to our people and the Israeli people. And we want peace that will give us both and the people of the region a new era where we enjoy just peace, stability, and prosperity.

Our determination stems to a great extent from your willpower, Mr. President, and your firm and sweeping drive with which you engulfed the entire world from the day you took office to set the parties on the path for peace, and also this same spirit exhibited by Secretary Hillary Clinton and Senator George Mitchell and his team.

The presence of His Excellency President Mubarak and His Majesty King Abdullah is another telling indication of their substantial and effective commitment and role, where Egypt and Jordan have been playing a supportive role for advancing the peace process. Their effective role is further demonstrated by the Arab Peace Initiative, which was fully endorsed by all of the Arab States. This initiative—and the Islamic countries as well—this initiative served a genuine and sincere opportunity to achieve a just and comprehensive peace on all tracks in our region, including the Syrian-Israeli track and the Lebanese-Israeli track, and provided a sincere opportunity—and valuable—to make peace.

The presence here today of the envoy of the Quartet, Mr. Tony Blair, is a most telling signal, especially since he has been personally involved in the Palestinian Authority for many years and in the efforts for state building in Palestine.

Excellencies, time has come for us to make peace, and it is time to end the occupation that started in 1967 and for the Palestinian people to get freedom, justice, and independence. It is time that a independent Palestinian state be established with sovereignty, side by side with the State of Israel. It is time to put an end to the struggle in the Middle East.

The Palestinian people, who insist on the rights and freedom and independence, are in most need for justice, security, and peace, because they are the victim, the ones that were harmed the most from this violence. And it is sending message to our neighbors, the Israelis, and to the world that they are also careful about supporting the opportunities for the success of these negotiations and the just and lasting peace as soon as possible.

With this spirit, we will work to make these negotiations succeed. And with this spirit, we are—trust that we are capable to achieve our historical, difficult mission: making peace in the land of peace.

Mr. Netanyahu, what happened yesterday and what is happening today is also condemned. We do not want at all that any blood be shed, one drop of blood, on the part of the—on the Israeli—from the Israelis or the Palestinians. We want people between the two—in the two countries to lead a normal life. They want them to live as neighbors and partners forever. Let us sign an agreement, a final agreement, for peace and put an end to a very long period of struggle forever.

And peace be upon you.

President Obama. I want to thank all the leaders for their thoughtful statements. I want to thank the delegations that are represented here, because they are the ones who oftentimes are doing a lot of the work. This is just the beginning. We have a long road ahead, but I appreciate very much the leaders who are represented here for giving us such an excellent start.

And I particularly want to commend Prime Minister Netanyahu and President Abbas for their presence here. This is not easy. Both of them have constituencies with legitimate claims, legitimate concerns, and a lot of history between them. For them to be here, to be willing to take this first step, the most difficult step, is a testament to their courage and their integrity and, I think, their vision for the future.

And so I am hopeful—cautiously hopeful, but hopeful—that we can achieve the goal that all four of these leaders articulated.

Thank you very much, everybody.

NOTE: The President spoke at 7:05 p.m. in the East Room at the White House. In his remarks, he referred to former Prime Minister Tony Blair of the United Kingdom, Quartet Representative in the Middle East. In their remarks, Prime Minister Netanyahu and President Abbas referred to U.S. Special Envoy for Middle East Peace George J. Mitchell. Prime Minister Netanyahu also referred to Yitzhak Ames, Tayla Ames, Kochava Even Chaim, and Avishai Shindler, Jewish settlers who were killed in Hebron on August 31. President Mubarak and President Abbas spoke in Arabic, and their remarks were translated by an interpreter.

Remarks on the National Economy and an Exchange With Reporters
September 3, 2010

The President. Good morning, everybody. As we head into Labor Day weekend, I know many people across this country are concerned about what the future holds for themselves, for their families, and for the economy as a whole.

As I've said from the start, there's no quick fix to the worst recession we've experienced since the Great Depression. The hard truth is, is that it took years to create our current economic problems, and it will take more time than any of us would like to repair the damage. Millions of our neighbors are living with that painfully every day.

But I want all Americans to remind themselves there are better days ahead. Even after this economic crisis, our markets remain the most dynamic in the world. Our workers are still the most productive. We remain the global leader in innovation, in discovery, in entrepreneurship.

Now, the month I took office, we were losing 750,000 jobs a month. This morning new figures show the economy produced 67,000 private sector jobs in August, the eighth consecutive month of private job growth. Additionally, the numbers for July were revised upward to 107,000.

Now, that's positive news, and it reflects the steps we've already taken to break the back of this recession. But it's not nearly good enough. That's why we need to take further steps to create jobs and keep the economy growing, including extending tax cuts for the middle class and investing in the areas of our economy where the potential for job growth is greatest. In the weeks ahead, I'll be discussing some of these ideas in more detail.

But one thing we also have to do right now, one thing we have a responsibility to do right now is to lift up our small businesses, which accounted for over 60 percent of job losses in the final months of last year. That's why once again I'm calling on Congress to make passing a small-business jobs bill its first order of business when it gets back into session later this month.

Now, here's why this is so important. Up until this past May, we were not only waiving fees for entrepreneurs who took out Small Business Administration loans, we were also encouraging more community banks to make loans to responsible business owners. Now, these steps are part of the reason about 70,000 new Small Business Administration loans have been approved since I took office. And I thank Karen Mills for the outstanding job she's been doing as Administrator of the Small Business Administration.

We've also been extending—fighting to extend these loan enhancements with a small-business jobs bill. It's a bill that will more than double the amount some small-business owners can borrow to grow their companies. It will completely eliminate capital gains taxes on key investments so small-business owners can buy new equipment and expand. And it will accelerate $55 billion in tax cuts for businesses, large and small, that make job-creating investments in the next 14 months.

And keep in mind, it is paid for. It will not add one dime to our deficit. So put simply, this piece of legislation is good for workers, it's good for small-businesspeople, it's good for our economy. And yet Republicans in the Senate have blocked this bill, a needless delay that has led small-business owners across this country to put off hiring, put off expanding, and put off plans that will make our economy stronger.

I've repeated since I ran for office, there is no silver bullet that is going to solve all of our economic problems overnight. But there are certain steps that we know will make a meaningful difference for small-business men and women, who are the primary drivers of job creation. There are certain measures that we know will advance our recovery. This small-business jobs bill is one of them.

And I'm confident that if we're willing to put partisanship aside and be the leaders the American people need us to be, if we're willing to do what's next not for the next—what's best not for the next election, but for the next generation, then we are not only going to see America's hard-working families and America's small businesses bounce back, but we'll rebuild America's economy stronger than it's been before.

Okay? Thank you very much.

Job Growth

Q. Mr. President, what are the other incentives that you mentioned Monday, sir?

The President. Well, I will be addressing a broader package of ideas next week. We are confident that we are moving in the right direction, but we want to keep this recovery moving stronger and accelerate the job growth that's needed so desperately all across the country.

Q. What about a poverty agenda, Mr. President? What about a poverty agenda for all classes——

Public Perception of Economic Recovery/Job Growth

Q. Mr. President, to what degree do you regret the administration's decision to call this "Recovery Summer"?

The President. I don't regret the notion that we are moving forward because of the steps that we've taken. And I'm going to have a press conference next week where, after you guys are able to hear where we're at, we'll be able to answer some specific questions.

But the key point I'm making right now is that the economy is moving in a positive direction. Jobs are being created. They're just not being created as fast as they need to, given the big hole that we experienced. And we're going to have to continue to work with Republicans and Democrats to come up with ideas that can further accelerate that job growth.

I'm confident that we can do that. And the evidence that we've seen during the course of this summer and over the course of the last 18 months indicate that we're moving in the right direction. We just have to speed it up.

All right? Thank you very much, everybody.

NOTE: The President spoke at 10:16 a.m. in the Rose Garden at the White House. The Office of the Press Secretary also released a Spanish language transcript of these remarks.

The President's Weekly Address
September 4, 2010

On Monday, we celebrate Labor Day. It's a chance to get together with families and friends, to throw some food on the grill, and have a good time. But it's also a day to honor the American worker, to reaffirm our commitment to the great American middle class that has for generations made our economy the envy of the world.

That is especially important now. I don't have to tell you that this is a very tough time for our country. Millions of our neighbors have been swept up in the worst recession in our lifetimes. And long before this recession hit, the middle class had been taking some hard shots. Long before this recession, the values of hard work and responsibility that built this country had been given short shrift.

For a decade, middle class families felt the sting of stagnant incomes and declining economic security. Companies were rewarded with tax breaks for creating jobs overseas. Wall Street firms turned huge profits by taking, in some cases, reckless risks and cutting corners. All of this came at the expense of working Americans, who were fighting harder and harder just to stay afloat, often borrowing against inflated home values to pay their bills. Ultimately, that house of cards collapsed.

So this Labor Day, we should recommit ourselves to our time-honored values and to this fundamental truth: To heal our economy, we need more than a healthy stock market; we need bustling Main Streets and a growing, thriving middle class. That's why I'll keep working day by day to restore opportunity, economic security, and that basic American Dream for our families and future generations.

First, that means doing everything we can to accelerate job creation. The steps we've taken to date have stopped the bleeding: investments in roads and bridges and high-speed railroads that will lead to hundreds of thousands of jobs in the private sector; emergency steps to prevent the layoffs of hundreds of thousands of teachers and firefighters and police officers; and tax cuts and loans for small-business owners, who create most of the jobs in this country. We also ended a tax loophole that encouraged companies to create jobs overseas. Instead, I'm fighting to pass a law to provide tax breaks to the folks who create jobs right here in America.

But strengthening our economy means more than that. We're fighting to build an economy in which middle class families can afford to send their kids to college, buy a home, save for retirement, and achieve some measure of economic security when their working days are done. And over the last 2 years, that has meant taking on some powerful interests who had been dominating the agenda in Washington for far too long.

That's why we've put an end to the wasteful subsidies to big banks that provide student loans. We're going to use that money instead to make college more affordable for students.

That's why we're making it easier for workers to save for retirement, with new ways of saving their tax refunds and a simpler system for enrolling in retirement plans like 401(k)s. And we're going to keep up the fight to protect Social Security for generations to come.

That's why we stopped insurance companies from refusing to cover people with preexisting conditions and dropping folks who become seriously ill.

And that's why we cut taxes for 95 percent of working families and passed a law to help make sure women earn equal pay for equal work in the United States of America.

This Labor Day, we are reminded that we didn't become the most prosperous country in the world by rewarding greed and recklessness. We did it by rewarding hard work and responsibility. We did it by recognizing that we rise or fall together as one Nation, one people, all of us vested in one another. That's how we have succeeded in the past, and that is how we will not only rebuild this economy but rebuild it stronger than ever before.

Thank you. And I hope you have a great Labor Day weekend.

NOTE: The address was recorded at approximately 5:35 p.m. on September 2 in the Blue Room at the White House for broadcast on September 4. The transcript was made available by the Office of the Press Secretary on September 3, but was embargoed for release until 6 a.m. on September 4.

Remarks at Laborfest in Milwaukee, Wisconsin
September 6, 2010

The President. Hello, Milwaukee! Oh, hello, Milwaukee. Thank you. It is good to be back in Milwaukee. It is good to be—I'm almost home. I just hop on the 94 and I'm home. Take it all the way to the South Side.

It is good to be here on such a beautiful day. Happy Labor Day, everybody. I want to say thank you to the Milwaukee Area Labor Council and all of my brothers and sisters in the AFL–CIO for inviting me to spend this day with you, a day that belongs to the working men and women of America.

I want to acknowledge your outstanding national president, a man who knows that a strong economy needs a strong labor movement, Rich Trumka. Thank you to the president of Wisconsin AFL–CIO, Dave Newby; our host, your area labor council secretary-treasurer, Sheila Cochran. I hear it's Sheila's birthday tomorrow. Where is she? Happy birthday, Sheila.

I'm proud to be here with our Secretary of Labor, a daughter of union members, Hilda Solis. And our Secretary of Transportation, Ray LaHood, is in the house. And I want everybody to give it up for people who are at the forefront of every fight for Wisconsin's working men and women: Senator Herb Kohl; Congresswoman Gwen Moore. Your outstanding mayor and I believe soon-to-be outstanding Governor, Tom Barrett's in the house. And I know your other great Senator, Russ Feingold, was here earlier standing with you and your families, just like he always has. Now he's in his hometown of Janesville to participate in their Labor Day parade.

So it is good to be back. Now, of course, this isn't my first time at Laborfest. Some of you remember, I stood right here with you 2 years ago, when I was still a candidate for this office. And during that campaign, we talked about how for years the values of hard work and responsibility that had built this country had been given short shrift and how it was slowly hollowing out our middle class. Listen, everybody who has a chair, go ahead and sit down, because everybody's all hollering. Just relax; I'm going to be talking for a while now. Everybody take—

[*applause*]—got a lot of hard-working people here; you deserve to sit down for a day. You've been on your feet all year working hard.

But 2 years ago, we talked about some on Wall Street who were taking reckless risks and cutting corners to turn huge profits while working Americans were fighting harder and harder just to stay afloat. We talked about how the decks all too often were stacked in favor of special interests and against the interests of working Americans.

And what we knew even then was that these years would be some of the most difficult in our history. And then 2 weeks later—2 weeks after I spoke here, the bottom fell out of the economy, and middle class families suddenly found themselves swept up in the worst recession of our lifetimes.

So the problems facing working families, they're nothing new. But they are more serious than ever. And that makes our cause more urgent than ever. For generations, it was the great American working class, the great American middle class that made our economy the envy of the world. It's got to be that way again.

Milwaukee, it was folks like you that built this city. It was folks like you that built this State. It was folks like you who forged that middle class all across the Nation.

It was working men and women who made the 20th century the American century. It was the labor movement that helped secure so much of what we take for granted today: the 40-hour work week, the minimum wage, family leave, health insurance, Social Security, Medicare, retirement plans. The cornerstones of the middle class security all bear the union label.

And it was that greatest generation that built America into the greatest force of prosperity and opportunity and freedom that the world has ever known, Americans like my grandfather, who went off to war just boys and then returned home as men, and then they traded in one uniform and set of responsibilities for another. And Americans like my grandmother, who rolled up her sleeves and worked in a factory on the homefront. And when the war was over, they studied under the GI bill, and they bought a home under the FHA, and they raised families supported by good jobs that paid good wages with good benefits.

It was through my grandparents' experience that I was brought up to believe that anything is possible in America. But Milwaukee, they also knew the feeling when opportunity is pulled out from under you. They grew up during the Depression, so they'd tell me about seeing their fathers or their uncles or—losing jobs; how it wasn't just the loss of a paycheck that hurt so bad, it was the blow to their dignity, their sense of self-worth. I'll bet a lot of us have seen people who've been changed after a long bout of unemployment. It can wear you down. Even if you've got a strong spirit, if you're out of work for a long time, it can wear you down.

So my grandparents taught me early on that a job is about more than just a paycheck. The paycheck's important, but a job's about waking up every day with a sense of purpose and going to bed at night feeling like you've handled your responsibilities. It's about meeting your responsibilities to yourself and to your family and to your community. And I carried that lesson with me all those years ago when I got my start fighting for men and women on the south side of Chicago after their local steel plant shut down. And I carried that lesson with me through my time as a State senator and a U.S. Senator, and I carry that lesson with me today.

And I know—I know that there are folks right here in this audience, folks right here in Milwaukee and all across America who are going through these kinds of struggles. Eight million Americans lost their jobs in this recession. And even though we've had 8 straight months of private sector job growth, the new jobs haven't been coming fast enough.

Now, here's the honest truth, the plain truth: There's no silver bullet; there's no quick fix to these problems. I knew when I was running for office—and I certainly knew by the time I was sworn in—I knew it would take time to reverse the damage of a decade worth of policies that saw too few people being able to climb into the middle class, too many people falling behind. We all knew this. We all knew that it would take more time than any of us want to dig ourselves out of this hole created by this economic crisis.

But on this Labor Day, there are two things I want you to know.

Number one, I am going to keep fighting every single day, every single hour, every single minute to turn this economy around and put people back to work and renew the American Dream, not just for your family, not just for all our families, but for future generations. That I can guarantee you.

Number two, I believe this with every fiber of my being: America cannot have a strong, growing economy without a strong, growing middle class and the chance for everybody, no matter how humble their beginnings, to join that middle class, a middle class built on the idea that if you work hard, if you live up to your responsibilities, then you can get ahead; that you can enjoy some basic guarantees in life—a good job that pays a good wage, health care that will be there when you get sick, a secure retirement even if you're not rich, an education that will give your children a better life than we had. These are simple ideas. These are American ideas. These are union ideas. That's what we're fighting for.

I was thinking about this last week. I was thinking about this last week on the day I announced the end of our combat mission in Iraq. And I spent some time, as I often do, with our soldiers and our veterans. And this new generation of troops coming home from Iraq, they've earned their place alongside the greatest generation. Just like that greatest generation, they've got the skills, they've got the training, they've got the drive to move America's economy forward once more.

We've been investing in new care and new opportunities and a new commitment to our veterans, because we've got to serve them just the way they served us. But Milwaukee, they're coming home to an economy hit by a recession deeper than anything we've seen since the 1930s. So the question is, how do we create the same kinds of middle class opportunities for this generation as my grandparents' generation came home to? How do we build our economy on that same strong, stable foundation for growth?

Now, anybody who thinks that we can move this economy forward with just a few folks at the top doing well, hoping that it's going to trickle down to working people, who are running faster and faster just to keep up——

Audience member. You'll never see it.

The President. ——you'll never see it. If that's what you're waiting for, you should stop waiting, because it's never happened in our history. That's not how America was built. It wasn't built with a bunch of folks at the top doing well and everybody else scrambling. We didn't become the most prosperous country in the world just by rewarding greed and recklessness. We didn't come this far by letting the special interests run wild. We didn't do it just by gambling and chasing paper profits on Wall Street. We built this country by making things, by producing goods we could sell. We did it with sweat and effort and innovation. We did it on the assembly line and at the construction site. We did it by investing in the people who built this country from the ground up: the workers, middle class families, small-business owners. We outworked folks, and we outeducated folks, and we outcompeted everybody else. That's how we built America.

And, Milwaukee, that's what we're going to do again. That's been at the heart of what we've been doing over these last 20 months: building our economy on a new foundation so that our middle class doesn't just survive this crisis, I want it to thrive. I want it to be stronger than it was before.

And over the last 2 years, that's meant taking on some powerful interests, some powerful interests who had been dominating the agenda in Washington for a very long time. And they're not always happy with me. They talk about me like a dog. That's not in my prepared remarks, it's just—[*laughter*]—but it's true.

You know, that's why we passed financial reform, to provide new accountability and tough oversight of Wall Street, stopping credit card companies from gouging you with hidden fees and unfair rate hikes, ending taxpayer bailouts for—of Wall Street once and for all. They're not happy with it, but it was the right thing to do.

That's why we eliminated tens of billions of dollars in wasteful taxpayer subsidies, handouts to the big banks that were providing student loans. We took that money, tens of billions of dollars, and we're going to go to make sure that your kids and your grandkids can get student loans and grants at a cheap rate and afford a college education. They're not happy with it, but it was the right thing to do. [*Applause*] Yes, we're using those savings to put a college education within reach for working families.

That's why we passed health insurance reform, to make coverage affordable; reform that ends the indignity of insurance companies jacking up your premiums at will, denying you coverage just because you get sick; reform that gives you control, gives you the ability, if your child is sick, to be able to get an affordable insurance plan, making sure they can't drop it.

That's why we're making it easier for workers to save for retirement, with new ways of saving your tax refunds, a simpler system for enrolling in plans like 401(k)s, and fighting to strengthen Social Security for the future. And if everybody is still talking about privatizing Social Security, they need to be clear: It will not happen on my watch, not when I'm President of the United States of America.

That's why we've given tax cuts, except we give them to folks who need them. We've given them to small-business owners. We've given them to clean energy companies. We've cut taxes for 95 percent of working Americans, just like I promised you during the campaign. You all got a tax cut. And instead of giving tax breaks to companies that are shipping jobs overseas, we're cutting taxes to companies that are putting our people to work right here in the United States of America.

See, we want to invest in growth industries like clean energy and manufacturing. You've got leaders here in Wisconsin—Tom Barrett, Jim Doyle—they've been fighting to bring those jobs to Milwaukee, fighting to bring those jobs here to Wisconsin. I don't want to see solar panels and wind turbines and electric cars made in China. I want them made right here in the United States of America.

I don't want to buy stuff from someplace else. I want to grow our exports so that we're selling to someplace else, products that say, "Made in the U.S.A."

Audience members. U.S.A.! U.S.A.! U.S.A.!

The President. That's right. There are no better workers than American workers. I'll put my money on you any day of the week. And when the naysayers said, well, you can't save the auto industry, just go ahead and let hundreds of thousands of jobs vanish, we said, we're going to stand by those workers. If they're—if the management's willing to make tough choices, if everybody's willing to come together, I'm confident that the American auto industry can compete once again. And today, that industry is on the way back. They said no; we said yes to the American worker. They're coming back.

Now, let me tell you, another thing we've done is to make long-overdue investments in upgrading our outdated, our inefficient national infrastructure. We're talking roads. We're talking bridges. We're talking dams, levees. But we're also talking a smart electric grid that can bring clean energy to new areas. We're talking about broadband Internet so that everybody's plugged in. We're talking about high-speed rail lines required to compete in a 21st-century economy. I want to get down from Milwaukee down to Chicago quick—avoid a traffic jam.

We're talking investments in tomorrow that are creating hundreds of thousands of private sector jobs right now.

Because of these investments and the tens of thousands of projects they spurred all across the country, the battered construction sector actually grew last month for the first time in a very long time.

But you know, the folks here in the trades know what I'm talking about. Nearly one in five construction workers are unemployed—one in five. Nobody's been hit harder than construction workers. And a lot of those folks, they had lost their jobs in manufacturing and went into construction; now they've lost their jobs again.

It doesn't do anybody any good when so many hard-working Americans have been idled for months, even years, at a time when there's so much of America that needs rebuilding. So that's why, Milwaukee, today I am announcing a new plan for rebuilding and modernizing America's roads and rails and runways for the long term. I want America to have the best infrastructure in the world. We used to have the best infrastructure in the world; we can have it again. We are going to make it happen.

Over the next 6 years, we are going to rebuild 150,000 miles of our roads. That's enough to circle the world six times; that's a lot of road. We're going to lay and maintain 4,000 miles of our railways, enough to stretch coast to coast. We're going to restore 150 miles of runways. And we're going to advance a next-generation air traffic control system to reduce travel time and delays for American travelers. I think everybody can agree on that. Anybody want more delays at airports?

Audience members. No!

The President. No, I didn't think so. That's not a Republican or a Democratic idea. We all want to get to where we need to go. I mean, I've got Air Force One now; it's nice. [*Laughter*] But I still remember what it was like. [*Laughter*]

This is a plan that will be fully paid for. It will not add to the deficit over time; we're going to work with Congress to see to that. We want to set up an infrastructure bank to leverage Federal dollars and focus on the smartest investments. We're going to continue our strategy to build a national high-speed rail network that reduces congestion and travel times and reduces harmful emissions. We want to cut waste and bureaucracy and consolidate and collapse more than 100 different programs that too often duplicate each other. So we want to change the way Washington spends your tax dollars. We want to reform a haphazard, patchwork way of doing business. We want to focus on less wasteful approaches than we've got right now. We want competition and innovation that gives us the best bang for the buck.

But the bottom line is this, Milwaukee: This will not only create jobs immediately, it's also going to make our economy hum over the long haul. It's a plan that history tells us can and should attract bipartisan support. It's a plan that says even in the aftermath of the worst reces-

sion in our lifetimes, America can still shape our own destiny. We can still move this country forward. We can still leave our children something better. We can still leave them something that lasts.

So these are the things we've been working for. These are some of the victories you guys have helped us achieve. And we're not finished. We've got a lot more progress to make. And I'm confident we will.

But there are some folks in Washington who see things differently.

Audience members. Boo!

The President. You know what I'm talking about. [*Laughter*] When it comes to just about everything we've done to strengthen our middle class, to rebuild our economy, almost every Republican in Congress says no. Even on things we usually agree on, they say no. If I said the sky was blue, they'd say no. [*Laughter*] If I said fish live in the sea, they'd say no. [*Laughter*] They just think it's better to score political points before an election than to solve problems. So they said no to help for small businesses, even when the small businesses said, we desperately need this. This used to be their key constituency, they said. They said no—no to middle class tax cuts. They say they're for tax cuts; I say, okay, let's give tax cuts to the middle class. "No." [*Laughter*] No to clean energy jobs, no to making college more affordable, no to reforming Wall Street. They're saying right now no to cutting more taxes for small-business owners and helping them get financing.

I—you know, I heard—somebody out here was yelling, "Yes, we can." Remember that was our slogan? Their slogan is "No, we can't." No, no, no, no. It——

Audience members. Yes, we can! Yes, we can! Yes, we can!

The President. Now, I mean, I personally think "yes, we can" is more inspiring than "no, we can't." To steal a line from our old friend Ted Kennedy, what is it about working men and women that they find so offensive? [*Laughter*]

When we passed a bill earlier this summer to help States save jobs, the jobs of hundreds of thousands of teachers and nurses and police officers and firefighters that were about to be laid off, they said no. And the Republican who thinks he's going to take over as Speaker— [*laughter*].

Audience members. Boo!

The President. I'm just saying, that's his opinion. [*Laughter*] He's entitled to his opinion. But when he was asked about this, he dismissed those jobs as "government jobs" that weren't worth saving.

Audience members. Boo!

The President. That's what he said. I'm quoting, "government jobs."

Now, think about this. These are the people who teach our children. These are the people who keep our streets safe. These are the people who put their lives on the line, who rush into a burning building. Government jobs? I don't know about you, but I think those jobs are worth saving. I think those jobs are worth saving.

By the way, this bill that we passed to save all those jobs, we made sure that bill wouldn't add to the deficit. You know how we paid for it? By closing one of these ridiculous tax loopholes that actually rewarded corporations for shipping jobs and profits overseas.

I mean, this was one of those loopholes that allowed companies to write off taxes they paid to foreign governments, even though they weren't paying taxes here in the United States. So middle class families were footing tax breaks for companies creating jobs somewhere else. I mean, even a lot of America's biggest corporations agreed that this loophole didn't make sense, agreed that it needed to be closed, agreed that it wasn't fair. But the man who thinks he's going to be Speaker, he wants to reopen this loophole.

Audience members. Boo!

The President. Look, the bottom line is this: These guys, they just don't want to give up on that economic philosophy that they have been peddling for most of the last decade. You know that philosophy: You cut taxes for millionaires and billionaires, you cut all the rules and regulations for special interests, and then you just cut working folks loose. You cut them loose to fend for themselves.

You remember they called it the "ownership society," but what it really boiled down to was, if you couldn't find a job, you couldn't afford college, you were born poor, your insurance company dropped you even though your kid was sick, that you were on your own.

Well, you know what? That philosophy didn't work out so well for middle class families all across America. It didn't work out so well for our country. All it did was rack up record deficits and result in the worst economic crisis since the Great Depression. I mean, think about it. We have tried what they're peddling. We did it for 10 years. We ended up with the worst economy since the 1930s and record deficits to boot. It's not like we haven't tried what they're trying to sell us.

Now, I'm bringing this up not because I'm trying to relitigate the past; I'm bringing it up because I don't want to relive the past.

It'd be one thing, Milwaukee, if Republicans in Washington had some new ideas, if they had said, you know what, we really screwed up, and we've learned from our mistakes; we're going to do things differently this time. That's not what they're doing.

When the leader of their campaign committee was asked on national television what Republicans would do if they took over Congress, you know what he said? He said, "We'll do exactly the same thing we did the last time." That's what he said. It's on tape.

So basically, here's what this election comes down to: They're betting that between now and November, you're going to come down with amnesia. [*Laughter*] They figure you're going to forget what their agenda did to this country. They think you'll just believe that they've changed.

These are the folks whose policies helped devastate our middle class. They drove our economy into a ditch. And we got in there and put on our boots, and we pushed, and we shoved. And we were sweating, and these guys were standing, watching us and sipping on a Slurpee. [*Laughter*] And they were pointing at us saying: "How come you're not pushing harder? How come you're not pushing faster?" And then when we finally got the car up—and it's got a few dings and a few dents, it's got some mud on it; we're going to have to do some work on it—they point to everybody and say, "Look what these guys did to your car"—[*laughter*]—after we got it out of the ditch. And then they got the nerve to ask for the keys back. [*Laughter*] I don't want to give them the keys back. They don't know how to drive.

I mean, I want everybody to think about it here. When you want to go forward in your car, what do you do?

Audience members. "D"!

The President. You put it in "D." They're going to pop it in reverse. [*Laughter*] They'd have those special interests riding shotgun, then they'd hit the gas, and we'd be right back in the ditch. [*Laughter*]

Milwaukee, we are not going backwards. That's the choice we face this fall. Do we want to go back, or do we want to go forward?

Audience members. Forward!

The President. I say we want to move forward. America always moves forward. We keep moving forward every day.

Let me say this, Milwaukee. I know these are difficult times. I know folks are worried. I know there's still a lot of hurt out there. I hear it when I travel around the country. I see it in the letters that I read every night from folks who are looking for a job or lost their home. It breaks my heart, because those are the folks that I got into politics for. You're the reason I'm here.

And when times are tough, I know it can be easy to give in to cynicism, I know it can be easy to give in to fear and doubt. And you know, it's easy sometimes for folks to stir up stuff and turn people on each other, and it's easy to settle for something less, to set our sights a little bit lower.

But I just want everybody here to remember, that's not who we are. That's not the country I know. We do not give up. We do not quit. We face down war. We face down depression. We face down great challenges and great threats. We have lit the way for the rest of the world.

Whenever times have seemed at their worst, Americans have been at their best. That's when we roll up our sleeves. That's when we remember we rise or fall together, as one Nation and as one people. That's the spirit that started the labor movement, the idea that alone, we may be weak; divided, we may fall; but we are united, we are strong. That's why they call them unions. That's why we call this the United States of America.

I'm going to make this case across the country between now and November. I am asking for your help. And if you are willing to join me and Tom Barrett and Gwen Moore and Russ Feingold and Herb Kohl, we can strengthen our middle class and make this economy work for all Americans again and restore the American Dream and give it to our children and our grandchildren.

God bless you, and God bless the United States of America.

NOTE: The President spoke at 2:11 p.m. at Henry W. Maier Festival Park. In his remarks, he referred to Gov. James E. Doyle, Jr., of Wisconsin; House Republican Leader John A. Boehner; and Rep. Pete Sessions, in his capacity as chairman of the National Republican Congressional Committee.

Statement on the Death of Jefferson Thomas
September 6, 2010

Michelle and I are saddened by the passing of Jefferson Thomas, who, as one of the Little Rock Nine, took a stand against segregation and helped open the eyes of our Nation to the struggle for civil rights.

Mr. Thomas was just a teenager when he became one of the first African American students to enroll in Little Rock Central High School.

Yet even at such a young age, he had the courage to risk his own safety, to defy a Governor and a mob, and to walk proudly into that school, even though it would have been far easier to give up and turn back. And through this simple act of pursuing an equal education, he and his fellow members of the Little Rock Nine helped open the doors of opportunity for their generation and for those that followed. The searing images of soldiers guarding students from those days will forever serve as a testament to the progress we've made, the barriers that previous generations have torn down, and the power of ordinary men and women to help us build a more perfect Union.

Our Nation owes Mr. Thomas a debt of gratitude for the stand he took half a century ago and the leadership he showed in the decades since. Our thoughts and prayers are with his family.

Videotaped Remarks on the Observance of Rosh Hashanah
September 7, 2010

As Jews in America and around the world celebrate the first of the High Holy Days, I want to extend my warmest wishes for the New Year. *L'shana Tova Tikatevu*—may you be inscribed and sealed in the Book of Life.

Rosh Hashanah marks the beginning of the spiritual calendar and the birth of the world. It serves as a reminder of the special relationship between God and his children, now and always. And it calls us to look within ourselves, to repent for our sins, recommit ourselves to prayer, and remember the blessings that come from helping those in need.

Today, those lessons ring as true as they did thousands of years ago. And as we begin this New Year, it is more important than ever to believe in the power of humility and compassion to deepen our faith and repair our world.

At a time when too many of our friends and neighbors are struggling to keep food on the table and a roof over their heads, it is up to us to do what we can to help those less fortunate.

At a time when prejudice and oppression still exists in the shadows of our society, it is up to us to stand as a beacon of freedom and tolerance and embrace the diversity that has always made us stronger as a people.

At a time when Israelis and Palestinians have returned to direct dialogue, it is up to us to encourage and support those who are willing to move beyond their differences and work towards security and peace in the Holy Land. Progress will not come easy, it will not come quick. But today we had an opportunity to move forward, toward the goal we share: two states, Israel and Palestine, living side by side in peace and security.

The Scripture teaches us that there is "a time to love and a time to hate, a time for war and a time for peace." In this season of repentance and renewal, let us commit ourselves to a more hopeful future.

Michelle and I wish all who celebrate Rosh Hashanah a sweet year full of health and prosperity.

NOTE: The President's remarks were videotaped at approximately 5:35 p.m. on September 2 in the Blue Room at the White House for later broadcast.

Statement on Chicago Mayor Richard M. Daley's Decision Not To Seek Reelection
September 7, 2010

No mayor in America has loved a city more or served a community with greater passion than Rich Daley. He helped build Chicago's image as a world-class city and leaves a legacy of progress that will be appreciated for generations to come.

Remarks at Cuyahoga Community College Western Campus in Parma, Ohio
September 8, 2010

The President. Hello, everybody! Hello! Thank you very much. Thank you, Ohio. Thank you, Cleveland. Everybody, please have a seat. Have a seat. We've got some business to do today. Thank you very much.

Audience member. We love you!

The President. I love you back. Thank you.

Before I get started, I want to just acknowledge some outstanding public servants who are here. First of all, somebody who I believe is one of the finest Governors in this country, Ted Strickland is here. The Lieutenant Governor and soon-to-be junior Senator from the great State of Illinois—or Ohio—I was thinking about my own—Lee Fisher is here.

Yes, I used to hear that line all the time about "Senator from Illinois"—that would be me. [*Laughter*]

Outstanding mayor of Cleveland, Frank Jackson is here; the mayor of Parma, Dean DePiero. Somebody who's fighting for working families each and every day, Senator Sherrod Brown is here; and three of the hardest working and finest Members of the House of Representatives: Dennis Kucinich, Marcia Fudge, and John Boccieri.

Well, good afternoon, everybody. It is good to be back in Ohio.

You know, in the fall of 2008, one of the last rallies of my Presidential campaign was right here in the Cleveland area. It was a hopeful time, just 2 days before the election. And we knew that if we pulled it off, we'd finally have the chance to tackle some big and difficult challenges that had been facing this country for a very long time.

We also hoped for a chance to get beyond some of the old political divides—between Democrats and Republicans, red States and blue States—that had prevented us from making progress. Because although we are proud to be Democrats, we are prouder to be Americans, and we believed then and we believe now that no single party has a monopoly on wisdom.

Now, that's not to say that the election didn't expose deep differences between the parties. I ran for President because for much of the last decade, a very specific governing philosophy had reigned about how America should work: Cut taxes, especially for millionaires and billionaires; cut regulations for special interests; cut trade deals, even if they didn't benefit our workers; cut back on investments in our people and in our future, in education and clean energy, in research and technology. The idea was that if we just had blind faith in the market, if we let corporations play by their own rules, if we left everyone else to fend for themselves, that America would grow and America would prosper.

And for a time, this idea gave us the illusion of prosperity. We saw financial firms and CEOs take in record profits and record bonuses. We saw a housing boom that led to new homeowners and new jobs in construction. Consumers bought more condos and bigger cars and better TVs.

But while all this was happening, the broader economy was becoming weaker. Nobody understands that more than the people of Ohio. Job growth between 2000 and 2008 was slower than it had been in any economic expansion since World War II, slower than it's been over the last year. The wages and incomes of middle class families kept falling while the cost of everything from tuition to health care kept on going up. Folks were forced to put more debt on their credit cards and borrow against homes that many couldn't afford to buy in the first place. And meanwhile, a failure to pay for two wars and two tax cuts for the wealthy helped turn a record surplus into a record deficit.

I ran for President because I believed that this kind of economy was unsustainable for the middle class and for the future of our Nation. I ran because I had a different idea about how America was built. It was an idea rooted in my own family's story.

You see, Michelle and I are where we are today because even though our families didn't have much, they worked tirelessly without complaint so that we might have a better life. My grandfather marched off to Europe in World War II, while my grandmother worked in factories on the homefront. I had a single mom who put herself through school and would wake before dawn to make sure I got a decent education. Michelle can still remember her father heading out to his job as a city worker long after multiple sclerosis had made it impossible for him to walk without crutches. He always got to work; he just had to get up a little earlier.

Yes, our families believed in the American values of self-reliance and individual responsibility, and they instilled those values in their children. But they also believed in a country that rewards responsibility, a country that rewards hard work, a country built on the promise of opportunity and upward mobility.

They believed in an America that gave my grandfather the chance to go to college because of the GI bill, an America that gave my grandparents the chance to buy a home because of the Federal Housing Authority, an America that gave their children and grandchildren the chance to fulfill our dreams thanks to college loans and college scholarships.

It was an America where you didn't buy things you couldn't afford, where we didn't just think about today, we thought about tomorrow. An America that took pride in the goods that we made, not just the things we consumed. An America where a rising tide really did lift all boats, from the company CEO to the guy on the assembly line.

That's the America I believe in. That's the America I believe in. That's what led me to work in the shadow of the shuttered steel plant on the south side of Chicago when I was a community organizer. It's what led me to fight for factory workers at manufacturing plants that were closing across Illinois when I was Senator. It's what led me to run for President. Because I don't believe we can have a strong and growing economy without a strong and growing middle class.

Now, much has happened since that election. The flawed policies and economic weaknesses of the previous decade culminated in a financial crisis and the worst recession of our lifetimes. And my hope was that the crisis would cause everybody, Democrats and Republicans, to pull together and tackle our problems in a practical way. But as we all know, things didn't work out that way.

Some Republican leaders figured it was smart politics to sit on the sidelines and let Democrats solve the mess. Others believed on principle that Government shouldn't meddle in the markets, even when the markets are broken. But with the Nation losing nearly 800,000 jobs the month that I was sworn into office, my most urgent task was to stop a financial meltdown and prevent this recession from becoming a second depression.

And, Ohio, we have done that. The economy is growing again. The financial markets have stabilized. The private sector has created jobs for the last 8 months in a row. And there are roughly 3 million Americans who are working today because of the economic plan we put into place.

But the truth is, progress has been painfully slow. Millions of jobs were lost before our policies even had a chance to take effect. We lost 4 million jobs in the 6 months before I took office. It was a hole so deep that even though we've added jobs again, millions of Americans remain unemployed. Hundreds of thousands of families have lost their homes. Millions more can barely pay the bills or make the mortgage. The middle class is still treading water, and those aspiring to reach the middle class are doing everything they can to keep from drowning.

And meanwhile, some of the very steps that were necessary to save the economy, like temporarily supporting the banks and the auto industry, fed the perception that Washington is still ignoring the middle class in favor of special interests.

And so people are frustrated, and they're angry, and they're anxious about the future. I understand that. I also understand that in a political campaign, the easiest thing for the other side to do is to ride this fear and anger all the way to election day.

And that's what's happening right now. A few weeks ago, the Republican leader of the House came here to Cleveland and offered his party's answer to our economic challenges. Now, it would be one thing if he had admitted his party's mistakes during the 8 years that they were in power, if they had gone off for a while and meditated and come back and offered a credible new approach to solving our country's problems.

But that's not what happened. There were no new policies from Mr. Boehner. There were no new ideas. There was just the same philosophy that we had already tried during the decade that they were in power, the same philosophy that led to this mess in the first place: Cut more taxes for millionaires and cut more rules for corporations.

Instead of coming together like past generations did to build a better country for our children and grandchildren, their argument is that we should let insurance companies go back to denying care for folks who are sick or let credit card companies go back to raising rates without any reason. Instead of setting our sights higher, they're asking us to settle for a status quo of stagnant growth and eroding competitiveness and a shrinking middle class.

Cleveland, that is not the America I know. That is not the America we believe in.

A lot has changed since I came here in those final days of the last election, but what hasn't is the choice facing this country. It's still fear versus hope, the past versus the future. It's still a choice between sliding backward and moving forward. That's what this election's about. That's the choice you will face in November.

Now, we have a different vision for the future. See, I've never believed that government has all the answers to our problems. I've never believed that government's role is to create jobs or prosperity. I believe it's the drive and the ingenuity of our entrepreneurs, our small businesses, the skill and dedication of our workers that's made us the wealthiest nation on Earth. I believe it's the private sector that must be the main engine for our recovery.

I believe government should be lean; government should be efficient. I believe government should leave people free to make the choices they think are best for their—themselves and their families, so long as those choices don't hurt others.

But in the words of the first Republican President, Abraham Lincoln, I also believe that government should do for the people what they cannot do better for themselves. And that means making the long-term investments in this country's future that individuals and corporations can't make on their own, investments in education and clean energy, in basic research and technology and infrastructure.

That means making sure corporations live up to their responsibilities to treat consumers fairly and play by the same rules as everybody else, their responsibilities to look out for their workers as well as their shareholders and create jobs here at home.

And that means providing a hand up for middle class families so that if they work hard and meet their responsibilities, they can afford to raise their children and send them to college, see a doctor when they get sick, retire with dignity and respect.

That's what we Democrats believe in, a vibrant free market, but one that works for everybody. That's our vision. That's our vision for a stronger economy and a growing middle class. And that's the difference between what we and Republicans in Congress are offering the American people right now.

Now, let me give you a few specific examples of our different approaches. This week, I proposed some additional steps to grow the economy and help businesses spur hiring. One of the keys to job creation is to encourage companies to invest more in the United States. But for years, our Tax Code has actually given billions of dollars in tax breaks that encourage companies to create jobs and profits in other countries.

I want to change that. I want to change that. Instead of tax loopholes that incentivize investment in overseas jobs, I'm proposing a more generous, permanent extension of the tax credit that goes to companies for all the research and innovation they do right here in Ohio, right here in the United States of America.

And I'm proposing that all American businesses should be allowed to write off all the investment they do in 2011. And this will help small businesses upgrade their plants and equipment and will encourage large corporations to get off the sidelines and start putting their profits to work in places like Cleveland and Toledo and Dayton.

Now, to most of you, I'll bet this just seems like common sense. [*Laughter*] But not to Mr. Boehner and his allies. For years, Republicans have fought to keep these corporate loopholes open. In fact, when Mr. Boehner was here in Cleveland, he attacked us for closing a few of these loopholes and using the money to help States like Ohio keep hundreds of thousands of teachers and cops and firefighters on the job.

Mr. Boehner dismissed these jobs we saved—teaching our kids, patrolling our streets, rushing into burning buildings—as, quote, "government jobs," jobs I guess he thought just weren't worth saving. And I couldn't disagree more. I think teachers and police officers and firefighters are part of what keeps America strong.

And, Ohio, I think if we're going to give tax breaks to companies, they should go to companies that create jobs here in America, not that create jobs overseas. That's one difference between the Republican vision and the Democratic vision. That's what this election is all about.

Now, let me give you another example. We want to put more Americans back to work rebuilding America: our roads, our railways, our runways. When the housing sector collapsed and the recession hit, one in every four jobs lost were in the construction industry. That's partly why our economic plan has invested in badly needed infrastructure projects over the last 19 months, not just roads and bridges, but high-speed railroads and expanded broadband access. All together, these projects have led to thousands of good private sector jobs, especially for those in the trades.

Mr. Boehner and the Republicans in Congress said no to these projects, fought them tooth and nail. Though I should say it didn't

stop a lot of them from showing up at the ribbon cuttings—[*laughter*]—trying to take credit. That's always a sight to see. [*Laughter*]

Now, there are still thousands of miles of railroads and railways and runways left to repair and improve. And engineers, economists, Governors, mayors of every political stripe believe that if we want to compete in this global economy, we need to rebuild this vital infrastructure. There is no reason Europe or China should have the fastest trains or the most modern airports. We want to put America to work building them right here in America.

So this week, I've proposed a 6-year infrastructure plan that would start putting Americans to work right away. But despite the fact that this has traditionally been an issue with bipartisan support, Mr. Boehner has so far said no to infrastructure. That's bad for America. And that too is what this election is all about.

I'll give you one final example of the differences between us and the Republicans, and that's on the issue of tax cuts. Under the tax plan passed by the last administration, taxes are scheduled to go up substantially next year—for everybody. By the way, this was by design. When they passed these tax cuts in 2001 and 2003, they didn't want everybody to know what it would do to our deficit, so they pretended like they were going to end, even though now they say they don't.

Now, I believe we ought to make the tax cuts for the middle class permanent—for the middle class permanent. These families are the ones who saw their wages and incomes flatline over the last decade. You deserve a break; you deserve some help. And because folks in the middle class are more likely to spend their tax cut on basic necessities, that strengthens the economy as a whole.

But the Republican leader of the House doesn't want to stop there. Make no mistake: He and his party believe we should also give a permanent tax cut to the wealthiest 2 percent of Americans.

Audience members. No!

The President. With all the other budgetary pressures we have, with all the Republicans' talk about wanting to shrink the deficit, they would have us borrow $700 billion over the next 10 years to give a tax cut of about a hundred thousand dollars each to folks who are already millionaires. And keep in mind, wealthy Americans are just about the only folks who saw their incomes rise when Republicans were in charge. And these are the folks who are less likely to spend the money, which is why economists don't think tax breaks for the wealthy would do much to boost the economy.

So let me be clear to Mr. Boehner and everybody else: We should not hold middle class tax cuts hostage any longer. We are ready this week, if they want, to give tax cuts to every American making $250,000 or less. That's 98—97 percent of Americans. Now, for any income over this amount, the tax rates would just go back to what they were under President Clinton.

This isn't to punish folks who are better off; God bless them. It's because we can't afford the $700 billion price tag. And for those who claim that our approach would somehow be bad for growth and bad for small businesses, let me remind you that with those tax rates in place under President Clinton, this country created 22 million jobs and raised incomes and had the largest surplus in our history.

In fact, if the Republican leadership in Congress really wants to help small businesses, they'll stop using legislative maneuvers to block an up-or-down vote on a small-business jobs bill that's before the Senate right now—right now. This is a bill that would do two things: It would cut taxes for small businesses and make loans more available for small businesses. It is fully paid for, won't add to the deficit, and it was written by Democrats and Republicans. And yet the other party continues to block this jobs bill, a delay that small-business owners have said is actually leading them to put off hiring.

Look, I recognize that most of the Republicans in Congress have said no to just about every policy I've proposed since taking office. I realize in some cases that there are genuine philosophical differences. But on issues like this one—a tax cut for small businesses supported by the Chamber of Commerce—the only reason they're holding this up is politics, pure and

simple. They're making the same calculation they made just before my Inauguration: If I fail, they win. Well, they might think that this will get them to where they want to go in November, but it won't get our country going where it needs to go in the long run. It won't get us there. It won't get us there. It won't get us there.

So that's the choice, Ohio: Do we return to the same failed policies that ran our economy into a ditch, or do we keep moving forward with policies that are slowly pulling us out? Do we settle for a slow decline, or do we reach for an America with a growing economy and a thriving middle class? That's the America that I see. We may not be there yet, but we know where this country needs to go.

We see a future where we invest in American innovation and American ingenuity; where we export more goods so we create more jobs here at home; where we make it easier to start a business or patent an invention; where we build a homegrown clean energy industry, because I don't want to see new solar panels or electric cars or advanced batteries manufactured in Europe or Asia. I want to see them made right here in the U.S. of A. by American workers.

We see an America where every citizen has the skills and training to compete with any worker in the world. That's why we've set a goal to once again have the highest proportion of college graduates in the world by 2020. That's why we're revitalizing community colleges like this one. That's why we're reforming our education system based on what works for our children, not what perpetuates the status quo.

We see an America where a growing middle class is the beating heart of a growing economy. That's why I kept my campaign promise and gave a middle class tax cut to 95 percent of working Americans. That's why we passed health insurance reform that stops insurance companies from jacking up your premiums at will or denying coverage because you get sick. That's why we passed financial reform that will end taxpayer-funded bailouts, reform that will stop credit card companies and mortgage lenders from taking advantage of taxpayers and consumers.

1287

That's why we're trying to make it easier for workers to save for retirement and fighting the efforts of some in the other party to privatize Social Security, because as long as I'm President, no one is going to take the retirement savings of a generation of Americans and hand it over to Wall Street. Not on my watch.

That's why we're fighting to extend the child tax credit and make permanent our new college tax credit, because if we do, it will mean $10,000 in tuition relief for each child going to 4 years of college. And I don't want any parent not to be sending their kids, in good time or bad, to college because they can't afford it.

And finally, we see an America where we refuse to pass on the debt we inherited to the next generation. Now, let me spend just a minute on this issue, because we've heard a lot of moralizing on the other side about this: Government spending and debt. Along with the tax cuts for the wealthy, the other party's main economic proposal is that they'll stop Government spending.

Now, it's right to be concerned about the long-term deficit. If we don't get a handle on it soon, it can endanger our future. And at a time when folks are tightening their belts at home, I understand why a lot of Americans feel it's time for Government to show some discipline too. But let's look at the facts. When these same Republicans—including Mr. Boehner—were in charge, the number of earmarks and pet projects went up, not down.

These same Republicans turned a record surplus into a record deficit. When I walked in, wrapped in a nice bow was a $1.3 trillion deficit sitting right there on my doorstep—[*laughter*]—a welcoming present.

Just this year, these same Republicans voted against a bipartisan fiscal commission that they themselves had proposed. Once I decided I was for it, they were against it. [*Laughter*] And when you ask them what programs they'd actually cut, they don't have an answer. That's not fiscal responsibility. That's not a serious plan to govern.

Now, I'll be honest, I refuse to cut back on those investments that will grow our economy in the future, investments in areas like educa-

tion and clean energy and technology. I don't want to cut those things. And that's because economic growth is the single best way to bring down the deficit, and we need these investments to grow. But I am absolutely committed to fiscal responsibility, which is why I've already proposed freezing all discretionary spending unrelated to national security for the next 3 years.

And once the bipartisan fiscal commission finishes its work, I'll spend the next year making the tough choices necessary to further reduce our deficit and lower our debt, whether I get help from the other side or not.

Of course, reducing the deficit won't be easy. Making up for the 8 million lost jobs caused by this recession won't happen overnight. Not everything we've done over the last 2 years has worked as quickly as we had hoped, and I am keenly aware that not all of our policies have been popular.

So no, our job is not easy. But you didn't elect me to do what was easy. You didn't elect me to just read the polls and figure how to keep myself in office. You didn't elect me to avoid big problems. You elected me to do what was right. And as long as I'm President, that's exactly what I intend to do.

This country is emerging from an incredibly difficult period in its history, an era of irresponsibility that stretched from Wall Street to Washington and had a devastating effect on a lot of people. We have started turning the corner on that era. But part of moving forward is returning to the time-honored values that built this country: hard work and self-reliance; responsibility for ourselves, but also responsibility for one another. It's about moving from an attitude that said, "What's in it for me?" to one that asks: "What's best for America? What's best for all our workers? What's best for all of our businesses? What's best for all of our children?"

These values are not Democratic or Republican. They are not conservative or liberal values. They are American values. As Democrats, we take pride in what our party has accomplished over the last century: Social Security and the minimum wage, the GI bill and Medicare, civil rights and workers' rights and women's rights. But we also recognize that throughout our history, there has been a noble Republican vision as well of what this country can be. It was the vision of Abraham Lincoln, who set up the first land-grant colleges and launched the transcontinental railroad; the vision of Teddy Roosevelt, who used the power of Government to break up monopolies; the vision of Dwight Eisenhower, who helped build the Interstate Highway System; and yes, the vision of Ronald Reagan, who, despite his aversion to Government, was willing to help save Social Security for future generations, working with Democrats.

These were serious leaders for serious times. They were great politicians, but they didn't spend all their time playing games or scoring points. They didn't always prey on people's fears and anxieties. They made mistakes, but they did what they thought was in the best interests of their country and its people.

And that's what the American people expect of us today—Democrats, Independents, and Republicans. That's the debate they deserve. That's the leadership we owe them.

I know that folks are worried about the future. I know there's still a lot of hurt out here. And when times are tough, I know it can be tempting to give in to cynicism and fear and doubt and division and just settle our sights a little bit lower, settle for something a little bit less. But that's not who we are, Ohio. Those are not the values that built this country.

We are here today because in the worst of times, the people who came before us brought out the best in America, because our parents and our grandparents and our great-grandparents were willing to work and sacrifice for us. They were willing to take great risks and face great hardship and reach for a future that would give us the chance at a better life. They knew that this country is greater than the sum of its parts, that America's not about the ambitions of any one individual, but the aspirations of an entire people, an entire nation.

That's who we are. That is our legacy. And I'm convinced that if we're willing to summon those values today and if we're willing to choose hope over fear and choose the future over the past and come together once more around the great project of national renewal, then we will restore our economy and rebuild our middle class and reclaim the American Dream for the next generation.

Thank you. God bless you, and may God bless the United States of America.

NOTE: The President spoke at 2:06 p.m.

Statement on the Terrorist Attack in Vladikavkaz, North Ossetia
September 9, 2010

The United States strongly condemns the terrorist bombing that occurred today in Vladikavkaz, North Ossetia. Our hearts go out to the people of North Ossetia, who have already suffered so much from horrific acts of terrorism. We offer our deepest condolences and stand with the people of Russia in this time of tragedy. This bombing further underscores the resolve of the United States and Russia to work together in combating terrorism and protecting our people.

Statement on the Observance of Eid al-Fitr
September 9, 2010

As Ramadan comes to an end, Michelle and I extend our best wishes to Muslims in the United States and around the world on the occasion of Eid al-Fitr. For Muslims all over the world, Eid al-Fitr marks the end of a holy month of fasting and prayer. It is a time of self-reflection focusing on the values that Muslims and people of all faiths share: charity, community, cooperation, and compassion. This year's Eid is also an occasion to reflect on the importance of religious tolerance and to recognize the positive role that religious communities of all faiths, including Muslims, have played in American life.

On this Eid, those devastated by the recent floods in Pakistan will be on the minds of many around the world. To help in the tremendous relief, recovery, and reconstruction effort for the floods, all Americans can participate by donating to the Pakistan Relief Fund at www.state.gov.

On behalf of the American people, we congratulate Muslims in the United States and around the world on this blessed day. *Eid Mubarak*.

The President's News Conference
September 10, 2010

The President. Have a seat, everybody. Good morning. Before I take your questions, I just want to talk a little bit about our continuing efforts to dig ourselves out of this recession and to grow our economy.

As I said in Cleveland on Wednesday, I ran for President because I believed the policies of the previous decade had left our economy weaker and our middle class struggling. They were policies that cut taxes, especially for millionaires and billionaires, cut regulations for corporations and for special interests, and left everyone else pretty much fending for themselves. They were policies that ultimately culminated in a financial crisis and a terrible recession that we're still digging out of today.

We came into office with a different view about how our economy should work. Instead of tax cuts for millionaires, we believe in cutting taxes for middle class families and small-business owners. We've done that.

Instead of letting corporations play by their own rules, we believe in making sure that businesses treat workers well and consumers friendly and play by the same rules as everyone else. So we've put in place commonsense rules that accomplish that.

Instead of tax breaks that encourage corporations to create jobs overseas, we believe in tax breaks for companies that create jobs right here in the United States of America. And so we've begun to do that.

We believe in investments that will make America more competitive in the global economy, investments in education and clean energy, in research and technology. And we're making those investments.

So these are the principles that have guided us over the last 19 months. And these are the principles that form the basis of the additional economic proposals that I offered this week. Because even though the economy is growing again and we've added more than 750,000 private sector jobs this year, the hole the recession left was huge, and progress has been painfully slow. Millions of Americans are still looking for work. Millions of families are struggling to pay their bills or the mortgage. And so these proposals are meant to both accelerate job growth in the short term and strengthen the economy in the long run.

These proposals include a more generous, permanent extension of the tax credit that goes to companies for all the research and innovation that they do here in America. And I've proposed that all American businesses should be allowed to write off all the investments they do in 2011. This will help small businesses upgrade their plants and equipment and will encourage large corporations to get off the sidelines and start putting their profits to work in our economy.

We also announced a 6-year plan to rebuild America's roads and railways and runways. Already our investments in infrastructure are putting folks in the construction industry back to work. And this plan would put thousands more back to work, and it would help us remain competitive with countries in Europe and Asia that have already invested heavily in projects like high-speed railroads.

But one thing we can do next week is end a month-long standoff on a small-business jobs bill that's been held up in the Senate by a partisan minority. I realize there are plenty of issues in Washington where people of good faith simply disagree on principle. This should not and is not one of those issues.

This is a bill that does two main things: It gives small-business owners tax cuts, and it helps them get loans. It will eliminate capital gains taxes for key investments in 1 million small businesses. It will provide incentives to invest and create jobs for 4 million small businesses. It will more than double the amount some small-business owners can borrow to grow their companies. It's a bill that's paid for, a bill that won't add to the deficit. It has been written by Democrats and Republicans. It's a bill that's been praised by the Chamber of Commerce. And yet a minority of Republican Senators have been using legislative tactics to prevent the bill from even getting to a vote.

Now, I was pleased to see that yesterday Republican Senator George Voinovich of Ohio said he would refuse to support this blockade any longer. Senator Voinovich said, "This country is really hurting," and, "We don't have time anymore to play games." I could not agree more.

I understand there's an election coming up. But the American people didn't send us here to think about our jobs. They sent us here to think about theirs. And there are small businesses right now who are putting off plans to hire more workers because this bill is stalled. That's not the kind of leadership this country deserves. And I hope we can now move forward to get small-business owners the relief they need to start hiring and growing again.

And while we're on the subject of economics, I also want to make an announcement about my economic team. This week, Christina Romer returned to Berkeley after a tireless, outstanding tenure as Chair of the Council of Economic Advisers. Christy is brilliant, she is dedicated, and she was part of the team that helped save this country from a depression. So we're going to miss her dearly. But today I'm happy to announce Austan Goolsbee as her replacement.

Austan has been one of my good friends and close economic advisers for many years. He's one of the finest economists in the country, and he's worked as a member of the Council of Eco-

nomic Advisers since we arrived here in Washington. He's not just a brilliant economist, he's someone who has a deep appreciation of how the economy affects everyday people, and he talks about it in a way that's easily understood. He already knows and works with the rest of the team very well. I have complete confidence he's going to do an outstanding job as CEA Chair.

And finally, tomorrow we will commemorate not only the heartbreak of September 11th, but also the enduring values and resilient spirit of America. Both Michelle and I will be joining our fellow citizens in remembering those who were lost on that day and honoring all who exhibited such extraordinary heroism in the midst of tragedy. I'll have further remarks tomorrow, but for now, let me just note that tomorrow is a National Day of Service and Remembrance, and I hope each of us finds a way to serve our fellow citizens, not only to reaffirm our deepest values as Americans, but to rekindle that spirit of unity and common purpose that we felt in the days that followed that September morning.

And now I'd be happy to take some questions, and I'm going to start with Darlene Superville of AP [Associated Press].

Midterm Elections/National Economy

Q. Thank you, Mr. President. You said this week that Democrats wouldn't do well in the November elections if it turns out to be a referendum on the economy. But with millions of people out of work and millions of people losing their homes, how could it not be a referendum on the economy and your handling of it, and why would you not welcome that?

The President. Well, the—what I said was that if it was just a referendum on whether we've made the kind of progress that we need to, then people around the country would say, we're not there yet. If the election is about the policies that are going to move us forward versus the policies that will get us back into a mess, then I think the Democrats will do very well, and here's why.

As I just indicated, middle class families had been struggling for a decade, before I came into office. Their wages and incomes had flatlined. They were seeing the cost of everything from health care to sending their kids to college going up. Job growth was the weakest of any economic expansion between 2001 and 2008 since World War II. The pace was slower than it's been over the last year.

So these policies of cutting taxes for the wealthiest Americans, of stripping away regulations that protect consumers, running up a record surplus to a record deficit, those policies finally culminated in the worst financial crisis we've had since the Great Depression. And for 19 months, what we have done is steadily worked to avoid a depression, to take an economy that was contracting rapidly and making it grow again; a situation where we were losing 750,000 jobs a month, and now we've had 8 consecutive months of private sector job growth; and made investments that are going to strengthen the economy over the long term.

But we're not there yet. I mean, we lost 4 million jobs in the 6 months before I was sworn in, and we lost 8 million jobs total during the course of this recession. That is a huge hole to dig ourselves out of. And people who have lost their jobs around the country and can't find one, moms who are sending out resumes and not getting calls back, worried about losing homes and not being able to pay bills, they're not feeling good right now. And I understand that.

And I ran precisely because I did not think middle class families in this country were getting a fair shake. And I ran because I felt that we had to have a different economic philosophy in order to grow that middle class and grow our economy over the long term.

Now, for all the progress we've made, we're not there yet. And that means that people are frustrated, and that means people are angry. And since I'm the President and Democrats have controlled the House and the Senate, it's understandable that people are saying, what have you done?

But between now and November, what I'm going to remind the American people of is that the policies that we have put in place have moved us in the right direction and the policies that the Republicans are offering right now are the exact policies that got us into this mess. It's not a situation where they went and reflected and said to themselves, you know what, we didn't do some things right, and so we've got a whole bunch of new ideas out here that we want to present to you that we think are going to help put us on the path of strong growth. That's not what happens. The chairman of their committee has said, we would do the exact same things as we did before Obama took office. Well, we know where that led.

And a perfect example is the debate we're having on taxes right now. I have said that middle class families need tax relief right now. And I'm prepared to work on a bill and sign a bill this month that would ensure that middle class families get tax relief. Ninety-seven percent of Americans make less than $250,000 a year or less. And I'm saying we can give those families—97 percent—permanent tax relief. And by the way, for those who make more than $250,000, they'd still get tax relief on the first $250,000; they just wouldn't get it for income above that.

Now, that seems like a commonsense thing to do. And what I've got is the Republicans holding middle class tax relief hostage, because they're insisting we've got to give tax relief to millionaires and billionaires to the tune of about $100,000 per millionaire, which would cost, over the course of 10 years, $700 billion, and that economists say is probably the worst way to stimulate the economy. That doesn't make sense, and that's an example of what this election is all about.

If you want the same kinds of skewed policies that led us to this crisis, then the Republicans are ready to offer that. But if you want policies that are moving us out, even though you may be frustrated, even though change isn't happening as fast as you'd like, then I think Democrats are going to do fine in November.

Okay. Caren Bohan [Reuters].

Tax Reform

Q. Thank you, Mr. President. You're looking for Republican help on the economic proposals that you unveiled this week, and you also mentioned the small-business bill. But you're at odds with them over tax cuts. Is there room for a middle ground whereby, for example, the tax cuts on the wealthy could be extended for a period of time and then allowed to expire?

The President. Well, certainly there is going to be room for discussion. My hope is, is that on this small-business bill that is before the Senate right now, that we actually make some progress. I still don't understand why we didn't pass that 2 months ago. As I said, this was written by Democrats and Republicans. This is a bill that traditionally you'd probably get 90 percent or 100 percent Republican support. But we've been playing politics for the last several months. And if the Republican leadership is prepared to get serious about doing something for families that are hurting out there, I would love to talk to them.

Now, on the high-income tax cuts, my position is, let's get done what we all agree on. What they've said is they agree that the middle class tax cut should be made permanent. Let's work on that. Let's do it. We can have a further conversation about how they want to spend an additional $700 billion to give an average of $100,000 to millionaires. That, I think, is a bad idea. If you were going to spend that money, there are a lot better ways of spending it. But more to the point, these are the same folks who say that they're concerned about the deficits. Why would we borrow money on policies that won't help the economy and help people who don't need help?

But setting that aside, we've got an area of agreement, which is, let's help families out there who are having a tough time. As I said, we could, this month, give every American certainty and tax relief up to $250,000 a year. Every single American would benefit from that. Now, people who make $250,000 a year or less, they'd benefit on all their income. People who make a million dollars would benefit on a quarter of their income. But the point is, is that that's something that we can all agree to. Why hold it up? Why hold the middle class hostage in order to do something that most economists don't think makes sense?

Q. So are you ruling out a deal with Republicans on tax cuts for the wealthiest?

The President. What I'm saying is, let's do what we agree to and that the Americans—people overwhelmingly agree to, which is, let's give certainty to families out there that are having a tough time.

Chip Reid [CBS News].

Economic Reform Agenda

Q. Thank you, Mr. President. On the economic package that you rolled out earlier this week, first on the business tax cuts. Why did you wait until this superheated campaign season to roll it out? A lot of your critics and even some Democrats say, well, clearly he's just using this for political purposes, he doesn't have any expectation it's actually going to be passed, it's a political weapon. Why did you wait so long to bring that out?

And on the stimulus part, we can't get people in the White House to say it is a stimulus—$50 billion for roads and other infrastructure, but they avoid the word "stimulus" like the plague. Is that because the original stimulus is so deeply unpopular? And if so, why is it so unpopular?

The President. Well, let me go back to when I first came into office. We had an immediate task, which was to rescue an economy that was tipping over a cliff. And we put in place an economic plan that 95 percent of economists say substantially helped us avoid a depression.

A third of those were tax cuts, by the way. A third of that economic plan was tax cuts for individuals and for small businesses. So we haven't—this notion that we waited until now to put forward a series of plans, Chip, we've—just on the small-business issue alone, we have cut taxes for small businesses eight times during the course of the last 18 months. So we're hardly Johnny-come-latelies on this issue.

Now, when you put all the things we've done together, it has made a difference. Three million people have jobs that wouldn't have them otherwise had we not taken these steps. The economy would be in much worse shape. But as I said before, we're not where we need to go yet, which means that if we're not there yet, what else can we do?

And the proposals that we've put forward are ones that historically, again, have garnered bipartisan support: a research and development tax credit so that companies that are investing in research here in the United States, which is part of what's going to keep us growing and keep us innovative, let's make sure that companies are strongly incentivized to do that; making sure that their expensing accelerated business depreciation is happening in 2011 so that if companies are sort of sitting on the sidelines right now, not sure whether they should invest, let's give them incentive to go ahead and invest now to give that a jumpstart.

On infrastructure, we've got a highway bill that traditionally is done every 6 years. And what we're saying is, let's ramp up what we're doing, let's beef it up a little bit, because we've got this infrastructure all across the country that everybody from Governors to mayors to economists to engineers of all political stripes have said is holding us back in terms of our long-term competitiveness. Let's get started now rebuilding America.

And in terms of paying for some of these things, let's stop giving tax breaks to companies that are shipping jobs overseas. Let's stop incentivizing that. Let's give tax breaks to companies that are investing right here in the United States of America.

Those are all commonsense approaches. Historically, as you know—you've been around this town for a long time—usually, Republicans and Democrats agree on infrastructure. Usually, Republicans and Democrats agree on making sure that research and development investments are made right here in the United States. And so let's get it done.

It has nothing to do with the notion that somehow what we did previously didn't work. It worked. It just hasn't done as much as we need it to do. We've still got a long ways to go, and we're going to keep on doing it.

Q. So this is a second stimulus? [*Laughter*]

The President. Here's how I would—there is no doubt that everything we've been trying to do—everything we've been trying to do is designed to stimulate growth and additional jobs in the economy. I mean, that's our entire agenda. So I have no problem with people saying, the President is trying to stimulate growth and

hiring. Isn't that what I should be doing? I would assume that's what the Republicans think we should do, to stimulate growth and jobs. And I will keep on trying to stimulate growth and jobs for as long as I'm President of the United States.

Hans Nichols [Bloomberg News].

Consumer Financial Protection Bureau

Q. Thank you, Mr. President. I'd ask you to—[*inaudible*]—so I'll ask my real question. It's now been more than 2 months since the financial regulatory reform bill has passed. A centerpiece of that was what you talked about as a Consumer Financial Protection Bureau. And yet you haven't named a head. Is Elizabeth Warren still a leading candidate? And if not, are you worried about some sort of Senate hurdle for her confirmation? Thank you.

The President. Yes, this is a great opportunity to talk to the American people about what I do think is going to be hugely helpful to middle class families in the years and decades to come, and that is an agency that has been set up, an independent agency, whose sole job is to protect families in their financial transactions. So if you are getting a credit card, we are going to have an agency that makes sure that that credit card company can't jack up your rates without any reason—including on old balances. And that could save American consumers tens of billions of dollars just in the first couple of years.

If you are out there looking for a mortgage— and we all know that part of the problem with the financial crisis was that folks were peddling mortgages that were unstable, that had these huge balloon payments that people didn't fully understand—well, now there's going to be some oversight in terms of how mortgages are shaped, and people are going to actually have to know what they're getting and what they're buying into. That's going to protect the economy as well as individual consumers.

So this agency, I think, has the capacity to really provide middle class families the kind of protection that's been lacking for too long.

Now, the idea for this agency was Elizabeth Warren's. She's a dear friend of mine. She's somebody I've known since I was in law school.

And I have been in conversations with her. She is a tremendous advocate for this idea. It's only been a couple of months, and this is a big task standing up this entire agency, so I'll have an announcement soon about how we're going to move forward. And I think what's fair to say is, is that I have had conversations with Elizabeth over the course of these—over these last couple of months. But I'm not going to make an official announcement until it's ready.

Senate Confirmations

Q. Are you unofficially concerned about a Senate confirmation?

The President. I'm concerned about all Senate confirmations these days. I mean, if I nominate somebody for dogcatcher——

Q. But with respect to Elizabeth Warren, are you——

The President. Hans, I wasn't trying to be funny. I am concerned about all Senate nominations these days. I've got people who have been waiting for 6 months to get confirmed who nobody has an official objection to and who were voted out of committee unanimously, and I can't get a vote on them.

We've got judges who are pending. We've got people who are waiting to help us on critical issues like homeland security. And it's very hard when you've got a determined minority in the Senate that insists on a 60-vote filibuster on every single person that we're trying to confirm, even if after we break the filibuster, it turns out that they get 90 votes. They're just playing games. And as I think Senator Voinovich said very well, it's time to stop playing games.

All right. Chuck Todd [NBC News].

Administration Accomplishments/Bipartisanship

Q. Given the theme, I think, of all of your answers, I've just got a short question for you. How have you changed Washington?

The President. Well, I'll tell you how we've changed Washington. Prior to us getting here, as I indicated before, you had a set of policies that were skewed towards special interests, skewed towards the most powerful, and ordinary families out there were being left behind.

And since we've gotten here, whether it's making sure that folks who can't get health insurance because of preexisting condition can now get health insurance or children who didn't have coverage now have coverage; whether it's making sure that credit card companies have to actually post in understandable ways what your credit card rates are and they can't jack up existing balances in arbitrary ways; whether it's making sure that we've got clean water and clean air for future generations; whether it's making sure that tax cuts go to families that need it, as opposed to folks who don't—on a whole range of issues over the last 18 months, we've put in place policies that are going to help grow a middle class and lay the foundation for long-term economic growth.

Now, if you're asking, why haven't I been able to create a greater spirit of cooperation in Washington, I think that's fair. I'm as frustrated as anybody by it. I think part of it has to do with the fact that when we came into office, we came in under very tough economic circumstances, and I think that some of the Republican leaders made a decision: We're going to sit on the sidelines and let the Democrats try to solve it. And so we got a lot of resistance very early.

I think what's also true is, is that when you take on tough issues like health care or financial regulatory reform, where special interests are deeply entrenched, there's a lot of money at stake for them, and where the issues are so complicated that it drags on for a long time, you end up having a lot of big fights here in town. And it's messy, and it's frustrating and——

Q. [*Inaudible*]

The President. Well, the—and so there is no doubt that an option that was available to me when I came in was not to take on those issues. I mean, we could have decided, you know what, even though we know that the pace of accelerating health care costs is going to bankrupt this economy and bankrupt businesses and bankrupt individuals, and even though we know that there are 30 million people—and that's a growing number of people—who don't have health insurance, we could have said, you know what, that's just too controversial, let's not take it on. And we could have said with respect to financial regulatory reform, you know what, we're just going to get too much resistance from Republicans, we shouldn't take that on.

I don't think that's the kind of leadership that the American people would want from their President. And are there things that I might have done during the course of 18 months that would at the margins have improved some of the tone in Washington? Probably. Is some of this just a core difference in approach, in terms of how we move this country forward, between Democrats and Republicans? I'd say the answer is a lot more the latter.

Anne Kornblut [Washington Post].

Muslim World/Religious Freedom and Tolerance

Q. Thank you, Mr. President. Nine years after the September 11th attacks, why do you think it is that we are now seeing such an increase in suspicion and outright resentment of Islam, especially given that it has been one of your priorities to increase—to improve relations with the Muslim world?

The President. I think that at a time when the country is anxious generally and going through a tough time, then fears can surface, suspicions, divisions can surface in a society. And so I think that plays a role in it.

One of the things that I most admired about President Bush was after 9/11, him being crystal clear about the fact that we were not at war with Islam. We were at war with terrorists and murderers who had perverted Islam, had stolen its banner to carry out their outrageous acts. And I was so proud of the country rallying around that idea, that notion that we are not going to be divided by religion, we're not going to be divided by ethnicity. We are all Americans. We stand together against those who would try to do us harm.

And that's what we've done over the last 9 years. And we should take great pride in that. And I think it is absolutely important now for the overwhelming majority of the American people to hang on to that thing that is best in us, a belief in religious tolerance, clarity about who our enemies are. Our enemies are Al Qaida and their allies who are trying to kill us, but have killed more Muslims than just about anybody on

Earth. We have to make sure that we don't start turning on each other.

And I will do everything that I can as long as I am President of the United States to remind the American people that we are one Nation under God, and we may call that God different names, but we remain one Nation. And as somebody who relies heavily on my Christian faith in my job, I understand the passions that religious faith can raise. But I'm also respectful that people of different faiths can practice their religion, even if they don't subscribe to the exact same notions that I do, and that they are still good people and they are my neighbors and they are my friends and they are fighting alongside us in our battles.

And I want to make sure that this country retains that sense of purpose. And I think tomorrow is a wonderful day for us to remind ourselves of that.

Natasha Mozgovaya of Haaretz. Is she here? Natasha—there you are back there.

Middle East Peace Process

Q. Mr. President, back in the region, the Palestinian and the Israeli leaders, they sound a bit less ready for this historic compromise. President Abbas, for example, said the Palestinians won't recognize Israel as a Jewish state. The question is, if these talks fail at an early stage, will this administration disengage? Or maybe you're ready to step up and deepen your personal involvement.

The President. President Abbas and Prime Minister Netanyahu were here last week, and they came with a sense of purpose and seriousness and cordiality that, frankly, exceeded a lot of people's expectations. What they said was that they were serious about negotiating. They affirmed the goal of creating two states living side by side in peace and security. They have set up a schedule where they're going to meet every 2 weeks. We are actively participating in that process. Secretary of State Hillary Clinton will be flying to the Middle East for the first series of next meetings on September 14 and 15.

And so what we've done is to bring the parties together to try to get them to recognize that the path for Israeli security and Palestinian sovereignty can only be met through negotiations. And these are going to be tough negotiations. There are enormous hurdles between now and our end point, and there are going to be a whole bunch of folks in the region who want to undermine these negotiations. We saw it when Hamas carried out these horrific attacks against civilians and explicitly said, we're going to try to do this to undermine peace talks. There are going to be rejectionists who suggest that it can't happen, and there are also going to be cynics who just believe that the mistrust between the sides is too deep.

We understood all that. We understood that it was a risk for us to promote these discussions. But it is a risk worth taking, because I firmly believe that it is in America's national security interests, as well as Israel's national security interests, as well as in the interests of the Palestinian people, to arrive at a peace deal.

Part of the reason that I think Prime Minister Netanyahu was comfortable coming here was that he's seen, during the course of 18 months, that my administration is unequivocal in our defense of Israel's security. And we've engaged in some unprecedented cooperation with Israel to make sure that they can deal with any external threats. But I think he also came here understanding that to maintain Israel as a Jewish state that is also a democratic state, this issue has to be dealt with.

I think President Abbas came here, despite great misgivings and pressure from the other side, because he understood the window for creating a Palestinian state is closing. And there are a whole bunch of parties in the region who purport to be friends of the Palestinians and yet do everything they can to avoid the path that would actually lead to a Palestinian state, would actually lead to their goal.

And so the two parties need each other. That doesn't mean it's going to work. Ultimately, it's going to be up to them. We can facilitate; we can encourage; we can tell them that we will stand behind them in their efforts and are willing to contribute as part of the broader international community in making this work. But ultimately, the parties have to make these decisions for themselves.

And I remain hopeful, but this is going to be tough. And I don't want anybody out there thinking that it's going to be easy. The main point I want to make is it's a risk worth taking because the alternative is a status quo that is unsustainable.

And so if these talks break down, we're going to keep on trying. Over the long term, it has the opportunity, by the way, also to change the strategic landscape in the Middle East in a way that would be very helpful. It would help us deal with an Iran that has not been willing to give up its nuclear program. It would help us deal with terrorist organizations in the region. So this is something in our interests. We're not just doing this to feel good. We're doing it because it will help secure America as well.

Jake Tapper [ABC News].

Religious Tolerance/Health Care Reform/Midterm Elections

Q. Thank you, Mr. President. A couple questions: First, were you concerned at all when you—when the administration had Secretary of Defense Gates call this pastor in Florida that you were elevating somebody who is clearly from the fringe?

And then more substantively, on health care reform, this is 6 months since health care passed. You pledged, A, that you would bend the cost curve and, B, that you Democrats would be able to campaign on this. And CMS reported yesterday that the cost curve is actually bending up, from 6.1 percent to 6.3 percent, post-health care legislation. And the only Democrats I've seen talking about health care legislation are running TV ads saying that they voted against it.

Thank you.

The President. With respect to the individual down in Florida, let me just say—well, let me repeat what I said a couple of days ago. The idea that we would burn the sacred texts of someone else's religion is contrary to what this country stands for. It's contrary to what this country—this Nation was founded on. And my hope is, is that this individual prays on it and refrains from doing it.

But I'm also Commander in Chief, and we are seeing today riots in Kabul, riots in Afghanistan that threaten our young men and women in uniform. And so we've got an obligation to send a very clear message that this kind of behavior or threats of action put our young men and women in harm's way. And it's also the best imaginable recruiting tool for Al Qaida.

And although this may be one individual in Florida, part of my concern is to make sure that we don't start having a whole bunch of folks all across the country think this is the way to get attention. This is a way of endangering our troops—our sons and daughters, fathers and mothers, husbands and wives who are sacrificing for us to keep us safe. And you don't play games with that.

So I hardly think we're the ones who elevated this story. But it is, in the age of the Internet, something that can cause us profound damage around the world, and so we've got to take it seriously.

With respect to health care, what I said during the debate is the same thing I'm saying now, and it's the same thing I will say 3 or 4 years from now. Bending the cost curve on health care is hard to do. We've got hundreds of thousands of providers and doctors and systems and insurers. And what we did was we took every idea out there about how to reduce or at least slow the costs of health care over time.

But I said at the time it wasn't going to happen tomorrow, it wasn't going to happen next year. It took us decades to get into a position where our health care costs were going up 6, 7, 10 percent a year. And so our goal is to slowly bring down those costs.

Now, we've done so also by making sure that 31 million people who aren't getting health insurance are going to start getting it. And we have now implemented the first phase of health care in a way that, by the way, has been complimented even by the opponents of health care reform. It has been smooth. And right now middle class families all across America are going to be able to say to themselves, starting this month, if I've got a kid who is under 26 and doesn't have health insurance, that kid can stay on my health insurance; if I've got a child with a preexisting condition, an insurer can't deny me coverage; if I get sick and I've got health insurance, that insurance company can't arbitrarily drop my coverage.

There are 4 million small businesses around the country who are already eligible and in some cases will be receiving a 35-percent tax break on health care for their employees. And I've already met small businesses around the country who say, you know, because of that, I'm going to be able to provide health care for my employees, I thought it was the right thing to do. So——

Q. ——the CMS study from February predicted a 6.1-percent increase, and now, posthealth care, 6.3 percent. So it seems to have bent it up.

The President. No, as I said, Jake, if the—I haven't read the entire study. Maybe you have. But if you—if what—the reports are true, what they're saying is, is that as a consequence of us getting 30 million additional people health care, at the margins, that's going to increase our costs. We knew that. We didn't think that we were going to cover 30 million people for free, but that the long-term trend in terms of how much the average family is going to be paying for health insurance is going to be improved as a consequence of health care.

And so our goal on health care is, if we can get, instead of health care costs going up 6 percent a year, it's going up at the level of inflation, maybe just slightly above inflation, we've made huge progress. And by the way, that is the single most important thing we could do in terms of reducing our deficit. That's why we did it, that's why it's important, and that's why we're going to implement it effectively.

Q. Sorry, and then the House Democrats running against health care—if you could comment on that.

The President. Well, there are—we're in a political season where every candidate out there has their own district, their own makeup, their own plan, their own message. And in an environment where we've still got 9.5 percent unemployment, people are going to make the best argument they can right now. And they're going to be taking polls of what their particular constituents are saying and trying to align with that oftentimes. That's how political races work.

April Ryan [American Urban Radio Networks].

Department of Agriculture Class-Action Lawsuit Settlements/National Economy/Education Reform

Q. Thank you, Mr. President. I want to ask a couple questions. On the economy, could you discuss your efforts at reviewing history as it relates to the poverty agenda, meaning LBJ and Dr. King?

And also, since Senate Republicans are holding up the issue of *Cobell* and *Pigford* too, can you make any assurances before you leave office that you will make sure that those awards are funded?

The President. Let me take the second question first. For those who aren't familiar, *Cobell* and *Pigford* relate to settlements surrounding historic discrimination against minority farmers who weren't oftentimes provided the same benefits as everybody else under the USDA.

It is a fair settlement. It is a just settlement. We think it's important for Congress to fund that settlement. We're going to continue to make it a priority.

With respect to the history of fighting poverty, I got my start in public service as a community organizer working in the shadow of steel plants that had been closed in some of the poorest neighborhoods on the south side of Chicago. That's what led me to want to serve. And so I am constantly thinking about how do we create ladders for communities and individuals to climb into the middle class.

Now, I think the history of antipoverty efforts is, is that the most important antipoverty effort is growing the economy and making sure there are enough jobs out there—single most important thing we can do. It's more important than any program we could set up. It's more important than any transfer payment that we could have. If we can grow the economy faster and create more jobs, then everybody is swept up into that virtuous cycle. And if the economy is shrinking and things are going badly, then the folks who are most vulnerable are going to be those poorest communities.

So what we want to focus on right now is broad-based job growth and broad-based economic expansion. And we're doing so against some tough headwinds, because as I said, we are coming out of a very difficult time. We've started to turn the corner, but we're not there yet.

And so that is going to be my central focus: How do I grow the economy? How do I make sure that there's more job growth?

That doesn't mean that there aren't some targeted things we can do to help communities that are especially in need. And probably the most important thing we can do, after growing the economy generally, is, how can we improve school systems in low-income communities? And I am very proud of the efforts that we've made on education reform, which have received praise from Democrats and Republicans. This is one area where actually we've seen some good bipartisan cooperation.

And the idea is very simple: If we can make sure that we have the very best teachers in the classroom, if we can reward excellence instead of mediocrity and the status quo, if we can make sure that we're tracking progress in real, serious ways, and we're willing to make investments in what goes on in the classroom and not the school bureaucracy, and reward innovation, then schools can improve. There are models out there of schools in the toughest inner-city neighborhood that are now graduating kids, 90 percent of whom are going to college. And the key is, how do we duplicate those?

And so what our Race to the Top program has done is, it's said to every State around the country, instead of just getting money based on a formula, we want you to compete. Show us how you are reforming your school systems to promote excellence, based on proven ideas out there. And if you do that, we're going to reward you with some extra money. And just the competition alone has actually spurred 46 States so far to initiate legislation designed to reform the school system.

So we're very proud of that. And that, I think, is going to be one of the most important things we can do. It's not just, by the way, K through 12. It's also higher education. And as a consequence of a battle that we had—and it was a contentious battle—in Congress, we've been able to take tens of billions of dollars that were going to banks and financial intermediaries in the student loan program and said, we're going to give that money directly to students so that they get more help going to college. And obviously, poor kids are the ones who are going to benefit most from those programs.

Helene Cooper [New York Times].

U.S. Military Operations in Afghanistan/Middle East Peace Process

Q. Thank you, Mr. President. Two questions—one on Afghanistan. How can you lecture Hamid Karzai about corruption when so many of these corrupt people are on the U.S. payroll?

And on the Middle East, do you believe that Israeli Prime Minister Benjamin Netanyahu should extend the settlement moratorium as a gesture to peace? And if he doesn't, what are you prepared to do to stop the Palestinians from walking?

The President. Okay. On Afghanistan, we are in the midst of a very difficult but very important project. I just want to remind people why we're there, the day before September 11th. We're there because that was the place where Al Qaida launched an attack that killed 3,000 Americans. And we want to make sure that we dismantle Al Qaida and that Afghanistan is never again used as a base for attacks against Americans and the American homeland.

Now, Afghanistan is also the second poorest country in the world. It's got an illiteracy rate of 70 percent. It has a multiethnic population that mistrusts, oftentimes, each other. And it doesn't have a tradition of a strong, central Government.

So what we have done is to say, we are going to—after 7 years of drift, after 7 years of policies in which, for example, we weren't even effectively training Afghan security forces, what we've done is to say, we're going to work with the Afghan Government to train Afghan security forces so they can be responsible for their own security. We are going to promote a political settlement in the region that can help to re-

duce the violence. We are going to encourage a Afghan Government that can deliver services for its people. And we're going to try to make sure that as part of helping President Karzai stand up a broadly accepted, legitimate Government, that corruption is reduced.

And we've made progress on some of those fronts. I mean, when it comes to corruption, I'll just give you an example. Four years ago, 11 judges in the Afghan legal system were indicted for corruption. This year, 86 were indicted for corruption. We have seen Afghan-led efforts that have gone after police commanders, significant businesspeople in Afghanistan. But we're a long way from where we need to be on that.

And every time I talk to President Karzai, I say that as important as it is for us to help you train your military and your police forces, the only way that you are going to have a stable Government over the long term is if the Afghan people feel that you're looking out for them, and that means making sure that the tradition of corruption in the Government is reduced.

And we're going to keep on putting pressure on them on that front. Is it going to happen overnight? Probably not. Are there going to be occasions where we look and see that some of our folks on the ground have made compromises with people who are known to have engaged in corruption? We're reviewing all that constantly, and there may be occasions where that happens.

And I think you're certainly right, Helene, that we've got to make sure that we're not sending a mixed message here. So one of the things that I've said to my national security team is, let's be consistent in terms of how we operate across agencies. Let's make sure that our efforts there are not seen as somehow giving a wink and a nod to corruption. If we are saying publicly that that's important, then our actions have to match up across the board. But it is a challenging environment in which to do that.

Now, with respect to Prime Minister Netanyahu and the Middle East, a major bone of contention during the course of this month is going to be the potential lapse of the settlement moratorium. The irony is, is that when Prime Minister Netanyahu put the moratorium in place, the

Palestinians were very skeptical. They said, ah, this doesn't do anything. And it turns out, to Prime Minister Netanyahu's credit and to the Israeli Government's credit, the settlement moratorium has actually been significant. It has significantly reduced settlement construction in the region. And that's why now the Palestinians say, you know what, even though we weren't that keen on it at first or we thought it was just window dressing, it turns out that this is important to us.

What I've said to Prime Minister Netanyahu is that given so far the talks are moving forward in a constructive way, it makes sense to extend that moratorium so long as the talks are moving in a constructive way. Because ultimately, the way to solve these problems is for the two sides to agree what's going to be Israel, what's going to be the state of Palestine. And if you can get that agreement, then you can start constructing anything that the people of Israel see fit, in undisputed areas.

Now, I think the politics for Prime Minister Netanyahu are very difficult. His coalition—I think there are a number of members of his coalition who've said, we don't want to continue this. And so one of the things that I've said to President Abbas is, you've got to show the Israeli public that you are serious and constructive in these talks so that the politics for Prime Minister Netanyahu—if he were to extend the settlements moratorium—would be a little bit easier.

And one of the goals I think that I've set for myself and for my team is to make sure that President Abbas and Prime Minister Netanyahu start thinking about how can they help the other succeed, as opposed to how do they figure out a way for the other to fail. Because if they're going to be successful in bringing about what they now agree is the best course of action for their people, the only way they're going to succeed is if they are seeing the world through the other person's eyes. And that requires a personal relationship and building trust. Hopefully, these meetings will help do that. Okay?

Ann Compton [ABC Radio].

Guantanamo Bay Detention Center/Trials for Terrorist Suspects

Q. Mr. President, what does it say about the status of American system of justice when so many of those who are thought to be plotters for September 11th or accused or suspected terrorists are still awaiting any kind of trial? Are you—why are you still convinced that a civilian trial is correct for Sheikh—Khalid Sheikh Mohammed? And why has that stalled? And will Guantanamo remain open for another year?

The President. Well, we have succeeded on delivering a lot of campaign promises that we made. One where we've fallen short is closing Guantanamo. I wanted to close it sooner. We have missed that deadline. It's not for lack of trying. It's because the politics of it are difficult.

Now, I am absolutely convinced that the American justice system is strong enough that we should be able to convict people who murdered innocent Americans, who carried out terrorist attacks against us. We should be able to lock them up and make sure that they don't see the light of day. We can do that. We've done it before. We've got people who engaged in terrorist attacks who are in our prisons—maximum security prisons all across the country.

But this is an issue that has generated a lot of political rhetoric, and people, understandably, are fearful. But one of the things that I think is worth reflecting on after 9/11 is, this country is so resilient, we are so tough, we can't be frightened by a handful of people who are trying to do us harm, especially when we've captured them and we've got the goods on them.

So I've also said that there are going to be circumstances where a military tribunal may be appropriate, and the reason for that is—and I'll just give a specific example. There may be situations in which somebody was captured in theater, is now in Guantanamo. It's very hard to piece together a chain of evidence that would meet some of the evidentiary standards that would be required in an Article III court. But we know that this person is guilty; there's sufficient evidence to bring about a conviction. So what I have said is, the military commission system that we set up—where appropriate for certain individuals that would make it—it would be difficult to try in Article III courts for a range of reasons—we can reform that system so that it meets the highest standards of due process and prosecute them there.

And so I'm prepared to work with Democrats and Republicans. And we, over the course of the last year, have been in constant conversations with them about setting up a sensible system in which we are prosecuting, where appropriate, those in Article III courts. We are prosecuting others, where appropriate, through a military tribunal. And in either case, let's put them in prisons where our track record is they've never escaped. And by the way, just from a purely fiscal point of view, the costs of holding folks in Guantanamo is massively higher than it is holding them in a super-maximum security prison here in the United States.

Q. How long for Khalid Sheikh Mohammed? Will that trial ever happen?

The President. Well, I think it needs to happen. And we're going to work with Members of Congress—and this is going to have to be on a bipartisan basis—to move this forward in a way that is consistent with our standards of due process, consistent with our Constitution, consistent also with our image in the world of a country that cares about rule of law. You can't underestimate the impact of that.

Al Qaida operatives still cite Guantanamo as a justification for attacks against the United States—still, to this day. And there's no reason for us to give them that kind of talking point when, in fact, we can use the various mechanisms of our justice system to prosecute these folks and to make sure that they never attack us again. Okay?

Ed Henry [CNN].

Al Qaida Leadership

Q. Mr. President, you were talking about some of the Al Qaida leaders that you have captured. One that you have not is Usama bin Laden. Tomorrow is going to be 9 years since he was the mastermind of 3,000 Americans being killed. And what you said—obviously, the last administration had 7 years and couldn't do it. But what you said as President-elect to CBS is,

quote: "I think capturing or killing bin Laden is a critical aspect of stamping out Al Qaida. He is not just a symbol. He is also the operational leader of an organization planning attacks against the U.S."

Do you still believe it's a critical part of your policy to capture or kill him? And do you think it's—isn't it a failure of your administration that here it's almost 2 years in—you campaigned saying you were going to run a smarter war on terror than the Bush administration. You haven't captured him, and you don't seem to know where he is.

The President. Well, Ed, I think capturing or killing bin Laden and Zawahiri would be extremely important to our national security. It doesn't solve all our problems, but it remains a high priority of this administration.

One of the things that we've been very successful at over the last 2 years is to ramp up the pressure on Al Qaida and their key leaders. And as a consequence, they have been holed up in ways that have made it harder for them to operate. And part of what's happened is, is bin Laden has gone deep underground. Even Zawahiri, who is more often out there, has been much more cautious.

But we have the best minds, the best intelligence officers, the best special forces, who are thinking about this day and night. And they will continue to think about it day and night as long as I'm President.

Q. But, sir, do you think Americans are going to face another 9 years of this terror threat, another generation? What's your message to them?

The President. Here's what I think. I think that in this day and age, there are going to be—there is always going to be the potential for an individual or a small group of individuals, if they are willing to die, to kill other people. Some of them are going to be very well organized, and some of them are going to be random. That threat is there. And it's important, I think, for the American people to understand that and not to live in fear. It's just a reality of today's world that there are going to be threats out there.

We have, I think, greatly improved our homeland security since 9/11 occurred. I am constantly impressed with the dedication that our teams apply to this problem. They are chasing down every thread, not just from Al Qaida, but any other actor out there that might be engaging in terrorism. They are making sure that even a—what might appear to be a lone individual who has very little organizational capacity—if they make a threat, they follow up.

But one of the things that I want to make sure we do as long as I'm President and beyond my Presidency is to understand America's strength in part comes from its resilience, and that we don't start losing who we are or overreacting if, in fact, there is the threat of terrorism out there.

We go about our business. We are tougher than them. Our families and our businesses and our churches and mosques and synagogues and our Constitution, our values, that's what gives us strength. And we are going to have this problem out there for a long time to come. But it doesn't have to completely distort us. And it doesn't have to dominate our foreign policy. What we can do is to constantly fight against it. And I think ultimately we are going to be able to stamp it out. But it's going to take some time.

White House Press Secretary Robert L. Gibbs. Last question.

The President. Wendell [Wendell Goler, FOX News Channel].

Religious Freedom and Tolerance

Q. Thank you, Mr. President. I wonder if I can get you to weigh in on the wisdom of building a mosque a couple of blocks from Ground Zero. We know that the organizers have the constitutional right. What would it say about this country if they were somehow talked out of doing that? And hasn't the Florida minister's threat to burn a couple hundred copies of the Koran, hasn't the threat itself put American lives in danger, sir?

The President. Well, on the second—on your second question, there's no doubt that when someone goes out of their way to be provocative in ways that we know can inflame the passions of over a billion Muslims around the world, at a time when we've got our troops in a lot of Muslim countries, that's a problem. And it has made

life a lot more difficult for our men and women in uniform who already have a very difficult job.

With respect to the mosque in New York, I think I've been pretty clear on my position here, and that is, is that this country stands for the proposition that all men and women are created equal, that they have certain inalienable rights—one of those inalienable rights is to practice their religion freely. And what that means is that if you could build a church on a site, you could build a synagogue on a site, if you could build a Hindu temple on a site, then you should be able to build a mosque on the site.

Now, I recognize the extraordinary sensitivities around 9/11. I've met with families of 9/11 victims in the past. I can only imagine the continuing pain and anguish and sense of loss that they may go through. And tomorrow we as Americans are going to be joining them in prayer and remembrance. But I go back to what I said earlier: We are not at war against Islam. We are at war against terrorist organizations that have distorted Islam or falsely used the banner of Islam to engage in their destructive acts.

And we've got to be clear about that. We've got to be clear about that because if we're going to deal with the problems that Ed Henry was talking about, if we're going to successfully reduce the terrorist threat, then we need all the allies we can get. The folks who are most interested in a war between the United States or the West and Islam are Al Qaida. That's what they've been banking on.

And fortunately, the overwhelming majority of Muslims around the world are peace loving, are interested in the same things that you and I are interested in: How do I make sure I can get a good job? How can I make sure that my kids get a decent education? How can I make sure I'm safe? How can I improve my lot in life? And so they have rejected this violent ideology for the most part—overwhelmingly.

And so from a national security interest, we want to be clear about who the enemy is here. It's a handful, a tiny minority of people who are engaging in horrific acts and have killed Muslims more than anybody else.

The other reason it's important for us to remember that is because we've got millions of Muslim Americans, our fellow citizens, in this country. They're going to school with our kids. They're our neighbors. They're our friends. They're our coworkers. And when we start acting as if their religion is somehow offensive, what are we saying to them?

I've got Muslims who are fighting in Afghanistan in the uniform of the United States Armed Services. They're out there putting their lives on the line for us. And we've got to make sure that we are crystal clear, for our sakes and their sakes, they are Americans and we honor their service. And part of honoring their service is making sure that they understand that we don't differentiate between them and us. It's just us.

And that is a principle that I think is going to be very important for us to sustain. And I think tomorrow is an excellent time for us to reflect on that.

Thank you very much, everybody.

NOTE: The President's news conference began at 11:02 a.m. in the East Room at the White House. In his remarks, the President referred to Rep. Pete Sessions, in his capacity as chairman of the National Republican Congressional Committee; Elizabeth Warren, Leo Gottlieb Professor of Law, Harvard University; President Mahmoud Abbas of the Palestinian Authority; Terry Jones, pastor, Dove World Outreach Center in Gainesville, FL; and Ayman Al-Zawahiri, founder of the Egyptian Islamic Jihad and senior Al Qaida associate. A reporter referred to Khalid Sheikh Mohammed, a former senior leader of the Al Qaida terrorist organization in U.S. military custody. The Office of the Press Secretary also released a partial Spanish language transcript of this news conference.

Letter to Congressional Leaders on Continuation of the National Emergency With Respect to Certain Terrorist Attacks
September 10, 2010

Dear Madam Speaker: (Dear Mr. President:)

Section 202(d) of the National Emergencies Act, 50 U.S.C. 1622(d), provides for the automatic termination of a national emergency unless, prior to the anniversary date of its declaration, the President publishes in the *Federal Register* and transmits to the Congress a notice stating that the emergency is to continue in effect beyond the anniversary date. Consistent with this provision, I have sent to the *Federal Register* the enclosed notice, stating that the emergency declared with respect to the terrorist attacks on the United States of September 11, 2001, is to continue in effect for an additional year.

The terrorist threat that led to the declaration on September 14, 2001, of a national emergency continues. For this reason, I have determined that it is necessary to continue in effect after September 14, 2010, the national emergency with respect to the terrorist threat.

Sincerely,

BARACK OBAMA

NOTE: Identical letters were sent to Nancy Pelosi, Speaker of the House of Representatives, and Joseph R. Biden, Jr., President of the Senate. The notice is listed in Appendix D at the end of this volume.

The President's Weekly Address
September 11, 2010

Today we pause to remember a day that tested our country. On September 11th, 2001, nearly 3,000 lives were lost in the deadliest at-

tack on American soil in our history. We will never forget the images of planes vanishing into buildings, of photos hung by the families of the missing. We will never forget the anger and the sadness that we felt. And while 9 years have come and gone since that September morning, the passage of time will never diminish the pain and loss forever seared in the consciousness of our Nation.

That is why on this day, we pray with the families of those who died. We mourn with the husbands and wives, the children and parents, friends and loved ones. We think about the milestones that have passed over the course of 9 years—births and christenings, weddings and graduations—all with an empty chair.

On this day, we also honor those who died so that others might live: the firefighters and first-responders who climbed the stairs of two burning towers, the passengers who stormed a cockpit, and the men and women who have in the years since borne the uniform of this country and given their lives so that our children could grow up in a safer world. In acts of courage and decency, they defended a simple precept: I am my brother's keeper; I am my sister's keeper.

And on this day, we recall that at our darkest moment, we summoned a sense of unity and common purpose. We responded to the worst kind of depravity with the best of our humanity.

So each year at this time, we renew our resolve against those who perpetrated this barbaric act of terror and who continue to plot against us, for we will never waver in defense of this Nation. We renew our commitment to our troops and all who serve to protect this country and to their families. But we also renew the true spirit of that day: not the human capacity for evil, but the human capacity for good; not the desire to destroy, but the impulse to save.

That's why we mark September 11th as a National Day of Service and Remembrance. For if there is a lesson to be drawn on this anniversary, it is this: We are one Nation, one people, bound not only by grief, but by a set of common ideals, and that by giving back to our communities, by serving people in need, we reaffirm our ideals, in defiance of those who would do us grave harm. We prove that the sense of responsibility that we felt for one another that day 9 years ago was not a fleeting passion, but a lasting virtue.

This is a difficult time for our country. And it's often in such moments that some try to stoke bitterness, to divide us based on our differences, to blind us to what we have in common. But on this day, we are reminded that at our best, we do not give in to this temptation. We stand with one another; we fight alongside one another. We do not allow ourselves to be defined by fear, but rather, by the hopes we have for our families, for our Nation, and for a brighter future. So let us grieve for those we've lost, honor those who have sacrificed, and do our best to live up to the shared values that we have, on this day and every day that follows.

Thank you.

NOTE: The address was recorded at approximately 2:30 p.m. on September 10 in the Diplomatic Room at the White House for broadcast on September 11. The transcript was made available by the Office of the Press Secretary on September 10, but was embargoed for release until 6 a.m. on September 11. The Office of the Press Secretary also released a Spanish language transcript of this address.

Remarks at a Wreath-Laying Ceremony at the Pentagon Memorial in Arlington, Virginia
September 11, 2010

Secretary Gates, Admiral Mullen, and members of the Armed Forces; my fellow Americans; most of all, to you, survivors who still carry the scars of tragedy and destruction, to the families who carry in your hearts the memory of the loved ones you lost here: For our Nation, this is

a day of remembrance, a day of reflection, and, with God's grace, a day of unity and renewal.

We gather to remember, at this sacred hour, on hallowed ground, at places where we feel such grief and where our healing goes on. We gather here at the Pentagon, where the names of the lost are forever etched in stone. We gather in a gentle Pennsylvania field, where a plane went down and a Tower of Voices will rise and echo through the ages. And we gather where the Twin Towers fell, a site where the work goes on so that next year, on the 10th anniversary, the waters will flow in steady tribute to the nearly 3,000 innocent lives.

On this day, it's perhaps natural to focus on the images of that awful morning, images that are seared into our souls. It's tempting to dwell on the final moments of the loved ones whose lives were taken so cruelly. Yet these memorials and your presence today remind us to remember the fullness of their time on Earth.

They were fathers and mothers raising their families; brothers and sisters pursuing their dreams; sons and daughters, their whole lives before them. They were civilians and servicemembers. Some never saw the danger coming; others saw the peril and rushed to save others, up those stairwells, into the flames, into the cockpit.

They were White and Black and Brown, men and women and some children, made up of all races, many faiths. They were Americans and people from far corners of the world. And they were snatched from us senselessly and much too soon, but they lived well, and they live on in you.

Nine years have now passed. In that time, you have shed more tears than we will ever know. And though it must seem some days as though the world has moved on to other things, I say to you today that your loved ones endure in the heart of our Nation, now and forever.

Our remembrance today also requires a certain reflection. As a nation and as individuals, we must ask ourselves how best to honor them, those who died, those who sacrificed. How do we preserve their legacy, not just on this day, but every day?

We need not look far for our answer. The perpetrators of this evil act didn't simply attack America; they attacked the very idea of America itself, all that we stand for and represent in the world. And so the highest honor we can pay those we lost—indeed, our greatest weapon in this ongoing war—is to do what our adversaries fear the most: to stay true to who we are as Americans, to renew our sense of common purpose, to say that we define the character of our country and we will not let the acts of some small band of murderers who slaughter the innocent and cower in caves distort who we are.

They doubted our will, but as Americans, we persevere. Today, in Afghanistan and beyond, we have gone on the offensive and struck major blows against Al Qaida and its allies. We will do what is necessary to protect our country, and we honor all those who serve to keep us safe.

They may seek to strike fear in us, but they are no match for our resilience. We do not succumb to fear, nor will we squander the optimism that has always defined us as a people. On a day when others sought to destroy, we have chosen to build, with a National Day of Service and Remembrance that summons the inherent goodness of the American people.

They may seek to exploit our freedoms, but we will not sacrifice the liberties we cherish or hunker down behind walls of suspicion and mistrust. They may wish to drive us apart, but we will not give in to their hatred and prejudice. For Scripture teaches us to "get rid of all bitterness, rage and anger, brawling and slander, along with every form of malice."

They may seek to spark conflict between different faiths, but as Americans, we are not and never will be at war with Islam. It was not a religion that attacked us that September day; it was Al Qaida, a sorry band of men which perverts religion. And just as we condemn intolerance and extremism abroad, so will we stay true to our traditions here at home as a diverse and tolerant nation. We champion the rights of every American, including the right to worship as one chooses, as servicemembers and civilians from many faiths do just steps from here, at the very spot where the terrorists struck this building.

Those who attacked us sought to demoralize us, divide us, to deprive us of the very unity, the very ideals that make America America, those qualities that have made us a beacon of freedom and hope to billions around the world. Today we declare once more, we will never hand them that victory. As Americans, we will keep alive the virtues and values that make us who we are and who we must always be.

For our cause is just, our spirit is strong, our resolve is unwavering. Like generations before us, let us come together today and all days to affirm certain inalienable rights, to affirm life and liberty and the pursuit of happiness. On this day and the days to come, we choose to stay true to our best selves as one Nation under God, indivisible, with liberty and justice for all.

This is how we choose to honor the fallen—your families, your friends, your fellow servicemembers. This is how we will keep alive the leg-acy of these proud and patriotic Americans. This is how we will prevail in this great test of our time. This is how we will preserve and protect the country that we love and pass it, safer and stronger, to future generations.

May God bless you and your families, and may God continue to bless the United States of America.

NOTE: The President spoke at 9:34 a.m. at the Pentagon. The Office of the Press Secretary also released a Spanish language transcript of these remarks.

Telephone Remarks to A123 Systems in Livonia, Michigan
September 13, 2010

The President. Good morning, everybody.

Governor Jennifer M. Granholm of Michigan. Good morning. Is that a familiar voice we hear?

The President. Governor Granholm, this is your friend Barack Obama.

Gov. Granholm. Mr. President, we're so happy to welcome you to our celebration of A123. I was just explaining how great it is that the Recovery Act provided jobs for Michigan. Maybe you have a few words to those who are assembled here.

The President. Well, look, I wish I could be there in person to celebrate with you today. But I am calling to congratulate A123 Systems on this tremendous milestone. As you said, thanks to the Recovery Act, you guys are the first American factory to start high-volume production of advanced vehicle batteries.

I met with David and some of the A123 team here at the White House back in April, and it's incredibly exciting to see how far you guys have come since we announced these grants just over a year ago. And this is important not just because of what you guys are doing at your plant, but all across America, because this is about the birth of an entire new industry in America, an industry that's going to be central to the next generation of cars. And it's going to allow us to start exporting those cars, making them comfortable, convenient, and affordable. It helps our manufacturing industry to thrive, and with it, that means our communities and our States and our country are going to thrive.

For a long time, our economic policies have shortchanged cutting-edge projects like this one, and it put us behind the innovation race. And I don't have to tell folks in Michigan that fewer parts of the economy have been harder hit by this recession than manufacturing. But what I said when you guys were in the White House was, I do not see a decline in manufacturing as inevitable for the United States. And I know you don't either.

And so we're starting to reverse that slide. And anybody who doubts that has to go and see what you guys are achieving. And I want everybody to understand, just a few years ago, American businesses could only make 2 percent of the world's advanced batteries for hybrids and electric vehicles—just 2 percent. But because of your extraordinary work, thanks to the Recovery Act, we're going to get up to 40 percent of the world's capacity. And that means when folks lift up their hoods on the cars of the future, I want them to see engines and batteries that are stamped "Made in America." And that's what you guys are helping to make happen.

So I want to thank your great Governor, Jennifer Granholm, for her vision in jump-starting a homegrown clean energy industry. I want to thank your congressional delegation, Senator Levin and Stabenow and Chairman Dingell and

Chairman Levin, for their leadership and their support of the Recovery Act. I also want to thank my Secretary of Energy, Steven Chu, for his extraordinary work to get the money out the door quickly and wisely.

But most of all, I want to congratulate and thank all the men and women of A123 Systems. You guys are making us proud. The work you're doing will help power the American economy for years to come. And so everybody there should just feel very, very good about what you

guys are doing. And I am looking forward to continuing to see the great work that you guys do in the years to come.

So thank you very much, everybody. And good luck.

NOTE: The President spoke at 10:15 a.m. from the Oval Office at the White House to A123 Systems employees. In his remarks, he referred to David Vieau, president and chief executive officer, A123 Systems.

Remarks at a Reception for Presidents of Historically Black Colleges and Universities
September 13, 2010

The President. Hello, everybody!

Audience members. Hello!

The President. Welcome. Welcome to the White House. It is good to see some old friends and familiar faces. And I want to especially welcome three of our newest board members of the President's Board of Advisers on Historically Black Colleges and Universities. I am so grateful that they've agreed to join, and I'm looking forward to working with all of you.

Now, last February, I saw some of you here when I signed the Executive order to strengthen the White House Initiative on HBCUs. And this is allowing the Government to collaborate with educational associations, with philanthropic organizations, and with the private sector to increase your capacity to offer a college degree to as many students as possible.

And we've also declared this week to be National HBCU Week. And we do this for two reasons: first of all, to remember our history. We remember all the men and women who took great risks and made extraordinary sacrifices to ensure that these institutions that you lead could exist. We remember that at a critical time in our Nation's history, HBCUs waged war against illiteracy and ignorance and won. You've made it possible for millions of people to achieve their dreams and gave so many young people a chance they never thought they'd have, a chance that nobody else would give

them. And that's something to celebrate, and that's something to be very, very proud of.

But we also use this week as an opportunity to look forward towards the future and to take stock of the work that we've got left to do. As many of you know, I set a goal that by 2020, the United States would once again lead in the number of college graduates, have the highest proportion of college graduates in the world. I set that goal because our success in a 21st-century economy is going to depend almost entirely on having a skilled workforce, how well trained our young people are.

We cannot reach that goal without HBCUs. We can't get there unless all of you are improving your graduation rates. We can't get there unless all of you are continuing to make the dream of a college education a reality for more students. We want to help you do that in every way that we can. Already, we've eliminated billions of dollars of unnecessary subsidies to banks and financial institutions so that that money could go directly to your students. And that is incredibly important. And as a consequence of that, we're making it possible for millions of more students to attend colleges and universities and community colleges all across the country.

We also want to keep strengthening HBCUs, which is why we're investing $850 million in these institutions over the next 10 years. And as I said in February, strengthening your institutions isn't just a task for our advisory board or for the Department of Education, it's a job for the entire Federal Government. And I expect all agencies to support this mission.

Now, none of this is going to be easy. I know—I'm sure you know that. As leaders of these institutions, you are up against enormous challenges, especially during an economic crisis like the one that we are going through. But we all have to try. We have to try. We have to remain determined. We have to persevere.

That's what the first founders of HBCUs did. They knew that even if they succeeded, that inequality would persist for a very, very long time. They knew that the barriers in our laws, the barriers in our hearts would not vanish overnight. But they also recognized a larger and distinctly American truth, and that is that the right education might one day allow us to overcome barriers, to let every child fulfill their God-given potential. They recognized, as Frederick Douglass once put it, that education means emancipation. And they recognized that education is how

America and its people might fulfill our promise.

That's what helped them get through some very difficult times. It's what kept them fighting and trying and reaching for that better day, even though they might not be able to live to see that better day. That's the kind of commitment that we're going to need today from everybody here at the White House, from all of you at your respective institutions.

We are extraordinarily proud of what you've done. But we've got a lot more work to do. And I just want everybody here to understand that you've got a partner in me and you've got a partner in the Department of Education and you've got a department with everybody here at the White House who's absolutely committed to making sure that you can succeed in your mission.

So thank you very much, everybody. God bless you. Thank you.

NOTE: The President spoke at 10:36 a.m. in the Grand Foyer at the White House.

Remarks and a Question-and-Answer Session in Fairfax, Virginia
September 13, 2010

The President. Thank you so much, all of you, for being here, and I want to say a special thanks to John and Nicole. Trevor and Olivia are back there.

Nicole Armstrong. They're going to turn the A/C unit off for you.

The President. Yes, exactly. That's all right. But I'm so grateful for their hospitality. They are just a wonderful family, and for them to open up their backyard for us is just terrific. So we really——

[*At this point, the President was handed a microphone.*]

The President. Oh, I've got a mike. So thank you to the entire family for opening up, and thanks to all of you for taking the time to be here. Because I want to—I was telling John and Nicole that a lot of times, when you're in Washington, you're busy, you've got a lot of stuff to

do, and you're in a bubble when you're President. And sometimes, you just don't have the opportunity to have the kinds of interactions that I used to have even when I was a Senator.

And so these kinds of formats are terrific for me. And my hope is, is that despite all these people who are here with cameras and microphones and all that stuff, that people won't be shy, because the whole point of this is for me to hear directly from you and to answer your questions, hear about your concerns, hear about your hopes, and hopefully, that will translate itself into some of the things that we're doing at the White House.

I obviously want to make some introductions that—I think all of you know that you've got some Members of Congress who are working very hard here in Northern Virginia, and I want to acknowledge them. First of all, Congressman Jim Moran, who's been doing great work for a very long time. Congressman Gerry Connolly has been doing terrific work here locally and now on Capitol Hill. We've got Sharon Bulova, who is the chairwoman of the Fairfax County Board of Commissioners.

And we've also got a couple of small-business owners, because one of the things I want to talk about is how we can grow the economy and get people back to work, and so who better to hear from than a couple of small-business owners. Don't worry, I'm not going to call on you, but I'm just glad you're here.

First of all, we've got Cherrelle Hurt, who is the owner of As We Grow Learning Center. Hey, Cherrelle. Thanks for being here. And Larry Poltavtsev—did I say that right, Larry?—who is the CEO of Target Labs, Inc. And so we're glad that you guys could join us.

Now, I'm only going to say a few things at the top. And I want to talk a little bit about why I decided to run for President in the first place, back in 2007, 2008.

Having served as a State senator, having then served as a United States Senator, I had had a chance to see how economic policies were having an effect on working class families and middle class families for a long time. And my wife and I, we came out of hard-working families who didn't have a lot, but because the economy was growing, because there was an emphasis on what was good for the middle class, we were able to get a great education, we were able to get scholarships. Michelle's dad worked as a blue-collar worker, but just on that one salary he was able to provide for his family and make sure that they always had enough and the kids had opportunities.

And what it seemed like was, for about a decade there, middle class families were losing more and more ground. And some of that had to do with changes in the global economy and greater competition from around the world. But a lot of it had to do with the policies that had been put in place, which really boiled down to cutting taxes, especially for millionaires and billionaires; cutting regulations that made consumers and workers more vulnerable; failing to make investments that were so critical in growing our middle class over the long term.

And so when I ran for President, my goal was to make sure that we get a set of economic policies in place that would lay the foundation for long-term growth in the 21st century so that the 21st century would be an American century, just like the 20th century had been.

And that's what we've tried to do over the last 19 months, in the midst of the worst financial crisis that we've seen since the Great Depression. The first thing we had to do was just stop the bleeding, stabilize the financial system, and make sure we didn't trip into a Great Depression. And we have done that.

So when I was sworn in on that very cold day in January—some of you may remember—we lost 750,000 jobs in that month alone. Now we've seen 8 consecutive months of private sector job growth because of the policies we've put in place.

We were on the verge of financial meltdown. Anybody who was involved in business at that time remembers banks were not lending at all. You couldn't even get an auto loan or a consumer loan. And now the financial systems have stabilized, although they're not completely where we need them to be. The economy was shrinking at a pace of—an astounding pace of about 6 percent annually. And now the economy has been growing.

So we stopped the bleeding, stabilized the economy, but the fact of the matter is, is that the pace of improvement has not been where it needs to be. And the hole that we had dug ourselves in was enormous. I mean, we lost 4 million jobs in the last 6 months of 2008, when I was still running. We lost 4 million jobs. And all told, we've lost 8 million jobs. And so even though we've grown jobs this year, we haven't been able to yet make up for those 8 million jobs that had been lost. And that's an enormous challenge.

Now, the second part of the challenge, though, is to make sure that even as we're digging ourselves out of this hole, we start making some better decisions so that long term we don't find ourselves in this circumstance again and we start creating the kind of economy that's working for middle class families.

So a couple of things that we did on that front. We cut taxes for middle class families, because we understand that people's incomes and wages have not gone up, have not kept pace with increases in health care, increases in college, and so forth.

The second thing that we felt was very important was to start creating some rules of the road again. So in financial services, for example, we passed a financial regulatory bill that makes sure that we're not going to have taxpayer bailouts, makes sure that banks have to operate a little bit more responsibly and take less risks with the money that they're investing. And we also made sure that consumers are treated more fairly, because part of what happened in this financial crisis was people were getting mortgages that they didn't understand. Suddenly, the bottom fell out of the housing market, and banks found themselves in a crisis situation.

So what we've said is, let's make sure that consumers know exactly the kinds of mortgages they're getting. Let's make sure that they can't be steered into these balloon-type payments where there's no chance that over the long term they're going to be able to make their payments.

Let's make sure that credit card companies have to notify you if they're going to increase your interest rates. And let's make sure that they can't increase your interest rates on your existing balances, only on future balances, so that they're not tricking you into suddenly paying exorbitant fees and putting you in the hole over the long term.

Gerry likes that one. [*Laughter*]

So we set up a bunch of rules both in the financial services area, in the housing sector, and in health care. And I know that a lot of people here heard a lot about the health care bill. One of the most important things that that was about was making sure that insurance companies treated you fairly. So if you've got health insurance, companies are not going to be able to drop you from coverage when you get sick, which is part of what had been happening. They couldn't deny you insurance because of a preexisting condition or if your child had a preexisting condition, which obviously makes families enormously vulnerable.

So a set of rules of the road for how companies interact with consumers, how they interact with workers.

And then the final thing that we've tried to do to lay this foundation for long-term economic growth is to put our investments in those things that are really going to make us more competitive over the long term. So we have made the largest investment in research and development, in basic research and science, in our history, because that's going to determine whether we can compete with China and India and Germany over the long term. Are we inventing stuff here that we can then export overseas?

We're making investments in our infrastructure, because we can't have a second-class infrastructure and expect to have a first-class economy. Just an interesting statistic over the last decade: China spends about 9 percent of its gross domestic product on infrastructure. Europe spends about 5 percent. We've been spending 2 percent. And that's part of the reason why we no longer have the best airports, we no longer have the best rail systems, we don't have the best broadband service. South Korea has better broadband service and wireless service than we do. And over time, that adds up. It makes us less competitive. So what we've said is, we've got to make investments in infrastructure.

A third area: education. A generation ago, we had the highest proportion of college graduates of any country in the world. We now rank 11th or 12th in the proportion of college graduates. Well, we can't win in an information society, in a global, technologically wired economy, unless we're winning that battle to make sure our kids can compete.

So what we've said is, we're going to put more money into higher education and through K through 12, but here's the catch: The money is only going to those communities that are serious about reforming their education system so they work well. Because it's—education is not just a matter of putting more money into it. You also have to make sure that we've got the best teachers, that we've got accountability, that the way we're designing our schools help our kids actually succeed over the long term, especially in areas of math and science, where we're lagging even further behind than we were a generation ago.

So those are the things that we've been trying to do over the last 19 months. Now, as I said before, the economy is growing, but it's not growing as fast as we would like. So over the last week, I've put forward a few more things that I think can really make a difference.

Number one, instead of giving tax breaks to companies that are investing overseas, which our Tax Code does right now, what I've said is, let's close those tax loopholes, and let's provide tax breaks to companies that are investing in research and development here in the United States. That's a smart thing to do. We want to incentivize businesses who actually are making profits right now to say, we should go ahead and take a chance, and let's invest in that next new thing.

Second is—what I've proposed is, is that we allow companies to write off essentially their new investments early if they make those investments here in 2011, so essentially accelerating the depreciation that they can take on their taxes to encourage them to front-load making investments now.

The third thing that we've proposed—and this is actually pending right now in the Senate, the United States Senate, because Gerry and Jim have already voted on it—is a small-business package that would eliminate capital gains taxes for small businesses, would help small businesses obtain loans. It is a commonsense bill that traditionally would have garnered a lot of bipartisan support, but we're in the political silly season right now so it's been blocked up by the Senate Republicans for the last month and a half, 2 months.

Small businesses are still having trouble getting loans. And what we want to do, even though we've already given them eight different tax breaks, is we want to say we're going to give you just a little bit more incentive, because if we can get small businesses growing and investing and opening their doors and hiring new workers, that's probably going to be the area where we can make the most progress over the next

year in terms of accelerating employment and reducing the unemployment rate.

So these are all steps that we're taking right now to try to move the economy forward. Now, I have never been more confident about the future of our economy, if we stay on track and we deal with some of these longstanding problems that we hadn't dealt with for decades.

If we make investments and improve our education system; if we make investments in research and development; if we make investments in things like clean energy so that we've got an energy policy that's not just tied to importing oil from the Middle East, but instead start figuring out how can we develop our homegrown industries; if we have a tax system that is fair and helps the middle class and that also attends to our long-term deficit problems; if we regulate, but not with a heavy hand, just regulate enough to make sure that we don't have a collapse of the financial system and consumers aren't taken advantage of and health insurance companies are responsive to ordinary families—if we do those things, there's no reason why we can't succeed.

And I've traveled all around the world, and I've looked at all the economic data. If you had a choice of which country you'd want to be, you still want to be the United States of America. We still have a huge competitive edge, and we've got the best workers in the world. And we've got the most dynamic economy in the world. We've got the best universities, the best entrepreneurs in the world.

But we've got to tackle these longstanding problems that have been getting in the way of progress, and we've got to do it now. We can't wait another 20 years or another 30 years, because other countries are catching up. That's what we've been trying to do over the last 2 years.

Now, some of these things, I got to admit, are hard. They cause great consternation. When we tried to get some commonsense rules in the financial sector, for example, that means billions of dollars that were going to profits to some of the banks are not going to be going there because you're getting a better deal on your credit card, and they're not happy about it. So that ends up creating a lot of drama on Capitol Hill. And it means that we've had some very contentious debates.

But I just want to close by saying this. Ultimately, when I get out of Washington and I start talking to families like yours, what I'm struck by is not how divided the country is, but I'm actually struck by how basically people have common values, common concerns, and common hopes. They want to be able to find a job that pays a decent wage; give their family, and their children in particular, a bright future; be able to retire with some dignity and respect; not get bankrupt when they get sick.

And that cuts across region, it cuts across racial lines, it cuts across religious or ethnic lines. People—there's a core set of American values that I think people across the country respond to.

And what I want to do is make sure that the Government is on the side of those values, of responsibility and hard work and thinking about future generations and not just thinking about the next election. And I think we've made progress, but we've got more progress to make.

So with that, I thank you all for being here. And what I want to do is, I just want to answer questions. And I know folks in the sun are hot, so I'm going to stand in the sun to make sure that you know that I feel—[*laughter*]—I feel your pain, as they—absolutely. I wouldn't mind having that hat, though. [*Laughter*] That's helpful. I should have thought ahead.

All right, anybody want to—John, go ahead. Yes. Here, hold on a second. I'll give you a mike, so—oh, we've got one.

Medical Research

Q. Mr. President, thank you very much for coming. We really appreciate it. It's a great opportunity. I'm an engineer. And you talked a lot about R&D and infrastructure and every—I love every dollar spent on that, by definition. I'm also a paraplegic. And we—I have a great interest in stem cell research and how it gets furthered. And so how do we get this issue to be a scientific issue instead of a political issue?

The President. Well, John, as you know, I have been a huge supporter of stem cell research for a very long time. When I came into office, we said that what's going to govern our decisionmaking here is sound science.

There are legitimate ethical issues involved in all this—the biotech industry—and those are going to continue as time goes on. I mean, there are some very tricky questions. And we've got to make sure that our values and our ethical standards are incorporated in everything we do. But we've also got to make sure that we're making decisions not based on ideology, but based on what the science is.

Now, the Executive order that I signed would say that we are not going to create embryos to destroy for scientific research. We're not going to do that.

On the other hand, when you've got a whole bunch of embryos that were created because families were trying to—couples were trying to start a family, and through in vitro fertilization, they're frozen in some canister somewhere and are going to be discarded anyway, then it makes sense for us to take those who—that are going to be destroyed and use them to advance our scientific knowledge to see if at some point we can start making huge progress on a whole set of issues.

Obviously, spinal cord injuries are an example, but Parkinson's disease, Alzheimer's disease, diabetes, juvenile diabetes. There's not a single family here who has not in some way been touched by a disease that could end up benefiting from the research that's done on stem cells.

Now, recently, a District Court judge said that not only—well, essentially said that our Executive order, he felt, went too far beyond what the guidelines that Congress had provided before I came into office. Although, the way he had written the order, it made it seem like even Bush's orders were out of line and that you have to stop stem cell research altogether.

We are appealing that. We're challenging it. And what we're going to keep on doing on a whole range of these decisions is to make sure that I'm talking to scientists and ethicists and others and try to build a commonsense consensus that allows us to make progress over the long term. Okay? Go ahead.

Small-Business Loans/Job Growth Legislation

Q. Mr. President, it's a privilege for me to be here. You talk about the small-business loans. My company is a high-tech company. And we are growing, and we are providing high-tech jobs for Americans. How can we ensure that banking and lending institutions are going to actually lend money to small businesses? There have been numbers of steps done in that way, but so far I've been denied a loan twice and only got the—for the third time after I asked for SBA-backed loan.

The President. Right. Tell me more about your business, by the way. I've actually read about it. But tell—people here, I think, would be interested, because you're working in—on clean energy issues and——

Q. This is correct, yes. I have two lines of business. Clean energy part, where we are actually trying to get companies to become green and change their practices so that they follow a sustainability practice as the regular ways, and the second part of my business is high tech. We are doing IT consulting and IT services for Federal Government and Fortune 500 companies.

The President. How many employees do you have right now?

Q. About 94.

The President. Ninety-four?

Q. Yes.

The President. Well, look, part of the answer is what you already spoke about, which is SBA, the Small Business Administration. We have doubled the number of small-business loans that we've been giving through the SBA. We've waived a lot of fees on those loans, because we knew that small businesses were getting harder hit than just about anybody during the financial crisis. They were the ones where the banks were pulling back the most. So we tried to fill that void as the banks were getting well, making sure the small businesses could keep their doors open.

But even by doubling the number of SBA loans, there's still not enough capital to meet all the demand for small businesses across the country.

That's why this bill that we're looking to pass this week out of the Senate, and that Gerry and Jim already voted for, is so important, because what it would do is it would take funding authorization to provide to community banks, who are most likely to give loans to small businesses, but it would say to those banks, you know what, we're going to hold you accountable for actually lending the money. So—because what we don't want to do is just help the banks boost their balance sheets, but they're never getting the money out of the door.

Over the long term, we think that there are going to be enormous opportunities for banks to make money with businesses like yours, because yours are the ones that grow. But they're still feeling gun shy because of what happened on Wall Street.

And in fairness to a lot of the community banks, they weren't the ones who were making big bets on derivatives, but they were punished nonetheless. They've been hit really hard in the housing market. They've been hit on their portfolios. They've been trying to strengthen their portfolios. But when we provide these loan guarantees through the SBA, or we provide cheaper money to them that they can then lend out, and as long as we're monitoring them to make sure that they actually lend those monies to small businesses, they're the ones that are most likely to get that money out the door.

This bill is very important. It has been held up now for a couple of months unnecessarily. There was an article in the USA Today just about 3 weeks ago that said small businesses were actually holding off on hiring because they weren't sure whether some of these tax cuts that they were going to get, as well as some of these lending facilities, would actually be set up.

And you hear some of my friends on the Republican side complaining that, well, we'd get more business investment if we had more certainty. Well, here's an example where we could give some certainty right away. Pass this bill. I will sign it into law the day after it's passed or the day it is passed. And then right away I think a lot of small businesses around the country will feel more comfortable about hiring and making investments.

Q. Well, this is what's happening right now is that, you know, I have contracts, and I am ready to hire 20 more people.

The President. Right.

Q. But nobody is going to give me additional loan right now. I mean, I had an off-the-record conversation with the vice president of one bank, and they said, it's simply we've made a decision not to loan to small businesses; it's simply more profitable to us to invest this money elsewhere.

The President. Well, that's why it's so important to make sure that if they are getting help from us in terms of having more money to lend, that they actually lend it out and they lend it to small businesses. And we've got to make a direct link between the help that they're getting and them actually lending the money. That's going to be critical.

All right, who's next? Yes, over here.

Preserving U.S. Historic Sites and Natural Resources/Energy-Efficient Buildings

Q. I'm John's sister Wendy.

The President. Hey, Wendy. How are you?

Q. I'm so honored and delighted to be here. Thank you.

The President. You must be John's younger sister.

Q. Yes, definitely, definitely. [*Laughter*]

The President. That's what I figured.

Q. No, he's my kid brother. And I actually am the stringer in from Boston with that hockey team you're meeting with this afternoon.

The President. There you go. Yes, I'm looking forward to congratulating them.

Q. I would tell you just a little story, which is, when I was in high school here at Woodson High School, I got involved in historic preservation. And I worked on an archeology dig. I researched the history of an old house. I helped move the one-room Legato schoolhouse from out in the country into town hall to restore it as a piece of our county's history. And that launched my lifelong career in historic preservation. And so I guess—and I know you are interested in history and have studied particularly, I think I've read, President Lincoln and the way he created a Cabinet and so on. So I know you

value our Nation's history. And I guess my question for you is, what are your thoughts about what we're doing in your administration to invest in preserving our Nation's history and our historic places?

And one little job-generating idea I'd give you is that all the studies show that renovating existing buildings, restoring historic buildings is more labor intensive than materials intensive. It creates more jobs. They're local jobs for local people. So I hope that might be part of your jobs strategy.

The President. Well, I am a huge booster of historic preservation. If I wasn't, Michelle would get on me, because she used to actually used to—in Chicago, used to be on the historic—on the landmark commission there. And we live in a landmark district in Chicago. So this is something that we care deeply about.

I guess I'd broaden the point to say that not only should we be thinking about historic preservation, but we should also be thinking about our national parks, our national forests. There's this treasure that we inherited from the previous generation, dating back to Teddy Roosevelt. And that requires us to continually renew that commitment to our historic structures and our natural resource base, so that when Trevor and Olivia and those guys have their kids, when you guys have your grandkids, that that stuff is there for them too.

So we have actually tried to ramp up our commitment to these issues. We've, where we can, put a little bit more money into it. But a lot of it's not just more money, it's also more planning. And the Recovery Act gave a range of grants to State and local governments in some cases around preservation issues.

Now, one point—one other point I want to make, though—and you were mentioning how renovation oftentimes will actually generate more jobs than new construction. A related idea is what we can do to make our existing buildings and housing stock more energy efficient, because it turns out that we could probably cut about a third of our total energy use just on efficiency. We wouldn't need new technologies. We wouldn't need to invent some fancy new fusion energy or anything. If we just took our existing building stock in homes and insulated them, had new windows—schools, hospitals, a lot of big institutions—we could squeeze huge efficiencies out of that.

There's a lot of ways to be had, and that would benefit everybody. It would mean that over time, we were helping to save the planet by reducing our carbon footprint. People would be paying less on their electricity bills and their heating bills and their air-conditioning bills. So it helps consumers.

The problem—the reason we haven't done more of this is because it requires some capital on the front end. I mean, a lot of school districts, for example, would love to retrofit their schools, but they're having problems just keeping teachers on payroll right now, so they always put off those investments.

And one of the things that we tried to do through the Recovery Act, and something that I know that Gerry and Jim have been interested in, is something called Home Star that we've been working on, is to essentially provide families as well as small businesses as well as institutions like schools or hospitals grants up front, where we say, all right, we're going to give you $10,000 to retrofit your building or your house. And then you're going to pay us back through your savings on utilities over a 5-year period, for example, so that over time, it doesn't cost taxpayers a lot of money, but we're essentially giving some money up front that's going to then be recouped.

And I think there are a lot of ideas that we can pursue on that front that could really make a difference and put a lot of people back to work, whether they're the folks selling the insulation at Home Depot or the small contractor that for a long time was remodeling kitchens or putting in home additions—maybe that business has dried up. This would be a new area for them to get put to work.

And about one out of four construction—one out of four jobs that have been lost during this recession are related to the construction industry in some fashion. Those folks have been hit harder than just about anybody else. This would be an important boost for them.

Q. If I could add to that just one thing, which is, it's really not necessary to replace the windows to get that energy efficiency. Didn't somebody write about the caulking gun?

The President. They—caulking is——

Q. It's a lot less expensive. [*Laughter*]

The President. Absolutely. Cash for caulkers. [*Laughter*] Good point.

All right, gentleman right there.

Labor Unions/U.S. Business Competiveness

Q. Mr. President, my name is Mark Murphy. I'm a neighbor of John and Nicole. Welcome to our neighborhood.

The President. Thank you. It's a beautiful neighborhood.

Q. And before I say anything more, I'd be remiss, and my children would be not letting me back home, if I didn't say hi to you.

The President. What are their names?

Q. Andrew, Tim, and Ellie, and my beautiful wife Shannon.

The President. Tell everybody I said hi.

Q. Thank you. Now, the question I have for you is, I'm a union-side labor attorney in DC. And I know you have some background in that. And your comments here today and both—your Labor Day comments struck me and my colleagues about the shrinking middle class and those jobs that were lost and how you're going to and your administration is going to replace those jobs.

I work every day with working class, blue-collar workers; I deal with a lot of different issues. One of the issues that is dear to my heart and, I know, a lot of my colleagues and union members is the Employee Free Choice Act. And for people who don't know about that, it's just basically an act, a law that would make it easier to unionize. And it's proven that unions—unionized employees get better wages and better benefits. And unfortunately, that act hasn't been passed yet, and I just wanted to hear your thoughts on that. Thank you.

The President. Well, the—a little bit of background, for those who aren't as familiar with it. The Employee Free Choice Act is in response to 20, 30 years where it's become more and more difficult for unions to just get a fair election and have their employers actually negotiate with them.

I mean, the laws that have been on the books have gotten more and more difficult to apply. A lot of times, companies who may be good employers, but just don't want the bother of having a union will work very hard to make sure a union doesn't develop. And they will drag out the process for a very long time, and in some cases, workers who are joining unions or want to join a union or are helping to organize one may get intimidated.

And so the idea behind the Employee Free Choice Act is, let's just make the playing field even. We don't have to force anybody to be in a union, but if they want to join a union, let's make it a little easier for them to go ahead and sign up.

Now, the answer—the short answer to your question is, we are very supportive of this. Frankly, we don't have 60 votes in the Senate. So the opportunity to actually get this passed right now is not real high. What we've done instead is try to do as much as we can administratively to make sure that it's easier for unions to operate and that they're not being placed at an unfair disadvantage.

Let me speak more broadly, though, about the point that you just made. So many things we take for granted came about because of the union movement. Minimum wage, 40-hour work week, child labor laws, you name it—weekends—a lot of these things came about because people were fighting for them. They didn't come about automatically and naturally.

The other thing that unions did, particularly in the manufacturing sector, was it gave a base for blue-collar workers to get a middle class wage, which meant that essentially the guys working at the Ford plant could afford to buy a Ford. And so it increased demand overall, and ironically, it meant that businesses had more customers and could make more money.

Now, we now live in an era of international competition. And that makes it harder for businesses. I mean, I think we should acknowledge that the business environment now is much more competitive than it was back in the 1960s or seventies. Technology has made it more diffi-

cult for businesses to compete. Transportation has made it more difficult to compete. The costs for shipping big, manufactured goods from China to the United States or high volumes of goods from Japan or Korea or Malaysia or Indonesia to the United States is a lot cheaper now than it was. So what that means is, we've got to be sympathetic to business concerns that they don't get priced out of the market if they're competing internationally.

And I think the best way to balance that is to make sure that business interests here in the United States and labor interests—workers' interests—here in the United States are aligned, make sure that businesses are looking after their workers and giving them a good deal. But workers and unions also have to think about businesses and not put them in a position where they're potentially priced out of the marketplace.

Now, I think that that balance is tilted way too far against unions these days. And I think that actually if we had some of these businesses with employees who were there for a longer term, were more loyal, they weren't worried about their jobs being shipped overseas, that that would actually be good for the economy as a whole and would be good for businesses here as a whole.

But we have to acknowledge that competition means that businesses and workers here in the United States have to be better trained, better skilled, more competitive, leaner, meaner. And we've got to invent more stuff so that we constantly are working on high-end jobs as opposed to the low-end jobs, because the truth is, the low-end jobs, we're never going to be able to compete on the basis of price. I mean, there's always going to be a country—actually, wages are starting to go up a little bit in China. Our problem is not China. The next is going to be Vietnam, or it's going to be Bangladesh or—there's always going to be someplace in the world where they pay lower wages.

Our advantage is going to be if we have higher skills, we have a workforce that works together more effectively, that our businesses are better organized—if we have that, then I think that we can compete against anybody.

And one of—a good example is actually Germany, which has a much higher rate of unionization than we do. But they've actually been able to continue to export at very high levels and compete all around the world, mainly because they've got such a highly skilled workforce; they're putting together high-end products that can compete with anybody.

Yes, right here. A mike is coming.

Education Jobs and State Funding Legislation

Q. Hi, Mr. President. It's an honor. I'm so nervous.

The President. Don't be nervous.

Q. Oh, I am so nervous. I love everything you're doing. I love your vision. I'm so glad you got into office. I love medical—health care reform. Where I come from, where—when we had to go to the doctor, we went to the doctor. If we needed surgery, we got surgery. And then I came here and found out, oh, my gosh, you need insurance—you need this, you need that—which I could never afford on the salary I make now. I'm very lucky. My husband, unfortunately, he is in the construction business, but hopefully, that's going to come back.

So my question is also—I work for Fairfax County Public Schools, and I haven't had a raise in 2 years, and I may not even have a job next year, because I hear it's going to get worse before it's going to get better. Do you agree with that? Like, I mean, I know it's—we're starting to improve and jobs are starting to come back, but how long do you think this is going to take? It sounds wonderful.

The President. Well, first of all, you have a better chance of keeping your job in the public school systems now because Gerry and Jim voted to close a pretty egregious tax loophole that was incentivizing jobs going overseas and that even some corporations that stood to benefit thought was ridiculous. They closed that loophole in order to fund teacher jobs and police officer jobs and firefighter jobs all across the country. So that's been very helpful in providing assistance to school districts that are strapped.

The economy is improving. But one of the headwinds that the economy is experiencing is actually that State and local governments have been getting really hard hit. Now, we gave States a lot of help at the beginning of this crisis because their budgets were just imploding. And typically, State and local governments, they get hit faster by declines in tax revenues and property tax. Obviously, they're relying on property taxes, and with the housing market collapsing, that was really hitting them hard. And so they were looking at possibly laying—slashing 30 percent of jobs in school districts or in social services.

And one of the most effective ways of preventing this from tipping over into a Great Depression was giving them help. The problem is, some of that help is running out. And property tax revenues haven't improved yet; sales tax revenues haven't improved yet as much as they'd like. So local districts, States are still having big budget problems, and they'll probably have those big budget problems next year.

Now the challenge we have is, ironically, that if you start laying off a whole bunch of teachers or a whole bunch of police officers or firefighters, now they don't have a job, which means they spend less, which means that there's less tax revenue. And you start getting into a vicious, downward spiral.

So that's why the steps that we took were so important. And I've got to say, this is an example of where you've just got a fundamental disagreement between Republican leadership right now and Democrats. John Boehner, who stands—wants to be the Speaker of the—the next Speaker of the House if the Republicans take over, he specifically said, well, these are just government jobs, and they're not worth saving. And he fought—he voted no on closing this tax loophole that was incentivizing jobs from going overseas.

Now, it's just not smart from an economic perspective for us to allow a whole bunch of those jobs that are right here in the United States to go away while we're giving tax revenue away to companies that are creating jobs somewhere else. It just doesn't make sense.

And so we're going to continue to have some of these battles over the next several years. And I think that, frankly, how State and local governments are able to deal with these budget challenges next year is in part going to depend on whether the people who are making the decisions are Jim and Gerry or whether they're John Boehner, because they've just got a different set of priorities. And I don't know about you, but I like these guys making these decisions more than the other folks. But that's just my unbiased opinion.

All right. Yes, go ahead.

Bipartisan Cooperation

Q. Mr. President, thank you so much for visiting us here in Mantua. It's quite an honor.

The President. Thank you.

Q. I think my question is kind of a good segue on that. We do face—the political environment has changed a lot since you were elected. And I think with the upcoming midterm elections, you can certainly expect a lot of new faces in Congress, and certainly a lot of the new Representatives and Senators are going to have been elected on platforms that are really opposed to Government intervention in the economy. What's your plan for working with the new Congress to make sure we get the actions that are—you see are necessary to end the recession? And what do you see as really common ground with Republicans in Congress for some of the solutions that can bring the recession to an end?

The President. Well, let me just say that I don't believe in wholesale Government intervention in the economy. My starting point is, is that what makes us the wealthiest, most dynamic country on Earth is a free-market system where small-business owners are creating jobs, and what start off as small businesses like AOL end up being big businesses, and some kid at Harvard starts something called Facebook, and the next thing you know, it's revolutionized part of our economy. That's our strength.

So that's a starting point where Republicans and Democrats should be able to come together. We all believe in that.

But there are some fundamental differences. At the beginning of the crisis, for Government not to intervene when the financial system was on the verge of meltdown and we were shedding hundreds of thousands of jobs a month and the credit markets had just frozen completely— for us not to intervene in that situation would have been simply irresponsible. And I don't know a economist, Democrat or Republican, who would suggest otherwise. It would have been simply irresponsible.

So that's—so some of these steps that we had to take had to do with emergency situations. A great example is the auto industry. When we decided to intervene—keep this in mind: We had been bailing out the auto industry for years under the previous administration. The difference was, we hadn't ever asked them anything in return. So they kept on with their bad practices, creating cars that, frankly, in this kind of energy environment, weren't the cars of the future. And they never changed their practices.

So what we said was, you know what, we're going to help you, but this time we're going to help you by also restructuring. And we're going to bring all the stakeholders together—the workers, management, shareholders—and we're going to say, if taxpayers are going to help you out, you've got to change how you do business. And they have. And they emerged from bankruptcy, and now you've got all three U.S. auto companies operating at a profit.

If we had not taken that step, we would have lost a million jobs in the auto industry. You would not have an auto—maybe Ford might have survived. GM and Chrysler definitely would not have. And the ripple effects on the economy would have been devastating.

So sometimes you make these decisions not because you believe in Government intervention, per se. You make these decisions because we've got a crisis, and we've got to respond.

Now, right now we've got a disagreement also on taxes. Jim, Gerry, the vast majority of Democrats think that because wages and incomes had flatlined for middle class families, which we define as less than $250,000 a year, that they should definitely get an extension of the tax cuts that were instituted in 2001, 2003.

Now, keep in mind that if you make more than $250,000 a year, you'd still get a tax cut. It's just you'd only get it up to your first $250,000. So if you make half a million dollars a year, you'd still get tax relief on the first half of your income. If you made a million, it would be the first quarter of your income. After that, you'd go back to the rates that were in place when Bill Clinton was President, which I just want to remind everybody, at that time we had 22 million jobs created, much faster income and wage growth; the economy was humming pretty good.

We could get that done this week. But we're still in this wrestling match with John Boehner and Mitch McConnell about the last 2 to 3 percent, where, on average, we'd be giving them $100,000 for people making a million dollars or more, which in and of itself would be okay, except to do it, we'd have to borrow $700 billion over the course of 10 years. And we just can't afford it.

Now, I wanted to lay out those differences before I talked about where I think we can work together. Where I think we have a great opportunity to work together is on the issue of our long-term debt.

Our big challenge right now is creating jobs and making sure the economy takes off. And the steps that we've been taking, including cutting taxes for small businesses, providing loans for small businesses, accelerating depreciation, those steps can encourage investment right now. They cost some money, but they're wise investments because right now our number-one focus has to be jobs, jobs, jobs, and encouraging business investment. But on the horizon, sort of in the middle term and the long term, we do have a very real problem with debt and deficits.

And I have to say that I understand a lot of people who are upset on the other side. And some of them were rallying in DC today—or yesterday. I do understand people's legitimate fears about are we hocking our future to—because we're borrowing so much to finance debt and deficits. I understand that. They saw the Recovery Act. They saw TARP. They saw the auto bailout. They look at this and—God, all these huge numbers adding up. So they're right to be concerned about that.

And I think that there's an opportunity for Democrats and Republicans to come together and to say, what are the tough decisions we've got to make right now that won't squash the re-covery, won't lead to huge numbers of teacher layoffs—short term we don't want to constrict too much early, but how can we get ourselves on a trajectory where midterm and long term we're starting to bring our debt and deficits slowly under control?

Now, I set up a bipartisan fiscal commission that's designed to start coming up with answers. And they're supposed to report back to me right after the election. That was on purpose, by the way. We said, don't give us the answer before the election because nobody will have an honest conversation about it, everybody will posture politically. But as soon as the election is over, report to us, and let's see if Democrats and Republicans can come together to make some tough decisions. And by the way, they are going to be some tough decisions.

People, I think, have a sense that somehow if we just eliminated a few pork projects and foreign aid, that somehow we would solve our debt. The big problem with our debt is actually the costs of Medicare and Medicaid. Our health care system is by far the thing that is exploding faster than anything. And as the population gets older and it's using more health care services, if we don't get control of that, we can't control our long-term debt. That's why health care reform was so important, because we're trying to rationalize and make the system smarter, but that's only one piece of it. We've also got to look at everything from defense budgets to food stamps. You name it, we've got to look at it and see are there ways that we can reduce our costs over the long term.

But we can't give away $700 billion to folks who don't need it and think somehow that we're going to balance our budget. It's not going to happen. That's one area where I think we can make progress.

A second area where I hope we can still make progress is on energy. Everybody agrees our energy policy doesn't make sense. We don't have an energy policy. We've talked about it since Richard Nixon. Remember OPEC, '73, and oil lines at the gas station? And every President has said this is a national security issue, this is a crisis, we've got to do something about it. But we don't do anything about it.

So my suggestion is, let's both do—let's join hands, Democrats and Republicans, and go ahead and take the leap and try to solve this problem. And there's not a silver bullet, there's not one magic solution to our energy problems. We're going to have to use a bunch of different strategies.

I already mentioned efficiency. That has to be a huge push. With respect to transportation sector, one of the things that we did without legislation—nobody has really noticed this, but this was huge—we increased fuel efficiency standards on cars for the first time in 30 years—cars and trucks. And we got the car companies and auto workers to agree to it, not just environmentalists. That's going to help.

We've got to look at nuclear energy. Historically, a lot of environmentalists have said, oh, we don't like nuclear energy. There are real problems with storage, et cetera. But if we're concerned about global warming and greenhouse gases, nuclear energy is a legitimate fuel—energy source that the Japanese and the French have been using much more intelligently than we have. We've got huge reservoirs of natural gas that are relatively clean, but we've got to use those in a environmentally sound way. We've got to develop those in a environmentally sound way. So that's an area where I think that we can still, hopefully, make some progress.

And the last thing I'll say—and some people disagree with me on this. They think it's too incendiary, it's too politically difficult, et cetera. I think we need to reform our immigration system, and we should be able to find a way that secures our borders and provides people who are already here a pathway so that they are out of the shadows. They're paying a fine. They're learning English. They're getting assimilated, but they're not living in fear. We should be able to do that.

And we had 11 Republican Senators who voted for it, including John McCain was a cosponsor of the bill. We should be able to get that done again, because everybody agrees that the system we've got right now is broken.

And one last thing I wanted to mention is actually education. The reason I didn't mention it up front is this has been one of the few areas where I've actually gotten some compliments from Republicans. I think the strategy that we have right now, which is to maintain high standards, work with States in a smart way to develop a—curriculums, teacher-training strategies, to boost our higher education—institutions of higher education, that's an area where we should all agree. Because it's indisputable that if we are working smarter, if our kids are better trained, then we will succeed. And if they're not, it doesn't really matter what else we do. Over time, we're going to decline.

All right, I've got time for one more question. I'm going to call on this young lady right here.

National Economy

Q. I'm really nervous. Thank you, Mr. President, for being here. There's a lot of people sending you a lot of good energy, one being my 82-year-old aunt. She wanted me to make sure I told her—told you that.

The President. Tell her I said hi.

Q. Okay. I'm a massage therapist, and I'm——

The President. I've got a crick in my neck right here. [*Laughter*]

Q. Yes, I bet you do.

The President. A lot of tension has been building up. [*Laughter*]

Q. Do you get regular massage? [*Laughter*]

The President. Go ahead, go ahead.

Q. One prevailing theme that comes here in my practice is fear. And on an energetic level, what I would like to see you institute or get started, bipartisan, is to alleviate people's fears of spending $5. I know this is like—it sounds so basic. But if we go out there and spend a little bit, it's going to come back around. It works. I mean, you've got a program here where you've got—you're giving a tax break to those companies that hire the returning vets.

The President. Right.

Q. You have a $2,400 tax break.

The President. Right.

Q. Well, who are those companies? I would patronize a company that's making the effort of going out and hiring these people. I mean, you've got to spend it to get it back.

The President. Well, the—look——

Q. And there's just this prevailing fear all the time, and it doesn't have—it comes down to $5, $10, whatever, you got to put it out there, and it will start the momentum going.

The President. Right.

Q. It would also be some good news.

The President. Well, look, I think you are absolutely right that some of this is psychology. Look, the country went through a huge trauma. The body politic is like an individual in the sense that if they go through a really bad accident and you're in a cast and got a little whiplashed and bruised and battered, it takes some time to recover. And that's what happened to our economy. We went through a really bad accident.

It was a preventable one, by the way. If we had had some more rules of the road in place, if we'd had better economic policies, we could have prevented it. But it is what it is. We went through this.

You're absolutely right, though, that now part of what's holding us back is us needing to go ahead and feel confident about the future. Now, that's not the only thing holding us back. Let's be realistic. Part of the reason people aren't spending is they had maxed out on their credit cards, and people, quite sensibly, said to themselves, you know what, this is probably a good time for us to reflect on the fact that we were buying a bunch of stuff that maybe we should get in the future but we weren't quite there yet and we should run down our debts. And people have done that. People have been paying down their debts a lot more over the last year than they had in the previous 5 or 10 years.

A lot of people were borrowing against their homes—home equity loans. One of the things that I always—Michelle and I always laugh about is when people talk about us, I think they forget that we were basically living the same lives as John and Nicole, just—it wasn't that long ago. It was like 6, 7 years ago. I still remember the first time I refinanced our—we had a condo, and we had gotten higher—initially, we had gotten higher rates. And then—because we bought it in 1993. And sometime around '97 or '98—I don't remember exactly when—the rates had gone down like a couple of percent. And we said, well, it makes sense for us to go to refinance.

And I still remember talking to the bank. And they said, you can refinance, and you can take some money out. And I said, well, what does that mean? They said, well, your house—your condo has appreciated so much that you can take—it's like found money.

And I remember thinking at the time, well, that doesn't sound right. [*Laughter*] But it was—but that was—everybody, I think, was so certain that homes were appreciating and they would always appreciate, and so it just made everybody feel a lot richer.

Now, homes suddenly start dropping in value. You don't have that kind of equity. And so people feel a little bit less wealthy; 401(k)s still haven't fully recovered; 529s, the college portfolios that people put together, they still haven't fully recovered. So there are legitimate and real reasons why people have pulled back a little bit.

But having said all that, I want to end on the point that you're making, which is that we have averted the worst. The economy is now growing. There are enormous opportunities out there. There are people who are inventing stuff that will be the new products of the future all across this country. There are young people who, when I meet them, they are talented and they're energetic and they feel confident about America.

If you travel overseas, as tough as this recession has been for us, the truth of the matter is, is that most countries still envy the United States. And there are billions of people around the world who would die to be here and have that opportunity to prosper and be part of this great middle class of ours.

And so my hope is—and this goes to the question of the previous gentleman—what can Republicans and Democrats do together after this election is stop spending so much time attacking the other side and spend a little more time focusing on what's good and what's right about America and what opportunities we have. And if we do that, then I'm absolutely confident that we're going to move forward for a long time to come.

Thank you very much, everybody. God bless you.

NOTE: The President spoke at 1:55 p.m. at the residence of Nicole Armstrong and John Nicholas. In his remarks, he referred to Trevor and Olivia Nicholas, children of Ms. Armstrong and Mr. Nicholas; Royce C. Lamberth, chief judge, Federal District Court for the District of Columbia; and Mark E. Zuckerberg, founder and chief executive officer, Facebook.

Remarks to NCAA Championship Teams
September 13, 2010

Hello, everybody. Well, it's good to see—boy, this is a healthy-looking group here. [*Laughter*] It is wonderful to see you. Welcome to the White House.

I want to thank all the teams that have traveled from all over the country to be here, and congratulations on being NCAA champions. We've got over 650 athletes and almost 150 coaches and staff here today. This is the most athletic talent we've ever had on the South Lawn.

We've got the sharpshooters from TCU rifle squad. Where are they? There they are down there. I think they might be able to give Secret Service a run for their money. [*Laughter*] We've got the Fairleigh Dickinson bowling team here. I need some tips, guys. [*Laughter*] You might be able to tell me how to get my score up.

I want to recognize Ambassador Ron Kirk, who's a big Texas Longhorns fan. He's our Ambassador for trade. We've got a lot of Members of Congress who are here, local officials who are with us. And I know they are incredibly proud of the trophies that all of you brought home. I want to thank the NCAA interim president, Jim Isch, for everything he's doing to support so many outstanding student-athletes. Give Jim a big round of applause.

Now, that term, "student-athlete," is the thing that makes me so proud to stand before you here today, because when each of you won the titles that you won, whether it was in lacrosse or gymnastics or wheelchair basketball, you didn't do it as professionals. You didn't have multimillion-dollar contracts or huge endorsement deals. You woke up early. You put in countless hours of practice for the love of the game and for the pride of your school. You rode those buses and you carried those bags because you knew what it was going to take to be the best and because every one of you has a competitive streak that's about a mile wide.

And most impressive of all, you did this while shouldering a full load of classes, sometimes grabbing a few minutes to study in airports or locker rooms, because you understand that "student-athlete" emphasizes "student" and not just "athlete."

So this is a group that knows what it means to be a champion. You also understand that being a champion means giving back to the folks who gave so much to you: the fans and the students who braved the heat and the rain and the snow to see you play, the communities that adopted you as one of their own.

And that's why I'm so proud to hear about all the ways that you've found to improve the lives of those around you. I know that one team here cooks dinner for the families of children suffering from serious illnesses. Another holds a track meet every year for more than 300 students with physical and mental disabilities. Together, you guys have organized blood drives, built houses, cleaned up beaches, and reached out to senior citizens. One young man even donated bone marrow to a little girl he had never met. And as he said, "Saving someone's life is a lot more important than a football game."

It's the kind of selfless attitude that's going to stay with you for the rest of your lives. And that's incredibly important, because for the vast majority of you, the day will come, and it will probably be sooner than you like, when you won't be known primarily as a hockey player or a tennis player or a baseball player anymore. Instead, you're going to be known as a doctor or a lawyer or a teacher or a nurse, a businessperson, a mom or a dad. And I'm confident that you're going to excel at that just as you've excelled at everything that you do.

No matter what you do, no matter where you end up, you will always know in your heart what it means to be the best there is at what you do. You'll always know what it's like to set a goal and then reach it, what it feels like to hit your limit and then go beyond it, to get to the top and turn around and give others a hand.

In other words, you're always going to know what it means to compete and what it means to be a champion. That's something that nobody will ever be able to take away from you. And that is something that you should be extraordinarily proud of.

So I'm thrilled to have a chance to meet all of you. You guys don't just make your communities proud, but you make America proud. God bless you. God bless the United States of America.

Thank you very much, everybody. Thank you.

NOTE: The President spoke at 5:46 p.m. on the South Lawn at the White House. In his remarks, he referred to Matthew Szczur, wide receiver, Villanova University football team.

Letter to the Speaker of the House of Representatives Transmitting Fiscal Year 2011 Budget Amendments
September 13, 2010

Dear Madam Speaker:

I ask the Congress to consider the enclosed Fiscal Year (FY) 2011 Budget amendments for the Department of the Interior. Overall, the discretionary budget authority proposed in my FY 2011 Budget would not be increased by these requests.

These amendments are necessary to strengthen oversight of offshore oil and gas operations, address deficiencies in mineral revenue collec-

tion, and facilitate the reorganization of the Bureau of Ocean Energy Management, Regulation, and Enforcement—formerly known as the Minerals Management Service.

The details of these requests are set forth in the enclosed letter from the Acting Director of the Office of Management and Budget.

Sincerely,

BARACK OBAMA

Remarks at Julia R. Masterman Laboratory and Demonstration School in Philadelphia, Pennsylvania
September 14, 2010

Thank you. Well, hello, Philadelphia, and hello, Masterman. It is wonderful to see all of you. What a terrific introduction by Kelly. Give Kelly a big round of applause. I was saying backstage that when I was in high school, I could not have done that. [*Laughter*] I would have muffed it up somehow. [*Laughter*] So we are so proud of you and everything that you've done. And to all the students here, I'm thrilled to be here.

Now, we've got a couple introductions I want to make. First of all, you've got the outstanding Governor of Pennsylvania, Ed Rendell, in the house. The mayor of Philadelphia, Michael

Nutter, is here. Congressman Chaka Fattah is here. Congresswoman Allyson Schwartz is here. Your own principal, Marge Neff, is here. The school superintendent, Arlene Ackerman, is here and doing a great job. And the Secretary of Education, Arne Duncan, is here.

And I am here. And I am thrilled to be here. I am just so excited. I've heard such great things about what all of you are doing, both the students and the teachers and the staff here.

Today is about welcoming all of you and all of America's students back to school, even though I know you've been in school for a little bit now. And I can't think of a better place to do it than at Masterman, because you are one of the best schools in Philadelphia. You are a leader in helping students succeed in the classroom. Just last week, you were recognized by a National Blue Ribbon—as a National Blue Ribbon School because of your record of achievement. And that is a testament to everybody here, to the students, to the parents, to the teachers, to the school leaders. It's an example of excellence that I hope communities across America can embrace.

Over the past few weeks, Michelle and I have been getting Sasha and Malia ready for school. And they're excited about it. I'll bet they had the same feelings that you do. You're a little sad to see the summer go, but you're also excited about the possibilities of a new year: the possibilities of building new friendships and strengthening old ones, of joining a school club or trying out for a team; the possibilities of growing into a better student and a better person and making not just your family proud, but making yourself proud.

But I know some of you may also be a little nervous about starting a new school year. Maybe you're making the jump from elementary to middle school or from middle school to high school and you're worried about what that's going to be like. Maybe you're starting a new school. You're not sure how you'll like it, trying to figure out how you're going to fit in. Or maybe you're a senior and you're anxious about the whole college process, about where to apply and whether you can afford to go to college.

And beyond all those concerns, I know a lot of you are also feeling the strain of some difficult times. You know what's going on in the news, and you also know what's going on in some of your own families. You've read about the war in Afghanistan. You hear about the recession that we've been through. And sometimes maybe you're seeing the worries in your parents' faces or sense it in their voice.

So a lot of you as a consequence, because we're going through a tough time as a country, are having to act a lot older than you are. You got to be strong for your family while your brother or sister is serving overseas, or you've got to look after younger siblings while your mom is working that second shift, or maybe some of you who are a little bit older, you're taking on a part-time job while your dad's out of work.

And that's a lot to handle. It's more than you should have to handle. And it may make you wonder at times what your own future will look like, whether you're going to be able to succeed in school, whether you should maybe set your sights a little lower, scale back your dreams.

But I came to Masterman to tell all of you what I think you're hearing from your principal and your superintendent and from your parents and from your teachers: Nobody gets to write your destiny but you. Your future is in your hands. Your life is what you make of it. And nothing, absolutely nothing is beyond your reach. So long as you're willing to dream big, so long as you're willing to work hard, so long as you're willing to stay focused on your education, there is not a single thing that any of you cannot accomplish, not a single thing. I believe that.

And that last part is absolutely essential, that part about really working hard in school, because an education has never been more important than it is today. I'm sure there are going to be times in the months ahead when you're staying up late doing your homework or cramming for a test or you're dragging yourself out of bed on a rainy morning and you're thinking, oh, boy, I wish maybe it was a snow day. [*Laughter*]

But let me tell you, what you're doing is worth it. There is nothing more important than what you're doing right now. Nothing is going to have as great an impact on your success in life as your education, how you're doing in school.

More and more, the kinds of opportunities that are open to you are going to be determined by how far you go in school. The farther you go in school, the farther you're going to go in life. And at a time when other countries are competing with us like never before, when students around the world—in Beijing, China, or Bangalore, India—are working harder than ever and doing better than ever, your success in school is not just going to determine your success, it's going to determine America's success in the 21st century.

So you've got an obligation to yourselves and America has an obligation to you to make sure you're getting the best education possible. And making sure you get that kind of education is going to take all of us working hard and all of us working hand in hand.

It takes all of us in government, from the Governor to the mayor to the superintendent to the President, all of us doing our part to prepare our students, all of them, for success in the classroom and in college and in a career. It's going to take an outstanding principal, like Principal Neff, and outstanding teachers like the ones you have here at Masterman, teachers who are going above and beyond the call of duty for their students. And it's going to take parents who are committed to your education.

Now, that's what we have to do for you. That's our responsibility. That's our job. But you've got a job too. You've got to show up to school on time. You've got to pay attention in your class. You've got to do your homework. You've got to study for exams. You've got to stay out of trouble. You've got to instill a sense of excellence in everything that you do. That kind of discipline, that kind of drive, that kind of hard work is absolutely essential for success.

And I can speak from experience here, because unlike Kelly, I can't say I always had this discipline. See, I can tell she was always disciplined. I wasn't always disciplined. I wasn't always the best student when I was younger. I made my share of mistakes. I still remember a conversation I had with my mother in high school. I was kind of a goof-off. And I was about the age of some of the folks here. And my grades were slipping. I hadn't started my college applications. I was acting, as my mother put it, sort of casual about my future. I was doing good enough. I was smart enough that I could kind of get by. But I wasn't really applying myself.

And so I suspect this is a conversation that will sound familiar to some students and some parents here today. She decided to sit me down and said I had to change my attitude. My attitude was what I imagine every teenager's attitude is when your parents have this conversation with you like that. I was like, you know, I don't need to hear all this. I'm doing okay; I'm not flunking out.

So I started to say that, and she just cut me right off. She said, you can't just sit around waiting for luck to see you through. She said, you can get into any school you want in the country if you just put in a little bit of effort. And she gave me a hard look, and she said, you remember what that's like? Effort? [*Laughter*] Some of you have had that conversation. [*Laughter*] And it was pretty jolting hearing my mother say that.

But eventually, her words had the intended effect, because I got serious about my studies. And I started to make an effort in everything that I did. And I began to see my grades and my prospects improve.

And I know that if hard work could make the difference for me, then it can make a difference for all of you. And I know that there may be some people who are skeptical about that. Sometimes you may wonder if some people just aren't better at certain things. You know, well, I'm not good at math, or I'm just not really interested in my science classes.

And it is true that we each have our own gifts, we each have our own talents that we have to discover and nurture. Not everybody is going to catch on in certain subjects as easily as others. But just because you're not the best at something today doesn't mean you can't be tomorrow. Even if you don't think of yourself as a math person or a science person, you can still excel in those subjects if you're willing to make the effort. And you may find out you have talents you never dreamed of.

Because one of the things I've discovered is excelling, whether it's in school or in life, isn't mainly about being smarter than everybody else. That's not really the secret to success. It's about working harder than everybody else. So don't avoid new challenges, seek them out. Step out of your comfort zone. Don't be afraid to ask for help. Your teachers and your family are there to guide you. They want to know if you're not catching on to something, because they know that if you keep on working at it, you're going to catch on.

Don't feel discouraged. Don't give up if you don't succeed at something the first time. Try again, and learn from your mistakes. Don't feel threatened if your friends are doing well. Be proud of them, and see what lessons you can draw from what they're doing right.

Now, I'm sort of preaching to the choir here, because I know that's the kind of culture of excellence that you promote at Masterman. But I'm not just speaking to all of you. I'm speaking to kids all across the country. And I want them to all here that same message: That's the kind of excellence we've got to promote in all of America's schools.

That's one of the reasons why I'm announcing our second Commencement Challenge. Some of you may have heard of this. If your school is the winner, if you show us how teachers and students and parents are all working together to prepare your kids and your school for college and a career, if you show us how you're giving back to your community and your country, then I will congratulate you in person by speaking at your commencement.

Last year, I was in Michigan at Kalamazoo and had just a wonderful time. Although I got to admit, their graduating class was about 700 kids, and my hands were really sore at the end of it— [*laughter*]—because I was shaking all of them.

But the truth is, an education is about more than getting into a good college. It's about more than getting a good job when you graduate. It's about giving each and every one of us the chance to fulfill our promise and to be the best version of ourselves we can be. And part of that means treating others the way we want to be treated, with kindness and respect. So that's something else that I want to communicate to students not just here at Masterman, but all across the country.

Sometimes, kids can be mean to other kids. Let's face it, we don't always treat each other with respect and kindness. That's true for adults as well, by the way.

And sometimes that's especially true in middle school or high school, because being a teenager isn't easy. It's a time when you're wrestling with a lot of things. When I was in my teens, I was wrestling with all sorts of questions about who I was. I had a White mother and a Black father, and my father wasn't around; he had left

when I was 2. And so there were all kinds of issues that I was dealing with. Some of you may be working through your own questions right now and coming to terms with what makes you different.

And I know that figuring out all of that can be even more difficult when you've got bullies in a class who try to use those differences to pick on you or poke fun at you or to make you feel bad about yourself.

And in some places, the problem is even more serious. There are neighborhoods in my hometown of Chicago and there are neighborhoods right here in Philadelphia where kids are doing each other serious harm.

So what I want to say to every kid, every young person, what I want all of you—if you take away one thing from my speech, I want you to take away the notion that life is precious, and part of what makes it so wonderful is its diversity, that all of us are different. And we shouldn't be embarrassed by the things that make us different. We should be proud of them, because it's the thing that makes us different that makes us who we are, that makes us unique. And the strength and the character of this country has always come from our ability to recognize—no matter who we are, no matter where we come from, no matter what we look like, no matter what abilities we have—to recognize ourselves in each other.

I was reminded of that the other day when I read a letter from Tamerria Robinson. She's a 12-year-old girl in Georgia. And she told me about how hard she works and about all the community service she does with her brother. And she wrote, "I try to achieve my dreams and help others do the same." "That," she said, "is how the world should work." That's a pretty good motto: I work hard to achieve my goals, and then I try to help others to achieve their goals.

And I agree with Tamerria. That's how the world should work. But it's only going to work that way if all of you get into good habits while you're in school. So yes, each of us need to work hard. We all have to take responsibilities for our own education. We need to take responsibility for our own lives. But what makes us who we are is that here, in this country, in the United States of America, we don't just reach for our own dreams, we try to help others do the same. This is a country that gives all its daughters and all of its sons a fair chance, a chance to make the most of their lives and fulfill their God-given potential.

And I'm absolutely confident that if all of our students here at Masterman and across this country keep doing their part, if you guys work hard and you're focused on your education and you keep fighting for your dreams and then you help each other reach each other's dreams, then you're not only going to succeed this year, you're going to succeed for the rest of your lives. And that means America will succeed in the 21st century.

So my main message to all of you here today: I couldn't be prouder of you. Keep it up. All of you, I know, are going to do great things in the future. And maybe some time in the 21st century, it's going to be one of you that's standing up here speaking to a group of kids as President of the United States.

Thank you. God bless you, and God bless the United States of America. Thank you.

NOTE: The President spoke at 1:05 p.m. In his remarks, he referred to Kelly Ca, student body president, Julia R. Masterman Laboratory and Demonstration School.

Statement on the Iranian Government's Release of Sarah Shourd
September 14, 2010

I am very pleased that Sarah Shourd has been released by the Iranian Government and will soon be united with her family. All Americans join with her courageous mother and family in celebrating her long-awaited return home. We are grateful to the Swiss, the Sultanate of Oman, and other friends and allies around the world who have worked tirelessly and admirably over the past several months to bring about this joyous reunion.

While Sarah has been released, Shane Bauer and Josh Fattal remain prisoners in Iran who have committed no crime. We remain hopeful that Iran will demonstrate renewed compassion by ensuring the return of Shane, Josh, and all the other missing or detained Americans in Iran. We salute the courage and strength of the Shourd, Bauer, and Fattal families, who have endured the unimaginable absence of their loved ones. We have gained strength from their resolve and will continue do everything we can to secure the release of their loved ones.

NOTE: The statement referred to Nora Shourd, mother of Sarah Shourd, an American citizen detained by Iranian authorities since July 31, 2009.

Statement on Senate Action on Small-Business Legislation
September 14, 2010

Today's vote brings us one step closer to ending the months-long partisan blockade of a small-business jobs bill that was written by both Democrats and Republicans. This is a bill that would cut taxes and help provide loans to millions of small-business owners, who create most of the new jobs in this country. It is fully paid for, it won't add to the deficit, and small businesses across the country have been waiting for Washington to act on this bill for far too long. I am grateful to Senators Reid, Baucus, and Landrieu for their leadership on this issue, as well as the two Republican Senators who put partisanship aside and joined Democrats in overcoming this filibuster. I urge all Members of the Senate to support final passage as soon as possible.

NOTE: The statement referred to Sens. George V. Voinovich and George S. LeMieux. The statement also referred to H.R. 5297.

Memorandum on the Accountable Government Initiative
September 14, 2010

Memorandum for the Senior Executive Service

Subject: Accountable Government Initiative

When I first campaigned for President, I said I wanted to change the way Washington works so that it works for the American people. That is why my Administration has undertaken the Accountable Government Initiative—to cut waste and make Government more open and responsive to the American public.

This is not just about lines on a spreadsheet or numbers in a budget. When Government does not work like it should, it has a real effect on people's lives—on small business owners who need loans, on young people who want to go to college, on the men and women in our Armed Forces who need the best resources when in uniform and deserve the benefits they have earned after they have left.

As the most senior managers in the Federal Government, you know how essential the work you and your colleagues do is to the Nation. You also are aware what happens when your best efforts are thwarted by outdated technologies and outmoded ways of doing business. You understand the consequences of accepting billions of dollars in waste as the cost of doing business and of allowing obsolete or under-performing programs to continue year after year.

Working together, we can change that, and the attached memo gives you an update on those efforts.

I have tasked our Chief Performance Officer, Jeff Zients, with leading the Accountable Government Initiative, and I have asked him to give me regular updates about our progress in making Government more efficient and effective. I know the Office of Management and Budget will be looking to you for feedback on how our efforts are faring, and what more we can do to cut waste and modernize Government.

Thank you for your work on this initiative and for your service to our country.

BARACK OBAMA

Remarks on Small-Business Legislation and Tax Reform
September 15, 2010

Good afternoon, everybody. I just met with my Cabinet and members of my economic team, and I wanted to speak about a few developments concerning our ongoing efforts to strengthen the economy and the middle class.

After months of partisan blockade in the Senate, we are finally on the verge of passing a small-business jobs bill that will cut taxes and provide loans for millions of small-business owners across America.

And while I am grateful for this progress, it should not have taken this long to pass this bill. At a time when small-business owners are still struggling to make payroll and they're still holding off hiring, we put together a plan that would give them some tax relief and make it easier for them to take out loans. It's a bill that's paid for; it won't add a dime to the deficit. It's a bill that was written by both Democrats and Republicans.

But for months, the Republican leadership in the Senate has said no. For months, they've used legislative maneuvers to prevent this bill from even coming up for a vote. And all the while, small-business owners kept waiting for help. They kept putting off plans to hire more workers and grow their businesses.

Now, thankfully, two Republican Senators— Senators George Voinovich and George LeMieux—have refused to support this blockade any longer. And because of their decision, this small-business jobs bill will finally pass. And I want to thank them for their efforts, because they understand that we simply don't have time anymore to play games—not just on this small-business jobs bill. Let me give you another example.

Right now we could decide to extend tax relief for the middle class. Right now we could decide that every American household would receive a tax cut on the first $250,000 of their income. But once again, the leaders across the aisle are saying no. They want to hold these middle class tax cuts hostage until they get an additional tax cut for the wealthiest 2 percent of Americans.

We simply can't afford that. It would mean borrowing $700 billion in order to fund these tax cuts for the very wealthiest Americans, $700 billion to give a tax cut worth an average of 100,000 to millionaires and billionaires. And it's a tax cut economists say would do little to add momentum to our economy.

Now, I just don't believe this makes any sense. Even as we debate whether it's wise to spend 700 billion on tax breaks for the wealthy, doesn't it make sense for us to move forward with the tax cuts that we all agree on? We should be able to extend, right now, middle class tax relief on the first $250,000 of income, which, by the way, 97 percent of Americans make less than $250,000 a year. So right off the bat, 97 percent of all Americans would get tax relief on all their income. People who are making more than $250,000 a year—say you're making a half a million dollars, you'd still get tax relief on half your income.

And everybody agrees that this makes sense. Middle class families need this relief. These are the Americans who saw their wages and incomes flatline over the last decade, who've seen the costs of everything from health care to college tuition skyrocket, and who have been hardest hit by this recession.

Extending these tax cuts is right. It is just. It will help our economy because middle class folks are the folks who are most likely to actually spend this tax relief, for a new computer for the kids or for maybe some home improvement.

And if the other party continues to hold these tax cuts hostage, these are the same families who will suffer the most when their taxes go up next year. And if we can't get an agreement with Republicans, that's what will happen.

So we don't have time for any more games. I understand there's an election coming up, but the American people didn't send us here to just think about our jobs; they sent us here to think about theirs. They sent us here to think about their lives and their children's lives and to be responsible and to be serious about the challenges we face as a nation.

That's what members of both parties have now done with the small-business jobs bill. And I hope we can work together to do the same thing on middle class tax relief in the weeks to come.

Thanks very much, everybody.

NOTE: The President spoke at 4:43 p.m. in the Rose Garden at the White House. In his remarks, he referred to H.R. 5297.

Remarks at the Congressional Hispanic Caucus Institute Annual Awards Gala
September 15, 2010

The President. Thank you very much. Thank you to Senator Menendez and to the chairwoman of the Congressional Hispanic Caucus, Congresswoman Velazquez, for those extraordinary introductions, but more importantly, for the outstanding work that you do each and every day. Please give them a huge round of applause. Thank you to the Congressional Hispanic Caucus Institute for inviting us this evening. Mi-

chelle and I are thrilled to be here with so many friends to kick off Hispanic Heritage Month.

I want to acknowledge a few people before I begin my remarks. First, somebody who I believe is going to go down in history as one of the greatest Speakers of the House of all time, Nancy Pelosi is here. Two of our outstanding Cabinet Secretaries are in the house, Secretary of the Interior Ken Salazar and our wonderful Secretary of Labor, Hilda Solis.

I want to thank our mistress of ceremonies, Soledad O'Brien. I want to congratulate Eva Longoria Parker and Arturo Sandoval and Lin-Manuel Miranda on your well-deserved awards this evening.

Audience member. We love you, Obama!

The President. I love you back! And I want to thank all the Members of Congress, the local elected officials, the CHCI alumni, and all who work day in and day out to advance the Hispanic community and America as a whole.

I also want to acknowledge and thank all of the outstanding Latino leaders serving across my administration, because I am proud that the number of Latinos I've nominated to Senate-confirmed positions at this point far exceeds any administration in history. And I'm especially proud that a whole bunch of them are Latinas. And as I've said before, one of my proudest moments of my Presidency was the day Justice Sonia Sotomayor swore an oath and ascended to our Nation's highest court and sparked new dreams for countless young girls all across America.

Now, some of you may remember, I first joined you here 2 years ago, as a candidate for this office. And we spoke then about how, after years of failed policies here in Washington, after decades of putting off the toughest challenges, we had finally reached a tipping point, a point where the fundamental promise of America was at risk.

We talked about how these challenges impacted the Latino community, but also about how they're bigger than any one community. I said then that if a young child is stuck in an overcrowded and underperforming school, it doesn't matter if she is Black or White or Latino, she is our child, and we have a responsibility to her; that if millions of Latinos end up in the emergency room because they don't have health care, it's not just a problem for one community, it's a problem for all of America. When millions of immigrants toil in the shadows of our society, that's not just a Latino problem, that is a American problem. We've got to solve it.

As Dr. King told Cesar Chavez all those years ago: Our separate struggles are really one. And that truth became painfully clear when, less than a week after I had appeared before the CHC, some of the biggest Wall Street firms collapsed and the bottom fell out of our economy. Millions of families across America were plunged into the deepest recession of our lifetimes. And a Latino community that had been hard hit before the recession was hit even harder.

So when I took office, I insisted that we could only rebuild our economy if we started growing the economy for all of our people, not just some of our people; if we provided economic security for all of our working families all across America. We had to renew the fundamental idea that everybody in America—everybody in America—has a chance to make it if they try, no matter who they are, no matter what they look like, no matter where they come from or where they were born.

That's the idea that drives us: the chance to make of our lives what we will. And I know that many of you are thinking tonight about a task that is central to that idea, and that's our fight to pass comprehensive immigration reform.

Now, I know that many of you campaigned hard for me, and understandably, you're frustrated that we have not been able to move this over the finish line yet. I am too. But let me be clear: I will not walk away from this fight. My commitment is getting this done as soon as we can. We can't keep kicking this challenge down the road.

Now, there's no doubt the debate over how to fix all this has been a fractured and sometimes painful one in this country. And let's face it, there are some who seek political advantage in distorting the facts and in dividing our people. We've seen it before. Some take advantage of the economic anxiety that people are feeling to stoke fear of those who look or think or worship differently, to inflame passions between "us" and "them."

I have news for those people. It won't work. There is no "us" and "them." In this country, there is only "us." There is no Latino America or Black America or White America or Asian America. There is only the United States of America—all of us. All of us joined together, indivisible.

If we appeal to the American people's hopes over their fears, we'll get this done. We already know what this reform looks like. Just a few years ago, when I was a Senator, we built a bipartisan coalition around a basic framework under the leadership of Senator Kennedy and Senator McCain and President Bush. We rallied with leaders from the business community and the labor communities and the religious communities. Many of you were there. And the bill we forged wasn't perfect. It wasn't what any one person might think was optimal.

But because folks were willing to compromise, we came up with a commonsense, comprehensive reform that was so far from the false debates, the notion that somehow on the one hand there's mass amnesty or on the other hand there's some unworkable mass deportation. That wasn't what we were talking about. And the American people, I think, were ready to embrace a commonsense solution. And we passed that bill through the United States Senate.

But since that effort fall apart—fell apart, we have seen how broken and bitter and divisive our politics has become. Today, the folks who yell the loudest about the Federal Government's long failure to fix this problem are some of the same folks standing in the way of good faith efforts to fix it. And under the pressures of partisanship and election-year politics, most of the 11 Republican Senators who voted for that reform just 4 years ago have backed far away from that vote today.

That's why States like Arizona have taken matters into their own hands. And my administration has challenged that State's law, not just because it risks the harassment of citizens and legal immigrants, but it is the wrong way to deal with this issue. It interferes with Federal immigration enforcement. It makes it more difficult for law—local law enforcement to do its job. It strains State and local budgets. And if other States follow suit, we'll have an unproductive and unworkable patchwork of laws across the country.

We need an immigration policy that works, a policy that meets the needs of families and businesses while honoring our tradition as a nation of immigrants and a nation of laws. We need it for the sake of our economy, we need it for our security, and we need it for our future.

And I understand it may not be the easy thing to do politically. It's easier to grandstand. But I didn't run for President to do what's easy. I ran to do what's hard. I ran to do what's right. And when I think something is the right thing to do, even my critics have to admit I'm pretty persistent. I won't let it go. They can call me a lot of things, but they know I don't give up.

Now, the Senate is going to have a chance to do the right thing over the next few weeks when Senator Reid brings the "DREAM Act" to the floor. Keep in mind, in the past, this was a bill that was supported by a majority of Democrats and Republicans. There's no reason why it shouldn't receive that same kind of bipartisan support today. I've been a supporter since I was in the Senate, and I will do whatever it takes to support the Congressional Hispanic Caucus's efforts to pass this bill so that I can sign it into law on behalf of students seeking a college education and those who wish to serve in our country's uniform. It's the right thing to do. We should get it done.

Now, I want to be straight with you. To make real progress on these or any issues, we've got to break the Republican leadership's blockade. Let's be clear about this: Without the kind of bipartisan effort we had just a few short years ago, we can't get these reforms across the finish line. Their leadership has made reaching 60 votes the norm for nearly everything the Senate has to do. The American people's business is on hold because, simply put, the other party's platform has been "no."

For example, consider the public servants I've nominated to carry out the people's business. Most of them had been supported widely and approved unanimously by Senate committees. But they've been held up for months by the Republican leadership. We can't even get an up-or-down vote on their confirmation. I nominated a man that you all know well.

Audience member. Salazar!

The President. Well, I did nominate Salazar. I got him confirmed. [*Laughter*] Raul Yzaguirre, to be our Ambassador to the Dominican Republic—Raul is right here. Now, Raul has been waiting for 10 months to be the Ambassador to the Dominican Republic. Right now there are 21 judges who've been held up for months while their courts have sat empty. Three of them are outstanding Latinos, like Judge Albert Diaz, who I nominated to the Fourth Circuit Court. He's been waiting for 10 months. This is a widely respected State court judge, military judge, and Marine Corps attorney. He was approved unanimously by the Judiciary Committee. But just last month, the Senate Republican leader objected to a vote on his confirmation yet again. And when he was asked why, he basically admitted it was simply partisan payback. Partisan payback.

We can't afford that kind of game-playing right now. We need serious leaders for serious times. That's the kind of leadership this moment demands. That is what we need right now. Because when I get out of this town and I'm meeting with people, talking to folks, nobody is asking me, "Hey, Barack, which party is scoring more points?" Nobody is saying, "Oh, don't worry about us, I just want you to do what's best for November."

What they're interested in is how they're going to find a job when they've only known one trade their whole life; how are they going to put their kids through school; how are they going to pay the bills if they get sick; how are they going to retire when their savings have plunged after this financial crisis. They're the folks we're here for. They're the folks we're fighting for.

That's why we passed Wall Street reform for every hard-working family who's tired of taken—getting taken advantage of every time they opened their credit card bill or mortgage payment or tried to send a remittance—send a payment to help their parents or families abroad.

That's why we're reforming America's schools so that all our children have a chance to learn the skills they need for today's economy. We eliminated tens of billions of dollars in wasteful subsidies to big banks that provide student loans, and we're taking that money to make college affordable for millions of students, including more than a hundred thousand Latino students. That's what the CHC did. That's what this administration did.

That's why we passed health insurance reform for Americans who are sick of being gouged by insurance companies that jack up rates and deny coverage because you've got a preexisting condition. Now millions of Americans with insurance can get free preventive care. Now 9 million Latinos and tens of millions of Americans will be able to afford quality health care for the first time.

That's why we cut taxes for small-business owners and 95 percent of working Americans.

Audience member. Puerto Rico bless you, Obama!

The President. Thank you. Instead of giving tax breaks to corporations to create jobs overseas, we're cutting taxes for companies that put our people to work here at home. Instead of tax breaks for the wealthiest Americans who don't need them and weren't even asking for them, we're fighting to cut taxes for you, middle class folks all across the country. That's what we're about. That's what we're fighting for.

And when it comes to just about everything we've tried to do, almost every Republican in Congress has folded their arms and said no. Even where we usually agree, they say no. They're thinking about the next election instead of the next generation, trying to score political points instead of solving problems. They said no to help for small businesses, no to middle class tax cuts, no to making college affordable, no to comprehensive immigration reform. Their platform, apparently, is *"No, se puede."* [*Laughter*] Is that a bumper sticker you want on your car?

Audience members. No! [*Laughter*]

The President. In fact, the chairman of their campaign committee said that if they take over, they'd go back to "the exact same agenda"—that's a quote—"the exact same agenda" they had when they were in power. They're saying they'll repeal Wall Street reform. They'll try to repeal health insurance reform. They'll give the special interests a pen and let them write the rules again.

And right now, because of that Republican blockade, those special interests—even foreign corporations—can spend tens of millions of dollars on campaign ads without even having to disclose who they are. You've seen some of these ads. You know, they call themselves Americans for Apple Pie or Moms for Motherhood. [*Laughter*]

And then they use their voice to drown out yours, to let Wall Street write rules that take advantage of Main Street, to let insurance companies write rules that let them cover or drop folks whenever and however they please, to go back to that "exact same agenda."

Well, let me tell you something. That agenda didn't work out so well for the Latino community. It didn't work out for anybody here in America. It is not going to solve the challenges we face. We can't go backwards. We've got to go forwards.

So let me say this, not just to the folks who are in this room, but to the Latino community across this country. You have every right to keep the heat on me and keep the heat on the Democrats, and I hope you do. That's how our political process works.

But don't forget who is standing with you and who is standing against you. Don't ever believe that this election coming up doesn't matter. Don't forget who secured health care for 4 million children, including the children of legal immigrants. Don't forget who won new Pell grants for more than 100,000 Latino students. Don't forget who fought for credit card reform, a new agency to protect consumers from predatory lending, and protections for folks who send remittances back home. Don't forget who cut taxes for working families. Don't forget who your friends are. *No se olviden.* Don't forget.

We can't go back now. Not when there is so much work to be done. We've got to move forward. We've got to move forward on jobs and on the economy and on immigration reform and all the unfinished business of our time. These are serious times. They require serious leaders and serious citizens, and your voice matters. Your voice can make the difference.

So let me close by saying this. Long before America was even an idea, this land of plenty was home to many peoples, to British and French, to Dutch and Spanish, to Mexican, to countless Indian tribes. We all shared the same land. We didn't always get along. But over the centuries, what eventually bound us together, what made us all Americans, was not a matter of blood, it wasn't a matter of birth. It was faith and fidelity to the shared values that we all hold so dear: "We hold these truths to be self-evident, that all men are created equal, endowed with certain inalienable rights: life and liberty and the pursuit of happiness."

That's what makes us unique. That's what makes us strong. The ability to recognize our common humanity, to remember that in this country, equality and opportunity are not just words on a piece of paper, they're not just words in the mouths of politicians, they are promises to be kept.

And that is our calling now: to keep those promises for the next generation. No matter which way the political winds shift, I will stand with you for that better future. And if you stand with me, and if we remember that fundamental truth—that divided we fall, but united we are strong, and out of many, we are one—then you and I will finish what we have started. We will make sure that America forever remains an idea and a place that's big enough and bold enough and brave enough to accommodate the dreams of all our children and all our people for years to come. *Si, se puede.*

Thank you. God bless you, and God bless the United States of America. Thank you.

NOTE: The President spoke at 8:34 p.m. at the Washington Convention Center. In his remarks, he referred to Soledad O'Brien, anchor, CNN; actor Eva Longoria Parker; musician Arturo Sandoval; lyricist and composer Lin-Manuel Miranda; and Rep. Pete Sessions, in his capacity as chairman of the National Republican Congressional Committee.

Remarks During a Meeting With the President's Export Council
September 16, 2010

Everybody, please have a seat. Have a seat. Well, good morning, everybody. And I want to thank all of you for being here today. This is a terrific kickoff on the President's Export Council. And I want to thank the Cabinet Secretaries, the senior officials in my administration who are here and have helped to pull this together, the members of my Export Council. I appreciate all of you being here to discuss next steps in growing America's exports and our economy. And I want to thank Jim McNerney and Ursula Burns, who are serving as Chair and Vice Chair of this council, for their outstanding work.

From the day that I took office, my administration's highest priority has been to pull our economy out of the deepest recession of our lifetimes, to put people back to work, and to position our economy on a path of long-term and sustainable growth.

In the immediate term, we've had to act across many fronts to get folks back on their feet and get our economy moving again. And one of the things that we've been trying to do is to help create the conditions necessary for our small businesses to grow and to hire. And a few hours from now, after months of delay, the Senate will finally have an up-or-down vote on a package of tax cuts and lending initiatives to help small businesses, some of which will be exporters.

Reinvigorating our economy in the short run and rebuilding it over the long term is not a one-step process; there are going to be many steps we have to take in the months and years ahead. But this is a critically important one. And I am grateful to those Senators on the Republican side of the aisle willing to take this vote on behalf of America's small-business owners.

But even as we're working to get our economy moving today, we are also laying a new foundation for growth tomorrow. And that's where you come in. We've been working to increase America's competitiveness in a global economy. After all, one of the reasons we got into the mess we've been in over the last couple of years is because, let's face it, we grew complacent. We allowed too much of our prosperity to be based on fleeting bubbles of consumption and risk and artificial gain. We spent too much; we saved too little. We allowed our economy to become bloated with debt both in the private sector and public sectors. We failed to fully harness the talents and skills and creativity of the American people. And we put off investments in technology and innovation that are critical to helping our businesses compete in the 21st century.

That's not a path we could afford to continue down. And that's why we've been working so hard to try to reverse those trends. We're upgrading our national infrastructure for tomorrow. We're investing in science and technology, research and development, and clean energy projects that will strengthen our global leadership. We're reforming our schools, making college more affordable, and investing in the skills and education of our people.

In fact, later today I'll be meeting with CEOs of a hundred of America's biggest companies who've joined together in common cause to make sure we're preparing all our students today with the science, technology, engineering, and math skills that they'll need for the high-tech jobs of today's high-tech industries. And by the way, Ursula is participating in that. And she is almost as overexposed as me today. [*Laughter*]

Because the best way we know to compete and win in the global marketplace is by doing what we do best: harnessing the talents and ingenuity of our people to lead the world in new industries. And we're building an economy where America's businesses and American workers once again do what they do best, which is build great products and sell them around the world.

We were just talking before we came in, and one of the things that I think is so critical is to realign the interests of business and workers here in America so that everybody is fighting on the same side, everybody is out there with a united front competing to make sure that America succeeds.

In this year's State of the Union Address, I set a goal for America: We will double our exports of goods and services over the next 5 years. Because the more American companies export, the more they produce. And the more they produce, the more people they hire. And that means more jobs, good jobs that often pay as much as 15 percent more than average. The world wants to buy goods and services made in the United States and our workers are ready to produce them.

That's why 6 months ago, we launched the National Export Initiative, the first-ever Governmentwide export promotion strategy with focused attention at the Presidential and Cabinet level.

America is going to bat as a stronger partner and a better advocate for our businesses abroad. We're increasing trade missions. We're removing barriers to help businesses gain a foothold in new markets. We're increasing export financing for small and medium-sized businesses. We hope to move forward on new trade agreements with some of our key partners in a way that doesn't just advance the interests of our businesses, workers, and farmers, but also upholds our most cherished values. And finally, we continue to coordinate with other nations around the world to promote strong, balanced, and sustainable growth.

So we're 6 months into what's going to be a 5-year-long process. And despite some strong economic headwinds this year, we've already seen some progress. Obviously, working off a low baseline given the crisis last year, exports are expected to be up, but we're very pleased to see that they're up 18 percent to where they were a year ago. And manufacturing exports are up 20 percent. And that's helping put a lot of our people back to work.

And there's more we can do to keep that growth going. Yesterday my export cabinet submitted a report detailing the progress that's been made and additional steps that our agencies intend to take to deliver on our goals. And I look forward to seeing these steps implemented.

It's also why 2 months ago, I announced the formation of this council to seek the expertise of private sector business and labor leaders who know what it takes to succeed. Earlier this morning, in a meeting with Vice President Biden as well as Jim and Ursula about some of the recommendations you've devised, we were encouraged that we think we can move forward rapidly on some of these fronts. And we're pleased to see the fresh and innovative strategies that we can pursue to help small and medium-sized companies sell their goods and services abroad.

With companies like yours in mind, we've been looking at our export control system and working to streamline the process in a manner that helps our high-tech companies stay competitive, while strengthening our national security. We're also working to resolve outstanding issues with our free trade agreements with our key partners, like Korea, and to seek congressional approval as soon as possible.

And as our troops come home from Iraq and Afghanistan and reenter the workforce, I think it's terrific that we are going to look at a veterans retraining initiative that would help them translate their remarkable leadership skills, but also their technical skills, skills they've honed in the military, into careers in the high-demand science and technology fields that will keep America economically strong and globally competitive well into the future.

So these are some of the steps we'll pursue to double America's exports over the next 5 years. When I made this initial announcement, some were skeptical, but the truth of the matter is, is that if we are increasing our exports by 14, 15 percent per year—something that is achievable—then we can meet our goal. And that's one of the ways that we're going to make this economy in the 21st century what it was in the 20th century: an unparalleled force for opportunity and prosperity for all our people.

So I look forward to seeing your recommendations and our continued work together to make that happen. I am very grateful, because this is a group of very busy people, that you're willing to invest the time and energy that you already have and will continue to invest in the future to make sure that this council is productive as possible. This is one of my top priorities. I'm going to be paying close attention to it. My Cabinet and my economic team are going to be working diligently on this.

So I am very confident this is going to be a worthwhile endeavor that may indirectly help your companies but is certainly going to help the country and the American people.

Thanks very much, everybody.

NOTE: The President spoke at 9:54 a.m. in the East Room at the White House.

Remarks on Education Reform
September 16, 2010

Thank you, everybody. Please have a seat. Thank you very much. Thank you to Ursula and all the board members here. We are so excited about this initiative. And I want everybody to also know that I've got one of the finest Secretaries of Education, I think, in the history of this country in Arne Duncan, and he is excited about it as well, so—[*applause*].

I hope you don't mind, before I begin, I just want to comment on a vote that just took place a little while ago in Congress. I want to thank the Senate for finally passing the small-business jobs bill that had been held up for months by partisan delay. It's going to make a difference in millions of small-business owners across the country who are going to benefit from tax breaks and additional lending so companies have the capital to grow and hire. And this is really welcome news.

Now, these tax breaks and loans are going to help create jobs in the short term. But the reason all of us are here, companies large and small, is to talk about an issue with far-reaching consequences for our economy in the long run, and that's the education of our children.

It's an incredibly impressive gathering that we have here. We've got dozens of leaders from the business community who are part of today's announcement. We're joined by talented and enterprising students. Where are the students? Raise your hands. Yes, we're very proud of you guys. We have some passionate and dedicated teachers. Teachers, raise your hands. Proud of you.

I want to recognize all the Members of Congress who are with us, as well as the top scientists from my administration, including my science adviser, John Holdren, who is here. Where's John? There he is right there. As well as—[*applause*]—and in addition, we've got—and this is obviously the coolest thing—we've got two trailblazing astronauts in Sally Ride and Mae Jemison, who are here. So we are just honored to have all of you here at the White House.

We're here for a simple reason. Everybody in this room understands that our Nation's success depends on strengthening America's role as the world's engine of discovery and innovation. And all the CEOs who are here today understand that their companies' future depends on their ability to harness the creativity and dynamism and insight of a new generation and that leadership tomorrow depends on how we educate our students today, especially in science, technology, engineering, and math.

We know how important this is for our health. It's important for our security. It's important for our environment. And we know how important it is for our economy. As I discussed this morning with my Export Council, our prosperity in a 21st-century global marketplace depends on our ability to compete with nations around the world. And we are never going to win that competition by paying the lowest wages or simply by trying to offer the cheapest products. We're going to win by offering the most innovative products. We're going to win by doing what we do best, which is harnessing the talents and ingenuity of our people to lead the world in new industries. That's how we can create millions of new jobs exporting more of our goods around the world.

Now, as any one of the scientists, CEOs, and teachers here will tell you, this kind of innovation isn't born in the boardroom or on the factory floor. It doesn't begin in a basement workshop or a research laboratory. That's where the payoff happens, but it starts long before. It starts in a classroom. It starts when a child learns that every star in the night sky is another Sun, when a young girl swells with accomplishment after solving a tough math problem, when a boy builds a model rocket and watches it soar, when an eager student peers through a microscope and discovers a whole new world. It's in these moments that a young person may discover a talent or a passion that might lead to a career. It's in these moments every day that our Nation—our promise as a nation is realized. And it is in these moments that we see why a quality science and math education matters, why it is absolutely critical to us.

Now, despite the importance of education in these subjects, in recent years, we have been outpaced by our competitors. There is no disputing that. One assessment shows American 15-year-olds ranked 21st in science and 25th in math when compared to their peers around the world. Yet for years, we've failed to address this challenge. There's been some talk about it. There have been some white papers and some reports about it. But we haven't solved it.

And instead, we've oftentimes gotten into tired arguments traded across old divides. And parents and students and teachers have been basically left to accept that mediocrity was the best that America could do. And we've got some islands of excellence, but we assume that we can't substantially turn this around.

The cost of this inaction is immeasurable: the inventions that are never built, the businesses never started, the cures never discovered, the sparks of imagination never lit, the brimming potential squandered because we failed to come together for the sake not just of our children, but for the sake of our future.

Now, I ran for President because I believe we cannot accept this failure of responsibility. I believe, as all of you do—and that's why you're here today—that America doesn't play for 2d place, and we certainly don't play for 25th. And that's why soon after I took office, I set this goal for our Nation: We will move from the middle to the top of the pack in math and science education over the next decade. And we are on the way to meeting this goal.

Under the leadership of Arne Duncan, a man who has devoted his life to the idea that every single child deserves a world-class education, we launched an initiative called Race to the Top. Under Race to the Top, States are actively competing to produce innovative math and science programs, raising standards, turning around struggling schools, recruiting and retaining more good teachers.

At a difficult time for our Nation, when budget cuts across America have threatened the jobs of countless teachers, we've also fought some tough opposition to save hundreds of thousands of educator and school-worker jobs. These are folks in the classroom right now because we refused to accept a lesser education for our children, even at a time of economic hardship.

Today my science advisory board, which is represented here by Eric Lander and Jim Gates, released a set of recommendations to recruit and train more great teachers over the next decade and to promote breakthrough innovation in math and science education. And it was a terrific report. I sat with Eric this morning and got a full briefing on it. And there are so many promising ideas out there, proven ideas that can work if we apply the will to it. And I'm asking Arne Duncan and Dr. Cora Marrett, Acting Director of the National Science Foundation, to take a look at all these recommendations closely and then start figuring out how can we implement them.

What I've also said for a long time is that our success will not be attained by government alone. It depends on teachers and parents and students and the broader community. It depends on us restoring an insistence on excellence in our classrooms and from our children. And that's why last year, I challenged scientists and business leaders to think of creative ways to engage young people in math and science. And now they are answering the call.

All across this country, companies and nonprofits are coming together to replicate successful science programs. New public-private partnerships are working to offer additional training to more than 100,000 teachers and to prepare more than 10,000 new teachers in the next 5 years. Media companies are creating content to inspire young people in math and science. And businesses are working with nonprofits to launch robotics competitions and other ways for kids to make things and learn with their hands.

So now we're building on this effort. The business leaders gathered in this room, with this board at the helm, are launching a new organization called Change the Equation to help our country reach the goal of moving to the top in math and science education. It brings together a coalition of more than a hundred CEOs from the Nation's largest companies who are committed to bring innovative math and science programs to at least a hundred high-need communities over the next year.

And by the way, they're doing this not only out of a sense of duty to the country, not only because it's the right thing to do, but they've got a self-interest in it. Xerox is going to do really well if we've got a whole bunch of engineers and scientists and math majors who are clamoring to work for some of America's most innovative businesses.

We're also announcing other commitments from companies and foundations and nonprofits that will create fun and educational programs for students in science museums and build hands-on learning centers and 21st-century libraries, make sure that the students of military families have access to AP courses, and improve professional development for math and science teachers.

And I think the teachers here will acknowledge that one of the challenges is making sure that those folks who are teaching these subjects in the classroom, that they're up to date, up to speed in getting the best professional training possible.

And this coalition is also going to extend opportunities to all of our young people, and that includes efforts to open doors for women and minorities, who all too often have been underrepresented in scientific fields, but who are no less capable of success in scientific careers.

So I want to thank all the leaders who are here today for their outstanding commitment to this cause, for lending their resources, their expertise, and their enthusiasm to the task of strengthening America's leadership in the 21st century by improving education. And I want to encourage others to be part of this growing movement, to harness the incredible potential for our young people, for while this may be a difficult time for our Nation and we face some tough challenges, it's that potential that ought to give us hope.

We need no better example than the students who are here today from West Philadelphia High School. These students, under the direction of some terrific teachers, entered a global competition against serious corporate and college challengers to build a production-ready car that runs on very little fuel. So as part of an after-school program, they worked to get their vehicles ready. They tweaked the hybrid engine. They figured out how to make their cars run more efficiently.

At first, the adults didn't really think their team had a chance. Admit it. [*Laughter*] But then something strange happened. Where older and more seasoned teams failed, they succeeded, even making it through an elimination round.

Now, they didn't win the competition. They're kids, come on. [*Laughter*] But they did build a car that got more than 65 miles per gallon. They went toe to toe with car companies and big-name universities. They went against big-name universities, well-funded rivals. They held their own. They didn't have a lot of money. They didn't have the best equipment. They certainly didn't have every advantage in life. What they had was a program that challenged them to solve problems and to work together, to learn and build and create. And that's the kind of spirit and ingenuity that we have to foster. That's the potential that we can harness all across America. That's what will help our young people to fulfill their promise, to realize their dreams, and to help this Nation succeed in the years to come.

And I just have to editorialize. This is the kind of thing that just isn't going to get a lot of attention initially. This will not lead the nightly news. You won't see this on the cover of Roll Call or Politico. It's not—doesn't have conflict and controversy behind it. [*Laughter*]

But these are actually the kinds of things that 10 years from now, 20 years from now, we're going to look back and say, this is something that made a difference. These are the kinds of things I'm really proud of. It doesn't get a lot of fanfare, but from the bottom up, it's making a huge difference in our country.

And so I just want to thank all of you who are here for your participation. And I wasn't sure, by the way, whether all the folks on the stage here were introduced, so I just want to make sure that everybody gets introduced. In addition to Ursula Burns from Xerox, I want to thank Rex Tillerson of ExxonMobil, Craig Barrett, who's the former Intel CEO, Antonio Perez of Kodak, Glenn Britt from Time Warner, and somebody who's not on the stage but is going to be the CEO of Change the Equation, Linda Rosen, and obviously, one of my heroes, Sally Ride. We are just so grateful to them. We're grateful to you. Let's go get this thing done.

Thank you very much, everybody.

NOTE: The President spoke at 3:43 p.m. in the South Court Auditorium of the Dwight D. Eisenhower Executive Office Building. In his remarks, he referred to Ursula M. Burns, chairman and chief executive officer, Xerox Corporation; Eric S. Lander, Cochair, and S. James Gates, Jr., member, President's Council of Advisers on Science and Technology; Rex W. Tillerson, chairman and chief executive officer, ExxonMobil; Antonio M. Perez, chairman of the board and chief executive officer, Eastman Kodak Company; and Glenn A. Britt, chairman, president, and chief executive officer, Time Warner Cable.

Statement on the Release of Census Bureau Data on Income, Poverty, and Health Insurance Coverage
September 16, 2010

Our economy plunged into recession almost 3 years ago on the heels of a financial meltdown and a rapid decline in housing prices. Last year, we saw the depths of the recession, including historic losses in employment not witnessed since the Great Depression. Today the Census Bureau released data that illustrates just how tough 2009 was: Along with rising unemployment, incomes failed to rise for the typical household, the percentage of Americans without health insurance rose to 16.7 percent, and the percentage of Americans living in poverty increased to 14.3 percent.

But the data released today also remind us that a historic recession does not have to translate into historic increases in family economic insecurity. Because of the Recovery Act and many other programs providing tax relief and income support to a majority of working families, and especially those most in need, millions of Americans were kept out of poverty last year.

The substantial expansion of the Children's Health Insurance Program (CHIP) helped inoculate our children from the economic distress experienced by their parents, as there was little change in the percentage of children without health insurance. The Affordable Care Act will build on that success by expanding health insurance coverage to more families.

Even before the recession hit, middle class incomes had been stagnant and the number of people living in poverty in America was unacceptably high, and today's numbers make it clear that our work is just beginning. Our task now is to continue working together to improve our schools, build the skills of our workers, and invest in our Nation's critical infrastructure.

For all of our challenges, I continue to be inspired by the dedication and optimism of America's workers, and I am confident that we will emerge from this storm with a stronger economy.

Statement on Senate Action on the Strategic Arms Reduction Treaty
September 16, 2010

I want to acknowledge an important step forward today that will advance our national security. This afternoon the Senate Foreign Relations Committee voted in favor of the new START Treaty, and I am pleased that it did so with strong bipartisan support. I called the committee chairman, Senator Kerry, and Senator Lugar, the ranking member, to express my gratitude for their leadership, and I commend the members of the committee for their thoughtful review of this Treaty.

Leaders from across the political spectrum, including Secretaries of State and Defense from Republican and Democratic administrations, have endorsed this Treaty. They recognize that it is in our national security interest. It reduces the deployed nuclear forces of both the United States and Russia, provides strong verification measures, and continues to improve relations between our two nations, the world's two largest nuclear weapon powers and key partners in global security. Indeed, ratification of this Treaty will reinforce our cooperation with Russia on a range of issues, including one of our highest priorities, preventing the spread of nuclear weapons.

Today I urge the full Senate to move forward quickly with a vote to approve this Treaty. I encourage Members on both sides of the aisle to give this agreement the fair hearing and bipartisan support that it deserves and that has been given to past agreements of its kind. For like those efforts, this Treaty will advance American leadership in the world, while strengthening our national security in the 21st century.

Message to the Congress on Continuation of the National Emergency With Respect to Persons Who Commit, Threaten To Commit, or Support Terrorism
September 16, 2010

To the Congress of the United States:

Section 202(d) of the National Emergencies Act (50 U.S.C. 1622(d)) provides for the automatic termination of a national emergency unless, prior to the anniversary date of its declaration, the President publishes in the *Federal Register* and transmits to the Congress a notice stating that the emergency is to continue in effect beyond the anniversary date. In accordance with this provision, I have sent to the *Federal Register* for publication the enclosed notice, stating that the national emergency with respect to persons who commit, threaten to commit, or support terrorism is to continue in effect beyond September 23, 2010.

The crisis constituted by the grave acts of terrorism and threats of terrorism committed by foreign terrorists, including the terrorist attacks on September 11, 2001, in New York and Pennsylvania, and against the Pentagon, and the continuing and immediate threat of further attacks on United States nationals or the United States that led to the declaration of a national emergency on September 23, 2001, has not been resolved. These actions pose a continuing unusual and extraordinary threat to the national security, foreign policy, and economy of the United States. For these reasons, I have determined that it is necessary to continue the national emergency declared with respect to persons who commit, threaten to commit, or support terrorism, and maintain in force the comprehensive sanctions to respond to this threat.

BARACK OBAMA

The White House,
September 16, 2010.

NOTE: The notice is listed in Appendix D at the end of this volume.

Remarks at a Reception for Senatorial Candidate Richard Blumenthal in Stamford, Connecticut
September 16, 2010

Thank you. Everybody, please have a seat. Have a seat. Well, hello, Stamford. It is good to be back in Connecticut, and it is an honor to stand here with your attorney general and the next United States Senator from Connecticut, Dick Blumenthal.

I also want to acknowledge your candidate for Governor, Dan Malloy, who is here, or he may have slipped out right before—there he is. Not sure—when you're campaigning, you can't be in one place too long. [*Laughter*]

And I also want to just say thank you to Cynthia and the kids for lending Dick to Connecticut and to the country. I know it is hard to be the spouse of a candidate and the spouse of an attorney general, and it's going to be tough being the spouse of a United States Senator. I promised that I would not let Michelle talk to Cynthia before the election. [*Laughter*] It's hard work. But we are extraordinarily grateful. And the fact that David and Matthew and Claire and Mike are doing so well is a testament I know Dick agrees with Mom. So please give her a big round of applause.

Now, Connecticut, let's face it, this decision in this election should be a no-brainer. [*Laughter*] Right? I mean, it should be. Should be a no-brainer. Here you've got a man who's been fighting for the people of Connecticut since the day he walked into the attorney general's office. He's got the record to prove it. He's taken on the tobacco industry and helped stop those companies from targeting our kids. He's taken on utility companies to try to beat back electricity rate increases and skyrocketing costs of heating oil. He's taken on the auto industry to help keep family dealerships open that have been around for almost a century.

There is no—there's no fight too big or too small for Dick Blumenthal to take on. He was there to help a mother get her insurance company to pay for her baby's special formula. He was there to help a family rebuild after their home was destroyed by fire. He's there at county fairs and Rotary Club meetings and PTA meetings, talking with people of this State, listening to your concerns.

This is the kind of leader you want representing you. Somebody you know. Somebody who shares your values. Somebody who doesn't just show up and try to get a victory by writing a big check and flooding the airwaves with negative ads. Now, I have to say, Dick say—said his opponent may have more money. Dick, she has more money than you. [*Laughter*] I mean, it's—[*laughter*]—just in case there's any confusion. [*Laughter*]

And I understand she has promised a smackdown. [*Laughter*] Right? This is what she said. And look, there's no doubt, I can see how somebody who's been in professional wrestling would think that they're right at home at the United States Senate—[*laughter*]—if they were watching some of the behavior that's been going on. [*Laughter*]

But the truth is—and Dick understands this—public service is not a game. At this moment, we are facing challenges we haven't seen since the Great Depression. And facing serious challenges requires serious leaders: leaders who are willing to take on the status quo, leaders who are willing to take on special interests, leaders who are willing to fight for our people and our future. And Dick Blumenthal is that leader. And that's why I need all of you to make him your next United States Senator. That's the choice in this election.

I want to give you a sense of the contexts of this election, what's at stake. See, for the last decade, there was a very specific philosophy that reigned in Washington: You cut taxes, especially for millionaires and billionaires. You cut regulations for special interests. You cut back on investments in education and clean energy and research and technology.

The idea was that if we put blind faith in the market, if we let corporations play by their own rules, if we left everybody else to fend for themselves, somehow America would automatically grow and would prosper.

And over the last 10 years, that philosophy has not worked out well. It didn't work for middle class families who saw their incomes go down while their costs of everything from school tuition to health care go up. It didn't work for an economy that experienced the slowest job growth since World War II; this was before the financial crisis. It didn't work when a record surplus turned into a record deficit. It didn't work when the recklessness of some on Wall Street led to the worst economic crisis since the Great Depression.

So I ran for President because I had a different idea about how this country was built. And it was an idea rooted in my own family's story. My parents, my grandparents, they never had much. They worked tirelessly so that I might have a better life. They believed in the American values of self-reliance and individual responsibility, and they instilled those values in their children.

But they also believed in a country that rewards hard work, a country that rewards responsibility, a country where we look after one another.

They believed in the America that gave my grandfather the chance to go to college because of the GI bill, an America that gave my grandparents a chance to buy a home because of the Federal Housing Authority, an America where a rising tide really does lift all boats, from the CEO to the newest guy on the assembly line.

That's the America I believe in. That's the America Dick Blumenthal believes in. We don't think that government has all the answers to our problems. We don't think government's main role is to create jobs or prosperity. We believe government should be lean and it should be efficient.

But in the words of the first Republican President, Abraham Lincoln, we also believe that government should do for the people what they can't do as well for themselves. And that means it should invest in our common future.

It means the powerful—special interests, corporations—that they need to live up to their responsibilities. It means government should help make the middle class more secure and give ladders for people to climb into that middle class. That's what we believe. That's the future that we see.

We see a future where we encourage American innovation and American ingenuity. And that's why we want to end tax breaks for companies that ship jobs overseas and give those tax breaks to companies that are investing in research and development and hiring right here in the United States of America.

That's why we're investing in research and technology and a homegrown clean energy industry, because I don't want to see new solar panels or electric cars or wind turbines, advanced batteries manufactured in Europe or Asia. I want to see them made right here in America, with American workers.

We see an America where every citizen has the skills and training to compete with any worker in the world. Today I had, down in Washington, a meeting with a hundred CEOs who are now partnering with our Department of Education and our National Science Foundation to improve math and science training in schools, because we need more engineers and more scientists. That's how we're going to keep our cutting edge.

And that's why we've set a goal to once again have the highest proportion of college graduates in the world by 2020. We used to be number 1; we're now around number 12. We're going to get back to number one by the end of this next decade.

And that's why we're revitalizing our community colleges and reforming our education system based on what works, not what perpetuates the status quo. That's why we're fighting to make permanent our new college tax credit. This is a tax credit that will mean $10,000 in tuition relief for each child going to 4 years of college.

So we see an America where a growing middle class is the beating heart of a growing economy. That's why I kept my promise and gave a middle class tax cut to 95 percent of working Americans. That's why we passed health insurance reform that stops insurance companies from jacking up your premiums or dropping coverage because you're sick or have a preexisting condition. That's why we passed financial reform to end taxpayer-funded bailouts, reform that will stop credit card companies and mortgage lenders and Wall Street banks from taking advantage of the American people. We want them to compete. We want a thriving financial services area. We want to compete on service, on good products and good prices.

That's why we're trying to make it easier for workers to save for retirement and fighting the efforts of some in the other party to privatize Social Security, because as long as I'm President, nobody is going to take the retirement savings of a generation of Americans and bet it on the market.

That's the America that we see. That's the America we believe in. That's the choice in this election.

Now, obviously, we've been through a incredibly difficult time as a nation. I never imagined that when I walked into the White House, preventing a second depression would be at the top of my to-do list. And even though we've done that, even though the economy is growing again and we're adding private sector jobs again, there is no doubt that because the hole was so deep, progress has been painfully slow.

Millions of Americans remain unemployed. Millions more can barely pay the bills. Hundreds of thousands of families have lost their homes. And behind each of these numbers is a story of heartache and struggle, and I read about that heartache and struggle in letters that I receive every single night and whenever I'm traveling around the country.

So I know that people are frustrated and they're angry and they're anxious about the future. And I also know that in a political campaign, the easiest thing for the other side to do is to try to ride that anger and fear all the way to election day, especially when you got millions of dollars that you can burn on negative ads.

That's what's happening right now. Look, let's face it, it would be one thing if Dick's opponent and other Republican candidates had looked back on the last decade and said: "You know what, our policies really didn't work very well, did they? They kind of screwed up." And they go—they went away, they meditated. [*Laughter*] They contemplated. And then they

finally said: "You know, everything we did ended up in this terrible recession. Let's try something new." And they came back, and they said: "We're going to propose something different. This time we think we've got the answer."

But that's not what they're doing. They're not offering any new ideas. I would challenge anybody here to name a single new idea that they're putting forward. They don't have one. They're not offering new policies. The chair of the Republican campaign committee said that if they take over Congress, they will pursue the exact same agenda as they did before I took office. Now, keep in mind, we lost 4 million jobs in the 6 months before I took office. And they'd pursue what they say are the exact same policies.

So here's what it comes down to. These folks spent a decade driving our economy into a ditch. And as soon as we took office, we put on our boots. We climbed down into the ditch. It was muddy down there. [*Laughter*] It was dusty, bugs. [*Laughter*] And we're pushing on the car, and we're trying to get it out and slipping and sliding. And the whole time, the Republicans are standing there, sipping on a Slurpee—[*laughter*]—just watching us, saying: "You're not pushing hard enough. You're not pushing the right way."

And we tell them: "Come on down here. Help. We could use a hand." "No, that's okay." And so finally—finally—after 2 years of toil, we get this car back on the road, and we can see the way forward. And we get a tap on our shoulder, and we turn around, and it's the Republicans. [*Laughter*] And they say, "Can we have the keys back?" [*Laughter*]

No, you can't have the keys back! [*Laughter*] You don't know how to drive! You don't know how to drive. You can't have the keys. You don't know how to drive.

All those—it's not just them, either. All those special interests, they're all lining up—"Yes, we're going to ride shotgun." [*Laughter*]

We can't give them the keys back. Have you ever noticed, by the way, that if you want to go forward in a car, you put your car in "D"? [*Laughter*] And if you want to go backwards, you put it in "R"? [*Laughter*] We'd end up right back in the ditch. It's true. You think that's a co-incidence. [*Laughter*] It's not.

If we gave them the keys back, they've told exactly what they plan to do. They want to go back to the days when credit card companies can jack up your rates without reason and insurance companies can deny you coverage just because you got sick. They want to stand by and do nothing while States are forced to lay off teachers and firefighters and cops, because, in the words of the Republican leader of the House, those are just, quote, "government jobs," apparently not worth saving.

They want to give more tax breaks to companies that ship jobs overseas instead of giving them to companies that are investing here in the United States. They want to borrow $700 billion to give a tax break worth an average of $100,000 to every millionaire and billionaire in America.

Now, these are the people who lecture us on fiscal responsibility, the same people who refused to pay for two wars, two tax cuts for some of the wealthiest Americans, and left me a—as a welcoming present—a $1.3 trillion deficit when I took office. And now they want to spend another $700 billion that 98 percent of Americans will never see.

That's their agenda. That's the sum total of their agenda. That's what they're offering the American people, a future that looks just like the past, one where special interests get free rein to play by their own rules and where middle class families are left to fend for themselves.

Now, that's not a future I accept for the United States of America. That is not a future that Dick Blumenthal accepts for the United States of America.

This is a tough election season. People are hurting, and they are understandably frustrated. And a lot of them are scared, and a lot of them are anxious. And that means that even when people don't have ideas, if they've got enough money behind them, they may be able to convince some folks that, you know what, just cast a protest vote, throw the bums out. That's a mentality that has an appeal. And you can't blame folks for feeling that way sometime. But that's not a future for our country, a country that's

more divided, that's more unequal, that's less dynamic, where we're falling behind in everything from investment in infrastructure to investment in R&D. That's not a vision for the future.

And if that's not a future you accept for this Nation, if that's not the future you want for your kids and for your grandkids, then we are asking you for help in this election.

Because if you don't think the stakes are large—and I want you to consider this—right now, all across the country, special interests are planning and running millions of dollars of attack ads against Democratic candidates. Because last year, there was a Supreme Court decision called *Citizens United*. They're allowed to spend as much as they want without ever revealing who's paying for the ads. That's exactly what they're doing—millions of dollars. And the groups are benign sounding: Americans for Prosperity. Who's against that? [*Laughter*] Or Committee for Truth in Politics. Or Americans for Apple Pie, Moms for Motherhood—I made those last two up. [*Laughter*]

None of them will disclose who's paying for these ads. You don't know if it's a Wall Street bank. You don't know if it's a big oil company. You don't know if it's an insurance company. You don't even know if it's a foreign-controlled entity.

In some races, they are spending more money than the candidates. Not here, because here the candidate's spending a lot of money. [*Laughter*]

They're spending more money than the parties. They want to take Congress back and return to the days where lobbyists wrote the laws. It is the most insidious power grab since the monopolies of the Gilded Age. That's happening right now. So there's a lot of talk about populist anger and grassroots, but that's not what's driving a lot of these elections.

We tried to fix this, but the leaders of the other party wouldn't even allow it to come up for a vote. They want to keep the public in the dark. They want to serve the special interests that served them so well over the last 19 months.

We will not let them. We are not about to allow a corporate takeover of our democracy. We're not about to go back to the days when special interests took advantage of Main Street families. We're not going to go back to the days when insurance companies wrote the rules that let you languish without health care because you had a preexisting condition. We're not going to go back to the exact same agenda we had before I took office.

A lot has changed since that last election, but what hasn't changed is the choice facing this country. It is still fear versus hope. It is still the past versus the future. It is still a choice between sliding backwards and moving forward. That is what this election's about. That's the choice you will face in November.

So I need you to knock on some doors for Dick Blumenthal. I need you to talk to your neighbors about Dick Blumenthal. I need you to make phone calls for Dick Blumenthal. We need you to write some more checks for Dick Blumenthal. We need you to do this for candidates all across the country, because the only way we'll match their millions of dollars is if we've got millions of people making their voices heard.

And none of this will be easy. It's going to be hard. But you didn't elect me to do what was easy. And you're not going to elect Dick to do what was easy. You elect us to do what is right. So help me get Dick elected. And let's keep on moving forward, Connecticut.

Thank you very much. God bless you, and God bless the United States of America.

NOTE: The President spoke at 6:36 p.m. at the Stamford Marriott Hotel & Spa. In his remarks, he referred to Thomaston, CT, resident Laura Austin and her son Skyler; Connecticut senatorial candidate Linda E. McMahon; Rep. Pete Sessions, in his capacity as chairman of the National Republican Congressional Committee; and House Republican Leader John A. Boehner. He also referred to his sister Maya Soetoro-Ng.

Remarks at a Democratic National Committee Reception in Greenwich, Connecticut
September 16, 2010

Well, listen, Richard and Ellen, I'm so grateful to you guys for opening up this extraordinary home.

And just a couple of quick acknowledgments. Obviously, we've got races all across the country that are important, but there are very few races that are more important to me than the race for U.S. Senate here, and Dick Blumenthal, I think, is just an outstanding candidate who is going to be a terrific U.S. Senator. We've got Dan Malloy, who is going to be the next Governor of Connecticut. And we've got somebody who is probably the only person who is putting in more miles than me, Tim Kaine.

It is great to be here with some new friends, but also some old friends. Richard and Ellen were some of my earliest supporters. They actually supported me when I ran for United States Senate, before people could pronounce my name. [*Laughter*] And so for them to open up their house like this is just terrific.

I'm not going to give a long speech because I want to take the opportunity to sit with each of you and hear what you're thinking, answer your questions. But let me just say generally, we came into office back in January of 2009 at a historic time: the worst financial crisis that we've seen since the Great Depression, on the verge of a Great Depression, in the midst of two wars. And so the challenges that we've confronted over these last 2 years have been extraordinary. And we've got a long way to go. This country received a body blow, and it was already having difficulties competitively. It was already falling behind educationally. We had a health care system that was broken, a middle class that hadn't seen its incomes or wages go up at the same time as their costs were skyrocketing for everything from college tuition to health care.

And so the recovery has been painfully slow. We've got millions of people who are still out of work, hundreds of thousands of people who've lost their homes. People are anxious about the future; they're fearful about the future. And we're in a very competitive environment, where other countries like China and India have now caught up—in some indicators—and are going to keep on moving, because they are hungry and they've got some very talented people.

Having said that, after being in this job for 2 years, I have never been more optimistic about America. I am optimistic partly because we did some really tough things that aren't always popular, but were the right things to do. We had initiated an education reform agenda that is shaking up the education system all across the country. And I've got a terrific Secretary of Education who's been able to get teachers, principals, students—sometimes there's some contentiousness about it, but everybody focused on how are we going to lift up performance for all our kids so they can compete in a global economy.

We have finally started digging into our health care system in a way that is not just providing health insurance to 31 million people who didn't have it before. I spoke to a woman today who was the first person to sign up for an insurance pool that allows people with preexisting conditions to finally get health insurance. She lives up in New Hampshire, had lymphoma, could not get treatment, could not get health insurance. And we signed that bill just as she was about to give up—and is now in the midst of treatment, and her prognosis is good.

But that's not the only reason that we initiated reform. We're now digging in to see what we can do so that our costs for businesses and families start getting under control and we can bend that cost curve.

We initiated a financial regulatory reform bill that was obviously contentious. And a lot of folks in Connecticut work on Wall Street, and so they're folks who at some point felt like, are we attacking Wall Street? No. What we want to do is to create a financial system that is vibrant and dynamic and innovative, but also create some rules of the road so we don't go through what we went through over the last 2 years. And if we had smart rules that treat consumers fairly and that promotes transparency, that's going to allow us to stay the leader in financial services for years to come. And it means that we're going to be able to finance businesses all around the country and around the world that help grow our economy.

So we made the largest investment in research and development in our history. We'd been falling behind, and now we are back at the forefront of R&D. We made the largest investment in green energy in our history so that we could start building solar panels and wind turbines all around the country.

So all these long-term investments that we made are going to be bearing fruit not just next year, not just the year after, but for a couple decades to come. And that's what makes me optimistic.

That's just on the domestic front. In foreign policy, we've reset our relations around the world so that—a lot of people who travel will come back and say to me, you know, folks are once again looking to America for leadership in a way that they haven't for a long time. We have ended our combat mission in Iraq. We are initiating Middle East peace once again; I had the parties at the table. Old adversaries like Russia are now cooperating with us, and we just got a nuclear arms reduction treaty out of the Senate committee today, and we hope to get it ratified before the end of the year.

Across the board, we are making progress. Now, I'm making this point for two reasons. Number one, the changes we've made are ones that will take some time to bear fruit. And folks who are out of work right now, whose homes are underwater right now, who are trying to figure out how to pay the bills or send their kids to college right now, they don't have 5 or 10 years to wait. And so we've got to still work very hard in the short term to dig ourselves out of this enormous hole.

And that's why having public servants like Dick Blumenthal in Washington is so important. Because the other side, all they are going to be feeding us is anger and resentment and not a lot of new ideas. But that's a potent force when people are scared and they're hurting. And so for all of you to support candidates like Dick all across the country is absolutely vital, because our job is not yet finished. And the agenda of the other side is essentially to roll back progress that we've made. And they're doing so, by the way, not just by self-financed candidates like the one here in Connecticut, but because of the Supreme Court decision from the Roberts Court called the *Citizens United*. You now have special interests spending—outspending candidates and parties all across America, spending millions of dollars without disclosing who they're spending it—who they are and what interests lie behind all these negative TV ads.

So we are going to be in some tough fights everywhere, and all of you are going to be desperately needed in order for us to keep moving in a positive direction.

Now, the second reason I'm telling you this is because Democrats, just congenitally, tend to get—to see the glass as half empty. [*Laughter*] If we get an historic health care bill passed—oh, well, the public option wasn't there. If you get the financial reform bill passed—then, well, I don't know about this particularly derivatives rule; I'm not sure that I'm satisfied with that. And gosh, we haven't yet brought about world peace,

and I thought that was going to happen quicker. [*Laughter*] You know who you are. [*Laughter*]

We have had the most productive, progressive legislative session in at least a generation. And so I want everybody here to—when you are talking to your friends and your neighbors and your coworkers, I want you to feel good about the support that you've provided. Because you didn't send me there to do what was easy, you sent me there to do what was hard. We have tackled some of the hardest problems facing this country, and we did so in the midst of crisis, and we are succeeding.

And so as long as you keep that in mind, not only will you feel good about writing checks, but you're also going to be feeling good as you go around the country making the case to ensure that people like Dick Blumenthal are elected to the U.S. Senate.

All right? So thank you very much, everybody. I look forward to talking to you.

NOTE: The President spoke at 7:52 p.m. at the residence of Richard Richman and Ellen Schapps Richman. In his remarks, he referred to Timothy M. Kaine, chairman, Democratic National Committee; cancer patient Gail O'Brien of Keene, NH; and Connecticut senatorial candidate Linda E. McMahon. Audio was not available for verification of the content of these remarks.

Remarks on the Appointment of Elizabeth Warren as Assistant to the President and Special Adviser to the Secretary of the Treasury on the Consumer Financial Protection Bureau
September 17, 2010

Good afternoon, everybody. Before we begin, I just want to mention a report that was released by the Census Bureau yesterday about what happened to wages during the last decade. It revealed that between 2001 and 2009, the incomes of middle class families fell by almost 5 percent. I want to repeat that: Between 2001 and 2009, the incomes of middle class families fell by 5 percent.

In the words of today's Wall Street Journal, this "lost decade" was the worst for families in half a century, a decade that obviously ended in a devastating recession that made things even worse.

We know that a strong middle class leads a strong economy. And that's why as we dig our way out of this recession, we've set our sights on policies that grow the middle class and provide a ladder for those who are struggling to join it. And that's why I'm urging the leaders of the other party to stop holding middle class tax cuts hostage and extend this relief to families immediately. They need it. They need our help. And that's why we're here today.

Part of what led to the financial crisis were practices that took advantage of consumers, particularly when too many homeowners were deceived into taking out mortgages on their homes that they couldn't afford. But we also know that these practices predated the crisis, and we also know that these practices don't just exist in the housing market.

For years, banks and mortgage lenders and credit card companies have often used fine print and confusing language and attractive, front-end offers to take advantage of American consumers. We've seen banks charge unreasonable overdraft fees. We've seen credit card companies hit folks with unfair rate hikes. We've seen mortgage lenders offer cheap initial monthly payments and interest rates that later skyrocketed. All this has cost middle class families billions of dollars—tens of billions of dollars—that they could have used to pay the bills or make the mortgage or send their kids to college.

And I have to say, when Michelle and I were first starting a family, we had to navigate a lot of these financial decisions, whether it was buying a first home or paying off our college loans or putting a lot of debt on credit cards. And obviously, we were better off than a lot of families, but we still often found ourselves confused or finding ourselves in tough situations as a consequence. So we've got an idea—a pretty good idea—I've got a personally good idea of how this can be difficult and sometimes confusing for the average consumer.

And that's partly why, even when I was still in the U.S. Senate, I took such a great interest in the work of the woman standing next to me. I have known Elizabeth Warren since law school. She's a native of Oklahoma. She's a janitor's daughter who has become one of the country's fiercest advocates for the middle class. She has seen financial struggles and foreclosures affect her own family.

Long before this crisis hit, she had written eloquently, passionately, forcefully about the growing financial pressures on working families and the need to put in place stronger consumer protections. And 3 years ago, she came up with an idea for a new, independent agency that would have one simple overriding mission:

standing up for consumers and middle class families.

Thanks to Elizabeth's efforts, as well as the dedication and persistence of the person to my right, Secretary of Treasury Geithner, as well as leaders in Congress like Chris Dodd and Barney Frank, that agency will soon become a reality.

The Consumer Financial Protection Bureau, which was one of the central aspects of financial reform, will empower all Americans with the clear and concise information they need to make the best choices, the best financial decisions for them and their families.

Never again will folks be confused or misled by the pages of barely understandable fine print that you find in agreements for credit cards or mortgages or student loans. The Bureau's going to crack down on the abusive practices of unscrupulous mortgage lenders. It will reinforce the new credit card law that we passed banning unfair rate hikes and ensure that folks aren't unwittingly caught by overdraft fees when they sign up for a checking account. It will give students who take out college loans clear information and make sure that lenders don't game the system. And it will ensure that every American receives a free credit score if they are denied a loan or insurance because of that score.

Basically, the Consumer Financial Protection Bureau will be a watchdog for the American consumer, charged with enforcing the toughest financial protections in history.

Now, getting this agency off the ground will be an enormously important task, a task that can't wait. And that task is something that I've asked Elizabeth to take on. Secretary Geithner and I both agree that Elizabeth is the best person to stand this agency up. She was the architect behind the idea for a consumer watchdog, so it only makes sense that she'd be the—she should be the architect working with Secretary of Treasury Geithner in standing up the agency.

She will help oversee all aspects of the Bureau's creation, from staff recruitment to designing policy initiatives to future decisions about the agency. She will have direct access to me and to Secretary Geithner, and she will oversee a staff at the Treasury Department that has already begun to work on this task.

She will also play a pivotal role in helping me determine who the best choice is for Director of the Bureau. And given the importance of these economic issues, I also want Elizabeth to have a role as a White House adviser, as well as adviser to Secretary Geithner, on consumer issues.

Elizabeth understands what I strongly believe, that a strong, growing economy begins with a strong and thriving middle class. And that means every American has to get a fair shake in their financial dealings.

For years, financial companies have been able to spend millions of dollars on their own watchdog—lobbyists who look out for their in-terests and fight for their priorities. That's their right. But from now on, consumers will also have a powerful watchdog, a tough, independent watchdog whose job it is to stand up for their financial interests, for their families' future. And I am proud that we got this done, and I'm equally proud that Elizabeth Warren will be helping to make her original vision a reality.

So we are extremely proud of you, Elizabeth. Good luck.

NOTE: The President spoke at 1:37 p.m. in the Rose Garden at the White House. The Office of the Press Secretary also released a Spanish language transcript of these remarks.

The President's Weekly Address
September 18, 2010

Back in January, in my State of the Union Address, I warned of the danger posed by a Supreme Court ruling called *Citizens United*. This decision overturned decades of law and precedent. It gave the special interests the power to spend without limit and without public disclosure to run ads in order to influence elections.

Now, as an election approaches, it's not just a theory. We can see for ourselves how destructive to our democracy this can become. We've seen it in the flood of deceptive attack ads sponsored by special interests using front groups with misleading names. We don't know who's behind these ads or who's paying for them. Even foreign-controlled corporations seeking to influence our democracy are able to spend freely in order to swing an election toward a candidate they prefer.

We've tried to fix this with a new law, one that would simply require that you say who you are and who's paying for your ad. This way, voters are able to make an informed judgment about a group's motivations. Anyone running these ads would have to stand by their claims. And foreign-controlled corporations would be restricted from spending money to influence elections, just as they were before the Supreme Court opened up this loophole.

This is common sense. In fact, this is the kind of proposal that Democrats and Republicans have agreed on for decades. Yet the Republican leaders in Congress have so far said no. They've blocked this bill from even coming up for a vote in the Senate. It's politics at its worst. But it's not hard to understand why.

Over the past 2 years, we've fought back against the entrenched special interests, weakening their hold on the levers of power in Washington. We've taken a stand against the worst abuses of the financial industry and the health insurance companies. We've rolled back tax breaks for companies that ship jobs overseas. And we've restored enforcement of common-sense rules to protect clean air and clean water. In other words, we've refused to go along with business as usual.

Now the special interests want to take Congress back and return to the days when lobbyists wrote the laws. And a partisan minority in Congress is hoping their defense of these special interests and the status quo will be rewarded with a flood of negative ads against their opponents. It's a power grab, pure and simple. They're hoping they can ride this wave of unchecked influence all the way to victory.

What's clear is that Congress has a responsibility to act. But the truth is, any law will probably come too late to prevent the damage that's already been done this election season. And that's why any time you see an attack ad by one of these shadowy groups, you should ask yourself, who is paying for this ad? Is it the health insurance lobby, the oil industry, the credit card companies?

More than that, you can make sure that the tens of millions of dollars spent on misleading ads don't drown out your voice. Because no matter how many ads they run, no matter how many elections they try to buy, the power to determine the fate of this country doesn't lie in their hands, it lies in yours. It's up to all of us to defend that most basic American principle of a government of, by, and for the people. What's at stake is not just an election; it's our democracy itself.

Thanks.

NOTE: The address was recorded at approximately 4:30 p.m. on September 17 in the Library at the White House for broadcast on September 18. In the address, the President referred to H.R. 5175. The transcript was made available by the Office of the Press Secretary on September 17, but was embargoed for release until 6 a.m. on September 18. The Office of the Press Secretary also released a Spanish language transcript of this address.

Remarks at the Congressional Black Caucus Foundation Phoenix Awards Dinner
September 18, 2010

The President. Hello, CBC! Well, it is wonderful to be back with all of you. I want to acknowledge, first of all, chair of the CBC Barbara Lee for the outstanding work that she has done this year. Somebody who not only is a passionate defender of our domestic agenda, but also somebody who knows more about our foreign policy than just about anybody on the Hill, the chair of the CBC Foundation, Donald Payne, thank you. Our ALC Conference cochairs, Elijah Cummings and Diane Watson, thank you. To Dr. Elsie Scott, president and CEO of the CBC Foundation, thank you for your outstanding work.

We've got a couple of very special guests here today. I want to give a shout-out to my friend, somebody who all of us rely on for his wisdom, his steadiness, the House majority whip, Jim Clyburn. A couple of folks who are working tirelessly in my Cabinet: the Attorney General of the United States, Eric Holder, is in the house; the woman who is charged with implementing health care reform, HHS Secretary Kathleen Sebelius, is here; our United States Trade Representative, Ambassador Ron Kirk, is here.

And obviously, it is a great honor to have been able to speak backstage to this year's Phoenix Award honorees: Judith Jamison, Harry Belafonte, Sheila Oliver, and Simeon Booker. Thank you for everything that you've done for America.

I know you've spent a good deal of time during CBC weekend talking about a whole range of issues and talking about what the future holds not just for the African American community, but for the United States of America. I've been spending some time thinking about that too. [*Laughter*] And at this time of great challenge, one source of inspiration is the story behind the founding of the Congressional Black Caucus.

I want us all to take a moment and remember what was happening 40 years ago when 13 Black Members of Congress decided to come together and form this caucus. It was 1969. More than a decade had passed since the Supreme Court decided *Brown* versus *Board of Education*. It had been years since Selma and Montgomery, since Dr. King had told America of his dream, all of it culminating in the passage of the Civil Rights Act and the Voting Rights Act.

The founders of this caucus could look back and feel pride in the progress that had been made. They could feel confident that America was finally moving in the right direction. But they knew they couldn't afford to rest on their laurels. They couldn't be complacent. There were still too many inequalities to be eliminated, too many injustices to be overturned, too many wrongs to be righted.

That's why the CBC was formed: to right wrongs, to be the conscience of the Congress. And at the very first CBC dinner, the great actor and activist Ossie Davis told the audience America was at a crossroads. And although his speech was magnificent and eloquent, he boiled his message down to a nice little phrase when it came to how America would move forward. He said, "It's not the man, it's the plan." It's not the man, it's the plan. That was true 40 years ago. It is true today.

We all understood that during my campaign. This wasn't just about electing a Black President. This was about a plan to rescue our economy and rebuild it on a new foundation. Statistics just came out this week: From 2001 to 2009, the income of middle class families in this country went down 5 percent. Think about that. People's incomes during that period, when the economy was growing, went down 5 percent. That's what our agenda was about: making sure that we were changing that pattern. It was about giving every hard-working American a chance to join a growing and vibrant middle class and giving people ladders and steps to success. It was about putting the American Dream within the reach of all Americans, not just some. No matter who you are, no matter what you look like, no matter where you come from, everybody would have access to the America Dream.

I don't have to tell you we're not there yet. This historic recession, the worst since the Great Depression, has taken a devastating toll on all sectors of our economy. It's hit Americans of all races and all regions and all walks of life. But as has been true often in our history, as has been true in other recessions, this one came down with a particular vengeance on the African American community.

It added to problems that a lot of neighborhoods had been facing long before the storm of this recession. Long before this recession, there were Black men and women throughout our cities and towns who'd given up looking for a job and kids standing around on the corners without any prospects for the future. Long before this recession, there were blocks full of shuttered stores that hadn't been open in generations. So yes, this recession made matters much worse, but the African American community has been struggling for quite some time.

It's been a decade in which progress has stalled. And we know that repairing the damage, climbing our way out of this recession, we understand it will take time. It's not going to happen overnight. But what I want to say to all of you tonight is that we've begun the hard work of moving this country forward. We are moving in the right direction.

When I took office, our economy was on the brink of collapse. So we acted immediately, and the CBC acted immediately, and we took steps to stop the financial meltdown and our economic freefall. And now our economy is growing again. The month I was sworn in, we had lost 750,000 jobs. We've now seen 8 months in a row in which we've added private sector jobs. We're in a different place than we were a year ago or 18 months ago.

And let's face it, taking some of these steps wasn't easy. There were a lot of naysayers, a lot of skepticism. There was a lot of skepticism about whether we could get GM and Chrysler back on their feet. There were folks who wanted to walk away, potentially see another million jobs lost. But we said, we've got to try. And now U.S. auto industries are profitable again and hiring again, back on their feet again, on the move again.

There were folks who were wondering whether we could hold the banks accountable for what they had done to taxpayers or were skeptical about whether we could make infrastructure investments and investments in clean energy and investments in education and hold ourselves accountable for how that money was spent. There was a lot of skepticism about what we were trying to do. And a lot of it was unpopular.

But I want to remind everybody here, you did not elect me to do what was popular, you elected me to do what was right. That's what we've been fighting together for: to do what's right. We don't have our finger out to the wind to know what's right.

That's why we passed health insurance reform that will make it illegal for insurance companies to deny you coverage because of a preexisting condition, historic reforms that will give over 30 million Americans the chance to finally obtain quality care, tackles the disparities in the health care system, puts a cap on the amount you can be charged in out-of-pocket expenses. Because nobody should go broke because they got sick in a country like the United States of America, not here.

That's why we passed Wall Street reform to finally crack down on the predatory practices of some of the banks and mortgage companies so we can protect hard-working families from abusive fees or unjustified rates every time they use a credit card or make a mortgage payment or go to a payday loan operation or take out a student loan or overdraw on their account at an ATM. Laws that will help put an end to the days of Government bailouts so Main Street never again has to pay for Wall Street's mistakes.

That's why we made historic investments in education, including our HBCUs, and shifted tens of billions of dollars that were going to subsidize banks and made sure that money was giving millions of more children the chance to go to college and have a better future. That's what we've been doing.

That's why we're keeping the promises I made on the campaign trail. We passed tax cuts for 95 percent of working families. We expanded national service, from AmeriCorps to the Peace Corps. We recommitted our Justice Department to the enforcement of civil rights laws. We changed sentencing disparities as a consequence of the hard work of many in the CBC. We started closing tax breaks for companies that ship jobs overseas so we can give those tax breaks to companies that invest right here in the United States of America.

We ended our combat mission in Iraq and welcomed nearly 100,000 troops home. In Afghanistan, we're breaking the momentum of the Taliban and training Afghan forces so that next summer, we can begin the transition to Afghan responsibility. And in the meantime, we're making sure we take care of our veterans as well as they have taken care of us. We don't just talk about our veterans, give speeches about our veterans; we actually put the money in to make sure we're taking care of our veterans.

And even as we manage these national security priorities, we are partnering with developing countries to feed and educate and house their people. We're helping Haiti rebuild, following an unprecedented response from the United States Government and the United States military in the wake of the devastation there. In Sudan, we're committed to doing our part—and we call on the parties there to do their part—to fully implement the Comprehensive Peace Agreement and ensure lasting peace and accountability in Darfur. As I said in Ghana, it is in America's strategic interest to be a stronger partner with the nations throughout Africa. That's not just good for them, that's good for us.

That's what we've been doing, CBC, at home and abroad. It's been an important time. We've had a historic legislative session. We could have been just keeping things quiet and peaceful around here, because change is hard. But we decided to do what was hard and necessary to move this country forward. Members of the CBC have helped deliver some of the most significant progress in a generation, laws that will help strengthen America's middle class and give more pathways for men and women to climb out of poverty.

But we've still got a long way to go: too many people still out of work, too many families still facing foreclosure, too many businesses and neighborhoods still struggling to rebound. During the course of this recession, poverty has gone up to a 15-year high.

So it's not surprising, given the hardships we're seeing all across the land, that a lot of people may not be feeling very energized, very engaged right now. A lot of folks may be feeling like politics is something that they get involved with every 4 years when there's a Presidential election, but they don't see why they should bother the rest of the time, which brings me back to Ossie Davis. Ossie Davis understood, it's not the man, it's the plan. And the plan is still unfinished.

For all the strides we've made in our economy, we need to finish our plan for a stronger economy. Our middle class is still shaken, and too many folks are still locked in poverty.

For all the progress on education, too many students aren't graduating ready for college and a career. We still have schools where half the kids are dropping out. We've got to finish our plan to give all of our children the best education the world has to offer.

We've still got to implement health care reform so that it brings down costs and improves access for all people.

And we've got to make sure that we are putting people to work rebuilding America's roads and railways and runways and schools. We've got more work to do. We've got a plan to finish.

Now, remember, the other side has a plan too. [*Laughter*] It's a plan to turn back the clock on every bit of progress we've made. To paraphrase my friend Deval Patrick, the last election was a changing of the guard; now we've got to guard the change. Because everything that we are for, our opponents have spent 2 years fighting against. They said no to unemployment insurance, no to tax cuts for ordinary working families, no for small-business loans, no to providing additional assistance to students who desperately want to go to school. That's their motto: "No, we can't." [*Laughter*] Can you imagine having that on your bumper sticker? [*Laughter*] It's not very inspiring. [*Laughter*]

In fact, the only agenda they've got is to go back to the same old policies that got us into this mess in the first place. I'll give you an example. They want to borrow $700 billion—keep in mind, we don't have $700 billion—they want to borrow $700 billion, from the Chinese or the Saudis or whoever is lending, and use it on tax cuts—more tax cuts for millionaires and billionaires. Average tax cut: $100,000 for people making a million dollars or more.

Now, the next few years are going to be tough budget years, which is why I've called for a freeze on some discretionary spending. If we are spending $700 billion, we're borrowing $700 billion, not paying for it, it's got to come from somewhere. Where do you think it's going to come from? Who do you think is going to pay for these $100,000 checks going to millionaires? Our seniors, our children, hard-working families all across America that are already struggling?

We shouldn't be passing tax cuts for millionaires and billionaires right now. That's not what we should be doing. We should be helping the middle class grow. We should be providing pathways out of poverty. And yet the man with the plan to be Speaker of the House, John Boehner, attacked us for closing corporate tax loopholes and using the money to keep hundreds of thousands of essential personnel on the jobs all across the States. He called these jobs, and I quote, "government jobs," suggested they weren't worth saving—teacher jobs, police officer jobs, firefighter jobs.

Ask your sister who's a teacher if her job is worth saving. Ask your uncle who's a firefighter if his job was worth saving. Ask your cousin who's a police officer if her job was worth saving. Ask your neighbors if their jobs were worth saving. Because I think a job is worth saving if it's keeping Americans working and keeping America strong and secure. That's what I believe. That's what's at stake in this. They want to hand Washington back over to special interests. We're fighting on behalf of the American people. They want to take us backwards. We want to move forward.

Their main strategy is they're betting you'll come down with a case of amnesia—[*laughter*]—that you'll forget what happened between 2001 and 2009, what that agenda did to this country when they were in charge. And they spent almost a decade driving the economy into the ditch. And now we've been down in that ditch, put on our boots—it's hot down there—we've been pushing the car, shoving it—[*laughter*]—sweating. They're standing on the sidelines, sipping a Slurpee—[*laughter*]—watching us, saying: "You're not pushing fast enough. You're not pushing hard enough." [*Laughter*]

Finally, we get the car out of the ditch; it's back on the road. They tap us on the shoulder. They say, "We want the keys back." We tell them: "You can't have the keys back. You don't know how to drive. You can't have it back." [*Applause*] That's right.

Audience member. Can't give them the keys!

The President. You can't give them the keys. [*Laughter*] I mean, I just want to point out, if you want your car to go forward, what do you do?

Audience members. "D"!

The President. You put it in "D." You want to go backwards, what do you do? That's all I'm saying. That's not a coincidence. That's not a coincidence.

All right, all right, I get it. We've got to move this program along. [*Laughter*]

There are those who want to turn back the clock. They want to do what's right politically instead of what's right, period. They think about the next election. We're thinking about the next generation. We can't think short term when so many people are out of work, not when so many families are still hurting. We need to finish the plan you elected me to put in place.

And I need you. I need you because this isn't going to be easy. And I didn't promise you easy. I said back on the campaign that change was going to be hard. Sometimes it's going to be slower than some folks would like. I said sometimes we'd be making some compromises and people would be frustrated. I said I could not do it alone. This wasn't just a matter of getting me elected and, suddenly, I was going to snap my fingers and all our problems would go away. It was a matter of all of us getting involved, all of us staying committed, all of us sticking with our

plan for a better future until it was complete. That's how we've always moved this country forward.

Each and every time we've made epic change, from this country's founding to emancipation to women's suffrage to workers' rights, it has not come from a man. It has come from a plan. It has come from a grassroots movement rallying around a cause. That's what the civil rights movement made possible. Foot soldiers like so many of you, sitting down at lunch counters, standing up for freedom—what made it possible for me to be here today—Americans throughout our history making our Union more equal, making our Union more just, making our Union more perfect, one step at a time.

That's what we need again. So I need everybody here to go back to your neighborhoods, to go back to your workplaces, to go to churches and go to the barbershops and got to the beauty shops and tell them we've got more work to do. Tell them we can't wait to organize. Tell them that the time for action is now and that if each and every person in this country who knows what is at stake steps up to the plate, if we are willing to rise to this moment like we've always done, then together, we will write our own destiny once more.

Thank you. God bless you, and may God bless the United States of America.

NOTE: The President spoke at 8:47 p.m. at the Walter E. Washington Convention Center. In his remarks, he referred to dancer and choreographer Judith Jamison; musician and activist Harry Belafonte; Sheila Y. Oliver, speaker, New Jersey General Assembly; journalist Simeon Booker; and Gov. Deval L. Patrick of Massachusetts.

Statement on the Oil Spill in the Gulf of Mexico
September 19, 2010

Today we achieved an important milestone in our response to the BP oil spill, the final termination of the damaged well that sat deep under the Gulf of Mexico. I commend Admiral Thad

Allen, Secretaries Salazar, Chu, Napolitano, Administrators Jackson and Lubchenco, Carol Browner, the Federal science and engineering teams, and the thousands of men and women who worked around the clock to respond to this crisis and ultimately complete this challenging but critical step to ensure that the well has stopped leaking forever.

However, while we have seen a diminished need for our massive response that encompassed more than 40,000 people, 7,000 vessels, and the coordination of dozens of Federal, State, and local agencies and other partners, we also remain committed to doing everything possible to make sure the Gulf Coast recovers fully from this disaster. This road will not be easy, but we will continue to work closely with the people of the Gulf to rebuild their livelihoods and restore the environment that supports them. My administration will see our communities, our businesses, and our fragile ecosystems through this difficult time.

Remarks at CNBC's "Investing in America" Town Hall Meeting and a Question-and-Answer Session
September 20, 2010

John Harwood. Good afternoon from Washington, DC. I'm John Harwood. It is noon on the East Coast. The Dow Jones average stands around 10,700 points. Fifteen million Americans are out of work. And we're spending the next hour talking about how to fix the troubled American economy.

Please welcome the President of the United States.

The President. Hey, John. Thank you. Thank you very much.

Mr. Harwood. Now, Mr. President, thanks for being here.

The President. That was quite a lead-in, by the way. [*Laughter*]

Continued Economic Stabilization

Mr. Harwood. Yes, wasn't it? You like that dramatic pause? [*Laughter*] We have got a cross section of people from around the country: CEOs, union workers, teachers and students, small——

The President. It's a good-looking group, I have to say. [*Laughter*] I'm——

Mr. Harwood. ——yes—small-business owners, people who don't have a job. Every one of them has a stake——

The President. Right.

Mr. Harwood. ——in the American Dream. And they got some good news over the weekend. The National Bureau of Economic Research, as you know, has said that the recession ended in June 2009, a few months after you took office. And yet here's the problem you find yourself with: Many leaders in business think you and your policies are hostile to them, and many ordinary Americans think your policies are helping Wall Street and big business. How did that happen?

The President. Well, first of all, even though economists may say that the recession officially ended last year, obviously for the millions of people who are still out of work, people who have seen their home values decline, people who are struggling to pay the bills day to day, it's still very real for them.

And I think we have to go back to what was happening when I was first sworn in as the 44th President of the United States. We went through the worst recession since the Great Depression. Nothing's come close. In fact, if you look at the consequences of the recession in the eighties, the recession in the nineties, and the recession in 2001, and you combine all three of those, it still wasn't as bad as this recession that we went through.

So the month I was sworn in, we lost 750,000 jobs; the month after that, 600,000; the month after that, 600,000. This is before any of our plans had a chance to take effect. The financial markets were on the verge of meltdown, and the economy was contracting about 6 percent, by far the largest contraction we've seen since the thirties.

You combine all that, and what that meant was that we had to take some steps very quickly just to make sure that the financial system was not collapsing, that people could get auto loans, could get student loans, that businesses large and small could get some financing to keep their doors open and to keep their payrolls on track. And in addition, we had to make sure that we didn't slip into a Great Depression.

Now, we've done that. Those programs that we put in place worked. So now you've got a financial system that is stable. It's still not as strong as it was back in 2006, 2007, but it is stabilized. You've got now 8 consecutive months of private sector job growth. Businesses are able to borrow again, they're investing again, they're making profits again.

That's all the good news. The challenge is, is that the hole was so deep that a lot of people out there are still hurting, and probably some folks here in the audience are still having a tough time. And so the question then becomes, what can we now put in place to make sure that the trend lines continue in a positive direction, as opposed to going back in the negative direction?

Last week, we got some good news. After fighting for several months, we finally got a small-business tax cut bill in place so that we're eliminating capital gains for small businesses and startups, making sure that they can get loans, because small businesses are the ones that have been hardest hit in terms of not being able to get capital. We have put forward proposals, for example, to accelerate investment here in the United States instead of overseas in research and development and plants and equipment that could put people back to work.

So there are a lot of plans in place that can make improvement, but it's slow and steady, as opposed to the kind of quick fix that I think a lot of people would like to see. But the thing I've just got to remind people of is the fact that it took us a decade to get into the problem that we're in right now.

The Wall Street Journal came out with a report based on census information that the years from 2001 to 2009, the middle class actually saw their wages decline by 5 percent. This was be-

fore the financial crisis. So these have been some long-term trends of the middle class having a lot of problems out there.

Mr. Harwood. Now——

The President. And what we've got to do now is to reverse it, but something that took 10 years to create, it's going to take a little more time to solve.

Mr. Harwood. Now, I've heard you give that turnaround message you just gave——

The President. Right.

Mr. Harwood. ——many times.

The President. Right.

Public Perception of Economic Stabilization/Midterm Elections

Mr. Harwood. Let me ask about your assessment of the challenge in and the problem in communicating that to the American people. We all identify with people like ourselves.

The President. Right.

Mr. Harwood. Do you think it's possible that because of your style or the unusual things about your background—your racial heritage, where you grew up, Ivy League education—that the fearful voters who are about to go to the polls in November think, yes, I hear him, he may get it intellectually, but he doesn't feel what I'm feeling?

The President. Well, here's my suspicion. I think that when the unemployment rate is still high and people are having a tough time, it doesn't matter if I was green—[*laughter*]—it doesn't matter if I was purple. I think people would still be frustrated, and understandably so.

Look, I can describe what's happening to the economy overall, but if you're out of work right now, the only thing that you're going to be hearing is, when do I get a job? If you're about to lose your home, all you're thinking about is, when can I get my home?

So I don't think that those are the issues. And by the way, I think most people understand—because I spent 2 years running around the country talking about my life and why I was running for President—they understand that I was the kid of a single mom and I got my education through scholarships and I lived in a small apartment with my grandparents and they were helped by the GI bill and FHA in terms of being able to climb into the middle class.

The whole reason I ran was because my life is a testimony to the American Dream. And everything that we've been doing since I came into office is designed to make sure that that American Dream continues for future generations.

I think the challenge right now is that I'm thinking about the next generation and there are a lot of folks out there who are thinking about the next election. If I were making decisions based on November, then I wouldn't have done some of the things that I did, because I knew they weren't popular. But they were the right thing to do. And that's got to be my top priority.

Mr. Harwood. Now, let's go to the real jury who will decide whether they were the right things to do with an audience question right here.

Education Reform/Financial Regulatory Reform/Health Care Reform

Q. Thank you very much, and, quite frankly, good afternoon, President Obama. I am deeply honored to finally be in this forum and so grateful for CNBC making the forum available so that you can speak to American citizens just like myself.

The President. Well, thank you.

Q. I am a chief financial officer for a veterans service organization, AMVETS, here in Washington. I'm also a mother, I'm a wife, I'm an American veteran, and I'm one of your middle class Americans. And quite frankly, I'm exhausted. I'm exhausted of defending you, defending your administration——

The President. Right.

Q. ——defending the mantle of change that I voted for——

The President. Right.

Q. ——and deeply disappointed with where we are right now.

I have been told that I voted for a man who said he was going to change things in a meaningful way for the middle class. I'm one of those people, and I'm waiting, sir. I'm waiting. I don't feel it yet. And I thought, while it wouldn't be in

great measure, I would feel it in some small measure.

I have two children in private school, and the financial recession has taken an enormous toll on my family. My husband and I joked for years that we thought we were well beyond the hot-dogs-and-beans era of our lives.

The President. Right.

Q. But quite frankly, it's starting to knock on our door and ring true that that might be where we're headed again. And quite frankly, Mr. President, I need you to answer this honestly: Is this my new reality?

The President. Well, first of all, I think that you describe exactly what is the bedrock of America: the—a veteran who's working for veterans, somebody who's a CFO and I am sure knows how to manage their money, have made good decisions.

Q. Some days. [*Laughter*]

The President. Well, I'm not saying once in a while you don't want to get a new pair of shoes, you know? [*Laughter*]

Q. Today even, sir. [*Laughter*]

The President. So the life you describe—one of responsibility, looking after your family, contributing back to your community—that's what we want to reward.

Now, as I said before, times are tough for everybody right now, so I understand your frustration. But I would just—when you say there are things that you'd like to see happen or you're hoping to see happen that haven't happened yet, let me just give you a couple of examples.

Q. Okay.

The President. I right now have two children; it sounds like you've got kids as well.

Q. Two girls.

The President. Two girls. You're going to be thinking about college soon.

Q. Next year.

The President. Okay. Now, part of what we did over the last year and a half is to make sure that billions of dollars that were going to subsidize financial service industries under the Federal student loan programs are now going to be going directly to students so that millions more students are going to be able to get loans and grants and scholarships to go to college. Now, that's going to have an impact on a whole bunch of kids out there, including maybe yours.

If you have a credit card, which I assume you do——

Q. No.

The President. Well, see, now you're really—now you've shown how responsible you are. [*Laughter*] But if you have a mortgage or a credit card or any kind of financial dealings out there, as a consequence of the changes we made, the credit card companies can't increase your interest rate without notifying you, and they can't increase your interest rate on your previous balances. In terms of getting a mortgage, they—you can't have a mortgage broker steer you to a mortgage that ultimately is going to cost you more money, because maybe they're getting a financial incentive to do so. Those things are now against the law. So there are a whole host of protections in there.

You are a parent who has children—if your child, heaven forbid, had a preexisting condition, before I took office, you were out of luck in terms of being able to get health insurance for that child. Now insurance companies have to give you health insurance for that child, and by the way, that health insurance company can't drop you if you get sick.

So there are a whole host of things that we've put in place that do make your life better. But the bottom line is, if your 401(k) is still down substantially from where it was a while back, if you haven't seen a raise in a long time, if your home value went down——

Q. Keep going. [*Laughter*]

The President. ——depending on where you live, all those things still make you feel like, gosh, I'm treading water.

Q. Still struggling, that's right.

The President. And so my goal here is not to try to convince you that everything is where it needs to be. It's not. That's why I ran for President. But what I am saying is, is that we're moving in the right direction. And if we are able to keep our eye on our long-term goal, which is making sure that every family out there, if they're middle class, that they can pay their bills, have the security of health insurance, retire with dignity and respect, send their kids to

college; if they're not yet in the middle class, that there are ladders there to get into the middle class if people work hard and get an education and apply themselves—that's our goal. That's the America we believe in. And I think that we are on track to be able to do that.

Revitalizing Business/Financial Regulation

Mr. Harwood. Mr. President, let me go at this from a different direction——

The President. Sure.

Mr. Harwood. ——from the direction of psychology, business confidence.

The President. Right.

Mr. Harwood. You just mentioned things that credit card companies and health insurance companies used to do.

The President. Right.

Mr. Harwood. There are some people in business who think—to use a phrase that you used recently about your critics—who think you talk about them like dogs. Let's listen to Ken Langone, a billionaire businessman.

The President. I'm sorry, billionaire businessman?

Mr. Harwood. Yes.

The President. Okay.

Q. What should they stop doing? Well, I think the one thing to do is to not make people in business feel like we're villains or criminals or doing something wrong. I think anytime we can create a job that puts somebody to work, the country's better served. So I think that there's got to be a need to understand that America, our democracy, is based on a strong, vibrant private economy.

Mr. Harwood. Are you vilifying business?

The President. Absolutely not. Look, let's look at the track record here. When I came into office, businesses, some of the same commentators who are on CNBC, were crying, "Do something," because as a consequence of reckless decisions that had been made, the economy was on the verge of collapse. Those same businesses now are profitable. The financial markets are stabilized. We haven't increased taxes on businesses. Actually, we have instituted about 50 tax cuts, many of them going to businesses large and small.

And so the only thing that we've said is that we've got to make sure that we're not doing some of the same things that we were doing in the past that got us into this mess in the first place.

So when I mentioned, for example, changes in the financial services industry, it is very important for us not to find ourselves in a position in which banks get too big to fail, and if they make bad decisions, taxpayers have to bail them out or we let the entire economy collapse. That's not a choice that I want any future President to have to make. And we instituted those changes.

And the fact is, when FDR in—put in place deposit insurance in banks, banks said at the time, this is going to destroy capitalism. When Medicare was instituted, there were a whole bunch of people who said, this is socialized medicine. Now we take it for granted. But there oftentimes is this response that somehow these modest reforms that make the free market work better for consumers and for workers as well as for businesses, on the front end are resisted.

Mr. Harwood. Let me take it, though, to a level that's beyond policy, and it goes to what you value and you don't value.

The President. Sure.

Mr. Harwood. I think some of those in business may think that deep down, you think that working for profit is morally inferior to the kind of work you used to do as a community organizer. Is that how you feel?

The President. No, it isn't. Look, the—in every speech, every interview that I've made, I've constantly said that what sets America apart, what has made us successful over the long term, is we've got the most dynamic free market economy in the world. And that has to be preserved. That has to be preserved. We are—we benefit from entrepreneurs and innovators who are going out there and creating jobs, creating businesses.

Government can't create the majority of jobs. And in fact, we want to get out of the way of folks who've got a great idea and want to run with it and are going to be putting people to work.

Mr. Harwood. Maybe we've got one of those people right here.

The President. I'd love to hear from him.

Revitalizing the American Dream

Q. Thank you, Mr. President. My name is Ted Brassfield. I'm 30 years old. I recently graduated law school. And I went back to law school in order to pursue a life of public service, like you have. And what I found was that I simply—there aren't jobs out there right now. I took advantage of the loans that you were just speaking about, but I can't make the interest payments on those loans today, let alone thinking—think about getting a mortgage, having a family, having even a marriage—it's awfully expensive. [*Laughter*] And so——

The President. I'm not going to comment on that. [*Laughter*] The—it's—let me just say that whatever the expense, it's worth it. [*Laughter*] I want that on record.

Q. Like a lot of people in my generation, I was really inspired by you and by your campaign and the message that you brought——

The President. Right.

Q. ——and that inspiration is dying away. It feels like the American Dream is not attainable to a lot of us. And what I'm really hoping to hear from you is several concrete steps that you're going to take moving forward that will be able to reignite my generation, reignite the youth who are beset by student loans. And I really want to know, is the American Dream dead for me?

The President. Absolutely not. Look, we still have the best universities in the world. We've got the most dynamic private sector in the world. We've got the most productive workers in the world. There is not a country in the world that would not want to change places with us. For all the problems that we've got, as tough as things are right now, we are still the country that billions of people around the world look to and aspire to. And I want everybody to always remember that.

Now, as I said before, what we saw happening during 2001 to the time I took office was wages actually declining for middle class families, people treading water, young people having more trouble getting their foot in the door in terms of businesses. And so we are now having to go back to the fundamentals that made America great.

And that means we've got to improve our education system. That means that we have to make sure that our markets are working in a way that is good for a broad base of people and not just a narrow base of people. It means that, let's say—you used the example of student loans—one of the things that I just mentioned was, is that we put billions of dollars more into student loans. This was paid for, now. We took this out of financial service industries that were getting essentially unjustified subsidies; they're now going to students so that your debt would be lower. And by the way, part of that law also capped your debt at 10 percent of your income so that you knew that you could actually afford to take out this debt and pay for it even if you had a modest salary.

So we are taking these steps. But the most important thing we can do right now is to grow our economy. That's the single most important thing that we can do. And some of the measures that we've put forward and I'm going to be fighting for are designed to exactly do that.

For example, we've said, let's accelerate business investment in the year 2011 to give a further jump-start to the economy. That's something that, by the way, doesn't add to the deficit, necessarily, long term, because this is depreciation that could be taken in the out-years. We're just saying, you invest now, you can take it now. And that gives businesses incentives to do it.

We want to give tax breaks to companies that are investing in research and development here in the United States, because the key to our long-term growth is technology and innovation. And if we can get more of those investments here, that's going to improve. The reforms we've made on education, which, by the way, have received bipartisan support, are designed to make sure we've got the best engineers and the best scientists in the world right here in the United States.

So if we're doing all those things, I am confident that the American Dream will continue for the next generation. What we can't do, though,

is go back to the same old things that we were doing, because we've been putting off these problems for decades. And that is something that I refuse to do.

Public Perception of President's Agenda/President's Cabinet

Mr. Harwood. Mr. President, let me ask you a question about course correction. Sometimes a leader, even if you think you've done the right things——

The President. Right.

Mr. Harwood. ——but if the people you're trying to lead don't think so, you've got to somehow accommodate that, just like you would in a relationship. He was talking about marriage. [*Laughter*]

As you go forward, is there any way in which you want to signal to the American people that you're going to change your approach? And specifically—we're coming up to the midterm election—have you asked your Treasury Secretary, Tim Geithner, and your top economic adviser, Larry Summers, to stay with you through the end of your term, or might you make some changes?

The President. Well, look, I have not made any determinations about personnel. I think Larry Summers and Tim Geithner have done an outstanding job, as have my whole economic team. This is tough, the work that they do. They've been at it for 2 years, and they're going to have a whole range of decisions about family that will factor into this as well. But the bottom line is, is that we're constantly thinking, is what we're doing working as well as it could? Do we have other options and other alternatives that we can explore?

I think one of the things that's on a lot of people's minds right now obviously, for example, is the issue of deficits and debt. That has fanned a lot of people's concerns, because we had to take a lot of emergency decisions last year that cost money. Now, they were the right things to do. Had we not taken them, the economy would be in a much worse position. Even John McCain's former economist during the campaign has said that if we hadn't taken these steps, that we might have lost another 8 million jobs and we would be in an even deeper hole.

Federal Budget Deficit/Tax Reform

Mr. Harwood. And we know you have that commission——

The President. But——

Mr. Harwood. ——that reports in December——

The President. Right.

Mr. Harwood. ——but I think a lot of Americans may wonder how serious you are about what that commission is going to do.

The President. Well, let me tell you. We've already identified $250 billion in cuts on the discretionary side of our budget. We've identified $300 billion worth of loopholes in our Tax Code that are not helping economic growth. If we just did those two things, as I've already proposed, that would make a huge difference. We've proposed to freeze discretionary spending for 3 years to start whittling down some of the debt that I inherited.

Mr. Harwood. Peter Orszag, as you know, your former budget director, says that we can't afford to extend the Bush tax cuts for anyone after a year or two. Is he right?

The President. Well, I want to make sure I get this gentleman's question in, but I will say this. The debate that we're having about tax cuts right now, I think, really speaks to the choices that everybody here is going to be facing as we go forward. I think all of us are concerned about the deficit, all of us are concerned about the debt. Now, what we've said is that we should extend tax cuts, tax relief, for middle class Americans—like most of the audience here—because, first of all, you're the ones who didn't see your wages or income rise. Second of all, you're the folks who are most likely to spend it on a new computer for your kids or in some other fashion that would boost demand in the economy.

Everybody agrees that this should be done. All we've said is that you get those tax breaks up to $250,000 a year. After that, if you make more than $250,000 a year, you still get a tax break; it's just you only get it up to 250,000.

Mr. Harwood. House Speaker Pelosi said last week——

The President. And let me finish this, John, because I just think it's very important that everybody understand this. What the Republicans are proposing is that we, in addition to that, provide tax relief to primarily millionaires and billionaires. It would cost us $700 billion to do it. On average, millionaires would get a check of $100,000.

And by the way, I would be helped by this, so I just want to be clear, I'm speaking against my own financial interests. This is a—it is a irresponsible thing for us to do. Those folks are the least likely to spend it and—*[applause].*

Mr. Harwood. Well, let me ask you from this angle. House Speaker Pelosi last week said you can get 80 percent of the revenue if you simply take away the tax cuts for people over a million dollars. Are you open to any sort of compromise that would capture most of that revenue, but those people between $250,000 and a million would get to keep that tax cut?

The President. Here's the basic principle. Here's what I can't do as President. I'm—I think I've worked pretty hard, and I have a pretty good grasp of the challenges that we're facing. But here's what I can't do: I can't give tax cuts to the top 2 percent of Americans, 86 percent of that money going to people making a million dollars or more, and lower the deficit at the same time. I don't have the math. *[Laughter]*

I would love to do it. Every—anybody in elected office would love nothing more than to give everybody tax cuts, not cut services, make sure that I'm providing help to student loans, make sure that we're keeping our roads safe and our bridges safe, and make sure that we're paying for our veterans who are coming back from Iraq and Afghanistan. At some point, the numbers just don't work.

So what I've said is very simple: Let's go ahead and move forward on what we agree to, which is tax relief for 97 percent of Americans—in fact, actually, everybody would get tax relief, but just up to $250,000 a year or more—and let's get the economy moving faster, let's get it growing faster. At some point in the future, if we want to have discussions about further lowering tax rates, let's do so at a time when we can actually afford it.

Mr. Harwood. All right, we've kept this gentleman waiting long enough.

The President. He's—thank you very much. What's your name?

U.S. Auto Industry/Revitalizing Business

Q. Mr. President, it is an honor to be in front of you. My name is Walt Rowen. I am a small-business owner. I'm a third-generation business owner in Pennsylvania. We are actually celebrating our hundredth-year anniversary, because we were founded in 1910.

The President. Congratulations.

Q. Thank you.

The President. What's the business?

Q. Something called Susquehanna Glass, and we do monogrammed glasswork.

The President. Outstanding.

Q. Yes. If you ever pick up a Williams-Sonoma catalog——

The President. Absolutely.

Q. ——and buy a monogrammed glass, you're getting the stuff from me. [*Laughter*]

The President. Well, congratulations. And your grandfather started this?

Q. My grandfather and his brother started the business, yes.

The President. That's outstanding.

Q. Three generations.

The President. That's great.

Q. Two World Wars, one Great Depression, and a lot of economic recessions, so we've been through a lot. What I have learned in running a small business over that period of time is that to succeed, to survive, you have to reinvest in your business.

The President. Right.

Q. It simply is imperative. The single greatest economic challenge that I face today is a public that is fearful and negative.

You—when you first came into office, your stimulus package actually funded a very ailing financial system, which was essential for small-businesspeople.

The President. Right.

Q. You turned around and invested in the auto industry and I believe saved millions of jobs, and I think you're actually going to make a profit on them.

The President. We are. That's true.

Q. We'll keep our fingers crossed. And yet your critics continue to paint you as a dramatically antibusiness President. I believe you are investing in this country, as small businesses invest. And yet for some reason, the public just doesn't get it. I need you to help us understand how you can regain the political center, because you're losing the war of sound bites, you're losing the media cycles.

I have a son that just graduated from college. He was just commissioned as a second lieutenant in the Army. He wants to make a career of the Army. I want to have a business for him to come back to when he gets out of the Army.

The President. Well, first of all, let me say to your son, thank you for your service to our country.

Q. Thank you.

The President. And we want to make sure we've got a strong economy for him to come back to.

As I said before, I think that if you look at what we've done over the last 2 years, it's very hard to find evidence of anything that we've done that is designed to squash business, as opposed to promote business.

You mentioned the auto industry. This is a great example of something that we did. We knew it wasn't popular. I mean, people just—the last thing folks wanted to see was us helping the auto industry. Now, keep in mind, the previous administration had been helping them, giving them billions of dollars and just asking nothing in return. But we were at a point where two of the big three automakers were about to liquidate, in the midst of this huge recession, and we would have lost an additional million jobs as a consequence, but also lost what is a signature manufacturing industry in this country. I mean, we built the world auto industry.

And so what we did was we said to the auto companies, we are going to help you, but you've got to make some changes. You've got to make sure that we see a restructuring of how you do business. And by the way, some of the folks who made the biggest concessions were actually the workers there. It wasn't—they took huge cuts in terms of pay and benefits because they understood that their wage structures could no longer support the auto industry in a competitive era.

We are now seeing the top three—the three U.S. automakers making a profit for the first time in a long time. They are hiring for the first time in a long time. And that has huge ramifications, because there are suppliers and the restaurant next to the plant that's open, and so it has provided a lot of confidence in a lot of these communities. But it wasn't popular at the time.

Now, there were some folks in—on CNBC— [*laughter*]—who were unhappy with our decision, partly because they had made bets, essentially, against the auto industry or they had senior debt. And we said, you know what, if the workers are giving up something, if management's giving up something, if the Federal Government's giving up something, and taxpayers are giving something, you're not going to get a hundred percent of what you bargained for in terms of some of the investments that you made here. You're going to have to take a haircut too. And they got very mad about it. I still remember some of the fulminating that was taking place on CNBC about it. [*Laughter*]

We didn't do that because we were antibusiness. We were doing it because we wanted to make sure that these businesses would continue. And by the way, some of the same folks who complained were some of the same folks who, if we hadn't taken some of those actions on Wall Street, would have lost everything they had. And they didn't mind us intervening when it was helping them. But they did mind it when we were helping some other folks.

So the point, I guess, I'm making is this. I think that American businesses like yours are what makes this country go. We have passed eight tax cuts for small businesses so far. We have made it easier for you to invest in plants and equipment. We have already taken down your capital gains, and we want to reduce capital gains for small businesses down to zero. All of these things are what historically have been considered probusiness agendas.

Even on health care—a lot of small businesses couldn't provide health care. We are now saying, we're giving you a tax break if you provide health care to your workers. And 4 million small businesses out there are in a position to potentially take advantage of it.

So—but what is absolutely true—and this goes to the point you were making earlier, John, about midcourse corrections—the rhetoric and the politicizing of so many decisions that are out there has to be toned down. We've got to get back to working together. And my hope is—and this is part of my job as leader. It's not just a matter of implementing good policies, but also setting a better tone so that everybody feels like we can start cooperating again, instead of going at loggerheads all the time. And I'm going to have to do more additional outreach to the business community on that front.

Mr. Harwood. You mentioned fulminating. One of my colleagues, Rick Santelli, was one of those who complained about your policies early—some of the Government interventions— and here's a question that he submitted on the issue of spending.

Federal Budget Deficit

Q. Mr. President, if I was to ask an investor would he invest in a company that for every dollar spent, it had to borrow 42 cents, I think that investor would think long and hard. Now, if you look at the amount of money the Government takes in and what we are spending, those are pretty much the numbers for our Government right now. Does it bother you that 42 cents of every dollar we are spending is borrowed? Even understanding that we have to deficit-spend during tough times, how long can the U.S. continue to spend in that fashion without potentially hurting our long-term financial health?

The President. Well, it bothers me a lot. It bothered me when I was running for office, and it bothered me when I arrived and I had a $1.3 trillion deficit wrapped in a bow waiting for me at the Oval Office. [*Laughter*] So the answer to Rick's question is, we're going to have to do something about it. And we've got to do it—do something about it fairly rapidly.

The first thing you do when you're in a hole is not dig it deeper. That's why this tax debate is important. We can't give $700 billion away to some—America's wealthiest people. We've got to make sure that we are responsible stewards for our budget. That's point number one.

As I've said before, I've already instituted a budgetary freeze for 3 years on nonsecurity discretionary spending. That can make a difference. We've identified over half a trillion dollars in changes to the budget that could make a difference.

The one thing I do have to say, though, to the public is that about 60 percent of our budget is entitlements: Social Security, Medicare, and Medicaid. And a lot of the discretion that I have is somewhat limited on some of these programs.

Now, part of the reason, for example, that health care reform was so important is because the biggest driver of our long-term deficits is Medicare. If health—if our economy is growing at 2 or 3 or 4 percent, but health care costs are going up 6 or 7 or 8 percent, then the budget will blow up no matter how many cuts I make in other programs.

Mr. Harwood. So everybody in this room needs to buckle up and be prepared for lower Social Security benefits and lower Medicare benefits in the future?

The President. What we have to do is make sure that we take in—the amount of money that we're taking in and the amount of money that we're going out matches up. And all of us have to have a conversation.

If we think it's important, for example, to treat our veterans fairly after they've served us and they come back with posttraumatic stress disorder—[*applause*]—then—and obviously, everybody here does—well, that costs money.

If we think it's important for us to invest in research and development—our R&D spending in this country had flatlined over the previous decade—if we think that us being at the cutting edge in science and technology is the key to our economic future, well, we've got to make those investments.

On infrastructure—I've proposed, as I said, that we expand infrastructure. Europe spends 5 percent of their GDP, their gross domestic product, their total economic output, on infrastructure. China spends 9 percent on infrastructure. We're spending 2 percent, which is why our bridges fall down and our roads are messed up and our sewer systems and our airports, all these things are in a bad way.

So there's no such thing as a free lunch. We've got to make long-term investments, and we've got to do so at a time when the economy is in a tough situation. We've got to identify those things that don't work, programs that aren't working the way they're supposed to, tax loopholes that aren't encouraging economic growth, and we've got to eliminate those. And we've got to do it—and here's the biggest challenge—we've got to do it in a way that doesn't risk the current recovery.

So we've got to think medium and long term and look at these long-term projections and say to ourselves, are there some changes we can make that may not take effect this year, but will take effect 5 years from now or 10 years from now so that we've got a better budget situation?

Mr. Harwood. Let's go to our audience.

The President. All right.

U.S. Political Environment/Tax Reform

Q. Good afternoon, Mr. President. Thank you for coming to speak with us today. My name is Andy Conti. I am a full-time MBA student at Georgetown University right here in the District. And my question is with regards to those individuals that feel like Federal Government is getting too large, specifically the Tea Party movement.

The President. Right.

Q. My dad and I were talking about the election—midterm elections just last night. He was asking who he should vote for. And the question was, what will the administration do if these activists are elected?

The President. Well, let me say this about the Tea Party movement—which your friend Rick helped to name. I think that America has a noble tradition of being healthily skeptical about government. That's in our DNA, right? I mean, we came in because the folks over on the other side of the Atlantic had been oppressing folks without giving them representation. And so we've always had a healthy skepticism about government, and I think that's a good thing.

I think there's also a noble tradition in the Republican and Democratic Parties of saying that government should pay its way, that it shouldn't get so big that we're leaving debt to the next generation. All those things, I think, are healthy.

The problem that I've seen in the debate that's been taking place and in some of these Tea Party events is I think they're misidentifying sort of who the culprits are here. As I said before, we had to take some emergency steps last year. But the majority of economists will tell you that the emergency steps we take are not the problem long term. The problem long term are the problems that I talked about earlier. We've got—we had two tax cuts that weren't paid for, two wars that weren't paid for. We've got a population that's getting older. It's—we're all demanding services, but our taxes have actually substantially gone down.

And so the challenge, I think, for the Tea Party movement is to identify specifically what would you do. It's not enough just to say, get control of spending. I think it's important for you to say, I'm willing to cut veterans' benefits, or I'm willing to cut Medicare or Social Security benefits, or I'm willing to see these taxes go up.

What you can't do—which is what I've been hearing a lot from the other side—is saying, we're going to control Government spending, we're going to propose $4 trillion of additional tax cuts, and that magically somehow things are going to work.

Now, some of these are very difficult choices. We were talking earlier about the business community and how it feels. We haven't raised corporate tax rates since I've been in office. People keep on saying that I might. But we haven't. We haven't proposed it.

Mr. Harwood. They want you to cut them.

The President. The—and what I've said is, if you can lower corporate tax rates by eliminating loopholes so that it's tax-neutral, I'm happy to work with you.

We've said, for example, that we don't want—right now dividends are taxed at 15 percent. They used to be taxed at 39 percent under the Clinton administration. And what we've said is, let's take them up to 20. That would be a reasonable position that would still be probusiness but wouldn't be so draining on the Treasury.

So we've got a bunch of these decisions that have to be made. I think we can all have a reasonable argument. And we're going to have some difference in terms of how to go about it. Some of us may want a few more cuts; some of us may want higher revenues. But understand that there are facts and a reality there that go beyond the political rhetoric, and we're not going to be able to solve this problem just by yelling at each other.

Federal Government's Regulatory Authority

Mr. Harwood. Let me ask you about one more specific thing the Tea Party argues that you're very well positioned to speak to. There are some in the Tea Party who argue that the Constitution has been perverted in a way that gives Government license to get involved in any activity—the commerce clause. You're a former constitutional law professor.

The President. Yes.

Mr. Harwood. What's your analysis of that?

The President. Well, look, the truth of the matter is that the Federal Government is probably less intrusive now than it was 30 years ago. Our tax rates are lower now than they were under Ronald Reagan. They're much lower than they were under Dwight Eisenhower.

It is true that there are some areas that we regulate more. But you know what? The truth is, everybody here probably thinks it's a pretty good idea that we regulate the food industry, for example, so we don't get E. coli and Salmonella. Well, that requires somebody overseeing businesses, most of whom are trying to do a good job, but some of them may not have the safety provisions in place to do that.

I think most people here think it is a good idea to make sure that you're not cheated if you are seeking a mortgage. Well, that requires some oversight.

So we're always going to try to balance regulation with making sure that people can go about their business and go about their lives without a bunch of people meddling in it.

Continued Economic Stabilization

Mr. Harwood. Having enacted a lot of stimulus and realizing the political appetite is drained, are you prepared now to say that in terms of getting the economy going, the era of big government's over, and it's time to stand up the private sector, and that's the focus of your policy?

The President. My entire focus right now is to make sure that the private sector is thriving, is growing, is investing. As I said, that's why we haven't increased taxes on corporations. We are not proposing dividends to go up—taxation on dividends to go up above 20 percent. I think we've been very responsible stewards.

I do believe that we've got to make sure that basic rules of the road in—are in place and that consumers, workers, ordinary folks out there aren't taken advantage of by sharp business practices. And I don't think that there's anything about that that's inherently antibusiness. Some of the business owners that we heard today, they are making a profit by offering a good service at a good price.

Mr. Harwood. All right, let's go to Anthony——

The President. And that's who we want to see rewarded.

Mr. Harwood. Let's go to Anthony Scaramucci, who is familiar to some viewers of our network because he appears on CNBC as a hedge fund manager.

Q. And I also went to law school with you, with Brian Mathis——

The President. It's great to see you.

Q. ——back in the day.

The President. You've done very well. [*Laughter*] Congratulations. That's great.

Q. And if I fouled you on the hoop court, it wasn't intentional.

The President. I remember that. [*Laughter*]

Public Perception of Financial System/Job Growth

Q. You would remember if I fouled you. I got a low center of gravity. [*Laughter*] The question I have, sir, and this is something I really—a lot of my friends are thinking about. Listen, I represent the Wall Street community. We have felt like a pinata. Maybe you don't feel like you're whacking us with a stick, but we certainly feel like we've been whacked with a stick. So I certainly think that Main Street and Wall Street are connected, and if we're going to heal the society and make the economy better, how are we going to work towards that, healing Wall Street and Main Street? Question number one.

And then question number two has to do with job growth. I was doing a calculation. I run SkyBridge Capital. It's got $7.4 billion under management, and I'm thinking about hiring new people. A $50,000 worker in New York City, if I want to pay the full freight on the health care plus the FICA and all the other stuff, it's about $90,000, sir. That woman—man or woman is going to take home about $35,000. It seems very, very disconnected, and I think that's one of the main reasons why we don't have a lot of job growth.

So two questions: When are we going to stop whacking at the Wall Street pinata? And how are we going to fix that arbitrage so that we can create jobs in our society?

The President. Great. Well, on the first issue——

Q. And I promise not to foul you if we play hoops again. [*Laughter*]

The President. The—on the first question, I think it would be useful to go back and look at the speeches that I've made, including a speech, by the way, I made back in 2007 on Wall Street before Lehmans had gone under, in which I warned about a potential crisis if we didn't start reforming practices on Wall Street.

At the time, I said exactly what you said, which is Wall Street and Main Street are connected. We need a vibrant, vital financial sector that is investing in businesses, investing in jobs, investing in our people, providing consumers loans so they can buy products. All that's very important, and we want that to thrive. But we've got to do so in a responsible way.

Now, I have been amused over the last couple years—this sense of somehow me beating up on Wall Street. I think most folks on Main Street feel like they got beat up on, and they—and I'll be honest with you, there's probably a big chunk of the country——

Q. But they are connected, sir.

The President. Hold on a second—there's a big chunk of the country that thinks that I have been too soft on Wall Street. That's probably the majority, not the minority.

Now, what I've tried to do is just try to be practical. I'm sure that at any given point over the last 2 years, there have been times where I have been frustrated, and I'll give you some examples. I mean, when I hear folks who say that somehow we're being too tough on Wall Street, but after a huge crisis, the top 25 hedge fund managers took home a billion dollars in income that year—a billion. That's the average for the top 25. I'm not—I—you're—which is——

Mr. Harwood. And yet Forbes magazine puts on their cover a story saying, "He has an anticolonial attitude," or Steve Schwarzman, a big figure on Wall Street, says, "Their approach to the financial regulation and taxation is like Hitler"——

The President. Right.

Mr. Harwood. ——"invading Poland." Where does that come from?

The President. I don't know where that comes from. That's my point. I guess—it is a two-way street. If you're making a billion a year, after a very bad financial crisis where 8 million people lost their jobs and small businesses can't get loans, then I think that you shouldn't be feeling put upon. The question should be, how can we work with you to continue to grow the economy?

A big source of frustration—this quote that you just said, this was me acting like Hitler going into Poland, had to do with a proposal to change a rule called carried interest, which basically allows hedge fund managers to get taxed at 15 percent on their income. Now, everybody else is getting taxed at, you know, a lot more. [*Laughter*] The secretary of the hedge fund is probably being taxed at 25, 28, right? What—and these folks are making—getting taxed at 15.

Now, there are complicated economic arguments as to why this isn't really income, this is more like capital gains, and so forth, which is a fair argument to have. I have no problem having that argument with hedge fund managers, many of whom I know and went to school with.

[*Laughter*] And I respect their business acumen. But the notion that somehow me saying maybe you should be taxed more like your secretary when you're pulling home a billion dollars or a hundred million dollars a year, I don't think is me being extremist or being antibusiness. And that's the confusion we get into.

I do want to be fair about your other point, which is the costs of workers. One of the things—one of the laws that we passed this year was the HIRE Act, which said, we'll give you a tax break if you hire a new worker so—to try to reduce some of those costs. And in some highcost places like New York City, the costs for the average worker may be even higher than it is if you are in some other places.

Tax Reform

Mr. Harwood. Why not a payroll tax holiday for exactly the issue that he mentioned?

The President. Well, this is something that we've examined. And we are going to be working with businesses to see, does it make sense for us to initiate some additional incentives in order to hire?

The one thing that I want to make clear about, though, is, is our health care bill didn't substantially add to employers' health care costs. It exempts from any kind of costs for employers folks who have 50 employees or less. What we've said is, if you've got more than 50 employees, then you should be able to give them health care. And we will give you tax incentives. Basically, we'll pay for—we'll give you a break that's as much of a third of your costs for their health care premiums. And the reason we're doing that is because if you're not paying for it, then taxpayers are paying for it. We're all paying for it, because, on average, these emergency room visits for people who don't have health insurance add up to an extra thousand dollars on each of our premiums who do have health insurance.

Housing Market

Mr. Harwood. Did I understand you just to say a moment ago that you are continuing to examine a payroll tax holiday and may be open to that as a way of spurring hiring?

The President. I—John, I think—here's what you can rest assured, is we are willing to look at any idea that's out there that we think will help. But we've got to do so in a responsible way. We've got to make sure that whatever it is that we're proposing gives us the best bang for the buck. A lot of ideas that look good on paper, when you start digging into them, it turns out that they're more complicated and they may end up not working the way they're supposed to.

And we've got to be self-critical. There are times where, for example, in the housing market, we were very successful in keeping the housing market alive at a time when it had completely shut down. But a lot of folks are still losing their homes because they've lost their job; they're just having trouble making their mortgage payments. And what we've been trying to do is to get the banks to work with the borrower to see, can you adjust the mortgage so that if they're willing to make a payment, that they can stay in their homes? That——

Mr. Harwood. Hasn't experience proven, though, that those interventions haven't worked, and basically, the housing market has got to find its bottom and then get back up?

The President. Well, this was the argument that Rick Santelli made. This is when he went on that rant about the Tea Party. [*Laughter*] And it is a fair economic argument that some people make that say, you know what, just leave it alone, and if people are losing their homes, they got to lose their homes, and if the housing market has to go down another 10 percent, just let it go down another 10 percent, and eventually it will find bottom. That's an argument that's being made out there.

I guess my job as President is to think about those families that are losing their home not in—as some abstract numbers. I mean, these are real people who worked really hard for that house. And we think it's very important that speculators, people who are just trying to flip condos, et cetera, that they're not getting help. We think it's very important to acknowledge that some people just bought too much house;

they couldn't afford it. And it's not fair for the rest of us to have to subsidize them because of bad judgments and mistakes that they made.

On the other hand, we also think it's important to recognize that if you've got communities where you've got—every other house is foreclosed, that that's bad for the economy as a whole.

So these are all tough decisions. But the main point I want to make is, is that we are going to constantly reexamine what we're doing. We are open to new ideas that are out there, and if we think something's going to work to put people to work, then absolutely we're going to try to make it happen.

Iran

Mr. Harwood. Let me ask you about two national security issues that are relevant to economic performance. One is Iran.

The President. Yes.

Mr. Harwood. Markets watch very closely for evidence of stability or lack of stability in the Middle East.

The President. Right.

Mr. Harwood. Colin Powell said yesterday that even though we can't take any option off the table, the stars are not lining up for an attack on Iran by the United States, by Israel, or the two countries in combination. Has he got that right?

The President. Well, General Powell is a very smart man. And I don't want to have a discussion about all the plans that we have in place to deal with Iran.

Iran having a nuclear weapon would be a real problem. We passed the toughest sanctions against Iran ever. They are having an effect. We continue to be open to diplomatic solutions to resolve this. We don't think that a war between Israel and Iran or military options would be the ideal way to solve this problem. But we are keeping all our options on the table.

China/Trade

Mr. Harwood. China—the—a very quick way to improve the competiveness of U.S. exports would be if the value of China's currency rises.

Is it time for you to be tougher than you have been so far on pressing the Chinese?

The President. This is a real problem. And I want to just give everybody some background on this. China—its currency is valued lower than market conditions would say it should be. And what that means is essentially that they can sell stuff cheaper here, and our stuff, when we try to sell there, is more expensive. So it gives them an advantage in trade.

What we've said to them is, you need to let your currency rise in accordance to the fact that your economy is rising, you're getting wealthier, you're exporting a lot. There should be an adjustment there based on market conditions. They have said yes in theory, but in fact, they have not done everything that needs to be done. We are going to continue to insist that on this issue and on all trade issues between us and China, that there—it's a two-way street.

Look, it's good for us that China does well, in the sense that, first of all, having millions of people get out of poverty is a good thing for the world. It makes them more stable. It buys them into a world economy that can reduce tensions and allow our businesses to thrive. It's a huge market where we should be able to export a lot of goods. I mean, eventually, I want some of those nice monogrammed glass things—[*laughter*]—to be in Shanghai and Beijing. But it's got to be fair. Our trade relationship has to be fair. You can't just sell to us and we can't sell to you.

And so we have been bringing more actions against China before the World Trade Organization. We are going to enforce our trade laws much more effectively than we have in the past—not because I'm antitrade; I'm protrade. I just want to make sure that trade is good for American businesses and American workers. And over the last several years, it hasn't always been.

Mr. Harwood. Mr. President, final question, because we're out of time and you've got to go.

The President. I'm having so much fun, though. [*Laughter*] Thanks a lot, John. It's been a great conversation.

Midterm Elections/President's Agenda

Mr. Harwood. Fifteen years ago, at a similar point in his Presidency, Bill Clinton took the stage at a town hall in New Hampshire with Newt Gingrich, who was then the Speaker of the House. Are you willing to and would you like to debate John Boehner, the House Republican leader, before the election to lay out your two visions for the economy?

The President. Well, I think that it's premature to say that John Boehner's going to be Speaker of the House. I do think it is very important for the country, as we go into these midterm elections, to understand that there's a choice in front of us. The other side, their basic argument is that if we go back to doing what we were doing before the financial crisis and before I was President, that we'd be in a better place.

Now, think about this: From 2001 to the time I took office, your average wages went down 5 percent. We took a record surplus under Bill Clinton and took it to record deficits. We had two tax cuts that weren't paid for, two wars that weren't paid for, that were hugely expensive. We put off solving health care costs that were skyrocketing. We didn't solve college tuition costs that were skyrocketing. We didn't have an energy policy. We were seeing jobs being shipped overseas because of the way our tax structure gave them incentives. Now, that was the agenda. We have tried what they're offering.

Now, I stay up every night and I wake up every morning thinking about the people who sent me into this job. And the single most important task I have is to make sure that the dreams of you and your families are realized. And so everything I'm doing is thinking about how do we grow this economy and how we grow this middle class. It has not happened fast enough. I know how frustrated people are. I know in some cases how desperate people are.

But I also know this, that an economy that was shrinking is now growing. We have finally tackled tough challenges like health care that we had been putting off for decades. I have put forward proposals that are going to require bipartisan cooperation in order for us to get Government spending under control.

And I am confident that if we stay on a course that gets us back to old-fashioned values of hard work and responsibility and looking out for one another, that America will thrive, that the 21st century will be an American century again. But I'm going to need everybody's support. I'm happy to have that debate over the course of the next several weeks and for months to come.

Thank you very much, everybody. Thanks, John.

Mr. Harwood. Thank you, Mr. President.

NOTE: The President spoke at 12:03 p.m. at the Newseum. In his remarks, he referred to Mark Zandi, chief economist, Moody's Analytics, in his former capacity as chief economic adviser to 2008 Republican Presidential nominee Sen. John S. McCain III; Rick Santelli, on-air editor, CNBC; and former Secretary of State Colin L. Powell. A participant referred to Brian P. Mathis, comanaging member, Provident Group Asset Management LLC. Mr. Harwood referred to Stephen A. Schwarzman, chairman, chief executive officer, and cofounder, the Blackstone Group.

Remarks at a Reception for Senatorial Candidate Joseph A. Sestak, Jr., in Philadelphia, Pennsylvania
September 20, 2010

The President. Hello, Philadelphia! Thank you. Thank you so much. Thank you, everybody. It is good to be back in Philly. First of all, I noticed everybody is in a better mood after the game yesterday.

Audience member. Go Bears!

The President. The Bears did well too, I just want to point out—[*laughter*]—2–0. But congratulations on the Eagles. You guys got a win.

It's also good to be back in Philly because I had to stop by the Reading Terminal Market. Got a couple of cheesesteaks that are waiting for me back there, so—[*laughter*]—but I didn't want to keep you all waiting. I also bought some apples so that Michelle would feel like I was eating healthy. [*Laughter*]

I've got some great friends who are here. I know the Governor, Ed Rendell, had to leave, but give him a big round of applause, because he's doing outstanding work. In the audience, we've got one of my favorite people. As excellent a person as he is a public servant, Senator Bob Casey is in the house. Your outstanding Member of Congress, Bob Brady, is here. Your mayor, Michael Nutter, is here.

And I want to thank Pat Croce. We were talking a little bit about the Bulls and the 76ers—[*laughter*]—and I like our chances. [*Laughter*] But no, I've been a big admirer of Pat's. He just

exudes enthusiasm about everything he does, and that's part of what I'm going to be talking about today: enthusiasm, having that spirit, even when things are tough, that pushes through to the victory line.

Now, it is great to be back in Pennsylvania because the main reason I'm here is to stand beside your next United States Senator, Joe Sestak.

Audience members. Joe! Joe! Joe!

The President. Joe! Joe! Joe!

And Joe is right. In me, he's got a friend. And I'm not the only one. Look, this is a friendly crowd. Everybody here loves Joe. Everybody here is supporting Joe. But I want to talk a little bit about enthusiasm, energy; why you need to work for Joe; why, between now and November, I need everybody here to knock on some doors and write some more checks and make some more phone calls and talk to your neighbors about Joe. That's what we need.

And you need to do this because the choice in this election could not be clearer and the stakes could not be higher. On the one hand, we have a candidate in Joe Sestak who is not a career politician. Everybody has been talking about insiders in Washington. Well, Joe is not one of the insiders who's been part of the problem. Instead, he's been solving problems in

Washington. He didn't go there with a liberal agenda or a conservative agenda. He went to serve the people of Pennsylvania, just like he's served his country for the last three decades.

This is somebody who's always working for you, whose door is always open, who's helped pass 10 pieces of legislation in just 3 years: the first new Federal funding for autism treatment in 12 years, student loan assistance for U.S. troops called to active duty, support for troops who come home with PTSD, more help and more contracts for Pennsylvania's small businesses. He has been doing the work. In Washington, you know, they make the distinction between show horses and workhorses. And Joe is a workhorse. He's been working, not talking.

And this is somebody who's been pragmatic. He will work with Democrats, he'll work with Republicans, he'll work with Independents. He's willing to work with anybody who's interested in actually getting the job done, and that's the kind of person that you want representing you in Washington. That's who Joe Sestak is. That's why you need to work for him to make him your next Senator.

On the other side, we've got a candidate who was in Washington for years, ran a special interest group whose main function has been to pull the Republican Party to the right—even farther to the right. [*Laughter*] Now, I guess you could say he's—they've done a good job—[*laughter*]—at that. This is somebody who, when he had a chance, voted to cut help for small businesses, who wants to make trade deals that send jobs out of Pennsylvania, who seems more concerned about the folks he used to trade with on Wall Street than the Pennsylvanians here on Main Street. It's someone who is telling us he'll do everything he can to return to the exact same policies that led us to this horrible recession that we're in in the first place.

We can't afford to let that happen. We cannot afford more of the same rigid ideology that led us—in this place. We can't afford to go backwards. We've got to move forward. We need Joe Sestak to move forward. That's the choice in this election.

I want to set the context for this, because for the last decade, a very specific philosophy

reigned in Washington. And it does have the advantage that it's simple to describe. You cut taxes, especially for millionaires and billionaires. You cut regulations for special interests. You cut back on investments in education and clean energy and research and technology. The basic idea was that if we put our blind faith in the market and if we let corporations play by their own rules and we leave everybody else to fend for themselves, that somehow America would grow and prosper.

We know how that philosophy worked out. It didn't work for middle class families, who saw their incomes go down and their costs go up. I'm—there was a report—this isn't from me, this is the Wall Street Journal, not known for—[*laughter*]—you know, pushing the Obama agenda. [*Laughter*] The Wall Street Journal said that from 2001 to 2009, when the other sides was in power, the average wage for middle class families went down 5 percent. That's before the crisis hit. So your wages and incomes flatlined, your costs of everything from health care to college tuition skyrocketed.

Their philosophy didn't work for an economy that experienced the slowest job growth of any decade since World War II. They took record surpluses, turned them into record deficits. And then finally, recklessness on the part of some on Wall Street led to the worst economic crisis since the Great Depression. That's their track record.

Now, I ran for President because I had a different idea about how this country was built. And it was an idea rooted in my own family's story. My parents, grandparents, they never had much. I was raised by a single mom who worked tirelessly so that I might have a better life. Her and my grandparents, they believed in the American values of self-reliance and individual responsibility, and they instilled those values in their children.

But they also believed in a country that rewards hard work and rewards responsibility and a country where we look after one another, where we say, I am my brother's keeper, I am my sister's keeper. They believed in that America.

They believed in an America that gave my grandfather the chance to go to college because of the GI bill, an America that gave my grandparents the chance to buy a home because of the Federal Housing Authority, an America where a rising tide really does lift all boats, from the CEO to the newest guy on the assembly line. That's the America I believe in, and that's the America Joe Sestak believes in.

I had a town hall on the economy today on CNBC. And I explained to people, we don't believe government has all the answers to our problems. We don't think government's main role is to create jobs or prosperity. Joe, I know, believes this, that government should be lean. It should be efficient. But in the words of the first Republican President, Abraham Lincoln, we also believe that government should do for the people what they can't do better for themselves.

And that means a future where we encourage American innovation and American ingenuity. That's why we want to end tax breaks going to companies that are shipping jobs overseas and start giving those tax breaks to companies that are investing in jobs and research and plants and equipment right here in the United States of America.

That's why we're investing in research and technology and a homegrown clean energy industry, because I don't want solar panels and electric cars and advanced batteries manufactured in Europe or in Asia. I want them made right here in the United States of America, in the U.S. of A., by American workers.

We see an America where every citizen has the skills and training to compete with any worker in the world. That's why we've set a goal to once again have the highest proportion of college graduates in the world by 2020. We used to be number 1; we're now number 12. We are going to get back to number one because that is our future.

That's why we're revitalizing our community colleges and reforming our education system based on what works best for our children, not what works to perpetuate the status quo. That's why we're fighting to make our new college tax credit permanent, a tax credit that will mean $10,000 in tuition relief for each child going to 4 years of college.

Most of all, we see an America where a growing middle class is the beating heart of a growing economy. That's why I kept my campaign promise and gave a middle class tax cut to 95 percent of working Americans. That's why we passed health insurance reform that stops insurance companies from jacking up your premiums at will or denying you coverage because you get sick.

While I was over at Reading Terminal, a woman came up to me. She says, "Thank you so much for health care reform. I've got two young people graduating from college. My children right now, they don't have health insurance, but because of your bill, they're going to be able to stay on my health insurance until they're 26 years old." And I told them, it was the right thing to do then, it's the right thing to do now, and we've got to keep it in place for the future.

That's why we passed financial reform: to end taxpayer bailouts, but also to stop credit card companies and mortgage lenders from taking advantage of the American people by jacking up rates without any notice.

That's why we're trying to make it easier for workers to save for retirement, fighting the efforts of some in the other party to privatize Social Security, because as long as I'm President, nobody is going to take the retirement savings of a generation of Americans and hand it over to Wall Street. We're not going to do that. This is the America we see. This is the America we believe in. That's the choice in this election.

Now, we've been through an incredibly difficult time as a nation. When I walked into the White House, preventing a second depression was not what I expected to be at the top of my to-do list. [*Laughter*]

And even though we've done that, even though the economy is now growing again and we're adding private sector jobs again, the hole was so deep that progress has been painfully slow. You still have millions of Americans who are unemployed, millions more who can barely pay the bills, hundreds of thousands of families who have lost their homes. These aren't just statistics. Behind each of those numbers, there's a face, there's a story, there's heartache, there's struggle. I see it in the letters I receive each night. I see it when I have town hall meetings or I travel around the country.

So I know people are frustrated and they're angry. And they're anxious about the future. And I also know that in a political campaign, the easiest thing for the other side to do is not to put forward any specifics, not to put forward any plans, but just try to ride that anger and fear all the way to election day. And that's what's happening right now.

I mean, look, it'd be one thing if Joe's opponent, the other Republican candidates, had looked back on the last decade and said to themselves: "You know what, our policies didn't work. We ended up in a terrible recession. We need to try something new."

But that's not what they're doing. They are not offering any new ideas. They're not offering any new policies. We're not engaged in some honest debate where they say, oh, we're going to get control of Government spending, and we're going to create jobs, and here's how we'll do it: We're going to do it one, two, three, four, five. That's not what they're doing.

The chair of one of their campaign committees said that if they take over Congress, they will pursue—I'm quoting now—"the exact same agenda" as they did before I took office—the exact same agenda.

Audience members. Boo!

The President. So here's an analogy I've used. I think you guys will understand it. They drove the economy into a ditch. And so me and Joe and others, we went down into the ditch, and we put on our boots. And it's muddy down there and slippery, and it's hot, and there are bugs. [*Laughter*] And we're pushing, and we're shoving to get the car out of the ditch. And the whole time, the Republicans are standing up there comfortable, sipping on a Slurpee, watching us. [*Laughter*]

They're saying, you got to push harder; you're not pushing the right way. [*Laughter*] But we keep on at it. Every once in a while we ask them to come down and help, and they say, no, no, we're not going to help. [*Laughter*]

Finally, we get this car back on level ground. It's a little dented. You know, it's got a few holes in the fender. But we're finally moving in the right direction. And suddenly, we get a tap on the shoulder. And they say, excuse me, we want the keys back. [*Laughter*]

You can't have the keys back because you don't know how to drive. They don't know how to drive the car. They can't have the keys back. You can't have it. And I just want to point out, when you want to drive and you want to go forward, what do you do? You put the car in what? In "D." If you're going backwards, what do you do? You put it in "R." [*Laughter*] That's not a coincidence.

They have told us exactly what they would do if we give them the keys back. Credit card companies, they'll be able to jack up the rates without reason. Insurance companies can deny you coverage because you're sick. They want to stand by and do nothing when States are forced to lay off teachers or firefighters or cops. According to the Republican leader of the House, those are just, quote, "government jobs" that presumably aren't worth saving.

They want to give more tax breaks to companies that ship jobs overseas. And they want to borrow $700 billion—$700 billion that we don't have—to give a tax break that is worth, on average, $100,000 to every millionaire and billionaire in America. Now, these are the folks who are lecturing us on fiscal responsibility. The same folks who refused to pay for two wars, two tax cuts for the wealthy, left me a $1.3 trillion deficit all wrapped up in a bow when I walked into the Oval Office. Now they want to spend another $700 billion that 98 percent of Americans will never see.

I believe we need a serious plan to reduce our deficit. That's why I've already proposed a 3-year freeze on all discretionary spending outside national security. It's why we've already identified $300 billion worth of tax loopholes that aren't serving our economy well that could be closed and a couple hundred billion dollars' worth of cuts that we could make in programs that aren't working anymore. That's why we launched a bipartisan fiscal commission to come up with real solutions to reduce our long-term deficit. But these folks aren't serious about the deficit, not if they want to spend another $100 billion without paying for it to give tax breaks to folks who don't need it and weren't even asking for it.

That's their agenda. That's what they're offering the American people, a future that looks like a recent past that did not work for you, one where special interests got rein to play by their own rules and where middle class families were left to fend for themselves.

Philadelphia, that's just not a future I accept for the United States of America. That is not a future that Joe Sestak accepts for the United States of America. And if you don't accept that future for this Nation, then we've got to have your help in this election.

If you don't think the stakes are large, I want you to consider this. This is worth thinking about. Right now, all across this country, special interests are running millions of dollars of attack ads against Democratic candidates. And the reason for this is last year's Supreme Court decision in *Citizens United*, which basically says that special interests can gather up millions of dollars—they are now allowed to spend as much as they want without limit, and they don't have to ever reveal who's paying for these ads.

And that's what they're doing all across the country. They're doing it right here in Pennsylvania—millions of dollars being spent. And the names always sound very benign. It's the Americans for Prosperity, Committee for Truth in Politics, Americans for Apple Pie. [*Laughter*] I made that last one up. [*Laughter*]

None of them will disclose who is paying for these ads. You don't know whether it's some big financial interest. You don't know if it's a big oil company or an insurance company. You don't even know if it's foreign controlled.

And we tried to fix this, but the leaders of the other party wouldn't even allow it to come up for a vote. They want the public to be in the dark. But we cannot allow a special interest takeover of our democracy. We can't go back to the days when just because you had a lobbyist, that you could write the Tax Code the way you wanted it, taking advantage of middle—Main

Street families, middle class families. We're not going to go back to the days when insurance companies wrote rules that said if your child had a preexisting condition, you might never be able to get him health insurance. We're not going back to the exact same agenda because we know what happened.

So a lot has changed since this last election, but what hasn't changed is the choice that we face in this country. It is still fear versus hope. It's still past versus future. It's still the choice between sliding backwards or moving forward. That's what this election is about. That's the choice you'll face in November.

Now, let me just close by saying this. Look, this is not going to be easy. Electing Joe is not going to be easy. He's going to be outspent, not just by the other candidate, but by these special interests. It's—but also because it's never easy. The challenges we're facing aren't easy. But you didn't elect me to do what's easy. You didn't elect me just to read the polls and figure out how to keep myself in office. You elected me to do what is right. That's why I ran. That's why Joe Sestak is running.

That's why you got to work hard in these next few weeks and knocking on doors for Joe and talking to your friends and neighbors about Joe and making phone calls for Joe and writing some checks for Joe. We need you to do this here in Pennsylvania and all across the country, because we can defeat those millions of dollars if we got people power on our side, millions of Americans making their voices heard. And if we do that, then hope will beat fear every time and the future will beat the past.

That's what this election is about. We need to come together around the great project of American renewal. We will restore our economy and rebuild our middle class and reclaim the American Dream for the next generation.

Thank you very much, everybody. God bless you. God bless the United States of America.

NOTE: The President spoke at 5 p.m. at the Pennsylvania Convention Center. In his remarks, he referred to Pat Croce, former president and co-owner, Philadelphia 76ers; Pennsylvania senatorial candidate Patrick J. Toomey;

Rep. Pete Sessions, in his capacity as chairman of the National Republican Congressional Com- mittee; and House Republican Leader John A. Boehner.

Remarks at a Dinner for Senatorial Candidate Joseph A. Sestak, Jr., in Philadelphia
September 20, 2010

The President. Thank you. Everybody, have a seat. Take a load off. Relax a little bit. It is wonderful to see all of you. It is great to be back in Philadelphia. I was mentioning, it's great to be back, especially after the Eagles just won.

Audience member. And the Phillies—[*inaudible*].

The President. The Phillies are looking pretty good. [*Laughter*] My White Sox are fading. [*Laughter*] I'm not happy about that. I'm also happy because I stopped by Reading Terminal Market and got a cheesesteak, so I am going to be—which is waiting for me as we speak. [*Laughter*]

But the main reason I'm pleased to be here is because I'm next to somebody who has served this country so well for so long. He's only been an elected official for a brief time, but he has served this country with extraordinary distinction for years and for the right reasons. He helped to keep this country safe, but he also understood—which is why he's running for the United States Senate—that America is only safe if our core foundation is strong. And Joe understands, just as I understood when I ran back in 2008, that for a long time, our foundation had been weakening. And that's really what this election is about, just as much as what the election back in 2008 was about.

When I started running, we didn't know yet that we were going to experience the worst financial crisis since the Great Depression. We didn't know the full magnitude of what could have been a second Great Depression. But here's what we knew, that for a decade, America had been losing ground. From 2001 to 2009, middle class families had actually lost 5 percent of their wages. So job growth was the most sluggish, the slowest since World War II.

The economy was not working for ordinary folks. And there was a economic philosophy that reigned that could be described pretty simply: Cut taxes for millionaires and billionaires, cut regulations and rules that help protect consumers and workers and our environment, and then leave everybody else to fend for themselves. And the notion was that if we had blind faith in the market, that somehow America would grow and prosper.

It was a very particular ideology, and we tried it for 8 years. And the result was that middle class families all across America lost ground, and those aspiring to climb into the middle class found that hard work and responsibility were not always rewarded. And a lot of people started losing faith in the possibilities of the American Dream.

That's what the election in 2008 was all about. We had a very clear choice between continuing to do the things that we had been doing that weren't working or trying something different.

Now, as it so happens, by the time I was sworn in, in January of 2009, we were in the midst of this extraordinary crisis, losing 750,000 jobs that month. We had lost 4 million jobs in the preceding 6 months. Ultimately, we'd lose 8 million jobs—nothing like it since the thirties. In fact, if you take the recessions of the early eighties, the recessions of the early nineties, and the recession of the early 2000s, this was worse in its effect than all three of those other recessions combined.

And so my first task, working with folks like Joe in Congress, was to make sure that we stopped the bleeding, make sure that we stabilized the financial markets, making sure that we didn't tip into a Great Depression. And we have succeeded in doing that.

But the hole that we dug was deep, and millions of people are still out of work. Hundreds of thousands of people have lost their homes.

People have trouble paying their bills. Young people have trouble when they get out of school finding a job. And so it wasn't enough just to stop the bleeding. We also had to lay that new foundation to make this economy stronger. And that's what we've been doing.

We made the largest investment in education at the Federal level in history and freed up tens of billions of dollars to go directly to young people so they could go to school. We made the largest investment in research and development in our history, because we knew that we had to regain our competitive advantage in a 21st-century global marketplace. We started investing in infrastructure, because it turns out that we used to have the best infrastructure in the world and we don't anymore. And China is spending 9 percent of its GDP on infrastructure, and Germany and Europe are spending 5 percent, and we were spending 2 percent, which is why our bridges were falling down and our airports were constantly delayed. And by the way, all these steps that we took were putting people back to work.

And we decided we had to change our health care system—even though it was hard, even though it was not always the popular thing to do—because businesses and families and ultimately the Federal Government were on a path that was unsustainable. It was going to break our backs if we did not finally do something. And we did something that not only helps people get health insurance, but makes sure that all of us who have health insurance can keep our kids on our health insurance plan until they're 26 and makes sure that if you've got a preexisting condition or your child has a preexisting condition, that they're still able to get health care. Because in a country as wealthy as ours, with the values that we have, nobody should go bankrupt just because they get sick.

We initiated financial regulatory reform to make sure that taxpayers don't have to pay for bailouts because of the recklessness of a few. And we also made sure that consumers were protected in their financial dealings.

And so step by step, what we've tried to do is to—even as we were dealing with the immediate crisis—look at not the next election, but

look at the next generation; and say to ourselves, what's really going to make a difference in terms of growing a middle class that is the backbone, that is the beating heart of our economy; and giving access to people so that if they work hard, they know that they can find a job that pays a living wage, and they know that they won't be bankrupt because they get sick, and they can send their children to college to aspire to something even greater than they achieved, and that they can retire with dignity and respect.

Now, I am so proud of the work that we've done over the last 20 months. And Joe Sestak has helped every step of the way on a whole range of issues: making sure that our veterans coming home are treated for PTSD and traumatic brain injuries; making sure that we update our GI bill so that the same GI bill that my grandfather went to school on and helped him enter into the middle class, well, now a post-9/11 GI bill is able to help this next generation of incredible young men and women who are coming home from Iraq and Afghanistan find their foothold in our economy; making sure that businesses here in Pennsylvania—we were just meeting a couple of businesses next door that are investing in solar panels and wind panels—wind turbines and clean energy—making sure that our energy policy is aligned with the technologies of the future; making sure that we remain at the cutting edge.

Joe has been at the forefront of all of these measures. But here's the thing: The other side pushes back. All the special interests that had dominated Washington for so long, they're not pleased that suddenly they're not writing the rules for their industries. The health insurance industry is not happy that they can't drop people with coverage who may not be economical, from their perspective, to cover. Some of the financial industries that we're now regulating, they see that maybe they've lost sources of profits. And so they are pouring millions of dollars in negative ads against candidates like Joe Sestak.

They want to go back to what we had before 2008. I'm not making this up. This is not a situation where Republicans went off into the desert after 2008 and said, "Boy, we really screwed up. We need to meditate here, and let's see if we can do something new." [*Laughter*] And finally, the eureka moment came, and they went out there and said, "Boy, have we got a whole bunch of new ideas." That's not what they're saying. They're saying, "We want to go back to the exact same agenda that got us into this mess in the first place."

And so we've got a big fight on our hands. It's a fight for what this country is about—about our core values. And in an environment in which people are understandably still frustrated and angry and confused about the depths of this crisis, what they're counting on is they can ride fear and anger all the way to victory in November. They're counting on amnesia. They're counting on the fact that nobody remembers it was their policies that got us into this mess in the first place.

So the way I describe it, just to make it a little more vivid, essentially they drove our economy into a ditch. And for the last 2 years, Joe and me and others, we put on our boots, we went down into the ditch. It's muddy, it's dusty. We're hot. Bugs are swarming all over the place. We're going in there. We're pushing up against the car. We're tugging and pulling. And every once in a while, we'd look up and we'd ask if the Republicans want to come down and help. And they'd be standing there with their Slurpees, and they'd say, "No, but you should push harder." [*Laughter*] "You're not pushing the right way."

And finally, we get the car up on the—on level ground, and it's a little dented, it needs a good wash, but the engine is still sound. And we're ready to move it forward. And suddenly, we get a tap on the shoulder, and we look back, and it's the Republicans. And they say, "We want the keys back." [*Laughter*]

And what we have to tell them is, you can't have the keys back because you don't know how to drive. We cannot afford to give you the keys to the car back. You don't know how to drive it.

And if you want to move forward, you got to put the car in "D," because when you put the car in "R," you end up going backwards, not forwards. And we can't afford to go backwards.

That's what this election is about, everybody. That is what this election is about.

Let me just describe for you one specific debate that we're having right now about tax cuts. Now, they instituted two tax cuts that were not paid for, along with two wars that were not paid for, which contributed to taking a record surplus to a record deficit. You now have a whole bunch of folks out there understandably and legitimately concerned about deficits and debt. And so the Republicans are trying to ride this wave: We are opposed to Government spending, and we are going to take our country back.

And then they propose a $700 billion extension of tax cuts for the top 3 percent of the country—top 2 percent of the country, a tax cut that 86 percent of it would go to people making a million dollars a year or more, would average a $100,000 check for people making a million dollars or more. That's their growth agenda—$700 billion, which we don't have, so we would have to borrow, from China or the Saudis or somebody, because we don't have it.

And if you don't think $700 billion is real money even in Washington, understand: That is the budget for Veterans Affairs over the course of 10 years. Everything we spend on our veterans—we would have to figure out how to come up with that much money. That's the amount of money we spend on the Department of Homeland Security. All this for folks who don't need a tax cut, weren't even looking for a tax cut. Well, that means you're not serious about the deficit. That means this is just talk and rhetoric.

So I want everybody to understand, these are serious times, and we need serious leaders. We can't have sound-bite leaders. We can't have folks who are thinking about the next election instead of the next generation. We need people who are willing to not just do what's easy, not just look at a poll or figure out which way the cable chatter is going and rush over to try to get at the front of the line. We need people who have the guts and the backbone to stand up and say, this is what's right.

You did not elect me to do what was popular. You elected me to do what was right. And that's what I've been trying to do, and that's what Joe Sestak is all about.

So final point. We were next door meeting with a few folks, and a gentleman said to me, "You've got to come back to Philadelphia." I pointed out I was just here last week. [*Laughter*] "You've got to come back to Philadelphia, get folks fired up. I know we can elect Joe if you come back to Philadelphia."

I said, you know what, you've got to get them fired up. This is not just me. This is not a spectator sport. The reason that I was elected President was because people like you all across this country were willing to knock on doors and talk to your friends and talk to your neighbors, and let's face it, in some cases, your kids came to you and said, you know what, we finally believe that maybe this country can change, and we want you to support Obama. And suddenly, people started meeting each other and talking to each other and thinking about what was possible. And you built something, something that we hadn't seen in this country for so long.

You generated the excitement. It wasn't about me. It was about you. And because we've gone through a difficult time over the last 2 years, there are a lot of people who are suddenly saying, well, you know what, maybe our hopes were too high. Maybe it's not worth getting involved. Change didn't happen as quickly as I expected. Maybe this is the best we can do.

Well, I am here to say that change is always hard. Things that are worthwhile are always hard. They always take time. And because we live in a big, messy democracy with a diverse population of people from every walk of life and because we have freedom of speech and freedom of the press and freedom of assembly, sometimes democracy can look just tough.

But that's what makes America so extraordinary, as long as all of you are willing to engage. So don't wait for me to come back to Philadelphia. Don't wait for me to elect Joe Sestak. You go out there and elect Joe Sestak.

You believe in yourselves. You believe in your own ability and the ability of Americans all across this country to change the country they love. If each and every one of you are knocking on doors and making phone calls and talking to your friends and talking to your neighbors, I guarantee you, Joe Sestak will be Senator. And he will join with Bob Casey, and he will join with me, and together, we are going to continue moving this country forward.

Thank you very much, everybody. God bless you. God bless the United States of America.

NOTE: The President spoke at 5:57 p.m. at the Pennsylvania Convention Center.

Remarks at a Democratic National Committee Dinner in Philadelphia
September 20, 2010

The President. Thank you. I am getting older, so I've got to make sure I have a card in case I forget anybody. First of all, I want to thank Mark and Ken for helping to pull this together. Thank you so much. You guys did an outstanding job.

To my dear friend Bob Casey, who was out there campaigning with me in Pennsylvania when our campaign was just full of ups and downs, and the Caseys were such great friends, continue to be such great friends. And Bob is not only a great Senator, he's just a fine, fine man and a good person to anybody who knows him.

We've got Arlen Specter in the house. And I want to thank him for his extraordinary service to this country. Representative Joe Sestak, who's going to be the next Senator from the great State of Pennsylvania, is here, or at least he was here. Where is he? Now, I just want to say, by the way, if he left, that's a smart thing to do. I want him out there going out and getting votes. [*Laughter*]

Congressman Chaka Fattah is in the house, doing outstanding work each and every day. Mayor Michael Nutter is helping to lead this city, and we are grateful to him. Dan Onorato, the next Governor of the great State of Pennsylvania, is here as well. Thank you all for being here.

When I was sworn in on that very cold day in January—some of you were there. Remember?

It was cold. But the spirits were warm. We had run a historic campaign against great odds at a time when the country understood that the path we were on was not tenable.

Between 2001 and 2009—this is according to the Wall Street Journal and according to the census—between 2001 and 2009, middle class families actually lost 5 percent of their income. Their wages and income had flatlined. And job growth was more sluggish during that period than any time since World War II. As tough as we're having it right now in terms of job growth, job growth was actually slower coming out of that recession after 2001. In the meantime, families were seeing their costs of health care, costs of sending their kids to college, you name it, were skyrocketing. And so people desperately felt that they were losing ground.

And a lot of this had to do with a very specific set of policies, an ideology that reigned in Washington that essentially said, we're going to cut taxes, regardless of its impact on deficits. We're going to cut taxes, especially for millionaires and billionaires. We're going to cut rules and regulations that protect consumers and workers and the environment. And we're basically going to cut loose middle class families and families aspiring to be in the middle class. We're going to cut them loose and let them fend for themselves. And if we do all that, then somehow prosperity is assured.

And for a while, on paper at least, I think some people thought it might work. Stock market was booming. We had a big housing bubble. Because housing prices kept on going up, people felt like they could borrow against their homes to make up for flatlining wages and incomes. People maxed out on their credit cards. And then the bottom began falling out, so that by the time I took office on that cold day, a hopeful day, that month we were going to lose 750,000 jobs. In the preceding 6 months before I took office, we had already lost 4 million jobs, and we were going to lose another 600,000 in February and another 600,000 in March, all before any of our economic policies would have a chance of taking effect.

Ultimately, as you all remember, we were on the verge of slipping into a Great Depression.

And I still remember the work that we had to do in the White House in March when the stock market was crashing, credit was completely locked up. People—and we've got some terrific businesspeople here—you remember, you could not get a loan. You could not get a line of credit. People couldn't borrow for—to buy a car. You couldn't borrow to get a student loan. And there were a lot of economists out there who thought we were going to go back into the kind of depression that we hadn't seen since 1930.

So our first task was to stop the bleeding, to stabilize the economy. And we've done that. The financial markets are now stable. The economy that was contracting 6 percent in that first quarter when I took office is now growing again. We've seen 8 consecutive months of private sector job growth. But even though we stabilized the situation, the devastation that had been wrought as a consequence of this crisis—which, by the way, is worse than the recession in the eighties, the nineties, and at the beginning of 2000, worse than all three of those combined—we've begun to dig ourselves out of that hole, but all those problems that existed before the crisis haven't gone away.

So even though things are getting better, you still have millions of people who are out of work. You still have hundreds of thousands of homes that have been lost. People are still having trouble paying their bills and financing a college education.

And so what we knew was, what we had to not only do is to deal with the immediate crisis before us, but go back to what we talked about during that campaign. How are we going to set a foundation for long-term, sustained economic growth? How can we make sure that the growing middle class that is at the heart of a healthy economy, that that was a reality again for people all across this country?

That's our project. And over the last 20 months, I have not been spending time thinking about the next election, I've been spending time thinking about the next generation.

And that means sometimes we've done some things that were very unpopular. And I always try to remind people, we actually have very good pollsters who work with the White House, so I know when something is going to be unpopular. But you didn't work so hard on my behalf simply to do what was popular. You elected me to do what was right, and that's what we've done. From finally reforming our health care system, a health care system that was fundamentally broken, and doing so not just in a way that gives people access to health care, not only allows young people to stay on their parents' health care until they're 26, not only allows people with preexisting conditions to finally get health care, but also stands the best chance of reducing our long-term health care costs, which is ultimately the single most important thing we can do to reduce the deficit. And we did that with the help of Bob Casey and Arlen Specter.

And then we reformed our financial system so we would not have a circumstance again in which taxpayers were faced with the choice of either bailing out folks for irresponsible behavior or risking a complete meltdown of the financial system.

And then we made modifications to our higher learning and student loan program so that now we've got billions of dollars that are now flowing to young people all across this country, millions of kids who are now going to be able to afford college, and their debt will not be more than 10 percent of their income.

And we made the largest investment in research and development in our history, because we know that the most important thing we can do to ensure that the economy is growing is ensure that the next big thing is right here in the United States of America. And we made investments in clean energy, the largest in our history, so that solar panels and wind turbines and green cars and advanced battery technology is all manufactured right here in the United States of America, because we don't want those jobs going overseas, we want them here.

So we have, over the last 20 months, laid the tracks, the foundation for us to finally solve problems that had been plaguing us for decades and to ensure that the 21st century is the American century, just like the previous century was.

Now, all this was difficult because we had the other side saying no to every single thing we could propose: no to tax cuts for small businesses, no to infrastructure projects that would put people back to work, no to health care, no to financial regulatory reform. Their motto was "No, we can't." [*Laughter*] But we got it done anyway.

But look, we've got to admit that there was a price to getting that stuff done, because their unwillingness to work with us, their decision to stand on the sidelines in the midst of this crisis, allowed them then to point and say, well, this is not our problem, this is their problem. And understanding that we had a big hole to dig ourselves out of, understanding that the public was going to be angry and frustrated with what had happened, I understand the politics behind what they did. The question now is, will they be rewarded for that kind of politics that focuses on the next election and not the next generation? And that's going to be in large part up to folks like you.

I mean, the truth of the matter is, is that there is no reason why we can't take our case directly to the American people and win. And we've got terrific candidates all across the country who are prepared to do so. And the biggest impediment we have right now is that independent expenditures coming from special interests—who we don't know because they're not obligated to disclose their contributions under a Supreme Court decision called *Citizens United*—means that in some places, you've got third parties that are spending millions more than the candidates combined, more than the parties in these States.

That's the biggest problem that we have all across the country right now. We've got great candidates who are taking their case directly to the American people, but they are being drowned out by groups like Americans for Prosperity. Nobody knows who they are. Well, we know who they are, but nobody knows where the money is coming from, and they certainly don't appear on those ads.

So I believe that if we are able to get our message out, if we have the same energy and focus and determination that we had in 2008 and 2006, then we will do fine. But that requires us to understand the stakes involved in this election. And I want everybody to understand, especially those who supported me, we are just in the first quarter here. We've gotten a lot of stuff done, but we've got a lot more work to do.

And the other side wants to go back—this is very explicit on their part—they want to go back exactly to the agenda that got us into this mess in the first place. That's—I'm not making that up. The chairman of their committee, when asked, "Well, what's your plan?"—"Well, we're going to go back to the exact same agenda that we had before Obama was elected." Think about that. This is the agenda that resulted in the worst financial crisis since the Great Depression. That's their agenda.

And if you need an illustration of it, look at the debate we're having with respect to tax cuts right now. Now, this is generally a fairly well-to-do group. And by the way, I include myself, as a consequence of selling a lot of books, in that category. [*Laughter*] Right now what we've said is, let's extend tax relief to 98 percent of the American people—actually, 100 percent of the American people, just up to $250,000. So even if you make a million dollars, you'd still get tax relief, but you'd only get it up to $250,000. After that, the rates would go up to what they were under Bill Clinton.

There's nobody in this room who would be hurt by that. And the economy would be helped, because the alternative is, we'd have to borrow $700 billion that we do not have in order to give people who make more than a million dollars an average of a $100,000 check. And obviously, somebody like Warren Buffett would get a much bigger check. He doesn't need it, and he doesn't want it, because he knows it's irresponsible. And yet the other side is willing to hold tax relief for 98 percent of the American people hostage purely for ideological reasons, because this is their only idea. They don't have another idea.

I'm not exaggerating. Think about it. What are they standing for? They say they are concerned about deficits: "We're going to get control of Government spending." What specific proposal have you heard from them in terms of what they would cut, what programs would they eliminate? Are they going to get rid of the work

that we've done to make sure that veterans with PTSD are getting help when they come home? Are they going to say to the millions of kids who are now receiving student loan help, you know what, sorry, you can't afford to go to school? What's their agenda? They don't have one.

And so the stakes in this election could not be higher. Their message is, whatever it is that Obama was for, we'll be against. We'll try to roll back health care. We'll try to roll back financial regulatory reform. And all those folks who were financing these third parties all across the country, all those special interests, they're going to be looking to be able to write the rules again if these folks are back in power.

So when I hear Democrats griping and groaning and saying, "Well, you know, the health care plan didn't have a public option," and, "I don't know, the financial reform—there was a provision here that I think we should have gotten better," or, "You know what, yes, you ended the war in Iraq, the combat mission there, but you haven't completely finished the Afghan war yet," or this or that or the other, I say, folks, wake up—[*laughter*]—this is not some academic exercise. As Joe Biden put it, "Don't compare us to the Almighty, compare us to the alternative." [*Laughter*] That's what's at stake in this election.

I've been using this analogy around the country. The other side drove the economy into the ditch, and we've been down there and putting on our boots, and it's muddy, and it's hot, and there are bugs swarming, and we've been pushing and shoving and sweating, trying to get this car out of the ditch. And the Republicans have been standing there, sipping on a Slurpee, watching us—[*laughter*]—and saying, "You're not pushing hard enough," or, "You're not pushing the right way." "Well, come down and help." "No, no, no, you go ahead." Finally, we get the car up on level ground, and it is—it's kind of dinged up. You know? I mean, it wasn't good for the car to be driven into the ditch. [*Laughter*] And it needs some bodywork, it needs a tuneup, it needs a carwash, but it's moving.

And suddenly, we get a tap on the shoulder, and the Republicans say, "We want the keys back." You can't have the keys back. You can't drive. That's why we were in the ditch. [*Laughter*] And as soon as they get into power, they will throw that car right back in reverse. There's a reason why when you want to go forward, you put it into "D," and when you go backwards, it goes into "R." [*Laughter*] They—that's not a co-incidence. They will drive it right back into the ditch, and they'll have those special interests riding shotgun in that process.

There is a lot at stake in this election. And everybody here who believed in what we were doing in 2008 and who believed in what we were doing in 2006 and understood that we were moving in the wrong direction for the previous 8 years, this is the time that counts. It is easy to support candidates and go to events when everybody is really popular. It was easy showing up to the Inauguration, even if it was cold. [*Laughter*] Right? I'm polling at 70 percent, and Beyonce and Bono are singing. [*Laughter*] Yes, well, I mean—but I believe that the reason you got involved at the outset was not because we had cool posters, not because it was the trendy thing to do, not just because my predecessor had become unpopular, but because at some level, we understood that the American Dream had served each of us very well and that we had to make sure the next generation was served just as well.

And that required us making some hard decisions. And that required us making some sacrifices. And that required us buckling down and taking responsibility for solving problems that had plagued us for decades. And that's what

change is. This is what change looks like. In a big, messy democracy like ours, a country that's huge and diverse, you know, it's not smooth. But it's worthwhile.

And so over the next 6 weeks, but over the next 2 years, over the next 6 years, over the next decade, whatever it is, I want all of you to remind yourselves why you got involved and why you care deeply, and not lose heart, but gird yourself for a battle that's worth fighting. Take pride in the fact that, yes, what we're trying to do here is finally take responsibility and move this country in a better direction and change our politics. And that's not going to be easy. But it can be done.

And for those of you who don't think it can be done, I just will remind you that it was just a few years back where I was a State senator in Illinois named Barack Hussein Obama, and I stand now addressing you as the President of the United States. Don't tell me it can't be done.

Thank you very much, everybody. God bless you.

NOTE: The President spoke at 7:04 p.m. at the Pyramid Club. In his remarks, he referred to Mark L. Alderman, member, Cozen O'Connor law firm; Kenneth M. Jarin, partner, Ballard Spahr, LLP; Allegheny County Executive Dan Onorato; Warren E. Buffett, chief executive officer and chairman, Berkshire Hathaway Inc.; and musicians Beyonce G. Knowles and Paul D. "Bono" Hewson.

Remarks on Presenting Posthumously the Congressional Medal of Honor to Chief Master Sergeant Richard L. Etchberger
September 21, 2010

Please be seated. Good afternoon, and on behalf of Michelle and myself, welcome to the White House. And I thank you, General Cyr, for that wonderful invocation.

Of all the military decorations that our Nation can bestow, the highest is the Medal of Honor. It is awarded for conspicuous gallantry, for risking one's life in action, for serving above and beyond the call of duty. Today we present the

Medal of Honor to an American who displayed such gallantry more than four decades ago, Chief Master Sergeant Richard L. Etchberger.

This medal reflects the gratitude of an entire nation. So we are also joined by Vice President Biden and Members of Congress, including Congressman Earl Pomeroy and, from Chief Etchberger's home State of Pennsylvania, Congressman Tim Holden.

We are joined by leaders from across my administration, including Secretary of Veterans Affairs Ric Shinseki, Secretary of Defense Robert Gates, vice chairman of the Joint Chiefs of Staff General Jim "Hoss" Cartwright, and leaders from across our Armed Services, including Air Force Secretary Michael Donley and Chief of Staff General Norton Schwartz.

I want to acknowledge a group of Americans who understand the valor we recognize today, because they displayed it themselves, members of the Medal of Honor Society. Most of all, we welcome Dick Etchberger's friends and family, especially his brother Robert and Dick's three sons, Steve, Richard, and Cory.

For the Etchberger family, this is a day more than 40 years in the making. Cory was just 9 years old, but he can still remember that winter in 1968 when he, his brothers, and his mom were escorted to the Pentagon. The war in Vietnam was still raging. Dick Etchberger had given his life earlier that year. Now his family was being welcomed by the Air Force Chief of Staff.

In a small, private ceremony, Dick was recognized with the highest honor that the Air Force can give, the Air Force Cross. These three sons were told that their dad was a hero, that he had died while saving his fellow airmen, but they weren't told much else. Their father's work was classified, and for years, that's all they really knew.

Then, nearly two decades later, the phone rang. It was the Air Force, and their father's mission was finally being declassified. And that's when they learned the truth, that their father had given his life not in Vietnam, but in neighboring Laos. That's when they began to learn the true measure of their father's heroism.

Dick Etchberger was a radar technician, and he had been handpicked for a secret assignment. With a small team of men, he served at the summit of one of the tallest mountains in Laos, more than a mile high, literally above the clouds. They manned a tiny radar station, guiding American pilots in the air campaign against North Vietnam.

Dick and his crew believed that they could help turn the tide of the war, perhaps even end it. And that's why North Vietnamese forces were determined to shut it down. They sent their planes to strafe the Americans as they worked. They moved in their troops. And eventually, Dick and his team could look through their binoculars and see that their mountain was surrounded by thousands of North Vietnamese troops.

Dick and his crew at that point had a decision to make: ask to be evacuated or continue the mission for another day. They believed that no one could possibly scale the mountain's steep cliffs, and they believed in their work. So they stayed; they continued their mission.

There were 19 Americans on the mountain that evening. When their shift was over, Dick and his four men moved down to a small, rocky ledge on a safer side of the mountain. And then, during the night, the enemy attacked. Somehow, fighters scaled the cliffs and overran the summit. Down the side of the mountain, Dick and his men were now trapped on that ledge.

The enemy lobbed down grenade after grenade, hour after hour. Dick and his men would grab those grenades and throw them back or kick them into the valley below. But the grenades kept coming. One airman was killed, and then another. A third airman was wounded, and then another. Eventually, Dick was the only man standing.

As a technician, he had no formal combat training. In fact, he had only recently been issued a rifle. But Dick Etchberger was the very definition of an NCO, a leader determined to take care of his men. When the enemy started moving down the rocks, Dick fought them off. When it looked like the ledge would be overrun, he called for airstrikes within yards of his own position, shaking the mountain and clearing the way for a rescue. And in the morning light, an American helicopter came into view.

Richard Etchberger lived the Airman's Creed to never leave an airman behind, to never falter, to never fail. So as the helicopter hovered above and lowered its sling, Dick loaded his wounded men, one by one, each time exposing himself to enemy fire. And when another airman suddenly rushed forward after eluding the enemy all night, Dick loaded him too and, finally, himself. They had made it off the mountain.

And that's when it happened. The helicopter began to peel away, a burst of gunfire erupted below, and Dick was wounded. And by the time they landed at the nearest base, he was gone.

Of those 19 men on the mountain that night, only 7 made it out alive. Three of them owed their lives to the actions of Dick Etchberger. Today we're honored to be joined by one of them, Mr. John Daniel.

Among the few who knew of Dick's actions, there was a belief that his valor warranted our Nation's highest military honor. But his mission had been a secret, and that's how it stayed for those many years. When their father's mission was finally declassified, these three sons learned something else. It turned out that their mother had known about Dick's work all along, but she had been sworn to secrecy. And she kept that promise—to her husband and her country—all those years, not even telling her own sons. So today's also a tribute to Catherine Etchberger and a reminder of the extraordinary sacrifices that our military spouses make on behalf of our Nation.

Now, this story might have ended there, with the family finally knowing the truth. And for another two decades, it did. But today also marks another chapter in a larger story of our Nation finally honoring that generation of Vietnam veterans who served with dedication and courage, but all too often were shunned when they came home, which was a disgrace that must never happen again.

A few years ago, an airman who never even knew Dick Etchberger read about his heroism and felt he deserved something more. So he wrote his Congressman, who made it his mission to get this done. Today we thank that airman, retired Master Sergeant Robert Dilley, and that Congressman, Earl Pomeroy, who, along with Congressman Holden, made this day possible.

Sadly, Dick's wife Catherine did not live to see this moment. But today, Steve and Richard and Cory, today your Nation finally acknowledges and fully honors your father's bravery.

Because even though it has been 42 years, it's never too late to do the right thing. And it's never too late to pay tribute to our Vietnam veterans and their families.

In recent years, Dick's story has become known, and Air Force bases have honored him with streets and buildings in his name. And at the base where he trained so long ago in Barksdale in Louisiana, there's a granite monument with an empty space next to his name, and that space can finally be etched with the words "Medal of Honor."

But the greatest memorial of all to Dick Etchberger is the spirit that we feel here today, the love that inspired him to serve, love for his country and love for his family. And most eloquent—the most eloquent expression of that devotion are the words that he wrote himself to a friend back home just months before he gave his life to our Nation. "I hate to be away from home," he wrote from that small base above the clouds, "but I believe in the job." He said, "It is the most challenging job I'll ever have in my life." And then he added, "I love it."

Our Nation endures because there are patriots like Chief Master Sergeant Richard Etchberger and our troops who are serving as we speak, who love this Nation and defend it. And their legacy lives on because their families and fellow citizens preserve it. And as Americans, we remain worthy of their example only so long as we honor it, not merely with the medals that we present, but by remaining true to the values and freedoms for which they fight.

So please join me in welcoming Steve, Richard, and Cory for the reading of the citation.

NOTE: The President spoke at 1:35 p.m. in the East Room at the White House. In his remarks, he referred to Brig. Gen. David H. Cyr, USAF, Deputy Chief of Chaplains, Headquarters U.S. Air Force, Washington, DC; Robert L. Etchberger, brother, and G. Steven Wilson, Richard C. Etchberger, and Cory R. Etchberger, sons, of Mr. Etchberger. Following the President's remarks, Lt. Cmdr. Matthew Maasdam, USN, Navy Aide to the President, read the citation.

Statement on Armenian National Day
September 21, 2010

The people of the United States join the people of Armenia in celebrating Armenia's day of independence today. On this occasion, we recognize and pay tribute to the spirit and accomplishments of the Armenian people and to their achievements around the world. The United States is proud of the historic ties and friendship between our countries and honored by the many contributions Americans of Armenian ancestry have made to our Nation. We congratulate the people of Armenia on their national day.

Remarks and a Question-and-Answer Session in Falls Church, Virginia
September 22, 2010

The President. Thank you, everybody. Thank you. Well, it is great to see you. Thanks, all, for taking the time to be here. I know it's a little warm under the Sun, so if anybody at some point wants to shift their chairs into the shade, I'm fine with that. I won't be insulted.

I want to just make a couple of acknowledgments of people who are here. First of all, I've got the Secretary of Health and Human Services—so she's charged with implementing the Affordable Care Act—Kathleen Sebelius. She's doing a great job—former Governor of Kansas, former insurance commissioner, knows all about this stuff. We're very proud to have her on the team.

Somebody who helped to champion the kinds of reforms and patients' rights that we're going to talk about here today, Congressman Jim Moran is here. Thank you so much, Jim; and Falls Church Mayor Nader Baroukh. I was just mentioning, Baroukh means "blessings" in Hebrew, one who's blessed. And Barack means the same thing. So he and I, we're right there. [*Laughter*] And I know he feels blessed to be the mayor of this wonderful town.

When I came into office, obviously we were confronted with a historic crisis, the worst financial crisis since the Great Depression. We had lost 4 million jobs in the 6 months before I was sworn in, and we had lost almost 800,000 the month I was sworn in. Obviously, the economy has been uppermost on our minds, and I had to take a series of steps very quickly to make sure that we prevented the country from going into a second Great Depression, that the financial markets were stabilized. We've succeeded in doing that, and now the economy is growing again.

But it's not growing as fast as it needs to, and you still have millions of people who are unemployed out there. You still have hundreds of thousands of people who have lost their homes. There's a lot of anxiety and there's a lot of stress out there. And so so much of our focus day to day is trying to figure out how do we just make sure that this recovery that we're slowly on starts accelerating in a way that helps folks all across the country.

But when I ran for office, I ran not just in anticipation of a crisis. I ran because middle class families all across the country were seeing their security eroded, partly because between the years 2001 and 2009, wages actually went down for the average family by 5 percent. We had the slowest job growth of any time since World War II. The Wall Street Journal called it the "lost decade."

And part of the challenge for families was, is that even as their wages and incomes were flatlining, their costs of everything from college tuition to health care was skyrocketing.

And so what we realized was we had to take some steps to start dealing with these underlying chronic problems that have confronted our economy for a very long time. And health care was one of those issues that we could no longer ignore.

We couldn't ignore it because the cost of health care has been escalating faster than just about anything else, and I don't need to tell you all that. Even if you have health insurance, you've seen your copayments and your premiums skyrocket. Even if you get health care from your employer, that employer's costs have skyrocketed, and they're starting to pass more and more of those costs on to their employees. More people don't get health care from their employers.

And in addition, what you were seeing was that at the State level and at the Federal level, the costs of health care, because people weren't getting it on the job and were trying to get it through the CHIP program or Medicaid or disability or what have you—all those costs were driving our Government bankrupt. I mean, anybody who's out there who's concerned about the deficit, the single biggest driver of our deficit is the ever-escalating cost of health care. So it was bankrupting families, companies, and our Government. So we said we had to take this on.

And most of all, as I traveled around the country, I'd hear stories from families in every single State, you know, they had a child who had a preexisting condition and they couldn't get health insurance, or they thought they had insurance, only to find out that in the fine print, there was some sort of lifetime limit of the sort that Paul described. They bump up next—against it, and suddenly they're out of luck and potentially going to lose their home or lose whatever savings they have because the insurance that they thought they were getting wasn't going to fully cover them.

Some people would tell me stories about how just as they got sick, the insurance company would have gone through their form and saw some innocuous mistake and just dropped their coverage because they hadn't listed—in some extreme cases, we had folks who had a gall bladder problem 15 years ago that had nothing to do with the sickness that they were now experiencing, but the insurance company said, ah, you forgot to list that. and so we're going to drop you from your insurance.

I met young people all across the country who, starting off in life, getting their first job,

weren't getting health insurance and couldn't stay on their parents' policies.

So the amount of vulnerability that was out there was horrendous. And what I said to myself and what I said to my team was, even as we were dealing with this big crisis—immediate crisis with respect to the economy, we've got to start doing something to make sure that ordinary folks who are feeling insecure because of health care costs, that they get some relief.

So the reason we're here today is that thanks to outstanding work by people like Jim, thanks to outstanding implementation by folks like Kathleen, we are now actually able to provide some help to the American people. Essentially, part of the Affordable Care Act that we can implement right now and will take effect—is it today or tomorrow?

Frances Brayshaw. Tomorrow.

The President. Tomorrow. See, Frances knows—[*laughter*]—that we can—that will take effect tomorrow is the most important patient's bill of rights that we've ever seen in our history. And let me just tick off some of the things that are going to be the case starting tomorrow.

Number one, Paul already mentioned the issue of lifetime limits. That is not going to be the rule anymore after tomorrow. If you've got a policy, you get sick, the insurance company covers you.

Number two, preexisting conditions for children: Children who have preexisting conditions are going to be covered.

Number three, we're going to make sure that if young people don't have health insurance through their employer, that they can stay on their parents' health insurance up to the age of 26, which is obviously a huge relief for a lot of parents who are seeing their young people just coming out of college and not being able to get insurance.

You're going to be able to make sure that the insurance company doesn't drop you because of an innocent mistake on your insurance form. This rule of rescission, they are not going to be able to drop you arbitrarily, which gives you more security.

Number four, you're going to be able to choose your doctor and not have to go through some network in an emergency situation as a consequence of these rules. So it gives customers more choice and more options.

There are so many good things about this. I may have forgotten one. Kathleen, anything else?

Secretary of Health and Human Services Kathleen Sebelius. [*Inaudible*]—and preventive care—[*inaudible*].

The President. Right, and preventive care. I knew there was one more. Preventive care will now be offered under your policy, which, over the long term, can actually save people money because you get diagnosed quicker.

So all these things are designed not to have Government more involved in health care. They're designed to make sure that you have basic protections in your interactions with your insurance company; that you're getting what you paid for; that you have some basic measures of protection in interacting with the health care system, which means that you're not going to go bankrupt, you're not going to lose your house if, heaven forbid, you end up having an accident; and you're able to get the quality care that you need.

Now, obviously, there are a whole host of other things involved in the health care reforms that we initiated. Small businesses, 4 million of them are going to get a huge tax break if they start providing health insurance to their employees. We've got measures that make sure that Medicare—that the life of Medicare is extended. And in fact, we just got a report today that the Medicare Advantage program that we have modified and scrutinized more carefully, that in fact rates are going to be lower for that than they were before.

I just met with State insurance commissioners from all across the country. They are newly empowered to look after consumers. And I'll just give you one example. In North Carolina, in part because of the new leverage that insurance commissioners have, the insurance commissioner there was able to get a $125 million rebate for 200,000 customers in North Carolina, and they are seeing the lowest rate increases ever.

All this is going to lower premiums. It's going to make health care more affordable. It's going to give you more security. That's the concept behind what we're implementing.

But rather than me do all the talking, I want to make sure that some people who have struggled in the past with the health care system have an opportunity to tell their story, because basically, the reason we did this was because of the stories I had heard from folks like you all across the country. And I want to make sure that a couple of you have a chance to tell your stories before I take some questions.

So we're going to start with Dawn. Where's Dawn? Dawn's right here. Dawn's already got her own mike. [*Laughter*] Introduce yourself, Dawn, and tell us a little about yourself and your situation.

Dawn Josephson. Thank you. I'm Dawn Josephson from Jacksonville, Florida. And I've been a self-employed entrepreneur since 1998. During that time, the majority of those years I didn't even have insurance because it was simply too expensive. In 2006, my son Wesley was born, little guy——

The President. Is this Wesley right here?

Mrs. Josephson. This is Wesley.

The President. Hey, Wes. Come on over here and give me a high five.

Mrs. Josephson. Go say hi. There you go.

The President. This is Wesley here.

Mrs. Josephson. That's Wesley. He was born in 2006, and that's when we got—we finally got health insurance. We had a few different policies over the years, always had something excluded from it, even something as silly as ear infections. And I mean, what kid does not get ear infections? So I mean, silly stuff.

In July of '09, he had eye surgery. We discovered he had sudden onset of a condition called strabismus in the eyes, and his right eye needed surgery. So we had the surgery, and less than a year later, we said we needed new insurance. What we had was killing us for our premium. And this was right around the time—right after the act passed.

The insurance company gave us an affordable rate. We were looking for a very affordable plan. And when she told us we were approved, my immediate response was, "But what's not covered?" And I knew full well we were going to have an exclusion for my son's eye. And she said: "You're covered. Nothing is not covered." And I said: "Okay, I'm not being very clear here with my questioning. What about my son?" She said, "Yes, your son is covered." I said: "No, you don't understand. What if he needs another surgery on his eye? Are you going to pay for it?" They said, "Yes, he's covered." And I was shocked. And she said, "We can no longer exclude preexisting conditions for children."

And it didn't hit me until later that night when I was talking with my husband as to why she said that, and we started talking about it. And I said, wow, something affected me personally from the Government—was really shocking.

So not only do we have a more affordable plan, but my son is now covered no matter what happens. It is routine for children with strabismus to need multiple surgeries. And I know now that that's not going to have to come out of our pocket, which was a big fear. So we're very thankful and very grateful. Thank you so much for everything you've done, President Obama, and everything that you've—everyone has done to push this through, because it's really made our life so much less stressful. It's just an average American family.

The President. That's a wonderful story. Thank you, Dawn.

Next, I want to talk to Gail, who flew down here from New Hampshire. And I had a chance to talk to Gail a couple of days ago. I had actually received—a letter had been passed on to us from Gail's husband telling their story. And so I just was so touched by it. And it was wonderful to have a chance to speak to her personally. But, Gail?

Gail O'Brien. That was awesome too. You made my day. Yes, in March of this year, I was diagnosed with high-grade, stage II non-Hodgkin's lymphoma, and I was uninsured. I work full time as a preschool teacher at a Montessori school that does not offer insurance to their employees. So I was scared to death—more—not as much, "Oh, I've got cancer, what am I going to do?" It was, "How am I going to pay for these outrageous bills that are going to come our way?"

So then we would have to have gone into our retirement fund and used all that up, and we have one son in college and one on the way to college in 2 years. We would have had to use all the money that we saved for those to pay for my medical bills.

And then when we heard about the high-risk pool and that it was in effect in July 1, we got right onto it. We called people. We got all of the criteria in order so that we were actually insured on July 1. My doctor let me wait for 3 months to start chemotherapy and radiation. And on July 5, I started chemo, and I am doing radiation right now. I'm feeling great. And if it wasn't for this bill, I would've probably not been feeling great because I would've been so stressed out and worried about paying for my medical bills, that now I can focus on my health instead of focusing on how am I going to pay to get better.

So I personally thank all of you and President Obama so much. I mean, you do not know what—how this has changed my life and how grateful I am to you.

The President. Well, I really appreciate that. And I should have mentioned, just for Gail, children are—with preexisting conditions are covered. We had to phase in the adult side of preexisting conditions because it's more complicated trying to get that whole pool of adults.

But what we did in the interim—by 2014, we're going to have in place a rule for insurance companies that they can't bar people—anybody, not just kids, but anybody with preexisting conditions—from getting insurance. But in that interim, over the next several years, over the next 4 years, we want to make sure that folks like Gail got help. And so we've set up these preexisting insurance pools, State by State. And Gail, I think, was the first person to sign up in New Hampshire. [*Laughter*]

Mrs. O'Brien. Told you I was on the ball. [*Laughter*]

The President. Right. So we've got thousands of people across the country who are now signing up, and States are working with Kathleen's office to get this set up so that they're able to get the coverage they need in a way that's actually affordable.

I mean, in some cases, you had situations where you could get, theoretically, insurance if you had a preexisting condition, but the costs were so exorbitant that it was just——

Mrs. O'Brien. I couldn't even get insurance.

The President. ——it was just impossible. And then some people, in certain markets, you just couldn't get insurance at all. And so now we're able to provide an interim step that helps directly people like Gail, and we're really proud of that.

So with that, what I want to do is I just want to open it up for any questions, comments, concerns that people have. We're focused mostly on health care, but if you want me to talk about what happened to the Redskins on Sunday, I can talk about that too. [*Laughter*]

Yes. Here, and let's make sure everybody gets a mike so that we can hear folks. And introduce yourself, if you don't mind.

Prescription Drug Program/Medicare

Q. Norma Byrne, I'm from Vineland, New Jersey. I'm very curious to know what can be done about the insurance companies and medication. As it stands now, the insurance companies rule when the doctors order. They either refuse, or it's a generic, or they have to go back to the doctor and argue with his office as to whether or not you can have it.

The President. Well, under Medicare, prescription drugs are covered under Part D. But for a lot of seniors, they still haven't been affordable, even under Part D. And so one of the things that was part of the reform act was us slowly phasing out something called the doughnut hole, which I'm sure you're familiar with. Essentially, the way the thing was set up when they set up the prescription drug plan program under Medicare under the previous administration, you were covered up to was—what was it, a couple thousand—$3,000, $2,000. Then once you hit that threshold, there was a hole—that's—hence the term "doughnut hole"—where you weren't covered for another several thousand dollars, and then it became so extreme that you had to still buy more drugs, then you would end up being covered again. So you had this doughnut hole. A lot of seniors fell into it.

One of our main priorities was saying, let's close the doughnut hole. And we are beginning to do that now, first by providing some supplemental assistance to seniors. Several—a couple of million seniors have already received—or is it about a million and a half seniors have already received checks of $250?

Q. I was able to get my heart medication once that check got there.

The President. Well—so you've already received it?

Q. Yes.

The President. And it helped you get some heart medication?

Q. Medicine I couldn't afford.

The President. Well, that's a wonderful story. And that's exactly what we want to make sure of is, is that you don't have to make decisions about do I get this medication or not.

Q. And I thank you from the bottom of my heart.

The President. Well, I appreciate that. But you're making, in addition to that, another point, which is that a lot of times, there's a process of decisionmaking between doctors and Medicare about what drugs are going to be covered. And one of the things that Kathleen is trying to do is to make sure—I don't want you to have to use your health care plan right now. [*Laughter*] But one of the things that we want to do is to make sure that we're trying to figure out how can we simplify and make it easier to understand what prescription drug plans are out there so that you know ahead of time—if you are primarily concerned about your heart condition and the drugs you need there, are you able to find the plan that you need that covers the drugs that your doctor is recommending. And that's something where I think we can still make some significant improvements.

Kathleen, do you want to add something to that?

[*At this point, Secretary Sebelius made brief remarks.*]

The President. Good.

Yes.

Health Insurance Coverage/Preventive Care/Cost of Health Care Reform

Q. Hi, President Obama.

The President. How are you?

Q. Good. My name is Nia Heard-Garris. I'm a fourth-year medical student at Howard. And I'm one of the people that has not been able to go the doctor, ironically, because I'm in medical school and I can't even go. So I just wanted to know what steps are we going to take after it's passed and goes into full effect to encourage young people to go see the doctor and to take preventative steps, just as older people? Because I feel like a lot of times we're left out.

The President. Well, first of all, as I said, up to the age of 26 you're going to be able to stay on your parents' coverage, and that's important for a lot of people. You look like you're, what, 22?

Q. Yes, I wish—24.

The President. Okay. [*Laughter*] Well, I mean, I wasn't that far off. [*Laughter*] "I wish." Let me tell you, 24 is just fine. [*Laughter*] But—so first of all, you'll be able to stay on your parent's policy for another couple years, and that gives you obviously some peace of mind.

The second thing that we're already doing is all the policies now are going to cover preventive care. So getting a mammogram, that's got to be part of your policy, and you no longer have to pay significant out-of-pocket costs that may dissuade you from getting the kind of preventive care that you need. And if you're a medical student, you know better than I do that so much of keeping ourselves healthy is knowing what's going on and going in and getting regular checkups and being able to monitor your health.

My mother died of ovarian cancer, and she did not have steady health insurance during her life because she was essentially a self-employed consultant. And ovarian cancer is a tough cancer once you get it. It's tough mainly because it's typically diagnosed very late.

Now, I can't say for certain that if she had been diagnosed earlier she might be with us here today, but I know that the fact that she did not have regular insurance meant that she was not getting the kinds of regular checkups that might have made a difference.

And so that's true for young people as well as old people, the provision that I just talked about—preventive care. If you've got insurance, then those—that preventive care is going to be covered, and that should make a difference.

And by the way, that should save us all a lot of money. I mean, one of the toughest things about this health care debate was—and sometimes I fault myself for not having been able to make the case more clearly to the country—we spend—each of us who have health insurance spend about a thousand dollars of our premiums on somebody else's care.

What happens is, you don't have health insurance, you go to the emergency room. You weren't getting a checkup; something that might have been curable with some antibiotics isn't caught. By the time you get to the hospital, it's much more expensive. The hospital cares for you because doctors and nurses, they don't want to just turn somebody away. But they've got to figure out how do they keep their doors open if they're treating all these people coming into the emergency room.

Well, what they do is they essentially pass on those costs in the form of higher premiums to the people who do have health insurance. And so we are already providing these subsidies, but it's the most inefficient possible subsidy we could provide. We're a lot better off if we are making sure that everybody is getting preventive care, we're encouraging wellness programs where people have access to doctors up front.

And that's why we feel pretty confident that over the long term, as a consequence of the Affordable Care Act, premiums are going to be lower than they would be otherwise; health care costs overall are going to be lower than they would be otherwise. And that means, by the way, that the deficit is going to be lower than it would be otherwise.

Understand, I want to make sure everybody is clear: The Congressional Budget Office, which is made—is independent, it's historically bipartisan; this is sort of the scorekeeper in Washington about what things costs—says that as a consequence of this act, the deficit is going to be over a trillion dollars lower over the course of the next two decades than it would be if this wasn't passed.

And the reason this is so important is because right now there's a political debate going on about should we maybe repeal the health care act or—because this is part of big government. And you've heard the Republican leader in the House saying that's going to be one of our priorities, chipping away at the health care act.

Well, first of all, I want to see them come and talk to Gail or talk to Dawn or talk to any of you who now have more security as a consequence of this act. And I want them to look you in the eye and say, sorry, Gail, you can't buy health insurance, or, sorry, little Wes, he's going to be excluded when it comes to an eye operation that he might have to get in the future.

I don't think that's what this country stands for. But what they're also going to have to explain is why would you want to repeal something that Congressional Budget Office says is going to save us a trillion dollars, if you're serious about the deficit? It doesn't make sense. I mean, it makes sense in terms of politics. It doesn't—and polls. It doesn't make sense in terms of actually making people's lives better.

Okay. Anybody else? Yes, go ahead. Here, Kathleen has got a mike.

Cost of Health Insurance for Small Businesses

Q. Thank you. Yes, I want to thank you, first of all. I have a son with intractable seizures, and this bill is going to make a huge difference in our lives personally. But I also want to speak on behalf of small business, because small business has been used as an argument against this bill, and I find it very hard to understand. I think there's a huge campaign of misinformation.

In fact, we were about ready to make a choice between not insuring our employees anymore because we simply couldn't afford it— it was $90,000 a year and a third of our payroll—or close our doors, because we had no choice anymore. And this bill and the tax increment that I get back takes that statistic from 30 to about 18 percent. It makes a massive difference in the fate of our business and in the fate of all of our employees who are insured. We did

not want to drop our policy—and in the fate of our son.

And I guess my question is, what can we do about this misinformation? It seems so pervasive everywhere, and it's so wrong. I think this bill is really affordable for small business, and I want some way to get that word out.

The President. Well, I appreciate that. Tell me what kind of business you got.

Q. I own a bookstore, The King's English.

The President. Oh, do you?

Q. Yes, in Utah.

The President. Well, that's wonderful.

Q. Thank you.

The President. I love bookstores.

Q. I know you do. I follow your career as you go from one to another. [*Laughter*]

The President. I used to be able to roam around in bookstores. Now it's a little more noticeable when I go in there.

Q. We read about it.

The President. And so you've been providing health insurance to your employees, but what you were seeing was because you're not Xerox or General Motors, you don't have this big pool, so you're essentially in the small-pool insurance market. And like the individual market, you were seeing your premiums just going up and up and up.

What were they—what was happening to them over the last several years?

Q. Well, in 2008, three of us hit 60. And of course, that's the place where they really go up. And our premiums shot up to well over 30 percent of our payroll, which shot our payroll up to 30 percent of our gross, which is totally unsustainable.

The President. Right. That's basically your margin.

Q. That's it—way more than the margin.

The President. Way more, right. I mean, it eats up whatever profits that you're making.

Q. Yes.

The President. So as a consequence of the Affordable Care Act, we've got 4 million businesses like yours that are now eligible for significant tax reductions, that'll pay for up to a third of the premiums that you're paying for yourselves and your employees. I mean, that goes directly to a small business's bottom line.

Now, what you'll hear is, well, but some businesses, they're now mandated to provide insurance, and if I have to provide insurance, then I'm going to—I'll hire fewer people. But it turns out that actually—and Kathleen will correct me if I'm wrong on the statistics here—it turns out that because employers with 50 employees or less are not subject to any penalty for not providing health insurance, about 96 percent of small businesses, they don't have any requirement on them, but they can take advantage of it.

Now, it is true that if you've got a business that has a thousand employees, you're not providing them any insurance whatsoever, what we're saying is, you know what, that's not fair, because all the rest of us are going to be paying for those folks when they go to the emergency room or they apply for Medicaid or what have you.

And so we're going to say, look, if you provide insurance we'll provide you help. If you don't, then we're going to charge you for the fact that somebody else is going to have to cover those costs. But for the vast majority of small businesses, this is a great deal. And we've got testimony here to show it.

Now, in terms of how to get the word out, nobody is more effective than you. So I hope that all the reporters who are here—[laughter]—will record what you just said and will help get that word out. But it's a challenge because, frankly, there was opposition from the Chamber of Commerce and some other small—and some other large lobbying organizations in Washington that said they were speaking for small businesses, but when you looked at the facts, this was good for small business.

In fact, probably nobody benefited more, because nobody is getting hurt more by health care costs than small business. So thanks for sharing your story.

Q. Thank you.

The President. Anyone else? I know it's warm out here, but I want to hear from as many people as I can. Go ahead.

Q. Hi. Thank you so much, Mr. President, for having us here. I want to thank you. I just

have a comment. My son Sami, who was here, is 7, and he has neurofibromatosis. I don't know—have you ever heard of it?

The President. You know, I've heard of it. But you should describe for us what that means.

Q. It means that he had a spontaneous mutation on his chromosome. And he was diagnosed 2½ years ago. And it just basically means your tumor suppressor doesn't work properly, so every nerve cell has the potential of becoming a tumor. So—and there's a wide——

The President. Which is pretty nerve racking for Mom.

Q. Oh, it's unbelievable, but—and there's a wide spectrum, so some people end up with minor complications, but others have serious problems. And he's already had surgeries and things of that nature. So I just want to thank you and the Secretary and Congressmen and Senators, because it's life changing for a parent.

The President. Well, Sami looks terrific. I saw him running around here.

Q. He is terrific.

The President. And I'm just glad to give you peace of mind.

Look, people ask me, sort of, how do I stay calm in my job. The reason I stay calm in my job is that every night at 6:30, no matter how busy I am, I go upstairs—I've got a very short commute—[laughter]—and I go upstairs and I have dinner with my wife and my daughters. And as long as they're doing good, as long as they're healthy and happy and running around and telling me stories about the crazy things that happened at school today, then there's a certain baseline that just gives you that sense, well, I can take anything, right?

Now, the flip side is when Malia or Sasha get a sniffle or an ear infection or a scrape or a bruise, I'm over there just miserable. And I still remember Sasha, when she was 3 months old, one night she just wasn't crying right. As a parent, you start recognizing, that's not how she cries. She wasn't hungry; it wasn't a diaper change. Something was going on.

So we called our pediatrician, and he said, "Well, why don't you bring her down?" And this was in the middle of the night. This is, like, 1 o'clock in the morning. And he was willing to see her, and he pressed on top of her head, and he said: "You know, she may have meningitis. I want you to go to the emergency room."

And it turned out she had meningitis, and she had to get a spinal tap, and they had to keep her there for 3 or 4 days. And the doctor was talking about if this didn't—if her temperature didn't come down and if we didn't solve this, she could have permanent damage to her hearing or other effects.

But I still remember that feeling of just desperation, watching the nurse take her away to provide treatment for her. But I was thinking, what if I hadn't had insurance? What if I was looking at my bank account and I didn't have the money to cover her? How would I be able to face my wife, and how would I be able to look in the mirror if I didn't feel like I could somehow make sure they were okay?

And that's what this is about, ultimately. I mean, we've got to make sure that health care—our health care dollars are used smartly. We've got to make the system work better for consumers. We've got to make it more responsive. But ultimately, the thing that's most important is we've just got to give people some basic peace of mind. And I'm just so glad that I'm able to stand here before you and hear these stories, and hopefully, it gives you a little more peace of mind.

So, all right, well, thank you, everybody. Appreciate you. And if anybody else has any questions, they can come up and we can chat in the shade here—[*laughter*]—while I—because I don't have to go right away, and maybe we can—these guys will take some pictures. So thank you.

NOTE: The President spoke at 11:59 a.m. at the residence of Paul and Frances Brayshaw. In his remarks, he referred to Wayne Goodwin, North Carolina Insurance Commissioner; Matt O'Brien, husband of Keene, NH, resident Gail O'Brien; House Republican Leader John A. Boehner; and neurofibromatosis patient Sami Wirtanen-DeBenedet and his mother Tracy Wirtanen.

Remarks at the Millennium Development Goals Summit in New York City
September 22, 2010

Good afternoon, Mr. Secretary-General, fellow delegates, ladies and gentlemen.

In the Charter of this United Nations, our countries pledged to work for "the promotion of the economic and social advancement of all peoples." In the Universal Declaration of Human Rights, we recognize the inherent dignity and rights of every individual, including the right to a decent standard of living. And a decade ago, at the dawn of a new millennium, we set concrete goals to free our fellow men, women, and children from the injustice of extreme poverty. These are the standards that we set. And today we must ask, are we living up to our mutual responsibilities?

I suspect that some in wealthier countries may ask, with our economies struggling, so many people out of work, and so many families barely getting by, why a summit on development? And the answer is simple. In our global economy, progress in even the poorest countries can advance the prosperity and security of people far beyond their borders, including my fellow Americans.

When a child dies from a preventable disease, it shocks all of our consciences. When a girl is deprived of an education or her mother is denied equal rights, it undermines the prosperity of their nation. When a young entrepreneur can't start a new business, it stymies the creation of new jobs and markets in that entrepreneur's country, but also in our own. When millions of fathers cannot provide for their families, it feeds the despair that can fuel instability and violent extremism. When a disease goes unchecked, it can endanger the health of millions around the world.

So let's put to rest the old myth that development is mere charity that does not serve our interests. And let's reject the cynicism that says certain countries are condemned to perpetual poverty, for the past half century has witnessed more gains in human development than at any time in history. A disease that had ravaged the generations, smallpox, was eradicated. Health care has reached the far corners of the world, saving the lives of millions. From Latin America to Africa to Asia, developing nations have transformed into leaders in the global economy.

Nor can anyone deny the progress that has been made toward achieving certain Millennium Development Goals. The doors of education have been opened to tens of millions of children, boys and girls. New cases of HIV/AIDS and malaria and tuberculosis are down. Access to clean drinking water is up. Around the world, hundreds of millions of people have been lifted from extreme poverty. That is all for the good, and it's a testimony to the extraordinary work that's been done both within countries and by the international community.

Yet we must also face the fact that progress towards other goals that were set has not come nearly fast enough. Not for the hundreds of thousands of women who lose their lives every year simply giving birth. Not for the millions of children who die from agony of malnutrition. Not for the nearly 1 billion people who endure the misery of chronic hunger.

This is the reality we must face: that if the international community just keeps doing the same things the same way, we may make some modest progress here and there, but we will miss many development goals. That is the truth. With 10 years down and just 5 years before our development targets come due, we must do better.

Now, I know that helping communities and countries realize a better future is not easy. I've seen it in my own life. I saw it in my mother, as she worked to lift up the rural poor from Indonesia to Pakistan. I saw it on the streets of Chicago, where I worked as a community organizer trying to build up underdeveloped neighborhoods in this country. It is hard work. But I know progress is possible.

As President, I have made it clear that the United States will do our part. My national security strategy recognizes development not only as a moral imperative, but a strategic and economic imperative. Secretary of State Clinton is leading a review to strengthen and better coordinate our diplomacy and our development efforts. We've reengaged with multilateral development institutions. And we are rebuilding the United States Agency for International Development as the world's premier development agency. In short, we're making sure that the United States will be a global leader in international development in the 21st century.

We also recognize, though, that the old ways will not suffice. That's why in Ghana last year, I called for a new approach to development that unleashes transformational change and allows more people to take control of their own destiny. After all, no country wants to be dependent on another. No proud leader in this room wants to ask for aid. No family wants to be beholden to the assistance of others.

To pursue this vision, my administration conducted a comprehensive review of America's development programs. We listened to leaders in government, NGOs and civil society, the private sector and philanthropy, Congress, and our many international partners.

And today I'm announcing our new U.S. global development policy, the first of its kind by an American administration. It's rooted in America's enduring commitment to the dignity and potential of every human being, and it outlines our new approach and the new thinking that will guide our overall development efforts, including the plan that I promised last year and that my administration has delivered to pursue the Millennium Development Goals. Put simply, the United States is changing the way we do business.

First, we're changing how we define development. For too long, we've measured our efforts by the dollars we spent and the food and medicines that we delivered. But aid alone is not development. Development is helping nations to actually develop, moving from poverty to prosperity. And we need more than just aid to unleash that change. We need to harness all the tools at our disposal, from our diplomacy to our trade policies to our investment policies.

Second, we are changing how we view the ultimate goal of development. Our focus on assistance has saved lives in the short term, but it hasn't always improved those societies over the long term. Consider the millions of people who have relied on food assistance for decades. That's not development, that's dependence, and it's a cycle we need to break. Instead of just managing poverty, we have to offer nations and peoples a path out of poverty.

Now, let me be clear: The United States of America has been and will remain the global leader in providing assistance. We will not abandon those who depend on us for lifesaving help, whether it's food or medicine. We will keep our promises and honor our commitments.

In fact, my administration has increased assistance to the least developed countries. We're working with partners to finally eradicate polio. We're building on the good efforts of my predecessor to continue to increase funds to fight HIV/AIDS, increasing those funds to record levels, and that includes strengthening our commitment to the Global Fund for AIDS, TB, and Malaria. And we will lead in times of crisis, as we've done since the earthquake in Haiti and the floods in Pakistan.

But the purpose of development—what's needed most right now—is creating the conditions where assistance is no longer needed. So we will seek partners who want to build their own capacity to provide for their people. We will seek development that is sustainable.

And building in part on the lessons of the Millennium Challenge Corporation, which has helped countries like El Salvador build rural roads and raise the incomes of its people, we will invest in the capacity of countries that are proving their commitment to development.

Remembering the lessons of the Green Revolution, we're expanding scientific collaboration with other countries and investing in game-changing science and technology to help spark historic leaps in development.

For example, instead of just treating HIV/AIDS, we've invested in pioneering research to finally develop a way to help millions of women actually prevent themselves from being infected in the first place.

Instead of simply handing out food, our food security initiative is helping countries like Guatemala and Rwanda and Bangladesh develop their agriculture and improve crop yields and help farmers get their products to market.

Instead of simply delivering medicine, our Global Health Initiative is also helping countries like Mali and Nepal build stronger health systems and better deliver care.

And with financial and technical assistance, we'll help developing countries embrace the clean energy technologies they need to adapt to climate change and pursue low-carbon growth.

In other words, we're making it clear that we will partner with countries that are willing to take the lead, because the days when your development was dictated by foreign capitals must come to an end.

Now, this brings me to a third pillar of our new approach. To unleash transformational change, we're putting a new emphasis on the most powerful force the world has ever known for eradicating poverty and creating opportunity. It's the force that turned South Korea from a recipient of aid to a donor of aid. It's the force that has raised living standards from Brazil to India. And it's the force that has allowed emerging African countries like Ethiopia and Malawi and Mozambique to defy the odds and make real progress towards achieving the Millennium Development Goals, even as some of their neighbors, like Cote d'Ivoire, have lagged.

The force I'm speaking about is broad-based economic growth. Now, every nation will pursue its own path to prosperity. But decades of experience tell us there are certain ingredients upon which sustainable growth and lasting development depend.

We know that countries are more likely to prosper when they encourage entrepreneurship, when they invest in their infrastructure, when they expand trade and welcome investment. So we will partner with countries like Sierra Leone to create business environments that are attractive to investment, that don't scare it away. We'll work to break down barriers to regional trade and urge nations to open their markets to developing countries. We will keep pushing for a Doha round that is ambitious and balanced, one that works not just for major emerging economies, but for all economies.

We also know that countries are more likely to prosper when governments are accountable to their people. So we are leading a global effort to combat corruption, which in many places is the single greatest barrier to prosperity, and which is a profound violation of human rights. That's why we now require oil, gas, and mining companies that raise capital in the United States to disclose all payments they make to foreign governments. And it's why I urged the G–20 to put corruption on its agenda and make it harder for corrupt officials to steal from their own people and stifle their nation's development.

The United States will focus our development efforts on countries like Tanzania that promote good governance and democracy, the rule of law and equal administration of justice, transparent institutions with strong civil societies, and respect for human rights. Because over the long run, democracy and economic growth go hand in hand.

We will reach out to countries making transitions from authoritarianism to democracy and from war to peace. The people of Liberia, for example, show that even after years of war, great progress can be achieved. And as others show the courage to put war behind them—including, we hope, in Sudan—the United States will stand with those who seek to build and sustain peace.

We also know that countries are more likely to prosper when they tap the talents of all their people. And that's why we're investing in the health, education, and rights of women and working to empower the next generation of women entrepreneurs and leaders. Because when mothers and daughters have access to opportunity, that's when economies grow, that's when governance improves.

And it's why we're partnering with young people, who in many developing countries are more than half the population. We're expanding educational exchanges, like the one that brought my father here to America from Kenya. And we're helping young entrepreneurs succeed in a global economy.

And as the final pillar of our new approach, we will insist on more responsibility, from ourselves and from others. We insist on mutual accountability.

For our part, we'll work with Congress to better match our investments with the priorities of our partner countries. Guided by the evidence, we will invest in programs that work; we'll end those that don't. We need to be big-hearted, but also hardheaded in our approach to development.

To my fellow donor nations: Let's honor our respective commitments. Let's resolve to put an end to hollow promises that are not kept. Let's commit to the same transparency that we expect from others. Let's move beyond the old, narrow debate over how much money we're spending, and instead, let's focus on results, whether we're actually making improvements in people's lives.

Now, to developing countries: This must be your moment of responsibility as well. We want you to prosper and succeed; it is not only in your interests, it is in our interests. We want to help you realize your aspirations as a nation and the individuals in each of your countries. But there is no substitute for your leadership. Only you and your people can make the tough choices that will unleash the dynamism of your country. Only you can make the sustainable investments that improve the health and well-being of your people. Only you can deliver your nations to a more prosperous and just future. We can be partners, but ultimately, you have to take the lead.

Finally, let me say this. No one nation can do everything everywhere and still do it well. To meet our goals, we must be more selective and focus our efforts where we have the best partners and where we can have the greatest impact. And just as this work cannot be done by any one government, it can't be the work of governments alone. In fact, foundations and private sector and NGOs are making historic commitments that have redefined what's possible.

And this gives us the opportunity to forge a new division of labor for development in the 21st century. It's a division of labor where, instead of so much duplication and inefficiency, governments and multilaterals and NGOs are all working together. We each do the piece that we do best, as we're doing, for example, in support of Ghana's food security plan, which will help more farmers get more goods to market and earn more money to support their families.

So that's the progress that's possible. Together, we can collaborate in ways unimaginable just a few years ago. Together, we can realize the future that none of us can achieve alone. Together, we can deliver historic leaps in development. We can do this, but only if we move forward with the seriousness and sense of common purpose that this moment demands.

Development that offers a path out of poverty for that child who deserves better; development that builds the capacity of countries to deliver the health care and education that their people need; development that unleashes broader prosperity and builds the next generation of entrepreneurs and emerging economies; development rooted in shared responsibility, mutual accountability, and, most of all, concrete results that pull communities and countries from poverty to prosperity—these are the elements of America's new approach. This is the work that we can do together. And this can be our plan, not simply for meeting our Millennium Development Goals, but for exceeding them and then sustaining them for generations to come.

Thank you very much, everyone. Thank you.

NOTE: The President spoke at 4:49 p.m. at United Nations Headquarters. In his remarks, he referred to Secretary-General Ban Ki-moon of the United Nations. The Office of the Press Secretary also released a Spanish language transcript of these remarks.

Remarks at a Democratic Congressional Campaign Committee and Democratic Senatorial Campaign Committee Reception in New York City
September 22, 2010

The President. Thank you! Hello, New York! Thank you very much.

Audience members. Yes, we can! Yes, we can! Yes, we can!

The President. It is good to be back in the Big Apple. Thank you so much. I'm here this week to meet with world leaders at the United Nations to talk about our efforts over the past year to make this a more peaceful and prosperous world. But it's also nice just to stop by and see some friends.

Now, you've got a couple of great friends in these two right here: One of the finest Speakers in history, I believe, Nancy Pelosi is here; chairman of the DSCC, Senator Bob Menendez is here. And they are doing outstanding work. Chairman of the DCCC, Chris Van Hollen is here. And we've got just an unbelievable New York delegation—Charlie Rangel, Scott Murphy, Steve Israel, Nita Lowey, Jerry Nadler, and Greg Meeks—in the house. [*Applause*] Yes, it's fun being here. [*Laughter*]

Audience member. We love you!

The President. I love you back. That's why I'm here.

Tonight I want to talk a little bit about our efforts here at home——

[*At this point, there was a disruption in the audience.*]

Audience member. President Obama—[*inaudible*].

The President. ——where this country is——

Audience member. President Obama, one, two, three! President Obama——

The President. All right.

Audience members. Boo!

The President. No, no, it's all right. It's all right. It's okay. You don't have to rip them down. That's okay.

Audience members. Obama! Obama! Obama!

The President. All right. We're okay. It's all right. It's okay.

Audience members. Obama! Obama! Obama!

The President. Wait, wait. Hey, hey, hey, hold on a second. Hold on. Hold on, it's okay. Look, the young lady—you don't need to yell. The—apparently you're interested in funding AIDS. We've increased AIDS funding. I don't know why you're putting the sign up. We've increased HIV/AIDS funding. So—but your message was delivered. We have increased AIDS funding at a time when the budget's going down.

[*The disruption in the audience continued.*]

Now, look, we are here to talk about what's at stake—I—we listened to you. We heard your point. And as I said before, we increased AIDS funding. Now, if you want to have a conversation later about how we can increase it even more, it's a conversation I'm happy to have.

But what I want to do is talk about what's coming up. I want us to talk about what's at stake in this election, because the people that potentially will take over if we don't focus on this election, I promise you, will cuts AIDS funding, and they'll cut every priority that you care about. So don't—so this is not the time or the place to do what you're talking about.

Now, over 3 years ago, I decided to run for President because I believed there were some very big challenges and some very difficult decisions that this Nation had ignored for too long. I ran because I believed our economy was on a path that was unsustainable for the middle class and for our future.

In the last decade, we had experienced the slowest job growth of any decade since World War II, even slower than it's been over the last year. I want to repeat that: slowest job growth since World War II. Between 2001 and 2009——

Audience member. Don't ask, don't tell!

The President. ——the incomes of middle class families——

Audience member. Don't ask, don't tell!

The President. ——fell by almost 5 percent—5 percent. I'm going to repeat that: Incomes for working families fell by almost 5 percent. All the while, middle class families saw everything from tuition bills to health care bills skyrocket. And for too many hard-working families, the American Dream was slowly slipping away.

Now, it was not any accident during this same period a very specific philosophy reigned in Washington: You cut taxes, especially for millionaires and billionaires; you cut regulations for special interests; you cut back on investments in education and clean energy, in research and

technology. The idea was, if we put blind faith in the market, if we let corporations play by their own rules, if we left everybody to fend for themselves, America would grow and America would prosper.

That was the philosophy that was put forward. For 8 years, we tried that. And that experiment failed miserably. We know what happened as a consequence of these policies. It made it harder for middle class families to get ahead. These policies turned record surpluses into record deficits. And ultimately, these policies led to the worst economic crisis since the Great Depression.

That's what we faced when I took office in January of 2009. Millions of jobs had already been lost. Hundreds of thousands more would be lost before our economic policies even had a chance to take effect.

I want everybody to understand this: Four million jobs had been lost in the 6 months before I took office, half of the total job losses during this recession. We lost 800,000 jobs almost the month I was sworn in.

So my most urgent task as President was to prevent a second depression. Now, 19 months later, we've done that. The economy is growing again. The financial markets have stabilized. The private sector has created jobs for the last 8 months in a row. There are 3 million Americans who wouldn't be working today if not for the economic plan we put in place. That is a fact.

But look, because we're climbing out of such a deep hole, there are still millions of Americans without work. There are millions more who can barely pay the bills or make the mortgage. And the middle class is still treading water. I hear these stories every day. I heard some today from folks who had been struggling with health care. I read them in heartbreaking letters that I receive every single night, and the worst are ones that come from children who say, "We're worried about losing our house," or, "My parents lost their job. What can you do?"

Folks are struggling, and as a consequence, they're impatient. People are frustrated with the pace of change, and so am I. But I'm also here to tell you this: We cannot lose heart. We cannot give up. Don't ever forget that this Nation has been through far worse, and we have come out stronger. We've been through war and depression and struggles for equal rights and civil rights. In each instance, we have made progress. Progress took time. Progress took sacrifice. Progress took faith. But progress came. And it will come for us if we work for it and if we fight for it and if we believe in it.

And that's where this upcoming election comes in. That's where we need your energy and enthusiasm, the energy and enthusiasm of everybody in this room and everybody you can reach.

Audience member. You got it!

The President. So—well, no—but no—but I want to make this point. This young lady here, she wants increases in AIDS funding. That's great. We increased AIDS funding. She'd like more? I'm sure we could do more if we're able to grow this economy again and if we continue on the policies that we're on.

Young man back there shouted, "Don't ask, don't tell." As President, I have said we're going to reverse it. I got the Chairman of the——

Audience member. That's right!

The President. ——Joint Chiefs of Staff and I got the Secretary of Defense to say that we're going to reverse it. [*Applause*] But hold on a second. But hold on a second. Think about what happened in Congress 2 days ago, where you got 56 Democrats voting to debate this issue and zero Republicans. And as a consequence, some of those signs should be going up at the other folks' events, and folks should be hollering at the other folks' events. Because the choice in November could not be clearer, a choice about what you want for the next 2 years, what you want the next 2 years to look like in this country.

You know what the other side's offering. It'd be one thing if the Republican candidates looked back at the last decade and they said: "You know what? Our policies didn't work. We ended up in a terrible recession. Let's try something new"—if they were championing your issues. Right? And you said, "Well, you know, maybe we've got an option here."

That's not what they're doing. Here's an illustration. A while back, they set up a web site where they asked Americans to speak out and offer their ideas about how to get the economy moving again. Well, it turns out that one of the most popular ideas posted on their web site— this is not—I'm not making this up—is ending tax breaks for corporations that ship jobs overseas and giving those tax breaks to companies that invest here in the United States of America—a sensible idea.

Here's the thing: That's exactly the policy the Republicans have been fighting against for years. [*Laughter*] That's a policy they've been fighting me and Nancy and Bob on for the last few months. So the problem is not that Americans aren't speaking out; it's that the other party isn't listening. And that's because they refuse to let go of the failed philosophy that they've been peddling for the last decade.

So make no mistake: The Republicans running for Congress, they want the next 2 years to look like the 8 years before I took office. They might be announcing some new details tomorrow—[*laughter*]—but the chair of one of their campaign committees already told us their intentions. He said that if the other party takes control of Congress, they plan to pursue—and I'm quoting here—the "exact same agenda" as they did during the last administration. The exact same agenda.

Audience members. Boo!

The President. So here's—look, here's what this comes down to. These folks spent a decade driving our economy into a ditch. And so me and Nancy and Bob and Chris Van Hollen and—we all put on our boots, and we went down into the ditch. It was muddy. It was hot. [*Laughter*] We're sweating. There are bugs. We're down there, and we're pushing on this car. We're pushing it up, and we're slipping and sliding, but we know we've got to get it up there.

And the Republicans are standing on level ground, and they're watching us. [*Laughter*] And they're sipping on a Slurpee—[*laughter*]— and they're saying, "You know, you're not pushing hard enough," or, "That's not the right way to push." And we—every once in a while, we'd look up to them and say, "Do you guys want to help?" They said: "No, no. No, we can't." [*Laughter*]

And so finally—finally—we get that car out of the ditch. Now, it's a little banged up. It's a little dented. It needs a tuneup. [*Laughter*] It's not moving as fast as we wanted, but it's on level ground, and we're ready to move forward. And suddenly we get a tap on the shoulder, and we look back, and it's the Republicans. [*Laughter*] They said, "Excuse me, we want the keys back." You can't have the keys back. You don't know how to drive. We cannot give them the keys back. We can't give them the keys back.

Look, if you want to go forward, what do you do? You put it in "D." If you want to go backwards, you put it in "R." We can't afford to go backwards. That's not a coincidence. We've got to go forward.

Democrats, I don't know about you, but I do not want to spend the next 2 years watching them try to drive our economy back into the ditch. I mean, we have seen this. We have seen this movie before, and we can't afford to go back to what they were doing. Not now. Not when we've come this far. I don't accept that future for the United States of America.

So we have a different idea about what the next 2 years should look like. It's an idea rooted in our belief about how this country was built. We know that government doesn't have all the answers to our problems. And we don't believe that government's main role is to create jobs or prosperity. I believe government should be lean and efficient. And that's why I've proposed a 3-year spending freeze and set up a bipartisan fiscal commission to deal with our deficit.

But in the words of the first Republican President, Abraham Lincoln, I also believe that government should do for the people what they can't do for themselves. I believe in a country that rewards hard work and responsibility, a country that invests in its people and its future, and yes, a country where we look after one another, where we respect everybody's dignity, where we say, I am my bother's keeper, I am my sister's keeper. That's what we believe in. That's what Democrats stand for. That's the choice in this election.

If we hand the keys over to the other side, we will spend the next 2 years fighting to keep those tax breaks for companies that create jobs and profits overseas, hundreds of billions of dollars in taxpayer subsidies we lose each year.

Over the last 19 months, we've closed several of these tax loopholes. Over the next 2 years, we'll fight to give tax breaks to companies that actually create jobs within our borders: to small businesses, to clean energy companies, to American manufacturers, to entrepreneurs that are researching and investing and innovating right here in the United States of America. That's who we want to help. That's the choice in this election.

If we give them back the keys, the other side will spend the next 2 years fighting for a $700 billion tax cut that only 2 percent of Americans will ever see. They want to borrow $700 billion. They say that they're about cutting deficits, but they want to spend—borrow $700 billion and give millionaires and billionaires an average tax cut of $100,000.

This is the party that lectures us on fiscal responsibility. That's what they're fighting for. I don't know about you, but I've got a different set of priorities for the next 2 years.

When I took office, I kept a campaign promise to cut taxes for 95 percent of working Americans. And we're fighting to make those middle class tax cuts permanent.

Over the last 19 months, we've passed a new college tax credit worth $10,000 in tuition relief for each child going to 4 years of college. We want to make that permanent too, because in good times or bad, no family should have to stop investing in their children's future. That's what we believe. That's what we stand for as Democrats. Those are our priorities. That's the choice in this election.

If we hand the other side the keys, they've promised to spend the next 2 years chipping away at the new rules we've put in place for special interests. And I refuse to let them do that. I refuse to go back to the days when insurance companies could deny you coverage or drop your coverage just because you're sick.

I was down with a group of families today because starting tomorrow, we've got a whole bunch of consumer protections, a patient's bill of rights, that goes into effect as a consequence of the Affordable Care Act. And I want you to know, I met a woman from New Hampshire who had gotten cancer, could not get insurance, and because of that legislation, she now is getting treatment, is feeling better, feeling optimistic about the future.

We had—[*applause*]—we met two moms whose children had preexisting conditions. And they were worried they couldn't get insurance for their children. And now they have the security of knowing that those kids are going to be safe.

Two small businesses who were there saying, we provide health insurance to our workers, but one guy, he said his premiums had gone up a hundred percent in 7 years. He said, "Basically, I could no longer afford it. Either I was going to have to lay off workers or stop giving them insurance—until this bill passed." And now that small-business owner is able to keep providing health insurance to his workers. That's what we're fighting for.

We had—we've had reform in the financial sector to make sure that if you've got a credit card or you're getting a mortgage, that you aren't being cheated. And the other side is basically saying, we want to take those protections away.

To paraphrase a friend of mine, Deval Patrick up in Massachusetts, the last election was about a changing of the guard; this election is about guarding the change. That's exactly what we've got to do over the next few weeks.

So if you don't think the stakes are large, I want you to consider this. If you don't think the stakes are large, I want you to understand, right now all over this country, special interests are planning and running millions of dollars of attack ads against Democratic candidates. Because of last year's Supreme Court decision in *Citizens United*, they are now——

Audience members. Boo!

The President. ——they are now allowed to spend as much as they want, unlimited amounts of money, and they don't have to reveal who's paying for these ads. And that's what they're doing; millions of dollars being spent by groups

with harmless-sounding names: Americans for Prosperity, the Committee for Truth in Politics, or Moms for Motherhood. [*Laughter*] I made that last one up. [*Laughter*]

But they pose as non-for-profit, social welfare, and trade groups. Every single one of them, virtually, is guided by seasoned Republican political operatives. None of them will disclose who is paying for these ads. They are spending tens of millions of dollars against Democratic candidates without telling the American people where that flood of money is coming from. You don't know if it's coming from big oil or insurance companies. You don't even know if it's coming from a foreign-controlled corporation.

And we tried to fix this, but the leaders of the other party wouldn't even let it come up for a vote. They want to keep the public in the dark. But we won't let them. We're not about to allow special interests to take over our democracy. We're not going to go back to the exact same agenda we had before I took office. We remember what it's like. They're counting on amnesia, but we remember exactly the policies that got us into a mess, and we're not going to go back to them.

So here's the bottom line. A lot has changed since the last election. But what hasn't changed is the choice facing the country. It's still fear versus hope. It's still the past versus the future. It's still a choice between sliding backward and moving forward. That is what this election's about, and that's the choice you'll face in November. And it won't be easy.

None of it will be easy, and that's because the challenges we face right now are not easy. None of this is easy. But you didn't elect me to do what's easy. You didn't elect me just to read the polls and figure out how to keep myself in office. You elected me to do what's right. And as long as I'm President, that's exactly what I will do—do what's right, not what's convenient.

But I need your help.

Audience member. You got it!

The President. Look, when I—but I want everybody to listen up on this—when I see all the polls, hear all the pundits, here's what I take away from them: The single biggest threat to our success is not the other party; it's us. It's complacency. It's apathy. It's indifference.

It's people feeling like: "Well, we only got 80 percent of what we want. We didn't get the other 20, so we're just going to sit on our hands. We're not going to go out there. It turns out bringing about change is hard." [*Laughter*] "I thought it was going to be easy. I liked the cute posters of the Obama campaign. I enjoyed the Inauguration. It was great when Beyonce and Bono was singing." [*Laughter*] "I didn't know that we were actually going to have to grind it out, that sometimes we'd have setbacks." [*Laughter*]

You know, the only way we fall backwards is if we don't get mobilized, if we don't get energized—because I promise you, the other side is energized—if we don't turn out our friends and our neighbors to vote. And that's what I need you to do. I need you to knock on some doors. I need you to talk to your neighbors. I need you to make some phone calls. I need you to remember that that election was not about me, it was about you.

If we do that, if we understand what's at stake and we step up to the plate and we realize that change is not a spectator sport and that no, it won't come easy and you're not going to get it all in one fell swoop and you won't even then get a hundred percent, if you remember that every bit of progress we've made from emancipation to women's suffrage to civil rights to So-

cial Security to Medicare—each and every one of those steps were laborious and difficult, and there were people who were trying to block that progress and people who were saying, that's socialism, and people who were saying this was undermining the country—every step of the way, there were people who were fighting it. But people didn't lose heart. Instead, people stood up and they said, you know what, we're just going to keep on pushing; we're going to keep on fighting.

Dr. King made famous a saying that "the arc of the moral universe is long, but it bends towards justice." We are moving in the direction of justice. We are moving in the direction of prosperity. But we've got to keep on moving. We can't stop now. And if we are out there working hard, if we are out there rekindling that spirit of hope, we won't just win this election, we will restore our economy, rebuild the middle class, reclaim the American Dream for the next generation.

Thank you, New York. God bless you. God bless the United States of America. Thank you.

NOTE: The President spoke at 6:46 p.m. at the Roosevelt Hotel. In his remarks, he referred to Rep. Pete Sessions, in his capacity as chairman of the National Republican Congressional Committee; Gov. Deval L. Patrick of Massachusetts; and musicians Beyonce G. Knowles and Paul D. "Bono" Hewson.

Remarks at a Democratic Congressional Campaign Committee and Democratic Senatorial Campaign Committee Dinner in New York City
September 22, 2010

Hello, New York! Thank you. Thank you so much. Everybody, please have a seat. It is wonderful to see so many friends, colleagues, people who have done so much for the country and so much for New York City. It is wonderful to be back in the Big Apple. And this is kind of an intimate affair, so I hope you don't mind, I'm going to occasionally go off script.

But the first thing I want to do is just say that we truly have the good fortune of having one of

the finest Speakers of the House, I think, in our history, and that's Nancy Pelosi, here tonight. She is doing outstanding work.

A terrific Senator who has taken on what is always a thankless task, and that is being head of the DSCC, and doing it with tremendous energy, Bob Menendez. I'm grateful for him. I'm grateful for chairman of the DCCC Chris Van Hollen, who's been working tirelessly. And then the whole New York delegation—Carolyn

Maloney, Charlie Rangel, Scott Murphy, Steve Israel, Nita Lowey, Jerry Nadler, and Greg Meeks—thank you guys for the great work that you've done each and every day.

We are at, I think, a critical, fascinating, difficult time in our history. Two years ago, when I came into office, we were coming on a surge of enormous energy, because people understood that we couldn't keep doing things the way we had been doing them.

And I want everybody to look back at the track record of 2001 to 2009 and what was happening in this country. We had not only entered into two wars that weren't paid for, not only had we turned record surpluses to record deficits, but what had happened to the middle class in this country or those aspiring to be part of the middle class—that beating heart of our economy, that representative of the American Dream, the notion that if you worked hard and you took responsibility, that not only could you provide for your family, but you could be assured that the next generation was going to do better than you did—they had taken hit after hit after hit.

This is not my opinion. The Wall Street Journal, a great champion of the Obama agenda— [*laughter*]—had an article just last week based on census data showing that middle class wages went down 5 percent from 2001 to 2009—went down 5 percent.

We had the slowest job growth during that period of any time since World War II. In fact, the pace of job creation was slower than it's been over the last year coming out of this horrific recession. At the same time, ordinary families were seeing their health care costs go up. They were seeing their college tuition for their kids go up.

And all of this was brought to you by, was underwritten by a very specific ideology that basically said, we're going to cut taxes, especially for millionaires and billionaires. We're going to cut rules for the most powerful interests in our society. We're going to cut ordinary folks loose to fend for themselves. And somehow, magically, we're going to grow and we're going to prosper.

And for a few years, at least, there was the illusion that maybe this might work, because we had a housing bubble and people were maxing out on their credit cards and spending. And so the sense was, well, maybe we can keep this thing going.

Although all across the country, people were struggling. They were seeing plants move out of their towns and suddenly empty out. Main Streets start getting boarded up. And then all of it finally culminated in the worst financial crisis since the Great Depression and the worst recession since the 1930s.

That was the context in which I was sworn into office in January of 2009. Six months leading up to the election, we actually lost 4 million jobs—4 million jobs in the last 6 months of 2008. We lost 750,000 the month that I was sworn in.

So my first responsibility as President, Nancy's first responsibility as Speaker, Bob's first responsibility, all the Members of Congress here today, our first responsibility was to make sure that we did not slip into a second Great Depression.

And we've succeeded at doing that. The financial markets are stabilized. The economy that was contracting 6 percent in the quarter in which I took office is now growing again. We've had 8 consecutive months of private sector job growth. We're making progress. But—[*applause*]—we are making progress.

But the fact is that the devastation that was caused by this recession lingers on. There are millions of people out there who are still looking for work. There are hundreds of thousands of people who have lost their homes, millions more who aren't sure if they're going to be able to make their mortgage payments or pay the bills. People are scared. People are anxious. People are uncertain about the future. And people are angry, because they feel at some fundamental level that they've been betrayed, that they've been betrayed by Washington, that they've been betrayed by folks who somehow had the inside line and the inside scoop.

And so they're frustrated. And essentially, what the other side has done over the last 2 years is count on amnesia. They're counting on the fact that people forget who got us into the mess and that they can ride anger and frustration all the way until November.

Essentially, they made a tactical decision that they would sit on the sidelines, and they'd let us try to clean up after them. And if it didn't work, then the politics would work for them. They were thinking about the next election instead of the next generation.

You know, I've been using an analogy that I think works. Essentially, they drove the economy into the ditch. And so Nancy and Bob and me, we all put on our boots, and we went down into the ditch. And it's dusty and muddy down there and hot and sweaty and bugs swirling around. And we're pushing and shoving, and we've got our shoulder to the bumper there, and we're pushing and yanking. And every so often, we look up, and there are the Republicans standing up on the road, sipping a Slurpee—[*laughter*]—looking down at us. And we say, "You want to come down and help?" And they say: "No, no, no, we can't. But you're not pushing hard enough. You're not pushing the right way."

And finally, after all this work, we finally get the car back on the road. It's pointing straight. It's banged up, it's dented, needs a tuneup, needs some bodywork, needs a paint job, but it's pointing in the right direction. And we feel this tap on our shoulders, and it's the Republicans. They say, "We want the keys back." And we have to explain to them: "You can't have the keys back. You don't know how to drive. We don't want to go back into the ditch. We're sorry, but you can't have them back."

Now, it would be one thing if they had meditated after the 2008 election and they said, boy, we really screwed up. Our ideology doesn't work. It's not serving the interests of the American people. And so they had come back and they had said, boy, we've got a whole bunch of new ideas. We realize the error of our ways. We'll work with the President where we can. Where we disagree with him, we'll be part of the loyal opposition.

That's not what happened. That's not what's happening now. The chairman of the other side's committee, when asked, "Well, what exactly would you do if you guys ended up taking over the House?" he said, "We're going to go back"—and I'm quoting—"to the exact same agenda that we had before the President took office." The exact same agenda.

And you can see it now in the proposals that they've got. They've said, well, you know, where are the jobs? We've got to grow the economy faster. We've got better ideas.

Here's their idea. Their primary idea, their principal idea is we're going to borrow $700 billion—borrow it because we don't have it—and we're going to give tax cuts that won't go to 98 percent of the American people. Ninety-eight percent won't get a dime of those tax cuts. And we will borrow $700 billion to do it.

And that's their principal agenda. This is the same crew that says that they're all about fiscal responsibility. They don't have new ideas. They don't have an agenda that would move the country forward.

Now, we've got a lot to be proud about over the last 2 years because not only did we prevent a Great Depression, but we moved forward a set of issues that so many people in this room had been hungry to see action on for years, because you understood that it wasn't good enough just to solve the crisis, we also had to start laying the foundation for moving this country forward over the long term.

And so after decades, we've finally tackled health care and passed the most important piece of legislation that ensures that 30 million people get health care, but also ensures that we're going to lower the cost of health care in years to come.

And I was at a little town hall—actually, a little backyard discussion with a group today, before I came up to New York. There was one woman who had been stricken by cancer at a time when she did not have insurance. She now is able to buy insurance because of the Affordable Care Act. Two small businesses who were about to discontinue health care for their employees because their costs had gone up a hundred percent over the last 7 years, who are now not only still able to provide health insurance but have seen $15,000 worth of tax breaks; two moms whose kids had preexisting conditions who could not get health care, and now have the security of knowing that their kids are covered. Every parent out there whose child doesn't have health insurance is going to be able to keep their kids on their insurance until they're 26 years old. That's a consequence of the majorities in the House and the Senate, the incredibly important and difficult work that they did.

On financial regulatory reform, not only have we made sure that we're looking out for systemic risks and preventing the kind of crisis that forces us a choice between bailouts or financial collapse, not only are we in a position now to prevent that, but we've also got a consumer protection agency that is long overdue that makes sure that people out there who are getting credit cards or mortgages, that somebody out there is looking for them—somebody out there is looking out for them, that they can't just have their interest rates jacked up for no reason, that they're not steered to mortgages that they can't afford. That's because of the outstanding work of these majorities in the House and the Senate.

We have made changes in how tobacco companies can market to their kids—to our kids. We have expanded national service more than at any time since the Peace Corps. We've provided—before the health care act—4 million children health insurance, including the children of legal immigrants.

On issue after issue—on education, we've probably initiated more changes in education across the country than at any time in the last 50 years. And for good measure, we shifted billions of dollars that were going to subsidies to financial industry through the student loan program, and now millions of young people are able to get scholarships that weren't able to get it before.

We made the largest investment in clean energy in our history so that you've got solar panels and wind turbines and advanced batteries and green cars being made right here in the United States of America, all across the country.

The largest investment in education in our history, the largest investment in our infrastructure since Dwight Eisenhower, the largest investment in research and basic science in a generation, and we did all this while we were making sure that we didn't go into a Great Depression and while we were ending one war and

making sure that we were in a position to start bringing our troops home and stabilizing Afghanistan at the same time.

Now, I tick all these things off because ultimately, when you look at what's going to happen in this election, it's not going to depend on me; it's going to depend on you. The other side is energized. As I said, they are surfing anger and frustration. And some of that anger is legitimate, although misplaced, misdirected. But people are feeling what they're feeling, and that is that we've been slipping and that they've gotten the brunt of some very bad decisions over the last several years. And the question is, are we as energized? Are we as motivated?

I was just talking to a larger crowd out there, and I had to remind them, you know, when I was running for office, in some ways, maybe we gave people the wrong impression about how change happens in a democracy. Everybody saw those nice Obama posters. It was kind of cool and trendy, that whole Internet thing. [*Laughter*] You have these big rallies and Barbra is singing and, you know, then the Inauguration, you had Bono and Beyonce.

And so I think people maybe got the impression that somehow change in this country is easy. Change in this country has never been easy. Emancipation was not easy. Women's suffrage wasn't easy. Medicare, Medicaid, Social Security, the civil rights movement, basic worker protections, basic consumer protections, each and every one of those issues we had to fight for. And sometimes you'd get 50 percent of it done or maybe 60 percent, and then you'd have to go back, and folks would try to chip away at it, and you'd have to push and try to get some more done the next year and the year after that.

And what was sustaining was that sense, that north star, that sense that, you know what, if we stay true to our values, if we believe that all people are created equal and everybody is endowed with certain inalienable rights and we're going to make those words live, that we're going to give everybody opportunity, everybody a ladder into the middle class, every child able to go as far as their dreams will take them, if we stay true to that, then we're going to be able to maintain the energy and the focus, the fight, the gumption to get stuff done. And it may not always happen in our lifetimes. And we may sometimes experience disappointments. And sometimes compromises are going to be made. But we know where we're going.

Well, people, this is what change looks like. This is what the elections of 2008 and 2006 were about. It wasn't about it happens one time and suddenly it's over and everybody can go home and relax. It's about everybody going out there and doing what needs to get done.

So I want to say to all of you, I am grateful for the extraordinary support that you provided me and that you provided House and Senate candidates all across the country. But don't stop now. There is too much at stake. There are other Supreme Court appointments to be made. There are other decisions in terms of how we're dealing with the international community to be made.

We're going to have to—if the last election was about changing the guard, this is about guarding the change that we've initiated. We've got to implement health care reform. We've got to implement financial regulatory reform.

There are still kids in this country that are hungry. There are still families in this country that are homeless. There are still people out there looking for work. And if we're compla-cent, if we're lethargic, we're letting those folks down and we're letting ourselves down and we're letting the country down.

So I don't know about you, but I'm still fired up. I am still ready to go. And I am going to need every single person out here not just to write checks, but to knock on doors, talk to your neighbors, talk to your friends, talk to your co-workers. If you got a business, talk to your employees; if you work at a business, talk to your employer. And tell them that even though times are tough, we're making progress. We remember that north star. We remember what we're about. We remember what this country is about. If we do that, I'm confident not only are we going to do well in this election, more importantly, we are going to serve the next generation.

Thank you, everybody. God bless you. God bless America.

NOTE: The President spoke at 7:50 p.m. at the Roosevelt Hotel. In his remarks, he referred to Rep. Pete Sessions, in his capacity as chairman of the National Republican Congressional Committee; and musicians Barbra Streisand, Beyonce G. Knowles, and Paul D. "Bono" Hewson. The transcript was released by the Office of the Press Secretary on September 23.

Remarks to the United Nations General Assembly in New York City
September 23, 2010

Mr. President, Mr. Secretary-General, my fellow delegates, ladies and gentlemen, it is a great honor to address this Assembly for the second time, nearly 2 years after my election as President of the United States.

We know this is no ordinary time for our people. Each of us comes here with our own problems and priorities. But there are also challenges that we share in common as leaders and as nations.

We meet within an institution built from the rubble of war, designed to unite the world in pursuit of peace. And we meet within a city that for centuries has welcomed people from across the globe, demonstrating that individuals of every color, faith, and station can come together to pursue opportunity, build a community, and live with the blessing of human liberty.

Outside the doors of this hall, the blocks and neighborhoods of this great city tell the story of a difficult decade. Nine years ago, the destruction of the World Trade Center signaled a threat that respected no boundary of dignity or decency. Two years ago this month, a financial crisis on Wall Street devastated American families on Main Street. And these separate challenges have affected people around the globe. Men and women and children have been murdered by extremists from Casablanca to London, from Jalalabad to Jakarta. The global economy suffered an enormous blow during the financial crisis, crippling markets and deferring the dreams of millions on every continent. Underneath these challenges to our security and prosperity lie deeper fears: That ancient hatreds and religious divides are once again ascendant; that a world which has grown more interconnected has somehow slipped beyond our control.

These are some of the challenges that my administration has confronted since we came into office. And today I'd like to talk to you about what we've done over the last 20 months to meet these challenges, what our responsibility is to pursue peace in the Middle East, and what kind of world we are trying to build in this 21st century.

Let me begin with what we have done. I have had no greater focus as President than rescuing our economy from potential catastrophe. And in an age when prosperity is shared, we could not do this alone. So America has joined with nations around the world to spur growth and the renewed demand that could restart job creation.

We are reforming our system of global finance, beginning with Wall Street reform here at home, so that a crisis like this never happens again. And we made the G–20 the focal point for international coordination, because in a world where prosperity is more diffuse, we must broaden our circle of cooperation to include emerging economies, economies from every corner of the globe.

There is much to show for our efforts, even as there is much work to be done. The global economy has been pulled back from the brink of a depression and is growing once more. We have resisted protectionism and are exploring ways to expand trade and commerce among nations. But we cannot and will not rest until these seeds of progress grow into a broader prosperity, not only for all Americans but for peoples around the globe.

As for our common security, America is waging a more effective fight against Al Qaida, while winding down the war in Iraq. Since I took office, the United States has removed nearly 100,000 troops from Iraq. We have done so responsibly, as Iraqis have transitioned to lead responsibility for the security of their country. We are now focused on building a lasting partnership with the Iraqi people, while keeping our commitment to remove the rest of our troops by the end of next year.

While drawing down in Iraq, we have refocused on defeating Al Qaida and denying its affiliates a safe haven. In Afghanistan, the United States and our allies are pursuing a strategy to break the Taliban's momentum and build the capacity of Afghanistan's Government and security forces so that a transition to Afghan responsibility can begin next July. And from South Asia to the Horn of Africa, we are moving toward a more targeted approach, one that strengthens our partners and dismantles terrorist networks without deploying large American armies.

As we pursue the world's most dangerous extremists, we're also denying them the world's most dangerous weapons and pursuing the peace and security of a world without nuclear weapons.

Earlier this year, 47 nations embraced a work plan to secure all vulnerable nuclear materials within 4 years. We have joined with Russia to sign the most comprehensive arms control treaty in decades. We have reduced the role of nuclear weapons in our security strategy. And here at the United Nations, we came together to strengthen the Nuclear Non-Proliferation Treaty.

Now, as part of our effort on nonproliferation, I offered the Islamic Republic of Iran an extended hand last year and underscored that it has both rights and responsibilities as a member of the international community. I also said—in this hall—that Iran must be held accountable if it failed to meet those responsibilities. And that is what we have done.

Iran is the only party to the NPT that cannot demonstrate the peaceful intentions of its nuclear program, and those actions have consequences. Through U.N. Security Council Resolution 1929, we made it clear that international law is not an empty promise.

Now, let me be clear once more: The United States and the international community seek a resolution to our differences with Iran, and the door remains open to diplomacy should Iran choose to walk through it. But the Iranian Government must demonstrate a clear and credible commitment and confirm to the world the peaceful intent of its nuclear program.

As we combat the spread of deadly weapons, we're also confronting the specter of climate change. After making historic investments in clean energy and efficiency at home, we helped forge an accord in Copenhagen that for the first time commits all major economies to reduce their emissions. We are keenly aware this is just a first step. And going forward, we will support a process in which all major economies meet our responsibilities to protect the planet while unleashing the power of clean energy to serve as an engine of growth and development.

America has also embraced unique responsibilities with come—that come with our power. Since the rains came and the floodwaters rose in Pakistan, we have pledged our assistance, and we should all support the Pakistani people as they recover and rebuild. And when the Earth shook and Haiti was devastated by loss, we joined a coalition of nations in response. Today we honor those from the U.N. family who lost their lives in the earthquake and commit ourselves to stand with the people of Haiti until they can stand on their own two feet.

Amidst this upheaval, we have also been persistent in our pursuit of peace. Last year, I pledged my best efforts to support the goal of two states, Israel and Palestine, living side by side in peace and security, as part of a comprehensive peace between Israel and all of its neighbors. We have traveled a winding road over the last 12 months, with few peaks and many valleys. But this month, I am pleased that we have pursued direct negotiations between Israelis and Palestinians in Washington, Sharm el-Sheikh, and Jerusalem.

Now, I recognize many are pessimistic about this process. The cynics say that Israelis and Palestinians are too distrustful of each other and too divided internally to forge lasting peace. Rejectionists on both sides will try to disrupt the process with bitter words and with bombs and with gunfire. Some say that the gaps between the parties are too big, the potential for talks to break down is too great, and that after decades of failure, peace is simply not possible.

I hear those voices of skepticism. But I ask you to consider the alternative. If an agreement is not reached, Palestinians will never know the pride and dignity that comes with their own state. Israelis will never know the certainty and security that comes with sovereign and stable neighbors who are committed to coexistence. The hard realities of demography will take hold. More blood will be shed. This Holy Land will remain a symbol of our differences instead of our common humanity.

I refuse to accept that future. And we all have a choice to make. Each of us must choose the path of peace. Of course, that responsibility begins with the parties themselves, who must answer the call of history. Earlier this month at the White House, I was struck by the words of both the Israeli and Palestinian leaders. Prime Minister Netanyahu said, "I came here today to find a historic compromise that will enable both people to live in peace, security, and dignity." And President Abbas said, "We will spare no effort, and we will work diligently and tirelessly to ensure these negotiations achieve their cause."

These words must now be followed by action, and I believe that both leaders have the courage to do so. But the road that they have to travel is exceedingly difficult, which is why I call upon Israelis and Palestinians and the world to rally behind the goal that these leaders now share. We know that there will be tests along the way and that one test is fast approaching.

Israel's settlement moratorium has made a difference on the ground and improved the atmosphere for talks. And our position on this issue is well known. We believe that the moratorium should be extended. We also believe that talks should press on until completed. Now is the time for the parties to help each other overcome this obstacle. Now is the time to build the trust and provide the time for substantial progress to be made. Now is the time for this opportunity to be seized so that it does not slip away.

Now, peace must be made by Israelis and Palestinians, but each of us has a responsibility to do our part as well. Those of us who are friends of Israel must understand that true security for the Jewish state requires an independent Palestine, one that allows the Palestinian people to live with dignity and opportunity. And those of us who are friends of the Palestinians must understand that the rights of the Palestinian people will be won only through peaceful means, including genuine reconciliation with a secure Israel.

I know many in this hall count themselves as friends of the Palestinians. But these pledges of friendship must now be supported by deeds. Those who have signed on to the Arab Peace Initiative should seize this opportunity to make it real by taking tangible steps towards the normalization that it promises Israel.

And those who speak on behalf of Palestinian self-government should help the Palestinian Authority politically and financially, and in doing so, help the Palestinians build the institutions of their state.

Those who long to see an independent Palestine must also stop trying to tear down Israel. After thousands of years, Jews and Arabs are not strangers in a strange land. After 60 years in the community of nations, Israel's existence must not be a subject for debate.

Israel is a sovereign state and the historic homeland of the Jewish people. It should be clear to all that efforts to chip away at Israel's legitimacy will only be met by the unshakeable opposition of the United States. And efforts to threaten or kill Israelis will do nothing to help the Palestinian people. The slaughter of innocent Israelis is not resistance, it's injustice. And make no mistake: The courage of a man like President Abbas, who stands up for his people in front of the world under very difficult circumstances, is far greater than those who fire rockets at innocent women and children.

The conflict between Israelis and Arabs is as old as this institution. And we can come back here next year, as we have for the last 60 years, and make long speeches about it. We can read familiar lists of grievances. We can table the same resolutions. We can further empower the forces of rejectionism and hate. And we can waste more time by carrying forward an argument that will not help a single Israeli or Palestinian child achieve a better life. We can do that.

Or we can say that this time will be different; that this time, we will not let terror or turbulence or posturing or petty politics stand in the way. This time, we will think not of ourselves, but of the young girl in Gaza who wants to have no ceiling on her dreams or the young boy in Sderot who wants to sleep without the nightmare of rocket fire.

This time, we should draw upon the teachings of tolerance that lie at the heart of three great religions that see Jerusalem's soil as sacred. This time, we should reach for what's best within ourselves. If we do, when we come back here next year, we can have an agreement that will lead to a new member of the United Nations, an independent, sovereign state of Palestine, living in peace with Israel.

It is our destiny to bear the burdens of the challenges that I've addressed: recession and war and conflict. And there is always a sense of urgency, even emergency, that drives most of our foreign policies. Indeed, after millennia marked by wars, this very institution reflects the desire of human beings to create a forum to deal with emergencies that will inevitably come.

But even as we confront immediate challenges, we must also summon the foresight to look beyond them and consider, what are we trying to build over the long term? What is the world that awaits us when today's battles are brought to an end? And that is what I would like to talk about with the remainder of my time today.

One of the first actions of this General Assembly was to adopt a Universal Declaration of Human Rights in 1948. That declaration begins by stating that "recognition of the inherent dignity and of the equal and inalienable rights of all members of the human family is the foundation of freedom, justice, and peace in the world."

The idea is a simple one: that freedom, justice, and peace for the world must begin with freedom, justice, and peace in the lives of individual human beings. And for the United States, this is a matter of moral and pragmatic necessity. As Robert Kennedy said, "[T]he individual man, the child of God, is the touchstone of value, and all society, groups, the state, exist for his benefit." So we stand up for universal values because it's the right thing to do. But we also know from experience that those who defend these values for their people have been our closest friends and allies, while those who have denied those rights, whether terrorist groups or tyrannical governments, have chosen to be our adversaries.

Human rights have never gone unchallenged, not in any of our nations and not in our world. Tyranny is still with us, whether it manifests itself in the Taliban killing girls who try to go to school, a North Korean regime that enslaves its own people, or an armed group in Congo-Kinshasa that use rape as a weapon of war.

In times of economic unease, there can also be an anxiety about human rights. Today, as in past times of economic downturn, some put human rights aside for the promise of short term stability or the false notion that economic growth can come at the expense of freedom. We see leaders abolishing term limits. We see crackdowns on civil society. We see corruption smothering entrepreneurship and good governance. We see democratic reforms deferred indefinitely.

As I said last year, each country will pursue a path rooted in the culture of its own people. Yet experience shows us that history is on the side of liberty, that the strongest foundation for human progress lies in open economies, open societies, and open governments. To put it simply, democracy, more than any other form of government, delivers for our citizens. And I believe that truth will only grow stronger in a world where the borders between nations are blurred.

America is working to shape a world that fosters this openness, for the rot of a closed or corrupt economy must never eclipse the energy and innovation of human beings. All of us want the right to educate our children, to make a decent wage, to care for the sick, and to be carried as far as our dreams and our deeds will take us. But that depends upon economies that tap the power of our people, including the potential of women and girls. That means letting entrepreneurs start a business without paying a bribe, and governments that support opportunity instead of stealing from their people. And that means rewarding hard work instead of reckless risk-taking.

Yesterday I put forward a new development policy that will pursue these goals. Recognizing that dignity is a human right and global development is in our common interest, America will partner with nations that offer their people a path out of poverty. And together, we must unleash growth that powers by individuals and emerging markets in all parts of the globe.

There is no reason why Africa should not be an exporter of agriculture, which is why our food security initiative is empowering farmers. There is no reason why entrepreneurs shouldn't be able to build new markets in every society, which is why I hosted a summit on entrepreneurship earlier this spring, because the obligation of government is to empower individuals, not to impede them.

The same holds true for civil society. The arc of human progress has been shaped by individuals with the freedom to assemble and by organizations outside of government that insisted upon democratic change and by free media that held the powerful accountable. We have seen that from the South Africans who stood up to apartheid to the Poles of Solidarity to the mothers of the disappeared who spoke out against the "dirty war" to Americans who marched for the rights of all races, including my own.

Civil society is the conscience of our communities, and America will always extend our engagement abroad with citizens beyond the halls of government. And we will call out those who suppress ideas, and serve as a voice for those who are voiceless. We will promote new tools of communication so people are empowered to connect with one another and, in repressive societies, to do so with security. We will support a free and open Internet so individuals have the information to make up their own minds. And it is time to embrace and effectively monitor norms that advance the rights of civil society and guarantee its expansion within and across borders.

Open society supports open government, but it cannot substitute for it. There is no right more fundamental than the ability to choose your leaders and determine your destiny. Now, make no mistake: The ultimate success of democracy in the world won't come because the United States dictates it, it will come because individual citizens demand a say in how they are governed.

There is no soil where this notion cannot take root, just as every democracy reflects the uniqueness of a nation. Later this fall, I will travel to Asia. And I will visit India, which peacefully threw off colonialism and established a thriving democracy of over a billion people. I'll continue to Indonesia, the world's largest Muslim-majority country, which binds together thousands of islands through the glue of representative government and civil society. I'll join the G–20 meeting on the Korean Peninsula, which provides the world's clearest contrast between a society that is dynamic and open and free and one that is imprisoned and closed. And I will conclude my trip in Japan, an ancient culture that found peace and extraordinary development through democracy.

Each of these countries gives life to democratic principles in their own way. And even as some governments roll back reform, we also celebrate the courage of a President in Colombia who willingly stepped aside or the promise of a new constitution in Kenya.

The common thread of progress is the principle that government is accountable to its citizens. And the diversity in this room makes clear, no one country has all the answers, but all of us must answer to our own people.

In all parts of the world, we see the promise of innovation to make government more open and accountable. And now we must build on that progress. And when we gather back here next year, we should bring specific commitments to promote transparency, to fight corruption, to energize civic engagement, to leverage new technologies so that we strengthen the foundations of freedom in our own countries, while living up to the ideals that can light the world.

This institution can still play an indispensable role in the advance of human rights. It's time to welcome the efforts of U.N. Women to protect the rights of women around the globe. It's time for every member state to open its elections to international monitors and increase the U.N. Democracy Fund. It's time to reinvigorate U.N. peacekeeping so that missions have the resources necessary to succeed and so atrocities like sexual violence are prevented and justice is enforced, because neither dignity nor democracy can thrive without basic security.

And it's time to make this institution more accountable as well, because the challenges of a new century demand new ways of serving our common interests.

The world that America seeks is not one we can build on our own. For human rights to reach those who suffer the boot of oppression, we need your voices to speak out. In particular, I appeal to those nations who emerged from tyranny and inspired the world in the second half of the last century, from South Africa to South Asia, from Eastern Europe to South America. Don't stand idly by, don't be silent when dissidents elsewhere are imprisoned and protesters are beaten. Recall your own history, because part of the price of our own freedom is standing up for the freedom of others.

That belief will guide America's leadership in this 21st century. It is a belief that has seen us through more than two centuries of trial, and it will see us through the challenges we face today, be it war or recession, conflict or division.

So even as we have come through a difficult decade, I stand here before you confident in the future, a future where Iraq is governed by neither tyrant nor a foreign power, and Afghanistan is freed from the turmoil of war; a future where the children of Israel and Palestine can build the peace that was not possible for their parents; a world where the promise of development reaches into the prisons of poverty and disease; a future where the cloud of recession gives way to the light of renewal and the dream of opportunity is available to all.

This future will not be easy to reach. It will not come without setbacks, nor will it be quickly claimed. But the founding of the United Nations itself is a testament to human progress. Remember, in times that were far more trying than our own, our predecessors chose the hope of unity over the ease of division and made a promise to future generations that the dignity and equality of human beings would be our common cause.

It falls to us to fulfill that promise. And though we will be met by dark forces that will test our resolve, Americans have always had cause to believe that we can choose a better history, that we need only to look outside the walls around us. For through the citizens of every conceivable ancestry who make this city their own, we see living proof that opportunity can be accessed by all, that what unites us as human beings is far greater than what divides us, and that people from every part of this world can live together in peace.

Thank you very much.

NOTE: The President spoke at 10:01 a.m. at United Nations Headquarters. In his remarks, he referred to Joseph Deiss, President, 65th Session of the U.N. General Assembly; Secretary-General Ban Ki-moon of the United Nations; Prime Minister Benjamin Netanyahu of Israel; President Mahmoud Abbas of the Palestinian Authority; and former President Alvaro Uribe Velez of Colombia. The Office of the Press Secretary also released a Spanish language transcript of these remarks.

Remarks Prior to a Meeting With Premier Wen Jiabao of China in New York City
September 23, 2010

President Obama. I want to welcome Premier Wen to the United States and once again say what an outstanding partner he's been over the last 21 months since I've been in office.

Along with President Hu, Premier Wen, I think, has exhibited extraordinary openness and cooperation with us as we try to strengthen the relationship between our two countries, a relationship that is based on cooperation, on mutual interest, on mutual respect.

We have worked together on a whole range of issues. Obviously, one of the most important issues has been to deal with the financial crisis and the recession that traveled around the world over the last several years. In the G–20, our cooperation, I think, has been absolutely critical.

I should probably actually let somebody translate now. [*Laughter*]

[*At this point, an interpreter translated President Obama's initial remarks.*]

Even as we've stabilized the world economy so that it is growing again and trade is growing again, we've also been working on a host of other issues that are of common interest. For example, we've cooperated extensively on issues of nuclear nonproliferation, and we have also had very frank discussions and cooperated on issues of climate change.

Obviously, we continue to have more work to do. On the economic front, although the world economy is now growing again, I think it's going to be very important for us to have frank discussions and continue to do more work cooperatively in order to achieve the type of balance and sustained economic growth that is so important and that we both signed up for in the context of the G–20 framework.

And we also, I think, have to work cooperatively together in order to achieve regional peace and stability, because the world looks to the relationship between China and the United States as a critical ingredient on a whole range of security issues around the world.

Fortunately, the Strategic and Economic Dialogue that we've set up provides an excellent forum for us to work through a range of bilateral as well as multilateral issues.

I have great confidence in the interest of both President Hu and Premier Wen to continue on the path of cooperation and mutually beneficial policies. I look forward to seeing them at the G–20 and APEC this fall. And I'm looking forward, hopefully, to the possibility of President Hu visiting us for an official state visit some time in the near future.

So, Premier Wen, to you and your delegation, welcome. And let me once again express on behalf of the American people our desire to continue to build a growing friendship and strong relationship between the peoples of China and the United States.

Premier Wen. It's a great pleasure to meet President Obama and all our American friends here. I always believed that China-U.S. relationship has gone beyond the bilateral scope and has important influence internationally.

Our common interests far outweigh our differences. In spite of the disagreements of one kind or another between our two countries, I believe these differences can be well resolved through dialogue and cooperation. So the China-U.S. relationship will always forge ahead. I have confidence in this.

Just now, you, Mr. President, referred to a host of areas where our two countries have co-operated, and I have come to the United States with such a cooperative spirit too. Our two countries can have cooperation on a series of major international issues and regional hotspot issues. We have cooperation on tackling the financial crisis and meeting the climate challenge. China and the United States can also embrace an even closer and bigger relationship in the fields of public finance, financial industry, and economic cooperation and trade.

I have come to this meeting with President Obama with a candid and constructive attitude. In the past couple of days here in my stay in New York, I have been saying such a message far and wide, that is, I'm sure I'm going to have a wonderful discussion with the President.

And I think our meeting today will also achieve the result that we will foster favorable conditions for the visit to the United States by President Hu Jintao at an appropriate time next year.

[*Inaudible*]—I want to thank you, Mr. President, for taking time.

NOTE: The President spoke at 11:27 a.m. at United Nations Headquarters. Premier Wen Spoke in Chinese, and his remarks were translated by an interpreter.

Remarks at a Luncheon Hosted by Secretary-General Ban Ki-moon of the United Nations in New York City
September 23, 2010

Good afternoon, everybody. I have already subjected you to one long speech today, so I will not do it again. But I do want to, as the President of the host country, the United States, thank all of you for your participation. And I want to thank Secretary-General Ban for hosting us. To all my fellow delegates and all the distinguished guests who are with us today, thank you for your leadership.

Mr. Secretary-General, I especially want to thank you for your dedication to pursuing peace, expanding security, protecting human rights, and advancing democracy and development.

Standing here, I am reminded of something President Franklin Roosevelt said shortly before the United Nations was founded. He said, "Peace can endure only so long as humanity really insists upon it and is willing to work for it and sacrifice for it." Over the last 2 years, our nations have come together in that spirit. We've shown the possibilities of working together in common purpose, from responding to terrible earthquakes in Haiti and floods in Pakistan, to carrying out peacekeeping missions, to focusing the world's attention on the upcoming referenda in Sudan.

But as we all know, our work is far from over. And in the months and years ahead, the challenges we face will require the work of all nations and all peoples. That's how real change happens. It will require the leadership of everybody in this room, because despite our differences, our people, I believe, share common aspirations: to live in security free from fear, to live in dignity free from want, to provide for our families, and to realize a better tomorrow. And as leaders, each of us has a responsibility to answer those aspirations and to leave our children a better world.

And so I want to propose a toast to Secretary-General Ban and to the spirit that brings us here today; that we insist not only upon peace and progress, but that we are also willing to work for it and to sacrifice for it.

Cheers.

NOTE: The President spoke at 1:58 p.m. at United Nations Headquarters.

Remarks at the Clinton Global Initiative Annual Meeting in New York City
September 23, 2010

President Obama. Thank you, everybody. Thank you. Please have a seat. Well, I am thrilled to be here. I want to thank President Clinton for the kind, although protocol-busting, introduction. [*Laughter*] And I want to thank him for inviting me back to join you at this year's meeting.

It was an extraordinary pleasure to be here at CGI last year. It's a pleasure to be back today, not only because of my highest regard for President Clinton personally, not just because of my gratitude to him for putting up with long hours away from our Secretary of State—[*laughter*]——

Former President William J. Clinton. Thank you for being grateful, though.

President Obama. I am grateful. [*Laughter*] But also because of the tremendous work he's doing through GCI [CGI].°

For the past 5 years, President Clinton has applied the full force of his energy and his influence—and it is formidable—to the work of this initiative. And with that passion and with that determination and that charm of his that makes it so darn hard to say no, he has marshaled $57 billion worth of commitments from folks like you, and that's bringing hope and opportunity to more than 200 million people around the world. It's a remarkable record of achievement.

But I'm not just here today to sing President Clinton's praises or to commend all of you for the terrific work that each of you have done, although I am grateful for that. I am here to play an even more important role, and that is to introduce my better half: my extraordinary wife, and America's extraordinary First Lady, Michelle Obama.

Now, Bill Clinton understands where I'm coming from here. [*Laughter*] He knows what it's like to be married to somebody who's smarter—[*laughter*]—somebody who's better looking—[*laughter*]—somebody who's just all around a little more impressive than you are. [*Laughter*] Right? It's—this is not news to people. [*Laughter*]

Since Michelle and I first started dating 22 years ago, pretty much everybody I know who's met her at some point comes up to me and says, "You know, Barack, you're great and all, I like you, but your wife, now, she's really something." [*Laughter*] And I, of course, agree. They're right. And I feel grateful that Michelle so far, at least, has not run for any offices I've been running for. [*Laughter*] She would beat me thoroughly.

Fortunately for me, as much as she cares deeply about public service, she hasn't shown much interest in the political chatter. She doesn't think about who's winning or losing, what the polls say, or who gets the best headline in the papers. No matter what the issue, there's only one thing that she wants to know, and that's: Who are we helping? That's what she

---

° White House correction.

asks. Who is this going to make a difference for? Whose life is this going to improve?

And while I get plenty of good advice from a lot of people during the course of the day, at the end of each day, it is Michelle—her moral voice, her moral center—that cuts through all the noise in Washington and reminds me of why I'm there in the first place.

She reminds me with her work to tackle childhood obesity so our kids can have healthy lives and the futures they deserve. She reminds me by throwing open the doors of our White House to young people from all different backgrounds, letting them know that we believe in their promise, letting them know that the White House is the people's house, and letting young people know that they're not that far away from all the power and prestige and decisions that are made, that, in fact, this is something they can aspire to, they can be a part of, because we are a government of and by and for the people.

She reminds me with her work to be a voice for America's military families and veterans, using her platform as First Lady to make sure they get support and respect and the appreciation that they deserve.

And while I am tremendously proud of the First Lady that she's been for this country, at the end of the day I'm most grateful that she's been such a partner to me and the best mother that I know.

Every moment that I spend with my daughters, I am thankful for all that she's done to make them who they are. Every day, I see her strength and her kindness and her character reflected in the two of them. And there is no greater gift, and I know Bill feels the same way about when he looks at Chelsea, he sees this incredible force that a mother can bring.

To this day, I still don't know how I talked her into marrying me, but I know that I am the luckiest guy in the world that she did. So it is with that that I would like to introduce you to my first lady, America's First Lady, Michelle Obama.

NOTE: The President spoke at 4:10 p.m. at the Sheraton New York Hotel & Towers. In his remarks, he referred to Chelsea Clinton, daughter of former President Clinton and Secretary of State Hillary Rodham Clinton. The transcript released by the Office of the Press Secretary also included the remarks of First Lady Michelle Obama.

Remarks Prior to a Meeting With Prime Minister Naoto Kan of Japan in New York City
September 23, 2010

Let me officially welcome the opportunity to speak again with Prime Minister Kan. We had an opportunity for intensive dialogue when we met together at the G–8 in Toronto. And once again, we have reaffirmed the importance of the U.S.-Japan alliance not only to regional stability, not only to the security of both our countries, but we believe it's one of the cornerstones of peace and security throughout the world.

So we look forward to discussing further how we can strengthen this alliance in the 21st century, how our economic relationship can continue to improve for the prosperity of both our peoples, how we can address regional hotspots and tensions that may arise, but also how we can work as leaders together in dealing with international problems like climate change and nuclear nonproliferation.

Japan will also be hosting the APEC meeting this year, and I'm looking forward to traveling to Yokohama, and I'm looking very much to finding ways that we can work together to shape an architecture for prosperity and economic development in the Pacific region, where obviously both the United States and Japan have a deep and longstanding interest.

So welcome. I hope you enjoy your stay in New York. And I look forward to my stay in Japan later this year.

NOTE: The President spoke at 5:12 p.m. at the Waldorf-Astoria Hotel.

Statement on Senate Passage of Small-Business Jobs Legislation
September 23, 2010

The small-business jobs bill passed today will help provide loans and cut taxes for millions of small-business owners without adding a dime to our Nation's deficit. After months of partisan obstruction and needless delay, I'm grateful that Democrats and a few Republicans came together to support this commonsense plan to put Americans back to work. I look forward to signing the bill on Monday.

NOTE: The statement referred to H.R. 5297.

Statement on Senate Action on Election Spending Disclosure Legislation
September 23, 2010

I am deeply disappointed by the unanimous Republican blockade in the Senate of the "DISCLOSE Act," a critical piece of legislation that would control the flood of special interest money into our elections. Today's decision by a partisan minority to block this legislation is a victory for special interests and U.S. corporations—including foreign-controlled ones—who are now allowed to spend unlimited money to fill our airwaves, mailboxes, and phone lines right up until election day, and it comes at the expense of the American people, who no longer have the right to know who is financing these ads in an attempt to influence an election for their preferred candidate. Wall Street, the insurance lobby, oil companies, and other special interests are now one step closer to taking Congress back and returning to the days when lobbyists wrote the laws. But despite today's setback, I will continue fighting to ensure that our democracy stays where it belongs, in the hands of the American people.

NOTE: The statement referred to S. 3628.

Interview With Bahman Kalbasi of BBC Persian in New York City
September 24, 2010

Mr. Kalbasi. Mr. President, thank you very much for your time.

The President. Thank you for having me.

U.N. General Assembly Address by President Mahmud Ahmadi-nejad of Iran

Mr. Kalbasi. If I could just begin with getting your reaction to the remarks Mr. Ahmadi-nejad made yesterday, faulting America for 9/11.

The President. Well, it was offensive. It was hateful. And particularly for him to make the statement here in Manhattan, just a little north of Ground Zero, where families lost their loved ones—people of all faiths, all ethnicities, who see this as the seminal tragedy of this generation—for him to make a statement like that was inexcusable.

And it stands in contrast with the response of the Iranian people when 9/11 happened, when there were candlelight vigils and, I think, a natural sense of shared humanity and sympathy was expressed within Iran. And it just shows once again sort of the difference between how the Iranian leadership and this regime operates and how, I think, the vast majority of the Iranian people, who are respectful and thoughtful, think about these issues.

Iran-U.S. Relations/U.N. Security Council Sanctions

Mr. Kalbasi. When your first video message to be sent in March of 2009, on the occasion of the Persian New Year, you spoke to the Government of Iran and people of Iran, and you talked about how you are committed to diplomacy. And you also said that this process of talking about all the issues on the table will only succeed if there is no threats, and with threats, this will not go forward. Yet your administration in much of this year not only threatened Iran with sanctions, but finally enacted sanctions that have been branded as "crippling." What do you say to those who see this as a departure from that promise of no threats and diplomacy only?

The President. Oh, I think we have to be—we have to look at what we've done this year, and it's very consistent. What I've said consistently is, is that we are willing to reach out with an open hand to the Iranian Government and the Iranian people, because we believe that there's nothing inevitable that should cause Iran and the United States to be enemies.

There's a history there that is difficult. But it can be bridged with mutual understanding, mutual respect. And we want to see the people of Iran ultimately succeed. But the Government has taken Iran on a path that has led to international condemnation. I mean, I think it's very important to understand that the sanctions that arose this year had to do with the fact that alone among signatories to the Nuclear Non-Proliferation Treaty, Iran has not been able to convince the international community that its nuclear program is peaceful. That's not just my judgment; that's the judgment of the international community, including countries like Russia and China that generally are very hesitant to impose sanctions on other countries. But they have consistently seen a behavior on the part of the Iranian Government that indicates that it has a nuclear program that does not abide by international rules and that potentially poses a threat to the region as well as the world.

Now, that's a choice that the Iranian regime has made. They can make another choice, and we would welcome them making another choice, which would be to act responsibly. They would then be able to have their rights for a peaceful nuclear program under the Nuclear Non-Proliferation Treaty. And that would remove the sanctions and would allow them to fully enter the international community in a way that would tremendously benefit the Iranian people. But we have not seen them make that choice yet.

So this is not a matter of us choosing to impose punishment on the Iranians. This is a matter of the Iranians' Government, I think, ultimately betraying the interests of its own people by isolating it further.

U.N. Security Council Sanctions

Mr. Kalbasi. This Government has lived through three decades of sanctions. What convinces you that this time it's any different, that it will, you know, end in some result for diplomacy or for resolution?

The President. Well, there are no guarantees. This regime has shown itself to be very resistant to observing basic international norms and being willing to engage in serious negotiations around a nuclear program that has generated great fear and mistrust in the region and around the world.

But we do think that the sanctions raise the costs for the Government. Most of these sanctions are targeted at the regime, at its military. And we think that over time, hopefully, there's enough reflection within the Iranian Government that they say to themselves, you know, this is not the best course for our people, this is not the best course for Iran—which is rooted in an incredible civilization. It has some of the highest literacy rates in the world. The potential for Iran to succeed economically, to open itself up to exchange and commerce with other countries, is enormous. But in order to do that, the Iranian regime, I think, has to take a different course than the one that it's been on of late.

Mr. Kalbasi. You speak of increasing cost, but many would argue that this is also impacting ordinary people in Iran. We get reports every day, from a small-businessman who can't import a spare part, mainly because of the banking system now not providing services to them, all the way to medicine and food prices going up because shipment lines are not being ensured, all the way to old-standing sanctions like planes that are not sold to the Iranians, that we have had 2,000 people die in plane crashes—all of these. Are you not worried that this might backfire, that people of Iran would be looking at America and wondering why they're being punished in this process?

The President. Well, I—look, I am obviously concerned about the Iranian people. And they are trying to live their lives, and there is so much promise in the country. The question is, can the Iranian regime take a different approach that would help its people as opposed to harm its people?

Right now it's not taking that approach. Right now what the Iranian Government has said is, it's more important for us to defy the international community, engage in a covert nuclear weapons program, than it is to make sure that our people are prospering. And the international community I don't think prefers the choice that has been taken.

As you noted, at the beginning of my term, I came in—at some political cost, by the way, because obviously outrageous, disgusting statements of the sort that Mr. Ahmadi-nejad just made makes the American people understandably wary of any dealings with the Iranian Government—but I said, you know, there should be a way for us to change the dynamic that has been in place since 1979, since you were born. And it turns out that so far, at least, the Iranian regime has been unwilling to change its orientation.

So when people inside of Iran are asking themselves, why is it that we can't get spare parts or food prices are going up or other basic necessities are harder to come by, they have to look at the management of their own Government, both in terms of the economic management, but also in terms of them deciding that it's a higher priority to pursue a covert nuclear program than it is to make sure that their people have opportunity.

I think they're moving down the wrong course, and they continue to have the option of moving down the right course.

Mr. Kalbasi. If these sanctions fail, what are your options, Mr. President?

The President. Well, I think there are a whole host of options, and these options would be exercised in consultation with the international community. Our strong preference is to resolve these issues diplomatically. I think that's in Iran's interest. I think that is in the interest of the international community. And I think it remains possible, but it is going to require a change in mindset inside the Iranian Government.

Iran/Nuclear Nonproliferation

Mr. Kalbasi. For—a lot of Iranians are looking at the—how this scenario is playing out. Many see similarities to the runup to the Iraq war, you know, the succession of U.N. resolutions, toughened economic sanctions, on-and-off talk about war and a military strike. What do you say to them that are worried that they'll wake up to a military attack by America or Israel?

The President. Well, I think what people should remember is that I don't take war lightly. I was opposed to the war in Iraq. I am somebody who's interested in resolving issues diplomatically. I think that we have been very clear that the Iranian Government has—and the nation of the Islamic Republic of Iran—have a right to peaceful nuclear programs and peaceful nuclear power. That is a right that all NPT members have.

So the Iranian Government itself has said, we are not interested in nuclear weapons. That's their public statement. If that's the case, there should be a mechanism whereby they can assure and prove to the international community, including the IAEA, that that is in fact the case. And if they take those constructive steps in serious negotiations, then not only should there not be a threat of war, but there also won't be the sanctions that are currently in place.

Again, the United States here is not operating unilaterally. There may have been strong objections to the United States going into Iraq. This is a situation where we've got the U.N. Security Council and countries that have significant business dealings with Iran making decisions not to do business with Iran, despite the fact that Iran is a significant oil producer. When a country like Japan or South Korea or China or Russia—all of whom have commercial dealings with Iran—make these decisions, they do so at great cost to themselves.

And the reason they're doing it is not simply because we're pressuring them. The reason they're doing it is because they too see a threat of destabilization if you have an Iranian regime pursuing nuclear weapons and potentially triggering an arms race in the region that could be dangerous for everybody.

Israel/Iran

Mr. Kalbasi. What if, during this process of diplomacy, Israel decides to attack Iran? Will you stop them?

The President. Well, I'm not going to engage in hypotheticals. I think that, understandably, Israel is very concerned when the President of a country, a large country near them, states that they should be wiped off the face of the Earth.

And so again, this is an example of where the Iranian people, I believe, are ill served. To have a President who makes outrageous, offensive statements like this does not serve the interests of the Iranian people, does not strengthen Iran's stature in the world community.

And there is an easy solution to this, which is, is to have a Iranian Government act responsibly in the international community, along the lines of not just basic codes of conduct or diplomatic norms, but just basic humanity and common decency.

Again, for Ahmadi-nejad to come to somebody else's country and then to suggest somehow that the worst tragedy that's been experienced here, a attack that killed 3,000 people, was somehow the responsibility of the Government of that country, is something that defies not just common sense, but basic sense—basic senses of decency that aren't unique to any particular country, they're common to the entire world.

Human Rights in Iran

Mr. Kalbasi. Mr. President, if I may, I want to move on to the human rights issue.

The President. Sure.

Mr. Kalbasi. After the disputed Presidential election, we saw the birth of a Green Movement in Iran, brutally oppressed by the Government.

The President. Right.

Mr. Kalbasi. We've all seen the images of young men and women dying on the streets, be-

ing shot at, many being taken into custody and dying in custody, journalists, politicians, students being taken to jail and staying there for years. For a lot of these human rights activists, when they look at United States, even though they've heard you talk about "arc of justice," and you talked about Neda, they see this sense of obsession with the nuclear issue, as if, if that is resolved, human rights is not the big problem for America in its relations with Iran. Are you—what's your response to them? You know, in the streets in Tehran, there was that chanting, "Mr. Obama, are you with us, or are you against us?" Are you with them, or are you against them?

The President. Well, I just made a speech this week in the U.N. General Assembly in which I said that not just my administration, but I think all of America, sees human rights, basic freedoms, the freedom to speak, the freedom to—freedom of the press, freedom of assembly, freedom to choose your own government, freedom from fear and abuse from government, as central to who we are, central to our values, central to our foreign policy. And that applies around the world, and it certainly applies in Iran.

I think all of us were moved by the demonstrations of courage and hope that were expressed in Iran after these elections. We have no interest in meddling in the rights of people to choose their own government, but we will speak out forcefully when we see governments abusing and oppressing their own people. And I think this is another example in which the Iranian Government delegitimized itself in ways that continue to reverberate around the world.

Had you seen an election that was abiding by basic rules, basic norms, in which the current regime had won, it might not have been an ideal outcome from my perspective, but we could have respected it. When we see instead a reaction in which people are imprisoned and beaten and shot and harassed and opposition figures are imprisoned, that, I think, violates the norms that need to be upheld all around the world.

So the answer is, is that for those who aspire to have their voices heard, to participate in a democracy that recognizes their human dignity, we will always stand with them.

U.S. Military Operations in Afghanistan

Mr. Kalbasi. On Afghanistan, we have a large Persian audience in Afghanistan who watch BBC, and they're hearing all these mixed messages, competing statements about what, really, July 2011 means. And they're worried about the commitment that America has to Afghanistan. Will you stay there until the job is done?

The President. Well, we are going to stay there until the job is done. The job is to provide Afghans themselves the capacity to secure their own country. And so the July 2011 date is a date in which, having ramped up our armed presence in Afghanistan in order to provide space and time for the Afghan security forces to develop and strengthen and to blunt the momentum of the Taliban, we will then start gradually reducing the number of U.S. troops and coalition troops that are inside of Afghanistan.

That's something that I think the Afghan people want. Afghans are a very proud people, and this is a sovereign Government. So we are providing them assistance. And in the short term, I increased our troop levels because, frankly, we had neglected the security situation, and Taliban had been able to regain momentum and control of vast portions of the country.

But now we're seeing Afghan security forces trained, we're seeing Afghan police trained, and we've got a very effective civilian effort there in order to help build infrastructure and improve the day-to-day lives of people within Afghanistan. So on—starting in July '11, we'll begin to draw down those additional troops.

But we're not going to suddenly leave, turn off the lights and go home on that date. What will happen was, as we are training up more and more Afghan security forces, they're becoming more effective, we will transition so that they are starting to take over more responsibility for security. And slowly, the United States troop presence, as well as coalition troop presence, will diminish.

That, I think, is something that is in the interests not just of the United States, but it's also in the interests of the Afghan people.

Afghanistan/Iran-U.S. Relations

Mr. Kalbasi. I have very short time, Mr. President.

The President. Yes.

Mr. Kalbasi. Iran, you've said, could play a constructive role in Afghanistan. And you have a common enemy, being Taliban. Is there a sense that you would take Iran up on its offer that it's publicly announced that they would— they're ready to assist. Would you take them up on that offer?

The President. Well, I think that Iran and all the countries in the region can play a constructive role in Afghanistan. Look, this is a country that's been war-torn. Most Afghans, like people around the world, simply want an opportunity to make a living, support their families, provide an education for their children.

And so I think the entire region would benefit from a stable, peaceful Afghanistan. And we are willing to work with Iran and all the other countries in the region to achieve that goal.

Now, I have to say that there have been times where the Iranian Government, I think, has said publicly it wants to work on these issues. Behind the scenes, we see evidence that occasionally they have actually helped insurgents in ways that end up harming our troops. But we will continue to explore ways in which we can work with all the countries in the region, including Iran, to stabilize Afghanistan.

I think this is one more example of where potentially the United States and Iran could end up working together on a whole range of issues. In order to do that, though, the Iranian regime has to make a decision that it is not simply maintaining power based on animosity towards the United States, based towards outrageous statements in the international community, but rather, is looking for constructive ways to improve the lives of ordinary people inside of Iran.

And if that shift in orientation takes place, I think the opportunities for tremendous progress for a great nation and a great civilization exist. If it doesn't, then it's going to continue to be isolated, and it's going to continue, I think, to cause friction not just with the United States, but with the world community.

Middle East Peace Process

Mr. Kalbasi. Yesterday you talked about the naysayers when it comes to the Middle East peace process. But, Mr. President, a lot of this pessimism comes from people who want peace, but they're looking at the makeup of the Israeli Government, they're looking at the divisions on the Palestinian side, and they don't think it's possible at this stage for them to take that bold step. What makes you so confident that this time is different? And if so, how would that geo-politically change the region, including Iran?

The President. Well, let me say, I wouldn't consider myself so confident that we can get this done. I think it's necessary. I—and the point I was making was for decades now, we have seen this conflict not only consume the politics of the region, but also hamper the ability of Israeli children to feel safe, Palestinian children to succeed and thrive.

And if we cannot begin to actually move towards a Palestinian state living side by side in peace and security with a Jewish—the Jewish State of Israel, then what we are going to see, I think, is more and more conflict, more and more bloodshed, and the prospects of any peaceful resolution will dissolve. So I'm moving on the—out of a sense of urgency, not because it's easy. I think it's going to be very difficult for us to achieve these goals.

What I am optimistic about is I think that President Abbas is a man who sincerely desires peace as well as a sovereign Palestinian state. I think Prime Minister Netanyahu has undergone an evolution in his thinking, and I think that he genuinely would like to see a peaceful Palestinian state and a secure Israeli state that's at peace with its neighbors.

We, as an international community, then have to support those efforts, acknowledging that it's very difficult. It may not be possible, but we have to try. And now's the time to try.

And I think that if we were able to achieve the goal of a peaceful settlement between the Israelis and the Palestinians, then that would change the dynamic of the region in a very positive way. What I think most Iranian people are looking for is that Palestinians have their right to a sovereign state. Well, there's only one way to achieve that, and that is by peace through Israel. It's not going to be achieved through violence.

And again, this is an example of where the Iranian regime has a choice. It can be supportive of peace efforts that result in concrete benefits for the Palestinian people, or it can choose to engage in rhetoric and fund terrorist activity that ensures continued conflict, which may serve their political interests, but certainly doesn't serve the interests of a Palestinian family on the West Bank who would prefer to have a country of their own in which they can start a business or send their children to school. That's, I think, the vision that we have to keep in mind.

Mr. Kalbasi. Thank you so much, Mr. President.

The President. I enjoyed it.

Mr. Kalbasi. Thank you for your time.

The President. Thank you very much.

NOTE: The interview began at 10:08 a.m. at the Waldorf-Astoria Hotel. In his remarks, the President referred to President Mahmoud Abbas of the Palestinian Authority; and Prime Minister Benjamin Netanyahu of Israel.

Remarks Prior to a Meeting With President Juan Manuel Santos Calderon of Colombia in New York City
September 24, 2010

President Obama. Well, I want to welcome President Santos here. This is the first time that we've met face to face, although we had a wonderful conversation on the phone.

He has already, I think, in the short time that he's been in office, shown remarkable leadership. Yesterday was a big day for the people of Colombia and those who are seeking peace in the region. Because of outstanding work by Colombian security forces, they were able to embark on a mission that resulted in the death of the leader of FARC.

The people of Colombia have been plagued by this terrorist insurgency for a very long time, and as a consequence of the success of Colombian security forces, I think we now have the chance to see continued stability in Colombia and in the region. And that will create the prospects for peace and development under President Santos's leadership. So we want to congratulate him.

The friendship between our two countries is extraordinarily important to us. We are working not just in dealing with things like drug interdiction, but we're also interested in figuring out how we can continually improve our economic cooperation, our political cooperation, and our people-to-people exchanges so that we continually deepen these bilateral ties.

And I think that President Santos also likes to boast about the fact that his Kansas Jayhawks have won a number of championships in basketball. And I was a little disappointed with them last year because I bet on them winning it all, and they lost. [*Laughter*] But he's already apologized to me for that. [*Laughter*]

So I want to welcome the President. Again, congratulations on a great start. We are confident that you're going to do well and we'll be able to strengthen the cooperation between our two nations.

President Santos. Thank you.

President Obama. Thank you.

President Santos. All right, I want to thank President Obama for his warm welcome and his generous words. We value in Colombia very much our very special relations with the United States. We're coming, ourselves, into a new era. Now that the security problem is more or less solved, we can now turn to a more progressive agenda. Social development, the prosperity of our people, climate change, the environment, those are the type of issues that we can now include in our agenda. And we want to enhance our relation to a true partnership where Colombia and the U.S. can work together in the region and outside the region for our mutual benefit.

I am proud of being a graduate from the University of Kansas. [*Laughter*] As President Obama knows that we are very good in basketball. But I told him, when he called me, what the Republicans say about my education, that I was—afterwards, I went to Harvard. And they say I was educated in Kansas and corrupted in Harvard. [*Laughter*] And I think that's something that we both are—also graduated from Harvard, and I'm sure that that's only a Republican point of view, not a Democratic one. [*Laughter*]

President Obama. Well, actually, they all—they think I was corrupted somewhere. [*Laughter*]

Welcome. Thank you so much.

President Santos. Thank you very much.

President Obama. Thank you.

NOTE: The President spoke at 12:26 p.m. at the Waldorf-Astoria Hotel. In his remarks, he referred to Victor Julio Suarez Rojas, chief of military operations of the Revolutionary Armed Forces of Colombia (FARC), who was killed by Colombian military forces on September 23. The Office of the Press Secretary also released a Spanish language transcript of these remarks.

Remarks at a United States-Association of Southeast Asian Nations Leaders Meeting in New York City
September 24, 2010

President Obama. Well, good afternoon, everyone. To all the leaders who are here as well as the delegations, welcome. I want to thank my fellow leaders for being here and for making this the first U.S.-ASEAN leaders meeting to take place in the United States. This reflects ASEAN's growing importance and the unprecedented cooperation between ASEAN and the United States.

As a Pacific nation, the United States has an enormous stake in the people and the future of

Asia. The region is home to some of our largest trading partners and buys many of our exports, supporting millions of American jobs. We need partnerships with Asian nations to meet the challenges of our growing economy, preventing proliferation, and addressing climate change.

As President, I've therefore made it clear that the United States intends to play a leadership role in Asia. So we've strengthened old alliances, we've deepened new partnerships, as we are doing with China, and we've reengaged with regional organizations, including ASEAN.

Last year in Singapore, I was proud to become the first American President to meet with all 10 ASEAN leaders. Today I'm pleased to host our second meeting as we elevate our partnership to meet the shared challenges and opportunities of the 21st century.

We'll focus on creating sustainable economic growth. Our trade with ASEAN countries is growing. In fact, America exports to ASEAN countries are growing twice as fast as they are to other regions, so Southeast Asia will be important to reaching my goal of doubling American exports.

Through APEC and initiatives like the Trans-Pacific Partnership, we're pursuing trade relationships that benefit all our countries. And we will continue to support ASEAN's goal of creating a more effective and integrated community by 2015, which would advance regional peace and stability.

We'll also focus on deepening our political and security cooperation. ASEAN countries are increasingly playing a leadership role in the region, and ASEAN itself has the potential to be a very positive force in global affairs. That is why the United States has accepted ASEAN's invitation to join the East Asia summit, which will help us meet regional and global challenges together. And I look forward to attending the East Asia summit in Jakarta next year.

So again, I want to thank my fellow leaders for being here. And I look forward to sustaining our momentum on my visits in November to Indonesia, Korea, and Japan, where we'll work together at the APEC summit to ensure strong, sustainable, and balanced economic growth.

With that, I'd invite President Triet of Vietnam, the ASEAN chair this past year, to offer a few words as well. And during that time, I suspect that lunch will be served.

President Nguyen Minh Triet of Vietnam. Your Excellency, President Obama, Excellenicies, ASEAN leaders, on behalf of my fellow colleagues from ASEAN countries, I want to thank Your Excellency President Obama for inviting us to the second ASEAN-U.S. leaders meeting in New York. And thank you so much for giving us the wonderful hospitality.

Over the years, and especially recently, the relations between ASEAN and the U.S. have been growing very well. And I remember the first meeting in Singapore in November 2009, and we come up with a lot of important outcomes to create favorable conditions for the growing of the relations between ASEAN and the U.S. And this time, I believe this a great opportunity for us to share the views and exchange our views on how to enhance the dialogue partnership between ASEAN and the U.S. in the coming years.

Your Excellencies, the relations between ASEAN and U.S. plays a very important role to the security, peace, and development in the region. Vietnam and ASEAN always support the deepening of the relations between ASEAN and the U.S., bilaterally and multilaterally. And we want to take our relations to the next level to greater comprehensiveness and more sustenance for the peace, stability, and development of our region.

I look forward to very fruitful and productive discussions that we are going to have today in order to bring about great benefits and to lay the foundation for the growing of the relations and cooperation between our two sides.

Thank you so much.

NOTE: The President spoke at 1:08 p.m. at the Waldorf Astoria Hotel. President Triet spoke in Vietnamese, and his remarks were translated by an interpreter. A portion of these remarks could not be verified because the audio was incomplete.

Joint Statement of the Second United States-Association of Southeast Asian Nations Leaders Meeting
September 24, 2010

1. We, the heads of State/Government of Brunei Darussalam, the Kingdom of Cambodia, the Republic of Indonesia, the Lao People's Democratic Republic, Malaysia, the Union of Myanmar, the Republic of Philippines, the Republic of Singapore, the Kingdom of Thailand and the Socialist Republic of Viet Nam, the Member States of the Association of Southeast Asian Nations (ASEAN), and the United States (U.S.), held our Second ASEAN-U.S. Leaders' Meeting on September 24 in New York. The Meeting was co-chaired by H.E. Nguyen Minh Triet, President of Viet Nam, in his capacity as Chairman of ASEAN, and H.E. Barack Obama, President of the United States of America. The Secretary-General of ASEAN was also in attendance.

2. ASEAN appreciated the United States' sustained engagement at the highest level with ASEAN Member States. We reaffirmed that U.S. participation in the annual Post Ministerial Conference (PMC) meetings, the ASEAN Regional Forum (ARF), the upcoming ASEAN Defense Ministers Meeting Plus (ADMM Plus) process, sustained engagement through the U.S.-ASEAN Trade and Investment Framework Arrangement (TIFA), U.S. accession to the Treaty of Amity and Cooperation in Southeast Asia (TAC), and the establishment of a permanent Mission to ASEAN have all demonstrated the United States' firm commitment to continue to strengthen comprehensive relations with ASEAN. We welcomed the appointment of the first resident U.S. Ambassador to ASEAN in Jakarta.

3. We recognized these elements of greater engagement between ASEAN and the United States. We agreed to further deepen our current partnership in order to provide the framework for continued growth in ASEAN-U.S. relations and to expand the significant contributions our cooperation already has made to peace, stability and prosperity in Southeast Asia and the broader East Asia region. We welcomed the idea to elevate our partnership to a strategic level and will make this a primary focus area of the ASEAN-U.S. Eminent Persons Group and will task it to develop concrete and practical recommendations to that end by 2011. We also looked forward to the adoption of the new five-year Plan of Action for 2011–2015.

4. ASEAN Leaders welcomed the United States' support for ASEAN Community and Connectivity. We will strengthen cooperation with the United States in addressing issues related to human rights, trade and investment, energy efficiency, agriculture, educational, cultural and people-to-people exchanges, interfaith dialogue, science and technology, disaster risk management and emergency response, health and pandemic diseases, environment, biodiversity conservation, climate change, combating illicit trafficking in persons, arms and drugs and other forms of transnational crimes. We resolved to deepen cooperation against international terrorism under the framework of the ASEAN-U.S. Joint Declaration for Cooperation to Combat International Terrorism.

5. We discussed the growing efforts to promote regional cooperation in East Asia and reaffirmed the importance of ASEAN centrality in the EAS process. ASEAN welcomed the U.S. President's intention to participate in the East Asia Summit (EAS) beginning in 2011 and Secretary Clinton's attendance as a guest of the chair at the Fifth EAS meeting on October 30, 2010 in Ha Noi. ASEAN and the United States expect to continue to

1425

exchange views with all stakeholders to ensure an open and inclusive approach to regional cooperation in the future.

6. We reviewed our discussion from our first historic meeting in Singapore last year and noted with satisfaction the substantial accomplishments of the U.S.-ASEAN Enhanced Partnership. We reaffirmed the importance of our common goals, and tasked our officials to continue to pursue programs and activities to achieve the Millennium Development Goals, enhance regional integration, and support the realization of an ASEAN Community by 2015.

7. We committed to further enhance cooperation on sustainable agriculture development and food security through the L'Aquila Food Security Initiative, in particular to promote investment in country led-plans, greater efficiency of production and distribution, capacity building, sharing of experience and best practices, research and development as well as infrastructure development. In particular, we pledged to strengthen food security through support for the ASEAN Integrated Food Security (AIFS) Framework and Strategic Plan of Action on Food Security (SPA–FS) and through the promotion of agricultural and fisheries trade.

8. We acknowledged the continued relationship on technical assistance and capacity-building for intellectual property protection and enforcement matters through a Letter of Arrangement between the ASEAN Secretariat and the U.S. Patent and Trademark Office, in place since 2004 and recently extended for another five years, and commended the results from previous training under this arrangement.

9. Building on our decision at the First ASEAN-U.S. Leaders Meeting, further consultations between relevant U.S. Cabinet Secretaries and their ASEAN counterparts should be explored and encouraged to develop areas of mutual cooperation.

10. ASEAN and the United States have learned valuable lessons from the crises of 1997 and 2008 and resolved to contribute to the reforms in the global financial architecture to safeguard the global economy from future crises, and committed to establish a durable foundation for future growth that is more balanced in its sources of demand and provides for development in line with the G–20 Framework for Strong, Sustainable, and Balanced Growth. In this respect, the United States acknowledged ASEAN's constructive role in multilateral fora, including its contributions to the G–20 process.

11. We welcomed the rebound in trade between ASEAN and the United States and remained committed to further enhance economic cooperation in order to sustain the recovery and create jobs and additional economic opportunities in each of our countries. Two-way ASEAN-U.S. trade in goods reached $84 billion in the first six months of this year, an increase of 28-percent over last year. In addition, the stock of U.S. foreign direct investment in ASEAN totaled $153 billion in 2008 and the stock of ASEAN foreign direct investment in the United States was $13.5 billion.

12. We supported the intensification of efforts to advance new initiatives identified by all Parties under the ASEAN-U.S. Trade and Investment Framework Arrangement (ASEAN-U.S. TIFA), including completion of a trade facilitation agreement, continued development of trade finance and trade and environment dialogues, and continued cooperation on standards under the ASEAN Consultative Committee on Standards and Quality (ACCSQ). We welcomed that our Finance Ministers have met, for the first time, to discuss issues of mutual concern in the global economy, and regional developments.

13. We recognized that corruption and illicit trade undermine development, invest-

ment, tax revenues and legitimate business in the region, creating insecurity in our communities and long-term barriers to growth. For this reason, we underscored the importance of ratification and full implementation of the UN Convention against Corruption. We also recognized the need to deepen our cooperation, especially in regard to discussions on achieving more durable and balanced global growth, increasing capacity building activities in the key areas such as combating corruption and illicit trade, preventing bribery, enhancing transparency in both public and private sectors, denying safe haven, extradition and asset recovery. We also welcomed the G–20's efforts to advance the fight against corruption.

14. We welcomed continued progress on regional trade and investment liberalization and facilitation, including through the Asia-Pacific Economic Cooperation (APEC) process, as well as ongoing negotiations on the Trans-Pacific Partnership involving several members of ASEAN as well as the United States.

15. We recognized that climate change is a common concern of humankind. In line with the Bali Roadmap, we reaffirmed that all countries should protect the climate system for the benefit of present and future generations in accordance with the principles and provisions of the UN-FCCC, including the principle of common but differentiated responsibilities and respective capabilities. We agreed to strengthen our cooperation on addressing the climate change issues including on adaptation, finance, technology transfer, and capacity building. We recognized the important contribution of the Copenhagen Accord and are committed to work together towards a successful outcome of the 2010 United Nations Climate Change Conference in Cancun, Mexico.

16. We appreciated the United States' support for the ASEAN Intergovernmental Commission on Human Rights and the of-

fer to support the Commission on the Promotion and Protection of the Rights of Women and Children through capacity building programs. We looked forward to the outcomes from the AICHR study tours that are to take place in the United States later this year and the visit of the ASEAN Commission on Women and Children planned next year.

17. ASEAN Leaders welcomed the continued U.S. engagement with the Government of Myanmar. We expressed our hope that ASEAN and U.S. engagement encourages Myanmar to undertake political and economic reforms to facilitate national reconciliation. We welcomed the ASEAN Chair's Statement of 17 August 2010. We reiterated our call from the November 2009 Leaders Joint Statement that the November 2010 general elections in Myanmar must be conducted in a free, fair, inclusive and transparent manner in order to be credible for the international community. We emphasized the need for Myanmar to continue to work together with ASEAN and the United Nations in the process of national reconciliation.

18. We reaffirmed the importance of regional peace and stability, maritime security, unimpeded commerce, and freedom of navigation, in accordance with relevant universally agreed principles of international law, including the United Nations Convention on the Law of the Sea (UNCLOS) and other international maritime law, and the peaceful settlement of disputes.

19. ASEAN Leaders welcomed the signing of the Treaty between the United States of America and the Russian Federation on Measures for the Further Reduction and Limitation of Strategic Offensive Arms on 8 April 2010 in Prague. ASEAN and the United States consider this an important step towards a world without nuclear weapons. In addition, ASEAN and the United States reaffirmed that the establishment of the South-East Asia Nuclear Weapons Free Zone (SEANWFZ) contributes

towards global nuclear disarmament, nuclear non-proliferation, regional peace and stability. We encouraged Nuclear Weapon States and State Parties to the SEANWFZ to conduct consultations, in accordance with the objectives and principles of the Treaty. In this regard, ASEAN welcomed the U.S. announcement at the 2010 Review Conference of the Nuclear Non-Proliferation Treaty that it is prepared to consult and resolve issues that would allow the United States to accede to the SEANWFZ Protocol. ASEAN congratulated the United States on the successful outcomes of the April 2010 Nuclear Security Summit, in which several ASEAN countries participated, and will work together implement the pledges and commitments they made there, and to engage others in the global effort to prevent nuclear terrorism.

20. We reiterated our commitment to prevent the use and spread of weapons of mass destruction (WMD), in an effort to build a world free of their threats. We congratulated the Philippines for its able and effective Presidency of the May 2010 Review Conference of the Nuclear Non-Proliferation Treaty (NPT), and stressed the necessity for all NPT Parties to continue to fulfill our respective obligation under the NPT. We reiterated the importance of a balanced, full and non-selective application and implementation of the Treaty's three pillars—nuclear disarmament, nuclear non-proliferation, and peaceful uses of nuclear energy.

21. We reaffirmed the importance of continuing to implement UN Security Council Resolutions 1929 on Iran as well as 1718 and 1874 on Democratic Peoples' Republic of Korea (DPRK). We called on both countries and the international community to implement their obligations under the aforementioned resolutions. We further called on DPRK to implement its commitments under the September 19, 2005 Joint Statement of the Six Party Talks to abandon all nuclear weapons and existing nuclear programs and return, at an early date, to the NPT and to IAEA safeguards. We also urged the DPRK to comply fully with its obligations in accordance with the relevant United Nations Security Council resolutions.

22. The Leaders of ASEAN and the United States welcomed the ADMM-Plus as a framework that could help strengthen the existing cooperation on regional defense and security between ASEAN and its partners in accordance with ADMM's open, flexible and outward-looking orientation. ASEAN welcomed the planned participation of the Secretary of Defense in the inaugural meeting of the ADMM-Plus in October.

23. We welcomed the continuation of the U.S.-Lower Mekong Initiative to promote cooperation in the areas of environment, health, education and infrastructure development. We supported the continued convening of the ministerial meetings between the United States and Lower Mekong Basin countries. We encouraged U.S. engagement and support to Brunei Indonesia Malaysia Philippines-East Asia Growth Area (BIMP-EAGA), Indonesia Malaysia Thailand-Growth Triangle (IMT-GT), Ayeyawady-Chao Phraya-Mekong Economic Cooperation Strategy (AC-MECS), Cambodia Laos Myanmar Viet Nam (CLMV), Heart of Borneo, and other sub-regional cooperation frameworks.

24. We recognized the importance of cooperation among ASEAN educational and research institutions and encouraged more such academic linkages. In this regard, we noted with appreciation the ERIA-Harvard University Cooperation in academic exchanges and research collaboration, particularly their joint-sponsored Symposium in Ha Noi on 26 October 2010 entitled "Evolving ASEAN Society and Establishing Sustainable Social Security Net."

25. We stressed the importance of sustaining dialogue at the highest level between the two sides and committed to hold our third

meeting next year in conjunction with the 2011 East Asia Summit.

NOTE: An original was not available for verification of the content of this joint statement.

Remarks at a United Nations Ministerial Meeting on Sudan in New York City
September 24, 2010

Good afternoon. Mr. Secretary-General, on behalf of us all, thank you for convening this meeting to address the urgent situation in Sudan that demands the attention of the world.

At this moment, the fate of millions of people hangs in the balance. What happens in Sudan in the days ahead may decide whether a people who have endured too much war move towards peace or slip backwards into bloodshed. And what happens in Sudan matters to all of sub-Saharan Africa, and it matters to the world.

I want to thank Vice President Taha and First Vice President Kiir for being here. To my fellow leaders from Africa, the Middle East, Europe, and Asia, your presence sends an unmistakable message to the Sudanese people and to their leaders that we stand united. The comprehensive peace agreement that ended the civil war must be fully implemented. The referenda on self-determination scheduled for January 9 must take place peacefully and on time. And the will of the people of south Sudan and the region of Abyei must be respected, regardless of the outcome.

We are here because the leaders of Sudan face a choice. It's not the choice of how to move forward to give the people of Sudan the peace they deserve. We already know what needs to be done. The choice is—for Sudanese leaders is whether they will have the courage to walk the path. And the decision cannot be delayed any longer.

Despite some recent progress, preparations for the referenda are still behind schedule. Now the vote is only a little more than a hundred days away. And tragically, as has already been referred to, a recent spike in violence in Darfur has cost the lives of hundreds of more people.

So the stakes are enormous. We all know the terrible price paid by the Sudanese people the last time north and south were engulfed in war: some 2 million people killed—2 million people; millions more left homeless; millions displaced

to refugee camps, threatening to destabilize the entire region. Separately, in Darfur, the deaths of hundreds of thousands shocked the conscience of the world. This is the awful legacy of conflict in Sudan, the past that must not become Sudan's future.

And that is why since I took office, my administration has worked for peace in Sudan. In my meetings with world leaders, I've urged my counterparts to fully support and contribute to the international effort that is required. Ambassador Susan Rice has worked tirelessly to build a strong and active coalition committed to moving forward. My special envoy, General Gration, has worked directly with the parties in his 20 visits to the region.

Now, we've seen some progress. With our partners, we've helped to bring an end to the conflict between Sudan and Chad. We've worked urgently to improve humanitarian conditions on the ground. And we're leading the effort to transform the Sudan People's Liberation Army into a professional security force, including putting an end to the use of children as soldiers.

Recognizing that Southern Sudan must continue to develop and improve the lives of its people, regardless of the referendum's outcome, we in the U.N. mission are helping the Government of Southern Sudan improve the delivery of food and water and health care and strengthen agriculture.

And most recently, we've redoubled our efforts to ensure that the referenda takes place as planned. Vice President Biden recently visited the region to underscore that the results of the referenda must be respected. Secretary Clinton has engaged repeatedly with Sudanese leaders to convey our clear expectations. We've increased our diplomatic presence in Southern Sudan, and mobilized others to do the same, to prepare for the January 9 vote and for what comes after.

But no one can impose progress and peace on another nation. Ultimately, only Sudanese leaders can ensure that the referenda go forward and that Sudan finds peace. There's a great deal of work that must be done, and it must be done quickly.

So two paths lay ahead: one path taken by those who flout their responsibilities and for whom there must be consequences—more pressure and deeper isolation; the other path is taken by leaders who fulfill their obligations, and which would lead to improved relations between the United States and Sudan, including supporting agricultural development for all Sudanese, expanding trade and investment, and exchanging Ambassadors and eventually working to lift sanctions—if Sudanese leaders fulfill their obligations.

Now is the time for the international community to support Sudanese leaders who make the right choice. Just as the African nations of the Intergovernmental Authority on Development rose to the challenge and helped the parties find a path to peace in 2005, all of us can do our part to ensure that the comprehensive peace agreement is fully implemented.

We must promote dignity and human rights throughout all of Sudan, and this includes extending the mandate of the U.N. independent expert of Sudan, because we cannot turn a blind eye to the violations of basic human rights. And as I said, regardless of the outcome of the referenda, we must support development in Southern Sudan, because people there deserve the same dignity and opportunities as anyone else.

And even as we focus on advancing peace between north and south, we will not abandon the people of Darfur. The Government of Sudan has recently pledged to improve security and living conditions in Darfur, and it must do so. It need not wait for a final peace agreement. It must act now to halt the violence and create the conditions—access and security—so aid workers and peacekeepers can reach those in need and so development can proceed. Infrastructure and public services need to be improved. And those who target the innocent—be they civilians, aid workers, or peacekeepers—must be held accountable.

Progress towards a negotiated and definitive end to the conflict is possible. And now is the moment for all nations to send a strong signal that there will be no time and no tolerance for spoilers who refuse to engage in peace talks.

Indeed, there can be no lasting peace in Darfur and no normalization of relations between Sudan and the United States without accountability for crimes that have been committed. Accountability is essential not only for Sudan's future, it also sends a powerful message about the responsibilities of all nations that certain behavior is simply not acceptable in this world, that genocide is not acceptable. In the 21st century, rules and universal values must be upheld.

I saw the imperative of justice when I visited one of the camps in Chad several years ago. It was crowded with more than 15,000 people, most of them children. What I saw in that camp was heartbreaking: families who had lost everything, surviving on aid. I'll never forget the man who came up to me, a former teacher who was raising his family of nine in that camp. He looked at me, and he said very simply, "We need peace." We need peace.

Your Excellencies—Vice President Taha, First Vice President Kiir—the Sudanese people need peace. And all of us have come together today because the world needs a just and lasting peace in Sudan.

Here, even as we confront the challenges before us, we can look beyond the horizon to the different future that peace makes possible. And I want to speak directly to the people of Sudan, north and south. In your lives, you have faced extraordinary hardship. But now there's the chance to reap the rewards of peace. And we know what that future looks like. It's a future where children, instead of spending the day fetching water, can go to school and come home safe. It's a future where families, back in their homes, can once again farm the soil of their ancestors. It's a future where, because their country has been welcomed back into the community of nations, more Sudanese have the opportunity to travel, more opportunity to provide education, more opportunities for trade. It's a future where, because their economy is tied to the global economy, a woman can start a small business, a manufacturer can export his goods, a growing economy raises living standards, from large cities to the most remote village.

This is not wide-eyed imagination. This is the lesson of history, from Northern Ireland to the Balkans, from Camp David to Aceh, that with leaders of courage and vision, compromise is possible and conflicts can be ended. And it is the example of Africans, from Liberia to Mozambique to Sierra Leone, that after the darkness of war, there can be a new day of peace and progress.

So that is the future that beckons the Sudanese people, north and south, east and west. That is the path that is open to you today. And

for those willing to take that step, to make that walk, know that you will have a steady partner in the United States of America.

Thank you very much.

NOTE: The President spoke at 3:37 p.m. at United Nations Headquarters. In his remarks, he referred to Secretary-General Ban Ki-moon of the United Nations; Vice President Ali Osman Taha and First Vice President Salva Kiir Mayardit of Sudan; U.S. Special Envoy to Sudan Maj. Gen. J. Scott Gration, USAF (Ret.); and Mohamed Chande Othman, United Nations Independent Expert on the Situation of Human Rights in Sudan.

The President's Weekly Address
September 25, 2010

This week, the economists who officially decide when recessions start and end declared the recession of 2008 to be over. But if you're one of the millions of Americans who lost your home, your job, or your savings as a consequence of the recession, this news is of little comfort or value.

Yes, the economy is growing instead of shrinking, as it was in 2008 and the beginning of 2009. We're gaining private sector jobs each month instead of losing 800,000, as we did the month I took office.

But we have to keep pushing to promote growth that will generate the jobs we need and repair the terrible damage the recession has done. That's why I've proposed a series of additional steps: accelerated tax breaks for businesses who buy equipment now, a permanent research and development tax break to promote innovation by American companies, and a new initiative to rebuild America's roads, rails, and runways that will put folks to work and make our country more competitive.

Taken together with the small-business tax cut and lending plan we passed through Congress last week, these steps will help spur jobs in the short run and strengthen our economy for the long run.

Now, the Republicans who want to take over Congress offered their own ideas the other day.

Many were the very same policies that led to the economic crisis in the first place, which isn't surprising, since many of their leaders were among the architects of that failed policy.

It's grounded in the same, wornout philosophy: cut taxes for millionaires and billionaires, cut the rules for Wall Street and the special interests, and cut the middle class loose to fend for itself. That's not a prescription for a better future. It's an echo of a disastrous decade we can't afford to relive.

The Republicans in Washington claimed to draw their ideas from a web site called America Speaking Out. It turns out that one of the ideas that's drawn the most interest on their web site is ending tax breaks for companies that ship jobs overseas. The funny thing is, when we recently closed one of the most egregious loopholes for companies creating jobs overseas, Republicans in Congress were almost unanimously opposed. The Republican leader, John Boehner, attacked us for it and stood up for outsourcing instead of American workers.

So America may be speaking out, but Republicans in Congress sure aren't listening. They want to put special interests back in the driver's seat in Washington. They want to roll back the law that will finally stop health insurance companies from denying you coverage on the basis of a preexisting condition. They want to repeal reforms that will finally protect hard-working families from hidden rates and penalties every time they use a credit card, make a mortgage payment, or take out a student loan.

And for all their talk about reining in spending and getting our deficits under control, they want to borrow another $700 billion and use it to give tax cuts to millionaires and billionaires. On average, that's a tax cut of about $100,000 for millionaires.

Instead of cutting taxes for the wealthiest few—tax breaks we cannot afford—I've called for tax cuts for middle class families who saw their incomes shrink by 5 percent during the last, lost decade. We've already cut eight different taxes for small-business owners to help them hire and grow, and we're going to cut eight more. We're challenging our States and schools to do a better job educating our kids and making college more affordable so America can once more lead the world in the proportion of our children graduating from college. And we're putting an end to the days of taxpayer-funded bailouts so Main Street never again has to pay for Wall Street's mistakes.

America is a great country. Our democracy is vibrant, our economy is dynamic, and our workers can outcompete the best of them. But the way for us to remain the greatest country on Earth isn't to turn back the clock and put the special interests back in charge. It's to make sure all our people are getting a fair shake. It's to make sure everyone who's willing to work for it still has a chance to reach for the American Dream. And that will remain my mission every single day so long as I have the honor of serving as President.

Have a nice weekend, everybody.

NOTE: The address was recorded at approximately 2:20 p.m. on September 22 in the Map Room at the White House for broadcast on September 25. The transcript was made available by the Office of the Press Secretary on September 24, but was embargoed for release until 6 a.m. on September 25. The Office of the Press Secretary also released a Spanish language transcript of this address.

Remarks and a Question-and-Answer Session With College and University Student Journalists
September 27, 2010

The President. Hey, everybody. Thanks for joining me today. Before I get to the questions, I want to just take a minute to underscore something that is probably going to make as big of a difference in our success as a nation as anything we do, and that's what we're trying to achieve to strengthen our Nation's higher education system. Our classrooms, our professors, our administrators, our students, you guys are going to drive future success of the United States.

I've been talking about this a lot lately. We have fallen behind. In a single generation, we've fallen from 1st to 12th in college graduation rates for young adults. And if we're serious about building a stronger economy and making sure we succeed in the 21st century, then the single most important step we can take is to make sure that every young person gets the best education possible, because countries that outeducate us today are going to outcompete us tomorrow.

So what I've done, starting with this past year's State of the Union Address, is proposed that by 2020, we once again are number one and have the highest proportion of college graduates in the world. And we're trying to put in place some policies to help us meet this goal.

First of all, we're making college more affordable. For example, we've changed the way Federal student loans are administered. Instead of handing over $60 billion in unwarranted subsidies to big banks that were essentially getting this money even though the loans were guaranteed by the Federal Government, we're redirecting that money so that it goes directly to students. And that's allowing us to support community colleges and make college more affordable for nearly 8 million students and families.

We're tripling the investment in college tax credits for middle class families. We're raising the value of Pell grants, and we're going to make sure that they keep up with inflation. What we've also done is made sure that future borrowers are able to choose a plan so that you never have to pay more than 10 percent of your salary each month to service student loans that you've taken. And if you go into public service and you keep up with your payments, whatever leftover student debt that you have will be forgiven after 10 years. And finally, as part of this effort, we're simplifying financial aid forms.

Another important way we're making college more affordable, under the Affordable Care Act, my health care bill, is that young adults can now stay on their parents' health plans until they're 26 years old. And that obviously provides relief to a lot of young people who are looking maybe at their first job not providing health insurance.

Our second priority is making sure that higher education creates a workforce that's ready for the new jobs of the future. Community colleges are going to play a critical role in getting there, and I've asked Dr. Jill Biden to hold the first-ever White House Summit on Community Colleges. That way stakeholders are going to be able to discuss how community colleges can make sure we've got the most educated workforce in the world in relevant subjects that help people get jobs. That summit is going to be here next week.

A third part of our higher education strategy is where all of you have an important role, and that's making sure that more students complete college. We've done okay in terms of college enrollment rates, but more than a third of America's college students and more than half of our minority students don't earn a degree, even after 6 years. And that's a waste of potential, particularly if folks are racking up big debt and then they don't even get the degree at the end. They still have to pay back that debt, but they're not in a stronger position to be able to service it.

So obviously, it's up to students to finish, but we can help remove some barriers, especially

those who are earning degrees while working or raising families. So that's why I've long proposed what I call a College Access and Completion Fund, which would develop, implement, and evaluate new approaches to improving college success and completion, especially for kids from disadvantaged backgrounds. We're also making sure our younger veterans are supported through a post-9/11 GI bill.

The key here is, is that we want to open the doors of our colleges and universities to more people so they can learn, they can graduate, and they can succeed in life.

And while we had a setback last week, one last element that I want to mention is the need to get the "DREAM Act" passed. Some of you are probably aware this is important legislation that will stop punishing young people who—their parents brought them here. They may not have been documented, but they've for all intents and purposes grown up as American young people. This gives them the chance to obtain legal status either by pursuing a higher education or by serving in the U.S. Armed Forces for the country they've grown up in and love as their own, the same way that all of us do.

So these are all some of the steps that we're taking to help students fulfill their dreams, but also a key part of my economic platform in terms of making the country stronger.

With that, I'm ready to take questions on higher education issues or any other issue that you guys are interested in.

Employment Prospects for College Graduates/National Economy

Q. Hi, Mr. President. How are you today?

The President. I'm good, Colin. Where are you calling from?

Q. I'm calling from southwest Virginia, Radford University.

The President. Well, tell everybody I said hi there.

Q. I'll do that. Okay, so I've heard some of my professors call our generation the lost generation, because we're going to get out of school with a ton of debt due to student loans and not be able to pay them off really because, well, we don't—not going to get a steady job—it's not that likely to begin with—and the economy is in the shape it is currently in. So I guess my question is, do you think there's some truth to that? And do you think it will take a longer time than usual for our generation to get on our feet?

And I guess—I mean, you talked about in your health care plan and how we're able to stay on our parents' plans now until we're 26, and that's going to help us deal with, kind of, money issues and insurance. But what else are you—is your administration doing to, kind of, I guess, help us stand up when we get out of college?

The President. A couple points I'd make. First of all, I think your generation is going to be just fine. I mean, we've gone through the worst financial crisis since the Great Depression, and so things are real tough for young people right now. But having said that, if you are getting a college degree, if you've got skills in math and science or good, sound communication skills, there are still jobs out there, even in a tough environment. And 9 out of 10 people who are looking for work can still find work.

The key is for us to keep on improving the economy, and that's going to be my number-one priority over the next several years. If the economy is growing, if we're investing in small businesses so they can open their doors and hire more workers, if we're helping large businesses in terms of plants and equipment—a lot of the initiatives that I've put in place already—if we're building infrastructure, not just roads and bridges, but also broadband lines, if we're investing in clean energy, all those things are going to open up new opportunities for young people with skills and talent for the future.

So don't let anybody tell you that somehow your dreams are going to be constrained going forward. You're going through a slightly tougher period. But if you think about it, what we called the greatest generation, my grandparents' generation, they had a situation where unemployment reached 30 percent, and they ended up essentially building the entire American middle class to what it was and making this the most powerful economy in the world. So right now we're going through a tough time, but I have no doubt that you guys are going to be successful.

Now, in the meantime, some specific things that we can do to help, I already mentioned two of them. One was you being able to stay on your parents' health care until you're 26. That gives you a little bit of a cushion in the initial jobs that you're getting coming out of college. The second thing that I've already mentioned is that starting in 2014, we're going to be in a situation where young people can cap their debt at 10 percent of their salary, regardless of what that salary is.

And if you go into something like teaching, for example, or you're a police officer or firefighter, public service jobs of one sort or another, then that's forgiven after 10 years. That's obviously going to be a big boost that would have helped me out a lot, because I ended up having 10 years worth of loans I had to pay down after I got out of law school.

In the meantime, what we're also doing—and this is already in place, this doesn't wait till 2014—we have increased the Pell grant. We've made it available to more people. We've made it more reliable. And so hopefully, students who are studying now are going to be able to keep their student loan—their debt lower than I did when I went to school or Michelle did when we went to school. That's obviously going to help. That's a second thing.

A third thing we're trying to do is to make sure that we're giving young people a better sense of what jobs are out there in the future so that people end up gravitating towards the skills and the degrees that they need to get employed. That's especially important for young people who are going through a community college system, because a lot of times folks are going through programs that—where they're racking up debt, they're getting college credits, but these aren't ultimately giving them the kinds of skills that they need to get a job.

And so all those things can be helpful in moving us forward. But the single most important thing I've got to do is make sure that we get this economy back on track, and that's why I'm so focused on things like a bill I'm going to be signing today that provides small businesses further incentive to invest and gives them tax breaks and financing, because they're huge drivers of job creation over the long term.

All right? Who do we have next?

President's Visit to Wisconsin/Political Participation

Q. Hi, Mr. President. Thank you for taking the time to do this today.

The President. Well, it's great to talk to you. Where—which college are you calling from?

Q. I'm calling from the University of Wisconsin, where you will be tomorrow.

The President. I am looking forward to getting to Madison. [*Laughter*]

Q. Well, we're very excited to have you here. So I guess my question is, why are you so interested in Wisconsin? I mean, you've been here quite a few times, especially over the summer. I mean, why come to—why host a rally here tomorrow?

The President. Well, first of all, I'm a Midwest guy, and so whenever I get a chance to get back to the Midwest, I'm always happy about it.

Second, I love Madison because when I was just out of college and I moved to Chicago to work as a community organizer, I still had a couple of friends who were up going to school in Madison. So I used to drive up there and have fun times, which I can't discuss in detail with you. [*Laughter*]

And the third thing is, the reason we're going to Madison is because I want to send a message to young people across the country about how important this election is.

Look, back in 2008, a lot of young people got involved in my campaign because they felt like the path that we were on—where we were in a war in Iraq, a war in Afghanistan, no clear plan for us to get out of either one; we had run up huge deficits that people were going to have to pay off long term; the economy wasn't doing well; health care system was a mess—I think people just generally felt that we needed to bring about some fundamental changes in how we operate. And this was all before the financial crisis. And I think a lot of people felt that our campaign gave them a vehicle to get engaged and involved in shaping the direction of this country over the long term.

Now, I've been in office for 2 years. We've been in the midst of this big financial crisis. I've been having all these fights with the Republicans to make progress on a whole bunch of these issues. And during that time, naturally, some of the excitement and enthusiasm started to drain away because people felt like, gosh, all we're reading about are constant arguments in Washington, and things haven't changed as much as we would like, as quickly as we'd like, even though the health care bill got passed and financial regulatory bill got passed, and there have been—we've brought an end to our combat mission in Iraq, but still it seems as if a lot of the old politics is still operating in Washington.

And what I want to do is just to go speak to young people directly and remind them of what I said during the campaign, which was, change is always hard in this country. It doesn't happen overnight. You take two steps forward, you take one step back. This is a big, complicated democracy. It's contentious. It's not always fun and games. A lot of times, to bring about big changes like, for example, in our energy policy, you're taking on a lot of special interests—the oil companies and utilities—and some of them may not want to see the kinds of changes that would lead to a strong, green economy.

And the point is, though, you can't sit it out. You can't suddenly just check in once every 10 years or so, on an exciting Presidential election, and then not pay attention during big midterm elections where we've got a real big choice between Democrats and Republicans.

I mean, you've got a situation right now where the Republicans put out their "Pledge to America" that says we're going to give $4 trillion worth of tax breaks, $700 billion of those going to millionaires and billionaires, each of whom would get on average a $100,000 check. And to even pay for part of that, we're going to cut all the improvements that we just talked about making on student loans, so that 8 million young people would see less support on student loans. We'd cut back our education assistance through the higher education by 20 percent. Well, that's a big choice. That has big consequences.

And so even though this may not be as exciting as a Presidential election, it's going to make a huge difference in terms of whether we're going to be able to move our agenda forward over the next couple of years.

And I just want to remind young people, they've got to get reengaged in this process. And they're going to have to vote in these midterm elections. You've got to take the time to find out, where does your congressional candidate stand on various issues, where does your Senate candidate stand on various issues, and make an educated decision and participate in this process, because democracy is never a one-and-done proposition. It's something that requires sustained engagement and sustained involvement. And I just want to remind everybody of that.

Health Care Reform

Q. Hi, Mr. President. How are you?

The President. I'm good, Katrina. Where are you calling from?

Q. Penn State University, where Joe Biden will be tomorrow.

The President. Well, tell the Nittany Lions, congratulations. You guys won this weekend.

Q. Oh, yes, barely. [*Laughter*]

The President. Barely. It was a little scary there for a second.

Q. You're telling me. Anyway, so my question is actually about health care. So will our parents' employers be required to cover us after we graduate at their group rate that they're currently at? Or will the cost go up as a result of us being kept on our parent's plan? And are there any regulations on this as far as, like, how it's going to work?

The President. Your costs should not—your parents' costs should not go up substantially. Under this rule, you should be able to stay on your parent's plan until you're 26. The only caveat to the thing is that it assumes that your employer doesn't offer you health care. So if you find a job on graduation and your new employer offers you a health care plan, you can't say to yourself, you know what, I'd rather stay on my parent's plan and that will save me some money. You've got to take up the offer that your employer gives you for health care. But if your employer does not offer you health care or if you're having trouble finding a job, during that period when you're looking for a job, you will be covered under your parent's plan up to the age of 26.

Affordability of College Tuition/Midterm Elections

Q. Hi, Mr. President. I hope things are going well for you.

The President. They're going great. And now, congratulations to you guys. Beating Texas, that was big.

Q. Thank you very much. I don't think many of us expected it.

The President. No, I can't imagine you did. [*Laughter*]

Q. Well, my question is that I think there's a lot of concern, especially in public universities, that education is becoming increasingly less affordable. I know, like, at UCLA last year, they raised tuition by 32 percent to help make up for slashed funding from the State, which accounts for, like, $200 million at just our university this year. And student aid has increased some in this time, especially for lower income groups, but I think, especially in the middle class, a lot of families are just not being able to compensate. So my question is, how would you address this concern that public higher education is becoming more of a strain on families?

The President. Right. Well, I talked about what we're doing to increase financial aid to students, and obviously, that's important. But there's another part of the equation, and that is just the cost of college generally, both at the public and private institutions. If I keep on increasing Pell grants and increasing student loan programs and making it more affordable, but health care—or higher education inflation keeps on going up at the pace that it's going up right now, then we're going to be right back where we started, putting more money in, but it's all being absorbed by these higher costs.

You've identified one of the reasons that at public institutions costs have gone up. It has to do with the fact that State budgets are being so hard pressed that they're having to make severe cutbacks in the support they provide to public education.

So one of the things that I can do to help is to make sure that the economy is growing. States then are taking in more tax revenue, and if States are taking in more tax revenue, then they don't have to try to pass on increased costs to students, because they can maintain levels of support to institutions of higher learning.

So improving the economy overall is going to be critical. That will take some pressure off the States. We also, though, need to work with the States and public universities and colleges to try to figure out what is driving all this huge inflation in the cost of higher education, because this is actually the only place where inflation is higher than health care inflation. And some of it are things that are out of the control of the administrators at universities, health care costs being an example. Obviously, personnel costs are a big chunk of university expenses, and if their health care costs are going up 6, 8 percent a year, then they're going to have to absorb those costs some way. And that's why our health care bill generally should help, because what we're trying to do is to control health care costs for everybody.

But there are other aspects of this where, frankly, I think students as consumers, parents as consumers, and State legislators and Governors are going to need to put more pressure on universities. And I'll just give one example, which people may not want to hear, but when I go to some colleges and universities—public colleges and universities and I look at the athletic facilities that exist these days or the food courts or the other things that have to do with the quality of life at universities, it's sure a lot nicer than it was when I was going to college. Somebody has to pay for that.

And part of what I think we've got to examine is, are we designing our universities in a way that focuses on the primary thing, which is education. You're not going to a university to join a spa; you're going there to learn so that you can have a fulfilling career. And if all the amenities of a public university start jacking up the cost of tuition significantly, that's a problem.

How courses are taught, so that we're making sure that the teaching loads at universities continue to emphasize research and continue to give professors the opportunity to engage in work outside the classroom that advances knowledge, but at the same time reminding faculties that their primary job is to teach. And so you've got to structure how universities operate to give students the best deal that they can; that's important too.

And so one of the things that we're going to be doing is working with university presidents and college presidents to figure out how can we get control of costs generally and refocus our priorities and our attention on what the primary function of a university is, and that is to give students the knowledge and skills that they need to have a fulfilling career after they get out, not to provide the best situation for the 4 years that they're there.

Like I—as I said, when I was going to college, I mean, food at the cafeteria was notoriously bad. I didn't have a lot of options. We used to joke about what was for lunch that day, and there would be a bunch of nondescript stuff that wasn't particularly edible. But—now, I don't want to get in trouble with the First Lady here, because she's obviously big on improving nutrition, but I do think that you've got to think about what we can do to generally make universities more cost effective for students.

And you guys have to be good consumers, and your parents have to be good consumers, and we've got to offer you more information. You should know where your tuition is going. There should be a pie chart at every university that says, out of every dollar you spend in tuition, here's where your money is going. And you should have some good understanding of that and be able to make some better decisions as a consequence of that information.

Let me just close, because I know we're out of time. And hopefully, as I travel around the country, I'm going to be able to talk to you guys individually when I visit colleges or universities.

I know we've gone through a tough time these last 2 years. And I do worry sometimes that young folks, having grown up or come of age in difficult economic times, start feeling as if their horizons have to be lowered and they've got to set their sights a little bit lower than their parents or their grandparents. And I just want to remind people that you guys all have enormous challenges that you're going to have to face, but you continue to live in the most vibrant, most dynamic, wealthiest nation on Earth.

And if you are able to work together as a generation to tackle longstanding problems that you inherited but that are solvable, then there's no reason why the 21st century is not going to be the American century, just like the 20th century was. And there's still billions of people around the world who want to come here, and they want to come here because they know that this is, for all our problems, still the land of opportunity.

But it's going to require us to get involved around critical issues like education and health care and energy and our foreign policy. And we're going to have to have vigorous debates,

and we're going to have to hammer out consensus on these issues. And the energy that you were able to bring to our politics in 2008, that's needed not less now, it's needed more now.

And so I hope that everybody starts paying attention these last 5 weeks. We've got an election coming up. I want everybody to be well informed and to participate. If you do, then I feel very optimistic about the country's future.

All right? Thank you, guys. Bye-bye.

NOTE: The President spoke at 12:16 p.m. in the Oval Office at the White House. Participating in the session were Colin Daildea, student, Radford University; Jennifer Zettel, student, University of Wisconsin—Madison; Katrina Wehr, student, Pennsylvania State University; and Daniel Schonhaut, student, University of California, Los Angeles.

Remarks on Signing the Small Business Jobs Act of 2010
September 27, 2010

Thank you, everybody. Please have a seat. Thank you very much. I am thrilled to be here on what is an exciting day. I want to begin by recognizing the Members of Congress who fought so hard to pass this bill on behalf of America's small businesses. A lot of work was involved in this obviously, but there are a few folks who are here on stage I want to make sure to acknowledge.

First of all, my dear friend—and my Senator—from the great State of Illinois, Senator Dick Durbin. A champion for businesses in Louisiana and around the country, Senator Mary Landrieu is here. A champion of small businesses, Senator Maria Cantwell of Washington is here. And one of the deans of the Senate, and as thoughtful a person about industry and manufacturing as you'll find, Senator Carl Levin of Michigan is here. From the House side, we've got Representative Melissa Bean, also my neighbor from Illinois, and Congressman Al Green from Texas is in the house.

We've got a couple of Governors here: Governor O'Malley of Maryland; and somebody who has been working so hard on behalf of the great State of Michigan—we are proud of what

she's been doing, because it's really hard work in Michigan right now—but Governor Granholm, I think, coming to the end of her term, has just done outstanding work, and I want to acknowledge her.

We've also got some mayors in the house, and I'm not sure if they're all here, but I'm going to go ahead and announce them: Mayor Coleman of Columbus, Ohio; Mayor Dickert from Racine, Wisconsin; Mayor Foxx from Charlotte, North Carolina; Mayor Pawlowski of Allentown, Pennsylvania; and Mayor Ravenstahl—whose Steelers won last night—from Pittsburgh. [*Laughter*] Give them all a big round of applause.

Finally, I want to thank members of my administration who are with us, including our Small Business Administrator and just a terrific advocate for small businesses, Karen Mills is here. Please give her a big round of applause. And our Treasury Secretary, Tim Geithner, as well as one of my top economic advisers, Gene Sperling, who worked so hard to get this legislation done. Where's Gene? There he is back there.

And most of all, I want to thank and welcome all the small-business owners from across the country who have come to the signing of this bill, many of whom, over the course of the last several months, I've had a chance to meet. I visited their facilities, everything from—I've seen trucks to pizza—[*laughter*]—to web sites to signs. And we've talked about how essential it is that we got this bill done, that it was critical that we cut taxes and make more loans available to entrepreneurs.

And so today, after a long and tough fight, I am signing a small-business jobs bill that does exactly that. It's good news. It's good news.

Now, this is important because small businesses produce most of the new jobs in this country. They are the anchors of our Main Streets. They are part of the promise of America: the idea that if you've got a dream and you're willing to work hard, you can succeed. That's what leads a worker to leave a job to become her own boss. That's what propels a basement inventor to sell a new product or an amateur chef to open a restaurant. It's this promise that has drawn millions to our shores and made our economy the envy of the world.

Yet along with the middle class, small businesses have borne the greatest brunt of this recession. They—you—were hit by a one-two punch. The downturn has meant people are spending less, so there's less demand. And the financial crisis made it difficult for small businesses to get loans.

So when I took office, I put in place a plan—an economic plan to help small businesses. And we were guided by a simple idea: Government can't guarantee success, but it can knock down barriers to success, like the lack of affordable credit. Government can't replace—can't create jobs to replace the millions that we lost in the recession, but it can create the conditions for small businesses to hire more people, through steps like tax breaks.

That's why we cut taxes for small businesses eight times. We passed a new tax credit for companies that hire unemployed workers, which is benefiting several of the people with us here today. Guy Brami from Gelberg Signs is here in Washington. And he's making use of this

tax break after he hired six workers. Cherrelle Hurt, who runs the As We Grow Child Care & Learning Center in Virginia, has been able to add three new employees.

We also increased the exemption on capital gains taxes for key small-business investments to 75 percent. We passed a tax cut so companies could immediately write off more expenses like new equipment. And as part of health reform, 4 million small-business owners could be eligible this year for a health care tax credit worth perhaps tens of thousands of dollars.

Our economic plan has also helped to free up credit, supporting nearly 70,000 new loans to small businesses through expanded SBA lending. This includes some of the business owners who are here today, like Joe Fugere of Tutta Bella Pizzeria in Seattle. I still haven't tasted the pizza, but he promises I'm going to get some at some point. [*Laughter*]

We also waived fees on SBA loans to save folks money on payments. And the emergency steps we took to stabilize the financial system helped to get credit flowing again.

So all told, these steps have made a real difference. But as far as we've come, everybody in this room understands we've still got a long way to go. I don't have to tell folks here that small businesses still face hardships, and it's still too difficult for many creditworthy small-business owners to get loans. So there is more we can do to help them grow and to help them hire. And that's why I began fighting for months to pass this jobs bill, the most significant step on behalf of our small businesses in more than decade. And once I sign it, it's going to speed relief to small businesses across this country right away.

So let me just outline what's in here. First, on top of the eight tax breaks we've already passed, we're adding eight more, which will accelerate more than $55 billion in tax relief over the next year to businesses across the country. Capital gains taxes will be completely eliminated for key investments in small businesses, driving capital to as many as 1 million small firms across America and, by the way, honoring a promise that I made as a candidate for President.

Four and a half million small businesses and individuals will be immediately—will be eligible to immediately write off more expenses. And that may benefit Ruth Gresser, who is here today and who is opening another restaurant in Alexandria, Virginia.

Two million self-employed Americans will be able to receive a new deduction for health insurance. And we're also increasing the tax break for anyone looking to open up a business. That's a $10,000 deduction to help entrepreneurs afford what can often be pretty discouraging startup costs, because our future prosperity in part depends on whether or not we are creating an environment in which folks can test new ideas, bring new products to market, and generate new businesses.

And that's not just a challenge for government. It's a challenge that requires businesses and leaders and universities, others to seek out new ways to promote entrepreneurship across this country.

Now, the second thing this bill does is we're going to make more loans available to small businesses. Right now there is a waiting list for SBA loans more than 1,400 names long. These are people who are ready to hire and expand, who've been approved by their banks, but who've been waiting for this legislation to pass. Well, when I sign this bill, their wait will be over. Their wait will be over. Virtually every person on that list will receive the loan they need in a matter of weeks.

Several of the small-business owners standing with me today are on this list, including Tony Scovazzo of AJS Consulting Engineers. Where's Tony? Raise your hand. Tony is right here. [*Laughter*] With Tony's loan, he'll be able to buy new office space and hire three people to do energy-efficient HVAC work. Terry Dunlap of Tactical Network Solutions—Terry, raise your hand. Terry is on the list. He plans to use his loan to hire as many as five more people.

Noel and Glen Mouritzen are also here. They'll be able to use a loan to set up a repair shop for helicopters and hire four or five workers. Herb Caudill is on this list. And Herb's company, Caudill Web, has a good problem: They've got more work than they can accept. So with this loan from SBA, he'll be able to bring

one or two new web programmers and designers to take on some new projects.

On top of these loans that will be freed up right away, we're also more than doubling the size limits of the most popular SBA loans, like the ones that have benefited many of the business owners who are with us here today. Plus, through this bill, we'll take other steps to promote lending. And this includes our new Small Business Lending Fund, designed to help Main Street banks lend to Main Street small businesses across this country. And this bill will also encourage additional private sector lending through innovative efforts at the State level to promote small business and manufacturing, efforts that have too often been constrained by State budget cuts.

So this law will do two big things: It's going to cut taxes, and it's going to make more loans available for small businesses. It's a great victory for America's entrepreneurs. It is a great victory for America's entrepreneurs.

Now, I have to admit, I regret that this bill—which was based on ideas from both Democrats and Republicans, and drawing support from business groups that don't normally support me—[*laughter*]—I regret that this was blocked for months by the Republican minority in the Senate, and that needlessly delayed this relief. But I do want to thank the two Republican Senators who bucked this partisanship to help pass this bill, and obviously, I want to thank all the Democrats who worked so hard to get it passed.

At this difficult time in our country, it's essential that we keep up the fight for every job, for every new business, for every opportunity to strengthen this economy. That's what's being done at the State level by Governor Granholm and Governor O'Malley and Governors all across the country. That's what's being done by the mayors who are here today who are fighting day in, day out to help start new businesses that can bring prosperity to their communities.

We've got to keep moving forward. That's why I fought so hard to pass this bill. And that's why I'm going to continue to do everything in my power to help small businesses open up and hire and expand. And that's why, with these small-business owners standing with me today, I am extraordinarily proud to sign this bill into law. All right?

[*At this point, the President signed the bill.*]

This is the tricky part. [*Laughter*] You start running out of letters. [*Laughter*] There you go. It's done.

NOTE: The President spoke at 1:47 p.m. in the East Room at the White House. In his remarks, he referred to Ruth Gresser, owner and chef, Pizzeria Paradiso; and Noel and Glen Mouritzen, owners, Greystones Aviation Worldwide. H.R. 5297, approved September 27, was assigned Public Law No. 111–240.

Remarks and a Question-and-Answer Session in Albuquerque, New Mexico
September 28, 2010

The President. Well, everybody, it's been great to see you. First of all, I just want to thank Andy and Etta for hosting us here today. Can everybody hear me? There we go. I want to thank Andy and Etta for hosting us today, because not only did they open up their home to all these Secret Service people and all these press and the whole bit, but they also arranged for perfect weather. [*Laughter*] I know Bill Richardson tried to take credit for it, but it's actually Andy and Etta that did it. And so we are very grateful to them for their hospitality here today. And obviously, we're extraordinarily grateful to Andy for his service in the Marine Corps and for Etta doing what she's doing in our school system. And so thank you very much.

Everybody knows your Governor, Bill Richardson, and we are grateful to him. Your Lieutenant Governor, Diane Denish, who is, I believe, going to be also the next Governor of the great State of New Mexico. We've got Congressman Martin Heinrich, and I will say that Martin told me that if I was going to come to Albuquerque that I better visit the South Valley the next time I come. So he gets some credit for bringing me here today.

And to all of you, thank you so much for being here. We've been trying to do more of these, A, just to get me out of the house. It's a very nice house that they provide for me in Washington, but at times you do feel like you're in the bubble. And so every once in a while, I need to just get out of there and have a chance to talk to folks and listen to them and answer questions, but also get suggestions and advice about what's happening in the country.

And so instead of doing all the talking, what I want to do is maybe just provide a few opening remarks and then basically have a conversation with you about things that are important to you and important to this community, important to this State. There is one thing I want to focus on, though, if you don't mind, in my opening remarks, and that's the issue of education. We have gone through obviously the toughest economic situation since the Great Depression, and no State has been untouched, no group of people has been untouched by the devastation. We lost 8 million jobs. The financial sector almost completely melted down. We almost slipped into a Great Depression. And so we acted very quickly to try to stop the bleeding.

And we've had some success. An economy that was shrinking, was contracting by 6 percent when I was sworn in, it's now growing again. We were losing 750,000 jobs a month when I was sworn in; we've had 8 consecutive months of private sector job growth.

So we're making progress, and we're moving in the right direction. But in addition to the immediate crisis that we were dealing with, one of the challenges that I think everybody around the country, when I talk to them, recognizes is, we've got to have a long-term plan for how we make sure America remains the number-one economy in the world; and how we make sure that we still have opportunities for middle class Americans to prosper and to expand, to be able to support their families and send their kids to college and retire with dignity and respect; and how do we provide ladders for people who aren't yet in the middle class to be able to get into the middle class; and how do we help small businesses grow; how do we help make sure that our large businesses are the innovators that are designing the new products that we're able to sell overseas.

The issue of how we stay competitive and are able to succeed in the next generation the same way that previous generations have succeeded, that's a question that I think a lot of people have been asking themselves for a long time.

Because keep in mind, even before this financial crisis, we were slipping in a lot of ways. From 2001 to 2009, during that 8-year period, wages—average wages for middle class families actually fell by 5 percent. Think about that. People's real incomes were actually falling, and this was at a time before the crisis. So supposedly, the economy was growing and things were going pretty well. In fact, people's incomes were falling.

During that same period of time, job growth was the most sluggish that it's been since World War II. So part of the reason I decided to run for President was because we had all these problems that we hadn't been dealing with for a long time—even before the crisis hit—that we had to deal with if we want to stay competitive for the 21st century. And the number-one issue in terms of us succeeding as an economy is going to be how well we educate and how well we train our kids. Nothing else comes close.

Now, the truth of the matter is, we used to have by far the best education system in the world. We were the first nation in the world to have compulsory public education. And so as people were moving off the farms, moving into the cities, moving into industry, suddenly they were able to get the training and the skills they needed for an advanced industrial economy.

And we had the best universities in the world and the best colleges in the world, and we had the number-one—we ranked number one in the proportion of college graduates in the world. We now rank 12th, and that's just happened in a generation. We went from number 1 to number 12 in the number of college graduates that we have.

Even folks who didn't go to college still got a good education. My grandmother, she was an amazing woman. She passed away a couple of years ago. But she never went to college. She worked—when my grandfather went off to World War II, she worked on a assembly line making bombers. She was like Rosie the Riveter. And then when my grandfather came back, he got the GI bill to go to college, but she didn't get the GI bill, so she went to work. She started off as a secretary; she ended up as a vice president at a bank in Hawaii.

And despite the fact that she hadn't gone to college, she was so well prepared, in terms of math and reading and skills, that she could end up getting an executive position, working her way up from being a secretary.

Well, now we rank 21st in science education in the world, and we rank 25th in math education in the world. So the trend line is that we're not at the top in terms of college graduates, we're not at the top at science, we're not at the top at math. We've got a third of our students who enroll who never graduate from high school. And all this means that not only is it bad for the young people who aren't getting this education—typically, a high school grad gets paid about $10,000 less than a college grad, and over the course of the lifetime, it means hundreds of thousand dollars in lost income—but it's also bad for the country as a whole because we don't have as many engineers, and we don't have as many scientists, we're not inventing the new products that are going to make all the difference in terms of how well we succeed.

So the reason I want to raise this is because there are a lot of issues we've been working on in Washington, a lot of them get a lot of attention, but something that hasn't gotten as much attention is what we've been trying to do working with States and local school districts over the last 2 years to make sure that we're moving in a new direction in improving our education system.

Let me just tell you a couple of things that we've done.

First of all, we set up something called Race to the Top. And what we said was that if States wanted to get some additional money, some extra money to help their schools, they would have to compete for that money by showing us what it is that you're doing to reform the school system so that you get excellent teachers, you have high standards, the schools are accountable, that you're going after the lowest performing schools and not just sort of skimming off the top.

And as a consequence of this competition called Race to the Top—we had about $4 billion—we've ended up seeing 32 States change their laws to reform the system so that the whole education structure works better for our kids and makes it more accountable, and we start providing better training and better recruitment for our teachers and more professional development and additional resources.

So it's been a big boost for education all across the country, moving forward on a reform agenda that doesn't just dictate to States, here's how you have to do everything, but it says, here's some criteria for success; if you have a plan to match that, then we're going to help you. So that's number one.

Number two, we've been helping to make sure that more young people get early childhood education, because the studies show that if kids are well prepared when they get to school, then they are much likely to do better. If they know their colors and their numbers and their letters and they know how to sit still—I remember when Malia and Sasha were young; that was a key training point.

And so early childhood education is—when it's well designed, makes a big difference, and we've been doing that.

Third thing we've been doing is focusing on higher education. Now, it turns out that we've got—the lottery scholarship program here in New Mexico is terrific, but we've got a whole lot of States all across the country and a lot of young people who still rely on Pell grants and student loan programs in order to finance their overall education.

And what we've been able to do is, when we came into office, tens of billions of dollars were going to banks and financial intermediaries, who were essentially acting as middlemen for the student loan program, even though it was federally guaranteed. Right? So they weren't taking any risks, but it was passing through

them, and they would take—they would skim off tens of billions of dollars of profits.

So we said, well, that doesn't make any sense. Why don't we just have the money go directly from the Government to the student, and we'll save all that money? And now what we have, we've been able to save $60 billion that we're putting in now to make sure that millions more young people across the country are able to get the student loans and the Pell grants that they need. And starting in 2014, we're actually going to be able to say to young people that you will never have to pay more than 10 percent of your income in repaying your student loans. And if you go into public service, if you're like Etta and you go into teaching, for example, after 10 years, whatever's remaining on your debt will be forgiven.

So that will give young people a much better head start, because everybody here, if they haven't experienced it personally, somebody in your family has finished college with huge amounts of debt that they're having trouble repaying. I know Michelle and I did too.

So there are a whole range of things that we're trying to do, working with colleges, community colleges, universities to try to improve our education system. One of the things that I announced this week was, we're really going to focus on science and math because that's where our young people, I think, are falling the most behind. And we've made a commitment that we're going to hire over the next couple of years 10,000 new science and math teachers. And we're going to work with the schools to help redesign their math and science curriculums so that we start boosting—I want to get to the point where we're number one in science and math.

And I also want to make sure, by the way, that that's true for all students, because I'll be honest with you, African American students, Latino students, we're doing worse in science and math than the overall average. So America is the 21st and 25th, but if you actually looked at performance of Latino and African American students, it would be even lower. And that's inexcusable because that's the fastest growing portion of our population. That's our future. That's our future workforce.

And so we've got to have the most skilled, most highly trained workers in the world. And this is what we're going to be focusing on over the next couple of years.

Now, last point I'm going to make, and then I'm just going to open it up because I promised I wouldn't give a long speech: This election coming up in November is going to offer a choice on a whole range of different issues. And this issue of education gives you a sense of the choice that I think Democrats are trying to make and the choice that the Republicans are trying to make. The Republicans recently put out what they call their "Pledge to America." And it basically outlined what their priorities are.

Their number one economic priority is retaining $700 billion tax breaks to the wealthiest 2 percent of the country, millionaires and billionaires mostly. They—we'd have to borrow the $700 billion because we don't have it. All right? We've got these deficits and debt. So we'd have to borrow the $700 billion from China or the Saudis or whoever is buying our debt, and then we'd pass off, on average, a $100,000 check to people who are making a million dollars up to more than a billion dollars.

That's their main economic plan. And when you ask them, "Well, how would you pay for some of this stuff?" they don't really have good answers. But one way they would pay for it is to cut back our education spending by 20 percent and eliminate about 200,000 Head Start programs and reduce student aid to go to college for about 8 million students.

That's one of their answers. And I just have to say, look, China, that's not the decision they're making about their education system and their kids. South Korea, that's not the decision that they're making about their kids.

I was in Shanghai, and I talked to the mayor. He said, you know, teachers are the most respected of professions, as much as doctors or engineers, and they're paid to reflect how much we value them.

I was in South Korea, and I was talking to the President, having lunch, and he said, you know,

my biggest problem in education is, the parents are so demanding. They're insisting that I ship in English—people from the United States and other English-speaking countries because they want all their kids to learn English by the time they're in third grade.

I mean, that's the—that's their mindset. That's the competition that they're in. So they're not cutting back on education right when we know that that's going to be the most important thing in determining our success over the long term. And we can't either. And so I just want everybody to think about those kinds of issues as you go into the polling place in November: Who's going to prioritize our young people to make sure they've got the skills they need to succeed over the long term? Nothing's going to be more important in terms of our long-term success.

All right? So with that, let me just open it up to any comments or questions people may have about anything. I talked a lot about education, but people may have a whole bunch of different interests here, and I'd love to hear from you. And we've got mikes so that everybody can hear your questions, okay?

Let's start with this young lady right here. And introduce yourself again. Even though I got all your names, I'm getting older, so it's harder to remember these things.

Immigration Reform

Q. Good morning, Mr. President. Welcome to Albuquerque. My name is Katerina Sano-Antonini, and I have two questions for you this morning, if I may.

The first question has to do with the changing demographics here in our neighborhood as well as in the public school system. I grew up here in this neighborhood. I'm raising my own family here. I work at a local public school here. And I have seen over the years firsthand how recent immigrants have revitalized our local economy. They start small businesses, they hire locally, they live within the community. How do you envision a comprehensive immigration reform as one measure towards America's economic recovery and long-term vitality?

The President. I have consistently—even before I was a Presidential candidate, but when I was a U.S. Senator and when I was running for U.S. Senator—said that we have to move forward on comprehensive immigration reform. Bill Richardson and I have had a lot of conversations about this.

This is a nation of immigrants. It was built on immigrants, immigrants from every corner of the globe who brought their talent and their drive and their energy to these shores because this was the land of opportunity. Now, we're also a nation of laws, so we've got to make sure that our immigration system is orderly and fair.

And so I think Americans have a legitimate concern if the way we've set up our immigration system and the way we are securing our borders is such where people just kind of come and go as they please. Well, that means that folks who are waiting—whether it's in Mexico City or in Nairobi, Kenya, or in Warsaw, Poland—if they're waiting there filling out their forms and doing everything legally and properly and it takes them 5 years or 6 years or 10 years before they're finally here and made legal, well, it's not fair to them if folks can just come and ignore those laws.

So what we—I think is so important to do is for us to both be a nation of laws and affirm our immigrant traditions. And I think we can do that. So what I've said is, look, yes, let's secure our borders. Yes, let's make sure that the legal immigration system is more fair and efficient than it is right now, because if the waiting times were lessened, then a lot of people would be more prone to go through a legal route than through an illegal route. Let's make sure that we're cracking down on employers who are taking advantage of undocumented workers to not pay them overtime or not pay them minimum wage or not give them bathroom breaks. Let's make sure that we're cracking down on employers to treat all workers fairly. And let's provide a pathway to citizenship for those who are already here, understanding that they broke the law, so they're going to have to pay a fine and pay back taxes and, I think, learn English, make sure that they don't have a criminal record. There are some hoops that they're going to have to jump

through, but giving them a pathway is the right thing to do.

Now, unfortunately, right now this is getting demagogued. A lot of folks think it's an easy way to score political points, is by trying to act as if there's a "them" and an "us," instead of just an "us." And I'm always suspicious of a politics that is dividing people instead of bringing them together. I think now's the time for us to bring—come together.

And I think that economically, immigrants can actually be a huge source of strength to the country. It's one of our big advantages, is we've got a younger population than Europe, for example, or Japan, because we welcome immigrants and they generally don't. And that means that our economy is more vital and we've got more people in the workforce who are going to be out there working and starting businesses and supporting us when we're retired and making sure Social Security's solvent. All those things are important.

So this is a priority that I continue to have. Frankly, the problem I've had right now is, is that—and I don't want to get into sort of inside baseball about Washington—but basically, the rules in the United States Senate have evolved so that if you don't have 60 votes, you can't get anything through the United States Senate right now. And several years ago, we had 11 Republican Senators who were willing to vote for comprehensive immigration reform, including John McCain. They've all reversed themselves. I can't get any of them to cooperate. And I don't have 60 Democrats in the Senate.

And so we're going to have to do this on a bipartisan basis. And my hope is, is that the Republicans who have said no and have seen their party, I think, use some unfortunate rhetoric around this issue, my hope is, is that they come back and say, you know, this is something that we can work on together to solve a problem instead of trying to score political points. Okay?

All right, who's next? Yes, sir, right here.

Housing Market

Q. My name is David Pacheco, and I work for the New Mexico VA Health Care System. My question is that, I think as an integral part of being Hispanic, being from here, home is very integral to that, and not only for Hispanics, for all New Mexicans, for all Americans. And yet I hear stories of my family members' friends, veterans that I treat, of losing their homes due to this economy that we've been through or are going through. And I guess my question is, what are we doing to prevent people from losing their homes?

I know education is truly incredible, and it moves people beyond what we can ever expect, but if we don't have homes to go to, what good is the education?

The President. Well, the housing crisis helped to trigger the financial crisis. And it's a complicated story, but essentially what happened was, banks started seeing money in peddling what looked like these very low interest rate mortgages, no money down, started peddling these things to folks. A lot of people didn't read the fine print, where they had adjustable-rate mortgages or balloon payments, and they ended up being in situations where they were in homes that they couldn't necessarily afford.

The banks made a whole bunch of money on all these mortgages that were being generated. But what happened was, is that when the housing market started going down, then all these financial instruments that were built on a steady stream of payments for mortgages, they all went bust, and that helped to trigger the entire crisis.

So the housing issue has been at the heart of the economic crisis that we're in right now. It is a big problem because part of what happened over the last several years is, is that we built more homes than we had families to absorb them. And what's happened now is, is that housing values have declined around the country, in some places worse than others. In Nevada, in Arizona, they've been very badly hit. In New Mexico, I don't think we had the same bubble, and so prices have not been as badly affected here. But overall across the country, housing lost a lot of value.

Now, this is a multitrillion-dollar market, so there's no Government program where we can just make sure that whoever's losing their home, that we can just pick up the tab and make sure that they can pay. And frankly, there are some people who really bought more home than they could afford, and they'd be better off renting, or they're going to have to make adjustments in terms of their house.

What we have tried to do, though, is to make sure that people who have been making their payments regularly, who are meeting their responsibilities, if they could have a little bit of an adjustment with the banks, if some of the principal was reduced, if some of the interest was reduced on their mortgage payment, they could keep on making payments. The bank would be better off than if the home was foreclosed on, obviously they'd be better off, and as the housing market starts picking back up again—which it will do over time, although not in the same trajectory as it used to, right? It's going to be more much gradual—then potentially the bank could recoup some of the money that it had lost by making the adjustments on the mortgages.

So we've set up a number of these mortgage modification programs that are out there. But I don't want to lie to you. We've probably had hundreds of thousands of people who've been helped by it. I think there have been a couple of million who've applied. But that doesn't meet the entire need because this is such a huge housing market.

And what really is probably the most important thing I can do right now to keep people in their homes is to make sure the economy is growing so that they don't feel job insecurity. That's probably the thing that's going to strengthen the housing market the most over the next couple of years. If we've got a growing economy, unemployment is gradually being reduced, then people are going to feel more confident. They're going to be able to make their mortgage payments. New homeowners, people who are potentially buyers of homes, are going to say, you know what, I don't mind entering the market because I think things have sort of bottomed out. That starts lifting prices, and that gets us on a virtuous cycle instead of a negative cycle.

But it's going to take some time. We're working our way out of overbuilding in the housing market, a lot of not very sensible financial arrangements in the housing market. And we've got to get back to sort of a traditional, more commonsense way of thinking about housing, which is, if you want a house, you got to save for a while. You got to wait until you have 20 percent down. You should go for a mortgage that you know you can afford. You've got to—there shouldn't be any surprises out there, right? That kind of traditional thinking about saving and thinking about the house not as something that is always going up 20 percent every year and you're going to flip and take out home equity loans and all that—we've got to have a different attitude, which reflects what you talked about, more of an attitude that this is your home. This is not just a way to make quick money.

Okay. Yes, sir. I know it's a little warm in here, by the way, but——

Energy/Parenting

Q. You're right, Mr. President, it is a little warm, but it's all good.

The President. It's all good.

Q. Yes, I want to thank you again, Mr. President, for coming to Albuquerque, New Mexico.

The President. Thank you.

Q. I have several questions to ask you. I'll make them short and brief.

I am one of those persons that has been helped by that modification program on my house. And I want to say thank you, because it has helped my family, and I'm one of the persons that it's helped. And I want to say thank you.

The President. That's great. I appreciate that.

Q. It has helped me and my family.

The President. I'm glad to hear that.

Q. Yes, and it has helped several—I mean, it's helped my family; I just don't know how to say thank you.

Second question, we can't always depend on government to help us as far as education is concerned. I do think—my wife is a teacher in an elementary school—it all has to start at home. We as parents have to educate our children on how to get educated; it starts at home. And I want to thank you for everything you've done for public education. Thank you again. But we all have to understand it kind of starts at home, as parents.

And the last question is, Mr. Obama, I am a president of the board of a weatherization program here in New Mexico. And I heard you did the same thing in Chicago, and I thank you. It's a nonprofit organization that has helped a lot of New Mexicans here in New Mexico—Central New Mexico Housing Corporation's a nonprofit organization helping lower income people with their homes.

For example, you had mentioned that a lot of people can't afford to upgrade their homes, things that they need. Well, we are able to provide assistance through Washington, the State of New Mexico, and some other agencies to provide free assistance for a lot of elderly or people who are—meet certain criteria. So I want to say thank you for—again for that weatherization program. It has helped a lot of New Mexicans, as myself, as mortgage modification. As a personal friend of yours, I want to say thank you because it has helped my family.

The President. I appreciate that. The—that's——

Q. It has helped me. Thank you.

The President. You're welcome. And people sometimes ask, well, you know, boy, you—you're working pretty hard and got all these issues coming at you, and how do you sort of stay focused and sane? It's hearing stories like yours, where if we did something that actually helps a family stay in their home or you meet a mom who says, my kid's now getting health insurance, and they weren't getting it before, you feel a great satisfaction. And I know Diane and the Congressman and Bill all feel the same way about it. So it's great to hear.

Let me just say something about the weatherization issue, which I think is so important. We've got to change how we use energy in this country.

Q. Yes, sir.

The President. And I know that Bill's been committed to this; Diane's committed to continuing this enormous progress. New Mexico's been at the forefront in thinking about solar and wind.

One of the most important things that we can do is something that doesn't require all kinds of new technology, doesn't require huge, fancy investments. It's just making our buildings, our homes, our schools, our hospitals more energy efficient: putting up insulation, getting in new windows, caulking, getting a new energy-efficient HVAC system. These things, if we did it across the board across the country, it could not only drastically reduce people's electricity bills, drastically reduce their heating bills, their air-conditioning bills, their gas bills, it could also go about a third of the way in solving the problems of climate change and the pollution that is causing the temperatures around the globe to get warmer.

So it's an environmental win, and it's a pocketbook win. And it creates businesses, because you can have a whole bunch of mom-and-pop HVAC companies who suddenly, they're out there getting business retrofitting homes to make them energy efficient. And small businesses can grow into larger businesses, can grow into bigger businesses.

I met a business in Seattle, Washington, that started off as a small mom-and-pop plumbing operation. And they now have a thousand employees, and they're ranked as one of the top 10 companies to work for in the State of Washington. They've got unionized tradesmen working alongside computer experts who diagram how the entire energy system of a school or a hospital works, and then they go in there, and they redo it soup to nuts.

Now, we made a huge investment in the Recovery Act on this issue of clean energy and weatherization, but this is again an example of where there's just a strong difference between the two parties. The other side, they really have not shown much of an interest in promoting this.

The—and the irony is, is that you can actually get your money back on this. See, a lot of homeowners would love to do it. They'd get their money back over time; it would pay for itself. But if you don't have $5,000 upfront to do it, you can't do it, even though you know you'd get the $5,000 back over the course of 5 years.

So a lot of these programs are designed to say, we're just going to give you a loan upfront so that you can go ahead and do it, and as you then recoup your money, you can pay some of it back.

It is something that is smart to do. We're seeing States start to implement it, but we've got to, I think, keep on pushing harder. The more we do this, the more efficient our economy as a whole's going to be, and that's going to mean more growth and more jobs in the future.

So—and by the way, last point I'll make: I can't agree with you enough about the parent thing. I was on an interview with Matt Lauer yesterday, and they asked me about parents. I said, look, Malia and Sasha, as wonderful as they are, they are great students, but if Michelle and I weren't supervising them, they'd come home, they'd turn on the TV and watch TV all night or be on their computers or talking to their friends. Right? So even in the White House, the key ingredient is parenting and just making sure your kids are focused on school. Teachers can help, but parents, they've got to get those kids started in the right direction.

All right.

President's Faith/Reproductive Rights

Q. Thank you.

The President. Yes, right here.

Q. Hello, Mr. President. Thank you for coming to the South Valley.

The President. Yes, it's great to be here.

Q. It's really a great opportunity, and I thank the Cavalier family for inviting me and my husband. I have three questions, and they're kind of hot topic questions. And I'll just——

The President. All three of them?

Q. All three of them. [*Laughter*]

The President. You didn't slip in like a—sort of a easy, boring one in there with the three?

Q. No. [*Laughter*]

The President. All right, let's hear them.

Q. One of them is basically—Mother Teresa answered it in an article, and I was going to ask you the same because I loved her answer. The first one is: Why are you a Christian?

Second one is, there's really no laws about the abortion law and when a woman can and can't have an abortion, whether it's 2 months or 8 months, and what is your view on that?

And the third one—it's not as—it is a hot topic, but it's literally a hot topic, and it's about my husband's chili peppers. [*Laughter*] And that was my question: Would you please take some chili peppers home with you? One is a habanero.

The President. I will definitely check out these chili peppers. I like spicy food to go with your spicy questions. [*Laughter*]

Q. Spicy.

The President. You know, I'm a Christian by choice. My family didn't—frankly, they weren't folks who went to church every week. I mean, my mother was one of the most spiritual people I knew, but she didn't raise me in the church.

So I came to my Christian faith later in life, and it was because the precepts of Jesus Christ spoke to me in terms of the kind of life that I would want to lead: being my brother's and sister's keeper, treating others as they would treat me.

And I think also understanding that Jesus Christ dying for my sins spoke to the humility we all have to have as human beings, that we're sinful and we're flawed and we make mistakes, and that we achieve salvation through the grace of God. But what we can do, as flawed as we are, is still see God in other people and do our best to help them find their own grace.

And so that's what I strive to do. That's what I pray to do every day. I think my public service is part of that effort to express my Christian faith. And it's—but the one thing I want to emphasize, having spoken about something that obviously relates to me very personally, as President of the United States, I'm also somebody who deeply believes that the—part of the bedrock strength of this country is that it embraces people of many faiths and of no faith, that this is a country that is still predominantly Christian, but we have Jews, Muslims, Hindus, atheists, agnostics, Buddhists, and that their own path to grace is one that we have to revere and respect as much as our own. And that's part of what makes this country what it is.

Now, with respect to the abortion issue, I actually think—I mean, there are laws both Federal, State, and constitutional that are in place. And I think that—this is an area where I think Bill Clinton had the right formulation a couple of decades ago, which is, abortion should be safe, legal, and rare. I think that it's something

that all of us should recognize is a difficult, sometimes—oftentimes tragic situation that families are wrestling with.

I think the families and the women involved are the ones who should make the decision, not the government. But I do think, actually, that there are a whole host of laws on the books that after a certain period, the interests shift such that you can have some restrictions, for example, on late-term abortions, and appropriately so. So the—so there is, in fact, a set of rules in place.

Now, people still argue about it and still deeply disagree about it. And that's part of our—that's part of our democratic way.

All right? Next.

Q. [*Inaudible*]

The President. Oh, I want to make sure I get everybody in.

Religious Freedom

Q. [*Inaudible*]

The President. Okay.

Q. ——as far as the mosque in New York.

The President. Yes.

Q. I'm a Christian, but we base our faith on free will. And that's what we were founded on, was freedom. And I just thank you——

The President. Well, I——

Q. ——for taking a stand.

The President. I appreciate that. The—you're exactly right. We were founded on freedom of religion. That's how this country got started. That's why people came here, because there were a bunch of other folks who said, you can't worship the way you want.

And we have to constantly, I think, reaffirm that tradition, even when it sometimes makes us uncomfortable.

Yes.

Small-Business Assistance

Q. Okay.

The President. And I will try those chili peppers. [*Laughter*]

Go ahead.

Q. Just like the rest of everyone, we appreciate you being here. It's a big honor to have you here.

The President. Thank you.

Q. And I have three things also. Mine are simple, though—kind of. [*Laughter*]

First one is, I did a lot of research on you when you were running for President, and so again, I appreciate you being here, and you have come from the same place a lot of the rest of us have come from. Okay? We've worked our way to where we are now, and we're working harder to get further, higher up. So that's one thing—easy.

Second thing is, I did take my son—as I said, we did a lot of research on you—I took my—he was probably 4 years old at the time, and we took him to your rally up at UNM. So we snuck all the way up as far as we can go. It would have been an honor if he was able to see you yesterday; unfortunately, we weren't able to. But we were.

Now, you—we own a restaurant right down here in the South Valley.

The President. What's it called?

Q. It's called Matteo's.

The President. Well, the—where are some samples? [*Laughter*]

Q. You know what? We have some for you. [*Laughter*] We brought some for you.

The President. Okay, I'm going to check them out. What do we got?

Q. We got to get it past——

The President. Oh, I'll talk to Secret Service. We'll see what you got. [*Laughter*] Yes.

Q. But we did indeed bring you some.

The President. Okay, all right.

Q. Now, you have just recently signed a bill for small businesses and getting loans. Now, it is hard for us to receive a loan, only because the money—we count on our local people to support us, and we support them with our meals, obviously. Now, the funds are supposed to be available immediately. Now, what are the—is the criteria, what is—when will that be going into action, and how hard would that be for someone in our situation?

The President. Well, the—obviously, I haven't looked at your books, and I don't know what your expansion plans are and—so——

Q. No, I understand that.

The President. ——but let me describe for you what we did. Number one is, we set up loan facilities, both through the SBA as well as a new facility, so that if you want to expand your business, you're having trouble getting credit through your local community bank, we are now providing additional financing to the bank that they—that gives them an incentive to loan to you, and they only get these loans if they pass it on to small businesses.

So we're not helping the bank just to hold the money. We're saying, if you, South Valley Bank, decide that you want to lend to Matteo's restaurant because you think that—you've tasted their food, it's terrific, and they want to open a new one or they want to build an addition, then they now have a pool of money that is going to make it much easier for them to lend to you at low interest rates. That's number one.

SBA, the Small Business Administration, also has a whole host of lending programs that we have expanded. We've reduced the fees for them. We've made it easier to apply. So if you're interested in the lending program, then you should contact your local SBA Administrator here in New Mexico, and I'm assuming that they're—I'll bet your Congressman here could probably let you know immediately how to get in touch with them, and they would outline for you all the programs that were available. So that's on the lending side.

Now, what we've also done is, on the tax side, we have said that for companies that are starting up, small businesses that are starting up, we're going to give them a whole bunch of tax breaks. If you decide that you want—have to build a new oven, and you haven't been sure—should you invest in it this year, should you put it off, it's kind of expensive—well, we're giving you incentives to go ahead and buy that oven this year and put it in. And it will be cheaper for you because you can essentially take—you can write off the business expenses of purchasing that oven this year a lot faster than you would have otherwise been able to do. So that's an example of just one of the kinds of tax cuts that are provided in this bill.

And it builds off, by the way, eight tax cuts that we already passed as part of the Recovery Act that people don't talk about. Right now you can get a tax break if you hire an unemployed worker; we will give you a tax break on the payroll taxes that you have to pay for that person.

There are tax breaks right now for health care. I don't know if you're providing health care for your employees. It's oftentimes very hard for restaurants, who are operating on pretty slim margins, to provide health insurance for their employees, but what we're doing now is, because of health reform, we'll pay up to a third of the cost of your premiums in the form of tax credits so that it's much more affordable, much cheaper for you to be able to provide health insurance for your employees.

So we've got a whole basket of tax cuts and lending assistance to small businesses. And the reason this is so important is because small businesses create the majority of new jobs in this country. Big businesses are very important too, and we're trying to encourage them obviously to do more to invest. They actually have a lot of money right now. It's just they're sitting on the sidelines with it instead of investing it, and we've got to encourage them to invest more.

But small businesses, that's the beating heart of so many communities: restaurants like yours, small dry cleaners, a plumbing operation, a tent company, a flower shop, okay? So the—we've got a bunch of small-business owners here. You knit the community together, and you give people opportunity, as well as building something for your family. And you're so invested in it because it's yours.

And small businesses have been harder hit by this recession than just about anybody else because they had a harder time getting financing and because obviously customer demand was down. And that's why we have really tried to focus on making sure that small businesses on Main Street get help.

I've got to do a little bit of editorializing again, though, about the politics of this because this is something that—this bill that I signed this week drew on Republican and Democratic

ideas. Traditionally, this is something that's been completely bipartisan. The Chamber of Commerce, the association for small businesses, a whole bunch of different groups supported it. We could not get the Republicans to let this come up to a vote for months. And there were finally articles in the USA Today about how small businesses were holding off making investments or hiring because they were still waiting to see if this thing would pass.

And finally, we got 2 Republicans to vote for it, out of 41. And one of them had to just admit, he said, look, the time for playing games is over; this is too serious.

And I guess that's something that I just hope, as you are talking to your friends and your neighbors and your coworkers, I hope that's the one thing you come away from here today thinking about is, these are serious times. I mean, we've got tough competition out there. This is the greatest country on Earth and will continue to be the greatest country on Earth as long as we can go ahead and handle serious problems that we have, instead of playing political games all the time.

And when you look at the choices before you, I think you've got to ask yourself, who's offering serious answers? And I know you feel that way not just for your business, but also for this new son that's coming. Yes. Have you thought about Barack as a name? [*Laughter*]

Q. Yes. We have. [*Laughter*]

The President. That's good. I like that. All right, this gentleman right here.

Economic Stabilization/Education Reform

Q. My name is Dan Padilla. I'm the principal of Los Lunas High School.

The President. Well, it's great to see you.

Q. And—thank you, sir, and——

The President. Now, has somebody given you a pass——

Q. Yes, and——

The President. ——to be off campus? Okay.

Q. Yes, they do.

The President. All right.

Q. As a matter of fact, I'm really proud that Etta is my counselor at my high school. So thank you all, and welcome to New Mexico.

The President. Thank you.

Q. This statement—I promise my students every day—my students are my mission every day, and what they think and what they do is important to all of us. And I have a statement from Ms. Valerie Mayse's AP class. And it could be a statement or question from any high school group of students. And it says, "Welcome, President Obama, to New Mexico." And it says: "We are all concerned and sometimes scared that there will be no money for us to continue our education. While we seem to be the target and the gauge on how much monies our school and State gets, what assurance will we have that we will be rewarded for good work? There seems to be less monies that banks lend our families, and most of all, no jobs. We want to thank you for listening to us. Thank you for all you do for our country. We know that you are only one man, and we must all believe, have faith, and support you in your endeavors."

The President. Well, thank you so much. That's a wonderful letter. And I think it's part of what makes me so optimistic about the country. When you actually travel and meet young people around the country, they'll make you optimistic. I mean, they're smart, and they're ambitious, and they want to help their community, and they've got good values, and they've got good common sense.

But they are anxious right now, which is understandable. I mean, they're growing up in the shadow of a financial crisis that we hadn't seen in our lifetimes. Unless you were born in 1910, 1915, you wouldn't remember a crisis like this having happened.

And so they're seeing it firsthand, and they're seeing it in their families. I'm sure even though their parents are trying to hide their stress from them, if business is bad, if you're having trouble paying the bills, kids hear that. They know it. And some of the letters that are most heartbreaking for me when I'm—I get a group of letters every night that I read from people all across the country; it's selected from the 40,000 e-mails and letters that we get. And sometimes it's letters from children, and they'll write to you about, you know, my dad lost his job, and he just doesn't seem the same, and is there something you can do? And it's heartbreaking. They absorb all the pain that is going on out here right now.

But that is why it is so important for us to make sure that we are meeting our commitments to them not just individually as parents, but also as a society. So when we increase student aid so that these young people that just wrote to me are able to afford going to college, and you've then got the other side in this election pledging to reverse those increases so that they're less likely to be able to afford going to college, that should motivate you at the voting booth in terms of what your priorities are.

When we—when we're talking about—when we—here's a good example, and the Congressman will remember this. We had a debate in Washington because States were very hard strapped for cash and were starting to lay off teachers. And we said, let's close a corporate tax loophole that is incentivizing companies to ship jobs overseas. Let's close that loophole and use that money to help States keep teachers and firefighters and cops on the job, because there were a bunch of States—Hawaii, actually, had gone to a 4-day-a-week school week because they just couldn't afford teachers. Think about that. Four days a week you go to school. They are missing a fifth of the school year because of budget crunches.

And so we said, well, that's not acceptable. Let's just close this tax loophole that even the companies that were using the loopholes couldn't really defend.

So we closed it. The leader of the Republicans in the House, he fought us tooth and nail to do that. And then when we pointed out this is saving a whole bunch of teacher jobs and police officer jobs and firefighter jobs, he says, well, those are just government jobs.

Just government jobs? Well, these are people who are teaching our kids. These are folks who are rushing into burning buildings to save our families, putting their lives on the line. Government jobs?

But that is the ideology that the other side has been bringing to every problem out here for years now. And that's the choice that we've got in this election.

So look, those young people, they're going to succeed. But we've got to make sure that we make it easier for them, as opposed to harder for them, to succeed.

Ultimately, what's going to bring about their success is their determination and their talents and their pluck and their willingness to stick to it. But, you know, we can give them a hand up. We can make sure that college is affordable. We can make sure that they're able to stay on their parents' health insurance until they're 26 if the first job they get out of school doesn't have health insurance. We can make sure that they're not cheated the first time they buy their home, because now we've got a consumer finance protection agency that's going to monitor mortgage brokers and bank practices so that people don't have to get tricked because of fine print.

These are just basic things that we can do. We—if they decide they want to open a business, we can make sure that they can get some financing and that they don't have to pay capital gains on their startup business. These little things add up to big things. It means that they can focus their energy on their dreams and their vision and what they're trying to build and not spend all their time constantly just worrying about, am I going to be able to go to school or not. That should be a given in this country because it's good for all of us, not just for these young people individually.

Okay? How are we doing on time? I want to make sure that I'm not—last question? I've got to—you're going to refer to him? Okay. You're going to defer to him. Well, he is a good-looking young man, I got to admit. You wanted to hear from him. I understand.

All right, go ahead.

Caring for Veterans

Q. Thank you so much, Mr. President. My name is Andrew Cavalier; I'm his son. Got a couple questions for you. One really hits hard for me. Getting a little emotional here. My father, being a veteran, we appreciate everything that he's done for the country. And obviously, the VA does a lot for my father.

The President. Yes, we love your dad. Yes, we appreciate what he's done.

Q. Thank you.

The President. Absolutely.

Q. The reason I get emotional is because——

The President. Because he's your dad.

Q. Well, unfortunately, at the VA, sometimes he doesn't get the care and the service that he should.

The President. Right.

Q. I mean, he sacrificed his body. I mean, over 17 surgeries that he's had.

The President. Right.

Q. I really didn't want to do this on TV.

The President. That's all right.

Q. But you know, I see—he put his blood, his sweat, and his tears into this country and doesn't always get the type of care that he deserves because—and I just want to ask, I mean, do you have any plan for that? There's obviously lots of veterans out there——

The President. Right.

Q. ——feel the same way, not getting the treatments that they deserve. It's not just the medications, you know, it's really being treated like a human.

The President. Right.

Q. And, I mean, that's kind of the issue that I have is, we put in our taxpayer dollars, and you know, it's—I mean, I have a small business myself. We help provide people with legal services, stuff like that, you know, having access to their rights. But when you can't afford it, I mean, we're forced to just basically settle for what we got because of the fact that that's all we could afford.

The President. Well, let me—first of all, you don't have to apologize for being emotional about your dad who served our country as a Marine, man. That's—I get emotional when I think about our young men and women and our veterans who have served this country with such bravery and courage. We have a sacred trust for people who put on the uniform of the United States. They serve us. They're willing to put their lives on the line. And that means that when they come back, we've got to serve them.

Now, here's the good news. First of all, I've got what I think is one of the finest, if not the finest, Secretaries of Veterans Affairs ever,

General Ric Shinseki, who himself is a disabled veteran. And this guy just thinks day and night about how are we going to make sure that veterans services are provided in a timely, effective, respectful fashion, all right? So that's point number one.

Point number two: We actually—even in the midst of this very difficult budget situation that we're in, we have increased over the last 2 years funding for veterans more than any time in the last 30 years—more than any time in the last 30 years.

And the reason we did it was because a lot of VA facilities had gotten outdated. The backlog in terms of folks trying to get medical services or getting their claims processed had just gotten ridiculous. You had over a million young people who had served in Iraq and now Afghanistan who had come back, and they've got new problems like—well, they're not new problems, but now we're much more effective at diagnosing posttraumatic stress disorder, traumatic brain injury—they weren't getting services. We've got women who are now serving in a much more dangerous situation in a lot of these theaters, and yet a lot of VA facilities still did not have special services for women and their special needs as they return.

So we are in the process of investing more in the VA and reforming how business is done at the VA than at any time in the last 30 years.

Now, we've still got a ways to go, but this is again an example of where, come November, we've got to start making some choices, because if, for example, we give tax breaks to millionaires and billionaires that cost us $700 billion that we don't have, that money has to come from somewhere. And we've got to be able to provide for our veterans. I'd rather choose veterans. I'd rather choose these young people who are looking for scholarships.

Homeless veterans—I mean, the notion that we've got somebody who served our country and they're now on the streets, they don't have a house? So we've said, we're going to have zero tolerance for homeless veterans. We are going to do everything we can to make sure that every single person who has served our country, that

they've got proper medical care and they've got a roof over their heads. And oftentimes that means counseling. And the irony is, if you make the investments early, then it turns out that they're less expensive over the long term.

So this is something that you're right to be emotional about, and I think we should all be emotional about it. And we're grateful to your dad for his service, and we just need to remind ourselves that there are millions of folks across the country who deserve that same kind of respect, and we've got to meet our obligations to them.

One last point I'll make about veterans, because it ties in with the overall theme of education: Working with our terrific Members of Congress here, we were able to pass the post-9/11 GI bill, which means that this generation of veterans is going to be able to benefit the same way my grandfather benefited when he came back from World War II, that he was going to be able to get his college education paid for. And by the way, we made it transferable to the spouses of veterans and their family members if they weren't going to use it, because military families make huge sacrifices as well, and oftentimes they don't get the service and the attention that they need. And this has been a huge priority of the First Lady, and it's something that I am very, very proud of. But we've got to keep on fighting for these changes. They don't come by themselves.

And I hope everybody's going to pay attention and do their homework and find out about candidates. And I think what you'll find is, is that when you're making choices for Governor and you're making choices for Senate and Congress, that these choices are going to mean something.

And you got to ask yourselves, what direction do I want this country to go in? Do I want to invest in our people, in our middle class and making it stronger, and our infrastructure and our education system and clean energy? Is that one vision, or are we just going to keep on doing the same things that got us into this mess in the first place?

All right? Thank you so much, everybody. It was great spending time with you. Thank you.

NOTE: The President spoke at 10:09 a.m. at the residence of Andy and Etta Cavalier. In his re-marks, he referred to Mayor Han Zheng of Shanghai, China; President Lee Myung-bak of South Korea; Matt Lauer, coanchor, NBC's "Today" program; Sens. George S. LeMieux and George V. Voinovich; and House Republican Leader John A. Boehner.

Statement on Gulf Coast Recovery and Restoration Efforts
September 28, 2010

I appreciate the hard work, led by Navy Secretary Ray Mabus, to develop this recovery and restoration plan for the Gulf Coast. The BP oil spill has created significant environmental and economic challenges for the region. My administration is committed to working with the people of the Gulf to help them restore the ecosystems that support them, rebuild their livelihoods, and safeguard their health and safety.

The Mabus report offers a commonsense proposal for a path forward, relying on the ideas and coordination of efforts at the local, State, tribal, and Federal levels, as well as of nonprofits and the private sector. I will ask Congress to provide dedicated resources to bolster the re-covery effort, but we will not allow the recovery to wait for congressional action. I have asked EPA Administrator Lisa Jackson to lead a task force that will coordinate efforts to create healthier, more resilient ecosystems, while also encouraging economic recovery and long-term health issues. In the Gulf, the economy and the environment are locked intrinsically together.

We recognize that the recovery effort will take new thinking, cooperation, and creativity. But most of all, it will take time. In the days ahead, we will stand with the people of the Gulf to help restore, rehabilitate, and revitalize the region. And together, we will finish the job.

Remarks at a Democratic National Committee Rally in Madison, Wisconsin
September 28, 2010

The President. Hello, Wisconsin! Thank you. Thank you so much. I am—I don't know about you, but I'm fired up.

Audience member. Ready to go!

The President. And ready to go.

A couple of people I want to acknowledge. First of all, a great mayor, somebody who's fighting for working families each and every day, Tom Barrett. Please give him a big round of applause.

Somebody who is one of the consciences of the Senate, who's always independent, doesn't always agree with me, but always agrees with the people of his State and looking out for them, Senator Russ Feingold; one of the most courageous Members of Congress that we have, Tammy Baldwin in the house.

I want to thank Madison Mayor Dave Cieslewicz—doing a great job. University of Wisconsin System President Kevin Reilly is here; University of Wisconsin—Madison Chancellor Biddy Martin is in the house.

And I want to thank our terrific musical guests, Ben Harper, The National, and Mama Digdown's Brass Band.

It is good to be back in the State of Wisconsin. I was mentioning that when I first moved to Chicago—[*applause*]—I know we've got some Chicago folks in the house—[*applause*]—you know, every once in a while, I had some friends who were going to school up here, and I'd drive up to Madison. And I had some fun times up here in Madison. I can't give you all the details—[*laughter*]—but I have good memories here.

And may I say that you Badgers are looking pretty good this year. You delivered quite a beating on Saturday. Almost wasn't fair. [*Laughter*]

Now, I'm not going to say a word about the Bears and the Packers. I'm not going to say anything about it. My lips are sealed. I'm not going to say a word about it. Why spoil this great mood? [*Laughter*] Because it's just nice to see that you're as fired up today as you were on Saturday. [*Laughter*] So don't think about Sunday. [*Laughter*]

I need you, though, fired up, Badgers. I need you fired up. We need you to stay fired up because there is an election on November 2 that's going to say a lot about the future, your future and the future of our country.

Two years ago, you defied the conventional wisdom in Washington. The message out there was, "No, you can't." No, you can't overcome the cynicism of our politics. No, you can't overcome the power of special interests in Washington. No, you can't make real progress on the big challenges of our time. No, you can't elect a skinny guy with a funny name, Barack Hussein Obama. They said, no, you can't. But what did you say, Wisconsin?

Audience members. Yes, we can!

The President. You proved that the power of everyday people going door to door, neighbor to neighbor, friend to friend, was stronger than the forces of the status quo. It made more difference than PAC money. It made more difference than all the TV advertising. You tapped into something that this country hadn't seen in a very long time. You did that.

And every single one of you is a shareholder in that mission of rebuilding our country and reclaiming our future. And I'm back here today because on November 2, we face another test. And the stakes could not be higher.

Think about it. When I arrived in Washington 20 months ago, my hope and my expectation was that we could pull together, all of us as Americans—Democrats and Republicans and Independents—to confront the worst economic crisis since the Great Depression. I hoped and expected that we could get beyond some of the old political divides between Democrats and Republicans, blue States and red States, that

had prevented us from making progress for so long, because although we are proud to be Democrats, we are prouder to be Americans.

And this country was confronting a crisis. Instead, what we found when we arrived in Washington was the rawest kind of politics. What we confronted was an opposition party that was still stuck on the same failed policies of the past, whose leaders in Congress were determined from the start to let us deal with the mess that they had done so much to create.

Because their calculation was as simple as it was cynical. They knew that it was going to take a long time to solve the economic challenges we face. They saw the data. They were talking to the economists. They realized that Obama was walking in and we had just lost 4 million jobs in the 6 months before I was sworn in, 750,000 jobs the month I was sworn in, 600,000 jobs the month after that, 600,000 jobs the month after that. So before our economic policies could even be put into place, we'd already lost most of the 8 million jobs we would lose.

And they knew that people would be frustrated. And they figured, if we just sit on the sidelines and just say no and just throw bombs and let Obama and the Democrats deal with everything, they figured they might be able to prosper at the polls.

And that's what they've done for the last 20 months. They have said no to just about every idea and policy I've proposed, even ideas that historically, traditionally, they agreed with. So now the pundits are saying that the base of the Republican Party is mobilized. The prediction among the pundits is this is going to be a bloodletting for Democrats. That's what they're saying in Washington.

Audience members. Boo!

The President. And what they're saying is— and the basis of their prediction is that all of you who worked so hard in 2008 aren't going to be as energized, aren't going to be as engaged. They say there is an enthusiasm gap and that the same Republicans and the same policies that left our economy in a shambles and the middle class struggling might ride right back into power.

Audience members. No!

The President. Now, that's what they're saying. I'm not making this up. You guys read the papers. You guys are watching the television. They're basically saying that you're apathetic, you're disappointed, you're, "Oh, well, we're not sure that we're going to turn out."

Wisconsin, we can't let that happen. We cannot sit this one out. We can't let this country fall backwards because the rest of us didn't care enough to fight. The stakes are too high for our country and for your future, and I am going to get out there and fight as hard as I can—and I know you are too—to make sure we keep moving forward.

The other side would have you believe this election is a referendum on me or a referendum on the economy, a referendum on anything except them. But make no mistake: This election is a choice. And the choice could not be clearer.

Understand, for the last decade, the Republicans in Washington subscribed to a very simple philosophy. And I want to be clear: This is the Republican leadership in Washington. A whole bunch of Republicans out all across America are feeling pretty disaffected too by what they saw when the Republicans were in charge. But their basic theory of the Republican leadership was, you cut taxes, mostly for millionaires and billionaires.

Audience members. Boo!

The President. You cut regulations for special interests, whether it's the banks or the oil companies or health insurance companies. Let them write their own rules. You cut back on investments in education and clean energy and research and technology.

So basically, the idea was if you just put blind faith in the market, if we let corporations play by their own rules, if we leave everybody else to fend for themselves, then America would automatically grow and prosper.

But that philosophy failed. Because in the period when they were in power—understand this, from 2001 to 2009—job growth was slower than it had been in any decade since World War II. Between 2001 and 2009, middle class incomes fell by 5 percent. The cost of everything from health care to college tuition just kept going up. And a free-for-all on Wall Street led to

the very crisis that right now we're digging ourselves out of.

So it's not like we don't have a controlled experiment here. We have—they were in charge. We saw what happened. So I've got—I've had two main jobs since becoming President: to rescue the economy from this crisis, to clean up after their mess, and to rebuild our economy stronger than it was before. That's been my job.

And over the last 20 months, we've made progress on both these fronts. We're no longer facing the possibility of a second depression, and I have to say, Wisconsin, that was a very real possibility when I was sworn in. We had about 6 months where the economy was teetering on the edge, and we could have plunged into a second depression.

Now the economy is growing again. Now the private sector has created jobs for the last 8 months in a row. There are about 3 million Americans who wouldn't be working today if not for the economic plan that we put into place. Those are facts.

By the way, I emphasize those are facts because the other side isn't always interested in facts.

Audience members. Boo!

The President. To rebuild this economy on a stronger foundation, we passed Wall Street reform to make sure that a crisis like this never happens again, so that these reforms are going to end the era of taxpayer-funded bailouts forever, reforms that will stop mortgage lenders from taking advantage of homeowners, reforms that'll stop credit card companies from hitting you with hidden fees or jacking up your rates without any reason.

But we didn't stop there. We started investing again in American research and American technology and homegrown American clean energy because I don't want solar panels and wind turbines and electric cars of the future built in Europe or Asia. I want them built right here in the United States of America with American workers.

To help middle class families get ahead, we passed a tax cut for 95 percent of working families. I want to repeat that: We cut taxes for 95 percent of working families, because if you were listening to the other side, you'd think we raised taxes.

But again, we deal in facts. And the fact is, we cut taxes for 95 percent of working families. We passed 16 different tax cuts for America's small-business owners, who create the majority of jobs in this country. We passed health care reform that will stop insurance companies from denying you coverage or dropping your coverage because you're sick.

And by the way, Madison, let me just see a show of hands, how many people are under the age of 26 in this crowd? Every single one of you, when you get out of college, if you have not found a job that offers you health care, you're going to be able to stay on your parents' health care until you're 26 years old, so you don't end up taking the risk of getting sick and being bankrupt.

We finally fixed the student loan system so that tens of billions of dollars—tens of billions of dollars of taxpayer subsidies that were going to big banks—they were acting as middlemen, and the student loan programs were going through these financial intermediaries. They were taking billions of dollars of profits. We said, well, let's cut out the middleman. We'll give the loans directly to students, and that means million more students are going to be able to take advantage of grants and student loans.

And by the way, we also kept a promise I made on the day that I announced my candidacy. We have removed combat troops from Iraq, and we have ended our combat mission in Iraq.

Now, that's just some of what we've done. I haven't even mentioned the fact that we signed into law laws making sure that we enforce equal pay for equal work, because I think my daughters should be treated just like somebody else's sons. I haven't mentioned the fact that we had the largest expansion of national service so that young people can tap into their idealism and start working here in this country and around the world to make people's lives better. I haven't talked about the fact that we made sure that tobacco companies can't market their products to children.

We have made progress over the last 20 months. And that is the progress that you worked so hard for in 2008. Now, we didn't get everything done. Sometimes people say, "Well, you know, this item is not done and that item, I"—well, I've only been here 2 years, guys. [*Laughter*] If you look at the checklist, we've already covered about 70 percent, so I figured I needed to have something to do for the next couple of years.

And look, here's the fact. Here's the fact, is that we're not where we need to be, not even close. The hole that we're climbing out of is a deep one. People, I want you to understand the magnitude of what we've gone through. This is deeper than the last three recessions combined. Most of the jobs we lost took place before any of our economic policies had a chance to take effect. And on top of that, the middle class had been struggling for more than a decade and jobs had been getting shipped overseas and millions of families were still treading water. Millions are still barely able to make their bills or make the mortgage. I hear their stories every day. I read them in just heartbreaking letters that I receive each night.

So I understand that people are frustrated. I understand people are impatient with the pace of change. Of course they are. Look, I'm impatient, but I also know this: Now is not the time to lose heart; now is not the time to give up. We do not quit. And we cannot forget that this Nation has been through far worse and we have come out stronger, from war to depression to the great struggle for equal rights and civil rights. We do not quit.

In every instance, progress took time. In every instance, progress took sacrifice. Progress took faith. You know, the slaves sitting around a fire singing freedom songs, they weren't sure when slavery would end, but they understood it was going to end. When women were out there marching for the right to vote, they weren't sure when it was going to happen, but they kept on going. When workers were organizing for the right to organize and were being intimidated, they weren't sure when change was going to come, but they knew it was going to come. And I am telling you, Wisconsin, we are bringing about change, and progress is going to come, but you've got to stick with me. You can't lose heart.

Change is going to come. Change is going to come for this generation if we work for it, if we fight for it, if we believe in it. The biggest mistake we could make right now is to let disappointment or frustration lead to apathy and indifference. That is how the other side wins. And I want everybody to be clear, make no mistake: If the other side does win, they will spend the next 2 years fighting for the very same policies that led to this recession in the first place, the same policies that left the middle class behind for more than a decade, the same policies that we fought so hard for to change in 2008.

Just look at the agenda the other leaders—that the leaders of the other party unveiled last week. They call this "Pledge to America." That's what they called it. And in case you're wondering how serious they are about changing Washington, this pledge was actually written with the help of a former lobbyist for AIG and a former lobbyist for ExxonMobil.

Audience members. Boo!

The President. You can't make this stuff up. [*Laughter*] This is the truth.

Now, the centerpiece of their pledge, their central economic idea—this is it, this is their main idea for growing the economy and dealing with the 8 million jobs that were lost as a consequence of their earlier policies—their main idea is a $700 billion tax cut for the wealthiest 2 percent of Americans, right?

Audience members. Boo!

The President. So 98 percent of Americans would never see a dime of this $700 billion. Now, keep in mind, we don't have $700 billion. [*Laughter*] So we'd have to borrow it. And the party that lectures us on fiscal responsibility wants to borrow another $700 billion to give a tax cut worth an average of $100,000 to every millionaire and billionaire in America.

Audience members. Boo!

The President. And when you ask them, well, where do they plan to find the $700 billion, where is this money? Is it laying around? You didn't tell us about this. Where is it? [*Laughter*] They don't have an answer. But to pay for just a

tiny fraction of this tax cut, they want to cut education by 20 percent.

Audience members. Boo!

The President. They want to eliminate 200,000 children from an early childhood education program like Head Start.

Audience members. Boo!

The President. They want to cut financial aid for 8 million college students, including some of the people who are out here today.

Audience members. Boo!

The President. This for a tax cut for folks who don't need it and weren't even asking for it. At a time when the education of a country's citizens is the biggest predictor of its economic success, they think it's more important to give another tax break to people who made the Forbes 400 list. Now, I have to ask my Republican friends a question here: Do you think that China is cutting back on education?

Audience members. No!

The President. Do you think that South Korea is making it harder for their citizens to get a college education?

Audience members. No!

The President. These countries aren't playing for second place. And let me tell you something, the United States of America doesn't play for second place, either. We play for first place, Wisconsin. We play for first place.

This is an economic issue of our generation. And I will not allow politicians in Washington to sacrifice your future on another round of tax cuts that aren't paid for, that we don't need, and you can't afford. And that's the choice in this election. That's why you need to be involved. Your future is at stake here.

Look, we have a different idea about what the next 2 years should look like. And it's an idea rooted in our belief about how this country was built. We know that government doesn't have all the answers to our problems. We don't believe that government's main role is to create jobs or prosperity.

One of the things that the other side has been able to do is to hoodwink a whole bunch of folks all across the country, after we had to take emergency measures to clean up their mess, to say, look, he's for big government. The steps we took to make sure that the auto industry didn't go down the tubes or the financial system didn't go down the tubes was because they weren't minding the store when they were in charge.

It's not because I came in with a big government agenda. I believe government should be lean and efficient. And that's why I've proposed a 3-year spending freeze. That's why I set up a bipartisan fiscal commission to deal with our deficit. But in the words of the first Republican President, Abraham Lincoln, I also believe that government should do for the people what they can't do better for themselves. I believe in a country that rewards hard work and responsibility, a country where we look after one another, a country where I say, I'm my brother's keeper, I'm my sister's keeper.

I believe in an America that gave my grandfather the chance to go to college because of the GI bill. I believe in an America that gave my grandparents the chance to buy a home because of the Federal Housing Authority. I believe in an America that gave their children and grandchildren the chance to fulfill our dreams thanks to scholarships and student loans like some of you are on. That's the America I know. That's the choice in this election.

Instead of $700 billion tax breaks for millionaires and billionaires, we want to make permanent the tax cuts for middle class Americans. You deserve a break. Instead of cutting education and student aid, we want to make permanent our new college tax credit that's worth $10,000 of tuition relief for each young person going to 4 years of college. We want to make clear that in good times and in bad times, no young American should have to sacrifice the dream of a college education just because they can't afford it. That's what we believe. That's the choice in this election.

If we let the other side take control of Congress, they'll spend the next 2 years fighting to preserve tax breaks for companies that create jobs and profits overseas, billions of dollars in taxpayer subsidies that we lose each year. Over the last 20 months, we've had—we've taken the step of closing a lot of these tax loopholes. And over the next 2 years, we're going to fight to give tax breaks to companies that are actually creat-

ing jobs here in the United States of America: to small businesses, to clean energy companies, to American manufacturers, to entrepreneurs who are researching and investing and innovating right here in the United States. That's who we want to help. And that's the choice in this election.

If the other side takes back Congress, they've promised to give back power to the same special interests we've been fighting for the last 20 months. In every State, including right here in Wisconsin, you've got millions of dollars pouring in from special interests. I refuse to let that happen. I refuse to go back to the days when insurance companies could deny you coverage or drop your coverage just because you're sick.

Just the other day, I was talking to a woman who did not have health insurance, even though she was working at a school. Contracted cancer, was not sure whether she was going to have to use the entire college fund that she had saved for her kids in order to get treatment. Fortunately, because of the health reform we signed, she now has coverage. But they would want to roll it back. They don't think that makes sense.

I refuse to go back to the days when credit card companies can jack up your rates without reason. I refuse to go back to the days where taxpayer-funded Wall Street bailouts end up being necessary. We can't allow the special interests to take the reins again. We've got to keep on fighting. There's too much at stake right now.

So, Madison, it comes down to this. And I'm not just talking to Madison, by the way, because there are 200 campuses across the country who are plugged in through web cams and house parties, so I'm speaking to everybody out there. [*Laughter*] Many of the folks in the other party who are running today are the exact same people who spent the last decade driving our economy into the ditch.

So me and Russ Feingold and Tammy Baldwin, we all went down into the ditch. And we put on our boots, and it was muddy down there and dirty and dusty, and we were sweating, and we were pushing the car out of the ditch. And every so often, we'd look up and see the Republicans standing there. They're just standing there, sipping on a Slurpee—[*laughter*]—and waving at us. And we'd say, "Well, come on down and help." They'd say: "No, no, no, but you should push harder. You're not pushing the right way."

But we understood we had to get the car out of the ditch, so we're pushing and we're pushing. Finally—finally—we get it up on level ground. Finally, we get it up on level ground. And look, let's face it, it's a little dented and a little busted, and it needs a tuneup—[*laughter*]—and the fenders all need to be hammered out a little bit, new paint job. But we're finally on level ground, we're moving forward. Suddenly, we get a tap on the shoulder, and we look behind us and who is it? It's the Republicans. And they're asking for the keys back. And we've got to tell them, you can't have the keys back. You don't know how to drive. You don't know how to drive. You don't know how to drive. You can't have them back.

I mean, I hope everybody has noticed, when you want to go forward in your car, what do you do? You put it in "D." When you want to go backwards, you put it in "R." Don't go back into the ditch. That's not a coincidence. That's not a coincidence, people.

So ultimately, whether they get the keys back is up to you. Look, there is no question the other side is excited. They have been pumped up to think that Obama is a Socialist, and he's this and he is that, and he's for big government, and he's responsible for all the—look, they have been fed a lot of information.

And there's some well-meaning people out there who are understandably scared of debt and deficits, and they see what's going on. They see jobs being shipped overseas, and they're not sure what's happening. And we are in charge. And they're saying, "Well, why hasn't change happened faster?"

And so you can persuade them maybe to give the Republicans the keys back if they're not hearing the other side of the argument. So a lot of them are fired up. And thanks to a recent Supreme Court decision, they are being helped along this year, as I said, by special interest groups that are allowed to spend unlimited amounts of money on attack ads. They don't

even have to disclose who's behind the ads. You've all seen the ads. Every one of these groups is run by Republican operatives. Every single one of them, even though they're posing as nonprofit groups with names like Americans for Prosperity or the Committee for Truth in Politics or Americans for Apple Pie. [*Laughter*] I mean, I made that last one up, but—[*laughter*]—but this is why—look, this is why we've got to work even harder in this election. This is why we've got to fight their millions of dollars with millions of our voices, voices who are ready to finish what we started in 2008.

Because if everybody who fought for change in 2008 shows up to vote in 2010, we will win. We will win. The polls say the same thing: We will win.

So what the other side—you know what the other side is counting on this time around? They're counting on you staying home. They're counting on your silence. They're counting on amnesia. [*Laughter*] They're betting on your apathy, especially because a lot of you are young folks.

So, Madison, you've got to prove them wrong. Let's show Washington one more time, change doesn't come from the top. It doesn't come from millions of dollars of special-interest-funded attack ads. Change happens from the bottom up. Change happens because of you. Change happens because of you. Change happens because of you.

I know times are tough right now. I know times are tough. I know a lot of folks are anxious about the future. And I know that during the campaign, especially after we had already started winning, the feeling was, well, this is just exciting. You got those nice "Hope" posters, and then there was the Inauguration, and Beyonce singing—[*laughter*]—and Bono.

And I know sometimes it feels a long way from the hope and excitement that we felt on election day or the day of the Inauguration. But I've got to say, we always knew this was going to take time. We always knew this was going to be hard. I said it was going to be hard, remember?

Audience members. Yes!

The President. I said I was going to tell you some things you didn't want to hear. I said that we were going to have to make some difficult choices. I said not everybody was going to be happy with every single decision I made.

You did not elect me to do what was easy. You didn't just elect me to read the polls and figure out how to keep myself in office. Whenever you read the media in Washington, all they're concerned about is, boy, his polls numbers are down, so that must mean that he didn't do the right thing. Just because your poll numbers are down, that's how everything is measured.

But you didn't elect me to look at the polls. You elected me to do what was right. You elected me to do what was right. That was change you could believe in, that I was going to do what was right, not what was expedient, not what was convenient.

And you got involved. What was different about this campaign was because you believed this was the moment to solve the challenges that the country had ignored for far too long.

That involvement can't end with the vote that you cast in 2008. That election was not just about putting me in the White House. It was about building a movement for change that went beyond any one campaign or any one candidate. It was about remembering that in the United States of America, our destiny is not written for us, it is written by us. That is the blessing of this country. The power to shape our future lies in our hands, but only if we're willing

to keep working for it and fighting for it and keep believing that change is possible.

So that's what's being tested right now. That's what's being tested. We are being tested here. The question is, are we going to have the courage to keep moving forward even in the face of difficulty, even in the face of uncertainty? This election is not about what we've done; it's about the work we have left to do. It's what—it's about what you want this country to look like over the next 2 years. It's about your future.

So, Madison, get out there and shape it. Get out there and fight for it. I need your help, Madison. We need you to commit to vote. We need you to pledge to vote. We need you to knock on doors. We need you to talk to neighbors. We need you to make phone calls. We need you to bring energy and passion and commitment. Because if we do, if you're willing to step up to the plate and realize that change is not a spectator sport, we will not just win this election, we are going to restore our economy, we are going to rebuild the middle class, we will reclaim the American Dream for this generation.

Thank you. God bless you. God bless the United States of America.

NOTE: The President spoke at 6:07 p.m. in the Kohl Center at the University of Wisconsin—Madison. In his remarks, he referred to former lobbyist Brian Wild; and musicians Beyonce G. Knowles and Paul D. "Bono" Hewson.

Message to the Congress on Blocking Property of Certain Persons With Respect to Serious Human Rights Abuses by the Government of Iran and Taking Certain Other Actions
September 28, 2010

To the Congress of the United States:

Pursuant to the International Emergency Economic Powers Act (50 U.S.C. 1701 *et seq.*) (IEEPA), I hereby report that I have issued an Executive Order (the "order") that takes additional steps with respect to the national emergency declared in Executive Order 12957 of March 15, 1995.

In Executive Order 12957, the President found that the actions and policies of the Government of Iran threaten the national security, foreign policy, and economy of the United States. To deal with that threat, the President in Executive Order 12957 declared a national emergency and imposed prohibitions on certain transactions with respect to the development of

Iranian petroleum resources. To further respond to that threat, Executive Order 12959 of May 6, 1995, imposed comprehensive trade and financial sanctions on Iran. Finally, Executive Order 13059 of August 19, 1997, consolidated and clarified the previous orders.

I have determined that the actions and policies of the Government of Iran on or after its presidential election of June 12, 2009, including its violent response to peaceful demonstrations and its commission of serious human rights abuses, warrant the imposition of additional sanctions.

The prohibitions contained in the new order implement section 105(a) of the Comprehensive Iran Sanctions, Accountability, and Divestment Act of 2010 (Public Law 111–195) (CISADA) concerning, *inter alia*, the imposition of sanctions pursuant to IEEPA with respect to each person on the list referred to in section 105(b). I applaud the efforts of the Congress to demonstrate the strong and sustained commitment of the United States to advancing the universal rights of all Iranians, and to sanction those who have abused their rights. The order, however, goes beyond the scope of section 105 of CISADA by imposing sanctions pursuant to IEEPA on persons who meet a broader set of criteria than those specified in section 105(b).

The order blocks the property and interests in property of persons listed in the Annex to the order, who I have determined meet the first of the three criteria set forth below. The order also provides criteria for designations of persons determined by the Secretary of the Treasury, in consultation with or at the recommendation of the Secretary of State:

- to be an official of the Government of Iran or a person acting on behalf of the Government of Iran (including members of paramilitary organizations) who is responsible for or complicit in, or responsible for ordering, controlling, or otherwise directing, the commission of serious human rights abuses against persons in Iran or Iranian citizens or residents, or the family members of the foregoing, on or after June 12, 2009, regardless of whether such abuses occurred in Iran;

- to have materially assisted, sponsored, or provided financial, material, or technological support for, or goods or services to or in support of, the activities described in section 1(a)(ii)(A) of the order or any person whose property and interests in property are blocked pursuant to the order; or

- to be owned or controlled by, or to have acted or purported to act for or on behalf of, directly or indirectly, any person whose property and interests in property are blocked pursuant to the order.

I have delegated to the Secretary of the Treasury the authority, in consultation with the Secretary of State, to take such actions, including the promulgation of rules and regulations, and to employ all powers granted to the President by IEEPA and the relevant provisions of CISADA, as may be necessary to carry out the blocking-related purposes of the order and to take such actions, including the promulgation of rules and regulations, and to employ all powers granted to the President by IEEPA, as may be necessary to carry out section 104 of CISADA. I have delegated to the Secretary of State the functions and authorities related to visa sanctions conferred upon the President by the relevant provisions of CISADA. I have also delegated to the Secretary of State, in consultation with the Secretary of the Treasury, the function of submitting to the appropriate congressional committees referred to in section 105(b) of CISADA the initial and updated lists of persons who are subject to visa sanctions and whose property and interests in property are blocked pursuant to the order. All executive agencies of the United States Government are directed to take all appropriate measures within their authority to carry out the provisions of the order.

The order, a copy of which is enclosed, became effective at 12:01 a.m. eastern daylight time on September 29, 2010.

BARACK OBAMA

The White House,
September 28, 2010.

NOTE: This message was released by the Office of the Press Secretary on September 29. The Executive order is listed in Appendix D at the end of this volume.

Remarks and a Question-and-Answer Session in Des Moines, Iowa
September 29, 2010

The President. Thank you so much for being here. And first of all, I just want to thank Jeff and Sandy and Tristan and Skyelar for letting us use their backyard. So please give them a big round of applause.

And since we are here, I should just say, go Bulldogs. I know how to work a crowd. [*Laughter*]

I want to make sure that everybody also acknowledges your outstanding Governor, Chet Culver is here; the mayor of Des Moines, Frank Cownie, who's here; and State Representative Janet Petersen is here—all of whom are doing great work and I had a chance to work with and get to know when I spent a few months here in Iowa a couple years ago.

It is wonderful to be back, and I thank all of you for coming. I am not going to give a long speech on the front end here. What I really want to do is hear from you. So what I'm going to do is just speak a little bit at the front end about where I think the country's at, how we move forward. It's relevant because there is an election coming up, although I'm going to try to avoid making just a straight political speech here.

When I started running for President back in 2008—2007, 2008—the reason I was willing to go into the race, even though Michelle was not crazy about politics and I had two young daughters who are the center of my world and I was going to be away from for quite a bit, was a feeling that the country was at a crossroads, that we had some fundamental decisions to make that we had been putting off for decades.

And there are a whole host of individual issues—education and energy and what we do in terms of our foreign policy—a whole bunch of discrete issues that concerned me. What concerned me most, I think, was the nature of our economy and how the American Dream seemed as if it was slipping away for too many people.

From 2001 to 2009, the average wage of middle class families in America actually declined by 5 percent. Job growth was slower during that period than at any time since World War II, at the same time as the costs of everything from health care to college tuition were skyrocketing.

And so what you had was a situation in which the very top was getting very wealthy, but the middle class, which is the beating heart of our economy, and those aspiring to get into the middle class were finding it harder and harder to get ahead.

And there were a range of reasons for that, but a lot of it had to do with the set of policies that had been put in place, whose basic premise was that if we cut taxes, especially for millionaires and billionaires, and if we cut back on rules and regulations for how our industries and companies operate, and then we cut everybody loose to sort of do—to fend for themselves, that somehow the economy would automatically grow. And it didn't work.

The other thing that was happening was that we were becoming less competitive internationally, so manufacturing jobs were moving overseas. You saw countries like China and India and Brazil investing heavily in their education systems and in infrastructure. And where we used to be ranked number one, for example, in the proportion of college graduates, we now rank number 12; where we used to have—had the best public school system in the world, now our kids rank 21st in science and 25th in math. And so slowly, all the things that had made us the most productive country on Earth were starting to slip away, and we were losing that competitive position.

So what I said was, I'm going to run for President because there are some long-term things that we can do that will start growing our economy from the bottom up, make sure that the middle class is expanding, make sure that innovation and entrepreneurship is taking place in this country and not someplace else, that we can start rebuilding our economy so that it works for everybody. And that was really the platform that I ran on in 2008.

And that meant that we had to have a school system that was serious about training our young people for the jobs of the future, which wasn't just a function of more money, by the way; it also meant reforming our school system so that it worked better. It meant that we made sure that every young person who worked hard and took responsibility was able to afford to go to college without accumulating some huge mountain of debt.

It meant that we put much more emphasis on math and science and how we could develop new technologies in our economy and innovation. It meant that we started investing more in research and development. We used to typically invest about 3 percent of our gross domestic product in research and development. That started slipping. I said we had to get it back up.

It meant that we invested in infrastructure that would lay the groundwork for a 21st-century economy—not just roads and bridges, but also broadband lines and a smart electric grid that could make us more energy efficient. It meant that we had a new energy policy that would focus on clean energy: solar and wind and biodiesel.

And it meant we had to fix our health care system, which was a huge drag on businesses and families and the Federal Government. It meant that we had to also get control of our spending and align what we take in and how much we spend at the Federal Government level so that it was sustainable.

Now, that was just on domestic policy. We had a whole bunch of things we had to do on foreign policy too.

It turns out that we were in more trouble than we had even imagined in 2008, so that by the time I was sworn in, in January of 2009, a lot of these economic policies had culminated in the worst financial crisis since the Great Depression. And I don't need to tell you how devastating that's been for people all across the country and here in Iowa. I mean, in the 6 months before I was sworn in, we'd lost 4 mil-

lion jobs. The month I was sworn in, we lost 750,000 jobs; the month after that, 600,000; the month after that, 600,000.

So we had already lost most of the 8 million jobs that we were going to end up losing in this recession before any of my economic policies even had a chance to take effect. And the financial system was on the verge of meltdown, so that we—people couldn't even get loans to buy a car. I mean, credit was just shut down.

So we had to take a number of emergency measures. We stepped in, and we stopped the bleeding. Now the economy is growing again. We've had private sector job growth for the last 8 months. Credit is now flowing again, although small businesses are still having a tough time getting credit, and so we've been focused—we signed a bill actually this week to help small businesses get credit and cut some of their taxes.

And so I'm very proud of the fact that we've been able to prevent the economy from going into a second depression. But not only do we have a big hole that we've got to climb ourselves out of—we still have those 8 million jobs that were lost, and that's a lot of jobs to make up—the economy's still not growing as fast as it needs to. A lot of small businesses are still struggling. A lot of large businesses are just sitting on a lot of cash because they're still uncertain about whether to invest in the future. But all those other problems that we had, those didn't go away, the foundational problems, the structural problems in the economy that had led us to slip relative to other countries. So we've had a real challenge over the last couple of years of dealing with a crisis but not taking our eye off the ball in terms of some of the policies that we've got to change.

And that's why financial reform was so important, so we never have to engage in taxpayer-funded bailouts again. That's why health reform was so important, because we had the opportunity not only to help ordinary folks have a better handle on their health care costs, but also that over time, we could make the health care system as a whole more efficient and effective.

That's why we've put so much emphasis on education reform. And this is one area where I think that we've actually gotten some compliments from Republicans, because we're—we are not taking an ideological approach. We're saying: How do we create more accountability in the system? How do we encourage better teachers in the classroom? How do we break through some of the bureaucracy to make sure our kids are learning what they need to learn?

This is all by way of saying that the challenges the economy faces are still great, and they're not going to go away tomorrow or the next day. But we're on the right path, we're on the right track, as long as we stay focused on two things: number one, that our economy only works when folks who are working hard, middle class families, ordinary folks have opportunity so that if they're doing the right thing, they're going to be able to support a family, they're going to be able to send their kids to a good school and send them to college, they're going to be able to retire with some dignity and respect, they're going to be able to afford health care and not go bankrupt when they get sick.

That has to be the orientation. And everything we think about in terms of economic policy is, how do we make sure that if people are out here working hard and taking responsibility for themselves and their families, that they are rewarded? That's the essence of the American Dream.

And the second thing that we've got to keep in mind is that we've got to make tough choices if we're going to solve some of these long-term problems that we've been putting off. And that means putting aside some of the politics as usual. And it also means sometimes telling folks things they don't want to hear.

Now, we're in election season, so that second part of the formula is very hard to apply. And I just want to say—and then I'm just going to open it up for comments and questions—when you look at the choice we face in this election coming up, the other side, what it's really offering is the same policies that from 2001 to 2009 put off hard problems and didn't really speak honestly to the American people about how we're going to get this country on track over the long term.

And I just want to use as an example the proposal that they put forward with respect to tax policy. They want to borrow $700 billion to provide tax cuts for the top 2 percent of Americans, people making more than $250,000 a year. It would mean an average of a $100,000 check to millionaires and billionaires. That's $700 billion we don't have, so we'd either have to borrow it, which would add to our deficit, or we'd have to cut, just to give you an example, about 20 percent of the amount of money that we spend on education. We'd have to cut investments we've made in clean energy. We'd have to cut investments we've made in Head Start. We'd have to cut improvements in terms of student loans for kids going to college that would affect about 8 million kids.

So that's an example of where you've got a choice to make. You can't say you want to balance the budget, deal with our deficit, invest in our kids, and have a $700 billion tax cut that affects only 2 percent of the population. You just can't do it.

And so I hope that as you go forward, not just over the next 6 weeks before the election, but over the next 2 years or next 6 years or next 10 years, as you're examining what's taking place in Washington, that you just keep in mind that we're not going to be able to solve our big problems unless we honestly address them.

And it means that we've got to make choices and we've got to decide what's important. And if we think our kids are important and the next generation's important, then we've got to act like it. We can't pretend that there are shortcuts or that we can cut our taxes, completely have all the benefits that we want and balance the budget and not make any tough choices. That's, I think, more than anything, the message that I want to be communicating to the American people in the months and years ahead.

Anyway, with that, I just want to open it up. I know that there are microphones somewhere in the audience. We got these terrific young people who have volunteered. They'll—so just raise your hand, and they'll find you.

Here you go. Why don't we start right here? And please introduce yourself.

National Economy/Job Growth

Q. Good morning, Mr. President. My name's Mary Stier. Welcome back to Iowa.

The President. Thank you, Mary.

Q. We're thrilled to have you back here.

The President. It's great to be back.

Q. I have a 24-year-old son who campaigned fiercely for you and was very inspired by your message of hope. He graduated from Simpson College about a year and a half ago with honors.

The President. Congratulations.

Q. And he's still struggling to find a full-time job. And he and many of his friends are struggling. They are losing their hope, which was a message that you inspired them with. Could you speak to that—how you would speak to the young men and women in our country who are struggling to find a job, and speak to that message of hope?

The President. Well, I was in Madison, Wisconsin, yesterday, and we had about 25,000 mostly young people come out. And it was a terrific reminder of the fact that young people still have so much energy and so much enthusiasm for the future. But they're going through a tough time. Look, this generation that is coming of age is going through the toughest economy of any generation since the 1930s. That's pretty remarkable.

Most of us—in fact, I'm just looking around the room—I think it's fair to say nobody here remembers the economy of the Great Depression. So the worst economy we had gone through—maybe one—*[laughter]*—maybe one, maybe a couple. But you guys look really good for your age, though, so—*[laughter]*.

But for most of us, the worst we had seen before was the 1980—'81 recession, the 1991 recession, and then the recession in 2001. This recession had more impact on middle class families than those other three recessions combined in terms of job loss and how it's affected people's incomes. So that's going to have an effect on an entire generation. It means that they're worried about the future in a way that most of us weren't worried when we got out of college.

Now, here's the good news, and I've said this to young people. I think that this generation—your son's generation—is smarter, more sophisticated, more passionate, have—has a broader worldview. I think that they don't take things for granted, they're willing to work hard for whatever they can achieve. I think they think about the community and other people, and they don't just have a narrow focus on what's in it for me. When I meet young people these days, I am very impressed with them. I think they've—they are terrifically talented.

And so their future will be fine. But in the short term, what I'd say to them is that, first of all, we're doing everything we can to make sure that they can get the best education possible.

One of the things that we did this year that didn't get a lot of attention was we were able to change the student loan program out of the Federal Government to save about $60 billion that's going to go directly to students in the form of higher grants, reduced loan burdens—debt burdens when they get out of college. It's going to make a difference to them. So we're going to do everything we can to make sure they can succeed educationally.

Number two, obviously, we're doing everything we can to grow the economy so that if they've got the skills, they're going to be able to find a job in this new economy. And as I said, we've seen private sector job growth 8 consecutive months now.

The economy is growing; it's just not growing as fast as we'd like it, partly because there are still some headwinds. We had some overhang because of all the problems in the housing market, and the housing market's a big chunk of our economy. All that excess inventory of houses that were built during the housing bubble, they're getting absorbed, and slowly, that will start improving. So the expectation is, is that although we're not growing as fast as we can, if we're making some good choices about providing small businesses tax breaks and helping to shore up the housing market, that over the next couple of years, you're going to start seeing steadily the economy improving.

And if young people like your son are prepared, if they're focused and equipped, they're going to be able to find a good job.

In the meantime, what we've also done is made sure, for example, that your son can stay on your health insurance until the age of 26, which—because of health care reform, and that is going to relieve some of the stress that they're feeling right now.

And then finally, what I'd tell your son is, is that we're trying to make some tough decisions now so that by the time he has his own son or daughter, that we are back to number one in research and development, back to number one in the proportion of college graduates, back to number one in terms of innovation and entrepreneurship, that we have succeeded in creating a competitive America that will ensure this 21st century is the American century, just like the 20th century was.

But it's going to take some time, and so the main message I have to young people—in some ways, this generation may be less fixed on immediate gratification than our generation was, partly because they've seen how—some hardship in their own families and in their own careers.

Okay, who's next? Gentleman right here.

U.S. Military Operations in Afghanistan/Cost of U.S. Military Operations

Q. My name's Bob Brammer. I live about five or six blocks away in Beaverdale, and we're really glad you came here, Mr. President.

The President. Thank you. It's not hard to come here. This is a nice neighborhood, by the way.

Q. It's great.

The President. I love these big trees.

Q. Hear, hear!

The President. It's beautiful.

Q. Now, my question relates to things halfway around the world and how they affect the economy, particularly the wars and the enormous amount of spending that has gone into that and the—over the last decade, not just the last couple years. So this is what I'd ask. Those decade-long conflicts have had an enormous cost in terms of people killed and wounded—our men and women and other peoples who are killed—and they've had a gigantic cost in terms of money and resources and people diverted to

the war. When can we look forward to reducing the huge spending on these wars, and is it possible that kind of funds could help us square up our budget and give us crucial resources to strengthen our economy right here at home?

The President. Well, I said at a speech I made at West Point talking about Afghanistan that I'm interested in nation-building here at home. That's the nation I want to build more than anything else.

As you know, because it was a big issue when I was campaigning here in Iowa, I was opposed to the war in Iraq from the start. I made a commitment that I would bring that war to a responsible end. We have now ended our combat mission in Iraq, and we've pulled out 100,000 troops out of Iraq since I was in office. So that's a commitment we've followed up on.

Now, Afghanistan was a war that most people right after 9/11, I think, overwhelmingly understood was important and necessary. We had to go after those who had killed 3,000 Americans. We had to make sure that Al Qaida did not have a safe haven inside Afghanistan to plan more attacks. And you can speculate as to whether if we hadn't gone into Iraq, we had just stayed focused on Afghanistan, whether by now we would have created a stable situation and we would not have a significant presence there. But that's not what happened.

So when I walked in, what we had was a situation in Afghanistan that had badly deteriorated over the course of 7 years and where the Taliban was starting to take over half of the country again. You had a very weak Afghan Government. And in the border region between Afghanistan and Pakistan, you had Al Qaida still plotting to attack the United States.

Now, I had said during the campaign, we need to make sure that we're getting Afghanistan right. And what I committed to when I came into office was, we'll put additional resources, meaning troops and money on the civilian side, to train up Afghan forces, make sure that the Afghan Government can provide basic services to its people.

But what I also said is, we're not going to do it in an open-ended way. We're going to have a time frame within which Afghans start having to take more responsibility for their own country. And I said that on July of next year, we're going to begin a transition of shifting from U.S. troops to Afghan troops in many of these areas.

Now, the situation there is very tough. Afghanistan is the second poorest country in the world. There are a lot of countries in the world; this is the second poorest. It has a 70-percent illiteracy rate. Afghanistan was much less developed than Iraq was. And it had no significant traditions of a strong central government that could provide services to its people or a civil service or—just the basic infrastructure of a modern nation-state.

So we're not going to get it perfect there. It is messy, it is hard, and the toughest job I have is when I deploy young men and women into a war theater, because some of them don't come back, and I'm the one who signs those letters to family members offering condolences for the enormous sacrifice of their loved ones.

But I do think that what we are seeing is the possibility of training up Afghan forces more effectively, keeping pressure on Al Qaida so that they're not able to launch big attacks, and that over the next several years, as we start phasing down, those folks start lifting up.

Here's the impact it will have on our budget. There are going to be still some hangover costs from these two wars, the most obvious one being veterans, which we haven't always taken care of as well as we should have, and I've had to ramp up veterans spending significantly because I think that's a sacred trust. They've served us well; we've got to serve them well. And that means services for posttraumatic stress disorder, reducing backlogs in terms of them getting disability claims, help specifically for women veterans, who are much more in the line of fire now than they'd ever been before. All those things cost some money.

So there's—even as we start winding down the war in Afghanistan, it's not as if there's going to be a huge peace dividend right away. But what it does mean is, we'll be able to more responsibly manage our military budget, and this is another example of where you can't say you want to balance the budget and not take on reform in the Pentagon. I mean, we've already pushed hard to eliminate some weapons programs in the Pentagon budget that the generals, the people who actually do the fighting, say we don't need. But getting those programs shut down is very difficult because typically, there's not a single weapons program out there that doesn't have some part being built in 40 different congressional districts in 10 or 20 different States, so that everybody has a political vested interest in keeping it going.

And Bob Gates, my Defense Secretary, has been really good about pushing hard on that. And we've won some battles, but that's going to be an area that we're going to have to take a serious look at as well when we put forward a plan for getting a handle on our long-term debt and deficits.

Okay? All right, I'm going to go boy, girl, boy, girl, just to make sure everybody knows I'm fair here. [*Laughter*] Right here.

Health Care Reform

Q. Hi. My name is Jeannette McKenzie, and my mother lives with my husband and I. We take care of her. She's been with us for 6 years now. She is currently in a nursing home getting rehab.

The President. Right.

Q. I have great concerns over your health bill. One of the ladies in admissions over there whom I was talking with the other week started—she's from England, and her family is still in England.

The President. Right.

Q. And she was explaining to us how—telling us what we had to look forward to here. Her sister worked as a nurse in the same hospital for 20 years. She was 55. She was told she needed open-heart surgery. She was put on a 10-year waiting list. Three years later, she had a major heart attack, and they were forced to give her that surgery that she needed.

I realize you're saying the 26-year-olds will have health insurance; they don't have to worry about that. My mother always told me the older you get, the faster time goes. And when she said that to me years back, I thought she was crazy.

The President. Yes, I've noticed this too. [*Laughter*]

Q. Yes. And these 26-year-olds in a heartbeat are going to be 50, 55. When you're young, you're supposed to be able to work hard for what you want. You build up your income. You further yourself so you can retire and have peace of mind.

The President. Right.

Q. It's hard to—I can't fathom now, how can you be excited in your youth when you have to save, save, save just to protect yourself health insurance-wise when you reach our age?

The President. Let me ask you a question, though. The—I mean, because you said you're worried about my health reform bill, and the nurse said, here's what you have to look forward to. Is your mom on Medicare?

Q. Yes.

The President. Yes.

Q. Yes, she's——

The President. So the—there's nothing in our health reform bill that is going to impact whether your mom can get heart surgery if she needed it. The—we didn't change the core Medicare program. So unless there's something specific that you're worried about——

Q. Medicare doesn't start until you're 65.

The President. No, no, I understand.

Q. I'm talking about 50, 55——

The President. Okay.

Q. ——years old.

The President. All right, so if you're not on Medicare——

Q. Yes, right.

The President. And do you have health insurance?

Q. Yes.

The President. Okay.

Q. Right now, yes.

The President. Right. So the—there's nothing in the bill that says you have to change the health insurance that you've got right now. I just want to identify what your worry is, because I want to say, you shouldn't be worried about it. But what is it that you think might happen to your health insurance as a consequence of health care reform?

Q. Okay, what I'm concerned about is, say, if my—just say if my husband got laid off.

The President. Right.

Q. Say we had no health——

The President. You had no health insurance, okay?

Q. ——care insurance. Okay.

The President. Now, right now, before reform, if you had no health insurance, you'd just be out of luck, okay?

Q. All right. And then we'd get the Government-run health insurance, right?

The President. Well, no——

Q. Is that what you're saying?

The President. No, here's the way it would work. So let me just kind of map it out for you. If you are already getting health insurance on your job, then that doesn't change. Health insurance reform was passed 6 months ago. I don't know if anybody here has gotten a letter from their employer saying you now have to go into Government-run health care because we can't provide you health insurance anymore. I mean, that hasn't happened, right?

So you're keeping the health insurance that you had through your job. And the majority of people still get health insurance through your job.

The only changes we've made on people's health insurance who already have it was to make it a little more secure by saying there are certain things insurance companies can't do. It's a patient's bill of rights, basically.

So insurance companies can no longer drop your coverage when you get sick, which was happening. Sometimes there were some insurance companies who were going through your policy when you got sick to see if you had filled out the form wrong, you hadn't listed some infection that they might call a preexisting condition, et cetera, a bunch of fine print that led to people not having health insurance. So that was one thing that we said.

We said also, you can keep kids on your health insurance till they're 26; that children with preexisting conditions had to be covered under health insurance.

So there were a handful of things that we said insurance companies have to do, just as good business practices to protect consumers. But otherwise, you can stay on your employer's health care. So that's if you have health insurance.

The other thing we did was we said, if you're—a lot of people who don't have health insurance, it's because they work for small businesses, who have trouble affording health insurance because they're not part of a big pool. They're not like a big company that has thousands of employees and they can negotiate because the insurance companies really wants their business. So what we said was, let's provide tax breaks to small businesses so they can—they're more likely to buy health insurance for their employees. And right now about 4 million businesses across the country are now getting a tax break—a tax credit if they provide health insurance for their employees that can save them tens of thousands of dollars. So that's the second thing.

And the third thing we said was, okay, if you don't have health insurance—let's just say your job doesn't offer you health insurance or you lose your job—then what we're going to set up is what's called an exchange, which is basically a big pool; you become part of this big group of people, just like as if you were working for a big company or a big university like Drake. You become part of this pool, and you'll be able to buy your own insurance through this pool, but the rates will be lower, and you'll get a better deal because you've got the bargaining power of these thousands or millions of people who you're buying it with. You'll still have a choice of plans. You'll be—have a choice of BlueCross, or you'll have a choice of this plan or that plan, but you'll be buying it through a pool. And if you can't afford it, then we'll provide you some subsidies to see if we can help you buy it—so make it affordable.

So that's essentially what health reform's about. Now, what that means is, is that you're not going to be forced to buy a, quote, "Government-run health care plan." The only thing that we have said is, is that there—if you can afford to get health care and you're not getting health care, well, that's a problem because that means when you get sick and you have to go the emergency room, everybody else here has to pay for it. And that's not fair.

So we've said, if you can afford to get health care, we're going to make sure that you can afford it, but you've got to have some basic coverage so that we're not subsidizing—everybody else isn't paying an extra thousand dollars on their premiums to cover you.

Q. All right. We're all—we all agree health—there needs to be health reform, okay? We just moved out here a year ago from Las Vegas.

The President. Right.

Q. Okay. There are illegal immigrants that are getting free health care right now, okay? The doctor we had, clinics and stuff, close up because they couldn't even afford to stay open because of all the illegal immigrants that were getting health care.

The President. Well, let me do this because—I'll answer this question, and then I want to make sure everybody else gets a chance too. But the—no, I think this is important for me to be able to clear up some stuff. There's no doubt that there are probably a number of hospitals in every major city, doctors in every major city, who are providing uncompensated care to a whole lot of people, including some illegal immigrants.

I mean, basically, most doctors and nurses that I meet, their whole reason for being in the profession is to help people. And so if they see somebody coming into the emergency room, if there's some child who is badly injured or sick, they're going to not check on their immigrant status; they're going to say, this is somebody who needs help.

And I think that's the right thing to do for our society generally. I don't—I think it is very important for us to make sure that we have compassion as part of our national character.

Now, the thing I want to point out, though, is, is that first of all, there's nothing in my health care plan that covers undocumented workers, right? So that's not part of health reform.

And the second thing is, it turns out, actually, illegal immigrants probably underutilize the health care system. They—the only time they go to the health care system is if they have an emergency, because for the most part, they're worried about getting caught.

So that's not to say that there's not a portion of that population that is getting uncompensated care that's adding to our costs. But there are a lot more Americans who don't have health insurance, as a consequence don't get regular checkups, aren't getting preventive care, are more likely to end up in the emergency room, are more likely to add to the costs of the hospitals or the doctors.

And so if we can provide them with basic checkups, basic preventive care, affordable health care so they've got some peace of mind, that will actually over time make the system more efficient as a whole, because emergency room care is the most expensive kind of care.

But I guess the main message I just want to communicate—because there was a lot of misinformation during the health care debate—I just want to communicate that the—if you're happy with what you've got, nobody's changing it. And you and your mom are going to be able to have—your mom is going to have her Medicare, and the core benefits of Medicare aren't changing. And if you've got health care through your employer, that's not going to change, except to make it a little bit safer and more secure.

If you don't have health care, then it's just going to help. And overall, independent estimates say that this is not going to add to our deficit; it's actually going to reduce our deficit because we're making the health care system more efficient over time.

But I understand why people are concerned, because this is a very personal thing, and nothing's scarier than when you don't have health care and you're sick.

I've told the story of when Sasha was 3 months old, she got meningitis. And I still remember going to the hospital. And she had to get a spinal tap, and I never felt so helpless and scared in my life. And I was lucky to have health insurance, but we were in the emergency room looking around and thinking, well, what if I was one of these other parents who didn't have it and my daughter was going through this? And I was thinking, I'm going to get a $20,000 or $30,000 bill after this, and I have no way of paying for it. What is—or what if my child has a chronic illness? And so it's not just a one-time

trip, but it's trip after trip. And I don't think any parent should have to go through that, not in a society as rich as ours, so—but thank you for the question. It was—it's helpful.

Yes, sir. Got a mike right behind you.

Taxes/Small Businesses/National Debt/Federal Budget/China-U.S. Relations

Q. President Obama, first, thanks for allowing us the opportunity to meet with you here in Iowa.

The President. You bet.

Q. And especially since I'm a Drake graduate, I'm especially thrilled to be here; it's like testing my education, my graduate degree at least.

Anyways, I moved here from Chicago about 30 years ago.

The President. You still got a little——

Q. It's a nice town.

The President. You still got a little Chicago in you.

Q. Yes, it's still going to be there. I won't argue with you on anything. But I think the reason I stayed here was, it was a wonderful place to start a business. I got a master's here, and I started a small business with $200 and a big dream. And I was 25 years old.

I'm 53 now. I've been in business 28 years. We went from what was myself to now almost 100-and-some employees and about 200,000 square foot of manufacturing.

The President. That's—what kind of business is it?

Q. We manufacture promotional products, and we actually make those bag signs you see in all the political yards.

The President. Right, right.

Q. We do all the printed T-shirts for every juvenile diabetes walk.

The President. That's great.

Q. And the beauty of my background is, I actually came from a medical background. My father, my father-in-law, my brother, my brother-in-law—everybody's a doctor, all in Chicago. So I was supposed to be a doctor, but I came here, and I said, well, you know, I sort of like business, I like making deals. So we got started in business, and we started out as an ad agency.

And I guess as we got into it, we realized that the key thing is to have a product to sell so you could sell truckloads of something rather than just sell one thing at a time. And so we did wholesale the way most people would like to do wholesale. And part of that meant importing, it meant trips to China 25 years ago, and it meant 25 years of growing the business.

I always hear—I'm never confrontational, I'm sure everybody here will tell you that—but I always hear that we're trying not to tax anybody but the people that make over that 250,000, that elitist 2 percent. Any viable, strong, competitive business—and the name of our business is Competitive Edge, 30 years ago, before CNN ever used it as a term—the hope is that you're supposed to grow profitability so you can grow your business.

When I went in as a young man of 25 and said, "How about a bank loan?"—it was a bank right across the street, and they really weren't interested in myself unless I was buying a boat or a car and I was going to make payments. They didn't understand the business.

Twenty-five years go by very quickly, unfortunately, and you find yourself looking around, proud of what you've built, but at the same time realizing there are new threats that, besides what, unfortunately, you have to deal with on your plate, on a macro level, which is mindboggling, we each have our own little niche.

We also pay that health insurance for our employees—always did. I remember paying for an employee who said, "What are my benefits?" I said, "You're going to get health insurance, you're going to get a profit-sharing possibility here, you're going to be able to grow with us." And the goal was, lock up the person, because you don't want people changing jobs.

That insurance for that individual was $32, $32 a month, and I more than happily picked that up. Today that amount is like $500. They don't even get the same level of service. They get all generics. They don't get the products; they don't get anything.

I guess what my commentary comes down to is, as the Government—it gets more and more involved in business and gets more involved in taxes to pay for an awful lot of programs, what

you're finding is, you're strangling those job-creation vehicles that are available; you're sort of strangling the engine that does create the jobs. We have jobs that we offer, I mean, regularly. There's always an opportunity for somebody that wants to work hard. I don't care what the background is. I don't care what the health level, what the education is, or where they came from.

But the fundamentals are profit. Two hundred and fifty thousand dollars—well, if you're two people and a family, that's not a lot. It seems like a lot, but not when you have the family, the kids, the cars, the college, and all the other things that go—plus you have to grow the engine. You have to grow it to continue to provide more jobs and to create the dream.

Yes, there's a lot of wealth, but it's trapped in the buildings, the 200,000 square feet. It's trapped in millions of dollars in inventory. It's trapped in accounts receivable, which can run millions of dollars, people that are saying: "You know, I don't have it right now. I can't pay yet." But the Government comes along every quarter, and the tax checks do go out on imaginary profits that you hope you won't write off as bad debts in a year later, on things that really, from my perspective, are the thrills of owning a small business, you know? Having the whole plate on a micro level that you would have and having to constantly keep the balls in the air.

One of the things that concerns me is that repeal the Bush, quote, "tax cuts." The repeal, I don't care if it's 5 percent; that's 5 percent that would create a job. Five percent on millions of dollars of profit creates many jobs. Nobody's putting it in their pocket. On a corporate level, they can sit with their piles of cash. But on a small-business level, which is the essence of this country, and it is the foreign Ambassador for countries around the world to meet us. When I go to China and I spend all my time, I have a one-on-one relationship.

I sent an e-mail out to all the people we do business with: Did you have any questions for our President? If I'm blessed and I have the opportunity to spend the 4 hours under the trees, I'd like to present your arguments. First one was, from China, why are you pressuring them for the renminbi? Why are you pressuring——

The President. All right, we're going way afield now. I mean, the—so let me focus on your question——

Q. ——the job creation and the taxes.

The President. ——and I'll be happy to talk about it. And then if you want, I can tell you, if you're making an argument on behalf of China about their currency, I'm happy to make that argument, to push back on that. But let me focus on the issue you raised about your business.

And first of all, we're—I'm thrilled that you've been able to build this success. I have signed eight small-business tax cuts since I came into office. And the package that we signed this week cut taxes in eight more ways. So your taxes haven't gone up in this administration; your taxes have gone down in this administration.

So I just want to be clear about this, because this is something that I know a lot of times there's—I just think the notion that, well, he's a Democrat, so your taxes must have gone up—well, that's just not true. Taxes have gone down for you, the small-businessperson, and by the way, for 95 percent of working families. That was part of the Recovery Act, was reducing people's taxes.

Now, with respect to the debate that's now taking place on the Bush tax cuts, keep in mind that what we've proposed is to extend the Bush tax cuts for all income up to $250,000. So it's not just sort of the person who is making $60,000 who would get a tax break or who is making $100,000 who would make a tax break—who would get a tax break. If you're making $300,000, you'd still get a tax break on the first $250,000 worth of income. You'd pay a slightly higher rate on the $50,000 above that. If you make half a million dollars, you'd still be having tax relief on the first half of your income. On the other half above 250, you'd have a slightly higher rate—a rate, by the way, that is back to the level it was under Bill Clinton, at a time when there were a lot of small businesses and, in fact, the economy was doing much better.

The reason I think it's important for us to do this is not because I'm not sympathetic to small businesses. It has to do with the fact that 98 percent—98 percent—of small businesses actually have a profit of less than $250,000. So it's not just individuals who generally don't make that much money; most small businesses don't make that much money, either. But it costs $700 billion.

And so I've got to figure out, well, how do I pay for $700 billion? Because everybody is also concerned that our deficit's out of control. So then folks will say, "Well, let's cut Government spending."

Well, most Government spending is Medicare, Medicaid, veterans funding, defense. When people look at the budget, a lot of times they say, "Well, why don't you just cut out foreign aid?" for example. Foreign aid is 1 percent of our budget; not 25 percent, it's 1 percent.

People say, "Well, why don't you eliminate all those earmarks, all those pork projects that Members of Congress are getting out there?" Now, I actually think that a lot of that stuff needs to end, but even if I eliminated every single earmark, pork project by Members of Congress, that's 1 percent of the budget. I mean—so finding $700 billion is not easy.

And when we borrow $700 billion, we're adding to our deficit and debt, and then we've got to pay interest to China or whoever else is willing to buy our debt.

So these are the choices. So it's not that when it comes to small businesses or big businesses, that I have any interest in raising taxes. I'd like to keep taxes low so that you can create more jobs. But I also have to make sure that we are paying our bills and that we're not adding—putting off debt for the future generation.

And that's what happened in the Bush tax cuts in 2001 and 2003. We lopped off taxes, and we did not pay for it. And that is the single largest contributor to the debt and the deficit. It's not anything that we did last year is—in emergency spending. It's not the auto bailout. It's not the health care bill. That's not what's added to our deficit. The single biggest reason that we went from a surplus under Bill Clinton to a deficit of record levels when I walked into office had to do with these Bush tax cuts, because they weren't paid for and we didn't make cut—we didn't cut anything to match them up.

So I think that to say to the top 2 percent of businesses—which, by the way, includes hedge fund managers who've set up an S corporation but are pulling down a billion dollars a year, but they're still considered a small business under the criteria that are set up there—that to say to them, you've got to pay a modestly higher amount to help make sure that our budget over time gets balanced, I think that's a fair thing to do.

And I think—when I talk to a lot of businesses, they just don't want super high rates of the sort that existed before Ronald Reagan came into office. And I'm very sympathetic to that. And on capital gains and dividends, for example, we want to keep those relatively level. We don't want—I would like to see a lower corporate tax rate. But the way to do that is to eliminate all the loopholes, because right now on paper, we've got a high corporate tax rate. But in terms of what people actually pay, they've got so many loopholes that they've larded up in the Tax Code that, effectively, they pay very low rates. So this is a challenge. But I want to do everything I can to make sure that your business succeeds.

I will say, I'm—the reason that I'm pushing China about their currency is because their currency is undervalued. And that effectively means that their—goods that they sell here cost about 10 percent less and goods that we try to sell there cost about 10 percent or—now, let me not say 10 percent, because I don't want the financial markets to think I've got a particular—there is a range of estimates. But I think people generally think that they are managing their currency in ways that make our goods more expensive to sell and their goods cheaper to sell here. And that contributes—that's not the main reason for our trade imbalance, but it's a contributing factor to our trade imbalance.

All right. Over here.

U.S. Poverty Rate/National Economy/Education

Q. Thank you. Good morning, Mr. President.
The President. Good morning.

Q. I'm a proud Iowa social worker who works with crime victims. And my question is about the poverty rate. We currently have a rate of 14 percent poverty. That's one out of seven people are in poverty. And I believe that that's the highest rate since the 1960s. And there's a lot of reasons why people go into poverty who weren't in poverty before, things like medical emergencies and losing jobs, being a crime victim, and, especially for women, a divorce.

My question is, what are we going to do—or I guess, more specifically, what are you going to do—[*laughter*]—to help one out of six or seven people get out of poverty?

The President. It's a profound question. I'm—the poverty rate, I think, is the highest it's been in 15 years. It's still significantly lower than it was back in the 1960s, but it's—look, it's unacceptably high.

The single most important thing I can do to drive the poverty rate down is to grow the economy. What has really increased poverty is folks losing their jobs and being much more vulnerable. So everything we can do to provide tax breaks for small businesses that are starting up, to make sure that we are encouraging—for example, trying to accelerate investment in plants and equipment this year and letting people write it off more quickly so that companies that are on the sidelines that are thinking about investing, they say, you know what, why don't we go ahead and take the plunge now and start hiring now, instead of later—all that can make a big difference in terms of growing the economy, reducing the unemployment rate. That'll reduce the poverty rate.

The second most powerful thing I can do to reduce the poverty rate is improve our education system, because the single biggest indicator of poverty is whether or not you graduated from high school and you're able to get some sort of postsecondary education. And right now too many of our schools are failing.

So this week we spent a lot of time talking about the education reforms we've already initiated. As I said, we set up something called Race to the Top. And it was a simple idea: The Federal Government sends education dollars to schools all across the country to help them, particularly poorer schools. But what we said is, we're going to take a portion of that money—$4 billion—and we're going to say to the States, you're going to have a competition for this money. You're not automatically going to get it because of some formula. You've got to show us that you are initiating reforms that are going to recruit better teachers and train them more effectively; that are going to have greater accountability measures so you're able to track how students are doing during the course of the school year and make adjustments so that they're not just being passed along from grade to grade even though they can't read and—or do arithmetic at their grade level. We're going to encourage more charter schools and more experiments in learning across the country.

All these reform efforts that we triggered through this competition have meant that 32 States actually changed their laws. It's probably the biggest set of reforms that we've seen nationwide on public education in a generation.

Then what we're trying to do is make sure that we're working with community colleges and ensuring that they are providing a great pathway for young people who do graduate from high school. They may not go to 4-year colleges right away, but the community college system can be just a terrific gateway for folks to get skills. Some start at a community college and then go on to 4-year colleges. Some just get technical training, get a job, and then come back maybe 5 years later to upgrade their skills or adapt them to a new business.

So we're putting a lot of resources and effort into making sure that community colleges are constantly improving, and they're adapting their curriculum to the jobs of the future. So education and growing the economy generally, those are the most important things I can do for poverty.

Now, there are other things like, for example, health reform so that people don't lose their homes if they get sick that will keep—help keep people out of poverty; making sure that we're dealing with domestic violence, which can have an impact on women that then drives them out of homes and puts them into difficult situations; dealing with our veterans so that if they've got posttraumatic stress disorder, we are treating them quickly before it compounds itself and eventually they end up on the streets and it's very hard for them then to get back on their feet.

Those are all things that are important, and we're going to keep on doing them. But if we can grow this economy and improve our education system, that's going to be the most important thing we can do.

Am I—I'm getting the signal? One more question? Okay.

I'm going to have to call on the guy with the collar. What can I do? [*Laughter*] The—I didn't mean to outrank you here, but——

Job Growth/Manufacturing Industry/Education

Q. Sorry, Matt. [*Laughter*] Mr. President, Father Michael Amadeo, pastor of Holy Trinity Catholic Church here in Beaverdale, as well as the school that in 2008 was recipient of the Department of Education's Blue Ribbon award.

The President. Congratulations.

Q. So thank you for being here.

The President. Congratulations. Congratulations.

Q. Secondly, thank you for your leadership. These are very tough economic times, tough times for our country in regards to men and women being deployed.

My question for you comes from a member of my congregation who is 55 years of age, has a wife, two children who are freshmen in high school. A year ago, he lost his job in manufacturing. He's been unemployed now for a year-plus. What will your economic policies do for him within the next year and, hopefully, to be able to secure a job and have that American Dream again, which has now been lost?

The President. Well, obviously that story is duplicated all across the country, and I get letters—I get about 40,000 letters or e-mails from constituents across the country every single day. And my staff selects out about 10 of them for me to read each night, sort of a representative sampling.

I know this is a representative sampling because about half the letters call me an idiot— [*laughter*]—so they—they're not screening them out. [*Laughter*] But a bunch of those letters talk about: "I'm 50 years old, I've worked hard all my life, I've looked after my family, the plant closed or the office shut down, and it's very hard for me now to find work. The jobs that are available pay 20, 30 percent less than what I was making before."

Sometimes the parents write about them feeling ashamed that they can't provide for their kids the way they wanted to.

Sometimes I get letters from kids who aren't at all ashamed of their parents. They love their parents. They're proud of them. But they know that their parents are feeling bad. And so they write to me saying, I wish you could just do something, because my dad or my mom, they look like they're losing hope and they're lost, and I feel bad.

So what you're hearing is what a lot of folks are going through all across the country. And I think—I've spoken generally about what we can do long term for our economic competitiveness. There are some things that we're doing immediately to try to improve the business climate. So as I already mentioned, trying to get businesses—who actually have a lot of cash, they're making profits now—to invest those profits now as opposed to sitting on the sidelines or holding them.

And in plant and equipment and research and development, we're trying to change sort of the incentive structures and the Tax Codes to spur on additional business investment.

If your—the member of your congregation, your parishioner, was in manufacturing, one of the things that we think holds a lot of promise is the whole clean energy sector, because some of the manufacturing jobs that have been lost just won't come back, partly because manufacturing has become much more efficient.

I mean, a lot of people think that the reason manufacturing has gone down so fast is because all these jobs have been shipped overseas. Well, that's a contributing factor. There's no doubt China took a whole lot of our manufacturing jobs; prior to that, Mexico. Next will be Vietnam or Malaysia or other countries, just because their wages are much lower.

But—and frankly, it's also because sometimes our trade deals weren't enforced very well. And one of the things that I'm saying is, I believe in free trade. I think that it can grow our economy. We already heard from a businessman who is involved in international trade. But I think it is very important to make sure that trade is fair and that each side is being treated equally. And right now that's not always the case.

But it turns out that a lot of manufacturing has declined just because it's gotten so much more efficient. You go into a steel plant now that used to take 10 folks to put out 1 unit of steel; now you need 1 person with a computer. When you go into just about any manufacturing plant these days, so much of it is automated. You've got these robot arms, and it's all clean and pristine, and it's just—it's a different type of industry now. So that's where a lot of jobs have been lost.

But here's the good news. The clean energy sector, I think, is going to be a huge growth sector. And what we did during the Recovery Act was we invested in companies, including companies here in Iowa. I was out at a wind farm—where was that? Out in Fort Madison, Siemens—where you go here and what was just a shutdown factory, they've reopened. They're building the blades for these massive windmills. And they had just hired several hundred people and were looking at hiring several hundred more because they are seeing some certainty in the renewable energy industry.

And so you—they had actually hired a lot of folks who were coming off traditional manufacturing industries, applying their new skills to these new jobs.

The same is happening in advanced battery manufacturing. I don't know how many people here have a hybrid car—you've got a couple of folks. It turns out that we weren't making the batteries that are going into these hybrid and electric cars; we were—they were all being made elsewhere. We had about 2 percent of the market.

So as part of the Recovery Act, what we said was, let's invest in creating our own homegrown advanced battery manufacturing. And we're on track now by 2015 to have 40 percent of the market.

And we were in Michigan and looking at one of these plants. A lot of the folks who were there are folks who used to work as suppliers for the auto industry. They had gotten laid off, and now they're back helping to build what will be the cars of the future. These advanced batteries that they're building are going into the Chevy Volt, which is a American-built clean energy car, a car of the future.

So there are still going to be opportunities for skilled tradesmen, people who've worked in manufacturing, but it's not going to be in just these massive factories of the 1950s. It's going to be in these new factories focusing on new industries, and this is where innovation and research and development is so important.

The one thing that's going to happen, though, is, is that parishioner is going to need probably to update some of their skills, because as I said, the fact that they know manufacturing, they know machines and tools, all that's going to be helpful, but they're also probably going to need to work a computer better. They're going to need to know how to diagnose a big, complicated system, looking at a flat screen inside the factory as opposed to tooling around and opening things up to see what's going on. And that may require some retraining. And that's again why the community college system can be so important.

A lot of folks at the age of 50, they don't need 2 years of education, but they may need 6 months where they're able to retool and get some help paying the bills and making the mortgage while they are retooling. And those are the kinds of programs that I think we need to set up.

Well, listen, this has been terrific. I am so grateful to all of you for taking the time to be here. As I listen to the questions, it's a good reminder, we've got a long way to go.

But I do want everybody to feel encouraged about our future. This goes to the first question that was asked about the next generation. America is still the wealthiest country on Earth. We have the best colleges and universities on Earth. It still has the most dynamic entrepreneurial culture on Earth. We've got the most productive workers of just about any advanced nation. We still have huge advantages, and people—billions of people around the world would still love the chance to be here.

And so I don't want everybody to forget that we've been through tougher times before, and we're going to get through these times. But typically, when we've gotten through tough times, it's because we all buckled down and we refocused and we came together and we made some tough but necessary adjustments and changes in how we approach the future. And I'm confident we're going to do that again.

But it's going to happen not just because of me, the President. It's going to be—happen because of individual small businesses. It's going to happen because of what's happening in congregations. It's going to happen because of what young people are doing—thinking about their future and how they're applying themselves to their studies.

All of us are going to have to be pulling together and refocusing on the future and not just the present. If we do that, we're going to do fine.

So thank you very much, everybody. Appreciate it.

NOTE: The President spoke at 10:06 a.m. at the residence of Jeff Clubb and Sandy Hatfield Clubb. In his remarks, he referred to Tristan Clubb, son, and Skyelar Clubb, daughter, of Mr. Clubb and Ms. Hatfield Clubb; Ryan Stier, son of Des Moines, IA, resident Mary P. Stier; and David Greenspon, owner, Competitive Edge Advertising Specialty Mfg. Co.

Remarks and a Question-and-Answer Session in Richmond, Virginia
September 29, 2010

The President. Well, everybody have a seat, have a seat. I just want to—first of all, I want to thank Matt and Stephanie who were making their backyard available until it got really wet, and Matthew and Lucy, who are our official hosts today. And I'm so appreciative of them.

I want to acknowledge our mayor, Dwight Jones. Thank you so much for being here. And of course, I've got to say thanks again to Ms. Shelton for being here. We are graced by your presence.

This is really a casual setting, so I hope that we just open it up for a good conversation about where the country is at, where it's going, how folks are feeling down here in Richmond. I want to hear from you at least as much as you're hearing from me.

I find this really useful to me, because when you're in Washington all the time and you're in these battles, sometimes you're in what's called the bubble. And I'm always doing—trying to do what I can to break out of it and be able to get back with folks and have a conversation.

What I want to do is just speak briefly about what's going on in the economy, and then just open it up.

Obviously, we're going through a tough time. And these last 2 years have been as tough as any that we've seen in most of our lifetimes, except for Ms. Shelton. [*Laughter*] Because the truth is, is that the financial crisis that we experienced was the worst since the Great Depression. We lost about 4 million jobs in the 6 months before I was sworn into office. We lost 750,000 jobs the month I was sworn into office, 600,000 jobs the 2 months after I was sworn in. So before any of my economic policies were put into place, we had already lost most of the 8 million jobs that we ended up losing in this recession.

And my first job was to make sure that the banking system did not completely collapse and to make sure that we didn't dip into a second depression. And we've done that. The economy that was contracting is now growing. We've had 8 straight months of private sector job growth. So we're making some progress.

But the truth is, is that people were having a tough time even before the crisis hit. We had gone—from 2001 to 2009, there was a period in which the average middle class family lost 5 percent of their income—5 percent of their wages—during that period. At the same time, the costs for health care and college tuitions

were skyrocketing. It was the slowest period of job growth since World War II, from 2001 to 2009.

So middle class families were generally having a very difficult time even before the crisis hit. And obviously, the crisis just made things worse. And this is all at a time when we've got increased global competition. I mean, you've got countries like China and India and Brazil that are really moving. They're educating their kids much more aggressively than they ever were. They are exporting much more than they ever were. And so we're having to compete at levels that we didn't have to compete before.

And so part of the reason I ran for President was because I felt it was very important for us to start grappling with some longstanding issues that we've been putting off for way too long.

We had to stop a health care system that was broken from bankrupting families and businesses and the Federal Government, so we initiated health reform so that we could start getting a better bang for our health care dollar.

And it's estimated that we'll end up saving over a trillion dollars because we make the system more efficient over time, even though we're going to be insuring more people. We had to reregulate the financial system so we never have a system where we've got taxpayer bailouts again. And so we passed financial regulatory reform. We had to transform our education system.

And one of the things I'm most proud of, although it hasn't gotten some of the fanfare that some of these other issues have gotten, is we've initiated reforms across the country through a program called Race to the Top where we're encouraging States to reform how they do business, emphasizing more math, emphasizing more science, making sure that we've got the very best teachers in the classroom, making sure that we're focusing on low-performing schools, because it's unacceptable where you've got schools in which a third of the kids or half of the kids drop out, and even the kids who graduate aren't graduating at grade level.

We use to be at the top in terms of math and science performance. Now our kids typically rank around 21st in science and 25th in math. That's just not acceptable.

We used to have the highest proportion of college graduates in the country; now we rank around 12th. And that's going to affect how we can compete long term, so part of what we did was to shift tens of billions of dollars that were going to subsidies to financial services groups in the direct student loan program, give those dollars directly to students, and we've got millions more students who are now getting grants and cheaper student loans.

Now, the other thing that we had to do is we had to confront all these problems—a financial crisis, people losing their jobs, small businesses not getting the financing they need to open or expand their businesses—we had to all do this in the context of a really bad budget.

When Bill Clinton left office, we had a record surplus. We hadn't had a surplus since World War II. And suddenly by the time I took office, we had a $1.3 trillion deficit. And this was a direct result of some policies that thought only about the present and didn't think about the future.

So we had tax cuts, mostly for millionaires and billionaires, in 2001 and 2003 that weren't paid for, and there weren't the cuts to go with it. So that ballooned the deficit. Then we had two wars that weren't paid for. That further ballooned the deficit. We had a prescription drug plan that was put into place that cost about $800 billion. That wasn't paid for. So you add all those things up, by the time I got into office we already had a $1.3 trillion deficit and we had exploded the national debt.

So one of the challenges now that I've got, having stabilized the economy, but we still need it to grow, we still need small businesses to get help, we still have to help people find work, we want to invest in research and development and technology. We've got to do all that, but we've also got to think, how are we going to get our budget under control over the long term.

And I was amused as I was driving in, there were some signs there that said cut spending, which sounds plausible, and I know your Congressman here, I think, has strong ideas about what he says he wants to do. Last week, the Re-publicans put forward what they called a "Pledge to America," which purported to say we're going to cut your taxes and we're also going to control spending and we're going to somehow balance the budget. But when you actually looked at the numbers, it was hard to figure out how they all added up.

Now, I'm not a math teacher. [*Laughter*] But I know a little bit about math. They're proposing about $4 trillion worth of tax cuts. About $700 billion of those tax cuts are for people who typically are millionaires and billionaires and on average would get $100,000 in tax relief, $700 billion that we don't have; we'd have to borrow in order to provide these tax cuts. And 98 percent of Americans wouldn't see any benefit from it.

And keep in mind that because we don't have it, it would actually end up costing more than $700 billion, because we'd end up having— since we're borrowing it, we'd have to pay interest on it.

Now, just to give you some sense of how they are proposing to pay for this, they're recommending a 20-percent cut in education spending. They are proposing essentially that we lower our support to students on student loans who want to go to college and grants for students who want to go to college, which would affect millions of students all across the country. They are proposing to roll back tax cuts that we had put in place during the Recovery Act that give 95 percent of working Americans tax relief.

So when you add it all up, essentially their proposal would drastically expand the deficit instead of shrinking it. Now, what they'll say is, well, we're going to have additional cuts. But they don't specify what those cuts would be. And one of the things I'm here to tell you—and then I want to sort of hear from you in terms of what your priorities are—is, I've got some very smart people working for me in my budget office. But they will tell me that one thing they can't do is cut taxes for the wealthiest Americans by $700 billion, protect Social Security, protect Medicare, protect veterans funding, and balance the budget. They just can't do it. The math doesn't add up.

And so part of the challenge, I think, particularly if we're thinking about the next generation, is making sure, as we move forward over the next couple of years, that we have an honest and serious conversation about how we're going to get control of our budget. That is going to be a big challenge.

And the choice that you make in this election, I think, should be based on facts and making sure that whatever politicians are saying, that they can back it up with some actual figures and numbers that work.

I know that here in Virginia and all across the country, there are a lot of people who are genuinely, legitimately, and sincerely concerned about the deficit and the debt. And no matter how much I say to them, well, this really has to do with problems that we inherited, it's not because of the emergency measures we took last year, their attitude is, okay, but it's still your job to solve it.

And I think that's a legitimate point of view. But if you are genuinely and sincerely concerned about debt and deficits, then you have to understand the other side just is not presenting a serious idea of how to balance our budgets and put us on a stable fiscal footing.

What they're selling is the same thing that they sold back in 2000 and 2001, which is you could slash taxes, including for the wealthiest Americans, and somehow that's not going to affect anything. And that's just not how it works. It's not how it works in your household, right? So it's not going to work for the country either. And we've got to have an honest conversation about it. All right?

So with that—I know it's a little warm in here, but if anybody wants to pull out their fans, feel free. If gentlemen want to take off their jackets, I'm sure nobody will mind. And let's just open it up for questions and comments.

And as I said, I don't—it doesn't have to be a question. You can give me a suggestion. If you've got good ideas, I need to hear them.

And we'll start with this gentleman. Please introduce yourself.

Employee Stock Ownership Plans/Small Businesses/Taxes

Q. Thanks, Mr. President. My name is Tom Roback. I manage a small business. We serve ESOP companies, hundreds of ESOP companies. And I've just found it extraordinary in visiting many of these ESOP companies with the culture that they've developed and the productivity and competitiveness, and it's a good model for keeping jobs here in the U.S.

The President. You want to just explain to everybody what ESOPs are? These are employee-owned businesses. I just want to make sure everybody understands.

Q. Exactly, exactly. And I wanted to just—the ESOP laws that have been in place for over 35 years have allowed employee owners to share a piece of the action of the business while not having to get in their—dig in their own pockets for that, so it's helped them get to retirement, which is tough these days long term.

My main question is just, with your good initiatives here—you're for focusing on small business in the new act—will you consider encouraging or expanding the law to help more small privately held companies look to the ESOP model? Thank you.

The President. I would absolutely be interested in taking a look at it. The idea behind these ESOPs is that if employees have a piece of the action—they're essentially shareholders in these companies—then you are aligning the interests of workers with the interests of the company as a whole.

Now, what that means is, is that when a company has a tough time, workers have to take a hit because they're owners, essentially. On the other hand, when things are going well, they're getting a share of the profits. And so theoretically, at least, it's something that can help grow companies, because the workers feel like they're working for themselves and they're putting more of themselves into their job each and every day.

I think that it's something that can be encouraged. I have not seen specific proposals that are out there legislatively, but I'm sure you can share them with me.

Q. Yes, there actually has been a lot of strong research recently.

The President. Good. So I'll be interested in taking a look at that stuff.

But let me say something more generally about small businesses. As part of the Recovery Act, we actually cut taxes for small businesses eight different ways. And I make mention of that because—and then I just signed a bill this week on Monday, before I went on the road, that further cuts taxes for small businesses, including eliminating capital gains for investments in startup businesses, making sure that small businesses can invest in inventory or in plant and equipment now and be able to take these deductions now so it gives them an incentive to start investing earlier on.

We have provided tax breaks for small companies who are providing health insurance to their employees, because typically it's—small businesses are the hardest folks to be able to provide health insurance because they're not part of a big pool. And what we've said is, let's give them a tax break; they can get up to a third of the premiums that they're paying for their employees as a credit so that it's just cheaper for them to provide health insurance.

So I wanted to point that out because somehow there's a myth out there I think that we have raised taxes on small businesses. If you listened to the other side, you'd be thinking, boy, Obama is just trying to crush small businesses with these high taxes. We've lowered taxes on small businesses over the last 2 years. In fact, we've lowered taxes on just about everybody over these last 2 years. And—but when you look at the polls, there's a decent number of folks who still think that somehow their taxes have gone up instead of gone down.

And that debate is going to be coming to a head now. I mentioned this $700 billion in tax cuts that they want to provide to the top 2 percent. We're in danger of seeing lapse tax breaks that everybody here probably is getting on their paychecks every 2 weeks. A lot of people didn't notice that they were getting a tax break because we did it incrementally, paycheck—it wasn't in one lump sum; it was like each paycheck you had a little bit less taken out in taxes.

That's going to lapse if we don't renew it, and the proposal—the Republicans are proposing to eliminate it.

So this is an example of where we've got to know what the facts are in order to make sure that the broadest base of people are getting the broadest base of help. Okay?

Yes, sir.

Role of Federal Government

Q. President Obama, my name is Dan Ream. I'm a librarian at Virginia Commonwealth University here in Richmond, the State's largest public university.

The President. We love libraries.

Q. We thank you. Libraries love the love. [*Laughter*] VCU, where I work, has benefited tremendously from your stimulus program. In fact, there are countless librarians, faculty, and staff members there who have their jobs today thanks to the stimulus program. So thank you for that. It's very important to us.

The President. Thank you. I appreciate it.

Q. My son, by the way, is a student at Davidson College. He is a swim coach here at the Southampton swim team, and he is in Madrid today. And he said, "This is the most exciting thing that has ever happened on my street, and I'm out of the country." [*Laughter*] "So, Dad and Mom, would you ask my question?"

The President. Okay, go ahead.

Q. May I?

The President. Although I have to say being in Madrid is not that bad. [*Laughter*]

Q. It's not.

The President. I mean, that's a pretty good deal. [*Laughter*]

Q. He loves it. Anyway, this is from Paul Ream, who is probably watching this on TV somewhere in Madrid.

The President. Good.

Q. His question is this: "In this public discussion of the economic crisis and in the Nation's political discourse in general, I feel like Democrats have lost hold of the populist attitude and rhetoric that truly embody the party's foundations.

"Our swim team community here at Southampton provides a wonderful example of that attitude. Like politics, it's a sport that focuses on individual performance. But what leads to success is a team-oriented, sportsmanlike approach. Respect for each other and respect for one's opponents are key to the success. And I think those are important elements of the Democratic Party.

"With that in mind, what are the ways we can change the dialogue to really emphasize this? Doing what's best for the people is not characterized by doing what's best for some individuals at the cost of others, which is the interpretation of some citizens today, especially with regard to the economy. How can we reframe the debate and really highlight the respectful and sportsmanlike nature of policies directed at benefiting the American people as a whole?"

The President. Well, that's a pretty good question.

Q. It's from Paul Ream.

The President. I like that. [*Laughter*] And you read it very well too. So I'm sure he'll——

Q. Thank you. I have my own question too, if we have time.

The President. ——he'll be very happy with your presentation.

Q. Thank you.

The President. Look, I think he makes a terrific point, and I've tried to make this point in most of my speeches when I talk about the economy. Part of what makes America the greatest country on Earth and what has made our economy the envy of the world for the last hundred years is that we combine this incredible sense of individual freedom and entrepreneurship and the profit motive and dynamic capitalism so that if you've got a good idea, if you want to start a whitewater rafting company or you want to open a new restaurant because you've got this great recipe, you can do it. And you don't have to go through a lot of bureaucracy, and you don't have to pay a bribe. And that is the wellspring of our wealth and how well we do.

Now, at the same time, part of what our strength has been is what we do in concert, in common, just like a team. Dwight Eisenhower built the Interstate Highway System. Nobody individually could build a highway system. So we pool our resources together to build the highway system, and that then provides opportunity and a platform for businesses to grow and prosper.

The Internet was a direct result of a investment in research and science, through the Government, that created the initial platforms that evolved into the Internet. And now there are all kinds of Internet companies that are starting, and you've got Facebook, and—a lot of wealth has been generated, a lot of jobs have been created. But those individual initiatives couldn't have happened if we hadn't made that initial investment, through our Government, in the research and development, because there was no sure thing. It wasn't like there was money to be made tooling around with these computers, trying to figure out how to communicate with each other more efficiently.

Clean energy is a good example as we move forward. Right now all of us would benefit if we had a cleaner, more efficient energy policy in this country. But nobody individually has that much incentive to do it. The oil companies, they've got tons of money, but they're making tons of money by selling oil. And the more oil they sell, the better off they're going to be. So they're not making huge investments in solar or wind or biodiesel.

A lot of people, I think, would benefit from retrofitting their homes or their buildings or hospitals. But it turns out that even though they'll recoup their money, they might not be able to afford up front to make the investment without some help. And so they don't do it, which means that we probably use 30 percent more energy because we've got buildings that are poorly insulated or poorly designed. And it would make sense for us to help small businesses and individuals make that investment.

If we gave them some loans on the front end, then all of us would benefit, and individually, each of us would benefit. But the point is, is that Abraham Lincoln, the first Republican President, I think had it right. He basically said, we should never do things for people that they can do for themselves. But government's role is to do what people can't do better by themselves, whether it's our collective defense, whether it's our firefighters, whether it's our libraries, whether it is our infrastructure or investments in research and development.

And I think that that's part of what the choice we're making in this election and over the next several years is going to be: Are we still able to make those decisions together about how to move the country forward? Or are we each going to just be looking out for ourselves? In which case, what's going to happen is, is that if you've got enough money that you an afford to live in a gated community, then you don't have to worry about police. If you can afford to have private schools, then you don't have to worry about public schools.

But over time what happens is, as a group, we're going to get poorer, even though some people do very well. All right?

Education Reform/Financial Regulatory Reform

Q. Thank you.

The President. Thank you. Yes.

Q. Hello, Mr. President. My name is Devin Wilder, and I'm a teacher at Albert Hill Middle.

The President. What do you teach?

Q. I teach civics. I teach eighth graders.

The President. This is a good thing. You'll be able to tell your class tomorrow that you——

Q. Yes. Actually, I have some questions——

The President. Oh, no——

Q. ——that I would love to give to you from my students.

The President. All right. I will try to respond to some of them.

Q. Okay. Especially if you can send a picture and some autographs to them.

The President. Okay. [*Laughter*] All right, sounds good.

Q. I'm from a education family—my mother is a teacher, my husband is a teacher also for the city at Thomas Jefferson High School, and I'm a mother of three. And the main focus has been on the middle class and the poor, but what about working class families? They seem to be on the fringe, not able to get a lot of these incentives and other programs of help. Childcare is a major issue, education for our children; proper nutrition, being able to afford proper food is an issue for working families. What is the Government going to do for that?

And then I also have another question, if I could ask about the education reforms that you're going to do. A lot of my students are concerned about those education reforms, and they would like some explanations about how is an extended day and how is going to school for an extra month going to make them more competitive in the global world.

The President. Well, let me take the second question first, because I want to be clear: I haven't passed a law that everybody has got to go to school for an extra month. I was asked about this on the "Today" show, and I made the observation, which is absolutely true, that most of our competitors, most other advanced countries, have their kids go to school about a month longer every year than we do. The 3-month summer is a direct result of public schools having been started when most of us still lived on farms, and so you took 3 months off because you had to help on the harvest.

But there's nothing written in stone that says we've got to have the organization, the school year the way we have it. There is a—studies show that kids lose something during that 3-month period. Poorer kids lose more during that 3-month period because they may not have as many books at home, supplemental activities. They may not be going to the museum or on field trips during the summer. And so they tend to lose more of what they've learned. And that's part of what contributes probably to the achievement gap and them falling behind.

So I think it's important for States to look at what they're doing and finding ways that potentially kids don't lose ground compared to kids in China or South Korea or other parts of the country.

Now, it's going to cost some money if we decide to make the school year longer because teachers and custodial workers, that means that they're in—they're working even longer than they're already working. And so we'd have to make some choices budgetarily.

Keep in mind, though, that this is why the choice in this election is so important. I'll give you an example. During—just a couple months ago, we had a debate in the House of Representatives. The Democrats decided to—because they were worried about States laying off teachers, decided to close a corporate tax loophole that actually incentivized investment overseas instead of investment here in the United States. So they decided to close one of these loopholes.

And that saved enough money to send several billions of dollars to the States so that they could keep their workforce intact. This is at a time, by the way, where there are States like Hawaii that had gone down to a 4-day-a-week school week because they couldn't afford to pay teachers for the fifth day.

Now, I promise you we can't compete against other countries if our kids are going to school 4 days a week. We can't compete if teachers are being laid off and classrooms get more crowded and teachers are having to dig more into their pockets for basic supplies in their classroom.

But when we had this proposal, we could not get any Republicans to support this position. And they had the usual rhetoric about Obama's trying to kill business and raise taxes, et cetera. No, we're just trying to make sure that we're making investments in the long term for our kids, which will be good for business, because businesses in this country aren't going to succeed if we don't have engineers and scientists developing new products and so forth.

So I don't want to lose the votes of all your kids by saying that they need to be in school another month. [*Laughter*] I do think that we have to have a debate, State by State in local school districts, about making sure what we can do to ensure our kids keep up.

Now, in terms of the issue that you raised about sort of middle class versus poor versus working class, my attitude is that everybody who is working hard, who's meeting their responsibilities, trying to raise a family, trying to send their kids to college, trying to retire with dignity and respect, trying to get health care— those folks—that's what it means to be middle class in this country.

This is who Michelle and I came from. I mean, I was raised by a single mom. I lived most of my formative years in an apartment that probably was smaller than this room right here,

living with my grandparents, and sometimes when my mother was—when I was living with her, it definitely was an apartment smaller than this.

Michelle, her dad worked as a blue-collar worker for the city of Chicago. And he had multiple sclerosis, but he never missed a day of work. He never graduated from college. Her mom never graduated from college. And yet somehow they were able to—both of our families were able to give us the best education in the world, and we grew up to be President and First Lady.

Now, that's what the American Dream is about. So I don't make a distinction between middle class, working class, poor folks who are trying to get into the middle class. As long as you're working hard, trying to meet your responsibilities, trying to better yourself and your family, that's what the American Dream is about.

All the policies that we've put in place have been designed to help those folks. So if you are a working family, whether you're making—your family income is $100,000 a year or $50,000 a year or $30,000 a year, if you've got a kid with a preexisting condition and you can't get health insurance, because of health reform that child is going to be able to get insurance. And if you can't afford it because your boss doesn't offer health insurance, you're going to be able to be part of a big pool and buy the same health insurance that Members of Congress get.

Regardless of where you fall on that income spectrum, if you've got a credit card, then the new financial reform bill says credit card companies can't jack up your interest rates without letting you know. And they can't increase your interest rates on your existing balances. They can't run a bait and switch and say you're on— this is a zero-percent interest credit card, then you get $5,000 on your credit card, and you get a letter saying suddenly interest is 29 percent. Can't do that.

Mortgage brokers can't steer you into interest rates on buying a house that are more expensive than what you could have gotten because they're getting a kickback. A lot of the consumer protections that we put in place, they affect everybody out here.

The student loan programs that we put into place, that impacts families across the board, because, again, whether you're making $100,000 or $50,000 or $30,000, if you're trying to send your kid to college, they're going to probably have to take out some debt. And what we did to take billions of dollars that were going to banks in unjustified subsidies and us saying, no, we're going to give that money directly to young people in the form of more grants or cheaper loans, capping how much they're going to have to repay in college to 10 percent of their income. That helps everybody.

So I think that that—what will make our economy grow is if this beating heart of our economy, the middle class folks who are working hard, pushing to improve their lot in life, if they're given some hands up to help them get to where they want to go, then I think our economy as a whole will do well.

Okay. Yes, sir.

Environment/Alternative Fuel Sources

Q. I'd like to ask you about a local and regional issue: the James River that runs through Richmond here and the Chesapeake Bay into which it goes. The Perrys depend on the James River to make a living with their outfitting company. Your EPA has very thankfully initiated a wonderful effort to finally clean up all the waters that enter the Chesapeake Bay.

However, our State government is resisting playing its part, whereas going ahead with this cleanup would create thousands of private sector jobs as well as the benefits from clean water and better fish. They're saying that we can't afford to do this in this economy, when actually doing it would be the kind of thing that would help the economy and our waters recover. Do you have anything to say about that?

The President. Well, I agree with you, and I'll pass on your suggestions to Mr. McDonnell— [*laughter*]—because—look, the point you make I think is important as sort of a general point, which is for a long time we tended to think of the environment in conflict with the economy, right? The notion was clean air, clean water is

nice to have, but if it comes down to it, it's more important that we have jobs.

The point you're making is that clean air and clean water can improve the economy and create new jobs if we think about it in creative ways. And that's part of the argument that I've been making about clean energy.

Let me give you an example. When I came into office, we were producing about 2 percent of the advanced batteries that are used in hybrid cars and electric cars—2 percent of the market. And we were probably just barely hanging on. Eventually, if you only got 2 percent of the market, you're going to end up with zero percent of the market.

So what we did was we said, as part of the Recovery Act, let's invest in a made-in-America, homegrown battery manufacturing effort. And we now have across the country people working in factories making advanced batteries that are going into American-made cars, because what we also did at the same time was we raised fuel efficiency standards on cars and trucks for the first time in 30 years. We didn't do that, by the way, through legislation. We actually got autoworkers and auto companies and environmentalists and all the stakeholders to agree on raising fuel efficiency standards nationally. So it didn't get a lot of attention, because there wasn't a big ruckus in Washington, we just did it.

And so automakers now want to make more fuel-efficient cars, and we now have the advanced battery manufacturing here in the United States to take advantage of that new market. We estimate that by 2015, we're going to have 40 percent of the advanced battery market.

So you've got a homegrown manufacturing industry here in the United States, putting people to work in good jobs and good wages. But that wouldn't have happened if there wasn't a market for clean cars.

[*At this point, the audio equipment produced feedback.*]

That's one of these guy's—one of those mikes is going off, so I think we're good. [*Laughter*]

But I want everybody to understand there are going to be some times where we do have to make some choices. I mean, coal is a good example, where—coal is a dirty-burning fuel, and mining coal can often be environmentally really destructive, particularly to rivers and waterways. On the other hand, we've got tons of coal. We're the Saudi Arabia of coal.

So what I've said is, well, let's invest in research and development to see if we can burn coal cleanly. And if we have regulations that provide incentives for coal companies to burn coal cleanly and mine coal cleanly, they'll adapt, and they'll start using new technologies, and that will create a more future-oriented growth industry.

But a lot of folks resist it. Their attitude is, well, no, we don't want to change anything. We just want to keep on doing what we've been doing.

Sooner or later, the world passes you by. China, India, Japan, all these countries are all thinking about new ways to find clean energy. And if we're not the ones who get there first in terms of figuring this stuff out, then they're the ones who are going to get the jobs of the future. And I don't want them to get those jobs. I want us to have those jobs right here in the United States.

So yes, sir.

Interest Rates

Q. My name is Bob Duvell. I'm retired.

The President. Here, Bob, why don't you grab a mike, although you've got a good strong voice.

Q. And I had one question for you regarding interest rates. The Federal Government's current policy seems to be to keep interest rates at a historical low level. The impact this has on retired seniors is the loss of income they receive on interest on CDs and IRAs. When do you see this policy changing so rates can get back to more normal levels?

The President. Well, first of all, I just want to make clear the administration doesn't make decisions on interest rates. The Federal Reserve makes decisions on interest rates. And so the—they really are an independent agency. I have to be very careful when I have a conversation with Ben Bernanke, the head of the Federal Re-

serve. I can talk generally about the economy, but I can't tell him, lower or jack up interest rates. So I want to make that clear.

But your general point I think is an important one. Interest rates are at a historic low because that was part of the way to avoid us tipping into a depression. By keeping interest rates very low, that meant that businesses that had seen consumer demand really shrink were still able to service their debt and to keep their doors open. And so it was the right thing to do to keep interest rates low.

You are absolutely right that that does have an adverse impact on savers and particularly seniors on fixed incomes because they're not getting as much of a return on their savings. The flip side of it is, though, is that inflation is also at a historic low. And so in terms of actual purchasing power, inflation is still low enough that savers are not losing a whole lot of money; they're just not seeing sort of the compounded interest expand their nest egg like it once did.

I think that you will see a return to higher, more normal interest rates when the economy gets stronger; you naturally start seeing more inflation than you're currently seeing. And when that happens, that will, I think, change the position of the Federal Reserve Bank. But as I said, this is not—this is one of those areas—the President has got a lot of power, a lot of juice. This is not one area where he's got juice.

Taxes

Q. What about the over-70½ mandatory deduction you have to take from your savings, IRA savings? Last year you changed it; we didn't have to do it.

The President. Yes, we did that temporarily as part of an effort because we understood that people were really going through a tough time and might have to dip into savings. We wanted to make sure they weren't penalized for it.

Q. But we're still doing that.

The President. Yes, the—well, things don't always get through Congress the way you want them. But we're going to be working on this. We're going to have to examine a lot of these issues moving forward as part of how we think about simplifying the Tax Code, making it fairer, and also making sure that folks in fixed incomes aren't harmed in this environment where it's harder and harder to save for retirement. So thank you for the question.

Q. Mr. President, my name is Darius——

The President. Well, hold on a second, though, Darin—just because—I'll get to you, but this gentleman had his hand up first. Or somebody over here did. It was over here.

Bipartisanship/Inclusive Political Process

Q. President Obama, I'm Scott Turner, a small-business owner, and one thing for sure about small-business owner, tremendously busy.

The President. What kind of business you got?

Q. It's an arborist firm, tree care. And get home at night, I feel like now I'm one of the few Americans who doesn't think he can watch a little bit of cable TV and tell everything you know about how to run the economy. [*Laughter*]

I don't have time to watch it. It's over my head. A good percentage of what we talk about here, the economy, I know I'm too busy working to understand how to tell you how to fix the economy.

So what I like to do is elect an official and send him to Washington and have all you smart guys figure that out. Returning to Dan's question that we didn't get all the way through—and a young person can recognize it, and I certainly recognize it trying to build team in small business—what—is there hope for us returning to civility in our discourse to healthy legislative process to something that I can trust, so as I strap on the boots again tomorrow morning, I know you guys got it under control? Because I'm not smart enough to fix it. I'd love to send you guys to Washington and have you do it. And it's hard to have that faith right now.

The President. Well, look, the—first of all, I think you give everybody too much credit when you say everybody in Washington is smart guys. [*Laughter*] I—we might dispute that.

But you're making such a powerful point. I think a lot of people were inspired by our campaign because we tried to maintain a very civil tone throughout the campaign. And part of my agenda was changing Washington, right? I mean, I came into national notice when I made a speech in Boston talking about there aren't red States and blue States, there's the United States of America. I believe that so profoundly.

I will tell you that changing the culture in Washington is very hard, and I've seen it these last 2 years, because I think that folks in Washington tend to think about how to stay in power more than they think about how to solve problems.

Now, if you look at what happened over the course of these last 2 years—and look, I'm sure I made some mistakes—but essentially, what happened was the other side made a calculated decision. They said: "You know what, we really got beat in 2008 bad. The economy is a mess. It's probably going to take us a while to dig our way out of it. We've got two choices. One choice would be to cooperate with the President and work with him to kind of solve these problems, in which case if things don't work, we get to share the blame, and if things do work, he gets all the credit, and he'll stay in power."

So just from a pure political calculation, they said: "We're better off just saying no to everything, blocking everything. If things don't work, then Obama will get all the blame. And if things get a little bit better, we won't be any worse off than we would have been." That, I think, was the political calculation.

Now, I have to give them credit that from just a raw political point of view, it's been a pretty successful strategy, right? Because right now people are frustrated. All the good feeling that we had coming into the campaign is dissipated. Everybody is thinking to themselves, "Well, gosh, you know, we sent Obama up there, we thought the tone would change, folks are arguing just as much as they were before, so we've kind of lost hope, and we're a little discouraged." And that means a lot of the people who were supporting me may stay—are talking about maybe just staying home in the election. And meanwhile, the other side is all ginned up: We can take power back.

I think that the only way this is going to change is if the same folks who supported me in 2008—not just Democrats, but Independents and Republicans who want to see the country move forward—if they don't sit on the sidelines, they don't give up, you don't give up, but you say I'm going to keep on looking for folks who are trying to offer serious solutions to problems. And you know, we don't expect our elected officials to be perfect but we do expect them to be honest and real with us about what we're going to do about education or what we're going to do about energy or what we're going to do about this problem or that problem.

And I've just got to assume that if people more and more insist and demand on that kind of attitude and are willing to punish folks when they go over the top, whether it's on the left or the right, in being not so civil, that eventually politicians adapt because they start saying to themselves, "Well, you know what, this is what voters want."

Now, there's one last aspect of this that makes it tough, and that is, the media has gotten very splintered. So what happens is these cable shows and these talk show hosts, they figure—a lot of them have figured out, the more controversial I can be, if I'm going out there and I'm calling Obama this name or that name or saying he wasn't born in this country or—that will get me attention. I will then write a book, I'll go and sell it, I get—right?

And there are folks on the left who do the same thing, trying to be purposely provocative, saying the meanest, nastiest things you can say about the other side. They get rewarded in the way our media is set up right now.

So part of the challenge is figuring out how to create a space for people saying we're all Americans, and we're just going to try to solve our problems, and we're going to have some differences, because some of these issues are hard—is there a way where those voices get heard, because right now they're not really getting heard.

I was amused—Jon Stewart, the host of "The Daily Show," apparently he is going to host a rally called something like "Americans in Favor of a Return to Sanity" or something like that. And his point was, you know, 70 percent of the people—it doesn't matter what their political affiliation are—70 percent of the folks are just like you, which is they're going about their business, they're working hard every day, they're looking after their families. They don't go around calling people names. They don't make stuff up. They may not be following every single issue, because they just don't have time. But they are just expecting some common sense and some courtesy in how people interact. And having those voices lifted up is really important. So hopefully, since they've got a whole bunch of cameras here, somebody was just listening to you.

Q. We're counting on you, because if you can't do it, I'm not sure who is going to.

The President. Well, I appreciate that.

Q. So my wife and I are counting on you.

The President. Thank you so much. It means a lot. All right, you get—I'm going to have to make this the last question. Go ahead.

National Economy/Consumer Confidence

Q. Okay, lucky me. Mr. President, my name is Darius Johnson. I'm the president of a very small community bank locally. And my question is this. Do you believe that our country, our Nation, is stronger as a result of your leadership, having been elected President? And the reason I ask this question is, I was reading earlier today that the consumer confidence index is down almost to the lowest point this year in the last September reading. And the expectations index is also trending downward. And I wonder if you think our Nation is strong—which I would hope you do—the question is, what is the disconnect between consumers' perception of the Nation, of our economy, and yours?

The President. Right. Well, it's a great question. There is no doubt in my mind that the country is stronger now than it was a year ago. And so the policies we put in place have reversed a contracting economy. It's now growing.

As I said before, we were losing hundreds of thousands of jobs a month; now each month we're adding jobs in the private sector.

Businesses are very profitable, which is why the stock market has actually recovered a lot of its value is because companies are making a profit. But I think that the reason there is a disconnect has to do with a couple of things.

Number one, it's the point that—I'm sorry, what was your name?

Q. Scott.

The President. The point that Scott made. I think people just—it seems like everybody is out there yelling at each other and angry, and so that kind of is disquieting. It makes people feel like the country just is pulling apart as opposed to coming together.

And then that adds to an atmosphere——

[The lights flickered.]

The President. ——oops—remember I talked energy-efficient buildings, we got to— *[laughter].* So I think that's part of it. But obviously, the most important part of it is just that people are still hurting economically. Even though things have gotten modestly better, you've still got millions of people out there who are out of a job.

You've still got hundreds of thousands of folks out there who are losing their homes. I hear from them every day in settings like this. I hear from them because I get letters every night from folks who are asking me, why aren't we seeing faster progress in terms of the economy picking up.

And so, you know, this has been now—this was the longest recession and the deepest recession by far that we've experienced since the Great Depression. Basically, unless you were of age during the Great Depression, folks have never seen anything like this.

So understandably, people are nervous. And I think those two things combine because if you don't have confidence that the country can pull together and you know that the problems are hard to solve and you know that we've got competition from China and Japan, India and Brazil and Europe, then you start thinking, well, maybe we're not going to be the same land of opportunity 20 years from now or 30 years from now as we were. And I think even people who are doing okay right now are anxious about the future of the country.

And I guess my response then to people is to say, look, in our own individual lives each of us go through times where it just seems like we get—it feels like we get some bad breaks or we make some mistakes, something happens in our life where we're kind of in a hole. And the deeper the hole sometimes the harder it is to muster up the energy and the go-get-'em attitude to be able to climb out of it.

But if you persist—at least I've found in my life and I'm sure everybody here has found in their lives—if you persist, if you stay with it, if you have a positive attitude that doesn't ignore problems, but says: "I can solve these problems, as long as I apply myself, and if something doesn't work I don't brood on the fact that it doesn't work; I'm going to try something different. But I'm just going to keep my eye on a better future," then eventually you get out of the hole. You figure it out. And America has always done that. We've been in tough times before, but we've always figured it out. Eventually—this isn't the first time we've had such contentious politics. I mean, shoot, I was—some people may remember when Bill Clinton was President, folks were going nuts, calling him names, and Hillary names, and frankly, when Ronald Reagan was President, the first couple of years, they were—the economy went through a very tough time.

And even though now everybody remembers him as a great communicator, at the time, everybody was saying, "Oh, the country is falling apart." We had inflation and high unemployment. But we got our way—we found our way through it.

And I think we'll find our way through this as well. We're just going to have to be persistent. And the one thing I think everybody has to admit about me, even my detractors, is I'm stubborn. I just—I stay with it. And I'm not going to lose heart about this country because I know what this country has given to me in my own life.

This is the only country in the world where somebody born in my circumstances could stand before you as the President of the United States—or as the President of their country. There's no other country that can provide that kind of opportunity. And if that was true for me, that's going to be true for the next generation. But we're just going to have to keep on pushing.

And being with families like all of yours gives me great confidence in the future.

So thank you very much, everybody. Appreciate it.

NOTE: The President spoke at 4:10 p.m. at the Southampton Recreation Association. In his remarks, he referred to Matthew Perry, president, Southampton Recreation Association, his wife Stephanie, and their children Matthew and Lucy; retired nurse Virginia Shelton of Ashland, VA; Rep. Eric Cantor; and Gov. Robert F. McDonnell of Virginia. He also referred to his mother-in-law Marian Robinson.

Statement on House of Representatives Passage of Legislation To Provide Health Care Services and Compensation for 9/11 Victims
September 29, 2010

We will never forget the searing images of September 11, 2001. And we will never forget the selfless courage demonstrated by the firefighters, police officers, and first-responders who risked their lives to save others. In the face of unspeakable brutality and evil, these brave men and women demonstrated the enduring strength of our values and the American spirit. Many who survived did not emerge from the dust and debris unscathed, facing continuing health problems as a result of their service. The "James Zadroga 9/11 Health and Compensation Act" would ensure that rescue and recovery workers, residents, students, and others suffering from health consequences related to the World Trade Center disaster have access to the medical monitoring and treatment they need. It is a critical step for those who continue to bear the physical scars of those attacks. I applaud the House for its support of this bill and for standing up on behalf of these heroes who served our country in its time of greatest need. I look forward to Congress completing consideration of this legislation so I can sign it into law.

NOTE: The statement referred to H.R. 847.

Statement on Senate Action on Immigration Reform Legislation
September 30, 2010

I was pleased to see that Senator Menendez introduced a bill in the Senate to fix our Nation's broken immigration system. I look forward to reviewing it in detail, and I'm pleased that the bill includes important building blocks laid out in the bipartisan framework presented earlier this year addressing the urgent need for reform. Senator Menendez and others in Congress have shown critical leadership on this issue, which is vital to moving this debate forward. As I told Senator Menendez and other members of the Congressional Hispanic Caucus when we met a couple of weeks ago, we cannot continue to allow partisan politics and divisive rhetoric to dominate and delay action on this critical issue. The American people expect their elected officials from both parties to work together to tackle the greatest challenges confronting our Nation, and that's what fixing the broken immigration system is all about. The status quo is simply unacceptable for both our economy and our security. Comprehensive immigration reform would provide lasting and dedicated resources for our border security, while restoring accountability and responsibility to the broken system. I look forward to working with members of both parties to get this done.

NOTE: The statement referred to S. 3932.

Statement on National Voter Registration Month
September 30, 2010

I join all those observing National Voter Registration Month and renew the call for all qualified citizens to register to vote if they haven't done so already. Many States have early deadlines and registration requirements for those wishing to participate in this fall's elections, and I encourage everyone to get informed and get involved. A healthy, vibrant democracy depends on the full participation of its citizens, and that's something we can all agree should transcend party or ideology. Every qualified citizen not only has the right to vote, but also a greater civic responsibility to exercise that right and play your part in the life of this country.

Remarks at a Democratic National Committee Dinner
September 30, 2010

Thank you. Thank you, everybody. It is great to see all of you. I am not going to give a long speech because I'm going to have a chance to sit at each table and talk to you in a smaller, more intimate setting. But I just want to, first of all, say thank you to John and Linda. I want to thank them, first of all, because they've taken some time off from the resort operation that they're running. [*Laughter*]

Those of you who may be aware that they have this spectacular situation in Italy, every one of my staff have rotated through there except me. [*Laughter*] And I don't know what it takes for me to get an invitation, but I'd appreciate a little break and some Tuscan sun and wine and—[*laughter*]—you know, pasta. [*Laughter*] I could use it. So it's not going to come immediately, but I'm holding out hope.

I am also thankful that John is still talking to me because for about a year and a half he never saw his wife. And Linda just was unbelievable for us, first during the campaign, helping us to navigate through a, at times, challenging press situation, with her extraordinary experience, and then helping to guide us through all the choppy waters that were required to get health care reform passed. So these guys have just been great friends for a very, very long time, as have many people in this room.

I'm just coming off 3 days on the road, and I want to report what's going on outside of Washington, because I think it's a useful corrective to what you may be reading and hearing on a day-to-day basis.

As John indicated, we're going through a very tough time. This is the toughest economy that most of us have experienced in our lifetimes; the toughest economy since World War II, since the Great Depression. And so people are feeling it. There are millions of people who are still out of work and are looking for work every day. There are hundreds of thousands of people who've lost their homes. There are millions of people who've seen their home values decline, their 401(k)s decline, their college savings fund for their kids declined. People haven't seen a lot of wage growth, and they feel anxious about the future.

That's a reality, and that means that this election cycle is going to be tough because of that reality. I always am reminded of what Michelle told me a while back. I had mentioned some poll where we were having some difficulty, and she said, look, let me tell you something. If somebody calls me at 8:00 p.m., right after dinner, and I spent my whole day thinking about getting my kids to school, worrying about whether my job is going to be there next week, my house is $100,000 underwater, and somebody asks me, how are things going in Washington? I promise you, I'm going to say, not very well.

And she's right. I mean, that's people's natural, understandable instinct. Having said all that, what you find when you go on the road is people absolutely understand that—the magnitude of this crisis, but it could have been much worse. They are glad to see that an economy that was shrinking by 6 percent is now growing again. They're glad to see that where we were losing 750,000 jobs the month I was sworn in, that we're now seeing 8 consecutive months of job growth.

They feel as if things have stabilized somewhat. The real question now is less looking backwards than it is looking forward. What they're concerned about predates this crisis. It has to do with a sense that our position in the world has slipped and that if we don't act like adults, get serious and start moving forcefully to deal with our education system so that we're producing more engineers and scientists and skilled workers; if we're not moving forward seriously on an energy policy that frees us from dependence on foreign oil and makes sure that our economy is not vulnerable; if we're not serious about controlling our health care costs both for families and businesses and for the Federal Government; and if we're not serious about making sure that here in Washington whatever money going out is matched by money coming in, if we're not serious about those things, then they're worried.

On the other hand, they genuinely believe, and are rooting for us coming up with a plan that can rally the country together and move us forward. And I think they're—when it comes to me, what they're most concerned about is, is that having come in with so much hope, it seems as if we're still having the same arguments here in Washington that we were having 5 years ago and that we were having 10 years ago and that we were having 15 years ago. And they just understand that we can't afford to have the same arguments over and over again.

And so one of the things that I've tried to say not just to Democrats, but also to Independents and Republicans, is that that hope you were feeling when I came in, there's no reason to lose it because the answers are still within our grasp. We know how to create schools that work for kids. We know what we need to do on the energy front that would put us at the—as a leader in clean energy and would mean that hybrid cars and electric vehicles and advanced battery technology was made here in the United States in-

stead of some other country. We know what we need to do to shore up Social Security.

The problem is not that we don't know how to do it, the question is do we have the will to do it. And all of that depends on whether you, the American people, are willing to stay engaged, understanding that democracy is messy and it's tough, but that if we keep on moving forward and we stay with it, that there's no reason why we can't deliver on the change that so many people believed in back in 2008.

And when people are reminded of that, that this never was going to be easy but when people come together they can make a difference, you can see them get a little more pep in their step.

We had a rally in Madison, Wisconsin, where we had 27,000 people show up. I was amused. One of the press reports was, well, people greet Obama happily, but without the euphoria of 2008. [*Laughter*] And I was there in 2008, and I was—[*laughter*]—and I was there 2 days ago, and I have to say, they seemed equally euphoric. [*Laughter*] They were pretty energized. They were fired up and ready to go.

And so they're hungry to get reengaged. And in these backyard meetings that we've had with families, there are serious questions about, look, what are you going to be able to do to make sure that my son who's graduating from college is going to be able to find a job; or I'm still kind of worried about the health care law, what can we do about that; or a senior citizen asking how are my savings going to be affected by your current economic policies. They're pointed questions. But so many of the questions have to do with we want to continue to believe that the American Dream is alive and well.

And they are not persuaded by the other side. They really aren't. I mean, the polling confirms this. And I forgot to mention how hard Tim Kaine is working as our chairman of the Democratic Party. But they're not persuaded by the other folks' arguments. They haven't gone through complete amnesia here. I mean, they remember that between 2001 and 2009, we had the most sluggish job growth since World War II, and that we took record surpluses to record deficits, and that a rash of deregulation resulted in many of the crises that we've seen over the last several years, and that the average wages of middle class families went down 5 percent during that period.

So it's not as if they are persuaded by the other side. But they do want an affirmative vision from us about how we can move forward.

Now, one last point I'll make. Both myself and Joe Biden, I think, have been recorded as saying to Democrats, you guys got to buck up a little bit. I want to be very clear what I mean here. I think one of the healthy things about the Democratic Party is we've got a big tent, and unlike the other side, if you take a look at our coalition, it is entirely representative of America, regionally, racially—across the board. And that means that sometimes we're going to have some vigorous arguments. Some Blue Dog from Arkansas is not going to believe the same thing as a liberal from Oakland, California. And it means that on any single issue that we've moved forward on, people want to shade it a little bit this way or shade it a little bit that way.

But what I'm reminding folks of is, if you take a look at what we said we were going to do when we were campaigning in 2008, and you now look 2 years later, despite that fact that we're going through the worst economic crisis since the Great Depression, we have fulfilled so many of these promises in a way that is unmatched by just about any Congress and any Democratic administration since at least the 1960s, and maybe before that.

And what that means is—I said this in an interview a while back—part of being a Democrat, I guess, is kind of looking at the glass half empty sometimes and thinking, oh, gosh, we didn't get this, and we didn't get that, and I'm still dissatisfied that that hasn't happened. But you know what, now is the time to remind ourselves of what we have accomplished and to recognize that all those things that remain undone will not get done unless we are just as focused, just as energized, just as excited as we were in 2008 or 2006. And that is going to make the difference in the race.

We already got news back that just that rally in Wisconsin had a significant impact in what's going on in Russ Feingold's campaign and Mayor Barrett's campaign for Governor. What it was, was really just Democrats kind of waking up. They're saying, gosh, we've got a race to run here. And by the way, we should be excited about what we've done. And we've got a serious choice to put before the American people.

Well, if we can duplicate that same kind of energy and motivation and focus, then I'm absolutely confident that we can not only maintain our majorities in the House and the Senate, but we can continue to deliver for middle class Americans out there, and folks who aspire to be in the middle class, who really are the beating heart of our economy and the beating heart of the Democratic Party.

So I am so grateful to all of you for staying committed and staying engaged. I'm going to need all of you to keep it up. And I'm going to need each and every one of you to make sure that you're talking to your friends, your neighbors, your coworkers, your family members to make sure that they're fired up and energized, and that they understand the stakes in this election.

And if you do, and if we get that kind of coalescing around our vision for a brighter future, then I'm absolutely confident that we're going to do well. And I know Tim is too.

So thank you. But don't rest. You'll have time to rest on November 3, okay? [*Laughter*] And hopefully it will be a rest that will be well deserved because we'll take satisfaction in understanding that we're going to be able to keep on moving this country forward.

Thank you very much, everybody.

NOTE: The President spoke at 7:40 p.m. at the residence of John Phillips and Linda Douglass. In his remarks, he referred to Mayor Thomas M. Barrett of Milwaukee, WI. The transcript was released by the Office of the Press Secretary on October 1. Audio was not available for verification of the content of these remarks.

Remarks at a Democratic National Committee Gen44 Summit
September 30, 2010

The President. Hello, DC! Thank you, DC. Thank you so much. I'm fired up! Thank you.

Let me, first of all, thank one of the finest DNC chairmen we've ever had, Tim Kaine. Please give it up for him. Tim Kaine—I want to just point this out, Tim Kaine supported me. He was the first statewide elected official outside of Illinois to endorse my candidacy for President. That's the kind of person—he supported me when nobody could pronounce my name. [*Laughter*] There was nothing in it for him, except he thought it was the right thing to do. And that's the kind of leader that you remember.

I know you heard from David Plouffe, my former campaign manager and great friend of mine. And I understand B.o.B was in the house. I will not do my version of "Airplane." [*Laughter*]

Audience member. We love you!

The President. I love you back.

It is good to see this crowd so fired up. I need you to be fired up. I need you to stay fired up, all the way to November 2. All the way to November 2. Because November 2 is going to say a lot about your future: a lot about your individual futures, but also about the future of our country.

Two years ago, with the help of a lot of you, some of you getting involved in politics for the first time, you defied the Washington conventional wisdom. I mean, you remember. Folks did not think we were going to win; let's face it. Because they didn't know about you. They said, no, you can't overcome the cynicism of our politics. No, you can't overcome the special interests. No, you can't make real progress on the big challenges of our time. They said, no, you can't. What did you say?

Audience members. Yes, we can!

The President. You said, yes, we can.

You proved that the power of everyday people going door to door, neighbor to neighbor, friend to friend, using networks, using the Internet, that that was stronger than the forces of the status quo. And every single one of you is a shareholder in that mission to rebuild our country and reclaim our future.

So I'm back here today just in case you've forgotten what that feels like, to change the country. Because on November 2, we face another test, and the stakes could not be higher.

When I arrived in Washington about 20 months ago, some of you were there. It was really cold. It was a cold day. It was a cold day, but the spirit was warm. And our hope was that we could pull together, Democrats and Republicans and Independents, to confront the worst economic crisis since the Great Depression. What we hoped was that we could get beyond some of the old political divides—red States, blue States—that had prevented us from making progress for so long. And we came into this with that spirit because we understood that we're proud to be Democrats, but we're prouder to be Americans.

And instead, what we confronted when we arrived was just politics, pure and simple, an opposition party that was still stuck in the same failed policies of the past, whose leaders in Congress were determined from the start to just let us deal with the mess that they had done so much to create.

Their calculation was simple and cynical. They knew that it was going to take a long time to solve the economic challenges we were facing. It was the worst economic crisis since the Great Depression. They understood that because it was going to take a long time, people would be frustrated. They'd feel anxious. They'd be fearful. And so what the other side calculated was, you know, if we just sit on the sidelines, we let Obama and the Democrats in Congress deal with everything, then we can do well in the polls. That was their theory.

And that's what they did for the last 20 months. They've said no to just about every idea I've proposed, every policy I've proposed, even ideas they've traditionally agreed with. [*Laughter*] I'm not exaggerating. I mean, we had situations where they would sponsor bills, I'd say okay, and then they'd say, oh, well, if you're okay with it, we must be against it. [*Laughter*] Happened a bunch of times. That's true.

And because they understood that folks were going to be anxious and fearful, they've been tapping into that fear. And now the pundits are saying that the base of the Republican Party is mobilized and energized and excited, and that all of us who worked so hard in 2008, well, maybe we're not as energized, maybe we're not as engaged.

Audience members. No!

The President. That's what they're saying. I'm just the messenger here. [*Laughter*] They say that there is an enthusiasm gap, and that the same Republicans and the same policies that left our economy in a shambles and the middle class struggling year after year, that those folks might all ride back into power. That's the conventional wisdom in Washington.

Audience members. Boo!

The President. We cannot let that happen. We cannot sit this out. We can't let this country fall backwards. The stakes are too high. We have to move this country forward for you and your future. So there better not be an enthusiasm gap, people. Not now. Not this time.

The other side would like you to believe that this election is a referendum on me or on the economy, on anything but them. They are counting on amnesia. [*Laughter*] They're counting that folks don't remember them. But make no mistake: This election is a choice. And the choice could not be clearer.

For the last decade, the Republicans in Washington subscribed to a very simple philosophy: You cut taxes, mostly for millionaires and billionaires. You cut regulations for special interests, whether it's oil companies or banks or insurance companies. You cut back on investments in education and clean energy and research and technology. And basically, the idea was that if you had blind faith in the market, if you let corporations play by their own rules, if you let everybody else fend for themselves, including young people, including the next generation, then somehow America would grow and prosper. That was the theory.

Now, look, here's what we know. The philosophy failed. We tested it. We tried it. We tried it for 8 years; it didn't work. When they were in charge, job growth was slower than it's been in any decade since World War II. Between 2001 and 2009, middle class incomes fell by 5 percent. This is when they were in charge. The cost of everything from health care to college tuition just kept on going up. A free-for-all on Wall Street led to the very crisis we're still digging out of today. And by the way, we went from record surpluses to record deficits.

These are the folks who say that they care about wasteful spending. They took us from a surplus when a Democrat was in charge to big deficits when they were in charge. That's the truth. Those are the facts.

They're counting on amnesia. They think you all forgot. So I've had two main jobs since I was President: to rescue this economy from crisis, and then to rebuild it stronger than it was before, so that you look forward to the 21st century as being the American century, just like the 20th century was the American century.

And over the last 20 months, we've made progress on both these fronts. There's no longer a possibility of a second depression. The economy is growing again. Private sector jobs we've created for 8 consecutive months. There are about 3 million Americans who would not be working today if it weren't for the economic plan we put in place.

We passed Wall Street reform to make sure a crisis like this never happens again. No more taxpayer-funded bailouts. We set up reforms that will stop mortgage lenders from taking advantage of homeowners. We reformed credit card practices so they won't hit you up with hidden fees or jack up your rates without reason.

We've started investing again in American research, American technology, homegrown American clean energy, because I don't want solar panels or wind turbines or electric cars built in Europe or built in Asia. I want them built right here in the United States of America, because we're all about making it in America.

To help middle class families get ahead, we passed a tax cut for 95 percent of working families in this country. We passed 16 different tax cuts for America's small-business owners. We passed health care reform to make sure insurance companies won't deny you coverage and you can stay on your parents' coverage until you're 26 years old.

We finally fixed up the student loan system so that tens of billions of dollars in taxpayer subsidies that were going to banks now go where it should to help you get an education. That's what we're about.

And along the way, we kept a promise that I made on the day I announced my candidacy. We have removed all combat troops from Iraq, and we are ending that war.

So that's the progress that we've made. That's a testimony to you. That's the progress that we worked so hard for in 2008. But we're not done. We're not close to being finished. The hole we're climbing out of is a deep one—deeper than the last three recessions combined. We lost 8 million jobs. Almost all of them—all those jobs—were lost before my economic policies had any chance to take effect. We lost 4 million jobs before I was sworn in, in this recession; 750,000 the month I was being sworn in.

And on top of that, the middle class has been struggling for more than a decade. So there are millions of families out there who are still treading water, millions still barely able to make their mortgage payments or pay the bills. I hear about these folks every day because they write me letters or they tell me when I'm on the road. And people are frustrated, they're anxious, they're scared about the future.

And they have a right to be impatient about the pace of change. I'm impatient. But I also know this: Now is not the time to quit. Now is not the time to give up. We've been through worse as a nation. We've come out stronger, from war to depression to the great struggles for equal rights and civil rights. It took time to free the slaves. It took time for women to get the vote. It took time for workers to get the right to organize.

But if we stay on focus, if we stay on course, then ultimately, we will make progress. It takes time. Progress takes sacrifice. Progress takes faith. But progress comes. And it will come for your generation, for this generation, if we work for it and fight for it and if we believe in it. That's something I believe.

The biggest mistake we could make is to let impatience or frustration lead to apathy and indifference, because that guarantees the other side wins. And if they do win, they will spend the next 2 years fighting for the very same policies that led us into this recession in the first place, the same policies that left middle class families behind for more than a decade, the same policies you fought hard to change in 2008.

Just look at the agenda of the leaders of the other party. They unveiled it last week, called it their "Pledge to America."

Audience members. Boo!

The President. That's what they called it. Now, their pledge was actually written with the help of a former lobbyist for AIG and Exxon-Mobil. So that gives you how much——

Audience members. Boo!

The President. ——a sense of how much change they intend.

The centerpiece of their pledge is a $700 billion tax cut. This is their main economic policy, their main jobs program, their main focus, a $700 billion tax cut for the wealthy that 98 percent of Americans will never see a dime of. I'd get a tax break under their plan. [*Laughter*] That would be good for me, but not for most of you all.

Now, keep in mind, we don't have $700 billion, so we'd have to borrow this from China or from some other country. And then we would be giving a tax cut worth an average of $100,000 to every millionaire and billionaire in America.

Audience members. Boo!

The President. Wait, wait, no, hold on, it gets worse. [*Laughter*]

When you ask them, well, where are you going to get this $700 billion? Do you have some magic beans somewhere? Are you going to— [*laughter*]—I mean, what's—how is this going to come about? They don't have an answer. Now, they will say, well, we're going to cut spending. So you say, okay, what are you going to cut? And then what they say is, well, we'll cut education by 20 percent. We'll eliminate 200,000 children from early childhood education programs like Head Start.

Audience members. Boo!

The President. We'll cut financial aid for 8 million college students.

Audience members. No!

The President. At a time when the education of our country's citizens is probably the best predictor of that country's economic success, they think it's more important to give another tax break to folks who are on the Forbes 400 list.

Now, I want to ask my Republican friends: Do you think China is cutting back on education?

Audience members. No!

The President. Do you think South Korea is making it harder for its citizens to get a college education?

Audience members. No!

The President. These countries aren't playing for second place. And guess what, the United States doesn't play for second place. We play for first place.

And I will not allow politicians in Washington to put your future at risk for another tax cut we can't afford and don't need. That's the choice in this election. That's why you need to be involved. Your future is at stake.

In fact, here's another thing they want to do to pay for this tax cut for the wealthy. They want to roll back what's remaining of our Recovery Act that gave a tax break to working and middle class families, 110 million people out there. So they want to roll back your tax cut to give their buddies a tax cut.

Look, we have a different idea than they do about what the next 2 years should look like. And it's an idea rooted in our belief about how this country was built. Government doesn't have all the answers to our problems. Government doesn't have the main role in creating jobs or prosperity. Government should be lean and efficient. Look, we're—we've proposed a 3-year spending freeze. We've set up a bipartisan fiscal commission to deal with our deficit.

But the first Republican President, my favorite Republican, Abraham Lincoln, here's what he said about government. Here's what he said about government. He said, "I believe that government should do for the people what they cannot do better for themselves." I believe in a country that rewards hard work and responsibility, a country where we look after one another, a country that says, I am my brother's keeper, I am my sister's keeper. I'm going to give a hand up. I'm going to join hands with folks and try to lift all of us up so we all have a better future, not just some, but all of us, every child in America. That's what I believe.

I believe in an America that gave my grandfather the chance to go to college because of the GI bill, and that gave my grandparents a chance to buy a house because of the Federal Housing Authority, an America that gave their children and grandchildren the chance to get the best education in the world through scholarships and student loans. That's the America I know. And that's the choice in this election.

Instead of giving tax breaks to millionaires and billionaires, we want to make permanent tax cuts for middle class Americans, because you deserve a break. Instead of cutting education and student aid, we want to make permanent our new college tax credit, so that you can get $10,000 worth of tuition relief—everybody who's going to 4 years of college. We want to make clear that in good times or in bad, no young American should have to sacrifice the dream of a college education just because they can't afford it. That's what we believe. That's the choice in this election.

If the other side takes control of Congress, they'll spend the next 2 years to preserve tax breaks for companies that create jobs and profits overseas. We want to shut down those subsidies. We want to give those tax breaks to companies that are creating jobs right here in the United States of America—that's what we believe in—to American manufacturers, to clean energy companies, to entrepreneurs who are researching and investing and making it here in the United States of America. That's what we believe. That's who we want to help.

If the other side takes back Congress, they've promised to give back power to the same special interests we've been fighting for the last 20 months. We can't let them do that. We can't go back to the days when insurance companies can drop your coverage just when you get sick, or credit card companies can jack up your rates whenever they feel like it. We can't go back to a system that results in taxpayer-funded bailouts. We can't allow special interests to take the reins again. We have to keep fighting. There is too much at stake right now.

So listen, Generation44. It comes down to this: Many of the folks in the other party, they're running to go back to the exact same things they were doing before.

I've used this analogy before; some of you may have heard it. Imagine they were driving a car—[*laughter*]—and they drove it into the ditch. And I put on my boots, and the Democrats put on their boots, Tim Kaine put on his boots. We all went down into the ditch. We were expecting the Republicans to come help. It's muddy down there and dusty. And they drove down there. In fact, we pulled some of them out of the car. [*Laughter*] Now they're standing up on the road, sipping a Slurpee, watching us. [*Laughter*]

And we're pushing and we're shoving and we're sweating, and there are bugs flying around. [*Laughter*] And we look up and say, "How about coming down and helping us out?" They say: "No, that's all right. But you all should push harder. You're not pushing the right way." [*Laughter*]

So we just keep pushing. Finally, we get the car up on level ground. It's a little dented. It needs a tuneup, needs a wash. [*Laughter*] Fender's all bent up. But it's pointing in the right direction. We're ready to move forward. Suddenly, we get a tap on the shoulder, and you look back, and it's the Republicans. [*Laughter*] And we say, "Well, what do you want now?" "We want the keys back," they say.

Audience members. Boo!

The President. But guess what, you can't have the keys back. You don't know how to drive. We don't want to end up back in the ditch. We can't afford to go back in the ditch. I don't want to have to push again. [*Laughter*] I want us to move forward.

I hope all of you notice that when you want to go forward in your car, what do you do?

Audience members. "D"!

The President. You put it in "D." When you want to go backwards, what do you do?

Audience members. "R"!

The President. You put it in "R." There's no coincidence there. We got to put it in "D." We got to go forward. We got to go forward, not backwards. We've got to go backwards—we got to go forwards. We can't go backwards.

At the end of the day, whether they get the keys back or not will depend on you. Because, look, look, the other side is excited. And thanks to a recent Supreme Court decision called *Citizens United*——

Audience members. Boo!

The President. ——they're being helped along this year by special interest groups. They are allowed to spend unlimited amounts of money on attack ads. And they don't have to disclose who's behind these ads. They have these innocuous names like Americans for Prosperity or Americans for Apple Pie—[*laughter*]—Moms for Motherhood. And you look back, and it's like "The Wizard of Oz." You look behind the curtain and there's some Republican operative, and it's insurance companies or the banks or all the folks that were fighting change.

I mean, why do you think they're giving up all this money? I mean, it's possible that maybe they're doing it because they want good government.

Audience members. No!

The President. But I got to admit, I'm kind of skeptical. [*Laughter*]

So that's why we've got to work even harder in this election. That's why we've got to fight their millions of dollars with millions of voices who are ready to finish what we started in 2008. Because if everybody who showed up in 2008 shows up in 2010, then we will win.

All of you are being tested. All of you are being tested. I know times are tough. I know that we're a long way from that cold day when we had a couple million people out on the Mall, and everybody felt excitement. But you know what? That was the easy part. You know, you had the "Hope" poster. [*Laughter*] You had Bono and Beyonce singing at the concert. You know, that was the celebration. But I told you guys when we were campaigning that change was going to take time, that power concedes nothing without a fight, that it was always going to be hard.

And by the way, you did not elect me to do what was easy. You did not elect me to go out there and put my finger out to the wind and figure out how to keep myself in office. You elected me to do what is right. You elected me to do what is true. And you got involved because you believe that this was the moment to do what is right and take on the challenges that had been ignored for too long.

So now is not the time to quit. Now is not the time to lose heart. That involvement can't end in 2008. That election was not just about putting me in the White House. It was about building a movement for change that went beyond one campaign or any one candidate. It was about remembering that here in the United States, our destiny is not written for us, it is written by us. We have the power to shape our future. Our future is in our hands.

And that's what's being tested right now: whether we've got the courage to keep going forward in the face of difficulty, in the face of uncertainty. And if you are willing to work hard and knock on doors and make phone calls and call up your friends and neighbors and coworkers and family, I promise you, we will not stop until we have finally made the American Dream true for every American out here.

God bless you, and God bless the United States of America.

NOTE: The President spoke at 9:12 p.m. at DAR Constitution Hall. In his remarks, he referred to musicians Bobby Ray "B.o.B" Simmons, Beyonce G. Knowles, and Paul D. "Bono" Hewson; and former lobbyist Brian Wild. The transcript was released by the Office of the Press Secretary on October 1.

Remarks on the Resignation of White House Chief of Staff Rahm I. Emanuel and the Appointment of Peter M. Rouse as Interim White House Chief of Staff
October 1, 2010

Good morning, everybody, and welcome to the least suspenseful announcement of all time. [*Laughter*] As almost all of you have reported— [*laughter*]—my Chief of Staff, Rahm Emanuel, has informed me that he will be leaving his post today to explore other opportunities. [*Laughter*]

This is a bittersweet day here at the White House. On the one hand, we are all very excited for Rahm as he takes on a new challenge for which he is extraordinarily well qualified. But we're also losing an incomparable leader of our staff and one who we are going to miss very much.

When I first started assembling this administration, I knew we were about to face some of the most difficult years this country has seen in generations. The challenges were big and the margin for error was small: two wars, an economy on the brinks of collapse, and a set of tough choices about issues that we had put off for decades, choices about health care and energy and education, how to rebuild a middle class that had been struggling for far too long.

And I knew that I needed somebody at my side who I could count on, day and night, to help get the job done. In my mind, there was no candidate for the job of Chief of Staff who would meet the bill as well as Rahm Emanuel. And that's why I told him that he had no choice in the matter. He was not allowed to say no. It wasn't just Rahm's broad array of experiences in Congress and in the White House, in politics and in business. It was also the fact that he just brings an unmatched level of energy and enthusiasm and commitment to every single thing that he does.

This was a great sacrifice for Rahm, Amy, and the family to move out here. Rahm gave up one of the most powerful positions on Capitol Hill to do this. And in the last 20 months, Rahm has exceeded all of my expectations. It's fair to say that we could not have accomplished what we've accomplished without Rahm's leadership, from preventing a second depression to passing historic health care and financial reform legislation to restoring America's leadership in the world.

So for nearly 2 years, I've begun my workday with Rahm. I've ended my workday with Rahm. Much to Amy's chagrin, I've intruded on his life at almost any hour of the day, any day of the week, with just enormous challenges. His advice has always been candid; his opinions have always been insightful; his commitment to his job has always been heartfelt, born of a passionate desire to move this country forward and lift up the lives of the middle class and people who are struggling to get there.

He has been a great friend of mine and will continue to be a great friend of mine. He has been a selfless public servant. He has been an outstanding Chief of Staff. I will miss him dearly, as will members of my staff and Cabinet with whom he's worked so closely and so well.

Now, I don't think anybody would disagree that Rahm is one of a kind. I am very fortunate to be able to hand the baton to my wise, skillful, and longtime counselor, Pete Rouse. Pete, who has more than 30 years of experience in public service, will serve as Interim Chief of Staff as we enter the next phase of our administration.

Many of you remember Pete as the top aide to then Senator—Senate Majority Leader Tom Daschle. Pete was affectionately known as the 101st senator. From the moment I became a U.S. Senator, he's been one of my closest and most essential advisers. He was my chief of staff in the Senate. He helped orchestrate and advise my Presidential campaign. He has served as one of my senior advisers here at the White House.

And in that role, he's taken on a series of management and legislative challenges with his customary clarity and common purpose. There is a saying around the White House: Let's let Pete fix it. [*Laughter*] And he does. Pete's known as a skillful problemsolver, and the good

news for him is that we have plenty of problems to solve. [*Laughter*]

So I am extraordinarily grateful to him that he's agreed to serve as our Interim Chief of Staff, and I look forward very much to working with him in this new role.

Obviously, these two gentlemen have slightly different styles. [*Laughter*] I mentioned, for example—this was a couple of years ago—I pointed out that Rahm when he was a kid had lost part of his finger in an accident, and it was his middle finger, so it rendered him mute for a while. [*Laughter*] Pete has never seen a microphone or a TV camera that he likes. [*Laughter*]

And yet there's something in common here. You know, as President of the United States you get both the credit and the blame for what happens around here. And the blame is usually deserved, or at least I happily accept it because that comes with the territory. But the credit really goes to the men and women who work in this building.

It goes to people like Rahm and Pete and the hundreds of others who are here today, who sometimes get some attention and sometimes don't, but these are folks who give up incredibly lucrative opportunities, sacrifice enormously, and their families sacrifice enormously. They come here every day to do the best possible job on behalf of the American people, and oftentimes, they don't get the thanks that they deserve.

As your President and as a fellow American, I want to take this moment to say to all the staff, all the Cabinet members, how proud I am of you and how grateful I am of you, and how particularly proud and grateful I am to my outgoing Chief of Staff, Rahm Emanuel.

NOTE: The President spoke at 11:22 a.m. in the East Room at the White House. The transcript released by the Office of the Press Secretary also included the remarks of White House Chief of Staff Emanuel.

Statement on California's Health Benefits Exchange Legislation
October 1, 2010

I want to congratulate Governor Schwarzenegger, Speaker Perez, President Pro Tempore Steinberg, and the members of the California State Legislature for passing and signing the bipartisan California Health Benefits Exchange legislation. They are taking an important early step toward reforming our private insurance marketplace so that California families and small businesses will have high-quality and affordable health insurance choices in 2014, when reform is fully implemented. I look forward to continuing to work with and provide resources and support for all States as we work toward creating a new competitive health insurance system that lowers costs for consumers and businesses, increases quality, and reduces our deficits.

Statement on the 50th Anniversary of the Founding of Cyprus
October 1, 2010

The people of the United States join the people of the Republic of Cyprus in celebrating its 50 years of independence today. This year also marks the 50th anniversary of bilateral relations between our countries, which are united by ties of kinship and common ideals. Our partnership is strengthened by the long history of friendship between our peoples and the many contributions Americans of Cypriot ancestry have made to our Nation. We look forward to deepening our relationship and strengthening cooperation in our many areas of mutual interest.

On this occasion, we recognize not just this history, but also the hopes for future security and prosperity. We applaud the determined efforts to achieve a comprehensive Cyprus settlement and support the reunification of the island as a bizonal, bicommunal federation. The United States is confident that a resolution meeting the aspirations of both communities is attainable.

We congratulate the people of the Republic of Cyprus on this historic anniversary.

Statement on Thad W. Allen's Service as Deepwater Horizon Oil Spill Incident Commander
October 1, 2010

I am profoundly grateful to Admiral Thad Allen for his years of dedicated service to America and particularly his outstanding leadership of the BP oil spill response effort. At a time when he could have enjoyed a well-deserved retirement from the United States Coast Guard, Admiral Allen stepped up to the plate and served his country when his skills and experience were urgently needed. This unprecedented response effort simply could not have succeeded without Admiral Allen at the helm, and the Nation owes him a debt of gratitude. As we continue to help the people of the Gulf Coast return to their lives and livelihoods, my administration's work will continue to benefit from Admiral Allen's selfless service and dedicated leadership. I wish him well in all of his future endeavors.

NOTE: The Office of the Press Secretary also released a Spanish language version of this statement.

The President's Weekly Address
October 2, 2010

Over the past 20 months, we've been fighting not just to create more jobs today, but to rebuild our economy on a stronger foundation. Our future as a nation depends on making sure that the jobs and industries of the 21st century take root here in America. And there is perhaps no industry with more potential to create jobs now and growth in the coming years than clean energy.

For decades, we've talked about the importance of ending our dependence on foreign oil and pursuing new kinds of energy, like wind and solar power. But for just as long, progress had been prevented at every turn by the special interests and their allies in Washington.

So year after year, our dependence on foreign oil grew. Families have been held hostage to spikes in gas prices. Good manufacturing jobs have gone overseas. And we've seen companies produce new energy technologies and high-skilled jobs not in America, but in countries like China, India, and Germany.

That's why it was essential, for our economy, our security, and our planet, that we finally tackle this challenge. That's why, since we took office, my administration has made an historic commitment to promote clean energy technology. This will mean hundreds of thousands of new American jobs by 2012: jobs for contractors to install energy-saving windows and insulation; jobs for factory workers to build high-tech vehicle batteries, electric cars, and hybrid trucks; jobs for engineers and construction crews to create wind farms and solar plants that are going to double the renewable energy we can generate in this country. These are jobs building the future.

For example, I want share with you one new development made possible by the clean energy incentives we have launched. This month, in the Mojave Desert, a company called BrightSource plans to break ground on a revolutionary new type of solar power plant. It's going to put about a thousand people to work building a state-of-the-art facility. And when it's complete, it will turn sunlight into the energy that will power up to 140,000 homes, the largest such plant in the world. Not in China, not in India, but in California.

With projects like this one and others across this country, we are staking our claim to continued leadership in the new global economy. And we're putting Americans to work producing clean, homegrown American energy that will help lower our reliance on foreign oil and protect our planet for future generations.

Now, there are some in Washington who want to shut them down. In fact, in the pledge they recently released, the Republican leadership is promising to scrap all the incentives for clean energy projects, including those currently underway, even with all the jobs and potential that they hold.

This doesn't make sense for our economy. It doesn't make sense for Americans who are looking for jobs. And it doesn't make sense for our future. To go backwards and scrap these plans means handing the competitive edge to China and other nations. It means that we'll grow even more dependent on foreign oil. And at a time of economic hardship, it means foregoing jobs we desperately need. In fact, shutting down just this one project would cost about a thousand jobs.

That's what's at stake in this debate. We can go back to the failed energy policies that profited the oil companies but weakened our country. We can go back to the days when promising industries got set up overseas. Or we can go after new jobs in growing industries. And we can spur innovation and help make our economy more competitive. We know the choice that's right for America. We need to do what we've always done: put our ingenuity and can-do spirit to work to fight for a brighter future.

Thanks.

NOTE: The address was recorded at approximately 2:30 p.m. on October 1 in the Diplomatic Reception Room at the White House for broadcast on October 2. The transcript was made available by the Office of the Press

Secretary on October 1, but was embargoed for release until 6 a.m. on October 2. The Office of the Press Secretary also released a Spanish language transcript of this address.

Statement on the 20th Anniversary of the Reunification of East and West Germany
October 2, 2010

On Sunday, October 3, the people of the United States join with the people of the Federal Republic of Germany in celebrating the Day of German Unity and the 20th anniversary of the unification of East and West Germany. This was an historic achievement, as Germans peacefully reunited and advanced our shared vision of a Europe, whole and free, anchored in the Euro-Atlantic institutions of NATO and the European Union. The United States commemorates today that spirit and the many accomplishments of Germany, one of our closest allies and greatest friends. We pay tribute to the countless contributions Germans have made to our own history and society. We honor the courage and conviction of the German people that brought down the Berlin Wall, ending decades of painful and artificial separation. It unleashed a spirit of hope and joy and opened the door to unprecedented freedom throughout the European Continent and around the world. The American people are proud of our role in defending a free Berlin and in supporting the German people in their quest for human dignity. We remain proud of our partnership with our German allies to advance freedom, prosperity, and stability around the world. We congratulate the people of Germany on this national day, and we express our gratitude for our vital friendship.

Letter to Congressional Leaders Transmitting a Report Related to Afghanistan and Pakistan
September 30, 2010

Dear _____:

In response to the requirement of section 1117 of the Supplemental Appropriations Act, 2009 (Public Law 111–32, the "Act"), and in order to keep the Congress fully informed, I am providing the attached report related to Afghanistan and Pakistan. This is the second report submitted under section 1117 of the Act and follows my March 2010 submission.

As I wrote in March, my Administration completed a thorough policy review last November, and I announced a new approach at West Point on December 1, 2009. As you are aware, I named and the Senate approved General David Petraeus to lead our military efforts in Afghanistan. Beyond that change, we are continuing to implement the policy as described in December and do not believe further adjustments are required at this time. Consistent with the Act and given the time necessary to accumulate data, the attached report covers the period ending June 30, 2010. To the extent possible, the report provides an update on our assessment since that date.

As the Congress continues its deliberations on the way ahead in Afghanistan and Pakistan, I want to continue to underscore our Nation's interests in the successful implementation of this policy.

Sincerely,

BARACK OBAMA

NOTE: Identical letters were sent to Vice President Joseph R. Biden, Jr., President of the Senate; Senate Majority Leader Harry M. Reid; Senate Minority Leader A. Mitchell McConnell; Daniel K. Inouye, chairman, and W. Thad Cochran, vice chairman, Senate Committee on Appropriations; Carl Levin, chairman, and John S. McCain III, ranking member, Senate Committee on Armed Services; John F. Kerry, chairman, and Richard G. Lugar, ranking member, Senate Committee on Foreign Relations; Joseph I. Lieberman, chairman, and Susan M. Collins, ranking member, Senate Committee on Homeland Security and Governmental Affairs; Patrick J. Leahy, chairman, and Jefferson B. Sessions III, ranking member, Senate Committee on the Judiciary; Diane Feinstein, chairman, and Christopher S. "Kit" Bond, vice chairman, Senate Select Committee on Intelligence; Speaker of the House of Representatives Nancy Pelosi; House Majority Leader Steny H. Hoyer; House Republican Leader John A. Boehner; David R. Obey, chairman, and Jerry Lewis, ranking member, House Committee on Appro-

priations; Isaac N. "Ike" Skelton IV, chairman, and Howard P. "Buck" McKeon, ranking member, House Committee on Armed Services; Howard L. Berman, chairman, and Ileana Ros-Lehtinen, ranking member, House Committee on Foreign Affairs; Bennie G. Thompson, chairman, and Peter T. King, ranking member, House Committee on Homeland Security; John Conyers, Jr., chairman, Lamar S. Smith, ranking member, House Committee on the Judiciary; and Silvestre Reyes, chairman, and Peter Hoekstra, ranking member, House Permanent Select Committee on Intelligence. This letter was released by the Office of the Press Secretary on October 4.

Remarks in a Discussion With the President's Economic Recovery Advisory Board and Business Leaders
October 4, 2010

The President. Have a seat, everybody. Good afternoon. Before we begin today's meeting of my economic advisory board, I wanted to say a few words about one of the topics that we'll be discussing, and something that's one of our most important economic issues of our time: the skills and education of our workforce, because every business leader in this room knows that the single most important predictor of America's success in the 21st century is how well our workers can compete with workers all around the world.

All of our education institutions, from our preschools to our universities, have a critical role to play here. But one of our most undervalued assets as a nation is our network of community colleges. These colleges don't just serve as a gateway to good jobs for millions of middle class Americans, community colleges also serve as a pool of talent from which businesses can draw trained, skilled workers. Unfortunately, because of the burden the recession has placed on State and local budgets, community colleges have been forced to cap enrollments and scrap courses. And even in the best of times, they receive far less funding than 4-year colleges and universities.

Not only is that not right, I think it's not smart. Not at a time when so many Americans are still looking for work. And not at a time when so many other nations are trying to outeducate us today so they can outcompete us tomorrow. We need to be doing more, not less, to equip our workers with the skills and training they need in the 21st century. It's an economic imperative.

And so I've said that by the year 2020, I want to see an additional 5 million community college degrees and certificates in America. To reach this goal, we're making an unprecedented investment in our community colleges, upgrading them, modernizing them, and challenging these schools to pursue innovative, research-oriented approaches to education. And I've asked Dr. Jill Biden, a community college educator for more than 17 years, who's with us here today, to help promote community colleges around the country and lead the first-ever White House Summit on Community Colleges, which will be taking place tomorrow. And I've asked this economic advisory board to reach out to employers across the country and come up with new ways for businesses, community colleges, and other job training providers to work together.

The results of their effort is an initiative called Skills for America's Future, which we'll be talking about today. And I want to thank Penny Pritzker and, I believe, Anna Burger and perhaps some other folks around this table for putting in enormous amounts of time on this initiative.

The idea here is simple: We want to make it easier to connect students looking for jobs with businesses looking to hire. We want to help community colleges and employers create programs that match curricula in the classroom with the needs of the boardrooms.

We've already seen cases where this can work. Cisco, for example, has been working directly with community colleges to prepare students and workers for jobs ranging from work in broadband to health IT. And all over the country, we know that the most successful community colleges are those that partner with the private sector. So Skills for America's Future would help build on these success stories by connecting more employers, schools, and other job training providers and helping them share knowledge about what practices work best.

The goal is to ensure that every State in the country has at least one strong partnership between a growing industry and a community college. And already, companies from UTC to Accenture to the Gap have announced their support for this initiative, as well as business leaders like my friend Penny Pritzker and Aspen Institute's Walter Isaacson.

I hope other business leaders will follow suit, and I'm also setting up a task force to work directly with the business community on this effort.

This is one of those ideas that just makes sense. Investing in the skills and education of our workers and connecting them with potential employers is something that we should all be able to agree upon, whether we're Republicans or Democrats, business leaders or labor leaders.

But it can only happen if we maintain our commitment to education. And so let me just make one last point before we start a broader discussion. I realize that we're facing an unten-

able fiscal situation. There was a $1.3 trillion deficit staring at me when I took office, and although the economic crisis and the steps we took to stop the freefall temporarily added to our fiscal challenges, it's clear that we're going to have to get serious about the deficit.

And that's why I've proposed a 3-year freeze on nonsecurity discretionary spending. That's why I've launched a bipartisan deficit reduction commission, which will be reporting in a few months.

What I won't do is cut back on investments like education that are directly related to our long-term economic performance. Now is not the time to sacrifice our competitive edge in the global economy. And that's why I disagree so strongly with the proposal from some on the other side of the aisle to cut education by 20 percent in next year's budget. It's a cut that would eliminate 200,000 children from Head Start programs, would reduce financial aid for 8 million college students. It would leave community colleges without the resources they need to meet the goals that we've talked about today. And that just doesn't make sense to me.

So I'm happy to have a debate about this issue in the coming months, but one thing I know is that this country will be stronger if all of our children get a world-class education. That means, by the way, not just money; it also means reform. And I'm glad to see Arne Duncan sitting here today, who's done as much to promote significant reform across the board than just about any Education Secretary in recent memory.

Our businesses will be more successful if they can find skilled, trained workers here in America. Our future will be more secure if anybody who's willing to work hard is able to achieve their dream of getting a college education. And those are priorities that we all share. Those are investments that can benefit the entire Nation. And that's what we need to focus on right now: what will grow our economy, fuel our businesses, rebuild our middle class, and keep the American Dream alive for the 21st century.

So I look forward to working with all of you toward that common goal, and now let's get down to the business of this meeting. I think they're going to remove this big thing here, and I'm going to be able to sit down, and we'll have a good conversation.

So—all right? Is somebody going to break this down? And I'll use this time to come around and say hello to everybody.

[*At this point, the President greeted participants while the podium was removed. The discussion then continued, as follows.*]

The President. Well, let's dive in. My understanding is that—and you tell me, Mr. Chairman, but I think that you are going to open up and introduce the subject, and then we're going to hear from Penny and Anna, both of whom worked very diligently on the Skills for America's Future.

Chairman Paul A. Volcker. Well, let me say first of all, we appreciate your presence and welcome your Secretaries and advisers here, Secretary——

The President. We got a bunch of big cheeses around here. [*Laughter*]

Chairman Volcker. ——Geithner and Duncan and Locke. I tell you, we ought to have some impact on something. And we have a feeling that we've made some contributions in the past. I might even mention regulatory reform, infrastructure bank, which you've just been talking about, and weatherization, Home Star; we had this nice program of tax review, which we arrived at no conclusion, but rather demonstrated the problems in the tax system.

But anyway, today is on, as you know, Skills for America. You've already introduced it. Penny was the driver, so far as we were concerned. We approved the program and its specifics a few—an hour or so ago. So Penny is—the floor is yours.

[*Penny S. Pritzker, chairman and founder, Pritzker Realty Group, made brief remarks, concluding as follows.*]

Ms. Pritzker. The goals that we've set out for Skills for America's Future are several. First is to create a certification for best-in-class partnerships that develop career pathway and training programs. The second is to recruit addition-al private sector and labor leaders to build a national network of high-impact partnerships at community colleges. Basically, we want to scale the program. We also want to provide a national voice for the effectiveness of these partnerships and therefore to convene stakeholders to share best practices.

Our fourth objective is to work with the interagency task force to align workforce programs funded by the Department of Labor and the Department of Education with market demands to help the task force identify and develop stackable credentials in high-demand industries and to increase the use of technology to improve training.

Finally, we want to ensure that every State has at least one high-impact partnership between industry and a community college, and our hope is that every State will have more than one.

Mr. President, this entire effort supports your goal for an additional 5 million community college degrees and certificates by 2020. And the initiative—we're very excited—the initiative will be part of what's called the Economic Opportunities Program at the Aspen Institute, led by an executive director and a core team, but the work will be nationwide. And our goal is that Skills for America's Future will launch a national movement to strengthen America's workforce, to optimize job training programs, and ultimately job placement.

So we ask you, Mr. President, as you said earlier, to endorse Skills for America's Future. And we just can't begin soon enough. We believe putting the resources into training and development of workers, as you believe, is one of the best investments that we can make in our country. So thank you.

The President. Well, the—thank you, Penny. Anna, do you want to chime in, because I know you worked on this. And then I actually—I know traditionally, sometimes people feel a little constrained in these conversations, but I'm going to make sure that I ask a couple questions. I just want some top lines on where we think we can have the most impact most quickly on this. But go ahead, Anna.

[*Anna Burger, secretary-treasurer, Service Employees International Union, made brief remarks, concluding as follows.*]

Ms. Burger. We have the opportunities through the work that we've done through Home Star and really thinking about how we can use the training centers that the laborers and others have across this country to bring people out of the community and retrofit our communities. At the same time, move them through the economy and give them greater skills so they can be building engineers and take on greater responsibilities as well.

And we heard from manufacturers about all the possibilities that we have in terms of turning our economy around and being a manufacturing base again if we have the workers who have the skills that we need. And we saw collaboration in a way that I had not seen it before. And we think that this opportunity, this initiative, gives us a way of being able to have a real public-private partnership, where workers and employers can be at the table, where we can actually bring our resources together and think about how we get from where we are today to the 21st century as quickly as possible.

So I was honored to be able to be part of this, and I think that this initiative that we all voted on today, that we hope that we can all embrace, can make a difference for working people today and in the future.

The President. I'm very encouraged, and I fully endorse it. I'm looking forward to being behind it 100 percent. I am interested—and maybe folks like Jim Skinner or others who are already doing this kind of work, and you guys may have already gone over this—but I'd be interested just in figuring out, when we look at the best practices, Penny, what two or three elements stand out, so that if we're planning to scale up, what are some indicators that this is the kind of workforce training that's going to work; this is the kind that's a waste of money and time that we have to revamp. Is it primarily businesses having spoken to the community colleges ahead of time and designed—helped them design it so that they know what skills are needed? Is a lot of it simply a matter of remedi-

ation, in which case we've got to do more work K–12 to make sure that folks are up to speed? What—and obviously, this will vary industry by industry, but I don't know if either Jim or Glenn or somebody who are already doing this, whether you guys have any thoughts on this, or Penny, based on all the conversations you had.

McDonald's Corporation President and Chief Executive Officer Jim Skinner. Well, I'd be happy to speak up. The selfish viewpoint of McDonald's, of course, around talent management leadership development, because we're a growing company, is making sure we have the skill sets in our workforce that are capable of delivering on our strategies.

Now, that has an enormous impact on America, because if you look at the work that we're doing, which is centrally focused on English Under the Arches, it's not about our people being able to speak English, it's about them being able to communicate more effectively, be more competitive in the workforce, and be associated with community colleges so that they can further their education. And we're going to expand that by 30 sites and another thousand managers. We've impacted a thousand or plus managers already.

And the opportunity for them then to further their education—Roger, you asked earlier the question about the connection to 4-year colleges—this gives them the opportunity to get credit in community colleges. We're willing to give our intellectual property to the community colleges and put these programs to work. And they're all audited and supported by community college professors. And it's 110 hours, 22 weeks, and it already is showing a dividend, certainly for us in the workforce. And not all these people stay with McDonald's their entire working life. They go somewhere else. And so I think we're contributing to the growth of these individuals for the workforce beyond what they might be doing today at McDonald's. And that's how we're connected with the current program, and we do a lot more, as you know, around talent management and leadership development.

The President. Good. Glenn, you want to——

Gap Inc. Chairman and Chief Executive Officer Glenn K. Murphy. A little different than

Jim's. I'd say the investment we're making is really focused on leadership. And if you look at Jim's business and our business, it's not uncommon that we have 26-, 27-year-old men and women who are running $5, $6 million businesses and they have 70, 80 employees. So we've really tried to work with the community colleges. We're going to be making investments in these seven cities.

And part of that is job shadowing, having them spend quality time with our managers. Of our workforce, we have 125,000 people of the business actually work in the stores. Everything happens in the stores. People like me have ceremonial jobs in offices, and we do what we do, but the reality is, we deal with millions of customers every single day inside our stores, and that comes down to phenomenal leadership.

And the community colleges can only do so much. I think they understand it, and I think that we've been working through high schools to get people through a program we have in New York and Chicago to get them ready to work in our stores. But the real angle on the community college is how do they get the leadership they need to feel confident that they can actually move forward in the business, deal with people, deal with difficult situations, lead, and get the pride that comes with providing great leadership.

So at the Gap, our angle is really, in the seven-city test we're going to do—which I was saying earlier to Penny, and Penny obviously has a lot of passion around this issue—is to build it out to many more cities over the next couple years and really get deep with these community students, these men and young women, future store managers of our business, and give them the one skill that ultimately will separate them from being successful in our industry, which is how to lead.

The President. Penny, do you want to add anything?

Ms. Pritzker. Well, I think that one of our objectives, Mr. President, is—through this effort—is to do exactly what you've asked us, which is to better understand what makes a successful partnership so that we can be replicating successful partnerships and sharing that information more efficiently. It's ad hoc at this point right now. So those are the kinds of efforts that we'll undertake.

The President. Good. Robert, you have some thoughts about sort of unemployment generally and how that connects with worker training, potential skills mismatches that are out there right now. You want to share some thoughts in terms of just the data that you've been looking at?

[Robert Wolf, chairman and chief executive officer, UBS Group Americas, made brief remarks, concluding as follows.]

Mr. Wolf. Now to the second point. If you look at the hardest hit States across factors such as unemployment, mortgage foreclosures, and industry sector job losses, you will see a direct correlation.

For example, Nevada, Florida, Michigan, and California rank in the top five States for both unemployment and the share of mortgages underwater. These four States have also lost a disproportionate amount of jobs in construction or manufacturing or both, way above the national levels. These two industries, construction and manufacturing, have lost the most jobs during the downturn. Construction's around 20 percent, and manufacturing's around 15 percent.

Mr. President, the PERAB wants you to know that this reinforces the need to ramp up two of your key initiatives, infrastructure spending and Home Star. It's critical that in this changing trend that for us to create new jobs, these are the two key initiatives that we need to continue.

Now, I've been asked to pass to John Doerr, who'll discuss in a little more detail the Home Star program.

The President. John.

[John Doerr, partner, Kleimer Perkins Caufield & Byers, made brief remarks, concluding as follows.]

Mr. Doerr. But I think it's of relevance today because the—one of the two tracks involves training workers to upgrade their skills and to create a new industry in America, which would be a professional home retrofit industry, and it's just not very often you get the chance, with a small Federal program, to kick-start what I estimate is a $30 to $40 billion new American industry whose jobs are never going to be outsourced.

So I know your administration is working very hard to push this forward. That's our status, and perhaps it could be part of an oil spill bill or some other action before the Congress adjourns.

The President. As you know, I've been sold on this for a long time. When we announced our desire to move aggressively for this, we went over to Home Depot, and what was striking was not only the enthusiasm, obviously, of a big national company like Home Depot, but talking to the—I met a young man who had been unemployed for 16 months, was retrained over the course of 2 to 3 months to lay down insulation, had proven to be just a terrific employee. He was working for a small contractor who had seen his business collapse after the housing bubble burst and now was seeing a significant pickup in his work around this notion.

So this can have a terrific impact at retail level among small businesses and among young people, who can be trained fairly rapidly to take on this work and to do a terrific job. So we're going to push hard. And obviously, it also cut our Nation's electricity bill, which we're all concerned about for energy and environmental reasons as well. This is going to be a top priority.

Jeff, do you want to talk a little bit about how you see this from a—for a company that operates internationally? And obviously, you and I have spoken a lot about how we can boost exports. One of my main goals is boosting exports. We're going to need a good workforce to do it.

General Electric Company Chairman and Chief Executive Officer Jeffrey R. Immelt. Mr. President, the exports markets remain strong. I was in Asia the last couple of weeks, and again, the economy has remained very strong. I think the work that Secretary Locke and State and USTR is really being felt, so I want to say thanks for that. Our exports continue to grow, as I know Jim's do and other—UTC and others. So we very much are supportive of the export initiative.

Our work is really around really recruiting high-tech manufacturing resources that help us make jet engines and gas turbines. The community colleges provide a very good asset that we work with labor in our communities to train people. Typically, we design a 2-year course with the community colleges and actually hire the people so they have on-the-job training; they come to work at GE, they get training in the afternoon, at night. And by the end of that 2-year time period, they can do precision machining and the other types of high-tech work that I think we want to have in this country.

The last thing I would say is that well-trained, this workforce remains the most competitive in the world. We can drive quality, cost, speed that is second to none. And we have big faith that that can be done here with the right level of education. And the community colleges are incredibly flexible to work with us on designing our own curriculum, which I think is a real asset as well.

The President. I think this last point is really important. I've never spoken to a community college president who would not happily redesign just about any program to meet the needs of an employer who says, I've got a thousand folks that I'm willing to hire if they get the right training. And obviously, at the Federal level, this is an area where we've got to exhibit maximum flexibility.

So where our resources go from the Department of Education or from Department of Labor, we are willing to modify any bureaucratic tangles to make sure that that training matches up with jobs as quickly as possible.

Jim, you got—you guys are also selling a lot of stuff. I'm glad to see it.

[*James W. Owens, chairman and chief executive officer, Caterpillar, Inc., made brief remarks, concluding as follows.*]

Mr. Owens. So there are a lot of skilled people ready to go to work that don't have an opportunity. There's clearly a lack of demand in this area. And I think we have a deficit in terms of investment in this country in the infrastructure we need to help us compete in the world market in the future.

So doing more of this on an emergency basis, with the extreme unemployment levels that we have, I think will help our economy and better position it to compete in the world market a decade or two ahead. And the welfare of our citizenry is really a function of our ability to compete in global markets. And we need to be really consciously thinking about that now. We need a different kind of recovery this time. It can't be retail-driven so much as it's got to be investment and really global competitiveness, export-oriented to give us the kind of sustainable recovery we're looking for.

So let's—I know you've made some proposals on infrastructure. Anything we can do to help you move those things forward——

The President. Thank you.

Mr. Owens. ——we'd be delighted.

The President. Rich, I know that obviously you're hearing some of this—what Jim said—from your own membership. Folks in the trades right now who were doing well when the housing market was booming have been devastated over the last couple of years, and so I'm assuming that ideas like infrastructure are ones that would garner strong support from your members.

[*Richard L. Trumka, president, AFL–CIO, made brief remarks, concluding as follows.*]

Mr. Trumka. And the last point is, we think we need to rebalance our economy in order to succeed globally, because if the United States is going to be a high-wage, high-performance, export-led economy, it needs to do three things that the other successful wealthy industrialized exporting countries have done. First, invest much more in education and lifelong training, which is what we're recommending that you do today; second, continue to invest in modern infrastructure, as Jim Owens has discussed earlier, including transportation, communications, and clean energy for the 21st century; and the third is to support labor law reforms that will allow workers the freedom to choose a union without fear of reprisal, because in a cutting-edge economy, unions are an essential partner for fast-paced innovative business. And successful high-wage export economies around the world have empowered workers, not treated them like costs to be cut.

So, Mr. President, we really applaud you for all the efforts you've made to, first, save the economy, and then turn it around and start to create jobs and build a foundation where the economy can grow and the jobs that we need can be created. And all of us look forward to working with you in that endeavor.

The President. Thank you. All my economic team—Tim, Larry, now Austan as the head of the CEA, my Cabinet Secretaries at Commerce and Education, Labor—we've spend a big chunk of each week, and have for the last 2 years, trying to optimize the Nation's economic performance and the recovery in light of a couple of things that have already been mentioned. Obviously, the severity of the downturn: Historically, financial crises bring about recessions that are deeper and longer lasting than the normal business-cycle recessions. There is a sense on the part of consumers that a—that they have to start saving more and cutting back on their debt levels, and that means that the prospect of a consumer-driven V-shaped recovery is less likely.

And we're in a fiscal environment in which we were already in debt, which means that some of the traditional tools that we have are more difficult to apply. We essentially have to apply the accelerator and the brakes at the same time.

But two things that I think might be worth focusing on in the remainder of our time would be, one, the issue of—that's already been raised—the issue of aggregate demand. Are there ways that, in a cost-effective fashion, we can boost aggregate demand? And the second thing we should talk about is uncertainty, because one of the things that we do hear—obviously, this has been prominent in the business press—is the notion that, well, companies are now making a profit again, they're sitting on a lot of cash, but they're unwilling to put that cash to work investing because they're concerned about uncertainty, whether it's legislative, health care, financial regulatory reform, or taxes and the outlook there.

So I'd be interested in hearing some thoughts from the group on both those items. Martin, I will start with you and see if there are some strategies for boosting aggregate demand that would garner your support, knowing that you are obviously concerned about our long-term fiscal outlook.

[*Martin S. Feldstein, president emeritus, National Bureau of Economics Research, made brief remarks, concluding as follows.*]

Mr. Feldstein. And the third thing deals with the tax rates. As you know, I think that the current tax rates should be continued for 2 years for everybody, but with no legislative commitment after that. I think the 2-year extension would help to keep demand alive at a time when the economy is weak, and the notion that it would not continue after that would take some 10—some $2 trillion off the size of the national debt at the end of the decade. And that would give a boost to confidence that the administration is really focusing on bringing down the out-year fiscal deficit.

So I think all three of those can help to move in the right direction, and they do so without increasing the fiscal deficit.

The President. Obviously—we may not have time to pursue it today—if you've got some specific ideas on the housing front I think we should hear them, and I'll make sure that our team follows up. The small business—it does sound like you've got something worked out that—with some specificity. I'd be interested in seeing how it might fit with some of the work we're already doing to help get small businesses loans.

The tax debate's a long one. [*Laughter*] I mean, I think the interesting question would be whether you felt the same way if you knew that there was—if you extended all the tax cuts for 2 years, that you couldn't hold the floodgates back and you'd then be extending them in perpetuity, whether you'd feel the same way.

[*Mr. Feldstein made further remarks.*]

The President. Bill, do you have some thoughts on this issue of either aggregate demand or uncertainty—or both?

[*William H. Donaldson, former chairman, Securities and Exchange Commission, made brief remarks, concluding as follows.*]

Mr. Donaldson. I subscribe to all that's been said here before in terms of the amalgamation and working together with community colleges and so forth and so on. But that's not going to happen overnight. And so what I would suggest with—is that your administration, and particularly you, step forward with a statement that you're not going to, at this time, increase taxes for anybody, and relieve that uncertainty.

That isn't to say that you're not going to do something about taxes—you and the Congress—but you're going to delay that. And I think the spark that would come from that—you're going to delay that, and then weave it into an overall tax reform, but not until you provide that spark to get us off this dead center.

And I think that prolonged arguments in the Congress about this after people come back is going to be counterproductive to this issue of uncertainty. I think that that will heighten it. And I think you have within your power and the power of this administration to put a pin into that uncertainty with a view toward putting the whole tax problem together in a more thought through, complete package.

The President. Let me just address this because both you and Martin raised this. I mean, it's interesting, sort of the focus is on uncertainty with respect to tax policy. Keep in mind that my administration's already been very unequivocal in saying that we will not change taxes at all for 98 percent of Americans, which you'd think would provide some level of certainty; that with respect to aggregate demand, I don't know any economist—including, I think, Martin—who would argue that we are more likely to get a bump in aggregate demand from $700 billion of borrowed money going to people like those of us around this table, who I suspect if we want a flat-screen TV can afford one right now and are going out and buying one.

If we were going to spend $700 billion, it seems that we'd be wiser having that $700 billion go to folks who would spend that money right away, if we were going to boost aggregate demand. And the consequences of extending the upper-income tax cuts, based on what we've heard fairly explicitly in the political environment, is that you do that now, you're going to do it forever. There's not going to be, necessarily, a deal that says—as Martin, I think—an entirely respectable position is to say, extend them all for 2 years, and then they go away. I mean, that's an intellectually consistent position. But that's not really the position that is being promoted up on Capitol Hill.

And so the question is, if I can achieve certainty for 98 percent of the people affected by the Tax Code, and there's an argument about the 2 percent, primarily because there's also great uncertainty about our deficits and how we're going to pay for those over the long term, why wouldn't I go ahead and promote certainty on the bulk of these taxes and also in that way preserve some flexibility to do something about a deficit, which everybody says is out of control and that we're going to have to do something with immediately?

I will allow Martin to respond, only because I named him in my comment. And then I'm going to bring in the big guns; I'm going to have Laura come in. [*Laughter*] So go ahead. Go ahead.

[*Mr. Feldstein made further remarks, concluding as follows.*]

Mr. Feldstein. As we've talked during the PERAB discussion earlier, before you joined us, there's this concern about the business community's attitude about the administration. And it's not just the business community, it's high-income individuals, entrepreneurs, and others. And so the increase in the tax on those individuals is a signal that the administration——

The President. They have to pay slightly higher taxes. [*Laughter*]

Mr. Feldstein. ——that they're going to have to pay higher taxes——

The President. That's what—that's the signal. [*Laughter*]

Mr. Feldstein. ——and it may be even more going forward.

The President. Right. I understand. I mean——

Mr. Feldstein. So it's more than just the mechanical—whether they can afford another flat-screen TV, but how they think about their business life and economic life going forward.

The President. I understand your point. And we can't belabor this. I just think it's a very interesting discussion, because essentially what the argument comes down to is that the psychology of those of us—and I'm in this category—those of us who are wealthy and make a lot of decisions that determine whether investments are made or not—that our psychology is sufficiently important; that even if we don't need a tax cut, we should give them a tax cut, we should give us a tax cut in order to induce us to play ball, because otherwise we're going to take the ball and go home.

And I understand the argument, and it may be true, but I think that you might understand how folks who have, as you pointed out, seen their home go underwater by $100,000 or have lost their jobs or are having trouble making ends meet, and they're thinking, boy, I could use tax relief right now, they might feel like they're being held hostage here; and that they also know that down the road, we're going to have to make decisions about spending cuts to offset whatever tax breaks or expenditures we put out there and that they, in the weaker position, are going to be ones who are really hurting.

And so this is something that we're going to have to wrestle with as a society, particularly given, Martin, that the group that you're talking about that you said psychologically might need a tax cut are the folks who disproportionately have been benefiting over the last two or three decades from all the growth in productivity so that they have a larger share—we have a larger share—of income and wealth than we have at any time since, what, the 1920s. You probably know the statistics better than I do.

So, Laura, do you want to—let me actually get some economic help here. [*Laughter*]

[*Laura D'Andrea Tyson, dean, Haas School of Business, University of California at Berkeley, made brief remarks, concluding as follows.*]

Ms. Tyson. So I would urge you to think about leverage, where a dollar of fiscal spending—and this is spending money, primarily, or targeted tax relief—can leverage a lot of private money. And of course, what we're talking about, how we started the program today, is exactly that. We're talking about partnership where the Government isn't putting in many resources at all; it's putting in some, but you mobilize the private sector.

So that's—aggregate demand is the issue. We have limited fiscal tools, but I think if we focus on infrastructure, you focus on education, you focus on R&D, alternative energy, places where the private sector really wants to be with you, you'll get a lot of leverage and you'll get some jobs.

The President. I'm going to let—I'd like to hear Paul chime in. And then, Mark, maybe you can address another source of uncertainty that's at least been expressed, and that's regulatory uncertainty. And then I think we can wrap up. So——

Chairman Volcker. I'm going to demonstrate that the chairman of this committee faces an unruly membership—[*laughter*]—has their own mind. But I want to show you that my psychology will not be affected—[*laughter*]—by turning to the tax rate which you expect that are in existing law. And given the deficit we have—I'm just repeating the arguments—if you're looking for the priorities of where to provide some stimulus, the most unlikely place to apply stimulus would be for those that already have so much of the wealth of the country that has been accumulated over two decades, when the people under $250,000 have had no increase in real income during this period of time.

And it seems to me the argument—whatever the precise number is—is very strong. In fact, I don't understand the opposite argument. But that's beside the point, maybe.

The President. All right. Mark?

[*Mark T. Gallogly, founder and managing partner, Centerbridge Partners, L.P., made brief remarks, concluding as follows.*]

Mr. Gallogly. On regulation for a second, one suggestion that I've heard, I didn't come up with—another fellow mentioned to me—is that if you look at the aggregate economy and you say, for a variety of reasons, this administration's had to deal with health care and energy and education and financial—reregulation of all four of these, and that by definition, when you reregulate whole sectors of the economy, in this case, four huge sectors of the economy, you do create uncertainty, particularly when the rules need to then be rethought, that if it's—could you possibly think about this in the context of a PAYGO, where for every incremental regulation you're putting in place, you're looking at the last few decades of regulation that are already in place, and you're taking something off the table?

A practical example of that today, I think, is Secretary Geithner must be dealing with the whole issue of mortgages and how you regulate mortgages on a go-forward basis, and there are multiple constituencies within that, including, we decided for a variety of reasons not to consolidate regulatory bodies in the United States. And each of—several of them have their mandate for how they want mortgages to be regulated. Well, is that a good idea?

You're going to ultimately have at least two, possibly three major forms of mortgage opportunity or mortgage forms or mortgage regulation in the U.S. And it seems that if you couldn't get rid of—because for whatever reason, politically, it wasn't the right thing to do—these multiple agencies, if the objective is to provide clarity to the consumer and to the financial institutions of how a mortgage is done, then maybe you could come up with one mortgage—one way to approach that, as opposed to three separate ones, which is probably where it's going today.

So whether the concept of PAYGO could completely apply or not, if you were to provide a clarity to the administration that it's not just added regulation, there's something else that has to come off the table, I think that would go a long way to—or at least part way—to dealing with some of Bill and Marty's comments.

The President. Well, I want to pick up on this because I think, Mark, you did a masterful summary of some of the challenges we've faced.

The reforms that we saw—let's just take the financial sector—I think most of us would agree that the rules that had been in place weren't working. If they had been working, then we wouldn't have found ourselves in the mess that we were in.

By definition, if you are reworking the rules for a financial sector that had grown to 30 percent of our economy, then that's going to be disruptive, and that's challenging. I think you are absolutely right that having taken a series of steps that were necessary, it's important now that there is a period of healing and consolidation and implementation that is less disruptive.

And I also think that part of that process involves going through what's already on the books to see are there areas that have outlived their usefulness, that no longer serve a function, particularly if you've got a new set of rules in place that are going more directly to current economic arrangements. And so OIRA, the agency that's charged with looking through rules—I mean, part of what we've been in discussions with them about is, how do we take old rules off the books, not just add new rules on? And that's something that we want to move forward very aggressively on.

In fact, when the Business Roundtable came to us with a list of things that they felt were adding uncertainty, I mean, I will tell you, some of the things they had on the list, which were equal-pay-for-equal-work laws, our attitude was, you know, feel certain that I think women should be paid as much as men—[*laughter*]—and you should just take that to the bank. That's something that I think is the right thing to do.

There were other areas where they had some legitimate concerns: that you had contradictory regulations that were working at odds with each other and really at this point didn't make sense. And what we're trying to do is go through very systematically to see where we can eliminate unnecessary redtape, unnecessary bureaucracy, regulations that have outlived their usefulness.

And what we're also trying to do is make sure that in the implementation of the new rules that have been put in place, that there's a collaborative process so that people have input and have—can get some confidence that these aren't just being put together willy-nilly.

I will tell you that there are some examples—the one you just raised, for example, if we've got too many forums that are regulating mortgages—where we fought pretty hard to try to streamline it. It's—it was tough. There are a whole host of jurisdictional and political issues that come up. And we'll continue to try to work on that front.

But I think your general point, that you can't just add new laws without taking away some that don't make sense, is important.

I also want to pick up on the point Laura made about taxes. We'll have to have a longer conversation about why we think businesses choose to invest or don't invest; where the sources of uncertainty are. I've said publicly, and Tim and I and Larry and Austan and others have talked extensively both in private and publicly, we would be very interested in finding ways to lower the corporate tax rate so that companies that are operating overseas are—can do so effectively and aren't put at a competitive disadvantage. We'd like to do so and figure out a way to do it that's revenue-neutral because, as you pointed out, just as some of Martin's prescriptions might in some cases add uncertainty and so we end up having contradictory imperatives, the same's true on tax policy.

Look, I'd be the most popular President on Earth if I could just eliminate all taxes, except then people want to pay for stuff and also want to make sure that we're closing our deficit and make sure that Social Security and Medicare are there for future generations and make sure that our kids are learning and make sure that we have good roads so that we can drive to the Gap or McDonald's and spend our money. And that means we're going to have to make some choices.

But I do want to say to this group—and I know that there was a subgroup that already worked on this and it was somewhat inclusive, but I'd like to continue to drive forward—if there are ideas whereby we can lower corporate tax rates in a way that does not massively add to our deficit but instead revolves around closing loopholes, much in the way the last major tax overhaul in '86 was able to square the circle, that is something that we would be very interested in, we think could eliminate uncertainty, might reduce each of your bills for accounting and legal services, and could be a win-win for everybody. And that's an area that we'd like to collaborate on.

So, Mr. Chairman, anything you want to close with?

Chairman Volcker. Well, just on this thought of uncertainty, there are two things on my list that I give priority to. One is the corporate tax situation, which is a mess. And the other is getting those trade agreements—those little trade agreements through, which disturb people when, obviously, protectionist measures are rising. And I think both of those agreements are in our interests. They're small, they're minor, but they give a signal, an important signal right now.

The President. I agree. And Korea is not so minor, especially when the EU and Canada have already wrapped up trade agreements with Korea.

Chairman Volcker. So it's more important to do it, yes.

The President. Yes. So—see, this was a fun conversation. It went a little off-script, which is good. [*Laughter*] I liked it. I enjoyed it.

Thank you very much, everybody. And I'm looking forward to—I like the fact, by the way, that our Cabinet members were able to join us. I think this is a format that will work better for future meetings. Thank you.

NOTE: The President spoke at 2:10 p.m. in the State Dining Room at the White House. In his remarks, he referred to Walter Isaacson, president and chief executive officer, Aspen Institute; and Austan D. Goolsbee, Chair, Council of Economic Advisers. Mr. Skinner referred to Advisory Board member Roger W. Ferguson, Jr., president and chief executive officer, TIAA–CREF.

Remarks at the White House Summit on Community Colleges
October 5, 2010

Thank you very much. Everybody please have a seat. Thank you so much.

I want to acknowledge some of the folks who are here who are making an incredible contribution to this effort. First of all, our Secretary of Education, Arne Duncan, is here. Our Secretary of Labor, Hilda Solis, is here. Someone who cares deeply about our veterans and the education that they receive, our chairman of the Joint Chiefs of Staff, Admiral Mike Mullen, and his wife Ms. Mullen, are here. Representative Brett Guthrie, Republican of Kentucky, is in the house and has been doing great work on this. And obviously, I am thrilled to not only see Jill Biden here, but also Albert Ojeda, who introduced Jill Biden, because I think the story he tells is representative of so many incredible stories all across the country.

I'm so grateful for Jill being willing to lead today's summit, first of all because she has to spend time putting up with Joe. [*Laughter*] And

that's a big enough task. Then to take this one on too on behalf of the administration is extraordinarily significant. I do not think she's doing it for the administration. She's doing it because of the passion she has for community colleges.

Jill has devoted her life to education. As she said, she's been a teacher for nearly 3 decades, although you can't tell it by looking at her— [*laughter*]—a community college professor for 17 years. I want it on the record Jill is not playing hooky today. The only reason she's here is because her college president gave her permission to miss class. [*Laughter*] And this morning, between appearing on the "Today" show, receiving briefings from her staff, and hosting the summit, she was actually grading papers in her White House office. [*Laughter*]

So I think it's clear why I asked Jill to travel the country visiting community colleges, because, as she knows personally, these colleges are the unsung heroes of America's education system. They may not get the credit they deserve, they may not get the same resources as other schools, but they provide a gateway to millions of Americans to good jobs and a better life.

These are places where young people can continue their education without taking on a lot of debt. These are places where workers can gain new skills to move up in their careers. These are places where anyone with a desire to learn and to grow can take a chance on a brighter future for themselves and their families, whether that's a single mom or a returning soldier or an aspiring entrepreneur.

And community colleges aren't just the key to the future of their students. They're also one of the keys to the future of our country. We are in a global competition to lead in the growth industries of the 21st century. And that leadership depends on a well-educated, highly skilled workforce.

We know, for example, that in the coming years, jobs requiring at least an associate's degree are going to grow twice as fast as jobs that don't require college. We will not fill those jobs or keep those jobs on our shores without community colleges.

So it was no surprise when one of the main recommendations of my economic advisory board, who I met with yesterday, was to expand education and job training. These are executives from some of America's top companies. Their businesses need a steady supply of people who can step into jobs involving a lot of technical knowledge and skill. They understand the importance of making sure we're preparing folks for the jobs of the future.

In fact, throughout our history, whenever we've faced economic challenges, we've responded by seeking new ways to harness the talents of our people. And that's one of the primary reasons that we have prospered. In the 19th century, we built public schools and land-grant colleges, transforming not just education, but our entire economy. In the 20th century, we passed the GI bill and invested in math and science, helping to unleash a wave of innovation

that helped to forge the great American middle class.

But in recent years, we've failed to live up to this legacy, especially in higher education. In just a decade, we've fallen from first to ninth in the proportion of young people with college degrees. That not only represents a huge waste of potential; in the global marketplace it represents a threat to our position as the world's leading economy.

As far as I'm concerned, America does not play for second place, and we certainly don't play for ninth. So I've set a goal: By 2020, America will once again lead the world in producing college graduates. And I believe community colleges will play a huge part in meeting this goal by producing an additional 5 million degrees and certificates in the next 10 years.

That's why last year I launched the American Graduation Initiative. I promised that we would end wasteful subsidies to big banks for student loans, and instead use that money to make college more affordable and to make a historic investment in community colleges. And after a tough fight, we passed those reforms, and today we're using this money towards the interest of higher education in America.

And this is helping us modernize community colleges at a critical time, because many of these schools are under pressure to cut costs and to cap enrollments and scrap courses even as demand has soared. It's going to make it possible for colleges to better harness technology in the classroom and beyond. And it's going to promote reform, as colleges compete for funding by improving graduation rates and matching courses to the needs of local businesses and making sure that when a graduate is handed a diploma it means that she or he are ready for a career.

We're also helping students succeed by making college more affordable. So we've increased student aid by thousands of dollars. We've simplified the loan application process. And we're making it easier for students to pay back their loans by limiting payments to 10 percent of their income. But reaching the 2020 goal that I've set is not just going to depend on government. It also depends on educators and students doing their part. And it depends on businesses and non-for-profits working with colleges to connect students with jobs.

So that's why we're holding this summit. That's why I'm asking my economic advisory board to reach out to employers across the country and come up with new ways for businesses and community colleges to work together. Based on this call to action, yesterday we announced a new partnership called Skills for America's Future. And the idea is simple: Businesses and community colleges work together to match the work in the classroom with the needs of the boardroom. And already, businesses from PG&E to UTC to the Gap have announced their support, as have business leaders like my friend Penny Pritzker and the Aspen Institute's Walter Isaacson. I hope that the companies, schools, and nonprofits that all of you lead will take part.

Today we can also announce the Gates Foundation is starting a new 5-year initiative to raise community college graduation rates. This is critically important because more than half of those who enter community colleges fail to either earn a 2-year degree or transfer to earn a 4-year degree. So we want to thank Melinda Gates, who's here, for that terrific contribution. And the Aspen Institute and several leading foundations are launching a competitive prize for community college excellence. It's going to shine a spotlight on community colleges delivering truly exceptional results, places that often don't get a lot of attention, but make a huge difference in their students' lives.

So we're investing in community colleges. We're making college more affordable. And we're bringing together businesses, nonprofits, and schools to train folks for the jobs of a new century. Now, all of this will help ensure that we continue to lead the global economy, but only if we maintain this commitment to education that's always been central to our success.

That's why I so strongly disagree with the economic plan that was released last week by the Republican leaders in Congress, which would actually cut education by 20 percent. It would reduce or eliminate financial aid for 8 million college students. And it would leave community colleges without the resources they need to meet the goals we've talked about today.

Instead, this money would help pay for a $700 billion tax cut that only 2 percent of the wealthiest Americans would ever see, an average of $100,000 for every millionaire and billionaire in the country. And that just doesn't make sense, not for students, not for our economy.

Think about it. China isn't slashing education by 20 percent right now. India is not slashing education by 20 percent. We are in a fight for the future, a fight that depends on education. And cutting aid for 8 million students or scaling back our community—our commitment to community colleges, that's like unilaterally disarming our troops right as they head to the frontlines.

So we obviously have to get serious about our deficit. That's why, after decades of profligacy, my administration report pay-as-you-go rules, proposed a 3-year freeze on nonsecurity spending. That's why we've formed a bipartisan deficit reduction commission.

But what we can't do is fund tax cuts for those who don't need it by slashing education for those who do. There's a better way for us to do this. And I want to work together with everybody concerned—Republican and Democrat—to figure that out.

To use an expression familiar to those of you who are from the Midwest: You don't eat your seed corn. [*Laughter*] We can't accept less investment in our young people if our country is going to move forward. It would mean giving up on the promise of so many people who might not be able to pursue an education, like the millions of students at community colleges across this country.

So I just want to use as an example Derek Blumke, who's here today. Where's Derek? Right here. Derek spent 6 years in the Air Force, three deployments in the Afghan theater, putting his life at risk to keep this country safe. And when he returned, he started classes at his local community college in northern Michigan. Now, apparently, what I'm told is, he wasn't sure whether he was smart enough to do the work, and he also was concerned that he wouldn't get the support that he needed.

And he was wrong on both fronts. His professors not only helped him transition from the military—even as he continued to serve in the Michigan Air National Guard—but also helped him to earn his associate's degree with honors. Then he transferred to the University of Michigan—go Blue!—[*laughter*]—where he graduated just a few weeks ago. And while he was there, he cofounded Student Veterans of America to help returning veterans like himself. So congratulations, Derek.

Or we can look to the example set by Albert Ojeda, who just spoke to you. He didn't have any advantages in life; grew up in a tough neighborhood in Phoenix, lost his father to violence, lost his mother to prison. But that didn't stop him from pursuing an education. It didn't stop him from attending community college, become an honor student, become the first member of his family to graduate from college.

There are so many folks out there like Derek and Albert. And I think about the many community college students who've written letters to me or e-mails through whitehouse.gov about how important community college has been to them. One person said he had been laid off and decided to return to school after 17 years. And attending community college "literally helped

save my life"—that's what he said. "I can not only see an associate's degree next year, but a new future filled with possibilities for the first time."

A new future filled with possibilities. That's why we're here today. That's the promise of an education not just for any one student, but for our entire country. And that's why it's so important that we work together on behalf of community colleges and an education system that harnesses the talents and hard work of every single American.

So thank you for the incredible work that each and every one of you do out there in schools, business folks who are supporting these community colleges, the students who are doing so much to contribute to our country. Let's get busy. Thank you very much.

Note: The President spoke at 12:17 p.m. in the East Room at the White House. In his remarks, he referred to Albert Ojeda, student, Arizona State University; Penny S. Pritzker, chairman and founder, Pritzker Realty Group; Walter Isaacson, president and chief executive officer, Aspen Institute; and Melinda French Gates, cochair, Bill & Melinda Gates Foundation. The transcript released by the Office of the Press Secretary also included the remarks of Jill T. Biden, wife of Vice President Joe Biden.

Remarks at a Reception Honoring World Ambassadors
October 5, 2010

Hello, everybody. Good afternoon, and welcome on behalf of Michelle and myself. We are thrilled to have you at the White House. It's good to see all of you, including the Dean of the Diplomatic Corps, from Djibouti, Ambassador Olhaye. It's wonderful to see you again.

Like our reception last year, this is an opportunity to thank you for your partnership, for the cooperation between our nations, and for the hospitality that your countries show our diplomats each and every day.

As Ambassadors, I know you all have a very difficult job. You have to understand the com-

plexities of other cultures and countries—unlike diplomats of a century ago who—for example, there was a diplomat who, when planning an international ceremony, invited Switzerland to send its navy. [*Laughter*]

You have to adapt to quickly changing events around the world—unlike President Jefferson, who said of an American Ambassador to Europe: "We haven't heard from him in 2 years. If we don't hear from him next year, I'll have to write him a letter." [*Laughter*]

Today, our nations and peoples are more interconnected than at any time in human history.

We've got extraordinary opportunities to advance our national interests and our common interests, which can reinforce each other. We can advance the aspirations of our people, who, despite any differences, basically seek the same things: to live in security and dignity, to seek progress and justice, and to realize a better future for their children.

And that's why, since I've taken office, I've pursued a new era of engagement with the world, a new commitment to diplomacy and partnership based on mutual interest and mutual respect. Today I want to thank you and your countries for joining us and for the progress that we've made together.

Together, we've strengthened old alliances, we have forged new partnerships, we have pursued an international order where the rights and responsibilities of all nations are upheld. We've put the global economy back on the path of growth so we can create jobs and opportunity for all of our people.

Together, we're working to confront violent extremism, to prevent the spread of nuclear weapons, and to secure vulnerable nuclear materials. We're engaged in the hard work of pursuing peace, from the Middle East to Sudan, and promoting development to give people and nations a path out of poverty. In short, we are doing together what none of us can achieve by ourselves.

But as I've said in my visits around the world, building the future we seek cannot be the work of governments and diplomats alone. It must also be the work of our societies and our people. That's why we're expanding partnerships and exchanges between our business leaders and entrepreneurs, students and scientists, civil society and faith communities.

And it's why I am so pleased that many of you are embracing the opportunity to experience America beyond Washington, visiting cities and towns across our country, like Atlanta next week, just like I understand that you visited my hometown of Chicago. I understand that you took in the incredible architecture, the culture,

the people, even our world-famous Chicago-style hot dogs. [*Laughter*] They are hard to resist. I noticed, though, that you did not go in January to experience our wonderful January weather in Chicago. [*Laughter*] That is easy to resist. [*Laughter*]

The spirit you felt across America is the spirit we need in our work: the idea that no matter where you come from or who you are, we can come together and work together. It's the same spirit I've seen in all the young people that I've met, from Strasbourg to Ankara to Cairo to Shanghai; in civil society leaders in Moscow and the extraordinary young African leaders that I welcomed to this very room here in the White House.

One of them—a young woman—stood up and looked at me and asked just how committed the United States is to this new era of partnership. I want to conclude by telling you exactly what I told her. I said, yes, as President of the United States, my first responsibility is to look out for the people and interests of the United States. And I always will. But I also said America wants all of you to succeed as well, whether it's in Africa or in Latin America, in Europe or in Asia, because when your nations and people succeed and prosper, it's not only in your interests, it's in America's interests. And that's why our commitment to this new era of engagement will remain a cornerstone of my foreign policy.

So in that spirit, Michelle and I are honored to welcome all of you. I'm mindful of that old saying about diplomacy, that sometimes more can be accomplished at 1 party than 20 serious conversations. [*Laughter*] So have a wonderful evening, have a wonderful party, and I look forward to all that we can accomplish together, tonight and beyond.

Thank you very much, everybody.

NOTE: The President spoke at 5 p.m. in the East Room at the White House. In his remarks, he referred to Shamima Muslim, a participant at the White House Young African Leaders Forum.

Remarks at the Fortune Most Powerful Women Summit
October 5, 2010

The President. Thank you very much. Thank you, everybody. Please, please have a seat. Thank you.

Well, I am just thrilled to be here tonight with some of the most brilliant, accomplished, influential women in this country. As Michelle Obama's husband, I feel very much at home. [*Laughter*]

I have three tall, good-looking, strong-willed women. That's just on the second floor. Then I've got my mother-in-law on the third floor. [*Laughter*]

So it's a thrill to be here. I want to thank Ann for that kind and brief introduction—[*laughter*]—and for her extraordinary leadership. And I want to thank all the people who helped to organize this spectacular event.

And I'm especially pleased to see the young people who are here. We are thrilled to have you.

I also see that my friend Warren Buffett is here. I understand that even though he is a man, he has been invited back year after year—[*laughter*]—because he knows that the surest path to success is to surround yourself with brilliant women. He's a smart guy.

I happen to share that belief. And I'm pleased to see some of the extraordinary women in my administration who are also here tonight, because I rely on their wise advice every single day, and I'm tremendously grateful for their service.

But being here isn't just meaningful to me as President. It's also meaningful to me personally. As some of you know, I was raised in part by my grandmother. She just passed away a couple of years ago. When I was born, she got a job as a secretary to help provide for our family. Now, she only had a high school education. She had grown up in a generation where women weren't necessarily encouraged to pursue a college degree, and certainly not after they had gotten married and had had a child. But she had an incredible mind and sound judgment. And so over the years she worked her way up—without a college degree, just a high school degree—to

become one of the first woman bank vice presidents in the State of Hawaii. And that was an amazing accomplishment, but that position was also her glass ceiling. For nearly two decades, she watched as men no more qualified than she was—in fact, usually men who she had trained—would get promoted up the corporate ladder ahead of her.

Now, I know that if given the chance, she would have run that bank better than anybody. But she never got that opportunity. And she never complained. She hardly ever took a vacation. She just kept getting up and giving her best every single day.

So tonight I'm inspired to be with so many women who have reached the pinnacles of their professions. That's a credit to all of you, and your individual drive and fortitude, because I know you've overcome plenty of obstacles of your own. And while we still have a ways to go, it's also a testament to the progress that we've made as a country, certainly since my grandmother was a young woman.

The 75 young leaders who are here tonight are another testament to that progress, because as you know, these young women went through a citywide selection process to attend this event. And on their applications, they were asked to list their career aspirations. And I've got a list of what they said. See, we've got "cultural anthropologist"——

Audience member. Woo!

The President. That's a good choice. My mother was an anthropologist, so thumbs up on that. "Classical singer."

Audience member. Woo! [*Laughter*]

The President. "U.S. Senator."

[*At this point, there was modest applause.*]

The President. Oh, were there some people who were saying like, "Oh, I don't know." [*Laughter*] "Professional race car driver." One stated that she intends to become "the next Bill Gates." I don't know why Buffett was skipped over, but—[*laughter*].

Another wrote, "Environmental scientist and work on ways to find new fuel resources"—important. And one—this is my favorite—one said, "Doctor, lawyer, and an engineer." This young lady said, "I know this is ambitious, but not impossible." [*Laughter*]

So when we talk about the theme of this year's conference, "Building a Legacy," that's exactly what we're talking about. That's what's at stake: that spark, that passion. All those ambitions and aspirations expressed by these young people.

And the question is, what are we doing to nurture that promise? How do we ensure that 10 or 20 or 30 years from now, these young women will be sitting where all of you are sitting tonight, with their own mentees, passing the torch to a next generation? What are we doing to build a dynamic, competitive, opportunity-rich economy so that they have successful lives and careers of their own?

Now, as some of our Nation's top business leaders and nonprofit leaders and leaders in so many different fields, the answers to these questions are going to be largely determined by you, because part of the competitiveness of America's economy, the richness of its cultural life, it's always depended on the innovation and enterprise of American businesses and American institutions and organizations, on the products you develop, and the jobs you create, and the growth that you drive.

Now, this doesn't relieve government of its responsibility to create the conditions for businesses to succeed. That's what government does best, those things that no individual or business will do on their own, but that create an environment where everybody can compete. So that means funding the basic research that drives new discoveries and sparks new industries. It means upgrading our infrastructure, including things like high-speed rail and Internet, so that you can get your products and services to your customers. It means promoting exports, because the more our businesses export, the more they produce and the more jobs they create.

And it means making sure that our people have what it takes to actually do those jobs. That's what we've been discussing during your conference today, and it's what I'd like to focus on tonight, because you know, as I do, that our businesses, our institutions, our economy cannot compete unless our workforce can compete, unless we harness the potential of every American and ensure that their skills match up to the work of the future.

And that starts with education, especially in fields like science and technology and engineering and math. We cannot sustain——

[*The Presidential Seal fell from the podium.*]

The President. Whoops, was that my—[*laughter*]—oh, goodness. That's all right. [*Laughter*] All of you know who I am. [*Laughter and applause*] But I'm sure there's somebody back there that's really nervous right now. [*Laughter*] Don't you think? They're sweating bullets back there right now. [*Laughter*]

Where were we? [*Laughter*] We cannot sustain high-tech, high-wage jobs here in America when our young people are lagging far behind competitors around the world. That's one of the reasons we launched a national competition called Race to the Top, designed to raise standards in our schools. And it's based on a simple idea: Instead of just funding the status quo, we're only going to invest in reform.

And with the help of business leaders like Ursula Burns, the CEO of Xerox, we've created a new partnership called Change the Equation, which is a coalition of more than 100 CEOs from our Nation's largest companies who've committed to bringing innovative math and science programs to at least 100 high-need communities over the course of the next year. And it includes a special focus on girls, who are often underrepresented in our scientific fields. And I know, by the way, from talking to Malia and Sasha, it's just a matter of giving them a little bit of confidence, and they will thrive and succeed in math and science. But somebody's got to be there to say to them, you know what, you can do this.

We also know that in today's economy, every American will need more than a high school diploma. And back when I took office, I set a goal: By 2020, America will once again have the highest proportion of college graduates in the world.

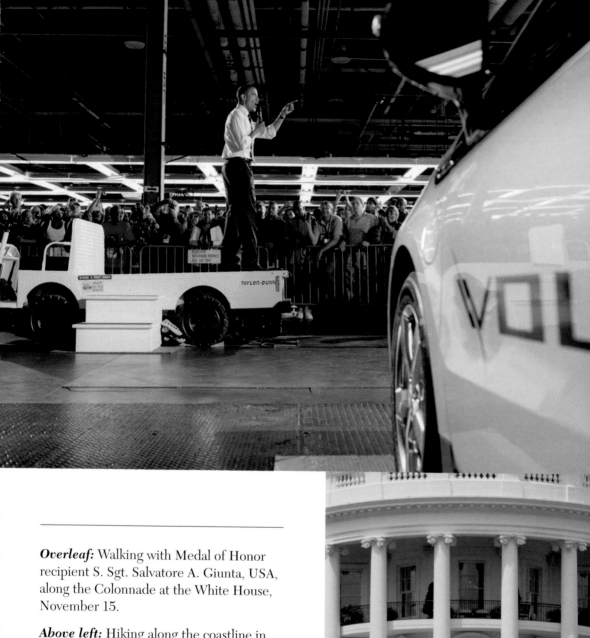

Overleaf: Walking with Medal of Honor recipient S. Sgt. Salvatore A. Giunta, USA, along the Colonnade at the White House, November 15.

Above left: Hiking along the coastline in Arcadia National Park in Bar Harbor, ME, July 17.

Left: Stopping for treats at the Gingerbread House Bakery in Kokomo, IN, November 23.

Above: Addressing employees at the General Motors Detroit-Hamtramck Assembly Center in Hamtramck, MI, July 30.

Right: Walking with Prime Minister David Cameron of the United Kingdom on the South Lawn at the White House, July 20.

Above left: Conferring with Warren E. Buffett, chief executive officer and chairman, Berkshire Hathaway Inc., in the Oval Office at the White House, July 14.

Left: Speaking with Rep. Eric Cantor at the conclusion of a bipartisan meeting with congressional leadership in the Private Dining Room at the White House, November 30.

Below: Chatting with Prime Minister Manmohan Singh of India during a state dinner at the Rashtrapati Bhavan in New Delhi, India, November 8.

Right: Participating in an arrival ceremony with President Susilo Bambang Yudhoyono of Indonesia at the Istana Merdeka in Jakarta, Indonesia, November 9.

Below right: Walking with President Lee Myung-bak of South Korea following a bilateral meeting at the Blue House in Seoul, South Korea, November 11.

Above left: Speaking with Secretary of the Treasury Timothy F. Geithner at the United Nations in New York City, September 23.

Left: Meeting with former President Jimmy Carter in the office of National Security Adviser Thomas E. Donilon at the White House, November 30.

Above: Attending a funeral ceremony for Sen. Robert C. Byrd with Governor Joseph Manchin III of West Virginia, left, Vice President Joseph R. Biden, Jr., right, and former President William J. Clinton, far right, at the State Capitol in Charleston, WV, July 2.

Right: Talking with former President William J. Clinton in the hallway outside the James S. Brady Press Briefing Room at the White House, December 10.

Overleaf: Walking with Vice President Joseph R. Biden, Jr., at the Chrysler Indiana Transmission Plant II in Kokomo, IN, November 23.

That's why we've increased student aid and tuition tax credits, and we've eliminated tens of billions of dollars in wasteful subsidies, and we're now using that money to make college more affordable to millions of students. We've made historic investments in community colleges, which are a pathway to opportunity not just for children of so many working families, but for millions of women returning to the workforce or who are raising children of their own and so need some flexibility in terms of a course of study and advancing careers.

And just yesterday we launched a new initiative called Skills for America's Future to connect students looking for jobs with businesses looking to hire. And the idea is very simple: Businesses and community colleges work together to match the curricula in the classroom with the needs of the boardroom. Companies then hire the graduates, who show up on their first day with precisely the skills that you need, and that they need to succeed. We've already got businesses from PG&E to United Technologies to the Gap who are supporting this initiative, as have business leaders like my friend who is helping to spearhead this, Penny Pritzker, and the Aspen Institute's Walter Isaacson. So we want to get these partnerships going in all 50 States. And I hope that companies that are represented here all decide to be a part of this program.

Now, let's not forget that most of your businesses did not start out as national or multinational corporations. They began as tiny startups, dreamed up in garages and around kitchen tables by folks who were willing to take a chance on an idea. So when we're talking about building a more competitive workforce, that doesn't just mean developing more competitive workers. It also means developing more competitive entrepreneurs. It means helping them translate those good ideas into successful businesses that create jobs and strengthen our economy.

And as any entrepreneur will tell you, one of the biggest roadblocks they face is access to capital. It turns out that's particularly true for women. A recent study by the Kauffman Foundation found that women high-tech entrepreneurs raised nearly 70 percent less capital when

starting their firms than men did. For all we know, one of those women could have had the idea for the next Google or Apple or HP. But that doesn't mean much if she can't get the cash to bring the idea to market.

So Theresa Daytner knows what that's like. She's one of the entrepreneurs that you're honoring this year. Is she here? Theresa? Where are you? Way back there. Hey, you. I love Theresa's story. She struggled at first to get capital for her construction company, partly because she was providing for her six kids and caring for her aging parents. So eventually she ran out of options. She applied for a home equity loan. And this resonates with me, this story. She handed her husband the application, and she said to him, "Here, honey, sign this, but don't read it." [*Laughter*]

Now, her company took off, bringing in more than $16 million in revenue so far this year. So we're very proud of what you've accomplished. But folks like Theresa, they shouldn't have to mortgage their family home to build their family business. That's why we're working to help entrepreneurs like Theresa with new tax cuts and more loans.

Yesterday the White House Council on Women and Girls hosted a Women's Entrepreneurship Summit to seek solutions to some of the challenges that women face. And I'm pleased that the Small Business Administration, under the leadership of Karen Mills, has announced a new effort to level the playing field for women entrepreneurs in industries where they're underrepresented, from computer technology to telecommunications to scientific research.

So we're working to support our entrepreneurs. We're working to better train and educate our workers. But as we seek to harness the talents and skills of the American people, there's another factor that I believe is too often overlooked, and that's the structure of our workplaces, whether our workplaces are mobile and flexible and accommodating enough to give people the opportunities they need to contribute and raise a family.

And I want to talk to all of you about this, not as women, not as women business leaders, but simply as business leaders, because while this issue may disproportionately affect women, I don't think it makes sense to label it as a woman's issue. Not just because plenty of men wish they had flexibility to be better fathers to their kids or better sons to their aging parents, but because we know that companies with flexible work arrangements can actually have lower turnover and absenteeism and higher productivity. So this is not just a woman's issue. It's not just a work-family balance issue. It's an economic competitiveness issue.

That's why so many of your companies are already leading the way, embracing things like telecommuting and flextime and onsite childcare. And my administration is committed to supporting efforts like these. Not just by investing in paid leave programs and childcare tax credits, but also by making the Federal Government a model for the policies that we're encouraging.

We're creating mobile workplaces and flexible work schedules, and we're judging employees by the results they get, not the face time they log, because this doesn't just provide a better experience for our employees, it helps us attract and retain the top talent and provide better service for the American people.

In the end, that's really our goal here, to get all our people doing the very best work that they can. That's how we've always moved forward in this country: breaking down barriers, being inclusive, setting aside the outdated assumptions that keep us from appreciating what each of us has to offer.

And obviously, that work's not finished. I'm not naive about that. But I also know that thanks to decades of struggle and sacrifice, a lot of it quiet, a lot of it behind the scenes, many of the obstacles that my grandmother faced no longer exist.

Today, women make up half of America's workforce. They are primary or cobreadwinners in two-thirds of our families. Their contributions are vital to the success of our economy. Today, girls like my daughters, young women like the ones at this dinner, have opportunities that my grandmother never dreamed of for herself.

So I want to conclude by telling you a little bit about one of these young women—I believe she may be here, Markela Izlar. Is Markela here? She's a senior—well, stand up, wave. She's a senior at Ballou High School.

Now, Markela has faced some pretty serious challenges in her life. Her father was killed in an act of violence before she was born. And in her essay, she wrote, "Life growing up in southeast DC hasn't been easy." She says, "I recently lost count of how many friends and family members I had to say goodbye to before it seemed like it was time."

But it turns out Markela loves math, and I hear you're pretty good at math. And she is determined to one day become either an engineer or an algebra teacher. And she concluded her essay by saying, "When I think about the disadvantages I have in my life, it motivates me to be successful. Because I understand that in life"—[*applause*]—she says, "I understand that in life everyone has a purpose and a plan, and every day, I see myself getting closer and closer to college, and one day, a career."

So, Markela, we are proud of you. We're proud of all the young women who are here in this room. And I want to make sure that our legacy to them is an America where they can fulfill every last bit of their promise and pursue every last one of their dreams and become powerful, accomplished women. And so many of you are setting such a great example for them.

So thank you. God bless you. God bless the United States of America. Thank you.

NOTE: The President spoke at 7:58 p.m. at the Andrew W. Mellon Auditorium. In his remarks, he referred to his mother-in-law Marian Robinson; Ann S. Moore, chairman, Time Inc.; Warren E. Buffett, chief executive officer and chairman, Berkshire Hathaway Inc.; William H. Gates III, chairman, Microsoft Corporation; and Penny S. Pritzker, chairman and founder, Pritzker Realty Group.

Remarks on Presenting Posthumously the Congressional Medal of Honor to Staff Sergeant Robert J. Miller
October 6, 2010

Please be seated. Good afternoon. And on behalf of Michelle and myself, welcome to the White House. And thank you, General Carver, for that beautiful invocation.

We are a nation of more than 300 million Americans. Of these, less than 1 percent wears the uniform of our Armed Services. And of these, just a small fraction has earned the badges of our special operations forces.

In the finest military the world has ever known, these warriors are the best of the best. In an era that prizes celebrity and status, they are quiet professionals, never seeking the spotlight. In a time of war, they have borne a burden far beyond their small numbers: training foreign militaries to stand on their own, bringing schools and medicine to remote villages, and taking to the terrorists and insurgents who plot against us.

Few Americans ever see their service, but all Americans are safer because of it. And our hearts swell with pride just hearing their names, including the legendary Green Berets. Today it is my privilege to present our Nation's highest military decoration, the Medal of Honor, to one of these remarkable soldiers, Staff Sergeant Robert J. Miller.

To do so, we are joined by Vice President Biden and, from the Miller's family's home State of Florida, a leader who helped make this day possible, Congresswoman Suzanne Kosmas.

We are joined by leaders from across my administration, including Secretary of Defense Robert Gates; chairman of the Joint Chiefs of Staff Admiral Mike Mullen; and leaders from our Armed Forces, including Army Secretary John McHugh and Chief of Staff General George Casey, as well as Commander of Special Operations Command, Admiral Eric Olson.

We are honored to be joined by Rob's fellow soldiers in whose ranks he served, his teammates from Alpha Company, 3d Battalion, 3d Special Forces Group from Fort Bragg, and those who now welcome him into their ranks, members of the Medal of Honor Society.

Most of all, we welcome more than 100 of Rob's friends and family, especially his father Phil, his mother Maureen, and his many brothers and sisters.

It has been said that courage is not simply one of the virtues, but the form of every virtue at the testing point. For Rob Miller, the testing point came nearly 3 years ago, deep in a snowy Afghan valley. But the courage he displayed that day reflects every virtue that defined his life.

Rob was wise beyond his years. Growing up in Wheaton, Illinois, outside of Chicago, he was the boy in school who penned a poem about American GIs in World War II, men—like the soldier Rob would become himself—who he said "fought day and night, fighting for what they thought was right."

Rob was born to lead—the high school gymnast who trained so hard his coach had to kick him out at night so they could close the gym. He was the Army recruit who pushed himself to his limits, both physically and mentally, to earn the title Green Beret. He was the Special Forces soldier who, on his first tour in Afghanistan, earned two Army Commendation Medals for his valor.

Devotion to duty, an abiding sense of honor, a profound love of country: These were the virtues that found their ultimate expression when Rob, just 24 years old and on his second tour, met his testing point on January 25, 2008.

Rob and his team were in the remote northwest of Afghanistan. Their mission: clear a valley of insurgents who had been attacking Afghan forces and terrorizing villagers. So when they came across an insurgent compound, Rob and his men made their move, unleashing their fire and calling in airstrikes.

Now, they were on foot, heading over to that destroyed compound to assess the damage and gather intelligence. It was still dark, just before dawn. It was freezing cold and silent, except for the crackle of their radios and the crunch of snow under their boots. Like so many times before, Rob was up front, leading a patrol of two dozen Afghans and Americans on a narrow trail along the valley floor, the steep mountains towering over them.

First, it was just a single insurgent, jumping out from behind a boulder. Then, the whole valley seemed to explode with gunfire. Within seconds, Rob and his patrol were pinned down with almost no cover, bullets and rocket-propelled grenades raining down from every direction. And when enemy reinforcements poured in, the odds were overwhelming. Rob's small patrol of two dozen men was nearly surrounded by almost 150 insurgents.

With the enemy just feets away—some so close he could see their faces—Rob held his ground. Despite the chaos around him, he radioed back enemy positions. As the only Pashto speaker on his team, he organized the Afghan soldiers around him. But the incoming fire, in the words of one soldier, was simply "astounding."

Rob made a decision. He called for his team to fall back. And then he did something extraordinary. Rob moved in the other direction, toward the enemy, drawing their guns away from his team and bringing the fire of all those insurgents down upon himself.

The fighting was ferocious. Rob seemed to disappear into clouds of dust and debris, but his team could hear him on the radio, still calling out the enemy's position. And they could hear his weapon still firing as he provided cover for his men. And then, over the radio, they heard his voice. He had been hit. But still, he kept calling out enemy positions. Still, he kept firing. Still, he kept throwing his grenades. And then they heard it: Rob's weapon fell silent.

This is the story of what one American soldier did for his team, but it's also a story of what they did for him. Two of his teammates braved the bullets and rushed to Rob's aid. In those final moments, they were there at his side, American soldiers there for each other.

The relentless fire forced them back, but they refused to leave their fallen comrade. When reinforcements arrived, these Americans went in again, risking their lives, taking more casualties, determined to bring Rob Miller out

of that valley. And finally, after fighting that raged for hours, they did.

When the dust settled and the smoke cleared, there was no doubt Rob Miller and his team had struck a major blow against the local insurgency. Five members of his patrol had been wounded, but his team had survived. And one of his teammates surely spoke for all of them when he said of Rob, "I would not be alive today if not for his ultimate sacrifice."

This is the valor that America honors today. To Rob's family and friends, I know that no words can ease the ache in your hearts. But I also know this: Rob's life and legacy endures.

Rob endures in the pride of his parents. Phil and Maureen, you raised a remarkable son. Today and in the years to come, may you find some comfort in knowing that Rob gave his life doing what he loved, protecting his friends and defending his country. You gave your oldest son to America, and America is forever in your debt.

Rob endures in the love of his brothers and sisters, all seven of whom join us today. Your brothers laid down his life so you could live yours in security and freedom. You honor him by living your lives to the fullest, and I suspect Rob would be especially proud of his younger brother Tom, who, inspired by his big brother, is now training to be a Green Beret himself.

Rob endures in the Afghans that he trained and he befriended. In valleys and villages half a world away, they remember him, the American who spoke their language, who respected their culture, and who helped them defend their country. They welcomed him into their homes and invited him to their weddings. And in a sign of their lasting gratitude, they presented Rob's parents with a beautiful Afghan flag—Afghan rug, which hangs today in the Miller home, a symbol of the partnership between the people of America and Afghanistan.

Rob Miller endures in the service of his teammates, his brothers in arms who served with him, bled with him, and fought to bring him home. These soldiers embody the spirit that guides our troops in Afghanistan every day: the courage, the resolve, the relentless focus on their mission to break the momentum of the Taliban insurgency and to build the capacity of

Afghans to defend themselves and to make sure that Afghanistan is never again a safe haven for terrorists who would attack our country. That is their mission, that is our mission, and that is what we will do. And I would ask Rob's team, who were with him that day, to please stand and be recognized. [*Applause*]

Finally, Rob Miller—and all those who give their lives in our name—endure in each of us. Every American is safer because of their service. And every American has a duty to remember and honor their sacrifice.

If we do, if we keep their legacy alive, if we keep faith with the freedoms they died to defend, then we can imagine a day, decades from now, when another child sits down at his desk, ponders the true meaning of heroism, and finds inspiration in the story of a soldier, Staff Sergeant Robert J. Miller, and a generation that "fought day and night, fighting for what they thought was right."

That is the meaning of this medal, and that is our summons today, as a proud and grateful nation. So please join me in welcoming Phil and Maureen Miller for the reading of the citation.

NOTE: The President spoke at 1:52 p.m. in the East Room at the White House. In his remarks, he referred to Maj. Gen. Douglas L. Carver, USA, Chief of Chaplains; and Philip Miller, father, and Maureen Miller, mother, of Mr. Miller. Following the President's remarks, Lt. Cmdr. Matthew R. Maasdam, USN, Navy Aide to the President, read the citation.

Remarks at a Democratic National Committee Dinner in Cresskill, New Jersey
October 6, 2010

A couple people I want to first of all acknowledge. Tim Kaine is here from the Democratic Committee. John Wisniewski is here, the New Jersey Democratic chairman.

Obviously, my main thanks go to Michael and Jackie, Zach, Melissa, Olivia for opening up their spectacular home, for being such incredible friends.

Michael basically took all the words out of my mouth. [*Laughter*] I don't really know what to say. [*Laughter*] Those of you who are interested in the Randy Moss trade—[*laughter*]—I have some opinions about that.

Look, one of the wonderful things about these events is I get the chance to spend some time just sitting with you individually, so I'm not going to give a long speech.

But let me just echo a couple of themes that Michael raised. You know, we're in a very tough election season. And we're in a tough election season because the country is going through a very difficult time. It's hard I think sometimes to appreciate the magnitude of what we faced when we came into office.

But this was the worst recession by far since the Great Depression. In fact, if you add up the recession in '91, the recession in 2000, the recession when Ronald Reagan came into office—the three previous recessions—this one had a bigger impact than all three of those combined. We lost 4 million jobs in the 6 months before I took office, 750,000 the month I was sworn in, 600,000 in the 2 subsequent months. We had lost most of the 8 million jobs that we lost before any of our economic policies were put into place.

And so our first job was to stop the crisis. And we've done that. The economy is now growing again. We've had 8 consecutive months of private sector job growth. The credit markets are now functioning. World trade is now expanding again.

And so, as Michael said, we're moving in the right direction. But one of the reasons I ran for President was not just to put a tourniquet around the crisis. It was the fact that for a long time, I think everybody had a sense that we weren't doing everything we needed to make sure we can compete in a new 21st-century economy, that we had lost ground, and that there was a foundation that had to be rebuilt just to make sure that the next generation and the generation after that can continue to live in the strongest economy in the world.

I want the 21st century to be the American century just like the 20th century was the American century. And in order to do that, we've had to make some tough choices, not all of which were popular. We had to fix a broken health care system because it was bankrupting the Government, it was bankrupting families, and bankrupting businesses.

That change of a system that large takes time, but we are now moving in the right direction to change it. We had to change a financial system that, frankly, if we did not reregulate, stood to create another round of crises.

This last one was the worst one, but keep in mind that we had seen every 4 or 5 years a world financial crisis. And we had to initiate, both in this country and internationally, a strategy so that risk-taking and the dynamism of our capitalist system is healthy and strong, but we weren't going to be facing crises in which taxpayers had a choice of either bailing out the system or watching it collapse.

We had to revamp our education system. And we are now in the process of making more changes across the country with our Race to the Top program than we've seen in decades, making sure that every young person has a chance to graduate from high school. They can read, they can write, they can do arithmetic, they're going on to college.

We used to be number one in college graduation rates; we're now number nine. We are going to reverse that so that by 2020, we're back on top.

We had to make sure that we're reinvesting in research and development and all the things that encourage innovation in our economy because that's going to be the basis of our long-term competiveness. So we've had to make a lot of tough decisions. But I am extraordinarily confident that we're moving in the right direction.

And as Michael indicated, many of you are a testament to the continuing strength and vitality of American democracy and the American economy. But in order for us to continue going in the right direction, we've got to sustain it.

And the election right now is really a choice between the policies that got us into the mess and the policies that have started to bring us out.

Now, when unemployment is still at 9.5, 9.6 percent, that gives an enormous advantage to whoever is not in power because they can simply point at the status quo regardless of causation and say, you know what, it's the folks who are in power that are at fault. And so that gives sort of a natural momentum behind their arguments.

What we have to do is to make sure that we maintain our focus on the long game; that we're not just thinking tactically, that we're not just thinking about what's convenient for us next month or in the next election, but what's good for the next generation. That's what we've tried to do over the last 20 months, and we've got to make that argument robustly over the remaining 4 weeks of this midterm.

I was joking at, I think, a dinner that Michael was at. One of the strengths of the Democrats is that we don't walk—march in lockstep. You know, we like to have internal dissent and arguments. We've very self-critical. We tend to look at the glass as half empty. And that makes us better because we're always asking ourselves tough questions. But that's also a weakness, particularly 4 weeks before an election. And right now all the reports out there are that the main challenge we have is closing an enthusiasm gap between the Democrats and the Republicans.

Well, Michael just listed the reasons you should be enthusiastic. We didn't just save this economy from a Great Depression. We also moved forward substantially on everything that we've said Democrats stood for, for years.

And we're not finished—unless we lose sight of that long game and we start sulking and sitting back and not doing everything we need to do in terms of making sure that our folks turn out.

Joe Biden has a useful saying. He says, don't compare me to the Almighty, compare me to the alternative. [*Laughter*] And I think Democrats would be well served right now to just keep that uppermost in their minds. If everyone here, and your friends and neighbors and coworkers and colleagues, are constantly focused on the choice before us and understanding that we're not finished, but unless we are able to maintain Democrats in the House and the Senate, then we're going to be stalled for 2 years or 4 years, and we could even start going backwards. As long as people keep that in mind, then I'm absolutely confident that we're going to do fine.

And so I just want to again thank Mike and Jackie for hosting us. I want to thank all of you for coming here. And I want you guys to make sure that you understand this country is the greatest country on Earth. We still have the best workers on Earth, the best universities on Earth, the most innovative economy on Earth. We're the most diverse on Earth. There's no advanced economy that has the same constant influx of energy from immigrants, and new ideas and the same core freedoms that we enjoy. There is not another country on Earth that

would not willingly trade places with us right now.

But we do have some tough decisions to make. I'm willing to make them. I need help in Congress in order to make them. And they need your help in order for us to be able to move forward.

So thank you so much, everybody.

NOTE: The President spoke at 6:15 p.m. at the residence of Michael and Jacqueline Kempner. In his remarks, he referred to Timothy M. Kaine, chairman, Democratic National Committee; Zach, Melissa, and Olivia Kempner, children of Mr. and Mrs. Kempner; and New England Patriots wide receiver Randy Moss, who was traded to the Minnesota Vikings on October 5. The transcript was released by the Office of the Press Secretary on October 7.

Remarks at a Rally for Governor Martin J. O'Malley of Maryland in Bowie, Maryland
October 7, 2010

The President. Hello, Bowie! Oh, it is good to see you all. Thank you. Thank you so much. It is——

Audience members. Obama! Obama! Obama!

The President. Thank you. Thank you. Thank you, BSU. Thank you. Thank you so much. It's good to be back in Maryland.

It is an honor to be standing here with one of the best Governors in the United States of America, Martin O'Malley. It's great to be with someone who has always had my back, your Congressman and our majority leader, Steny Hoyer, in the house. I'm proud to be here with your outstanding Senators, Barbara Mikulski and Ben Cardin, some of your outstanding Congressmen, Chris Van Hollen and Elijah Cummings and Donna Edwards and John Sarbanes. I'm proud to be here with Lieutenant Governor Anthony Brown.

Anthony and I went to law school together. He looks younger than me though. [*Laughter*] Doesn't have as much gray hair. [*Laughter*]

And I want to thank the president of Bowie State, Mickey Burnim. Thank you so much for your hospitality.

Now, let me say up front a few words about Martin. Here is a man who made tough choices in tough times to move Maryland forward. His rock-solid support for public education has made Maryland schools the best in America 2 years in a row, the best in America—not the best on the East Coast, not the best in the Mid-Atlantic States, the best in America.

His innovative policies have helped drive violent crime down to its lowest level since 1975. His smart leadership helped turn around Chesapeake Bay. And thanks to decisions that he made, along with my good friend Tim Kaine in Virginia, the blue crab population is up 60 percent over last year. And that's good news to folks who make their living on the Bay, and it's good news to folks who like good eating.

So Martin has been a great Governor for a great State, which is why I hope you are fired up in these last few weeks. I hope you're ready to fight for Martin so he can keep fighting for you. Because there's an election coming up that's going to say a lot about the future—your future, but also the future of this country.

Audience members. We love you, Obama!

The President. I love you back. But I've got a good—[*applause*]—but I want to talk about this election now. [*Laughter*] I do love you, though.

Two years ago, you defied the conventional wisdom in Washington. You remember. They said, you can't overcome the cynicism of our politics. You can't overcome the power of the special interests. You can't make progress on the big challenges of our time.

Audience members. Yes, we can!

The President. You can't elect an African American with a funny name. They said, no, you can't.

Audience members. Yes, we can!

The President. I'm sorry, what did you say?

Audience members. Yes, we can!

The President. You said, yes, we can.

Audience members. Yes, we can! Yes, we can! Yes, we can!

The President. Now, here's the thing, though, here's the trick. Because I know everybody here remembers the Inauguration, and even though it was cold, everybody was having a great time. And Beyonce was singing and—[*laughter*]—and Bono. And everybody thought, this is great.

But our victory in that campaign, that wasn't the end of the road. That was the beginning. The campaign by itself didn't deliver the change that we needed. It just gave us the chance to make change happen. And it made each of you shareholders in the mission of rebuilding our country and reclaiming our future. And I'm back today, 2 years later, because the success of that mission is at stake. We've got a lot at stake right now. On November 2, I'm going to need you just as fired up as you were in 2008. Just as fired up.

I want to just go down memory lane here for the last 20 months so we understand where we've been, what we have to do, and where we're going. After that last election, it was my hope that we could pull people together, Democrats and Republicans, because we had to confront the worst economic crisis since the Great

Depression, the worst by far in most of our lifetimes. Because although we're proud to be Democrats, we're prouder to be Americans. We wanted to bring everybody together. And I know there are plenty of Republicans who feel the same way in this country.

But unfortunately, when we arrived in Washington, the Republicans in Congress, they had a different idea. They knew it would take more than a couple of years to climb out of this unbelievable recession that they had created. They knew that by the time the midterm rolled around that people would still be out of work; that people would still be frustrated. And they figured that if we just sat on the sidelines and opposed every idea, every compromise that I offered, if they spent all their time attacking Democrats instead of attacking problems, that somehow they would prosper at the polls.

So they spent the last 20 months saying no, even to policies that they'd supported in the past. No to middle class tax cuts, no to help for small businesses, no to a bipartisan deficit reduction commission that they had once sponsored. I said yes, they said no. I'm pretty sure if I said the sky was blue, they'd say no. [*Laughter*] If I said there are fish in the sea, they'd say no. See, their calculation was if Obama fails, then we win.

Audience members. Boo!

The President. That was their calculation. Well, they might have thought that playing political games would get them through an election, but I knew it wasn't going to get America through our crisis. So I made a different choice. Instead of playing politics, I took whatever steps were necessary to stop an economic freefall. I did what we needed to do even if it wasn't popular, even if it wasn't easy. Because you all did not elect me to do what was easy. You didn't elect me to spend all day looking at the polls and figuring out how to keep me in office. You elected me to do what was right. That's why you elected me, to do what's right.

And 20 months later, 20 months later, we no longer face the possibility of a second depression. Our economy is growing again. Private sector jobs have grown 8 months in a row. Thanks to Martin O'Malley's leadership, Maryland has gained over 33,000 jobs since January, the best start of a year since 2000, which, by the way, was the last time Democrats were in charge. There are 3 million Americans who wouldn't be working today if it weren't for the economic plan we put in place.

But the truth is we've still got a long way to go. We all know that. The hole we were in was so deep. There are still millions of Americans without work. There are still millions of families who can barely pay the bills or make a mortgage, middle class families who were struggling even before the crisis hit and now they're just treading water.

So of course people are frustrated. People are impatient with the pace of change. They want things to move a little quicker. I understand that. I'm impatient too. But the other side, they don't have an answer. All they have decided to do is to ride that frustration and that anger all the way to the ballot box. And right now you've got pundits who are saying, well, the other party's supporters are more excited. They're saying they're going to turn out at higher levels.

Audience members. No!

The President. They say that all of you who worked so hard in 2008, you might not be as pumped up, might not as be as energized.

Audience members. No!

The President. You might not care as much; that you might be willing to let the other folks who left the economy in a shambles go back to Washington and go back to Annapolis.

Audience members. No!

The President. Well, Maryland, I think the pundits are wrong. But it's up to you to prove them wrong. Don't make me look bad, now. [*Laughter*] I'm betting on you, not on them. But it's up to you to defy the conventional wisdom. It's up to you to show the pundits that you care too much to let this country fall backwards. You want it to keep moving forward; that you're ready to fight for our future.

So make no mistake: This election is a choice. And that choice could not be clearer. I mean, think about it. This is not as if candidates in the other party were offering new ideas. They didn't go meditate and say, boy, we really

messed up, let's try to figure out if we can do some things better. That's not what happened. It's not as if they've changed their agenda since the last time they ran Washington or the last time they ran Annapolis.

In fact, the chairman of one of their campaign committees promised that if Republicans take control of Congress, they will follow the exact same agenda they pursued during the last administration.

Audience members. Boo!

The President. That's what they said. And we all know what that agenda was. Basically, you've been there, done that. [*Laughter*] Basically, what they're saying is we're going to cut taxes, mostly for millionaires and billionaires. Then we're going to cut regulations for special interests. We're going to cut back on investments in education and clean energy, in research and technology. And basically, the idea is if we just put blind faith in the marketplace and if we let corporations play by their own rules, and we leave everybody else to fend for themselves, then America is going to somehow grow and prosper. What did this young lady say? Been there, done that.

I mean, there is a problem with their approach, which is we tried it, and it didn't work. It didn't work for middle class families who saw their incomes fall by 5 percent when they were in power. Middle class incomes fell. That's not—don't take my word for it. That's the Wall Street Journal. Meanwhile, your costs for everything from health care to college tuition went up when they were in charge. Job growth, when they were in charge, was slower than any time since World War II. Think about that. They weren't creating jobs. They're going around talking about jobs now. They had 8 years. They took a record surplus left by President Bill Clinton, they came back with a record deficit by the time I took office. Now, they're out there talking about deficit reduction. We saw what you had to do with the deficit. It didn't work when there was a free-for-all on Wall Street that led to a crisis that we're still struggling through today.

Now, I bring this up not to relitigate the past. I just don't want to relive the past. I don't want to go through that mess again. That's the philosophy the other side wants to bring to Washington and wants to bring to Annapolis if they win in November. That's the philosophy that Martin's opponent espouses. Republicans might have given it a new name—they called it the "Pledge to America"—but it's the same old snake oil they've been peddling for years. Same old stuff. Same old stuff.

Now, I want everybody to take a look at this "Pledge to America." It's interesting. They put it out with great fanfare, but now nobody is really talking about it. But let's examine their pledge. For starters, it turns out the pledge was actually written in part by a former lobbyist for AIG and ExxonMobil.

Audience members. Boo!

The President. You can't make this stuff up. [*Laughter*] So they helped write this thing. The centerpiece of the pledge, their big idea, is a $700 billion tax cut for the wealthiest 2 percent of Americans. That's their big idea. So how many folks here make more than $250,000 a year? Just a show of hands here. All right. You need to donate to Martin O'Malley's campaign. [*Laughter*] For the rest of you, their idea isn't much. I mean, these are the folks who want to lecture us on fiscal responsibility. They want to borrow $700 billion, and then they want to give out tax cuts worth an average of $100,000 to millionaires and billionaires.

And when you ask them, "Well, where are going to get this $700 billion?" they don't have an answer. They don't have an answer. They don't know. I guess we'd have to borrow it from China. [*Laughter*]

But when you look at the "Pledge to America," it turns out they do have an idea about how to pay for a small portion of it. They want to cut education by 20 percent.

Audience members. Boo!

The President. That's a cut that would reduce financial aid for 8 million college students, including a whole bunch of college students right here at BSU.

Audience members. Boo!

The President. Now, I want to just focus on this for a minute, because here in Maryland, you understand how important education is to

our economy, how important it is to our future. Martin O'Malley knows that too. His opponent raised college tuition in this State by 40 percent when he was in charge. This is at a time when the economy was doing better. Now, even in the toughest of times, over the last 2 years, Martin O'Malley froze in-State tuition, so he kept the cost of this school and other schools affordable for Maryland's families. And thanks to his unprecedented investment in Maryland's education, as I said before, you've been ranked the best when it comes to public schools the last 2 years in a row. That's what Martin O'Malley does. He walks the walk, doesn't just talk the talk.

But we can't maintain this progress if our opponents have their way. At a time when the education of our country's citizens is one of the biggest predictors of economic success, they think it's more important to give another tax break to folks who don't need it and weren't even asking for them than to invest in our young people.

Let me ask you—I want to ask my Republican friends a question here: Do you think China is cutting back on education right now?

Audience members. No!

The President. Do you think South Korea is making it harder for its citizens to get a college education?

Audience members. No!

The President. Those countries aren't playing for second place. And guess what? The United States does not play for second place. We play for first place. We're going to make investments in you.

As long as I am President, and as long as Martin O'Malley is your Governor, we will not allow politicians in Washington or Annapolis sacrifice your education for tax cuts we can't afford. That is the choice in this election.

Martin, me, Barbara, Steny, the rest of the folks up on this stage, we've got a different idea about what the next 2 years should look like, and it's an idea rooted in our belief about how this country was built. We know government doesn't have all the answers to our problems. We don't believe that government's main role is to create jobs or prosperity. We think government should be lean; we think it should be efficient.

That's why Martin actually cut spending by $5 billion. He's reduced the size of government in this State. That's why I've proposed a 3-year freeze and set up a bipartisan fiscal commission to deal with our deficit.

But what we also understand, in the words of the first Republican President, Abraham Lincoln, is that government should do for the people what they cannot do better for themselves.

I think we might have had somebody faint down here. So if we got the paramedics—right here up front, everybody is pointing at him. Now—they'll be all right, just make sure you give him some space. And if somebody has a bottle of water, you might want to get it to him.

Look, we believe in a country that rewards hard work and responsibility. We believe in a country where we look after one another, where we say, I am my brother's keeper, I am my sister's keeper. That's the America I know. That's the America Martin cares about. That's the choice in this election.

Instead of tax breaks for millionaires and billionaires, we want to make permanent the tax cuts we gave to middle class Americans, because you deserve a break. [*Laughter*] Instead of the other side's plan to keep tax breaks for companies that ship jobs overseas, we want to give tax breaks to companies that invest right here in the United States of America, to small businesses, American manufacturers, American clean energy companies. I don't want solar panels and wind turbines and electric cars built in Asia or built in Europe. I want them made right here in the United States of America by American workers.

Audience members. U.S.A.! U.S.A.! U.S.A.!

The President. Instead of cutting education, cutting student aid, we want to make permanent our new college tax credit. This is a credit worth $10,000 in tuition relief for every young person going to 4 years of college. That means you, Bowie State.

We will fight to keep the reforms we've made to the student loan system. Thanks to those reforms, tens of billions of dollars in taxpayer subsidies that would have gone to big banks are now going to where they should, to students like you.

If the other side wins, they'll try their hardest to give free rein back to the insurance companies and the credit card companies and the Wall Street banks that we're finally holding accountable. We can't let them do that. We can't go back to the days of taxpayer-funded bailouts or when credit card companies could just jack up your rates without reason. We can't go back to the days when insurance companies could just drop your coverage because you're sick. We've got to keep in place the new law that says if you're out there looking for a job or have one that don't offer you coverage, you should be able to stay on your parent's insurance policy until you're 26 years old.

That's the choice in this election. That's what's at stake right now. So, Maryland, it comes down to this: A lot of folks running in the other party, these are the exact same people who spent the last decade driving this economy into a ditch. And so, for the last 20 months, me and Martin and Steny and Barbara and all these folks, we have gotten down into the ditch, put on our boots. We're down there. It's hot. We were sweating, bugs everywhere. We're down there pushing, pushing, pushing on the car. Every once in a while we'd look up and see the Republicans standing there. They're just standing there fanning themselves—[*laughter*]—sipping on a Slurpee. [*Laughter*] And we'd say, "Come on down and help." They'd say, "No, that's all right." [*Laughter*] They'd say, "You're not pushing the right way. You got to push faster."

And we just kept on pushing and pushing. And finally, we got this car up on level ground. Finally, we got it up on level ground. Now, this car is a little beat up now because they drove it into the ditch. It's got some dents, needs a tune-up. But it's pointing in the right direction.

We want to start back on that road to prosperity, but suddenly, we feel this tap on our shoulder. We look back. Who is it? It's the Republicans. And they say, "We want the keys back." And we got to tell them, you can't have the keys back because you don't know how to drive. You don't know how to drive. We'll give you a ride if you want, but you got to sit in the backseat. We'll take you to prosperity, but you got to sit in the backseat because you don't know how to drive.

Have you ever noticed, when you get in your car, if you want to go forward, what do you do? You got to put it in "D." If you want to go backwards, what do you do? You put it in "R." That is not a coincidence. We don't want to go backwards.

But it's up to you to make sure they don't get the keys back. See, the other side sees a chance to get back in the driver's seat. And by the way, thanks to a recent Supreme Court decision, they are being helped this year like we've never seen before by special interest groups that are spending unlimited amounts of money on attack ads. And then they don't disclose who is behind them. Because of the Supreme Court law, they don't have to disclose who is behind it.

It could be the oil companies. It could be the insurance industry. It could be Wall Street. You don't know. Their lips are sealed. The floodgates are open, though. And almost every one of these independent organizations is run by Republican operatives. They're posing as nonprofit, nonpolitical groups. They've got names like Americans for Prosperity or the Committee for Truth in Politics or Moms for Motherhood. Actually, the last one I made up. [*Laughter*]

But you'd think—there was a recent report that in recent weeks, conservative groups like this have outspent Democratic groups by 7 to 1.

There's another one up here who got a little hot. Let him sit down. Let him sit down. All right, you got another bottle of water? If we can get another bottle of water up here and a medic up here.

Now, I want to remember, next time you guys come out here, make sure you drink something and eat something before you're standing here, especially when you got a bunch of politicians talking. [*Laughter*]

But I want you to understand this, because this is important. It is estimated that Democratic groups are being outspent 7 to 1. In Indiana's Senate race, it's nearly 6 to 1. In a House race there, a conservative group has spent nearly as much as both parties combined. In Colorado, they're outspending the Democratic Party near-

ly 2 to 1. In Missouri, the Republicans' Senate committee hasn't spent a dime, but outside groups have dropped $2 million of negative ads to help the Republican candidate.

Just this week, we learned that one of the largest groups paying for these ads regularly takes in money from foreign corporations. So groups that receive foreign money are spending huge sums to influence American elections, and they won't tell you where the money for their ads come from.

So this isn't just a threat to Democrats. All Republicans should be concerned. Independents should be concerned. This is a threat to our democracy. The American people deserve to know who's trying to sway their elections. And if we just stand by and allow the special interests to silence anybody who's got the guts to stand up to them, our country is going to be a very different place.

So here's the bottom line. We're going to need to work even harder in this election. We're going to need to fight their millions of dollars with millions of voices, everybody here who is ready to finish what we started in 2008. Because if everybody who fought for change in 2008 shows up on November 2, I am absolutely confident we will win.

What the other side is counting on, the other side is counting on, is that this time around you're going to stay home. They're counting on your silence. They're counting on amnesia. They're counting on your apathy, especially the young people here. They don't believe you're going to come out and vote. They figure Obama is not on the ballot, you're not going to come out and vote.

Maryland, you've got to prove them wrong. Let's show Washington one more time change doesn't come from the top. It doesn't come from millions of dollars of attack ads funded by special interests. Change happens from the bottom up. Change happens because of you.

So I know times are tough. And I know we're a long way from the hope and the excitement we all felt on election night and Inauguration Day. But we always knew this was going to take time. We always knew it was going to be hard. I said it was going to be hard. Change has always been hard.

From the first days of our Nation, every time Americans have tried to bring about real, meaningful change, we faced setbacks and disappointments. From the founding of this country—George Washington experienced setbacks and disappointments. We've had to face fear and doubt. Harriet Tubman had fear and doubt. But as Americans, we have always moved forward. We have always kept fighting. We've always remembered that in the United States of America, our destiny is not written for us, it is written by us. That's how we got through war. That's how we got through depression. That's what civil rights workers understood. That's how we got women's rights and workers' rights. And that's what's being tested right now.

And if we've got the courage to keep moving forward, even in the face of difficulty, even in the face of uncertainty, I guarantee, if all of you are out there knocking on doors and making phone calls and voting for Martin O'Malley and Barbara Mikulski and the rest of the Democratic ticket, then we are not just going to win this election, but we are going to make sure that the American Dream is alive and well for future generations.

Thank you, everybody. God bless you, and God bless the United States of America.

NOTE: The President spoke at 3:25 p.m. at Bowie State University. In his remarks, he referred to former Gov. Timothy M. Kaine of Virginia, in his capacity as chairman of the Democratic National Committee; musicians Beyonce G. Knowles and Paul D. "Bono" Hewson; Rep. Pete Sessions, in his capacity as chairman of the National Republican Congressional Committee; and former lobbyist Brian Wild.

Statement on Archbishop Desmond Tutu's Retirement From Public Life
October 7, 2010

It is with deep appreciation that I note Archbishop Desmond Tutu's retirement from public life today on the occasion of his 79th birthday. This event invites us to celebrate his many accomplishments, from which we have all benefited. For decades he has been a moral titan: a voice of principle, an unrelenting champion of justice, and a dedicated peacemaker. He played a pivotal role in his country's struggle against apartheid and extraordinary example of pursuing a path to forgiveness and reconciliation in the new South Africa. He has also been an outspoken voice for freedom and justice in countries across the globe; a staunch defender of the rights of lesbian, gay, bisexual, and transgender persons; and an advocate for treatment and prevention programs to stop the spread of HIV/AIDS. We will miss his insight and his activism, but will continue to learn from his example. We wish the Archbishop and his family happiness in the years ahead.

Statement on Signing the Intelligence Authorization Act for Fiscal Year 2010
October 7, 2010

Today I have signed into law H.R. 2701, the "Intelligence Authorization Act for Fiscal Year 2010." This is the first intelligence authorization act enacted in nearly 6 years, and it includes a number of provisions that will assist in the effective and efficient execution of Intelligence Community (IC) programs. One such provision would facilitate information sharing by IC elements with the National Counterterrorism Center and the Office of the Director of National Intelligence (ODNI).

In a September 27, 2010, letter to Congress, the ODNI summarized my Administration's understanding of how sections 331 and 348 of the bill would be interpreted. In particular, section 331 addresses the fundamental compact between the Congress and the President regarding the reporting of sensitive intelligence matters as embodied in title V of the National Security Act. Section 331's requirement to provide a "general description" of a covert action finding or notification provides sufficient flexibility to craft an appropriate description for the limited notification, based on the extraordinary circumstances affecting vital interests of the United States and recognizing the President's authority to protect sensitive national security information. Also, as previously indicated, my Administration understands section 331's requirement to provide to the intelligence committees "the legal basis" under which certain intelligence activities and covert actions are being or were conducted as not requiring disclosure of any privileged advice or information or disclosure of information in any particular form.

In a March 15, 2010, letter to Congress, the Department of Justice summarized my Administration's understanding of a number of provisions. In particular, section 405 establishes an Inspector General of the Intelligence Community in the ODNI. In accordance with long-standing executive branch policy, my Administration understands section 405's requirement that the Inspector General make an immediate report to congressional committees regarding investigations focused upon certain current or former IC officials as not requiring the disclosure of privileged or otherwise confidential law enforcement information. Moreover, the whistleblower protection provisions in section 405 are properly viewed as consistent with President Clinton's stated understanding of a provision with substantially similar language in the Intelligence Authorization Act for Fiscal Year 1999. See *Statement on Signing the Intelligence Authorization Act for Fiscal Year 1999*: Public Papers of the Presidents of the United States, William J. Clinton, 1998 (p. 1825).

BARACK OBAMA

The White House,
October 7, 2010.

NOTE: H.R. 2701, approved October 7, was assigned Public Law No. 111–259.

Remarks at a Reception for Senatorial Candidate Alexi Giannoulias in Chicago, Illinois
October 7, 2010

The President. Hello, Chicago! Oh, it's good to be home! It is good to be home. Got all my friends—all my friends—in the house.

Audience member. Long time no see.

The President: Long time no see.

It is wonderful to see—I see so many familiar faces here. Just a couple of people I've got to make mention of. First of all, he may be in my remarks, but I just want to say that there is nobody who was a better partner to me when I was in the United States Senate, nobody who is a better friend to working families here in Illinois, and nobody who is a better debater on the floor of the United States Senate than the man to my left, Dick Durbin. So love Dick Durbin. Love Dick Durbin. I love Loretta Durbin more. [*Laughter*] But Dick Durbin I love.

We also—if I'm not mistaken, we've got the junior Senator from Illinois, Roland Burris, in the house. Where's Roland? There he is right there. Appreciate Roland for his outstanding service.

We've got the next Lieutenant Governor of the great State of Illinois, Sheila Simon, who, by the way, knows a little bit about good Senators. Congressman Danny Davis is in the house. Congresswoman Jan Schakowsky is here—love Jan. Attorney General Lisa Madigan is here. Comptroller Dan Hynes is here. Senate President John Cullerton is here. The next treasurer, Robin Kelly, is in the house. The next comptroller, David Miller, is in the house.

Now, I see everybody else here. [*Laughter*] But if I started naming everybody I know, I'm in trouble. So I've just got to stop—[*laughter*]—except to say that it's also nice to be standing here with the next Senator from the great State of Illinois, Alexi Giannoulias.

Alexi is my friend. I know his character. I know how much he loves this country. I know how committed he is to public service. He has been a great advocate on behalf of the people of Illinois, and he's in this for the right reasons. He's not in it for the special interests; he's in it for your interests. You may not always agree with him, but you always know where he stands. He's comfortable in his own skin. He doesn't shift with the wind. He doesn't pretend to be something that he's not. You know who he is today and who he'll be tomorrow, and that's important. You can trust him. You can count on him.

And let me just also say—because I play basketball with him—[*laughter*]—and I have still some sore ribs to prove it—he's a competitor. And we've seen that in this campaign. He just keeps on plowing ahead, because he knows that he wants to serve. In some very tough circumstances, in a tough political season, he has not wavered. And that's the kind of person that you want. That's the kind of person that you know, when the going gets tough in Washington, will be fighting for you.

So I hope you're fired up in these last few weeks. I need you to be fired up. Fired up and ready to go. I need it. I need that because there is an election—in case you were curious—[*laughter*]—on November 2—an election—you can begin voting next week—that's going to say a lot about the future, your future and the future of our country. So you've got to be fired up.

Now, this is Chicago, so I know politics is—this is sport right here. [*Laughter*] I mean, I know everybody is paying attention. By the way, have you seen my Chief of Staff? [*Laughter*] I was like, looking around, it's like, what happened? [*Laughter*]

Two years ago, you defied the conventional wisdom in Washington, because they said you couldn't overcome the cynicism of our politics. You couldn't overcome the special interests. You can't make big progress on big issues. Can't happen. They said, no, you can't.

What did you say?

Audience members. Yes, we can!

The President. You said, yes, we can.

But sometimes, I feel as if we had such a high on election night, and then there was the Inauguration and Bono was singing and Beyonce and—[*laughter*]—everybody from Chicago

went to Washington and was having a big party. But I have to remind you that the victory in that campaign didn't deliver the change that we needed. It just gave us the chance to make change happen. That was the start, not the finish, of the journey. And it made each of you a shareholder in the mission of rebuilding our country and reclaiming our future. And I'm back today because 2 years later, the success of that mission is at stake.

After that last election, it was my hope that we could pull together, Democrats and Republicans, and start dealing with the worst crisis we had seen since the Great Depression. That was my fervent hope because we may be proud Democrats, but we're prouder to be Americans. And there are Republicans across the country who feel the same way.

But the Republicans in Washington, they had a different idea. They knew it was going to take more than 2 years to climb out of this mess that they had created. They knew that by the time of this election, the midterm election, that there would still be people out of work, that people would be frustrated. And they figured if they just sat on the sidelines and just said no, opposed every idea I offered or Dick offered or Jan offered or Danny offered, if they spent all their time attacking Democrats instead of attacking our problems, then they'd have a chance to prosper at the polls. That was their calculation.

And they just spent the last 20 months saying no, even to policies that they had supported in the past. They said no to middle class tax cuts. They said no to help for small businesses. They said no to a bipartisan deficit reduction commission that they had cosponsored. And when I was for it, suddenly, they were against it. If I said the sky was blue, they said no. [*Laughter*] If I said there were fish in the sea—no. Their calculation was if Obama fails, we win. They were very explicit about it.

Now, they figured that that political game would get them through an election. But I knew it wasn't going to get America through the crisis. So I made a different calculation. I made a different choice. I took whatever steps were necessary to stop the economic freefall—with the help of people like Dick, with the help of people like Jan and Danny—even if those measures were not popular, even if they were not easy. Because you did not send me to Washington to do what was easy. You didn't send me to put my finger out to the wind and measure which way the wind was blowing and try to figure out how to stay in office. You elected me to do what was right. That's why you sent me.

So 20 months later, we no longer face the possibility of a second depression. Our economy is growing again, The private sector has created jobs for 8 months in a row. There are 3 million Americans who wouldn't be working today if it weren't for the economic plan we put into place.

When we came in, when I flew in on Air Force One and we landed at O'Hare, there were a group of folks greeting us there. And there were a group of folks who had gotten jobs directly as a consequence of the Recovery Act. And so we know that we did the right thing.

But look, we've still got a long way to go. Because the hole that we're climbing out of is so deep, there are still millions of Americans without work. The 6 months before I was sworn in we had lost 4 million jobs. We lost 750,000 the month I was sworn in, 600,000 the 2 months subsequent after that. And so most of the 8 million jobs we lost were before any of our economic plans took effect. And that means we've got a big hole to fill. There are still millions of families who can barely pay the bills or make a mortgage. Middle class families who were struggling to get by before the crisis hit are still treading water.

So of course people are frustrated. Of course people are impatient. I'm impatient. But the other side decided, we're just going to try to ride that anger, that frustration, to the ballot box, without offering any serious ideas about how to solve our problems. And now the pundits are saying, well, the other party's supporters, they're more excited. They say all of you who worked so hard in 2008 might not be as excited this time, you might not be as energized, you might not care as much; that you don't mind if the same politicians and policies that created this mess, left the economy in a sham-

bles, return to Washington. That's what the pundits are predicting. They're basically counting on you all having amnesia. [*Laughter*]

But I think they're wrong, Chicago. And it's up to you to prove them wrong. It's up to you to defy the conventional wisdom once again. It's up to you to show the pundits that you love this country too much to let it fall backwards; you are ready to move forward. You've got to show them that you're ready to fight for our future.

Because this election is a choice. Don't—no mistaking the situation here. The choice could not be clearer. Because it's not as if the Republicans, they went off into the desert and meditated after 2008, and they said: "Boy, what did we do wrong? We got this—as a consequence of our stewardship, the whole economy is in meltdown." That's not what they did. They didn't come back with a set of new ideas. They haven't changed their agenda since the last time they ran Washington. The chairman of one of their campaign committees promised that if Republicans take control of Congress, they will follow—and I'm quoting—"the exact same agenda" they pursued during the last administration.

And we know what that agenda was: You cut taxes, mostly for millionaires and billionaires; you cut regulations for special interests; you cut investments in education and clean energy, in research and development and technology. So basically, you just put blind faith in the market, we let corporations play by their own rules, we leave everybody else to fend for themselves, and somehow America is going to prosper.

Here's the thing, though. We know what happened. It's not as if we didn't try that. We tried it for 8 years. It didn't work. It didn't work for middle class families who saw their incomes fall—wages went down 5 percent between 2001 and 2009—when they were in power. That's not according to me; that's according to the Wall Street Journal. Job growth was slower during that period than any decade since World War II.

These guys are talking about jobs now? They had 8 years and it didn't work. They took a record surplus left by President Bill Clinton and it became a record deficit by the time I took office, a big $1.3 trillion present they left me as I walked in the Oval Office. They set up a free-for-all on Wall Street that led to a crisis that we're still grappling with today.

Now, I bring up all these things not to relitigate the past. I just don't want to relive the past. And I bring this up because that is the philosophy that Republicans like Alexi's opponent intend to bring back if they win in November. Now, they might have a new name for it. They call it the "Pledge to America." [*Laughter*] The "Pledge to America," it's the same stuff they've been peddling for years. [*Laughter*] They're trying to hoodwink you once again.

Let's take a look at the "Pledge to America." Some of you may not have examined it. [*Laughter*] Now, for starters, it turns out that part of the pledge was actually written by a former lobbyist for AIG and ExxonMobil. You cannot—yes—[*laughter*]—you can't make this stuff up. [*Laughter*] So that gives you a clue of who they're making the pledge to.

Then the centerpiece of this pledge is a $700 billion tax cut for the wealthiest 2 percent of Americans. That is their big idea. Now, these are the folks who lecture us on fiscal responsibility, so I have to point out we don't have $700 billion. We'd have to borrow $700 billion—from the Chinese or the Saudis—and then use it to provide tax cuts worth an average of $100,000 to millionaires and billionaires.

When you ask them, "Well, where are you going to find the $700 billion?" they don't have an answer. But when you look at the fine print, it turns out that a small portion of the tax cut they want to pay for by cutting education by 20 percent—20 percent—which would translate into reduce financial aid for 8 million college students. At a time when education is the biggest predictor of a country's economic success, they think it's more important to provide these tax breaks to folks who don't need them, weren't asking for them, than it is to make sure that our young people can get to college, which makes me want to ask our Republican friends, do you think China is cutting back on education? Do you think South Korea is making it harder for its citizens to get a college education? These countries are not playing for second place. And the United States of America does

not play for second place. We play for first. That's what this election is about. That's what this election is about.

See, Alexi and I have a different idea about what the next 2 years should look like. It's an idea rooted in our belief about how this country was built. We know government doesn't have all the answers to all of our problems. We don't believe government's main role is to create jobs or prosperity. We believe government should be lean and efficient and that the private sector should be creating jobs. We want to reduce the deficit, which is why we've proposed a 3-year spending freeze and we set up that bipartisan fiscal commission to deal with our deficit that the other side voted against.

But we also believe in America we reward hard work and responsibility. We believe this is a country where we look after one another; that we are our brother's keeper, our sister's keeper. That's the America I know. That's the choice in this election.

So instead of tax cuts for millionaires and billionaires, we want to make permanent tax cuts for middle class Americans because folks who work hard every day, they deserve a break. Instead of the Republican plan to keep tax breaks for companies that are shipping jobs overseas, we want to give tax breaks to companies that are investing here in the United States of America, to small businesses and American manufacturers and clean energy companies. I don't want solar panels and wind turbines and electric cars made in Europe and Asia. I want them built here, in the United States, by American workers.

If Republicans take back Congress, they will try their hardest to give back power to the same special interests that me and Dick and Jan and Danny have been fighting for the last 20 months. We can't let them do that. We can't go back to the days when insurance companies could drop your health insurance when you got sick. We can't go back to the day when credit cards could jack up your rates for no reason. We can't go back to the days of taxpayer-funded bailouts. We can't allow special interests to take free rein again.

That's why I'm proud to be standing next to Alexi. He's made it clear he'll fight for you in the United States Senate. He's not funding his campaign with Federal PACs or lobbyist money. On his first day in office, he enacted the most sweeping ethics reforms of any Illinois State treasurer, ensuring that contractors and banks couldn't "pay to play" for State business. He took on credit card companies and banned them from aggressively marketing on college campuses, so that our kids don't graduate with credit card debt on top of tuition debt.

And a lot of you know what he did for Hartmarx, which, by the way, made this suit. It's a company that's employed people in this State for more than a hundred years. And when it fell on hard times, and a big bank threatened to pull its credit, risking more than 600 jobs, Alexi stepped in. He told that bank if they did that they'd no longer manage the money of Illinois taxpayers. He helped save that company, those jobs. They can testify about who he's going to fight for, who he cares about.

That's the kind of person you want in the United States Senate, somebody who doesn't forget where they came from, why they're in this, who they're fighting for. Somebody who does not stop fighting, period, because there's too much at stake right now to give up the fight.

So it comes down to this, Chicago. There are a lot of folks in the other party who are running today who are the same folks who drove this economy into the ditch. And me and the rest of the Democrats here in Washington, we climbed down into that ditch. We put on our boots. It was muddy. It was hot. [*Laughter*] There's bugs. [*Laughter*] But we pushed and we pushed and we pushed. And every once in a while we'd look up and see the Republicans up there, looking comfortable, fanning themselves, sipping on Slurpees. [*Laughter*] And we'd say, "Why don't you come down and help?" And they'd say: "No, but you're not pushing hard enough. You're not pushing the right way." [*Laughter*] And we just kept on pushing. And finally, we got the car up on level ground. Finally, we got it on level ground.

Now, it's gone through some trauma, so the fender is all dented, needs a tuneup. [*Laughter*]

But it's on level ground, it's pointing in the right direction. And suddenly, we feel this tap on our shoulder, and we look back and it's the Republicans. And we say, "What do you want?" They say, "We want the keys back." [*Laughter*]

And you tell them: "No, you can't have the keys back. You don't know how to drive!" You do not know how to drive. You can join us. You can hop in the backseat. [*Laughter*] But we're not giving you the keys back.

Have you ever noticed when you drive, you want to go forward, what do you do? You put the car in "D." If you want to go backwards, you put it in "R." [*Laughter*] That's not a coincidence. Not a coincidence.

But whether they get the keys back is ultimately up to you. They see a chance to get back in the driver's seat with the special interests riding shotgun. And thanks to a recent Supreme Court decision, they're being helped along by special interest groups that are spending unlimited amounts of money all on attack ads, and they don't disclose who's behind the ads. It could be an oil industry, could be an insurance company, could be Wall Street, you don't know. Almost every one of them is run by Republican operatives. They're posing as nonprofits, nonpolitical groups. They've got these innocuous-sounding names like Americans for Prosperity or the Committee for Truth in Politics or Moms for Motherhood. [*Laughter*] I made that last one up. [*Laughter*] But you wouldn't know. [*Laughter*]

According to one recent report, conservatives—conservative groups like these have outspent Democrats 7 to 1. Right here in Illinois, in this Senate race, two groups funded and advised by Karl Rove have outspent the Democratic Party 2 to 1 in an attempt to beat Alexi—2 to 1. Funded and advised by Karl Rove. Just this week, we learned that one of the largest groups paying for these ads regularly takes in money from foreign sources.

So the question for the people of Illinois is, are you going to let special interests from Wall Street and Washington and maybe places beyond our shores come to this State and tell us who our Senator should be?

Audience members. No!

The President. That's not just a threat to Democrats. That's a threat to our democracy. The American people deserve to know who's trying to sway their election. And if we just stand by and allow special interests to silence anybody who's got the guts to stand up against them, our country is going to be a very different place. That's not how our democracy operates.

So that's why we've got to work even harder in this election. That's why we need to fight their millions of dollars with millions of voices who are ready to finish what we started in 2008. Because if everybody who fought for change in 2008 shows up to vote in 2010, we will win. And by the way, most of the polls say the same thing. Alexi will win. Pat Quinn will win. The entire ticket will win.

So they are counting on you staying home and being apathetic. They're counting on your silence. They are counting on your amnesia. That's what they're counting on.

So, Chicago, prove them wrong. Let's show Washington one more time change doesn't come from the top, it doesn't come from mil-lions of dollars of attack ads. Change happens from the bottom up. Change happens because of you.

And if you get fired up one more time, if you're knocking on doors and making phone calls and talking to your friends and going in the barbershops, going in the beauty shops, I promise you we will have Alexi as the next Senator from the great State of Illinois.

Thank you very much. God bless you, and God bless the United States of America.

NOTE: The President spoke at 6:15 p.m. at the Drake Hotel. In his remarks, he referred to Loretta S. Durbin, wife of Sen. Richard J. Durbin; former White House Chief of Staff Rahm I. Emanuel; musicians Paul D. "Bono" Hewson and Beyonce G. Knowles; Rep. Pete Sessions, in his capacity as chairman of the National Republican Congressional Committee; Sen. Mark S. Kirk; former lobbyist Brian Wild; former White House Deputy Chief of Staff Karl C. Rove; and Gov. Patrick J. Quinn III of Illinois.

Remarks at Ernest Maier Inc. in Bladensburg, Maryland
October 8, 2010

Good morning, everybody. It is good to be here at Ernest Maier Block. I just had a chance to take a quick tour, a look around with Brendan Quinn, president and CEO of Ernest Maier, and it's a remarkable story. Brendan came here initially to help a family business, turn it around; it was experiencing losses. He ended up purchasing the company and now has grown it enormously—has terrific employees here. He provides full health insurance to them. They are supporting their families, and even during this difficult downturn, he hasn't had to lay anybody off and is still confident about its growth. So we're just very proud of him and what this company has accomplished.

These are the guys that build serious stuff: concrete blocks, bricks for walls that are thick, difficult to move, and can stop anything in their path—sort of like the way I feel about Congress sometimes. But this is a family business that's been here over 80 years. They believe in invest-ing in their workers. They care about the environment, so they collect and process using cooking oil from local restaurants to power some of their equipment. Their community cares about them, so business is growing. Brendan has hired folks this year, and with the smart investments he's made, he hopes to continue that growth.

Small businesses like this one are the bricks and blocks of our entire economy. And over the past 2 years, my administration has been doing everything we can to help encourage more success stories like this, because it is small businesses that will power our growth and put our people back to work.

This morning we learned that in the month of September our economy gained 64,000 jobs in the private sector. July and August private sector job numbers were revised upwards. So we've now seen 9 straight months of private sector job growth; in all, more than 850,000 private sector jobs gained this year, which is in sharp contrast to the almost 800,000 jobs that we were losing when I first took office. But that news is tempered by a net job loss in September, which was fueled in large measure by the end of temporary census jobs and by layoffs in State and local governments.

I should point out that these continuing layoffs by State and local governments—of teachers and police officers and firefighters and the like—would have been even worse without the Federal help that we've provided to States over the last 20 months, help that the Republicans in Congress have consistently opposed. I think the Republican position doesn't make much sense, especially since the weakness in public sector employment is a drag on the private sector as well. So we need to continue to explore ways that we can help States and local governments maintain workers who provide vital services.

At the same time, we have to keep doing everything we can to accelerate this recovery. Yes, the trend line in private sector job growth is moving in the right direction. But I'm not interested in trends or figures as much as I am interested in the people behind them, the millions of honest, hard-working Americans swept up in the most devastating recession of our lifetimes. As I've said before, the only piece of economic news that folks still looking for work want to hear is, "You're hired." And everything we do is dedicated to make that happen.

Last week, for example, I signed into law the Small Business Jobs Act, a small-business bill that does some big things. And I want to mention three of them today.

First, within the 11 days since it took effect, more than 2,000 small-business owners have already received more than a billion dollars' worth of new loans, with more to come. And beginning today, the Small Business Administration is offering larger loans for folks who need them.

Second, it expands the tax cut for all the equipment investment small businesses make this year, something that Brendan is planning to take advantage of here at Maier Block. And we were just talking about his belief that the more we can accelerate depreciation, the more likely

we're going to see businesses like his make these investments.

It's going to help small-business owners upgrade their plants and equipment, it will encourage large corporations to get off the sidelines and start putting their profits back into the economy, and it will accelerate $55 billion in tax cuts for businesses that make job-creating investments over the next year.

Third, it creates a new initiative to strengthen State programs that spur private sector lending to small businesses, a step that will support $15 billion in new small-business loans across the country. Maryland, for example, will be able to support $250 million in new lending for businesses that are expanding and creating jobs in communities like this one.

Thousands of small-business owners across America had been waiting for months for this bill to pass, for the loans and tax cuts they have badly needed to grow their businesses and hire new employees. Unfortunately, it was held up all summer by a partisan minority until a few courageous Republican Senators put politics aside. Just imagine the difference it could have made for small businesses and our economy had it happened months before.

Putting the American people back to work, expanding opportunity, rebuilding the economic security of the middle class is the moral and national challenge of our time. It is too important to fall prey to pure partisanship or blind ideology. This bill's rapid results prove that when we work together, we can get a lot done. And that's what the great debate we're having today is all about.

I believe that instead of extending tax loopholes that encourage investments in overseas jobs, we should permanently extend the tax credit that goes to companies for all the research and innovation they do right here in America.

I believe that instead of borrowing another $700 billion we don't have to give tax cuts to the wealthiest 2 percent of Americans who don't need them, we should permanently extend the tax cuts for middle class families. They're the folks who saw their wages and incomes flatline over the past decade, and they're the ones who deserve a break.

And I believe that instead of sitting still, we should invest in rebuilding America's roads and railways and runways. Too many American workers have been out of work for months, even years, and that doesn't do anybody any good when there is so much of America to rebuild. Our infrastructure is falling far behind what the rest of the world is doing, and upgrading it is vital to our economy and our future competitiveness. This is a project worthy of America's efforts. It's something that engineers, economists, Governors, and mayors of every political stripe support, and many of them issued a sobering report about this challenge last week. And on Monday, I will be meeting with some of them at the White House to discuss how we can put Americans to work doing what they do best, building America.

As I've said many times before, it took us a long time to get out of where we are right now. And the damage left by this recession is so deep that it's going to take a long time to get out. It will take determination, persistence, and most importantly, the will to act, all elements that the American people have in abundance. And if we summon that spirit now, if we keep moving forward, I'm absolutely convinced that we will rebuild our economy, we will put our people back to work, and we'll come through these tough days to brighter and better days ahead.

And I want to thank Brendan not only for his hospitality here today, but somebody who's got the courage and the foresight and the skills to create a terrific business that's supporting so many families. Thank you very much.

NOTE: The President spoke at 11:40 a.m.

Remarks on the Resignation of James L. Jones, Jr., as National Security Adviser and the Appointment of Thomas E. Donilon as National Security Adviser
October 8, 2010

The President. Good afternoon, everybody. When I took office, I pledged to do whatever was required to protect the American people and restore American leadership in the world. And over the past 20 months, that's exactly what we've done. During this time, I've relied every day on the advice and counsel of my National Security Adviser, General Jim Jones.

When I talked to Jim about taking this job shortly after the election, it was a difficult decision for him. He had just retired from the military, had a wide range of family obligations. But because of his patriotism, his dedication to keeping America safe, we were able to agree that he would serve, but he asked that we would—he would serve for about 2 years. I am extraordinarily thankful that both he and his wife Diane agreed to make that additional sacrifice for our country.

Today, as we approach that 2-year mark, I'm announcing that Jim has decided to step aside as National Security Adviser later this month

and that he will be succeeded by his very capable deputy, Tom Donilon.

The American people owe Jim an unbelievable debt of gratitude for a lifetime of service. As a marine in Vietnam, he risked his life for our country and was highly decorated for his courage. As Commandant of the Marine Corps, he led our Marines into the 21st century and won widespread admiration within the Corps and beyond. As Supreme Allied Commander in Europe, he helped the NATO alliance prepare for the new missions of our time. And given the multiple crises that we inherited, Jim has drawn on all of these experiences as National Security Adviser.

The list of challenges that our country has faced these last 2 years is daunting. Since my administration took office, we have removed nearly 100,000 troops and ended our combat mission in Iraq. We've refocused on the war against Al Qaida and subjected its leadership to relentless pressure. We are pursuing a new strategy that finally devotes the resources we need in the fight against extremism in Afghanistan and Pakistan.

We've reset relations with Russia and signed a historic new START Treaty. And after years of drift, we have built a broad international coalition to hold Iran accountable and applied unprecedented pressure through tough new sanctions.

We have renewed the push for peace in the Middle East, charted a course to secure vulnerable nuclear materials within 4 years, and reestablished our leadership in the Pacific rim, while taking the lead in forging a response at the global level to the economic crisis.

And in between, we've responded to a range of crises like Haiti and the floods now in Pakistan that are required from us as leaders in the world.

In short, we've spared no effort to keep the American people safe, while also repairing old alliances, building new partnerships, and restoring America's leadership in the 21st century.

Through these challenges, Jim has always been a steady voice in Situation Room sessions, daily briefings, and with meetings with foreign leaders, while also representing our country abroad with allies and partners in every region of the world. At the same time, he has led an unprecedented reform of our national security staff here at the White House. Reflecting the new challenges of our time, he put new emphasis on cybersecurity, development, and climate change and made sure that homeland security is fully integrated into our efforts.

Serving as National Security Adviser is one of the most difficult jobs in our Government. But through it all, Jim—like the marine he has always been—has been a dedicated public servant and a friend to me. After a lifetime of service, I know this was also an enormous sacrifice for the Jones family. Many of them are here today, and I want to thank them as well. Jim, like your father and uncle and generations of Joneses who served before you, you complete this assignment knowing that your country is safer and stronger. I thank you, and the American people thank you.

National Security Adviser Jones. Thank you, Mr. President.

The President. I am also proud to announce that General Jones will be succeeded by his deputy, and one of my closest advisers, Tom Donilon.

Tom has a wealth of experience that will serve him well in this new assignment. He has served three Presidents and been immersed in our national security for decades. Over the last 2 years, there's not a single critical national security issue that has not crossed Tom's desk. He has helped manage our national security team and the policymaking process and won the respect and admiration of his colleagues in the White House and across the administration. He has a probing intellect and a remarkable work ethic, although it's one that depends on a seemingly limitless quantity of Diet Coke. [*Laughter*]

Tom, however, is not the only valuable member of the Donilon team who works here at the White House. His wife Cathy, who's here, has done an extraordinary job as Jill Biden's Chief of Staff. I'm grateful to the Donilon family for all the work that they've already done for our Nation and for agreeing to take on this additional responsibility.

We have some huge challenges ahead. We remain a nation at war, and we will not rest in our efforts to disrupt, dismantle, and defeat Al Qaida. And above all, we are committed to forging the kind of American leadership that can shape the world in the 21st century just as we shaped the world in the 20th: a world of greater peace, a world of growing markets and expanding prosperity, a world of shared security, a world where American leadership enlists the support of old allies and new partners while advancing the values that help keep us safe and make America a beacon to the world.

That is the kind of American leadership that Jim Jones has always stood for and the kind of leadership that Tom and my entire national security team will continue to work for in the years to come.

So with that, I want to once again personally thank Jim for his outstanding service and offer the mike to him to say a few words.

NOTE: The President spoke at 1:05 p.m. in the Rose Garden at the White House. In his remarks, he referred to Catherine M. Russell, Chief of Staff to Jill T. Biden, wife of Vice President Joe Biden. The transcript released by the Office of the Press Secretary also included the remarks of National Security Adviser Jones.

Remarks on Signing the Twenty-First Century Communications and Video Accessibility Act of 2010
October 8, 2010

Hello, everybody. Good to see you. Everybody, please have a seat. Well, it is wonderful to see all of you here today, to be with all of you. I want to make some special acknowledgements. We've got some legislators here who have been fighting on behalf of the disabilities community for a very long time. We're so proud of the legislation I'm signing today, as well as legislation we signed earlier this week. So I want to acknowledge all of them.

First of all, responsible in large part for guiding this process through in the Senate, Senator Mark Pryor of Arkansas; Representative Ed Markey, Democrat from Massachusetts. We also have here Senator Jay Rockefeller of West Virginia; Senator Barbara Mikulski, Democrat of Maryland. We've got Kent Conrad, as well as Byron Dorgan, the Dakota boys from North Dakota. [*Laughter*]

We've got Representative Henry Waxman, who's on so many important pieces of legislation this year, and we're grateful to him. Mr. Julius Genachowski is here, who's the chairman of the FCC. Where's Julius? There he is right there, a classmate of mine, somebody who has just been a great friend for a long time.

And finally, we've got this guy. [*Laughter*] Some of you may know him. I happened to be listening to him this morning when I woke up. He's what I work out to. [*Laughter*] He's what I sweet-talk Michelle to. [*Laughter*] Mr. Stevie Wonder is in the house. I was doing a little rendition of some of his music to him, and he was kind enough not to laugh. [*Laughter*]

Now, earlier this year, we celebrated the 20th anniversary of the Americans with Disabilities Act right here in the White House. Many of you were here. And it was a moment for every American to reflect not just on one of the most comprehensive civil rights bills in our history, but what that bill meant to so many people. It was a victory won by countless Americans who refused to accept the world as it is and, against great odds, waged quiet struggles and grassroots crusades until finally change was won.

The story of the disability rights movement is enriched because it's intertwined with the story of America's progress. Americans with disabilities are Americans first and foremost and, like all Americans, are entitled to not only full participation in our society, but also full opportunity in our society.

So we've come a long way. But even today, after all the progress that we've made, too many Americans with disabilities are still measured by what folks think they can't do, instead of what we know they can do.

The fight for progress isn't about sympathy, by the way; it's about opportunity. And that's why all of us share a responsibility to keep building on the work of those who came before us, one life, one law, one step at a time.

So today we're here to take two more steps on that journey. First of all, on Tuesday I signed Rosa's Law. This is named for a 9-year-old girl, right there. Rosa, wave to everybody. That's some good waving there, Rosa. [*Laughter*]

Rosa Marcellino, it's so inspiring to have her here. As one of hundreds of thousands of Americans with Down syndrome, Rosa worked with her parents and her siblings to have the words "mentally retarded" officially removed from the health and education code in her home State of Maryland.

Now, Rosa's Law takes her idea a step further. It amends the language in all Federal health, education, and labor laws to remove that same phrase and instead refer to Americans living with an "intellectual disability." Now this may seem to some people like a minor change, but I think Rosa's brother Nick put it best. Where's Nick? You right there, Nick? You can wave too. Go ahead. [*Laughter*]

But I want everybody to hear Nick's wisdom here. He said, "What you call people is how you treat them. If we change the words, maybe it will be the start of a new attitude towards people with disabilities." That's a lot of wisdom from Nick.

Nick and Rosa's parents are all choking up because they're really proud of their kids, and appropriately so.

Now, the bill I'm signing today into law will better ensure full participation in our democracy and our economy for Americans with disabilities. The Twenty-First Century Communications and Video Accessibility Act will make it easier for people who are deaf, blind, or live with a visual impairment to do what many of us take for granted, from navigating a TV or DVD menu to sending an e-mail on a smart phone. It sets new standards so that Americans with disabilities can take advantage of the technology our economy depends on. And that's especially important in today's economy, when every worker needs the necessary skills to compete for the jobs of the future.

So together, these changes are about guaranteeing equal access, equal opportunity, and equal respect for every American. And they build on the progress that we've already made as an administration over the last 20 months.

Together, we put in place one of the most important updates to the ADA in 20 years by prohibiting disability-based discrimination by government entities and private businesses and by updating accessibility standards.

I issued an Executive order focused on establishing the Federal Government as a model employer of Americans with disabilities.

We passed the Christopher and Dana Reeve Paralysis Act, the first piece of comprehensive legislation aimed at addressing the challenge faced by Americans living with paralysis.

We reauthorized the Children's Health Insurance Program, covering an additional 2.6 million children in need in 2009, including children with disabilities.

And the Affordable Care Act we passed will give every American more control over their health care and will do more to give Americans with disabilities control over their own lives than any legislation since the ADA.

So equal access, equal opportunity, the freedom to make of our lives what we will, living up to these principles is an obligation we have as Americans, and to one another. Because, in the end, each of us has a role to play in our economy, each of us has something to contribute to the American story, and each of us must do our part to continue on this never-ending journey towards building a more perfect Union.

So I am so proud of the legislators here today. I want to thank all the advocates who helped bring this legislation about. And now I'm very proud to sign the bill.

NOTE: The President spoke at 2:06 p.m. in the East Room at the White House. In his remarks, he referred to Nina and Paul Marcellino, parents, and Madeline and Gigi Marcellino, sisters, of Rosa Marcellino. He also referred to Rosa's Law, S. 2781, which was approved on October 7 and assigned Public Law No. 111–256. S. 3304, approved October 8, was assigned Public Law No. 111–260.

Statement on the Awarding of the Nobel Peace Prize to Liu Xiaobo
October 8, 2010

I welcome the Nobel Committee's decision to award the Nobel Peace Prize to Mr. Liu Xiaobo. Last year, I noted that so many others who have received the award had sacrificed so much more than I. That list now includes Mr. Liu, who has sacrificed his freedom for his beliefs. By granting the prize to Mr. Liu, the Nobel Committee has chosen someone who has been an eloquent and courageous spokesman for the advance of universal values through peaceful and nonviolent means, including his support for democracy, human rights, and the rule of law.

As I said last year in Oslo, even as we respect the unique culture and traditions of different countries, America will always be a voice for those aspirations that are universal to all human beings. Over the last 30 years, China has made dramatic progress in economic reform and improving the lives of its people, lifting hundreds of millions out of poverty. But this award reminds us that political reform has not kept pace and that the basic human rights of every man, woman, and child must be respected. We call on the Chinese Government to release Mr. Liu as soon as possible.

Memorandum of Disapproval on the "Interstate Recognition of Notarizations Act of 2010"
October 8, 2010

It is necessary to have further deliberations about the possible unintended impact of H.R. 3808, the "Interstate Recognition of Notarizations Act of 2010," on consumer protections, including those for mortgages, before the bill can be finalized. Accordingly, I am withholding my approval of this bill. (The Pocket Veto Case, 279 U.S. 655 (1929)).

The authors of this bill no doubt had the best intentions in mind when trying to remove impediments to interstate commerce. My Administration will work with them and other leaders in Congress to explore the best ways to achieve this goal going forward.

To leave no doubt that the bill is being vetoed, in addition to withholding my signature, I am returning H.R. 3808 to the Clerk of the House of Representatives, along with this Memorandum of Disapproval.

BARACK OBAMA

The White House,
October 8, 2010.

Letter to Congressional Leaders Certifying Exports to the People's Republic of China
October 8, 2010

Dear Madam Speaker: (Dear Mr. President:)

Pursuant to the authority vested in me by section 902(b)(2) of the Foreign Relations Authorization Act, Fiscal Years 1990 and 1991 (Public Law 101–246) (the "Act"), and as President of the United States, I hereby report to the Congress that it is in the national interest of the United States to terminate the suspensions under section 902(a)(3) of the Act with respect to the issuance of temporary munitions export licenses for exports to the People's Republic of China insofar as such restrictions pertain to the C–130 cargo aircraft to be used in oil spill response operations at sea. License requirements remain in place for these exports and require review and approval on a case-by-case basis by the United States Government.

Sincerely,

BARACK OBAMA

NOTE: Identical letters were sent to Nancy Pelosi, Speaker of the House of Representatives, and Joseph R. Biden, Jr., President of the Senate.

The President's Weekly Address
October 9, 2010

The other day, I was talking about education with some folks in the backyard of an Albuquerque home, and someone asked a question that's stayed with me. He asked, "If we don't have homes to go to, what good is an education?" It was a heartfelt question, one that could be asked by anyone who's lost a home or a job in this recession.

Because if you're out of work or facing foreclosure, all that really matters is a new job. All that really matters is a roof over your head. All that really matters is getting back on your feet. That's why I'm fighting each and every day to jump-start job creation in the private sector, to help our small-business owners grow and hire, to rebuild our economy so it lifts up a middle class that's been battered for so long.

But even as we focus on doing all that, even as we focus on speeding up our economic recovery, we also know that when it comes to jobs, opportunity, and prosperity in the 21st century, nothing is more important than the quality of your education. At a time when most of the new jobs being created will require some kind of higher education, when countries that outeducate us today will outcompete us tomorrow, giving our kids the best education possible is an economic imperative.

That's why, from the start of my administration, we've been fighting to offer every child in this country a world-class education, from the cradle to the classroom, from college through a career. Earlier this week, I announced a new Skills for America's Future initiative that will help community colleges and employers match what's taught in the classroom with what's needed in the private sector, so we can connect students looking for jobs with businesses looking to hire.

We're eliminating tens of billions of dollars in wasteful subsidies for banks to administer student loans and using that money to make college more affordable for millions of students. And we've launched a Race to the Top in our States to make sure our students, all of them, are graduating from high school ready for college, so we can meet our goal of graduating a higher proportion of students from college than any other country in the world by 2020.

And yet if Republicans in Congress had their way, we'd have had a harder time meeting that goal. We'd have had a harder time offering our kids the best education possible, because they'd have us cut education by 20 percent. Cuts that would reduce financial aid for 8 million students; cuts that would leave our great and undervalued community colleges without the resources they need to prepare our graduates for the jobs of the future.

Now, it is true that when it comes to our budget, we have real challenges to meet. And if we're serious about getting our fiscal house in order, we'll need to make some tough choices. I'm prepared to make those choices. But what I'm not prepared to do is to shortchange our children's education. What I'm not prepared to do is undercut their economic future, your economic future, or the economic future of the United States of America.

Nothing would be more detrimental to our prospects for success than cutting back on education. It would consign America to second place in our fiercely competitive global economy. But China and India aren't playing for second. South Korea and Germany, they aren't playing for second. They're playing for first, and so should the United States of America.

Instead of being shortsighted and shortchanging our kids, we should be doubling down on them. We should be giving every child in America a chance to make the most of their lives, to fulfill their God-given potential. We should be fighting to lead the global economy in this century, just like we did in the last. And that's what I'll continue fighting to do in the months and years ahead. Thanks, everybody, and have a great weekend.

NOTE: The address was recorded at approximately 2:15 p.m. on October 8 in the Map Room at the White House for broadcast on October 9. The transcript was made available by the Office of the Press Secretary on October 8, but was embargoed for release until 6 a.m. on October 9.

The Office of the Press Secretary also released a Spanish language transcript of this address.

Statement on the International Civil Aviation Organization's Declaration on Aviation Security
October 9, 2010

I commend the International Civil Aviation Organization for adopting yesterday's declaration on aviation security, which forges a historic new foundation for aviation security that will better protect our world from evolving terrorist threats. Following the attempted December 25th terrorist attack, at my direction, the Department of Homeland Security has worked with ICAO, our international partners, and representatives ranging from airline CEOs to avia-

tion industry trade associations in an unprecedented effort to strengthen international aviation security. The extraordinary global collaboration demonstrated by the nearly 190 ICAO countries during the ICAO General Assembly in Montreal has helped to bring about a truly 21st-century international aviation security framework that will make air travel safer and more secure than ever before.

Remarks at a Democratic National Committee Rally in Philadelphia, Pennsylvania
October 10, 2010

The President. Hello, Philadelphia!

Audience members. Yes, we can! Yes, we can! Yes, we can!

The President. Thank you. Thank you. Oh, this is—thank you. Joe, this is a good-looking crowd, man. This is a beautiful crowd on a beautiful day. It's good to be back here in Pennsylvania.

Vice President Joe Biden. And they're all the way back in the parking lot. They can't even see you.

The President. It is good to be back in Pennsylvania, good to be back in Philly. I know part of the reason you're fired up is because you've just heard from one of the finest Vice Presidents we will ever see in this country's history, Joe Biden. Plus, Joe looks cool in those glasses too, doesn't he?

You know, I want you to know, when I was still campaigning, right after I selected Joe, I—we went out and we were doing some events and small town hall meetings. And everywhere we went with Joe, some woman would come by and say, you know, I think Joe's kind of cute. Can you introduce me to Joe? [*Laughter*] That

was true. And I had to inform this woman that Joe is married to a wonderful Jill Biden.

In addition to hearing from Joe, I know you've heard from Governor Ed Rendell. Senator Arlen Specter's in the house. Senator Bob Casey is in the house. State Treasurer Rob McCord is here. Congressman Chaka Fattah is here. Congressman Joe Sestak is here. Congressman Bob Brady is here. Mayor Michael Nutter is in the house. And we've got Allegheny County Executive Dan Onorato is here. I want to thank Pastor Kevin Johnson for the invocation. DJ Diamond Kuts, and give it up for the Roots.

Now, I'm glad to see that this crowd is fired up. Are you fired up?

Audience members. Fired up!

The President. Are you ready to go?

Audience members. Ready to go!

The President. I've got to make sure you stay fired up. I promise you'll be out of here to catch the Phillies and the Eagles. I don't want to get between Philly fans and their sports teams.

Now, Philadelphia, 2 years ago, you defied the conventional wisdom in Washington. They said, no, you can't. They said, no, you can't overcome the cynicism of politics. No, you can't overcome the special interests and the big money. No, you can't take on the big challenges of our time. No, you can't elect a skinny guy with a funny name to the Presidency of the United States. What did you say?

Audience members. Yes, we can! Yes, we can! Yes, we can!

The President. That's what you said.

But, Philly, I've got this message for you today. I want everybody to understand, our victory in that campaign, that wasn't the end of the road. That was just the beginning of the road. That was just the start of the journey. By itself, it does not deliver the change that we need. I know a lot of you thought, just because of election night and the Inauguration, everybody was having fun and Beyonce was singing and Bono, and so everybody thought, boy, this is it.

But that was just the start, because we understood what we were going up against. The only thing that the election did was, it gave us the chance to make change happen. It made each of you a shareholder in the mission of rebuilding our country and reclaiming our future. And Philly, I'm back here 2 years later because our job is not yet done, and the success of our mission is at stake right now. On November 2, I need you as fired up as you were in 2008, because we've got a lot of work ahead of us.

After that last election, it was my hope that we could pull together, Democrats and Republicans, to confront the worst economic crisis since the Great Depression. I hoped that we could get beyond the divisions of red States and blue States. That's what we thought. Because although we are proud to be Democrats, we are prouder to be Americans, and I know there are plenty of Republicans out there in this country who feel the exact same way.

But when we arrived in Washington, the Republicans in Congress, they had a different idea. They knew it would take more than 2 years to climb out of this recession. They knew that by the time of this election, people would still be out of work. They knew people would still be frustrated. And so what they figured was, if we just sat on the sidelines, if Republicans just opposed everything we said we could do, if they

rejected every compromise we offered, if they spent all their time attacking Democrats instead of attacking problems, they figured they might be able to do well in the polls.

So they sent—they spent the last 20 months saying no, even to policies that they had supported in the past. They said no to middle class tax cuts. They said no to help for small businesses. They said no to a bipartisan deficit reduction commission that they had once cosponsored. If I said the sky was blue, they said no. If I said there were fish in the sea, they said no. They figured, if Obama fails, then we win. Am I wrong, Joe? That's exactly what they said.

Now, they made a—they may have thought that playing political games would help them win an election, but I knew it wouldn't get America through the crisis. So I made some different decisions. I took whatever steps were necessary to stop the economic freefall, to stop a second depression, even if those decisions were not popular, even if they were not easy. Because you didn't elect me to do what was easy. You elected me to do what was right. That's why you sent me to Washington. You didn't send me to Washington to put my finger to the wind and figure out which way the wind was blowing, to spend all my time reading the polls. You sent me there to solve problems.

And 20 months later, we no longer face the possibility of a second depression. Our economy is growing again. The private sector created jobs 9 months in a row now. There are 3 million Americans who would not be working today if not for the economic plan that Joe and I put into place. That's the truth.

Now, what's also the truth is we've still got a long way to go. The hole we're climbing out is so deep, the Republicans messed up so bad, left a—such a big mess, that there are still millions of Americans without work. I want everybody to understand this, just in case there's still some undecideds out there. Before I was inaugurated and before Joe was inaugurated, we had lost 4 million jobs in the 6 months before that. We lost almost 800,000 jobs the month I was sworn in, 600,000 the month after that, 600,000 the month after that. Before any of our economic plans were put into place, we had lost almost 8 million jobs—because of their policies.

And that means that it's going to take us a while to get out of this hole. There are still millions of Americans who can barely pay their bills, millions of Americans who are just barely hanging on, millions of middle class families who were struggling even before this crisis hit and are out there treading water. I know.

So of course people are frustrated. Of course people are impatient with the pace of change. And believe me, so am I. But here's the thing I need everybody to remember. No matter how angry you get, no matter how frustrated you are, the other side has decided to ride that frustration and anger without offering any solutions.

And the other—and you know, a lot of folks in Washington think that they're running a smart strategy. They're saying the other party's supporters are more enthusiastic, more excited. They say all y'all are going to stay home. You might not come out like you did in 2008. They say you might not care as much. They think, oh, well, Obama's name is not on the ballot; maybe they're not going to turn out. They think you're going to be willing to let the same politicians and the same policies that left our economy in a shambles back to Washington.

Well, Philadelphia, I think the pundits are wrong. I think the pundits are wrong. I think we're going to win, but you got to prove them wrong. It's up to you to show the pundits that you care too much about this country to let it fall backwards, that you're going to keep us moving forward, that you're ready to fight for the future.

Just look, everybody, I need you to understand, this election is a choice. And the choice could not be clearer. It's not as if the Republicans are offering new ideas. It's not as if the Republican leaders have changed their agenda since the last time they ran Washington. In fact, the chairman of one of their campaign committees promised that if the Republicans take control of Congress, they will follow the exact same agenda they pursued the last time they were in power.

We know what that agenda was. We know what this agenda was. You cut taxes, mostly for millionaires and billionaires. You cut regulations for special interests. You try to bust the unions. You cut back on investments in education and clean energy and research and technology. The basic idea is that if we put our blind faith in the market and we let corporations do whatever they want and we leave everybody else to fend for themselves, then America somehow automatically is going to grow and prosper.

Well, let me tell you something. The problem with their theory is, it didn't work. We tried it for 8 years. It didn't work for middle class families who saw their incomes fall and their costs go up when Republicans were in charge. I want everybody to understand, between 2001 and 2009, the wages of middle class families went down 5 percent. They didn't go up, they went down. Job growth was the slowest that it had been at any time since World War II, slower than it's been over the last year. When they were in charge, they took a record surplus from Bill Clinton, and by the time I got there, we had a record deficit. And because of that free-for-all that they had on Wall Street, we're still digging our way out of the crisis. That's their track record.

Now, listen, everybody, I don't bring this up because I want to relitigate the past. I bring it up because I don't want to relive the past. I don't want to go through what we already gone through. I bring it up because this is the other—this philosophy that the other side intends to bring if they win in November. Republicans might have a new name for it—they call it the "Pledge to America"—but it's the same old stuff they've been peddling for years.

Let's take a look at the "Pledge to America." Anybody read the "Pledge to America"? Let me tell you, for starters, it turns out that the pledge was actually written in part by a former lobbyist for AIG and ExxonMobil. That should tell you something right there. You can't make that stuff up.

And the centerpiece of the pledge is a $700 billion tax cut that would only go to the top 2 percent, the wealthiest 2 percent of Americans. Ninety-eight percent of you would not get this tax cut, but they would borrow $700 billion from the Chinese or from the Saudis or somebody. That's their big idea to get the economy moving again. These are the same folks who lecture us on fiscal responsibility, but now they want to borrow $700 billion to give a tax cut worth an average of $100,000 to millionaires and billionaires.

When you ask them, "Where are you going to get the money?" they say, "Well, we don't have it." But mostly, they're going to borrow it from other countries. And just to pay for a small part of it, they want to cut education by 20 percent. They would reduce financial aid for 8 million college students.

Now, Philadelphia, at a time when the education of our country's citizens is one of the most important things for economic success, the notion that we would give out tax cuts to folks who don't need them and sacrifice the next generation, that does not make any sense at all.

I want to ask my Republican friends, do you think China's cutting back on education? Do you think South Korea or Germany or India are cutting back on education? Those countries aren't playing for second place. They're playing for first place. Guess what? America does not play for second place either. We pay—we play for first place.

So, Philly, as long as I'm President, we're not going to let Washington politicians sacrifice your education for a tax cut we can't afford. And that is a choice in this election.

Joe and I, we've got a different idea about what the next 2 years should look like, and it's an idea rooted in our belief about how this country was built. We know government doesn't have all the answers to all our problems. We know the private sector is primarily responsible for creating jobs and prosperity. I believe government should be lean and efficient, and I don't want anybody in Washington wasting your taxpayer dollars. That's why I proposed a 3-year spending freeze, set up a bipartisan fiscal commission to deal with our deficit.

But in the words of our first Republican President, named Abraham Lincoln, we also believe that government should do what people can't do better by themselves. We believe in a country that rewards hard work and responsibility. We believe in a country where we look after

one another. We believe in a country where working people can come together so they can get a minimum wage and better working conditions. We believe that I am my brother's keeper, I am my sister's keeper; that everybody deserves a fair shot at the American Dream. That's the America I know. That's the choice in this election.

We want to make permanent tax cuts for the middle class, because you deserve a break. Instead of the other side's plan to keep giving tax breaks to companies that are shipping jobs overseas, I want to give those tax breaks to companies that are investing right here in the United States of America. I want to give it to small businesses and to American manufacturers and to clean energy companies. I don't want solar panels and wind turbines and electric cars built in Europe or Asia. I want them built here in the United States of America by American workers.

Instead of cutting education and student aid, we want to make our new college tax credit permanent: $10,000 in tuition relief for every young person who goes to college. We're going to fight to keep the reforms we've made to the student loan system, because thanks to those reforms, tens of billions of dollars in taxpayer subsidies that would be going to banks right now are going to students. That's where they belong.

If the other side wins, they'll try their hardest to give rein back to the insurance companies and the credit card companies and the Wall Street banks that we're finally holding accountable. We can't let them do that. We can't go back to the days of taxpayer-funded bailouts. We can't go back to the day when credit card companies could just jack up your rates without any reason or insurance companies could deny or drop your coverage just because you get sick.

We need to keep that new law in place that says if you're looking for a job or have a job that doesn't offer you coverage and you're a young person, you can stay on your parents' insurance until you're 26 years old, and that they can't drop your coverage just because you get sick. That's the choice in this election, Philadelphia. That's what at stake right now.

So, Philly, it comes down to this. Many of the Republicans who are running right now, these are the exact same folks who spent the last decade driving our economy into a ditch. And once we were elected, Joe and I, we put on our boots; we went down into that ditch. It was muddy and dusty down there, and it was hot. And we started pushing on that car to get it out of the ditch. And we had a whole bunch of folks like Joe Sestak helping us push that car out of the ditch.

And every once in a while, we'd look up at the Republicans. They were—they had driven into the ditch, but they had gotten out, and they were kind of taking a break, fanning themselves and sipping on a Slurpee, watching us do all the work. And every once in a while, they'd say: "Why don't you push harder? You're not pushing the right way, Obama." But they didn't help.

And after pushing and pushing over these last 20 months, finally we've got that car out of the ditch. Now, the car is a little dented up. The fender's a little busted. It needs a tuneup. But it's moving. It's pointing in the right direction. We're on level ground now. We're starting to make repairs. And suddenly, we get a tap on our shoulder, and we look back, and who is it? It's the Republicans. And they say—what are they saying?—they say, "We want the keys back."

Philadelphia, they can't have the keys back. They don't know how to drive. They don't know how to drive. They can ride with us if they want, but they got to get in the backseat. Because we want to go forward. We don't want the special interests riding shotgun. We want working families, middle class families, up front. They're our priority.

I just want everybody to notice, when you get in your car and you want to go forward, what do you do? You put the car in "D." If you're going backwards, what do you do? You put the car in "R." That's not a coincidence. You want to ride forward; put it in "D" on November 2.

But listen, listen, can I just say, at the end of the day, Philly, whether the Republicans get the keys back or not's going to depend on you. There is no question—there's no question the other side sees a chance to get back in the driver's seat.

And thanks to a Supreme Court decision called *Citizens United*, they are being helped along this year by special interest groups that are spending unlimited amounts of money on attack ads—attacking folks like Patrick Murphy, attacking folks like Joe Sestak—just attacking people without ever disclosing who's behind all these attack ads. You don't know. It could be the oil industry, could be the insurance industry, could even be foreign-owned corporations. You don't know because they don't have to disclose.

Now, that's not just a threat to Democrats; that's a threat to our democracy. Every American business and industry deserves a seat at the table, but they don't get a chance to buy every chair. We've seen what happens when they do. They put the entire economy at risk, and every American might end up suffering.

So you can't let it happen. Don't let them hijack your agenda. The American people deserve to know who's trying to sway their elections. And you can't stand by and let special interests drown out the voices of the American people.

So, Philadelphia, that's why I need you working even harder in this election than you did in the last election. We need you to fight their millions of dollars with our millions of voices. I look out on this crowd, and I see millions of voices all across the country. We've got to finish what we started in 2008. Because if everybody who fought so hard for change in 2008 shows up to vote in 2010, I'm absolutely confident we will win. And most of the polls say the same thing.

See, what the other side is counting on, what they're counting on is you're going to stay home. They're counting on your silence. They're counting on your amnesia. They're counting on your apathy. They're counting on young people staying home and union members staying home and Black folks staying home and middle class families staying home. They're counting on the fact that they made the argument so ugly in Washington that you just completely turned off and you're not going to vote for anybody. And if that happens, they win.

Philly, let's prove them wrong. Let's show Washington one more time, change doesn't come from the top, it comes from the bottom. It doesn't come from millions of dollars of ads; it comes because people are out there knocking on doors, making phone calls, going into the beauty shops, going into the barber shops. We have come—I know we're a long way from the day—the hope and excitement we all felt on election night. We're far from Inauguration Day. But I always told you it was going to take time. I always told you it was going to be hard because change has always been hard.

But from the first days of our Nation, every time Americans have tried to bring about real, meaningful change, we've faced down setbacks, we've faced down disappointments. We have faced fear, and we have faced down doubt. As Americans, we've always moved forward. We've always kept fighting. We've always remembered that in the United States of America, our destiny is not written for us, it is written by us.

That's how we came through war. That's how we came through depression. That's how we got civil rights legislation. That's how we got workers' rights. That's how we got women's rights. It's being tested right now, but if you keep mov-

ing forward in the face of difficulty, I promise you we will not lose this election. We will win this election. And we will make sure that every American has the opportunity to live out the American Dream.

God bless you, and God bless the United States of America.

NOTE: The President spoke at 4:57 p.m. at Morton Field. In his remarks, he referred to Kevin R. Johnson, senior pastor, Bright Hope Baptist Church; musicians Tina "DJ Diamond Kuts" Dunham, Beyonce G. Knowles, and Paul D. "Bono" Hewson; Rep. Pete Sessions, in his capacity as chairman of the National Republican Congressional Committee; former lobbyist Brian Wild; and Rep. Patrick Murphy. The transcript released by the Office of the Press Secretary also included the remarks of Vice President Joe Biden.

Statement on the Death of Albertina Walker
October 10, 2010

Michelle and I are saddened by the passing of gospel great Albertina Walker. Ms. Walker was known for her Grammy Award winning voice and recognized by many as the Queen of Gospel. Growing up on the South Side of Chicago, she started singing in her church youth choir at just 4 years old, where she learned to spread the Good News through song. She also performed before President Bill Clinton and was honored at the White House by President George W. Bush for her contributions to gospel

music. And she never forgot to give back, impacting her community through the Albertina Walker Scholarship Fund and many other charitable endeavors.

Ms. Walker's voice and message has touched congregations across the Nation. Though we have lost an American icon, her influence on gospel music will continue for generations. Our thoughts and prayers are with her family and the countless lives she touched.

Remarks Following a Meeting on Infrastructure Investment
October 11, 2010

Good morning, everybody. I just had a meeting with Treasury Secretary Tim Geithner, Secretary of Transportation Ray LaHood, and Governors like Ed Rendell, mayors like Antonio Villaraigosa, and economists and engineers from across the country to discuss one of America's greatest challenges: our crumbling infrastructure and the urgent need to put Americans back to work upgrading it for the 21st century.

We're also joined today by two former Transportation Secretaries of both political parties: Sam Skinner, who served under President George H.W. Bush, and Norm Mineta, who served in the Cabinets of both President Clinton and President George W. Bush. They're here today because they are passionate about this task.

Their cooperation—and indeed, this country's very history—proves that this is something for which there has traditionally been broad bipartisan support. So Sam and Norm have been leading a bipartisan group of more than 80 experts who, just last week, released a call to action demanding a fundamental overhaul of how America approaches funding and building our infrastructure. And today my Treasury Department and my Council of Economic Advisers have released our own study.

And these reports confirm what any American can already tell you: Our infrastructure is woefully inefficient, and it is outdated. For years, we have deferred tough decisions, and today, our aging system of highways and byways, air routes and rail lines hinder our economic growth. Today, the average American household is forced to spend more on transportation each year than food. Our roads, clogged with traffic, cost us $80 billion a year in lost productivity and wasted fuel. Our airports, choked with passengers, cost nearly $10 billion a year in productivity losses from flight delays. And in some cases, our crumbling infrastructure costs American lives. It should not take another collapsing bridge or failing levee to shock us into action.

So we're already paying for our failure to act. And what's more, the longer our infrastructure erodes, the deeper our competitive edge erodes. Other nations understand this. They are going all in. Today, as a percentage of GDP, we invest less than half of what Russia does in their infrastructure, less than one-third of what Western Europe does. Right now China's building hundreds of thousands of miles of new roads. Over the next 10 years, it plans to build dozens of new airports. Over the next 20, it could build as many as 170 new mass transit systems. Everywhere else, they're thinking big. They're creating jobs today, but they're also playing to win tomorrow. So the bottom line is our shortsightedness has come due. We can no longer afford to sit still.

What we need is a smart system of infrastructure equal to the needs of the 21st century: a system that encourages sustainable communities with easier access to our jobs, to our schools, to our homes, a system that decreases travel time and increases mobility, a system that cuts congestion and ups productivity, a system

that reduces harmful emissions over time and creates jobs right now.

So we've already begun on this task. The Recovery Act included the most serious investment in our infrastructure since President Eisenhower built the Interstate Highway System in the 1950s. And we're not just talking new and restored roads and bridges and dams and levees, but we're also talking a smart electric grid and the high-speed internet and rail lines required for America to compete in the 21st-century economy. We're talking about investments with impacts both immediate and lasting.

Tens of thousands of projects employing hundreds of thousands of workers are already underway across America. We're improving 40,000 miles of road and rebuilding water and sewer systems. We're implementing a smarter, more stable, more secure electric grid across 46 States that will increase access to renewable sources of energy and cut costs for customers. We're moving forward with projects that connect communities across the country to broadband internet and connect 31 States via a true high-speed rail network. And what's more, a great many of these projects are coming in under budget.

By investing in these projects, we've already created hundreds of thousands of jobs. But the fact remains that nearly one in five construction workers is still unemployed and needs a job. And that makes absolutely no sense at a time when there is so much of America that needs rebuilding.

So that's why, last month, I announced a new plan for upgrading America's roads, rails, and runways for the long term. Over the next 6 years, we will rebuild 150,000 miles of our roads, enough to circle the world 6 times. We will lay and maintain 4,000 miles of our railways, enough to stretch from coast to coast. And we will restore 150 miles of runways and advance a next-generation air traffic control system that reduces delays for the American people.

This plan will be fully paid for. It will not add to our deficit over time. And we are going to work with Congress to see to that. It will establish an infrastructure bank to leverage Federal dollars and focus on the smartest investments. We want to cut waste and bureaucracy by consolidating and collapsing more than 100 different, often duplicative programs. And it will change the way Washington works by reforming the Federal Government's patchwork approach of funding and maintaining our infrastructure. We've got to focus less on wasteful earmarks, outdated formulas. We've got to focus more on competition and innovation; less on shortsighted political priorities and more on our national economic priorities.

So investing in our infrastructure is something that members of both political parties have always supported. It's something that groups ranging from the Chamber of Commerce to the AFL–CIO support today. And by making these investments across the country, we won't just make our economy run better over the long haul; we will create good, middle class jobs right now.

So there is no reason why we can't do this. There is no reason why the world's best infrastructure should lie beyond our borders. This is America. We've always had the best infrastructure. This is work that needs to be done. There are workers who are ready to do it. All we need is the political will. This is a season for choices, and this is the choice: between decline and prosperity and between the past and the future.

Our future has never been predestined. It has been built on the hard work and sacrifices of previous generations. They invested yesterday for what we have today. That's how we built canals and railroads and highways and ports that allowed our economy to grow by leaps and bounds. That's how we led the world in the pursuit of new technologies and innovations. That's what allowed us to build the middle class and lead the global economy in the 20th century. And if we're going to lead it in the 21st, that's the vision we can't afford to lose sight of right now. That's the challenge that's fallen to this generation. That's the challenge that this country is going to meet. And with the help of these gentlemen behind me, and I hope strong bipartisan support, I have no doubt that we will meet these challenges.

Thank you very much, everybody.

NOTE: The President spoke at 11:08 a.m. in the Rose Garden at the White House. In his remarks, he referred to Gov. Edward G. Rendell of Pennsylvania; and Mayor Antonio R. Villaraigosa of Los Angeles, CA. The Office of the Press Secretary also released a Spanish language transcript of these remarks.

Remarks at a Democratic Congressional Campaign Committee Reception and Fundraiser for Representative Ron Klein in Miami, Florida
October 11, 2010

The President. Hello, everybody. Well, it is wonderful to be here. I want to thank a few people at the outset. First of all, I want to thank the Mourning family, who are opening up this beautiful home and arranged this fantastic weather. We're so grateful to them. Yes, you can give them a big round of applause.

Chris Van Hollen, this is the only guy who puts in more miles than me. [*Laughter*] He has been working so hard as the chairman of the Democratic Congressional Campaign Committee. He is a great Congressman in his own right, a great leader inside the House, but he's also just been doing a bang-up job in what is one of the more difficult posts in politics.

Debbie Wasserman Schultz is here. Where's Debbie? She was here. She was here. Well, we love her, so give her a round of applause. Ron Klain——

Audience member. Klein.

The President. No, I've got a—Biden's chief of staff is Ron Klain, and I just talked to him on the phone so I slipped up.

Ron Klein is here, and one of the main reasons that we're here—but—if he's not here, I know—is he? Where is he? He's inside. All right, we love him. Kathy Castor is here. Ted Deutch is here and his family.

Anybody that I miss? You all are here, and we love you.

Now, the main reason we're here is for Ron, who has done such an unbelievable job in Congress, but more importantly, in the community. They've made south Florida their home for the last 25 years. This is where they raised their family, where Ron helped run a small business. That's exactly who Ron has been fighting for since he came to Washington: the families and small-business owners that he grew up with, all of you. Those are the folks he cares about.

He fought to bring down the skyrocketing cost of homeowner's insurance. He's fighting to protect and strengthen Medicare and Social Security. He helped write tough new sanctions to crack down on Iran as they try to develop nuclear weapons, something I know that everybody here cares deeply about and my administration has made one of our top priorities. He has made the security of our ally, Israel, a constant theme in his work. He knows the people of south Florida because he's spent so much time listening to your concerns, and he's one of you.

And so this election, I think, is representative of what's happening all across the country. We've got wonderful candidates like Ron who are working so hard and have, over the last 20 months, done more to get this country back on track than any Congress in my lifetime—any Congress at least since 1965.

You know, 2 years ago, a lot of you worked your hearts out for Ron's campaign and for my campaign. And we knew at that point that the country was on the wrong track. What we didn't realize was how bad it was going to be by the time we took office. We have gone through the worst financial crisis since the Great Depression. We have made sure that as a consequence of a bunch of tough actions that we took we didn't slip into the second Great Depression.

As Chris was just saying, we now have an economy that is stabilized. An economy that was shrinking by 6 percent when I came into office is now growing. We have seen 9 consecutive months of private sector job growth. Businesses are profitable again and investing again. And all of that is because Members of Congress like Ron and Chris and Ted and Kathy were willing to take tough votes, even in the face of enormous criticism, because they knew it was the right thing to do.

And so at a certain point, the reason you send folks to represent you in Washington is not just to put their fingers up to the wind; it's not just to figure out what's going to help keep them in office. You send them there to do what's right and to make sure that they are thinking about you and your families each and every day.

And that's what Ron has done, and that's what Chris has done, and that's what I intend to do as long as I have the great honor of being your President. That is our number-one priority.

Audience member. Thank you.

The President. Now, of course, things aren't where we want them to be. We've got a lot more work to do. The question in this election is not whether or not things are where we want them to be, the question is who is going to help us get to where we want to be. And on that choice, the answer is absolutely clear.

Look at what the Republicans have been offering out here. I mean, they have now been out of power for 2 years, and they had a chance over the last 2 years to try to work with us to figure out how we could move the country forward. And instead, their basic philosophy was, we are just going to say no to everything. We're going to say no to help to small businesses. We're going to say no to putting people back to work. We're going to say no to helping young people get student loans. We're going to say no to making sure that folks aren't thrown off their health care when they get sick or because they have a preexisting condition. They said no each and every time.

And now they come before you and they say, we want to lead again. And yet the ideas they're offering are the exact same ideas that got us into this mess in the first place. It's not as if they've gone off and meditated and decided, you know what, we really screwed up; here's a whole bunch of new ideas. [*Laughter*] They don't have new ideas.

The same philosophy that got us into this mess, that you basically give tax cuts mostly to millionaires and billionaires and you cut regulations in the banking industry and in the health care industry and in the oil industry, that you basically leave everybody else to fend for themselves, that philosophy is the same philosophy that produced the most sluggish job growth since World War II, that saw the wages of middle class families decline by 5 percent when they were in power, that resulted in the worst crisis that we've seen in the financial markets that has an impact far beyond Wall Street, and that took a record surplus left by Bill Clinton and got us into record deficits that I inherited when I walked into the White House.

Now, that same philosophy is what they're peddling right now. They put a new name on it. What did they'd call it? "Pledge to America." And when you actually take the time to read it, it turns out that they are peddling the same snake oil they were before. They put some different names on it, but it's the same concepts.

Their big idea for putting people back to work, their main economic proposal is to provide $700 billion in tax cuts to the top 2 percent of the income bracket. The other 98 percent of American people won't get a dime of it. And it's not money that we've got. We'd have to borrow that $700 billion from China or the Saudis. And they don't pay for it, but the proposals that they've talked about to start paying for it include cutting education by 20 percent.

Think about that. Here we are trying to compete with China and South Korea and Germany, countries that are investing and as a consequence have created a higher proportion of college graduates than we have, and we're going to cut education? We're going to create a situation where 8 million young people across the country are getting fewer student loans, less help because we want to give tax cuts to folks who don't need them, weren't even asking for them, and won't spend them, so they won't have any impact in terms of boosting demand in our economy. That does not make sense. But that's an example of the lack of ideas that we're seeing from the other side.

Now, Ron, myself, others, we've got a different idea of how we need to move this country forward. We envision a situation in which instead of giving tax breaks to companies that are shipping jobs overseas, we give tax breaks to companies that are investing right here in the United States of America.

We have a vision where we're rebuilding our infrastructure—I talked about this—so that we're not just rebuilding our roads and our bridges and our rail systems, but we're laying broadband lines, and we're making sure that we have the best Internet service in the world.

We want to invest in our young people to make sure that we have the highest proportion of college graduates of any country. We used to be number one; we're now number nine. I want us to get back to number one by the year 2012.

I want to invest in clean energy so that solar panels and wind panels—wind turbines and the electric cars and advanced batteries of the future, that those are made not in Asia, not in Europe, but they're made right here in the United States of America with American workers. And by the way, that means we're also saving our environment in the bargain.

And yes, I want to get our budget under control, but I don't want to do it on the backs of folks who need it most. I want to make sure that we do it in a responsible way.

And again, when you look at the hypocrisy of the other side—we set up a bipartisan fiscal commission that originated as a bipartisan idea, Democrats and Republicans. And when I decided this was a good idea and I endorsed it, and I said, let's vote for it, you know what happened? The Republicans voted against it.

So there's a fundamental lack of seriousness in terms of how they want to move this country forward. And these are serious times. And we've got to have people in Congress who are not thinking about the next election but are thinking about the next generation.

The analogy I've been using as I've traveled across the country—the other folks, they drove this economy into a ditch. And we decided, even though we hadn't driven it in the ditch, it was our responsibility to get us out of the ditch. So Ron and myself and Chris and Debbie and others, we all went down into the ditch. We put on our boots. It's muddy down there. It's hot. We're sweating. [*Laughter*] We're pushing and pulling to get that car out of the ditch. And every once in a while we'd look up, and the Republicans would be standing there, waving at us. [*Laughter*]

And we'd say, "Why don't you come on down and help?" And they'd say: "No, thanks, but you're not pushing hard enough. You're not pushing the right way."

But despite the lack of help, we kept on pushing, until finally we've got that car on level ground. Finally it's just sitting there ready to go forward. It's a little banged up. It's got to go to the body shop. It needs a tuneup. But we're pointing in the right direction. And we get a tap on our shoulders, and we look, and lo and behold, it's the Republicans. And they want the keys back. [*Laughter*]

We've got to tell them, in this election, you can't have the keys back. You don't know how to drive. You don't know how to drive. You can get in the car, but you got to ride in the backseat. [*Laughter*]

Audience member. In the trunk!

The President. In the trunk. [*Laughter*] No, we wouldn't do that. We got room in the back. But we don't want their hands on the wheel. [*Laughter*]

And that's why all of you are so important. Look, when I won, when Ron won, we didn't win because of us. We won because of you. We won because you guys believed in something. You decided that you didn't have to have big money, you didn't have to be connected to special interests, you didn't have to be well connected in order to win. You just had to believe in the American Dream and want to align our Govern-ment on the side of people who wake up every day, work hard, and just want that piece of that dream for themselves and their family; want to make sure they can have a job that pays a living wage; make sure that they're not bankrupt when they get sick; make sure they can send their kids to college and aspire to things that they didn't dream of; retire with dignity and respect.

That's the essence of what Ron's campaign was about, the essence of what my campaign was about. That's why you worked so hard. We're not finished. That day that we got elected on election night and then the Inauguration, that was a lot of fun, but that wasn't the end of the journey. That was just the beginning of the journey. We've got a long ways to go. And we can't get there without you.

So I'm grateful for you all being here today, but I'm going to be even more grateful if over the next 3 weeks, you're out there talking to your friends, you're talking to your neighbors, you're talking to your coworkers, you're talking to family members, and you remind them that as frustrating as things are right now, we have come so far in the last 20 months. And if you remind them, we've got so much more to do, if you do that, I'm convinced Ron is going to win. I'm convinced that the American people are going to win.

Go bless you. God bless the United States of America.

NOTE: The President spoke at 5:54 p.m. at the residence of Alonzo and Tracy Mourning.

Statement on the Awarding of the Nobel Memorial Prize in Economic Sciences to Peter A. Diamond and Dale T. Mortensen
October 11, 2010

I congratulate Peter Diamond and Dale Mortensen on winning the Nobel Prize in Economics for their groundbreaking economic research that has applications in a wide range of areas, like unemployment and housing, where we need our best and brightest minds. I have nominated Peter to the Board of Governors of the Federal Reserve to help bring his extraordinary expertise to our economic recovery. I hope he will be confirmed by the Senate as quickly as possible.

Statement on Parliamentary Elections in Kyrgyzstan
October 11, 2010

I congratulate the people and Government of the Kyrgyz Republic for carrying out orderly parliamentary elections yesterday. Above all, I congratulate the voters of Kyrgyzstan, who demonstrated by their participation in yesterday's historic election that they are committed to selecting their government through peaceful, democratic means.

Election observers have reported some flaws and irregularities in the voting process, which must be investigated and corrected. Yet the election also demonstrated important and positive attributes of a genuine democracy: The campaign period was competitive and lively, domestic and international observers freely monitored the voting process on election day, and the outcome was still not known on the day of the vote. Through our assistance programs to the Kyrgyz Government and civil society and our participation in the election monitoring mission, I am pleased that the United States has played an active role in facilitating this democratic achievement.

Elections are only one instrument of democratic governance. The next phase in Kyrgyzstan's democratic restoration should be the formation of a coalition government that can govern the country effectively and peacefully. Given recent tragic events in Kyrgyzstan, there are serious challenges ahead. Yet yesterday's vote should give supporters of democracy in Kyrgyzstan, Central Asia, and around the world hope and renews our conviction to help the courageous people of Kyrgyzstan consolidate their democracy, jump-start their economy, and maintain peace and security.

Remarks at a Dinner for the Democratic Congressional Campaign Committee and Representative Ron Klein in Miami
October 11, 2010

Hello, everybody. Please have a seat, have a seat. It is good to be back, Miami. This is quite a view, Alonzo. [*Laughter*]

To the entire Mourning family, Tracy and Alonzo, Trey, Myka, Alijah, thank you so much for your hospitality and this spectacular setting. We are grateful to you.

To Representative Chris Van Hollen, who is here, the chairman of the DCCC, everybody give him a big round of applause. Congresswoman Debbie Wasserman Schultz is here. Representative Ron Klein is here. And we're going to get him back in Congress. Representative Kathy Castor—is Kathy here? Give her a round of applause anyway, even if she's not here. And I know Representative Ted Deutch is here, and his beautiful family.

In addition, I want to say that Dwyane Wade, Chris Bosh, I wish you the best of luck when you're not playing the Bulls. [*Laughter*] I just want to be clear about that. I like you. [*Laugh-ter*] But when you're playing the Bulls, I'm rooting against you. [*Laughter*]

I am stunned that Alonzo let a Laker in here. [*Laughter*] But he said that Magic transcends party lines—and so we're glad to have Magic in the house.

Now, I want to just say a little bit about Ron, because so much of the reason we're here is to make sure that he continues to do the outstanding work that he's doing on behalf of south Florida. They have lived here for 25 years. This is where they raised their family. This is where Ron helped run a small business. That's who he's been fighting for since he got to Washington—families and small-business owners—because he's part of them, he understands them. He's fought to bring skyrocketing costs of homeowner's insurance down. He's fighting to protect and strengthen Medicare and Social Security. He was one of the leaders in helping to make sure that we impose sanctions on Iran, to provide more security for us, but also to provide more security for our ally, Israel.

He knows the people of south Florida, has been listening to them, has been working with them, is fighting for them. And he's an example of the kinds of unbelievable public servants that we've got all across the country, who have been doing heroic work under the most difficult circumstances.

So I just want to spend a little bit of time talking about what those circumstances are and why this election is so important. When people think about elections, they tend to think back to 2008, and they remember the Inauguration Day, and Beyonce was singing, and everybody was looking nice, or they think about election day, and everybody with the signs, and—"Yes We Can." They don't remember when we were walking around in the snow in Iowa, knocking on doors and nobody knew who we were. And it was tough.

And what I said to people at that time was that the reason I was running for President was because I felt that the country had gone off-track, that it wasn't working on behalf of the ordinary families where so many of us started— families in Lansing or families in Chicago or families in south Florida—families that didn't have a lot, but they had a lot of love, they had a work ethic, they wanted to make sure their kids got ahead. And they figured if they lived up to their responsibilities, then they would be able to get a good job that pays a living wage. They could buy a house. They could send their kids to school so they could aspire to things they never hoped for themselves.

They believed that they shouldn't get bankrupt if they get sick. They should be able to retire with some dignity and some respect. They believed in the American Dream. It didn't matter what color you were, what race you were, what religion you were, there was a notion that we could all make it if we did the right thing by ourselves, our families, our communities. And people had lost that belief, and that's why I decided to run.

But I also said that the problems we were experiencing had been going on for a decade. The years between 2001 and 2009 had seen the slowest job growth since World War II. The years between 2001 and 2009, middle class families, on average, lost 5 percent of their wages. Their incomes actually went down during those years. And so what I said was the election will not be the end of the journey; that will be the beginning, because then we're going to have to work hard to try to make sure that we rebuild this economy on a solid foundation.

Now, what we didn't know when I started running, and what we discovered only in the few months before I won was that we were about to enter into the worst financial crisis since the Great Depression. We lost 4 million jobs in the 6 months before I took office; lost almost 800,000 jobs the month I was sworn in, 600,000 the month after that, 600,000 the month after that. Businesses couldn't get credit. The banking system locked up. And people were talking seriously that we were about to go into a second Great Depression.

And so my first job coming into office was to make sure that we stabilized the economy. And we have done that. An economy that was shrinking by 6 percent is now growing. An economy that was shredding jobs, we've had 9 months straight of private sector job growth. Businesses can now get loans again. Corporations are now profitable again. We have the opportunity to move the country forward.

But we are still digging ourselves out of a enormous hole. When you lose 8 million jobs, even if you've created 800,000 this year, and even if we save 3 million, we've still got a deep hole to climb out of. And so, understandably, people are frustrated and they are angry. And what the other side is trying to do is to ride that anger and that frustration all the way to the ballot box.

They're not counting on the need to offer good ideas. They're just counting on people being angry and figuring that is sufficient for them to get elected. And when I came in, and Ron and Chris and Debbie and others who work in Washington, when we came in, our hope was that in the midst of crisis we could bring everybody together to work on the challenges that confronted us, because we may be proud Democrats, but we're prouder Americans. And our attitude was we are happy to work across the aisle to solve problems.

That was not the attitude that we confronted. Basically, they said no to everything. If I said that the ocean was blue, they'd say no. If I said there were fish in the sea, they'd say no. Their attitude was, if Obama fails, then we win.

Now, I couldn't play that game because my responsibility was to make sure that even when the decisions were tough, we took the decisions that were required to get us on the right track. And we have now done that. But moving forward, I can only succeed if I've got help. Now, I know this is a little too obvious, but I've got to use the basketball metaphor for you. [*Laughter*]

There's a reason why Dwyane is really excited to have Chris Bosh and LeBron James, because he remembers the last time he won the championship, he had a guy named Shaq running around. Now Shaq is going to try to stop you this time. But he remembers what it was like to have teammates. As great as Magic was, he couldn't do it without Worthy and Jabbar and all those tremendous stars from "Showtime."

Well, the same is true in politics. I'm pretty good—[*laughter*]—I'm a pretty good point guard, but I can't do it on my own. If I don't have Ron there, if I don't have a Debbie there, doing the hard work each and every day to move this country's agenda forward, we are not going to succeed.

I mean, there are folks right now in Washington, some of the pundits who actually say, you know, Obama might be better off with what happened with Clinton; you lose the House, you lose the Senate, or you lose some seats, and then you can pivot because the Republicans finally have to take responsibility. That may be short-term political thinking in the minds of pundits; that's not how I think because I'm thinking about how do I move the country forward.

I've got to make sure that we have an energy policy where we're investing in clean energy here in the United States of America, so that we're building wind turbines and solar panels and electric cars right here in the United States.

So I've got to have partners to do that with. I can't do it alone.

I've got to make sure that we've got the best education system in the world right here in the United States of America. And that requires continuing to make investments in our young people. And I can't do that by myself. If we're going to help small businesses succeed, then we've got to make sure that we are providing them the loans and the tax cuts that are going to help them, because those startups, that's what creates the vibrancy and the dynamism that helps this economy grow. I can't do that by myself.

On every important issue out there, I am going to need help. And the Members of Congress who are here today, they've shown the courage of their convictions. They're willing to take tough votes because they're the right thing to do.

If we're going to protect Medicare and Social Security at the same time as we're reducing our deficit, then we're going to have some very difficult budget choices. And we've got to make sure that the folks who are there have the kind of values that say, we're going to make sure that our seniors are always protected, and we're not going to go back to the days where the poverty rate was higher for people in their golden years. That's not acceptable. So we're going to need some help.

Now, I hope that we can get help from the other side. But I'm not optimistic right now. I've seen what they call the "Pledge to America." And it would have been one thing if after the disaster of their economic policies, they had gone off and gone to a think tank or gone into the desert to meditate and come back and said, you know what, we really screwed up; we've got a whole new set of answers here. But that's not what happened.

They have said they will do the exact same thing. The centerpiece of their economic agenda, their big plan for jobs is to borrow $700 billion that we don't have, to give an average $100,000 tax cut to millionaires and billionaires. Ninety-eight percent of the country would not get these tax breaks, and as a consequence, they wouldn't spend them. So it would do nothing to boost the economy in any significant way. And we'd be borrowing the money to do it.

And you know how they've proposed paying for it? They haven't—with the exception of a few suggestions like cutting education spending by 20 percent. Think about that. And think about the folks back in your old neighborhood, Magic, all those kids who are working hard, thinking, maybe I can go to go college if I can get a scholarship, if I can get a Pell grant. And we're going to cut support for them at a time when we know that the single most important thing to determine whether we are winners or losers in the global economy is how well our workforce is educated?

Imagine that. You think China is cutting back on their education investments? You think South Korea or Germany are saying let's invest less in our young people right now? Of course not. They're not playing for second. And the United States does not play for second either. We play for first place. That's what we're about, and that's what this election is about.

I should point out, by the way, that a whole lot of people in this room would get a tax cut under that plan. But the question is—and that includes me, by the way—is that really what's most important to us right now? Or is it more important that we get this country back on track so that it's there for future generations? Are we going to reach back and make sure that somebody else is getting a helping hand?

So as I've traveled the country I've been using this analogy: Essentially, the other side drove the car into the ditch. And me and Ron and the rest of the outstanding Democrats here, we all climbed down into that ditch. It was muddy down there and hot. We had to put on boots. There were bugs. But we started pushing, pushing that car out of the ditch. Every once in a while, we'd look up and the Republicans would be standing there fanning themselves, sipping on Slurpees, looking all comfortable. [*Laughter*]

We'd say, "Why don't you come down and help?" "No, that's all right, but you all aren't pushing fast enough. You're not pushing the right way."

And even though we did not get any help, we kept on pushing, until finally we got that car up on level ground. Now, it's a little banged up, needs some bodywork, needs a tuneup, but we are pointing in the right direction and we are ready to move forward again. And suddenly, we get this tap on our shoulders. We look back, and it's the Republicans. And they're saying, we want the keys back. You can't have the keys back. You don't know how to drive. [*Laughter*] Now, if you want to ride, you can ride in the backseat. But we're not going to give you— [*laughter*]—give you the wheel. [*Laughter*]

That's what this election is about. It is a fundamental choice about the direction of our future. We cannot do it alone. And in the same way that I need a team, Ron needs a team, members of the Democratic delegation here need a team. You are that team. And I need you guys to be as excited as you were in 2008.

You know, this is just the first quarter. And we've put up a lot of points, under very adverse circumstances. But we've got three more quarters to play. And if suddenly everybody is acting like, "well, that's it, I'm tired," we'll lose. And when I say "we," I mean the country will lose. One of the marks of a champion is not just talent, it's not just skill, it's heart. It's perseverance. Are you willing to stick with something until it's finished.

The project of bringing about change so that this country is more just and more prosperous and we are growing faster and we can compete in the global stage and our young people are prepared for the 21st century, that project is not done. And it is hard. But we need heart. We need character. And I believe that's what we've got. I believe in this team. I hope you believe in it too. If you do, then I promise you that not only are we going to win this election, we are going to restore the American Dream for every American.

Thank you very much, everybody. God bless you. God bless the United States of America. Thank you.

NOTE: The President spoke at 6:16 p.m. at the residence of Alonzo and Tracy Mourning. In his remarks, he referred to Alonzo "Trey," Myka, and Alijah Mourning, children of Mr. and Mrs. Mourning; Dwyane Wade, shooting guard, Chris Bosh, power forward, and

LeBron James, small forward, National Basketball Association's Miami Heat; former NBA players Earvin "Magic" Johnson, Jr., James Worthy, and Kareem Abdul-Jabbar; musician Beyonce G. Knowles; and Shaquille O'Neal, center, Boston Celtics.

Statement on the 10th Anniversary of the Terrorist Attack on the USS *Cole*
October 12, 2010

We remember today the 17 U.S. sailors who lost their lives 10 years ago as a result of an Al Qaida terrorist attack against the USS *Cole* off the coast of Yemen. These brave men and women were serving their country and helping to maintain security in the Gulf region when Al Qaida launched this outrageous attack.

We pay tribute on this day to the courage and sacrifice of those who lost their lives in this attack and to their families. We remain steadfast in our support for the brave men and women of our Armed Forces who continue to risk their lives around the world to defeat these terrorists and to keep our Nation safe, and we stand with our military families who sacrifice so much to support them.

I will never forget meeting with some of the families of the victims of this bombing in February 2009. I am deeply grateful to them for their sacrifice and their efforts to keep the memory of this tragic event alive in our Nation's conscience. The families and loved ones of those we lost are in our hearts and prayers, and the American people stand with them on this solemn day of remembrance.

Al Qaida continues to use Yemen, as well as other places around the world, as platforms from which to pursue its murderous agenda, and we continue to work closely with our Yemeni and other global partners to counter the Al Qaida threat. As we do, we will always remember those we lost on the USS *Cole*, and we will honor their legacy of selfless service by advancing the values that they stood for throughout their lives.

Statement on Rescue Efforts at the San Jose Mine in Copiapo, Chile
October 12, 2010

Our thoughts and prayers are with the brave miners, their families, and the men and women who have been working so hard to rescue them. While that rescue is far from over and difficult work remains, we pray that by God's grace, the miners will be able to emerge safely and return to their families soon. We are also proud of all of the Americans who have been working with our Chilean friends on the ground to do everything that we can to bring these miners home.

Remarks at a Town Hall Meeting and a Question-and-Answer Session
October 12, 2010

The President. Well, hello, everybody. Hello. Thank you, everybody. Please, please have a seat. Thank you so much.

First of all, Sarah, I think you've got a future. You sounded really good. I was persuaded. [*Laughter*] So thank you for the wonderful introduction.

I want to thank Tim Kaine and Paul Hodes, who are up in New Hampshire and doing great work. Jeremy, thank you for helping to moderate. And I also want to thank Steve Knapp and—the president of GW—and all the GW family for helping to host us here today. Please give them a big round of applause. Thank you.

Now, one thing about being President is that you hear yourself talk all the time. [*Laughter*] So I do not want to spend a whole bunch of time with a long opening speech. Let me just make a few remarks at the top, and then I really want to hear from you. And I know we're not only getting questions from the audience, but we're also going to be getting questions through the Internet and Skype and a whole bunch of other things that Malia and Sasha understand and I'm still trying to sort out.

You know, when you think back to almost 2 years ago, election night when I stood in Grant Park in Chicago or the Inauguration here in Washington, DC, there was just such an incredible sense of possibility and promise. We had run a very unlikely campaign. It was a campaign based on not fancy endorsements and big special interest money, but it was all based on grassroots participation, ordinary folks who had decided that the country was on the wrong track and we needed to get involved.

And one of the most inspiring things about the campaign was how so many young people like Sarah got involved in public life for the first time, because what that signaled was a reaffirmation of a central American truth, which is our destiny is not written for us by somebody else. Our destiny is written by us. When we decide to join together and make common cause, then there's nothing we can't accomplish. And so we overturned a lot of conventional wisdom in this town as a consequence of that election.

What we understood, but maybe didn't fully appreciate, was that I was taking office at a time of extraordinary crisis in this country. We had just gone through a decade in which job growth had been sluggish and in which middle class families had seen their wages and incomes actually go down rather than go up. People had seen their health care costs rise, their college tuition rise. They had a sense that maybe the American Dream was increasingly out of reach for so many people.

But what we found out when I was sworn in was that we were possibly down a path to a second Great Depression. The financial system had melted down. We had lost 4 million jobs in the 6 months prior to me taking office. We lost 750,000 jobs the month I took office, 600,000 after that, 600,000 the month after that.

And so the hole that had been dug was very deep. And my first challenge was to make sure that we didn't slide any further. And we had to take a whole set of emergency actions, some of which frankly were unpopular, some of which I hadn't talked about in the campaign because we

hadn't anticipated having to take these drastic emergency steps. But my first job was to make sure that we stopped the slide, and we did.

And so now we have an economy that's growing again. We have seen 9 consecutive months of private sector job growth. The financial system has stabilized. And yet because of that hole, we've got millions of people across the country who are struggling. And some of you know in your own families those struggles: people who can't find work despite sending resume after resume out, small-business owners who still are having trouble getting loans, young people who are still having trouble financing their college educations, people who are worrying about losing their homes to foreclosure.

So there's a lot of anger and there's a lot of frustration and a lot of fear across the country. And one of the challenges of this election is to make sure that we understand that as difficult as things are and have been over the last 2 years, we are moving in the right direction. And the question is going to be whether once again hope overcomes fear. Because what essentially the other side has decided is that they're going to try to ride fear and anxiety all the way to the ballot box on November 2. And frankly, and I'm just going to be blunt, some on our side have said to themselves, well, you know what, everything that we thought was going to happen hasn't happened immediately in 20 months, and so maybe we don't have the same enthusiasm and excitement and energy as we did that first time around.

The most important message I can deliver to all of you today is, number one, over the last 20 months not only have we prevented America from slipping into a Great Depression, but we finally started tackling those structural, fundamental issues that all of you cared so much about and that we campaigned on. So we now have a health care reform in place that can make sure that young people all across America can stay on their parents' health insurance until they're 26 years old; that makes sure that seniors have a Medicare system that they can count on and don't have over time a doughnut hole that leaves them in the terrible choice of do I buy my prescription drugs or do I instead pay the rent.

We have also set it up so that over time the cost of health care can go down, which will be an enormous relief for small businesses and families, as well as the Federal Government, because frankly, we couldn't afford the trajectory that we were on.

We have reformed our education system in fundamental ways. All across the country you're seeing investments in science and math education and teacher recruitment, and clearing away some of the redtape and bureaucracy that was preventing us from making sure that our kids got the best possible start in life. And we also transformed the student loan system so that a lot of young people here at GW and all across the country are now receiving billions of dollars of additional assistance that previously had been going to banks in unwarranted subsidies.

We, across the country, have seen investments in clean energy, in solar panels and wind turbines and biodiesel plants that promise a clean energy future, something that I know this next generation in particular is concerned about, not only for economic reasons, but also for environmental reasons.

So we have made some huge changes over the last 20 months and we can make more. But we're not there yet. We're not where we need to be yet. And this election is going to help determine whether we can continue on this path so that America finally takes on these tough challenges, we finally start making sure that the American Dream works for everybody and not just some, and that we're able to compete on a global stage that is more competitive than it has been at any time in my lifetime—and I'm a lot older than a bunch of you guys.

So that's the challenge. Now, the only way this is going to work is if hope defeats fear, and that manifests itself in you guys committing to vote. So I need everybody here and everybody who's listening to commit to vote. But I also need you to talk to your friends and neighbors, coworkers, aunts, uncles, relatives, whoever it is that you can get your hands on, and tell them November 2 matters.

If you were excited in 2008, that was the beginning of the journey; that's not the end of the journey. Or to use a sports metaphor, we just finished the first quarter. We've got a whole bunch more work to do. If all of you, a little wiser, a little older after these past 22 months—I'm certainly older, I've got more gray hair here—if you can muster and sustain that same effort and energy, then I'm absolutely confident that we will do well in the election. We will win all across the country. And the polls bear that out. But more importantly, America will win because we will not have retreated from the progress that we've started. Rather, we will advance and build off the progress that we've started.

So it's going to be up to you. The future is going to be in your hands. And I have to say, the other side right now is excited because they see the opportunity to—in the midst of some still very difficult economic times, they see the opportunity to take advantage of that politically.

The only thing that is going to counteract their enthusiasm, their excitement, and the millions of dollars that are pouring in from special interests into races all across the country, are your voices. We've overcome those forces before; there's no reason why we can't again. But it's going to require that commitment on your part, not only to vote, but to make sure that you get other folks to vote as well.

So with that, Jeremy, why don't we open it up to some questions.

Organizing for America Deputy Director Jeremy Bird. Well, thank you, Mr. President, for joining us. As you said, we have questions from—that we took from different mediums. We've got a Skype question we're going to get to you later.

But first—and we'll put it up on the screen for you in the room as well——

The President. Okay.

Election Spending Disclosure

Mr. Bird. We have a question online. The question is from James in California, and he asks: "Mr. President, how best can citizens work to mitigate the effect of corporate money on elections?"

The President. Well, this is a big challenge. Now, let me first of all say that throughout the history of America, money has always influenced elections. That's always been the case, starting from the very first Presidential election.

And the truth is also that Democrats, just like Republicans, have to get their message out. And that means we've got to send out direct mail and we've got to run television ads.

In a big, complicated democracy like ours, it requires resources to get out your message. And there's nothing wrong with that, per se. But what's happening in this election is unprecedented because what we're seeing, partly as a consequence of a Supreme Court decision called *Citizens United,* is the ability of special interests to mobilize millions of dollars from donors who are undisclosed to run negative ads at levels that are outspending, in some cases, the candidates themselves or the parties.

And when I say negative ads, there was a recent study done estimating that 86 percent of these ads that are being run by these so-called third-party organizations are negative. Eighty-six percent of them are negative ads that are just bombarding candidates all across the country, and we don't know where this money is coming from. We don't know if it's being paid for by oil companies who don't like some of our environmental positions. We don't know if they're being run by banks who are frustrated by some of our financial positions. We don't know if they're being funded by foreign corporations because they're not disclosed.

And so this poses an enormous challenge. And one of the most frustrating things is that these ads, when they run, the names of these groups are all really innocuous sounding, right? There's Americans for Prosperity and Moms for Motherhood. I made that one up, but—[*laughter*]—but you get the idea.

So if you're just watching the screen, you think, well, gosh, Americans for Prosperity—I'm for prosperity and they're saying all these horrible things about the Democratic candidate. Maybe the Democratic candidate is not for prosperity.

Now, they have every right under the First Amendment to let their voices be heard, but I think all of us would agree that it would make a difference if you were watching these ads and you found out, well, Americans for Prosperity actually are bankrolled by a bunch of very wealthy special interests that are opposed to legislation that you support. That might have an influence in terms of how you interpret that ad. This is a huge problem.

Now, for this election we're not going to be able to change the law. I hope that the Supreme Court at some point looks at the evidence that's accumulated over the next—over the past several months and says, this is really hijacking our democracy, this is not a healthy thing.

In the meantime, though, the most important thing we can do is make sure that we vote and make sure that we're talking to our friends and neighbors and getting out facts and information.

I am confident that if people have good information and can make up their own minds, that we will do well. The people, by the way, who have the most credibility in delivering that message are you. Because the truth of the matter is, no matter how negative an ad it may be, it's sort of background noise. Most people kind of tune out, especially in these States where they're getting it every 2 seconds. I mean, heaven forbid that you live in a competitive congressional district. I mean, it must just be nonstop. So at a certain point, people tune those things out.

But if they hear from their friend who they respect, their neighbor who they respect, here are the facts about what President Obama did with financial regulation to make sure that credit card companies can't jack up your rates without any reason or without any notice; here's—it turns out that because of health reform, you're going to be able to get health insurance even though you've got a preexisting condition; when they hear those things from you directly, that has more credibility than any television ad.

And that's how you overcome all this money that's pouring into the elections. You are the most powerful messengers possible. And that's how democracy ultimately should work.

Mr. Bird. Thank you, Mr. President. And thank you, James, for your question.

All right, now we're going to try something new.

The President. All right.

Mr. Bird. So we're going to try a different medium here. We're going to go to Skype for the first time ever.

The President. I'm very excited.

Mr. Bird. We're going to actually have someone calling in from their computer here. And we actually have Paula calling in from the great city and your hometown, Chicago, Illinois.

Paula?

Midterm Elections

Q. Good evening, Mr. President. In this last push to get out the vote, is there an overarching message or approach that you think volunteers could best take to persuade voters to get back to the polls on November 2?

The President. Great question, although I don't think she can hear me, right? This is not a two-way Skype?

Mr. Bird. I don't think it's two-way here.

The President. Okay.

Mr. Bird. She's watching you online right now.

The President. Well, hello, everybody. [*Laughter*] I think the most important message to deliver in this election is that it is a choice. Because what the other side is counting on is—understanding the economy is still weak, even though it's growing; a lot of people are still unemployed, even though we've seen private sector job growth—in that kind of environment, the easiest thing to do is to say things aren't good enough now, throw the bums out. That's going to be their message, particularly since we have control of the House and the Senate, as well as the White House.

We have to make sure that we are delivering a choice to people. And so the most effective message is to say that this is what Democrats stand for. We stand for tax cuts for middle class families who have seen their incomes declining over the last several years. We stand for giving tax breaks to companies that are investing in research and development here in the United States, not those who are investing in research and development overseas and jobs overseas. We stand for making sure that every young person in this country is getting a good, quality ed-

ucation K through 12 and that they can afford to go to college without taking on so much debt that they could never hope to pay it back.

This is what we stand for: innovation, research and development, skilled workers, lifelong learning, all the things that are required to make sure that this a competitive 21st-century America that is playing for number one on the global stage.

And what the other side stands for are the same failed policies that got us into this mess in the first place. It's not as if we didn't try the other side's theories. We tried them for 8 years. We had massive tax cuts, much of those tax cuts going to millionaires and billionaires. We deregulated across the board in every field imaginable, from the financial sector to oil and gas companies to you name it. We didn't take the challenges that middle class families were going through seriously. We said, you know what, fend for yourselves, you don't need help from the Government; the market will solve all problems.

We tried that, and it didn't work. And so when this election is posed as a choice, then I think people—sort of the light bulb goes on, "Oh, yes, now I remember; that didn't work." And that then gives us an opportunity to say what we've been doing isn't enough, we're only halfway there, but what we're doing is starting to work, and we've got to stay on that path.

And for a lot of people here, depending on who you're talking to, you should tailor a message to speak to those persons' concerns. If the young people who are here, if you're talking to a classmate, it's not that hard to say, what's your student loan debt going to be when you graduate? And they've probably calculated, boy, I'm going to owe 50,000, 60,000, 70,000, 100,000. And you say to them, you know what, the President passed a tax credit for young people that will be worth $10,000 for anybody going to 4 years of college, and that could be repealed if Republicans take over. They've already proposed to cut education spending by 20 percent. Well, that will get people's attention because that's a pocketbook issue, that's a bread-and-butter issue.

If you're talking to a senior, and you say, I know you've heard a lot of nonsense about the health reform bill, but do you know that the trustees of Medicare said that as a consequence of our reforms we extended the life of Medicare, and by the way, if you're in that zone called the doughnut hole where you're having trouble paying for your prescription drugs, you're going to be receiving a $250 check to help pay for those prescription drugs. And over time, by next year, we're going to cut your costs for prescription drugs in half, according to the reform law.

So you want to speak to people in terms of what it is that they're going through right now in their lives. And I think that across the board, if they see what the choice is, then I think that we'll do very well.

National Economy/Job Creation and Growth/Alternative Energy Sources

Mr. Bird. Thank you, Mr. President. We're going to—before we open it up to the crowd, we're going to take one more from folks online. And this one comes from Twitter. This is from Maureen in New Jersey. You'll also see it up on the screen here. And Maureen asks: "Can we inform people that the campaign slogan was 'Yes, we can,' not 'Yes, we can in 21 months'?" [*Laughter*] "It took 8 years to get us into this mess."

The President. Well, that's sort of a softball. [*Laughter*] But I appreciate it, Maureen.

Look, people have good reason to feel frustrated. If you're having trouble making your mortgage right now, and you've seen your home value go down by $100,000, or you've seen your 401(k) drop in value by 20 percent and you're about to retire, if you've had to put off your college education because your family can't quite afford to help you out now and you're having trouble, you know, that's tough.

And so I don't blame the American people for feeling frustrated and impatient. But I do think it is important to make sure that we're communicating that the problems that we have are problems that can be solved, but they're not going to be solved overnight. And what we want

to make sure of is, is that we're on the right path.

So let's take the example of American manufacturing. We've seen manufacturing leave our shores for years now. Plants closed all across this country. Some of it has to do with them just shifting to places like China that had lower labor costs; some of it had to do with automation. And so those are a lot of well-paying jobs that helped to build our middle class that over the last 20, 30 years have been gutted.

Now, I think the American worker is the most productive worker on Earth. I think we have the most creative and dynamic entrepreneurial culture on Earth. We still have more innovation than any country on Earth, but we haven't harnessed it. And especially we're not harnessing it for the jobs of the future.

So when you look at clean energy, for example, when we came into office, we were producing 2 percent of the world's advanced batteries that go into electric cars and hybrid cars.

Now, you think about it. This is where the industry is going. We were making all our money, to the extent that any of our automakers were making money, making them on SUVs. So what we said was let's jump-start an American advanced battery industry. And we have seen advanced battery plants open throughout the Midwest, and we're on pace now to have 40 percent of the market by 2015, in 5 years time.

Now, that's just one example of how we can rebuild American manufacturing using innovation, using research, using the skills and talents of our workforce. But we're not going to completely replace all the jobs that were lost in manufacturing in 2 years time or 3 years time. What we have to do is nurture and build on these successes in solar panels and wind turbines and electric cars. Over time we're creating a whole new industry that can absorb skilled workers. And then if we're training those workers effectively for those jobs, then as those industries grow, opportunities for Americans grow. And that's always been how this middle class has been built here in this country.

So I guess my main response to Maureen is, on the one hand, I think you've got to be sympathetic to the fact that people need help now, and we're doing everything we can to make sure that job growth is here now, that we're helping small businesses get loans right now so they can keep their doors open or they can expand. We're making sure that teachers aren't getting laid off as much as we can by providing help to the States and local governments that are hard strapped. There are a lot of things that we're doing right now.

But those big structural changes that a lot of folks are worried about, those can be solved but it's going to require persistent effort. It's going to require imagination and stick-to-it-ness over the course of several years in order for us to get back to where we were.

I'm confident we'll get there, but we've got to make sure that we don't start going back to the policies that resulted in American manufacturing decline. And I'm confident we can do that.

Mr. Bird. Thank you. Now what we'd like to do is just open it up to you to take questions from the audience here.

The President. All right. Let's see who we got. This young man right here, he's all ready. Introduce yourself.

President's Time in Office/Congressional Voting

Q. Hi. I'm Daniel Lippman from Massachusetts and I thank you for coming to GW.

The President. Thank you.

Q. And my question is, what are some of the surprises that you've encountered in Washington and what lessons have you learned in your 21 months here? Thank you.

The President. Well, where do I start? [*Laughter*] You know, let me tell you something. On the one hand, I've been surprised by how the news cycle here in Washington is focused on what happens this minute as opposed to what needs to happen over the course of months, years. The 24-hour news cycle is just so lightning fast and the attention span, I think, is so short that sometimes it's difficult to keep everybody focused on the long term.

The things that are really going to matter in terms of America's success 20 years from now when we look back are not the things that are being talked about on television on any given day or appear on the Internet on a blog on any given day. And so that's challenging.

And I've got to constantly figure out how to work with this new media environment to make sure that we stay focused on what's important. Are we educating our kids over the long term? Are we putting enough money into research and development? Are we helping grow startup businesses and small businesses that are going to create the jobs of the future? Are we competitive in terms of how we deal with our export sector?

Those big questions, a lot of times they're kind of dull, they're wonkish, and so they don't attract as much attention as you'd like.

On the other hand, let me tell you something that I've been surprised about is how courageous a lot of Members of Congress have been on some of the big, tough issues that we've worked on over the last 20 months.

I know it's fashionable to get down on Congress. Congress is right now very unpopular, both parties, because people just see the arguments all the time, and the noise, and then they're absorbing all those negative ads, and they just feel like, gosh, you know, these folks, they don't care about us. And I get that.

But there are a lot of folks who took some really tough votes over the course of the last 20 months, knowing that it was bad for them politically; who voted for health care reform even though the polls said this would cause them problems in the next election; who voted for financial regulatory reform, even though they knew that by supporting it, it might attract big money pouring in and directing negative ads against them. And they did it anyway. And that was risky for them.

And so part of the reason why I think this election is so important is I want to make sure that when somebody does the right thing, they get rewarded. I'm a strong believer in accountability in politics. And when somebody does the wrong thing, including somebody in my own party, I think they should be held to account.

But I also think that there have been a surprising number of folks who have been willing to stand up. There's a candidate in Virginia, Tom Perriello, who's a great guy, who has worked—he comes from—his is not a traditionally Democratic district. But he's just done what's right. And there have been times where he disagreed with me and he criticized me, but he always did so from a place of principle.

John Boccieri in Ohio, Betsy Markey in Colorado—I mean, there just have been some folks who really stood up, knowing that they might be putting their congressional careers at risk. And that's been a pleasant surprise.

So, all right? Next. Let's see, I'm going to go boy, girl, boy, girl, so that I don't—okay, go ahead. And we've got a microphone for you.

Education/Taxes

Q. Hi, my name is Francesca. I live in DC, but I'm originally from Dallas, Texas.

The President. Great to see you, Francesca.

Q. Mr. President, you have pointed out that U.S. students have fallen from the top 20 nations in math and science in test scores, and jobs and contracts are going overseas. You've called education funding a national priority. But do you think it's time to label education funding a national security priority?

The President. I think it's a national security priority. Look, there has never been a nation on Earth that lost its economic edge and maintained its military edge. And the reason that we have the most effective military on Earth in the history of the world is first and foremost because we have unbelievable men and women in uniform who make sacrifices on our behalf every single day, and are extraordinary.

But the second reason is because we've had the biggest economy in the world that can support this incredible Armed Forces that we have. And if we start falling behind economically, we will fall behind from a national security perspective. There's no doubt about it.

And the single most important determinant of how we do economically is going to be the skills of our workforce. And you're exactly right. We used to be at the top of the heap when it came to math and science education. We're now 21st and 25th, respectively, in science and math. We used to be number one in the proportion of college graduates in the world. We're now ranked around ninth.

Other countries are making huge investments. I mean, China is doubling, tripling, quadrupling the number of college graduates it's generating. I mean, it is putting huge resources into it because it understands that unless they want to build low-wage manufacturing plants for the duration of the 21st century, they've got to start moving up the value chain in the economy. They've got to start producing more engineers and scientists. India understands that; Germany has long understood that. And yet here we are, losing that first-place position. That is unacceptable.

So here's the thing. We know what works. There are schools out there that do great even with kids who come from the most disadvantaged backgrounds, in the poorest neighborhoods, still producing outstanding results. And it requires having great teachers; it requires cutting through some of the bureaucracy to make sure that innovative learning is taking place; it means having accountability and the ability to measure the progress that students are making.

And one of the things I'm very proud that we've done is institute this program called Race to the Top that basically says to States all across the country, you know what, you can compete for some special funding, some additional funding for your school district if you start instituting these reforms that we know work.

And by the way, this is not a Democratic or Republican issue. Some of the things that we've been doing have not always been popular among some Democratic constituencies, but this is an example of doing what's hard because it's right. I'm not interested in us funding the perpetuation of the status quo; I want to fund what works.

Math and science education—making sure that we are focused on building excellence in school districts all across the country that can produce more scientists, engineers—absolutely critical. And we can do it. We know how to do it, but it does require some investment. It requires us making some good choices.

So when my friends across the aisle propose a tax cut for not just the middle class, right, because we're in favor of tax cuts for middle class families, but also then want to give tax cuts that would only go to the top 2 percent of Americans income-wise—which, by the way, includes me, so I'd get a tax break, despite living in this really nice house right down the street—when they make that argument, I say to them, you know what, I would love to keep taxes low for everybody. And by the way, taxes are a lot lower under an Obama Presidency than they were under Ronald Reagan's Presidency. But I'm not willing to borrow $700 billion that we don't have, that will then require me to cut investments that could produce more math and science teachers, or more scientists and engineers. That doesn't make sense.

And that's an example of the kind of choice that exists on November 2. And when you're talking to your friends and neighbors and asking them to commit to vote, that's what you got to be talking about, is our long-term future depends on us making good choices now because this is a more competitive environment than it's ever been and we're digging ourselves out of a big hole and we've got this big deficit that we inherited, and because of the emergency measures that we've taken that has added more pressure on our budget. And all this means that we've got to make smart choices. We can't just do everything we want. We've got to do the things that are necessary to make sure that America can compete. That's got to be our top priority.

Mr. Bird. Mr. President, I'm sad to say this, but we have time for one more question.

The President. One more question. All right. So it's a guy's turn, this gentleman in the purple shirt.

Global Competitiveness

Q. Thank you, Mr. President. My name is Matt Verghese from the great State of Maryland, very close. A lot of times when I talk to my friends who are looking for jobs for the first time, they're very anxious about the future, they're very anxious about finding jobs, about settling down, about owning their first home. And their parents are also worried about my generation as well. What can you tell them to reassure them to make sure that they aren't overcome by fear and can remain hopeful in the future?

The President. Well, one of the great strengths of America is our adaptability. Now, this is not the first time we've gone through difficult times, obviously. This country was founded on defying the odds. Nobody thought that you could start this country, of and by and for the people, and that everybody would be treated equally, and that over time not only would women win the right to vote and slaves be emancipated and become full citizens, but we'd be attracting people from all corners of the Earth, and somehow the whole thing would work.

I mean, that defies imagination that we were able to pull this off. But that core idea embodied in the Declaration of Independence, in our Constitution, contains such a profound truth about the worthiness of every individual and our ability to come together around a set of principles and laws, that we have been able to overcome slavery, depressions, world wars. There have been moments where it looked like we were going to be overtaken, and yet somehow we adapted and renewed ourselves and got back on track.

That's true even in recent history. I mean, a lot of the young people here won't remember this, but back in the 1980s, it wasn't China that everybody was worried about, it was Japan. And people were having almost the exact same conversation now—or back in the 1980s that they're having now: Japan was cleaning our clock, they're taking over, they're buying Rockefeller Center, and there's no way we can compete. And yet American businesses got leaner and they got more efficient, and people started working harder, and we were more innovative, and we improved quality control and we made a series of decisions that over time got us in a very strong position.

So we tend to meet these challenges. But every once in a while, having gone through sort of the wrenching economic turmoil that we've gone through, we have to adjust to new realities. And we have to be honest and critical about where we're falling short.

And so right now we have to be honest that our education system has slipped. We've got to be honest about the fact that competition is rising around the world and that means our businesses have to be more competitive. We've got to focus more on exports.

I think families, as well as the Federal Government, have understood that you can't just operate on the basis of debt and consumption; there's got to be savings and production. I think we now recognize, painfully, that an economy that's just built on a financial sector that is thinking about gaming the system all the time instead of actually just financing businesses that are actually producing goods and services for people is not the best way to organize our economy and it means that we've got to have more effective regulations. I think we recognize that if our health care system keeps on gobbling a bigger and bigger percentage of our economy, that we're not going to be competitive with other countries.

So there a whole bunch of decisions that we're having to make right now, but we'll make them. We will make them because we've made them in the past. Sometimes it's painful because this is a big, diverse democracy. There are a lot of arguments. People yell at each other and are very passionate about different ideas about how we solve those problems.

But eventually, I think the instincts of the American people are good. The instincts of the American people are sound. I think they know that nobody is promising us that this experiment of ours in democracy is going to be easy, but what we know is, is if we work hard, if we're unified, if we're respectful of one another, if we stay focused on not just the short term but on the next generation, that we can solve our problems.

And so I think letting your friends know that America has gone through tougher problems than this and we've solved them, and we're going to solve these problems in our generation, communicating that confidence about the future is going to be really important. And what makes me confident is all of you, because I get a—one of the great things about being President is I get to meet the American people from every State, every walk of life, every station. And you guys give me confidence. You guys give me hope.

But I really need you to get out on November 2 because then you'll—[*applause*]—if all of you vote, I promise we're going to do just great. Thank you very much, everybody. Appreciate it.

NOTE: The President spoke at 7:06 p.m. at George Washington University. In his remarks, he referred to Arlington, VA, resident Sarah Hinkfuss; and former Gov. Timothy M. Kaine of Virginia, in his capacity as chairman of the Democratic National Committee.

Remarks on the American Opportunity Tax Credit
October 13, 2010

Rescue Efforts at the San Jose Mine in Copiapo, Chile

Good afternoon, everybody. Before we get to what we're here to talk about, which is education, I just want to say a quick word about what so far appears to be a successful rescue of the trapped Chilean miners.

This is obviously something that's captivated the world's attention, and this rescue is a tribute not only to the determination of the rescue workers and the Chilean Government, but also the unity and resolve of the Chilean people, who have inspired the world. And I want to express the hopes of the American people that the miners who are still trapped underground will be returned home safely as soon as possible.

Let me also commend so many people of good will—not only in Chile, but also from the United States and around the world—who are lending a hand in this rescue effort, from the NASA team that helped design the escape vehicle to American companies that manufactured and delivered parts of the rescue drill to the

American engineer who flew in from Afghanistan to operate the drill.

Last night, the whole world watched the scene at "Camp Esperanza" as the first miner was lifted out from under more than 2,000 feet of rock and then embraced by his young son and family. And the tears they shed, after so much time apart, expressed not only their own relief, not only their own joy, but the joy of people everywhere. So it was a thrilling moment, and we're hopeful that those celebrations duplicate themselves throughout the rest of today.

Behind me I've got the Mohan family: Edward, Kathleen, and Sarah. Raise your hands—there we go. [*Laughter*] I've got the O'Mealia family: Mary Ellen with her sons Sean and Tom and her daughters Kelly and Leigh Anne. And we've got the Maynard family: Philip and Joanne with son Gregory and daughters Katherine and Elizabeth.

We just had a wonderful visit. And the reason we're here today, all of us, is that one of the most important things that's going to determine our long-term success is education. Over the past 21 months, as we've climbed our way out of this recession, I've often said that if we want Americans—and America itself—to succeed in the 21st century, we need to offer all of our young people the best education the world has to offer.

At a time when the unemployment rate for folks who've never gone to college is almost double what it is for those who have gone to college, when most of the new jobs being created will require some higher education, when countries that outeducate us today will outcompete us tomorrow, offering our children a world-class education isn't just a moral obligation, it's an economic imperative.

And that's why, from the start of my administration, we've been doing everything we can to make that kind of education possible, from the cradle to the classroom, from college through a career. We're reforming Head Start and challenging weak programs to compete for funds, because if you're receiving tax dollars, you should be delivering results for our kids. We're launching a Race to the Top in our States, which is raising standards and promoting excellence in teaching so our students, all of them, can graduate ready for college and a career.

We're upgrading our undervalued community colleges so we can link students looking for work with businesses that are looking to hire. We're eliminating tens of billions of dollars in wasteful subsidies for banks to profit as middlemen administering student loans, and we're using that money to make college more affordable for millions of additional students.

And we're offering middle class families what's called an American Opportunity Tax Credit, a college tuition tax credit worth up to $2,500 a year. I am calling on Congress to make this tax credit permanent so it's worth up to $10,000 for 4 years of college, because we've got to make sure that in good times or bad, our families can invest in their children's future and in the future of our country.

Today the Treasury Department is putting out a report showing what a difference these college tuition tax credits are making. Over our first year in office, we've increased tax cuts for higher education by over 90 percent. We're helping the dream of a college degree—putting that dream within reach of more than 12 million students from working families.

And so I'm pleased that the families standing behind me could join me here today. Mary Ellen O'Mealia is a single mom who's been working hard to put each of her four kids, Sean, Kelly, Leigh Anne, and Tom, through college. And it hasn't been easy, but it's been a little easier thanks to what we've done. Like Mary Ellen, Joanne and Philip Maynard are able to put their son Gregory and their daughters Katherine and Elizabeth through UMass Amherst in part because of this American Opportunity Tax Credit. And this tax credit is making possible Kathleen and Edward Mohan to give their daughter Sarah the education she needs to pursue her dream of becoming a nurse.

So all these families have benefited directly from this tax credit, and they represent families all across the country from every State. What we need to do is to make it possible for all America's working families to do what the O'Mealias, the Maynards, and the Mohans have been able to do, and that's to send their kids to college.

Now, if the Republicans in Congress had their way that would be more difficult. They've proposed cutting back on education by 20 percent. That means reducing financial aid for 8 million students and leaving our community colleges without the resources they need to prepare our students for the jobs of the future.

Nothing would be more shortsighted. There's an educational arms race taking place around the world right now, from China to Germany to India to South Korea. Cutting back on education would amount to unilateral disarmament. We can't afford to do that. The nation that educates its children the best will be the nation that leads the global economy in the 21st century.

Now, ultimately, this is not just about making our economy more competitive. It's not just about preparing our kids for the jobs of the future, though all those things are absolutely es-

sential. It's also about who we are as a people. It's about building a brighter future where every child in this country has a chance to rise above any barriers of race or faith or station and they can fulfill their God-given potential, where the American Dream is a living reality. By opening the doors of college to anyone who wants to go, that's a future we can help build together.

These three families represent those core values, represent those beliefs. The parents who are standing here have worked extraordinarily hard to make sure that their children have opportunities. And we need to reward that sense of responsibility, that sense of commitment to the next generation, by making sure they're not having to do it alone.

So thank you all for being here. Thank you very much, everybody.

NOTE: The President spoke at 1:50 p.m. in the Rose Garden at the White House.

Remarks at an MTV/BET Town Hall Meeting and a Question-and-Answer Session
October 14, 2010

MTV Correspondent Sway Calloway. Ladies and gentlemen, it's our honor to welcome the President of the United States, Barack Obama.

The President. It's good to see you.

Mr. Calloway. Good to see you as well, Mr. President.

The President. Thank you.

Rescue Efforts at the San Jose Mine in Copiapo, Chile

Mr. Calloway. Looking bright, that's right. Before we take our first question from the audience, I wanted to talk about a issue that's been in global news: the Chilean miners who have just been rescued. The whole entire world was glued to their television sets, as well as their laptops. It was a very emotional story, very compelling story. I watched it from my hotel room. And I wanted to know, where did you watch it? And what went through your mind as you did?

The President. Well, I was watching it at the White House, and I think so many of you have seen the joy of the families as these miners were coming out. It was a testament to their personal strength. It was a testament to the way the Chilean people came together. But it was also a testament to how the world came together, because I think some of you may be aware that some of the drilling machinery that was used to get them out was made here in the United States of America; that NASA scientists helped design the mechanisms to get the miners out. And so the fact that we played some small part, I think, in this terrific story is a testament to American know-how and ingenuity, but also how we try to help other people across the globe during trying times.

Mr. Calloway. Okay, thank you, Mr. President.

The President. It was very inspiring.

Mr. Calloway. Very inspiring. Great. Your first question is coming from April. She's right there.

BET Correspondent April Woodard. Hello, Mr. President. Here's our first question.

Bipartisanship in Politics/Health Care Reform

Q. Thank you so much for taking my question, Mr. President. My name is Cynthia Meyer, I'm from Austin, Texas, and I am a Republican.

So here's my question: In 2008, you campaigned heavily on the issue of bipartisanship and reaching across the aisle, and as a Republican, I very much respected that. But, to be frank, when all was said and done, I don't think that was—that actually happened. Specifically with health care, I think Republicans had a lot of really good ideas that were very reasonable, and a lot of the American people agreed. And so my question for you is, how are you going to improve the dialogue among the two parties?

The President. Well, it's a great question. And by the way, I love Austin, Texas. One of my favorite towns in the country.

When I ran, it was based on the notion that Washington was broken. We were having arguments that had more to do with who would win an election than how we were going to solve the country's problems. And I continue to believe that that is holding us back.

So on a whole range of issues, my hope was, is that we could come together, Democrats and Republicans, to find practical, commonsense solutions to health care, to education, to energy issues, because although I'm a proud Democrat, I'm a prouder American. And I think all of us believe, regardless of our party affiliations, that this is a critical time, where we've got to solve big problems.

Now, I will tell you that with respect to health care, we actually spent months trying to obtain cooperation from Republicans to see if we could negotiate a commonsense solution. This is not, by the way, something that I'm just making up. I think the record will show that we had repeated meetings, hopeful that they would meet us halfway in terms of shaping legislation that would preserve the private insurance market, wouldn't be disruptive so that people could

still get the health care that they were currently obtaining if they were happy with it, but that we would also deal with some longstanding problems about skyrocketing costs and the fact that there were 30 million people without health insurance, and people were being dropped when they got sick, and we just couldn't get there.

Partly—and I'll be honest with you, part of it had to do with the fact that some folks made a decision that politically it would be useful for me to suffer this political defeat in terms of running against me the next time out. And some of them were pretty explicit about saying it.

Now, that's all past history. Health care passed. I'm proud of the fact that a lot of the young people here are going to benefit very directly. If you are under 26 years old and you don't have a job, or the job that you have doesn't offer you health care, you can now stay on your parents' health insurance till you're 26 years old.

If you have a preexisting condition, you are going to be able to get health insurance. Insurance companies can't deny it. We've eliminated things like lifetime limits, allowing insurance companies to drop you for your coverage when you get sick.

We're doing a whole bunch of things to emphasize prevention so that you can get regular checkups and mammograms and things like that so that you don't wait until you're sick and have to go to the emergency room. And that can help drive down costs.

So there are a lot of things we've done well, but here's the broader point. I do think that there are a lot of good Republican ideas out there. In fact, there were a number of them that were incorporated in this health care bill. And my hope is, is that as we look forward, let's say on education or on energy, some of the things that we haven't yet finished, that we're going to have a greater spirit of cooperation after this next election.

And elections are always a little bit funny. People start saying things and emphasizing differences. After the election, my hope is, is that people start emphasizing what we have in common.

Ms. Woodard. Thank you, Mr. President. We have another question from Sway, across the aisle.

Mr. Calloway. Thank you.

Jobs/National Economy/Infrastructure Investment/Tax Reform

Q. Hello, my name is Adam Hunter. I live here in the District by way of Somerset, New Jersey. When you were first elected, it seemed as though the sky was falling in terms of the economy. There was a bailout that you supported. There was stimulus that added to our deficit. But yet it seems as though our unemployment rate still rises—you said it was going to go past 8 percent; now it's at 9.4 percent. There were jobs added to the economy by the Census Bureau, by temporary workers, but now they're out of work, back on our unemployment rolls.

Now we have young people who are out of college, out of grad school, who don't have the most experience, like myself, still trying to find work, but it's hard. And then we're looking towards our private industry to employ us, the young people, but they're uncertain about it because of their tax policies about to change not in their favor, because they're looking at their tax rates going back up.

So my question to you is, why should we still support you going forward with your monetary and economic policies? And if the economy does not improve over the next 2 years, why should we vote you back in?

The President. Well, that was a—there's a lot of stuff in there, so let me try to unpack that. [*Laughter*] First of all, with respect with unemployment, we lost 4 million jobs before I took office. The 6 months before I took office, we lost 4 million jobs. The month I took office, we lost 750,000 jobs; the month after that, 600,000; the month after that, 600,000 more. So most of the 8 million jobs that we lost during this recession were lost before my economic policies were even put into place. That's point number one.

Point number two is that as a consequence of the Recovery Act that we put into place, there is no doubt that 3 million folks are working now that would not otherwise be working. That's point number two.

So it worked in terms of helping to cushion the fall. But we went through the worst financial crisis since the Great Depression, something that didn't happen on my watch, although we have managed it in a way that prevented a second Great Depression and prevented the banking system from melting down completely.

Now, whereas the economy was contracting when I came into office, it's now growing. With respect to the private sector, we've seen job growth 9 consecutive months in the private sector. Where we're actually losing jobs right now has to do with State and local governments who are having to lay off workers because at the State and local level, they've seen a huge drop in their tax revenues. And so they've got to lay off teachers and firefighters and police officers. And last month, that was where most of the job losses happened.

Now, that's, again, behind us. What we have to do moving forward is to make sure that small businesses that account for most of the job growth in our economy are getting the kind of financing that they need. And that's why I passed legislation just a couple of months ago that helps small businesses get loans and lowers their taxes, eliminates capital gains for startup companies, so that if you're young entrepreneurs out here and want to start a business, you're going to be able to do so with a lot more advantages than before we made some of these changes.

We've got to make sure that we rebuild the infrastructure in this country, because we used to be—have the best bridges, the best roads, the best airports. And now, when you go to China or you go to Europe, you see that they are outstripping us in terms of infrastructure. And if we put people back to work, that would be good not only in the short term, but it would also lay the foundation, the framework for long-term economic and job growth.

And in terms of tax policy, what we've said is we're going to provide tax cuts to 98 percent of the American people. Corporate taxes are not higher than they were when I came in. They're actually—they've been lower because we passed a whole bunch of tax cuts. Ninety-five percent of Americans got a tax break under the Recovery Act that I passed. So taxes aren't higher. The reason that there's the possibility that taxes may go up is because the previous administration had put into place a tax policy that is supposed to run out at the end of 2010 and they never paid for it. And now we've got to figure out what to do.

What we've said is we'll give tax cuts to 98 percent of Americans. Anybody who's making $250,000 a year or less, we are going to continue the tax breaks that you're receiving.

If you make more than $250,000, then you only get your tax breaks up to $250,000. And above that, if you're a millionaire or a billionaire, then your taxes go back to the old rates that they were under Bill Clinton. And we could pass that tomorrow. I'm ready to pass that tomorrow. And that would provide businesses with certainty about what's going to happen.

But keep in mind that taxes are not higher since I took office. Taxes are generally lower than since I took office.

Mr. Calloway. Thank you, Mr. President. We're going to go to April for your next question on the other side of the room.

Education Reform

Q. Good afternoon, Mr. President. My name is Tiara Washington, and I am from Washington, DC. And I'm a student at Montgomery College in Takoma Park, Maryland. I have a pretty personal story for you. Growing up, I was a victim of domestic violence, and even though there were physical and emotional signs of abuse, none of my teachers ever reached out and questioned if I was okay. Aside from that, after graduating from high school and entering college, I realized that the DC public school system didn't properly prepare me for college-level coursework. And on top of that, I got into the school of my dreams, but I couldn't afford to stay there.

My question is, what is your administration planning to do to improve comprehensive primary education and address college affordability?

The President. Well, first of all, I can tell that you have just been working so hard to overcome all these disadvantages, and so I just want to say how proud I am of you. And we're going to get you back into school, if you're not in school right now. There's no reason why you shouldn't be able to afford to go to college.

There are two steps in terms of education. And keep in mind that what has made America the wealthiest, most successful country on Earth historically has been our commitment to education. We started the public school system very early in the century, and as a consequence we had more skilled workers than any nation on Earth, which meant that we were more productive than any nation on Earth. We then made a commitment, particularly after World War II with the GI bill, to massively expand our commitment to college education, and that meant we had more engineers and we had more scientists and that meant we had better technology, which meant that we were more productive and we could succeed in the global marketplace.

And what's happened in a generation is that our lead has slipped. We're now—we rank 21st when it comes to math education. We rank 25th when it comes to science. We used to be number one in the proportion of college graduates. We now rank ninth. And at an age where knowledge, skills, are the determinant of how successful we're going to be, unless we reverse that we're going to keep slipping behind economically to a lot of other countries. I mean, China is not playing for second place. Germany, South Korea—these are all countries that are investing massively in education. We've got to do the same thing.

Now, it's not just a matter of money. It's a matter of reform. So what we've done is at the K–12 level, the most important thing we can do is to make sure that we've got very high standards, we expect a lot out of all of our young people, and we make sure that we have the best teachers possible in every classroom. And so we're working with States all across the country to invest in talented young people like some of you going into the teaching profession, getting the best professional skills possible. We want every math teacher to know math. We want every science teacher to have expertise in science. We want them to know how to inspire and engage young people.

And so we're working to create an atmosphere where the best and the brightest are going into teaching, teachers are getting paid well, they have freedom within the classroom to do creative things, but they're also held accountable.

And through something called Race to the Top, we've been inspiring reforms all across the country, using relatively little amounts of money, but we give them an incentive. We say, if you want some additional money for your school, we'll give it to you. But you've got to compete, show us that you're going to reform your education system so that our children are performing better. Now, that's at the K–12 level.

We're also emphasizing, by the way, math and science education, especially for women, young girls, and for minorities who oftentimes underperform in those fields. And we want to generate more math and science teachers, and we're getting the private sector to help us by paying for the training and the scholarships for more math and science teachers.

Now, at the college level, this is something that many of you may not be aware of, so relative to the earlier question about what our Recovery Act did, part of the Recovery Act was to institute a American opportunity tax credit that has benefited 12 million young people across the country. It gives a enormous tax break to those of you who are going to college.

On average, folks save about over $1,000 a year using this tax credit. We've combined that with doubling the Pell grant program. Part of what was happening before we passed some of this legislation was that the student loan program, which many of you may have used, was going through banks or financial intermediaries, and so they were siphoning off billions of dollars of profits before the loan went to the student.

But the problem was, these loans were guaranteed by the Federal Government, so they weren't taking any risk. It was an unwarranted subsidy. We said, let's just make these loans directly to students. That way we saved about $40

billion that is now going into the expansion of loan programs, grant programs.

And the final thing we did is, is that in a couple of years, we've set up a system whereby when you take on college debt, you will never have to pay more than 10 percent of your income in repayments. And what that will do is make sure that you will never be prevented from going to school just because of money. We want to make sure that you and others like you can succeed.

Q. Thank you, Mr. President.

The President. Thank you.

Ms. Woodard. Thank you, Mr. President. Sway has a question behind you.

The President. Okay.

Mr. Calloway. Thank you, I'm over here.

Bullying and Harassment Prevention Efforts

Q. Hello, my name is Allie Vonparis. I'm a junior at University of Maryland in College Park and also—this is more of a personal question—but I'm also a victim of anonymous, hurtful, degrading harassment over the Internet. Police and university officials have been unable to help put a stop to it. My question to you is, what can you do, if anything, to put a stop to these vicious attacks over the Internet while preserving our rights to freedom of speech? I also ask this in light of the recent—the tragic deaths recently on the news of young people who are bullied and harassed online. Thank you.

The President. Well, it's a great question. And obviously, our heart breaks when we read about what happened at Rutgers, when we read about some of these other young people who are doing nothing to deserve the kind of harassment and bullying that just completely gets out of hand.

And so we—actually, the Department of Education has initiated a—we had a summit a couple of weeks ago just to talk about this issue: How can we help local and State officials set up structures where young people feel safe, where there's a trigger that goes off when this kind of bullying starts taking place so that immediately school officials can nip it at the bud? So there are a range of cooperative efforts that we can initiate.

Now, in terms of the Internet, you're right, it is a challenging thing because the Internet—

part of the power of the Internet is, is that information flows out there and it's generally not censored and it's generally not controlled by any single authority.

But at your school, for example, I think there is nothing wrong with instituting policies that say that harassment of any form, whether it comes through the Internet or whether it happens to you face to face, is unacceptable; that we've got zero tolerance when it comes to sexual harassment, we have zero tolerance when it comes to harassing people because of their sexual orientation, because of their race, because of their ethnicity.

And I think that making sure that every institution, whether it's our schools, our government, our places of work, take these issues seriously and know that in some cases there are laws against this kind of harassment and that prosecutions will take place when somebody violates those laws. Sending that message of seriousness is something that I think we all have to do.

Now, the last point I would make is that the law is a powerful thing, but the law doesn't always change what's in people's hearts. And so all of us have an obligation to think about how we're treating other people. And what we may think is funny or cute may end up being powerfully hurtful. And I've got two daughters, 12 and 9, and Michelle and I spend a lot of time talking to them about putting themselves in other people's shoes and seeing through other people's eyes. And if somebody is different from you, that's not something you criticize, that's something that you appreciate.

And so I think there's also a values component to this that all of us have to be in a serious conversation about. Because ultimately peer pressure can lead people to bully, but peer pressure can also say bullying is not acceptable.

Mr. Calloway. Thank you, Mr. President, very much. Your next question is coming from April right in front of you.

U.S. Military's "Don't Ask, Don't Tell" Policy

Q. Hello, Mr. President.
The President. How are you?
Q. I'm good, thanks. How are you?

The President. I'm doing great.
Q. Good. My name is Bridget Todd. I'm from Richmond, Virginia. I'm a faculty member at Howard University. I teach English.
The President. You look like a student. [*Laughter*]
Q. Oh, thank you. [*Laughter*]
The President. It's true.
Q. I get that a lot.
The President. Right.
Q. I voted for you in the last elections based on your alleged commitment to equality for all Americans, gay and straight, and I wanted to know where you stood on "don't ask, don't tell." I know that you've mentioned that you want the Senate to repeal it before you do it yourself. My question is, you as the President can sort of have an Executive order that ends it once and for all, as Harry—as Truman did for the integration of the military in '48. So I wonder why don't you do that if this is a policy that you're committed to ending.
The President. First of all, I haven't "mentioned" that I'm against "don't ask, don't ask"— I have said very clearly, including in a State of the Union Address, that I'm against "don't ask, don't tell," and that we're going to end this policy. That's point number one.

Point number two: The difference between my position right now and Harry Truman's was that Congress explicitly passed a law that took away the power of the executive branch to end this policy unilaterally. So this is not a situation in which with a stroke of a pen I can simply end the policy.

Now, having said that, what I have been able to do is for the first time get the chairman of the Joint Chiefs of Staff, Mike Mullen, to say he thinks the policy should end. The Secretary of Defense has said he recognizes that the policy needs to change. And we, I believe, have enough votes in the Senate to go ahead and remove this constraint on me, as the House has already done, so that I can go ahead and end it.

Now, we recently had a Supreme Court—a district court case that said "don't ask, don't tell" is unconstitutional. I agree with the basic principle that anybody who wants to serve in our Armed Forces and make sacrifices on our behalf, on behalf of our national security, anybody should be able to serve. And they shouldn't have to lie about who they are in order to serve.

And so we are moving in the direction of ending this policy. It has to be done in a way that is orderly, because we are involved in a war right now. But this is not a question of whether the policy will end. This policy will end, and it will end on my watch. But I do have an obligation to make sure that I am following some of the rules. I can't simply ignore laws that are out there. I've got to work to make sure that they are changed.

Ms. Woodard. Thank you so much. Thank you, Mr. President. We're going to head over to Katie at our feedback station.

CMT Correspondent Katie Cook. Thank you so much, April.

Mr. President, hi.

The President. Hi, Katie. How are you?

Ms. Cook. Hi, I'm fabulous. Thank you. I wanted to give you an idea, first of all, of some of our trending topics we've been seeing on Twitter. Pretty much number one for the last couple of days has been jobs, education in the second category there. LGBT issues have been kind of floating between third and fourth position, obviously a very, very important issue.

And also, just to update you, we've had over 100,000 tweets come in, in the last couple of days, and over 10,000 since we went live. And I have this one for you here now.

Sexual Orientation

Q. "Dear President Obama, do you think being gay or trans is a choice?"

The President. I am not obviously—I don't profess to be an expert. This is a layperson's opinion. But I don't think it's a choice. I think that people are born with a certain makeup and that we're all children of God. We don't make determinations about who we love. And that's why I think that discrimination on the basis of sexual orientation is wrong.

Ms. Cook. All right, well, thank you very much. Thank you for being here, answering our questions.

And we just want to remind everyone at home that you can continue to submit questions

for President Obama via Twitter by simply using the hash tag and then "Ask," followed by the issue you care most about.

And for the last 24 hours or so, we've also been asking people to share with us their greatest hopes and their greatest fears. Use the hash tag "My greatest hope" and "My greatest fear" to join the discussion, and we'll be revealing what people are saying shortly after the break. We'll be right back.

[*At this point, there was a break in the town hall meeting, and the meeting resumed as follows.*]

Ms. Woodard. We have a question here, Mr. President.

Social Security

Q. Mr. President, my name is Joe San Georgio. I'm a senior at George Washington University. And my question is about Social Security. The Congressional Budget Office projects that Social Security could go into the red as early as 2018. And it seems to me there are only three options if we want to fix it: raise the retirement age, raise payroll taxes, or reduce benefits.

I know in the past you've said that all options are on the table, but do you have a limit for what would be acceptable changes for each of those three things?

The President. Well, first of all, let me just say something about these projections. According to the Congressional Budget Office, what'll happen is around 2018, we'll start taking in less money than we're sending out. So right now Social Security generally runs a surplus; that surplus will start getting drained around 2018.

Now, that doesn't mean that Social Security is going bankrupt. It doesn't mean that Social Security is going away. What it does mean is if we don't do anything about it, right around the time—you guys are a little young for you to retire, but let's say when I'm retired—[*laughter*]—what's going to end up happening is, is that if you expected a dollar of benefits, you'll only get about 75 cents, so people won't get the full bargain that they thought they were getting when they paid into Social Security.

That's why we've got to strengthen it. And I have said that all options are on the table. I think we've got to look at how we preserve it for the next generation. I do think that the best way to do it would be to look at the fact that right now you only pay Social Security taxes up to about $106,000, and after that, you don't pay any Social Security tax. So that means Warren Buffett, who makes more than $100,000 a year, the vast bulk of his income, he doesn't pay Social Security taxes on it. That could be modified or changed in a way that would help extend the solvency of Social Security.

But this is an area where—I'm sorry, what was the young lady from Austin—this is where Cynthia's point about bipartisanship is so important. I set up a bipartisan fiscal commission that is made up of Republicans and Democrats to sit and meet over the last several months to start looking at how we generally start reducing our debt and our deficit so we're not leaving it to the next generation. They're supposed to report back to me after the election because we specifically designed it so they wouldn't get caught up with silly season and would be able to just focus on what makes sense.

They're going to provide that report to us around the 1st of December, and my hope is from there that we can get a Republican-Democratic agreement on how we strengthen Social Security as well as looking at some of these other major expenditures that we have that we've got to deal with to make sure that we're not just leaving you guys with a mountain of debt.

Political Participation

Ms. Woodard. Thank you, Mr. President. I want to talk to you for a moment about the Tea Party. We have the Speaker of the House, Nancy Pelosi, who said the Tea Party is "Astroturf," a false grassroots movement that is bankrolled by the wealthy conservatives. I want to know if you agree with that assertion, or do you believe the young people here today should say that the Tea Party is legitimate and be looking to participate in the fall with them?

The President. Well, look, this is a democracy, so political participation generally is legiti-

mate. I want to encourage people to get involved. That's point number one.

Point number two is I think there are a lot of people who are involved in the Tea Party who have very real and sincere concerns about spending that's out of control or generally philosophically believe that the Government should be less involved in certain aspects of American life rather than more involved. And they have every right and obligation as citizens to be involved and engaged in this process.

I do think that what has happened is, layered on top of some of that general frustration that has expressed itself through the Tea Party, there is an awful lot of corporate money that's pouring into these elections right now. I mean, you've got tens of millions of dollars in what are called third-party expenditures that are being spent basically on negative ads. I mean, about 86, 90 percent of them are negative ads. And you guys have probably seen them more than I do, because I don't watch that much TV.

But if you're in a battleground State right now, you are being bombarded with negative ads every single day and nobody knows who is paying for these ads. They've got these names like Americans for Prosperity or Moms for Motherhood or—actually that last one I made up. [*Laughter*] But you have these innocuous-sounding names, and we don't know where this money is coming from. I think that is a problem for our democracy. And it's a direct result of a Supreme Court decision that said they didn't have to disclose who their donors are.

And so you don't know is there—is an oil company that is unhappy about some environmental rules that we put in place funding these? Are the insurance companies that aren't happy about some of the restrictions we've placed on insurance companies being able to drop your coverage—are they paying for them? We don't know that. And I think it's important for us to make sure that disclosure is available so that you guys can make your own decisions about if you see an ad, you know who is paying for it and you can make your own judgments about whether it's true or not.

Ms. Woodard. Thank you, Mr. President. We're going to Sway, to your right.

Mr. Calloway. Thank you, April.

Drug Control Policy/Immigration Reform

Q. Mr. President, my name is Nathan Martin. I actually help produce a conservative talk radio show, and I'm getting married in 2 weeks.

The President. Congratulations.

Q. Thank you very much. And my question for you deals with an issue that I saw back in my home State of Mississippi, and something that came up earlier this year. First I just want to say, like, my next-door neighbors are illegal immigrants, and I play soccer with them. This is not an issue of race. But, Mr. President, at the same time, I've seen the drugs pour into my community, coming through Mexico. I've seen the cartels become more powerful. And I've also seen a State in Arizona that, when they tried to do something about it because they didn't see anything coming out of Washington the last 2 years, that when they tried to do something about it they felt cut off. They were attacked. They were accused of some human rights infringements.

So my question for you is this: When Arizona passed a law, the Justice Department said it infringed upon their jurisdiction and struck it down. However, when California passed the legalization of marijuana, an issue with drugs—which also ties into Federal policy—the Federal Government said that they would stay out of the way. How do you reconcile those two things, particularly how they relate to the border and the security of our country?

The President. Well, let me first of all be clear. When it comes to our approach to Federal drug enforcement, we take Federal drug enforcement extraordinarily seriously, spend a lot of money on it. But obviously, we have to figure out who is it that we're going after, because we've got limited resources. And so decisions that are made by the Justice Department or the FBI about prosecuting drug kingpins versus somebody with some small amount in terms of possession, those decisions are made based on how can we best enforce the laws that are on the books.

When it comes to immigration, I have actually put more money, under my administration, into border security than any other administration previously. We've got more security resources at the border—more National Guard, more border guards, you name it—than the previous administration. So we've ramped up significantly the issue of border security.

What I have also said, though, is that if we're going to solve the problem, then given the massive border that we have on the south—and by the way, a massive border on the north that nobody talks about—that the best way for us to solve it is in a comprehensive way. That means, number one, that we have serious border security. And we want to work with States like Arizona so that border security is meaningful.

Number two, it means that we're going after employers who are hiring and then taking advantage of and exploiting undocumented workers, which happens a lot. Undocumented workers can't report if they're not being paid overtime, or if their health and safety laws are being violated, or if they're not getting the minimum wage. And so a lot of times companies prefer to hire them in order to take advantage of them. We've got to crack down on those employers.

The third thing I think we have to do is to make sure that the undocumented workers who are living here today, that they have to take responsibility. They've got to register, pay a fine, pay their back taxes, learn English, and then get on a pathway in which they could have the prospect of being here legally.

If we can do that, that allows us then to focus our attention on folks who have violated laws, who are here illegally, drug cartels who are trying to take advantage of turmoil at the border in order to peddle their wares. That's got to be the strategy—a comprehensive strategy. That's something we're committed to. And we've got to work with States to do it. It's something that I welcome not only with Arizona, but with every State down on those borders.

Mr. Calloway. Okay, thank you, Mr. President. Your next question is over your left shoulder, actually on the other side of the room.

Ms. Woodard. Right here.

Race Relations in America

Q. Hi, Mr. President. My name is Kishor Nagua. I'm a graduate student at the Johns Hopkins School of Advanced International Studies. And my question has to do with race relations with respect to the country.

Over the past several months, the racial climate seems to have deteriorated, manifested through the commentary from the Arizona immigration law, from the commentary with respect to the Republican candidacy for Governorship in South Carolina, and through the commentary from the speculated Islamic center near Ground Zero.

This seems to run in utter contrast to the idealism that the country was endowed with after your election. So my question to you is, what's happened?

The President. Well, historically, when you look at how America has evolved, typically we make progress on race relations in fits and starts. We make some progress, and then there's maybe some slippage.

Oftentimes, misunderstandings and antagonism surfaces most strongly when economic times are tough. And that's not surprising. If everybody is working and feeling good and making money and buying a new house and a big screen TV, you're less worried about what other folks are doing.

And when you're out of work and you can't buy a home or you've lost your home and you're worried about paying your bills, then you become more worried about what other folks are doing. And sometimes that organizes itself around kind of a tribal attitude and issues of race become more prominent.

Having said that, I think we've got to keep things in perspective. You look at this audience. This audience just didn't exist 20 years ago. The amount of interaction, the amount of understanding that exists in your generation among people of different races and different creeds and different colors is unprecedented. And by the way, that goes—that cuts across party lines, that cuts across partisan lines.

I mean, the fact of the matter is, is that in your generation, everybody is constantly bombarded with all kinds of different input from different cultures, and that's a strength, that's a positive thing. That's why I remain confident about America's ability to compete in the world, precisely because we've got a little bit of everybody in this country.

But what is important is that we make sure to work together, that we understand our strength comes from unity and not division. And that's going to be something that I think your generation is going to be especially important, because if all of you lead, then your parents and your grandparents tend to follow. If you say, well, Mom or Dad, actually, I don't agree with your opinion about such and such group, they listen.

I will be 50 next year, and I will tell you, as you get older, your mind gets a little more set. And it needs the poking and prodding and breaking through of stereotypes that I think young people provide. So you guys are going to be the messengers of this continued strengthening of the diversity in this country.

But you shouldn't be down about it. I think actually that the trend lines continue to be good.

Ms. Woodard. Thank you, Mr. President. We're going to get some feedback. We're going to head over to our feedback station and Katie.

Ms. Cook. All right, thank you, April. Mr. President, as you can probably see on the screen there, we've had almost 15,000 tweets since we went live, so a lot of great interaction. And now we're moving on to an issue that we've heard a lot about from our Twitter audience, and that is Sudan.

Situation in Sudan/Southern Sudan Independence Referendum

Q. "Mr. President, the January referendum in Sudan could lead to an outbreak of war. How will you prevent this?"

The President. Well, first of all, this is an example of where young people have taken the lead. Sudan is where the genocide in Darfur took place. So many young people on college campuses across the country got engaged and involved in it. It helped to surface attention on the issue. And I actually think that the previous administration did some good work on this in helping to broker a peace deal between northern Sudan and southern Sudan. That's one conflict. We have then worked to make sure that in Darfur, the violence against civilians was drastically reduced. We helped to stop an outbreak of war between Chad and Sudan.

But this is a tumultuous area. This is a dangerous area. The last time there was a war between north and south, 2 million people were killed. And so right now what we're trying to do is organize a referendum where the south, in a peaceful, legal fashion, could decide to break off and form their own nation separate from what is currently all of Sudan. We've only got about 90 days to get this done.

So when I went up to the United Nations during the General Assembly, I helped to organize a forum in which we got the north and the south together to try to broker a deal. I've got Hillary Clinton, my U.N. Ambassador, Susan Rice, Special Envoy General Scott Gration, all working together. This is one of our highest priorities.

But it's something that we all have to pay attention to, because if you have an outbreak of war between the north and south in Sudan, not only could that erupt in more violence that could lead to millions of deaths, but solving the problem in Darfur becomes that much more difficult, because Khartoum, the seat of government for northern Sudan, could end up feeling more threatened and not being willing to deal with some of the continuing violence that exists in western Sudan and Darfur.

So this is a huge issue, something that we're paying a lot of attention to. I hope all of you continue to pay attention to it and put pressure on your elected representatives to get involved, because we're going to need to give these countries help.

And it's important for us to prevent, by the way, these wars not only out of charitable reasons, but also out of self-interest, because if war explodes there, it could have a destabilizing effect that creates more space for terrorist activity that could eventually be directed at our homeland.

Ms. Cook. It's certainly a very difficult situation. Thank you.

The President. Thank you.
Ms. Cook. April has your next question.
Ms. Woodard. Okay, Mr. President.

"Development, Relief, and Education for Alien Minors (DREAM) Act of 2009"

Q. Good afternoon, Mr. President, my name is Alejandro Gonzales. I'm a junior at Georgetown University. And I came from Cuba when I was 6 years old. Since coming from Cuba, I have been able to live the American Dream, because I've been able to get a higher education. Others haven't been as lucky as I am, and there's a lot of immigrants in this country today who unfortunately can't do that. How will your administration take concrete steps to make sure that legislation like the "DREAM Act" gets passed before the end of your term, so that these immigrants don't live the dream—don't dream the dream, live the reality?

The President. Well, for those of you who aren't familiar with the "DREAM Act," this is a concept that I think is central to the American story. Each wave of immigrants that have come in have been able to assimilate, integrate, and then rise up and become part of this great American Dream.

We've now got a group of young people in this country who for all practical purposes are American. They grew up here. They've gone to school here. They don't know anything other than being American kids. But their parents may have brought them here without all the proper paperwork—might have brought them here when they were 3, might have brought them here when they were 5.

And so, lo and behold, by the time they finish school, and they're ready to go to college, they find out they can't go to college and, in fact, their status as Americans are threatened.

And so what we've said is for those young people, who didn't break any laws, they didn't have a choice when they came here, give them a chance by getting an education or serving in our military, having a series of standards that they have to meet in terms of showing good character. And if they do that, then give them a pathway for finally getting their paperwork straight and being full-fledged American citizens.

It's the right thing to do. It has received bipartisan support in the past. My strong hope is that we can get bipartisan support for this in the future. And this is something that I've been a cosponsor of this legislation on. I'm going to keep on pushing.

I actually feel somewhat optimistic that we can get it done in the next legislative session.

Q. Thank you.

Ms. Woodard. Thank you, Mr. President. We're going to go back to the feeding station and Katie.

Ms. Cook. All right, thank you so much for all of these answers once again. And I just want to remind everybody that is watching at home that we want to know your greatest hope and we want to know your greatest fear. Please share your thoughts now via Twitter using the hash tag "My greatest hope" and "My greatest fear."

We're going to be discussing your answers with the President when we come back.

[There was a break in the town hall meeting, and the meeting resumed as follows.]

Ms. Woodard. Welcome back to our conversation with President Barack Obama. We have another question right here, Mr. President.

Environmental Justice

Q. Hi, Mr. President. My name is Adrian. I'm from Butner, North Carolina. I just wanted to ask you a question about environmental justice. I am a big fan of the city of New Orleans. It's my favorite city in the country. And obviously, Katrina devastated the Gulf Coast, and not only just the land but the people there as well, and they are still struggling. Hopefully, that will not happen again. I don't think it will, especially under your administration. However, there are still quite a few landfills and there are nuclear power plants that are in low-income communities. And this is definitely not just an environmental issue, but also a civil rights issue. It's also, aside from a civil rights issue, it's a public health issue because these people are getting sick and they cannot afford to get the health care they need to get well.

So my question is, what sort of steps is your administration planning to take to address the issue of environmental justice?

The President. Well, let me say first of all that this is an example of where the issue probably has more to do with income than it has to do with race or ethnicity. Generally speaking, in this country a lot of environmentally problematic facilities tend to be located in places where poor folks live because wealthier folks have the ability to say "not in my backyard."

And I got firsthand experience of this when I was a community organizer. I was working in Chicago in a place called Altgeld Garden. It was down at the tip of Chicago. It had a landfill on one side; it had a polluted river on another; it had a sewage treatment plant on another. And folks who were living there had higher cancer rates and they had asbestos in their buildings. And it was just a toxic soup down there because they didn't have power.

And so part of what we have to do is to make sure, number one, that we are enforcing generally our environmental policies. Without regard to whether some place is wealthy or poor, everybody should have the chance at clean air and clean water.

Number two, we've got to identify new strategies to use cleaner energy, because that is a recipe for reducing the overall amount of pollution that's out there. And one of the things that we've done during the course of the last 20 months that I've been in office that I'm very proud of is generating more investment in clean energy—solar panels, wind turbines, biodiesel. The more we are using clean energy, renewable energy sources, the less this ends up being a problem for everybody, but particularly for folks who have to suffer the consequences of some of these facilities.

Ms. Woodard. Thank you, Mr. President. We're going over to Katie in the feedback station.

Katie, what do you got?

Bipartisanship in Politics

Ms. Cook. All right, thank you, April.

Mr. President, of course we asked people to send in their greatest hopes and their greatest fears. I'll read a couple of the fears here first. "My greatest fear is that we are turning into a communist country." And another one here: "My greatest fear is that Obama will be reelected."

The President. Oh, no. [*Laughter*]

Ms. Cook. Would you like to respond to those?

The President. Well, look, I mean, this is an example of how our political rhetoric gets spun up. Twitter and all these things are very powerful, but it also means sometimes that instead of having a dialogue, we just start calling folks—calling each other names. And that's true on the left or the right.

That's something I think we've got to avoid. We've got to be able to have a conversation and recognize we're all Americans; we all want the best for this country. We may have some disagreements in terms of how to get there, but all of us want to make sure that our economy is strong, that jobs are growing. All of us want to make sure that people aren't bankrupt when they get sick. All of us want to make sure that young people can afford an education.

And I'm pretty confident that if we work together over the next several years, that the political temperature will go down, the political rhetoric will go down, because we'll actually be making progress on a lot of these issues.

But we've got to stop the name-calling and we've got to stop looking at the next election. We've got to be focused on figuring out what we're doing for the next generation.

Ms. Cook. All right, well, thank you very much. I believe Sway has your next question.

Mr. Calloway. I'm over here behind you.

Ms. Cook. There you are.

Mr. Calloway. Mr. President.

Immigration Reform

Q. Hi, Mr. President, my name is Anna, and I want to share with you my greatest fear. I moved here when I was 14 in 2003, and I followed every legal step. I come from Colombia, and I'm waiting for my green card, and I have been waiting for it for about 3 years. My grandma turned 92, and I'm afraid that my green card

will not get here in time for me to see her for a last time. Sorry.

The President. No, no. Well, look, first of all, say hi to your grandma for me.

Q. On the phone, yes.

The President. And second of all, one of the things that we're trying to do to deal with the immigration issue is to accelerate the process for legal immigration. This is something that we don't talk about a lot. A lot of the focus is on illegal immigration. But we're a nation of immigrants. And so the question is, how do we make legal immigration faster, less bureaucratic, cut the redtape?

And so I'll be interested in finding out after maybe this session from you, what your experience has been with the office, because what we're trying to do is reduce the backlog so that those people like yourself that are doing things the right way and the legal way, that you don't get so tangled up in a bunch of bureaucracy that you end up being discouraged. There's no reason why you should be discouraged. We want you here, because I can tell you've got a great deal to contribute to the country.

Q. Thank you so much.

The President. Thank you.

Mr. Calloway. Thank you, Mr. President. We're going to go back to Katie over there.

Education Reform/Gun Control Policy

Ms. Cook. All right, thank you, Sway. And let's move on to some hope, what do you say? Let's see, I've got a couple tweets here. "My greatest hope is that my children will have better teachers than I had." And the second one here: "My greatest hope is something will be done about young kids having guns. I live in South Jersey and the crime rate is crazy down here."

The President. Well, we've already addressed the teachers issue. That's one of my greatest hopes. We've got to make sure that teachers are respected, that they are rewarded, that young people like yourself who have talent and want to work with people, that you're able to support yourself and live out a great life being a teacher. And so we're doing everything we can to encourage it.

In terms of guns, obviously school violence is still a big problem. We're spending a lot of time, the Department of Justice, working with local school districts to figure out how can we keep guns out of the hands of kids. It's a top priority, especially in a lot of urban districts.

Ms. Cook. Yes, it is. All right, thank you. April.

Ms. Woodard. I just wanted to let you look at this form that you filled out. We gave them an opportunity to fill out their greatest hope. Did you want to express to the President what your greatest hope is?

Reducing Minority Incarceration Rates

Q. Hello, Mr. President, my name is Alicia Thompson. I'm a communication sciences and disorders major from Howard University. I'm from Edison, New Jersey. My greatest hope would be that basically right now through a lot of research I've realized that there is more Black men incarcerated than in college. So my greatest hope is that by 10 years from now, that there will be more Black men enrolled in college than incarcerated.

The President. Well, it is a goal that you and I share. And as I said, it starts young. I mean, African American boys oftentimes fall behind in school early, start feeling discouraged, check out, drop out, end up on the streets, and then get into trouble.

And if we can make sure that that young boy starting at the age of 3 or 4 already knows their colors and their letters and are getting good preschool, and by the time they get into school, they've got a good teacher and are getting the support that they need and are able to keep up with their classwork, that is going to do more to reduce the incarceration rate at the same time, obviously, as it increases the college enrollment rate.

That's why we've got to prioritize education going forward. Thank you.

Ms. Woodard. Thank you, so much. Thank you, Mr. President. We want to thank you on behalf of everyone, on behalf of BET, MTV, and CMT. Thank you so much for joining us.

And thank you all and everyone in the world that is watching here today.

The President. Oh, thank you very much, April. Thank you so much.

Ms. Woodard. Sure.

The President. Thank you.

NOTE: The President spoke at 4:02 p.m. at BET Studios. In his remarks, he referred to Warren E. Buffett, chief executive officer and chairman, Berkshire Hathaway Inc.

Letter to Congressional Leaders on Continuation of the National Emergency With Respect to Significant Narcotics Traffickers Centered in Colombia
October 14, 2010

Dear Madam Speaker: (Dear Mr. President:)

Section 202(d) of the National Emergencies Act, 50 U.S.C. 1622(d), provides for the automatic termination of a national emergency unless, prior to the anniversary date of its declaration, the President publishes in the *Federal Register* and transmits to the Congress a notice stating that the emergency is to continue in effect beyond the anniversary date. In accordance with this provision, I have sent to the *Federal Register* for publication the enclosed notice stating that the emergency declared with respect to significant narcotics traffickers centered in Colombia is to continue in effect beyond October 21, 2010.

The circumstances that led to the declaration on October 21, 1995, of a national emergency have not been resolved. The actions of significant narcotics traffickers centered in Colombia continue to pose an unusual and extraordinary threat to the national security, foreign policy, and economy of the United States and cause an extreme level of violence, corruption, and harm in the United States and abroad. For these reasons, I have determined that it is necessary to maintain economic pressure on significant narcotics traffickers centered in Colombia by blocking their property and interests in property that are in the United States or within the possession or control of United States persons and by depriving them of access to the U.S. market and financial system.

Sincerely,

BARACK OBAMA

NOTE: Identical letters were sent to Nancy Pelosi, Speaker of the House of Representatives, and Joseph R. Biden, Jr., President of the Senate. The notice is listed in Appendix D at the end of this volume.

Remarks at a Rally for Senatorial Candidate Christopher A. Coons and the Democratic Senatorial Campaign Committee in Wilmington, Delaware
October 15, 2010

The President. Thank you so much. Thank you. Everybody, please have a seat. It is good to be back in Wilmington. Last time I was here, it was a day just like today, spectacular day. We were outside. Some of you were there. And it was just beautiful.

It is great to be back here in Delaware. It is an extraordinary honor to be here to campaign for the next great Senator from the State of Delaware, Chris Coons.

I want to just acknowledge some of the extraordinary public servants who are here. You've already heard from them or about them, but all these folks have been such great friends of mine and such terrific workers on behalf of Delaware, I want to make sure to make mention of them.

Governor Jack Markell is here, and he's just doing a great job. Where's Jack? There he is. Lieutenant Governor Matt Denn is here, along with Zachary; Senator Ted Kaufman, done extraordinary work over the last 2 years—thank you, Ted; and my great friend Tom Carper, senior Senator from Delaware.

Delaware Attorney General Beau Biden—we are so thrilled with the work that he's done, but also his extraordinary service to our country. We are proud of him and grateful for him. And former Lieutenant Governor and soon-to-be Member of Congress John Carney is in the house.

And then there's this guy. [*Laughter*] I've had to make a lot of decisions over the last 24 months, both before I was President and since. The single best decision that I have made was selecting Joe Biden as my running mate—single best decision I've made. I mean that. It's true.

Joe has been an extraordinary Vice President, a great friend, a fighter, somebody who knows what our core mission is, which is making sure that we are growing this economy on behalf of a middle class so they can aspire to live out the American Dream. Joe has lived out that dream. He hasn't forgotten where he came from.

And so I know that me taking him out of Delaware for a while was frustrating, but I assure you, it was worth it at least for me—[*laughter*]—and I think for you. So I am grateful to all of you.

Now, that's why it's so important, in filling these enormous shoes of Joe, that we get somebody who represents those same Delaware values. And Chris is the kind of leader that you want representing you in the United States Senate.

He knows this State. He knows its values. When he talks about cleaning up Washington, it's from the standpoint of somebody who's cleaned house as a county executive, somebody who's balanced a budget, somebody who's cracked down on wasteful spending, somebody who even cut his own pay. Believe me, you won't see too many Members of Congress willing to do that.

Chris has traveled all across this State, talking to people, finding out what's on their minds, listening to their hopes for the future. He wants Delaware to be a leader on clean energy because he knows it will lead to new jobs and new industries. And he's got a plan to make it happen. Chris isn't looking to be a voice for special interests. He wants to be a voice for Delaware. This is where he grew up. This is the community he's going to fight for if you send him to Washington.

Now, in a little more than 2 weeks, you have the opportunity, right here in Delaware, to set the direction of this State and this country for the next several years. In 2 weeks, you can continue the journey that we started in 2008. And just like you did in that election, you can defy the conventional wisdom that says you can't change Washington, you can't overcome the cynicism of politics, you can't overcome all the special interest money, you can't solve tough problems. That has always been the conventional wisdom.

It was the conventional wisdom 2 years ago. You remember that? Everybody said, "No, you can't." And 2 years ago, you said, "Yes, we can." And you can say that same thing 2 weeks from now.

I want everybody to be clear: There is no doubt this is a difficult election. It is difficult here, and it is difficult all across the country. And although I think Chris has so far run an extraordinary race, I don't want anybody here taking this for granted. This is a tough political environment. This is a tough political environment right now. This is a difficult election because we've been through an incredibly difficult time as a nation.

For most of the last decade, middle class families saw their costs rise and their incomes fall. They saw too many jobs disappear overseas. There were too many parents who couldn't afford to send their kids to college or see a doctor when they got sick, or Americans working two jobs, three jobs just to make ends meet. And all these problems were compounded when we had the worst economic crisis since the Great Depression, the worst in most of our lifetimes, a recession that cost us more than 4 million jobs in the 6 months before I took office, 750,000 jobs lost the month I was sworn in, 600,000 the month after that, 600,000 the month after that. All told, 8 million jobs lost, most of them lost before any of our economic had plans an opportunity to take effect.

It was a once-in-a-generation challenge. And I'll be honest with you—Joe will recall this—our hope was that because this was such a unique challenge, that it would cause both parties to put politics aside for the sake of the country. That was our expectation. Our hope was that we could move beyond the division and the bickering and the game-playing that had dominated Washington for so long, because although we are proud to be Democrats, we're prouder to be Americans.

But you know what happened. The Republican leaders in Washington made a different decision. And I want to be clear, it was the decision of Republicans in Congress, because I think there were a whole lot of Republicans all across the country who, in fact, wanted the same thing, but that's not what they saw in Washington. Their attitude—it was tactical on their part—was that we were climbing out of such a deep hole, they had made such a big mess, that they figured it was going to take some time to repair the economy, longer than any of us would like. They knew that people would be frustrated. They knew people would be angry. And they figured if they just sat on the sidelines and opposed us every step of the way, if they said no even to policies that they could agree with, that historically they had supported, then people might forget that they were the ones who had caused the mess, and that people's anger and frustration would lead them to success in the next election. That was their strategy.

And you have to give them credit. In terms of short-term tactics, it wasn't a bad strategy. In terms of what was good for the country, it didn't work out so well.

So the other side wants you to believe that this election is simply a referendum on the current state of the economy. But make no mistake: This election is a choice. This election is a choice, and the stakes couldn't be higher.

If they win this election, the chair of the Republican campaign committee has promised to pursue the exact same agenda as they did before I took office. And we know what that agenda was: You cut taxes, mostly for millionaires and billionaires, you cut rules for special interests, and then you cut middle class families loose to fend for themselves.

We also know the results of that agenda. It's not as if we didn't try it. [*Laughter*] This isn't—we don't have to guess in terms of how their theories might work out.

From 2001 to 2009, slowest job growth since World War II; 2001 to 2009, incomes for middle class families went down by 5 percent. Those aren't my claims. That was trumpeted in the Wall Street Journal. Took a record surplus and turned it to a record deficit, an agenda that let Wall Street run wild at the expense of folks on Main Street, an agenda that nearly destroyed our economy.

That's what they say they want to go back to, the exact same agenda. If they take over Congress, the other side has promised to roll back health reform so that insurance companies can go back to denying you coverage when you get sick or denying your child coverage if they've got a preexisting condition.

They want to roll back Wall Street reform so that taxpayers are on the hook again for Wall Street bailouts and credit card companies can hit you with hidden fees and penalties and mortgage brokers can steer you to the most expensive mortgage or a mortgage you can't afford.

They want to cut back on education spending by 20 percent to help pay for a $700 billion tax break that only the wealthiest 2 percent of Americans will ever benefit from.

Audience member. No!

The President. My sentiments exactly. [*Laughter*]

This is the same theory they've been peddling for years. This is not as if they went off into the desert after 2008 and they said, "Boy, we really screwed up; let's meditate here a little bit, and let's try to figure out what we did wrong," and then they came back and they said, "We realize the error of our ways, and we've got some new idea"—that's not what's happening. They're just pretending as if all that stuff didn't happen.

And so it's up to you to remind your friends and your neighbors and your coworkers, we've tried that stuff. It didn't work. We've been there

before, and we're not going back. We're moving forward, not backwards.

We don't want to keep giving tax breaks to companies that ship jobs overseas. We want to give tax breaks to companies that are investing right here in Wilmington, right here in Delaware. We don't want tax cuts for folks who don't need them by borrowing from—the money from China to pay for them and cut education in the process. We want to invest in young people right here in the United States of America, because we know that the countries that outeducate us today are going to outcompete us tomorrow. And so we're going to invest in our young people.

We don't want to go back. We don't want to go back to the days where insurance companies and Wall Street banks had free rein to run roughshod over the middle class. We don't want to see 2 more years of gridlock and game-playing and point-scoring in Washington. We want to solve problems. We want to move forward. That's why Chris is running. That's why his family is putting up with him running, because we want to solve problems for the families of Delaware and people all across America.

We want a growing middle class and an economy that's built to compete in the 21st century. And because of the steps we've taken, we no longer face the possibility of a second depression. As Joe said, the economy is now growing again. The private sector—we've seen job growth in the private sector 9 months in a row now. But we still have a long way to go. We've still got a lot of work to do. There are a lot of people hurting out there. I hear from them every day, families hanging on by a thread. That's what's keeping me up at night. That's what keeps me fighting.

And I know this: The biggest mistake we could make right now as a country is to go back to the same policies that caused this hurt in the first place. The last thing we should do is return to a philosophy that nearly destroyed our economy and decimated the middle class over the course of years. And that's what this election is about: not where we are right now, but where we want to go 2 years from now and 5 years from now and 10 years from now and 20 years from now. It's not about the work we've done, but the work we have left to do.

And I bring this up not because I want to re-litigate the past. It's because I don't want to re-live the past. I want to reach for a better future.

And this election is a choice between our fears and our hopes. That's what's at stake right now. Look, Chris and I and Joe, we've got a different idea about what the next 2 years should look like. It's an idea rooted in our belief about how this country was built. We know government doesn't have the answer to all our problems. We believe government should be lean and efficient. And you've seen Chris's track record on that front as a county executive.

But in the words of Abraham Lincoln, the first Republican President, we also believe government should do for the people what they cannot do better for themselves. We believe in a country that rewards hard work and responsibility, a country where we look after one another, a country where we say, I am my brother's keeper, I am my sister's keeper. I'm not just thinking about myself, I'm thinking about everybody. I want every child to succeed. I want everybody to climb that ladder to success. That's the choice in this election. That's what we're about. That's why we're Democrats. That's why we're going to win this election.

You're fired up?

Audience members. Yes!

The President. We see a future where the next century is driven by American innovation and American ingenuity. We want to give tax breaks to companies that are creating jobs and investing in research and development right here in the United States, to small businesses, to American manufacturers, to clean energy companies. I don't want solar panels and wind turbines and electric cars and advanced batteries made in Europe or Asia. Chris Coons and I want them built here in the United States of America, by American workers. I want us to take the lead in energy independence. That's the choice in this election.

We see an America where every citizen has the skills and training to compete with any worker in the world. The other side might think it's a good idea to cut education by 20 percent, but let's think about this. Do you think that China is cutting education by 20 percent? Is South Korea cutting education spending, or India or Germany? These countries, they're not cutting back on education. Those countries are not playing for second place, and neither should we. The United States of America, we play for first. We play for first place.

And that's why we took tens of billions of dollars—with the help of Tom and Ted and others—we took tens of billions of dollars in taxpayer subsidies that used to go to big banks; they're now going where they should be going, to students and families, millions of young people out there getting a break on their student loans so they can go to college. That's why we want to make our new college tax credit permanent. This is a tax credit worth $10,000 in tuition relief for each student who's going to college. That's the America we believe in.

That's the America we believe in, where the middle class is growing and where opportunity is shared and the only limit to your success is how hard you are willing to work. That's why the tax cuts we want to make permanent would go to middle class families. That's why we'll fight the efforts of some in the other party to privatize Social Security, because as long as I'm President, no one is going to take the retirement savings of a generation of Americans and hand it over to Wall Street. Not on my watch. That's why we're going to keep fighting to keep the new protections we put in place for patients and consumers, so insurance companies can't drop you when you're sick, credit card companies can't jack up your rates without notice on your bill. That's the choice in this election. That's what we're fighting for.

Now, right now the same special interests that would profit from the other side's agenda, they are fighting hard, they're fighting back. To win this election, they are plowing tens of millions of dollars into front groups that are running misleading, negative ads all across America. Tens of billions of dollars are pouring in. And they don't have the courage to stand up and disclose their identities. They could be insurance companies or Wall Street banks or even foreign-owned corporations. We will not know because there's no disclosure. They've got these innocuous-sounding names: Americans for Prosperity and Moms for Motherhood. [*Laughter*] I made that last one up. [*Laughter*].

But this isn't just a threat to the Democrats, it's a threat to our democracy. And the only way to fight it, the only way to match their millions of dollars is with millions of voices who are ready to finish what we started in 2008. And that's where you come in.

A lot of you got involved in 2008 because you believed we were at a defining moment in our history, a crossroads. You believed this is a time where the decisions we make won't just affect us; they're going to affect and shape the lives of our children and our grandchildren for decades to come. And that's the reason you knocked on doors and made phone calls and waited in line to cast your vote, some of you for the very first time, because you believed that your actions could make a difference, that you might play some small role in making big change.

Now we are in the midst not just of advocating for change, not just calling for change, but doing the grinding and sometimes frustrating work of delivering change inch by inch, day by day. And it's not easy. Believe me, Joe and I know. And I understand that some of the excitement has faded since election night or Inauguration Day. You know, that was fun. Beyonce was singing, and Bono. [*Laughter*] But that's not what the election was about.

I also know it's hard to keep faith when a family member still hasn't found a job after months of trying or another foreclosure sign is hung on the house down the street. And it doesn't help when you turn on the television and you see politicians tearing each other down or pundits who treat politics like a sport.

But I'm here to tell you, don't let anybody tell you that this fight is not worth it. Don't let them tell you that we're not making a difference. Because of you, there is a woman in New Hampshire right now who no longer has to choose between losing her home and treating her cancer. Because of you, there are parents right now who can look their children in the eye and guarantee that those kids are going to college. Because of you, there are small-business owners

and clean energy entrepreneurs who can keep their doors open and put out "Help Wanted" signs in the window. Because of you, there are nearly 100,000 brave men and women who are no longer at war in Iraq—because of you. So don't let them tell you change isn't possible.

Don't let them convince you that we have not made progress. We have made progress. I've been using this analogy as I travel across the country. Now, these folks drove the car into the ditch. And Joe and I, Tom and Ted and others, we all put on our boots, and we went down into that ditch. And it was muddy, and it was nasty and hot. And there were bugs. [*Laughter*]

But we decided we were going to get that car out of the ditch. We kept on pushing. We kept on shoving. Every once in awhile, we'd look up, and the Republicans, they'd just be standing there—[*laughter*]—fanning themselves, sipping on a Slurpee. [*Laughter*] And we would say, "Why don't you come down and help?" They'd say, "No, no, that looks muddy down there. No." [*Laughter*]

So we pushed anyway. We kept on pushing. We kept on pushing. And finally, we got this car up on level ground, pointing in the right direction. And you know, look, the car is a little dented up. It needs to go to the body shop. It needs a tuneup. But it's running, and it's ready to go forward.

And suddenly, we get this tap on our shoulder, and we look back, and who is it? The Republicans. They say, "Excuse me, can we have the keys back?" And we got to tell them: "No, you can't have the keys back. You don't know how to drive." You can't have them back. Can't have them back. You can ride with us, but you got to ride in the backseat. We're not going to have special interests riding shotgun. We want the American people in the front.

You've noticed when you want your car to go forward, what do you do? You put it in "D." [*Laughter*] When you want it going backward, what do you do? You put it in "R." We want to go forward; we don't want to go back. Don't let them tell—don't let them take this country backwards.

Don't let them take this country backwards because you didn't care enough to fight for it.

Because if our parents and grandparents and great-grandparents had made the same decision 50 years ago or 100 years ago, we would not be here tonight. The only reason we are is because past generations were unafraid to push forward. Even in the face of difficulty, even in the face of uncertainty, they were willing to do what was necessary, even when success was not promised and was sometimes slow and you had to grind it out. That's how we got through war. That's how we got through depression. That's why we have civil rights. That's why we have workers' rights. That's why we have women's rights. That's the spirit we need today.

The journey we started in 2008 was not about putting a President in the White House. It was never just about getting to election night. It was about every day after that and building a movement for change that endures. It's about realizing that in the United States of America, anything is possible if we're willing to work for it and fight for it and believe in it.

So I need you all to keep on fighting. I need all of you to knock on doors. I need all of you to talk to your neighbors. I need all of you to make phone calls. I need all of you to commit to vote for Chris Coons. Because if you are willing to step up to the plate, we won't just win this election, we're going to restore our economy and rebuild our middle class, and we will reclaim the American Dream for this generation.

Thank you. God bless you. God bless the United States of America.

NOTE: The President spoke at 1:46 p.m. at the Grand Opera House. In his remarks, he referred to Zachary Denn, son of Lt. Gov. Matthew P. Denn of Delaware; Rep. Pete Sessions, in his capacity as chairman of the National Republican Congressional Committee; and musicians Beyonce G. Knowles and Paul D. "Bono" Hewson. The transcript released by the Office of the Press Secretary also included the remarks of Vice President Joe Biden.

Statement on Signing the Coast Guard Authorization Act of 2010
October 15, 2010

Today I have signed into law H.R. 3619, the "Coast Guard Authorization Act of 2010." This Act strengthens the Coast Guard as a military service and branch of the Armed Forces in the Department of Homeland Security by providing organizational flexibility for the Coast Guard and allowing for improvements to its military housing. Additionally, the Act materially enhances the marine safety and maritime security missions of the Coast Guard, and it includes language to implement the International Convention on the Control of Harmful Anti-Fouling Systems on Ships, 2001.

Section 818 of the Act requires the Comptroller General to determine whether it is feasible to deliver securely a transportation security card to an approved applicant's place of residence. If such a determination is made, the Secretary of Homeland Security (Secretary) would be required to implement a process that allows for such delivery. This provision would impermissibly vest authority in the Comptroller

General, a congressional officer, to bind the Secretary in the performance of an Executive function. Therefore, the Secretary will need to treat the Comptroller General's findings as advisory and nonbinding.

Finally, certain provisions in section 401 may vest significant authority in the Coast Guard Chief Acquisition Officer, who is not appointed in conformity with the Appointments Clause of the Constitution. The Executive will therefore need to construe these provisions as requiring approval of any exercise of significant authority by a supervisor who is an officer of the United States.

BARACK OBAMA

The White House,
October 15, 2010.

NOTE: H.R. 3619, approved October 15, was assigned Public Law No. 111–281.

The President's Weekly Address
October 16, 2010

After a decade of hardship for middle class families and a recession that wiped away millions of jobs, we are in the middle of a tough fight to rebuild this economy and put folks back to work.

Winning this fight will not depend on government alone. It will depend on the innovation of American entrepreneurs, on the drive of American small-business owners, on the skills and talents of American workers. These are the people who will help us grow our economy and create jobs.

But government still has an important responsibility, and that's to create an environment in which someone can raise capital to start a new company, where a business can get a loan to expand, where ingenuity is prized and folks are rewarded for their hard work.

That's why I fought so hard to pass a jobs bill to cut taxes and make more loans available for entrepreneurs. It eliminated the capital gains taxes for key investments in small businesses. It increased the deduction to defray the costs of starting a company. And it's freeing up credit for folks who need it. In fact, in just the first 2 weeks since I signed the bill, thousands of business owners have been able to get new loans through the SBA.

But we need to do more, so I've proposed additional steps to grow the economy and spur hiring by businesses across America. Now, one of the keys to job creation is to encourage companies to invest more in the United States. But for years, our Tax Code has actually given billions of dollars in tax breaks that encourage companies to create jobs and profits in other countries.

I want to close these tax loopholes. Instead, I want to give every business in America a tax break so they can write off the cost of all new equipment they buy next year. That's going to make it easier for folks to expand and hire new people. I also want to make the research and experimentation tax credit permanent. Because promoting new ideas and technologies is how we'll create jobs and retain our edge as the world's engine of discovery and innovation. And I want to provide a tax cut for clean energy manufacturing right here in America, because that's how we'll lead the world in this growing industry.

These are commonsense ideas. When more things are made in America, more families make it in America, more jobs are created in America, more businesses thrive in America. But Republicans in Washington have consistently fought to keep these corporate loopholes open. Over the last 4 years alone, Republicans in the House voted 11 times to continue rewarding corporations that create jobs and profits overseas, a policy that costs taxpayers billions of dollars every year.

That doesn't make a lot sense. It doesn't make sense for American workers, American businesses, or America's economy. A lot of companies that do business internationally make an important contribution to our economy here at home. That's a good thing. But there is no reason why our Tax Code should actively reward them for creating jobs overseas. Instead, we should be using our tax dollars to reward companies that create jobs and businesses within our borders.

We should give tax breaks to American small businesses and manufacturers. We should reward the people who are helping us lead in the industries of the future, like clean energy. That's how we'll ensure that American innovation and ingenuity are what drive the next century. That's how we'll put our people back to work and lead the global economy. And that's what I'll be fighting for in the coming months.

Thanks.

NOTE: The address was recorded at approximately 4:35 p.m. on October 15 in the Library at the White House for broadcast on October 16. The transcript was made available by the Office of the Press Secretary on October 15, but was embargoed for release until 6 a.m. on October 16. The Office of the Press Secretary also released a Spanish language transcript of this address.

Remarks at a Rally for Governor Deval L. Patrick of Massachusetts in Boston, Massachusetts
October 16, 2010

The President. Hello, Boston! Are you fired up? You ready to go? You know, let me just say, Boston, before I get started, that I've been doing a lot of traveling, I've been campaigning for a lot of folks, and sometimes, you know, you get used to hearing politicians speak, and occasionally, I've got to admit, you're in the back and you're on your BlackBerry or—[*laughter*]—but when Deval speaks, I listen. I listen.

Massachusetts, it is great to be back. And I just want to say that I am so proud of your leadership here in this State, starting with your senior Senator, one of the outstanding public servants that we have, John Kerry.

Two of the best Members of Congress that I know, Ed Markey and Barney Frank, are in the house; your outstanding mayor, Tom Menino; one of my dearest friends, who has just been so outstanding since we came back, Vicki Kennedy—give Vicki Kennedy a big round of applause. Give it up for James Taylor, Lieutenant Governor Tim Murray, and I am so happy to be standing here with one of the best Governors this State has ever seen, my friend Deval Patrick.

Now, Deval and I, we go back a little ways. So I am a little biased here. But the reason I came today isn't just because Deval has been there for me as a friend, it's because he continues to inspire me as a leader. At a time when too many folks bow to the politics of the moment, he represents the politics of conscience and conviction. In an age of too much cynicism, he has matched unbending optimism with unyielding effort to move Massachusetts forward.

Now, Deval has steered this State through some very turbulent waters. He could have spent his time in office figuring out how to stay there. He could have spent his days looking at the polls and avoiding tough decisions. But you didn't elect him to do what was easy. You elected him to do what was right. And that is exactly what he has done.

Because he chose to invest in job creation, Massachusetts has created jobs faster than any other State in the Nation. Because he chose to invest in education, your students are first in the Nation. Because he chose to invest in clean energy, Massachusetts leads the Nation in clean energy initiatives and energy efficiency. Because of his dedication to expanding health care, 98 percent of the people in this State are insured. Because Deval Patrick chose to lead in the toughest of times, this State will lead in the future.

And that's why you've got to help him finish the work you all started in 2006. That's why you need him. That's why you need to help guard the change that you helped deliver in 2006, by giving Deval Patrick 4 more years.

Audience members. Four more years! Four more years! Four more years!

The President. Four more years.

Audience members. Four more years! Four more years! Four more years!

The President. Now, in a little more than 2 weeks——

Audience members. Fight global AIDS! Fight global AIDS! Fight global AIDS!

The President. In a little more than 2 weeks, you've got a chance to do just that. In 2 weeks——

Audience members. Fight global AIDS! Fight global AIDS! Fight global AIDS!

The President. We're all right. In 2 weeks, we can go 4 more years.

Audience members. Four more years! Four more years! Four more years!

The President. All right. In 2 weeks, you can set the direction of this State and this country for the next 2 years. And just like you did in 2006, just like you did again in 2008, you can defy the conventional wisdom, the kind that says, no, you can't. The conventional wisdom says, no, you can't overcome cynicism in our politics. It says, no, you can't overcome the special interests. It says, no, you can't tackle the biggest challenges. But in 2 weeks, you can say, "Yes, we can."

Now, there is no doubt that this is a difficult election. It's difficult here in Massachusetts, it's difficult all across the country. And that's because we've been through an incredibly difficult time as a nation.

For most of the last decade, middle class families saw their costs rise, their incomes fall. Between 2001 and 2009, the average wage of middle class families went down 5 percent. Between 2001 and 2009, we saw the most sluggish job growth since World War II. Between that period of time, too many jobs disappeared overseas. There were too many parents who couldn't afford to send their kids to college, too many parents who couldn't afford, in some cases, to let their kid see a doctor when they got sick; Americans working two jobs and three jobs just to make ends meet.

And all these problems were compounded by the worst economic crisis since the Great Depression, a recession that cost us more than 4 million jobs before I even took the oath of office, 750,000 jobs lost the month I was sworn in, 600,000 the month after that, 600,000 the month after that.

It was a once-in-a-lifetime challenge, a once-in-a-generation challenge. And I hoped, like many of you hoped, that we could have both parties put politics aside for the sake of the country. We all hoped that we could start moving beyond the divisions and the bickering and the game-playing that had dominated Washington for so long, because although we are proud to be Democrats, but we are prouder to be Americans. And so we weren't going to let party labels get in the way of progress.

And I know a lot of Republicans felt the same way all across the country, but the Republican leaders in Washington made a different decision. Because we were climbing out of such a deep hole, they knew that it was going to take time to repair the economy. They knew that you couldn't recover 8 million jobs overnight. Those folks that Deval was talking about, they knew that they were going to be going through struggles and hardships, and that the longer it took, the more frustrated and angry people would get. And so the Republican leadership made a calculation. It was a tactical decision that if they just sat on the sidelines, if they didn't lift a finger to help, if instead they opposed us every

step of the way, if they said no even to policies that historically they had agreed to, that historically they had sponsored and adopted, they figured they could ride people's anger and frustration all the way to the ballot box.

That is what's happened over the last 20 months. So I need all of you to be clear over these next 2 weeks: This election is a choice. And the stakes could not be higher, because if they win this election, the chair of a Republican campaign committee has already promised to pursue the "exact same agenda" as they did before they took office.

Audience members. Boo!

The President. That's what they said. The very same agenda that cut taxes for millionaires and billionaires, that cut rules for special interests, that cut middle class families loose to fend for themselves. It's an agenda that turned a record surplus into a record deficit, an agenda that let Wall Street run wild at the expense of folks on Main Street, an agenda that nearly destroyed our economy.

If they take over Congress, the other side has promised to roll back health reform so that insurance companies can go back to denying you coverage before—because you're sick. They want to roll back Wall Street reform so that taxpayers are on the hook for Wall Street bailouts and credit card companies can hit you with hidden fees and penalties.

And if they win in Congress, they will cut AIDS funding right here in the United States of America and all across the world. You know, one of the great things about being a Democrat is we like arguing with each other. [*Laughter*] But I would suggest to the folks who are concerned about AIDS funding, take a look at what the Republican leadership has to say about AIDS funding, because we increased AIDS funding.

They want to cut education by 20 percent to help pay for a $700 billion tax break that only the wealthiest 2 percent of Americans will ever see.

So that's what's happening at the national level. Here in Massachusetts, it's the same story. Deval's opponents, they've got a very different vision about where this State should go.

They want to let the insurance companies run wild. They want to eliminate unemployment benefits for thousands of people. They want to eliminate investments in education and clean energy. It is the same theory the other side has been peddling for years, and it is up to us to tell them we don't want what they are selling. We've been there, we've tried it, we don't like it, and we're not going back.

I mean, this is not a situation in which we haven't tried it. We tried what they're selling. We tried it for 8 years. It didn't work out so well. You know, I've been using an analogy across the country. Imagine them driving a car into the ditch. And Deval and me and Kerry and Markey and Frank, we've all put our boots on. We went down into the ditch and we started pushing that car out of the ditch.

And it was hot down there, muddy, and we kept on pushing. And every once in a while we'd look up and the Republicans are standing up there, fanning themselves—[*laughter*]—sipping on a Slurpee. And we'd ask, are you going to help? And they'd say, no, that's all right, but you all should push harder. You're not pushing the right way. [*Laughter*]

And so even though we got no help from them, even though they didn't lift a finger, we kept on pushing. And finally we've got this car on level ground. It's a little banged up. You know, it needs some bodywork. It needs a tune-up. But it's ready to move forward. And suddenly we get this tap on our shoulder. And we look back and, lo and behold, who is it? It's the Republicans. And they say, excuse me, can we have the keys back?

Massachusetts, they can't have the keys back. They don't know how to drive. They can get in and ride with us if they want, but they got to be in the backseat.

I don't know if any of you have noticed, but if you want to go forward in your car, what do you do? You put it into "D." You want to go backwards you put it into "R." Don't let us go backwards now. That's not a coincidence.

Because of the steps that we've taken—because of the steps we've taken, we no longer face the possibility of a second depression. The economy is growing again. Private sector job growth, we've seen 9 months in a row. But we still have a long way to go. We've still got a lot of work to do. I know there are people who are still hurting out there. Deval meets them and sees them every day. I see them and hear from them every day. There are families that are still hanging just by a thread. That's what keeps me awake at night. That's what keeps me fighting. That's what keeps Deval fighting.

But we also know this: that the biggest mistake we can make right now is to—is out of hurt and confusion, the worst thing we could do is to go back to the very same policies that caused this mess in the first place. The last thing we can do is go back to a philosophy that nearly destroyed our economy and decimated the middle class. And I say this not because I want to relitigate the past, it's because I don't want to relive the past.

So what this election's about is not where we are right now. It's where we want to be 2 years from now, where we want to be 5 years from now, where we want to be 10 years from now, where we want to be 20 years from now. It's not just about the work we've done, it's about the work we've got left to do. It's about moving forward, not moving backwards, but moving forward between our doubts and our hopes. That's what's at stake right now.

Look, Deval and I have a different idea about what the future holds, and it's an idea rooted in our belief about how this country was built. It's based not just on our reading of history, but our experience in our own lives. We have seen transformation in this country. And we know it didn't all come from government. We know government doesn't have all the answers to our problems. We know government should be lean and efficient.

But in the words of the first Republican President, Abraham Lincoln, we also believe that government should do for the people what they cannot do better for themselves. We believe in a country that rewards hard work. We believe in a country that encourages responsibility. We believe in a country where we look after one another. Where we say, I am my brother's keeper, I am my sister's keeper. That's the America we know. That's the choice in this election.

We see a future that's driven by American innovation and American ingenuity. We don't want to keep giving tax breaks to corporations that ship our jobs overseas.

We want to give tax breaks to companies that are creating jobs right here in Massachusetts, right here in the United States of America, to small businesses, to American manufacturers, to clean energy companies, because I don't want to see all the solar panels and wind turbines and electric cars built in Europe or in Asia. Deval and I want them built right here in America, by American workers. That's the choice in this election.

We see an America where every citizen has the skills and training to compete with any worker in the world. The other side might think it's a good idea to cut education by 20 percent, but you don't think it's a good idea. You know who else doesn't think it's a good idea? China and South Korea and Germany and India, they are boosting education spending, not cutting back. They understand that whoever is able to train their young people will be able to outcompete any other country in the world. Those countries are not playing for second place. And the United States doesn't play for second place. We play for first.

That's why tens of billions of dollars in taxpayer subsidies that used to go to big banks are now going where they should, to students and to families. That's why we want to make our new college tax credit permanent, which will be worth $10,000 in tuition relief for every student in America. That's the vision we see. That's the future we want, where the middle class is growing, where opportunity is shared, and where the only limit to your success is how hard you're willing to try.

That's why we want tax cuts for the middle class permanent. That's why we'll fight the efforts of some in the other party to privatize Social Security, because as long as I'm President, nobody is going to take the retirement savings of a generation and hand it over to Wall Street. That's why we won't go back to the days when insurance companies and Wall Street banks had free rein to run roughshod over the middle class. We don't want insurance companies dropping you when you get sick or credit card companies hitting you with hidden fees and penalties. We don't want taxpayers ever again to have to pay a bailout for Wall Street's mistakes. That's the choice in this election. That's what we're fighting for.

Now, let me say this, the same special interests that would profit from the other side's agenda, they are fighting back just as hard. To win this election, they are plowing tens of millions of dollars into front groups that are running misleading, negative ads all across America. They don't even have the courage to stand up and disclose their identity. They could be insurance companies, they could be banks, they could be even foreign-controlled corporations. We will never know.

This is not just a threat to Democrats. This is a threat to our democracy. And the only way to fight it, the only way to match their millions of dollars, is with millions of voices who are ready to start—who are ready to finish what we started in 2008. Only you can make a difference. Only you can roll back these efforts.

Look, let me say this, Massachusetts. This will be the largest get out the vote operation in the history of this State, but only if you do your part. We need all of you to sign one of the cards they're handing out. We need all of you to text the letters "GOTV" to the number 89800. It's on those signs. Lift one of those signs up right there. I don't even mind if you do it right now. Like I said, my staff is probably BlackBerrying right now in the back; they're not listening to my speech.

But the reason this is important is because a lot of you got involved in 2006 and 2008 because you believed that we're in a defining moment in our history. You believed this is a time when the decisions we make about the challenges we face, they're not just going to affect us; they're going to affect the lives of our children and our grandchildren and our great-grandchildren. They'll affect the trajectory of this country for decades to come. And the reason you knocked on doors and made phone calls and waited in line to cast your vote for Deval, for me—some of you for the very first time in your lives—was because you believed that your actions could make a difference, that you could play a role in making big change, that history was not predestined, that you could shape history.

Now we're in the midst of not just advocating for change, not just calling for change. We're doing the grinding, sometimes frustrating work of delivering change, inch by inch, day by day.

And Massachusetts, we know it's not easy. I know it's not easy. I know sometimes you think about election night or Inauguration Day when Beyonce was singing and Bono was singing and that was so much fun and you were feeling good and you think, well, gosh, I wish politics was that easy all the time. [*Laughter*]

I understand that sometimes hope may have faded as we've grinded out this work over the last several years. I know it's hard to keep faith when a family member still hasn't found a job after months of trying or another foreclosure sign is hung on the house down the street. And you're watching TV and all you see are politicians tearing each other down and pundits who treat politics like a sport. I know it can be discouraging.

But don't ever let anybody tell you this fight isn't worth it. Don't ever let them tell you you're not making a difference. Because of you, there is a woman in New Hampshire right now who no longer has to choose between losing her house and treating her cancer. Because of you, there are parents who can look their children in the eye and tell them, you're going to college. Because of you, there are small-business owners who can keep their doors open. Because of you, there are clean energy entrepreneurs right here

in Massachusetts who are hanging out the help wanted signs; they want to hire some folks. Because of you, there are 100,000 brave men and women who are no longer at war in Iraq. Don't let them tell you that change isn't possible. Don't let them take this country backwards because we did not have the conviction to fight.

Because here's what I know: If our parents and our grandparents and our great-grandparents had made the same decision 50 years ago or 100 years ago, we wouldn't be here tonight. The only reason we're here is because past generations have been unafraid to push forward, even in the face of difficulty, to do what was necessary, even when success was uncertain.

That's how we came through war. That's how we came through depression. That's why we've got civil rights. That's why we've got workers' rights. That's why we've got women's rights. That's the spirit that we need now. And if you have that spirit, I guarantee you, we will reelect Deval Patrick. We will win in November. And all of us together will rebuild the middle class and restore the American Dream.

God bless you, and God bless the United States of America.

NOTE: The President spoke at 3:45 p.m. at the Hynes Convention Center. In his remarks, he referred to musicians James Taylor, Beyonce G. Knowles, and Paul D. "Bono" Hewson; Victoria R. Kennedy, wife of the late Sen. Edward M. Kennedy; and Rep. Pete Sessions, in his capacity as chairman of the National Republican Congressional Committee.

Remarks at a Democratic Senatorial Campaign Committee Reception in West Newton, Massachusetts
October 16, 2010

Thank you very much. Well, first of all, to Ralph and Wing, thank you for opening up this extraordinary home, and we will not show up unannounced—[*laughter*]—whatever John may say. You guys have been extraordinarily gracious, and we really appreciate it.

To all of you who are here, thank you for being such stalwart supporters not just to the Democratic Party, but supporters of an idea about how America should be organized to make sure that everybody has an opportunity. There are core values that all of you stand for, and that's the reason that you're here today.

Now, I want to, obviously, speak about the two gentlemen who are here with me, two of the finest Senators I think the country has ever seen, one who's been there for a while, one who hasn't been there too long, but both John Kerry and Sheldon Whitehouse exemplify what we expect from our public servants: people who are smart and well informed and dedicated.

A counterpart in the House of Representatives, Ed Markey, is here, and he does extraordinary work. Marty Meehan is here, and we wish you would stay in the House, but I know that the University of Massachusetts is glad that they have him, and I know he's doing a great job of chancellor. And thank you very much for your service. And Setti, the best of luck to you in being mayor in this wonderful community.

Now, I think John gave you a pretty good sense of what's going on out there. So what I want to do is just share a little bit of perspective from the Oval Office in terms of what I've seen over the last 2 years.

The reason this is a difficult time politically is because the country has gone through a very difficult time generally. This is the worst crisis we've seen since the Great Depression, since most of our lifetimes.

I mean, if you think about—I am—I'll be 50 next year, so I came of age, entered into college just as Ronald Reagan came to power during the last recession that was anything approaching what we've gone through. We had then another recession at the beginning of the nineties, another recession at the beginning of 2000, 2001. If you combine those previous three recessions, the magnitude and impact they've had is less than what we've had just in this one recession. I mean, that gives you some scope, some scale. We had lost 4 million jobs in the 6 months prior to me taking office, and then another 750,000 the month that I was sworn in, and 600,000 several months subsequent to that.

So all told, we've lost 8 million jobs during the course of this recession. But that doesn't begin to measure, I think, the full impact of what people have experienced: the fear of suddenly seeing their 401(k)s plummet by 40 percent; the uncertainty of having your home values drop so that suddenly your mortgage is higher than the value of your home; the people who didn't lose their jobs but now are uncertain as to whether those jobs will still be there.

And this is all on top of what had been essentially what the Wall Street Journal, not just Democrats, called the lost decade, a decade in which, from 2001 to 2009, the average middle class family actually lost 5 percent of their income. And we had the most sluggish job growth since we had since World War II. In fact, the job growth we've had over the last year was at a faster clip than we had between 2001 and 2009.

So families were already struggling before the crisis hit. And obviously, once the crisis hit, it unsettled the entire country and the entire world in ways that we had not seen for a very, very long time.

Now, I say that to, first of all, remind us of how far we've come over the last 20 months. An economy that was contracting is now growing. We've had nine consecutive months of private sector job growth. The financial sector is stable.

And so in some ways what is remarkable is how, despite this body blow that the country took, the country once again has proven more resilient and more adaptable and more dynamic than I think a lot of folks give us credit for. But it's also to remind you that we've got so much more work to do. People out there are still hurting very badly, and they are still scared.

And so part of the reason that our politics seems so tough right now, and facts and science and argument does not seem to be winning the day all the time, is because we're hard-wired not to always think clearly when we're scared. And the country is scared, and they have good reason to be.

Our job, then, is to make sure that even as we make progress, that we are also giving people a sense of hope and a vision for the future; a sense that we will get through these tough times, and the country will come out stronger for it, having gone through this trauma.

And that's why this election is so absolutely critical, because essentially you can respond in a couple of ways to a trauma like this. I mean, one is to pull back, retrench, respond to your fears by pushing away challenges, looking backwards. And another is to say we can meet these challenges and we are going to move forward. And that's what this election is about.

Now, I am confident that if we move forward, that the worst is behind us. And we've got a lot of running room looking forward. It is true that we are in the toughest economic fight of our lives internationally. But you remember back in the eighties, everybody said Japan was going to be taking over? I mean, we periodically go through these moments where we question America's ability to compete. And what happens is we whip ourselves into shape, we stiffen our spines, we become more productive, we re-emphasize science and technology and education; we say to ourselves we can no longer do the things that are not productive, we're going to just focus on those things that help us grow for the future, and we adapt. And we're going to do so this time.

There is no reason why we won't rank, once again, number one in the proportion of college graduates. There's no reason why we're not going to be the leader in clean energy technology. When we came in, we were getting 2 percent of the world's advanced battery manufacturing. And through the Recovery Act and the help of these guys, we're now on track to have 40 percent of that market by 2015. Just over the course of 2 years, we have built an entire industry.

Well, we can duplicate that in every leading industry, whether it's solar panels or wind turbines. I have confidence that the health care reform bill that we passed, as painful as it was, is going to result in a system that is more efficient, more fair; where not only do we have 30 million people now suddenly having health insurance, but we're going to start working with hospitals and doctors to figure out how are we going to eliminate unnecessary tests and how are we going to make sure that we're reducing infection rates in hospitals and how are we going to be more effectively deploying providers so that people are getting better services for lower costs.

On every front, there are clear answers out there that can make this country stronger. But we're going to have to get—break through the fear and the frustration that people are feeling

right now. And that's going to require all of you not just to write checks, but also to help remind people that we've been through tougher times before and we've gotten through them, and to lift up people's spirits and make sure that they're not reacting just to fear.

Now, it also requires me to have a Congress that I can work with. And John is absolutely right when he says that the Republicans made a very calculated decision. And it was—look, I give them credit. It was a smart tactical decision. When I was sworn in with a lot of high spirits, they had two ways to go. They could have cooperated with us, in which case everybody would have ownership in solving problems, but if we were successful, then people would still—would probably give the Democrats' majority more credit. And if we weren't successful, they'd share the blame. So what they instead said was, we'll just let them try it out, and we're not going to lift a finger to help, and—because they figured, we had made such a mess, it's going to take them a really long time to clean it up.

But I served in the Senate, and it is true that the kind of obstructionism that we've seen is unprecedented, by every measure. I mean, we can't get Deputy Treasury Secretaries appointed at a time of crisis when we need Deputy Treasury Secretaries. We can't get district court judges called up for a vote, even when they're voted out of the committee unanimously on a bipartisan basis, we cannot overcome—we can't just call those judges up for a vote, a clean vote. We end up having to go through a cloture motion, and they will filibuster, make us wait for days, weeks, figuring out how to schedule it. And then when we finally actually get a vote, it turns out it will be 90 to nothing. They were just doing that just to play games, just to stall. Then that's on the House side—or on the Senate side. I mean, on the House side, we've got similar problems.

So I don't anticipate that getting better next year. I anticipate that getting worse. And that is why it is going to be absolutely critical that we do everything we can in the next 3 weeks to make sure that we have a Senate that cares about moving the country's business and is thinking about the next generation and not just the next election; that is operating on the basis of some conviction and not cynicism.

These two guys exemplify that, but they're going to need some help because every bit of progress that we need to make is going to be a matter of grinding it out. You know, and I'll just take one example. I mentioned earlier energy. Nobody has been working harder to move an energy policy, an energy agenda, forward than John Kerry; one that is necessary. It's one that's necessary not just for our economy, but it's also necessary for our environment.

Now, that is a piece of unfinished business that is going to require a lot of heavy lifting. And John will tell you that we may be able to get 4, 5, 6 Republicans, but it's going to be hard to get 20 Republicans. Our ability to actually map out an energy strategy that is good for our future is going to depend on how much help John Kerry has in that process. And probably nothing is going to have—make as big of a difference, in terms of our long-term economic competitiveness, as us getting this right.

The same is true, by the way, on foreign policy. You know, over the last 20 months, we've successfully removed 100,000 of our troops out of Iraq, as I promised and committed to doing. We're going to have a series of tough decisions to make on Afghanistan. We're going to have a series of tough decisions to make on how to sustain momentum in dealing with Iran. We've got a START Treaty that is coming up that would not only reduce nuclear weapons for both the United States and Russia but underpins an entire effort that we've made over the last 20 months to strengthen the nonproliferation treaty so that we can go after Iran and North Korea from a place of moral stature.

And that depends on us having some votes—67 to be precise—in the Senate. Again, we may be able to get 5, 6, 7 Republicans on some of these; we can't get 20.

So there's almost nothing this room cares about—from how well the financial regulatory reform bill is implemented, to how health care is implemented, to whether we have an energy policy, to whether the investments we've made in higher education continue, to our ability to manage these incredible international challenges—not one of these issues will we be able to make serious progress on if we do not have a strong Democratic Senate.

And that's why I need all of you, regardless of what cable news says, regardless of what you're reading in the papers, I need all of you to be hopeful and act with confidence that the American people, as shaken up as they've been, still want us to move forward.

And if we can get that message out, facilitated in part by the extraordinary contributions that you've made today and that you've been making for years, if we get that message out, then I think we are going to hold onto the Senate. I think we can win the House. And I think we will continue to make progress.

And we will look back on this difficult time, 5 years from now, 10 years from now, 15 years from now, 20 years from now, with extraordinary pride. We'll look back the same way that people look back who helped start Social Security; the same way that people felt when they looked back because they had helped lead the civil rights movement. We'll be able to look back in the same way those who were involved in the space program looked back and said, you know what, we did something that wasn't just out of short-term expedience, we did something that committed this country to greatness over the long term.

And you know, I guess I would just leave you with this thought. A lot of people ask me, they say, boy, how do you manage this? You know, you just—all this stuff on your desk and people hollering at you all the time and—[*laughter*]—and that's just the Democrats. [*Laughter*] And I'll tell you what keeps me going—two things.

Number one, I get enough stories, enough letters from people all across the country, talking about how tough it is for them, that I am reminded of what a great privilege it is for me to try to help, and that nothing I'm going through remotely compares to the courage and tenacity and hardship that the American people are going through.

And the other thing that gets me through is the humor and the resilience and the love people have for their children and the love people have for this country. When you hear the American people, they are so extraordinarily decent and there's a goodness at the heart of this country. That makes me confident that we will get through these times and we are going to get to where we need to go.

So thanks to all of you for helping us get to where we need to go. God bless you. Thank you.

NOTE: The President spoke at 5:19 p.m. at the residence of Ralph and Wing Cheung de la Torre. In his remarks, he referred to Mayor Setti Warren of Newton, MA.

Remarks at a Reception for Governor Theodore Strickland of Ohio in Chagrin Falls, Ohio
October 17, 2010

The President. Thank you, everybody. Thank you. Everybody, please have a seat. Have a seat. I've got a lot of thank yous. First of all, to Carole and David Carr, thank you so much for your extraordinary hospitality. Please give them a big round of applause. To John and Carolyn Climaco, who are also cohosts, thank you so much for this great event.

We're mainly here for this guy, but there are a couple other folks I want to make mention of. Yvette McGee Brown is going to be an outstanding Lieutenant Governor.

Current Lieutenant Governor, soon to be United States Senator, Lee Fisher is in the house. A champion of working people each and every day, Senator Sherrod Brown is here. He's around here somewhere. There he is, back there. He's grabbing some of the big shrimp back there. [*Laughter*]

We've got an outstanding congressional delegation, and I want every single one of them back with me: Marcia Fudge, Betty Sutton, John Boccieri, Tim Ryan.

I love this Ohio delegation. They have the courage of their convictions. I mean, they have—they get beat up. It's tough being a Member of Congress these days. Ted remembers.

Gov. Strickland. Right.

The President. And yet day in, day out, they consistently think what's best for the country, not what's best for my reelection—until 2 weeks before the reelection. [*Laughter*]

So right now I want to make sure everybody else is thinking about putting them back where they belong, in Congress.

I want to say a little something about Michelle. It is not true that more importantly I'm President of the United States. More importantly, I am Michelle Obama's husband and Malia and Sasha's father. And Michelle has put up with me through thick and thin, and I am grateful for her each and every day.

And it's fun having her along on this road trip. [*Laughter*] Usually, I'm all by myself, listening to my iPod. We had a wonderful conversation on the way here, and she was telling me what I should do. [*Laughter*] It's true. [*Applause*] It's true. You think I'm joking; I'm not. [*Laughter*] I have witnesses.

It is great to be back in Ohio, and it is great to be back in the Cleveland area. And it's a great honor to be helping somebody who I truly believe is one of the best Governors in this country, Ted Strickland. I truly believe that. They believe it too. [*Applause*] They believe it too. They believe it too.

Now, we all understand Ted took office during an enormously difficult time for Ohio. It was difficult even before this terrible financial crisis struck. Ohio had been hit harder than most States by the loss of manufacturing, jobs moving overseas. And then when the recession hit in 2007, 2008, times got even tougher. But from the day that he took office, Ted hasn't wasted a minute in fighting to make sure that he turned this economy around. Under Ted's watch, Ohio has invested in high-growth industries and new infrastructure. You've provided job training and new skills to more than 150,000 workers. There are over 65,000 more students in college today in Ohio because of the steps that Ted has taken.

He's cut redtape. He's kept taxes low so that businesses locate here in Ohio. And he's a fighter. He hasn't just been concerned about the next election, he's been thinking about the next generation. And his work is not yet done.

So I implore you to do everything you can over these final 2 weeks to make sure that we've got Ted Strickland in for another 4 years. It is absolutely critical. [*Applause*] It is absolutely critical.

When you have somebody of high character, who hasn't forgotten where he comes from and understands the essence of the American Dream, you make sure that guy gets back into office. And that requires work, because there is a lot of money being spent on the other side to try to defeat Ted. And there are a lot of special interests who would be more than happy to replace him. And the way we make up for that is by effort, by knocking on doors and making phone calls and talking to friends and talking to neighbors.

And I know everybody here has contributed to Ted's campaign. Go out and rustle up some more, because he's going to need some help in these last 2 weeks.

Now, I want to just speak a little bit about the broader political context, because obviously, this is a tough time for Democrats here in Ohio, but it's a tough time all across the country. We have gone through the worst economic crisis since the Great Depression. And so when times are that difficult, elections are going to be difficult, and understandably so.

You know, the 6 months before I took office, we lost 4 million jobs across the country—a lot of those were in Ohio—4 million jobs in the 6 months prior to me talking office. We then lost 750,000 jobs the month I was sworn in, 600,000 jobs the month after that, 600,000 jobs the month after that.

But it wasn't just the immediate crisis that has been weighing on people. It's the fact that for the previous decade, the middle class had been losing ground. That's not something I'm making up. The statistics are there, and they're clear. From 2001 to 2009, the average middle class family lost 5 percent of their income—lost 5 percent. We had the most sluggish job growth since World War II between 2001 and 2009. Slower, by the way, than it's been over the course of this last year. At the same time, costs of everything were skyrocketing: costs of health care, costs of sending your child to college.

And so the bills were piling up for a lot of families at a time when salaries and wages weren't going up. And a lot of families just barely stayed afloat by working the extra job, maxing out on their credit cards, taking out home equity loans. And when this crisis hit, all those efforts to barely stay above water became that much more difficult.

So my first job when I got into office, my very first job and the task of all the Members of Congress here, was to stop the bleeding and to prevent this economy from plunging into a second Great Depression. And we did it. And it wasn't always popular, the decisions that we made. Those decisions weren't always popular. There were a whole bunch of folks in Washington who said let the car companies go under, regardless of the impact it would have on States like Ohio. There were a lot of folks who said we don't need to worry about unemployment insurance for folks who had been laid off and were now experiencing long-term unemployment. There were a whole lot of arguments about doing nothing. And we said that's not an option, we can't play politics here.

And so we stood up. All these Members of Congress here stood up. Ted Strickland stood up. And we gave it everything we had. And as a consequence, an economy that was contracting is now growing again. An economy that was shedding millions of jobs, we've seen 9 consecutive months of private sector job growth—9 consecutive months.

But we've still got a lot of work to do. And part of what's so challenging is when I was first sworn in, the hope was that we'd have partners on the other side of the aisle that, despite some philosophical disagreements, would recognize the critical challenges we were facing and would decide, at least for a while, to put politics aside. That was our hope. Because although we are proud Democrats, we are prouder to be American, and we understood that everybody had to join together—[*applause*]—that everybody had to join together to make a difference.

Unfortunately, the Republican leaders in Washington and some of the Republican leaders in Ohio, they made a different decision. They were focused on the election. And they said to themselves, you know what, we screwed up so bad, the economy is in such a mess, that it's probably going to take a while to fully recover. And so rather than roll up our sleeves and help, we're going to be better off standing on the sidelines and letting the Democrats deal with these problems. Because people are going to be angry, and people are going to be frustrated. People are going to be disheartened. And if things aren't working, then it's Democrats who will end up suffering the political consequences.

That was the decision they made. That's not the decision Ted Strickland made. That's not the decision I made. Because there are some things that are more important than politics. And you didn't send me to Washington, you didn't send Ted to the statehouse, to do what was easy. You sent us to do what was right. And that's what we've tried to do over these last several months: do what was right.

Now—so make no mistake, the stakes at this point could not be higher. The stakes could not be higher. The chair of the Republican campaign committee said a while back—he was asked, what exactly would you propose to do if you ended up retaking power in Washington? He said, well, we're going to pursue the exact same agenda as before Obama came into power.

And they've got the same answer here in Ohio. And we know what that philosophy is. You give tax cuts mostly to millionaires and billionaires, folks who don't need it and weren't even asking for it. You cut regulations for special interests so that the financial system is unregulated, so that those who are polluting are unregulated, so that credit card companies are unregulated or mortgage brokers are unregulated. That's the essence of their agenda. And then you cut the middle class loose. You let them fend for themselves.

You call it the ownership society, but basically, what it means is you are on your own. If you don't have health care, tough luck, you're on your own. If you can't find a job, tough luck, you're on your own. If you're a child who showed the poor judgment of not choosing the right parents—[*laughter*]—so you're born in a poor neighborhood, tough luck, pull up—pull yourself up by your own bootstraps. You're on your own.

That's the philosophy that they have been peddling for decades. And it's not as if we haven't tried it. This is not an abstract argument that I'm having with the Republicans—because we did. We tried it for 8 years. And it resulted in the worst economic crisis in our history.

And what they're counting on right now is that all of you have forgotten. They are counting on amnesia. That is the essence of their campaign strategy. They're counting on you having forgotten.

If they take over Congress, the other side has promised to roll back health care, so that insurance companies can go back to denying coverage for folks who have gotten sick. They've already said they are going to cut back education funding by 20 percent to help pay for tax cuts that would only impact the top 2 percent of the country. We want to give tax cuts to middle class folks, the 98 percent. They're holding those tax cuts hostage for the top 2 percent. And to help pay for them, they want to cut education funding by 20 percent.

They're going to be making the same choices here in Ohio if Ted Strickland doesn't get elected because we are going to be in tough fiscal times. We're going to have to make tough decisions. And we're going to have to decide what is most important. And when you hear the national Republicans say the single most important economic agenda item that they have is providing $700 billion worth of tax cuts, an average of $100,000 to millionaires and billionaires at the same time as we're cutting student loans for kids to go to college or help for community colleges that can help bridge people who need to upgrade their skills to find that new job for the future, that is what this election is about. That's the choice in this election.

Here's how I've been putting it as I travel around the country. The Republicans drove the car into the ditch. And it was a pretty deep ditch. And so me and Ted and these Members of Congress, we put on our boots, and we went down into the ditch, doing the responsible thing. Let's get the car out of the ditch. And it was hot down there, muddy, bugs. [*Laughter*]

But we kept on pushing because we knew that that next generation of Americans is going to depend on us getting this car out of the ditch. So we push, and we push. Every once in a while we'd look up, and the Republicans would be standing there, fanning themselves, sipping on a Slurpee. [*Laughter*]

And every once—and we'd say, "Why don't you come down and help?" They'd say, "No, that's all right, but you're not pushing hard enough." [*Laughter*] "You're not pushing the right way."

That's okay. We decide we're going to push. We push, we push. Finally, we get this car up on level ground. Finally, we have this car pointing in the right direction. It's a little beat up, needs to go to the body shop, needs a tuneup. But we're moving in the right direction.

Suddenly, we get this tap on the shoulder. Who is it? It's the Republicans. They say, "Excuse me, we'd like the keys back." [*Laughter*] Well, you can't have the keys back. You don't know how to drive! [*Applause*] You don't know how to drive! You can't have them back. [*Applause*] You can't have them back. You can't do it.

You can ride with us if you want. [*Laughter*] But you all have to be in the backseat. [*Laughter*] You've noticed when you want to go forward, what do you do with your car? You put it in "D." [*Laughter*] You want to go backwards you put it in "R." [*Laughter*] We want to go forward, Ohio. We don't want to go backwards. We've tried that. [*Applause*] We've tried that.

Look, Ted and I have a different idea. Maybe it has to do with our backgrounds, because neither of us were born into fame or wealth or power. We came from working people, folks who worked hard to get into the middle class. We remember the trajectory of our own families. Michelle remembers the trajectory of her family. And so we we've got a different idea about how this country should be working.

We don't think that government can solve all our problems. We think government has to be lean and efficient. That's why Ted has consistently made tough decisions to streamline Ohio government, to make sure that it works. But in the words of the first Republican President, Abraham Lincoln, who'd have a great deal of trouble getting a nomination in the Republican Party right now. [*Laughter*] You know that's true. [*Laughter*] He said that government should leave to the people—let them do what they can do best for themselves. But government should also be there to do things that the people can't do so well for themselves.

There are some things we've got to do together: build an infrastructure, investing in clean energy, making sure our kids get the education that they need. The notion that I am my brother's keeper and I am my sister's keeper and that we are going to rise or fall together, that you are not on your own, that's what we believe.

We believe in an America that rewards hard work and responsibility, but also one where we look after one another. We believe in an America that prizes innovation and ingenuity. And that's why Ted has made such a push on clean energy. That's why we're seeing advanced battery manufacturing and solar panels and wind turbines. We don't want those jobs going to Europe or Asia.

We want the new electric car. We want the solar panel. We want that built right here in the United States of America with American workers. And I know that's what our Members of Congress want as well. That's the choice in this election.

For that same reason, we do not accept the notion of cutting education spending. You think China is cutting education spending right now or South Korea or Germany? Those countries aren't playing for second place. They are playing for first. And the United States of America doesn't play for second place either. We've got to invest in our young people.

That's why with the help of these Members of Congress, we completely transformed our student loan program so we've got tens of billions of dollars more going to millions of students all across the country so that they can afford their education. That's why we passed an American opportunity tax credit that provides up to $10,000 for young people to go to college.

And you combined that with the efforts Ted's made at the State level. That's why Ohio has been able to move forward on the education front. And we can't start moving backwards. That's the choice that we're making in this election. That's what this election is all about.

We see an America where the middle class is growing and opportunity is shared. And the only limit to your success is how hard you're willing to try. And we believe in an America that makes sure that it treats our seniors with the dignity and the respect that they deserve, which is why when I hear some folks in the other party still talking about privatization of Social Security, we say, not on my watch, because we're not going to allow a generation's savings to go get wasted on Wall Street.

We want to make sure that insurance companies are giving you a fair deal, that if you've been paying your premiums, that they're not dropping you suddenly when you get sick, and that you can still get health insurance even if your child has a preexisting condition. And if you're a young person graduated from college, that you can stay on your parent's policy until you can finally get a job that offers health insurance.

We want to make sure that credit card companies are treating you fairly and not jacking up your rates unnecessarily. We want to make sure that mortgage brokers aren't steering you into predatory loans. We do this not because we think that government has all the answers, but rather that the free market works best when it's got some basic rules of the road and consumers are protected and you're getting a fair deal.

We're promoting fair dealing all across America, and businesses are competing based on the best product and the best service and the best price. There's nothing antibusiness about that. That's the essence of how America got built.

We want to build our infrastructure. We used to have the best infrastructure in the world. And now suddenly, you've got countries in Asia that boast better trains and better airports. What happened? What happened to our sense of imagination, our sense of destiny?

That's what Ted and I and these Members of Congress, that's what we're fighting for. That's the choice in this election, not a small, cramped vision of what America should be, where each of us just worry about ourselves, but a big, large vision, a generous vision about what America can be. That's what's at stake in this election.

But look, I can give the most magnificent speeches, and Michelle can go travel around the country and campaign, and we can have the greatest candidates and an outstanding Governor with a great track record. None of this means anything if you don't believe, if you don't commit.

I know it's a long time since election night 2 years ago and Inauguration Day, and Beyonce singing and Bono. [*Laughter*] And everybody was having a fine old time. And because things have been so tough, because there are families out there still hanging on a thread, because you know family members who maybe are still looking for a job, because the news has been so tough, and frankly, because you have been inundated with millions of dollars of negative advertising day in, day out, I know that there are times where probably it's hard to recapture that sense of possibility.

It's hard sometimes to say, "Yes, we can." You start thinking, well, maybe, I don't know. [*Laughter*] It's not as inspiring a slogan.

But I said during the campaign, this has never been easy. This has never been easy. The idea of America has never been easy. The notion of 13 Colonies coming together and overthrowing the greatest empire in the world and then drafting a document that says we find these truths to be self-evident, that all men are created equal, endowed with certain inalienable rights, that's hard.

And then having to overcome the stain of slavery and figuring out how we are going to get everybody included, and how are we going give women the right to vote, and how are we going to make sure that workers aren't taken advantage of? And how are we going to grow this economy so that it works for everybody? And then after two world wars and veterans coming back, how do we make sure they get an education so that they can live out this idea of America, that you can make it if you try?

Every step of the way has been hard. And if our parents and our grandparents and our great-grandparents, if they hadn't had that stick-to-it-ness, if they had just gotten disheartened because some folks got grumpy and said some mean things about them and got cynical and told them you couldn't do it, we would not be here.

And now it's our turn. So yes, it's hard. That's okay. It's supposed to be hard because nothing worthwhile is easy. Ted Strickland understands that. These Members of Congress understand that. I want all of you to understand that. I want you to knock on some doors, make some phone calls, call in some chips, get organized, get mobilized. Because if you do, we're going to re-elect Ted Strickland as Governor of Ohio.

We're going to get all these Members of Congress back into Congress. I'm going to keep on working for you. I'm going to keep on fighting for you. We are going to grow this middle class, grow this economy, and make sure the American Dream is there for the next generation.

God bless you. God bless the United States of America.

NOTE: The President spoke at 5:01 p.m. at the residence of David and Carole Carr. In his remarks, he referred to John R. Climaco, founding partner, Climaco, Wilcox, Peca, Tarantino & Garofoli Co., LPA, and his wife Carolyn; Yvette McGee Brown, founder and president, Center for Child and Family Advocacy at Nationwide Children's Hospital; Rep. Pete Sessions, in his capacity as chairman of the National Republican Congressional Committee; and musicians Beyonce G. Knowles and Paul D. "Bono" Hewson. The transcript released by the Office of the Press Secretary also included the remarks of the First Lady.

Remarks at a Democratic National Committee Rally in Columbus, Ohio
October 17, 2010

The President. O–H!

Audience members. I–O!

The President. O–H!

Audience members. I–O!

The President. O–H!

Audience members. I–O!

The President. Oh, what do you think about Michelle Obama? [*Applause*] She's kind of cute, isn't she?

Audience members. Yes!

The President. Yes, indeed. It is good to be back in Columbus. Thank you so much. I am so proud to be here with Governor Ted Strickland, one of the finest Governors in this country; Lieutenant Governor Lee Fisher; Yvette McGee Brown; Michael Coleman; an outstanding congressional delegation—Mary Jo Kilroy, Tim Ryan, Marcia Fudge, John Boccieri; outstanding former Senator and astronaut, John Glenn; the Central State University Drumline in the house; and my friend John Legend; and about 35,000 of my closest friends.

It is good to be here with all of you Buckeyes. Now, let me just say, I am sorry about last night. [*Laughter*] But one thing I know about Buckeyes is, y'all don't quit. You get up, you keep fighting, you keep believing, and that's what we need from you right now.

We need you fired up. Because in a little more than 2 weeks, you can set the direction of this State and the direction of this country for not just the next 2 years, but the next 5 years, the next 10 years, the next 20 years. Just like you did in 2008, you can defy the conventional wisdom, the kind that says you can't overcome the cynicism of our politics, you can't overcome the special interests and the big money, you can't elect a skinny guy with a funny name, Barack Obama—[*laughter*]—you can't tackle our biggest challenges. Everybody said, no, you can't. And in 2008, you showed them, yes, we can.

So, in 2 weeks, you've got the chance to say once again, yes, we can. Now, look, let's be honest. This is a difficult election. This is hard. And it's hard because we've been through an incredibly difficult time as a nation. We've gone through a tougher time than anytime in the lifetimes of most of you. Think about it: For most of the last decade, middle class families saw their costs rise from everything from health care to college tuition while their incomes fell. Between 2001 and 2009, the incomes of middle class families fell by an average of 5 percent. Job growth was as sluggish it had been, most sluggish it had been since World War II. A lot of jobs moved overseas, especially here in Ohio. There were too many parents who couldn't afford to send their kids to college, too many people who couldn't afford to see a doctor when they got sick, Americans working two jobs and three jobs just to make ends meet.

And then all these problems were compounded with the worst economic crisis since the Great Depression. And I think sometimes we forget how scary it was, the magnitude of this crisis. We lost 4 million jobs in the 6 months before I was sworn in, 750,000 the month I was sworn in, 600,000 the month after that, 600,000 more the month after that. We lost 8 million jobs during the course of this recession, a once-in-a-generation challenge.

And when I was sworn in, it was my profound hope—and I know it was the hope of many of you, not just Democrats, but Republicans—it was the hope of so many people that it would cause both parties to put politics aside for the moment for the sake of the country.

The notion was that we could move beyond the division and the bickering and the game-playing that had dominated Washington for so long, because although so many of us are proud to be Democrats, we are prouder to be Americans. We are prouder to be Americans.

But the Republican leaders in Washington made a different decision. They made a tactical decision. Their basic theory was that we had gone into such a deep hole, the economy was so badly damaged, they knew it was going to take time for us to repair the economy. They knew it was going to take longer than anybody would

like. And they knew that people would be frustrated and they'd be angry. And some of the enthusiasm that we had seen in the 2008 election would start to dissipate as people looked at their friends losing jobs and their small businesses having to close their doors. And they figured if they just sat on the sidelines long enough and if they opposed everything that we did, if they said no even to policies that traditionally they had supported, then they figured that they could ride people's anger and frustration all the way to success in the next election. That was their working theory. In other words, they were basically counting on you forgetting who caused the mess in the first place.

And now they're sitting back, and they basically want you to believe that this election is a referendum on the economy, a referendum on me. They don't want you to understand this is a choice. But make no mistake, this election is a choice, and the stakes could not be greater. Because if they win this election, the chair of a Republican campaign committee has promised that they will pursue the exact same agenda as they did before they took office.

Now—so just understand, this is not like the Republicans went off and they said, boy, we really screwed up; we've got to rethink everything. And they went off into the desert, and they meditated, and then they finally came back with some new ideas. [*Laughter*] That's not what happened—the very same agenda.

And we know what that agenda is. You cut taxes for millionaires and billionaires. You cut rules for special interests, whether it's insurance companies that want to drop your coverage when you get sick or credit card companies that want to jack up your rates or Wall Street banks that are dealing in all kinds of derivatives that end up crashing the market. You cut the middle class loose to fend for themselves.

They'll tell you it's the ownership society, but basically, it's saying, you're on your own. If you lose your job, you're on your own. If your child doesn't have health care, tough luck, you're on your own. You're a young person, you can't afford to go to college, too bad. Lift yourself up by your own bootstraps. You're on your own.

It's an agenda that turned a record surplus into a record deficit, an agenda that produced slower job growth than we've had this past year, an agenda that let Wall Street run wild at the expense of folks right here on Main Street, an agenda that nearly destroyed the economy. Do they think that we have forgotten?

Audience members. No!

The President. I mean, it's not like we didn't try what they're peddling. We tried it for 8 years. It didn't work. And if they take over Congress, the other side has already promised to roll back health reform so that insurance companies can go back to denying you coverage when you get sick.

Audience members. Boo!

The President. They want to roll back Wall Street reform so that taxpayers can be on the hook for the next bailout.

Audience members. Boo!

The President. They want to let credit card companies hit you with hidden fees or penalties.

Audience members. Boo!

The President. They want to cut education by 20 percent to help pay for a $700 billion tax break for the wealthiest 2 percent of Americans, folks who don't need it and won't even——

Audience members. Boo!

The President. Look, this is the same theory they have been peddling for years. And, Ohio, it is up to you to tell them we do not want what they are selling. We've been there before, and we are not going back.

Let me—I've been explaining to people around the country, it's as if they drove America's car into the ditch. They drove it into the ditch, and it was a big ditch. And so I came along, and Ted Strickland came along, and we put on our boots, and we went down into the ditch. And it was hot down there, and it was muddy. [*Laughter*] There were bugs. [*Laughter*] But we said, that's okay. Even though we didn't drive it into the ditch, it's still our responsibility to get that car out of the ditch.

And so we pushed and we pushed. And every once in a while, we'd look up, and up on the road, you'd see the Republicans standing there, fanning themselves, sipping on a Slurpee, having a latte. [*Laughter*]

And we'd say: "Hey, why don't you come down and help push a little bit? We need some help down here." And they'd say, "No, that's all right." [*Laughter*] They said: "But you need to push harder. You're not pushing the right way."

And we just kept on pushing. We kept on pushing. Finally, we get this car up on level ground. It's pointing in the right direction. We're ready to move America forward. But the next thing we know, we get this tap on our shoulder, and we look back, and who is it? It's the Republicans. And they say, "We want the keys back." [*Laughter*] You can't have the keys back. You don't know how to drive!

Now, if you want, you can roll with us. [*Laughter*] But you got to be in the backseat. I don't know if you've noticed, if you want to take your car forward, you got to put it in what?

Audience members. "D"!

The President. In "D." If you want to go backwards, it goes what?

Audience members. "R"!

The President. We don't want to go backwards. We're moving America forward.

Because——

Audience member. [*Inaudible*]

The President. I love you back. Now, let's examine what's happened over the last 20-something months. Because of the steps we've taken, we no longer face the possibility of a second depression. The economy's growing again. The private sector's created jobs 9 months in a row. But you know what, we still have such a long way to go. We've got so much more work to do.

I know there are people out there who are just hanging by a thread, people who are hurting. It's what keeps me up at night. It's what keeps me fighting.

But I also know this: The biggest mistake we could make right now, Ohio, is to go back to the very same policies that caused all this hurt in the first place.

I mean, think about it for a second. It just doesn't make sense. The other side is counting on all of you having amnesia, just forgetting what happened here. We can't return to a philosophy that nearly destroyed our economy and decimated the middle class right here in Ohio. And I say this not to relitigate the past, I say it because we can't relive the past. And that's what this election's about, not just where we've been, but where we want to go. Not where we are right now, but where we want to be 10 years from now and 20 years from now. What does America's future look like? What's the work we've got left to do?

This election is not just about moving forward versus moving backwards. It's also a contest between our deepest hopes and our deepest fears. And the other side is playing on fear. That's what they do. That's what they do.

You see, we Democrats have a different idea about what the future should look like, and it's an idea rooted in our belief about how this country was built. It's a—it's based on not just ideas in books, it's based on the lived history of Ted Strickland and Michelle and myself. We didn't come from wealthy families. We didn't come from famous families. We came from working families. We came from some ordinary folks. We had to go to school on scholarships and grants. If we wanted some spending money, we had to work for it.

We—and so we remember the story of our families' lives, and it's the story of your lives. And we know that government doesn't have all the answers to our problems. We believe government should be lean and efficient. But in the words of the first Republican President, Abraham Lincoln—who, by the way, I'm not sure could win a nomination in the Republican Party right now—[laughter]—we also believe that government should be there to help people do what they cannot do better for themselves. That means we believe in a country that rewards hard work and responsibility, but also a country where we give each other a hand up, where we look after one another, where we say, I am my brother's keeper, I am my sister's keeper. That's the America I know. That's the choice in this election.

We see a future where the next century is driven by American innovation, American ingenuity. We don't want to give tax breaks to companies that ship jobs overseas. We want to give tax breaks to companies right here in the United States of America, to small businesses and American manufacturers and clean energy companies, because we want the solar panels and wind turbines and electric cars made right here in the U.S. of A. by American workers. That's the choice in this election.

We see an America where every citizen has the skills, the training to compete with any worker in the world. The other side might think it's a good idea to cut education by 20 percent, but let me tell you who doesn't think that. China doesn't think it's a good idea. South Korea, India, they don't think it's a good idea. They're not cutting back on education, because they're not playing for second place. And the United States of America doesn't play for second place. We play for first.

That's why tens of billions of dollars in taxpayer subsidies that used to go to big banks, you know where they're going now? Where they should, to students and families to help pay for their student loans, to help pay for their education.

That's why we're making a college tax credit permanent, worth $10,000 in tuition relief for every student who is going to college. We see an America where the middle class is growing, where opportunity is shared, where it's not just some people who make it, but everybody has got a chance to make it, where the only limit to your success is how hard you're willing to try.

That's why we want to give tax cuts and make them permanent for middle class families. That's why we'll fight efforts to privatize Social Security. That's not going to happen on my watch. We're not going to take the retirement savings of a generation of Americans and hand it over to Wall Street.

That's why we refuse to go back to the days when insurance companies or the banks or the oil companies had free rein to do whatever they wanted, running roughshod over the interests of middle class families. I want to make sure that insurance companies, if you're paying your premium, then they are paying for your health care when you get sick. I want to make sure that credit card companies aren't hitting you with hidden fees and penalties. I don't want taxpayers to be on the hook for Wall Street's mistakes.

I do that as somebody who profoundly believes in the free market. But the free market works when there are rules of the road in place and when the best businesses, the ones that are competing for your business on the basis of high quality and a good price and good customer service, when they're the ones who succeed because there are decent rules out there looking out for consumers, looking out for you. That's the choice in this election. That's what we're fighting for. That's what we're fighting for.

Now, I want to warn you about something—and by the way, I hope you don't mind I'm losing my voice, because I'm still fired up. But I've got some campaigning to do over the next couple weeks here.

Right now the same special interests that would profit from the other side's agenda, they're fighting back. The empire is striking back. [*Laughter*] To win this election, they are plowing tens of millions of dollars into front groups. They're running misleading, negative ads all across the country. They don't have the courage, they don't have the gumption to stand up and disclose their identity. They could be insurance companies, banks, we don't know. This isn't just a threat to Democrats. This is a threat to our democracy.

And the only way to fight it, the only way to match their millions of dollars is all of you, millions of voices who are ready to finish what we started in 2008. That's where you come in. That's where you come in. That's why you need to vote in this election.

Thanks to early voting here in Ohio, you can vote right now. Look, look, a lot of you got involved in 2008 because you believed we were in a defining moment in our history. You believed this was a time where the decisions we make, they're going to shape the lives of our children and our grandchildren for decades to come.

That's why you knocked on those doors. That's why you made those phone calls. That's why you stood in line, some of you, to cast your vote—some of you for the very first time in your lives—because you believed that your actions could make a difference, that you could play a role in making change.

And now we're not just advocating change. We're not just calling for change. We're doing the hard work of change; we're grinding it out. Sometimes it's frustrating. We're delivering change inch by inch, day by day. It's not easy. Believe me, I know it's not easy.

I understand that some of you, when you think back, you know, election night looked so good. Inauguration Day, Beyonce was singing. [*Laughter*] Bono was up there. Everybody had a good feeling.

And then you know what happens is, we start trying to solve these problems, and it doesn't happen as quick as we want. Suddenly, the other side is obstructing, and people start looking around and seeing a family member of mine's still losing a job or another foreclosure sign's gone up in my neighborhood. And you're seeing all these TV ads, and politicians are tearing each other down. And pundits are saying you can't really change politics.

I know it gets discouraging sometimes. But don't let anybody tell you this fight isn't worth it. Don't let them tell you you're not making a difference.

Ohio, because of you, right now there's a woman in New Hampshire who no longer has to choose between losing her home and treating her cancer. Because of you, there are parents who can look their children in the eye and say, yes, you are going to college. Because of you, there's some clean energy entrepreneur that is out there building some new plant somewhere and calling people, putting them to work, putting up "Help Wanted" signs. Because of you, 100,000 brave men and women are no longer at war in Iraq. That's all because of you.

So don't let them tell you that change isn't possible. Don't let them take this country backwards because we didn't fight for it. Because here's what I know: Nothing in America has ever been easy. The very founding of this country was hard. It required a revolution. And when you thought about those 13 Colonies coming together, how unlikely was it that they could gain their freedom from the most powerful empire on Earth and then draft a document based on principles that had never been tried before: We hold these truths to be self-evident, that all men are created equal, that we are endowed with certain inalienable rights?

And then we had to grapple with the legacy of slavery and a Civil War. And we had to fight to make sure that workers could get a decent deal on their job. And we had to fight to make sure that women got the right to vote. And then World War II came, and we had to fight to defeat fascism and overcome a depression.

And when folks came back, we had to invest in them with the GI bill to make sure we could grow a middle class that was the envy of the world and win a cold war and put a man on the Moon. Each and every one of those steps required struggle. And each and every time there was somebody out there who said, we can't do that. Each and every time, there was somebody who said, you know what, you're wasting your time. There was somebody who was saying, you know what, change isn't going to happen.

And if our parents and our grandparents and our great-grandparents had made the decision to sit it out 50 years ago, 100 years ago, 200 years ago, we wouldn't be here tonight. The only reason we're here is because past generations have been unafraid. They're unafraid to push forward even in the face of difficulty. They're unafraid to do what's necessary, even when things are uncertain. That's how we got through war. That's how we got through depression.

That's why we have civil rights and women's rights and workers' rights.

And if you will recapture that spirit, if you are out there knocking on doors and making phone calls, talking to your friends and neighbors, if you do not give up hope, then I guarantee you that not only are we going to win this election—because this was never just about putting a President in the White House; it was about building a movement for change that lasted for a long time—we will build a movement for change that will last 10 years from now and 20 years from now, and we will grow this economy and restore the middle class to its rightful place. And once again, the American Dream will be alive and well.

God bless you, Ohio, and God bless the United States of America.

NOTE: The President spoke at 8:08 p.m. at Ohio State University. In his remarks, he referred to Yvette McGee Brown, candidate for Lieutenant Governor of Ohio; Mayor Michael B. Coleman of Columbus, OH; Rep. Pete Sessions, in his capacity as chairman of the National Republican Congressional Committee; and musicians John Legend, Beyonce G. Knowles, and Paul D. "Bono" Hewson. The transcript released by the Office of the Press Secretary also included the remarks of the First Lady, who introduced the President.

Remarks at a White House Science Fair
October 18, 2010

Thank you, everybody. Everybody, please have a seat. I am having so much fun. [*Laughter*] It is great to see all of you here for our first White House science fair. I have been looking forward to doing this for a long time. One of the great joys of being President is getting to meet young people like all of you and some of the folks in the other room, who I just had a chance to see some of their exhibits and the work that they were doing. It's inspiring, and I never miss a chance to see cool robots when I get a chance. [*Laughter*]

We are joined by several Nobel laureates, including our Energy Secretary, Dr. Steven Chu. These are obviously the older folks who have helped to expand the frontiers of human knowledge. But we're also joined by a few people who inspire young people to pursue that knowledge. One of them is the one and only Science Guy, Bill Nye, who's in the house. I'm also pleased to welcome Jamie Hyneman and Adam Savage, known as the MythBusters. I can announce today that I taped a special guest appearance for their show, although I didn't get to blow anything up. [*Laughter*] I was a little frustrated with that.

I also want to welcome and congratulate Subra Suresh, who was sworn in this morning as the Director of the National Science Foundation, and who's here with his family. Please stand up. We are very grateful to have Subra taking this new task. He has been at MIT and has been leading one of the top engineering programs in the country, and for him now to be able to apply that to the National Science Foundation is just going to be outstanding. So we're very grateful for your service.

But the main reason I'm here is, I just want to recognize all the incredibly talented young men and women who've traveled here from every corner of this country to demonstrate their experiments and their inventions. And I just had a chance to meet with some of them, and it's hard to describe just how impressive these young people are. Their work—from cancer therapies to solar-powered cars, water purification systems, robotic wheelchairs—all of it is a testament to the potential that awaits when we inspire young people to take part in the scientific enterprise: tackling tough problems; testing new hypotheses; to try, and then to fail, and then to try again until they succeed.

And it's hard to single out any of the folks that I saw—who I met with, because everybody was so impressive. But just to give you one example, the last young lady that I talked to, between her freshman and sophomore years in high school, taught herself chemistry, and then decided that she wanted to see if she could create a new drug to deal with cancer cells using light activation and won the international science competition and is now being contacted by laboratories across the country to see if this might actually have applications in terms of curing cancer.

Now, if that doesn't inspire you—[*laughter*]—if that doesn't make you feel good about America and the possibilities of our young people when they apply themselves to science and math, I don't know what will.

And so that's just one example. Now, another example, in Tennessee, there was a team that decided—up in Appalachia, sometimes it's hard to get purified water. And so they constructed an entire system, self-contained system, powered by—with a water wheel that would purify water and could potentially be used for an entire community, so a very practical application of the knowledge that they had gained in the classroom.

You just saw example after example of that, and it's incredibly impressive. The importance of tapping this potential is why we're here. It's why I wanted to host this fair, which culminates this weekend in a science and engineering festival on the National Mall and across the country, where more than a million people are expected to participate.

So we welcome championship sports teams to the White House to celebrate their victories. I've had the Lakers here. I've had the Saints here, the Crimson Tide. I thought we ought to do the same thing for the winners of science fairs and robotic contests and math competitions, because often we don't give these victories the attention that they deserve. And when you win first place at a science fair, nobody is rushing the field or dumping Gatorade over your head. [*Laughter*] But in many ways, our future depends on what happens in those contests, what happens when a young person is engaged in conducting an experiment or writing a piece of software or solving a hard math problem or designing a new gadget.

It's in these pursuits that talents are discovered and passions are lit and the future scientists, engineers, inventors, entrepreneurs are born. That's what's going to help ensure that we succeed in the next century, that we're leading the world in developing the technologies, businesses, and industries of the future.

And this is the reason my administration has put such a focus on math and science education. Because despite the importance of inspiring and educating our children in these fields, in recent years, the fact is we've been outpaced by a lot of our competitors. One assessment shows that American 15-year-olds ranked 21st in science and 25th in math when compared to their peers around the world. Now, obviously, the young people who are here all boosted our averages considerably. [*Laughter*]

But the point is, is that there are tens of millions of talented young people out there who haven't been similarly inspired, and we've got to figure out how do we make sure that everybody who's got that same talent and inclination, how do we give them the tools that they need so that they can succeed, so that they're entering international science competitions, so that they're up to snuff when it comes to math.

It is unacceptable to me, and I know it's unacceptable to you, for us to be ranked, on average, as 21st or 25th, not with so much at stake. We don't play for second place here in America. We certainly don't play for 25th. So I've set this goal: We will move from the middle to the top in math and science education over the next decade. We are on our way to meeting this goal.

We're doing it in a couple of ways. Under the leadership of my Secretary of Education, Arne Duncan, we've launched an initiative called Race to the Top. And through Race to the Top, States are actively competing to produce innovative math and science programs, to raise standards, to turn around struggling schools, and to recruit and retain more outstanding teachers.

And when budget cuts across America threatened the jobs of countless teachers, we fought some tough opposition to save the jobs of hundreds of thousands of educators and school workers, because nothing is more important than the investment we're making in education. These are the folks in the classroom right now who are there because we refuse to accept a lesser education for our children, even when the economic times are tough.

But what I've said for a long time is, is that success is not going to be achieved just by government. It depends on teachers and parents and students and the broader community supporting excellence. And that's why last year, I challenged scientists and business leaders to think of creative ways that we can engage young people in math and science.

And it was interesting, when I was talking to some folks—how did you get interested in this? How did you first enter a robotics contest? And a lot of times it turned out that a young person had been inspired because they had seen some older kid involved in a robotics contest. Or there had been a teacher who had connected up with some international contest, and it gave them a focal point for their energy and their attention and their interest.

This is a challenge that will determine our leadership in the 21st-century global economy. So we need all hands on deck. Everybody has got to be involved. And I'm pleased that there are a lot of people out there who are answering the call. Companies, not-for-profits, they're coming together to replicate successful existing science programs.

We've got new public-private partnerships that are working to offer additional training to more than 100,000 current teachers and to prepare more than 10,000 new teachers in the next 5 years. Businesses are working with nonprofits to launch robotics competitions and other ways for kids to make things and learn things with their hands. And more than 100 leaders from some of the Nation's top companies have launched a new organization called Change the Equation to help us move to the top in math and science education.

As of this moment, more than $700 million has been committed by the private sector to this historic effort. And today I want to announce two new public-private initiatives.

The Defense Advanced Research Projects Agency, also known as DARPA—and I think those of you who are interested in science and technology know what an extraordinary role DARPA has played in all sorts of innovations that we now take for granted—DARPA is launching a campaign to inspire young people in science and engineering, to help create what DARPA Director Regina Dugan has called a "renaissance of wonder."

So, for example, teams of students in a thousand schools will be able to use advanced 3–D printers to manufacture unmanned vehicles and mobile robots for competitions. In addition, leading CEOs are going to be part of a new on-line campaign to show young people the array of jobs that their companies offer scientists and engineers. And they ought to know. This is an interesting statistic, particularly at a time when young people are thinking about their careers: The most common educational background of

CEOs in the S&P 500 companies—all right, the Nation's most successful, most powerful corporations—the most common study of CEOs is not business, it's not finance, it's not economics, it's actually engineering. It's engineering. So I want all the young people out there to think about that. Nothing can prepare you better for success than the education you're receiving in math and science.

And this is a difficult time for our country, and it would be easy to grow cynical and wonder if America's best days are behind us, especially at a time of economic hardship and when so many people, from Wall Street to Washington, seem to have failed to take responsibility for moving this country forward for so long. But when you have a chance to talk to these young people that I had a chance to meet with, these incredibly bright and creative young men and women, it can't help but leave you optimistic about our future.

They remind us that this country was not built on greed; it wasn't built on reckless risks; it wasn't build on short-term thinking; it wasn't built on shortsighted policies. It was forged of stronger stuff, by bold men and women who dared to invent something new or improve something old, who took chances, who crafted and built and who tested our assumptions, and who believed that in America, all things are possible.

We can think of Einstein, Edison, Franklin, Tesla, and the founders of Google and Apple and Microsoft. But now we've got some other people to think about, like Mikayla Nelson, who's here today. Where's Mikayla? Is she here? There she is, right there. Mikayla—I had a chance to—Mikayla is from Billings, Montana. She works with an entire team. I'm sorry to embarrass you here, Mikayla. [*Laughter*] She's like, "Oh, God, he called on me." [*Laughter*]

She's representing Will James Middle School. She and her classmates built a solar-powered car that won the design award in the National Science Bowl. She's in ninth grade. She's already trying to earn a pilot's license, and she's working on building an actual plane. She wants to be an engineer. There's no doubt we can expect great things from her.

We can think of Diego Vazquez and Antonio Hernandez, representing Cesar Chavez High School in Phoenix. Where are those guys? I met them earlier. There they are, right there. They developed a new motorized chair to help a classmate with disabilities and won a grant competition as a result. They did not have a lot of money to do this. They didn't have a lot of advantages in life. In fact, the first time they were ever on an airplane was when they flew to present their invention. But they did have a desire to work together to help a friend and to build something that never existed before.

And by the way, the way they funded their project—they had—they and their folks made tamales. They had a huge tamale-making session and were selling them. And they were showing me the video of how they raised the funds to be able to enter in this competition. Unbelievable.

That's not just the power of science. That's the promise of America. Anybody with a good idea can prosper. Anybody with talent can succeed. That's why we're here today. That's what we're all celebrating. And that's why it's so important that we promote math education and science education, on behalf of not just this generation, but all the generations to follow.

So to all the young people who are here, I could not be prouder of you. I expect some of you to be back here as Nobel Prize winners and whatnot. In the meantime, just keep on doing what you're doing.

And to the parents and the teachers who have helped to inspire these young people, thank you. What you're doing is paying huge dividends not just for the young people themselves, but for the country. We're very proud of you.

Thank you, everybody.

NOTE: The President spoke at 12:30 p.m. in the East Room at the White House. In his remarks, he referred to Nobel Prize winners Baruch S. Blumberg, John C. Mather, and Harold E. Varmus; William S. Nye, television personality and executive director of the Planetary Society; science fair student participants Amy Chyao of Plano, TX, Mathilda Lloyd of Kingston, TN, and Samuel Snodgrass and Sonja Solomon of Oak Ridge, TN; Sergey Brin and Larry Page, cofounders, Google Inc.; Steven P. Jobs and Stephen G. Wozniak, cofounders, Apple Inc.; and Paul G. Allen and William H. Gates III, cofounders, Microsoft Corporation.

Remarks at a Democratic Senatorial Campaign Committee Dinner in Rockville, Maryland
October 18, 2010

Good evening, everybody. Thank you so much. It is wonderful to see all of you. Rajeev and Seema and your wonderful children, thank you for your extraordinary hospitality and bringing your mom, who I love. It's wonderful to see her. And, Seema, your parents, it's wonderful to meet them as well.

I want to, before I begin, just say that, Maryland, you are graced with two of the finest Senators in the United States Senate in Barbara Mikulski and Ben Cardin. We are so proud of them. Everything that I've been able to accomplish over the last couple of years has been because I had just great partners. And these are two of the best partners, and they were also wonderful colleagues when I was in the United States Senate. And so I am just truly blessed to have them with me.

Rajeev's introduction was so eloquent, I almost don't want to add to it. But I think that he touched on the essence of what this upcoming election is about and what this historical moment is about.

Most of us here came from someplace else, or our parents came from someplace else, or our grandparents, our great-grandparents came from someplace else. And they were inspired by a particular idea, this idea of America. As wonderful as the land is here in the United States, as much as we have been blessed by the bounty of this magnificent continent that stretches from the Atlantic to the Pacific, what makes this place special is not something physical. It has to do with this idea that was started by Thirteen Colonies that decided to throw off the yoke of an empire and said, "We hold these truths to be self-evident, that all men are created equal, that each of us are endowed with certain inalienable rights, that among these are life, liberty, and the pursuit of happiness."

And that idea, over the course of 200-plus years, evolved into an understanding—not just here in America, but around the world—that in the United States, if you were willing to make the effort, if you're willing to apply the energy that your parents applied when they came here, if you were willing to make sacrifices for the future and not just think about short-term gain, that somehow it would be possible for you to achieve dreams that someplace else you might never imagine possible.

And that American Dream is what inspired me and, I suspect, inspired Barbara and Ben, to get into public service, because what we understood was that although the essence of the American Dream is that each individual can succeed, what underwrites that dream is also the understanding that we're all in this together and that it's incumbent upon us to make sure that we're creating the climate, the environment, the opportunity for everybody to succeed, not just some people to succeed. There's no caste system in the United States of America. Anybody who is willing to make the effort can succeed.

And part of why this is such an important historical moment is, frankly, over the last decade, that idea that ended up creating this emerging middle class that became the engine of our economic growth and the envy of the world has been pretty hard hit. Obviously, it's been hard hit by this recession, but I want to go before the recession. The period from 2001 to 2009, every middle class family lost about 5 percent of its income. During that same period, job growth was more sluggish than it had been at any time since World War II. There was a sense on the part of,

I think, a lot of ordinary Americans that no matter how hard they tried, it was becoming more and more difficult to make it.

And the things that helped to make America the envy of the world—our infrastructure, our education system, our health care systems—all those things had become—had begun to break down in pretty substantial ways, so that whereas we used to rank number one in the proportion of college graduates, by 2009, 2010, we ranked 9th or 10th. Our students now rank—15-year-olds typically rank 21st in science and 25th in math in the world, where we used to be number one.

Our health care system was broken, wildly expensive, leaving 30 million without health insurance and burdening families, businesses, and the Federal Treasury, as well as State treasuries.

Our infrastructure, which used to be the best in the world, suddenly we have bridges that are falling apart, airports that are outdated and making a very unpleasant experience for those of you who still have to travel through commercial flights. I've got to admit I've got my own plane now, so it's a little easier for me. [*Laughter*]

And so when I ran for President 2 years ago, we already knew that we had to change direction, that we had to deal with some of these fundamental challenges that we've been putting off for years: education, energy, health care, infrastructure. We had to make sure that we were creating an environment in which people could, in fact, succeed, and they were rewarded for their hard work and their responsibility, not for reckless risk-taking, not for short-term thinking.

This was all before the crisis hit, the worst financial crisis that we've experienced since the Great Depression. So my first job, Barbara's first job, Ben's first job when we got back in—when I was sworn in, in January of 2009, we had lost 4 million jobs in the 6 months that preceded me being sworn in, 750,000 the month that I was sworn in, 600,000 the month after that, 600,000 the month after that. My first job was to stop the crisis.

And we did that. And sometimes that took some unpopular decisions. But I wasn't elected to do what was easy, I was elected to do what

was right. And so since that time, over the course of 20 months, whereas we were—the economy was shrinking when I took office, the economy is now growing again. Where we were losing jobs, we've now seen 9 consecutive months of public sector job growth—of private sector job growth.

So not only did we deal with the crisis, but we also started finally making progress on all those things that we've been putting off. So Rajeev talked about clean energy and the efforts of his company. One of our first tasks in the Recovery Act was figuring out how do we not only boost demand and make sure that we're dealing with this crisis, but also how do we invest in some long-term thinking. And so we made the largest clean energy investment in our history.

Then we said if we really want to jump-start education, what do we need to do? And we started something called Race to the Top that is now investing in competition in States all across the country, making sure that they're focused on proven mechanisms to boost math learning and science learning and make sure that we've got the best possible teachers in the classroom.

And then we said, well, how do we make sure that every young person can go to college once they get through that high school? And we shifted billions of dollars that were going to banks in the form of unwarranted subsidies, and we took that money and we made sure that that money was going directly to student loans and Pell grants so that young people would never feel as if they were barred from opportunity simply because they didn't come from a wealthy family.

And yes, then we took on health care because we understood that if we didn't start taking it on now we would continue to see a system in which we were subsidizing a system that wasn't working for too many Americans and too many businesses. And because of those efforts we now can say to the American people that if you don't have health insurance, you're going to be able to get health insurance that's affordable. And if you do have health insurance, then insurance companies are going to have to treat you fairly. And in the process, we're going to start making the system overall more efficient so that suddenly doctors and hospitals are thinking in more innovative ways about how we can improve system deliveries, and we suddenly are investing in health information technology, so instead of having multiple tests, you can take one test and have it e-mailed to every doctor and specialist that you're dealing with, and that over time we're going to bring down the cost of health care for everybody.

All these efforts we made because we had folks like Ben and Barbara there who were willing to think not about the next election, but about the next generation. And that's a hard thing for politicians to do because we live in an environment in which politics has become meaner and coarser than it used to be; where millions of dollars of negative ads are thrown at candidates; where, frankly, what used to be a spirit of occasional bipartisanship in order to get things done has now given way to constant partisanship, so that over the last 2 years, we've had Republicans not supporting us even on issues that they used to sponsor simply because these were issues that we supported.

So it's not easy for elected officials to think long term. And yet because of the challenges we face, because or the emergency situation we were in, that's what we saw a whole bunch of legislators do. And I couldn't be prouder of what we accomplished together over the last 2 years.

What we also know, though, is our work is unfinished. We were just talking about clean energy. The fact of the matter is, we still don't have an overarching energy policy that makes sense for the future—for the 21st century. So we've got to make more investments in innovation, in research and development in clean energy, because I want the solar panels and the wind turbines and the biodiesel and other clean energy approaches that are available. I want those investments made right here in the United States of America. And in order for us to do that, I've got to have a Congress that again is willing to think long term.

We've still got a lot more work to do with respect to education reform. And when I see my Republican colleagues suggesting that we might cut education spending by 20 percent, at a time when I know that China and South Korea and Germany are not cutting education by 20 percent. They understand this is going to be the single most important determinant of how well we're able to compete in the 21st century. And I know that I've got to have some partners in Congress who understand what's at stake.

We've got to rebuild our infrastructure. We just got started with the Recovery Act. Even though I know that there's a lot of road work being done all across the country and here in Maryland as well, we still have $2 trillion worth of infrastructure that's crumbling, unattended to, that we're going to have to rebuild. And what an opportunity—at a time when interest rates are low, when contractors are coming in under budget, people are desperate for work, construction workers have been laid off because the housing bubble burst—for us to put those folks back to work doing the work that America needs done.

We've still got to get control of our deficit in a serious way. And that's going to require more than just platitudes, it's going to require tough choices. And the question is going to be, do we have people in place who are making those choices not based on what's politically expedient or what special interests are lobbying for, but rather what's good for America over the long term?

So we've got a lot of work to do. I try to explain to folks who, in a town like Washington where everybody is watching the polls day to day and everybody is obsessed with sort of short-term thinking, I try to explain, we're just in the first quarter. We've got a big chunk of the game left to play. And I need to have teammates who are thinking about that story that Rajeev told, that essential part of America that we have to make sure is there for the next generation, for these young people, an America in which everybody has opportunity.

And that's what this election is about. That's the choice in this election. Now, this is a difficult political environment right now. Unemployment is still 9.6 percent. And that means it doesn't matter how good of a job you've done, people want to know what are you going to do now.

And the way I've been describing it around the country, it's as if the Republicans drove the economy into the ditch. And Barbara and Ben and me, we've gone into the ditch, and we've been pushing the car out. [*Laughter*] And we finally got the car out, and the Republicans suddenly tap us on the shoulder and say, "Well, we want the keys back," after not having lifted a finger to help us get the car out of the ditch. And we have to explain to them, "Well, you know, you can't have the keys back because you don't know how to drive." [*Laughter*] You can drive with us. You can—we'll have to put you in the backseat. [*Laughter*]

But it's still a challenging environment. And so the support that you're providing is going to make a difference in us making the case for why we've got to keep moving forward, why we can't go backwards, why we can't go back to the economic policies that resulted in this mess in the first place.

And I am absolutely confident that if all of you are talking to your friends and talking to your neighbors and talking to your coworkers, if we have the resources to be able to get our message out—not just here in Maryland, but all across the country—that the American people, they still want to dream big. They still believe in that story that Rajeev told because they know that it was true for their family as well. It's been true for generations of Americans.

I'll close just by telling a quick story about the highlight not just of my day but probably of my week, maybe of my month.

We hosted a science fair today at the White House. This is the first time that we'd ever hosted a science fair at the White House. And the reason we did it was because I kept on having over these championship basketball teams and football teams. We had the Alabama Crimson Tide. We had the New Orleans Saints. We had the Los Angeles Lakers. And it's a lot of fun having these great sports teams come by. And I said, but how about all these kids who are involved in science and math and engineering? Why aren't we celebrating them?

So we hosted this science fair. And they actually set up exhibits in the State Dining Room. And this was just a sampling of some of the young people that we'd invited. And you walk through, and at each booth, you met the most amazing young people you would ever care to meet.

There was a team from Tennessee that had designed a self-powered water filtration plant. It had a water wheel on it, and it ran the battery that then filtered the water. And they explained that up in the Appalachian regions, a lot of homes still didn't have clean water and this was a cheap way to do it. For a thousand bucks, you could provide all the water that 60 or 70 families needed. Just designed it—high school kids.

You had robots that were running around doing all kinds of things. [*Laughter*] And there was a family—young children who had emigrated from Turkey that were now in public schools here, and they had designed a whole town that would be more energy efficient and had created a whole model for how it could be done.

And then there was this—the last person I spoke to was a young woman, looked like she was of Chinese heritage, lived in Dallas, 16 years old. When she was a freshman in high school, she studied biology and became interested in life sciences and became interested in cancer research. So she decided during the summer to teach herself chemistry—[*laughter*]—taught herself chemistry and designed as a science project exploration of the development of a new cancer drug, based on some experimental cancer drugs that are currently being put together that involve injecting the drug and then it's activated by light. And it allows a more localized treatment that isolates the cancer cells—kills the cancer cells, but leaves the healthy cells untouched.

And the problem is clinical trials and treatments have shown that it's okay for skin cancer and other diseases where they're close to the surface, but it's harder to penetrate. Bottom line is she decided she was going to design a new drug that would work better for harder-to-reach cancers, having taught herself chemistry—[*laughter*]—at 16 years old.

She went on to win the international science competition. And now she and her teacher, her high school science teacher, are being approached by laboratories all across the country who want to collaborate with them in thinking about this new potential breakthrough cancer drug.

So I'm talking to her, pretending like I understand everything that she's saying. [*Laughter*] And I'm thinking to myself, think about what this means. You've got the portrait of Lincoln in the State Dining Room looking down over us. You've got an African American President named Barack Obama. You've got a young Chinese American girl, 16 years old, who is designing cancer drugs, having taught herself chemistry in high school. That idea of America is alive and well. But we have to nurture it, and we have to sustain it.

And for all the meanness of our political season and the yelling and nonsense that we see day in and day out on television, that is something that is worth remembering, because I think sometimes during difficult times, some of us may get discouraged or lose heart.

I don't want you to be discouraged. Just think about those young people, think about the young people who are here. Think about Rajeev and his family and Seema and her family, and think about Barbara and Ben and their families, when they emigrated. That story continues. We just have to build on it. We have to have confidence in it.

And we have to remember that as long as we're unified as opposed to divided, as long as we think towards the future and not just toward the present, that America will prosper and that the 21st century will be the American century, just as the 20th was.

Thank you so much, everybody. God bless you.

NOTE: The President spoke at 8:03 p.m. at the residence of Rajeev and Seema Sharma. In his remarks, he referred to White House science fair student participants Mathilda Lloyd of Kingston, TN, Samuel Snodgrass and Sonja Solomon of Oak Ridge, TN, and Amy Chyao and her chemistry teacher, Vashka Desai, of T.H. Williams High School in Plano, TX. The transcript was released by the Office of the Press Secretary on October 19.

Remarks on Signing an Executive Order Renewing the White House Initiative on Educational Excellence for Hispanics
October 19, 2010

Excellent. Everybody, please be seated. Welcome to the White House, everybody. Thank you, Javier, for that outstanding introduction. I will not play you chess. [*Laughter*] You may not have won at the nationals, but you'd beat me. [*Laughter*] And then Malia and Sasha would laugh about it. [*Laughter*] We are very proud of you, and we're glad you are here.

Thank you also to the University of Texas-Pan American Mariachis that performed for us. And hello to everybody across the country participating in watch parties and in education reform efforts in your own communities. It's precisely that kind of participation—engaging the American people, giving all of you more say in the policies that affect your lives, and holding ourselves accountable to deliver real results in return—that is at the heart of a new Executive order I'm about to sign to strengthen the White House Initiative on Educational Excellence for Hispanics.

Now, before I sign this document, I'd like to acknowledge a few people who have been and will continue to be instrumental to our success: our Assistant Secretary for Elementary and Secondary Education, Thelma Melendez de Santa Ana; our Assistant Secretary for Post-Secondary Education, Eduardo Ochoa; and our Assistant Deputy Secretary, Rosalinda Barrera.

I also want to thank Eduardo Padron, the president of Miami Dade Community College, who has been a leader in my administration's efforts to strengthen America's community colleges. And because that's not enough, in addition to running a community college, he's also agreed to serve as the Chair of this initiative's Presidential advisory commission. So we are grateful to you. This will be a group of 30 Latino leaders who are going to make sure that, when it comes to our children's education, my administration hears the voices of the Latino community loud and clear.

And I also want to give a special recognition to our recently confirmed Ambassador to the Dominican Republic, Raul Yzaguirre. It was Raul's vision and tenacious commitment to equal education for all our people that helped this initiative become a reality back in 1990 under George H.W. Bush. And so we are very proud that he is here today to see that his work continues.

The question then back in 1990 is the same question we face now: How do we best improve educational opportunities and outcomes for our Hispanic students? Over the past year and a half, under Juan Sepulveda's leadership—and Juan, thank you for your outstanding work— over the last year and a half, this initiative has worked to gather the answers from those who know best, people in communities across this country. Juan hosted more than a hundred conversations. He's taken comments from more than 10,000 Americans. And he's worked with leaders from more than 30 States, as well as the District of Columbia and Puerto Rico, to come up with real solutions that work best for our kids.

We know why this is so important. Today, Latinos make up the largest minority group in America's schools—more than one in five students overall—and they face challenges of monumental proportions. Latino students are more likely to attend our lowest performing schools, more likely to learn in larger class sizes, more likely to drop out at higher rates. Fewer than half take part in early childhood education. Only about half graduate on time from high school. And those who do make it to college often find themselves underprepared for its rigors. In just a single generation, America has fallen from first to ninth in college completion rates for all our students.

Now, this is not just a Latino problem, this is an American problem. We've got to solve it because if we allow these trends to continue, it won't just be one community that falls behind, we will all fall behind together. At a time when the unemployment rate for Americans who've never gone to college is almost double what it is for those who have gone to college, when most of the new jobs that are being created require some higher education, when other countries are outeducating us today to outcompete us tomorrow, making sure that we offer all our kids, regardless of race, a world-class education is more than a moral obligation. It is an economic imperative if we want to succeed in the 21st century.

And that's why, when I took office, I set two big goals for American education. One was to make sure all our students, like the ones who are here with us today, receive a complete and competitive education from cradle to career. And number two, by the year 2020—the year Javier will graduate from college—America will once again have a higher share of college graduates than any other nation on Earth. That is our goal.

Now, improving educational outcomes for the Hispanic community is critical to reaching these overall goals. And reaching these goals is behind every battle that we've waged on behalf of our children's education since I took office.

We are expanding and reforming early childhood education so that our children aren't behind by the time they reach the schoolhouse door. We're challenging programs that don't measure up to compete for their funding, because if you're receiving tax dollars, you'd better be able to deliver results for our children.

We've launched a Race to the Top encouraging States to change their schools from the bottom up for all our children, Black, White, and Latino alike. Already, 48 States and DC have competed to raise standards, improve curricula, and turn around struggling schools. And we'll take steps to recruit and train more good teachers, including bilingual teachers.

We're tackling the dropout crisis that affects the Hispanic community more than any other community. And we're challenging States and communities to turn around our 5,000 worst schools, including many of the ones that produce the most Latino and African American dropouts.

To reach the second goal that I've set, leading the world in the proportion of college graduates, we're offering middle class families the American opportunity tax credit, which is a tax credit worth up to $2,500 a year that's already helped put the dream of a college degree within the reach of more than 12 million students from working families.

We're upgrading our community colleges so that we can link students looking for work with businesses looking to hire. We're funding and implementing the post-9/11 GI bill so our veterans, including our outstanding Latino veterans, can come home to the same chance to earn a college education as my grandfather had when he came back from World War II.

We're eliminating $60 billion over the next decade in wasteful giveaways to banks that profited from a broken student loan system, and we're using that money to make college more affordable for millions of students. In fact, we estimate that these steps will make college more affordable for more than 150,000 additional Latino students.

And as I've said before, Congress should finally pass the "DREAM Act." I've supported this bill—[*applause*]—I have supported this bill for years, and I'll do everything it takes to sign it into law on behalf of students seeking a college education and those who wish to serve in our country's uniform.

Turning around our troubled schools, putting the dream of a college education within the reach of working families, educating our kids—all of them—to graduate ready for college, ready for a career, ready to make the most of their lives, that's what we're doing. That is why we're here.

But while strengthening Hispanic education in America is the purpose of this initiative, it's not something that can fall on the Department of Education alone. I expect agencies across the Federal Government to take this initiative seriously and support its mission. And it's also not something the Government can do by itself. It's going to take all of us—public and private sectors, teachers and principals, all of you at home at those watch parties, parents getting involved in their kids' education and students giving their best—because the farther they go in school, the farther they will go in life, and that means the farther we'll go as a country.

Now I know there will be cynics out there who say that this improvement that we're seeking is not possible, that the reforms won't work, the problems in our education system are too entrenched. It's easy to think that way. This initiative, for example, has been around for 20 years, and we still face many of the same challenges. And it's true, as I've said ever since I ran for this office—and as everyone here knows firsthand—that change is hard. Change takes time. Fixing what is broken in our education system will not be easy. We won't see results overnight. It may take years, even decades, for all these changes to pay off.

But that's no reason not to get started. That's no reason not to strive for these changes. That's a reason for us, in fact, to start making them right now. It's a reason for us to follow through. And as long as I'm President, I will not give in to calls to shortchange any of our students.

So in the end, this is about building a brighter future where every child in this country—Black, White, Latino, Asian, or Native American; regardless of color, class, creed—has a chance to rise above any barrier to fulfill their God-given potential. It's about keeping the promise at the heart of this country that we love. The promise of a better life, the promise that our children will dream bigger, hope deeper, climb higher than we could ever imagine, that's the promise that so many of you work to advance each and every day in your own respective fields. And as long as I have the privilege of being your President, that's a promise that I intend to work to keep.

Thank you very much, everybody. Now I'm going to sign this initiative. Thank you.

NOTE: The President spoke at 2:11 p.m. in the East Room at the White House. In his remarks, he referred to Javier Garcia, student, Stell Middle School in Brownsville, TX; and Juan Sepulveda, Director, White House Initiative on Educational Excellence for Hispanic Americans. The Office of the Press Secretary also released a Spanish language transcript of these remarks. The Executive order is listed in Appendix D at the end of this volume.

Statement on the Settlement in the *Keepseagle* Class-Action Lawsuit on Discrimination by the Department of Agriculture
October 19, 2010

Today the Department of Agriculture and the Department of Justice announced a settlement agreement with the plaintiffs in the *Keepseagle* class-action lawsuit. This suit was originally filed in 1999 by Native American farmers alleging discrimination in access to and participation in USDA's farm loan programs. With today's agreement, we take an important step forward in remedying USDA's unfortunate civil rights history.

I applaud Secretary Vilsack and Attorney General Holder for their hard work to reach this settlement, a settlement that helps strengthen the nation-to-nation relationship and underscores the Federal Government's commitment to treat all citizens fairly. In light of that commitment, Congress must also act to implement the historic settlements of the *Pigford II* lawsuit brought by African American farmers and the *Cobell* lawsuit brought by Native Americans over the management of Indian trust accounts and resources. My administration also continues to work towards a resolution of the claims made by women and Hispanic farmers against the USDA.

Remarks at a Rally for Governor John Kitzhaber in Portland, Oregon
October 20, 2010

The President. Hello, Portland! Thank you! Thank you very much, everybody. It is good to be back in the State of Oregon. And it is an honor to be standing here with your next Governor, John Kitzhaber.

Audience member. We love you!

The President. I love you back. Great to be here.

Now, I have to first of all say, look, I've got a special place in my heart for Oregon. My best friend from high school lives in Eugene and is a big Ducks fan. So he's got season tickets. I'm always getting some e-mail from him about how good they're doing. Congratulations.

Now, on the other hand, my brother-in-law happens to be the coach of the Beavers. But I'm not confused. [*Laughter*] I root for them both. I've got the whole State covered.

We've got some wonderful guests here. You may have heard from a couple of them, but I want to make sure that you hear—that I have a chance to introduce them. First of all, your outstanding senior Senator, Ron Wyden, is in the house. Give him a big round of applause. Your outstanding junior Senator, Jeff Merkley, is here. My great friend and one of my earliest supporters who always has that little bike thing on his lapel—[*laughter*]—Earl Blumenauer is here. One of his outstanding partners in the House of Representatives, is doing a great job, David Wu is here.

Audience members. Wu! Wu! Wu!

The President. Wu! Wu, Wu, Wu. Just want everybody—I want all the press to be clear, they were saying, "Wu." [*Laughter*] Secretary of State Kate Brown is here. State Treasurer Ted Wheeler is here. And Attorney General Kroger is here.

Now, Portland, let's talk about this Governor's race for a second. This should not be a difficult choice. [*Laughter*] This should not be a difficult choice. I know you have a race where both candidates are talking about change. But there's only one candidate who's actually delivered change. And that's John Kitzhaber.

When John—you know John's track record. When John was Governor, this economy grew, created more than 120,000 new jobs. When John was Governor, he increased access to health care for thousands of children. When John was Governor, he invested in education and improved Oregon's public schools. When John was Governor, he protected the environment of one of the most beautiful States in the

Nation, brought clean energy industries to Oregon.

I have heard that John is an outstanding fly fisherman. Another reason to vote for him. That's why he cares about the environment so much. He's out there. And if you send in your ballot for John, this State will continue to be on the cutting edge of America's future. That's what you know.

I mean, look, here is a guy who has already done the job and done it well. After John last served as Governor, he was a national leader on health care. He could have gone anywhere. He could have done anything, but he chose to stay here because his commitment to Oregon is personal. As an emergency room doctor, as a legislator, as a Governor, as a father, he spent his life fighting for the people of Oregon. That's why you need him again. You need him one more time.

Now, I just want to say I'm getting a cold. I'm actually getting over it, but I would suspect by the end of this speech, I am going to be hoarse. [*Laughter*] But I know it won't matter because you are going to be fired up, even if you can't hear me.

You're going to be fired up. Because in less than 2 weeks—in less than 2 weeks, you can set the direction of this State and this country not just for the next 2 years, not for the next 4 years, not just for the next 10 years, for the next 20 years. Just like you did in 2008, you can defy the conventional wisdom. Yes, you can. Yes, you can.

Audience members. Yes, we can! Yes, we can! Yes, we can!

The President. I think they're fired up!

Audience members. Yes, we can! Yes, we can! Yes, we can!

The President. You can defy the conventional wisdom because you know what the conventional wisdom always is. They say you can't overcome the cynicism of politics. No, you can't overcome the special interests. No, you can't overcome the big money. No, you can't overcome the negative ads. No, you can't. No, you can't. No, you—there's always somebody out there saying, no, you can't. But in 2 weeks, you've got a chance to say, yes, we can.

There is—look, now, I want to be clear, though. There's no doubt this is a difficult election. I know you guys love your Trail Blazers. I understand. That's okay. And we've been through an incredibly difficult time as a nation. But I want you to think about how we got here.

For most of the last decade, middle class families saw their incomes actually fall. Between 2001 and 2009, the average middle class family saw their income fall 5 percent when the other party was in charge. We had the most sluggish job growth since the Great Depression in those 8 years when the other party was in charge. Meanwhile, your cost of health care skyrocketed. Your cost of sending your kids to college skyrocketed. Too many jobs were shipped overseas. Too many parents weren't sure whether if their child got sick they could send them to a doctor.

Americans were working two jobs or three jobs just to make ends meet. And then all of this finally culminated in the worst economic crisis since the Great Depression. And I want everybody to understand that this recession started long before I took office. We had lost—we lost 4 million jobs in the 6 months before I was sworn in, 750,000 the month I was sworn in, 600,000 the month after that, 600,000 the month after that. We lost almost 8 million jobs, most of them lost before any of our economic policies were put into place.

Now, you would have thought that given the crisis, when we got to Washington Democrats and Republicans would come together, we'd put politics aside and deal with this once-in-a-generation challenge. I hoped, I expected that we could move beyond the game-playing and the partisanship and the bickering that had dominated for Washington so long, roll up our sleeves, and get to work. Because although we are proud to be Democrats, we are prouder to be Americans. And all of us have a stake in creating a better future.

But the Republican leaders in Washington, they made a different decision.

Audience members. Boo!

The President. Look, now, here's what they calculated—and it was a clever political calculation. They said to themselves, boy, we made such a big mess—[*laughter*]—we are in such a deep hole that it's going to take everything Obama's got just to try to get us out of it. It's going to take some time to repair the economy. Folks are going to be frustrated and angry. And if we just sit on the sidelines and oppose Obama and Democrats every step of the way, if we say no even to the policies that traditionally we've supported to help small businesses or to cut taxes, then maybe we can ride people's anger and frustration; they'll forget that we were the ones who caused this thing in the first place.

In other words, Oregon, their working theory was—the basis of their campaign is amnesia. [*Laughter*] They figure you're going to forget because you're angry about the situation.

I understand that. But make no mistake, this election isn't about anger, it's not about fear. This election is a choice. And the stakes could not be higher. If they win this election, then you know that the other guy's priorities are going to be different than John's.

Nationally, if they win this election, the chair of the Republican campaign committee promised to pursue the "exact same agenda" that they did before I took office.

Audience members. Boo!

The President. No, no. And we know what this agenda is. I mean, there are no surprises here unless you've forgotten, unless you're suffering from amnesia.

Audience members. No!

The President. Let's see, we'll cut taxes for millionaires and billionaires; that's part of their agenda.

Audience members. Boo!

The President. We will cut rules for special interests, including polluters.

Audience members. Boo!

The President. We'll cut middle class families loose to fend for themselves.

Audience members. Boo!

The President. So if you're somebody with a preexisting condition, can't get health care, tough luck, you're on your own. That's their theory. If you can't find a job, tough luck, you're on your own. If you're a young person who can't afford a college education, tough luck, you're on your own. That's their theory.

Audience members. No!

The President. And by the way, these are the same folks who say that they're concerned about debt and the deficit. Except it turns out that they took a record surplus from a Democratic President and created a record deficit and helped nearly destroy our economy. You can't forget. This is similar to the agenda that John's opponent wants to pursue right here in Oregon.

And, Portland, it is up to you to tell them we haven't forgotten. We don't have amnesia. And we don't want what you're selling, because we've tried it before and we didn't like it because it didn't work.

We don't want them rolling back health reform, so insurance companies can deny you coverage because you're sick. We don't want them rolling back Wall Street reform, so now credit card companies can go back to hitting you with hidden fees and penalties. We don't want their plan to cut education by 20 percent so they can give a $700 billion tax break to the wealthiest 2 percent of Americans.

Audience members. No!

The President. We have tried that before, and we're not going back.

So look, obviously, we've got a long way to go. We've got a lot of work to do. That's why John wants to run. That's why John got in this race, because he knows Oregon needs you; he knows Oregon needs his experience, his wisdom, his compassion.

And look, we know we've got a lot of work to do, but the economy is growing again. The private sector has created jobs for 9 months in a row. But we've got a lot of work to do. There's still a lot of people hurting out there. And there are a lot of people hurting right here in Oregon. That's what keeps me up at night. That's what keeps me fighting. That's what keeps John up at night.

But I also—I know this: The biggest mistake we can do right now is go back to the same policies that caused all this hurt in the first place. And I say this not because I want to relitigate the past. I just don't want to relive the past.

Oregon, imagine the Republicans driving a car into the ditch. [*Laughter*] And it's a deep ditch. And so we decided, well, we got to go get that car out of the ditch. And so me and Wyden and Merkley and Wu and Blumenauer and the Democrats, we went down there, we put on our boots. It was muddy down there. It's hot. There are bugs everywhere. [*Laughter*] But we knew we had to get that car out of the ditch. So we start pushing on that car. We start pushing and pushing. And every once in a while we look and the Republicans are up there, just standing there. [*Laughter*] Not lifting a finger. [*Laughter*] And we—and we tell them, why don't you come down and help, because you all got the car into the ditch? They say, no, that's all right, but you need to push harder. You're not pushing the right way. [*Laughter*]

So we just kept on pushing. And finally, we get this car up on level ground. Finally, it's pointing in the right direction. It's a little banged up. It needs to go to the body shop. It needs a tuneup. But we're pointed in the right direction. And suddenly, we get this tap on our shoulder, and we look back, and who is it? It's the Republicans. And they're saying to us, Oregon, we want the keys back. And we got to tell them, you can't have the keys back because you don't know how to drive. You don't know!

Have you ever noticed, when you want to go forward in the car, you got to put your car in "D." [*Laughter*] When you go backwards, you put it in "R." We don't want to go back into the ditch. And the Republicans, they can come with us, but they're going to have to sit in the backseat.

Look, John and I, we've got a different idea about what the future should look like. And it's an idea rooted in our belief about how this country was built and what we've seen in our own lives. Look, we know that government doesn't solve every problem out there. We believe that government should be lean and efficient. But in the words of the first Republican President, Abraham Lincoln—who, by the way, would have trouble getting a nomination in the Republican Party right now—Honest Abe said that government should do for people what they cannot do better for themselves.

So we believe in a country that rewards hard work and responsibility. We believe in a country that prizes innovation and entrepreneurship.

But we also believe in a country where we look after one another, where we say, I am my brother's keeper, I am my sister's keeper. That's the America I know. That's the choice in this election.

We see a future where the next century is driven by American innovation, American ingenuity. We're investing in science and technology. And we no longer are giving tax breaks to companies that ship jobs overseas. We give our tax breaks to companies that are investing right here in Oregon, right here in the United States, to small businesses, to American manufacturers, to clean energy companies. I don't want solar panels or wind turbines or electric cars made in Europe or Asia. I want them made here in the United States of America with American workers. That's the choice in this election.

We see an America where every single American—every—everybody has the skills and the training to compete with any worker in the world.

Now, the other side might think it's a good idea to cut education by 20 percent. But you know what? China is not cutting its education budget by 20 percent. Korea is not cutting it by 20 percent. Germany is not cutting it by 20 percent. They're not playing for second place. The United States of America doesn't play for second place. We play for first place. And that means training our kids to compete.

That's why tens of billions of dollars in taxpayer subsidies that used to go to big banks, because they were the middlemen in the student loan program, even though they weren't taking any risks. That money we took and we sent it where it should be going, to students and to families. That's why we intend to make our new college tax credit permanent, worth $10,000 in tuition relief for every student, whether you are a Duck or a Beaver or any other college student here.

We see an America where opportunity is shared and the middle class is growing, where the only limit to your success is how hard you're willing to try. And that's why we want to give tax cuts to middle class families and make those permanent. That's why we believe in making sure Social Security is there not just for this generation, but for the next generation, and we will not privatize Social Security. The last thing we want to do is hand it over to Wall Street.

We believe—yes, we believe in making sure that we leave clean air and clean water for the next generation, that Oregon is as beautiful 50 years from now as it is today. And that means working with a partner in the statehouse to make sure that we're enforcing laws against pollution. That's the choice in this election. That's what we're fighting for.

But right now the same special interests that would profit from the other side's agenda, they're fighting back hard. To win this election, they are plowing tens of millions of dollars through front groups. They're running misleading negative ads all across America.

And these folks, they don't disclose who the donors are. They've got these innocent-sounding names—Americans for Prosperity or Moms for Motherhood. [*Laughter*] I made that last one up. [*Laughter*] But you don't know where this money is coming from. It could be insurance companies, Wall Street banks. It could be foreign-controlled corporations. We don't know.

This is not just a threat to Democrats, this is a threat to democracy. And the only way to fight it, the only way to match millions of dollars in negative ads is with millions of voices of people who care and want to finish what we started in 2008.

That's where you come in. That's where you come in. We need you all to mail in your ballots now. Mail them in. If everybody who fought for change in 2008 shows up to vote in 2010, then John is going to win his election.

But you got to mail in that ballot. Let me just see a show of hands. Who hasn't mailed in their ballots yet? Fess up. Come on, guys. Let's go. Let's go. You just got it? All right, well, go tomorrow then.

But you have to vote. You have to vote. Look, a lot of you got involved in 2008 because you believed that we were at a defining moment in our history. You believed that the decisions we make right now won't just affect us, they'll affect our kids and our grandkids, for decades to come. That's why you knocked on doors. That's why you made phone calls and talked to your

friends and neighbors. Some of you voted for the very first time, because you believed you could play a part in shaping history.

So now we're in the process—not just talking about change, now we're in the process of bringing about change. But you know what? It's hard. I said it was going to be hard during the campaign. Some of you didn't believe me. [*Laughter*] It's hard. We're grinding it out, inch by inch, day by day, week by week, month by month. There are—and this is a big, messy democracy. And so people get into arguments and folks push back. And the special interests, they don't go down without a fight. It is not easy.

And that means that sometimes it can wear you down. And all that hope that we felt when we had that 70,000-person rally in Portland on that beautiful day, or some of that hope that we had on election night, or some of that hope that we had on Inauguration Day when Beyonce was singing and Bono was singing and everything was great, sometimes that fades.

And then you see—some of you see family members who still haven't found a job, or you see another foreclosure sign in a house down the street. And you're seeing all these negative ads and you're seeing pundits tearing folks down and you just get discouraged and turned off.

But here's the thing I need you to remember. Don't ever let anybody tell you this fight isn't worth it. Don't let them tell you you're not making a difference. Because of you, there are folks all across the country who don't have to choose between losing their home or treating their cancer. Because of you, parents can look their kids in the eye and say, you're going to go to college. Because of you, a business owner got a small-business loan and keeping their doors open. Because of you, 100,000 brave men and women are no longer fighting a war in Iraq. That's because of you.

Don't let them tell you that change isn't possible, because here's what I know. If our parents, if our grandparents, if our great-grandparents listened to the cynics 50 years ago or 100 years ago or 200 years ago, we wouldn't be here tonight. Think about it. Those Thirteen Colonies wouldn't have the courage to start a revolution. Louis and Clark would have never made it out here.

The only reason we are here is because past generations have been unafraid to push forward, to do what's necessary, even in the face of uncertainty, even in the face of difficulty. That's how we came through war and came through depression. That's how we got civil rights and women's rights and workers' rights. That's the spirit we need today, Oregon. That's the spirit we need today, Portland.

The journey we began was not about putting me in the White House, it was about building a movement for change and realizing the promise of America. And if you are willing to keep fighting, and knocking on doors, and making phone calls, and mailing in your ballots, then not only are we going to elect John, but we are going to preserve that American Dream and American promise for centuries to come.

God bless you, and God bless the United States of America.

NOTE: The President spoke at 7:05 p.m. at the Oregon Convention Center. In his remarks, he referred to musicians Beyonce G. Knowles and Paul D. "Bono" Hewson; and Rep. Pete Sessions, in his capacity as chairman of the National Republican Congressional Committee. He also referred to his brother-in-law Craig Robinson, in his capacity as head coach of the Oregon State University men's basketball team.

Remarks and a Question-and-Answer Session in Seattle, Washington
October 21, 2010

The President. Hello, everybody. Have a seat, have a seat. Have a seat. Well, thank you so much for taking the time to be here. And I am just thrilled to be able to join you and have a little conversation in the backyard. And I want to obviously start by thanking the Fosses for their extraordinary hospitality. Give them a big round of applause, not only Cynnie and Erik, but also Anna and Elsa, although they said that since they get out of school today, it's okay. [*Laughter*] They thought that was a pretty good deal. They did not mind.

In addition, I want to make sure that everybody has had a chance to meet your outstanding Senator, Patty Murray, who's here. And I want to see if there are any other elected officials that I've got to introduce. We do have Jim McDermott, who's doing an outstanding job in the House of Representatives. The outstanding mayor of Seattle, Mike McGinn, is here. And one of my favorite Governors in the country, Christine Gregoire, is here.

So we really try to organize these as conversations, as opposed to me making a speech. I'll be making a big speech later. So if you guys want to tune in or anybody wants to come on over, you can check it out. But this is as much an opportunity for me to hear from you as it is a chance for me to speak. But I just want to say a few things up top.

My economic advisers actually put out a report today, and they put out a lot of pieces of paper, but this one we thought was really interesting because it had to do with reflections on what's happening to women in the economy. And obviously, the economy is something that's on everybody's minds right now. It's something that we've been struggling with for the last 2 years since I was first sworn into office.

We had a financial crisis that was unprecedented, the worst financial crisis we had seen since the Great Depression. It caused a massive recession. In the 6 months before I was sworn in, we lost 4 million jobs. We lost 750,000 the month I was sworn in, 600,000 the month after that, 600,000 the month after that. So we lost almost 8 million jobs before any of the economic policies we put into place were able to take effect.

And so we've got a big hole that we're digging ourselves out of, and obviously, everybody here in one way or another has either seen the impact of it or seen the impact on one of your family members or your friends, your community.

Now, it turns out that men have gotten really hard hit in this—during this recession. They've actually lost jobs a little bit faster than women have, particularly in the construction industry because so many of them were involved in the construction trades, and when the housing bubble burst, that really had a significant impact.

But what's interesting is that the economy has changed, where women have made such enormous strides that they now constitute fully half of the workforce. They actually constitute probably more than half of the money that's coming in to middle class families. And business—small-business owners are now a much higher proportion women than they used to be.

And so when you talk about what's happened to the middle class, part of what you're talking about is what's happening to women in the workforce.

We've made enormous strides since the 1960s, when my grandmother was a secretary at a bank and wasn't expected to go to college and had to work her way up until she finally became the vice president of the bank, but still hit a glass ceiling and could never quite go as far as her talents could take her. That's not as true as it used to be. But what is still true is, we still have a significant gender gap when it comes to wages.

Women, because they're running more and more small businesses, are now having a tougher time getting financing and loans than male-owned businesses are. And I think women, because—at least in my household—tend to have a better sense of the family budget, they're mindful of how tough not just this recession has been, but the last decade has been on middle class families. It turns out that from 2001 to 2009, the average middle class family lost 5 percent of their income. Their wages actually went down during that period. And between 2001 and 2009, job growth was actually more sluggish than at any time since World War II, even more sluggish than it's been over the past year.

And so as I travel around the country and I talk to families, what they're concerned about is not just the immediate recovery from the recession, but also what does the future hold in terms of middle class families being able to grow, being able to afford health care, being able to pay the bills, being able to send their kids to college.

Those are the challenges that I think we're going to have to continue to confront.

And we can't confront those unless we understand that our economy works only when everybody's participating. And that means that things like equal pay for equal work aren't just women's issues; those are middle class family issues, because how well women do is—will help determine how well our families are doing as a whole. It means that everybody's got to have access to financing for small businesses. And one of the things we're very proud of over the last couple of years, with the help of people like Patty and Jim, is that we've massively expanded lending to small businesses so that they can help create the kind of opportunities not only for themselves, but also for their workers, that ends up being the driver of our economy.

It means that we've got to make sure that our girls are getting as good of an education as our boys, particularly in math and science, where traditionally they've lagged. And as the father of two daughters, this is something that I spend a lot of time thinking about.

And so with, again, the help of Patty and Jim and others, we've been able to shift billions of dollars that were going to these unwarranted subsidies to banks and now put them directly into the student loan programs and to Pell grants so that more and more people are able to get the kind of higher level training that they need to compete in this new global economy.

So here's the bottom line: Where the economy was shrinking by 6 percent when I took office, the economy is now growing again; where we were losing 750,000 jobs a month, we've now seen 9 consecutive months of private sector job growth. So we've made progress, and we're moving in the right direction. But we've still got a lot of work to do.

And what I want to hear from you about is how you think we can be even more effective in helping you meet the challenges that your families face or your businesses face. We want to partner with the State, we want to partner with cities to figure out how are we fostering economic development that pulls everybody in, because one thing I'm absolutely certain about—and this is one of the reasons I ran for President in the first place—is that America succeeds best when everybody's got a shot, not just when a few are doing well. The beating heart of our economy has always been a growing and expanding middle class, where families are able to see a vision about where they might take their lives and pursue it, and if they work and they put effort into it, then they can succeed. If they—if that happens for everybody, then we all succeed.

And unfortunately, over the last decade, that wasn't what was happening. And it's going to take us some time to turn it around. But I'm confident that we're now moving in the right direction, but we've still got more work to do, which is part of the reason why this election coming up is so important.

But as I said, what I'm really interested in is hearing from you what are the day-to-day concerns and challenges and roadblocks that you see for your success, because that'll help shape how we move our agenda forward over the next couple of years.

Now, what I want to do, if you don't mind, is I'm going to start with a couple of small-business owners who are here, because I think they're indicative of the positive changes that have taken place in the economy. These are women-owned businesses that are doing outstanding work and hiring a lot of people here in the local economy. And then we're just going to open it up, and people can ask questions, give me comments, give me suggestions.

So what I want to do is start with Christina Lomasney, who is the owner of Modumetal. And she's also a physicist, so I think this is very cool because—and so, Christina, tell me a little bit about your business. And then tell me sort of how you think Government can be helpful in seeing Modumetal grow even faster.

Christina Lomasney. Mr. President, as you said, I'm Christina Lomasney. I'm the president of Modumetal, which is a company that's dealing in advanced metals manufacturing in Seattle. I started the company with my cofounder, John Whitaker, in 2007 as an outgrowth of an environmental restoration company called Isotron that I started in 2001.

[*At this point, Ms. Lomasney made brief remarks, concluding as follows.*]

Last year, Modumetal received a grant from the United States Department of Energy that was made possible by the American Recovery and Reinvestment Act, and that grant made it possible for us to conduct some important business development activity—or rather, product development activities inside of the company.

Today, Modumetal employs 25 people, including interns from the university, and we are actively hiring as a result of a collaboration that we recently announced with a major steel company in the United States. I am—I hope to grow the company by about 15 percent over the coming months and am very optimistic about what the future holds for us.

The President. That's great. Congratulations. Now, let me just—on the grant that you received, one of the things that is really important for our economy long term is making sure we're investing in research and development. And the Recovery Act contained probably the biggest increase in research and development funding that we have seen in a very long time.

Just how important is it for you to be able to get that kind of seed money to engage in the new research that you're doing? Because part of what your company is all about is cutting-edge technology, and you can't just keep on doing the same things and expect to be able to compete in the global economy, is that right?

Ms. Lomasney. Absolutely. So seed funding for us is absolutely critical to our ability to build this company. We're starting with, as I mentioned, a new manufacturing technology that we began from scratch from a research concept, and we're building it up now and scaling up the manufacturing.

So these—this investment, this kind of investment and other kinds of investment that occur in our economy are absolutely critical to a company like Modumetal.

The President. That's great. I think—a lot of times I think we get in these ideological arguments about what the Government's role is in the economy. Now, none of us think that Government alone creates jobs. That's not its task.

This economy has always thrived because of the private sector and entrepreneurship and people having an idea and running with it. But what historically has happened is, Government has had an important role in sparking, catalyzing new technologies, new research, that then the private sector is able to take over, part—some—partly because the private sector sometimes isn't willing to invest in really cutting-edge technologies on the front end. They're unproven; they don't want to take the risks.

And so whether it's the Internet or the bar code or you name it, a lot of that initial impulse has come from Government grants and Government funding like this. It doesn't mean that the Government then ends up creating the products or the technologies themselves, but it does give companies like yours a start in terms of being able to move forward.

And so we're very proud of the investments that we've made in research and technology, and we're going to have to keep on doing that in the years to come.

So now—next we've got Jody Hall, who is the owner of Cupcake Royale. I don't know if she brought any samples. [*Laughter*] But just in case any of you are hungry, you might want to pay attention here. Jody?

Jody Hall. Well, thank you so much. It's such an honor to be here. My business is called Cupcake Royale, and I did bring some samples. But you have some fierce security, so somebody might be enjoying them——

The President. They—I suspect Secret Service confiscated them and are now eating them as we speak. [*Laughter*]

Ms. Hall. I see Duncan with a little bit of frosting on his—[*laughter*]. So yes, I did bring you some treats for the First Family as well, because everybody loves cupcakes.

But—so I started my business in 2003. We were actually the first cupcake bakery that I know of that opened outside of Manhattan. And so it was a risky move. I came from corporate America and grew up there and decided to kind of spread my wings and give it a try. And we did really well.

[*Ms. Hall made brief remarks, concluding as follows.*]

So I guess the first thing I want to say is, just very quickly, I worked very hard with Senator Murray to pass and fight for small businesses for health care legislation reform, and you guys passed that, and I just have great respect for that. There is not one small-business owner that I know in the city of Seattle that I connect with that isn't looking forward to the implementation of the exchanges to reduce costs and bring higher quality insurance to small businesses. We need that. So thank you. Just have to say that.

The President. That's great. Good job, Patty.

[*Ms. Hall made further remarks, concluding as follows.*]

Ms. Hall. Patty was a great leader and took a very early start in the Senate, and obviously Congressman McDermott as well. So that said, I also worked with the Government to help me with my business. A year and a half ago, I had the opportunity to buy our fourth retail location in Capitol Hill. We were able to open a bakery and a cafe there. And it allowed us to really grow our business. I did this through the SBA 504 loan, so I was able to purchase a building in Capitol Hill in one of the hottest spots in the city. I was only—I only had to put down 10 percent, versus, if I walked into a bank, probably 25 or 30 percent for somebody in my position and length of business and that kind of thing.

[*Ms. Hall made further remarks, concluding as follows.*]

So in the last 18 months, starting with this loan, we've been able to add 30 jobs. And I'm very proud of that.

And that, plus adding the Salted Caramel the day you were inaugurated, has really helped our business to thrive. [*Laughter*] I hear you're a big fan of salted caramel.

The President. Absolutely. [*Laughter*]

Ms. Hall. And that's what I brought you. So——

The President. Wonderful. Well, thank you so much. This is a wonderful story, Jody. And I just wanted to underscore something: Women-owned businesses have grown significantly faster than small businesses overall. But one of the challenges still ends up being financing.

And one of the things that the Small Business Administration has done really well is that they are three times more likely to provide loans to women-owned businesses than regular banks have been. And so the story that you told about being able to access financing for what obviously is a great product and a great business model is something that we want to continue to emphasize.

We had a big fight, some of you may remember, about a month, month and a half ago, where for 6 months, we'd been advocating getting more financing to small businesses through the SBA and other mechanisms, as well as cutting taxes on small businesses. We finally were able to get that through the Senate thanks to the hard work of folks like Patty. And that means that there are going to be companies like yours all across the country that are really going to be able to benefit.

And I'm really looking forward to trying your cupcakes. [Laughter] So fantastic.

All right, the—now let's just open it up. So you can just raise your hands. We got a couple folks with mikes here. Don't be shy. Even though every word you say will be recorded— [laughter]—by those people back there.

Health Care Reform/Economic Stabilization

Q. Hi, I'm Jordan Royer, and my wife Julianna is here with us. We have two daughters as well. So obviously, what you're talking about—education reform, science, mathematics—all of that is very important to us.

The President. Right.

Q. One of the things that I wanted to ask you, though, is, it seems like in the media, the stuff we're talking about—the health care reform, which we've supported, and some of the other things, the Recovery Act—there's a distortion that's happening on the facts in the media. And the media, in our view—my view—should be a referee on that. And we're not getting that. And I'm just wondering how we can help you, how—what your plan is, and Senator Murray's and the

other elected leaders here. How do we get the facts out to people? Because it really is hurting us that these distortions continue in the public sphere.

The President. Well, look, I appreciate the question. First of all—I'll take health care first. Health care is just really big and complicated, and so the truth of the matter is, we knew going into the debate that it would be subject to distortions, particularly because there were a number of interests out there that were doing pretty well through the status quo.

And it's a multitrillion dollar business. And so if you're going to make significant changes to the system, it's going to have an impact on people's bottom lines. And they're going to fight back. And they did vociferously for a very long time. And that meant it was subject to some misleading information.

As we begin to implement, I think we're going to have a better chance of clarifying what health reform means. So let me be very specific. You've got about 4 million small businesses out there right now—even before we set up the exchanges—who stand to get a tax break of up to 35 percent of the premiums that they're paying if they're already providing health insurance to their employees. So right off the bat, that can mean tens of thousands of dollars that small businesses are able to reinvest in new plants, new equipment, hiring a few extra workers, just because of the tax provisions that were in the health reform act.

Once they start seeing those benefits, it's a little harder for them to argue, boy, this is a terrible thing. Senior citizens have already started receiving $250 checks as a downpayment on us closing the doughnut hole for those who have difficulty paying for their prescription drugs and have significant need. And so we've already got millions of people across the country who are receiving it. So instead of them thinking there are going to be death panels, now they connect health reform with the fact that this is helping them on their prescription drug coverage.

Everybody here who has health insurance, what you're going to start discovering is that you now have a patient's bill of rights which didn't exist before and makes your insurance more secure. So everything from, if you have somebody in your family with a preexisting condition, being able to know that you can get coverage for them; to, if you've got a young person who's graduating from college and they don't get health care on their first job, being able to stay on your coverage until they're 26 years old; to insurance companies not being able to drop you when you get sick just because of some fine print or you making some technical error in filling out your application—all those changes are suddenly going to mean something for people as they start using them more.

Now, it also requires, though, us constantly beating the drum and being very clear about what exactly is in the bill. And look, the challenge that Patty's facing, because she's in the middle of an election, Jim and others are facing, is that we've got now tens of millions of dollars in every media market that is just constantly sending out negative ads, not really specifying what it is exactly about the health care bill that they don't like, other than just sort of a knee-jerk assertion that it's socialized medicine or it's a Government takeover. And that, obviously, in the short term can have a negative impact on people's opinions.

Over the long term, as I said, when people start seeing its impact on folks, and I think as more and more people see that the traditional health care that they got through their employer is being threatened by higher premiums and higher deductibles and is less reliable than it might have been before, I think that we're going to look back 20 years from now and say this was absolutely the right thing to do.

When it comes to the Recovery Act, again, every specific provision in it people like. So if you say 40 percent of the Recovery Act were tax cuts—not tax hikes, but tax cuts—to small businesses, to 95 percent of working families, people say, well, that's a good idea.

Then we say, well, and then a big chunk of it was infrastructure so we can start rebuilding our roads and our bridges and our airport runways. And people say, well, I like that.

"Well, how about investment in clean energy so that the solar panels and wind turbines and

electric cars are built here in the United States?" "Well, we fully support that."

"Well, how about help to the States so that they didn't have to lay off tens of thousands of teachers and police officers and firefighters?" "Well, we support that."

Well, that's the Recovery Act. What I just listed, that's what this was. And so I think that one of the challenges we had 2 years ago was, we had to move so fast, we were in such emergency mode, that it was very difficult for us to spend a lot of time doing victory laps and advertising exactly what we were doing, because we had to move on to the next thing.

And I take some responsibility for that. I mean, our attitude was, we just had to get the policy right, and we did not always think about making sure we were advertising properly what was going on. But I think that we have the opportunity now that the economy is more stabilized to be as clear as possible with folks about what we've done.

Last point I'll make: People have a legitimate concern, I think, about the debt and the deficits. And a lot of the emergency steps that we took in 2009 and then the first half of this year, it cost money and added to the deficit. So the key issue here is that had we not taken those steps, had we dipped into a depression, had unemployment gone up to 12 or 13 percent, then the deficit would have been even worse.

But that's kind of a hard argument to make. And I think people have a legitimate concern, a legitimate worry, as to what are we doing to start—now that we're out of the immediate crisis, but we're only experiencing sluggish job growth at this point and sluggish economic growth—how do we get back to a point where we're living within our means? That's an entirely legitimate concern. It's a concern that I have. And we're going to have to have a serious debate over the next several years about how to do it.

The problem I have with the argument the way it's playing out right now in the country is that there's a suggestion on the other side that somehow the problem with our debt and our deficits all arose magically the minute I took office, whereas in fact, when I arrived at the

White House, I was inheriting a $1.3 trillion deficit. We had taken record surpluses last time there was a Democratic President and over the course of a decade moved to record deficits.

The big problems we have in terms of debt and deficits have to do with structural gaps between the amount of money we're taking in and the amount of money we're spending. And if we're going to get serious about the deficit, then we're going to have to look at everything: entitlements, defense spending, revenues. How do all those things fit together so that we can have a sustainable budget that invests in the things that we absolutely need for our long-term future and we stop funding some things that are nice to have but we can't afford.

And that's going to be a tough conversation, which is—it's interesting now when you listen to the Republicans talk about out-of-control Government spending, and then you ask them, "Well, what would you cut?" and there's this deafening silence. And they'll say things like, "Well, we'll roll back health care," except it turns out that, according to the Congressional Budget Office, the health care bill is actually going to reduce our deficit by over a trillion dollars over the next 20 years. So that would add to the deficit.

Then they'll say, "Well, we'll pull back the unused portion of the stimulus." Well, first of all, that's—most of it has already been spent, and a big chunk of what hasn't been spent are actually tax cuts, which they say they're for.

And then they'll say, "Well, we'll roll back spending back to 2008 levels," without being clear that that would mean, for example, a 20-percent cut in education spending.

So one of the things that I think, as voters, everybody here should be doing is constantly asking people, when you say you want to get the budget under control, what exactly do you mean? What exactly are you going to do? And if they can't answer the question, then it means they're not serious about it.

All right. Right here.

Community Planning/Infrastructure

Q. Hi, Mr. President. My name is Emily East. And it's such a privilege to have this opportunity to talk to you.

The President. Thanks, Emily.

Q. I want to ask you a question about a program you implemented early on in your Presidency that doesn't really make it to the top of the headlines, per se—the sustainable communities program. And this is more getting to quality of life for middle class families. It's the idea that the Federal Government is going to invest kind of more comprehensively by a partnership between Transportation, Housing and Urban Development, and sustainable communities.

You did a fantastic job of incorporating that in the stimulus act, and actually, Seattle has received the benefit of that just recently with funding through the TIGER program, with Senator Murray's support, on the South Park Bridge, which is helping a community that really needs it.

Are you going to be—are we going to be seeing more of that kind of innovation, having the bureaucracy, if you will, talk to each other and be more systemic and thorough in how they're addressing communities to help us kind of live and work and be sustainable and have access to transportation, which will make all of our lives a little bit easier?

The President. Absolutely. And I appreciate you asking the question. Look, part of my goal is to figure out how do we make Government smarter. I don't want Government bigger, I want Government smarter, because a lot of what we do is not as efficient as it should be.

And so the idea behind sustainable communities is pretty simple. If you've got Department of Transportation over here, and you've got the Environmental Protection Agency over here, and then you've got—the social service agency is over here, and they're not talking to each other, and they're not planning together, and there's no coordination regionally between the city of Seattle, surrounding suburbs, then what you end up with is the sum being less than the whole of—or the whole being less than the sum of its parts.

And so what we want to do is make sure that there's just more efficient coordination and we're thinking through, if we're spending money on transportation, how do we do it in a way that is encouraging economic growth? How are we doing it in a way that is reducing sprawl? How are we doing it in a way that makes commuting easier for people? How are we coordinating between various localities? And I think we've got a great opportunity to do more of this as we think about our future infrastructure needs.

One of the things that I've said would make a huge difference in us continuing the progress that we've made on economic growth and putting more people back to work is to finally tackle the huge backlog of infrastructure needs that we have, not just traditional infrastructure like roads and bridges and sewer lines and water mains, but also high-speed rail, also a smart grid that can help us get clean energy from one place to another in an efficient way where there's—we don't lose as much energy as we do right now with these old power lines that we have.

How do we make a air control system that reduces delays? I've got to admit, I don't fly commercial that much anymore. [*Laughter*] But from what I hear, it has not improved; it's not that pleasant of an experience.

So these are all areas where we've got a huge amount of progress to make. And if we have a serious agenda for infrastructure, and instead of politics determining where the money goes, we start giving some thought to how do we get the best bang for the buck, how do taxpayers get the best value for the money they're spending so that we don't build bridges to nowhere, but instead we're connecting people in the most effective way possible, then that can not only put people to work, but it also lays the foundation for long-term economic growth well into the future.

That's going to be a major focus that we have over the next couple of years. And my hope is we can get Republican support, because historically, the issue of infrastructure has always been bipartisan. And if we're thinking from a perspective of how do we make America competitive long term—people go to China right now, they come back, and they can't believe that China has better airports than us or they're building high-speed rail lines and we're not.

We used to have the best infrastructure in the world, and frankly, we can't make that claim any more. And I want us to get back to number one and put some people back to work in the process.

All right. Right here.

Energy

Q. Mr. President, I'm Nicey Hilton. I'm a neighbor down the street. And my question is regarding the future and being number one in the U.S. One of my fears is that we are not going to be competitive and we're going to shift our dependence from Mideast oil over to other countries that are innovating and manufacturing like crazy with alternative energy.

And I know we've done some work to encourage the U.S. to catch up, but I'm still concerned that we're already falling way behind, and that will affect the future for my children in terms of jobs and our economy.

The President. Well, it's a great question. Unfortunately, we haven't weaned ourselves off Middle East oil, so we're already—we're still sending the billions of dollars there. And we're falling behind when it comes to alternative energy.

We got a good start with the Recovery Act. We started investing in clean energy in projects all across the country. And I'll just give you one example of what we've been able to jump-start. When I came into office, the United States accounted for about 2 percent of the market in advanced battery technology. Now, these are the batteries that go into electric cars and electric trucks and hybrids. We had 2 percent of the market.

And I said, well, if we're going to make an investment in the cars of the future, we should be making the parts here in the United States too.

And so we've started looking at who's got capacity to start building these advanced batteries, and through an investment in the Recovery Act, we are now on pace to have 40 percent of the market by 2015. So in a relatively short period of time, we have created advanced battery manufacturing plants, privately owned, all across the country. We've got the expertise to do it. We just didn't have the wherewithal to do it.

That shows you how fast we can turn things around if we're making good, smart, strategic investments. And I think that there's more that we can do next year. Part of it has to do with things like a renewable energy standard, for example, that's—local governments and the Federal Government are big purchasers of energy. So us being good role models by saying, we're going to buy more fuel-efficient cars, and we are going to be customers for these new nascent industries, that can make a difference as well.

Another good example of an area where we can make progress right away is making buildings more energy efficient. We can probably solve, at least theoretically, a huge chunk of the greenhouse gas problem just by making our buildings more energy efficient. And Erik's a contractor, so I haven't talked to him about this, but one of the things that I'd love to do is to see more and more contractors just be in the business of retrofitting homes to make them better insulated, have better HVAC units.

When I was here a couple of years ago, I went to a company called McKintry—McKinstry, which is doing unbelievable work. It started off as a mom-and-pop operation and built itself up. It's got over a thousand employees now. And it goes to hospitals and schools and helps them figure out how can they save huge amounts of money by becoming more energy efficient.

A lot of families and businesses are interested in becoming more energy efficient, but the challenge they've got is finding the capital upfront. And so we've been talking about, at the legislative level, creating a program called Home Star, where families could get a tax credit or the money upfront to make these investments and then pay it back gradually as they saw their electricity bills go down.

So there are a lot of creative ways that we can jump-start this industry. I think people are really interested in it. But you're absolutely right; right now we're behind. We invented a lot of

technologies where we are now no longer the leader—solar energy, wind energy—and that's something that I'm determined to change.

But Government is going to have to play a role in helping to jump-start a lot of investment from the private sector that will eventually come in, once they know that there's going to be a market for this clean energy.

All right, yes, sir. You've got a mike right behind you.

Trade

Q. I'm Cliff Eckman. I'm Cynnie's father, and Erik is my son-in-law.

The President. You've got some cute granddaughters.

Q. And I have some very cute granddaughters. Yes, we're very proud of them. Anyway, we'd like to welcome you to the Northwest. And you may not hear this very often, but I would like to say we're very proud that you're our President.

The President. Well, I appreciate that. Thank you. Thank you very much. Thank you.

Q. Many of us feel that way.

The President. Thank you.

Q. But my question is, it seems like—I was just reading that our trade deficit, announced in August, was like $46 billion; $28 billion of that was with China. And it seems to me one of the big problems are import tariffs. We have—a lot of countries, such as China, Korea, Japan, many European countries, have import tariffs that protect their industries. That's one question, and what can we do about that. And the other is the export of jobs that happen with corporations, and they get tax benefits for it, which doesn't make a lot of sense to me.

The President. Well, look, they're both great questions. And I'll take the second one first. We've got a bunch of tax loopholes, a bunch of provisions in the Tax Code that actually encourage companies to invest and keep profits overseas. They've been on the books for a long time.

Jim, Patty, others have consistently voted to close these loopholes. It has been consistently resisted by the other side. In fact, one of the ways that we were able to get some help to local governments to keep teachers on the payroll this summer was by closing one of the most egregious loopholes that even some of the companies who were getting the benefit admitted really didn't have any logic to it. But the other side voted against us. We were able—we had to really fight to get it done.

So I want tax breaks to go to companies that are investing here in the United States—investing in research, investing in development. And that—that's common sense. And that's what every other country does. Every other country structures their tax code so that you have an incentive to invest there and create jobs there. We should be doing the exact same thing.

Now, when it comes to trade, I'm a big supporter of trade. And obviously, Seattle and the Pacific Northwest generally benefits greatly from trade. And we don't want to build a wall between ourselves and other countries. I think we've got the best workers on Earth; we've got the most innovative entrepreneurs here; we've got unbelievable universities. There's no reason why we can't compete with anybody on anything around the world.

But it's got to be structured so that it's fair. And frankly, because we were—we used to be so big and other countries were so far behind, when a lot of the trade rules were initially set up, I think we neglected to drive as tough of a bargain as we could have, just because the feeling was, well, if China is making low-wage—or low-skill, assembly-line toys, that's not a huge loss to the United States relative to our overall economy. But what we didn't understand was, if they're working hard, competing, advancing each and every year, then over time, they're going to try not just to be making toys, but then they want to make computers, and then they're going to want to make cars and, right? And they move up the value stream of the economy.

And if we have the same rules as we had, where they're able to keep our products out but we're wide open to any products they want to send in, then we're going to be at a huge disadvantage. And we have seen that disadvantage grow and grow over the last several decades.

So what I've said is, I am for trade, but it has to be reciprocal. If you want to sell cars here in the United States, then we've got to be able to sell cars in your markets. If you want to be able to sell manufacturing goods where having low-wage workers is a big advantage to you, then we've got to be able to sell services that take advantage of our knowledge and our high-skill workers, and we've got to be able to go into your markets, and you can't protect them.

And that's going to be, I think, a major debate that's going to be coming up over the next couple of years. Now, this is going to be a tough debate because I think a lot of people, their instinct is, well, trade just doesn't work for us generally, and so a lot of people are going to want to, I think, close our borders or slap on huge tariffs on other countries.

My attitude is not that I want to end trade; I want to grow trade, I want to expand trade, I want to double our exports. We've set a goal of doubling our exports, but I want to do so by driving a better bargain with our trading partners. And the truth of the matter is, they probably expect it. They're trying to figure out why we've been such pushovers for the last couple decades anyway. [*Laughter*] It doesn't make sense.

All right, yes. Go ahead.

Education Reform

Q. Mr. President, forgive me for having my notes. But first I want to let you know how much I applaud your efforts on behalf of this country.

The President. Thank you so much.

Q. And as a mother, former foster parent, and now a kindergarten teacher here in the Seattle area, I've seen the impact of limited resources on our educational system. Our schools are in disrepair. The teachers in my school, we work long hours. And throughout the district, we're dealing with crowded classrooms. And despite this effort, many students are not academically prepared to participate, innovate, and compete in this workforce.

And I realize the economy is in dire straits and our limited dollars are stretched pretty thin. But what can you do at a national level to support teachers at the regional and local level? And by the way, have you and Michelle seen—

or had a chance to see—"Waiting for 'Superman' "?

The President. Well, Michelle and I did see "Waiting for 'Superman.'" I got to admit, that's another good deal of being President, is, like, everybody sends you their movies ahead of time. [*Laughter*] And so we get them on DVD before they hit the theaters. [*Laughter*]

And it was a powerful movie. Not only did we see the movie, but we actually—I was so moved by the kids in the movie that I invited them to the Oval Office. And they came and visited, and we had a wonderful time. And they're all doing well. Not surprisingly, once they were in the movie, suddenly everybody rallied to make sure that they could get into a terrific school.

But of course, there are millions of kids like that who are talented, curious, energetic, and yet right now are still trapped in schools that don't work well.

Now, we're not going to transform our education system overnight. It took us decades to get to where we are; it's going to take us a while to get to where we need to be. But here's what we know. We used to rank number one in proportion of college graduates; we now rank ninth. We used to be at the top when it came to math and science education; we're now 21st and 25th, respectively, in the world when you test 15-year-olds. That's a recipe for disaster. So there's nothing more urgent than for us to make sure that our education system is working effectively.

Part of it is a resource issue. Part of it is also a reform issue. And unfortunately, over the last couple of decades, we've had a debate where some people argue, just give us more money, and other people argue, just blow up the system, instead of recognizing it's both. We've got to make investments in education, but we also have to make sure that the money is well spent.

So what we did was we designed something called Race to the Top, and the concept's pretty simple. Most Federal money going to education—and education accounts for about 7 percent of overall spending on education because most of it's locally funded—but most of that money is allocated through a standard formula, and it's designed to help particularly schools that have less of a resource base.

But what we said was, how about pulling out a few billion dollars and creating a competition? So schools are still going to get their formula-based funding, but if you want some extra money, then we want you to show us that you're pursuing aggressively a reform agenda that focuses on what we know works, which is having high standards, making sure that there's accountability, making sure that we are investing in great teachers and focusing on low-performing schools and making them transform themselves so that they're not just accepting, year after year, 50 percent dropout rates or kids reading at 3 grade levels behind where they should be.

And lo and behold, with this relatively small pot of money, because schools all across the country were so interested in competing, we saw already 46 States have initiated legislative changes to move forward on reform. And not every State has won the competition—it's designed to be a competition—but what it's done is made everybody look more carefully at are we doing things smart, are we doing things right when it comes to educating our kids.

We want to continue that Race to the Top agenda. And as I said, the single most important ingredient for improving our education system is our teachers, making sure we're investing in them. And my sister is a teacher. She's taught in some very tough public schools. So I know how hard teachers work. And the vast majority of them go into it not for the money; they go into it because they care deeply about kids and they love their jobs.

But a lot of them don't get the training that they need. They don't get the support they need. They don't have the professional development that they need. A lot of math teachers didn't major in math in school; a lot of science teachers didn't major in a scientific subject in school. And so we've got to make sure that we're constantly investing in them and also holding them accountable.

If we're not seeing a good enough performance, then we've got to say, you know what, here's how you can improve, and give them concrete ways so that they can up their game, because that has the single biggest impact in terms of kids.

Now, the last thing I'll say is just on higher education—I already mentioned this. We have shifted, in a deficit-neutral way, billions of dollars into our student loan programs, into our community colleges. It is making a huge difference for millions of students all across the country.

And it was a pretty simple proposition. For years, we had a system in which the student loan program went through banks and financial intermediaries who would take a fee, even though they were taking no risk, because these were all federally guaranteed loans.

And so we said, well, why would we do that? Why wouldn't we just send these loans directly to the students? If these banks and these financial intermediaries want to help administer the program, then we can hire them for that purpose, but they shouldn't be making a profit off the loans themselves.

And we're—we've saved $40 billion now that is going to go, over the next several years, directly to students who—in the form of bigger loans, more students getting loans. It can make a huge difference. And that's an example of not making Government bigger, just making it work smarter.

And those are the kinds of agendas that I think Patty and I and Jim and others want to pursue further over the next couple of years. All right?

How much time do we have? I just want to make sure. Sometimes I get scolded by my team. [*Laughter*] Time for one more. There he is. There's Marvin. I'm going to go back here.

Health Care Reform/Education

Q. Thank you so much for being here today and doing this. And I apologize for reading, but this is so very personal and so very important for the women that I work and care for. And I'm a nurse practitioner, nurse midwife, working at a community health center, Planned Parenthood. My clients range between 13 and 16 years of age.

The women I see, about three-quarter, rely on State programs or pay out of pocket, and a quarter have health insurance in varying degrees, mostly catastrophic. As a health clinic, we are reimbursed 50 percent or less for DHHS Medicaid patients. We are one of the few providers who do not cap our Medicaid patients, even though the reimbursement is so low.

How will coverage between now and 2014, when more patients will need to be on government programs, not bankrupt our community public health clinics?

The President. Well, first of all, part of our goal is to make sure that there are more people who are able to get health insurance for the job—through their job, or through these health exchanges that we're going to be setting up by 2014. So ideally, that will drive down the number of folks who are uninsured and where you are giving uncompensated care. So that is important.

Right. This notion that somehow we did something radical because we shouldn't have Government-run health care, the fact is, is that right now there's all kinds of Government-run health care. There's Medicare, there's Medicaid, and then there's emergency room care that indirectly we pay for, one way or another, either because we are subsidizing hospitals that have a lot of uncompensated care or because all of our premiums are higher since hospitals have to figure out some way of paying for it or clinics have to figure out some way of paying for it. So what they do is they just charge people who do have insurance a little bit higher. On average, everybody pays $1,000 per family in higher premiums to pay for other people. It's a tax; you just don't know it. And it's administered not through the Government, but through your insurance premiums.

So part of our goal is to make sure, A, that more people have basic coverage; B, that means that more people have preventive care. And if some of your clients have preventive care—I mean, you know this better than I do—then they're not coming in with diseases that could have been managed very early and much less expensively.

And diabetes is a classic example. The number of people who have diabetes because they're grossly overweight, they didn't catch it fast enough, they haven't changed their eating habits and that, had they gotten some effective care on the front end, could have avoided it entirely, is astronomical. It adds huge amounts of money to our health care bill overall.

So we want to emphasize prevention. We want to give people more options in terms of being able to be covered in the first place. And then we also have to make sure that Medicaid and Medicare doctors and providers are effectively reimbursed.

And frankly, what's happened historically is, when States or the Federal Government run short on money, what they do is they just say, well, you know what, we'll just pay 70 percent or 60 percent of what the costs are, and we'll make the providers figure it out.

And as a consequence, you got more and more providers who are not taking Medicaid patients. And if we don't fix the reimbursement formula for Medicare, you're going to have a bunch of doctors and hospitals who are going to start declining Medicare patients too, which is a scary proposition.

So—now, that's—keep in mind, that's expensive. And so part of what health reform is about is figuring out how can we make sure that every provider gets every dollar that they need for quality care that they are providing.

On the other hand, let's make sure that the care that's actually being provided is improving the health of the patients, as opposed to just being a hidden way for providers to get more money.

And what I mean by that is—let me—and I don't want to get too technical here, but I'll try to give you a simple example. It turns out that there are a lot of tests that are done that probably aren't needed, but because the system is so inefficient and because providers get reimbursed for a lot of these tests, that we're probably paying more than we should just on testing that doesn't improve the quality of care.

And part of the health reform act is going to have doctors and medical experts say, what's the best way to care for a patient with a particular ailment? And let's start reimbursing doctors for the overall outcome, as opposed to the number of procedures that they're doing.

That way, it may turn out we'll have fewer procedures, but overall, a better outcome. And providers will get full reimbursement for those things that are effective. They may not get reimbursement for things that have been shown to be less effective.

Now, all these changes are not going to happen overnight. They're going to take some time because this system has been such a mess for such a long time, that making it more rational is something that will take several years. But I'm optimistic we can do it. And I appreciate the great work that you're doing. So tell everybody, all your coworkers, help's on the way. [*Laughter*]

This has been a terrific conversation. I want to close just by telling you something that happened this week that was, I think, the highlight of my week.

I had a—we hosted the first White House science fair at the White House because we realized, when the Lakers win the NBA championship, we have them over to the White House. And when the Alabama Crimson Tide wins the national championship, we have them over to the White House. And when these incredible young people are winning international science competitions or participating in these national competitions, nobody's acknowledging them. And that's sending the wrong message about what's going to be the most important thing to allow us to compete into the future.

So we had this national science competition. And a select group of them set up displays in the State Room in the White House. And it was unbelievable watching these kids. I mean, you had a young woman who was—had designed a energy-efficient car and had a scale model that was made out of some material that I had never heard of before.

You had a group from Tennessee that had designed this water purification system that was self-generating through a water wheel. And the whole thing was only about yea big, but it could provide filtered water for 60 families very cheaply.

These are all high school kids, by the way. You had this—a couple of these Latino kids who had designed this chair for doing therapy for people who are disabled that they had designed from scratch because they had seen a friend of theirs who was disabled and not had the equipment that he needed. And they didn't have a lot of money in the school, so they actually sold tamales to finance this project. First time they had ever been on a plane was actually to fly to the competition that they ended up doing so well on.

And then the last person I met—and there were others who were doing unbelievable stuff—but the last young woman I met, she was 16 years old. In her freshman year, she had taken biology, had gotten interested in the life sciences, was particularly interested in cancer treatment. So she decided, between her freshman and sophomore year, to teach herself chemistry in the summer because she was so anxious to get started on learning more about cancer treatments.

And she decided as a science project to try to invent a new cancer drug, because right now there are clinical trials and experimental treatments where you inject the drug into the cancer, and then it's activated by light, and it potentially will just kill the cancer cells without killing the healthy cells, unlike chemotherapy or radiation treatments.

And so—but apparently, the ones that are being tested right now by all the big laboratories, they only can be used for skin cancer or places where the light can penetrate fairly close to the surface.

So she literally designed a new drug, won the international science competition, and now is being contacted by all these laboratories around the world who are working on this—these types

of drugs. She's very smart. [*Laughter*] She's 16 years old. She hasn't graduated from high school yet.

Here's the point: When you talk to these young people, you felt so optimistic about America. You felt like there's nothing that can stop us. If we can just harness that energy and that ingenuity, and if we're investing in those kids and we're giving them a chance and they're able to start their own businesses and their own engineering firms, and if they're in the classroom teaching younger kids that same sense of wonder and excitement, there's nothing we can't do.

And I think that's important to remember because we've gone through a very difficult time over the last couple years. But there are kids like that all across the country. And if we create the right conditions for them, they will make sure that the 21st century is the American century just like the 20th was.

Thank you so much, everybody. Appreciate you.

NOTE: The President spoke at 10:01 a.m. at the Foss residence. In his remarks, he referred to White House Trip Director Marvin Nicholson; and White House science fair participants Mikayla Nelson of Billings, MT, Mathilda Lloyd of Kingston, TN, Samuel Snodgrass and Sonja Solomon of Oak Ridge, TN, Diego Vazquez and Antonio Hernandez of Phoenix, AZ, and Amy Chyao of Plano, TX. He also referred to his sister Maya Soetoro-Ng. A portion of these remarks could not be verified because the audio was incomplete.

Remarks at a Rally for Senator Patricia L. Murray in Seattle
October 21, 2010

The President. Thank you, Huskies! It is great to see all of you. Look, I'm not going to give a long speech now because then you'll be listening to two long speeches. I just wanted to—the main reason I wanted to come out, because I thought it would be cool to run through the tunnel. [*Laughter*] I liked doing that.

But I also wanted to come out and just say thank you to all of you because there are a lot of you who worked on our campaign, there are a lot of you who voted, some for the very first time, because you realized that we're at a crossroads in history right now. America is the greatest country on Earth, but we didn't get here because it was preordained. We got here because our parents and our grandparents and our great-grandparents. They were all willing to roll up their sleeves and work, to work on behalf of freedom, to work on behalf of opportunity.

A lot of our parents, grandparents, great-grandparents came here from other countries to start a new life because they realized that if they worked hard here in America, then there was nothing that could stop them, and that there was a unique legacy in this Nation of being able to live out your dreams.

And over the last decade, some of those dreams felt like they were slipping away. People felt as if the economy was only for those at the very top and that no matter how hard you worked, you were treading water. And people were having trouble making ends meet and paying for health care and paying for college educations. And I think a lot of young people started feeling that maybe the 21st century wouldn't be the American century like the 20th century was.

And what our campaign was about in 2008 was reminding everybody that there is nothing we can't do when we join together as citizens from every walk of life, that there is nothing we can't accomplish when we dream big dreams and are willing to work for them.

And over the last 2 years, as difficult as things have been, as big as the problems that we inherited were, I have been so inspired because I've had the opportunity to work with people like Patty Murray to make sure that every American has decent health care, to make sure that an economy that was shrinking is growing again, to start putting people back to work, to make sure we've got equal pay for equal work, to make sure that we've got a couple of wonderful women on the Supreme Court, to make sure that young people can afford a college education, to make sure that we brought back 100,000 troops from Iraq, to make sure that we're respected around the world once again, to start investing in research and development so that our economy can thrive, to make sure that we're investing in clean energy so that we're at the forefront,

not only of growing our economy, but of saving the planet.

And I've been inspired by you, because wherever I go, traveling across this country, especially when I meet young people, I am reminded of your energy and your drive and your imagination. And for all the problems, we're going through right now, we still have the best workers on Earth; we've got the finest universities on Earth; we've got the best entrepreneurs on Earth; we've got the freest, most vibrant economy on Earth——

Audience member. And the best President on Earth!

The President. Well, I won't say that, but we've got a pretty good President. I—and so—[*applause*]—but here's what I need from you now, and this is the point that Patty was making. Look, Patty has worked so hard on behalf of Washington, worked so hard on behalf of this institution, worked so hard on behalf of you. I've got to have Patty as a partner in Washington.

So I am here to deliver one simple message: If you have not voted yet, you've got to get that ballot and put it in the mail. Don't delay. Do it right after this rally. You've got to then talk to your friends. You've got to talk to your neighbors. You've got to make phone calls. You've got to knock on doors. You have to make sure that you are as fired up and as excited now as you were 2 years ago, because the work is not yet done. And I have to have Patty Murray back in the United States Senate.

Can I get that promise from you guys? Are you going to vote? I need Patty Murray back in the United States Senate. And you need to send her there. If you do, I guarantee you, we're going to continue to work to make sure the American Dream is not just here for this generation, but for generations to come.

Thank you, everybody. God bless you. God bless the United States of America. Thank you.

NOTE: The President spoke at 11:42 a.m. at the University of Washington.

Remarks at a Rally for Senator Patricia L. Murray in Seattle
October 21, 2010

The President. Hello, Huskies! Thank you! Woof, woof! Give it up for Patty Murray! I am thrilled to be back in Seattle. It is great to be back in the State of Washington.

We've got some great friends here that I want to make sure everybody acknowledges. The Governor, Chris Gregoire, is here. Representative Jim McDermott is in the house. Representative Norm Dicks is here. Representative Joe [Jay]° Inslee is here. King County Executive Dow Constantine is here. And your great United States Senator, Patty Murray, is in the house.

Audience member. We love you!

The President. I love you back.

When this State sent Patty to the Senate, she wasn't one of those lifelong politicians who wanted the job for the fancy title or the nice office. She was the mom in tennis shoes who was just looking to help a few people and solve a few problems. All these years later, that's exactly what she has done. That's exactly what she's done. She's helped a lot of people. She's solved a lot of problems. And now she needs our help so she can keep on fighting for you in the United States Senate.

And, Washington, you know Patty Murray. You know what she's made of. You've seen her go to bat to keep Boeing jobs and aerospace jobs right here in Washington. You've seen her fight for clean energy jobs and new infrastructure jobs. You've seen her fight to make sure that this Nation keeps faith with our veterans because it is a sacred trust. This is a Senator who still flies across the country every weekend to come home. When we were in the Senate together, I used to think, poor Patty. [*Laughter*] I mean, I got my little hour-and-a-half flight to Chicago. And she had a lot longer way to go.

But she knew how important it was to come home and listen to the cares and concerns of her constituents. That's the kind of leader you need at a time like this, somebody who knows your lives.

° White House correction.

So look, if you haven't already voted for Patty Murray, let me be clear. You need to go right after this rally, fill out that ballot, and mail it in—today. Not tomorrow, not the next day, but today.

Let's get this done. Let's get Patty Murray back into the United States Senate.

Look, we need you fired up. We need you fired up, Seattle, because in just a few days your decision in this election is going to set the direction of this State and of this country for years to come.

And there are a lot of folks out there in Washington, DC—not in Washington State, but in Washington, DC—who are saying, you know what, it can't be done, just like they said in 2008. You can't—what they're saying is that you can't say no to the special interests, that you can't overcome the cynicism in politics.

Audience members. Yes, we can!

The President. That you can't overcome the millions of dollars in negative ads.

Audience members. Yes, we can!

The President. That you can't elect a Black guy with a funny name, Barack Obama.

Audience members. Yes, we can!

The President. That's what they always say.

Audience members. Yes, we can! Yes, we can! Yes, we can!

The President. They're always telling us what we cannot do, and you just keep on coming back and saying, yes, we can.

Now, look, let's be honest. There's no doubt this is a difficult election. And it's because we have been through an incredibly difficult time as a nation. And it didn't just happen a year ago or 2 years ago. For most of the last decade, middle class families saw their incomes fall. Between 2001 and 2009, which corresponds to when the Republicans were in charge, middle class incomes of families fell. Job growth was actually more stagnant than any time since World War II. Jobs were disappearing overseas. In the meantime, the costs of everything from health care to college tuition were going up.

There were too many parents who couldn't afford to send their kids to college, too many people who couldn't afford to go see a doctor when they got sick, too many Americans working two, three jobs just to make ends meet. And then all these problems culminated in the worst economic crisis since the Great Depression. We lost 4 million jobs in the 6 months before I was sworn into office, 750,000 the month I took the oath of office, 600,000 jobs lost the month after that, 600,000 jobs lost the month after that. We lost almost 8 million jobs before any of my economic policies were put into place.

Now, when I got to Washington, my hope was that both parties would put politics aside and that we would roll up our sleeves and meet this once-in-a-generation challenge. The hope was that we could start moving beyond the division and the bickering and the game-playing that had dominated Washington for so long, although—because although we are proud to be Democrats, we are prouder to be Americans. We are prouder to be Americans.

And let me tell you, there are a lot of Republicans in this country who felt the same way, but Republican leaders in Washington, they made a different calculation. They made a different decision because—here was their tactic, here was their theory. They realized, boy, we made a really big mess. [*Laughter*] And the economy is in such bad shape, we're going to be climbing out of such a deep hole, that we are better off standing on the sidelines because then maybe people will forget what a big mess we caused. And we'll just let Obama and Murray and the Democrats try to solve all these problems. And we're going to sit on the sidelines and carp and complain and obstruct and say no.

And their calculation was that because it was going to take a long time to dig ourselves out of this hole, longer than any of us would like, that all of you would get frustrated and would get angry. And they figured that if they just sat on the sidelines and opposed us every step of the way, that eventually—eventually, they could ride that anger and that frustration to success in this election. That was their calculation. That was their theory.

In other words, they were betting on amnesia. They were betting on the idea that you'd forget who caused this mess in the first place.

Well, let me tell you, Seattle, it's up to you to tell them you haven't forgotten.

It's up to you. It's up to you to remind everyone that this choice is an election between two different visions of America: a choice between falling backwards and moving forwards, a choice between an America that embraces opportunity for everybody and an America that's a cramped vision just for the few.

If they win this election, the chair of the Republican campaign committee has promised publicly, he said, we're going to pursue the exact same agenda as they did before I took office.

I mean, this is not a situation where the Republicans said, boy, we really screwed up, let's figure something new out to do. They want to pursue the same agenda: tax cuts mostly for millionaires and billionaires; cutting rules for special interests, whether it's the oil companies or the banks or the health insurance companies; cutting middle class families loose to fend for themselves. The same agenda that let Wall Street run wild. The same agenda that took record surpluses and turned them into record deficits. The same agenda that nearly destroyed our economy.

That's what they're promising—more of the same. It's not as if we didn't try it, Seattle. We tried it for 8 years. It did not work, and we can't afford to go back to that same agenda.

Let me just give you an example. They want to cut education by 20 percent. They want to use that money and then borrow more money from China and other countries to help pay for a $700 billion tax break that only the wealthiest 2 percent of Americans will ever see. That's their main economic agenda. They want to roll back health reform so insurance companies can deny you coverage when you're sick, or drop your coverage. They want to roll back Wall Street reform so taxpayers are once again on the hook for Wall Street bailouts and credit card companies can hit you with hidden fees and penalties.

Patty Murray's opponent has the distinction of being the first candidate in the country to call for repeal of Wall Street reform. Think about this. We almost had a financial meltdown that plunged America and the world into catastrophe, and he thinks we should go back to the old rules that got us into that problem.

He wants to eliminate the oversight that we desperately need. Look, this is the same theory these folks have been peddling for years. And it's up to you to say, we are not buying what you are selling.

We did it, we tried it before. It did not work. We are not going back. We're not going back. Yes, times are tough. But because of the steps we've taken, we're no longer facing the possibility of a second depression. The economy is growing again.

The private sector has created jobs for 9 months in a row now. Yes, we've still got a long way to go. Yes, we still have a lot of work to do. There are a lot of people hurting out there right now. There are some families that are just hanging on by a thread. That's what keeps me up at night. That's what keeps Patty up at night. That's what keeps us fighting.

But I also know this: The biggest mistake we could make is to go back to the very same policies that caused all this hurt in the first place. And I say this not because I want to reargue the past. It's because I don't want to relive the past.

Let me offer an analogy I've been using around the country. The Republicans took America's car and drove it into the ditch. [*Laughter*] And it was a really deep ditch. And it was really reckless driving. So Patty and I show up at the—we show up at the scene of the accident. The Republicans have climbed out of the car, abandoned the accident. Patty and I, we're putting on our boots, and we go down and into the ditch, and it's muddy down there, and it's hot, and it's dusty. But you know what, we know we've got to get the car out, so we just start pushing.

And Patty, even though she's small, she's tough, so she's pushing hard. She's pushing. And even though I'm skinny, I'm pretty tough, so I'm pushing. And sometimes our feet slip a little bit, and sometimes it's not budging, but we're just staying on it, and we're sweating. And every once in a while we look up, and the Re-

publicans are up there on the road, they're just waving. [*Laughter*] They're going around whispering to everybody: "They're not pushing hard enough. They're not pushing the right way."

And we say to them, "Well, why don't you come down here and help push?" "No, no, no, no." [*Laughter*] "But push harder, push harder."

So we just go ahead and push. And finally—finally—we get this car up on the road. Finally. The car is a little banged up. The car is banged up, it's got to go the body shop. We need to get a tuneup. But you know what, it's pointing in the right direction. It's ready to move.

And suddenly, we get this tap on our shoulders, and we look back. Who is it? It's the Republicans. And they say, "We want the keys back." [*Laughter*]

And you can't have the keys back. You don't know how to drive. I want Patty Murray driving the car. The Republicans can ride with us, but they've got to be in the backseat—[*laughter*]—where they can't do too much damage.

Have you ever noticed when you want your car going forward, what do you do? You put it in "D." When you go backwards, you put it in "R." Don't go back in the ditch. Don't go back in the ditch. I don't want to have to push us out again.

Patty and I, we've got a different idea about what the future should look like, and it's an idea rooted in our belief about how this country was built. Patty and I, we grew up understanding the sacrifices our families made to allow us to have opportunity. We grew up watching working parents struggle, and then make it and live out their American Dream. We know that government doesn't have all the answers to our problems. We've seen how hard our parents, grandparents had to work. We understand that self-sufficiency is part of what made America great. We believe that government has to be lean and efficient.

But in the words of the first Republican President, Abraham Lincoln—who, by the way, would have difficulty winning the Republican nomination today—[*laughter*]—we also believe that government should do for the people what the people cannot do better individually for themselves. So we believe in a country that rewards hard work and responsibility. We believe in individual initiative. But we also believe in a country that's investing in the future. We believe in a country that's investing in our young people. We believe in a country where we're looking out for one another. We believe in a country that supports our veterans when they come home. We believe in a country that says I am my brother's keeper, and I am my sister's keeper. That's the America I know. That's the America Patty knows. That's the choice in this election.

We see a future where the next century is driven by American innovation and American ingenuity. We don't want to keep giving tax breaks to companies that ship jobs overseas. We want to invest in companies that are investing in jobs right here in the United States of America, in small businesses, in American manufacturers, in American clean energy companies. We don't want solar panels and wind turbines and electric cars made in Europe and Asia. We want them made right here in the United States of America, with American workers. That's the choice in this election.

We see an America where every citizen has the skills and the training to compete with workers anywhere in the world. The other side might think it's a good idea to cut education by 20 percent, but you know what? China is not cutting education by 20 percent. South Korea is not cutting education by 20 percent. Germany is not cutting education by 20 percent. They're not playing for second place. And the United States of America doesn't play for second place. We play for first. We play for number one.

That's why tens of billions of dollars in taxpayer subsidies that used to go to big banks are now going where they should, to you, to students, to families. That's why we want to make our new college tax credit permanent, worth $10,000 in tuition relief for every student, because we want to invest in you. That's what this election is about.

We see an America where the middle class is growing and where opportunity is shared by everyone. And the only limit to your success is how hard you're willing to try. That's why when we designed tax cuts, they were for middle class

families. That's why we'll fight the efforts of some in the other party who think it's still a good idea to privatize Social Security, because as long as I'm President, no one is going to take the retirement savings of a generation of Americans and turn it over to Wall Street. Not on my watch. Not on Patty's watch. That's the choice in this election. That's what we're fighting for.

We want to create jobs through investments in research and development. We want to rebuild our infrastructure so it's the best in the world. We want to have the number-one college graduation rates of anyplace in the world. We want a financial system that works for consumers. We want enforcement of clean energy legislation, but also clean air legislation and clean water legislation.

Look, right now the same special interests who would profit from the other side's agenda, they are fighting back hard. They were fighting us tooth and nail on everything we did over the last two years. And now they see their opening, they see their chance. So to win this election, they are plowing tens of millions of dollars into front groups that are running misleading negative ads all across America. You've seen them. You've seen them.

Just flooding the airwaves with negative ads. And they don't have the courage to stand up and disclose the identity of the donors. They could be insurance companies. They could be Wall Street banks. We don't know. We don't know who it is.

But understand, this kind of politics, that's not just a threat to Democrats. It's a threat to our democracy. And the only way to fight it, the only way to match their millions of dollars in negative ads is with the millions of voices who are ready to stand up and finish what we started in 2008. That means you. That's where you come in.

That's why you need to mail in your ballots, Seattle. That's why you've got to vote in this election. If everybody who voted in 2008 shows up in 2010, we will win this election. We will win this election. But you've got to come out and vote.

A lot of you got involved in 2008 because you believed that we were at a defining moment in our history. And you believed that this was a time when the decisions we make would have an impact not just on us but on our children, our grandchildren, our future generations.

And you wanted to make sure that your voice was heard. The reason you knocked on doors and made phone calls and cast your vote, some of you for the very first time, was because you believed that your actions could make a difference and you'd play a role in bringing about historic change.

Now, we are in the midst not just of advocating for change, not just for calling for change, we are grinding it out. We are doing the hard, frustrating, inch-by-inch, day-by-day, week-by-week work of bringing about change.

And look, I understand that when you're watching it, you say to yourself, boy, this is hard. This isn't easy. This isn't happening as fast as I would like. And I understand how some of you might think back to election night or Inauguration night when Beyonce was singing and Bono. [*Laughter*] And you were saying, boy, that was exciting, that was fun, that was a big party. And now it just seems like we're working all the time and folks are arguing and everybody is mad. All these pundits are on TV. And this is just kind of discouraging.

And then maybe there's some of you who know it's hard to keep faith when a family member still hasn't found a job after months of trying or you see another foreclosure sign hanging on the house down the street. And of course, it doesn't help when you're seeing all these negative ads and people putting each other down.

But I want everybody to understand this. I want everybody to understand you can't let it get to you. Don't ever let anybody tell you that this fight is not worth it. Don't let them tell you that you're not making a difference.

Because of what you did, Seattle, because of what you did, there's a woman somewhere who no longer has to choose between losing her home and treating her cancer. Because of you, there are parents who can look their children in the eye and say, you are going to college. Because of you, there are small businesses that kept their doors open and folks who didn't lose their jobs. Because of you, there are teachers in the classroom who are still teaching. Because of you, there are firefighters who are still fighting fires. Because of you there are 100,000 brave men and women who are back from a war in Iraq. That's because of you.

So don't let anybody tell you change isn't possible. Don't let them get you down. Because if our—think about the founding of this country, what we—think about it. None of us would be here if it weren't for that extraordinary leap of faith that had been taken. Thirteen Colonies deciding to start a revolution based on an idea that had never been tried before: a government of and by and for the people, a government based on the simple proposition that all men are created equal, that we're endowed with certain inalienable rights.

Think about it. If our parents and grandparents and great-grandparents had listened to the cynics 50 years ago or 100 years ago or 200 years ago, we wouldn't be here today. They would have said, don't even try a revolution. The British Empire is too powerful. Don't try to liberate the slaves. It's too hard. Don't try to get women the right to vote. Don't try to initiate workers' rights or civil rights. Don't try. We can't.

The only reason we are here today is because past generations, they didn't listen to the cynics. They were unafraid to push forward even in the face of difficulty, even in the face of uncertainty. That's why we've come so far, through war and depression. That's why we have civil rights and workers' rights and women's rights. That's why we will end "don't ask, don't tell." That is the spirit we need today.

The journey we began together was not about putting a President in the White House. It was about building a movement for change that endures. It's about realizing that in America, anything is possible, if we're willing to work for it, if we're willing to fight for it.

That's what Patty Murray believes. That's what I believe. And if that's what you believe, I need you to knock on doors and make phone calls and talk to your friends and talk to your neighbors. And if you do that, I promise you, not only will we win this election, but we will restore the dream for the next generation.

God bless you, and God bless the United States of America.

NOTE: The President spoke at 12:15 p.m. at the University of Washington. In his remarks, he re-ferred to Rep. Pete Sessions, in his capacity as chairman of the National Republican Congressional Committee; Republican senatorial candidate Dino Rossi; and musicians Beyonce G. Knowles and Paul D. "Bono" Hewson.

Statement on the Death of Paul S. Miller
October 21, 2010

I was saddened to learn of the passing of one of my staffers and a leader in the disability rights movement, Paul Miller. In a world where persons with disabilities are still too often told, "You can't," Paul spent his life proving the opposite. A graduate of the University of Pennsylvania and Harvard Law School, Paul went on to become a law professor, disability law expert, one of the longest serving commissioners of the Equal Employment Opportunity Commission, an adviser to President Bill Clinton, and later, an invaluable adviser to me. But more important than any title or position was the work that drove him. He dedicated his life to a world more fair and more equal and an America where all are free to pursue their full measure of happiness, and all of us are better off for it.

My thoughts and prayers go out to his wife Jennifer, his daughters Naomi and Delia, and all whose lives Paul touched.

Remarks at a Democratic National Committee Dinner in Palo Alto, California
October 21, 2010

Please have a seat. I'm going to come to you, and I'm not going to bore you with a long speech because I'm going to be able to sit with each of you at your table and to have a terrific conversation.

My main message is to say thank you to Zachary and Marissa for opening up this wonderful home. I was especially thrilled to see the pumpkins—[*laughter*]—and the Halloween stuff out there because in the Obama household, Halloween is big. And in fact, for all the campaigning I'm going to be doing over the next 10 days, I will be home on Sunday night—[*laughter*]—when the girls get dressed up and do some trick-or-treating.

I see a lot of old friends here, people who have supported us for a very long time, and I see some new ones as well. Some of you I had a chance to meet around the same time I first met Marissa. I remember that first visit to Google very well. In fact, it made it into my second book. And I talked about how inspiring it was and how it spoke to the essence of America, the American idea that if we're innovating, if people have the tools to let their imaginations run, that there's nothing we can't do in this country.

And that's I think the spirit that all of us want to see recaptured after a decade in which, frankly, that can-do spirit had been lost. Obviously, we're going through a very difficult time right now, the worst financial crisis since the Great Depression, the worst recession since the Great Depression. But my task over the last 2 years hasn't just been to stop the bleeding. My task has also been to try to figure out how do we address some of the structural problems in the economy that have prevented more Googles from being created, prevented more Hewlett-Packards from being created, prevented more engineers from being trained in our schools; how do we unleash this incredible energy and dynamism that we know has always driven America, decade after decade.

We've made a start on all these fronts. I think our education reform agenda has been as innovative and aggressive as anything that we've seen, and we're now partnering with the private sector to figure out how do we get more math and science education so that we can train more engineers and more computer scientists and more mathematicians and more researchers to help drive the next wave of technology.

We have tackled things like health care that have been weights around the necks of not just individual families and businesses, but also our Federal budget. We're taking on clean energy in ways that we have not seen before. We've raised the national CAFE standards on cars and trucks for the first time in 30 years, made the largest investment in clean energy in history. We're seeing solar panels and wind turbines and advanced battery manufacturing all across the country because of the efforts that we've been making.

And so I'm optimistic about the future. But in the short term, we've got a long way to go. There are a lot of people out there who are hurting, a lot of families who are struggling to make a mortgage payment or pay the bills, a lot of kids who still aren't sure whether they can finance their college educations.

And so we're going to have a big choice in this election in an environment in which people are frustrated and hurting. And it's going to be very important that we're able to make the choice clear about going forwards or going backwards. And the only way we can get that message out effectively is if we've got the support of folks like you, because in a place like California, frankly, as many people as I meet when I travel here, I can't meet everybody. At some point, we're going to have to be able to get the message out, and you help us do that.

So I'm grateful to you. We are excited about these last 10 days. I've been traveling around the country. We had rallies in Portland and Seattle earlier over the last couple of days, I think 15,000 in each place; 35,000 in Columbus, Ohio; 30,000 in Madison, Wisconsin.

And as we travel around the country, although everybody recognizes that the last 2 years have been tough, what has been remarkable is the degree of resilience people feel and the sense that as hard as things have been, we're still going to keep on fighting to make sure that we have a better future for our kids and our grandkids.

Your presence here represents that. I am going to be quiet now because I want to make sure that I have a chance to talk to all of you and hear from all of you. And if at any time people want to come in here and provide an update on the Giants game—[*laughter*]—I am perfectly happy to hear from them.

So again, to our hosts, thank you very much. To all of you, it's great to see you again, and I look forward to a good conversation.

NOTE: The President spoke at 6:33 p.m. at the residence of Zachary S. Bogue and Marissa A. Mayer. Audio was not available for verification of the content of these remarks.

Remarks at a Rally for Senator Barbara Boxer in Los Angeles, California
October 22, 2010

The President. Thank you. Everybody, please have a seat. Thank you. Thank you so much. It is good to be back in L.A. It is good to be back in L.A. It is good to see such wonderful friends. I just want to make mention of a few of them. Congresswoman Jane Harman is here. Congresswoman Laura Richardson is here. Congressman Adam Schiff is in the house. Soon-to-be Congresswoman Karen Bass is here. State Controller John Chiang is here. I know Stevie Wonder was in the house. And, Sim Farar, thank you so much for doing an extraordinary job. And to all the other cochairs who helped put this together, thank you.

It is good to be back in L.A. And it is an honor to be standing here with one of my alltime favorite Senators, Barbara Boxer.

It was one of my great privileges to work with Barbara in the United States Senate. And during that time, we became good colleagues and even better friends. And I had a chance to see her at work, day in and day out. And I came to learn that while Barbara is somewhat vertically challenged—[*laughter*]—you should see the box I had to push out of the way here—[*laughter*]—

Barbara is somebody who's got more fight in her than anybody I know. And she's always fighting for the right reason, fighting for the right cause.

And today, Barbara is in a tough election, even though the choice should be easy, because there's only one candidate in this race who has spent her career fighting for California's families, and that is Barbara Boxer. There's just one candidate who's done that.

There's one candidate who fought for and helped pass the most progressive and largest middle class tax cut in history. There's only one candidate who is fighting to create thousands of construction jobs all throughout California, rebuilding its roads and its bridges and its highways so that this great State has the best infrastructure in the world.

There's only one candidate who stood up to the insurance companies so that every Californian can have accessible and affordable health care, making sure that insurance companies aren't dropping you when you get sick, making sure young people can stay on their parents' health insurance until they're 26 years old.

There is only one candidate who has consistently fought to protect our children's education and will protect a woman's right to choose. There is only one candidate who's fighting to make California the clean energy hub of America. Only one candidate who's championed clean air and clean water and the most beautiful coastline in the world.

And that candidate is your Senator, Barbara Boxer. So she's fought for you for a long time. Now she's got to see you fight for her over these last couple of weeks. We have to have Barbara back in the Senate. We have to have her back in the Senate.

And in 11 days, your decision will set the direction not just of this State, but of this country for the next 5 years, the next 10 years, the next 20 years, for generations to come. Some of you brought your kids here, and I love when I have a chance to see young people here, because it reminds us of why we do what we do.

And just like you did in 2008, you've got an opportunity here to defy the conventional wisdom and defy the pundits, defy all those talking heads who say you can't overcome cynicism in politics, you can't overcome special interests, that millions of dollars in negative ads are what determine the outcome of races.

In 11 days, you've got a chance once again to say, yes, we can. Yes, we can.

Now, look, let's not fool ourselves. This is a tough election. This is a difficult election because this country has gone through one of the most difficult periods in our Nation's history. And it didn't just start with the financial crisis. Over the last decade, between 2001 and 2009, middle class families had seen their incomes actually decline by 5 percent. Think about that. During that 8-year period, middle class families had less money. At a time—at the same time that their health care costs were shooting up, sending your kids to college was becoming more and more expensive. Job growth between 2001 and 2009 was the most sluggish since World War II, more sluggish than it's been over the last year.

And so you had folks who were out there working two jobs, three jobs just to make ends meet. You had parents who had to say to their kids, I'm not sure I can afford to send you to college, and families who had to make a decision, maybe we don't go to the doctor even though we're feeling sick. All that was happening before the crisis hit.

And then it culminated in the worst economy since the Great Depression. We lost 4 million jobs in the 6 months before I was sworn in, 750,000 the month I was sworn in, 600,000 after that, 600,000 after that. So we had lost almost 8 million jobs between—before any of the economic policies that Barbara and I helped to put into place had any chance to take an effect.

Now, when I got to Washington, my hope was that we were going to be able to bring the parties together to address this crisis, because although we are proud Democrats, we are prouder to be American. And every once in a while you'd think that folks would stand up and say, enough of the politics, enough of the game-playing, let's get to work.

That's my hope. That was my hope. But we know what actually happened. The Republicans made a tactical decision. I mean, they bragged about this, so this is not something I'm making up. They basically said to themselves, you know what, we created such a big mess, we have dug such a big hole, the economy is going to take so long to recover that we're better off not trying to solve the problems. We're better off standing on the sidelines and hoping people forget that we caused the problems—[*laughter*]—and then pointing our fingers and trying to place the blame on Barack Obama or Barbara Boxer.

That was their strategy. Their strategy was premised on amnesia. [*Laughter*] That was their approach.

Now, we made a different decision. We decided we can't afford to play politics. We understood that some of the decisions that had to be made might be unpopular. But what we said to ourselves was that we go to Washington not to have a fancy office and not to have a fancy title; we go there to do what's right. You did not elect me to do what was easy. You elected me to do what was right. And that's the same reason that you elected Barbara Boxer—to do what was right.

Now, it is now up to you to let the Republicans know that we haven't forgotten how we got here, that we don't have amnesia. It's up to you to be clear that this isn't a referendum on Barbara. This is a choice between the policies that got us into this mess and the policies that are going to lead us out of this mess.

This is a choice between the past and the future, between fear and hope, between moving backwards and moving forwards. And I don't know about you, but I want to move forward.

The chair of the Republican campaign committee was quoted in the newspaper a while back, Barbara. He was asked, well, what would you do if you took power in the House? He said, well, we're going to pursue the exact same agenda that we pursued before Obama took office.

Now think about this: This resulted in the worst economy in our lifetimes. So you could have imagined the Republicans going off into the desert and doing some reflection—[*laughter*]—and saying to themselves, boy, we really screwed up. We need some new ideas.

And then they might have come back and said, you know what, we got some great new ideas that we think can get the economy moving. That's not what happened. They are clinging to the same worn-out, tired, snake-oil ideas that they were peddling before.

I'm not—[*laughter*]—you know what they are. They do have the benefit of being simple. You cut taxes, mostly for millionaires and billionaires, regardless of the impact on the deficit. You cut rules for all manner of special interests. And you cut middle class families to fend for themselves. So if you're somebody who just lost your job, tough luck. You're on your own. You might not even get unemployment insurance, according to this philosophy. You're a young person who can't afford to go to college? Pull yourself up by your own bootstraps. Tough luck, you're on your own. You don't have health insurance? Too bad, you're on your own. This agenda that poses as conservatism is not conservative. It resulted in a radical shift from record surpluses to record deficits, allowed Wall Street to run wild, nearly destroyed our economy.

Now, I bring this up not to reargue the past. I bring it up because I don't want to relive the past. We have been there. We tried what they are trying to sell, and we're not buying this time.

I've been using an analogy that Barbara likes quite a bit, so I've got to make sure to use it here. Otherwise, she'll scold me. Imagine the Republicans driving our economy into the ditch. And it's a deep ditch. [*Laughter*]

Sen. Boxer. It's very deep.

The President. And they and their buddies somehow walk away from the accident, but the car is still down there. So Barbara and I, we put on our boots, and we rappel down into the ditch. [*Laughter*] And it's muddy and hot. And there are bugs there. And we're pushing on this car, trying to get it out of the ditch—pushing and pushing. And even though Barbara is small, she's tough. So she's pushing. [*Laughter*]

And every once in a while we look up, and there are the Republicans. They're up there, you know, sipping on a Slurpee and fanning themselves. [*Laughter*] And we'll ask them, "Why don't you come down here?" And they say: "No, no, but you guys aren't pushing hard enough. You're not pushing the right way."

Finally, we get the car up on level ground. We're ready to move forward. The car is banged up. It needs some bodywork. It needs a tuneup. But it's ready to move in the right direction. And we get this tap on our shoulders. We look back. Lo and behold, it's the Republicans. And what are they saying? They're saying, "We want the keys back." [*Laughter*] You cannot have the keys back. You don't know how to drive. You don't know how to drive. You don't know how to drive. No, no.

We—you can ride with us. But you'll have to be in the backseat. [*Laughter*] We're going to put middle class families in the front seat. We're driving for them.

Audience member. That's right.

The President. You notice, when you want to go forward, you put your car in what?

Audience members. "D"!

The President. "D." When you want to go backwards, what happens? You put it in "R." [*Laughter*] We don't want to go back into that ditch. Don't do it. Don't do it.

Because of the steps we've taken, because Barbara was there in the Senate, this country is no longer facing a second depression. Our economy is growing again. The private sector has created jobs 9 months in a row. But look, we still have a long way to go. We've still got a lot of work to do. There are still families out there that are hurting badly, some hanging on by a thread. That's what keeps me up at night. That's what keeps Barbara up at night. And that's why this election is so important. That's why the choice we make is so important.

Look, Barbara and I, we've got a different idea, a different vision about what our future should look like, and it's an idea rooted in our own experience, living out the American Dream, because we didn't come from plenty. We know government doesn't have all the answers to our problems. We want a government that is lean and efficient.

But in the words of the first Republican President, Abraham Lincoln—who, by the way, could not win a Republican nomination these days—[*laughter*]—no, seriously, can you imag-ine him trying to run with these folks? [*Laughter*] Lincoln said government should do for the people what they cannot do better for themselves. So we believe in an America that rewards hard work and responsibility and individual initiative. But we also believe in an America that invests in its future, that invests in its people, in the education of our children, in the skills of our workers. We believe in a country that looks after one another. Where we say I am my brother's keeper, I am my sister's keeper. That is the America that I know. That is the America that Barbara knows. That is the choice in this election.

So if we give them the keys back, they'll keep giving tax breaks to companies that ship jobs overseas. I want to give tax breaks. Barbara wants to give tax breaks. We already have to companies that are investing right here in the United States of America, to small businesses and American manufacturers and clean energy companies that are building solar panels and wind turbines and electric cars right here in the United States of America with American workers. That's the choice in this election. That's what we're about.

You give the keys to the other side, they want to have a $700 billion tax break that would only go to the top 2 percent—wealthiest 2 percent of Americans—and they'd cut education by 20 percent in the process.

Now, think about this. Let me tell you, China is not cutting education spending by 20 percent. South Korea is not cutting education by 20 percent. Germany is not cutting education by 20 percent. They understand that whoever outeducates us today will outcompete us tomorrow. They are not playing for second place. And the United States of America doesn't play for second place. We play for first place.

And that's why Barbara and I, working together, took away unwarranted subsidies to banks and have now provided tens of billions of dollars in additional aid to students so they can go to colleges. We're creating tax credits worth $10,000 in tuition relief for every student.

That is the choice in this election. That's the choice in this election. Yes, we want tax cuts going to middle class families, make those permanent. Yes, we believe in clean air and clean water. And we think that those laws should be enforced.

You give the keys to the other side, they're going to put those special interests right back sitting shotgun. They've already promised to roll back Wall Street reform, roll back health insurance reform. And we refuse to let that happen because we think that if you're paying an insurance premium, they shouldn't be able to drop you when you get sick. The whole point of having health insurance is to have it there when you need it.

We don't think credit card companies should be able to jack up your rates without any notice and without any reason. We want to make sure that taxpayers never again have to pay for bailouts because of reckless risks taken by a few. We don't believe in privatization of Social Security, because as long as I'm President we're not going to have our retirement savings handed over to Wall Street.

Those are all choices that we've got to make in this election. That's what we're fighting for.

We believe in making investments in infrastructure. We shouldn't be the country that is lagging behind when it comes to high-speed rail, when it comes to a smart electric grid. We should have the best airports in the world, the best roads in the world, the best bridges in the world, the best broadband access in the world. That is our legacy. That is our history.

But you know what, right now the same special interests that fought us every inch of the way, they are fighting just as hard in this election. They want to roll back the clock. Here in California, oil companies and the other special interests are spending millions on a campaign to gut clean air standards and clean energy standards, jeopardizing the health and prosperity of this State. All across America, special interests have poured millions of dollars into phony front groups. You've seen them. They're called Americans for Prosperity or Moms for Motherhood. [*Laughter*] I made that last one up.

They don't have the guts to say, we're funding this. So they hide behind these front groups. You don't know who these groups are. You don't know who's funding it, although we have a

pretty good idea—smearing Democratic candidates. This is thanks to a gigantic loophole. They can spend without limit, keep their contributions secret. It could be oil companies, Wall Street speculators, insurance companies. You don't know. They won't tell you. They won't say.

And by the way, those of you who don't think that the Supreme Court is important, this is a direct result of a ruling called *Citizens United*, which is why when Barbara and I make sure that we've got people like Sonia Sotomayor and Elena Kagan on the bench. The only way we're going to do that is if we've got a Senate majority that is serious.

These rulings are not just a threat to Democrats. They're a threat to our democracy. And the only way to fight, the only way to match their millions of dollars is your millions of voices, to finish what we started in 2008.

That's why it's wonderful that you're at this lunch, but I've got to ask more of you. You've got to go out there and talk to your friends and your neighbors and your coworkers, to your cousins and nephews and uncles and whoever is out there. You've got to talk to them. We've got to fight for this.

You fought in 2008 because you believed we were at a unique moment in our history, where the decisions we made now would have an impact for generations. But we just started. This is just the first quarter. We've got a lot more work to do. And I know that there are times over the course of the last 2 years where some of you may have thought back to election night or the campaign or the Inauguration and Beyonce was singing—[*laughter*]—and Bono. And it all seemed so wonderful and fun.

And then suddenly, the actual work of change, not just talking about change, but the actual work of change began. And we had to grind it out. And suddenly, we've got filibusters. And we've got distortions in the media. And suddenly, everybody starts feeling like, boy, this is harder than we expected.

Well, we knew it was going to be hard. I told you it was going to be hard. And yet—and yet—we've made a difference. Don't let anybody tell you that that work we've put in has not made a difference.

Because of you, because of the work that you did, because of the hope that you showed, there's a woman here in—somewhere in California who is going to be able to get treatment for her cancer instead of having to mortgage her house.

Because of you, somewhere here in California, there's going to be a young person who says, you know what, I can afford to go to college. Because of you, there's some small-business owner who was able to keep their doors open despite the worst possible recession.

Because of you, there's a clean energy company that has some magnificent idea that could end up leading to unbelievable innovation sometime in the future. That happened all because of you. Because of you, there are 100,000 young men and women who have come home from Iraq and are no longer at war. That's because of you. Don't let them tell you that what you did didn't make a difference. Don't let them tell you that what you did didn't make a difference.

Change is hard, but it's always been hard. That's been the history of this country, from its founding. And if our grandparents, our great-grandparents, our great-great-grandparents, if they had said to themselves, well, I can't do this because it's too hard, success is uncertain, there are people saying mean things about me—

[*laughter*]—we would have never gotten through a war, we would have never gotten through depression, we wouldn't have gotten civil rights or women's rights or workers' rights.

We got through those things and helped to perfect our Union because in the face of uncertainty, in the face of adversity, in the face of difficulty, people stood up. They said, "Yes, we can." They had the courage of their convictions. And we had leaders like Barbara Boxer.

What was true then is just as true now. And so if everybody here keeps that spirit alive and is out there knocking on doors and making phone calls and calling their friends and calling their neighbors and reminding everybody of the same hope, the same possibility that we did 2 years ago, we're not just going to reelect Barbara Boxer, we are going to make sure that the American Dream is alive and well for future generations.

Thank you, everybody. God bless you. God bless the United States of America.

NOTE: The President spoke at 12:38 p.m. in the Ronald Tutor Campus Center at the University of Southern California. In his remarks, he referred to musicians Stevie Wonder, Beyonce G. Knowles, and Paul D. "Bono" Hewson; and Sim Farar, finance chair for Sen. Boxer's reelection campaign committee.

Remarks at a Democratic National Committee Rally in Los Angeles
October 22, 2010

The President. Hello, L.A.! Oh, this is a Trojan kind of welcome right here. Fight on! Oh, I am fired up!

You know, Jamie Foxx is pretty good at this. We might have to recruit him. We'd have to make him shave his goatee, though. [*Laughter*]

It is wonderful to see all of you. Let me just say how proud I am to be here with some of the finest elected officials that I know: the next Governor of the great State of California, Jerry Brown; your outstanding mayor, Antonio Villaraigosa; Speaker of the California Assembly John Perez; L.A. City Council President Eric Garcetti; a dear, dear friend of mine, so I want everybody to do right by her, San Francisco

District Attorney Kamala Harris; an outstanding congressional delegation—Diane Watson, Judy Chu, Adam Schiff, Grace Napolitano, Xavier Becerra; an unbelievable Secretary of Labor, Hilda Solis; and somebody who has been fighting on your behalf for many, many years and needs to be—keep on fighting for us for the next 6 years, Senator Barbara Boxer.

It is great to be with all of you on this beautiful day.

Audience member. We love you!

The President. You know, we are going to need—I love you back.

We need all of you to fight on. We need all of you fired up. We need all of you ready to go, because in just 11 days, in just 11 days, you have the chance to set the direction of this State and of this country not just for the next 2 years, but for the next 5 years, the next 10 years, the next 20 years. And just like you did in 2008, you can defy the conventional wisdom, the conventional wisdom that says young people are apathetic, the conventional wisdom that says you can't beat the cynicism in politics, that you can't overcome the special interests, that all that matters is all the big money and the negative TV ads. You have the chance to say, yes, we can.

Audience members. Yes, we can! Yes, we can! Yes, we can!

The President. Yes, we can. Yes, we can. *Si, se puede.*

Look, now, look, I don't want to fool anybody, even though this is an incredible crowd, a magnificent crowd, but let me be clear: This is going to be a difficult election, because we've been through an incredibly difficult time as a nation.

For most of the last decade, the middle class has been hurting. Families saw their incomes, between 2001 and 2009—by about 5 percent. That's not my statistics. That's the Wall Street Journal talking. Job growth was more sluggish during that period than any time since World War II. Jobs were being shipped overseas. Parents couldn't afford to send their kids to college. Families couldn't afford to send somebody in their family to a doctor. Americans were working two, three jobs just to try to make ends meet. And all this culminated in the worst economic crisis since the Great Depression.

Understand, we lost 4 million jobs in the 6 months before I took office, 750,000 the month that I was sworn in, 600,000 the month after that, 600,000 the month after that. We hadn't seen anything like this since the 1930s. We lost 8 million jobs before any of my economic policies had a chance to be put into place.

Now, my hope was that in this moment of crisis, we could come together and both parties would put politics aside, that we would come together to meet this once-in-a-generation challenge, because although we are proud Democrats, we are prouder to be Americans. And you

know, there are plenty of Republicans who feel the same way out there.

But the Republican leaders in Washington, they made a different calculation. They looked around at the mess that they had made, at the mess that they had left me, and they said, boy, this is a really big mess. And they said it's going to take a long time to fix. Unemployment is probably going to be high for a while, and in the meantime, people are going to get angry and frustrated. So maybe if we just sit on the sidelines, say no to everything, and then point our fingers at Obama and say he's to blame, they figured that maybe you all would forget that they caused the mess in the first place, and they'd be able to ride anger all the way to election time. But, Los Angeles, as I look out on this crowd, this tells me you haven't forgotten.

Their whole campaign strategy is amnesia. And so you need to remember that this election is a choice between the policies that got us into this mess and the policies that are leading out of this mess, a choice between the past and the future, a choice between hope and fear, a choice between moving forward or going backwards. And I don't know about you, but I want to move forward, Trojans. I want to go forward.

Now, look, I understand it would be one thing if the Republicans, having made this mess, they went off into the desert or into some retreat somewhere and they meditated on, boy, we really screwed up, and now let's come up with some new ideas because we recognize the error of our ways. But that's not what's going on.

The Republican Campaign Committee chairman promised the exact same agenda if they win back the House and if they win back the Senate: the same agenda of cutting taxes for millionaires and billionaires, of cutting rules for the special interests, from cutting middle class families loose to fend for themselves. Their basic philosophy is, you're on your own. If you're sick, you don't have health care, too bad, you're on your own. You don't have a job, them's the breaks; you're on your own. You're a young person wants to go to USC, wants to get his education but can't afford it, tough luck, you're on your own. It's the same agenda that turned a record surplus into a record deficit, the same agenda that allowed Wall Street to run wild, the same agenda that nearly destroyed our economy.

And I bring all this up not because I want to reargue the past. I bring it up because I don't want to relive the past. We can't afford it. I bring it up because it's not as if we haven't tried what they're selling. We tried it. We didn't like it, and we're not going back to it.

I want you to think about it this way. Imagine that these folks drove the car into the ditch. And it was a really deep ditch. And somehow they were able to walk away from the accident, but they did nothing to get the car out of the ditch. And so me and Barbara and Jerry and Antonio, we all put on our boots, and we climbed down into the ditch.

And it's hot down there. It's—flies are down there—[laughter]—and we're sweating. But we're pushing; we're pushing to get the car out of the ditch. And even though Barbara Boxer is small, she is pushing too. And we're all pushing. And as we're pushing, we look up, and the Republicans are all standing there at the top of the ditch. They're all looking down. And we say, why don't you come down and help? And they say, no, that's all right. And then they kick some dirt down into the ditch. [Laughter] They're sipping on a Slurpee. They're fanning themselves. You're not pushing hard enough, they say. You're not pushing the right way.

And yet, despite all that, we still get the car out of the ditch. And it's finally on level ground. And I admit, the car is a little banged up. I mean, the fender is bent and it's going to have to go to the body shop, and it needs a tuneup. But it's on level ground, and it's pointing in the right direction. We're ready to move forward. And suddenly—suddenly—we get this tap on our shoulder and we look back, and who is it? It's the Republicans. And they say, we want the keys back.

And we've got to tell them, you can't have the keys back. You don't know how to drive. You can ride with us, but you got to be in the backseat, because we got middle class America in the front seat. We're looking out for them.

You ever notice when you want to go forward, what do you do? You put your car in "D." You want to go backwards, what do you do? You put it in "R." That's not a coincidence. We want to go forward. We don't want to go backwards.

Audience members. Yes, we can! Yes, we can! Yes, we can!

The President. Yes, we can.

Look, because of the steps that we've taken, we no longer face the possibility of a second depression. The economy is growing again. The private sector has seen job growth 9 months in a row. But we've still got a long way to go. We've still got a lot of work to do. There are a lot of people out there still hurting. I know there are a lot of families still hanging on by a thread. That's what keeps me up at night. That's what keeps me fighting. That's why all of you are here, because you know we've got more work to do.

But understand, we've got a different idea about what the future holds. It's an idea rooted in our belief about how this country was built. We know that the government doesn't have the answers to all our problems. We believe government should be lean and efficient. But in the words of the first Republican President, Abraham Lincoln—who, by the way, couldn't get a nomination in today's Republican Party—[laughter]—we also believe that government should do for the people what they cannot do better for themselves.

We believe in an America that rewards hard work and responsibility and individual initiative, but that also puts a hand up to help people live out their dreams. We believe in an America that invests in its people, in its future, the education of our children, the skills of our workers. We believe in a country where we look after one another, where I am my brother's keeper, where I am my sister's keeper. That's the America that I know. And that is the choice in this election.

This election is a choice. And if we give them the keys, which will happen if you don't vote, they'll keep giving tax breaks to companies that ship our jobs overseas. We want to give tax breaks to companies that create jobs right here in the United States, to small businesses and American manufacturers and clean energy companies. Because I don't want wind panels and—wind turbines and solar panels and electric cars made in Europe or Asia; I want them built right here in the United States, by American workers here in the United States of America. That's the choice in this election.

If we give them the keys back, and we will if you don't vote, the other side has said they are going to cut taxes for millionaires and billionaires, costing us $700 billion, and to help pay for it, they're going to cut education spending by 20 percent.

Now, think about this. This is at a time when the question of whether a country competes almost entirely depends on how well we educate our children. Do you think that China wants to cut education by 20 percent?

Audience members. No!

The President. Is South Korea cutting education by 20 percent?

Audience members. No!

The President. Those countries aren't playing for second place. America doesn't play for second place. We play for first place.

Audience members. U.S.A.! U.S.A.! U.S.A.!

The President. We play for first. And that's why, instead of giving unwarranted subsidies to the banks, we've taken tens of billions of dollars, and we're now putting them where they should go—to students like you—to make sure that you can afford a college education and a $10,000 tuition tax credit for every young person in America so you can get the education you deserve. That's the choice in this election.

We want tax cuts to middle class families. We don't want special interests back in the shotgun. You know, the other side has already promised to roll back Wall Street reform, roll back health insurance reform. We refuse to make that happen. We want to make sure that insurance companies can't deny you coverage when you get sick. We want to make sure that the law we passed to make sure that you can stay on your parents' health insurance till you're 26 years old, that that remains the law of the land.

We want to make sure that credit card companies can't hit you with hidden fees or jack up your rates without notice. We want to make sure that taxpayers aren't stuck with a Wall

Street bailout because somebody else took unwarranted risks.

We're going to fight the effort to privatize Social Security, because as long as I'm President, nobody is going to take a generation's worth of retirement savings and hand them over to Wall Street. Not on my watch.

We are going to make sure we continue to invest in clean energy and we enforce our clean air and clean water laws. You've seen what they're trying to do here in California, trying to roll back laws that will keep California at the cutting edge. And now that we've got special interests spending millions of dollars out there to gut these clean air standards and clean energy standards, and they're doing the same thing all across the country: millions of dollars in special interest money, using phony front groups. You don't know their names. They call themselves Americans for Prosperity or Mothers for Motherhood. I made that last one up, but—[*laughter*]—but it might as well be.

And you don't know who's behind it. You don't know, is it an insurance company? Is it a bank? Who is financing all these negative ads against Jerry Brown? Who's financing all these negative ads against Barbara Boxer?

And you know how they're able to do this without disclosing their donors is because of a Supreme Court ruling called *Citizens United*, which shows you how important it is who's making appointments on the Supreme Court. I'm proud I appointed Sonia Sotomayor. I appointed Elena Kagan.

All this money pouring into these elections by these phony front groups, this isn't just a threat to Democrats, it's a threat to our democracy. And the only way to fight it is all of you, all these voices matching those millions of dollars, all of you being committed to finish what we started in 2008. That's why it's so important all of you get out. All of you have got to vote, because if everybody who fought for change in 2008 turns out this time, we will win this election.

And so I want to remind you why you got involved. You didn't just get involved to elect a President. You got involved because you believed we were at a defining moment. You believed that this was a time when the decisions we make, the challenges we face, are going to shape the lives of our children and our grandchildren and our great-grandchildren for decades to come. That's why you knocked on doors. That's why you made phone calls. That's why some of you cast your vote for the very first time.

And look, I understand the last 2 years haven't been easy. I know that a lot of you, you're thinking back to election night or Inauguration Day and how much fun that was, and Beyonce was singing and Bono. [*Laughter*] And Jamie was there. And it felt like a big party. But I want everybody to understand, I told you this was going to be hard. I told you power concedes nothing without a fight.

Inch by inch, day by day, week by week, we've been grinding it out, because that's the nature of change in a big, complex democracy. And I recognize some of you may feel now that, gosh, it seems so distant from those wonderful memories and change is harder than I expected; we haven't gotten everything done that we hoped for yet. And maybe you know somebody in your family who's out of a job or maybe somebody in your neighborhood has put up a foreclosure sign, and you think, boy, we're not moving as quick as we want.

I understand that. But don't let anybody tell you that our fight hasn't been worth it. Don't let them tell you that we're not making a difference. Because of you, there are people right here in California who don't have to choose between getting treatment for their cancer or going bankrupt. Because of you, there are parents who are able to look their children in the eye and say, yes, you will go to college. We can afford it; we're getting some help. Because of you, there are small businesses who are able to keep their doors open, even in the midst of recession. Because of you, we have brought home nearly 100,000 brave men and women from Iraq.

Because of you, we are going to continue to fight to end "don't ask, don't tell." Because of you, we are going to make sure that we've got an energy policy for the future of America—because of you. So don't tell—don't let them tell you that change isn't possible. Because here's

what I know: Change is always hard. And if our parents, if our grandparents, if our great-grandparents, if they had listened to the cynics 50 years ago, 100 years ago, 200 years ago, we wouldn't be here today.

Think about it. This country was founded on 13 Colonies coming together to do what had never been done before: declaring a revolution, throwing off the yoke of tyranny, battling the biggest, baddest empire on Earth. And then they decided, you know, we're going to try to form a new type of government. And they wrote on paper, they said in their declaration, "We hold these truths to be self-evident, that all men are created equal, that we are all endowed by our Creator with certain inalienable rights, that among these are life, liberty, and the pursuit of happiness."

The cynics didn't believe it. And then, when we had to perfect that Union and fight a civil war, the cynics didn't believe it. They didn't think we could free the slaves. If our ancestors had given up, if they had given up to the cynics, we couldn't have gotten through war, we couldn't have gotten through depression, we would not have been able to battle and finally achieve civil rights and women's rights and workers' rights.

That is the spirit we have to summon today. The journey we began together was not just about putting a President in the White House. It was about building a movement for change. It was about realizing the promise of the United States of America and understanding that if we're willing to work for it, there's nothing we cannot achieve.

So I need you to keep on believing. I need you to keep hoping. And if you knock on some doors and make some phone calls and keep marching and keep organizing, we won't just win this election; we are going to restore the American Dream for not just some, but for every, every, everybody in this great land.

Thank you very much, everybody. God bless you, and God bless the United States of America.

NOTE: The President spoke at 2:06 p.m. in Alumni Park at the University of Southern California. In his remarks, he referred to actor Jamie Foxx; and musicians Beyonce G. Knowles and Paul D. "Bono" Hewson.

Statement on the Death of Bishop Arthur M. Brazier
October 22, 2010

Michelle and I were deeply saddened to learn of the passing of our dear friend, a stalwart of the city of Chicago and one of our Nation's leading moral lights, Bishop Arthur M. Brazier. Through his service as a pastor and his work on behalf of our communities, Bishop Brazier touched the lives of countless Americans.

Bishop Brazier grew up during the Great Depression and never forgot how the sting of poverty can shape a community and a nation. A committed patriot, Bishop Brazier served as a staff sergeant in the United States Army in India and Burma at the height of World War II. He returned to Chicago, where he promoted spiritual empowerment and economic develop-ment through his pastorate of Apostolic Church of God and leadership of numerous community organizations and charitable efforts.

There is no way that we can replace the gentle heart and boundless determination that Bishop Brazier brought to some of the most pressing challenges facing Chicago and our Nation. However, his spirit will live on through the parishioners, leaders, and friends that he touched each day. Michelle and I join the Brazier family, the Apostolic Church of God, and all of Chicago in this moment of prayer and mourning and in our commitment to ensure that Bishop Brazier's legacy lives on through our service to others.

Letter to Congressional Leaders on Continuation of the National Emergency With Respect to the Situation in or in Relation to the Democratic Republic of the Congo
October 22, 2010

Dear Madam Speaker: (Dear Mr. President:)

Section 202(d) of the National Emergencies Act (50 U.S.C. 1622(d)) provides for the automatic termination of a national emergency unless, prior to the anniversary date of its declaration, the President publishes in the *Federal Register* and transmits to the Congress a notice stating that the emergency is to continue in effect beyond the anniversary date. In accordance with this provision, I have sent to the *Federal Register* for publication the enclosed notice stating that the national emergency with respect to the situation in or in relation to the Democratic Republic of the Congo and the related measures blocking the property of certain persons contributing to the conflict in that country are to continue in effect beyond October 27, 2010.

The situation in or in relation to the Democratic Republic of the Congo, which has been marked by widespread violence and atrocities that continue to threaten regional stability, continues to pose an unusual and extraordinary threat to the foreign policy of the United States. For this reason, I have determined that it is necessary to continue the national emergency to deal with that threat and the related measures blocking the property of certain persons contributing to the conflict in that country.

Sincerely,

BARACK OBAMA

NOTE: Identical letters were sent to Nancy Pelosi, Speaker of the House of Representatives, and Joseph R. Biden, Jr., President of the Senate. The notice is listed in Appendix D at the end of this volume.

Remarks at a Democratic National Committee Rally in Las Vegas, Nevada
October 22, 2010

The President. Hello, Vegas! It is good to be back in Vegas. It is good to be back in Nevada. Oh, I am fired up. Are you fired up?

There are a couple of folks that I want to make mention of. First of all, Congresswoman Shelley Berkley is in the house. An outstanding freshman Congresswoman, Dina Titus is here. Senate Majority Leader Steven Horsford is in the house. Former Governor Bob Miller is here. My dear friend, my Senator from Illinois, Dick Durbin is here to help his partner Harry Reid.

And I want to say to all the folks from Orr school, thank you so much for your hospitality, and thanks to Principal George Leavens. Thank you.

I am happy to see all of you. And I have to say, for some reason, whenever I'm coming to Vegas, suddenly, a whole bunch of folks on my staff want to come with me. I don't know. [*Laughter*] Suddenly, there are no seats on Air Force One. It's all crowded. [*Laughter*] So I've already told them they've got to behave themselves a little bit while they're here.

But the main reason I'm here, the main reason I need you fired up, is because in just 11 days, you have the chance to set the direction of this State and this country, not just for the next 5 years, not just for the next 10 years, but for the next several decades.

And if I'm going to be able to help middle class families all across this country live out their dreams, then I want to have a partner in the United States Senate named Harry Reid.

You know, Harry's not the flashiest guy, let's face it. [*Laughter*] You know, Harry kind of speaks in a very soft voice. He doesn't move real quick. [*Laughter*] He doesn't get up and make big stemwinding speeches. But Harry Reid does the right thing.

Harry Reid has never forgotten what it's like to grow up in Searchlight, Nevada. [*Applause*] Got a Searchlight folk right here. He knows what it's like to be poor. He knows what it's like to work hard. He knows what it's like sometimes to hit some bumps in the road, to hit

some obstacles, to have to overcome some stuff, that things don't always work out perfectly.

But because of that, because he remembers where he came from, it means that he thinks every single day about how am I going to give the folks in Nevada a better shot at life.

And so I want everybody here to understand what's at stake.

Audience members. Obama! Obama! Obama!

The President. I appreciate everybody saying "Obama," but I want everybody to say "Harry! Harry! Harry!"

Audience members. Harry! Harry! Harry!

The President. That's right. I need partners like Harry. And I need partners like Dina Titus. And I need partners like Shelley Berkley. Look, but it all depends on you.

Just like you did in 2008, you can defy the conventional wisdom: the wisdom that said you can't overcome cynicism in politics; the wisdom that says the special interests always win; the wisdom that says somehow the folks with the big money who are running the most negative ads, somehow they're always going to be successful; the wisdom that says we can't tackle big challenges in America anymore.

In 11 days, you can say to them: "You may think, no, we can't. We think, yes, we can."

Audience members. Yes, we can! Yes, we can! Yes, we can!

The President. Yes, we can. *Si, se puede.* There is no doubt that this is going to be a difficult election. And that's because we've been through an incredibly difficult time as a nation. And nobody's been hit harder than Nevada.

But keep in mind, things were tough even before the financial crisis hit. Between 2001 and 2009, average middle class families in America lost 5 percent of income, when the Republicans were in charge. We had the slowest job growth since World War II when the Republicans were in charge. You saw your health care costs go up. You saw the cost of a college education go up. Too many jobs being shipped overseas, too many folks working two, three jobs and still barely making ends meet. And all this culminated in the worst financial crisis since the Great Depression.

So we know the results of the Republican philosophy when it comes to the economy. It's no secret. Basically, their theory was you cut taxes for millionaires and billionaires, you cut regulations for Wall Street and other special interests, and then you cut middle class families loose to fend for themselves.

That was their theory. And what happened was, before I took office, we had already lost 4 million jobs all across this country. A whole bunch of them were right here in Nevada. The first month that I was sworn in we lost 750,000 jobs; month after that, 600,000; the month after that, 600,000. We lost almost 8 million jobs before my policies, Harry Reid's policies, were put into effect.

And so our hope was that because we were in crisis, that we could come together, both parties, put politics aside, and deal with this once-in-a-generation challenge. I wanted to move beyond the bickering and the game-playing and the partisanship that had dominated Washington for so long, because although we are proud to be Democrats, we are prouder to be Americans.

I know there are a whole bunch of Republicans out there who felt the same way. But the Republican leaders in Washington, they made a different decision. Here's the thing, they realized what a big mess they had made. They said, boy, we screwed up so bad, it is going to take a really long time to recover those 8 million jobs that were lost. It's going to take a long time before the housing market fully recovers. So our best bet, instead of trying to help Obama and Harry Reid to solve problems, we're going to stand on the sidelines, sit on our hands, and basically, just say no to everything.

Their theory was, people will forget that we were the ones who caused all this stuff, and we'll be able to blame them, and people will be so angry and frustrated that we'll be able to ride this anger all the way to the ballot box. That was their theory.

In other words, they are basically betting on all of you having amnesia. [*Laughter*] They're basically—they're banking on the fact that you

might forget who got us in this mess in the first place. So let me tell you, Las Vegas, you have not forgotten. I have not forgotten. We are not going to buy what they are selling. That is the choice we've got in this election.

We've got a choice between the policies that got us into this mess and the policies that are helping to get us out of this mess. It's a choice between the past and the future, between falling backwards and moving forward, a choice between hope and fear. I don't know about you, but I want to move forward.

You know, the chair of the Republican campaign committee was asked, what would you do if you win back the Congress? And he said, "We're going to do the exact same thing, pursue the exact same agenda as before we took office." Now, think about this. Their policies resulted in the worst economic crisis since the 1930s, and they want to go back to that exact same set of policies. Does that make any sense to you?

Audience members. No!

The President. I mean, it would be one thing if they had kind of gone away and gone off into the desert—you know, there's some desert here. They could have gone off into the desert. They could have meditated and thought about, "Boy, how did we screw up so bad?" And they felt bad about it, and then they came back and they had some new ideas and they wanted to cooperate with us.

But that's not what happened. They want to do the exact same things they did before. And it's not as if we didn't try them. We tried them for 8 years, and it didn't work. So why would we buy that snake oil now? We're not going to.

Look, this is—imagine that the economy is a car, and the Republicans drove this car into a ditch. And it was a really deep ditch. And somehow they were able to walk away from the accident, from the scene of the crime, but they left the car down in the ditch.

So me and Harry and Dina and Shelley, we put on our boots, and we went down into the ditch. We had to rappel down, it was so deep down there. And when we got down there, it was muddy and dirty, and it was hot. [*Laughter*] We're sweating; there are bugs everywhere. But we had to make sure we get that car out of the ditch, so we start pushing. We're pushing, we're pushing, we're pushing.

And every once in a while we'd look up, and lo and behold, up on the hill there, there's the Republicans. They're just standing there, sipping on a Slurpee—[*laughter*]—fanning themselves.

And we'd say, "Why don't you come down and help?" And they'd say, "No," and then they'd kick some more dirt down into the ditch. [*Laughter*] But that's okay. We kept on pushing, we kept on pushing.

Finally, we get this car up on level ground. Finally, we get it out of the ditch. Now, the car is banged up. It's banged up, and it's got a bunch of dents. It's got to go to the body shop. It needs a tuneup. But it's pointed in the right direction. The engine is still turning.

And suddenly, as we're about to get in the car, we feel this tap on our shoulder, and we look back, and who is it? It's the Republicans. [*Laughter*] And they say, "Excuse me, we'd like the keys back." [*Laughter*]

And we got to tell them, "I'm sorry, you can't have the keys back. You don't know how to drive, you don't know how to drive. If you want, you can ride with us, but you've got to ride in the backseat." [*Laughter*] We're putting middle class families in the front seat where they belong.

You ever notice when you want to go forward in your car, what do you do? You put it in "D." If you want to go backwards, you put it in "R." I don't want to go backwards. Let's go forward, let's go forward. I want to go forward.

Look, because of the steps that we've taken, we no longer face the possibility of a second depression. The economy is growing again. Private sector job growth has happened 9 months in a row. But look, everybody here in Nevada knows we've still got a long way to go. We've got a lot of work to do. A lot of folks are hurting out there. Families are hanging on by a thread. A lot of folks are seeing their homes lose a lot of value, a lot of foreclosures out here.

It keeps me up at night; it keeps Harry Reid up at night. That's what keeps us fighting, because we've got a different idea about what the future should hold, and it's an idea rooted in our own lives, because neither Harry or I were born with a silver spoon in our mouths. Our families were working folk. And we understand how hard it is sometimes.

But we understand that government doesn't have all the answers to our problems. Government has got to be lean; it's got to be efficient. We believe in individual initiative, but we also believe, in the words of Abraham Lincoln, that government should do for the people what they cannot do better for themselves.

We believe in a country that rewards hard work and responsibility. We believe in an America that invests in its future and its people, in the education of our children, in the skills of our workers. We believe in an America where we look after one another, where I am my brother's keeper, I am my sister's keeper. That's the America we believe in. That's the choice in this election.

If we give them the keys back, the other side is going to keep giving tax breaks to companies that ship jobs overseas. We want to give tax breaks to companies that are investing right here in Nevada, companies creating jobs here in America, small businesses, American manufacturers, clean energy companies. We want solar panels built right here in the United States of America. We want wind turbines built right here in the United States of America. We want electric cars built here in the United States of America by American workers.

If the other side gets the keys, they say they want to give a $700 billion tax cut to the top 2 percent, millionaires and billionaires. They don't have the money. The only way to pay for it is to borrow some money from China and then to cut education spending by 20 percent.

Now, think about this. Here we are in the 21st century where everybody knows that the country that educates their people the best is going to succeed the most. Do you think China is cutting education by 20 percent?

Audience members. No!

The President. Do you think South Korea or Germany or India are cutting education by 20 percent?

Audience members. No!

The President. Those countries, they're not playing for second place, and neither does the United States of America. We play for first place.

And that's why Harry Reid and Dina Titus and Shelley Berkley, that's why Democrats in Congress helped to take away tens of billions of dollars that were going in unwarranted subsidies to banks, and they shifted those to fund college scholarships for young people all across the country, millions of young people getting more help to go to college. That's what this election is about. That's the choice that we face.

When we give tax cuts, we want to give tax cuts to middle class families who need help. They deserve relief. We don't want the special interests to be back in the shotgun seat. They've already promised to roll back Wall Street reform. They've promised to roll back health insurance reform.

We refuse to let that happen, because I don't want your health care denied just when you need it most because insurance companies are playing games. I don't want you to have to pay for another Wall Street bailout. I don't want credit card companies to be able to jack up your interest rates whenever they feel like it without giving you notice.

That's the old way of doing business. We've got a new way of doing business. We're moving forward; we're not moving backwards. That's the choice in this election.

We believe in rebuilding our infrastructure. I just came into Las Vegas Airport. We're doing work right there, putting people back to work because of Harry Reid, because of Dina Titus, because of Shelley Berkley.

We need to make sure that we've got the best infrastructure in the world. We're not going to have better airports in other countries than here in the United States. We can't have better roads and bridges and broadband lines. We've always had the best infrastructure. We need to continue that. That's the choice in this election.

And by the way, another choice in this election is making sure that Social Security is there, not just for this generation, but for the next generation. We're not going to privatize Social Se-

curity. Not on my watch and not on Harry Reid's watch. That's a choice in this election.

Now, let me say this, let me say this. We've got some big problems because the same special interests that we've been battling for the last 2 years, they're fighting back hard. They want to roll back the clock. And all across America they are pouring hundreds of millions of dollars into a bunch of phony front groups running negative ads. Have you seen some negative ads out here?

Audience members. Yes!

The President. You don't even know who's sponsoring these ads. They have all these names like Americans for Prosperity, Mothers for Motherhood. *[Laughter]* Actually, I made that last one up, but—*[laughter]*—but they're spending without limit, keeping their contributions secret. They don't even have the guts to stand up for what they say they believe in. And we don't know who's funding them. Is it the oil industry? Is it the insurance companies? Is it speculators? They won't tell you. They won't say. They don't want you to know who's bankrolling all these negative ads.

This is not just a threat to Democrats, this is a threat to our democracy. And, Nevada, the only way to fight it, the only way to match their millions of dollars, is with the millions of voices. All those folks who fought for change in 2008, we've got to fight for change in 2010.

So this is where all of you come in. You have to vote, everybody. Now, I just want everybody to know we've got early voting here in Nevada. And if you go right across the way to Boulevard Mall, if you get in line before 8 o'clock, you can cast your ballot right now. Don't wait. Don't wait, don't wait. If everybody who showed up in 2008 shows up in 2010, we will win this election.

So let me just say this. You know, in 2008, a lot of you got involved, some for the very first time. Some of you knocked on doors, some of you made phone calls, some of you talked to your neighbors, talked to your friends, because you understood we were at a defining moment in our history. You believed that this was a chance for you to make some history, to help finally move America in a better direction. You understood that what happened today was going to shape the lives of our children and our grandchildren. That's the reason you got involved. That's why you worked so hard, some of you for the very first time.

And I know sometimes over the last 2 years, as we've been grinding out change, doing battle, dealing with filibusters, dealing with obstruction, dealing with the "no, you can't" crowd, I know sometimes you might have gotten discouraged.

You think back to election night 2 years ago, you think back to the Inauguration, and Beyonce was singing and Bono, and you think, boy, that was so much fun. And then the work of bringing about actual change is so hard. And sometimes, you may get discouraged and lose heart.

And maybe, as you travel around Nevada, you see all the foreclosures. Somebody in your family still doesn't have a job, and you say, well, maybe what I did didn't really make a difference. But I'm here to tell you, Nevada, don't let anybody tell you that what you've done didn't matter.

Because of what you did, there's somebody in Nevada who's able to get their cancer treatments without mortgaging their house. Because of what you did, there's a small-business owner somewhere that kept their doors open in the depths of recession. Because of what you did, there's somebody who's going to work every day on that construction site. Because of what you did, there's a child somewhere that's getting health care. Because of what you did, there are 100,000 brave young men and women who have come back from Iraq. Because of what you did, America is a better place. But we've just begun. We're just in the first quarter. I can't have you tired now. I can't have you tired when we're just getting started.

Look, change has always been hard in this country. This country was founded when 13 Colonies came together in a revolution that no-

body believed could happen, except they believed. They founded this country on ideas that hadn't been tried before: "We hold these truths to be self-evident, that all men are created equal, that they are endowed by their Creator with certain inalienable rights, that among these are life, liberty, and the pursuit of happiness."

Nobody believed that the slaves could be free, except they believed. Folks didn't believe that women could win the right to vote, except women believed. Nobody believed that we could get workers' rights, except workers believed. There were a lot of folks who said we would never get civil rights. But we got civil rights because somebody out there believed.

Imagine if our parents, our grandparents, our great-grandparents had said, oh, this is too hard; oh, I'm feeling tired; oh, I'm feeling discouraged; oh, somebody is saying something mean about me. [*Laughter*] We would not be here today.

We got through war and depression. We have made this Union more perfect because somebody somewhere has been willing to stand up in the face of uncertainty, stand up in the face of difficulty. That is how change has come. And that's the spirit we have to restore in 2010.

And if all of you are going to go out and vote, all of you knock on doors, all of you are talking to your friends and neighbors, I promise you we will not just win this election, we just won't elect Harry Reid, but we are going to restore the American Dream, the Vegas dream, the Nevada dream, for families for generations to come.

God bless you, and God bless the United States of America.

NOTE: The President spoke at 6:15 p.m. at William E. Orr Middle School. In his remarks, he referred to Rep. Pete Sessions, in his capacity as chairman of the National Republican Congressional Committee; and musicians Beyonce G. Knowles and Paul D. "Bono" Hewson.

The President's Weekly Address
October 23, 2010

Over the past 2 years, we've won a number of battles to defend the interests of the middle class. One of the most important victories we achieved was the passage of Wall Street reform.

This was a bill designed to rein in the secret deals and reckless gambling that nearly brought down the financial system. It set new rules so that taxpayers would never again be on the hook for a bailout if a big financial company went under. And reform included the strongest consumer protections in history to put an end to a lot of the hidden fees, deceptive mortgages, and other abusive practices used to tilt the table against ordinary people in their financial dealings.

It was a tough fight. The special interests poured millions into a lobbying campaign to prevent us from reforming the system, a system that worked a lot better for them than for middle class families. Some in the financial industry were eager to protect a status quo that basically allowed them to play by their own rules. And these interests held common cause with Republican leaders in Washington who were looking to score a political victory in an election year.

But their efforts failed. And we succeeded in passing reform in the hopes of ensuring that we never again face a crisis like the one we've been through, a crisis that unleashed an economic downturn as deep as any since the Great Depression. Even today, we're still digging out of the damage it unleashed on the economy. Millions of people are still out of work. Millions of families are still hurting.

We're also seeing the reverberations of this crisis with the rise in foreclosures. And recently, we've seen problems in foreclosure proceedings, mistakes that have led to disruptions in the housing markets. This is only one more piece of evidence as to why Wall Street reform is so necessary. In fact, as part of reform, a new consumer watchdog is now standing up. It will have just one job: looking out for ordinary consumers in the financial system. And this watchdog will have the authority to guard against unfair practices in mortgage transactions and foreclosures.

Yet despite the importance of this law and despite the terrible economic dislocation caused by the failures in our financial system under the old rules, top Republicans in Congress are now beating the drum to repeal all of these reforms and consumer protections. Recently, one of the Republican leaders in the Senate said that if Republicans take charge of Congress, repeal would be one of the first orders of business. And he joins the top Republican in the House who actually called for the law to be repealed even before it passed.

I think that would be a terrible mistake. Our economy depends on a financial system in which everyone competes on a level playing field and everyone is held to the same rules, whether you're a big bank, a small-business owner, or a family looking to buy a house or open a credit card. And as we saw, without sound oversight and commonsense protections for consumers, the whole economy is put in jeopardy. That doesn't serve Main Street. That doesn't serve Wall Street. That doesn't serve anyone. And that's why I think it's so important that we not take this country backward, that we don't go back to the broken system we had before. We've got to keep moving forward.

Thanks.

NOTE: The address was recorded at approximately 2:10 p.m. on October 20 in the Diplomatic Reception Room at the White House for broadcast on October 23. In the address, the President referred to Sen. John Cornyn, in his capacity as chairman of the National Republican Senatorial Committee; and House Republican Leader John A. Boehner. The transcript was made available by the Office of the Press Secretary on October 22, but was embargoed for release until 6 a.m. on October 23.

Remarks at a Rally for Gubernatorial Candidate Mark B. Dayton in Minneapolis, Minnesota
October 23, 2010

The President. Hello, Minnesota! Hello, Gophers! Oh, it is good to be back in Minnesota! And it's an honor to be standing here next to your next Governor, Mark Dayton.

Let me just make mention of the other wonderful public servants who are here. Former Vice President Walter Mondale is in the house. Your terrific pair of Senators, Amy Klobuchar and Al Franken, are here; an outstanding congressional delegation—Keith Ellison, Betty McCollum, Jim Oberstar.

All the great candidates who are on the DFL ticket are here today, and we're thrilled to see them. And obviously, I am very honored to be here with Mark, because I served with Mark in the United States Senate. And so I know this man. And I know that he's been fighting for the people of this State his entire career. You know what kind of leader he is. You know what kind of fighter he is. Everybody else in this race might be talking about change. Here's the only candidate who can actually deliver change, who's actually delivered change before.

The only candidate who's helped grow this State's economy. The only candidate who's put people back to work. The only candidate who's saved taxpayer dollars by cutting waste and abuse. So you know Mark Dayton. He's got a track record. He's the only candidate in this race who will stand up for the middle class, who's got a plan to balance the budget without sacrificing our children's education. A candidate who has a plan to create jobs and help small-business owners grow and to thrive.

The point is, Mark Dayton has spent his life fighting for Minnesota, and now I need all of you to fight for Mark Dayton so we can keep this State moving forward.

Well, it looks like you're kind of fired up. And I need you fired up because in just 10 days, you have the chance not just to set the direction of this State, but also help to determine the direction of this country, not just for the next 2 years, but the next 5 years, the next 10 years, the next 20 years.

And just like you did in 2008, you have the chance to defy the conventional wisdom, because right now the conventional wisdom is that you can't overcome the cynicism of politics, that you can't overcome all the special interest money that Mark was talking about, that you can't tackle big challenges, that the political system just can't digest it. The same way that they said in 2008 that you can't elect a skinny guy with a funny name to the Presidency of the United States of America. And so, in 2008, you said, "Yes, we can." In 2010, you've got to say, "Yes, we can."

Audience members. Yes, we can! Yes, we can! Yes, we can!

The President. Yes, we can.

Look, there is no doubt that this is going to be a difficult election. And it's because we've been through an incredibly difficult time for our nation. For most of the last decade, the middle class in America was getting pounded.

I'll give you a few statistics. Between 2001 and 2009, when Republicans were in charge, the middle class saw their incomes go down by 5 percent during that period. That's not according to me; that's according to the Wall Street Journal. Between that same period we had the slowest, most sluggish job growth of any time since World War II. So this was a lost decade for middle class families. Costs of everything from health care to getting a college education were skyrocketing. Jobs were disappearing overseas. Too many parents had to say to their kids, you know, we might not be able to afford to send you to college. Too many families had to pass up going to the doctor when they got sick because they couldn't afford it, too many Americans having two, three jobs and still not being able to make ends meet.

And then all of this culminated in the worst financial crisis and the worst economic crisis since the Great Depression. I want everybody to think back to when I was first sworn in. We had lost 4 million jobs in the 6 months before I took office. We lost 750,000 the month I took the oath, 600,000 the month after that, 600,000 more the month after that. We lost almost 8 million jobs, almost all of them lost before any of our economic policies could be put into place.

And when I arrived in Washington, my hope was that we could put politics aside for a moment to meet this once-in-a-generation challenge. My hope was we could stop the division and the bickering and the partisanship that had dominated Washington and that we could come together to solve problems, because although we are proud Democrats, we are prouder to be Americans, Minnesota. And I believe there are a lot of Republicans out there that felt the same way.

But when we got to Washington, the Republican leaders in Congress, they had a different idea. Their basic theory was they looked around and said, boy, we really made a big mess, we really screwed up. It's going to take a long time to get those 8 million jobs back. People are going to be angry and frustrated. It's better if we refuse to cooperate, we say no to everything, we try to gum up the works in Congress, and we may be able to deflect the blame come the next election. We'll just pretend like we had nothing to do it, and we'll point our fingers at the Democrats. In other words, the other side was betting on amnesia. [*Laughter*] They're betting that you'll forget who caused this mess in the first place.

But, Minneapolis, it is up to you to show them that you have not forgotten. It's up to you to remember that this election is a choice between the policies that got us into this mess and the policies that are leading us out of this mess. It's a choice between the past and the future, a choice between hope and fear, a choice between falling backwards and moving forwards. And I don't know about you, but I want to move forward. I don't want to go backward.

And if you don't think this is a choice, if you think somehow there's a new and improved Republican Party out there, let me be clear: The chair of the Republican campaign committee was asked, well, what are you going to do if you take over Congress? He said, we'll pursue the exact same agenda as we did before Obama took office.

I mean, it's not as if they went off into the desert, they realized, boy, we really screwed up, and they went and meditated for a while and came up with some new ideas. All they've got is the same old stuff that they were peddling over the last decade: cut taxes mostly for millionaires and billionaires, cut rules for special interests, and then cut middle class families to fend for themselves. So if you're out of a job, tough luck, you're on your own. If you don't have health care, their philosophy says, tough luck, you are on your own. You're a young person trying to afford a college education, too bad, pull yourself up by your own bootstraps; you're on your own. This same agenda turned a record surplus into record deficits, allowed Wall Street to run wild and nearly destroyed our economy.

And I make these points not because I want to reargue the past. I just don't want to relive the past. We can't afford it. We can't afford it. We tried their way. It's not as if we didn't try it. We tried it for 8 years, and it didn't work. And you know the true sign of madness is if you do the same thing over and over again and expect a different result. We've tried what they're doing, and it didn't work. And we wouldn't get a different result if we went back to it. So we've got to move forward, not back.

I know that Al Franken talked to you a little bit about the analogy of a car being driven into the ditch, although I guess Al kind of embellished it a little bit. He said there were alligators down there—[*laughter*]—I didn't see the alligators. But it is true the car went into the ditch. [*Laughter*] And it is true that me and Al and Amy and Mark and others, we had to climb down into the ditch. And it is hot down there and dirty.

And we've been pushing that car, pushing it, pushing it, pushing it. The whole time the Republicans have been standing on the sidelines. [*Laughter*] They've been looking down, fanning themselves, sipping on a Slurpee—[*laughter*]—kicking dirt down into the ditch, kicking dirt in our faces. But we kept on pushing.

Finally we got this car up on level ground. And yes, it's a little beat up. It needs to go to the body shop. It's got some dents. It needs a tune-up. But it's pointing in the right direction. And now we've got the Republicans tapping us on the shoulder, saying, we want the keys back.

You can't have the keys back. You don't know how to drive. You can ride with us if you want, but you got to sit in the backseat. [*Laughter*] We're going to put middle class America in the front seat. We're looking out for them.

I mean, you have noticed, when you want to go forward, what do you do with your car? You put it in "D." If you want to go backwards, what do you do? You put it in "R." [*Laughter*] I don't want to go backwards. I'm going forwards, with all of you.

Minnesota, because of the steps we've taken, we no longer face the possibility of a second depression. The economy is growing again. We've seen 9 straight months of private sector job growth. But we've still got a long way to go. There are a lot of folks hurting out there, a lot of people hanging by a thread. There's still families who have members who are desperate for a job. There are still a lot of folks who are still worried about losing their home. That's what keeps me up at night. That's what keeps Mark up at night. That's what keeps us fighting.

Because we've got a different idea about what the future should hold for America, and it's an idea rooted in our belief about how this country was built. We understand government can't solve every problem. We know government has to be lean and mean. We know that everybody who pays taxes expects efficiency. They don't want to see their tax dollars wasted.

But in the words of the first Republican President, Abraham Lincoln—who, by the way, could not win the nomination of the Republican Party these days—[*laughter*]—we also believe that a government should do for the people what they cannot do better for themselves. We believe in an America that rewards hard work and responsibility and individual initiative, but also an America that invests in its people and its future, an America that invests in the education of our children, in the skills of our workers. We believe in an America in which we look after one another, where I say, I am my brother's keeper, I am my sister's keeper. That's our vi-sion. That's the America that I believe in and that Mark believes in and that you believe in. That's the choice in this election.

If you give the other side the keys, the other side will keep giving tax breaks to companies that ship jobs overseas. Mark and I, we want to give tax breaks to companies that are investing right here in Minnesota, right here in the United States, in small businesses and American manufacturers. We want to invest in clean energy companies, because I don't want solar panels and wind turbines and electric cars built in Europe or built in Asia. I want them built right here in America, with American workers. That's the choice in this election.

If we give them the keys, here's their big economic idea. This is their big job plan, is to cut taxes for the top 2 percent. It will cost $700 billion. It will be an average $100,000 check for millionaires and billionaires; 98 percent of folks would not see any of this money from this tax break. And to pay for it we'd have to borrow money from China. Oh, and by the way, we'd also have to cut education spending by 20 percent.

Now, why on Earth do we think that would be good for our future? Do you think that China is cutting education spending by 20 percent?

Audience members. No!

The President. Is South Korea or India or Germany, are they cutting education by 20 percent?

Audience members. No!

The President. They're not playing for second place. They understand that our competitiveness will be determined by how well we educate our workers for tomorrow. And America doesn't play for second place either. We play for first place.

That's why Amy, that's why Al, that's why we worked together—Keith, Patty—that's why we came together to make sure that we took tens of billions of dollars that were going to banks in unwarranted subsidies, and we sent that money where it should be going, to you. We are financing millions of young people's college educations more effectively now: higher Pell grants, better student loans, a $10,000 tax credit for every young person going to college. Those are the kinds of choices we're making. And that's the choice in this election.

That's why, when it comes to tax cuts, we gave 95 percent of working families a tax cut. We gave the tax cuts to families that needed them, not folks who didn't need them, because we know you're the ones that need relief. That's the choice in this election.

We give the other side the keys back and they, I promise you, will have those special interests sitting shotgun. The chair of one of the other party's committees has already promised that one of the first orders of business is to repeal Wall Street reform. Now, think about this. We just had the worst financial crisis since the 1930s, and one of their orders of business would be to eliminate protections for consumers, eliminate protections for taxpayers, go back to a system that resulted in us having to save the entire economy and take these drastic measures.

Why would we do that? Why would we do that? Why would we go back to the point where credit card companies could jack up your interest rates without any notice and could institute hidden fees? Why would we go back to the health care policies that they believe in, where insurance companies could drop your insurance when you get sick? Why would we do—why would we put those folks back in the driver's seat?

Let me tell you about health care reform. Because of health care reform, everybody here who is under 26 can stay on their parents' health care even if they don't have health insurance. Because of that reform, insurance companies can't drop somebody because they've got a preexisting condition. Because of health care reform, millions of small businesses are getting tax credits so they can afford to provide health insurance to their employees. That is their agenda, to repeal that?

Let me tell you something. We believe in making sure people don't get ripped off when they sign up for a mortgage. We believe in making sure that credit card companies treat you fairly. We believe taxpayers shouldn't ever be forced to pay for Wall Street's mistakes. We believe that insurance companies should cover you when you've been paying your premiums.

That's what we believe. That's the choice in this election. That's why you've got to elect Mark Dayton Governor, because he believes it too.

Whether you care about protecting Social Security or you care about protecting our environment, whether you care about having an energy policy that can start freeing ourselves from dependence on foreign oil or you believe in a foreign policy that fosters cooperation among other nations, there is a choice in this election. We know what we're fighting for.

But right now the same special interests that we've battled on your behalf, they're fighting back hard. Mark mentioned that they are spending millions of dollars. They want to roll back the clock. And they are pouring millions of dollars through a network of phony front groups, flooding the airwaves with misleading attack ads, smearing fine public servants like Mark.

And thanks to a gigantic loophole, these special interests can spend unlimited amounts without even disclosing where the money is coming from. We don't know where it's coming from. We don't know if it's from the oil industry. We don't know if it's from banks. We don't know if it's insurance companies. Could be coming overseas; we don't know. They won't tell you. They don't want you to know. They won't stand behind what they do. This isn't just a threat to Democrats. This is a threat to our democracy.

Minnesota has always had a tradition of clean, fair elections, a tradition of good government, and the only way to uphold that tradition, the only way to match their millions of dollars is with millions of voices, millions of voices who are ready to finish what we started in 2008.

And that's where all of you come in. That's why all of you have got to get out, all of you have to vote. If you are not registered to vote yet, you can walk in right now, you can register anytime between now and election day. There is no excuse. Because if everybody who fought for change in 2008 votes in 2010, then Mark will win his election.

A lot of you got involved in 2008 because you believed we were at a defining moment; that it was a time when the decisions we make now would have an impact across the decades, would impact our children and our grandchildren for decades to come. That's the reason you knocked on doors and you made phone calls and you—some of you cast your vote for the very first time—because you believed that in America, citizens who want to make their country better can make a difference.

And you know what, I told you then—2 years ago I told you that change is not easy; power does not give up without a fight. And I understand that some of you since election night and Inauguration Day—when it was a lot of fun; Beyonce was singing and Bono, and everybody had their "Hope" posters, and everything looked like it might be easy. And I warned folks then, this won't be easy. Power concedes nothing without a fight.

And so for the last 2 years, we have been grinding it out. We passed health care reform, but it was a hard fight. We passed Wall Street reform, but it was a hard fight. And now maybe some people are feeling discouraged, thinking, boy, this is harder than I expected. And maybe all that work that I did in 2008, maybe it didn't make as much of a difference as I had hoped.

But I want everybody here to understand: Don't let anybody tell you that what you did has not made a difference, that the fight isn't worth it. Because of you—because of you—there's somebody in Minnesota right now that, instead of going bankrupt, is able to get treatment for their cancer. Because of you, there's a young person who's going to be able to go to college. Because of you, some small business has stayed open in the depths of a recession. Because of you, there are 100,000 brave young men and women who we've brought home from Iraq. Because of you—because of you.

So don't let them tell you that change isn't possible. It's just hard, that's all. And that's okay. We've got to earn it. We're just in the first quarter. We've got a lot more quarters to play.

You know, this country was founded on a tough, difficult idea. Thirteen Colonies deciding to break off from the most powerful empire on Earth, and then drafting a document, a Declaration of Independence that embodied ideas that had never been tried before: "We hold these truths to be self-evident, that all men are created equal, endowed by our Creator with certain inalienable rights, that among these are life, liberty, and the pursuit of happiness." That's not an easy idea. And it had to be fought for, inch by inch, year by year.

Slowly, slaves were freed. Slowly, women got the right to vote. Slowly, workers got the right to organize.

Imagine if our grandparents and our great-grandparents and our great-great-grandparents had said, oh, this is too hard. Folks are saying mean things about us. I'm not sure if we can ever get to the Promised Land. We wouldn't be here today. But they understood that we are tested when we stand up in the face of difficulty, when we stand up in the face of uncertainty, when we're unafraid to push forward. Because we know we're doing it not just for ourselves, but for future generations.

That's how we came through war and depression. That's why we have civil rights and women's rights and workers' rights. That's why we've been able to clean up our air and clean up our water. That's why we've been able to end combat operations in one war.

The journey we began together was never about putting me in the White House; it was about building a movement for change that endures. It's about understanding that in America anything is possible if we're willing to work for it and fight for it and, most of all, believe in it.

So I need you to keep fighting. I need you to keep working. And I need you to keep believing. And if you knock on some doors again, if you make some phone calls again, if you talk to your neighbors again, if you go to vote again, then I promise you we won't just win this election, we won't just have Mark as Governor, but you and I together, we are going to restore the American Dream for future generations.

God bless you, and God bless the United States of America.

NOTE: The President spoke at 3:42 p.m. at the University of Minnesota. In his remarks, he referred to musicians Beyonce G. Knowles and Paul D. "Bono" Hewson.

Remarks at a Democratic Congressional Campaign Committee Dinner in Minneapolis
October 23, 2010

Thank you. Everybody, please have a seat, have a seat. You're going to make me blush. [*Laughter*] I am thrilled to see all of you here today. And let me, first of all, say that Minnesota has one of the finest congressional delegations of any in the country. I am grateful to your two wonderful Senators who I've gotten a chance to know over the last several years: Amy Klobuchar, who I served with—hey, Amy, how are you? And Al Franken, who we were very happy to see arrive in Washington. The outstanding Members of the House—Keith Ellison, Betty McCollum, Jim Oberstar, and Tim Walz—all who are here; we're thrilled to have them.

The great congressional candidates who are with us here today, we are proud of you. And Mark Dayton, who I had a chance to serve with as Senator. He was dedicated, he had a heart as big as this room, and he is going to be just an outstanding Governor for this State. So we are proud of you.

And what can I say about Nancy Pelosi, who will go down in history as one of the finest Speakers in the history of the United States of America? She is—Nancy is just so elegant and beautiful, and people just don't realize she is tough. [*Laughter*] She is tough. And she has to be tough, because we are in a very difficult political cycle.

And so I just want to give you a sense of—oh, I'm sorry, I didn't know you were here—a guy who has his own tough job—Chris Van Hollen, the head of the DCCC, who's doing great work each and every day. Almost missed Chris. Chris is working like a dog, so I want to make sure everybody knows what wonderful work he's doing.

Chris will tell you this is a difficult political environment we're in right now. And it's because we've gone through as tough a couple of years as this country has ever seen, certainly the toughest couple years since the 1930s. And Nancy alluded to it, but just to give people a sense of perspective here: We lost 4 million jobs in the 6 months before I was sworn in, 4 million

jobs in the 6 months before I was sworn in. We lost 750,000 jobs the month I was sworn in, 600,000 the month after that, 600,000 the month after that. Almost all of the 8 million jobs that would ultimately be lost during this recession were lost before any of the Democrats' economic policies were able to be put into place. Before the Recovery Act could really take root, before some of the other steps that we took in terms of small-business loans, tax cuts, could take seed.

And so we saw a massive hole. And that in and of itself would be sufficient to make this a difficult political environment, but what makes it worse is that crisis was really a culmination of what some have called the lost decade. Between 2001 and 2009, we had the slowest job growth in any time since World War II. Between 2001 and 2009, we actually saw the middle class lose 5 percent of their income—5 percent of their income. This is at a time when the costs of health care, the costs of a college education were all skyrocketing. People were watching manufacturing ship out to other countries.

And so you had a sense already, before the crisis on Wall Street, that we had not prepared ourselves for the future; that we had left too many challenges untended to; that our politics in Washington had become simply a mechanism for special interests to advance their narrow causes, but that we had lost the capacity to do big things and to finally tackle some of those structural issues that were impeding us from creating the kind of future that we want for our children and our grandchildren.

So we had a big job when we first came in. And our first job was obviously to stop the bleeding, and we did that. An economy that was shrinking is now growing again. An economy that was shedding hundreds of thousands of jobs every month, we've now seen 9 months of consecutive job growth in the public sector—in the private sector. That's in addition to all the jobs that we've saved for teachers and firefighters and social workers and police officers here in Minnesota and all across the country.

And so the good news is, is that we've been able to stabilize the economy. The bad news is, is that we're nowhere near done. We've got so much more work to do. There are still millions of people out of work who are desperate and just hanging on by a thread. There are hundreds of thousands of folks who are concerned about losing their homes. People are scared. People are nervous.

And that's why the tactics that were deployed by the other side, at the beginning of my Presidency, are so frustrating to so many of us, those of us who deeply care about the future of this country. Because their basic strategy was, boy, we made such a big mess that rather than take responsibility for it—which most of us would have hoped was going to happen, right? Our thinking was we're going to come in, and even though the other folks caused it, we're going to be part of the solution, not part of the problem. We're not going to play politics. We're not going to point fingers. We're going to roll up our sleeves and start getting to work, because although we are proud Democrats, we are prouder to be Americans. That was our hope and expectation.

And instead, the other side made a tactical decision which was, this is such a mess, it's probably going to take several years to solve. And so we're better off sitting on the sidelines saying no to everything, obstructing every possible bit of progress that could be made, so that we are well positioned by the time the next election rolls around to simply point our fingers and say the Democrats are to blame.

In other words, their political strategy was based on amnesia—[*laughter*]—based on the premise that people would not remember that they were the folks who were responsible for the devastation to our economy.

Now, we made a different decision. And because of the Members of Congress who are in this room, because of the leadership of Nancy Pelosi, because of the leadership of Harry Reid in the Senate, we didn't think about the next election, we thought about the next generation. And we also decided, even as we were going to

solve the immediate crisis, that it was time once and for all for us to tackle the big issues that were holding us back as a country.

And so we started off with education. We've seen a transformation of our education agenda. Not only did we save the jobs of teachers, but we also instituted a reform agenda that now has States all across the country raising standards, training teachers more effectively, going out there each and every day and finding out what are the best practices that can ensure that our kids can learn and compete in the 21st century. And that's K–12.

And then we said, that's not enough. We've got to make sure that every young person in America is prepared for college and then can afford to go to college. So we took tens of billions of dollars that were going to the banks in unwarranted subsidies, and we shifted those to our student loan programs and our Pell grant programs. And we've got millions of young people all across the country who are now able to afford college because of the steps that these courageous Members of Congress were willing to take during the course of this year.

That's on education. We took on health care. And obviously, health care is something that's been debated a lot. It's going to be very interesting, now that the other side says their main agenda is repealing health care. What exactly do they want to repeal? Do they want to repeal us saying to 30 million people, you now finally have affordable health care? Are they just going to say, you know what, tough luck, you're on your own? Are they going to want to repeal provisions that say young people can stay on their parents' health insurance until they're 26 years old if they can't get health insurance on the job? Do they want to repeal us closing the doughnut hole so that senior citizens can afford their prescription drugs when they get sick and don't have to choose between groceries and their medicine?

Are they going to want to repeal what essentially was the most robust patient bill of rights in our history that says to insurance companies, you can't drop coverage for people when they get sick, you can't preclude them from getting health insurance when they've got a preexisting condition, you can't impose arbitrary lifetime limits that leave people bankrupt even though they've been paying premiums all their lives?

What exactly are you going to repeal? And are you going to repeal all the mechanisms that Nancy alluded to, to lower the costs and improve the quality of care so that the Congressional Budget Office says we will actually save over a trillion dollars in deficits as a consequence of this program?

It's going to be an interesting exercise if they think that they can follow through on that, because the American people may have heard a lot of arguments on Capitol Hill, but when they see what actually is being delivered I don't think the Republicans are going to feel so good about this repeal call.

But the reason they're moving forward on it is because they're being driven by the special interests who have been paying for their campaigns over the course of the last several months.

The same is true on Wall Street reform. We said that we've got to have a financial system that is vibrant and dynamic, but also a financial system that has basic rules of the road, that works for everybody, not just for some. So we made sure that credit card companies can't jack up your interest rates arbitrarily, without notice. We made certain that mortgage brokers can't steer you to more expensive interest rate mortgages. We made sure that we got systems in place to guard against the kind of structural breakdowns that resulted in the taxpayer bailouts that all of us find unacceptable.

And now you've got folks on the other side who have said one of their first agenda items is to try to repeal Wall Street reform. Think about this. This is in the wake of the worst financial crisis since the 1930s, and they want to go back to the status quo, business as usual.

Across the board—energy, education, health care, our financial systems, consumer protections—their basic agenda is, we're going to do the things exactly as we were doing them before President Obama got into office. And that's an agenda that America simply can't afford. It is an agenda that folks simply can't afford.

We were at a rally right before we came here, and I've been using this analogy around the country. They drove this economy into a ditch. And Nancy and I, we've had to put our boots on—[*laughter*]—and the rest of the congressional delegation, we had to rappel down into the ditch, and we're trying to push to get that car out of there. And the Republicans are just standing on the sidelines watching us, fanning themselves, sipping on a Slurpee. [*Laughter*]. They're kicking dirt back into the ditch. [*Laughter*] We're getting it into our eyes. Didn't lift a finger to help. All they did was point and say, you're not pushing hard enough; you're not doing it the right way.

We finally have gotten this car out of the ditch, and it's taken a lot of effort. And yes, the car is banged up; it is dented, it is in need of some bodywork and a tuneup, but it's moving in the right direction. We're about to go forward.

And suddenly, we get this tap on our fingers, and we look back, and it's the Republicans asking for the keys back. And our basic attitude is, no, you can't have the keys back. You don't know how to drive. [*Laughter*] You don't know how to drive.

Now, I want to be clear, they are more than happy to join us for the ride, but they've got to sit in the backseat, because we want America's families in the front seat. We want them in shotgun, not special interests, not the folks who've been calling the shots in the past.

That's the challenge that we face. Because, look, every Democrat who is here—Al, Nancy, Chris, Tim, Keith, Betty, Jim—every—Amy— what binds us together as Democrats is a shared vision about what America is. We believe in hard work and responsibility and individual initiative. We know government can't solve every problem. We understand that government needs to be lean and efficient. Nobody here wants to waste taxpayer dollars.

In fact, one of our most important agendas is restoring people's confidence that, in fact, government in a serious way can do what it's supposed to be doing, nothing more, nothing less. But we also believe that part of being an American is, is that we look out for one another; that I am my brother's keeper, I am my sister's keeper;

that we are willing to invest not just in the here and now, but in the future; that we're investing in our kids' education, we're investing in our workers' skills; that we're investing in our infrastructure.

And frankly, that's not what we've been doing for a very long time. And that's part of the change in mindset that we've been undergoing over the last couple of years. We've got to be thinking about the next generation.

In the words of Abraham Lincoln, we believe that every individual should be able to do what they do best for themselves, but we also believe that government should be able to do what people can't do for themselves as well as government can do. And there are some basic things that we include in that

Right now the Republican agenda, what they call the promise for America, they want to cut education spending by 20 percent in order to pay for $700 billion worth of tax cuts that would only go to the top 2 percent. We don't have the $700 billion. We'd have to borrow from China to pay for it, and in part to pay for a tiny amount of that tax cut they would cut education by 20 percent.

Do you think China is cutting education by 20 percent right now? Do you think South Korea or Germany or India are cutting education spending by 20 percent? It makes no sense.

We want to restart rebuilding our infrastructure and putting people back to work right now. Yes, we've saved 3.5 million jobs. We've got a whole bunch more jobs that we could create out there, putting people to work doing the work that needs to be done. Anybody who's been to Beijing or Singapore, and you walk through their airports and you say, America used to have the best infrastructure. We used to have the best airports; we used to have the best roads, the best bridges. And now we're investing less than half of what Europe or Asia are investing in their infrastructure.

Where is that going to leave our children and our grandchildren 10 years from now, 20 years from now, 50 years from now? Why aren't the best railway lines, the best high-speed rails, the best broadband lines here in the United States of America?

We've got a race to see who's going to determine the clean energy future. And one of the things we did in the Recovery Act was invest in solar panels and wind turbines and advanced battery manufacturing here in the United States of America. I want those things made here. But right now we're getting our clock cleaned because we have not been serious about making those investments. And we haven't set the guideposts where private capital could come in and start making those investments. And that means losing that race. That's not acceptable.

And so we've got a lot of work to do. And as much progress as we've made over the last 2 years, the only way we're going to continue on that progress is if each and every one of you are out there talking to your friends and your neighbors, knocking on doors, making phone calls—yes, writing checks to these outstanding Members of Congress—because I've got to have a partner. I've got to have folks working with me who are willing to put aside their short-term political interests when it comes to the interests of the country.

And so let me just leave you with this thought. I know that because this has been a tough couple of years, I've had people come back—come up to me sometimes and say, gosh, when you were elected in 2008, that was so exciting. Election night was just unbelievable, and then Inauguration Day, you had Beyonce singing and—[*laughter*]—Bono. And I was at the Inauguration, and it was just so inspiring. And I've got to admit, Mr. President, sometimes over the last couple of years, with all the negative ads and all the money that's been pouring in, all the filibustering and obstruction in Congress, sometimes, I just start losing altitude, start losing hope. It just seems like change is so hard to bring about.

And I've got to remind people, first of all, I warned you it was going to be hard. I never said it was going to be easy. If it was easy, it would have already been done. We knew it was going to be hard. But what I also tell people is, don't let anybody tell you that what we've been fighting for hasn't made this country better, hasn't been worth it.

Because of the work that these Members of Congress did, because of the support that you've provided them, there are people right here in Minnesota who are able to get coverage for their cancer treatments instead of having to sell their house. Right now, today. Because of what you did, there are small businesses that are open right now that otherwise would have shuttered their doors.

Because of what you did, there are parents here in Minnesota who are able to look their kids in the eye and say, you know what, even though our savings got blasted by the economic downturn and the fall in the stock market, despite all that we can guarantee that you're going to go to college.

Because of what you did, there are 100,000 young men and women who've come home from Iraq, no longer involved in that combat mission. And because of what you did, when those 100,000 come home, they're getting the treatment they need, they're getting the benefits that they deserve. They got a post-9/11 GI bill that they can count on so that they can be part of this latest and greatest generation and help grow and expand and build our middle class.

Those are all the consequences of the work that you did. And so yes, things don't happen as quickly as we want; they're not always as smooth as people would want. This is a big, messy democracy. That's the nature of America. It's always been that way. This Nation was founded on hard. A revolution of Thirteen Colonies breaking away from the greatest empire on Earth, that was hard. It was hard to free the slaves and ensure that we weren't living half free and half slave. It was hard for all those immigrants, our grandparents and great-grandparents and great-great-grandparents, to come here and try to carve out a life for themselves. It was hard to overcome war and depression. And it was hard to fight for civil rights and women's rights and workers' rights.

But they did it because they understood that in America, when citizens join together and decide they've got a vision for the future; when they decide our destiny is not written for us, it is written by us; when they made that decision, we can't be stopped. And that's what this election is about: whether we continue with that trajectory, whether we continue with that tradition.

I'm absolutely confident we can. So I want everybody here to understand that we're just in the first quarter. We're just starting. We've got a lot more work to do. And the only way we're going to be able to do it is if each and every one of you had that same spirit of possibility, are undaunted in the face of uncertainty, are unafraid in the face of difficulty. If you will join with us, I promise you we will look back on this period and we will say, yes, we were tested, but we met that test for future generations.

Thank you very much, everybody. Thank you.

NOTE: The President spoke at 5:35 p.m. at Van Dusen Mansion. In his remarks, he referred to musicians Beyonce G. Knowles and Paul D. "Bono" Hewson.

Remarks at American Cord & Webbing Co., Inc., in Woonsocket, Rhode Island
October 25, 2010

Thanks so much. Please, everybody have a seat. It is just wonderful to be at American Cord and Webbing. And thank you. I just saw all the great work that's being done here. I want to acknowledge a few friends here in the first row. First of all, your outstanding senior Senator, Jack Reed; we're so proud of him. And your equally outstanding junior Senator, Sheldon Whitehouse, is here; we got my dear friend Congressman Patrick Kennedy. And I want to just say, right now Providence Mayor Dave Cicilline—soon could have another job. Congressman Jim Langevin is just a great friend and an inspiration to all of us. We've got Woonsocket mayor, Leo Fontaine is here. Where's Mr. Mayor? There he is, right there. And of course, somebody all of you know, Mark Krauss. Where's Mark? [*Applause*] And Ray Velino, right here. [*Applause*] Hey! You guys are pretty popular. [*Laughter*] That's nice.

It is great to be here in Rhode Island, and it is great to be here at American Cord and Webbing. I just had a chance to take a quick tour and see the outstanding work that so many of the workers are doing here. These guys make webbing, cords, buckles, plastic and metal hardware for sporting goods, outdoor goods, travel gear. They are also making customized leashes for Bo—[*laughter*]—that I am very proud of, and it is clear that they take enormous pride in what they do.

This is a third-generation company, and Mark was telling me how it got started with his grandfather and—1917? And it's just a testament to American ingenuity and American entrepreneurship. And now he's got four beautiful kids, along with his lovely wife. And one of them or two of them may end up continuing the business once Mark decides he's ready to retire. But that looks like a long ways off. [*Laughter*] He looks pretty young and pretty fit.

Like most small businesses, American Cord and Webbing has gone through some tough times in the past few years. Early in 2009, they lost customers and had to lay off some workers. But they buckled down—that was a pun. [*Laughter*] You got that? You catch that one? And they invested in new products and pursued new customers. And over the past year, they've hired back all the workers they had to lay off. And today business is going well. In fact—[*applause*].

So this year, Mark expects to turn a profit. He's going to invest in new machinery and new equipment. And just last month, this company was approved for an SBA loan that's going to help them expand this facility by nearly half, which is going to be very exciting.

Now, this is important, not just for this particular business and these particular workers, but for America. It's small businesses like this one, after all, that are the bricks and blocks, the cord and webbing, if you will, of our economy. But the financial crisis made it very difficult for them to get the loans that they needed to grow.

The recession meant that folks are spending less. And across the country, many small businesses that were once the cornerstones of their communities are now empty storefronts that haunt our Main Streets.

So the bottom line is, when our small businesses don't do well, America doesn't do well. So we all have a stake in helping our small businesses grow and succeed. And because small businesses create two out of every three new jobs in America, our economy depends on it.

And that's why, over the past 20 months, we've done everything we can to boost small businesses like this one. And what's guided us is a simple principle: Government can't guarantee your success, can't guarantee Mark's success—he doesn't expect it to—but government can knock down some of the barriers that stand in the way of small-business success and help create the conditions where small businesses can grow and hire and create new products and prosper.

That's why we've now passed, with the help of these outstanding Members of Congress, 16 different tax cuts for America's small businesses over the last couple years—16 tax cuts over the last couple years.

We've passed tax cuts for hiring back unemployed workers. We've passed tax cuts for investing in new equipment. There are 4 million small businesses right now that are poised to get a tax break of up to 35 percent of the premiums they pay if they are providing health insurance to their employees, and that's a tax break that can free up tens of thousands of dollars to upgrade facilities, buy new equipment, or hire a few new workers.

And last month, after plenty of political obstacles, after months in which thousands of small-business owners across America were waiting for the loans and tax cuts they badly needed to grow their business and hire new employees, I signed into law the Small Business Jobs Act.

Now, that act extended provisions that helped support tens of thousands of new SBA loans under the Recovery Act, and it waived fees on those loans to save owners money on their payments, something that saved this particular company more than $9,000.

In less than a month since that new law took effect, more than 3,600 small-business owners have already received more than $1.4 billion worth of new loans, with more to come, and the SBA has already begun offering larger loans for small businesses—small-business owners who need them.

The law also accelerates $55 billion in new tax cuts for businesses both large and small that make job-creating investments over the next year. It eliminates capital gains taxes on key new investments made in small businesses until the end of this year. It dramatically increases the amount small businesses can write off on new equipment investments, and we want to do more so that you can write it all off. These are tax cuts that can help America—help businesses like American Cord and Webbing that are making new investments right now. And it can help create jobs.

Finally, that—the law that we signed creates new initiatives to increase lending to small businesses. It strengthens State programs that spur private sector lending, and that's a step that will support $15 billion in new small-business loans across the country. And it sets up a new small-business lending fund that will support Main Street banks that lend to Main Street businesses.

We're doing all this because when times are tough, I believe we should be cutting taxes for small-business owners. We should be cutting taxes for companies that are investing here in Rhode Island and here in the United States of America.

When new loans are hard to come by, I believe we should help free up lending. When some companies are shipping jobs overseas, we should be helping companies like this one: our small businesses, our manufacturers, our clean energy companies. I think those are pretty commonsense values that we can all agree on.

Now, I will confess, I wish that Republican leaders in Congress had agreed earlier. They voted against these ideas again and again. They talk a good game about tax cuts and giving entrepreneurs the freedom to succeed, when, in fact, they also ended up voting against tax cuts for the middle class; they voted against tax breaks for companies creating jobs here in the United States.

Now, when you vote against small-business tax relief and you hold up a small-business jobs bill for months, that doesn't do anything to support small businesses like this one. It doesn't do anything to support the outstanding workers at this company. It's just playing politics. If you're going to talk a big game, then you need to deliver.

So I hope that my friends on the other side of the aisle are going to change their minds going forward, because putting the American people back to work, boosting our small businesses, rebuilding the economic security of the middle class, these are big national challenges. And we've all got a stake in solving them. And it's not going to be enough just to play politics. You can't just focus on the next election, you've got to focus on the next generation.

That's how Mark's company has succeeded, by focusing on the next generation. And that's how we have to think about our work in Washington.

So let me just again congratulate the company for doing the great work that you're doing. Thank you for your hospitality. I know it's always a big fuss when I show up. [*Laughter*]

And to all of you here in Rhode Island and all across the country, when I tour plants like this, it makes me optimistic. We've got big problems, and it's going to take some time to solve them. It took us a long time to get into this economic hole that we've been in.

And the recession that we inherited was so deep that it's going to take some time to get out. But we are going to get out. And I'm absolutely convinced that there are brighter days ahead for America, an America where businesses like this one aren't just thriving, but are powering our economic growth, where workers like the ones who are here are rewarded for the work that you do, where our middle class is growing, where opportunity is shared by all our people and the American Dream is back within the reach of those who are willing to work for it.

So that's what we're working for. That's the guiding principle behind all of my administration's activities, is how do we make sure that the economy is growing and that the middle class is growing, because that's the beating heart of this economy. What you do here is a great example of what we've got to be able to do all across this country.

We're proud of you, and I thank you so much for letting us join you here today and seeing the wonderful success that you've been able to accomplish.

Thank you very much, everybody. Thank you.

NOTE: The President spoke at 4:53 p.m. In his remarks, he referred to Mark J. Krauss, president, and Raymond J. Velino, general manager, American Cord & Webbing Co., Inc.; and Helene Krauss, wife of Mr. Krauss, and their children Bari, Sloane, Jordan, and Alex Krauss.

Statement on National Work and Family Month
October 25, 2010

National Work and Family Month serves as a reminder to all of us, especially working caregivers, their families, and their employers, that while we have made great strides as a nation to adopt more flexible policies in the workplace, there's more we can do. Millions of Americans continue to struggle day in and day out to balance work and family life, to juggle their job responsibilities with caring for a child, an elderly relative, or a loved one with a disability. This is something Michelle and I understand; it wasn't too long ago that we were both working full-time outside the home while raising two young daughters.

There are steps we can all take to help—implementing practices like telework, paid leave, and alternative work schedules—and my administration is committed to doing its part to help advance these practices across the country. And within the Federal Government, we have followed the lead of many private sector companies when it comes to increasing workplace flexibility. Because at the end of the day, attracting and retaining employees who are more productive and engaged through flexible workplace policies is not just good for business or for our economy, it's good for our families and our future.

Remarks at a Democratic Congressional Campaign Committee Reception in Providence, Rhode Island
October 25, 2010

The President. Hello, Rhode Island! Thank you so much. Thank you. Are you fired up?

Audience members. Woo!

The President. It is good to be back in Rhode Island. It is good to be here for an outstanding soon-to-be Member of Congress, Dave Cicilline.

Now, you already have some great Members of Congress, and so I just want to make quick mention of them. Your senior Senator, one of the finest Senators that I know, Jack Reed is in the house; his great partner, junior Senator Sheldon Whitehouse. A dear friend, Patrick Kennedy, is here. Outstanding legislator Jim Langevin is here. And somebody who's working so hard to maintain a Democratic majority across the country, the head of the DCCC, Chris Van Hollen, is here. Thank you, Chris. And all of you are here. And I'm really happy about that.

Now, Providence, 1 week from tomorrow, you have the chance to set the direction not just for this State, but for this country, not just for the next 2 years, but for the next two decades. And just like you did in 2008, you have the chance to defy the conventional wisdom.

Now, you remember in 2008, everybody looks back and says, oh, that was easy. No, it wasn't easy. [*Laughter*] In retrospect it looked easy. But at the time, everybody said, you can't overcome the cynicism in our politics. You can't overcome all the special interest money. You can't take on the biggest challenges that we face. You certainly can't elect a skinny guy named Barack Obama. And you said, "Yes, we can." And a week from tomorrow, we have a chance to say "Yes, we can" again. We've got a chance to say "Yes, we can" again.

Audience members. Yes, we can! Yes, we can! Yes, we can!

The President. Yes, we can! [*Laughter*]

Audience members. Yes, we can! Yes, we can! Yes, we can!

The President. Look, there is no doubt that this is going to be a difficult election. I'm confident that David is going to win. I feel good about it.

But look, this is going to be a difficult election because we've been through an incredibly difficult time as a nation. For most of the last decade, middle class families have just barely been treading water.

I want to give you a couple of statistics. Between 2001 and 2009, we had the slowest job growth of any time since World War II. In fact, job growth was slower during those 8 years than it has been over the last year.

Between that same period, 2001 to 2009, middle class families, on average, lost 5 percent of their income. Think about that. This is at a time when health care costs skyrocketed, college tuition off the charts, more jobs being shipped overseas, families just barely keeping up, working two jobs, three jobs to pay the mortgage, to pay the bills. Too many parents were saying to their kids, I'm not sure we can afford college; too many families saying, we can't afford to see a doctor when we get sick. It's just too expensive.

And then all these problems that had been building up for a decade culminated in the worst financial crisis and the worst economic crisis since the Great Depression. In the 6 months before I took office, we lost 4 million jobs in America—in 6 months. We lost 750,000 the month I took office, 600,000 the month after that, 600,000 the month after that. We lost almost 8 million jobs before any of the economic policies the Democrats had a chance to put

into place could take effect—almost 8 million jobs.

Now, our hope was that because of the magnitude of the crisis, that me and Jack and Sheldon, Jim, others, Patrick—our hope was that finally we'd be able to come together with the Republicans and start solving problems instead of playing politics. We figured this is a once-in-a-generation challenge, and so let's see if we can put the bickering aside and the gamesmanship that had dominated Washington for way too long, because, although we're proud to be Democrats, we are prouder to be Americans.

And there are a lot of Republicans that, I think, felt the same way. But Republican leaders in Congress, they made a different decision. Their basic strategy was, you know what, we really screwed up. This is such a big mess. We've lost so many jobs. The economy is so bad that it's going to take a while to fix all these problems. And if we're there helping, then, gosh, who knows, they might realize that we're to blame. So we're better off just standing on the sidelines and saying no to everything. And people are going to get angry and frustrated. And they may forget that, in fact, we were the folks in power when this crisis occurred. And we'll be able to point our fingers and pretend we had nothing to do with it.

That was their tactic. That was their strategy. In other words, their main electoral strategy, their political strategy was amnesia. [*Laughter*] They are banking on you forgetting who caused this mess in the first place. But, Providence, it is up to you to let them know we have not forgotten. We have not forgotten.

We have not forgotten, and it's up to you to remember that this is a choice in the election between the politics that got us into this mess and the politics that are getting us out: between hope and fear, between the past and the future, between moving forward and moving backwards. And I don't know about you, but I want to move forward. David, I want to move forward. I want to move forward.

Look, if they win this election, the chair of the Republican campaign committee has already promised to pursue—and I'm quoting here—"the exact same agenda" as they pursued before I took office.

And we know what that agenda is. It does have the virtue of simplicity. [*Laughter*] You cut taxes, mostly for millionaires and billionaires, you cut rules for special interests, and then you cut middle class families to fend for themselves.

So if you're a family that doesn't have health care, tough luck, you're on your own. If you're a young person who can't afford to go to college, too bad, you're on your own. If you've lost your job, you need a little help with unemployment insurance, you need a little help with some job training, tough luck, you're on your own.

And this is all done under the guise, under the banner of fiscal conservatism, except it turns out that this same agenda turned record surpluses under a Democratic President and converted them into record deficits that allowed Wall Street to run wild that nearly destroyed our economy.

Now, I bring all this up not because I want to reargue the past. I bring it up because I don't want to relive the past. It's not as if, Providence, we haven't tried what they're peddling. We tried it for 8 years. It didn't work. We can't go back.

Audience member. We can't go back. [*Laughter*]

The President. We can't go back. Look, I've been using this analogy as I travel the country. Imagine the Republicans driving the economy into a ditch. And it's a deep ditch. It's a big ditch. And somehow they walked away from the accident, and we put on our boots and we rappelled down into the ditch—me and Jack and Sheldon and Jim and Patrick. We've been pushing, pushing, trying to get that car out of the ditch.

And meanwhile, the Republicans are standing there, sipping on a Slurpee—[*laughter*]—fanning themselves. We're hot and sweaty and pushing, and they're kicking dirt into the ditch—[*laughter*]—getting it into our faces. But that's okay. We said—every once in a while we'd ask them, do you want to come down and help? They'd say, no, but you're not pushing the right way though; push harder.

Finally, we get this car out of the ditch, and it's banged up. It needs some bodywork, needs a tuneup. But it's pointing in the right direction. The engine is turning and it's ready to go. And we suddenly get this tap on our shoulders. We look back, who is it? The Republicans. And they're saying, excuse me, we want the keys back. You can't have the keys back. You don't know how to drive! You can't have them back; can't do it. Not after we've worked this hard.

We can't have special interests sitting shotgun. [*Laughter*] You know, we got to have middle class families up in front. We can't—we don't mind the Republicans joining us. They can come for the ride, but they got to sit in back. [*Laughter*]

Look, these 2 years have been incredibly difficult. And not every decision we've made has always been popular, but they've been the right things to do, because you sent me there not to do what was easy, but do what was right. That's why you sent me there.

And because of the steps we've taken, we no longer face the possibility of a second depression. The economy is growing again. We've seen private sector job growth for 9 months in a row. I just had a chance to visit with some of the elected officials at a wonderful small business here that is representative of small businesses all across the country. They survived the recession, and they're now ready to grow and expand.

And we've passed tax cuts and provided them additional financing so they can hire more workers. But you know what? We've still got a long way to go. We know we do. There are a lot of people hurting out there. There are a lot of folks who have been looking for work for months and still can't find it, a lot of families still hanging on by a thread.

That's what keeps me up at night. That's what keeps David up at night. That's what we're focused on, because we've got a different idea about what the future should look like. And it's an idea rooted in our own families, our own backgrounds, about our understanding about how this country was built.

I didn't come from money. I didn't have a famous, well-connected family. And I was raised by my parents to believe—and my grandparents to believe in self-reliance. We know government doesn't have all the answers to our problems. We know our young people—if our schools are going to succeed—our young people have to work hard in school. Parents have to do a good job parenting.

We believe government should be lean and efficient and that each of us should take responsibility for contributing to our community. But in the words of the first Republican President, Abraham Lincoln, we also believe that government should do for the people what they can't do better for themselves.

So we believe in hard work and responsibility and individual initiative. But we also believe in an America that invests in its future, invests in its people, in the education of our children, in the skills of our workers.

We believe in a country where we look out for one another, where I am my brother's keeper, I am my sister's keeper. That's the America I know. That's the choice in this election. That's the choice in this election.

If we give the other side the keys to the car, you know what they're going to do? They're going to keep on giving tax breaks to companies that ship jobs overseas. I believe in tax breaks for companies like the one that I just visited, companies that are investing here in the United States, small businesses, American manufacturers, clean energy companies.

I don't want solar panels and electric cars made in Europe or Asia. I want them made right here in the United States with American workers. That's the choice in this election.

I think a lot of Americans right now, what they're asking—they're seeing all the negative ads on TV. What they really want to know is, what's your plan to move America forward; what's your plan to put people back to work?

And we've put forward plans to rebuild our infrastructure. We used to have the best infrastructure in the world. But we don't now. We've got to invest in that. We've got to invest in research and development. We want to make sure that we're giving incentives to companies to push their investments forward into next year so that we can jump-start the economy and help move it forward. Very concrete plans about how

we're going to invest in education so every one of our young people have the skills to compete in this new global economy.

You know what the other side's big idea is? And I'm not exaggerating, they've got one idea. And their idea is to cut taxes for the top 2 percent wealthiest Americans—would mean an average $100,000 check to millionaires and billionaires; it would cost $700 billion that we do not have. We'd have to borrow it from China. And when you ask them, "Well, how else are you going to pay for it other than just borrowing?" they say, "Well, we'll cut some programs." It turns out part of what they're proposing is a cut of 20 percent in our education budget.

Audience members. Boo!

The President. Now, think about this. Do you think, at a time when education will probably make more of a difference in terms of how well our economy performs than any other single indicator, that we should be cutting education by 20 percent? Do you think China is cutting it by 20 percent? You think Germany and South Korea are cutting education by 20 percent? Of course not, because they're not playing for second place. They're playing for first place. And we need to play for first place. That's what we do in the United States of America.

That's why, with the help of a Democratic Congress, we took tens of billions of dollars that were being put into unwarranted subsidies for banks in the student loan program. We said, let's not do that. Let's have the money go where it belongs, to the students. And we now have millions more young people who are able to get student loans and Pell grants, higher levels of grants, a $10,000 tuition relief credit for each student. That's our agenda for economic growth. That's what's going to make a difference.

That's why when we talk about tax cuts, we want to give permanent tax relief to middle class families. They need the relief. That's the choice in this election.

Look—and let me just say, they've already said, the other side has already said, we're going to roll back regulations and put special interests back in charge in Washington. This is not me making it up. The person who would take over the energy committee in the House of Representatives is the guy who apologized to BP when we said, you've got to pay for all the small businesses and families that have been—and fishermen that have been hurt by the oil spill.

That's the head of the energy company [committee].° Another one of their members has already promised that one of their first orders of business would be to repeal Wall Street reform. Now, we just went through the worst financial crisis in our history, and we finally now have some rules of the road that are going to say no taxpayer bailouts; you got to have higher capital requirements. We're going to make sure that we've got tough overseers that protect consumers from everything from predatory mortgages to unwarranted credit card fees. And their main agenda is rolling these rules back? Why? Why would we do that?

We can't let that happen, Providence. Look, we believe in making sure that people don't get ripped off when they sign up for a mortgage. We believe credit card companies shouldn't be able to jack up your rates without notice. We believe that insurance companies, if you're paying your premiums, they actually have to pay when you get sick. They can't drop your health insurance when you get sick.

We think it's a good idea that young people should be able to stay on their parents' health insurance until they're 26 years old. We think it's a good idea that senior citizens see that doughnut hole closed so that they can actually afford their prescription drug coverage. Those are ideas that we believe can move America forward.

That's the choice in this election. We believe Social Security should never be privatized, not as long as I'm President. We're not going to take the retirement savings of a generation of Americans and hand it over to Wall Street. That's the choice in the election. That's what we're fighting for.

But understand, the other side is fighting back. The same special interests we've been battling on your behalf over the last 2 years, they are fighting back hard. And they are now using these phony front groups to funnel hundreds of millions of dollars in negative ads all across the country, distorting the records of Democrats. And you know what? They are not even willing to disclose where the money is coming from. You don't know. Could be from insurance companies, could be from oil companies, could be from Wall Street banks. You don't know.

This is all the consequence of a Supreme Court decision, so don't let anybody tell you that the Supreme Court doesn't matter. That's why I put Sonia Sotomayor and Elena Kagan there. We need to have some Supreme Court Justices who are looking out for you.

But because of this campaign finance loophole, you've got hundreds of billions of dollars. It's not just a threat to Democrats. It's a threat to our democracy. I mean, imagine if you can—if special interests can just spend as much money as they want and you don't know who they are. They've got these innocent sounding names: Americans for Prosperity or Moms for Motherhood. [Laughter] No, I made the last one up. [Laughter] But you don't know.

And that cheapens our discourse. It hurts our democracy. And there's only one way to fight back against those millions of dollars, and that's with the millions of voices of people like you. It's all of you saying—[applause]—it's all of you being willing to finish what we started in 2008.

I've got to have you come out in droves and vote in this election. You've got to come out and vote. And look, if everybody who voted in 2008 votes in 2010, we are confident we will win this election.

And a lot of you—[applause]—a lot of you got involved in 2008, some of you for the very first time, because you understood that we're at a crossroads in our history, that the decisions we make now don't just affect us, they affect our children and our grandchildren and our great-grandchildren. That's why some of you knocked on doors. That's why some of you made phone calls. That's why many of you stood in line to cast your ballots.

° White House correction.

And it turns out, you know what, actually delivering change is very hard. I warned you. [*Laughter*] I said it was going to be hard. And so over the last 2 years, we've been grinding it out. And sometimes I know it gets frustrating. Some of you may get discouraged. You say, gosh, we have these bigger majorities, and things are being filibustered, and there's all this nastiness on TV. And maybe you just can't change politics.

But I want everybody to understand we're just in the first quarter. We got a whole game to play. We've got a whole game to play. We've got a whole game to play.

And I want everybody here to understand that because I've had good teammates, like the folks you sent here from Rhode Island, we have made a huge difference. Don't let anybody tell you we haven't made a difference.

Because of you, there's somebody here in Rhode Island somewhere who is going to be able to get their treatment for cancer without having to give up their house or go bankrupt. Because of you, there are folks—small businesses right here in New Hampshire—who are able to keep their doors open in the depths of recession.

Because of you, there are young people right here in Rhode Island who are going to be able to go to college and otherwise couldn't go to college. Because of you, there are 100,000 young men and women who are returning home from Iraq—because of you. Because of the things that you did in 2008, we have made huge changes.

So don't let people tell you you're not making a difference. Yes, it's hard. But it's always been hard. The history of America has been hard, starting with a revolution to found this country. The idea of America is hard, based on a document and ideas that had never been tried before: "We hold these truths to be self-evident, that all men are created equal, endowed by their Creator with certain inalienable rights, that among these are life, liberty, and the pursuit of happiness."

That's a hard idea. And we had to overcome slavery. We had to fight for women's rights. And we had to fight for workers' rights. But each successive generation hasn't shied away just because it's hard. We kept on going. We kept moving forward.

And that's why we're here today. And we want 20 years from now, 30 years from now, 100 years ago—100 years from now, we want people to be able to look back and say, you know what, this generation did the same thing. That same spirit that got us through war and depression, that helped to perfect this Union, that same spirit is alive and well in 2010.

That's what I need all of you to show me. And if you do, I promise you David is going to Congress. And we will continue to help rebuild the American Dream for all people.

Thank you very much, Rhode Island. God bless you. God bless the United States of America.

NOTE: The President spoke at 6:03 p.m. at the Rhode Island Convention Center. In his remarks, he referred to Mayor David N. Cicilline of Providence, RI.

Remarks at a Democratic Congressional Campaign Committee Dinner in Providence
October 25, 2010

The President. Thank you so much. I was back in the kitchen making sure everything was going okay. [*Laughter*] It smells really good.

So first of all, I just want to thank Johnnie and Buff and the whole Chace family for opening up this spectacular home. And we are so grateful for your hospitality.

I want to make sure to recognize a couple of folks that are here. Obviously, Chris Van Hollen, this guy is the hardest working man in politics right now. [*Laughter*] He is having to run around all across the country, working so hard on our behalf. And we are really proud of what he's accomplished against daunting odds. I think we are going to end up doing really well, partly because of his leadership. So please give him a big round of applause.

Looking around here, I don't see the Rhode Island delegation. I don't know where—[laughter]—there they are. All right, there they are. All right. Sheldon, Jack, and Patrick, we could not have accomplished half of what we accomplished this year if it hadn't been for them. You guys have an outstanding congressional delegation. And so I am grateful to them not only for their hard work, but also for their friendship and good counsel. I really appreciate it.

We are 10 days away, is that right? Nine?

Audience member. Eight. [*Laughter*]

The President. I've been on the road a lot. [*Laughter*] Seems like it will be 10. But I have been traveling all across the country over the last several weeks, and the mood out there is interesting. I mean, this is going to be a difficult election, there's no doubt about it, because we've gone through one of the most difficult times in our Nation's history. I think the magnitude of the crisis isn't fully appreciated, partly because the terrific actions that were taken by Congress helped to stem the crisis fairly early on. But the devastation is something that we are feeling and will continue to feel for a while.

I was mentioning in a speech earlier, we lost 4 million jobs in the 6 months before I took office, before I was sworn in, 750,000 jobs the month I was sworn in, 600,000 the month after that, 600,000 the month after that. So most of the 8 million jobs that we ended up losing in this recession we had lost before any of the economic policies that we had a chance to put into place could take effect. And most economists estimate, including John McCain's economist, that had we not taken these steps, unemployment might be at 12 percent or 13 percent.

So an economy that was shrinking is now growing. We've seen 9 months straight of public sector job growth. But the fact is, people are still hurting. I mean, the consequences of that crisis are felt everywhere, here in Rhode Island and all across the country: people who have been looking for work in some cases for over a year and still can't find a job, families that have seen the values of their homes decline drastical-

ly. They're having trouble maybe financing their kid's college education because of what happened to their savings accounts or their investment accounts.

And so it's not surprising that the country is angry and the country is frustrated. And essentially the strategy of the Republicans when we came in was to try to ride that anger as long as possible. We had hoped that in this once-in-a-generation challenge that we were facing that we would see an end to some of the game-playing and posturing and politicizing of everything we did because there would be a recognition that this was an urgent time and we had to take some key steps not only for the next several years, but to ensure that we were going to be competitive in generations to come.

And frankly, the Republicans made a strategic decision which said, you know what, we are going to just step back, say no, do nothing, obstruct, and hopefully, then people will forget how we got into this mess in the first place. In other words, their electoral strategy is amnesia. And although it may have seemed like a smart political tactic, it wasn't right for the country.

And so we made a different decision, which was that we were going to do everything that we could not only to deal with the immediate crisis, but also to start finally tackling some of the structural problems that had been holding this country back for far too long.

And some of those decisions might not be popular, but we determined they were the right thing to do. And I know that Sheldon and Jack and Chris and Patrick and certainly I felt that you guys sent us there not to do what was easy, but to do what was right, and that we did not go to Washington for fancy offices or titles.

We went there because somewhere in our lives, somebody had helped us. Somewhere in our life stories, we had seen an America in which we looked after one another; we gave everybody an opportunity; that we made investments in education and worker training and infrastructure; we didn't just think about the next election, but we thought about the next generation.

And that's what we've done over the last 2 years. And I could not be prouder of the record of accomplishment in this Congress. A lot of it happened so fast people didn't realize it. I mean, within the first few months, not only had we made investments in clean energy that were unprecedented, not only did we significantly increase our research and development so that we could continue to be an innovation economy, not only did we make the largest investment in infrastructure since Eisenhower built the Interstate Highway System, not only did we make the largest investment in education in history, but we had made sure that 4 million children who hadn't previously gotten it had health insurance.

We had made sure that mortgage fraud was actually policed, that credit card companies couldn't abuse their customers. We expanded national service larger than any expansion since the Peace Corps. And this was all before we started tackling some of the enormous issues that we tackled, like health care reform and financial regulatory reform.

And it was interesting, Ira Magaziner is here; so he was there for the last round in '94 and remembers how tough this was. And I have to tell you, when it comes to health care reform, we knew how tough it was going to be, because it is a huge, complicated system with a lot of interests. And we had neglected it for so long that inevitably, it was going to be a contentious fight.

But what we also knew was if we didn't start tackling it now, that not only were you going to continue to see 30 million people without health insurance, not only were we going to continue to waste money on preventable diseases like diabetes because people weren't getting regular checkups, but there was no way that we could ever hope to deal with our deficit, because the primary driver of our deficit—almost by a magnitude of several times—the biggest driver of our deficit and our debt, long term, is our health care costs. And we've got to bring those costs down.

So we have taken steps that essentially encompass the biggest patient's bill of rights in our history, combined with measures that over time can actually make sure that we are bending the cost curve and making smarter health care investments that will result in higher quality and lower cots. And in the bargain, 30 million people are going to end up getting health care.

You've got young people who are able to stay on their health care up until the age of 26 if they're not getting it on the job. You've got folks with preexisting conditions who now have some hope of getting coverage and won't be bankrupted when they get sick.

Oh, and by the way, it turns that according to the Congressional Budget Office, it reduces our deficit by over a trillion dollars over the course of two decades. So we—[*applause*].

On financial regulatory reform, the other big project that we had, my general theory is, if you've gone through the worst financial crisis since the Great Depression, probably something's not working. And we rolled up our sleeves and put together a set of rules that allow for innovation in the financial markets; that allow Wall Street to do well, but not at somebody else's expense; make sure that we've got consumer protections; make sure there aren't taxpayer bailouts; make sure that if one company goes under, it's not too big to fail, because we've got a mechanism to let them go into bankruptcy without bringing the entire financial system down with it.

All of these things were huge battles, and this is just on the domestic front. By the way, I had two wars to deal with at the same time. And so we've brought home 100,000 troops from Iraq. We've got a strategy in Afghanistan that will allow us to start phasing down our troop levels next year at the same time as we're going to provide an opportunity for Afghans to stand up and start strengthening their own security capacity.

Incredibly proud of what we've done. But we've got so much more to do. I mean, not only do we have 9.5 percent unemployment, which is a huge drag on our economy and has just an enormous human toll that keeps me up at night every day, but there are a bunch of things that we're going to have to do to make sure that we can compete in what is going to be the most competitive global economy imaginable.

We used to have the best infrastructure in the world. We don't now. Anybody who has been to the airport in Beijing or in Singapore will tell you that we're losing ground.

We used to stitch the entire country together with our rail systems, and now our rail systems are 20th century—19th century in some cases—compared to the 21st-century high-speed rail around the world.

We still underinvest in research and development. We don't have an energy policy that will allow us to be the leaders in solar and wind and biodiesel that can not only help protect our environment, but also create the jobs of the future.

We've got so much work left to do, and the only way I can do it is if I've got good partners in Congress. The only way I can do it is if Chris and Jack and Sheldon are not in the minority, but are the majority, that they are the ones who are helping to guide these issues through.

I know that a lot of times people wonder, gosh, you know, why did it take—why did the health care take so long? Well, this is not a monarchy we live in. This is a democracy. And it's a big, messy democracy. And there's supposed to be debate, and there's supposed to be contentiousness, and it's supposed to be hard to make big changes.

But ultimately, we got those changes done because we had leaders in Congress who were willing not just to put their fingers up to the wind, but instead were committed to doing what was right. And we're going to need more of that in not just the next couple of years, but for the next decade if we want to make sure that finally we are positioning ourselves so that our kids can live out the American Dream and we're handing an America off that is stronger than the one we inherited.

That's going to require some very tough choices. And I'll just use as one example fiscal issues. We do have a big debt, and we've got a big deficit. Most of it was structural and inherited from the previous administration, where we went to—from record surpluses to record deficits. A bunch of it is a consequence of this huge economic crisis that we just went through. But it is real, and we're going to have to deal with it.

And that means choices. And so when you've got the other party saying, let's provide $700 billion worth of tax cuts to the top 2 percent—so, many of the people in this room, those of us

who don't need it and aren't asking for it and are not going to be making different decisions as a consequence of it—and we don't have this $700 billion, so we'd have to borrow it from China or Saudi Arabia or others, and when you've got the other side, in their "Pledge to America," saying that a portion of this will be paid for by cutting education by 20 percent at a time when we know that the biggest determinant of our success is going to be how well our workforce is educated, that's the choice that makes this election so absolutely critical.

I mean, we made a different choice when it comes to education. Not only have we been willing to reform education—in ways that sometimes offends some of our core base—because it's the right thing to do, but we also, for example, took tens of billions of dollars that were going in unwarranted subsidies to banks, and they're now going to students in direct student loans and in increased Pell grants and making college much more affordable and boosting up our community colleges, which serve as a gateway for so many working families.

There are going to be choices like that repeatedly over the next year, the next 2 years, the next 5 years, where you make decisions about are we going to invest in our future, are we going to invest in our infrastructure, are we going to invest in research and development?

When we cut spending, do we do so intelligently with a scalpel to make sure that it's not hurting the most vulnerable and to make sure that it's not essentially impacting our ability to compete over the long term? Or are we just doing it in a knee-jerk fashion because of whatever is politically fashionable?

That's what's at stake in this election. But it's going to be hard. The only way we succeed is if we've got the ability to get out the message, particularly in this last week. Because we are getting snowed under by unsupervised spending, undisclosed spending through these front groups that so many of you have read about: Americans for Prosperity and Moms for Motherhood. That last one I made up. [*Laughter*]

But there are a whole bunch of groups out there, mostly run and coordinated by Republican operatives, as a consequence of the Supreme Court *Citizens United* decision that are just spending millions of dollars in——

Audience member. And they're liars.

The President. Well, and these ads completely distort Democrats' records. But it's a powerful force. I mean, if you're in a competitive House race right now, if you're in a State like Colorado and you just watch this stuff, I mean, it is just a blizzard of negative ads.

And so we're going to have to do our best to match that, mostly with the—just by telling the truth. But also we're going to have to have enough money to be able to get that truth out. And that's where all of you come in.

So I am grateful to all of you for the kind of support that you've already shown us. I want to just close by saying this. I meet a lot of people who say, boy, I got really involved in politics for the first time in 2008. I was so inspired, and I was so excited. And I knocked on doors, and my kids, they talked to me about it. They got involved. It was just a magical time, and then election night and Inauguration, and Beyonce was singing. [*Laughter*] And Michelle looked so pretty in her dress. [*Laughter*]

And I understand that excitement. It was a good thing because I think it reminded us of what is possible when citizens get involved. It was a moment where we overcame the cynicism of our politics and the conventional wisdom of Washington, and we said, you know what, when people join together, we can do amazing things, unlikely things.

And I know that over the course of the 2 years, sometimes, people feel like, gosh, that magical moment now has given way to just the grinding it out and filibusters and cable chatter. And you just start feeling like, boy, this is exhausting. And a lot of people come up and say that to me.

And yet I just want everybody to understand, because of you being involved, right now there's a woman in New Hampshire somewhere who doesn't have to give up her house to get her cancer treatments. And right now there are young people around the country who didn't think they could finance their college educations that now can. And right now there are incredible scientific experiments and research being done in cutting-edge areas that otherwise

wouldn't be happening and might set the groundwork for amazing industries of the future. And right now there's small businesses here in Rhode Island that might have shut down in the middle of—in the depths of recession had we not made those investments. And right now there are 100,000 young men and women of incredible courage who are home because of what you've done.

So don't let people tell you you haven't made a difference. This is what change looks like. It is slow; it is methodical. There are times where we'll experience setbacks. But the trajectory is sound. We're going in the right direction. We just got to keep on going. So thank you, guys.

The last thing I have to do is to make sure that you all send your mayor to Congress. And I want to just say something special about David. I had a chance to meet him when I was still running—was I running for Senator or was I running for President at that point?

Mayor David N. Cicilline of Providence, RI. For President.

The President. I was already running for President. [*Laughter*] It all blurs together. [*Laughter*]

And when I came here, the interesting thing was, everybody I talked to said, boy, you should see our mayor. He's just like—he's exciting, and he's smart, and he's funny, and he's passionate. And I got to know David, and he was exactly as advertised—unless it's the other guy running them. [*Laughter*] None of that stuff is true.

Look, the truth of the matter is, we feel confident that David is going to be joining us in Congress because of the incredible support of all of you. But the key is making sure that when David gets there, he's able to get something done. And I promise you, it's a lot easier to get something done in the majority than in the minority. [*Laughter*]

So obviously, I need everybody. Don't take it for granted; run scared. I know he will. He's going to be knocking on doors and making phone calls. And you need to be doing the same on his behalf. But the fact that you're here tonight reminds us that even beyond this one particular race, we've got races all across the country with great candidates like David. And they need that support, and they need that help as well. And that's what you're showing here tonight.

So thank you so much to the Chaces. Thank you. I've got to get home because Michelle is on the road, so I've got to be home to tuck in the girls and walk the dog. [*Laughter*] And scoop the poop. [*Laughter*] So I apologize that I can't stay for dinner, but it looks simply spectacular. And again, I thank you all for being here tonight. All right?

NOTE: The President spoke at 7:09 p.m. at the residence of Johnnie C. Chace and Arnold B. "Buff" Chace, Jr. In his remarks, he referred to Mark Zandi, chief economist, Moody's Analytics, in his former capacity as chief economic adviser to 2008 Republican Presidential nominee Sen. John S. McCain III; Ira C. Magaziner, Special Adviser for Policy Development during the administration of President William J. Clinton; and musician Beyonce G. Knowles.

Statement on the Earthquake and Tsunami in West Sumatra, Indonesia
October 26, 2010

Michelle and I are deeply saddened by the loss of life, injuries, and damage that have occurred as a result of the recent earthquake and tsunami in West Sumatra. At the same time, I am heartened and encouraged by the remarkable resiliency of the Indonesian people and the commitment of their Government to rapidly assist the victims. As a friend of Indonesia, the United States stands ready to help in any way. Meanwhile, our thoughts and prayers are with the Indonesian people and all those affected by this tragedy.

Remarks on Domestic Violence Prevention
October 27, 2010

Thank you, everybody. Everybody, please have a seat. Thank you so much.

Let me just be clear: Biden's boss is Dr. Jill Biden. [*Laughter*] So let there be no confusion about that.

I want to begin obviously by recognizing my Vice President for the unbelievable leadership that he has shown for more than two decades on this issue, fighting alongside all the advocates who are here today. Great work.

He started holding hearings on domestic violence back in 1990. He wrote and gathered the support to pass the Violence Against Women's Act, a law that has saved countless lives, transformed how we address these all too pervasive crimes. And as Vice President, he hasn't let up. He is helping us to step up our efforts across all relevant Federal agencies. So nobody feels more passionately about this than Joe, and I am grateful to him for all of his leadership. We're really proud of him.

I also want to thank Valerie Jarrett, my Senior Adviser and Chair of our Council on Women and Girls. Valerie has helped to ensure that the issues that we're talking about today—the concerns of women and girls—are addressed at the highest levels of our Government.

I want to acknowledge Lynn Rosenthal, the first-ever adviser at the White House—[*applause*]. So we're proud of Lynn. I guess you know her. [*Laughter*] She's been calling you up a little bit. But she's doing great work helping to advise us on these issues.

I want to thank Judge Susan Carbon, the Director of the Office on Violence Against Women at the Department of Justice. We're proud of what we're doing here.

I want to thank my Secretary for Health and Human Services, Secretary Sebelius, who is helping to coordinate our efforts.

And finally, I want to thank everybody who is here today for the work that you're doing to stop domestic violence and to help its survivors. You've got champions like Senator Frank Lautenberg and Congresswoman Donna Edwards who have done extraordinary work in Congress. You've got leaders like Mayor Mitch Landrieu of New Orleans. And I think you already heard about some of the interesting work that they're doing down in that city.

There are so many organizations that are represented here today. We are very proud of you and what you do. I'm thrilled to see Joe Torre, who's here, who understands this issue personally and deeply, and for him to lend his name to this is extraordinarily important. And we hope that the Dodgers do better next year. [*Laughter*] My White Sox aren't doing so hot either, so—[*laughter*].

As you all know, domestic violence was for far too long seen as a lesser offense. As Valerie said, it was frequently treated like a private matter. Victims were often sent home from the hospital without intervention; children were left to suffer in silence. And as a consequence, abuse could go on for years. In many cases, this violence would only end with the death of a woman or a child.

And we've come an incredibly long way since that time. We have changed laws. We've made progress in changing the way people think about domestic abuse. As Joe pointed out, we've reduced the incidence of domestic violence. We've done so in no small part because of the advocacy of your organizations and the willingness of victims to tell their own stories, even when it's difficult.

And if there's one group that I want to thank, am grateful for, it's people who are willing to tell their stories, because it's hard. It's hard stuff. When Joe Torre stands up and talks about growing up in an abusive household, about being afraid to come home when he saw his dad's car parked in the front of the house, and finding a refuge in baseball, that connects in a way that no speech by a politician can connect.

As a consequence, he started Safe At Home, a foundation for children going through what he went through, and it's helping kids all across the country.

We're joined by Lori Stone and Ruth Glenn, both of whom were victims of years of violent abuse in their marriages. And they're sharing their stories in the hope that nobody else has to experience the pain and fear that they lived with every day.

Those stories remind us of how cruel, how menacing domestic violence can be because it happens at home, the place where you should feel safe; because the abuse comes at the hands of the people who are supposed to love you and trust you; because escaping domestic violence is not only associated with a great deal of fear, but also incredible financial and legal challenges that often leave victims of abuse feeling trapped.

That's what we have to change. And I say that not only as a President, but as a son, as a husband, as the father of two daughters. Now, we've made a great deal of progress in recent years. But everybody in this room understands that our work is not yet finished, not when there's more we can do to help folks looking to restart their lives and achieve financial independence; not when there's more to do to ensure that the victims of abuse have access to legal protection; not when children are trapped in abusive homes, especially when we know the lingering damage and despair that this can cause in a child's life; not when one in every four women experiences domestic violence and one in six women are sexually assaulted at some point in their lives.

It's not acceptable. And I know that Valerie and Joe spoke about some of our efforts in detail, but I just want to highlight a few key parts of what is a new, coordinated effort to protect victims and break the cycle of abuse.

We're helping the victims of violence to overcome the financial barriers they often face getting back on their feet. And Lori's experience serves as an example. Lori had not only—had suffered abuse at the hands of her husband physically, he also destroyed their credit. And she had to spend her limited savings on legal representation to keep custody of her children.

So we're going to start taking steps to connect survivors with jobs, to help them save, to make it easier for them to rebuild their credit, to make sure that no one has to choose between a violent home and no home at all. And—[*applause*].

Secretary Donovan at the Department of Housing and Urban Development is releasing new rules today to prevent the victims of domestic violence from being evicted or denied assisted housing because a crime was committed against them. That's not right, and we're going to put a stop to it.

We're also doing more to help the victims of domestic violence access legal services and protections. So today the Justice Department is releasing new tools and best practices to judges, to advocates, to law enforcement to help ensure that protective orders are issued and enforced. And the Vice President and the Justice Department are launching a new effort to help victims of domestic abuse find lawyers to represent them pro bono. You heard Joe talk about that. That's critical; that's important.

As the advocates in this room can attest, when a victim of abuse leaves a violent relationship, it's often a particularly vulnerable time. I know that's when Ruth Glenn was viciously attacked by her husband. And there are many stories like this—too many stories. We need to make sure that we're doing everything we can for victims in this critical period to ensure that folks who are seeking help and protection get that help and get that protection. That's our responsibility.

So these are just a few of the steps that we're taking. But the bottom line is this: Nobody in America should live in fear because they are unsafe in their own home—no adult, no child. And no one who is the victim of abuse should ever feel that they have no way to get out. We need to make sure every victim of domestic violence knows that they are not alone, that there are resources available to them in their moment of greatest need. And as a society, we need to ensure that if a victim of abuse reaches out for help, we are there to lend a hand.

This is not just the job of government, it's a job for all of us. So I want to thank all of you for the work that you do in your respective communities. And I want you to know that this administration is going to stand with you each and every step of the way.

So congratulations on your great work. We've got more work to do. And I couldn't be prouder to be part of this effort. Thank you very much, everybody.

NOTE: The President spoke at 4:25 p.m. in the East Room at the White House. In his remarks, he referred to Lynn Rosenthal, White House Adviser on Violence Against Women; and Joseph P. Torre, former manager, Los Angeles Dodgers.

Statement on the Death of Former President Nestor C. Kirchner of Argentina
October 27, 2010

On behalf of the American people, I offer my sincere condolences to the Argentine people and to President Cristina Fernandez de Kirchner upon the death of Nestor Kirchner, former President of Argentina and Secretary General of the Union of South American Nations (UNASUR). Nestor Kirchner played a significant role in the political life of Argentina and had embarked upon an important new chapter with UNASUR.

Michelle's and my thoughts and prayers are with President Fernandez de Kirchner and their children.

NOTE: The statement referred to Maximo, son, and Florencia, daughter, of President Cristina Fernandez de Kirchner and former President Nestor C. Kirchner of Argentina.

Statement on the Presidential Election in Cote d'Ivoire
October 28, 2010

The United States supports the people of Cote d'Ivoire as they prepare to express their

democratic voice and participate in Presidential elections on October 31, 2010. The Ivoirian

Government, the candidates, their supporters, and all political actors have an obligation to ensure that the long-delayed Presidential elections are held in a peaceful and transparent manner. The people of Cote d'Ivoire deserve a secure environment for elections and for their choice to be accepted by all candidates. These elections are a critical step to rebuilding Cote d'Ivoire. The United States stands with the Ivoirian people as they prepare for long-awaited democratic elections and move closer to lasting peace and prosperity in Cote d'Ivoire.

Remarks at Stromberg Metal Works, Inc., in Beltsville, Maryland
October 29, 2010

Hello, everybody. Good to see you. Thank you. Thank you so much. Everybody, please have a seat. It is wonderful to be here at Stromberg Metal Works. And I want to thank Bob Gawne and his lovely bride of 58 years, Patricia, for their incredible hospitality.

I also want to note that you've got your great Senator from the State of Maryland, Ben Cardin, in the house. Give him a big round of applause. Your other Senator, Barbara Mikulski, couldn't make it but wanted me to say hello on her behalf, as well as Majority Leader Steny Hoyer, who couldn't make it but wants to say hello as well. And I know they are all incredibly proud of this amazing facility.

I just took a tour with Bob and saw a little bit of what you guys do here, saw the workers turning raw metal into sheets, cutting it into shapes, banging it into finished products. Everybody here is proud of what they do, and it shows in the great work that you do. This is a company with a proud history. Paul Stromberg, a former Navy metalsmith, founded it in 1940. In 1958, a young former marine—Bob—came on as chief engineer. And nearly 30 years later, Bob bought the company. Today, it is in its 70th year of operation, it is employee owned, it continues to grow. We've got a unionized workforce that— where folks who put in a hard day's work get a living wage that allows them to support a family. This is a community business where even during downturns and tough times, people are looking out for each other.

So it just describes, I think, what's best about America and what's best about American business. And we are very, very proud of you. It's an all-American success story, and I'm proud to be here. [*Applause*] That's right.

Now, this morning we learned that our economy grew at a rate of 2 percent over the last 3 months. We've had 9 consecutive months of private sector job growth, after nearly 2 years of job loss. But as we continue to dig out from the worst recession in 80 years, our mission is to accelerate that recovery and encourage more rapid growth so that businesses like this one can continue to prosper and we can get the millions of Americans who are still looking for jobs back to work.

Now, I don't believe that government can or should guarantee the success of this company or any company. I don't think Bob or any business owner expects government to guarantee success. Success has to be earned. It has to be earned the old-fashioned way through great ideas and hard work and great employees. That's the American way.

But there are times, like in the past few years, when our economy is hit with as devastating a blow as we've seen—when credit is frozen, when demand is stalled—that we've got a responsibility to offer temporary and targeted incentives to spur investment, to knock down the barriers that stand in your way, and to help create the conditions you need to grow and to hire and to prosper. And that's what we've done.

Since I took office, we've cut taxes for small businesses 16 times, 16 different tax cuts for small businesses. Instead of providing tax breaks for companies that are shipping jobs overseas, we're giving tax breaks to encourage companies to invest right here in the United States of America, in small businesses, in clean energy firms, in manufacturers, in businesses like this one. And we've taken steps to expand lending to small businesses, which, even with good credit, continue to have difficulty borrowing the capital they need to grow.

It's been just over 1 month since I signed the Small Business Jobs Act into law. And in that month—just 1 month, through just one provision in that bill—the Small Business Administration, the SBA, has supported nearly $3 billion in new loans to more than 5,000 small businesses across the country. That's fast. And we expect that when all is said and done, these steps will help support tens of billions of dollars in loans to our entrepreneurs so they can expand, they can grow, and they can hire new workers in communities like this one.

Now, that same initiative also accelerated $55 billion in new tax relief for businesses that make job-creating investments over the next year, including by extending a provision in the Recovery Act called business expensing, or bonus depreciation. Now, this is a pretty simple concept. What it does is allow a business like this one to immediately deduct 50 percent of the cost of certain investments like new equipment.

And I was talking to Bob, and he says he's got to buy a new piece of equipment for this plant basically every year. The reason this company is able to compete against low-wage countries, against nonunion workforces, is because it's got better equipment and it's got more skilled, better workers. That's the reason that it's succeeding.

So what I want to do to accelerate this recovery is to allow businesses of all sizes to immediately deduct the entire cost of these investments—100 percent—all next year, through the end of 2011. And that means that business owners like Bob who decide to upgrade their plants, upgrade their equipment, that means that they are able to write off immediately that depreciation in 1 year. And that means that they're going to have additional money to invest in workers and in other plants and equipment.

So let's just take the example of Stromberg. Let's say that a similar business is thinking about buying $1 million worth of additional shop equipment next year. Typically, the business might only be able to deduct the value of that new equipment over the course of several

years. Under this proposal, a business like this one would be able to deduct all $1 million next year. That accelerates hundreds of thousands of dollars in tax cuts, real money that businesses can use to expand or hire new workers.

Now, this is not a shot in the dark. This is a proposal that works. A new report from the Treasury Department estimates that it will accelerate $150 billion in tax cuts for 2 million businesses large and small around the country.

It would temporarily lower the average cost of investment by more than 75 percent for companies like Stromberg, creating a powerful new incentive for businesses to invest more right now—perhaps about $50 billion—which will generate more jobs and more growth.

So this is a good idea. It's a proven idea. It's an idea that will allow more equipment to be purchased and, eventually, more folks to be hired. And it will put a dent in the jobless rate that we've got to keep on working on because it's way too high right now.

And look, I know we're at the height of political season. I just had my guy show me a little button showing that he had already voted—early voted. So I hope everybody else is using that as an example. But it is political season. Political season is going to be over soon. And when it does, all of us are going to have a responsibility, Democrats and Republicans, to work together wherever we can to promote jobs and growth.

And the idea I'm advancing today is one that both Democrats and Republicans should be able to support. In fact, Republicans have actually offered this idea in the past. It's a simple proposal that will make a serious difference for this company and others like it. It will encourage business investment right now. It will create jobs right now. It will help our economy grow right now. And when many of our friends and neighbors are still navigating through some tough times, that's what America needs right now.

When I hear Bob and Patricia talk about their lives together and building this—helping to build this company, I'm reminded that this country has been through tough times before. We've weathered tough times before. And it's precisely in those times that we regrouped, we reinvested, we retooled, and we rebuilt. It's in those times that we recaptured the ingenuity and the resilience that makes us a great people and makes this a great country.

And that's the spirit that we've got to recapture and unleash once again, a spirit of optimism and confidence and hope that has made America the most dynamic country in the world. And standing here with all of you, I am absolutely convinced that there are going to be brighter days ahead for America, an America where businesses like this one are leading our economy forward and workers like all of you are rewarded for the work that you do, where our middle class is growing again and investment is being made here in the United States again and the American Dream is back within the reach

for all who are willing to work for it, where we're forging our future the way you forge your steel right here, with hard work and sweat, with American know-how and ingenuity, cooperating together, working together. That's how the folks who came before us built the first American century in plants just like this one. That's how we're going to make sure that the 21st century is an American century as well.

So thank you very much, everybody. God bless you. God bless America. Bob and Patricia, thanks for the great work that you do. Thank you.

NOTE: The President spoke at 11:42 a.m. In his remarks, he referred to Robert B. Gawne, chief executive officer, Stromberg Metal Works, Inc.

Remarks on Explosive Devices Found Aboard Flights Bound for the United States
October 29, 2010

Good afternoon, everybody. I want to briefly update the American people on a credible terrorist threat against our country and the actions that we're taking with our friends and our partners to respond to it.

Last night and earlier today, our intelligence and law enforcement professionals, working with our friends and allies, identified two suspicious packages bound for the United States, specifically, two places of Jewish worship in Chicago. Those packages have been located in Dubai and East Midlands Airport in the United Kingdom. An initial examination of those packages has determined that they do apparently contain explosive material.

I was alerted to this threat last night by my top counterterrorism adviser, John Brennan. I directed the Department of Homeland Security and all our law enforcement and intelligence agencies to take whatever steps are necessary to protect our citizens from this type of attack. Those measures led to additional screening of some planes in Newark and Philadelphia.

The Department of Homeland Security is also taking steps to enhance the safety of air travel, including additional cargo screening. We will

continue to pursue additional protective measures for as long as it takes to ensure the safety and security of our citizens.

I've also directed that we spare no effort in investigating the origins of these suspicious packages and their connection to any additional terrorist plotting. Although we are still pursuing all the facts, we do know that the packages originated in Yemen. We also know that Al Qaida in the Arabian Peninsula, a terrorist group based in Yemen, continues to plan attacks against our homeland, our citizens, and our friends and allies.

John Brennan, who you will be hearing from, spoke with President Salih of Yemen today about the seriousness of this threat, and President Salih pledged the full cooperation of the Yemeni Government in this investigation.

Going forward, we will continue to strengthen our cooperation with the Yemeni Government to disrupt plotting by Al Qaida in the Arabian Peninsula and to destroy this Al Qaida affiliate. We'll also continue our efforts to strengthen a more stable, secure, and prosperous Yemen so that terrorist groups do not have the time and space they need to plan attacks from within its borders.

The events of the past 24 hours underscores the necessity of remaining vigilant against terrorism. As usual, our intelligence, law enforcement, and homeland security professionals have served with extraordinary skill and resolve and with the commitment that their enormous responsibilities demand. We're also coordinating closely and effectively with our friends and our allies, who are essential to this fight.

As we obtain more information, we will keep the public fully informed. But at this stage, the American people should know that the counterterrorism professionals are taking this threat very seriously and are taking all necessary and prudent steps to ensure our security. And the American people should be confident that we will not waver in our resolve to defeat Al Qaida and its affiliates and to root out violent extremism in all its forms.

Thank you very much.

NOTE: The President spoke at 4:22 p.m. in the James S. Brady Press Briefing Room at the White House.

Remarks at a Rally for Representative Thomas S.P. Perriello in Charlottesville, Virginia
October 29, 2010

The President. Hello, Cavaliers! Thank you! Are you fired up? Oh, it is good to be back in Charlottesville. Good to be back.

I want to thank Mayor Dave Norris for his hospitality. UVA, thank you. I was in the neighborhood and thought I'd stop by just to make sure you get out and vote on Tuesday for one of the best Congressmen Virginia has ever had, Tom Perriello.

Audience member. I love you!

The President. Now—I love you back. It's great to see you. Thank you.

Now, look, I am here for one reason. I'm not here because Tom votes with me on every issue. Sometimes he disagrees with me. There are times where I know that his first allegiance is not to party labels, it's not to the Democratic Party; it is to the people of his district and the people of Virginia.

The reason I am here is because in this day and age, let's face it, political courage is hard to come by. The easiest thing to do, especially when you're a first-term Congressman, the easiest thing to do is make your decisions based on the polls. You put your fingers up to the wind, you check which way the political wind is blowing before you cast every vote. That's how a lot of folks think they should do their jobs in Washington.

And that's not who Tom is. He did not go to Washington—he didn't go to Washington to do what was easy, to do what was popular. He went to do what was right.

Audience members. Go, Tom, go! Go, Tom, go! Go, Tom, go!

The President. Go, Tom, go! Go, Tom, go! Go, Tom, go!

Tom went to help make the tough decisions necessary to save this economy from a second depression. He went to fight for jobs in Virginia. And in the last 6 months, this district has seen the announcement of over 2,000 new jobs, including new clean energy jobs right here in this district.

Tom Perriello went—Tom went to Washington to make college more affordable for students and families. We got any students here today? The first bill Tom wrote was a $2,500 tuition tax credit that is now the law of the land, helping you.

Tom went to Washington to take on the insurance companies and the credit card companies and the Wall Street banks, to make sure they can't take advantage of his constituents or the American people. That's what Tom Perriello is about.

So Tom Perriello went to Washington to do what's hard. He went to do what is right. And now the lobbyists and the special interests are going after him. And the question I have for you is, when somebody like this has your back, do you have his back?

Audience members. Yes, we can! Yes, we can! Yes, we can!

The President. Sounds like you do. Look, Charlottesville, in 4 days, you have the chance to set the direction of this State and this country not just for the next 2 years, but for the next 10 years, for the next 20 years, just like you did in 2008.

You can defy the conventional wisdom. You know what that is: The conventional wisdom that says that you can't overcome the cynicism of our politics, that you can't overcome the special interests, you can't overcome the big money, you can't tackle our biggest challenges, you don't want to make waves.

We always say we want integrity from our elected officials. And you know what, this is a test case right here in Charlottesville, because this man has integrity. And in 4 days, you have the chance to say, yes, we can.

Now, there is no doubt this is a tough election. It's tough in Tom's district. It's tough all across the country because we have gone through an incredibly difficult time as a nation.

For most of the last decade, middle class families were hurting. Between 2001 and 2009, when the other party was in charge, we saw the slowest job growth of any time since World War II. The average middle class income went down 5 percent. This is when they were in charge.

Meanwhile, as your incomes were going down, your costs of living, health care, college tuition, groceries all were going up. Too many jobs were leaving this area and going overseas. Too many parents couldn't afford to send their kids to college or go to a doctor when they got sick. Americans were working two to three jobs just to make ends meet. All this was happening before the crisis. And it all culminated and was compounded by the worst economic situation since the Great Depression.

We lost 4 million jobs before Tom and I were even sworn into office, in the 6 months before we were sworn in, 750,000 the month we were sworn in, 600,000 the month after that, 600,000 the month after that. We were in a freefall.

We'd lost almost 8 million jobs before any of our economic policies had a chance to be put into effect.

And when Tom and I went to Washington, we both hoped that Republicans and Democrats would take some time to put politics aside because we had a once-in-a-generation challenge, because although we are proud to be Democrats, we are prouder to be Americans.

And there are plenty of Republicans around the country that feel the same way. But Republican leaders in Washington, they made a different decision. They realized—they looked around, they said: "Boy, we really made a big mess out of this economy, and it's going to take a long time to fix it, and in the meantime people will probably be angry and frustrated. So maybe if we just sit on the sidelines and say no to everything and don't lift a finger to help, knowing that unemployment will still be high, maybe we'll—maybe, just maybe, people will blame the Democrats instead of us." That was their basic strategy.

And so now in this election the other side is betting on amnesia. They're betting that you forgot who caused this mess in the first place. So, Charlottesville, it is up to you to let them know that we have not forgotten. It's up to you to remember this election is a choice between the policies that got us into this mess and the policies that are getting us out of this mess.

Let me tell you something. If they win this election, the chair of a Republican campaign committee has promised, quote, "the exact same agenda" as before Tom and I took office. In other words——

Audience members. Boo!

The President. No, no—now, this is the agenda that resulted in the worst economy since the Great Depression, an agenda of cutting taxes mostly for millionaires and billionaires. You cut the rules for special interests and big corporations. You cut middle class families loose to fend for themselves. It's the same agenda that turned a record surplus into a record deficit, the same agenda that allowed Wall Street to run wild, the same agenda that nearly destroyed our economy.

Now, look, this is not as if we had not tried their agenda. Charlottesville, we tried it for 8 years. It didn't work. And so I bring all this up not because I want to reargue the past. I just don't want to relive the past. We've been through it before. We're not going back there. We're not going back.

Think about what has happened over the last 20 months. Because of the steps we've taken, we no longer face the possibility of a second depression. The economy is growing again. Private sector jobs we've seen increase 9 months in a row.

Now, look, nobody knows better than Tom that we've still got a long way to go. We've still got a lot of work to do.

There are too many people hurting here and all across the country. There are families who are still hanging on by a thread. That's what keeps me up at night. That's what keeps Tom up at night. How can we help families who got hit hard during this recession? How can we make sure that they're back up on their feet?

But you know what, we've got a different idea about what the next 2 years should look like, what the next 10 and 20 years should look like. It's very different from what the Republicans are thinking.

It's an idea rooted in our belief about how this country was built. I just had a chance to meet Tom's mom and—[*applause*]—Tom's mom. And just talking to her, you can tell that this is somebody who understands what it means to work hard and to raise a family. And both Tom and I know what it's like to see our families struggle once in a while. And we know that government doesn't have all the answers to our problems. And we believe government should be lean and it should be efficient. And we believe that job growth is going to come from the private sector and that each of us have responsibilities to take individual initiative to make it.

But in the words of the first Republican President, Abraham Lincoln, we also believe that government should do for the people what the people can't do better for themselves. We believe in hard work and responsibility. But we also believe in a country that invests in its future, that invests in its children, that helps workers get retrained, where we look after one another, where we say, I am my brother's keeper, I am my sister's keeper. That's that America we love. That's the America we believe in. That's the choice in this election.

We believe in an America that invests in its future and its people, an America that's built to compete in the 21st century. We know the jobs and businesses of tomorrow will end up in the countries with the most educated workforce, the best infrastructure, the strongest commitment to research and technology. I want that nation to be the United States of America. Tom wants that nation to be the U.S. of A.

Audience members. U.S.A.! U.S.A.! U.S.A.!

The President. U.S.A.!

Audience members. U.S.A.! U.S.A.! U.S.A.!

The President. There is no reason that China should have faster railroads or newer airports than we do. We're the nation that built the transcontinental railroad. We're the nation that built the Interstate Highway System.

Today, we see an America where we've put—because of Tom's efforts, because of our efforts, we've put thousands of people, people right here in Virginia, to work building new railroads and runways and highways, an America where we build an infrastructure for the 21st century and put people to work doing the work that America needs doing.

We see an America where we invest in homegrown innovation and ingenuity, where we export more goods so we create more jobs here at home, where we make it easier to start a business or patent an invention.

We don't want to keep giving tax breaks to companies that ship jobs overseas. We want to give tax breaks to companies that are investing right here in Charlottesville, right here in Virginia, to small businesses and American manufacturers and clean energy companies. I don't want solar panels and wind turbines and electric cars made in Europe or made in Asia. I want them made here in the United States of America with American workers. That's the choice in this election.

We see an America where every citizen—not just some, but every citizen—have the skills and the training to compete with any worker in the world. We can't allow other countries to out-compete us when it comes to math or science or college graduation rates. We used to be number one in college graduation rates. Now we're number nine. We used to be number one in science and math. Now we're 21st and 25th. That makes no sense.

And that's why, working with Tom, we've made historic investments in education. That's why we set a goal that by 2020 we will once again have the highest proportion of college graduates in the world.

That's why Tom and I refuse to think it makes sense to pay for a $700 billion tax cut for millionaires and billionaires and then cut education by 20 percent to pay for it. Let me tell you, China is not cutting education. South Korea is not cutting its education spending. India is not cutting education spending. Germany is not cutting education spending. Those countries aren't playing for second place. And neither does the United States of America. We play for first place.

That's why, thanks to Tom, tens of billions of dollars in taxpayer subsidies that used to go to the big banks are now going where they should, to you, to students, to help support your college education. That's why we want to make permanent the college tax credit that Tom Perriello fought for, a tax credit worth $10,000 of tuition relief for each student. That is the choice in this election. That is the America that we believe in.

We see an America where corporations live up to their responsibilities to treat consumers fairly, to play by the same rules as everybody else. That's why we made sure insurance companies can't jack up your premiums for no reason or deny you coverage because you're sick. That's why we made sure credit card companies can't hit you with hidden fees and penalties. That's why we made sure taxpayers never again are on the hook for the irresponsibility of Wall Street.

We see an America where we don't pass on a mountain of debt to the next generation. And we will attack the trillion-dollar deficit that I inherited when I took office. But we will do it in a responsible way, not by cutting education. We won't do it by putting the burden on our children or our seniors or our veterans or our middle class families. We won't do it by borrowing another $700 billion to give tax cuts to folks who don't need them and weren't even asking for them. We'll do it by asking for shared sacrifice from all Americans. That's how we do things in America. That's the choice in this election.

So, Charlottesville, we've got a lot of work to do in these next few years.

Audience member. [*Inaudible*]

The President. Yes! [*Laughter*] Exactly. We've got a lot of work to do in the next few years. And we need to work together, Democrats and Republicans, Independents, all to get it done.

But the leaders of the other party, so far they don't see it that way. They're feeling kind of cocky right now. They're feeling a little cocky. And the Republican leader in the House says that "this is not the time for compromise." That's what he said. That's a quote. "This is not the time for compromise."

The Republican leader of the Senate said that his main goal for the next 2 years, this is his top priority, is to beat me in the next election.

That's his top priority. I mean, he didn't say, "My top priority is to create jobs for folks in Virginia." He didn't say, "My top priority is to make America more competitive." He's already thinking about the next election. This one is not even over yet. We haven't even finished this election. He's already thinking about the next election.

That's what's wrong with Washington. That doesn't make any sense. That's the kind of cynicism that we're fighting against. That's the kind of politics we need to change in this country; the kind of politics—you know, this kind of politics that puts scoring points ahead of solving problems. I mean, it's so prevalent it happens every day.

And the sad thing is sometimes that cynicism is rewarded. Sometimes, because of all the special interest money pouring in, all the negative ads, all the clout, sometimes folks who were operating in the best interests of their constituents, sometimes they don't win because folks don't turn out, because folks don't vote, because folks feel like, well, this is just too hard.

This is where all of you come in, because the only way to fight that cynicism, the only way to fight the millions of dollars of special interest attack ads that they're running is with the millions of voices who are ready to finish what we started in 2008.

See, 2008 was just—that wasn't the end goal. It wasn't just to put a President in. It wasn't just to put Tom in. It was to keep building a movement for change. And if everybody who fought for change in 2008 shows up in 2010, then we will win this election, and Tom is going back.

So I want you to think back to—some of you got involved in 2008 because you believed we were at a defining moment in our history. We still are. You believed this is a time where the decisions we make won't just affect us, but will affect future generations, our children and our grandchildren. That's still true.

You knocked on doors and you made phone calls and you cast your vote, some for the very first time, because you knew that if we didn't act now, then the opportunity to keep the American Dream alive might slip away. And that's still the case.

Actually delivering change isn't easy. Believe me, I know. So does Tom. [*Laughter*] I mean, we've got our lumps. We've been getting beat up pretty good. But the reason we're here is because the lumps we've taken are nothing like the lumps that people have been taking for so many years out there. Folks who have worked hard, done everything right and are at risk of losing their home or lost their job or suddenly aren't sure whether they can send their kids to college, we've got to remember those folks. We've got to remember what this is about.

I understand that some of the hoopla and the excitement of election night and Inauguration Day from a couple years ago, that fades. Beyonce was singing and Bono was there. All that stuff—all that stuff—fades away, but that spirit can't fade.

And it's still in each of you. Don't let anybody take that away from you. Don't let folks tell you that all that effort has not been worth it. Don't let them tell you we're not making a difference.

Because of you, right now there are folks in Virginia who don't have to choose between los-

ing their home and getting treatment for their cancer. Because of you, there are parents who can look their children in the eye and say, you are going to college. Because of you, there are small businesses who are able to keep their doors open during this great recession. Because of you, there are nearly 100,000 brave men and women who are coming back from Iraq—because of you.

So don't let them tell you change isn't possible. Here's what I know. This country was founded on what seemed impossible. We had 13 Colonies come together and have to battle the greatest empire on Earth. And then they drafted this document nobody had ever tried before, proclaiming, "We hold these truths to be self-evident"—a son of Virginia wrote those words—"that all men are created equal, and they are endowed by their Creator with certain inalienable rights, that among these are life and liberty and the pursuit of happiness."

And there were those that didn't believe, but the Founders understood, as imperfect as we were, as long as it would take, that we would be set on a journey to perfect this Union. And think of everything our forbears went through for us to be here tonight, those who braved oceans because they emigrated, those who fought slavery, those who made sure women had the right to vote, those who made sure that workers had the right to organize.

Imagine if they had given in to cynicism, if they had said, oh, this is too hard. Oh, we're being attacked. [*Laughter*] Oh, there are negative ads being run against us. [*Laughter*] Oh, this is taking too long. Oh, somebody is filibustering. [*Laughter*] They could have given up. They went through much tougher fights than we went through. They got beat up a lot; they got beat up, literally. [*Laughter*]

But they kept on going. They kept on dreaming. They kept on believing. They kept on pushing, even in the face of difficulty, even in the face of uncertainty. They understood that they had to do what was necessary.

And that's what brought us through war. And that's what brought us through depression. And that's what got us civil rights. And that's what got us women's rights. And that's what got us workers' rights. And that's what made this the greatest country on Earth. That's the spirit we need today. That's the journey that put me in the White House. That's what sent Tom Perriello to Congress. That is what we have to sustain, is that realization that in the United States of America, anything is possible if we're willing to work for it, if we are willing to fight for it and believe in it.

So I need you guys to keep on fighting. Tom needs you to keep on believing. In these last 4 days, I need you to knock on doors and make phone calls and talk to your neighbors and vote, because if you're willing to step up to the plate, we won't just win this election, we won't just send Tom back to Congress, but we will rebuild this middle class. And we will put people back to work, and we will reclaim the American Dream for future generations.

God bless you, and God bless the United States of America.

NOTE: The President spoke at 7:50 p.m. in Charlottesville Pavilion. In his remarks, he referred to Linda Perriello, mother of Rep. Perriello; House Republican Leader John A. Boehner; Senate Minority Leader A. Mitchell McConnell; and musicians Beyonce G. Knowles and Paul D. "Bono" Hewson.

The President's Weekly Address
October 30, 2010

Tuesday is election day, and here in Washington, the talk is all about who will win and who will lose, about parties and politics. But around kitchen tables, I'm pretty sure you're talking about other things: about your family finances, or maybe the state of the economy in your hometown; about your kids and what their futures will bring. And your hope is that once this election is over, the folks you choose to represent you will put the politics aside for a while and work together to solve problems. That's my hope too.

Whatever the outcome on Tuesday, we need to come together to help put people who are still looking for jobs back to work. And there are some practical steps we can take right away to promote growth and encourage businesses to hire and expand. These are steps we all should be able to agree on, not Democratic or Republican ideas, but proposals that have traditionally been supported by both parties.

We ought to provide continued tax relief for middle class families who have borne the brunt of the recession. We ought to allow businesses to defer taxes on the equipment they buy next year. And we ought to make the research and experimentation tax credit bigger and permanent to spur innovation and foster new products and technologies.

Beyond these near-term steps, we should work together to tackle the broader challenges facing our country so that we remain competitive and prosperous in a global economy. That means ensuring that our young people have the skills and education to fill the jobs of a new age. That means building new infrastructure, from high-speed trains to high-speed internet, so that our economy has room to grow. And that means fostering a climate of innovation and entrepreneurship that will allow American businesses and American workers to lead in growth industries like clean energy.

On these issues—issues that will determine our success or failure in this new century—I believe it's the fundamental responsibility of all who hold elective office to seek out common ground. It may not always be easy to find agreement; at times we'll have legitimate philosophical differences. And it may not always be the best politics. But it is the right thing to do for our country.

That's why I found the recent comments by the top two Republicans in Congress so troubling. The Republican leader of the House actually said that "this is not the time for compromise." And the Republican leader of the Senate said his main goal after this election is simply to win the next one.

I know that we're in the final days of a campaign, so it's not surprising that we're seeing this heated rhetoric. That's politics. But when the ballots are cast and the voting is done, we need to put this kind of partisanship aside, win, lose, or draw.

In the end, it comes down to a simple choice. We can spend the next 2 years arguing with one another, trapped in stale debates, mired in gridlock, unable to make progress in solving the serious problems facing our country. We can stand still while our competitors, like China and others around the world, try to pass us by, making the critical decisions that will allow them to gain an edge in new industries.

Or we can do what the American people are demanding that we do. We can move forward. We can promote new jobs and businesses by harnessing the talents and ingenuity of our people. We can take the necessary steps to help the next gen-eration, instead of just worrying about the next election. We can live up to an allegiance far stronger than our membership in any political party. And that's the allegiance we hold to our country.

Thanks.

NOTE: The address was recorded at approximately 4:05 p.m. on October 29 in the Blue Room at the White House for broadcast on October 30. In the address, the President referred to House Minority Leader John A. Boehner; and Senate Minority Leader A. Mitchell McConnell. The transcript was made available by the Office of the Press Secretary on October 29, but was embargoed for release until 6 a.m. on October 30.

Remarks at a Democratic National Committee Rally in Philadelphia, Pennsylvania
October 30, 2010

Hello, Philadelphia! Oh, this is a good-looking crowd here. Are you fired up? Are you ready to go?

First of all, thank you, Elliot, for the unbelievable introduction. We appreciate you. We've got a couple other special guests here. I want to make sure that I acknowledge them. Governor Ed Rendell is in the house; U.S. Senator Arlen Specter is here; U.S. Senator Bob Casey; Congressman Chaka Fattah; Congressman, soon-to-be Senator, Joe Sestak; Mayor Michael Nutter; Allegheny County Executive and soon-to-be Governor Dan Onorato.

I want to thank the first-time voters and Temple University Young Democrats for all the great work you guys have done. And give it up for Quincy Lyons for the great job he's doing organizing.

Now, I am not here to give a long speech, because I want everybody out there, not in here. I'm here to deliver two messages. The first message is thank you, because not only did all of you mobilize, organize, and energize in 2008 to help send me to the White House, but over the last 2 years, so many of you have continued to be involved each and every day to make sure that we could keep moving this country forward. It's be-cause of you that young people are getting college scholarships that weren't getting it before.

It's because of you that young people can now stay on their parents' health insurance till they're 26 and folks who have health insurance aren't dropped by insurance companies when they get sick.

And the fact that—and it's because of you that we're also going to be able to fund AIDS. It's because of you that we are going to be in a position to make sure that each and every person out there is able to find work after a devastating economic crisis that made such a difference to so many families all across this country.

Now, here's the thing, though, guys: You cannot stop now, because the fact of the matter is, we are in a difficult election. It's difficult here in Pennsylvania. It is difficult all across the country.

And unless each and every one of you turn out and get your friends to turn out and get your families to turn out, then we could fall short and all the progress that we've made over the last couple of years can be rolled back.

So the key right now is not just to show up here; it's not just to listen to speeches. It's to go out there and do the hard work that's going to be required to bring this home over the last few days. That's going to be the key.

And so I know that some of you may have been at the rally we had with 20,000 folks at Germantown. But you know what, coming to a rally, that's not the hard part. What I need this weekend is 20,000 doors knocked on by all the volunteers who are here today. Is that something that you think you can do, 20,000?

In order for Joe Sestak to be successful and Dan Onorato to be successful and the entire Democratic ticket to be successful, you're going to need to talk to folks everywhere you can and make sure that you describe to them the future that you see for this country.

You want a country where every young person can get a decent education. You want a country where nobody is bankrupt because they get sick. You want a country where our seniors can retire with dignity and respect and Social Security is there not just for this generation, but for future generations.

You want a country that has the best infrastructure in the world. We used to be number one. We can't have the best rail lines and the best airports built in China or Singapore. They need to be right here in the United States of America.

We don't want to be falling behind in math and science and technology. We've got to be first in research and development and technology to make sure that the new products and new services are developed right here in the United States.

We want clean energy here. We don't want solar panels and wind turbines and electric cars built in China or Europe. We want them built here in the United States with American workers.

And so it is absolutely critical that you go out there and you describe your hopes for the future, especially the young people here, because this election is not just going to set the stage for the next 2 years, it's going to set the stage for the next 10, for the next 20.

And for those of you who were so excited 2 years ago, I just want to remind you this: Two years ago was not about me, it was about you and it was about this country. And I said then that change was going to be hard. Now, we've been involved in some tough fights over the last 2 years. We can't move backwards now. We've got to keep moving forward now. And that's all going to be up to you.

So I want everybody to get out there, knock on doors, make phone calls, volunteer, talk to your friends, talk to your neighbors, go into the beauty shops, go into the barbershops, when you're in church or—you know, this weekend, I want everybody to be talking about have folks voted.

If you do that, then I am confident we're not just going to win this election, but we're going to keep on moving this country forward so that the American Dream is accessible for everybody, not just some.

Thank you very much, Philadelphia. I love you. God bless you. Let's get busy. Let's go to work. Thank you.

NOTE: The President spoke at 11:38 a.m. at Temple University. In his remarks, he referred to Elliot Griffin, student, Temple University.

Remarks at a Democratic National Committee Rally in Bridgeport, Connecticut
October 30, 2010

The President. Thank you! Thank you so much.

Audience members. Yes, we can! Yes, we can! Yes, we can!

The President. Thank you so much. Thank you, everybody. Well, I don't know about you, but this is getting me kind of fired up.

It is great to be back in Connecticut. I want to just say, I am so pleased to be joined here by the Attorney General and soon-to-be Senator, Dick Blumenthal; former Mayor of Stamford and soon-to-be Governor Dan Malloy; Congresswoman Rosa DeLauro; Congressman Jim

Himes; and Mayor of Bridgeport Bill Finch; and all of you.

Bridgeport, in 3 days, you've got the chance to set the direction not just for this State, but for this country, for years to come. And just like you did in 2008, you have the chance to defy the conventional wisdom. You've heard it all from the pundits. You've been hearing it on TV, the wisdom that says you can't overcome cynicism in politics, you can't overcome the special interests, you can't take on the biggest challenges. In 2008, they said you couldn't elect a skinny guy with a funny name. [*Laughter*] And just like you did in 2008, in 3 days you've got the chance to say what?

Audience members. Yes, we can!

The President. Yes, we can.

Now, there's no doubt this is a tough election. Even though you've got great candidates here in Connecticut, it is a tough election because we have been through an incredibly difficult time as a nation. And it didn't just start last year or 2 years ago. For most of the last decade, middle class families have been struggling.

Between 2001 and 2009, the average income of middle class families went down by 5 percent. Between 2001 and 2009, job growth was slower than any time since World War II. And this all culminated in the worst financial crisis and the worst economic crisis we've seen since the Great Depression.

And as a consequence, all across the country, there are too many parents who couldn't afford to send their kids to college, too many families who couldn't go see a doctor when they got sick, too many Americans working two or three jobs just to make ends meet, and too many Americans with no job at all.

I want to give you guys a sense of perspective. In the 6 months before I took the oath of office, we had lost 4 million jobs. We lost 750,000 jobs the month I was sworn in, 600,000 the month after that, another 600,000 the month after that. We lost almost 8 million jobs before we had even put our economic program in place.

Now, my hope was that we'd have both parties putting politics aside during this crisis to meet this once-in-a-generation challenge, be-cause although we are proud to be Democrats, we are prouder to be Americans. And we believe that we can bring people together.

And I know there are plenty of Republicans who feel the same way. But Republican leaders in Washington, they made a different decision. They realize, boy, we really made a big mess of this economy.

Audience members. Fund global AIDS! Fund global AIDS!

The President. Excuse me, excuse me, excuse me, everybody. Okay, let me just say this—excuse me, young people. Excuse me.

Audience members. Boo!

The President. Let me just say this—these folks have been—you've been appearing at every rally we've been doing. And we're funding global AIDS, and the other side is not. So I don't know why you think this is a useful strategy to take.

So what we would suggest—I think it would make a lot more sense for you guys to go to the folks who aren't interested in funding global AIDS and chant at that rally because we're trying to focus on figuring out how to finance the things that you want financed, all right? You guys, same thing. Now, it is going to take——

Audience members. Obama! Obama! Obama!

The President. All right. All right, you guys have made your point. You guys have made your point. Let's go. Now, look, let me just—understand—everybody, we're all right. Come on, guys.

[*At this point, there was a disruption in the audience.*]

The President. All right, everybody. Come on.

[*The disruption continued.*]

The President. All right, everybody. Hey! Listen up, listen up, listen up, listen up. Look, listen up, listen up, everybody.

First of all, this is one of the great things about Democrats, is we always like to be heard. And that's a good thing. That's part of what this democracy's all about.

The second thing is, it's very important to remember that an issue like global AIDS is very important. And the question we've got is, which party's most likely to actually fund it in ways that help people around the world. All right?

So—[*applause*]—but we're not going to be able to do anything unless we get the economy fixed, unless we can put people back to work, unless folks feel more confident about the future. It's going to be hard to move forward on all these initiatives.

And our hope was, when we came in, in the midst of crisis, that we could get all parties to come together to focus on these challenges. But, you know what happened was the other side, particularly the Republican leaders in Congress, their basic calculation was, look, this economy's so bad, we made such a mess of things that our best strategy is to stand on the sidelines, obstruct, say no. And since it probably won't be fixed completely in 2 years, we can just point the finger at the Democrats and pretend like they're to blame. Now, that was the strategy. In other words, they were counting on amnesia as a political strategy. That was their strategy.

We had a different strategy. Our strategy was, let's fix the problem. And as a consequence of the steps we've taken, an economy that was shrinking is now growing again. We've seen 9 consecutive months of job growth.

But here's the thing, folks. We've got to remind ourselves that our job is not yet done. We've got a lot of work to do, and this election is a choice, because the other side—basically, what they want to do is go back to the exact same policies that got us into this mess in the first place.

And we know, by the way, what those policies are: cut taxes mainly for millionaires and billionaires, cut regulations that curb special interests, and then cut middle class families loose to fend for themselves. So if you're out of a job, tough luck, you're on your own, according to this philosophy. If you don't have health care, too bad, you're on your own. If you're a young person who can't afford college, pull yourself up by your own bootstraps. You're on your own.

We know how that philosophy worked. It did not work. We have tried what they are selling right now. We tried it for 8 years. It did not

work. We are not going back to that. That is the choice in this election.

Imagine that the economy's a car and the Republicans drove it into a ditch. [*Laughter*] And it's a very steep ditch. So somehow the Republicans walked away from the scene of the accident. [*Laughter*] And we had to go in. And we put our boots on, us Democrats. We started pushing and shoving on that car, trying to get it out. And it's hot and dusty down there. And every once in a while we'd look up, and there are the Republicans standing up there, sipping on a Slurpee—[*laughter*]—fanning themselves.

And we'd say, why don't you come down and help? And they'd say, no, no, no; no, thank you. And they'd kick some dirt down into the ditch, make it a little harder for us. [*Laughter*] But we kept on pushing. We kept on pushing until finally we get this car up on level ground. Finally, we have this car pointing in the right direction. And suddenly we feel this tap on our shoulders; we look back, and lo and behold, who is it? It's the Republicans. [*Laughter*] And they said, excuse me, can we have the keys back?

And we got to say, no. You can't have the keys back. You don't know how to drive. You don't know how to drive. We can't give them the keys back.

Have you ever noticed, Connecticut, if you're in your car and you want to go forward, what do you do? You put your car in "D." If you want to go backwards, what do you do?

Audience members. Put it in "R"!

The President. Put it in "R." We don't want to go backwards. We're moving forward. That's what this election is all about.

Now, let me tell you, we have taken a lot of steps to move forward, but we've still got a long way to go. There are a lot of people hurting out there. There are folks who are just barely hanging on by a thread, too many folks losing their homes, too many folks out of work.

And so our challenge is how do we keep growing this economy so that once again ordinary families, middle class families, working families, that they can live out that American Dream.

You see, we've got a different idea than the other side about what the future holds, and it's an idea rooted in our belief about how this country was built. This is a country that has been built from the bottom up, not the top down. And we know government doesn't have all the answers to our problems. We believe government should be lean and efficient. We know that the foundation of a strong economy is a strong free market. We believe in entrepreneurship and individual initiative.

But in the words of the first Republican President, Abraham Lincoln, we also believe that government should do for the people what they cannot do better for themselves. We believe in an America that rewards hard work and responsibility for all people. We believe in an America where we look after one another. Where I am my brother's keeper, I am my sister's keeper. That's the America I know. That's what this election's about.

We believe in an America that invests in its future and its people, an America that's built to compete in the 21st century. We know the jobs and businesses of tomorrow, they'll end up in the countries that have the best educated workforce and the best infrastructure and the strongest commitment to research and technology. I want that nation to be the United States of America.

Dick Blumenthal wants that country to be America; Jim Himes wants that country to be America. There's no reason that China should have faster railroads, Singapore, newer airports, than us. We're the nation that built the transcontinental railroad. We're the nation that built the Interstate Highway System.

We're putting people to work right now in Connecticut and all across the country rebuilding our roads and our railways and our runways, putting people to work building an infrastructure that's adequate for the 21st century. That's the future we see.

We see an America where we invest in homegrown innovation and ingenuity so we can export jobs, not just import goods. We want to make it easier to start a business or patent an invention.

We don't want to keep giving tax breaks to companies that ship jobs overseas. We want those tax breaks to go to companies that are in-

vesting here in Bridgeport, small businesses and American manufacturers and clean energy companies, because we don't want electric cars or solar panels or wind turbines made in China or Asia or in Europe. We want them made right here in the United States of America with American workers. That's the choice in this election.

We see an America where every citizen has the skills and the training to compete with any worker in the world. We can't allow other countries to outpace us when it comes to math or science or college graduation rates. We used to be number one in college graduation rates. Now we're number nine. That's not acceptable.

That's why we made historic investments in education, set a goal that by 2020 we'd be number one again. That's why when the other side says, we want to cut taxes for millionaires and billionaires—$700 billion tax cut that would go only to the 2 percent wealthiest Americans—and they want to pay for it in part by a 20-percent cut in education, we have to reply to them, education is the key. China's not cutting education spending by 20 percent. Germany's not cutting education by 20 percent. They're not playing for second place. And the United States of America does not play for second place either. We play for first.

That's why we took tens of billions of dollars that were going in taxpayer subsidies, unwarranted subsidies to big banks, and sent that money to where it needed to go: to students and to families to help them pay for college. That's why we've got a new college tax credit worth $10,000 in tuition relief to every student. That's the future we believe in. That's the choice in this election. That's the America that we believe in.

We see an America where corporations live up to their responsibilities to treat consumers fairly, to play by the same rules as everybody else. That's why we made sure insurance companies couldn't jack up your premiums for no reason or deny you coverage just because you were sick. That's why we made sure credit card companies can't hit you with hidden fees or penalties and that taxpayers will never again be on the hook for the irresponsibility of a few on Wall Street.

That's the America we believe in, an America where we don't pass on a mountain of debt to the next generation. And that's why we're going to attack the trillion-dollar deficit I inherited when I took office. But we're going to do it in a responsible way.

We're not going to do it by cutting education by 20 percent. We won't do it by putting the burden only on our children or our seniors or our veterans or on middle class families. And we won't do it by borrowing another $700 billion for a tax cut we don't need.

We'll do it by asking for shared sacrifice from all Americans. And that's the choice in this election, Bridgeport. That's the America I see.

Now, we've got a lot of work to do in these next few years. And we need to work together, Democrats and Republicans, to get it done. But, you know, frankly, I've got to see some cooperation on the other side. The Republican leader of the House said, and I quote, "This is not the time for compromise." The Republican leader of the Senate said that his main goal over the next 2 years, his top priority, was beating me in the next election.

I mean, so he didn't say jobs was his top priority, improving the economy was his top priority. His top priority was beating me. He was thinking about the next election. This one's not even over yet.

That's the kind of attitude we're fighting against, Bridgeport. That's the kind of politics that we've got to change, a politics that says it's all about scoring point rather than solving problems.

And that's where all of you come in. Because the only way to fight this cynicism, the only way to match the millions of dollars of negative ads that special interests are pouring in, is with millions of voices—those of you who are ready to finish what we started in 2008.

So we need you to get out and vote. If everybody who voted in 2008 shows up 2010, then we will win this election. We will win this election. Dick will win his election, and Jim will win his election.

A lot of you got involved in 2008 because you believed we were at a defining moment in our history. You believed that this was a time where the decisions we make, they won't just affect us, they'll affect our children and our grandchildren for decades to come.

That's why you got involved. That's why you knocked on doors. That's why you made phone calls. That's why some of you voted for the very first time.

And you know what, delivering that change isn't easy. When we won 2 years ago, that was just the start. That wasn't about electing a President; that was about building a movement to change the country for the better.

And look, I understand some of the excitement has faded since election night and Inauguration night, Beyonce was singing and Bono was up there. I know I look a little older now. I got a little more gray hair than I did. [*Laughter*] I know.

Audience member. You're gorgeous!

The President. No, no, Michelle still looks good. I'm looking a little older. [*Laughter*] I know that. And sometimes, it may feel like, gosh, you know, for all the progress we've made, it's so hard. Folks get so angry, and maybe it's not worth it. But I want all of you to understand, don't let anybody tell you this fight isn't worth it. Don't let them tell you we're not making a difference.

Because of you, there's a woman who no longer has to choose between losing her home and treating her cancer. Because of you, there are parents who can look their children in the eye and say, you are going to college. Because of you, there are small businesses that were able to keep their doors open in the depths of recession. Because of you, there are 100,000 young, brave men and women who are now home because we're not fighting in Iraq. Because of you, because of you—don't let them tell you change isn't possible, because the truth is, change has always been hard.

This country was founded on hard. You know, 13 Colonies coming together, defying the British Empire, that's hard. And then drafting a document with principles that have never been tried in the world before: "We hold these truths to be self-evident, that all men are created equal, endowed by their Creator with certain inalienable rights, that among these are life, liberty, and the pursuit of happiness." That's a hard idea. Nobody was sure whether it was going to work.

We had to overcome slavery. And folks had to work for women's suffrage. They had to work and fight for workers' rights. Then they had to struggle some more to make sure that fascism was defeated and a depression was overcome.

And at each and every junction, success wasn't guaranteed. And there were setbacks. And there were people who said, maybe this won't work. There were naysayers.

Imagine if our parents and grandparents and great-grandparents had listened to the cynics 50 years ago or a hundred years ago or 200 years ago. We wouldn't be here today.

The only reason we are here is because they faced down their doubts. They faced down their fears. They pushed forward in the face of difficulty. They pushed forward in the face of uncertainty. That's why we came through war and depression and why we have civil rights and women's rights and workers' rights.

That's why, because we have veterans who are willing to fight for what they believed in. We need that spirit today. We need that spirit today. I need that here in Connecticut, Bridgeport.

I promise you—and I promise you this: If you bring that spirit over the next few days, if you are knocking on doors, if you are making phone calls, if you're going to barbershops and the beauty shops and talking to your friends and talking to your neighbors, if all the young people who came out in 2008 say "Yes, we can" again, I promise you, we will not just win an election. We are going to restore this economy. We are going to rebuild our middle class. We are going to deliver the American Dream to the next generation and the generation after that and the generation after that, all the way into the distant future.

God bless you, and God bless the United States of America.

NOTE: The President spoke at 3:19 p.m. in the Arena at Harbor Yard. In his remarks, he referred to House Republican Leader John A. Boehner; Senate Minority Leader A. Mitchell McConnell; and musicians Beyonce G. Knowles and Paul D. "Bono" Hewson.

Remarks at a Democratic National Committee Rally in Chicago, Illinois
October 30, 2010

The President. Hello, Chicago! It's good to be home. It is good to be home. You all organized some good weather for me too. Thank you.

I should mention to the national press that the weather's not always like this—[*laughter*]—in late October, early November. But it is a spectacular night, and you guys look beautiful. Thank you so much. Thank you.

I want to make sure that everybody knows the outstanding elected officials who are here. First of all, the current Governor and the next Governor of the great State of Illinois, Pat Quinn is in the house. One of the finest mayors in the history of America, Richard Daley is here. My—the senior Senator and great friend of mine from the great State of Illinois, Dick Durbin is in the house. The junior Senator who has served this State for so many years, Roland

Burris is here. A couple of wonderful Members of Congress, Jan Schakowsky and Bobby Rush are in the house. Senate President John Cullerton is here. Attorney General Lisa Madigan is here. Secretary of State Jesse White is here.

The alderwoman—we're in Chicago, you got to talk about your alderwoman—[*laughter*]—Leslie Hairston is in the house. Democratic nominee for Lieutenant Governor and my great friend, Sheila Simon is here; another wonderful friend, nominee for treasurer, Robin Kelly; outstanding young public servant, nominee for comptroller, David Miller. Alderman and Democratic nominee for Cook County Board president and my alderwoman, Toni Preckwinkle is here. I want to thank Common for doing such a great job in the opening—Chicago boy. [*Laughter*] And treasurer and soon-to-be Senator from the great State of Illinois, Alexi Giannoulias is here.

Are you—so you're fired up and ready to go? How about you? Are you fired up and ready to go? I can't think of—I can't——

Audience members. Obama! Obama! Obama!

The President. Thank you. Look, I can't think of anything better than being with a hometown crowd that is fired up. Plus, I'm going to sleep in my own bed tonight.

Now, Chicago, in 3 days, you have the chance to set the direction of this State and this country for years to come. And just like you did in 2008, you can defy the conventional wisdom, the kind that says you can't overcome cynicism in politics, you can't overcome the special interests, you can't overcome the big money, you can't overcome all the negativity, you can't overcome the big challenges any more, you can't elect a skinny guy with a funny name to the U.S. Senate or the Presidency. In 3 days, you've got the chance to once again say what?

Audience members. Yes, we can!

The President. Look, there is no doubt that this is a tough election. It's tough here in Illinois. It's tough all across the country. And the reason it's tough is because we've been through an incredibly difficult time as a nation. It didn't just start a year ago. It didn't just start 2 years ago. For the last decade, for the last 10 years, the middle class has been getting a tough time.

Between 2001 and 2009, the wage—the incomes of the average middle class family went down 5 percent. Between 2001 and 2009, job growth was slower than any time since World War II, so families were seeing their incomes go down even as their costs for health care, their costs for college education, their costs for groceries were all going up.

Folks were having to keep two, three jobs just to keep up. Meanwhile, too many jobs were disappearing overseas. And all this culminated in the worst financial crisis since the Great Depression and the worst economic crisis since the 1930s.

So families that were already worried, already having a tough time, already having to skip going to the doctor because they didn't have insurance, or already having to say to their kids, maybe you can't go to college this year because we don't have the money—things got even worse.

We lost 4 million jobs in the 6 months before I took the oath of office, 750,000 the month I took the oath, 600,000 the month after that, 600,000 the month after that. We'd lost almost 8 million jobs before any of our economic policies had a chance to take effect.

Now, when I got to Washington, my hope was that we could bring both parties together, that we could put politics aside to meet this once-in-a-generation challenge. That was my hope, because although we are proud to be Democrats, we are prouder to be Americans.

And I believe and—I believed then and I still believe now that there are a lot of Republicans around the country who feel the same way and a lot of Independents around the country who feel the same way.

But the Republican leaders in Washington, they made a different decision. Rather than roll up their sleeves and get to work, they looked around and they said, boy, we made a really big mess. We made such a big mess that it's going to take everything just to try to solve it. And it may not be solved in a couple of years. So many folks have already lost their jobs. So many businesses have already closed. We might be better off just sitting on our hands, sitting on the sidelines, and just going after Obama and saying no to every single thing he proposes, and then maybe the Democrats will get the blame when people get angry and frustrated for the lack of progress.

In other words, the other side, their political strategy was that all of you would get amnesia. [*Laughter*] That was their strategy. They're betting that everybody around the country would forget who caused this mess in the first place.

So, Chicago, it's up to you to let them know that we have not forgotten. We don't have amnesia. It's up to you to remember that this election is a choice between the policies that got us into this mess and the policies that are starting to lead us out of this mess.

If the other side wins this election, the chair of a Republican campaign committee promised the exact same agenda that we had before I took office. Now, we know what that agenda was. We know what that agenda is. They want to cut taxes, mostly for millionaires and billionaires. They want to cut the rules for special interests. They want to cut middle class families loose to fend for themselves.

So if you're out of work, tough luck, you're on your own. If you don't have health insurance or the—your insurance company drops you when you get sick, too bad, you're on your own. You're a young person trying to make it to college, but you don't have a lot of money, too bad. Pull yourself up by your bootstraps; you're on your own. It's the same agenda that turned record surpluses into record deficits, that allowed Wall Street to run wild, that nearly destroyed our economy.

So I bring this up—I wanted to just go down memory lane there for a moment not to reargue the past, but because we don't want to relive the past. We've been there before. We've tried what they're selling, and we're not buying it. We're not going back.

Around the country I've been trying to describe it this way. Imagine the American economy is a car. And the Republicans were at the wheel, and they drove it into a ditch. And it's a steep ditch; it's a deep ditch. And somehow they walked away.

But we had to go down there. So me and all the Democrats, we put on our boots, and we rappelled down into the ditch. [*Laughter*] It was muddy down there and hot. We're sweating, pushing on the car. Feet are slipping. Bugs are swarming.

We looked up, and the Republicans are up there, and we call them down, but they say, no, we're not going to help. They're just sipping on a Slurpee—[*laughter*]—fanning themselves. They're saying, you're not pushing hard enough; you're not pushing the right way. But they won't come down to help. In fact, they're kind of kicking dirt down into us—down into the ditch. [*Laughter*]

But that's okay. We know what our job is, and we kept on pushing, we kept on pushing, we kept on pushing until finally, we've got that car on level ground. Finally, we got the car back on

the road. Finally, we got that car pointing in the right direction.

And suddenly, we had this tap on our shoulder, and we look back, and who is it? It's the Republicans. And they're saying, excuse me, we'd like the keys back. And we've got to say to them, I'm sorry, you can't have the keys back. You don't know how to drive! You don't know how to drive. You can ride with us. [*Laughter*] But we're driving, and we're going to have the middle class sitting right beside us because they're the folks that we're fighting for.

Look, because of the steps we've taken, we no longer face the possibility of a second depression. The economy is growing again. We've seen private sector job growth for 9 months in a row.

But we've still got a long way to go. We've still got a lot of work to do. All across this State, from Carbondale to Elgin to Quincy to Chicago, folks are hurting. There are too many folks without jobs. Some families are hanging on by a thread.

That's what keeps me up at night. That's what keeps Pat up at night. It's what keeps Alexi up at night. That's what keeps us fighting, because we know that we've still got a long way to go.

See, we've got a different idea about what the future should hold for families across Illinois and across this country. And it's an idea rooted in our belief about how this country was built.

You know, we—you think about our stories. Pat came from humble beginnings, Alexi from an immigrant family. Me, you guys know my background. We didn't come to the scene with a silver spoon in our mouths here. Our families worked hard, and they knew that government doesn't have all the answers to our problems. We believe government has to be lean and efficient. We believe that free enterprise is the greatest engine for prosperity ever known to man.

But in the words of the first Republican President, Abraham Lincoln, we also believe that government should and must do for the people what they cannot do by themselves individually. We believe in America that rewards hard work and responsibility for everybody and creates ladders of opportunity. We believe in a country where we look after one another, where we say, I am my brother's keeper, I am my sister's keeper. That's the America we believe in. That's the America we know. That's the choice in this election.

We believe in an America that invests in its future and in its people. We believe in an America that's built to compete in the 21st century. We know the jobs and businesses of tomorrow will end up in the countries that have the best educational system, the best infrastructure, the strongest commitment to research and technology. I want that nation to be the United States of America.

There's no reason why China should have the fastest railroads or Singapore have better airports. We're the nation that built the transcontinental railroad right through Chicago. We're the nation that built the Interstate Highway System right through Chicago.

Today, we're seeing America put folks to work, thousands of people building new roads and railways and runways, because that's what America is about—we build; an America where we build an infrastructure for the 21st century, putting people back to work, doing the work that needs to be done.

We see an America where we invest in home-grown innovation and ingenuity; where we export goods, we don't just import goods; where we create jobs here at home; where we make it easier for somebody with a good idea to start a business or patent an invention. We don't want to keep on giving tax breaks to corporations that ship jobs overseas. We want to give tax breaks to companies that are investing right here in Illinois, right here in the Midwest, all across America, investing in small businesses and American manufacturers and clean energy companies. We don't want solar panels and wind turbines and electric cars made in Asia or in Europe. We want them made here in America by American workers. That's the choice in this election.

We see an America where every citizen has the skills and the training to compete with any worker in the world. We can't allow other countries to outpace us when it comes to math and science and our college graduation rates. We

used to be number one in college graduation rates. We used to be number one in math and number one in science. And now we're 9th in college graduation rates, 21st in math, 25th in science. That's not acceptable. And that's why we, over the last 2 years, made historic investments in education. That's why we set a goal: By 2020, we are going to be number one again in the proportion of college graduates.

And we didn't just talk about it. We put our money where our mouth was. And we stopped providing subsidies to the big banks and poured tens of billions of dollars into student loans and Pell grants to make college more affordable for students all across this country.

Millions of young people are seeing college more affordable because of the actions we took. And now we've got the other side saying that to pay for a $700 billion tax cut that would go to the top 2 percent—the wealthiest 2 percent—they want to cut education by 20 percent.

That makes no sense. It makes no sense. Do you think China is cutting back education spending by 20 percent?

Audience members. No!

The President. Do you think Germany is cutting back education spending by 20 percent?

Audience members. No!

The President. Those countries aren't playing for second place. And we don't play for second place. This is the United States of America. We play for first place. That's the choice in this election. That's what this election's all about.

That's why we have to continue to provide assistance to young people going to college. That's why we have to renew the tax credit we've instituted—$10,000 per young person who is going to college for 4 years—so that they're not loaded down with a mountain of debt and they can aspire to anything that their imagination leads them to. That's what this election is about.

Look, this election is also about not leaving a mountain of debt for the next generation. The other side talks a good game about deficits, except you will recall that the last time they were in charge, they took record surpluses from a Democratic President and left record deficits that I inherited.

And so when we make decisions about deficits, we're not going to do it on the shoulders—on the backs of students or seniors or veterans or the vulnerable. We're going to make sure that we do it in a sensible way that shares sacrifices. We're going to go after those deficits, but we're going to do it in a way that's fair and reflects the need to grow this economy over the long term. And that's what this election is about. And this election is making sure that we don't turn the keys back to the special interests in Washington.

You know, when we passed health care reform, let me tell you something: We did that because all across this country there were folks—hard-working folks—who paid their insurance premiums and then suddenly found insurance companies dropping them when they got sick, or folks who were working hard and wanted to get insurance, but had a preexisting condition and couldn't get it.

And so we said, anybody in America, anybody in America who is working hard, who's doing the right thing, they shouldn't go bankrupt when they get sick. And so we passed a law that made sure that insurance companies could no longer drop you when you got sick.

We passed a law that said everybody under the age of 26 could stay on their parents' health insurance. We passed a law to make sure that 30 million folks can get affordable, accessible insurance, and we did it in a way that will reduce our deficit by over a trillion dollars. And now the other side says they want to roll that back.

The same thing is true for financial reform. We just went through the worst crisis since the 1930s. And so we passed a bill that says you can't be cheated by your credit card company; they can't jack up your rates for no reason; that we're not going to have taxpayer bailouts again. And they said their number-one priority, they want to roll this back.

So look, we've got a lot of work to do, not only to move the country forward, but to make sure that the progress we've made continues. And we need to work together, Democrats and Republicans, to get it done.

But I've got to tell you, the other side, right now they're feeling kind of cocky, and they don't see it that way. The Republican leader of the House says that, quote, "this is not a time for compromise." The Republican leader of the Senate said that his main goal over the next 2 years, his number-one priority, is to beat me in the next election.

I mean, keep in mind, he didn't say his number-one priority was put more people back to work, help more small businesses succeed. It wasn't to reduce the deficit. His top priority was to win the next election. We haven't even finished this election yet.

But that's the kind of cynicism we're fighting. That's the kind of politics that we decided to change in this country, the kind of politics that puts scoring points ahead of solving problems. And that's where you come in.

And I want to speak not just to Chicago; I want to speak to everybody in Illinois. The only way to fight this cynicism, the only way to match the millions of dollars of special interests' money, all that money that's being poured in as attack ads against Alexi, against Pat, the only way to do it is with your voices, the millions of voices who are ready to finish what we started in 2008.

We need you to get out and vote. But we need you more than that. We need you to work to help get everybody out to vote, because if everybody who fought for change in 2008 shows up in 2010, we will win this election.

And you know, a lot of you got involved in 2008 because you believed we were at a defining moment in our history. A lot of you believed that this was a time when the decisions we made about the challenges we face wouldn't just affect us, they'd affect our children and our grandchildren and our great-grandchildren.

That's why you knocked on those doors. That's why you made those phone calls. That's why you cast, in some cases, your votes for the very first time, because you understood what was at stake.

And now, 2 years later, I know that some of the excitement that we had in Grant Park, you know, that fades away. Some of the excitement——

Audience members. No!

The President. ——some of the excitement of Inauguration Day—you know, Beyonce was singing—[*laughter*]—and Bono was up there, and everybody was feeling good—I know that good feeling starts slipping away. And you talk to your friends who are out of work, you see somebody lose their home, and it gets you discouraged. And then you see all these TV ads and all the talking heads on TV, and everything just feels negative. And maybe some of you, maybe you stop believing. Maybe you lose faith.

But I want everybody here to understand, don't let anybody tell you that this fight hasn't been worth it. Don't let them tell you that you haven't already made a difference. Because of you, there's a woman somewhere in Illinois who doesn't have to choose between losing her home and treating her cancer. Because of you, somewhere here in Illinois there's a parent who can look their child in the eye and say: "You are going to go to college. We can afford it." Because of you, somewhere in Illinois there's a small-business owner who is able to keep their doors open and keep all the families that were supported by jobs at that business—keep that company going. Because of you, somewhere in Illinois there is an outstanding veteran, one of the hundreds of thousand brave men and women who are no longer at war in Iraq because of you.

So don't let folks tell you that change isn't possible. Don't let that get you down. I know things are hard sometimes, but you know what, this country was founded on hard.

You know, this country started 13 Colonies, who folks said didn't have a chance against the British Empire. And then they drafted this document with ideas that had never been tried before: "We hold these truths to be self-evident, that all men are created equal, endowed by their Creator with certain inalienable rights, that among these are life and liberty and the pursuit of happiness."

But even after they drafted those documents, it was still hard. And we had to abolish slavery. And we had to win women the right to vote. And we had to win workers the right to organize. We had to battle through depression and the war against fascism and the divisions in our own country to perfect this Union. And we ha-

ven't gotten there yet, but at every stage we've made progress because somebody stood up.

And when one person stood up, then suddenly 10 people stood up, and then maybe a thousand people stood up, and then maybe a hundred thousand stood up, and then maybe a million stood up. That's what happens with change. It's infectious. And that's the spirit we need today.

You know, in the introductions, I think some people mentioned a dear friend of mine who passed this past weekend. Bishop Brazier had a church right down the street. Michelle and I used to go to church at Apostolic sometime. And here's somebody who knew me when I was a young lawyer, had just moved to Chicago. And I remember when I was making the decision to run for President, I called him, and I said: "You know, Bishop, I'm really not sure this is possible. I don't know if I'm going to make it, but I think it's worth trying." And he says, "I don't know what God has in store for you, Barack." But he did say, "You won't know either unless you try."

And that idea is what has motivated so many people across the decades. That idea is the quintessentially American idea that this journey is never easy, but we've got to try.

And the journey we began together 2 years ago was not about putting me in the White House; it was about building a movement for change that endures. It was about realizing that in the United States of America, anything is possible if we're willing to work for it, if we're willing to fight for it, if we're willing to believe in it.

So, Chicago, I need you to keep on fighting. Illinois, I need you to keep on believing. I need you to knock on some doors. I need you to talk to your neighbors. I need you to get out and vote in this election, because if you do, if you're willing to step up, if you're willing to try, we won't just win this election, Pat won't just win this election, Alexi won't just win this election, but we will restore our economy, we will rebuild the middle class, and we will reclaim the American Dream for another generation and generations to come.

God bless you, and God bless the United States of America.

NOTE: The President spoke at 7:13 p.m. at Midway Plaisance Park. In his remarks, he referred to musicians Lonnie R. "Common" Lynn, Jr., Beyonce G. Knowles, and Paul D. "Bono" Hewson; and Bishop Arthur M. Brazier, former pastor, Apostolic Church of God, who died on October 22. The transcript was released by the Office of the Press Secretary on October 31.

Remarks at a Democratic National Committee Rally in Cleveland, Ohio
October 31, 2010

The President. Hello, Cleveland! Thank you! Are you fired up? It is good to be back in Cleveland, good to be back in Ohio. And it's great to be with a crowd that looks like it's fired up and ready to go.

A few people I want to just thank because they are doing outstanding work each and every day: the Cleveland mayor, Frank Johnson—Frank Jackson. Thank you so much. Thank you, Frank. My dear friend Attorney General Rich Cordray; State Treasurer Kevin Boyce; some of the finest Members of Congress that we have, Senator Sherrod Brown is in the house; Congressman Dennis Kucinich; Congresswoman Betty Sutton; one of my favorite Members of Congress who couldn't be here because he just had a baby yesterday. Not—his wife had a baby. [*Laughter*] He is an outstanding young man, and we expect to send him back to Congress, John Boccieri. New baby girl is named Emma, by the way.

I want to thank President Ronald Berkman here at Cleveland State University. I want to thank Common for his wonderful performance. I want to thank—Congresswoman Betty Sutton is in the house, I believe. Is she here? Where is Betty? Hey, Betty. [*Laughter*] And most of all, folks who are going to be leading Ohio for many years to come—Lieutenant Governor Lee Fisher, who's going to be going to Washington, and one of the finest Governors in this country, Ted Strickland, and First Lady Frances Strickland.

We are here for Ted, and we're here for Lee and all the members of the congressional delegation.

Audience member. Marcia Fudge!

The President. Marcia Fudge—Marcia Fudge, of course. But I didn't—for some reason, Marcia wasn't on the list. Is Marcia here? Where is Marcia? We love Marcia—it's just she wasn't here, that's all. I love Marcia. That's my girl. [*Laughter*] We were acknowledging those folks who were in the crowd, but we love Marcia. And Marcia is going to do a great job.

Look, Joe Biden and I have been traveling all across the country, and there are a lot of places where we're doing a lot of great work, but there are very few places where we are doing as much good work as we were doing right here in Ohio. And, Cleveland, in just 2 days—in just 2 days—you've got the chance——

Audience members. Yes, we can! Yes, we can! Yes, we can!

The President. I can't hear you. Did you say, yes, we can?

Audience members. Yes, we can! Yes, we can! Yes, we can!

The President. In 2 days, you have the chance to set the direction of this country and this State for many years to come. Just like you did in 2008, you can defy the conventional wisdom. The kind of conventional wisdom, the stale wisdom that says you can't overcome cynicism in our politics; that says, no, you can't overcome all the special interests and the special interest money; that says, no, you can't tackle the biggest challenges in this country.

In 2 days, you've got the chance to once again say, yes, we can.

Now, Cleveland, there is no doubt that this is a difficult election. And that's because we've gone through an incredibly difficult time as a nation. And nobody knows that more than the folks in Cleveland and the folks in Ohio.

For most of the last decade, middle class families have been struggling. This didn't just start a year ago; it didn't just start 2 years ago. Between 2001 and 2009, the average middle class family saw their incomes across the country go down by 5 percent, when the other side was in charge. Between 2001 and 2009, job growth was slower than any time since World War II. Meanwhile, the costs of everything, from health care to sending a child to college, kept on going up and up and up. Too many families couldn't send their kids to college. Too many families couldn't visit a doctor when somebody got sick. Americans, too many of them were working two, three jobs and still couldn't make ends meet. And a whole lot of folks couldn't find a job at all.

And these problems were then compounded by the worst economic crisis, the worst financial crisis since the Great Depression. I mean, think about it, we had a recession that was so bad we lost 4 million jobs before Joe and I were even sworn into office. Then we had another 750,000 jobs lost the month we took office, 600,000 the month after that, 600,000 the month after that. We lost almost 8 million jobs before our economic policies could even be put into place.

Now, when Joe and I got to Washington, our hope was that both parties would put politics aside to meet this once-in-a-generation challenge. Because although we are proud to be Democrats, Cleveland, we are prouder to be Americans. And we had confidence, and continue to have confidence, that there are Republicans out there who feel the same way.

But the Republican leaders in Washington, they had a different calculation. Their basic theory was, you know what, the economy is so bad, we made such a mess of things, that rather than cooperate, we'll be better off just saying no to everything. We'll be better off not even trying to fix the economy. And people will get angry and they will get frustrated and maybe 2 years from now they will have forgotten that we were the ones who caused the mess in the first place.

In other words, their basic political strategy has been to count on you having amnesia. They're betting all of you forgot how we got here. Well, Cleveland, it's up to you to let them know we have not forgotten. It's up to you to remember that this election is a choice between the policies that got us into this mess and the policies that are leading us out of this mess.

If they win this election, the chair of a Republican campaign committee promised to pursue the exact same agenda as they did before I came into office. Now, think about that. We know what that agenda is. It does have the virtue of simplicity. You can describe it very quickly. You basically cut taxes for millionaires and billionaires, you cut rules for special interests, and then you cut middle class families loose to fend for themselves. You don't have a job? Tough luck, you're on your own. You don't have health care? Too bad, you're on your own. You're a young person who can't afford to go to college? Pull yourself up by your own bootstraps; you're on your own.

This is an idea, this notion of theirs, that turned a record surplus into record deficits. You hear them talking down about how they are going to cut debt and deficits? These are the folks who ran up the deficit. These are the folks that allowed Wall Street to run wild. These are the folks that nearly destroyed our economy.

Now, I bring this up not to reargue the past. I bring it up because I don't want to relive the past. We've been there before, we've tried what they're selling, and we are not going back. We are not going back.

Cleveland, imagine the Republicans were driving the economy like a car, and they drove it into the ditch. And this is a very deep, steep ditch. And Joe and I and Ted, we had to put on our boots; we had to rappel down. [*Laughter*] And it's muddy down there and dusty and hot. Somehow the Republicans, they fled the scene. And now they're up on the street, and they're looking down, and we call them down to help and they say, no, that's all right. [*Laughter*] They're sipping Slurpees. [*Laughter*] They're fanning themselves. They're saying, you're not pushing hard enough. Sometimes they're kicking dirt down into the ditch—[*laughter*]—making it a little harder for us.

But that's okay. We kept on pushing. We kept on pushing. We kept on pushing. And finally—finally—we got that car back on level ground. It's moving—it's pointing in the right direction. It's a little banged up. It needs to go to the body shop. It needs a tuneup. But it's pointing in the right direction.

And just as we're about to go, suddenly we get a tap on our shoulders. And we look back, who is it? It's the Republicans. And they're saying, we want the keys back.

Audience members. No!

The President. Cleveland, we can't give them the keys back. They don't know how to drive. You can't give them the keys back. They can ride with us, but we don't want to go back in the ditch.

Have you noticed when you want to go forward, what do you do with your car?

Audience members. "D"!

The President. You put it in "D." When you want to go backwards, what do you do?

Audience members. "R"!

The President. You put it in "R." That's not a coincidence. I don't know about you, but I want to move forward.

Look, because of the steps we've taken, we no longer face the possibility of a second depression. The economy is growing again. The private sector has created jobs 9 months in a row. And you heard Ted describe his track record here in the State of Ohio, massively expanding access to education, seeing job growth month after month, building infrastructure to put people back to work. That is Ted's record. That's Lee's record.

So at the Federal level and the State level, we have been working hard. But look, we understand we've got a long way to go. We've got a lot of work to do. I know there are a lot of people out there who are still hurting. I know there are families some of them still hanging by a thread. It keeps me up at night. It keeps Joe up at night. It keeps Ted up at night. That's what we're fighting to fix.

But you know what, the way to fix it is not to go back to what got us here. It's to move forward with the policies that are getting us out. See, Ted and Lee and Joe and I, we've got a different idea about what the next few years should look like. And it's an idea rooted in our belief about how this country was built. We didn't come from wealth. We didn't come from fame. But our families understood, in America if you work hard, if you're responsible, if you do the right thing, you've got a chance.

And our families taught us that government doesn't have all the answers to our problems.

Government should be lean and efficient. We can't waste taxpayer dollars, especially at a time as tough as this. But in the words of the first Republican President, Abraham Lincoln, we also believe that government should do for the people what they cannot do better for themselves.

We believe in an America that rewards hard work and responsibility and individual initiative; that believes in the free market. But we also believe in a country where we look after one another, where I am my brother's keeper, where I am my sister's keeper. That's the America I know. That's the America Joe knows. That's the America Ted knows. That's the America you know, an America that invests in its future and in its people, an America that's built to compete in the 21st century.

We know the jobs and businesses of tomorrow will end up in countries that educate their workers best, that build the best infrastructure, that have the strongest commitment to research and technology. I want that nation to be the United States of America. I want that taking place right here in Ohio, right here in Cleveland. That's how we're going to rebuild.

There is absolutely no reason that China should have faster railroads, that Singapore should have newer airports. We're the nation that built the transcontinental railroad. We're the nation that built the Interstate Highway System. Right now we are seeing thousands of people working to rebuild our roads and our railways and our runways, right here in Ohio and all across the country, trying to start to rebuild an infrastructure for the 21st century, putting people to work doing the work that America needs done.

We see an America where we invest in homegrown innovation and ingenuity, where we export more than we import, where we make it easier to start a business or patent an invention. We don't want to keep giving tax breaks to companies that are shipping jobs overseas. I want companies getting tax breaks that are investing in Cleveland and in Dayton and in Toledo and in Ohio and in the United States of America, in small businesses and American manufacturing—which is coming back—and in clean energy companies. I don't want solar panels and wind turbines built in Asia or Europe. I want them made right here in the U.S. of A. with American workers. That's the choice in this election.

We see an America where every citizen has the skills, the training to compete with any worker in the world. We can't allow other countries to outpace us when it comes to education. We used to be number one in the rate of college graduation rates. We used to be at the top in math and science. Now we're 9th in the proportion of college graduates, 21st and 25th in math and science. That's unacceptable.

And so we made historic investments in education, just like Ted has done here in Ohio. We set a goal that by 2020 we're going to be number one again in the proportion of college graduates.

Now, remember I said it is a choice this election. The other side, their main economic idea—this is their main idea—is to provide $700 billion worth of tax cuts to the top 2 percent of earners——

Audience members. No!

The President. ——the 2 percent of wealthiest Americans, an average of $100,000 for millionaires and billionaires. Now, look, I want people to succeed. I think it's wonderful if folks get rich. I want everybody to have a chance to get rich. You do too. This guy is raising his hand. I think that's great. That's part of the American Dream. But the way they want to pay for these tax cuts is to cut education by 20 percent and to borrow the rest from other countries.

Let me tell you, do you think China is cutting education spending by 20 percent?

Audience members. No!

The President. Is Germany cutting education by 20 percent?

Audience members. No!

The President. They're not because they're not playing for second place. They're playing for first place. And you know what, the United States of America, we don't play for second place. We don't play for 9th place or 21st place or 25th place. We play for number one. And that's what we've got to do in education.

And that's why we committed tens of billions of dollars that had been going in unwarranted

subsidies to big banks, and we steered that money to where it needed to be going, to students right here at Cleveland State and all across the country, increasing access to Pell grants, increasing college scholarships.

That's why we want to make permanent our new college tax credit, a tax credit worth $10,000 in tuition relief for each young person who is going to college. That's the choice in this election. That's what America is about. That's what we believe in.

We see an America where corporations are thriving and profitable but where they're also living up to their responsibilities to treat consumers fairly, to play by the same rules as everybody else. That's why we made sure insurance companies couldn't jack up your premiums for no reason or deny you coverage just because you're sick. That's why we made sure credit companies can't hit you with hidden fees or penalties. That's why we made sure taxpayers are never again on the hook for the irresponsibility of Wall Street banks.

And you know, we see an America where we don't pass on a mountain of debt to the next generation. We've got to go after this trillion-dollar deficit that I inherited when I took office, but we're going to do it in a responsible way. Not by cutting education by 20 percent. Not by burdening our children or our seniors or our veterans or middle class families. We won't do it by borrowing another $700 billion to give tax cuts to folks who don't need them. We'll do it by asking for shared sacrifice of all Americans. That's the choice in this election. That's the America that we believe in.

So look, we've got a lot of work to do over the next few years. Ted has got a lot of work to do here in Ohio. Lee has got a lot of work to do in Washington. And we're going to need to work together, Democrats and Republicans and Independents, to get it all done. But you know what, so far we're not seeing that from the other party. I guess they're feeling cocky, maybe. The Republican leader of the House says, "This is not a time for compromise." That's a quote. The Republican leader of the Senate said his main goal for the next 2 years, his top priority, is to win the next election and to beat me.

Think about this. His priority is not to get the economy moving. It's not to create jobs. It's not to reduce the deficit. His top priority is to win the next election. We haven't even finished this election.

But you know, that's the mentality that we're fighting against, Cleveland. That's the kind of politics that we've got to change. It's a politics that always puts scoring points ahead of solving problems. And that's where all of you come in, each and every one of you here. The only way to fight that kind of politics, the only way to match the millions of dollars of negative ads that have been pouring down, using these phony front groups—millions of dollars of ads—the only way to fight that is millions of voices who are ready to finish what we started in 2008.

We've got to get Cleveland out to vote. We've got to get everybody in Ohio out to vote. And in Ohio you can vote early. There is early voting just a few blocks from here, so you can go right after this rally if you haven't voted. Because if everyone who fought for change in 2008 shows up to vote in 2010, we will win this election. I am confident of that.

A lot of you got involved in 2008 because you believed we were at a defining moment in our history. That's what Joe believed. That's what I believed. You believed that we were in a time where the decisions we make won't just affect us, they'll affect our children, they'll affect our grandchildren for decades to come. That's the reason so many of you knocked on doors, made phone calls, and some cast your vote for the very first time.

And it turns out, as I said at the time, change isn't easy. Power concedes nothing without a fight. And so throughout the past 20 months we have been pushing and working, and I've had a great partner in Joe Biden, couldn't have a better Vice President. And I've had a great partner in Ted Strickland, couldn't have a better Governor than Ted. And we've made progress. But I know that sometimes as we're grinding out this change and there's all the negative ads and the pundits on TV and there's still a lot of unemployment out here and sometimes people feel discouraged.

And I know that some of the excitement of election night and Inauguration Day starts to fade. You know, Beyonce was singing, and Bono was up there. And I know people start to—oh, that was fun. Now it's just—seems like work all the time. And then you guys see me on TV and, boy, he's getting really gray. Did you see that? [*Laughter*] He's starting to look old. [*Laughter*]

But look—[*applause*]—look, Cleveland, I want you to remember this. Don't let anybody tell you this fight isn't worth it. Don't let anybody tell you you're not making a difference. Because of you, there's a woman somewhere in Ohio who no longer has to choose between losing her home and treating her cancer. Because of you, somewhere in Ohio there's a parent who can look their child in the eye and say, "Yes, you are going to college; we can afford it." Because of you, somewhere in Ohio there's a small-business owner who kept their doors open in the depths of recession. Because of you, there are nearly 100,000 brave men and women who are no longer at war in Iraq—because of you.

So don't let them tell you that change isn't possible. Because here's what I know: It's always been hard to bring about change in America. Think about it. This country was founded on hard. I mean, we started off as Thirteen Colonies having to battle the most powerful empire on Earth. And a lot of people said, well, you can't do that. And then they decided we're going to try a new form of government of and by and for the people. And they said, "We hold these truths to be self-evident, that all men are created equal, endowed by our Creator with certain inalienable rights, that among these are life and liberty and the pursuit of happiness."

That idea had not been tried before. There was no certainty of success. But they knew it was worth trying. And over decades, they had to work to make that idea real—had to abolish slavery, had to win women the right to vote, had to win workers the right to organize.

All that change was hard. Imagine if our parents, our grandparents, our great-grandparents, if they had said, ah, you know what, this is just too hard; I'm getting discouraged. What if they had just given up? What if people had been calling them names and worse and they had said, we can't do this?

They said, yes, we can.

Audience members. Yes, we can!

The President. They understood that the only thing that prevents us here in America from achieving our dreams, the only thing that might prevent us, is if we don't try. The only reason we are here is because past generations have been unafraid to push forward, even in the face of difficulty, even in the face of uncertainty. That's how we came through war. That's how we came through depression. That's why we have civil rights and workers' rights and women's rights, and that's the spirit we need today.

Cleveland, the journey we began together was never about just putting a President in the White House. It was about building a movement for change that endures. It was about realizing that in the United States of America, if we are willing to fight for it, if we're willing to work for it, if we believe in it, anything is possible.

So, Cleveland, I need you to keep on fighting. I need you to keep on believing. I need you to knock on some doors. I need you to talk to your neighbors. I need you to talk to your friends. I need you to go early vote. I need you to get your friends to vote. Because if you are willing to step up to the plate, Ted will win this election; Lee will win this election. We will restore our economy. We will rebuild our middle class. And we will reclaim the American Dream for future generations.

God bless you, and God bless the United States of America.

NOTE: The President spoke at 2:15 p.m. in the Wolstein Center at Cleveland State University. In his remarks, he referred to Rep. Marcia L. Fudge; House Republican Leader John A. Boehner; Senate Minority Leader A. Mitchell McConnell; and musicians Lonnie R. "Common" Lynn, Jr., Beyonce G. Knowles, and Paul D. "Bono" Hewson.

Statement on the Death of Theodore C. Sorensen
October 31, 2010

I was so saddened to learn that Ted Sorensen passed away. I got to know Ted after he endorsed my campaign early on. He was just as I hoped he'd be, just as quick witted, just as serious of purpose, just as determined to keep America true to our highest ideals.

From his early days desegregating a Nebraska pool to his central role electing and advising President Kennedy, to his later years as an international lawyer and advocate, Ted lived an extraordinary life that made our country and our world more equal, more just, and more se-

cure. Generations of Americans entered public service aspiring to follow in his footsteps.

Even as I mourn his loss, I know his legacy will live on in the words he wrote, the causes he advanced, and the hearts of anyone who is inspired by the promise of a new frontier. My heart goes out to his wife Gillian, his daughter Juliet, his sons Eric, Stephen, and Philip, and the entire Sorensen family.

NOTE: The statement referred to Juliet Sorenson Jones, daughter of Mr. Sorensen.

Letter to Congressional Leaders on Continuation of the National Emergency With Respect to Sudan
November 1, 2010

Dear Madam Speaker: (Dear Mr. President:)

Section 202(d) of the National Emergencies Act (50 U.S.C. 1622(d)) provides for the automatic termination of a national emergency un-

less, prior to the anniversary date of its declaration, the President publishes in the *Federal Register* and transmits to the Congress a notice stating that the emergency is to continue in effect beyond the anniversary date. In accordance with this provision, I have sent to the *Federal Register* for publication the enclosed notice stating that the Sudan emergency is to continue in effect beyond November 3, 2010.

The crisis constituted by the actions and policies of the Government of Sudan that led to the declaration of a national emergency in Executive Order 13067 of November 3, 1997, and the expansion of that emergency in Executive Order 13400 of April 26, 2006, and with respect to which additional steps were taken in Executive Order 13412 of October 13, 2006, has not been resolved. These actions and policies are hostile to U.S. interests and pose a continuing unusual and extraordinary threat to the national security and foreign policy of the United States. Therefore, I have determined that it is necessary to continue the national emergency declared with respect to Sudan and maintain in force sanctions against Sudan to respond to this threat.

Sincerely,

BARACK OBAMA

NOTE: The notice is listed in Appendix D at the end of this volume.

Statement on the 10th Anniversary of Crews Aboard the International Space Station
November 2, 2010

Today marks an important milestone in the history of human exploration. For the past decade, men and women from 15 nations have lived and worked together in space in the peaceful pursuit of science and exploration. The first crew of the International Space Station took up residence 200 miles above Earth on this date 10 years ago, and we have had a sustained human presence in space ever since.

Truly an international endeavor, the space station has brought disparate nations together for a common purpose, to better our lives on Earth. More than 600 experiments conducted in orbit aboard this amazing laboratory have contributed to important research designed to improve the quality of life for everyone.

Because of the extraordinary value of this orbiting research outpost, earlier this year, I proposed extending the life of the space station until at least 2020 so that NASA can pioneer new frontiers in education and international cooperation that will maximize the scientific return of this important foothold in space. Congress overwhelmingly agreed, and I was recently able to sign into law legislation that calls for extending the life of the space station for at least another 10 years.

As we look to the next 10 years, we can only imagine what's in store for our future astronauts, engineers, and scientists. I am committed to ensuring that NASA continues along a sustainable path as an international leader in space exploration and as an inspiration to a new generation of explorers to pursue careers in science, technology, engineering, and mathematics.

As we look to the future of America's continued leadership in space and think about the steps we will take in the months and years to come to extend humanity's reach beyond Earth orbit, I would like to say thank you and a job well done to the men and women who have contributed to this historic achievement.

The President's News Conference
November 3, 2010

The President. Good afternoon, everybody. Last night I had a chance to speak to the leaders of the House and the Senate and reached out to those who had both won and lost in both parties. I told John Boehner and Mitch McConnell that I look forward to working with them. And I thanked Nancy Pelosi and Harry Reid for their extraordinary leadership over the last 2 years.

After what I'm sure was a long night for a lot of you—and needless to say, it was for me—I can tell you that some election nights are more fun than others. Some are exhilarating. Some are humbling. But every election, regardless of who wins and who loses, is a reminder that in our democracy, power rests not with those of us in elected office, but with the people we have the privilege to serve.

Over the last few months, I've had the opportunity to travel around the country and meet people where they live and where they work, from backyards to factory floors. I did some talking, but mostly I did a lot of listening. And yesterday's vote confirmed what I've heard from folks all across America: People are frustrated. They're deeply frustrated with the pace of our economic recovery and the opportunities that they hope for their children and their grandchildren. They want jobs to come back faster, they want paychecks to go further, and they want the ability to give their children the same chances and opportunities as they've had in life.

The men and women who sent us here don't expect Washington to solve all their problems. But they do expect Washington to work for them, not against them. They want to know that their tax dollars are being spent wisely, not wasted, and that we're not going to leave our children a legacy of debt. They want to know that their voices aren't being drowned out by a sea of lobbyists and special interests and partisan bickering. They want business to be done here, openly and honestly.

Now, I ran for this office to tackle these challenges and give voice to the concerns of everyday people. Over the last 2 years, we've made progress. But clearly, too many Americans haven't felt that progress yet, and they told us that yesterday. And as President, I take responsibility for that.

What yesterday also told us is that no one party will be able to dictate where we go from here, that we must find common ground in order to set—in order to make progress on some uncommonly difficult challenges. And I told John Boehner and Mitch McConnell last night, I am very eager to sit down with members of both parties and figure out how we can move forward together.

I'm not suggesting this will be easy. I won't pretend that we will be able to bridge every difference or solve every disagreement. There's a reason we have two parties in this country, and both Democrats and Republicans have certain beliefs and certain principles that each feels cannot be compromised. But what I think the American people are expecting, and what we owe them, is to focus on those issues that affect their jobs, their security, and their future: reducing our deficit, promoting a clean energy economy, making sure that our children are the best educated in the world, making sure that we're making the investments in technology that will allow us to keep our competitive edge in the global economy.

Because the most important contest we face is not the contest between Democrats and Republicans. In this century, the most important competition we face is between America and our economic competitors around the world. To win that competition, and to continue our economic leadership, we're going to need to be strong and we're going to need to be united.

None of the challenges we face lend themselves to simple solutions or bumper sticker slogans, nor are the answers found in any one particular philosophy or ideology. As I've said before, no person, no party, has a monopoly on wisdom. And that's why I'm eager to hear good ideas wherever they come from, whoever proposes them. And that's why I believe it's important to have an honest and civil debate about the choices that we face. That's why I want to engage both Democrats and Republicans in serious conversations about where we're going as a nation.

And with so much at stake, what the American people don't want from us, especially here in Washington, is to spend the next 2 years refighting the political battles of the last two. We just had a tough election; we will have another in 2012. I'm not so naive as to think that everybody will put politics aside until then, but I do hope to make progress on the very serious problems facing us right now. And that's going to require all of us, including me, to work harder at building consensus.

You know, a little over a month ago, we held a town hall meeting in Richmond, Virginia. And one of the most telling questions came from a small-business owner who runs a tree care firm. He told me how hard he works and how busy he was, how he doesn't have time to pay attention to all the back-and-forth in Washington. And he asked, "Is there hope for us returning to civility in our discourse, to a healthy legislative process, so as I strap on the boots again tomorrow, I know that you guys got it under control?" "It's hard to have a faith in that right now," he said.

I do believe there is hope for civility. I do believe there's hope for progress. And that's because I believe in the resiliency of a nation that's bounced back from much worse than what we're going through right now, a nation that's overcome war and depression, that has been made more perfect in our struggle for individual rights and individual freedoms.

Each time progress has come slowly and even painfully. But progress has always come, because we've worked at it and because we've believed in it and, most of all, because we remembered that our first allegiance as citizens is not to party or region or faction, but to country, because while we may be proud Democrats or proud Republicans, we are prouder to be Americans. And that's something that we all need to remember right now and in the coming months. And if we do, I have no doubt that we will continue this Nation's long journey towards a better future.

So with that, let me take some questions. I'm going to start off with Ben Feller at AP [Associated Press].

Midterm Elections/National Economy/Bipartisanship

Q. Thank you, Mr. President. Are you willing to concede at all that what happened last night was not just an expression of frustration about the economy, but a fundamental rejection of your agenda? And given the results, who do you think speaks to the true voice of the American people right now, you or John Boehner?

The President. I think that there is no doubt that people's number-one concern is the economy. And what they were expressing great frustration about is the fact that we haven't made enough progress on the economy. We've stabilized the economy, we've got job growth in the private sectors, but people all across America aren't feeling that progress. They don't see it. And they understand that I'm the President of the United States, and that my core responsibility is making sure that we've got an economy that's growing, a middle class that feels secure, that jobs are being created. And so I think I've got to take direct responsibility for the fact that we have not made as much progress as we need to make.

Now, moving forward, I think the question's going to be, can Democrats and Republicans sit down together and come up with a set of ideas that address those core concerns? I'm confident that we can.

I think that there are some areas where it's going to be very difficult for us to agree on, but I think there are going to be a whole bunch of areas where we can agree on. I don't think there's anybody in America who thinks that we've got an energy policy that works the way it needs to, that thinks that we shouldn't be working on energy independence. And that gives opportunities for Democrats and Republicans to come together and think about, whether it's natural gas or energy efficiency or how we can build electric cars in this country, how do we move forward on that agenda.

I think everybody in this country thinks that we've got to make sure our kids are equipped, in terms of their education, their science background, their math backgrounds, to compete in this new global economy. And that's going to be an area where I think there's potential common ground.

So on a whole range of issues, there are going to be areas where we disagree. I think the overwhelming message that I hear from the voters is that we want everybody to act responsibly in Washington. We want you to work harder to arrive at consensus. We want you to focus completely on jobs and the economy and growing it, so that we're ensuring a better future for our children and our grandchildren.

And I think that there's no doubt that as I reflect on the results of the election, it underscores for me that I've got to do a better job, just like everybody else in Washington does.

Q. [Inaudible]

The President. Well, I think John Boehner and I and Mitch McConnell and Harry Reid and Nancy Pelosi are going to have to sit down and work together, because I suspect that if you talk to any individual voter yesterday, they'd say, there are some things I agree with Democrats on, there are some things I agree with Republicans on. I don't think people carry around with them a fixed ideology. I think the majority of people, they're going about their business, going about their lives. They just want to make sure that we're making progress. And that's going to be my top priority over the next couple of years.

Savannah Guthrie [NBC News].

President's Policymaking/Administration Accomplishments/Bipartisanship

Q. Just following up on what Ben just talked about, you don't seem to be reflecting or second-guessing any of the policy decisions you've made, instead saying the message the voters were sending was about frustration with the economy or maybe even chalking it up to a failure on your part to communicate effectively. If you're not reflecting on your policy agenda, is it possible voters can conclude you're still not getting it?

The President. Well, Savannah, that was just the first question, so we're going to have a few more here. I'm doing a whole lot of reflecting, and I think that there are going to be areas in policy where we're going to have to do a better job. I think that over the last 2 years, we have made a series of very tough decisions, but decisions that were right in terms of moving the country forward in an emergency situation where we had the risk of slipping into a second Great Depression.

But what is absolutely true is that with all that stuff coming at folks fast and furious—a recovery package, what we had to do with respect to

the banks, what we had to do with respect to the auto companies—I think people started looking at all this and it felt as if government was getting much more intrusive into people's lives than they were accustomed to.

Now, the reason was, it was an emergency situation. But I think it's understandable that folks said to themselves, you know, maybe this is the agenda, as opposed to a response to an emergency. And that's something that I think everybody in the White House understood was a danger. We thought it was necessary, but I'm sympathetic to folks who looked at it and said, this is looking like potential overreach.

In addition, there were a bunch of price tags that went with that. And so even though these were emergency situations, people rightly said: Gosh, we already have all this debt; we already have these big deficits; this is potentially going to compound it. And at what point are we going to get back to a situation where we're doing what families all around the country do, which is make sure that if you spend something, you know how to pay for it, as opposed to racking up the credit card for the next generation.

And I think that the other thing that happened is that when I won election in 2008, one of the reasons I think that people were excited about the campaign was the prospect that we would change how business is done in Washington. And we were in such a hurry to get things done that we didn't change how things got done. And I think that frustrated people.

I'm a strong believer that the earmarking process in Congress isn't what the American people really want to see when it comes to making tough decisions about how taxpayer dollars are spent. And I, in the rush to get things done, had to sign a bunch of bills that had earmarks in them, which was contrary to what I had talked about. And I think, folks look at that and they said: Gosh, this feels like the same partisan squabbling; this seems like the same ways of doing business as happened before.

And so one of the things that I've got to take responsibility for is not having moved enough on those fronts, and I think there is an opportunity to move forward on some of those issues. My understanding is Eric Cantor today said that he wanted to see a moratorium on earmarks continuing. That's something I think we can work on together.

Q. Would you still resist the notion that voters rejected the policy choices you made?

The President. Well, Savannah, I think that what, I think, is absolutely true is voters are not satisfied with the outcomes. If right now we had 5 percent unemployment instead of 9.6 percent unemployment, then people would have more confidence in those policy choices. The fact is, is that for most folks, proof of whether they work or not is, has the economy gotten back to where it needs to be? And it hasn't.

And so my job is to make sure that I'm looking at all ideas that are on the table. When it comes to job creation, if Republicans have good ideas for job growth that can drive down the unemployment rate and we haven't thought of them, we haven't looked at them, but we think they have a chance of working, we want to try some.

So on the policy front, I think the most important thing is to say that we're not going to rule out ideas because they're Democrat or Republican. We want to just see what works. And ultimately, I'll be judged as President as to the bottom line, results.

Mike Emanuel [FOX News].

Health Care Reform/Bipartisanship

Q. Thank you, Mr. President. Health care—as you're well aware, obviously, a lot of Republicans ran against your health care law. Some have called for repealing the law. I'm wondering, sir, if you believe that health care reform, that you worked so hard on, is in danger at this point and whether there's a threat as a result of this election?

The President. Well, I know that there's some Republican candidates who won last night who feel very strongly about it. I'm sure that this will be an issue that comes up in discussions with the Republican leadership. As I said before, though, I think we'd be misreading the election if we thought that the American people want to see us for the next 2 years relitigate arguments that we had over the last 2 years.

With respect to the health care law, generally—and this may go to some of the questions that Savannah was raising. When I talk to a woman from New Hampshire who doesn't have to mortgage her house because she got cancer and is seeking treatment, but now is able to get health insurance; when I talk to parents who are relieved that their child with a preexisting condition can now stay on their policy until they're 26 years old and give them a time to transition to find a job that will give them health insurance, or the small businesses that are now taking advantage of the tax credits that are provided, then I say to myself, this was the right thing to do.

Now, if the Republicans have ideas for how to improve our health care system, if they want to suggest modifications that would deliver faster and more effective reform to a health care system that has been wildly expensive for too many families and businesses and certainly for our Federal Government, I'm happy to consider some of those ideas.

For example, I know one of the things that's come up is that the 1099 provision in the health care bill appears to be too burdensome for small businesses. It just involves too much paperwork, too much filing. It's probably counterproductive. It was designed to make sure that revenue was raised to help pay for some of the other provisions, but if it ends up just being so much trouble that small businesses find it difficult to manage, that's something that we should take a look at.

So there are going to be examples where I think we can tweak and make improvements on the progress that we've made. That's true for any significant piece of legislation.

But I don't think that if you ask the American people, should we stop trying to close the doughnut hole, that will help senior citizens get prescription drugs? Should we go back to a situation where people with preexisting conditions can't get health insurance? Should we allow insurance companies to drop your coverage when you get sick even though you've been paying premiums? I don't think that you'd have a strong vote for people saying those are provisions I want to eliminate.

Midterm Elections/Health Care Reform

Q. According to some exit polls, sir, about one out of two voters apparently said that they would like to either see it overturned or repealed. Do you—are you concerned that that may embolden voters who are from the other party, perhaps?

The President. Well, it also means one out of two voters think it was the right thing to do. And obviously, this is an issue that has been contentious. But as I said, I think what's going to be useful is for us to go through the issues that Republicans have issues on, not sort of talking generally, but let's talk specifics. Does this particular provision—when it comes to preexisting conditions—is this something you're for or you're against? Helping seniors get their prescription drugs—does that make sense or not?

And if we take that approach, which is different from campaigning—I mean, this is now governing—then I think that we can continue to make some progress and find some common ground.

Chip Reid [CBS News].

National Economy/Bipartisanship

Q. Thank you, Mr. President. Republicans say, more than anything else, what this election was about was spending. And they say it will be when hell freezes over that they will accept anything remotely like a stimulus bill or any kind of the proposals you have out there to stimulate job growth through spending. Do you accept the fact that any kind of spending to create jobs is dead at this point? And if so, what else can Government do to create jobs, which is the number-one issue?

The President. Well, I think this is going to be an important question for Democrats and Republicans. I think the American people are absolutely concerned about spending and debt and deficits. And I'm going to have a deficit commission that is putting forward its ideas. It's a bipartisan group that includes Republican and Democratic Members of Congress. Hopefully, they were able to arrive at some consensus on some areas where we can eliminate programs that don't work, cut back on Government

spending that is inefficient, can streamline Government, but isn't cutting into the core investments that are going to make sure that we are a competitive economy that is growing and providing opportunity for years to come.

So the question I think that my Republican friends and me and Democratic leaders are going to have answer is, what are our priorities? What do we care about? And that's going to be a tough debate, because there are some tough choices here.

We already had a big deficit that I inherited, and that has been made worse because of the recession. As we bring it down, I want to make sure that we're not cutting into education that is going to help define whether or not we can compete around the world. I don't think we should be cutting back on research and development, because if we can develop new technologies, in areas like clean energy, that could make all the difference in terms of job creation here at home.

I think the proposal that I put forward with respect to infrastructure is one that, historically, we've had bipartisan agreement about. And we should be able to agree now that it makes no sense for China to have better rail systems than us and Singapore having better airports than us. And we just learned that China now has the fastest supercomputer on Earth; that used to be us. They're making investments because they know those investments will pay off over the long term.

And so in these budget discussions, the key is to be able to distinguish between stuff that isn't adding to our growth, isn't an investment in our future, and those things that are absolutely necessary for us to be able to increase job growth in the future as well.

Now, the single most important thing I think we need to do economically—and this is something that has to be done during the lame duck session—is making sure that taxes don't go up on middle class families next year. And so we've got some work to do on that front to make sure that families not only aren't seeing a higher tax burden, which will automatically happen if Congress doesn't act, but also making sure that business provisions that, historically, we have extended each year—that, for example, provide tax breaks for companies that are investing here in the United States in research and development—that those are extended. I think it makes sense for us to extend unemployment insurance because there are still a lot of folks out there hurting.

So there are some things that we can do right now that will help sustain the recovery and advance it, even as we're also sitting down and figuring out, okay, over the next several years what kinds of budget cuts can we make that are intelligent, that are smart, that won't be undermining our recovery, but, in fact, will be encouraging job growth.

Q. But most of those things that you just called investments they call wasteful spending and they say it's dead on arrival. It sounds like, without their support, you can't get any of it through.

The President. Well, what is absolutely true is, is that without any Republican support on anything, then it's going to be hard to get things done. But I'm not going to anticipate that they're not going to support anything. I think that part of the message sent to Republicans was, we want to see stronger job growth in this country. And if there are good ideas about putting people to work that traditionally have garnered Republican support and that don't add to the deficit, then my hope is and expectation is, is that that's something they're willing to have a serious conversation about.

When it comes to, for example, the proposal we put forward to accelerate depreciation for business, so that if they're building a plant or investing in new equipment next year, that they can take a complete writeoff next year, get a huge tax break next year, and that would then encourage a lot of businesses to get off the sidelines. That's not historically considered a liberal idea. That's actually an idea that business groups and Republicans, I think, have supported for a very long time.

So again, the question's going to be, do we all come to the table with an open mind and say to ourselves, what do we think is actually going to make a difference for the American people?

That's how we're going to be judged over the next couple of years.

Peter Baker [New York Times].

Bipartisanship/Energy

Q. Thank you, Mr. President. After your election 2 years ago, when you met with Republicans you said that, in discussing what policies might go forward, that elections have consequences and that you pointed out that you had won. I wonder what consequences you think this election should have then, in terms of your policies. Are there areas that you're willing—can you name today areas that you would be willing to compromise on that you might not have been willing to compromise on in the past?

The President. Well, I think I've been willing to compromise in the past and I'm going to be willing to compromise going forward on a whole range of issues. Let me give you an example, the issue of energy that I just mentioned.

I think there are a lot of Republicans that ran against the energy bill that passed in the House last year. And so it's doubtful that you could get the votes to pass that through the House this year or next year or the year after. But that doesn't mean there isn't agreement that we should have a better energy policy. And so let's find those areas where we can agree.

We've got, I think, broad agreement that we've got terrific natural gas resources in this country. Are we doing everything we can to develop those? There's a lot of agreement around the need to make sure that electric cars are developed here in the United States, that we don't fall behind other countries. Are there things that we can do to encourage that? And there's already been bipartisan interest on those issues.

There's been discussion about how we can restart our nuclear industry as a means of reducing our dependence on foreign oil and reducing greenhouse gases. Is that an area where we can move forward?

We were able, over the last 2 years, to increase, for the first time in 30 years, fuel efficiency standards on cars and trucks. We didn't even need legislation. We just needed the cooperation of automakers and autoworkers and investors and other shareholders. And that's going to move us forward in a serious way.

So I think when it comes to something like energy, what we're probably going to have to do is say, here are some areas where there's just too much disagreement between Democrats and Republicans. We can't get this done right now, but let's not wait. Let's go ahead and start making some progress on the things that we do agree on, and we can continue to have a strong and healthy debate about those areas where we don't.

Republican Party's Agenda/Administration Accomplishments

Q. Is there anything in the "Pledge to America" that you think you can support?

The President. I'm sure there are going to be areas, particularly around, for example, reforming how Washington works, that I'll be interested in. I think the American people want to see more transparency, more openness. As I said, in the midst of economic crisis, I think one of the things I take responsibility for is not having pushed harder on some of those issues. And I think if you take Republicans and Democrats at their word, this is an area that they want to deliver on for the American people. I want to be supportive of that effort.

Jake Tapper [ABC News].

Midterm Elections/Taxes/National Economy

Q. Thank you, Mr. President. I have a policy question and a personal one. The policy question is, you talked about how the immediate goal is the Bush tax cuts and making sure that they don't expire for those who earn under 200, 250,000. Republicans disagree with that strongly. They want all of the Bush tax cuts extended. Are you willing to compromise on that? Are you willing to negotiate at all, for instance, allow them to expire for everyone over $1 million? Where are you willing to budge on that?

And the second one is, President Bush, when he went through a similar thing, came out and he said, "This was a thumpin'." You talked about how it was humbling, or you alluded to it perhaps being humbling. And I'm wondering,

when you call your friends, like Congressman Perriello or Governor Strickland, and you see 19 State legislatures go to the other side, Governorships in swing States, the Democratic Party set back, what does it feel like?

The President. It feels bad. [*Laughter*] The toughest thing over the last couple of days is seeing really terrific public servants not have the opportunity to serve anymore, at least in the short term. And you mentioned—there are just some terrific Members of Congress who took really tough votes because they thought it was the right thing, even though they knew this could cause them political problems and even though a lot of them came from really tough swing districts or majority-Republican districts. And the amount of courage that they showed and conviction that they showed is something that I admire so much. I can't overstate it.

And so there's a—not only sadness about seeing them go, but there's also a lot of questioning on my part in terms of could I have done something differently or done something more so that those folks would still be here. It's hard. And I take responsibility for it in a lot of ways.

I will tell you, they've been incredibly gracious when I have conversations with them. And what they've told me is, you know, I—we don't have regrets because I feel like we were doing the right thing. And they may be just saying that to make me feel better, which, again, is a sign of their character and their class. And I hope a lot of them continue to pursue public service because I think they're terrific public servants.

With respect to the tax cut issue, my goal is to make sure that we don't have a huge spike in taxes for middle class families. Not only would that be a terrible burden on families who are already going through tough times, it would be bad for our economy. It is very important that we're not taking a whole bunch of money out of the system from people who are most likely to spend that money on goods, services, groceries, buying a new winter coat for the kids.

That's also why I think unemployment insurance is important. Not only is it the right thing to do for folks who are still looking for work and struggling in this really tough economy, but it's the right thing to do for the economy as a whole.

So my goal is to sit down with Speaker-elect Boehner and Mitch McConnell and Harry and Nancy sometime in the next few weeks and see where we can move forward in a way that, first of all, does no harm; that extends those tax cuts that are very important for middle class families; also extends those provisions that are important to encourage businesses to invest and provide businesses some certainty over the next year or two.

And how that negotiation works itself out, I think, is too early to say. But this is going to be one of my top priorities. And my hope is, is that given we all have an interest in growing the economy and encouraging job growth, that we're not going to play brinksmanship, but instead we're going to act responsibly.

Q. So you're willing to negotiate?

The President. Absolutely.

Laura Meckler [Wall Street Journal].

Bipartisanship/Environment

Q. Thank you, Mr. President. You said earlier that it was clear that Congress was rejecting the idea of a cap-and-trade program and that you wouldn't be able to move forward with that. Looking ahead, do you feel the same way about EPA regulating carbon emissions? Would you be open to them doing essentially the same thing through an administrative action, or is that off the table as well?

And secondly, just to follow up on what you said about changing the way Washington works, do you think that—you said you didn't do enough to change the way things were handled in this city. Some of—in order to get your health care bill passed, you needed to make some of those deals. Do you wish, in retrospect, you had not made those deals and even if it meant the collapse of the program?

The President. I think that making sure that families had security and that we're on a trajectory to lower health care costs was absolutely critical for this country. But you are absolutely right that when you are navigating through a House and a Senate in this kind of pretty partisan environment that it's a ugly mess when it

comes to process. And I think that is something that really affected how people viewed the outcome. That is something that I regret, that we couldn't have made the process more—healthier than it ended up being. But I think the outcome was a good one.

With respect to the EPA, I think the smartest thing for us to do is to see if we can get Democrats and Republicans in a room who are serious about energy independence and are serious about keeping our air clean and our water clean and dealing with the issue of greenhouse gases, and seeing are there ways that we can make progress in the short term and invest in technologies in the long term that start giving us the tools to reduce greenhouse gases and solve this problem.

The EPA is under a court order that says greenhouse gases are a pollutant that fall under their jurisdiction. And I think one of the things that's very important for me is not to have us ignore the science, but rather to find ways that we can solve these problems that don't hurt the economy, that encourage the development of clean energy in this country, that in fact may give us opportunities to create entire new industries and create jobs, that—and that put us in a competitive posture around the world.

So I think it's too early to say whether or not we can make some progress on that front. I think we can. Cap-and-trade was just one way of skinning the cat; it was not the only way. It was a means, not an end. And I'm going to be looking for other means to address this problem.

And I think EPA wants help from the legislature on this. I don't think that the desire is to somehow be protective of their powers here. I think what they want to do is make sure that the issue is being dealt with.

Ed Henry [CNN].

U.S. Military's "Don't Ask, Don't Tell" Policy/Administration Accomplishments/Bipartisanship/National Economy

Q. Thank you, Mr. President. I wanted to do a personal and policy one as well. On personal, you had a lot of fun on the campaign trail by saying that the Republicans were drinking a Slurpee and sitting on the sidelines while you were trying to pull the car out of the ditch. But the point of the story was that you said if you want to go forward, you put the car in "D"; if you want to go backwards, you put it in "R." Now that there are at least 60 House districts that seem to have rejected that message, is it possible that there are a majority of Americans who think your policies are taking us in reverse? And what specific changes will you make to your approach to try to fix that and better connect with the American people?

And just on a policy front, "don't ask, don't tell" is something that you promised to end. And when you had 60 votes and 59 votes in the Senate—it's a tough issue—you haven't been able to do it. Do you now have to tell your liberal base that with maybe 52 or 53 votes in the Senate, you're just not going to be able to get it done in the next 2 years?

The President. Well, let me take the second issue first. I've been a strong believer in the notion that if somebody is willing to serve in our military, in uniform, putting their lives on the line for our security, that they should not be prevented from doing so because of their sexual orientation. And since there's been a lot of discussion about polls over the last 48 hours, I think it's worth noting that the overwhelming majority of Americans feel the same way. It's the right thing to do.

Now, as Commander in Chief, I've said that making this change needs to be done in an orderly fashion. I've worked with the Pentagon, worked with Secretary Gates, worked with Admiral Mullen, to make sure that we are looking at this in a systemic way that maintains good order and discipline, but that we need to change this policy.

There's going to be a review that comes out at the beginning of the month that will have surveyed attitudes and opinions within the Armed Forces. I will expect that Secretary of Defense Gates and chairman of the Joint Chiefs of Staff Admiral Mullen will have something to say about that review. I will look at it very carefully. But that will give us time to act in—potentially, during the lame duck session to change this policy.

Keep in mind, we've got a bunch of court cases that are out there as well. And something that would be very disruptive to good order and discipline and unit cohesion is if we've got this issue bouncing around in the courts, as it already has over the last several weeks, where the Pentagon and the chain of command doesn't know at any given time what rules they're working under.

We need to provide certainty, and it's time for us to move this policy forward. And this should not be a partisan issue. This is an issue, as I said, where you've got a sizable portion of the American people squarely behind the notion that folks who are willing to serve on our behalf should be treated fairly and equally.

Now, in terms of how we move forward, I think that the American people understand that we're still digging our way out of a pretty big mess. So I don't think anybody denies they think we're in a ditch. I just don't think they feel like we've gotten all the way out of the ditch yet. And to move the analogy forward that I used in the campaign, I think what they want right now is the Democrats and the Republicans both pushing some more to get the car on level ground. And we haven't done that.

If you think I was engaging in too much campaign rhetoric, saying the Republicans were just sitting on the side of the road, watching us get that car out of the ditch, at the very least we were pushing in opposite directions. And so——

Q. ——the idea that your policies are taking the country in reverse. You just reject that idea altogether that your policies could be going in reverse?

The President. Yes. And I think—look, here's the bottom line. When I came into office, this economy was in a freefall, and the economy has stabilized. The economy is growing. We've seen 9 months of private sector job growth. So I think it would be hard to argue that we're going backwards. I think what you can argue is we're stuck in neutral. We are not moving the way we need to, to make sure that folks have the jobs, have the opportunity, are seeing economic growth in their communities the way they need to. And that's going to require Democrats and

Republicans to come together and look for the best ideas to move things forward.

It will not be easy, not just because Democrats and Republicans may have different priorities, as we were just discussing when it came to how we structure tax cuts, but because these issues are hard.

The Republicans throughout the campaign said they're very concerned about debt and deficits. Well, one of the most important things we can do for debt and deficits is economic growth. So what other proposals do they have to grow the economy? If, in fact, they're rejecting some of the proposals I've made, I want to hear from them what affirmative policies can make a difference in terms of encouraging job growth and promoting the economy, because I don't think that tax cuts alone would—are going to be a recipe for the kind of expansion that we need.

From 2001 to 2009, we cut taxes pretty significantly, and we just didn't see the kind of expansion that is going to be necessary in terms of driving the unemployment rate down significantly.

So I think what we're going to need to do and what the American people want is for us to mix and match ideas, figure out those areas where we can agree on, move forward on those, disagree without being disagreeable on those areas that we can't agree on. If we accomplish that, then there will be time for politics later, but over the next year I think we can solidify this recovery and give people a little more confidence out there.

Hans Nichols [Bloomberg News].

Private Sector/National Economy/Job Growth

Q. Thank you, Mr. President. I want to ask if you're going to have John Boehner over for a Slurpee, but I actually have a serious question.

The President. I might serve—they're delicious drinks. [*Laughter*]

Q. The Slurpee summit.

The President. The Slurpee summit—that's good, Chip. I like that. [*Laughter*]

Q. Since you seem to be in a reflective mood, do you think you need to hit the reset button with business? How do you plan to set that reset button with business? Would that—would you

include anything beyond your Cleveland speech, those proposals, to get them off the sidelines, get them off the cash they're hoarding, and start hiring again? Thank you.

The President. Yes, I think this is an important question that we've been asking ourselves for several months now. You're right, as I reflect on what's happened over the last 2 years, one of the things that I think has not been managed by me as well as it needed to be was finding the right balance in making sure that businesses have rules of the road and are treating customers fairly, and—whether it's their credit cards or insurance or their mortgages—but also making absolutely clear that the only way America succeeds is if businesses are succeeding.

The reason we've got a unparalleled standard of living in the history of the world is because we've got a free market that is dynamic and entrepreneurial, and that free market has to be nurtured and cultivated. And there's no doubt that when you had the financial crisis on Wall Street, the bonus controversies, the battle around health care, the battle around financial reform, and then you had BP, you just had a successive set of issues in which I think business took the message that, well, gosh, it seems like we may be always painted as the bad guy.

And so I've got to take responsibility in terms of making sure that I make clear to the business community, as well as to the country, that the most important thing we can do is to boost and encourage our business sector and make sure that they're hiring. And so we do have specific plans in terms of how we can structure that outreach.

Now, keep in mind, over the last 2 years, we've been talking to CEOs constantly. And as I plan for my trip later this week to Asia, the whole focus is on how are we going to open up markets so that American businesses can prosper and we can sell more goods and create more jobs here in the United States. And a whole bunch of corporate executives are going to be joining us so that I can help them open up those markets and allow them to sell their products.

So there's been a lot of strong interaction behind the scenes. But I think setting the right tone publicly is going to be important and could end up making a difference at the margins in terms of how businesses make investment decisions.

Q. But do you have new specific proposals to get them off the sidelines and start hiring?

The President. Well, I already discussed a couple with Chip that haven't been acted on yet. You're right that I made these proposals 2 months ago, but—or 3 months ago—but it was in the midst of a campaign season where it was doubtful that they were going to get a full hearing just because there was so much political noise going on.

I think as we move forward, sitting down and talking to businesses, figuring out what exactly would help you make more investments that could create more jobs here in the United States, and listening hard to them—in a context where, maybe, Democrats and Republicans are together so we're receiving the same message at the same time—and then acting on that agenda could make a big difference.

Matt Spetalnick of Reuters.

President's Leadership and Policymaking/Midterm Elections

Q. Thank you, Mr. President. How do you respond to those who say the election outcome, at least in part, was voters saying that they see you as out of touch with their personal economic pain? And are you willing to make any changes in your leadership style?

The President. There is a inherent danger in being in the White House and being in the bubble. I mean, folks didn't have any complaints about my leadership style when I was running around Iowa for a year. And they got a pretty good look at me up close and personal, and they were able to lift the hood and kick the tires. And I think they understood that my story was theirs. I might have a funny name, I might have lived in some different places, but the values of hard work and responsibility and honesty and looking out for one another that had been instilled in them by their parents, those were the same values that I took from my mom and my grandparents.

And so the track record has been that when I'm out of this place, that's not an issue. When

you're in this place, it is hard not to seem removed. And one of the challenges that we've got to think about is how do I meet my responsibilities here in the White House, which require a lot of hours and a lot of work, but still have that opportunity to engage with the American people on a day-to-day basis and know—give them confidence that I'm listening to them.

Those letters that I read every night, some of them just break my heart. Some of them provide me encouragement and inspiration. But nobody's filming me reading those letters. And so it's hard, I think, for people to get a sense of, well, how's he taking in all this information?

So I think there are more things that we can do to make sure that I'm getting out of here. But, I mean, I think it's important to point out as well that a couple of great communicators, Ronald Reagan and Bill Clinton, were standing at this podium 2 years into their Presidency getting very similar questions because the economy wasn't working the way it needed to be and there were a whole range of factors that made people concerned that maybe the party in power wasn't listening to them.

This is something that I think every President needs to go through, because the responsibilities of this office are so enormous and so many people are depending on what we do, and in the rush of activity, sometimes we lose track of the ways that we connected with folks that got us here in the first place.

And that's something that—now, I'm not recommending for every future President that they take a shellacking like they—like I did last night. [*Laughter*] I'm sure there are easier ways to learn these lessons. But I do think that this is a growth process and an evolution. And the relationship that I've had with the American people is one that built slowly, peaked at this incredible high, and then during the course of the last 2 years, as we've, together, gone through some very difficult times, has gotten rockier and tougher. And it's going to, I'm sure, have some more ups and downs during the course of me being in this office.

But the one thing that I just want to end on is getting out of here is good for me too, because when I travel around the country, even in the toughest of these debates—in the midst of health care last year during summer when there were protesters about, and when I'm meeting families who've lost loved ones in Afghanistan or Iraq—I always come away from those interactions just feeling so much more optimistic about this country.

We have such good and decent people who, on a day-to-day basis, are finding all kinds of ways to live together and educate kids and grow their communities and improve their communities and create businesses and work together to create great new products and services. The American people always make me optimistic.

And that's why, during the course of the last 2 years, as tough as it's been, as many some-times scary moments as we've gone through, I've never doubted that we're going to emerge stronger than we were before. And I think that remains true, and I'm just going to be looking forward to playing my part in helping that journey along.

All right. Thank you very much, everybody.

NOTE: The President's news conference began at 1:02 p.m. in the East Room at the White House. In his remarks, the President referred to House Minority Whip Eric Cantor. The Office of the Press Secretary also released a Spanish language transcript of the President's opening remarks.

Remarks Following a Cabinet Meeting
November 4, 2010

Hello, everybody. I just want to make a few quick remarks to expand on some things that I said yesterday. Obviously, Tuesday was a big election. I've congratulated the Republicans and consoled some of our Democratic friends about the results. And I think it's clear that the voters sent a message, which is, they want us to focus on the economy and jobs and moving this country forward. They're concerned about making sure that taxpayer money is not wasted, and they want to change the tone here in Washington, where the two parties are coming together and focusing on the people's business, as opposed to scoring political points.

I just had a meeting with my Cabinet and key staff to let them know that we have to take that message to heart and make a sincere and consistent effort to try to change how Washington operates. And the folks around this table have done extraordinary work in their agencies. They have cooperated consistently with Congress. I think they are interested in bipartisan ideas. And so they are going to be integral in helping me to root out waste in Government, make our agencies more efficient, and generate more ideas so that we can put the American people back to work.

Now, at the same time, obviously, what's going to be critically important over the coming months is creating a better working relationship between this White House and the congressional leadership that's coming in, as well as the congressional leadership that carries over from the previous Congress. And so I want everybody to know that I have already called Mitch McConnell, John Boehner, Harry Reid, and Nancy Pelosi to invite them to a meeting here at the White House in the first week of the lame duck on November 18. This is going to be a meeting in which I want us to talk substantively about how we can move the American people's agenda forward. It's not just going to be a photo op. Hopefully, it may spill over into dinner. And the immediate focus is going to be what we need to get done during the lame duck session.

I mentioned yesterday, we have to act in order to assure that middle class families don't see a big tax spike because of how the Bush tax cuts have been structured. It is very important that we extend those middle class tax provisions to hold middle class families harmless.

But there are a whole range of other economic issues that have to be addressed: unemployment insurance for folks who are still out there looking for work; business extenders, which are essentially provisions to encourage businesses to invest here in the United States, and if we don't have those, we're losing a very important tool for us to be able to increase business investment and increase job growth over the coming year. We've got to provide businesses some certainty about what their tax landscape's going to look like, and we've got to provide families certainty. That's critical to maintain our recovery.

I should mention that in addition to those economic issues, there are some things during the lame duck that relate to foreign policy that are going to be very important for us to deal with, and I'll make mention of one in particular, and that's the START Treaty. We have negotiated with the Russians significant reductions in our nuclear arms. This is something that traditionally has received strong bipartisan support. We've got people like George Shultz, who helped to organize arms control treaties with the Russians back when it was the Soviet Union, who have come out forcefully in favor of this.

This is not a traditionally Democratic or Republican issue, but rather, a issue of American national security. And I am hopeful that we can get that done before we leave and send a strong signal to Russia that we are serious about reducing nuclear arsenals, but also send a signal to the world that we're serious about nonproliferation. We've made great progress when it comes to sending a message to Iran that they are isolated internationally, in part because people have seen that we are serious about taking our responsibilities when it comes to nonproliferation, and that has to continue.

So there is going to be a whole range of work that needs to get done in a relatively short period of time, and I'm looking forward to having a conversation with the leadership about some agenda items that they may be concerned about.

Last point I'll make is that I've also invited the newly elected Democratic and Republican Governors here to the White House on December 2 because I think it's a terrific opportunity to hear from them, folks who are working at the State and local levels, about what they're seeing, what ideas they think Washington needs to be paying more attention to.

A lot of times things are a little less ideological when you get Governors together, because they've got very practical problems that they've got to solve in terms of how do they make sure that roads and bridges are funded and how do they make sure that schools stay open and teachers stay on the job. That kind of nuts-and-bolts stuff, I think, oftentimes yields the kind of commonsense approach that the American people, I think, are looking for right now.

So in sum, we've got a lot of work to do. People are still catching their breath from the election. The dust is still settling. But the one thing I'm absolutely certain of is that the American people don't want us just standing still and they don't want us engaged in gridlock. They want us to do the people's business, partly because they understand that the world is not standing still.

I'm going to be leaving at the—tomorrow for India, and the primary purpose is to take a bunch of U.S. companies and open up markets so that we can sell in Asia, in some of the fastest growing markets in the world, and we can create jobs here in the United States of America. And my hope is, is that we've got some specific announcements that show the connection between what we're doing overseas and what happens here at home when it comes to job growth and economic growth.

But the bottom line is, is that all around the world, countries are moving. They are serious about competing. They are serious about competing with us not just on manufacturing, but on services. They're competing with us when it comes to educational attainment, when it comes to scientific discovery.

And so we can't afford 2 years of just squabbling. What we need to do is make sure that everybody is pulling together, Democrats and Republicans and Independents, folks at the Federal level and the State levels, private sector with the public sector, to make sure that America retains it competitiveness, retains its leadership in the world. And that's something that I'm very much looking forward to helping to be a part of.

So thank you very much, everybody.

NOTE: The President spoke at 9:40 a.m. in the Cabinet Room at the White House. In his remarks, he referred to former Secretary of State George P. Shultz. The Office of the Press

Secretary also released a Spanish language transcript of these remarks.

Statement on the Observance of Diwali
November 4, 2010

Tomorrow Hindus, Jains, Sikhs, and some Buddhists here in America and around the world will celebrate the holiday of Diwali, the festival of lights. This is a day when members of some of the world's oldest religions celebrate the triumph of good over evil. Last year, I marked this holiday as many will this weekend by lighting the *diya*, or lamp. This lamp symbolizes the victory of light over darkness and knowledge over ignorance.

Diwali is a time for celebration, but it is also a time for reflection, a time when we must remember that there are always others less fortunate than ourselves. This holiday reminds us all that we should commit ourselves to helping those in need. For many, this is also a time to gather with family and to pray. To those celebrating Diwali in India, I look forward to visiting you over the next few days. And to all those who will celebrate this joyous occasion on Friday, I wish you, your families, and loved ones happy Diwali and *Saal Mubarak*.

Letter to Congressional Leaders on Continuation of the National Emergency With Respect to Weapons of Mass Destruction
November 4, 2010

Dear Madam Speaker: (Dear Mr. President:)

Section 202(d) of the National Emergencies Act (50 U.S.C. 1622(d)) provides for the automatic termination of a national emergency unless, prior to the anniversary date of its declaration, the President publishes in the *Federal Register* and transmits to the Congress a notice stating that the emergency is to continue in effect beyond the anniversary date. In accordance with this provision, I have sent to the *Federal Register* for publication the enclosed notice, stating that the national emergency with respect to the proliferation of weapons of mass destruction that was declared in Executive Order 12938, as amended, is to continue in effect for 1 year beyond November 14, 2010.

Sincerely,

BARACK OBAMA

NOTE: Identical letters were sent to Nancy Pelosi, Speaker of the House of Representatives, and Joseph R. Biden, Jr., President of the Senate. The notice is listed in Appendix D at the end of this volume.

Letter to Congressional Leaders on Notification Designating Irving A. Williamson as Vice Chair of the United States International Trade Commission
October 29, 2010

Dear Madam Speaker: (Dear Mr. President:)

Consistent with the provisions of 19 U.S.C. 1330(c)(1), this is to notify the Congress that I have designated Irving A. Williamson as Vice Chair of the United States International Trade Commission for the term expiring June 16, 2012.

Sincerely,

BARACK OBAMA

NOTE: Identical letters were sent to Nancy Pelosi, Speaker of the House of Representatives, and Joseph R. Biden, Jr., President of the Senate. This letter was released by the Office of the Press Secretary on November 5.

Remarks on the National Economy
November 5, 2010

Good morning, everybody. We are in the middle of a tough fight to get our economy growing faster so that businesses across our country can open and expand, so that people can find good jobs, and so that we can repair the terrible damage that was done by the worst recession in our lifetimes. Today we received some encouraging news.

Based on today's jobs report, we've now seen private sector job growth for 10 straight months. That means that since January, the private sector has added 1.1 million jobs. Let me repeat: Over the course of the last several months, we've seen over a million jobs added to the American economy. In October, the private sector has added 159,000 jobs. And we learned that businesses added more than 100,000 jobs in both August and September as well. So we've now seen 4 months of private sector job growth above 100,000, which is the first time we've seen this kind of increase in over 4 years.

Now, that's not good enough. The unemployment rate is still unacceptably high, and we've got a lot of work to do. This recession caused a great deal of hardship, and it put millions of people out of work. So in order to repair this damage, in order to create the jobs to meet the large need, we need to accelerate our economic growth so that we are producing jobs at a faster pace.

Because the fact is an encouraging jobs report doesn't make a difference if you're still one of the millions of people who are looking for work. And I won't be satisfied until everybody who is looking for a job can find one. So we've got to keep fighting for every job, for every new business, for every opportunity to get this economy moving. And just as we passed a small-business jobs bill based on ideas of both parties and the private sector, I am open to any idea, any proposal, any way we can get the economy growing faster so that people who need work can find it faster.

This includes tax breaks for small businesses, like deferring taxes on new equipment, so that they've got an incentive to expand and hire, as well as tax cuts to make it cheaper for entrepreneurs to start companies. This includes building new infrastructure, from high-speed trains to high-speed Internet, so that our economy can run faster and smarter. It includes promoting research and innovation and creating incentives in growth sectors like the clean energy economy. And it certainly includes keeping tax rates low for middle class families and extending unemployment benefits to help those hardest hit in—by the downturn while generating more demand in the economy.

It's also absolutely clear that one of the keys to creating jobs is to open markets to American goods made by American workers. Our prosperity depends not just on consuming things, but also on being the maker of things. In fact, for every $1 billion we increase in exports, thousands of jobs are supported here at home. And that's why I've set a goal of doubling America's exports over the next 5 years. And that's why on the trip that I'm about to take, I'm going to be talking about opening up additional markets in places like India, so that American businesses can sell more products abroad in order to create more jobs here at home.

And this is a reminder, as well, that the most important competition we face in this new century will not be between Democrats and Republicans, it's the competition with countries around the world to lead the global economy. And our success or failure in this race will depend on whether we can come together as a nation. Our future depends on putting politics aside to solve problems, to worry about the next generation instead of the next election.

We can't spend the next 2 years mired in gridlock. Other countries, like China, aren't standing still. So we can't stand still either. We've got to move forward.

I'm confident that if we can do that, if we can work together, then this country will not only recover, but it will prosper. And I'm looking very much forward to helping to pry some markets open, help American businesses, and put people back to work here at home during the course of this trip.

Thank you very much.

NOTE: The President spoke at 9:36 a.m. in the Roosevelt Room at the White House. The Office of the Press Secretary also released a Spanish language transcript of these remarks.

Remarks on the Second Anniversary of the Terrorist Attacks in Mumbai, India
November 6, 2010

On behalf of Michelle and myself, I want to say what an extraordinary honor it is to be here in India. I want to thank the people of Mumbai and all of you here today for your extraordinarily warm welcome. And I want to say to the people of India how much we are looking forward to spending the next 3 days in this remarkable country and to deepening the partnership between our two countries.

I know there's been a great deal of commentary on our decision to begin our visit here in this dynamic city, at this historic hotel. And to those who have asked whether this is intended to send a message, my answer is simply, absolutely. Mumbai is a symbol of the incredible energy and optimism that defines India in the 21st century. And ever since those horrific days 2 years ago, the Taj has been the symbol of the strength and the resilience of the Indian people.

So yes, we visit here to send a very clear message that in our determination to give our people a future of security and prosperity, the United States and India stand united.

A few moments ago, Michelle and I had the opportunity to visit the memorial here and to honor the memory of those who were lost. And we also had the privilege of meeting with some of their families, as well as some of the courageous survivors. I thank them all for joining us here today, along with so many others who endured the anguish of those 4 days in November.

We'll never forget the awful images of 26/11, including the flames from this hotel that lit up the night sky. We'll never forget how the world, including the American people, watched and grieved with all of India.

But the resolve and the resilience of the Indian people during those attacks stood in stark contrast to the savagery of the terrorists. The murderers came to kill innocent civilians that day. But those of you here risked everything to save human life.

You were strangers who helped strangers; hostages who worked together to break free and escape; hotel staff who stayed behind to escort guests to safety, including the hotel manager, even after he lost his own family; a nanny who braved the bullets to protect a young boy; and Indians in uniform who stopped the carnage and whose colleagues made the ultimate sacrifice.

The perpetrators wanted to pit believers of different faiths against one another, but they failed. Because here in Mumbai, the diversity that is India's strength was on full display: Hindus, Sikhs, Christians, Jews, and Muslims protecting each other, saving each other, living the common truth of all the world's great religions, that we are all children of God.

Those who attacked Mumbai wanted to demoralize this city and this country. But they failed, because the very next day, Mumbaikars came back to work. Hotel staff reported for their shifts; workers returned to their businesses. And within weeks, this hotel was once again welcoming guests from around the world.

By striking the places where our countries and people come together, those who perpetrated these horrific attacks hoped to drive us apart. But just as Indian citizens lost their lives on 9/11, American citizens lost their lives here on 26/11, along with the citizens of many nations. And just as our people prayed together at candlelight vigils, our Governments have worked closer than ever, sharing intelligence, preventing more attacks, and demanding that the perpetrators be brought to justice.

Indeed, today, the United States and India are working together more closely than ever to keep our people safe. And I look forward to deepening our counterterrorism cooperation even further when I meet with Prime Minister Singh in New Delhi.

We go forward with confidence, knowing that history is on our side. Because those who target the innocent, they offer nothing but death and destruction. What we seek to build— to welcome people of different faiths and backgrounds and to offer our citizens a future of dignity and opportunity—that is the spirit of the gateway behind us, which in its architecture reflects all the beauty and strength of different faiths and traditions and which has welcomed people to this city for a century.

That is the hope that in towns and villages across India, across this vast nation, leads people to board crowded trains and set out to forge their futures in this city of dreams. And that is the shared determination of India and the United States, two partners that will never waver in our defense of our people or the democratic values that we share.

For just as your first Prime Minister said the day that the father of your nation was taken from you, we shall never allow that torch of freedom to be blown out, however high the wind or stormy the tempest. We believe that in America, and we know you believe it here in India.

God bless you, and thank you very much.

NOTE: The President spoke at 2:25 p.m. at the Taj Mahal Palace and Tower Hotel. In his remarks, he referred to hotel manager Karambir Singh Kang.

The President's Weekly Address
November 6, 2010

This week, Americans across the country cast their votes and made their voices heard. And your message was clear. You're rightly frustrated with the pace of our economic recovery. So am I. You're fed up with partisan politics and want results. I do too.

So I congratulate all of this week's winners: Republicans, Democrats, and Independents. But now the campaign season is over, and it's time to focus on our shared responsibilities to work together and deliver those results: speeding up our economic recovery, creating jobs, and strengthening the middle class so that the American Dream feels like it's back within reach.

That's why I've asked to sit down soon with leaders of both parties so that we can have an extended discussion about what we can do together to move this country forward. And over the next few weeks, we're going to have a chance to work together in the brief upcoming session of Congress.

Here's why this lame duck session is so important. Early in the last decade, President

Bush and Congress enacted a series of tax cuts that were designed to expire at the end of this year. What that means is, if Congress doesn't act by New Year's Eve, middle class families will see their taxes go up starting on New Year's Day.

But the last thing we should do is raise taxes on middle class families. For the past decade, they saw their costs rise, their incomes fall, and too many jobs go overseas. They're the ones bearing the brunt of the recession. They're the ones having trouble making ends meet. They're the ones who need relief right now.

So something's got to be done, and I believe there's room for us to compromise and get it done together.

Let's start where we agree. All of us want certainty for middle class Americans. None of us want them to wake up on January 1 with a higher tax bill. That's why I believe we should permanently extend the Bush tax cuts for all families making less than $250,000 a year. That's 98 percent of the American people.

We also agree on the need to start cutting spending and bringing down our deficit. That's going to require everyone to make some tough choices. In fact, if Congress were to implement my proposal to freeze nonsecurity discretionary spending for 3 years, it would bring this spending down to its lowest level as a share of the economy in 50 years.

But at a time when we are going to ask folks across the board to make such difficult sacrifices, I don't see how we can afford to borrow an additional $700 billion from other countries to make all the Bush tax cuts permanent, even for the wealthiest 2 percent of Americans. We'd be digging ourselves into an even deeper fiscal hole and passing the burden on to our children.

I recognize that both parties are going to have to work together and compromise to get something done here. But I want to make my priorities clear from the start. One, middle class families need permanent tax relief. And two, I believe we can't afford to borrow and spend another $700 billion on permanent tax cuts for millionaires and billionaires.

There are new public servants in Washington, but we still face the same challenges. And you made it clear that it's time for results. This is a great opportunity to show everyone that we got the message and that we're willing, in this postelection season, to come together and do what's best for the country we all love.

Thanks.

NOTE: The address was recorded at approximately 5:20 p.m. on November 4 in the Blue Room at the White House for broadcast on November 6. The transcript was made available by the Office of the Press Secretary on November 5, but was embargoed for release until 6 a.m., e.d.t., on November 6. Due to the 9½-hour time difference, the address was released after the President's remarks at the Taj Mahal Palace and Tower Hotel in Mumbai, India. The Office of the Press Secretary also released a Spanish language transcript of this address.

Remarks During a Meeting With Business Leaders in Mumbai
November 6, 2010

President Obama. Well, thank you very much, everybody, for joining us. I'm going to be very brief here today. This is partly because I've got a long speech that will immediately follow this.

But as I emphasized before I left the United States, one of the biggest priorities on this trip is to highlight the degree to which U.S. economic success, U.S. job creation, U.S. economic growth is going to be tied to our working with, cooperating with, establishing commercial ties with the fastest growing economies in the world. And no country represents that promise of a strong, vibrant commercial relationship more acutely than India.

Obviously, anybody who comes to Mumbai is struck by the incredible energy and drive and entrepreneurial spirit that exists here. This is a commercial town, and this is a increasingly commercial nation. And it is so important for not just U.S. companies, but U.S. workers to recognize these incredible opportunities, and

hopefully, for Indian workers and Indian companies to recognize the opportunities for them as well.

So often, when we talk about trade and commercial relationships, the question is who's winning and who's losing. This is a classic situation in which we can all win. And I'm going to make it one of my primary tasks during the next 3 days to highlight all the various ways in which we've got an opportunity, I think, to put Americans back to work, see India grow its infrastructure, its networks, its capacity to continue to grow at a rapid pace. And we can do that together, but only if both sides recognize these opportunities.

So rather than speak about these possibilities in the abstract, I've been having a terrific conversation with some U.S. CEOs who are already doing a lot of work here in India. I just had a chance to meet some young Indian entrepreneurs, as well as U.S. and Indian companies that are joint venturing to take U.S. technology and apply it in new ways here in India, using new business and innovative business models.

But what I'm really excited about is the fact that we're actually doing some business while we're here. And so before I turn it over to some of the companies, I'd like Minister Sharma to just say a few words and thank him and the entire Indian Government for the incredible hospitality that's already been shown to me during the few hours since I've arrived, and I'm very much looking forward to the remaining days ahead.

Commerce and Industry Minister Anand Sharma of India. Thank you, Excellency, President Obama. I'm very privileged to welcome you on behalf of the Government and people of the Republic of India. Your visit has a special significance, because after many missed opportunities in our engagement as two nations, there has been a historic embrace.

We watched with admiration your election, your commitment, your references to the values espoused by the father of the Indian nation, Mahatma Gandhi, Martin Luther King, the civil rights movement, and to speak for human dignity and the values associated.

Our two countries share a lot. And in the 21st century, there are expectations that these two countries, which have a shared commitment to democracy, to human rights, pluralistic society, multicultural, multireligious, multiethnic, can define the course, as the global architecture, political and economic, changes.

We welcome what you have said as you embarked for India about doubling the trade, but also increase jobs. By enhanced economic engagement, both will happen. India has reached a stage where I can say not with optimism, but without any hesitation, that this is a country of limitless opportunities for your industry, for your investors to engage in.

At the same time, both our countries are fortunate that we have human resources. U.S. has institutions, U.S. has strengths in innovation, in high-end technologies, and it can be greatly rewarding for both our countries.

My Prime Minister, Dr. Manmohan Singh, and the chairperson of the ruling coalition, Sonia Gandhi, has specifically asked me to convey the warm greetings and welcome to you. We hope your visit will be a pathbreaking one, clearly defining the roadmap of the cooperation between the two big democracies of the world.

Thank you.

President Obama. Thank you so much.

With that, what I'd like to do is to provide an opportunity for Jeff Immelt and Anil Ambani to talk about work that General Electric and Reliance are going to be doing together. And then I'll turn it over to representatives of Boeing and SpiceJet to talk about the terrific partnership that they're forging. These are two wonderful examples of how the collaboration and commercial ties between India and the United States are resulting directly in economic benefits in both countries and jobs in both countries.

So, Jeff, why don't we start with you?

[*At this point, Jeffrey R. Immelt, chairman and chief executive officer, General Electric Company, made brief remarks. Anil Dhirubhai Ambani, chairman, Reliance Anil Dhirubhai Ambani Group, then made brief remarks, concluding as follows.*]

Mr. Ambani. But saying that apart, I still think that your being here today is a strong signal for us in India. And you've chosen to come at a time which is Diwali, which was yesterday. And there could not be a more auspicious moment because we believe in astrology and palmistry and history. But our new year is tomorrow, so this is the best way to begin our new year to have you here as our valued guest and to make this announcement with Jeff.

Thank you so much.

President Obama. Thank you so much, Anil. I appreciate that.

Christopher.

Boeing Military Aircraft President Christopher M. Chadwick. Well, thank you, Mr. President. I'm fortunate to represent Boeing, who has been doing business with India for 60 years now. Unfortunately, unlike Jeff I've only been coming here 5 years. But I've come 35 times in 5 years. [*Laughter*]

And so what I've found is there are a lot of similarities between India and the United States. The culture is the same. The work ethic is the same. And we all believe in commercial collaboration and partnerships.

We're here with SpiceJet today to commemorate a sale of 30 new 737 next-generation aircraft. We are proud as a Boeing company to be a partner with SpiceJet. And all the employees of Boeing—this is an honor for them.

President Obama. Mr. Kansagra.

SpiceJet Director Bhupendra "Bhulo" Kansagra. Thank you. Welcome, Mr. President, to India. As a fellow Kenyan, I'm very proud to see that you have made——

President Obama. Made something of myself. [*Laughter*]

Mr. Kansagra. ——India as the focus of your drive for exports out of the U.S. To that effect, the 30 aircraft order, which is the second of such orders we have placed with Boeing, will enhance SpiceJet's penetration into the Indian low-cost travel, low-cost transportation market, which really is the focus for SpiceJet.

Boeing has given us huge support together— and Fred also has extended his assistance to finance our forthcoming aircraft in the next year. That support and that partnership will take SpiceJet and Boeing to greater heights. And your coming here to India today will only help that day further. Thank you.

President Obama. Well, thank you very much.

So just to summarize, just around this table you're seeing billions of dollars in orders from U.S. companies, tens of thousands of jobs being supported. We're a potential that has barely been scratched. And this is, I think, why folks back home in the United States need to embrace the possible partnership with India, as a democracy, one that appreciates human rights and pluralism, one that has a entrepreneurial culture. We have an enormous possibility to partner with them for decades to come.

And by the way, it's not just big companies that we're emphasizing. We just had some terrific meetings with some startup ventures. And I'll just give a couple of examples. We have an Indian entrepreneur who has purchased water filtration equipment from a U.S. company. The U.S. company typically sold it to big plants around the country, but this Indian entrepreneur realized getting clean water is hard in India. And he's actually set up franchises using the U.S. filtration equipment and franchised a hundred franchisees around the country where they're selling clean water at a very, very cheap rate.

It's good for those communities. It's good for the businesses. And it's supporting jobs in the United States of America. We're seeing examples of that all across the board, but we haven't taken full advantage of these opportunities. And we need to.

On the Indian side, I just want to say to the people of India, every American businessperson who comes here is thrilled, Mr. Minister, with how rapidly India is growing and its increasing preeminence on the world stage. And I think that we want to place our bets with India as a strong partner. And that's true not only in the private sector, as you've already heard, but it's true with the U.S. Government as well, which is why I'm so looking forward to spending time here over the next several days.

Thank you very much, everybody.

NOTE: The President spoke at 5:10 p.m. at the Trident Nariman Point Hotel. Minister Sharma referred to Member of Parliament (lower House) Sonia Gandhi of India, in her capacity as chairperson of the ruling United Progressive Alliance parliamentary coalition. Mr. Kansagra referred to Fred P. Hochberg, chairman and president, U.S. Export-Import Bank. Audio was not available for verification of the content of these remarks.

Remarks at the United States-India Business and Entrepreneurship Summit in Mumbai
November 6, 2010

Thank you very much. Please, everyone, be seated. Good afternoon, everyone. *Namaste.* Thank you all for an extraordinarily warm welcome. And before I get started, I just want to acknowledge some outstanding public servants, some wonderful dignitaries who are in the room: Anand Sharma, our Commerce and Industry Minister here in India; Khurshid Salman, the Minister of Corporate Affairs and Minority Affairs, who's here; Dr. Montek Singh Ahluwalia, State Planning Commission deputy chairman; Gary Locke, who is the Secretary of Commerce for the United States; Terry McGraw, the chairman of the U.S.-India Business Council; Hari Bhartia, the president of the Confederation of Indian Industries; and Rajan Bharti Mittal, president of the Federation of Indian Chambers of Commerce and Industry.

On behalf of my wife Michelle and myself, thank you to the people of Mumbai and the people India for the incredible hospitality you have already shown just in the few hours since I've arrived in this magnificent country.

We are especially honored to be here as you celebrate Diwali. Now, last year I was—[*applause*]. Some of you may know this, last year, I was honored to become the first American President to help celebrate the Festival of Lights in the White House. And I know that today families are lighting their *diyas* and giving thanks for their blessings and looking ahead to the new year. So to all of you who are observing this sacred holiday here and around the world, happy Diwali and *Saal Mubarak*.

I want to thank all the organizations that have brought us together today, as well as the business leaders, the CEOs, the Government officials who have joined us here in Mumbai. I just had some incredibly productive discussions with American business leaders and Indian entrepreneurs, and today I want to speak with you about why we all benefit from the strengthening ties between our nations.

This is my first trip to India, but this will be my longest visit to another country since becoming President. And that's because I believe that the relationship between the United States and India will be one of the defining and indispensable partnerships of the 21st century.

Our nations are the two largest democracies on Earth. We are bound by a common language and common values, shared aspirations, and a shared belief that opportunity should be limited only by how hard you're willing to work, only by how hard you are willing to try. Trade and commerce between our people has been happening for centuries, even before we were independent nations. Indian immigrants crossed oceans to work on farms in the United States, and later generations came to practice medicine and do cutting-edge research and to start businesses. American researchers, in turn, partnered with Indian scientists to launch the Green Revolution that transformed life for generations of Indians. Americans have helped build India, and India has helped to build America.

Today, your country is one of the fastest growing economies in the world. And while there are many amazing success stories and rapidly expanding markets in Asia, the sheer size and pace of India's progress in just two decades is one of the most stunning achievements in human history. This is a fact. Since your reform of the Licensing Raj and embrace of the global economy, India has lifted tens of millions of people from poverty and created one of the largest middle classes on the planet.

You are now a nation of rapid growth and rising incomes and massive investments in infrastructure and energy and education. In the coming decades, you will be the world's most populous nation, with the largest workforce and one of the largest economies in the world. Now, undoubtedly, that means that the United States and India will engage in a healthy competition for markets and jobs and industries of the future. But it also offers the prospect of expanded commercial ties that strongly benefit both countries.

The United States sees Asia, and especially India, as a market of the future. We don't simply welcome your rise as a nation and a people, we ardently support it. We want to invest in it. And I'm here because I believe that in our interconnected world, increased commerce between the United States and India can be and will be a win-win proposition for both nations.

I realize that for some, this truth may not be readily apparent. I want to be honest. There are many Americans whose only experience with trade and globalization has been a shuttered factory or a job that was shipped overseas. And there still exists a caricature of India as a land of call centers and back offices that cost American jobs. That's a real perception. Here in India, I know that many still see the arrival of American companies and products as a threat to small shopkeepers and to India's ancient and proud culture.

But these old stereotypes, these old concerns ignore today's reality: In 2010, trade between our countries is not just a one-way street of American jobs and companies moving to India. It is a dynamic, two-way relationship that is creating jobs, growth, and higher living standards in both our countries. And that is the truth.

As we look to India today, the United States sees an opportunity to sell our exports in one of the fastest growing markets in the world. For America, this is a jobs strategy. As we recover from this recession, we are determined to rebuild our economy on a new, stronger foundation for growth. And part of that foundation involves doing what America has always been known for: discovering and creating and building the products that are sold all over the world. That's why I've set a goal of doubling America's exports over the next 5 years, because for every $1 billion in exports, thousands of jobs are supported at home.

And already, our exports to India have quadrupled in recent years, growing much faster than our exports to many other countries. The goods we sell in this country currently support tens of thousands of manufacturing jobs across the United States, from California and Washington to Pennsylvania and Florida. And that doesn't even include all the American jobs supported by our other exports to India, from agriculture to travel to educational services.

As we speak, American-made machinery is helping India improve its infrastructure, including the new airport here in Mumbai where I landed this morning. This year, there was a new sight on India's highways, American-made Harley-Davidson motorcycles. [*Laughter*] A growing number of American-made aircraft are taking flight in your skies. And soon there will be more.

That's because today, just moments before I arrived here, several landmark deals were sealed between the United States and India. Boeing, one of America's largest companies, is on track to sell India dozens of commercial and cargo aircraft. General Electric, another American company, will sell more than a hundred advanced jet engines. And I'm pleased that two U.S. firms are finalists for a major locomotive tender. Now, these are just a few of the more than 20 deals being announced today, totaling nearly $10 billion in U.S. exports.

From medical equipment and helicopters to turbines and mining equipment, American companies stand ready to support India's growing economy, the needs of your people, and your ability to defend this nation. And today's deals will lead to more than 50,000 jobs in the United States—50,000 jobs—everything from high-tech jobs in Southern California to manufacturing jobs in Ohio.

Now, these are major deals that are significant for both our nations. But our trade relationship is not just about what America sells India, it's also about what Indian investment in America is doing. Indian investment in America is among the fastest growing of any country. In recent years, Indian companies have invested billions of dollars in the United States: in American machinery, manufacturing, mining, research, technology. Today, these investments support tens of thousands of American jobs.

And at the same time, hundreds of American companies, including many small businesses, are investing in India, not just in telecommunications, but in industries from clean energy to agriculture. This means more choices for Indian consumers and more jobs for Indians and Americans.

Our relationship is also about more than the goods that we sell or the investments we make; it's about the innovative partnerships we forge in the name of progress. Before I came here, I had a fascinating meeting. I met with business leaders from both our countries, including some incredibly young Indian entrepreneurs. And what's fascinating is the way that they are now partnering to take technology that has had one application and use in the United States and found entirely new uses and new business models here in India.

They're working together to make cell towers across India that can run on solar and not diesel. They're putting American technology into Indian electric cars, they're trying to bring new filtration systems and clean drinking water to rural India, and they're trying to develop better drugs for diseases like malaria. These are examples of American companies doing well and Indian companies doing well.

And these partnerships remind us that by pursuing trade and commerce, we are unleashing the most powerful force the world has ever known for eradicating poverty and creating opportunity, and that's broad-based economic growth.

Now, despite all this progress, the economic relationship between the United States and India is still one of enormous untapped potential. Of all the goods that India imports, less than 10 percent come from the United States. Of all the goods that America exports to the world, less than 2 percent go to India. Our entire trade with your country is still less than our trade with the Netherlands; this is a country with a smaller population than the city of Mumbai. As a result, India is only our 12th largest trade partner.

I have no doubt we can do better than that; we can do much better. There's no reason this nation can't be one of our top trading partners. And that's why we want to work together with you to remove the barriers to increased trade and investment between our nations.

In the United States, we're committed to doing our part. With India and our other G–20 partners, we've resisted the protectionism that

would have plunged the global economy even deeper into recession. Today, our country remains one of the most open economies in the world. And while I make no apologies about doing whatever it takes to encourage job creation and business investment in America, I still work to make sure our efforts don't unfairly target companies and workers from this nation or any nation.

And to further increase our exports to places like India, we're marshalling the full resources of the United States Government to help our companies sell their goods and services in other markets. We're increasing export financing for small and medium-sized businesses. We're being a better advocate for our businesses. We're increasing our trade missions. In fact, my Secretary of Commerce, Gary Locke, will be leading another trade mission to India in the next few months. And we're reforming our export control system, so that even as we strengthen our national security, we make sure that unnecessary barriers don't stand in the way of high-tech trade between our countries. Today I'm pleased to announce that we will work with India to fundamentally reform our controls on exports, which will allow greater cooperation in a range of high-tech sectors and strengthen our nonproliferation efforts.

So we're taking the necessary steps to strengthen this relationship. India can also do its part. Over the past two decades, it has become much easier for companies to do business and invest here in India. It was striking talking to some of the American CEOs who are here who've come frequently over decades and seen the incredible progress that's been made. But I don't think it's any secret that infrastructure, regulatory barriers, and other issues of uncertainty still pose some serious challenges.

Today, India is making major investments in its infrastructure and creating greater transparency to support growth and entrepreneurship. Going forward, that commitment must be matched by a steady reduction in barriers to trade and foreign investment—from agriculture to infrastructure, from retail to telecommunications—because in a global economy, new growth and jobs flow to countries that lower barriers to trade and investment.

These are steps we can take together to strengthen the economic ties between our nations, ties that hold incredible promise for our people and our future: the promise of new jobs, new industries, and new growth. Whether or not that promise is fulfilled depends on us, on the decisions we make and the partnership we build in the coming years.

We must admit it won't always be an easy road, but as I stand here today, I can tell you that I'm absolutely confident we will meet this challenge, because in our two nations, I see the fundamental ingredients to success in the 21st century.

I'm confident because we both cherish the entrepreneurial spirit that empowers innovation and risk-taking and allows them to turn a good idea into a new product or company that changes the world. And we have examples of Indian entrepreneurs and American entrepreneurs sitting right here who've already begun to do that.

And I'm confident because we both know that for those businesses to thrive, our nations need to invest in science and technology, in research and development, and an infrastructure for the 21st century.

I'm confident because we both recognize that knowledge is the currency of the future and that we must give our children the skills and education that success requires in a global economy.

And I'm confident because our countries are blessed with the most effective form of government the world has ever known: democracy. Even if it can be slow at times, even if it can be messy, even if sometimes the election doesn't turn out as you'd like. [*Laughter*]

For we know that when governments are accountable to their people, their people are more likely to prosper and that, over the long run, democracy and economic growth, freedom in the political sphere and freedom in the economic sphere, go hand in hand. We believe that.

What gives me the most confidence about our future is our greatest resource, the drive and ingenuity of our people: workers and entrepreneurs, students and innovators, Indians and Americans, including the nearly 3 million Indian Americans who bind our nations together.

For despite all the sweeping changes of the last few decades, from the reform of the Licensing Raj to the technological revolutions that continue to shape our global economy, it has been people who have driven our progress. It is individual men and women like you who put their shoulder to the wheel of history and push: an American scientist who discovers an agricultural breakthrough; an Indian engineer who builds the next-generation electric car; a small-business owner in Detroit who sells his product to a new company in New Delhi; and all the Mumbaikars who get up every day in this "City of Dreams" to forge a better life for their children, from the boardrooms of world-class Indian companies to the shops in the winding alleys of Dharavi.

This is the spirit of optimism and determination that has driven our people since before we were nations, the same spirit that will drive our future. And that's why I'm thrilled to be in India and with you here today. And that's why I'm confident that we can and will forge new economic partnerships and deliver the jobs and broad-based growth that our peoples so richly deserve. And I am absolutely certain that the relationship between the United States and India is going to be one of the defining partnerships of the 21st century.

Thank you very much, everybody. Thank you.

NOTE: The President spoke at 5:43 p.m. at the Trident Nariman Point Hotel.

Remarks Following a Tour of an Agriculture Exposition and an Open Government and Technology Exposition in Mumbai
November 7, 2010

Well, here's the good news, is that in the United States we are trying to do some of the same things that you're doing: trying to make government more transparent, trying to make government more accountable, trying to make government more efficient. And one of the incredible benefits of the technology we're seeing right here is that in many ways India may be in a position to leapfrog some of the intermediate stages of government service delivery, avoiding some of the 20th-century mechanisms for delivering services and going straight to the 21st.

But many of the issues that you're talking about here are ones that we're trying to apply in the United States as well. For example, in many rural areas in the United States, it's hard sometimes to get to a hospital. Even though the infrastructure may be better developed, there's still significant distances. And to the extent that we can use technology to provide people with basic health information—in some cases, simple diagnoses—that can save people time, it can save the Government money, and we can end up with better health outcomes. And obviously, the same applies for all the services you mentioned.

So I want to congratulate all of you for doing the terrific work. And I look forward to watching this terrific experiment in democracy continue to expand all throughout India, and you'll be a model for countries around the world.

NOTE: The President spoke at 11:15 a.m. at St. Xavier College. Audio was not available for verification of the content of these remarks.

Remarks at a Town Hall Meeting and a Question-and-Answer Session in Mumbai
November 7, 2010

The President. Thank you very much. Everybody, please have a seat. Have a seat. *Namaste.*

Audience members. Namaste.

The President. It is such a pleasure to be here. Now, I have to say, first of all, I don't like speaking after Michelle—[*laughter*]—because she's very good. Also, because she teases me. You notice how she said for you to all ask tough questions. If you want to ask easy questions, that's fine. [*Laughter*]

But on behalf of Michelle and me, I want to thank St. Xavier's university. I want to thank Rector de Souza. I want to thank Principal—I want to get this right—Mascarenhas. [*Laughter*] But it's a little smoother than that when you say it. I want to thank Vice Principal Amonkar and all of you for being such gracious hosts.

And I know it's hot out here today. For you to be so patient with me, I'm very grateful to you. I also want to thank the city of Mumbai and the people of India for giving us such a extraordinary welcome.

In a few minutes, I'll take some questions. I come here not just to speak, but also to listen. I want to have a dialogue with you. And this is one of the wonderful things that I have a chance to do as President of the United States. When I travel, we always try to set up a town hall meeting where we can interact with the next generation, because I want to hear from you. I want to find out what your dreams are, what your fears are, what your plans are for your country.

But if you will indulge me, I also want to say a few words about why I'm so hopeful about the partnership between our two countries and why I wanted to spend some of my time here in India speaking directly to young people like yourselves.

Now, as Michelle said, we have both looked forward to this visit to India for quite some time. We have an extraordinary amount of respect for the rich and diverse civilization that has thrived here for thousands of years. We've drawn strength from India's 20th-century independence struggle, which helped inspire America's own civil rights movement. We've marveled at India's growing economy and it's dynamic democracy. And we have personally enjoyed a wonderful friendship with Prime Minister Singh and Mrs. Kaur over the last 2 years.

But of course, I'm not just here to visit, I'm here because the partnership between India and the United States, I believe, has limitless potential to improve the lives of both Americans and Indians, just as it has the potential to be an anchor of security and prosperity and progress for Asia and for the world.

The U.S.-India relationship will be indispensible in shaping the 21st century. And the reason why is simple: As two great powers and as the world's two largest democracies, the United States and India share common interests and common values, values of self-determination and equality, values of tolerance and a belief in the dignity of every human being.

Already on this trip, I've seen those shared interests and values firsthand. We share a commitment to see that the future belongs to hope and not fear. And I was honored to stay at the Taj Hotel, the site of the 26/11 attacks, and yesterday, in meetings with some of the survivors, I saw firsthand the resilience of the Indian people in overcoming tragedy, just as I reaffirmed our close cooperation in combating terrorism and violent extremism in all of its forms.

We also share struggles for justice and equality. I was humbled to visit Mani Bhavan, where Gandhi helped move India and the world through the strength and dignity of his leadership.

We share a commitment to see that this era after globalization leads to greater opportunity for all our people. And so yesterday at a summit of business leaders and entrepreneurs, we discussed the potential for greater economic cooperation between our two countries, cooperation that could create jobs and opportunity through increased trade and investment, unleashing the potential of individuals in both our countries.

And even as we are countries that look to the future with optimism, Americans and Indians draw strength from tradition and from faith.

This morning Michelle and I enjoyed the chance to join young people here in Mumbai to celebrate Diwali, a holiday that is observed not just here in India, but also in the United States, where millions of Indian Americans have enriched our country. I have to point out, by the way, those of you who had a chance to see Michelle dance, she was moving. And it was just an extraordinary gift for these young people to perform and share this wonderful tradition with us.

Tomorrow in New Delhi, I'll have the opportunity to meet with Prime Minister Singh and many other leaders, and I'll have the privilege to address your Parliament. And there I will discuss in greater detail our efforts to broaden and deepen our cooperation and make some specific announcements on important issues like counterterrorism and regional security, on clean energy and climate change, and on the advance of economic growth and development and democracy around the globe.

Now, just as the sites I've seen and the people I've met here in Mumbai speak to our common humanity, the common thread that runs through the different issues that our countries cooperate on is my determination to take the partnership between our two countries to an entirely new level. Because the United States does not just believe, as some people say, that India is a rising power, we believe that India has already risen. India is taking its rightful place in Asia and on the global stage. And we see India's emergence as good for the United States and good for the world.

But India's future won't simply be determined by powerful CEOs and political leaders, just as I know that the ties among our people aren't limited to contacts between our corporations and our Governments. And that's why I wanted to speak to all of you today, because India's future will be determined by you and by young people like you across this country. You are the future leaders. You are the future innovators and the future educators. You're the future entrepreneurs and the future elected officials.

In this country of more than a billion people, more than half of all Indians are under 30 years old. That's an extraordinary statistic, and it's one that speaks to a great sense of possibility, because in a democracy like India's—or America's—every single child holds within them the promise of greatness. And every child should have the opportunity to achieve that greatness.

Now, most of you are probably close to 20 years old. Just think how the world has changed in those 20 years. India's economy has grown at a breathtaking rate. Living standards have improved for hundreds of millions of people. Your democracy has weathered assassination and terrorism. And meanwhile, around the globe, the cold war is a distant memory, and a new order has emerged, one that's reflected in the 20 members of the G–20 that will come together in Seoul next week, as countries like India assume a greater role on the world stage.

So now the future of this country is in your hands. And before I take your questions, I want you to consider three questions I have for you, questions about what the next 20 years will bring. First, what do you want India to look like in 20 years? Nobody else can answer this question but you. It's your destiny to write. One of the great blessings of living in a democracy is that you can always improve the democracy. As our Founding Fathers wrote in the United States, you can always forge a more perfect Union.

But if you look at India's last 20 years, it's hard not to see the future with optimism. You have the chance to lift another several hundreds of millions of people out of poverty, grow even more this enormous middle class that can fuel growth in this country and beyond. You have the chance to take on greater responsibilities on the global stage while playing a leading role in this hugely important part of the world.

And together with the United States, you can also seize the opportunities afforded by our times: the clean energy technologies that can power our lives and save our planet, the chance to reach new frontiers in outer space, the research and development that can lead to new industry and a higher standard of living, the prospect of advancing the cause of peace and pluralism in our own countries, but also beyond our borders.

Which brings me to a second question: Twenty years from now, what kind of partnership do you want to have with America? Just before I came to speak to all of you today, I visited two expos right in another courtyard here that underscore the kind of progress we can make together. The first focused on agriculture and food security, and I was able to see innovations in technology and research, which are transforming Indian farming.

A farmer showed me how he can receive crop information on his cell phone. Another showed me how tools appropriately sized and weighted for women are helping her and other female farmers increase their productivity. Many of these innovations are the result of public and private collaborations between the United States and India, the same collaboration that helped produce the first Green Revolution in the 1960s.

And tomorrow I will be discussing with Prime Minister Singh how we can advance the cooperation in the 21st century, not only to benefit India, not only to benefit the United States, but to benefit the world. India can become a model for countries around the world that are striving for food security.

The second expo I toured focused on the ways that innovation is empowering Indian citizens to ensure that democracy delivers for them. So I heard directly from citizens in a village hundreds of miles away, through e-Panchayat. I saw new technologies and approaches that allow citizens to get information, or to fight corruption, monitor elections, find out whether their elected official is actually going to work, holding government accountable.

And while these innovations are uniquely India's, their lessons can be applied around the world. So earlier this year at the U.N., I called for a new focus on open societies that support open government and highlighted their potential to strengthen the foundation of freedoms in our own countries, while living up to the ideals that can light the world. And that's what India is starting do with some of this innovation.

We must remember that in some places the future of democracy is still very much in question. Just to give you an example, there are elections that are being held right now in Burma that will be anything but free and fair based on every report that we're seeing. And for too long the people of Burma have been denied the right to determine their own destiny.

So even as we do not impose any system of government on other countries, we, especially young people, must always speak out for those human rights that are universal and the right of people everywhere to make their own decisions about how to shape their future, which will bring me to my final question, and then you guys can start sending questions my way.

How do you—how do each of you—want to make the world a better place? Keep in mind that this is your world to build, your century to shape. And you've got a powerful example of those who went before you. Just as America had the words and deeds of our Founding Fathers to help chart a course towards freedom and justice and opportunity, India has this incredible history to draw on, millennia of civilization, the examples of leaders like Gandhi and Nehru.

As I stood in Mani Bhavan, I was reminded that Martin Luther King made his own pilgrimage to that site over 50 years ago. In fact, we saw the book that he had signed. After he returned home, King said that he was struck by how "Gandhi embodied in his life certain universal principles that are inherent in the moral structure of the universe, and these principles are as inescapable as the law of gravitation."

You have that power within you. You too must embody those principles. For even within this time of great progress, there are great imperfections: the injustice of oppression, the grinding punishment of poverty, the scourge of violent extremism and war. King and Gandhi made it possible for all of us to be here today, me as a President, you as a citizen of a country that's made remarkable progress. Now you have the opportunity and the responsibility to also make this planet a better place. And as you do, you'll have the friendship and partnership of the United States, because we are interested in advancing those same universal principles that are "as inescapable as the law of gravitation."

The lives that you lead will determine whether that opportunity is extended to more of the world's people, so that a child who yearns for a better life in rural India or a family that's fled from violence in Africa, or a dissident who sits in a Burmese prison, or a community that longs for peace in war-torn Afghanistan, whether they are able to achieve their dreams.

And sometimes the challenges may be incredibly hard, and in the face of darkness, we may get discouraged. But we can always draw on the light of those who came before us. I hope you keep that light burning within you, because together the United States and India can shape a century in which our own citizens and the people of the world can claim the hope of a better life.

So thank you very much for your patience. And now you can take Michelle's advice and ask me some tough questions. Thank you very much.

So we have, I think, people in the audience with microphones, and so when they come up, if you could introduce yourself—love to know who you are. And we'll start with that young lady right over there.

Religion/Combating Extremism

Q. Hi, good day, sir. Hi, my name is Anna, and I'm from St. Davis College. My question to you is, what is your take or opinion about jihad or jihadi? Whatever is your opinion? What do you think of them?

The President. Well, the phrase jihad has a lot of meanings within Islam and is subject to a lot of different interpretations. But I will say that, first, Islam is one of the world's great religions. And more than a billion people who practice Islam, the overwhelming majority view their obligations to their religion as ones that reaffirm peace and justice and fairness and tolerance. I think all of us recognize that this great religion in the hands of a few extremists has been distorted to justify violence towards innocent people that is never justified.

And so I think one of the challenges that we face is how do we isolate those who have these distorted notions of religious war and reaffirm those who see faiths of all sorts—whether you are a Hindu or a Muslim or a Christian or a Jew or any other religion or you don't practice a religion—that we can all treat each other with respect and mutual dignity and that some of the universal principles that Gandhi referred to, that those are what we're living up to, as we live in a nation or nations that have very diverse religious beliefs.

And that's a major challenge. It's a major challenge here in India, but it's a challenge obviously around the world. And young people like yourselves can make a huge impact in reaffirming that you can be a stronger observer of your faith without putting somebody else down or visiting violence on somebody else.

I think a lot of these ideas form very early. And how you respond to each other is going to be probably as important as any speech that a President makes in encouraging the kinds of religious tolerance that I think is so necessary in a world that's getting smaller and smaller, where more and more people of different backgrounds, different races, different ethnicities are interacting and working and learning from each other.

And those circumstances—I think all of us have to fundamentally reject the notion that violence is a way to mediate our differences. Okay?

All right. Yes, I may not get to every question. I'll call on this young man right here. Right there, yes.

Materialism/Community Service/Public Service

Q. Good morning, sir. My name is Jehan. I'm from H.R. College. Sir, my question is more about spirituality and moral values. As we see today in today's world, there's more of a materialistic frame of thought when it comes to generations—budding generations. So what do you believe is a possible methodology which governments, whether yours or any other governments in the world, they can adopt to basically incorporate the human core values, the moral values of selflessness, brotherhood, over the materialistic frame of thought which people work by today?

The President. It's a terrific question, and I'm glad you're asking it. India is making enormous progress in part because, like America, it has this incredible entrepreneurial talent, entrepreneurial spirit. And I think we should not underestimate how liberating economic growth can be for a country.

In the United States, I used to work with a lot of churches when I was still a community organizer, before I went to law school. And one of the common phrases among the pastors there was, "It's hard to preach to an empty stomach." It's hard to preach to an empty stomach. If people have severe, immediate material needs— shelter, food, clothing—then that is their focus. And economic growth and development that is self-sustaining can liberate people, allow them—it forms the basis for folks to get an education and to expand their horizons. And that's all for the good.

So I don't want any young person here to be dismissive of a healthy materialism, because in a country like India, there's still a lot of people trapped in poverty. And you should be working to try to lift folks out of poverty, and companies and businesses have a huge role in making that happen.

Now, having said that, if all you're thinking about is material wealth, then I think that shows a poverty of ambition. When I was visiting Gandhi's room, here in Mumbai, it was very telling that the only objects in the room were a mat and a spinning wheel and some sandals, a few papers. And this is a man who changed history like probably no one else in the 20th century in terms of the number of lives that he affected. And he had nothing, except an indomitable spirit.

So everyone has a role to play. And those of you who are planning to go into business, I think it's wonderful that you're going into business, and you should pursue it with all your focus and energy. Those of you, though, who are more inclined to teach or more inclined to public service, you should also feel encouraged that you are playing just as critical a role. And whatever occupation you choose, giving back to the community and making sure that you're reaching back to help people, lift up people who may have been left behind, that's a solemn obligation.

And by the way, it's actually good for you. It's good for your spirit. It's good for your own moral development. It will make you a happier person, knowing that you've given back and you've contributed something.

Last point I would make: I think this is another thing that India and the United States share, is there's a healthy skepticism about public servants, particularly electoral politics. In the United States, people generally have—hold politicians in fairly low esteem, sometimes for good reason, but some of it is just because the view is that somehow government can't do anything right. And here in India, one of the big impediments to development is the fact that in some cases the private sector is moving much faster than the public sector is moving.

And I would just suggest that I hope some of you decide to go ahead and get involved in public service, which can be frustrating. It can be, at times, slow to—you don't see progress as quickly as you'd like. But India is going to need you not just as businessmen, but also as leaders who are helping to reduce bureaucracy and make government more responsive and deliver services more efficiently. That's going to be just as important in the years to come. Because otherwise, you're going to get an imbalance where some are doing very well but broad-based economic growth is not moving as quickly as it could. Okay.

Excellent question.

I'm going to go boy, girl, boy, girl—or girl, boy, girl, boy, just to make sure it's fair. Let's see. This young lady right there. Yes.

President's Values/President's Decisionmaking

Q. Hello.

The President. Hello.

Q. My name is Siddhi Deshpande. I actually wanted to ask you, you mention Mahatma Gandhiji a lot, usually in your speeches. So I was just wondering how exactly do you implement his principles and his values in your day-to-day life, and how do you expect the people in U.S. to implement those values? Thank you.

The President. Well, it's a terrific question. Let me say, first of all, that he, like Dr. King, like Abraham Lincoln, are people who I'm constantly reading and studying, and I find myself falling woefully short of their example all the time. So I'm often frustrated by how far I fall short of their example.

But I do think that at my best, what I'm trying to do is to apply principles that fundamentally come down to something shared in all the world's religions, which is to see yourself in other people, to understand the inherent worth and dignity of every individual, regardless of station, regardless of rank, regardless of wealth, and to absolutely value and cherish and respect that individual, and then, hopefully, try to take that principle of treating others as you would want to be treated and find ways where that can apply itself in communities and in cities and in states and ultimately in the country—in a country and in the world.

As I said, I often find myself falling short of that ideal. But I tend to judge any particular policy based on, is this advancing that spirit, that it's helping individuals realize their potential, that it's making sure that all children are getting an education, so that I'm not just worrying about my children, that I'm thinking, first and foremost, about the United States of America, because that's my responsibility as President, but I'm also recognizing that we are in an interrelationship with other countries in the world and I can't ignore an abuse of human rights in another country. I can't ignore hardships that may be suffering—that may be suffered by somebody of a different nationality.

That, I think, more than anything is what I carry with me on a day-to-day basis. But it's not always apparent that I'm making progress on that front.

One of the other things I draw from all great men and women, like a Gandhi, though, is that on this journey you're going to experience setbacks and you have to be persistent and stubborn, and you just have to keep on going at it. And you'll never roll the boulder all the way up the hill, but you may get it part of the way up. Good.

This gentleman in the blue shirt. Right here. Do we have a microphone? Oh, here we go. Thanks.

U.S. Economy/Midterm Elections/U.S. Foreign Policy/India-U.S. Relations/Trade

Q. Good afternoon, Mr. President.

The President. Good afternoon.

Q. It's an honor to question you. What my question would be is, when you were being elected as President, one of the words you used a lot was "change." After your midterm election, the midterm polls that did take place, it seems that the American people have asked for a change. The change that you will make, how exactly is it going to affect young India, people from my generation?

The President. That's an interesting question.

Q. Thank you.

The President. The United States has gone through probably the toughest 2 years economically as we've gone through since the 1930s. I mean, this was a profound financial crisis and economic shock, and it spilled over to most of the world. India weathered it better than many countries. But most of the work that I did with Prime Minister Singh in the first 2 years in the G–20, we were focused on making sure that the world financial system didn't collapse.

And although we've now stabilized the economy, unemployment in the United States is very high now relative to what it typically has been over the last several decades. And so people are frustrated. And although we're making progress, we're not making progress quickly enough.

And one of the wonderful things about democracy is that when the people are not happy, it is their right, obligation, and duty to express their unhappiness, much to the regret sometimes of incumbents. But that's a good thing. That's a healthy thing.

And my obligation is to make sure that I stick to the principles and beliefs and ideas that will move America forward, because I profoundly believe that we have to invest in education, that that will be the primary driver of growth in the future, that we've got to invest in a strong infrastructure, that we have to make sure that we are

taking advantage of opportunities like clean energy.

But it also requires me to make some midcourse corrections and adjustments. And how those play themselves out over the next several months will be a matter of me being in discussions with the Republican Party, which is now going to be controlling the House of Representatives. And there are going to be areas where we disagree, and hopefully, there are going to be some areas where we agree.

Now, you asked specifically, how do I think it will affect policy towards India. I actually think that the United States has a enormous fondness for India, partly because there are so many Indian Americans and because of the shared values that we have. And so there is a strong bipartisan belief that India is going to be a critical partner with the United States in the 21st century. That was true when George Bush was President; that was true when Bill Clinton was President. It was true under Democratic and Republican control of Congress.

So I don't think that fundamental belief is going to be altered in any significant way. I do think that one of the challenges that we're going to be facing in the United States is in—at a time when we're still recovering from this crisis, how do we respond to some of the challenges of globalization? Because the fact of the matter is, is that for most of my lifetime—I'll turn 50 next year—for most of my lifetime, the United States was such a dominant economic power, we were such a large market, our industry, our technology, our manufacturing was so significant that we always met the rest of the world economically on our terms. And now because of the incredible rise of India and China and Brazil and other countries, the United States remains the largest economy and the largest market, but there's real competition out there.

And that's potentially healthy. It makes—Michelle was saying earlier I like tough questions because it keeps me on my toes. Well, this will keep America on its toes. And I'm positive we can compete because we've got the most open, most dynamic entrepreneurial culture, we've got some of the finest universities in the world, incredible research and technology. But it means that we're going to have to compete.

And I think that there's going to be a tug of war within the United States between those who see globalization as a threat and want to retrench and those who accept that we live in a open, integrated world which has challenges and opportunities and we've got to manage those challenges and manage those opportunities, but we shouldn't be afraid of them.

And so what that means, for example, is on issues of trade, part of the reason I'm traveling through Asia this week is I believe that the United States will grow and prosper if we are trading with Asia. It's the fastest growing region in the world. We want access to your markets. We think we've got good products to sell; you think that you've got good products to sell us. This can be a win-win situation.

So I want to make sure that we're here because this will create jobs in the United States and it can create jobs in India. But that means that we've got to negotiate this changing relationship. Back in the 1960s or seventies, the truth is the American economy could be open even if our trading partners' economies weren't open. So if India was protecting certain sectors of its economy, it didn't really have such a big effect on us. We didn't need necessarily reciprocity because our economy was so much larger.

Well, now things have changed. So it's not unfair for the United States to say, look, if our economy is open to everybody, countries that trade with us have to change their practices to open up their markets to us. There has to be reciprocity in our trading relationship. And if we can have those kinds of conversations, fruitful, constructive conversations about how we produce win-win situations, then I think we'll be fine.

If the American people feel that trade is just a one-way street, where everybody is selling to the enormous U.S. market, but we can never sell what we make anywhere else, then people in the United States will start thinking, well, this is a bad deal for us. And that could end up leading to a more protectionist instinct in both parties, not just among Democrats, but also among Republicans. So that's what we have to guard against. Okay.

All right, it's a young lady's turn. This young lady with the glasses. Yes.

Pakistan/India-Pakistan Relations

Q. A very warm welcome to you to India, sir.

The President. Thank you so much.

Q. My name is Afsheen Irani, and I'm from H.R. College of Commerce and Economics. We were the privileged college to host Mr. Otis Moss this January. Sir, my question to you is why is Pakistan so important an ally to America, so far as America has never called it a terrorist state?

The President. Well—no, no, it's a good question. And I must admit I was expecting it. [*Laughter*] Pakistan is an enormous country. It is a strategically important country not just for the United States, but for the world. It is a country whose people have enormous potential, but it is also right now a country that within it has some of the extremist elements that we discussed in the first question. That's not unique to Pakistan, but obviously, it exists in Pakistan.

The Pakistani Government is very aware of that. And what we have tried to do over the last several years, certainly—I'll just speak to my foreign policy—has been to engage aggressively with the Pakistani Government to communicate that we want nothing more than a stable, prosperous, peaceful Pakistan and that we will work with the Pakistani Government in order to eradicate this extremism that we consider a cancer within the country that can potentially engulf the country.

And I will tell you that I think the Pakistani Government understands now the potential threat that exists within their own borders. There are more Pakistanis who've been killed by terrorists inside Pakistan than probably anywhere else.

Now, progress is not as quick as we'd like partly because when you get into, for example, some of the northwest territories, these are very—this is very difficult terrain, very entrenched. The Pakistani Army has actually shifted some of its emphasis and focus into those areas. But that's not originally what their armed forces were designed to do, and so they're having to adapt and adjust to these new dangers and these new realities.

I think there is a growing recognition—but it's something that it doesn't happen overnight—of what a profound problem this is. And so our feeling has been to be honest and forthright with Pakistan, to say we are your friend, that this is a problem, and we will help you, but the problem has to be addressed.

Now, let me just make this point, because obviously the history between India and Pakistan is incredibly complex and was born of much tragedy and much violence. And so it may be surprising to some of you to hear me say this, but I am absolutely convinced that the country that has the biggest stake in Pakistan's success is India. I think that if Pakistan is unstable, that's bad for India. If Pakistan is stable and prosperous, that's good.

Because India is on the move. And it is absolutely in your interests, at a time when you're starting to succeed in incredible ways on the global economic stage, that you [don't]° want the distraction of security instability in your region. So my hope is, is that over time trust develops between the two countries, that dialogue begins—perhaps on less controversial issues, building up to more controversial issues—and that over time there's a recognition that India and Pakistan can live side by side in peace and that both countries can prosper.

That will not happen tomorrow. But I think that needs to be our ultimate goal. Okay. And by the way, the United States stands to be a friend and a partner in that process, but we can't impose that on India and Pakistan. Ultimately, India and Pakistan have to arrive at their own understandings in terms of how the relationship evolves.

Okay. I've got time for one more question. It's a guy's turn. This young man right here in the striped shirt.

° White House correction.

Afghanistan

Q. Good afternoon, Mr. President. It's an absolute honor to hear you, and I must say this, that one day I hope I'd be half as good as a leader as you are today.

The President. Well, you're very kind. Thank you.

Q. Mr. President, my question relates to your Afghanistan policy. In light of your statements that the troop withdrawal would start in 2011, there have been recent developments that would indicate that U.S.A. has been in talks with Taliban so as to strike out a stable government in Afghanistan as when you withdraw. Now, does this point to the acceptance of the inevitability of the U.S. to fulfill the vision which they had, with which they invaded Afghanistan in 2001? Does it point out to their inability to take a military control of all the tumultuous southern regions so that they can install a stable government? You'll notice that in Iraq where there's a lot of instability now. So does it point to a sort of tacit acceptance of U.S. inability to create harmony in Afghanistan?

The President. First of all, I want to just unpack some of the assumptions inside the question because they're broadly based in fact, but I want to be very precise here.

I have said that starting in the summer of next year, July 2011, we will begin drawing down our troop levels, but we will not be removing all our troops. Keep in mind that we ramped up significantly, because the idea was that for 7 years we had just been in a holding pattern; we'd had just enough troops to keep Kabul intact, but the rest of the countryside was deteriorating in fairly significant ways. There wasn't a real strategy. And my attitude was, I don't want to, 7 years from now or 8 years from now, be in the exact same situation. That's not a sustainable equilibrium.

So I said, let's put more troops in to see if we can create more space and stability and time for Afghan security forces to develop, and then let's begin drawing down our troops as we're able to stand up Afghan security forces.

Now, in fact, it turns out that in Iraq—you mentioned Iraq as a parallel—in Iraq, we have been relatively successful at doing that. The Government is taking way too long to get formed, and that is a source of frustration to us and, I'm sure, to the Iraq people. Having said that, though, if you think about it, it's been 7 months since the election, and violence levels are actually lower in Iraq than they've been just about any time since the war started, at a time when we pulled back our forces significantly. So it shows that it is possible to train effective, indigenous security forces so that they can provide their own security. And hopefully, politics then resolves differences, as opposed to violence.

Now, Afghan, I think, is actually more complicated, more difficult, partly because it's a much poorer country. It does not have as strong a tradition of a central government; civil service is very underdeveloped. And so I think that the pace at which we're drawing down is going to be determined in part by military issues, but it's also going to be determined by politics. And that is, is it possible for the—a sizeable portion of the Pashtun population in Afghanistan that may be teetering back and forth between Taliban or a central government, is it possible for them to feel that their ethnicity, their culture, their numerical position in the country is adequately represented, and can they do that within the context of a broader constitutional Afghan Government?

And I think that's a worthy conversation to have. So what we've said to President Karzai—because this is being initiated by him—what we've said is, if former Taliban members or current Taliban members say that they are willing to disassociate themselves with Al Qaida, renounce violence as a means of achieving their political gain—aims, and are willing to respect the Afghan Constitution so that, for example, women are treated with all the right that men are afforded, then, absolutely, we support the idea of a political resolution of some of these differences.

Now, there are going to be some elements that are affiliated to the Taliban that are also affiliated with Al Qaida or LT or these other organizations, these extremists that are irreconcilable. They will be there. And there will need to be a military response to those who would perpetrate the kind of violence that we saw here in Mumbai in a significant ongoing way or the kind that we saw on 9/11 in New York City.

But I think a stable Afghanistan is achievable. Will it look exactly as I might design a democracy? Probably not. It will take on an Afghan character.

I do think that there are lessons that India has to show not just countries like Afghanistan, but countries in sub-Saharan Africa. I mean, some of the incredible work that I saw being done in the agricultural sector is applicable to widely dispersed rural areas in a place like Afghanistan and could—I promise you, if we can increase farmers' yields in Afghanistan by 20 percent or 25 percent, and they can then get their crops to market, and they're cutting out a middleman and they're ending up seeing a better standard of life for themselves, that goes a long way in encouraging them to affiliate with a modern world.

And so India's investment in development in Afghanistan is appreciated. Pakistan has to be a partner in this process. In fact, all countries in the region are going to be partners in this process. And the United States welcomes that. We don't think we can do this alone.

But part of our—and this is probably a good way to end—part of my strong belief is that around the world, your generation is poised to solve some of my generation's mistakes and my parents' generation's mistakes. You'll make your own mistakes, but there's such incredible potential and promise for you to start pointing in new directions in terms of how economies are organized, in terms of how moral precepts and values and principles are applied, in how nations work together to police each other so that they're not—so that when there's genocide, or there is ethnic cleansing, or there are gross violations of human rights, that an international community joins together and speaks with one voice; so that economic integration isn't a source of fear or anxiety, but rather is seen as enormous promise and potential; where we're able to tackle problems that we can't solve by ourselves.

I went to a lower school—do you call them high schools here? It's sort of a high school. And Michelle and I saw this wonderful exhibit of global warming and the concerns that these young people had—and they were 14, 15. And their energy and their enthusiasm was infectious. And I asked them, which one of you are going to be scientists who are going to try to solve this problem? And all of them raised their hands. And I said, well, this is hugely important for India. And they said, no, not for India, for the world.

You see, they—their ambitions were not just to be great scientists for India. Their ambition was to be a great scientist for the world because they understood that something like climate change or clean energy, that's not an American problem or an Indian problem, that's a human problem. And all of us are going to have to be involved in finding solutions to it.

And as I listen to all of you, with your wonderful questions, I am incredibly optimistic and encouraged that you will help find those solutions in the years to come.

So thank you very much for your hospitality. Thank you, everybody.

NOTE: The President spoke at 11:45 a.m. at St. Xavier College. In his remarks, he referred to Gursharan Kaur, wife of Prime Minister Manmohan Singh of India; and President Hamid Karzai of Afghanistan. He also referred to the Lashkar-e-Taiba terrorist organization. A student referred to Otis Moss III, pastor, Trinity United Church of Christ in Chicago, IL. The transcript released by the Office of the Press Secretary also included the remarks of the First Lady.

Statement on the Parliamentary Elections in Burma
November 7, 2010

The November 7 elections in Burma were neither free nor fair, and failed to meet any of the internationally accepted standards associated with legitimate elections. The elections were based on a fundamentally flawed process and demonstrated the regime's continued preference for repression and restriction over inclusion and transparency.

One of the starkest flaws of this exercise was the regime's continued detention of more than 2,100 political prisoners, including Aung San Suu Kyi, thereby denying them any opportunity to participate in the process. The unfair electoral laws and overtly partisan Election Commission ensured that Burma's leading prodemocracy party, the National League for Democracy, was silenced and sidelined. The regime denied the registration of certain ethnic parties, cancelled elections in numerous ethnic areas, and stage-managed the campaign process to ensure that prodemocracy and opposition candidates who did compete faced insurmountable obstacles. Ultimately, elections cannot be credible when the regime rejects dialogue with opponents and represses the most basic freedoms of expression, speech, and assembly.

We will monitor the situation in Burma closely in the weeks and months ahead. The United States will continue to implement a strategy of pressure and engagement in accordance with conditions on the ground in Burma and the actions of the Burmese authorities. We renew our calls for the authorities to free Aung San Suu Kyi and all other political prisoners immediately and unconditionally, cease systematic violations of human rights, begin to hold human rights violators accountable, and welcome prodemocracy and ethnic minority groups into a long-overdue dialogue. Only genuine, inclusive dialogue can place Burma on the path to a truly representative democracy which upholds human rights and builds a better future for its citizens.

NOTE: The statement referred to Aung San Suu Kyi, leader of the National League for Democracy in Burma.

Remarks at a Welcoming Ceremony in New Delhi, India
November 8, 2010

Well, first of all, I want to thank all the people of India for the extraordinary hospitality and welcome that Michelle and I and my delegation have already received.

And we took this trip with the intention of strengthening what is already an incredible friendship between the United States and India. As I've said earlier during my visit, I believe that the partnership between the United States and India will be one of the defining partnerships of the 21st century. We are the two largest democracies in the world. We share extraordinary people-to-people contacts. Most importantly, we share a core set of values.

And my hope is that during the course of these discussions between myself and the Prime Minister, myself and the President, and other members of the Indian delegation, that we will be able to continue to build on the commercial ties that we already have to strengthen our cooperation in our bilateral relations in the international economy; that we'll be able to focus on issues like counterterrorism in order to assure that both the United States and India are secure

well into the future; that we can build on the people-to-people ties that are in part grounded in the millions of Indian Americans who contribute so much to our country and help give us an appreciation of Indian life; and that, given that India is not simply an emerging power, but now is a world power, that the United States and India will be able to work together to promote the international principles, the rules of interaction between nations that can promote peace and stability and prosperity not only for our two nations, but for the world as a whole.

So to all the people of India, Michelle and I express our extraordinary thanks for the wonderful hospitality that we've received, and also we want to send our warmest regards from the people of the United States to all the people of India.

Thank you so much.

NOTE: The President spoke at 9:57 a.m. at the Rashtrapati Bhavan. In his remarks, he referred to Prime Minister Manmohan Singh and President Pratibha Devisingh Patil of India.

The President's News Conference With Prime Minister Manmohan Singh of India in New Delhi
November 8, 2010

Prime Minister Singh. Your Excellency, President Barack Obama, distinguished representatives of the media, I'm delighted to welcome President Obama and his gracious wife on their first visit to our country. I welcome the President as a personal friend and a great charismatic leader who has made a deep imprint on world affairs through his inclusive vision of peace, security, and welfare for all peoples and all nations.

The President and the First Lady have made an abiding impression on the people of India with their warmth, with their grace, and with their commitment to promoting the relationship between our two great democracies.

President Obama yesterday characterized the India-U.S. partnership as one of the defining and indispensable partnerships of the 21st century. In my discussion with the President, we have decided to accelerate the deepening of our ties and to work as equal partners in a strategic relationship that will positively and decisively influence world peace, stability, and progress.

We welcome the decision by the United States to lift controls on exports of high-technology items and the technologies to India and support India's membership in multilateral export control regimes such as the Nuclear Suppliers Group. This is a manifestation of the growing trust and confidence in each other.

We have agreed on steps to expand our cooperation in space, civil nuclear defense, and other high-end sectors. We have announced specific initiatives in the areas of clean energy, health, and agriculture. These include a joint clean energy research and development center, the establishment of a global disease detection center in India, and an agreement for cooperation in weather and crop forecasting.

We have decided to hold a higher education summit next year. Cooperation in the field of education holds great promise because no two other countries are better equipped to be partners in building the knowledge economy of the future.

The United States is one of our largest trading partners. Our trade is balanced and growing. India is among the fastest growing sources of investment in the United States. Indian investments have helped to increase the competitiveness of the U.S. economy. We welcome increased U.S. investments and high-technology flows in key sectors of our economy, including the sector of nuclear energy.

We have agreed to facilitate trade and people-to-people exchanges, recognizing that protectionism is detrimental to both our economies.

I conveyed our gratitude to the President for the cooperation we have received in our counterterrorism measures post-Mumbai. We will start a new homeland security dialogue to deepen this cooperation.

We had a detailed exchange on the situation in our extended region, including East Asia, Afghanistan, Pakistan, and West Asia. We have a shared vision of security, stability, and prosperity in Asia based on an open and inclusive regional architecture. We have agreed to broaden our strategic dialogue to cover other regions and areas and initiate joint projects in Africa and Afghanistan.

As states possessing nuclear weapons, we have today put forth a common vision of a world without nuclear weapons and decided to lead global efforts for nonproliferation and universal and nondiscriminatory global nuclear disarmament. This is a historic and bold bilateral initiative.

We also decided to strengthen cooperation to tackle nuclear terrorism, and we welcome U.S. participation in the Global Center of Nuclear Energy Partnership, which will be set up in India.

President Obama is a sincere and a valued friend of our country, and our discussions have led to a meeting of minds. Ours is a partnership based on common values and interests, a shared vision of the world, and the deep-rooted ties of friendship among our two peoples. I look forward to working with the President to realize the enormous potential of this partnership of our two countries.

I now invite President Obama to make his remarks. And I thank you.

President Obama. Thank you very much, Prime Minister Singh, and good afternoon, everyone. I want to begin by saying how thrilled my wife Michelle and I and our entire delegation are to be here in India. We have been received with incredible warmth and incredible hospitality. And that includes the hospitality of our friends, Prime Minister Singh and his lovely wife Mrs. Kaur, who we thank for such graciousness and a wonderful dinner last night.

As I've said throughout my visit, I have come to India because I believe that the relationship between the United States and India is indispensable to addressing the challenges of our time, from creating economic opportunity for our people to confronting terrorism and violent extremism, from preventing the spread of nuclear weapons to addressing climate change, from the development that gives people and nations a path out of poverty to advancing human rights and values that are universal. None of this will be possible without strong cooperation between the United States and India.

Moreover, as Prime Minister Singh alluded to, ours is no ordinary relationship. As the world's two largest democracies, as large and growing free market economies, as diverse, multiethnic societies with strong traditions of pluralism and tolerance, we have not only an opportunity, but also a responsibility to lead.

And that's why I believe that the relationship between the United States and India will, in fact, be one of the defining partnerships of the

21st century. That's why I've worked with the Prime Minister, a man of extraordinary intellect and great integrity, to deepen and broaden the cooperation between our countries. And I very much look forward to addressing the Indian Parliament and the people of India later today to discuss how the United States and India can take our partnership to the next level, with a vision of how we can work together as global partners.

With the progress we've made today, we're seeing just how broad and deep our cooperation can be. As President, I've had the opportunity to appear with many of my foreign counterparts at press conferences such as this, but I cannot remember an occasion when we have agreed to so many new partnerships across so many areas as we have during my visit.

We've expanded trade and investment to create prosperity for our people. The major trade deals that were signed in Mumbai were an important step forward in elevating India to one of America's top trading partners. Today I'm pleased to welcome India's preliminary agreement to purchase 10 C–17 cargo planes, which will enhance Indian capabilities and support 22,000 jobs back in the United States.

We agreed to reform our controls on exports, and the United States will remove Indian organizations from the so-called entity list, which will allow greater cooperation in a range of high-tech sectors like civil space and defense. And we agreed to keep working to reduce trade barriers and resist protectionism.

As a result of this visit, we are already beginning to implement our civil nuclear agreement. We agreed to deepen our cooperation in pursuit of clean energy technologies, and this includes the creation of a new clean energy research center here in India and continuing our joint research into solar, biofuels, shale gas, and building efficiency. And we agreed to new partnerships including forestry and sustainable development of land to help meet the commitments we made at Copenhagen to combat climate change.

To ensure the safety of our citizens, we're deepening our efforts to prevent terrorism. Cooperation between our countries' intelligence and law enforcement communities has already reached unprecedented levels. And today we're taking another step, a new effort between our Department of Homeland Security and the Indian Ministry of Home Affairs to improve security at our ports, our airports, and our borders.

I also discussed with the Prime Minister our efforts in Afghanistan and once again thanked him and the Indian people for the generous contributions that India has made towards development and improving the lives of the Afghan people. We agreed on the need for all nations in the region to work together and ensure that there are no safe havens for terrorists.

We're expanding our efforts to prevent nuclear proliferation. In keeping with its commitment at our Nuclear Security Summit, India will build a new center of excellence for nuclear energy and security to help reach our goal of securing vulnerable nuclear materials in 4 years.

Given India's growing role in the region, we also agreed to deepen our consultations on East Asia. Given India's growing role on the world stage, we'll expand our dialogue on global issues. And we discussed the need for international institutions, including the United Nations, to reflect the realities of the 21st century, which I will discuss further in my address to Parliament.

Finally, we continue to expand partnerships between our peoples. To promote global health, we're moving ahead with a new disease detection center here in New Delhi. Building on our successful efforts to expand educational exchanges, including our Singh-Obama 21st Century Knowledge Initiative, we'll convene a summit to forge new collaborations in higher education. And we're announcing two initiatives today that harness technology to deliver progress for our people.

Building on the Indian and American agricultural collaboration that led to the Green Revolution, we're launching a new partnership for a Evergreen Revolution to improve food security around the world. We're also launching a new partnership to promote open government and to empower citizens. And in my address to Parliament, I'll be discussing why these efforts can be models for the kind of cooperation that not only benefits America and India, but benefits other nations as well.

So taken together, all of these partnerships, all these initiatives make it clear the relationship between the United States and India is stronger, deeper, and broader than ever before.

So, Mr. Prime Minister, again I thank you for your partnership and for your friendship. I am confident that as India's influence in the world continues to rise, so too will the opportunities for even closer cooperation between our two countries. And that will mean even greater security and prosperity for India, for the United States, for this region, and for the world.

Thank you very much, Mr. Prime Minister.

Moderator. Thank you, Mr. President.

The Prime Minister and the President would be happy to take two questions each from the Indian and the American media. You are requested to please restrict yourself to one question either to the Prime Minister or the President and indicate whom the question is addressed to. The first question goes to the American side.

White House Press Secretary Robert L. Gibbs. Scott Wilson from the Washington Post.

India-Pakistan Relations

Q. Thank you, Mr. President, Prime Minister.

Mr. President, as—after a difficult and violent summer in Kashmir, perhaps the chief flashpoint between your chief ally in the Afghanistan war and India, could you explain your administration's policy towards Kashmir and what role the United States might play in resolving that crisis? And if I might, could you please—this morning you called India a world power. Is it possible anymore to stand in the way of India's bid for a permanent seat on the U.N. Security Council?

And, Prime Minister——

Moderator. Sir, I will request you to please restrict yourself to one question.

Q. Not one each?

Moderator. Please one question, if it's possible. Please restrict yourself to one question to one of the leaders. Thank you.

Q. Okay. Prime Minister—may I address the Prime Minister?

Moderator. All right.

Q. Thank you. To follow on a question that was asked yesterday by a student in Mumbai, do you believe that the United States should refer to Pakistan as a terrorist state?

President Obama. With respect to Kashmir, obviously, this is a longstanding dispute between India and Pakistan. As I said yesterday, I believe that both Pakistan and India have an interest in reducing tensions between the two countries. The United States cannot impose a solution to these problems, but I've indicated to Prime Minister Singh that we are happy to play any role that the parties think is appropriate in reducing these tensions. That's in the interests of the region, it's in the interests of the two countries involved, and it's in the interests of the United States of America.

So my hope is that conversations will be taking place between the two countries. They may not start on that particular flashpoint. There may be confidence-building measures that need to take place. But I'm absolutely convinced that it is both in India's and Pakistan's interest to reduce tensions, and that will enable them, I think, to focus on the range of both challenges and opportunities that each country faces.

I do want to make this point, though, that I think Prime Minister Singh, throughout his career and throughout his Prime Ministership, has consistently spoken out both publicly and privately on his desire, his personal commitment, to reduce tensions between India and Pakistan. And for that, I very much commend him. I think Prime Minister Singh is sincere and relentless in his desire for peace.

And so my hope is, is that both sides can, over the next several months, several years, find mechanisms that are appropriate for them to work out what are these very difficult issues.

Mr. Prime Minister.

Q. [*Inaudible*]

President Obama. Oh, well, you know, I was instructed to only take one question. [*Laughter*] It looks like the Indian and the American press are collaborating. That's not the kind of partnership we were looking for. [*Laughter*] But I will be addressing that issue in my speech in Parliament today, so if you'll just have a little bit of patience.

Prime Minister Singh. Mr. President, as far as India's relations with Pakistan are concerned, I've always maintained that a strong, peaceful, moderate Pakistan is in the interest of India, is in the interest of South Asia and the world as a whole.

We are committed to engage Pakistan. We are committed to resolve all outstanding issues between our two countries, including the word "K"; we're not afraid of that. But it is our request that you cannot simultaneously be talking and at the same time the terror machine is as active as ever before. Once Pakistan moves away from this terror-induced coercion, we will be very happy to engage productively with Pakistan to resolve all outstanding issues.

India-U.S. Relations

Moderator. Smita Prakash of ANI [Asia News International].

Q. Mr. President, my question to you, sir, you've consistently said India, as an emerging power, has potential to be America's important—most important strategic partner. What is your vision for India in the next decade? And how vital is this relationship for your administration—in your administration's worldview? Thank you.

President Obama. Well, first of all, this relationship is extraordinarily important to me, and don't just take my word for it, I think, look at our actions. Obviously, this trip is—been of enormous significance. It's no accident that this is the longest time that I've spent in a foreign country since I've been President.

And both the Prime Minister and I have alluded to why I think this partnership can be so important. We are the world's two largest democracies. We have both a set of values and principles that we share that I believe are universal: the belief in individual liberty, in freedom of the press, in freedom of political assembly, in human rights. We both have large market economies.

And the person-to-person contacts between India and the United States are unparalleled.

We have millions of Indian Americans who are helping to grow our country each and every day. And we have hundreds of thousands of students from India who are studying in the United States and then bringing back what they've learned to help develop India.

And so on the commercial level, on the person-to-person level, the strategic level, I think this partnership is incredibly important.

As I said yesterday, I don't think India is emerging; it has emerged. India is a key actor on the world stage. And given that we have these values that we share, at a time when there are still too many conflicts, there are still too many misunderstandings between nations, when principles like democracy and human rights too often are not observed, for our two countries to be able to stand together to promote those principles—in international forums, by the example that we set, by the bilateral ties that we form—I think can be incredibly powerful and incredibly important.

And one last point I want to make on this: This is a belief that is shared by Republicans and Democrats in the United States. I mean, if you think about what's happened in our relationship, how it's evolved over the last 15 to 20 years—you had President Clinton, a Democrat; President Bush, a Republican; and now me, another Democrat—each of us reaffirming in a steady, committed way, why the U.S.-India relationship is so important.

And so we are going to continue to cultivate this. We will continue to nurture it. We have business leaders who are here today and have been working actively in the private sector to strengthen those ties. We want to make sure that our Governments are acting in that same constructive way. And if we do so, then I think that's not only going to benefit India and the United States, but I think ultimately will benefit the world as well.

Prime Minister Singh. The foremost concern of the Indian polity is to grapple with the problem of poverty, ignorance, and disease, which still afflict millions of our citizens. For that, we need a strong, resurgent, robust rate of economic growth. And it is a growth rate which is within our reach. Our objective is to sustain a growth rate of 9 to 10 percent per annum in the next three decades. And in that process, the help of the United States is of enormous significance.

We need a global trading system which is— does not encourage protectionism, which enables our entrepreneurs to make use of the enormous opportunities that processes of globalization now offer. We need the American assistance by way of export of capital. We welcome American investments in our economy.

I've mentioned earlier, also on several occasions, India needs an investment of a trillion dollars in the next 5 years in its infrastructure, and we would welcome American contribution in fulfilling that ambition of ours.

America is a home of high technology. We need that technology to upgrade our skills both in the civilian sector and also in the defense sector. So I attach great importance to strengthening in every possible way India's cooperation with the United States. This is truly a relationship which can become a defining relationship for this 21st blessed century of ours.

White House Press Secretary Gibbs. Christi Parsons with the Chicago Tribune.

U.S. Economy/Global Economic Stabilization

Q. Thank you very much. This question is for you, President Obama, but if the Prime Minister chooses to weigh in on it, that would be lovely.

Mr. President, the German Finance Minister says this of recent Fed decisions: "It doesn't add up when the Americans accuse the Chinese of currency manipulation and then, with the help of their central bank's printing presses, artificially lower the value of the dollar." Might this, in fact, look hypocritical to other world leaders as you head to the G–20 to talk about this and other issues? How do you address it? And do you expect support from the Indian Government in your press to get the Chinese Government to appreciate the value of the currency?

Thank you.

President Obama. First of all, Christi, as you're aware, the Federal Reserve is an independent body. It doesn't take orders from the White House, and it's important as a policy matter, as an institutional matter, that we don't comment on particular Fed actions.

I will say that the Fed's mandate, my mandate, is to grow our economy. And that's not just good for the United States, that's good for the world as a whole.

The United States has been an engine for growth, for trade, for opportunity for decades now. And we've just gone through an extraordinary economic trauma, which has resulted in some extraordinary measures. And the worst thing that could happen to the world economy, not ours—not just ours, but the entire world's economy—is if we end up being stuck with no growth or very limited growth. And I think that's the Fed's concern, and that's my concern as well.

Now, when we go to the G–20, we're going to be talking about a whole host of issues, including how do we start creating balanced and sustainable growth. And if you think about what's happened at the G–20 over the last couple of years, the first G–20 I participated in was all about putting out a fire. We had an immediate crisis in the financial sector that had to be dealt with. And working with outstanding leaders like Prime Minister Singh, we were able to deal with it, and that immediate crisis was contained.

Subsequently, we've talked about how do we maintain growth, how do we start looking at fiscal consolidation and making sure that countries that may have overextended themselves for a long time start getting their houses in order. But part of balanced growth is also a recognition that we can't continue to sustain a situation in which some countries are maintaining massive surpluses, others massive deficits, and there never is the kind of adjustments with respect to currency that would lead to a more balanced growth pattern.

Now, I should point out that India is—has been part of the solution and not part of the problem. As Prime Minister Singh mentioned, generally, there's a balanced growth pattern with respect to India. We've got a—excellent trade ties with India. India has been moving in a more liberal direction consistently under Prime Minister Singh's leadership. And India has been a very constructive partner with us in some of these international issues. I expect that will continue.

So I'm sure that we'll have more commentary at the G–20 when we get to Seoul. Every country, I think, is concerned right now about what other countries are doing at a time when the recovery is still fragile. But the bottom line is that every country that participates in the G–20 will benefit if the United States economy is growing.

Prime Minister Singh. Ladies and gentlemen, I don't claim to have any expert knowledge of the working of the American economies. But I do know one thing: that a strong, robust, fast-growing United States is in the interest of the world. And therefore, anything that would stimulate the underlying growth impulses of entrepreneurship in the United States would help the cause of global prosperity.

India-U.S. Relations/Commercial Relationship With India

Moderator. The fourth and last question to Maya Mirchandani of NDTV [New Delhi Television].

Q. Thank you. This question is for President Obama, but, Mr. Prime Minister, I'd request you as well to answer it if that's possible since you're taking the other questions as well.

But just taking forward, I think, what my colleague from the U.S. media just said, the American press has been full of headlines on this visit of yours, about the 50,000 jobs that have been created because of deals that have been struck around this visit. Critics argue that unemployment rates in India are also very high. So what does India get out of all these deals that have been struck and this visit? And also, isn't the outsourcing bogey a little misdirected, given that it's become such a hot-button issue? The job losses are really in the manufacturing sector, and they're going to China, which is the greater threat.

President Obama. Well, first of all, I don't think you've heard me make outsourcing a bogeyman during the course of my visit. In fact, I explicitly said in my address in Mumbai to the Business Council that I think both countries are operating on some stereotypes that have outlived their usefulness.

In every discussion that I've had with Indian businesses, what I've seen is that our countries are matched up in a way that allows for enormous win-win potential. So you mentioned that some of the deals that we have struck are ones that will create jobs in the United States. That's absolutely true. We're very proud of some of our high-tech industries, and we think that we make some of the best products in the world, and we want to sell them to a growing Indian market.

But it turns out that those same technologies are ones that will allow Indian entrepreneurs to grow and to thrive and to create jobs right here in India. And that's true at the large scale; if we're helping to build up Indian infrastructure, then that helps to knit the country together and get goods and products and services to market.

It's true of the small scale. I mean, I had these amazing conversations down in Mumbai with Indian businesspeople who had taken American technology—in one case it was solar cells; in another case it was some of the equipment designed to be used for electric cars—and they were using those technologies in new ways in India, using different business models that were—that applied uniquely to India, to make profits and to do good here in India, and to create jobs here in India.

So I think that the pattern that you're going to see is that U.S. companies are creating jobs in the United States with technologies where we've got a lead. Indian businesses are then going to take those technologies and apply them in India to grow Indian businesses as well. And that's going to be a win-win for both. Those are the kinds of patterns that, I think, make this relationship so important.

And when I go back home to the United States—part of the reason that I advertise these 50,000 jobs is I want to be able to say to the American people when they ask me, "Well, why are you spending time with India, aren't they taking our jobs?"—I want to be able to say, actually, you know what, they just created 50,000 jobs. And that's why we shouldn't be resorting to protectionist measures, we shouldn't be thinking that it's just a one-way street. I want both my—the citizens in the United States and citizens in India to understand the benefits of commercial ties between the two countries.

Prime Minister Singh. Well, as far as India is concerned, India is not in the business of stealing jobs from the United States of America. Our outsourcing industry, I believe, has helped to improve the productive capacity and productivity of American industry. And the new deals that have been struck, they all happen to be in infrastructure, and infrastructure today is the biggest bottleneck to the faster growth of India, to the faster growth of employment. And therefore, these deals that the President has mentioned are truly an example of trade being a win-win situation for both our countries.

In fact, I have a vision, when the G–20 meets later in the month in Seoul, that the world needs a new balance between deficit countries and surplus countries, and that balance has to be restored by paying more attention to the development—of the development potential, including infrastructure development and energy infrastructure, agricultural infrastructure in the poorer countries of the world.

That is the challenge before the global statesmanship. And I do hope that the Group of Twenty, when it meets in Seoul, with the active guidance and support of President Obama, who in a way is the father of the Group of Twenty— it was his initiative which led to the creation of the Group of Twenty—this group will, I sincerely hope, grapple with this issue of rebalancing growth by laying emphasis on faster growth in the countries which are described normally as developing world.

NOTE: The President's news conference began at 1 p.m. at the Hyderabad House. In his remarks, the President referred to Gursharan Kaur, wife of Prime Minister Singh. A reporter referred to Minister of Finance Wolfgang Schaeuble of Germany.

Joint Statement by President Barack Obama and Prime Minister Manmohan Singh of India
November 8, 2010

Reaffirming their nations' shared values and increasing convergence of interests, Prime Minister Manmohan Singh and President Barack Obama resolved today in New Delhi to expand and strengthen the India-U.S. global strategic partnership.

The two leaders welcomed the deepening relationship between the world's two largest democracies. They commended the growing cooperation between their governments, citizens, businesses, universities and scientific institutions, which have thrived on a shared culture of pluralism, education, enterprise, and innovation, and have benefited the people of both countries.

Building on the transformation in India-U.S. relations over the past decade, the two leaders resolved to intensify cooperation between their nations to promote a secure and stable world; advance technology and innovation; expand mutual prosperity and global economic growth; support sustainable development; and exercise global leadership in support of economic development, open government, and democratic values.

The two leaders reaffirmed that India-U.S. strategic partnership is indispensable not only for their two countries but also for global stability and prosperity in the 21st century. To that end, President Obama welcomed India's emergence as a major regional and global power and affirmed his country's interest in India's rise, its economic prosperity, and its security.

A GLOBAL STRATEGIC PARTNERSHIP FOR THE 21st CENTURY

Prime Minister Singh and President Obama called for an efficient, effective, credible and legitimate United Nations to ensure a just and sustainable international order. Prime Minister Singh welcomed President Obama's affirmation that, in the years ahead, the United States looks forward to a reformed UN Security Council that includes India as a permanent member.

The two leaders reaffirmed that all nations, especially those that seek to lead in the 21st century, bear responsibility to ensure that the United Nations fulfills its founding ideals of preserving peace and security, promoting global cooperation, and advancing human rights.

Prime Minister Singh and President Obama reiterated that India and the United States, as global leaders, will partner for global security, especially as India serves on the Security Council over the next two years. The leaders agreed that their delegations in New York will intensify their engagement and work together to ensure that the Council continues to effectively play the role envisioned for it in the United Nations Charter. Both leaders underscored that all states have an obligation to comply with and implement UN Security Council Resolutions, including UN sanctions regimes. They also agreed to hold regular consultations on UN matters, including on the long-term sustainability of UN peacekeeping operations. As the two largest democracies, both countries also reaffirmed their strong commitment to the UN Democracy Fund.

The two leaders have a shared vision for peace, stability and prosperity in Asia, the Indian Ocean region and the Pacific region and committed to work together, and with others in the region, for the evolution of an open, balanced and inclusive architecture in the region. In this context, the leaders reaffirmed their support for the East Asia Summit and committed to regular consultations in this regard. The United States welcomes, in particular, India's leadership in expanding prosperity and security across the region. The two leaders agreed to deepen existing regular strategic consultations on developments in East Asia, and decided to expand and intensify their strategic consultations to cover regional and global issues of mutual interest, including Central and West Asia.

The two sides committed to intensify consultation, cooperation and coordination to promote a stable, democratic, prosperous, and independent Afghanistan. President Obama appreciated India's enormous contribution to Afghanistan's development and welcomed enhanced Indian assistance that will help Afghanistan

achieve self-sufficiency. In addition to their own independent assistance programs in Afghanistan, the two sides resolved to pursue joint development projects with the Afghan Government in capacity building, agriculture and women's empowerment.

They reiterated that success in Afghanistan and regional and global security require elimination of safe havens and infrastructure for terrorism and violent extremism in Afghanistan and Pakistan. Condemning terrorism in all its forms, the two sides agreed that all terrorist networks, including Lashkar e-Taiba, must be defeated and called for Pakistan to bring to justice the perpetrators of the November 2008 Mumbai attacks. Building upon the Counter Terrorism Initiative signed in July 2010, the two leaders announced a new Homeland Security Dialogue between the Ministry of Home Affairs and the Department of Homeland Security and agreed to further deepen operational cooperation, counter-terrorism technology transfers and capacity building. The two leaders also emphasized the importance of close cooperation in combating terrorist financing and in protecting the international financial system.

In an increasingly inter-dependent world, the stability of, and access to, the air, sea, space, and cyberspace domains is vital for the security and economic prosperity of nations. Acknowledging their commitment to openness and responsible international conduct, and on the basis of their shared values, India and the United States have launched a dialogue to explore ways to work together, as well as with other countries, to develop a shared vision for these critical domains to promote peace, security and development. The leaders reaffirmed the importance of maritime security, unimpeded commerce, and freedom of navigation, in accordance with relevant universally agreed principles of international law, including the United Nations Convention on the Law of the Sea, and peaceful settlement of maritime disputes.

The transformation in India-U.S. defense cooperation in recent years has strengthened mutual understanding on regional peace and stability, enhanced both countries' respective capacities to meet humanitarian and other challenges such as terrorism and piracy, and contributed to the development of the strategic partnership between India and the United States. The two Governments resolved to further strengthen defense cooperation, including through security dialogue, exercises, and promoting trade and collaboration in defense equipment and technology. President Obama welcomed India's decision to purchase U.S. high-technology defense items, which reflects our strengthening bilateral defense relations and will contribute to creating jobs in the United States.

The two leaders affirmed that their countries' common ideals, complementary strengths and a shared commitment to a world without nuclear weapons give them a responsibility to forge a strong partnership to lead global efforts for nonproliferation and universal and non-discriminatory global nuclear disarmament in the 21st century. They affirmed the need for a meaningful dialogue among all states possessing nuclear weapons to build trust and confidence and for reducing the salience of nuclear weapons in international affairs and security doctrines. They support strengthening the six decade-old international norm of non-use of nuclear weapons.

They expressed a commitment to strengthen international cooperative activities that will reduce the risk of terrorists acquiring nuclear weapons or material without reducing the rights of nations that play by the rules to harness the power of nuclear energy to advance their energy security. The leaders reaffirmed their shared dedication to work together to realize the commitments outlined at the April 2010 Nuclear Security Summit to achieve the goal of securing vulnerable nuclear materials in the next four years. Both sides expressed deep concern regarding illicit nuclear trafficking and smuggling and resolved to strengthen international cooperative efforts to address these threats through the IAEA, Interpol and in the context of the Nuclear Security Summit Communiqué and Action Plan. The two sides welcomed the Memorandum of Understanding for cooperation in the Global Centre for Nuclear Energy Partnership being established by India.

Both sides expressed deep concern about the threat of biological terrorism and pledged to promote international efforts to ensure the safety and security of biological agents and toxins. They stressed the need to achieve full implementation of the Biological and Toxin Weapons Convention and expressed the hope for a successful BWC Review Conference in 2011. The United States welcomed India's destruction of its chemical weapons stockpile in accordance with the provisions of the Chemical Weapons Convention. Both countries affirmed their shared commitment to promoting the full and effective implementation of the CWC.

The two leaders expressed regret at the delay in starting negotiations in the Conference on Disarmament for a multilateral, non-discriminatory and internationally and effectively verifiable treaty banning the future production of fissile material for nuclear weapons or other nuclear explosive devices.

India reaffirmed its unilateral and voluntary moratorium on nuclear explosive testing. The United States reaffirmed its testing moratorium and its commitment to ratify the Comprehensive Test Ban Treaty and bring it into force at an early date.

The leaders reaffirmed their commitment to diplomacy to resolve the Iranian nuclear issue, and discussed the need for Iran to take constructive and immediate steps to meet its obligations to the IAEA and the UN Security Council.

TECHNOLOGY, INNOVATION, AND ENERGY

Recognizing that India and the United States should play a leadership role in promoting global nonproliferation objectives and their desire to expand high technology cooperation and trade, Prime Minister Singh and President Obama committed to work together to strengthen the global export control framework and further transform bilateral export control regulations and policies to realize the full potential of the strategic partnership between the two countries.

Accordingly, the two leaders decided to take mutual steps to expand U.S.-India cooperation in civil space, defense, and other high-technology sectors. Commensurate with India's nonproliferation record and commitment to abide by multilateral export control standards, these steps include the United States removing Indian entities from the U.S. Department of Commerce's "Entity List" and realignment of India in U.S. export control regulations.

In addition, the United States intends to support India's full membership in the four multilateral export control regimes (Nuclear Suppliers Group, Missile Technology Control Regime, Australia Group, and Wassenaar Arrangement) in a phased manner, and to consult with regime members to encourage the evolution of regime membership criteria, consistent with maintaining the core principles of these regimes, as the Government of India takes steps towards the full adoption of the regimes' export control requirements to reflect its prospective membership, with both processes moving forward together. In the view of the United States, India should qualify for membership in the Australia Group and the Wassenaar Arrangement according to existing requirements once it imposes export controls over all items on these regimes' control lists.

Both leaders reaffirmed the assurances provided in the letters exchanged in September 2004 and the End-Use Visit Arrangement, and determined that the two governments had reached an understanding to implement these initiatives consistent with their respective national export control laws and policies. The Prime Minister and President committed to a strengthened and expanded dialogue on export control issues, through fora such as the U.S.-India High Technology Cooperation Group, on aspects of capacity building, sharing of best practices, and outreach with industry.

The possibility of cooperation between the two nations in space, to advance scientific knowledge and human welfare, are without boundaries and limits. They commended their space scientists for launching new initiatives in climate and weather forecasting for agriculture, navigation, resource mapping, research and development, and capacity building. They agreed to continuing discussions on and seek ways to collaborate on future lunar missions, international space station, human space flight and data sharing, and to reconvene the Civil Space

Joint Working Group in early 2011. They highlighted the just concluded Implementing Arrangement for enhanced monsoon forecasting that will begin to transmit detailed forecasts to farmers beginning with the 2011 monsoon rainy season as an important example of bilateral scientific cooperation advancing economic development, agriculture and food security.

The two leaders welcomed the completion of steps by the two governments for implementation of the India-U.S. civil nuclear agreement. They reiterated their commitment to build strong India-U.S. civil nuclear energy cooperation through the participation of the U.S. nuclear energy firms in India on the basis of mutually acceptable technical and commercial terms and conditions that enable a viable tariff regime for electricity generated. They noted that both countries had enacted domestic legislations and were also signatories to the Convention on Supplementary Compensation. They further noted that India intends to ratify the Convention on Supplementary Compensation within the coming year and is committed to ensuring a level playing field for U.S. companies seeking to enter the Indian nuclear energy sector, consistent with India's national and international legal obligations.

India will continue to work with the companies. In this context, they welcomed the commencement of negotiations and dialogue between the Indian operator and U.S. nuclear energy companies, and expressed hope for early commencement of commercial cooperation in the civil nuclear energy sector in India, which will stimulate economic growth and sustainable development and generate employment in both countries.

Just as they have helped develop the knowledge economy, India and the United States resolved to strengthen their partnership in creating the green economy of the future. To this end, both countries have undertaken joint research and deployment of clean energy resources, such as solar, advanced biofuels, shale gas, and smart grids. The two leaders also welcomed the promotion of clean and energy efficient technologies through the bilateral Partnership to Advance Clean Energy (PACE) and expanded cooperation with the private sector. They welcomed the conclusion of a new MOU on assessment and exploration of shale gas and an agreement to establish a Joint Clean Energy Research Center in India as important milestones in their rapidly growing clean energy cooperation.

The leaders discussed the importance of working bilaterally, through the Major Economies Forum (MEF), and in the context of the international climate change negotiations within the framework of the UNFCCC to meet the challenge of climate change. Prime Minister Singh and President Obama reiterated the importance of a positive result for the current climate change negotiations at the forthcoming conference of the United Nations Framework Convention on Climate Change (UNFCCC) in Mexico and affirmed their support for the Copenhagen Accord, which should contribute positively to a successful outcome in Cancun. To that end, the leaders welcomed enhanced cooperation in the area of climate adaptation and sustainable land use, and welcomed the new partnership between the United States and India on forestry programs and in weather forecasting.

INCLUSIVE GROWTH, MUTUAL PROSPERITY, AND ECONOMIC COOPERATION

The two leaders stressed that India and the United States, anchored in democracy and diversity, blessed with enormous enterprise and skill, and endowed with synergies drawn from India's rapid growth and U.S. global economic leadership, have a natural partnership for enhancing mutual prosperity and stimulating global economic recovery and growth. They emphasize innovation not only as a tool for economic growth and global competitiveness, but also for social transformation and empowerment of people.

Prime Minister Singh and President Obama celebrated the recent growth in bilateral trade and investment, characterized by balanced and rapidly growing trade in goods and services. They noted positively that the United States is India's largest trading partner in goods and services, and India is now among the fastest grow-

ing sources of foreign direct investment entering the United States. The two leaders agreed on steps to reduce trade barriers and protectionist measures and encourage research and innovation to create jobs and improve livelihoods in their countries.

They also welcomed expanding investment flow in both directions. They noted growing ties between U.S. and Indian firms and called for enhanced investment flows, including in India's infrastructure sector, clean energy, energy efficiency, aviation and transportation, healthcare, food processing sector and education. They welcomed the work of the U.S.-India CEO Forum to expand cooperation between the two countries, including in the areas of clean energy and infrastructure development. They also encouraged enhanced engagement by Indian and American small and medium-sized enterprises as a critical driver of our economic relationship. They looked forward to building on these developments to realize fully the enormous potential for trade and investment between the two countries.

Recognizing the people-to-people dynamic behind trade and investment growth, they called for intensified consultations on social security issues at an appropriate time. The two leaders agreed to facilitate greater movement of professionals, investors and business travelers, students, and exchange visitors between their countries to enhance their economic and technological partnership.

To enhance growth globally, the Prime Minister and President highlighted both nations' interests in an ambitious and balanced conclusion to the WTO's Doha Development Agenda negotiations, and in having their negotiators accelerate and expand the scope of their substantive negotiations bilaterally and with other WTO members to accomplish this as soon as possible. They agreed to work together in the G–20 to make progress on the broad range of issues on its agenda, including by encouraging actions consistent with achieving strong, balanced, and sustainable growth, strengthening financial system regulation, reforming the international financial institutions, enhancing energy security, resisting protectionism in all its forms, reducing barriers to trade and investment, and implementing the development action plans.

Building on the historic legacy of cooperation between the India and the United States during the Green Revolution, the leaders also decided to work together to develop, test, and replicate transformative technologies to extend food security as part of an Evergreen Revolution. Efforts will focus on providing farmers the means to improve agricultural productivity. Collaboration also will enhance agricultural value chain and strengthen market institutions to reduce post-harvest crop losses.

Affirming the importance of India-U.S. health cooperation, Prime Minister and the President celebrated the signing of an MOU creating a new Global Disease Detection Regional Center in New Delhi, which will facilitate preparedness against threats to health such as pandemic influenza and other dangerous diseases.

Embracing the principles of democracy and opportunity, the leaders recognized that the full future potential of the partnership lies in the hands of the next generation in both countries. To help ensure that all members of that generation enjoy the benefits of higher education, the Prime Minister and the President agreed to convene an India-U.S. Higher Education Summit, chaired by senior officials from both countries in 2011, as part of a continued effort to strengthen educational opportunities. They welcomed the progress made in implementing the Singh-Obama 21st Century Knowledge Initiative that is expanding links between faculties and institutions of the two countries and the expansion in the Nehru-Fulbright Programme for Scholars.

Noting that the ties of kinship and culture are an increasingly important dimension of India-U.S. relations, President Obama welcomed India's decision to hold a Festival of India in Washington DC in 2011. Recognizing the importance of preserving cultural heritage, both governments resolved to initiate discussions on how India and the United States could partner to prevent the illicit trafficking of both countries' rich and unique cultural heritage.

A SHARED INTERNATIONAL PARTNERSHIP FOR DEMOCRACY AND DEVELOPMENT

Consistent with their commitments to open and responsive government, and harnessing the expertise and experience that the two countries have developed, the leaders launched a U.S.-India Open Government Dialogue that will, through public-private partnerships and use of new technologies and innovations, promote their shared goal of democratizing access to information and energizing civic engagement, support global initiatives in this area and share their expertise with other interested countries. This will build on India's impressive achievements in this area in recent years and the commitments that the President made to advance an open government agenda at the United Nations General Assembly. The President and Prime Minister also pledged to explore cooperation in support of efforts to strengthen elections organization and management in other interested countries, including through sharing their expertise in this area.

Taking advantage of the global nature of their relationship, and recognizing India's vast development experience and historical research strengths, the two leaders pledged to work together, in addition to their independent programs, to adapt shared innovations and technologies and use their expertise in capacity building to extend food security to interested countries, including in Africa, in consultation with host governments.

Prime Minister Singh and President Obama concluded that their meeting is a historic milestone as they seek to elevate the India-U.S. strategic partnership to a new level for the benefit of their nations and the entire mankind. President Obama thanked President Patil, Prime Minister Singh, and the people of India for their extraordinary warmth and hospitality during his visit. The two leaders looked forward to the next session of the U.S.-India Strategic Dialogue in 2011.

NOTE: An original was not available for verification of the content of this joint statement.

Remarks to the Indian Parliament in New Delhi
November 8, 2010

Mr. Vice President, Madam Speaker, Mr. Prime Minister, Members of Lok Sabha and Rajya Sabha, and most of all, the people of India: I thank you for the great honor of addressing the representatives of more than 1 billion Indians and the world's largest democracy. I bring the greetings and friendship of the world's oldest democracy, the United States of America, including nearly 3 million proud and patriotic Indian Americans.

Over the past 3 days, my wife Michelle and I have experienced the beauty and dynamism of India and its people, from the majesty of Humayun's Tomb to the advanced technologies that are empowering farmers and women who are the backbone of Indian society; from the Diwali celebrations with schoolchildren to the innovators who are fueling India's economic rise; from the university students who will chart India's future to you, leaders who helped to bring India to this moment of extraordinary promise.

At every stop, we have been welcomed with the hospitality for which Indians have always been known. So to you and the people of India, on behalf of me, Michelle, and the American people, please accept my deepest thanks. *Bahoot dhanyavad.*

Now, I am not the first American President to visit India, nor will I be the last. But I am proud to visit India so early in my Presidency. It's no coincidence that India is my first stop on a visit to Asia, or that this has been my longest visit to another country since becoming President. For in Asia and around the world, India is not simply emerging, India has emerged.

And it is my firm belief that the relationship between the United States and India, bound by our shared interests and our shared values, will be one of the defining partnerships of the 21st century. This is the partnership that I've come here to build. This is the vision that our nations can realize together.

My confidence in our shared future is grounded in my respect for India's treasured past, a civilization that's been shaping the world

for thousands of years. Indians unlocked the intricacies of the human body and the vastness of our universe. It's no exaggeration to say that our information age is rooted in Indian innovations, including the number zero.

Of course, India not only opened our minds, she expanded our moral imaginations with religious texts that still summon the faithful to lives of dignity and discipline, with poets who imagined a future "where the mind is without fear and the head is held high," and with a man whose message of love and justice endures, the father of your nation, Mahatma Gandhi.

For me and Michelle, this visit has therefore held special meaning. See, throughout my life, including my work as a young man on behalf of the urban poor, I've always found inspiration in the life of Gandhi and his simple and profound lesson to be the change we seek in the world. And just as he summoned Indians to seek their destiny, he influenced champions of equality in my own country, including a young preacher named Martin Luther King. After making his pilgrimage to India a half-century ago, Dr. King called Gandhi's philosophy of nonviolent resistance "the only logical and moral approach" in the struggle for justice and progress.

So we were honored to visit the residence where Gandhi and King both stayed, Mani Bhavan. And we were humbled to pay our respects at Raj Ghat. And I am mindful that I might not be standing before you today, as President of the United States, had it not been for Gandhi and the message he shared and inspired with America and the world.

An ancient civilization of science and innovation, a fundamental faith in human progress, this is the sturdy foundation upon which you have built ever since that stroke of midnight when the tricolor was raised over a free and independent India. And despite the skeptics who said this country was simply too poor or too vast or too diverse to succeed, you surmounted overwhelming odds and became a model to the world.

Instead of slipping into starvation, you launched a Green Revolution that fed millions. Instead of becoming dependent on commodities and exports, you invested in science and technology and in your greatest resource, the Indian people. And the world sees the results, from the supercomputers you build to the Indian flag that you put on the Moon.

Instead of resisting the global economy, you became one of its engines, reforming the Licensing Raj and unleashing an economic marvel that has lifted tens of millions of people from poverty and created one of the world's largest middle classes.

Instead of succumbing to division, you have shown that the strength of India—the very idea of India—is its embrace of all colors, all castes, all creeds. It's the diversity represented in this chamber today. It's the richness of faiths celebrated by a visitor to my hometown of Chicago more than a century ago, the renowned Swami Vivekananda. He said that "holiness, purity, and charity are not the exclusive possessions of any church in the world, and that every system has produced men and women of the most exalted character."

And instead of being lured by the false notion that progress must come at the expense of freedom, you built the institutions upon which true democracy depends: free and fair elections, which enable citizens to choose their own leaders without recourse to arms; an independent judiciary and the rule of law, which allows people to address their grievances; and a thriving free press and vibrant civil society, which allows every voice to be heard. This year, as India marks 60 years with a strong and democratic constitution, the lesson is clear: India has succeeded not in spite of democracy, India has succeeded because of democracy.

Now, just as India has changed, so too has the relationship between our two nations. In the decades after independence, India advanced its interests as a proud leader of the nonaligned movement. Yet too often, the United States and India found ourselves on opposite sides of a north-south divide, estranged by a long cold war. Those days are over.

Here in India, two successive Governments led by different parties have recognized that deeper partnership with America is both natural and necessary. And in the United States, both of my predecessors—one a Democrat, one a Republican—worked to bring us closer, leading to increased trade and a landmark civil nuclear agreement.

So since that time, people in both our countries have asked: What's next? How can we build on this progress and realize the full potential of our partnership? That's what I want to address today, the future that the United States seeks in an interconnected world, and why I believe that India is indispensable to this vision; how we can forge a truly global partnership, not just in one or two areas, but across many; not just for our mutual benefit, but for the benefit of the world.

Of course, only Indians can determine India's national interests and how to advance them on the world stage. But I stand before you today because I am convinced that the interests of the United States—and the interests we share with India—are best advanced in partnership. I believe that.

The United States seeks security: the security of our country, our allies, and partners. We seek prosperity, a strong and growing economy in an open international economic system. We seek respect for universal values. And we seek a just and sustainable international order that promotes peace and security by meeting global challenges through stronger global cooperation.

Now, to advance these interests, I have committed the United States to comprehensive engagement with the world, based on mutual interest and mutual respect. And a central pillar of this engagement is forging deeper cooperation with 21st-century centers of influence, and that must necessarily include India.

Now, India is not the only emerging power in the world. But relationships between our countries is unique, for we are two strong democracies whose Constitutions begin with the same revolutionary words: "We the people." We are two great republics dedicated to the liberty and justice and equality of all people. And we are two free market economies where people have the freedom to pursue ideas and innovation that can change the world. And that's why I believe that India and America are indispensable partners in meeting the challenges of our time.

Since taking office, I've therefore made our relationship a priority. I was proud to welcome Prime Minister Singh for the first official state visit of my Presidency. For the first time ever, our Governments are working together across the whole range of common challenges that we face. Now, let me say it as clearly as I can: The United States not only welcomes India as a rising global power, we fervently support it, and we have worked to help make it a reality.

Together with our partners, we have made the G–20 the premier forum for international economic cooperation, bringing more voices to the table of global economic decisionmaking, and that has included India. We've increased the role of emerging economies like India at international financial institutions. We valued India's important role at Copenhagen, where for the first time, all major economies committed to take action to confront climate change and to stand by those actions. We salute India's long history as a leading contributor to United Nations peacekeeping missions. And we welcome India as it prepares to take its seat on the United Nations Security Council.

In short, with India assuming its rightful place in the world, we have an historic opportunity to make the relationship between our two countries a defining partnership of the century ahead. And I believe we can do so by working together in three important areas.

First, as global partners we can promote prosperity in both our countries. Together, we can create the high-tech, high-wage jobs of the future. With my visit, we are now ready to begin implementing our civil nuclear agreement. This will help meet India's growing energy needs and create thousands of jobs in both of our countries.

We need to forge partnerships in high-tech sectors like defense and civil space. So we've removed Indian organizations from our so-called entity list. And we will work to remove—and reform our controls on exports. Both of these steps will ensure that Indian companies seeking high-tech trade and technologies from America are treated the same as our very closest allies and partners.

We can pursue joint research and development to create green jobs, give India more access to cleaner, affordable energy, meet the commitments we made at Copenhagen, and show the possibilities of low-carbon growth.

And together, we can resist the protectionism that stifles growth and innovation. The United States remains—and will continue to remain— one of the most open economies in the world. And by opening markets and reducing barriers to foreign investment, India can realize its full economic potential as well. As G–20 partners, we can make sure the global economic recovery is strong and is durable. And we can keep striving for a Doha round that is ambitious and is balanced, with the courage to make the compromises that are necessary so global trade works for all economies.

Together, we can strengthen agriculture. Cooperation between Indian and American researchers and scientists sparked the Green Revolution. Today, India is a leader in using technology to empower farmers, like those I met yesterday who get free updates on market and weather conditions on their cell phones. And the United States is a leader in agricultural productivity and research. Now, as farmers and rural areas face the effects of climate change and drought, we'll work together to spark a second, more sustainable Evergreen Revolution.

Together, we're improving Indian weather forecasting systems before the next monsoon season. We aim to help millions of Indian farmers—farming households save water and increase productivity, improve food processing so crops don't spoil on the way to market, and enhance climate and crop forecasting to avoid losses that cripple communities and drive up food prices.

And as part of our food security initiative, we're going to share India's expertise with farmers in Africa. And this is an indication of India's rise, that we can now export hard-earned expertise to countries that see India as a model for agricultural development. It's another powerful example of how American and Indian partnership can address an urgent global challenge.

Because the wealth of a nation also depends on the health of its people, we'll continue to support India's effort against diseases like tuberculosis and HIV/AIDS, and as global partners, we'll work to improve global health by preventing the spread of pandemic flu. And because knowledge is the currency of the 21st century, we will increase exchanges between our students, our colleges, and our universities, which are among the best in the world.

As we work to advance our shared prosperity, we can partner to address a second priority, and that is our shared security. In Mumbai, I met with the courageous families and survivors of that barbaric attack. And here in Parliament, which was itself targeted because of the democracy it represents, we honor the memory of all those who have been taken from us, including American citizens on 26/11 and Indian citizens on 9/11.

This is the bond that we share. It's why we insist that nothing ever justifies the slaughter of innocent men, women, and children. It's why we're working together, more closely than ever, to prevent terrorist attacks and to deepen our cooperation even further. And it's why, as strong and resilient societies, we refuse to live in fear. We will not sacrifice the values and rule of law that defines us, and we will never waver in the defense of our people.

America's fight against Al Qaida and its terrorist affiliates is why we persevere in Afghanistan, where major development assistance from India has improved the lives of the Afghan people. We're making progress in our mission to break the Taliban's momentum and to train Afghan forces so they can take the lead for their security. And while I have made it clear that American forces will begin the transition to Afghan responsibility next summer, I've also made it clear that America's commitment to the Afghan people will endure. The United States will not abandon the people of Afghanistan—or the region—to violent extremists who threaten us all.

Our strategy to disrupt and dismantle and defeat Al Qaida and its affiliates has to succeed on both sides of the border. And that's why we have worked with the Pakistani Government to address the threat of terrorist networks in the border region. The Pakistani Government increasingly recognizes that these networks are not just a threat outside of Pakistan, they are a threat to the Pakistani people as well. They've suffered greatly at the hands of violent extremists over the last several years.

And we'll continue to insist to Pakistan's leaders that terrorist safe havens within their borders are unacceptable and that terrorists behind the Mumbai attacks must be brought to justice. We must also recognize that all of us have an interest in both an Afghanistan and a Pakistan that is stable and prosperous and democratic, and India has an interest in that as well.

In pursuit of regional security, we will continue to welcome dialogue between India and Pakistan, even as we recognize that disputes between your two countries can only be resolved by the people of your two countries.

More broadly, India and the United States can partner in Asia. Today, the United States is once again playing a leadership role in Asia: strengthening old alliances; deepening relationships, as we are doing with China; and we're reengaging with regional organizations like ASEAN and joining the East Asia summit, organizations in which India is also a partner. Like your neighbors in Southeast Asia, we want India not only to Look East, we want India to Engage East, because it will increase the security and prosperity of all our nations.

As two global leaders, the United States and India can partner for global security, especially as India serves on the Security Council over the next 2 years. Indeed, the just and sustainable international order that America seeks includes a United Nations that is efficient, effective, credible, and legitimate. That is why I can say today, in the years ahead, I look forward to a reformed United Nations Security Council that includes India as a permanent member.

Now, let me suggest that with increased power comes increased responsibility. The United Nations exists to fulfill its founding ideals of preserving peace and security, promoting global cooperation, and advancing human rights.

These are the responsibilities of all nations, but especially those that seek to lead in the 21st century. And so we look forward to working with India and other nations that aspire to Security Council membership to ensure that the Security Council is effective, that resolutions are implemented, that sanctions are enforced, that we strengthen the international norms which recognize the rights and responsibilities of all nations and all individuals.

This includes our responsibility to prevent the spread of nuclear weapons. Since I took office, the United States has reduced the role of nuclear weapons in our national security strategy, and we've agreed with Russia to reduce our own arsenals. We have put preventing nuclear proliferation and nuclear terrorism at the top of our nuclear agenda, and we have strengthened the cornerstone of the global nonproliferation regime, which is the Nuclear Non-Proliferation Treaty.

Together, the United States and India can pursue our goal of securing the world's vulnerable nuclear materials. We can make it clear that even as every nation has the right to peaceful nuclear energy, every nation must also meet its international obligations, and that includes the Islamic Republic of Iran. And together, we can pursue a vision that Indian leaders have espoused since independence, a world without nuclear weapons.

And this leads me to the final area where our countries can partner: strengthening the foundations of democratic governance, not only at home, but abroad.

In the United States, my administration has worked to make government more open and transparent and accountable to people. Here in India, you're harnessing technologies to do the same, as I saw yesterday at an expo in Mumbai. Your landmark Right to Information Act is empowering citizens with the ability to get the services to which they're entitled and to hold officials accountable. Voters can get information about candidates by text message. And you're delivering education and health care services to rural communities, as I saw yesterday when I joined an e-Panchayat with villagers in Rajasthan.

Now, in a new collaboration on open government, our two countries are going to share our experience, identify what works, and develop the next generation of tools to empower citizens. And in another example of how American and Indian partnership can address global challenges, we're going to share these innovations with civil society groups and countries around the world. We're going to show that democracy, more than any other form of government, delivers for the common man and woman.

Likewise, when Indians vote, the whole world watches. Thousands of political parties, hundreds of thousands of polling centers, millions of candidates and poll workers, and 700 million voters: There's nothing like it on the planet. There is so much that countries transitioning to democracy could learn from India's experience, so much expertise that India can share with the world. And that too is what is possible when the world's largest democracy embraces its role as a global leader.

As the world's two largest democracies, we must never forget that the price of our own freedom is standing up for the freedom of others. Indians know this, for it is the story of your nation. Before he ever began his struggle for Indian independence, Gandhi stood up for the rights of Indians in South Africa. Just as others, including the United States, supported Indian independence, India championed the self-determination of peoples from Africa to Asia as they too broke free from colonialism. And along with the United States, you've been a leader in supporting democratic development and civil society groups around the world. And this too is part of India's greatness.

Now, we all understand every country will follow its own path. No one nation has a monopoly on wisdom, and no nation should ever try to impose its values on another. But when peaceful democratic movements are suppressed—as they have been in Burma, for example—then the democracies of the world cannot remain silent. For it is unacceptable to gun down peaceful protestors and incarcerate political prisoners, decade after decade. It is unacceptable to hold the aspirations of an entire people hostage to the greed and paranoia of bankrupt regimes. It is unacceptable to steal elections, as the regime in Burma has done again for all the world to see.

Faced with such gross violations of human rights, it is the responsibility of the international community—especially leaders like the United States and India—to condemn it. And if I can be frank, in international fora, India has often shied away from some of these issues. But speaking up for those who cannot do so for themselves is not interfering in the affairs of other countries. It's not violating the rights of sovereign nations. It is staying true to our democratic principles. It is giving meaning to the human rights that we say are universal. And it sustains the progress that in Asia and around the world has helped turn dictatorships into democracies and ultimately increased our security in the world.

So promoting shared prosperity, preserving peace and security, strengthening democratic governance and human rights, these are the responsibilities of leadership. And as global partners, this is the leadership that the United States and India can offer in the 21st century. Ultimately, though, this cannot be a relationship only between Presidents and Prime Ministers, or in the halls of this Parliament. Ultimately, this must be a partnership between our peoples. So I want to conclude by speaking directly to the people of India who are watching today.

In your lives, you have overcome odds that might have overwhelmed a lesser country. In just decades, you have achieved progress and development that took other nations centuries. You are now assuming your rightful place as a leader among nations. Your parents and grandparents imagined this. Your children and grandchildren will look back on this. But only this generation of Indians can seize the possibilities of the moment.

As you carry on with the hard work ahead, I want every Indian citizen to know: The United States of America will not simply be cheering you on from the sidelines. We will be right there with you, shoulder to shoulder, because we believe in the promise of India. We believe that the future is what we make it. We believe that no matter who you are or where you come

from, every person can fulfill their God-given potential, just as a Dalit like Dr. Ambedkar could lift himself up and pen the words of the Constitution that protects the rights of all Indians.

We believe that no matter where you live—whether a village in Punjab or the bylanes of Chandni Chowk—[*laughter*]—an old section of Kolkata or a new highrise in Bangalore—every person deserves the same chance to live in security and dignity, to get an education, to find work, to give their children a better future.

And we believe that when countries and cultures put aside old habits and attitudes that keep people apart, when we recognize our common humanity, then we can begin to fulfill these aspirations that we share. It's a simple lesson contained in that collection of stories which has guided Indians for centuries, the "Panchatantra." And it's the spirit of the inscription seen by all who enter this great hall: "That one is mine and the other a stranger is the concept of little minds. But to the large-hearted, the world itself is their family."

This is the story of India, this is the story of America: that despite their differences, people can see themselves in one another and work together and succeed together as one proud nation. And it can be the spirit of partnership between our nations, that even as we honor the histories which in different times kept us apart, even as we preserve what makes us unique in a globalized world, we can recognize how much we can achieve together.

And if we let this simple concept be our guide, if we pursue the vision I've described today, a global partnership to meet global challenges, then I have no doubt that future generations—Indians and Americans—will live in a world that is more prosperous and more secure and more just because of the bonds that our generation has forged today.

So thank you, and *Jai Hind*. And long live the partnership between India and the United States.

NOTE: The President spoke at 5:40 p.m. at the Parliament House. In his remarks, he referred to Vice President Mohammad Hamid Ansari, Lok Sabha Speaker Meira Kumar, and Prime Minister Manmohan Singh of India.

Remarks at a State Dinner Hosted by President Pratibha Devisingh Patil of India in New Delhi
November 8, 2010

Madam President, thank you for your very gracious words and for the example of your leadership that inspires so many women, as well as men, across this nation. I was observing that one of the reasons I think India is doing so well is because it has so many strong women leaders. And I want to thank you and Dr. Shekhawat for hosting us this evening and your extraordinary hospitality.

To our dear friends, Prime Minister Singh and Mrs. Kaur; to distinguished guests; ladies and gentlemen: On behalf of Michelle and I, we just want to thank you for this extraordinary expression of friendship between our two nations.

I've done a lot of speaking today, so I want to be relatively brief. We've learned several things from this trip in India. We've learned that despite geographic distances between our nations, we are now closer than ever before. We've learned that although we may have traveled different paths to reach this moment in history, that we can walk towards the future together. We've also learned that no matter how hard I try, Michelle will always be a better dancer. [*Laughter*]

Let me say, it's been a particular pleasure to be here during Diwali. And last year during the state visit when Prime Minister Singh and Mrs. Kaur came, it was during our Thanksgiving season. And the fact that we can share some of our most meaningful holidays with each other speaks to the closeness of our countries and the values that we share as well as the common hopes for the future.

To my good friend and partner, Prime Minister Singh, from humble beginnings to high office, your life reflects all the progress and possibility of this great nation. And so all of us thank you not only for leading this nation and our partnership to new heights, but for the spirit with which you've led your life, with compassion, truth, commitment, humility, and love.

And to all who are gathered here tonight and to the people of India, for the past 3 days you've opened your country to us. Like so many before, we learned that you don't simply visit India, you experience India, in the richness of its traditions, in its diversity, the optimism and the warmth of its people.

From extraordinarily difficult circumstances, India has achieved what many thought was impossible. And in doing so, you captured the imagination of the world. Now our two nations have a chance to do what many also thought was impossible, and that is to build a global partnership in a new century.

And so I'd like to close with the words that your President spoke in this building on the day that India declared itself a republic, words describing how this diverse nation has stayed united and strong and because they speak to the spirit that binds our two countries together as well.

I propose a toast, knowing that our ties subsist because they are not of iron or steel or even of gold, but of the silken cords of the human spirit. Cheers.

NOTE: The President spoke at 9:05 p.m. at the Rashtrapati Bhavan. In his remarks, he referred to Devisingh Ransingh Shekhawat, husband of President Patil; and Gursharan Kaur, wife of Prime Minister Singh.

Joint Declaration on the Comprehensive Partnership Between the United States of America and the Republic of Indonesia
November 9, 2010

1. On the occasion of his historic state visit to Indonesia, President Barack Obama and President Susilo Bambang Yudhoyono held talks today in Jakarta where they

officially inaugurated the Comprehensive Partnership between the Republic of Indonesia and the United States of America. Through this partnership, the two Presidents are opening a new era of bilateral relations between Indonesia and the United States for the long-term, based on mutual respect, common interests, and shared values.

2. President Yudhoyono welcomed the United States' leadership role in promoting multilateral diplomacy, promoting peace, addressing the threat of climate change, and expanding engagement in Southeast Asia. President Obama reaffirmed America's admiration for Indonesia's extraordinary democratic transformation and broad-based reforms, the success of which are critical both to the region and to the United States. He also reiterated the United States' support for Indonesia's national unity and territorial integrity, and respect for Indonesia's independent and active foreign policy.

3. The leaders welcomed the steady improvement in bilateral relations in recent years, but agreed it was timely and appropriate to elevate this strategic relationship to a higher level. The two Presidents share a vision of a relationship that must become deep, enduring, and forward-looking, while focusing on addressing the challenges of the 21st Century.

4. The spirit behind this new partnership is a shared desire to increase consultation and cooperation, reflecting warmer ties, significant shared interests, and a belief that partnership is critical not only to the bilateral relationship, but to addressing key regional and global challenges. The partnership is founded on the shared values of freedom, pluralism, tolerance, democracy and respect for human rights. It will be a dynamic 21st century partnership with a forward-looking agenda to advance the cooperation of both countries on a wide-range of issues: education, environment, security, science and technology, trade and investment, democracy, human rights, health, energy, food, entrepreneurship, and more.

5. As leaders of the world's second and third largest democracies, President Obama and President Yudhoyono are committed to building a democratic partnership that will promote peace, freedom, prosperity, rule of law, and tolerance in the region and around the world. In part, this will be accomplished by establishing bridges of dialogue, cooperation and mutual understanding within the international community, and between people and cultures of different religions and faiths. They will also seek to build even stronger relations and increased cooperation between the governments, civil societies, and people of the United States and Indonesia.

6. As leaders of two of the world's largest economies, President Yudhoyono and President Obama expressed confidence in the progress of Indonesia's economic reforms and the economic recovery in the United States, which create a strong foundation for expanded trade and investment in both directions. On trade, they recognized the importance of keeping markets open, as well as facilitation and capacity building programs to increase trade flows including creating and realizing opportunities for small businesses and entrepreneurs. In this regard, the leaders welcomed the creation of the Global Entrepreneurship Program in Indonesia. On investment, they resolved to promote investment flows by supporting efforts of Indonesia to improve its investment climate, and further build its infrastructure. They identified the recently signed Investment Support Agreement under the Overseas Private Investment Corporation and the United States Millennium Challenge Account as concrete vehicles to promote this goal.

7. The two leaders seek an enduring Partnership that transcends official exchanges and fully leverages the extraordinary tal-

ents of our strongest asset, the Indonesian and American people. The Comprehensive Partnership will thus have at its core strong people to people relations and dynamic collaboration with non-governmental groups. In this regard, the two leaders are pleased to welcome the formation of the U.S.-Indonesia Council for Higher Education Partnership, which seeks to harness the energies of the non-governmental, public, and private sectors in both countries in support of expanding bilateral programs in higher education including to help build Indonesia's capacity to provide world class university education and to double within five years the number of American and Indonesian students who study in each other's country. The leaders encouraged the formation of additional public-private partnerships to help address other complex challenges such as climate change.

8. President Yudhoyono welcomed President Obama's decision to join the East Asia Summit, which further integrates the United States into the evolving institutional architecture of the Asia-Pacific region and opens a new channel for expanding multilateral cooperation. They agreed to energetically harness the new Partnership so that it will contribute to the continued progress and prosperity of both countries, while also serving as an important pillar for growing U.S.-ASEAN cooperation, and for advancing regional peace and prosperity.

They also agreed to continue to work closely together in the Asia-Pacific Economic Cooperation forum to strengthen and deepen regional economic integration by addressing barriers to trade and investment.

9. The two leaders also committed to work together to strengthen the G–20 as the premier forum for the world economy, and to work towards progress of the Doha Round. President Obama welcomed Indonesia's co-chairmanship of the G–20's anti-corruption working group. The two leaders further pledged to support international efforts to reach the Millennium Development Goals, attain a world free from nuclear weapons, and promote UN reforms. They reaffirmed their strong commitment to combat climate change, including finding creative ways to support the new Norway-Indonesia REDD+ partnership, and agreed to enhance overall cooperation in this area.

10. Both leaders pledged to maintain close contacts and consultation. In this regard, the two Presidents welcomed the establishment of the Joint Commission Meeting and a dynamic Plan of Action under the Comprehensive Partnership, both of which will help ensure that the partnership produces tangible results and continues to strengthen in the future.

NOTE: An original was not available for verification of the content of this joint declaration.

Remarks Prior to a Meeting With President Susilo Bambang Yudhoyono of Indonesia in Jakarta, Indonesia
November 9, 2010

President Yudhoyono. Mr. President and the delegate, first of all, I would like to once again welcome you to Jakarta, Indonesia. Thank you for visiting us, and I am hoping that your visit will mark another milestone in our bilateral relations.

We have discussed many issues on our bilateral relation as well as on the regional and global affairs. And I am optimistic that we could further promote, deepen, and expand our bilateral friendships, partnerships, and cooperations.

I would like to give the floor to you firstly on how could we further expand and deepen our bilateral cooperations.

President Obama. Excellent. Well, thank you very much, Mr. President. And to your delegation and to the people of Indonesia, thank you for your hospitality and the warm greeting that we've already received.

We had an excellent conversation. It was so good that it ran over the scheduled time. And so I think the recommendation has been that we use this expanded bilateral just to try to summarize some of the discussion that we've already had and the meeting of the minds that we've had on a range of issues.

Obviously, the most important thing that comes out of this visit is finalizing the comprehensive partnership between our two countries. We are very invested in making this successful because it is our belief that Indonesia is not just a rising regional power, but a rising world power. And as the world's two most populous—two of the three most populous democracies, as countries that I think share a tradition of pluralism and diversity, for us to work together——

[*At this point, the press pool was escorted out of the room.*]

NOTE: The President spoke at 6:01 p.m. at the Istana Merdeka. Audio was not available for verification of the content of these remarks.

The President's News Conference With President Susilo Bambang Yudhoyono of Indonesia in Jakarta
November 9, 2010

President Yudhoyono. Your Excellency, President Barack Obama, today Indonesia has the honor of welcoming the state visit of President Obama for the first time, fulfilling my invitation to him. It is my hope that this visit that we have been waiting for so long by the people of Indonesia can further enhance the relations between Indonesia and the cooperation between Indonesia and the United States in the future.

In President Obama's state visit this time, it also coincides—we are launching the comprehensive partnership that we hope with its—this partnership all forms of cooperation between our governments can be enhanced in a concrete manner in the future.

We both agreed to enhance, increase cooperation the field—in various fields with the specific agenda and specific priority that we wish to enhance—that is in the area of trade and investment, in the area of education, energy, in the area of climate change and the environment, in the area of security and democracy and also civil society.

We earnestly hope that this partnership that we establish, that we can look to the future, and this partnership may build upon people-to-people relations between our two great nations, and furthermore, can contribute to the creation of global peace, stability, and the economy, be it at the regional or at the global level.

Ladies and gentlemen, there are many issues that we discussed earlier at the bilateral meeting, but I wish to convey a number of elements that became the commitment of both our governments—commitment of the United States and the Republic of Indonesia—to truly enhance and to build upon in the future.

First of all is in the area of trade and investment. At this time, the United States is the trade partner number three for Indonesia, with $21 billion in 2008, and also investor number three for Indonesia. We hope that—and I personally expect that—once again, the investment and trade between our two countries can be increased significantly in the future, bearing in mind that the magnitude of the economies of the United States and also the economic growth that is occurring in Indonesia right now.

We also discussed and agreed to enhance cooperation in the area of energy, especially clean energy, and invite the U.S. to participate in the development of geothermal energy that is also one of Indonesia's great sources of renewable energy and a high number of deposits.

We also discussed the opportunity to cooperate in the area of climate change, environment, and also management of the forest. Indonesia possesses the responsibility to manage our forests, to reduce the emissions of greenhouse gas effects from the forest. We also have a target to reduce 26 percent of our emissions by 2020, with the cooperation of the international community, the United States, and Indonesia, as developing country and developed country. Therefore, our hopes to attain this and this kind of commitment will contribute significantly and play an effective role.

It is our need to underscore the cooperation in education sector. Therefore, I thanked President Barack Obama for his assistance and cooperation all this time in the area of education. When we met in Toronto in June, the United States assisted $100 million to the development of education in Indonesia. This is a pillar of great importance for people-to-people contact, for cooperation between our two great nations, comprehensive partnership that we possess right now. We agreed to enhance this cooperation in the area of education in the future.

We also underscored the importance of cooperation in the area of counterterrorism, where terrorism is an enemy for all nations, and we must—and we desire to strengthen cooperation in the context of law enforcement. In this regard, it will be an effective focus in the efforts to eradicate acts of terrorism.

Ladies and gentlemen, we also discussed the issue of—global and regional issues of common concern. Among others, the future of the relations between ASEAN and the United States, the future of the East Asia summit, and also cooperation in regional—in the context of APEC, we both agreed to discuss efforts to ensure stability and security and peace in our region—specifically Asia-Pacific, including in the area of Asia, which currently is facing a lot of focus on many shifts in geopolitics in the recent times.

I conveyed to President Obama that Indonesia will chair ASEAN in 2011, and therefore, as host of the East Asia summit, we invite Obama to attend the meeting with other leaders in the East Asia summit, including the President of Russia, to together we discuss matters on the issue of security in our region, specifically Asia-Pacific.

And we also discussed the issue of G–20, where we must continue to promote G–20 as a premier forum for international economic cooperation so that efforts to develop global economic growth that is strong, balanced, and sustainable can be achieved. And also we must secure the balance of the global economy so that it will bring benefit to all humanity.

We also see the issue of Myanmar and hope that the process of democratization in Myanmar that is currently taking place as promised by the Government of Myanmar will take place in a good way.

Last but not least, we also discussed the issue of the situation in the Middle East, including the issue of Palestine and Israel. And also I conveyed the His Excellency that the position of Indonesia is clear that we need a resolution on Palestine-Israel in a permanent and sustainable manner, a two-state solution and independence for the people of Palestine who are living in peace with the people of Israel and must be supported by the international community.

Ladies and gentlemen, those are the key elements that I wish to convey that we discussed during our bilateral meeting this evening. And it is my big hope from Indonesia that—and I'm very optimistic that with the comprehensive partnership with the Government of the United States and cooperation and partnership between Indonesia and the United States in various fields will receive our effort to enhance and to improve.

Therefore, ladies and gentlemen, I wish to now invite President Barack Obama to convey his views to the Indonesian press and also to the U.S. press and the participants here. And I also truly hope that once again this framework for cooperation that is new can truly bring benefit, be it for the nation of the United States and Indonesia.

I welcome—I invite you, Mr. Barack.

President Obama. Selamat sore. Thank you, President Yudhoyono, for your kind words, your gracious welcome, and for your friendship and your partnership.

After more than one attempt, it is wonderful to finally be back in Indonesia. And I'm very pleased that my wife Michelle is joining me for her first visit to the country. I assure you, it won't be her last. And I want to thank the people of Jakarta for the wonderful reception when we arrived. Even in the rain, people were there to greet us. And we're very appreciative of that.

Of course, we're mindful that this is a difficult time for Indonesia: first, the recent earthquake and tsunami, and now the volcanic eruptions. And our thoughts and prayers are with those who have lost their loved ones or their homes. And I know that President Yudhoyono has been tireless in his efforts to make sure that people are safe and that this difficulty is dealt with in as effective way as possible. And so we are fully supportive of him.

The United States will continue to support the relief efforts in any way that we can. And I hope that my presence here today is a reminder that in good times and in bad times the United States stands as a friend with Indonesia.

Now, obviously, much has been made of the fact that this marks my return to where I lived as a young boy. I will tell you, though, that I barely recognized it. As I was driving down the streets, the only building that was there when I first moved to Jakarta was Sarinah. Now it's one of the shorter buildings on the road. [*Laughter*]

But today, as President, I'm here to focus not on the past, but on the future: the comprehensive partnership that we're building between the United States and Indonesia.

As one of the world's largest democracies, as the largest economy in Southeast Asia, and as a member of the G–20, as a regional leader, as a vast archipelago on the frontlines of climate change, and as a society of extraordinary diversity, Indonesia is where many of the challenges and the opportunities of the 21st century come together.

At the same time, the United States is leading again in Asia. We are strengthening our alliances. We're deepening relationships, as we're doing with China. We're reengaging with ASEAN and joining the East Asia summit, and we're forging new partnerships with emerging powers like Indonesia. So our comprehensive partnership is bringing our countries closer together. And I want to focus just on three key areas. And we discussed a wide range of issues during our meeting.

First, as President Yudhoyono mentioned, we are looking to expand our trade and invest-

ment and commercial relationships because it can create prosperity in both our countries.

Trade between us is growing fast, and that includes American exports to Indonesia. And that's why Indonesia is one of the growing markets that we're going to be focused on as part of my initiative to double U.S. exports. President Yudhoyono and I discussed ways to create the conditions that would encourage additional trade and investment. He mentioned that we're number three right now in terms of trade volume and investment. And I informed him we don't like being number three, we want to be number one. [*Laughter*]

And so we're going to be doing everything we can to expand this trading relationship. And I'm pleased to announce that the Overseas Private Investment Corporation, or OPIC, will host its annual conference this spring in Indonesia to highlight new opportunities for partnership here and across the region.

To strengthen cooperation in science and technology that fuels growth, we are going to be pursuing joint research in areas like energy and biodiversity conservation. And we are expanding educational partnerships between our young scientists, engineers, and doctors. And building on the entrepreneurship summit that I hosted in Washington, which was attended by some very talented young Indonesians, I'm pleased that Indonesia will be hosting a regional entrepreneurship conference next year.

As we prepare for the G–20 and APEC summits, President Yudhoyono and I discussed the need to ensure that the global economic recovery is strong and balanced and is creating jobs in all of our countries. So that's focus number one: trade, investment, and the economy.

Second, we're forging new ties between our people to address common challenges. We're expanding partnerships between our students and our universities. We aim to double the number of educational exchanges between our two countries within 5 years. And I thank President Yudhoyono's offer for additional scholarships for young Americans to study in Indonesia. I think that's a wonderful thing that needs to happen.

We're proud to support Indonesia's leadership under President Yudhoyono in confronting climate change. I understand there's been a lot of rain this year, and obviously, we can't look at 1 year as indicative of the future, but I think there's no doubt that as an archipelago, Indonesia will be on the frontlines when it comes to the potential impacts of climate change.

So we're glad to work with President Yudhoyono on this issue, and we welcome and will support the new partnership between Indonesia and Norway to slow emissions from deforestation and degradation of peat land.

We're bringing on—we're building on Indonesia's inspiring transition from dictatorship to democracy by launching a new effort to help Indonesian civil society groups who tackle corruption and promote human rights at home to share their experience with civil society groups across this region, because I think people can learn from the experiences of Indonesia.

And I would note that many of the partnerships I've mentioned are a direct result of my call in Cairo for a new beginning between the United States and Muslim communities around the world. And it involves the private sector as well, thanks to efforts like Partners for a New Beginning, which is forging partnerships around science, education, and entrepreneurship.

The third element of our comprehensive partnership is to deepen our political and security cooperation. As President Yudhoyono mentioned, we're already enjoying strong cooperation in preventing terrorism, preventing piracy. We look forward to Indonesia's leadership as the chair of ASEAN next year, and I look forward to returning to Jakarta next year for the East Asia summit.

One of the challenges ASEAN and the world will continue to face is Burma, and I commend Indonesia for standing up for the people of Burma and their rights. Last week's election in Burma was neither free, nor fair. And we will continue our efforts to move Burma toward democratic reform and protection of human rights. As a first step, the Burmese authorities should immediately and unconditionally release all political prisoners, including Aung San Suu Kyi.

So promoting prosperity, expanding partnerships between our people, and deepening political and security cooperation, these are the pillars of our new partnership, which owes so much to the leadership of my good friend President Yudhoyono. I believe that our two nations have only begun to forge the cooperation that's possible. And I say that not simply as someone who knows firsthand what Indonesia can offer the world, I say it as President, a President who knows what Indonesia and the United States can offer the world together if we work together in a spirit of mutual interest and mutual respect.

So *terima kasih* and *Assalamu alaikum.*

Asia-Pacific Region

Q. Good evening, Mr. President. I speak in Indonesian because Mr. President has been in Jakarta. Lately, Mr. President, the region of Asia-Pacific is developing, and the development is extraordinary. There's initiative, cooperation, and there is always promotion to a strategic partnership. What do you think is the role of the U.S. in the configuration of Asia-Pacific in the future? Thank you very much, Mr. President.

President Obama. Well, this is something that President Yudhoyono and I spent a lot of time discussing. Asia is the fastest growing part of the world. It's the fastest growing in terms of population. It's the fastest growing set of economies. And so there's enormous potential and enormous promise, but only if countries are cooperating, if they are observing basic rules of the road, if potential conflicts are resolved in a peaceful fashion.

And so it's very important, I think, to make sure that we have the kinds of multilateral institutions and architecture that can maximize the potential and minimize the challenges of a rapidly changing region.

I think Indonesia is going to be a critical partner in that, a critical leader in that, primarily because it is a country that has figured out how to create a genuine democracy despite great diversity, and so, I think, can promote the kinds of values that will help people all across this region maximize their potential.

What I'd like to see is that even as we continue to work through APEC on economic issues—

it's primarily an economic organization—that the East Asia summit becomes a premier organizational structure to work on political and security issues. And I think under President Yudhoyono's leadership next year, there's enormous potential for us to start looking at some specific areas of common interest.

One example that I mentioned in our bilateral meeting was the issue of the South China Sea and how various maritime issues, conflicts, can get resolved in a peaceful fashion. I think that's something that everybody has an interest in, everybody has a concern in. But there may be a whole host of other issues like that in which the East Asia summit is probably the ideal venue.

Regardless of whether we're talking about APEC or East Asia summit, or for that matter the G–20, Indonesia is going to have a seat at the table. And its leadership is going to be absolutely critical and the United States wants to make sure that we're coordinating closely on all these issues of critical concern.

Carol Lee of Politico. Where is Carol? There you go.

President Obama's Childhood in Indonesia/Outreach to Muslim World

Q. Thank you, Mr. President. How would you assess your outreach to the Muslim world at this point in your Presidency, particularly in light of some of the controversies back home? And if you could, give us some of your thoughts on what it's like to return here as President of the United States.

President Obama. Well——

Q. And may I, President Yudhoyono? Obviously, President Obama spent some time here as a child, and I wonder what your thoughts are and what special insights that gives him into the region. Thank you very much.

President Obama. Well, I'll take the second question first. I think it's wonderful to be here, although I have to tell you that when you visit a place that you spent time in as a child, as President it's a little disorienting. First of all, as I said before, the landscape has changed completely. When I first came here, it was in 1967, and people were on *becaks*, which for those of you who aren't familiar is sort of a bicycle rickshaw thing.

And if they weren't on *becaks*, they were on *bemos*, which were—[*laughter*]—they were sort of like little taxis, but you stood in the back, and it was very crowded.

And now, as President, I can't even see any traffic because they block off all the streets—[*laughter*]—although my understanding is that Jakarta traffic is pretty tough. But I feel great affection for the people here. And obviously, I have a sister who's half Indonesian. My mother lived and worked here for a long time. And so the sights and the sounds and the memories all feel very familiar. And it's wonderful to be able to come back as President and, hopefully, contribute to further understanding between the United States and Indonesia.

One of the things that's striking is because it's almost on the exact opposite side of the world, I think not enough Americans know about this great country. And hopefully, my visit here will help to promote additional interest and understanding. People have heard of Bali and they've heard of Java, but they don't always know how to locate it on a map back home. And I think that increasing awareness of Indonesia is something I'm very much looking forward to doing.

Obviously, this is a short visit. It's a shorter visit than I would like. My hope is, is that we're going to be able to come back and maybe bring the kids and visit some places outside of Jakarta. When you go to—inland, further into Java, there are just incredible places like Yogya, old ancient temples, and places that I have very fond memories of visiting when I was a kid. I'd love to do that.

With respect to outreach to the Muslim world, I think that our efforts have been earnest, sustained. We don't expect that we are going to completely eliminate some of the misunderstandings and mistrust that have developed over a long period of time. But we do think that we're on the right path.

So whether it's our more active communications to press in Muslim countries or exchange programs in which we're having U.S. scientists and other educators visit Muslim countries or that entrepreneurship summit that we had in Washington in which we invited young business leaders from Muslim countries all across—all around the world, what we're trying to do is to make sure that we are building bridges and expanding our interactions with Muslim countries so that they're not solely focused on security issues.

Because you come to a place like Indonesia, which is a large—the largest Muslim population in the world, but people here have a lot of other interests other than security. That security is important, but I want to make sure that we are interacting with a wide range of people on a wide range of issues. And I think by broadening the relationship, it strengthens it, it builds trust, creates more people-to-people contact. That will be good for our security, but it will also be good for the larger cause of understanding between the United States and the Muslim world.

So I think it's an incomplete project. We've got a lot more work to do. And it's not going to eliminate some—or replace some tough dialogue around concrete policy issues. Those are going to continue. There are going to be some policy differences that we can't avoid. But I do think it's helping.

President Yudhoyono. Could you repeat your questions to me?

Q. Sorry. Thank you. I wanted to ask you, obviously, President Obama spent some time here as a child, and I wonder what your thoughts are, and how that gives him special insight into the region. Thank you.

President Yudhoyono. Very good. I, a few times having met with President Barack Obama, up to now one thing that I felt during our meetings, the understanding of the situation in developing countries, an understanding on the issues faced by a country like Indonesia that is often very complex. That makes it possible for President Barack Obama to see in a more clear situation what are the true challenges faced by the developing world. And therefore, the cooperation that we build between Indonesia and the United States, for example, is more precise. He understands more the challenges, the situation, and the obstacles that is faced by countries like Indonesia.

That's what I really felt when I met with him. And now I too can feel more easy to convey to him the issues that we are faced, the challenges

faced by Indonesia, and therefore, the agenda that we discuss together, including comprehensive partnership that we have discussed will be more precise and accurate for the benefit not only for Indonesia, but also for the people of the United States.

Group of Twenty (G–20)/Global Economic Stabilization

Q. Good evening, President Obama and President Yudhoyono. I'm from ANTARA. My question is one, and it is to President Obama, regarding to the global economic crisis that still has impacts on the economy of the world today. The President of the United States, where you have created a lot of unemployment in this region, East Asia. Do you think this affects the economic cooperation between Indonesia and the United States?

And in the context of the G–20, how do you see the effectiveness of the G–20 to improving or the recovery efforts in the global economy? Because we still see many challenges faced by countries, especially in the area of currency.

President Obama. Well, I think that overall the G–20 has been very successful in stabilizing the world economy. When you think about where we were when I first entered office and attended my first G–20 meeting in April of 2009, at that point, there was great uncertainty as to whether the financial system was going to be melting down around the world.

The economies of a lot of countries, including the United States, were contracting at a severe pace. I think our economy contracted in that first quarter by 6 percent. World trade had drastically contracted. And in part because of the effective coordination between the G–20 countries—making sure that countries weren't resorting to protectionism, coordinating a package of recovery programs that increased world demand, effectively intervening in the banking system and stabilizing it—because of all those actions, what we've seen is that countries for the most part around the world are back on a growth pattern.

Now, you're absolutely right that we still have a lot of work to do. And I'm going to be joining

President Yudhoyono in Seoul, South Korea, to discuss the next steps that have to be taken.

One of the key steps is putting in place additional tools to encourage balanced and sustainable growth. One of the reasons that the crisis was so severe was, there were huge imbalances when it comes to surpluses and deficits. Our trading patterns were such where there was a lot of money floating around engaged in a lot of speculative activity.

And what we agreed to in previous meetings of the G–20 is, is that we need to establish a framework for more balanced growth. We have not yet achieved that balanced growth. You're seeing some countries run up very big surpluses and intervening significantly in the currency markets to maintain their advantage when it comes to their currency. We've got other countries that are in deficit. Both surplus and deficit countries would benefit if there was a more balanced program in which the surplus countries were focused on internal demand, there was a more market-based approach to their currencies, and the deficit countries thereby were able to export more, and that would also make it easier for them to deal with their unemployment issues.

So this is going to be something that we're going to be discussing extensively in Seoul. I'm confident we can make progress on it. It's not going to happen all at once. But I'm very much focused on creating a win-win situation in which everybody is invested in expanding world trade, everybody is invested in increased prosperity, but we're doing so in a way in which everybody is benefiting and not just some.

Last question on our side is Stephen Collinson of AFP [Agence France-Presse].

Middle East Peace Process/China/Asia-Pacific

Q. Thank you, Mr. President. As the President mentioned, events in the Middle East are watched very closely here. Does Israel's advanced planning for more than a thousand new homes in Jerusalem undermine trust between the parties and undermine your peace efforts?

And if I may just ask President Yudhoyono, is ASEAN ready for the more advanced role in world affairs the U.S. would like to see it play?

And should the U.S. engagement—renewed engagement be seen in any way as a counterbalance to a rising China?

President Obama. I have not—I've been out of town, so I'm just seeing the press reports. I have not had a full briefing on Israel's intentions and what they've communicated to our administration. But this kind of activity is never helpful when it comes to peace negotiations. And I'm concerned that we're not seeing each side make the extra effort involved to get a breakthrough that could finally create a framework for a secure Israel living side and side—side by side in peace with a sovereign Palestine.

We're going to keep on working on it, though, because it is in the world's interest, it is in the interest of the people of Israel, and it is in the interest of the Palestinian people to achieve that settlement, to achieve that agreement. But each of these incremental steps can end up breaking down trust between the parties.

Even though it wasn't directed to me, I do want to just chime in briefly on the issue of China. We want China to succeed and prosper. It's good for the United States if China continues on the path of development that it's on.

That means that, first of all, just from a humanitarian point of view, lifting millions of people out of poverty is a good thing. It is also a huge expanding market where America then can sell goods and services, and so we think China being prosperous and secure is a positive. And we're not interested in containing that process. We want China to continue to achieve its development goals.

We do want to make sure that everybody is operating within an international framework and sets of rules in which countries recognize their responsibilities to each other. That's true for the United States. That's true for China. That's true for Indonesia. It's true for all of us. And the more that we have international mechanisms in which people say we have rights, we also have responsibilities, we're going to abide by them, we're going to hold each other accountable, the better off we'll all be.

President Yudhoyono. Yes, the views that I have of the future of our region, the region of Asia, including East Asia and Southeast Asia, all wish to have a region that is experiencing development, including economic development. This region should continue to be a region that is stable, a region that is peaceful and a region that is safe.

In this regard, the community that is built upon in Asia, in East Asia also, and also a framework now through the East Asia summit framework, we have the responsibility to—in one area, to ensure that the cooperation in the region, especially in the area of economic cooperation, can contribute significantly to the development of the global economy that will bring benefit for all humanity.

On the other spot of the coin, we also have the responsibility to ensure stability and security in our region. I am not using any theory or the theory of one power to counterbalance the other powers. But I do have the view that there must be some form of dynamic equilibrium in Asia-Pacific, in East and Southeast Asia. And the formation of such regional cooperation such that is East Asia summit, where there are 10 countries from ASEAN and there is also China, Republic of Korea, Japan, India, Australia, New Zealand, and now Russia and the United States, therefore, I have faith that it will be more effective to ensure peace, stability, and order in this region.

And in this regard, with such a condition, such cooperation in the area of economic will go effectively, and it is Indonesia's hope that China and the U.S. relations will continue to flow well because if something happens between those two states, it will have severe impacts to not only countries in the region, in Asia, but also to the world.

For that reason, I hope that the economic relations between the U.S. and China will continue to proceed well, despite the geopolitical developments. We also hope to contribute to creating a region in East Asia, in Southeast Asia, and especially in Asia-Pacific, to become a region that is stable and productive.

That is my views in general on the regional architecture issues and the future cooperation in our region.

Thank you very much.

NOTE: The President's news conference began at 6:35 p.m. at the Istana Merdeka. In his remarks, the President referred to Aung San Suu Kyi, leader of the National League for Democracy in Burma; and his sister Maya Soetoro-Ng. President Yudhoyono and a reporter spoke in Bahasa Indonesia, and their remarks were translated by an interpreter. A portion of these remarks could not be verified because the audio was incomplete.

Remarks at a State Dinner Hosted by President Susilo Bambang Yudhoyono of Indonesia in Jakarta
November 9, 2010

President Yudhoyono, Mrs. Yudhoyono, to all the distinguished guests who are here today, thank you for this extraordinary honor. I am proud and humbled to accept this award on behalf of my mother. And although she could not be here in person, I know that my sister Maya Soetoro would be equally proud.

Now, I'm going to have the opportunity to speak tomorrow, and so I will try to keep my remarks brief. First of all, thank you for the *bakso*—[*laughter*]—and the *nasi goreng*, the *emping*, the *kerupuk*. [*Laughter*] *Semuanya enak.* [*Laughter*] Thank you very much.

But the fact, President, that you would choose to recognize my mother in this way speaks to the bonds that she forged over many years with the people of this magnificent country. And in honoring her, you honor the spirit that led her to travel into villages throughout the country, often on the back of motorcycles, because that was the only way to get into some of these villages.

She believed that we all share common aspirations: to live in dignity and security, to get an education, to provide for our families, to give our children a better future, to leave the world better than we found it. She also believed, by the way, in the importance of educating girls and empowering women, because she understood that when we provide education to young women, when we honor and respect women, that we are in fact developing the entire country. That's what kept bringing my mother back to this country for so many years, that's the lesson that she passed on to me, and that's the lesson that Michelle and I try to pass on to our daughters.

So on behalf of our entire family, we thank you. I am deeply moved. It is this same largeness of heart that compels us tonight to keep in our thoughts and prayers all those who are suffering from the eruptions and the tsunami and the earthquake. With so many in need tonight, that's one more reason for me to keep my remarks short.

As a young boy in Menteng Dalam 40 years ago, I could never imagine that I would one day be hosted here at Istana Negara—never mind as President of the United States. I didn't think I would be stepping into. this building ever. [*Laughter*]

And I know that much has been made about how a young boy could move between such different countries and cultures as Indonesia and the United States. But the truth is, is that our countries have far more in common than most people realize. We are two peoples who both broke free from colonial rule. We are both two vast nations that stretch thousands of miles. We are both two societies that find strength in our diversity. And we are two democracies where power resides in the people. And so it's only natural that we should be partners in the world.

I am fortunate to have a very strong partner in President Yudhoyono, Indonesia's first directly elected President, and a leader who has guided this nation through its journey into .democracy. And our two nations are fortunate that we are forging a partnership for the 21st century. And as we go forward, I'm reminded of a proverb: *Bagai air dengan tebing*—like bamboo and the river bank, we rely on each other.

And so I'd like to propose a toast. In the spirit of friendship between our two countries, we are reminded of the truth that no nation is an island, not even when you're made up of thousands of islands. We all rely on each other together, like bamboo and the river bank. And like my mother riding between villages on a motorcycle, we are all stronger and safer when we see our common humanity in each other.

So, President Yudhoyono, and to all the distinguished guests who are here, thank you for your extraordinary friendship and the warmth with which you have received Michelle and myself. And I promise that it won't take so long before I come back.

NOTE: The President spoke at 10:01 p.m. at the Istana Negara. In his remarks, he referred to Kristiani Herrawati, wife of President Yudhoyono.

Remarks at the University of Indonesia in Jakarta
November 10, 2010

The President. Terima kasih. Terima kasih. Thank you so much. Thank you, everybody. *Selamat pagi.*

Audience members. Selamat pagi!

The President. It is wonderful to be here at the University of Indonesia. To the faculty and the staff and the students, and to Dr. Gumilar Rusliwa Somantri, thank you so much for your hospitality.

Assalamu alaikum dan salam sejahtera. Thank you for this wonderful welcome. Thank you to the people of Jakarta, and thank you to the people of Indonesia.

Pulang kampung nih. I am so glad that I made it back to Indonesia and that Michelle was able to join me. We had a couple of false starts this year, but I was determined to visit a country that's meant so much to me. And unfortunately, this visit is too short, but I look forward to coming back a year from now when Indonesia hosts the East Asia summit.

Before I go any further, I want to say that our thoughts and prayers are with all of those Indonesians who are affected by the recent tsunami and the volcanic eruptions, particularly those who've lost loved ones and those who've been displaced. And I want you all to know that as always, the United States stands with Indonesia in responding to natural disasters, and we are pleased to be able to help as needed. As neighbors help neighbors and families take in the displaced, I know that the strength and the resilience of the Indonesian people will pull you through once more.

Let me begin with a simple statement: *Indonesia bagian dari diri saya*. I first came to this country when my mother married an Indonesian named Lolo Soetoro. And as a young boy, I was coming to a different world. But the people of Indonesia quickly made me feel at home.

Jakarta—now, Jakarta looked very different in those days. The city was filled with buildings that were no more than a few stories tall. This was back in 1967, '68—most of you weren't born yet. [*Laughter*] The Hotel Indonesia was one of the few high rises, and there was just one big department store called Sarinah. That was it. *Becaks* and *bemos*, that's how you got around. They outnumbered automobiles in those days. And you didn't have all the big highways that you have today. Most of them gave way to unpaved roads and the *kampungs*.

So we moved to Menteng Dalam, where—[*applause*]—hey, some folks from Menteng Dalam right here. And we lived in a small house. We had a mango tree out front. And I learned to love Indonesia while flying kites and running along the paddy fields and catching dragonflies, buying *sate* and *bakso* from the street vendors. I still remember the call of the vendors: "*Sate!*" [*Laughter*] I remember that. "*Bakso!*" [*Laughter*] *Enak, ya?* But most of all, I remember the people: the old men and women who welcomed us with smiles, the children who made a foreign child feel like a neighbor and a friend, and the teachers who helped me learn about this country.

Because Indonesia is made up of thousands of islands and hundreds of languages and people from scores of regions and ethnic groups, my time here helped me appreciate the common humanity of all people. And while my stepfather, like most Indonesians, was raised a Muslim, he firmly believed that all religions were worthy of respect. And in this way, he reflected

the spirit of religious tolerance that is enshrined in Indonesia's Constitution, and that remains one of this country's defining and inspiring characteristics.

Now, I stayed here for 4 years, a time that helped shape my childhood, a time that saw the birth of my wonderful sister Maya, a time that made such an impression on my mother that she kept returning to Indonesia over the next 20 years to live and to work and to travel and to pursue her passion of promoting opportunity in Indonesia's villages, especially opportunity for women and for girls. And I was so honored when President Yudhoyono last night at the state dinner presented an award on behalf of my mother, recognizing the work that she did. And she would have been so proud, because my mother held Indonesia and its people very close to her heart for her entire life.

Now, so much has changed in the four decades since I boarded a plane to move back to Hawaii. If you asked me—or any of my schoolmates who knew me back then—I don't think any of us could have anticipated that one day I would come back to Jakarta as the President of the United States. And few could have anticipated the remarkable story of Indonesia over these last four decades.

The Jakarta that I once knew has grown into a teeming city of nearly 10 million, with skyscrapers that dwarf the Hotel Indonesia and thriving centers of culture and of commerce. While my Indonesian friends and I used to run in fields with water buffalo and goats—[*laughter*]—a new generation of Indonesians is among the most wired in the world, connected through cell phones and social networks. And while Indonesia as a young nation focused inward, a growing Indonesia now plays a key role in the Asia-Pacific and in the global economy.

Now, this change also extends to politics. When my stepfather was a boy, he watched his own father and older brother leave home to fight and die in the struggle for Indonesian independence. And I'm happy to be here on Heroes Day to honor the memory of so many Indonesians who have sacrificed on behalf of this great country.

When I moved to Jakarta, it was 1967, and it was a time that had followed great suffering and conflict in parts of this country. And even though my stepfather had served in the army, the violence and killing during that time of political upheaval was largely unknown to me because it was unspoken by my Indonesian family and friends. In my household, like so many others across Indonesia, the memories of that time were an invisible presence. Indonesians had their independence, but oftentimes they were afraid to speak their minds about issues.

In the years since then, Indonesia has charted its own course through an extraordinary democratic transformation, from the rule of an iron fist to the rule of the people. In recent years, the world has watched with hope and admiration as Indonesians embraced the peaceful transfer of power and the direct election of leaders. And just as your democracy is symbolized by your elected President and legislature, your democracy is sustained and fortified by its checks and balances: a dynamic civil society, political parties and unions, a vibrant media, and engaged citizens who have ensured that in Indonesia, there will be no turning back from democracy.

But even as this land of my youth has changed in so many ways, those things that I learned to love about Indonesia, that spirit of tolerance that's written into your Constitution, symbolized in mosques and churches and temples standing alongside each other, that spirit that's embodied in your people, that still lives on: *Bhinneka Tunggal Ika*—unity in diversity. This is the foundation of Indonesia's example to the world, and this is why Indonesia will play such an important part in the 21st century.

So today I return to Indonesia as a friend, but also as a President who seeks a deep and enduring partnership between our two countries. Because as vast and diverse countries, as neighbors on either side of the Pacific, and above all, as democracies, the United States and Indonesia are bound together by shared interests and shared values.

Yesterday President Yudhoyono and I announced a new comprehensive partnership between the United States and Indonesia. We are increasing ties between our Governments in many different areas, and just as importantly, we are increasing ties among our people. This is a partnership of equals, grounded in mutual interests and mutual respect.

So with the rest of my time today, I'd like to talk about why the story I just told—the story of Indonesia since the days when I lived here—is so important to the United States and to the world. I will focus on three areas that are closely related, and fundamental to human progress: development, democracy, and religious faith.

First, the friendship between the United States and Indonesia can advance our mutual interest in development. When I moved to Indonesia, it would have been hard to imagine a future in which the prosperity of families in Chicago and Jakarta would be connected. But our economies are now global, and Indonesians have experienced both the promise and the perils of globalization, from the shock of the Asian financial crisis in the nineties to the millions lifted out of poverty because of increased trade and commerce. And what that means, and what we learned in the recent economic crisis, is that we have a stake in each other's success.

America has a stake in Indonesia growing and developing, with prosperity that is broadly shared among the Indonesian people, because a rising middle class here in Indonesia means new markets for our goods, just as America is a market for goods coming from Indonesia. So we are investing more in Indonesia, and our exports have grown by nearly 50 percent, and we are opening doors for Americans and Indonesians to do business with one another.

America has a stake in an Indonesia that plays its rightful role in shaping the global economy. Gone are the days when seven or eight countries would come together to determine the direction of global markets. That's why the G–20 is now the center of international economic cooperation, so that emerging economies like Indonesia have a greater voice and also bear greater responsibility for guiding the global economy. And through its leadership of the G–20's anticorruption group, Indonesia should lead on the world stage and by example in embracing transparency and accountability.

America has a stake in an Indonesia that pursues sustainable development, because the way we grow will determine the quality of our lives and the health of our planet. And that's why we're developing clean energy technologies that can power industry and preserve Indonesia's precious natural resources, and America welcomes your country's strong leadership in the global effort to combat climate change.

Above all, America has a stake in the success of the Indonesian people. Underneath the headlines of the day, we must build bridges between our people because our future security and prosperity is shared. And that is exactly what we're doing, by increasing collaboration among our scientists and researchers and by working together to foster entrepreneurship. And I'm especially pleased that we have committed to double the number of American and Indonesian students studying in our respective countries. We want more Indonesian students in American schools, and we want more American students to come study in this country. We want to forge new ties and greater understanding between young people in this young century.

These are the issues that really matter in our daily lives. Development, after all, is not simply about growth rates and numbers on a balance sheet. It's about whether a child can learn the skills they need to make it in a changing world. It's about whether a good idea is allowed to grow into a business and not suffocated by corruption. It's about whether those forces that have transformed the Jakarta I once knew—technology and trade and the flow of people and goods—can translate into a better life for all Indonesians, for all human beings, a life marked by dignity and opportunity.

Now, this kind of development is inseparable from the role of democracy. Today, we sometimes hear that democracy stands in the way of economic progress. This is not a new argument. Particularly in times of change and economic uncertainty, some will say that it is easier to take a shortcut to development by trading away the right of human beings for the power of the state. But that's not what I saw on my trip to India, and that is not what I see here in Indonesia.

Your achievements demonstrate that democracy and development reinforce one another.

Like any democracy, you have known setbacks along the way. America is no different. Our own Constitution spoke of the effort to forge a "more perfect Union," and that is a journey that we've traveled ever since. We've endured civil war, and we struggled to extend equal rights to all of our citizens. But it is precisely this effort that has allowed us to become stronger and more prosperous, while also becoming a more just and a more free society.

Like other countries that emerged from colonial rule in the last century, Indonesia struggled and sacrificed for the right to determine your destiny. That is what Heroes Day is all about, an Indonesia that belongs to Indonesians. But you also ultimately decided that freedom cannot mean replacing the strong hand of a colonizer with a strongman of your own.

Of course, democracy is messy. Not everyone likes the results of every election. You go through your ups and downs. But the journey is worthwhile, and it goes beyond casting a ballot. It takes strong institutions to check the power—the concentration of power. It takes open markets to allow individuals to thrive. It takes a free press and an independent justice system to root out abuses and excess and to insist on accountability. It takes open society and active citizens to reject inequality and injustice.

These are the forces that will propel Indonesia forward. And it will require a refusal to tolerate the corruption that stands in the way of opportunity, a commitment to transparency that gives every Indonesian a stake in their Government, and a belief that the freedom of Indonesians—that Indonesians have fought for is what holds this great nation together.

That is the message of the Indonesians who have advanced this democratic story, from those who fought in the Battle of Surabaya 55 years ago today, to the students who marched peacefully for democracy in the 1990s, to leaders who have embraced the peaceful transition of power in this young century. Because ultimately, it will be the rights of citizens that will stitch together this remarkable *Nusantara* that stretches from Sabang to Merauke, an insistence that every child born in this country should be treated equally, whether they come from Java or Aceh, from Bali or Papua, that all Indonesians have equal rights.

That effort extends to the example that Indonesia is now setting abroad. Indonesia took the initiative to establish the Bali Democracy Forum, an open forum for countries to share their experiences and best practices in fostering democracy. Indonesia has also been at the forefront of pushing for more attention to human rights within ASEAN. The nations of Southeast Asia must have the right to determine their own destiny, and the United States will strongly support that right. But the people of Southeast Asia must have the right to determine their own destiny as well. And that's why we condemned elections in Burma recently that were neither free nor fair. That is why we are supporting your vibrant civil society in working with counterparts across this region. Because there's no reason why respect for human rights should stop at the border of any country.

Now, hand in hand, that is what development and democracy are about, the notion that certain values are universal. Prosperity without freedom is just another form of poverty, because there are aspirations that human beings share: the liberty of knowing that your leader is accountable to you, that you won't be locked up for disagreeing with them, the opportunity to get an education and to be able to work with dignity, the freedom to practice your faith without fear or restriction. Those are universal values that must be observed everywhere.

Now, religion is the final topic that I want to address today, and like democracy and development, it is fundamental to the Indonesian story.

Like the other Asian nations that I'm visiting on this trip, Indonesia is steeped in spirituality, a place where people worship God in many different ways. Along with this rich diversity, it is also home to the world's largest Muslim population, a truth I came to know as a boy when I heard the call to prayer across Jakarta.

Just as individuals are not defined solely by their faith, Indonesia is defined by more than its Muslim population. But we also know that relations between the United States and Muslim communities have frayed over many years. As President, I've made it a priority to begin to repair these relations. As part of that effort, I went to Cairo last June, and I called for a new beginning between the United States and Muslims around the world, one that creates a path for us to move beyond our differences.

I said then and I will repeat now that no single speech can eradicate years of mistrust. But I believed then and I believe today that we do have a choice. We can choose to be defined by our differences and give in to a future of suspicion and mistrust, or we can choose to do the hard work of forging common ground and commit ourselves to the steady pursuit of progress. And I can promise you, no matter what setbacks may come, the United States is committed to human progress. That is who we are. That is what we've done. And that is what we will do.

Now, we know well the issues that have caused tensions for many years, and these are issues that I addressed in Cairo. In the 17 months that have passed since that speech, we have made some progress, but we have much more work to do.

Innocent civilians in America, in Indonesia, and across the world are still targeted by violent extremism. I made it clear that America is not and never will be at war with Islam. Instead, all of us must work together to defeat Al Qaida and its affiliates, who have no claim to be leaders of any religion, certainly not a great world religion like Islam. But those who want to build must not cede ground to terrorists who seek to destroy. And this is not a task for America alone. Indeed, here in Indonesia, you've made progress in rooting out extremists and combating such violence.

In Afghanistan, we continue to work with a coalition of nations to build the capacity of the Afghan Government to secure its future. Our shared interest is in building peace in a war-torn land, a peace that provides no safe haven for violent extremists and that provide hope for the Afghan people.

Meanwhile, we've made progress on one of our core commitments, our effort to end the war in Iraq. Nearly 100,000 American troops have now left Iraq under my Presidency. Iraqis have taken full responsibility for their security. And we will continue to support Iraq as it forms an inclusive government, and we will bring all of our troops home.

In the Middle East, we have faced false starts and setbacks, but we've been persistent in our pursuit of peace. Israelis and Palestinians restarted direct talks, but enormous obstacles remain. There should be no illusion that peace and security will come easy. But let there be no doubt: America will spare no effort in working for the outcome that is just and that is in the interests of all the parties involved. Two states, Israel and Palestine, living side by side in peace and security; that is our goal.

The stakes are high in resolving all of these issues. For our world has grown smaller, and while those forces that connect us have unleashed great opportunity and great wealth, they also empower those who seek to derail progress. One bomb in a marketplace can obliterate the bustle of daily commerce. One whispered rumor can obscure the truth and set off violence between communities that once lived together in peace. In an age of rapid change and colliding cultures, what we share as human beings can sometimes be lost.

But I believe that the history of both America and Indonesia should give us hope. It is a story written into our national mottoes. In the United States, our motto is *E pluribus unum*—out of many, one. *Bhinneka Tunggal Ika*—unity in diversity. We are two nations, which have traveled different paths. Yet our nations show that hundreds of millions who hold different beliefs can be united in freedom under one flag. And we are now building on that shared humanity, through young people who will study in each other's schools, through the entrepreneurs forging ties that can lead to greater prosperity, and through our embrace of fundamental democratic values and human aspirations.

You know, before I came here, I visited Istiqlal Mosque, a place of worship that was still under construction when I lived in Jakarta. And I admired its soaring minaret and its imposing dome and welcoming space. But its name and history also speak to what makes Indonesia great. *Istiqlal* means independence, and its con-

struction was in part a testament to the nation's struggle for freedom. Moreover, this house of worship for many thousands of Muslims was designed by a Christian architect.

Such is Indonesia's spirit. Such is the message of Indonesia's inclusive philosophy, *Pancasila*. Across an archipelago that contains some of God's most beautiful creations, islands rising above an ocean named for peace, people choose to worship God as they please. Islam flourishes, but so do other faiths. Development is strengthened by an emerging democracy. Ancient traditions endure, even as a rising power is on the move.

This is not to say that Indonesia is without imperfections. No country is. But here we can find the ability to bridge divides of race and region and religion, that ability to see yourself in other people. As a child of a different race who came here from a distant country, I found this spirit in the greeting that I received upon moving here: *Selamat datang*. As a Christian visiting a mosque on this visit, I found it in the words of a leader who was asked about my visit and said: "Muslims are also allowed in churches. We are all God's followers."

That spark of the divine lives within each of us. We cannot give in to doubt or cynicism or despair. The stories of Indonesia and America should make us optimistic, because it tells us that history is on the side of human progress, that unity is more powerful than division, and that the people of this world can live together in peace. May our two nations, working together, with faith and determination, share these truths with all mankind.

Sebagai penutup, saya mengucapkan kepada seluruh rakyat Indonesia: terima kasih atas. Terima kasih. Assalamu alaikum. Thank you.

NOTE: The President spoke at 9:30 a.m. In his remarks, he referred to Gumilar Rusliwa Somantri, president, University of Indonesia; President Susilo Bambang Yudhoyono of Indonesia; Masdar F. Mas'udi, deputy chairman of the Indonesian Islamic organization Nahdlatul Ulama. He also referred to his sister Maya Soetoro-Ng. No translation for the portion of the President's remarks delivered in Bahasa Indonesia was provided by the Office of the Press Secretary.

Letter to Congressional Leaders on Continuation of the National Emergency With Respect to Iran
November 10, 2010

Dear Madam Speaker: (Dear Mr. President:)

Section 202(d) of the National Emergencies Act (50 U.S.C. 1622(d)) provides for the automatic termination of a national emergency unless, prior to the anniversary date of its declaration, the President publishes in the *Federal Register* and transmits to the Congress a notice stating that the emergency is to continue in effect beyond the anniversary date. In accordance with this provision, I have sent to the *Federal Register* for publication the enclosed notice stating that the national emergency with respect to Iran that was declared in Executive Order 12170 of November 14, 1979, is to continue in effect beyond November 14, 2010.

Our relations with Iran have not yet returned to normal, and the process of implementing the January 19, 1981, agreements with Iran is still underway. For these reasons, I have determined that it is necessary to continue the national emergency declared on November 14, 1979, with respect to Iran, beyond November 14, 2010.

Sincerely,

BARACK OBAMA

NOTE: Identical letters were sent to Nancy Pelosi, Speaker of the House of Representatives, and Joseph R. Biden, Jr., President of the Senate. The notice is listed in Appendix D at the end of this volume.

Remarks at a Veterans Day Ceremony in Seoul, South Korea
November 11, 2010

Hello, Yongsan! Oh, it is wonderful to be here. Give another round of applause to Army Specialist Courtney Newby for the great introduction.

A few other people that I want to just make mention of. We are so proud and want to thank our outstanding representatives here in the Republic of Korea, Ambassador Kathleen Stephens and General Skip Sharp. Please give them a big round of applause.

A former colleague of mine in the Illinois State Senate who is now a Congressman from the great State of Illinois, Peter Roskam, is with us here today. So give him a big round of applause. Where's Peter? Where is he? There he is up there.

And our great friend and ally from the Republic of Korea is here—General Jung is here. Give him a big round of applause—deputy commander, Combined Forces. A few other people I want to give thanks to: Lieutenant General John Johnson, Command Sergeant Major Robert Winzenried.

We are so proud to have with us U.S. and Republic of Korea vets of the Korean war who are here, and we are greatly honored by their presence. And I want to make special mention of one of them, Congressional Medal of Honor recipient Hector Cafferata, Jr. Please give him an extraordinary round of applause.

It is an enormous honor to be here at Yongsan Garrison. As President of the United States, I have no greater privilege than serving as Commander in Chief of the finest military that the world has ever known. And on this Veterans Day, there's no place I'd rather be than right here with U.S. Forces Korea.

We've got 8th Army in the house. We've got members of the 7th Air Force. We've got U.S. Navy Forces Korea. We've got just about every marine in South Korea here today. Happy birthday, Marines, by the way. And we've got a whole lot of DOD civilians too. So we are very proud of you.

It's good to see some spouses and family members in the audience. You bear the burden of your loved ones' service in ways that are often immeasurable: an empty chair at the dinner table or another holiday where mom and dad are someplace far away. So I just want you to know that this Nation recognizes the sacrifices of families as well. And we are grateful for your service as well.

Now, on this day, we honor every man and woman who has ever worn the uniform of the United States of America. We salute fallen heroes and keep in our prayers those who are still in harm's way, like the men and women serving in Iraq and Afghanistan.

We recall acts of uncommon bravery and selflessness. But we also remember that honoring those who've served is about more than the words we say on Veterans Day or Memorial Day. It's about how we treat our veterans every single day of the year. It's about making sure they have the care they need and the benefits that they've earned when they come home. It's about serving all of you as well as you've served the United States of America.

This has been one of my highest priorities since taking office. It's why I asked for one of the largest increases in the VA budget in the past 30 years. It's why we've dramatically increased funding for veterans' health care. It's why we're improving care for wounded warriors, especially those with posttraumatic stress and traumatic brain injury. It's why we're working to eliminate the backlog at the VA and reforming the entire process with electronic claims and medical records. It's why there are fewer homeless veterans on the streets than there were 2 years ago. It's why there are nearly 400,000 veterans and their families who are going to college because of the post-9/11 GI bill.

So I want all of you to know, when you come home, your country's going to be there for you. That is the commitment I make to you as Commander in Chief. That is the sacred trust between the United States of America and all who defend its ideals.

It's a trust that's been forged in places far from our shores, from the beaches of Europe to the jungles of Vietnam, from the deserts of Iraq and the mountains of Afghanistan to the peninsula where we stand today.

Sixty years have come and gone since the Communist armies first crossed the 38th parallel. Within 3 days, they'd captured Seoul. By the end of the next month, they had driven the Korean Army all the way south to Pusan. And from where things stood in the summer of 1950, it didn't appear that the Republic of Korea would survive much longer.

At the time, many Americans had probably never heard of Korea. It had only been 5 years since we had finished fighting the last war. But we knew that if we allowed the unprovoked invasion of a free nation, then all free nations would be threatened. And so for the first time since its creation, the United Nations voted to use armed forces to repel the attack from North Korea.

And so on September 15, 1950, American forces landed at Inchon. The conditions they fought under were some of the worst that Americans had ever experienced. The temperatures reached more than 30 below zero in the winter, over 100 degrees in the summer. In many places, Americans and our Korean allies were outgunned and outmanned, sometimes by as much as 20 to 1. At one point, they were hit with 24,000 artillery shells a day. By the end, the fighting had sometimes devolved into trench warfare, waged on hands and knees in the middle of the night.

And yet our soldiers fought on. Nearly 37,000 Americans would give their lives in Korea— 37,000. But after 3 years of fighting, our forces finally succeeded in driving the invading armies back over the 38th parallel. One war historian said that while he believed Korea was "the greatest of all trials" for American troops, their performance was "nothing short of miraculous."

Many of the men responsible for this miracle were only teenagers. Others had just finished fighting in the Second World War. Most would go home to raise their families and live out their lives. And 62 veterans of the Korean war have returned to be with us here today.

Gentlemen, we are honored by your presence. We are grateful for your service. The world is better off because of what you did here. And for those who can, I would ask that, again, you receive the thanks of a grateful nation. If any—actually, they're all standing now, so it looks like they're doing great. But please give them a big round of applause.

I also want to recognize the Korean soldiers who battled side by side with our own. These men fought bravely and sacrificed greatly for their country, and some of them have joined us here as well. So thank you, friends. *Katchi kapshida*—we go together.

The veterans who have traveled here today saw battle at the Inchon landing and the Pusan Perimeter. They survived the bloodshed at Heartbreak Ridge and the ambush at Chosin Reservoir. At one point in that battle, the enemy tossed a grenade into a trench where multiple marines lay wounded. And that is where Private Hector Cafferata ran into that trench, picked up that grenade, and threw it back. It detonated in his hand and severely injured his arm. But because of what he did, Private Cafferata served the lives of his fellow marines. He received the Medal of Honor for his heroism. He is here today. Again, please give him an incredible—[*applause*].

Each of these men served their Nation with incredible courage and commitment. They left their homes and their families and risked their lives in what's often been called the forgotten war. So today we all want you to know this: We remember. We remember your courage; we remember your sacrifice. And the legacy of your service lives on in a free and prosperous Republic of Korea.

Real change comes slowly. Many people don't live to see the difference they've made in the lives of others. But for the men and women who have served on this peninsula, all you have to do is look around. Whether you're a veteran who landed in 1950 or one of the Yongsan troops today, the security you've provided has made possible one of the great success stories of our time.

There are Koreans who can still remember when this country was little more than rice paddies and villages that would flood during monsoon season. Not two generations later, highways and skyscrapers line the horizon of one of the most prosperous, fastest growing democra-

cies in all of the world. That progress has transformed the lives of millions of people.

And you should know, one of these people is a man who went from grinding poverty to the Presidency of this country. When I visited last year, I had lunch with President Lee, who I'll be seeing later today, and he shared with me his story of what it was like growing up poor as a child in Korea. And he said, "I hope the American people understand how grateful we are for what you've done, because we would not be the strong, prosperous nation we are were it not for the sacrifices made by the men and women of the United States military." That's from the President of this country.

Because the Korean war ended where it began geographically, some ended up using the phrase "die for a tie" to describe the sacrifices of those who fought here. But as we look around in this thriving democracy and its grateful, hopeful citizens, one thing is clear: This was no tie. This was victory.

This was a victory then, and it is a victory today. And 60 years later, a friendship that was forged in a war has become an alliance that has led to greater security and untold progress, not only in the Republic of Korea, but throughout Asia. That is something that everyone here can be extraordinarily proud of.

Now, it's also a reminder of what still lies on the other side of the 38th parallel. Today, the Korean Peninsula provides the world's clearest contrast between a society that is open and a society that is closed, between a nation that is dynamic and growing and a government that would rather starve its people than change. It's a contrast that's so stark, you can see it from space, as the brilliant lights of Seoul give way to the utter darkness of the North.

This is not an accident of history. This is a direct result of the path that's been taken by North Korea, a path of confrontation and provocation, one that includes the pursuit of nuclear weapons and the attack on the *Cheonan* last March.

And in the wake of this aggression, Pyongyang should not be mistaken: The United States will never waver in our commitment to the security of the Republic of Korea. We will not waver.

The alliance between our two nations has never been stronger, and along with the rest of the world, we've made it clear that the North Korea's pursuit of nuclear weapons will only lead to more isolation and less security for them.

There is another path available to North Korea. If they choose to fulfill their international obligations and commitments to the international community, they will have the chance to offer their people lives of growing opportunity instead of crushing poverty, a future of greater security and greater respect, a future that includes the prosperity and opportunity available to citizens on this end of the Korean Peninsula.

Until that day comes, the world can take comfort in knowing that the men and women of the United States Armed Forces are standing watch on freedom's frontier. In doing so, you carry on the legacy of service and sacrifice that we saw from those who landed here all those years ago. It's a legacy we honor and cherish on this Veterans Day.

At the Korean War Memorial in Washington, there's a plaque right near the inscription that lists the number of Americans who were killed, wounded, missing in action, and held as prisoners of war. And it says, "Our Nation honors her sons and daughters who answered the call to defend a country they never knew and a people they never met."

A country they never knew and a people they never met. I know of no better words to capture the selflessness and generosity of every man or woman who has ever worn the uniform of the United States of America. At a time when it has never been more tempting or accepted to pursue narrow self-interest and personal ambition, all of you here remind us that there are few things that are more fundamentally American than doing what we can to make a difference in the lives of others.

And that's why you'll always be the best that America has to offer the world. And that is why people who never met you, who never knew you, will always be grateful to the friend and ally they found in the United States of America.

So thank you for your service. May God bless you, and may God bless the United States of America. Thank you.

NOTE: The President spoke at 10:53 a.m. at U.S. Army Garrison—Yongsan. In his remarks, he referred to Gen. Walter L. "Skip" Sharp, USA, commander, United Nations Command, Combined Forces Command, and U.S. Forces Korea; Gen. Jung Seung-jo, Republic of Korea Army, deputy commander, Combined Forces Command; Lt. Gen. John D. Johnson, USA, commanding general, 8th U.S. Army, and chief of staff, United Nations Command, Combined Forces Command, and U.S. Forces Korea; CSM Robert A. Winzenried, USA, command sergeant major, United Nations Command, Combined Forces Command, U.S. Forces Korea, and 8th U.S. Army; and President Lee Myung-bak of South Korea.

The President's News Conference With President Lee Myung-bak of South Korea in Seoul
November 11, 2010

President Lee. Thank you, members of the press. On behalf of the Government and people of the Republic of Korea, I wish to welcome President Obama and his delegation on their second visit to Korea.

As you know, ladies and gentlemen, this year we are commemorating the 60th anniversary of the Korean war. The alliance between Korea and the United States was born out of the trenches of the war. Our brave soldiers fought together side by side against Communist aggression to defend peace and freedom. So I thank President Obama and the people of the United States.

And today is Veterans Day, and we are honored to remember those valiant soldiers and their families who sacrificed so much for their country defending freedom. I've been told that President Obama has personally visited the U.S. Forces Korea here to take part in the ceremony to celebrate the Veterans Day, and I thank President Obama.

President Obama and I agreed that our bilateral relationship is strong in every aspect, and we will continue to work so that we can make it even stronger. In particular, we agreed to carry on the future vision for the alliance that we adopted last June, which states that Korea and the U.S. will work to expand our strategic alliance in all areas. We renewed our pledge and common commitments, and we will make sure to carry them out with an eye toward our common future.

Furthermore, based on our firm security alliance, Korea and the U.S. will maintain a strong defense posture that will deter all provocations and threats, ensuring peace and stability on the Korean Peninsula.

President Obama and I agreed that the importance and responsibilities of the G–20 as the premier forum for international economic cooperation will continue to grow as it carries out its mandate. We will work together so that its legitimacy and credibility will be enhanced. President Obama recognized the role that Korea has played as chair, and we thank him for his kind remarks.

We both agreed that it's critically important that the G–20 is able to deliver on its promises. The G–20 must implement substantive and specific action plans that will ensure the sustainable and balanced growth of the global economy. This is our collective goal. We must place ourselves on the path to a more sustainable, prosperous future that will have far-reaching benefits for all of us.

Now, with regards to the Korea-U.S. free trade agreement, President Obama and I agreed that we will give my Trade Minister and the U.S. Trade Representative more time so that they can finalize the technical issues. And President Obama and I will continue to work together so that we can have a mutually acceptable agreement at the earliest possible date.

President Obama and I talked about the situation on the Korean Peninsula. We agreed to strengthen our cooperation in dealing with the North Korea nuclear issue. We recognize the close cooperation that was evident during the aftermath of the sinking of the *Cheonan* by North Korea. We also reaffirm that North Korea must fully and irrevocably give up all its nuclear weapons ambitions and work towards achieving denuclearization of the peninsula. This is an essential requirement if we are to bring about genuine and permanent peace and stability on the peninsula and beyond.

President Obama and I agreed that North Korea must display sincere and genuine intent to give up all its nuclear weapons ambitions and to back this up with action as soon as possible. They must work to fundamentally and comprehensively resolve their nuclear issue.

And for this, ladies and gentlemen, Korea and the U.S. will work with the members of the six-party talks, as well as with the larger international community who are committed to global peace and stability.

President Obama and I agree that North Korea should and must show sincerity towards the Republic of Korea and to assume responsibility for what they did to the *Cheonan*. Such could be the starting point for improving inter-Korean relations. We urge North Korea to make that strategic decision. We will continue our close cooperation on this matter.

And President Obama and I also talked in length about global issues such as nonproliferation, eradicating terrorism, how to tackle climate change, the future of green growth, and attaining stability in Afghanistan and other regional issues. These are important regional and international issues that require continued cooperation.

Ladies and gentlemen, I congratulated our American friends for joining the East Asia summit for the first time in Hanoi last month. Again, welcome. It's great to have the U.S. join us. And I look forward to the U.S. contributing more to peace, stability, and prosperity in East Asia.

And of course, we will continue to work closely for all this and more. Today's meeting has been a chance for us to reaffirm our close alliance and partnership in laying out the map for the future. I'm also pleased that our bilateral relationship has been strengthened and also pleased that President Obama and I have had a chance to foster our friendship.

Thank you.

President Obama. Thank you, President Lee, for your gracious welcome and for what you've done to express how much our alliance has meant to you and the people of this nation. And I can assure you that the sentiment you expressed is shared by the American people, especially by our veterans and servicemembers who've served here and have great affection for South Korea and its people.

It is wonderful to be back in Seoul. We are here for the G–20, and I want to thank President Lee and the people of the Republic of Korea for their hospitality. And I want to congratulate you on becoming the first non-G–8 country to host a G–20 summit. This is another example of what President Lee calls "Global Korea," a Korea that plays an increasingly active and leading role in the world. It is a role that the United States firmly supports and wants to encourage.

Any time we meet, it's an opportunity to reaffirm the unbreakable alliance between our two countries. This, however, is a special occasion. It's the United States Veterans Day. We celebrate veterans on this day. And this year, as President Lee noted, is also the 60th anniversary of the start of the Korean war. So I just had a wonderful opportunity at Yongsan not only to pay tribute to our American troops serving here, but to pay tribute to our veterans of the Korean war, Americans and Koreans.

Their service, through six decades, is a powerful reminder that security, democracy, and prosperity reinforce each other. As President Lee has said, security has allowed this country to become a great democracy and one of the economic miracles of our time. In turn, prosperity that is broadly shared, within countries and in regions, makes us safer and more secure. Advancing our shared prosperity and security was the focus of our meetings today.

As President Lee just noted, we discussed the need to keep moving forward towards a U.S.-Korea free trade agreement, which would create jobs and prosperity in both our countries. We believe that such an agreement, if done right, can be a win-win for our people. It could be a win for the United States because it would increase the export of American goods by some $10 billion and billions more in services, supporting more than 70,000 jobs back home.

It could be a win for South Korea, with more access to the American economy, which would support jobs, raise living standards, and offer more choices for Korean consumers. And it could be a win for the overall economic partnership between our two countries by bringing us closer together, allowing us to benefit from each other's innovations, and ensuring strong protections for workers' rights and the environment.

So we have asked our teams to work tirelessly in the coming days and weeks to get this completed, and we are confident that we will do so. And President Lee, in fact, asked his team to come to Washington in the near future to continue these discussions. So I appreciate all the efforts that he's making on this issue.

To advance our shared security, President Lee and I also discussed our ongoing efforts to strengthen and modernize our alliance, including our joint vision for meeting 21st-century challenges. And although I said it at Yongsan, we can never say it enough: The United States will never waver in our commitment to the security of the Republic of Korea.

I reaffirmed our conviction that in the aftermath of the sinking of the *Cheonan*, North Korea must address South Korea's concerns and end its belligerent behavior. Likewise, North Korea needs to fulfill its obligations to eliminate its nuclear weapons program. Only by meeting its responsibilities and not threatening others will North Korea find real security and respect.

And I want to reiterate that along with our South Korean and international partners, the United States is prepared to provide economic assistance to North Korea and help it integrate into the international community, provided that North Korea meets its obligations.

Finally, since this is "Global Korea," we discussed the whole range of issues before us.

Heading into the G–20, we discussed the need to create an approach where all of our economies, developed and emerging, can help achieve global growth that is balanced and sustained. We discussed common security challenges, including Afghanistan and Iran. And I told President Lee that we're very much looking forward to South Korea hosting the next nuclear security summit in 2 years, which is yet another example of South Korean leadership and another step toward our goal of securing all vulnerable materials around the world.

So again, I want to thank my good friend President Lee for his hospitality and leadership. And as we mark the 60th anniversary of the war that turned us into strong allies, I want to salute President Lee and the people of South Korea for the extraordinary progress that you've made—a strong and prosperous democracy that's an example to others, in this region and around the world.

Mr. President.

Moderator. Now we will be taking questions from the members of the press. First of all, a Korean press reporter will ask a question directed to President Lee.

South Korea-U.S. Free Trade Agreement

Q. A question going out to President Lee Myung-bak. You have just said that you discussed the KORUS FTA issue with President Obama, and we were very hopeful—hoping that a conclusion or an agreement would be reached between the two leaders. What was the obstacle, and what kind of effort do you intend to continue to employ in order to get this agreement?

President Lee. The talks will continue. The talks, like I said, will continue between Korea and the United States. And as you know, my Trade Minister as well as the U.S. Trade Representative have been engaged in extensive discussions, but President Obama and I agreed that we need to give them a bit more time so that they can iron out the technical issues between themselves. So once the G–20 summit here in Korea is over, I'm sure that the discussions will continue and the officials from both sides will meet. I expect it won't take too long.

Moderator. A member of the U.S. press will ask a question to President Obama.

President Obama. Patricia Zengerle.

Global Economic Stabilization

Q. Thank you, Mr. President. I'm Patricia Zengerle from Reuters. There's been much criticism of U.S. monetary policy in the runup to this G–20. And with old G–7 partners like Germany opposing you, does this not make it much harder for the United States to press China for yuan appreciation and persuade other G–20 partners to support your goals if they sense that the U.S. is being isolated at the summit?

President Obama. Well, I think that you will see at this summit a broad-based agreement from all countries, including Germany, that we need to ensure balanced and sustainable growth. And it is my expectation that the communique will begin to put in place mechanisms that help us track and encourage such balanced and sustainable growth.

The most important thing that the United States can do for the world economy is to grow, because we continue to be the world's largest market and a huge engine for all other countries to grow. Countries like Germany that export heavily benefit from our open markets and us buying their goods. That's true for every G–20 member.

And so the point that we have consistently made is that in a prudent, stable way, we want to make sure that we are boosting growth rates at home as well as abroad. It is difficult to do that if we start seeing the huge imbalances redevelop that helped to contribute to the crisis that we just went through. And I don't think this is a controversial proposition. In fact, we set up a framework back in Pittsburgh that discussed this, and this is just a follow-on to the work that we've already done.

Now, as I've said, I think, when I was first asked this in India, it's not our habit to comment on actions by the Federal Reserve. But as President of the United States, I can tell you that my instructions to my team, including Secretary Geithner, is to focus every single day on how we can grow our economy, how we can increase exports, how we can make sure that even as we're buying goods from places like South Korea, we're also selling goods to places like South Korea.

That's part of the reason why we think that getting this Korea-U.S. free trade agreement done is so important. And President Lee and I discussed this, and our instructions are we're not—we don't want months to pass before we get this done; we want this to be done in a matter of weeks.

So bottom line is, Patricia, I think that when you see the final communique, it will reflect a broad-based consensus about the direction that we need to go. There may be on any given—at any given moment disagreements between countries in terms of particular strategies. That's not surprising because each country has unique problems and finds itself in different positions. Countries like Germany historically are very sensitive to issues like inflation. But I don't think you'll get any objection to their belief that if the U.S. isn't growing, that's not good for the rest of the world.

It also doesn't negate the fact that if we—if individual countries are engaging in practices that are purposely designed to boost their exports at the expense of others, that that can contribute to problems as opposed to solving them.

Q. President Lee, on the same subject? President Lee, do you have any concerns about that U.S. policy might lead to a flood of hot money coming into the Korean economy?

President Lee. I think that kind of question should be asked to me when President Obama is not standing right next to me. [*Laughter*]

No, we get asked a very similar question. And I answer it this way: I tell those who ask me that question that, first and foremost, what's most important for us and for everyone around the world, including the Americans, is for the U.S. economy to be robust, to recover, and to continue to grow. That is critically important for the entire global economy if they wish to get on the path of sustainable and balanced growth.

Now, I know that there have been certain decisions taken by the U.S. Government and the Federal Reserve. And I know that those decisions were made with due consideration for everything else.

And you asked me a question about the influx of hot money into the Korean economy. I don't see any possibility of this happening or such an event becoming destabilizing for the Korean economy. But what I would want to emphasize is that such a measure—decision taken by the U.S. Government, we hope that it will be a positive contribution to the recovery and the revival of the U.S. economy. We know that this has been talked about in Pittsburgh. And that is, namely, the fact of adopting an indicative guideline or a framework for ensuring strong and sustainable growth.

And we know that these and other topics of interest will be included in the Seoul communique as well. And we know that are making progress on this through cooperation. I'd also emphasize another point, and that is the importance of international cooperation.

Moderator. And now we will have a Korean reporter ask a question to His Excellency President Obama.

North Korea

Q. I have a question to Mr. President Obama. Let me ask you about the North Korea nuclear threats. The six-party talks were launched in 2003 to resolve the North Korea nuclear issue. But it remains an issue of serious concern. There are even some reports about North Korea having several nuclear bombs already. So how you evaluate the past talks? Do you have any idea or plan to move the denuclearization process forward?

Thank you.

President Obama. The six-party talks provided a valuable forum to engage North Korea and encourage it to move towards more responsible behavior. And in 2005, we began to see some positive movement, but then there was backsliding. And since that time what we've seen is talk for the sake of talking, instead of talk for the sake of actually implementing changes that would resolve the tensions on the peninsula.

President Lee and I have been moving in complete agreement over the last couple of years in sending a message to the North

Koreans that they have a choice available to them. They can continue on a path of belligerence towards their neighbors, an unwillingness to denuclearize, engaging in provocative acts, and that will ensure their continued isolation from the world community. It will prevent them from developing, it will result in hardship for their people, and it will continue to create tensions in the region.

The preferred choice is for North Korea to say, we are going to meet our previous commitments; we are going to engage in a irreversible path towards denuclearization. And as I said in my opening statement, if they are willing to take those steps, then you will see a South Korea, a United States, and an international community that can give them substantial assistance to help develop their country and improve their security over the long term.

Now, President Lee and I have discussed this extensively and our belief is, is that there will be a appropriate time and place to reenter into six-party talks. But we have to see a seriousness of purpose by the North Koreans in order to spend the extraordinary time and energy that's involved in these talks. We're not interested in just going through the motions with the same result. And I think the North Koreans understand that.

So our expectation is, is that we will continue to engage. We will continue to look for signals from the North Koreans that they're serious. At the point where it appears that they are, in fact, prepared to move forward on the kind of path that all of us want to see, then we're going to be there ready to negotiate with them.

Moderator. As both Presidents have a subsequent meetings, so we will just take the final question, a question from the U.S. reporter.

U.S. Deficit and National Debt/South Korea-U.S. Free Trade Agreement

Q. Jonathan Weisman with the Wall Street Journal. The Speaker of the House and several members of your party partially condemned the initial proposals from the chairman of your Deficit Commission, calling them simply unacceptable. If the—as the Commission nears its final report, what message do you have to your party

to keep their powder dry? And are you preparing to make the difficult decisions that you have said are necessary to cut the deficit, even if that means raising the retirement age or cutting back on Medicare?

And if I may, to President Lee, to many Americans who see Hyundais on their roads, LG phones in their pockets, Samsung televisions on their walls, South Korea epitomizes the kind of one-way trade relationship that President Obama discussed in India. What assurances can you give the American people, many of whom whose parents fought and died for your country, that they will finally get the ability to freely and fairly compete for the South Korean consumers with your conglomerates?

And if President Obama wants to weigh in on that, we welcome it. Thank you.

President Obama. I have not seen the final report from the deficit commission. I have said very clearly that until I see the final report I'm not going to comment on it because I want them to have the space to do their work. They're still in negotiations. I think Chairmen Bowles and Simpson are trying to round up 14 votes for certain aspects of the recommendations, and I want to make sure that they've got the room and the space to do so.

I set up this Commission precisely because I'm prepared to make some tough decisions. I can't make them alone. I'm going to need Congress to work with me. There was a lot of talk during the course of this campaign season about debt and deficits. And unfortunately, a lot of the talk didn't match up with reality. If we are concerned about debt and deficits, then we're going to have to take actions that are difficult and we're going to have to tell the truth to the American people.

I'm somebody who's big on eliminating earmarks in Congress, but earmarks alone won't balance a budget. I think that we can root out more waste and abuse in Federal spending, but even the most optimistic estimates about the amount of waste and abuse that can be eliminated still leaves a huge deficit and a substantial debt.

So as you said, Jonathan, we're going to have to make some tough choices. The only way to make those tough choices, historically, has been if both parties are willing to move forward together.

And so before anybody starts shooting down proposals, I think we need to listen, we need to gather up all the facts. I think we have to be straight with the American people. If people are, in fact, concerned about spending, debt, deficits, and the future of our country, then they're going to need to be armed with the information about the kinds of choices that are going to be involved, and we can't just engage in political rhetoric.

There's one last point I want to make about debt and deficits, and that is that the single most important thing we can do to reduce our debt and our deficits is to grow. We increase our economic growth by 1 percentage point, and over time that could have as much of an impact as completely eliminating the Bush tax cuts. I mean, it makes a huge difference if we are growing an extra 1 percent or an extra 1.5 percent.

And so part of the discussion that we have to have on a bipartisan basis, in addition to getting serious about spending and making sure that the money that's coming in matches up with the money that's going out, is also what steps do we have to take to make sure that we're growing. And I'm not going to be favorably disposed towards recommendations or moves by Congress that don't take into account the needs for us to grow long term.

Just with respect to the free trade agreement, again, I think that President Lee is sincere in wanting to get this done. My goal is reciprocal trade; that is a win-win for both countries. I think that can be achieved.

But obviously, what you're alluding to, Jonathan, is a popular concern in the United States of America, and that's why President Lee and I agreed that we need to make sure that over the next several weeks, we are crossing all the t's, dotting all the i's, being able to make the case to both the Korean people and the United States population that this is good for both countries.

And if we rush something that then can't garner popular support, that's going to be a prob-

lem. We think we can make the case, but we want to make sure that that case is airtight.

President Lee. Thank you for the question, and I do understand the reason why you are asking that question. I think there's one thing that the U.S. consumers should understand. We know that in the past, the United States and the people of the United States should understand that many countries around the world, when they were developing, they were able to export a lot of their goods and manufactured goods to the United States. And the American consumers did a tremendous job of helping these developing countries develop their economies. And the Korean products that you talked about—the LG, Samsung, Hyundai cars, and some of these products—when you look at a cell phone made by the LG, the core technology and the goods that are used by these LG companies to build one single cell phone, most of them are imported goods or parts. And many of them come from the United States and other countries, so you cannot say that it is 100 percent Korean manufactured.

So the bilateral trade imbalance is about $8 billion between the U.S. and Korea. That figure has been continuously going down because in that, there's a lot of figures that is hidden, namely the royalty that the Korean companies have to pay the United States that they pay every year.

So one thing that I wish to point out is that—to the American consumers is that there is really no trade imbalance when you—when the U.S. talks about its trade relationship with the United—Republic of Korea.

Now, I know that it will be beneficial for everyone if we can create good jobs in the United States. And I said it before that that will be helpful not only to the American consumers, but to the Republic of Korea as well.

I believe that this can be a win-win agreement, this free trade agreement between the Korea and the United States. And that is the basic principle and the understanding that we've been working on. And I'm hopeful that we can reach an agreement on this.

And I just wanted to make sure that you understand this issue between—the trade imbalance between the two countries.

NOTE: The President spoke at 2:13 p.m. at the Blue House. In his remarks, he referred to Erskine B. Bowles and Alan K. Simpson, Cochairs, National Commission on Fiscal Responsibility and Reform. President Lee referred to Minister of Trade Kim Jong-hoon of South Korea. President Lee and a reporter spoke in Korean, and their remarks were translated by an interpreter.

Remarks Prior to a Meeting With President Hu Jintao of China in Seoul
November 11, 2010

President Obama. It's wonderful to see President Hu once again. We were just noting that it's the seventh time we've had an opportunity to meet. And the U.S.-China relationship, I think, has become stronger over the last several years.

We've been discussing a whole range of not only bilateral issues, but world issues. And as two leading nuclear powers, obviously, we have a special obligation to deal with issues of nuclear proliferation. As two of the world's leading economies, we've got a special obligation to deal with ensuring strong, balanced, and sustainable growth.

I am very much looking forward to hosting President Hu in Washington. And in the meantime, we have created a structure, a Strategic and Economic Dialogue, in which our teams have been working on a whole range of issues. And we're seeing significant progress.

So I look forward to this meeting, and I'm glad to see you again.

President Hu. The Chinese side stands ready to work with the U.S. side to increase dialogue, exchanges, and cooperation so that we can move forward the China-U.S. relationship on a positive, cooperative, and comprehensive track.

I'd like to thank President Obama for inviting me to visit the United States early next year. The competent departments in our two countries are making preparations for the visit. I hope and do believe that the visit will be successful.

This evening the G–20 Seoul summit will be opened. I believe that with the concerted efforts of all the parties, the summit in Seoul will produce positive outcomes.

NOTE: The President spoke at 3:47 p.m. at the Grand Hyatt Seoul hotel. President Hu spoke in Chinese, and his remarks were translated by an interpreter.

Remarks Prior to a Meeting With Chancellor Angela Merkel of Germany in Seoul
November 11, 2010

President Obama. It is a great pleasure to have a chance to meet with Chancellor Merkel. Not only do I have great personal admiration for her, but obviously, the strong alliance between our two countries is one of the cornerstones of prosperity and peace not just in the transatlantic relationship, but in the world.

And we are very proud of the work that we've been doing together. As NATO allies, we obviously have a lot to talk about with respect to issues like Afghanistan, on economic issues, as G–20 members, but also as two of the world's largest economies, making sure that we can continue with the balanced and sustainable growth that all of us seek.

So I'm looking forward to a productive meeting not just here with Chancellor Merkel, but as part of the G–20. And I'm confident that, as a consequence of the work that we have been doing and will continue to do, that we are going to be able to put the world on a path that ensures strong growth and opportunity for both of our peoples.

So it's wonderful to see you again.

Chancellor Merkel. Well, I too am very glad to have had the opportunity to meet again. I think we personally haven't met since the Toronto meetings, so I think it's a very good thing to yet again demonstrate that we are willing to share responsibility together and to use this meeting here to send a signal, really, a good signal for our global growth.

We have worked well together and continue to work well together on a number of areas, and I think in very crucial areas. And I think it's very necessary to work together because only together will we be able to tackle the crucial problems in the world today, problems and issues such as Afghanistan, the upcoming NATO summit meeting, and also obviously this meeting of the G–20.

So I am confident that here too we shall continue to share responsibility and to work well together.

NOTE: The President spoke at 5:22 p.m. at the Grand Hyatt Seoul hotel. Chancellor Merkel spoke in German, and her remarks were translated by an interpreter.

Remarks at a Ceremony Honoring the Group of Twenty Small and Medium-Sized Enterprises (SME) Finance Challenge Award Winners in Seoul
November 12, 2010

Well, thank you very much. Good afternoon, everybody. And again, to President Lee and the people of the Republic of Korea, thank you for your incredible hospitality.

I'm just going to be very brief. I think we all recognize that economic growth is critical for all our countries. And although it's the big companies that get most of the attention, when it comes to creating jobs and opportunity, oftentimes, it's the small and medium-sized enterprises that make all the difference in people's lives.

And one of the biggest challenges for such companies is to make sure that they receive the financing that they need. I am very pleased that we have been able through the G–20 to launch this concrete program that is making a difference in people's lives.

Between Koreans, Canadians, and the United States, we're going to contribute $528 million to put some of the extraordinary ideas that are represented by the winners into practice and to boost the excellent work that they're already doing.

So to all the winners who are here today, congratulations, keep up the outstanding work. And we look forward to—as a consequence of this award—seeing more and more creative mechanisms to finance worthy enterprises. And many of the lessons that are going to be learned from these projects are ones that, hopefully, can be expanded to a whole host of countries for years to come.

So thank you very much for your excellent work.

NOTE: The President spoke at 4:35 p.m. at the Coex Center.

The President's News Conference in Seoul
November 12, 2010

The President. Good afternoon, everybody. Before I discuss the G–20, I wanted to briefly comment on the agreement in Iraq that's taken place on the framework for a new government. There's still challenges to overcome, but all indications are that the Government will be representative, inclusive, and reflect the will of the Iraqi people who cast their ballots in the last election.

This agreement marks another milestone in the history of modern Iraq. Once again, Iraqis are showing their determination to unify Iraq and build its future and that those impulses are far stronger than those who want Iraq to descend into sectarian war and terror.

For the last several months, the United States has worked closely with our Iraqi partners to promote a broad-based Government, one whose leaders share a commitment to serving all Iraqis as equal citizens. Now Iraq's leaders must finish the job of forming their Government so that they can meet the challenges that a diverse coalition will inevitably face. And going forward, we will support the Iraqi people as they strengthen their democracy, resolve political disputes, resettle those displaced by war, and build ties of commerce and cooperation with the United States, the region, and the world.

Now, here in Seoul, once again, we are very grateful to our hosts—President Lee and the people of Seoul and South Korea—for your extraordinary hospitality.

We came to Seoul to continue the work that has taken us from London to Pittsburgh to Toronto. We worked together to pull the global economy back from catastrophe. To avoid the old cycles of boom and bust that led to that crisis, we committed ourselves to growth that is balanced and sustained, including financial reform and fiscal responsibility.

The actions we took were not always easy or popular, but they were necessary. As a result, the global economy is growing again. Some economies, especially emerging economies, are experiencing strong economic growth. Trade has risen. Jobs are being created, as in the United States, where we've had 10 consecutive months of private sector job growth and created more than 1 million private sector jobs this year alone.

In short, we succeeded in putting the global economy back on the path of recovery, but we also know that the progress has not come nearly fast enough, especially when it comes to my highest priority, which is putting Americans back to work.

Nor have we yet achieved the balanced global growth that we need. Many advanced economies are growing too slowly and not creating enough jobs. Some countries are running large surpluses, others running large deficits. Put

simply, we risk slipping back into the old imbalances that contributed to the economic crisis in the first place and which threaten global recovery.

So here in Seoul, the question was whether our nations could work together to keep the global economy growing. I know the commentary tends to focus on the inevitable areas of disagreement, but the fact is, the 20 major economies gathered here are in broad agreement on the way forward, an agreement that is based on a framework that was put forward by the United States. And for the first time, we spelled out the actions that are required, in four key areas, to achieve the sustained and balanced growth that we need.

First, we agreed to keep focusing on growth. At home, the United States has been doing our part by making historic investments in infrastructure and education, research and clean energy. And as a consequence, our economy is growing again, even as we must do more to ensure that that growth is sustained and translates into jobs for our people.

Here at Seoul, we agreed that growth must be balanced. Countries with large deficits must work to reduce them, as we are doing in the United States, where we're on track to cut our deficit in half by 2013 and where I'm prepared to make tough decisions to achieve that goal. Likewise, countries with large surpluses must shift away from unhealthy dependence on exports and take steps to boost domestic demand. As I've said, going forward, no nation should assume that their path to prosperity is paved simply with exports to the United States.

Second, we agreed that exchange rates must reflect economic realities. Just as the major advanced economies need to keep working to preserve stability among reserve currencies, emerging economies need to allow for currencies that are market driven. This is something that I raised yesterday with President Hu of China, and we will continue to closely watch the appreciation of China's currency. All of us need to avoid actions that perpetuate imbalances and give countries an undue advantage over one another.

Third, we took further steps to implement financial regulatory reform. At home, we are implementing the toughest financial reform since the Great Depression, and we are expecting the same sense of urgency, rather than complacency, among our G–20 partners. Here in Seoul, we agreed to new standards, similar to those that we've passed in the United States, to make sure that banks have the capital they need to withstand shocks and not take excessive risks that could lead to another crisis. And we agreed on an approach to ensure that taxpayers are not asked to pay for future bank failures.

Fourth, we agreed to focus on development as a key driver of economic growth. The work we did here today builds on a new development policy that I announced in September and recognizes that the most effective means of lifting people out of poverty is to create sustainable economic growth, growth that will create the markets of the future. We also agreed on an action plan to combat corruption, which in some countries is the single greatest barrier to economic progress.

Finally, we reaffirmed the need to avoid protectionism that stifles growth and instead pursue trade and investment through open markets. That's why, for example, we will continue to work towards a U.S.-Korea free trade agreement in the coming weeks, not just any agreement, but the best agreement to create jobs both in America and Korea.

And that's why I spoke very frankly to my G–20 partners today about the prospects of the Doha round. For just as emerging economies have gained a greater voice at international financial institutions, in part because of the work we've done here at the G–20, so too must they embrace their responsibilities to open markets to the trade and investment that creates jobs in all our countries.

So again I want to thank our South Korean hosts for a very successful summit. I want to thank my fellow leaders for their partnership. Here in Seoul, we've laid out the steps we must take to realize the balanced and sustained growth that we need. And now and in the days ahead, these are the commitments that we're going to have to meet.

So with that, let me take a few questions. And I'll start off with Julianna Goldman of Bloomberg.

South Korea-U.S. Free Trade Agreement

Q. Thank you, Mr. President. A question on the South Korea free trade agreement. If U.S. concerns on autos and beef aren't adequately addressed over the next few weeks, at that point would it be better to just have no deal at all?

The President. Well, I've always said that I'm not interested in signing a trade agreement just for the sake of an announcement, I'm interested in trade agreements that increase jobs and exports for the United States and, hopefully, also increase opportunities for our trading partners. I think that is achievable between the United States and Korea.

But the whole issue here from my perspective, and has always been over the last couple of years, is do we have a deal that works for us? That's my first obligation. President Lee's obligation obviously is to make sure it works for Korea. I think we can get a win-win, but it was important to take the extra time so that I am assured that it is a win for American workers and American companies as well as for Korean workers and Korean companies, because I'm the one who's going to have to go to Congress and sell it.

And from my perspective, again, I'm not interested in a announcement but then an agreement that doesn't produce for us. We've had a lot of those in the past, a lot of announcements, but at the same time, we see American manufacturing deteriorate and, as a consequence, a lot of concern back home. And understandably, I think there's a lot of suspicion that some of these trade deals may not be good for America. I think this one can be, but I want to make sure that when I present that trade agreement to Congress, I am absolutely confident that we've got the kind of deal that is good for both countries.

Dan Lothian of CNN.

Impact of Midterm Elections on U.S. Image Abroad/Tax Reform

Q. Thank you. After the midterm elections you said that you were open to compromise on the Bush tax cuts. I'm wondering if you're prepared today to say that you're willing to accept a temporary extension for the wealthiest Americans? And then on an unrelated question, do you feel that the election has weakened you on the global stage?

The President. The answer to the second question is no. I think what we've seen over the last several days as we've traveled through Asia is that people are eager to work with America, eager to engage with America on economic issues, on security issues, on a whole range of mutual interests. And that's especially true in Asia, where we see such enormous potential. This is the fastest growing part of the world. And we've got to be here, and we've got to work. And I'm absolutely confident that my administration, over the next 2 years, is going to continue to make progress in ensuring that the United States has a presence here not just for the next couple of years, but for decades to come.

With respect to the Bush tax cuts, what I've said is that I'm going to meet with the—both the Republican and Democratic leaders late next week, and we're going to sit down and discuss how we move forward. My number-one priority is making sure that we make the middle class tax cuts permanent, that we give certainty to the 98 percent of Americans who are affected by those tax breaks. I don't want to see their income taxes spike up, not only because they need relief after having gone through a horrendous recession, but also because it would be bad for the economy.

I continue to believe that extending permanently the upper income tax cuts would be a mistake and that we can't afford it. And my hope is, is that somewhere in between there we can find some sort of solution. But I'm not going to negotiate here in Seoul. My job is to negotiate back in Washington with Republican and Democratic leaders.

Ben Feller of AP [Associated Press].

U.S. Economy/Job Creation and Growth

Q. Thank you, Mr. President. You came to Asia talking about the deep frustration that Americans feel about the slow pace of recovery in the economy, and over your travels in the past 10 days, you've been talking a lot about sustainable growth. But the American people don't seem as interested in gradual growth as much as they want real, noticeable help right now. Can you promise them that there will be, in fact, noticeable job growth during your 4-year term? And do you think that the unemployment rate will still be north of 9 percent when you run for reelection?

The President. Well, I don't have a crystal ball, Ben, but I will say this. First of all, we've grown the economy by a million jobs over the last year. So that's pretty noticeable. I think those million people who've been hired notice those paychecks. And that's 10 consecutive months of private sector job growth.

In order to speed up job growth, we've put forward a range of proposals that I hope to discuss with Democratic and Republican leaders, because I don't think we can just stand pat. I continue to believe that we need to invest in a creaky infrastructure back home. And I think as you travel around Asia, you start seeing other countries investing in infrastructure. That's what the United States has done in the past, but we've been living off the investments that we made back in the thirties, forties, fifties, and sixties. And it's time for us to make sure that we've upgraded our roads and our railways and our airports. That will make us more productive and will put people back to work right now.

I continue to believe that it is important for us to work with businesses to see if we can incentivize them to invest now rather than holding cash waiting for the future. They've got cash to spend. And so we've put forward a series of tax proposals that historically Republicans have supported. And my expectation would be, there's no reason for them not to support it just because I'm supporting it. And so that's a conversation that I hope to have next week.

But we have a recovery. It needs to be speeded up. Government can't hire back the 8 million people who lost their jobs. Ultimately, that's up to the private sector. But I think we can set the conditions whereby we're seeing significant improvement during the course of the next year, the next 2 years, and we can chip away at the unemployment rate so that we get back to the kinds of levels that reflect a growing middle class and increased opportunity for all people.

Jake Tapper [ABC News].

China/U.S. Congress

Q. Thank you, Mr. President. This communique has a commitment that all countries will refrain from competitive devaluation of currencies. I'm wondering what you think that means concretely when it comes to China's behavior, what you expect from them?

And also, I'm wondering, when it comes to Congress, if you think your party, the Democratic Party, would benefit from new blood, new leadership?

The President. I've been very clear and persistent since I came into office that we welcome China's rise. We think the fact that China has grown as remarkably as it has, has lifted millions of people out of poverty, and that is ultimately good for the world and good for America, because it means that China has the opportunity to be a responsible partner. It means that China can be an enormous market for the United States, for Korea, for countries throughout Asia and around the world. And it's just good to get people out of poverty and give them opportunity.

What I've also said is that precisely because of China's success, it's very important that it act in a responsible fashion internationally. And the issue of the RMB is one that is an irritant not just to the United States, but is an irritant to a lot of China's trading partners and those who are competing with China to sell goods around the world. It is undervalued, and China spends enormous amounts of money intervening in the market to keep it undervalued.

And so what we've said is, it's important for China in a gradual fashion to transition to a market-based system. Now, this is something that China has done in the past. And China has also acknowledged that it needs to transition to

a more balanced growth strategy internally, where they're focusing on their enormous domestic market and giving their people the opportunity to buy goods and services and consume, all of which will promote their growth, but also will reduce some of the imbalances around the world.

And so what this communique, I think, communicates, not just to China, but to all of us, is letting currencies reflect market fundamentals, allowing your currency to move up and down, depending on the role that you're playing in the international trading system, is the best way to assure that everybody benefits from trade rather than just some. And the communique strongly communicates that principle.

My expectation is that China is going to make progress on this issue. President Hu is going to be visiting me in Washington in January, and our hope and expectation is, is that we will continue to see progress on this front.

It means some adjustments for China. And so we're—we understand that this is not solved overnight. But it needs to be dealt with, and I'm confident that it can be.

Sheryl Stolberg.

Oh, I think that what we will naturally see is a whole bunch of talented people rise to the top as they promote good ideas that attract the American people when it comes to jobs and investment and how to grow the economy and how to deal with our challenges. I think Speaker Pelosi has been an outstanding partner for me. I think Harry Reid has been a terrific partner in moving some very difficult legislation forward. And I'm looking forward to working with the entire leadership team to continue to make progress on the issues that are important to the American people.

Sheryl [Sheryl Gay Stolberg, New York Times].

U.S. Influence Abroad/President's Relationships With World Leaders

Q. Thank you, Mr. President. I'm hoping to get you in a little bit of a reflective mode. You spoke in your press conference in DC about your relationship with the American people. You said then that it had built slowly, it peaked at this incredible high, and then during the course of the last 2 years it had gotten rockier and tougher. And I'm wondering if you think the same could be said of your relations with foreign leaders, who maybe were just a teensy bit falling all over you when you first arrived on the world stage.

The President. That's not how I remember it. I remember our first G–20, you guys writing the exact same stories you're writing now about the exact same issues. Don't you remember that, Sheryl?

The United States obviously has a special role to play on the international stage, regardless of who is President. We are a very large, very wealthy, very powerful country. We have had outsized influence over world affairs for a century now. And you are now seeing a situation in which a whole host of other countries are doing very well and coming into their own, and naturally, they are going to be more assertive in terms of their interests and ideas. And that's a healthy thing. That's why we now have a G–20, because the old arrangements didn't fully reflect these new realities.

But let's just reflect on this summit. The framework for balanced and sustainable growth is one that we helped to originate. The financial reforms and Basel III are based on ideas that came out of our work and reflect many of the principles that are in Dodd-Frank. The development document that was set forward in this communique tracks the development ideas that I put forward several weeks ago in terms of how we can encourage not just aid, but also self-sufficiency. The corruption initiative that's reflected in the communique was prompted by recommendations and suggestions that we made.

So sometimes, I think, naturally, there's an instinct to focus on the disagreements, because otherwise, these summits might not be very exciting; it's just a bunch of world leaders sitting around intervening. And so there's a search for drama. But what's remarkable is that in each of these successive summits, we've actually made real progress.

And sometimes the progress—charting the progress requires you to go back and look at previous summits, starting off with—let's say, on financial regulatory reform. In Toronto, we

said, here's what we need to do; let's have this ready by the time we get to Seoul. It wasn't real sexy back in Toronto, and nobody really wrote about it, but it actually moved the ball forward in terms of a coordinated response to financial regulation.

IMF reform is something that the United States has said we need to get done. And in previous summits, we said we're going to find a way to get that done. And lo and behold, here we are at this summit, and we've actually achieved what is a huge shift in how power is assigned in these international financial institutions.

So the work that we do here is not always going to seem dramatic. It's not always going to be immediately world changing. But step by step, what we're doing is building stronger international mechanisms and institutions that will help stabilize the economy, ensure economic growth, and reduce some tensions.

Now, last point I'll make on this: Part of the reason that sometimes it seems as if the United States is attracting some dissent is because we're initiating ideas. We're putting them forward. The easiest thing for us to do would be to take a passive role and let things just drift, which wouldn't cause any conflict. But we thought it was important for us to put forward more structure to this idea of balanced and sustained growth. And some countries pushed back. They were concerned about what might this—is this somehow going to lock us in to having to change our growth patterns or our trade policies or what have you. And that resistance is natural. It arises out of the fact that the U.S. is showing leadership and we are pushing to try to bring about changes.

Q. [*Inaudible*]—foreign leaders and if you had noticed any change during your time in office——

The President. And I guess what I'm saying is, is that I actually think that my relationships have grown much stronger with the people who I've worked with here.

I mean, when I first came into office, people might have been interested in more photo ops because there had been a lot of hoopla surrounding my election. But I now have a genuine friendship with Prime Minister Singh of India, and I think that he and I share a level of understanding and interest in working together that didn't exist when I first came onto the scene. I think the same is true for Chancellor Merkel, the same is true for Prime Minister Erdogan, the same is true for President Lee.

That doesn't mean that there aren't going to be differences, but—the same is true for my relationship with President Hu. It wasn't any easier to talk about currency when I had just been elected and my poll numbers were at 65 percent than it is now. It was hard then, and it's hard now. Because this involves the interests of countries and not all of these are going to be resolved easily. And it's not just a function of personal charm; it's a function of countries' interests and seeing if we can work through to align them.

All right. Savannah Guthrie [NBC News].

U.S. Tax Reform/Deficit and National Debt

Q. A quick follow-up. Some are interpreting your senior adviser David Axelrod's comments to a newspaper back home that your compromise position is to temporarily extend the Bush tax cuts. Is that the wrong interpretation?

The President. That is the wrong interpretation, because I haven't had a conversation with Republican and Democratic leaders. Here's the right interpretation. I want to make sure that taxes don't go up for middle class families starting on January 1. That's my number-one priority for those families and for our economy.

I also believe that it would be fiscally irresponsible for us to permanently extend the high-income tax cuts. I think that would be a mistake, particularly when we've got our Republican friends saying that their number-one priority is making sure that we deal with our debt and our deficit.

So there may be a whole host of ways to compromise around those issues. I'm not going to negotiate here in Seoul on those issues. But I've made very clear what my priorities are. All right?

Q. Oh, sorry, that was actually my quick follow-up.

The President. Oh, I see. [*Laughter*]

Q. ——but this leads me right to my real question, which is, speaking of fiscal responsibility——

The President. Yes.

Q.——given the fact that the bulk of the expense of extending the tax cuts to the middle class would be trillions of dollars, in the interest of telling the truth to the American people, can we afford that? Thank you.

The President. Well, the middle class in the United States saw their real wages go down 5 percent over the period of 2001 to 2009, at the same time as all their costs were going up. And so giving them permanent relief is good for those families. I also believe strongly it is good for our economy right now, at a time when we are still in recovery.

The costs are significant, and we are going to have to have a discussion about, over the medium and long term, how do we match up our spending with our revenues, because right now they are way out of balance. That's why we have a deficit. That's why we have a debt. And it is our responsibility to the next generation to make sure that that gets solved.

I don't start thinking on the revenue side. I start thinking on the spending side—where can we potentially save money? I'm looking forward to getting the official Bowles-Simpson recommendations. I'm going to study those carefully, consult widely, and see what we can do on the spending side that will have an impact. And then we've got to see how much of a shortfall do we have. And then we're going to have to have a debate, which will probably be a tough debate and has to be an honest debate with the American people about how do we pay for those things that we think are really important.

I think it is really important for us to invest in research and development because that's going to be the key to innovation and our long-term economic success. But we've got to figure out how to pay for that. I think it's really important to invest in our education system. That's going to be a key to our long-term economic growth and competitiveness. How are we going to pay to make sure that young people can go to college? I think it's important to make sure that Social Security and Medicare are there, not just for this generation, but for the next. How do we make that sustainable?

So that's going to be a series of tough conversations. What I know is that if we're spending $700 billion—if we're borrowing $700 billion to pay for tax breaks for folks like me who don't need them and where I'm least likely to spend that money and circulate it in the economy, that's probably not a great approach.

But again, I know that the other side feels very strongly about it, and I'm willing to have a tough, hard-headed discussion with Democratic and Republican leaders about that issue.

Chip Reid [CBS News].

U.S. Federal Reserve System/National Economy

Q. Thank you, Mr. President. I know it's not your habit to comment on Fed decisions, but there's been quite a bit of reporting, if you believe it, and I'm sure you do, that there's quite a bit of unhappiness among G–20 countries over that decision. And I'm not asking you to comment on the decision. But did you get an earful from other leaders here on the Fed decision? Could you share with us what some of them said? And if you're not willing to delve too deeply into that, what was the number-one complaint, concern, or piece of advice that you got from foreign leaders about the U.S. economy and your stewardship of the economy?

The President. What about compliments? You didn't put that in the list. There was only complaints, concerns, or—[laughter]. You know, there was not a lot of discussion about the Fed decision in the leaders' meetings. I think a couple of times there were some veiled references to monetary policy that may have effect on other countries. But it wasn't central to any of the discussions that we had.

I know that on the margins, there was a lot of discussion, and in the press, there was a huge amount of discussion about it. But I have to tell you, that wasn't part of the discussion that we had inside the leaders' meetings.

Most of the discussion had to do with how do we translate this idea of rebalancing into concrete steps. And the communique accurately reflects the consensus. It's puzzling to me that the reporting is all talking about conflict when the communique actually reflects a hard-won consensus that the world's 20 largest economies signed up for and that gives us some mechanisms to start monitoring, looking at indicators, seeing how countries are doing on this front.

It doesn't provide an enforcement mechanism that says to Korea or the United States or Germany or Brazil, "You have to do something," but it does give the international community the ability to monitor and see exactly what countries are doing and to see if the policies they're pursuing are fair to their trading partners. And if they're not, then it gives a mechanism to apply at least some peer pressure on those countries to start doing something about it.

I think when people talk to me about the U.S. economy, their main concern is, is it growing fast enough. Because a lot of countries, including South Korea, depend a lot on exports, and the U.S. is the world's largest market. They want to see us grow. They want unemployment to go down in the United States. And so I think they're very interested in what are additional strategies that can be used to encourage takeoff in the U.S. economy. And I described to them some of the steps that we're taking and that we're going to be continuing to take in order to make that happen.

I guess the last point I would just make about the Fed decision, when I am asked about it my simple point is to say that, from everything I can see, this decision was not one designed to have an impact on the currency, on the dollar. It was designed to grow the economy.

And there's some legitimate concern that we've had very low inflation, that a huge danger in the United States is deflation, and that we have to be mindful of those dangers going forward because that wouldn't be good for the United States or for the rest of the world. Beyond that, that's just an observation about what I think the intent was.

Last question. Scott Horsley [National Public Radio].

Group of Twenty (G–20) Summit

Q. One of your top advisers said this morning that the challenges facing the G–20 now are much more manageable than they were at the height of the crisis. How does that affect the dynamic? Is there some taking the eye off the ball among your fellow leaders?

The President. I think what it means is that in the absence of crisis people probably are willing to hunker down a little bit more on some of the negotiations. Speed seems less of the essence, and so people think, well, if it doesn't get solved now, maybe we can put this off for another day.

What's remarkable to me, though, is despite some of those impulses, we're still getting stuff done. And as I emphasized before, we should not anticipate that every time countries come together that we are doing some revolutionary thing. Instead of hitting home runs, sometimes we're going to hit singles. But they're really important singles. And I just listed some of these out.

IMF reform, this is something that folks have been talking about for a decade or more. It's gotten done. Financial regulatory reform—huge lift that we talked about in my first G–20 summit—it is now coming to fruition. We've still got some more work to do, but we've made enormous progress in a huge—really short period of time. Basel II, I think, took a decade to negotiate. We got this done basically in a year and a half.

The development agenda that's been put forward will make a difference. This rebalancing is still a work in progress, but everybody is on record now saying surplus countries and deficit countries both have to be mindful of their policies and think about the adjustments that they need so that we can sustain economic growth and keep our borders open to goods and services over the long term.

So those are all positives, and I think that's an indication of the seriousness with which people take these meetings, even if, as I said, it's not always going to be revolutionary progress, but sometimes evolutionary progress.

I feel obliged to take maybe one question from the Korean press, since you guys have been such excellent hosts. Anybody? This gentleman right here. He's got his hand up. He's the only one who took me up on it. Go ahead. And I'll probably need a translation, though, if you're asking the question in Korean. In fact, I definitely will need a translation. [*Laughter*]

Q. Unfortunately, I hate to disappoint you, President Obama, I'm actually Chinese. [*Laughter*]

The President. Well, it's wonderful to see you.

Q. But I think I get to represent the entire Asia.

The President. Absolutely.

Q. We're one family here in this part of the world.

The President. Well, your English is better than my Mandarin also. [*Laughter*]

Q. Thank you.

The President. But—now, in fairness, though, I did say that I was going to let the Korean press ask a question. So the—I think that you held up your hand anyway.

Q. How about will my Korean friends allow me to ask a question on your behalf? Yes or no?

The President. Well, it depends on whether there's a Korean reporter who would rather have the question. No, no takers?

Q. [*Inaudible*]

The President. Oh, this is getting more complicated than I expected. [*Laughter*]

Q. Take quick, one question from an Asian, President Obama.

The President. Well, the—as I said, I was going to—go ahead and ask your question, but I want to make sure that the Korean press gets a question as well. Go ahead.

U.S. Perception of the President's Actions

Q. Okay. My question is very simple. You mentioned interpretation. I know part of the difficulty being the American President is that some of the decisions that you take, actions you make will be interpreted in a way that are not what you thought they would be or what you meant they would be. For instance, some of the actions you've taken were interpreted as antibusiness domestically in the United States. And as someone just mentioned, some of the actions taken by the U.S. Government that you represent as well were interpreted as sacrificing other countries' interests for America's own benefit. So it's—you find yourself constantly being interpreted in a thousand different ways. How do you address these interpretations?

The President. With wonderful press conference like this that give me the opportunity, hopefully, to provide my own interpretation. But look, you make a valid point. We live in a connected world. Everything I say, everything my administration does, anything one of my aides does is interpreted in one fashion or another. In America, we call it spin. And there's a spin cycle that is going on 24 hours a day, 7 days a week. And I think that in this media environment, it is in some ways more challenging to make sure that your message and your intentions are getting out in a consistent basis.

But I think that if I'm consistent with my actions and I'm consistent with my goals, then over time, hopefully, people look at my overall trajectory and they can draw accurate conclusions about what we're trying to do.

With respect to business, for example, we've had in the United States some battles between myself and some in the business community around issues like financial regulation or health care. At the same time, I've said repeatedly and I said on this trip, we can't succeed unless American businesses succeed. And I'm going to do everything I can to promote their ability to grow and prosper and to sell their goods both in the United States and abroad. And the fact that the economy is now growing and trade is expanding and the stock market is up, I think, is an indication that I mean what I say. And hopefully, by the end of my administration businesses will look back and say, you know what, actually the guy was pretty good for business, even if at any given point in the road they may be frustrated.

So all right, now I'm stuck with this last one, but I think I've got to go fly a plane.

South Korea-U.S. Free Trade Agreement

Q. [*Inaudible*]—some of the South Korean citizens have suggested——

The President. Right.

Q. What led your administration to decide to try and extract further concessions from Korea on imports of American beef? And did you miscalculate the extent that this appears to be non-negotiable here in Korea? Do you really think you can convince people living in Korea to buy more American beef?

The President. Well, first of all, beef was not the only issue that was of concern. In fact, a larger concern had to do with autos. And the concern is very simple. We've got about 400,000 Korean autos in the United States and a few thousand American cars here in Korea. And people are concerned about whether the standards, the nontariff barriers with respect to autos, is something that is preventing us from being able to compete with very good products.

Now, I think that we can find a sweet spot that works both for Korea and the United States. But I repeat, I'm not interested in trade agreements just for the sake of trade agreements. I want trade agreements that work for the other side, but my main job is to look out for the American people, American workers, and American businesses. And I want to make sure that this deal is balanced. And so we're going to keep on working on it. But I'm confident we can get it done.

All right, thank you very much, everybody. I'm late for my flight.

NOTE: The President spoke at 4:43 p.m. at the Coex Center. In his remarks, he referred to Chancellor Angela Merkel of Germany; Prime Minister Recep Tayyip Erdogan of Turkey; President Lee Myung-bak of South Korea; and Erskine B. Bowles and Alan K. Simpson, Cochairs, National Commission on Fiscal Responsibility and Reform.

Remarks at the Asia-Pacific Economic Cooperation CEO Summit in Yokohama, Japan
November 13, 2010

Thank you so much. Thank you. Good morning. And thank you to Mr. Yonekura for the kind introduction. And thanks to everyone at Nippon Keidanren for hosting APEC's CEO summit this year.

I also want to thank my good friend, Prime Minister Kan, and the Japanese people for their generosity and their hospitality in hosting APEC. It is wonderful to be back in this beautiful country. And we in America are very much looking forward to hosting APEC next year in my home State of Hawaii.

Now, Yokohama is my last stop on a journey that's taken me from Mumbai to New Delhi to Jakarta and to Seoul. And in each place, we have deepened friendships, we have strengthened partnerships, and we have reaffirmed a fundamental truth of our time: In the 21st century, the security and prosperity of the American people is linked inextricably to the security and prosperity of Asia. That's why this was not my first trip here and why it will not be my last. America is leading again in Asia, and today I'd like to talk about why.

Now, the story of Asia over the last few decades is the story of change that is so rapid and transformative that it may be without precedent in human history. The economic miracle that began here in Japan after the Second World War has now swept across the Pacific and throughout the wider region. Countries where people once lived on a few dollars a day are now some of the fastest growing economies in the world, with incomes and living standards that few could have imagined 40 or 50 years ago.

For example, when I lived in Jakarta as a young boy, I can remember the buildings being no more than a few stories tall. There was just one modern shopping center. On Tuesday, I returned to a teeming city of nearly 10 million, filled with skyscrapers and thriving centers of culture and commerce. In Seoul, I noted that there are Koreans who can still remember when their country was little more than rice paddies and small villages. And today, it is one of the most prosperous democracies in the world. When I was in Mumbai, I met with young entrepreneurs who were putting American technology into Indian electric cars and selling clean water to Indians from filtration equipment purchased from the United States. These are breakthroughs that will continue to fuel growth in a nation that has already lifted millions from poverty.

In barely two generations, these sweeping changes have improved the lives and fortunes of millions of people here in the Asia-Pacific. But in today's interconnected world, what happens in Japan or China or Indonesia also has a direct effect on the lives and fortunes of the American people. That's why I came here.

The Asia-Pacific is where the United States engages in much of our trade and our commerce, where our businesses invest and where we attract investment to our shores, where we buy and where we sell many of our goods and services, exports that support millions of jobs for our people.

Seven of America's 15 top trading partners are now APEC members. Sixty percent of the goods we export go to this region of the world. The United States is also the largest export market for Asia, which has led to more affordable goods and services for American consumers.

And what's more, this is a relationship that will only become more important as this region continues to grow. Within 5 years, Asia's economy is expected to be about 50 percent larger than it is today. And for at least the next 4 years, Asia-Pacific economies will grow faster than the world average.

Now, undoubtedly, this rapid growth will lead to a healthy competition for the jobs and industries of the future. And as President of the United States, I make no apologies for doing whatever I can to bring those jobs and industries to America. But what I've also said throughout this trip is that in the 21st century, there is no need to view trade, commerce, or economic growth as zero-sum games, where one country always has to prosper at the expense of another. If we work together and act together, strengthening our economic ties can be a win-win for all of our nations.

Now, that cooperation was on display yesterday at the first G–20 summit in an Asia-Pacific nation. Having successfully worked together to avoid global depression, our challenge now is a global recovery that is both balanced and sustained. Yesterday there was a broad agreement on the way forward, an agreement based on the framework that we put forward.

First, we agreed to keep focusing on growth. As the largest economy in the world, an engine for global growth, that's particularly important for the United States. As Prime Minister Singh of India said when I was visiting there, "A strong, robust, fast-growing United States is in the interests of the world" and "would help the cause of global prosperity."

And that's why we passed an economic plan that has led to 5 consecutive quarters of economic growth and 10 consecutive months of private sector job growth. That's why we passed and are implementing the toughest set of financial reforms since the Great Depression, something that our G–20 partners need to do with the same sense of urgency.

And that's why we're cutting back on nonessentials in the face of serious fiscal challenges. Already, we're on track to meet our goal of cutting our deficit in half by 2013. And I'm absolutely committed to making the tough choices necessary to get us the rest of the way there and bring down our deficits in the long run.

But we are not cutting back on the investments that are essential to America's long-term economic growth: education, clean energy, research, and infrastructure. We will make sacrifices, but everyone here should know that as long as I'm President, we are not going to sacrifice America's future or our leadership in the world.

The second major thing we agreed on in Seoul was that in order for the recovery to be sustained, economic growth must be balanced. One of the important lessons the economic crisis taught us is the limits of depending primarily on American consumers and Asian exports to drive economic growth.

Going forward, countries with large surpluses must shift away from an unhealthy dependence on exports and take steps to boost domestic demand. As I said, going forward, no nation should assume that their path to prosperity is simply paved with exports to America.

In the United States, we see the need for rebalancing as an opportunity to rebuild our economy on a new, stronger foundation for growth, where we save more and we spend less, where we're known not just for what we consume, but for what we produce. We want to get back to doing what American has always been known for: discovering, creating, and building the products that are sold all over the world.

And that's why I've set a goal of doubling U.S. exports over the next 5 years. This is a big part of what brought me to Asia this week. In this region, the United States sees a huge opportunity to increase our exports in some of the fastest growing markets in the world.

For America, this is a jobs strategy, because with every $1 billion we sell in exports, 5,000 jobs are supported at home. And jobs supported by exports pay up to 18 percent higher than the national average. Meanwhile, for Asia-Pacific nations, these U.S. goods and products also provide more choice for consumers who are enjoying higher standards of living throughout the region. This is a win-win for all of us.

Over the course of this trip, we've made good progress toward our export goals. While we were in India, I was pleased to announce a set of trade deals that total nearly $10 billion in U.S. exports. From medical equipment and helicopters to turbines and mining equipment, these deals support more than 50,000 jobs in the United States.

In Indonesia, a fast-growing market where we have been steadily increased our exports, President Yudhoyono and I discussed ways to encourage additional trade and investment between our nations.

And in South Korea, President Lee and I moved closer to completing a trade deal. There are some outstanding issues that are difficult, and we need to get a deal that is good for American workers and businesses. But completion of this deal could lead to billions of dollars in increased exports and thousands of American jobs for American workers. So I'm committed to seeing this through, and I'm pleased that President Lee offered to send a team of negotiators to Washington in the coming weeks so we can try to finish the job.

The United States is also looking to expand trade and commerce throughout the Asia-Pacific. Even though our exports in this region have risen by more than 60 percent over the last 5 years, our overall share of trade in the region has declined in favor of our competitors, and we want to change that. We don't want to lose the opportunity to sell our goods and services in fast-growing markets. We don't want to lose the opportunity to create new jobs back home. That's why we want to keep working with our fellow APEC economies to reduce trade barriers. And that's why we want to pursue the Trans-Pacific Partnership, which would facilitate trade and open markets throughout the Asia-Pacific.

Agreements like this will obviously benefit our economies and our people, but they will also send a strong signal that when it comes to this growing, sprawling region of the world, the United States is here to stay. We are invested in your success because it's connected to our own. We have a stake in your future because our destiny is shared. It was a Japanese poet who said: "Individually, we are one drop. Together, we are an ocean." So it must be with the billions of people whose lives are linked in the swirling currents of the Pacific.

In the last century, the American people have contributed greatly to the security and prosperity of this region. The strength of our alliances and the bravery of our men and women in uniform helped keep the peace. And the openness of our markets helped to fuel the rise of the Asian miracle.

In this young century, we stand ready to lead again. Yes, we've gone through a difficult time and there are challenges that remain that are great. There will be setbacks and disagreements, and we won't solve every issue in one meeting or one trip or even one term of my Presidency.

But I've never been more confident in what the United States of America has to offer the world at this moment in history: in our universities and our research centers that continue to produce the most promising minds and discoveries and innovations; in our businesses that keep developing products and technologies that are transforming the lives of millions; in the spirit of tolerance and diversity that sends a powerful example to a world that is smaller and more connected than at any time in human history; and in the most effective form of government the world has ever known, namely, democracy. For it will always be true that when leaders are accountable to their people, their people are more likely to prosper.

Indeed, what has characterized America from the start, the idea of America that endures, is particularly indispensable in times of great challenge and great change. It's the idea that led us westward and skyward, to roads and railways that cut through wilderness, to ships and planes and fiber-optic lines that carry American commerce around the world. It is the idea that through hard work and sacrifice, it is possible to end up in a better place than where you started, and it's possible to give your children chances you never had. And it's the idea that even when circumstances seem bleak and challenges seem daunting, it is possible to overcome, to persevere, and ultimately to succeed.

In different ways and different places over the last week, I've seen this idea alive in the teeming, thriving democracies of Asia. And that gives me great confidence in the ties that bind our people and great hope in our ability to move together towards the future not as drops, but with the strength of an ocean.

So I thank you for your hospitality. I congratulate all the outstanding businesses who are here today. And I look forward to our close cooperation in the months and years to come. Thank you very much. Thank you.

NOTE: The President spoke at 9:44 a.m. at the Royal Park Hotel. In his remarks, he referred to Hiromasa Yonekura, chairman, Nippon Keidanren.

Remarks Following a Meeting With Prime Minister Naoto Kan of Japan in Yokohama
November 13, 2010

Prime Minister Kan. First of all, I'd like to welcome President Obama warmly to Japan. Exactly 1 year ago, the President visited Japan on the first leg of his visit to Asia, and I'm very happy to welcome him here in Yokohama as he visits Japan once again, this time to wrap up his Asia trip, during which he's visited many Asian countries.

We were able to have a very fruitful discussion today. First, Japan and the United States, at this meeting of APEC, of pan-Pacific countries, we shall step up our cooperation. So we agreed on doing that. And in Japan's relations with China and Russia, recently we've faced some problems, and the United States has supported Japan throughout, so I expressed my appreciation to him for that.

For the peace and security of the countries in the region, the presence of the United States and the presence of the U.S. military, I believe, is becoming only increasingly important. And that is not only my sense, but I think the sense of many countries, many neighboring countries in this region. So that is one point that I made to him.

And we discussed various issues between Japan and the United States, including host-nation support, and we are producing agreements on Okinawa. Following the conclusion of the gubernatorial election in Okinawa, I shall be making my maximum efforts on the basis of the May 28 Japan-U.S. agreement and that I shall be making my utmost efforts. That is what I told the President as well.

On the economic front, with regard to comprehensive economic partnership agreement, I explained that Japan is steering significantly towards opening up itself and that he stated he would welcome this.

With regard to TPP, of course we have to also consider the other participating countries, but we would like to get down to consultations with the participating countries of TPP. And the President also expressed his support that—will

support our efforts or consultations in order to glean information about TPP.

We did engage in very broad-ranging discussions as the changes may take place around the world. I believe it is important that countries around the world comply with the internationally accepted rules. And the President suggested that Japan is a model country in that respect.

And on the question of permanent membership on the Security Council of the U.N. in the future, the President also stated his support for Japan.

Next year, sometime in the coming spring, the President kindly invited me to visit Washington, DC. This year marks the 50th anniversary of the Japan-U.S. Security Pact. By the time I visit Washington, DC, I hope I will be able to issue a joint statement which is very broad-ranging, and so we agreed that we'll launch working-level efforts towards that end.

Tomorrow the President will be visiting Kamakura to, I understand, enjoy his good, old memories. And I wish him a very pleasant stay so that he'll be able to return to the United States with pleasant memories of this trip.

President Obama. Thank you very much, Prime Minister Kan, for your warm welcome and hospitality. And to the people of Yokohama, it is wonderful to be here. Japan was my first stop in Asia as President last year, and it is a pleasure to be back for the APEC summit. And I'm very appreciative to all the people of Japan and send warm regards from the American people.

As allies for half a century, the partnership between Japan and the United States has been the foundation for our security and our prosperity, not only for our two countries, but also for the region. It's allowed us to become two of the world's largest economies. It has made Japan the second largest trading partner outside of North America.

We are bound by our people, our families, our businesses, students, and tourists, who bring us closer every day. We are partners in

Asia and around the world. And as Prime Minister Kan noted, I expressed my deep appreciation for the fact that Japan is really a model citizen internationally and works in support of international rules and norms that can make all of us more prosperous and more secure. And so I'm very grateful for this partnership.

And as Prime Minister said, we had a very productive meeting on a whole range of challenges that we face together. We are deepening our economic relationship. I'm pleased that the Open Skies agreement that enters into force today will expand air service between our two countries and strengthen the ties between our peoples and our businesses.

We're launching new partnerships in pursuit of the clean energy economies of the future. Following our work together at the G–20, the Prime Minister and I discussed our close cooperation in APEC, and I thanked him for the hard work that Japan has done in preparation for our meetings here.

I have a special interest in a successful summit, since I will be the host of the next APEC meeting in Honolulu next year.

We discussed the need to expand trade and open markets across the region. I very much welcomed the Prime Minister's interest in liberalizing trade and his promotion of domestic reforms. He explained that these steps could put Japan on the road to membership in the Trans-Pacific Partnership, and I very much welcomed Japan's interests. And we agreed that our Government will be consulting closely on these matters in the months to come.

With regard to our shared security, we affirmed our commitment to our alliance, which marks its 50th anniversary this year. Five decades of experience make this clear: Japan and the United States are stronger when we stand together. I'm pleased that our teams have completed an agreement in principle outlining Japan's commitment to host nation support, including continued financial investments in the alliance.

And, Mr. Prime Minister, I want to thank you for this important demonstration of Japan's commitment to our alliance and to regional peace and stability.

The commitment of the United States to the defense of Japan is unshakeable. Our alliances, bases, and forward presence are essential not only to Japan's security, but as Prime Minister noted, they help us ensure stability and address regional challenges across Northeast Asia.

For this reason, the Prime Minister and I agreed to keep moving forward on our roadmap on realignment so that we can meet Japan's defense needs and also address the needs of Japanese communities that host our bases. And I'm confident that we can continue to work together to ensure both.

As partners around the world, we reviewed the range of security challenges we face together, including our cooperation on the prevention of the spread of nuclear weapons and the need to secure the world's vulnerable nuclear materials. I discussed our progress in Afghanistan and expressed my appreciation to Japan. Japan is the largest donor of assistance for reconstruction and development. And I told the Prime Minister how much we value Japan's willingness to accept the obligations of leadership, including its contributions to the United Nations.

And as the Prime Minister noted, we discussed the issue of Security Council reform. I reiterated our longstanding view that Japan stands as a model of the kind of country we would want to see as a permanent member of the Security Council, and I look forward to a reformed Security Council that includes Japan as a permanent member.

Finally, I'm delighted that the Prime Minister has accepted my invitation to visit the United States in the first half of next year. We've instructed our governments to intensify their efforts to deepen and modernize our alliance, and I hope that by the time the Prime Minister arrives in Washington, we'll be able to lay out a joint vision that can guide our partnership for decades to come.

Just to close, the Prime Minister mentioned that as a young boy I had the occasion to visit Japan, including touring the Amida Buddha at Kamakura. I am looking forward to an opportunity to return tomorrow and again experience the extraordinary aspects of Japanese culture.

So again, to all the people of Japan, thank you so much for your hospitality and your friendship. And, Mr. President [Prime Minister],° I'm very much looking forward to us working together not only at this summit, but on a whole range of bilateral issues in the years to come.

Thank you.

Prime Minister Kan. Thank you.

NOTE: The President spoke at 11:32 a.m. at the InterContinental Yokohama Grand hotel. Prime Minister Kan spoke in Japanese, and his remarks were translated by an interpreter. Audio was not available for verification of the content of these remarks.

Remarks Following a Meeting With Prime Minister Julia E. Gillard of Australia in Yokohama
November 13, 2010

President Obama. Well, let me just say very briefly, I've had a chance to speak previously with Prime Minister Gillard on the phone. It is a wonderful opportunity for me to meet her during the course of both the G–20 and now in our first face-to-face meeting. The United States does not have a closer or better ally than Australia. We are grateful for all the work that we do together.

I expressed my personal thanks to the people of Australia through the Prime Minister for the enormous sacrifices that are being made in Afghanistan by Australian troops. We, I think, are going to be discussing these issues further when we see each other at the Lisbon summit. But obviously, all of us have an interest in bringing about a good outcome in that region that ensures our safety and security over the long term.

On the economic front, I reiterated to the Prime Minister how important the Asia-Pacific region is to our economy and to world economic growth. Australia is a central player in that economy. And so we are going to continue to explore ways that we can work together to expand trade, expand investment, ensure that everybody is playing by the rules of the road in the region and cooperating effectively. The Trans-Pacific Partnership is a good example of the kind of collaboration between our two countries that, I think, can expand opportunity for all peoples.

So I am just grateful to have this opportunity to speak with the Prime Minister. I've extended

an invitation to her to visit the United States sometime early next year, and we'll find a date, and hopefully, we can build on some of the discussions that we've already had to further enhance our bilateral cooperation.

So, Prime Minister, thank you and to your entire delegation for the good work that you've done. And I look forward to seeing you in Washington.

Prime Minister Gillard. Thank you. And I have to say to President Obama, we've had the opportunity to be at the G–20 over the last few days and had the opportunity for a few brief discussions there, and we will see each other in Lisbon next weekend. Our two countries are great mates, to use our terminology, and as great mates, we are continuing to work together in our region and beyond.

We have had the opportunity to talk about Afghanistan, and I do want to take this opportunity to pass on the condolences of the Australian people for the losses that you have suffered there. But we are working together there and will have time next weekend at Lisbon to talk about the transition strategy.

We've also had the opportunity to reflect on the discussions we had at AUSMIN about the American force posture review and the work that we are doing on new challenges like cybersecurity. And we've had the opportunity to talk about our engagement in the region, where the U.S. engagement is strengthening through forums like the East Asia summit.

° White House correction.

And we are on the same page on trade, so we very much look forward to the discussions of the Trans-Pacific Partnership during the course of the APEC meetings.

So a very good opportunity to have a good discussion about the areas where our two coun-tries are collaborating now and for the future. Thank you.

NOTE: The President spoke at 12:20 p.m. at the InterContinental Yokohama Grand hotel. Audio was not available for verification of the content of these remarks.

The President's Weekly Address
November 13, 2010

This weekend, I'm concluding a trip to Asia whose purpose was to open new markets for American products in this fast-growing part of the world. The economic battle for these mar-kets is fierce, and we're up against strong com-petitors. But as I've said many times, America doesn't play for second place. The future we're fighting for isn't as the world's largest importer, consuming products made elsewhere, but as the world's largest manufacturer of ideas and goods sold around the world.

Opening new markets will not only help America's businesses create new jobs for Amer-ican workers, it will also help us reduce our def-icits, because the single greatest tool for getting our fiscal house in order is robust economic growth. That kind of growth will require ensur-ing that our students are getting the best educa-tion possible, that we're on the cutting edge of research and development, and that we're re-building our roads and railways, runways and ports, so our infrastructure is up to the chal-lenges of the 21st century.

Given the deficits that have mounted up over the past decade, we can't afford to make these investments unless we're also willing to cut what we don't need. That's why I've submitted to Congress a plan for a 3-year budget freeze, and I'm prepared to offer additional savings. But as we work to reform our budget, Congress should also put some skin in the game. I agree with those Republicans and Democratic Mem-bers of Congress who've recently said that in these challenging days, we can't afford what are called earmarks. These are items inserted into spending bills by Members of Congress without adequate review.

Now, some of these earmarks support worthy projects in our local communities. But many others do not. We can't afford bridges to no-where like the one that was planned a few years back in Alaska. Earmarks like these represent a relatively small part of overall Federal spend-ing, but when it comes to signaling our commit-ment to fiscal responsibility, addressing them would have an important impact.

As a Senator, I helped eliminate anonymous earmarks and created new measures of trans-parency so Americans can better follow how their tax dollars are being spent. As President, time and again, I've called for new limitations on earmarks. We've reduced the cost of ear-marks by over $3 billion, and we've put in place higher standards of transparency by putting as much information as possible on earmarks.gov. In fact, this week, we updated the site with more information about where last year's ear-marks were actually spent and made it easier to look up Members of Congress and the earmarks they fought for.

Today, we have a chance to go further. We have a chance to not only shine a light on a bad Washington habit that wastes billions of taxpay-er dollars, but take a step towards restoring public trust. We have a chance to advance the interests not of Republicans or Democrats, but of the American people, to put our country on the path of fiscal discipline and responsibility that will lead to a brighter economic future for all. And that's a future I hope we can reach across party lines to build together.

Thanks, everybody, and have a great week-end.

NOTE: The address was recorded at approximately 9:40 a.m., k.s.t., on November 11 in the Namsan Room III at the Grand Hyatt Seoul in Seoul, South Korea, for broadcast on November 13. The transcript was made available by the Office of the Press Secretary on November 12, but was embargoed for release until 6 a.m., e.s.t., on November 13. Due to the 14-hour time difference, the address was broadcast after the President's remarks in Yokohama, Japan. The Office of the Press Secretary also released a Spanish language transcript of this address.

Statement on Elections in Tanzania and Zanzibar
November 13, 2010

On behalf of the United States, I congratulate the people of the United Republic of Tanzania on your recent national election and your continued commitment to a tradition of multiparty contests begun in 1992. I look forward to working with President Jakaya Kikwete and the members of the 10th Parliament as we build on the long, fruitful partnership between our nations to advance shared development goals and tackle the many global challenges before us.

I also extend my congratulations to Zanzibar's President Ali Mohamed Shein, First Vice President Seif Sharif Hamad, the new unity Government, and most especially the Zanzibari people, who have made history by conducting a peaceful contest after years of strife.

As I said to President Kikwete when we met at the White House in 2009, the people of the United States support all Tanzanians in your efforts to institutionalize democratic, transparent governance, to realize the full potential of your union, and to ensure that the steps you have taken together toward a lasting peace and prosperity cannot be reversed.

Statement on the Burmese Government's Release of Aung San Suu Kyi
November 13, 2010

While the Burmese regime has gone to extraordinary lengths to isolate and silence Aung San Suu Kyi, she has continued her brave fight for democracy, peace, and change in Burma. She is a hero of mine and a source of inspiration for all who work to advance basic human rights in Burma and around the world. The United States welcomes her long overdue release.

Whether Aung San Suu Kyi is living in the prison of her house or the prison of her country does not change the fact that she, and the political opposition she represents, has been systematically silenced, incarcerated, and deprived of any opportunity to engage in political processes that could change Burma. It is time for the Burmese regime to release all political prisoners, not just one.

The United States looks forward to the day when all of Burma's people are free from fear and persecution. Following Aung San Suu Kyi's powerful example, we recommit ourselves to remaining steadfast advocates of freedom and human rights for the Burmese people and accountability for those who continue to oppress them.

Remarks Following a Meeting With President Dmitry A. Medvedev of Russia in Yokohama
November 14, 2010

President Obama. Well, let me just say it is wonderful once again to meet with my friend Dmitry. I think we've built up an excellent relationship over the past 2 years, working on a whole range of issues. We had a very productive discussion here.

Obviously, the focus of APEC and our previous meeting in Seoul, the G–20, has been on international economic issues. And we stressed our interest in working with Russia on a range of bilateral and multilateral economic issues. I think that President Medvedev is doing an outstanding job trying to reform and move Russia forward on a whole range of economic issues, and we're working closely with them on Russia's interest in potentially joining the WTO.

In addition, we spoke about a range of security issues. I reiterated my commitment to get the START Treaty done during the lame duck session, and I've communicated to Congress that it is a top priority. We also discussed the fact that President Medvedev is personally going to be attending the NATO summit in Lisbon, and it allows us to restart the NATO-Russia Council and a host of consultations so that we can reduce tensions and increase cooperation on various security matters in the European theater.

I want to again thank President Medvedev on his cooperation with respect to Afghanistan. There has been excellent transit cooperation in recent months, and we think we can build on that in our discussions next week. And on a range of international issues and hotspots from Sudan to the Middle East, we think that Russia has been a excellent partner.

So we appreciate all the good work that President Medvedev and his team are doing, and I look forward to seeing him next week. Both he and I are racking up a lot of miles on our airplanes these days. But there's a lot of work to do. And I'm glad to have him as an excellent partner on a whole range of these issues.

President Medvedev. I would like also to say that it has been very pleasant for me to have this meeting and to discuss a whole range of bilateral and multilateral issues with my colleague, President of the United States of America Barack Obama.

Indeed, we have built on a very good relationship. We understand each other very well. It's very important to attain agreement on a whole range of issues. Those issues are always quite a few. We started with bilateral relations here. Of late, we have seriously moved forward the question of Russia WTO accession. And I

perceive this as a tribute to the acumen—to the team in effect in the U.S. of America, which has fulfilled all the agreements reached during my visit to Washington, DC. And I hope this process will continue and promptly Russia will join WTO.

Now, as regards other issues at hand, indeed, we certainly discussed regional matters, international issues. One of the important topics for the coming days will be the meeting in Lisbon, which will take place very shortly, and where the U.S.—the Russia-NATO summit will be held. We stated the improvement of relations between Russia and the North Atlantic Treaty Organization. And this is useful both to our countries and all parties involved.

And now we're discussing a whole range of issues involved, including the so-called European ABM. We have exchanged views as to what could be done here, and we have agreed to give instructions to our aides and ministers to pursue this work further. At the summit, certainly, we'll discuss this matter too.

Besides, we have been fruitfully cooperating in various regional fora such as G–20, which was to address international issues and to attain goals even if the situation in the economy of our countries still remains quite difficult. And I know that my friend Barack Obama has been involved in this 24 hours per day. I would like to wish him success in this area since the status of U.S. economy greatly affects the general state of the international economy.

And finally, we touched upon various international challenges which remain the same, and we agreed to coordinate our work in this field, and we'll work very actively and closely like we did recently.

Thank you.

President Obama. Okay. Thank you, everybody.

NOTE: The President spoke at 9:45 a.m. at the InterContinental Yokohama Grand hotel. President Medvedev spoke in Russian, and his remarks were translated by an interpreter. A portion of these remarks could not be verified because the audio was incomplete.

Exchange With Reporters Aboard Air Force One
November 14, 2010

The President. All right, what do you got?

President's Visit to Asia

Q. Highlight of trip for you, sir?

The President. What's that?

Q. What's your takeaway from the trip? What's your sense of——

The President. You know, the—a couple of things. Number one, I think all of Asia is eager for American engagement and leadership. We saw that in India, we saw it in Indonesia, we saw it in—during the G–20, and we saw it during APEC.

And it wasn't just from leaders. I was struck when I was at the first school that we went to in Mumbai, and those young kids who were talking about the environment and green technology. On the way down, I said, "Well, what are you guys' plans?" "Well, we're of course going to go to college." I said, "Where are you going to go?" "Well, America, of course."

And so I think that sometimes, because we've gone through a tough couple of years, there's a tendency for us to think that somehow Asia is moving and we're forgotten. And in fact, I think everywhere in Asia, what I heard from leaders and people is that we are still central and they want us there.

Now, the second strong impression is, those folks are moving. Korea, China, India, the entire Southeast Asian region, Japan—all of them recognize how competitive things are and that they are thinking each and every day about how to educate their workforce, rebuild their infrastructure, enter into new markets. And we should feel confident about our ability to compete, but we are going to have to step up our game.

Bipartisanship

Q. Sir, as you look ahead to the coming week, I'm wondering how do you sit down at the table——

The President. I'm sure it will be very relaxing.

Q. Yes. [*Laughter*] How do you approach a meeting with a Senate Republican leader whose life ambition seems to be to make sure you don't have a second term and an incoming House Speaker apparent whose mantra seems to be "no compromise"?

The President. Campaigning is very different from governing. All of us learn that. And they're still flush with victory, having run a strategy that was all about saying no. But I am very confident that the American people were not issuing a mandate for gridlock. They want to see us make progress precisely because they understand instinctually how competitive things are and how we have to step up our game.

So my expectation is, when I sit down with Mitch McConnell and John Boehner this week, along with the Democratic leaders, that there are a set of things that need to get done during the lame duck, and that they are not going to want to just obstruct, that they're going to want to engage constructively. There are going to be some disagreements. There may be some need for compromise. But we should be able at least to get through the lame duck, making sure that taxes don't go up for middle class families starting January 1, that some of the key business provisions that can assure economic growth get done. And then we're going to have a whole bunch of time next year for some serious philosophical debates. And they should welcome those debates next year.

Strategic Arms Reduction Treaty

Q. How do you get the START Treaty through the lame duck as well? Seems like an uphill battle right now.

The President. You know, actually, I feel reasonably good about our prospects. It was voted out of committee with strong bipartisan support. Senator Lugar is somebody who's made disarmament one of his signature issues. In fact, my first trip overseas was with Dick Lugar to Russia. And we've been in a series of conversations with Senator Kyl, whose top priority is making sure that the nuclear arsenal that we do have is modernized. I share that goal. We've heard from Senators like McCain and Graham who say they want to see this done.

And I think when we look at how important Russian cooperation has been on issues like Iran sanctions, on issues like transit into Afghanistan for our equipment for our troops, my hope and expectation is that, given this is a good treaty, given it has the support of previous Republican senior Government officials, that we should be able to get it done.

Tax Reform

Q. During the campaign season, you talked about the cost of extending the tax cuts, that that would actually make the U.S. less competitive. Now that you're indicating that you're open to some sort of compromise on the tax cuts, how do you do that and also ensure——

The President. Well, what I've said, Julianna [Julianna Goldman, Bloomberg News], is that I believe it is a mistake for us to borrow $700 billion to make tax cuts permanent for millionaires and billionaires. It won't significantly boost the economy, and it's hugely expensive. So we can't afford it.

Now, I know this is something that, during the campaign at least, the Republicans expressed some strong feelings about. I want to hear from them how strongly they feel about it, particularly given that they're also saying they want to control the deficit and debt.

And if they feel very strongly about it, then I want to get a sense of how they intend to spend—how they intend to pay for it.

President's Agenda

Q. Mr. President, you said it right after the election in the news conference that you were going to do some reflecting about what it meant. And now you've had this 10 days away, seeing a lot of different people. Can you reflect at all for us about how you might change your agenda, change your style, and how these travels might have affected your thinking?

The President. As I said in the press conference the day after the election, I spent the first 2 years trying to get policy right based on my best judgment about how we were going to deal with the short-term crisis and how we were going to retool to compete in this new global economy.

In that obsessive focus on policy, I neglected some things that matter a lot to people and rightly so: maintaining a bipartisan tone in Washington; dealing with practices like earmarks that are wasteful at a time of—where everybody else is tightening their belts; making sure that the policy decisions that I made were fully debated with the American people and that I was getting out of Washington and spending more time shaping public opinion and being in a conversation with the American people about why I was making the choices I was making.

So I think, moving forward, I'm going to redouble my efforts to go back to some of those first principles. And the fact that we are out of crisis—although still obviously in a difficult time—I think, will give me the capacity to do that.

Anything else?

Israeli Settlements in West Bank and East Jerusalem/Middle East Peace Process

Q. Did you get a chance to see the—look at the new Israeli plans for settlement freeze just yet?

The President. I think it's promising. And so we've been in contact with both the Israelis and the Palestinians to make sure that we use this opportunity to start negotiating as quickly as possible on some of the final status issues that would render the settlement issue moot.

But I commend Prime Minister Netanyahu for taking, I think, a very constructive step. It's not easy for him to do. But I think it's a signal that he's serious, and my hope is, is that he and President Abbas start negotiations immediately.

All right?

White House Press Secretary Robert L. Gibbs

Q. Is Gibbs in line for a Presidential Medal of Freedom for taking on the Indians back there, getting reporters in?

The President. I will say that his foot is still bruised. [*Laughter*] But it was all for a good cause.

All right, guys.

Q. Thanks a lot, sir.

NOTE: The President spoke at 2:17 p.m., e.d.t., while en route to Joint Base Andrews, MD. In his remarks, he referred to Prime Minister Benjamin Netanyahu of Israel; and President Mahmoud Abbas of the Palestinian Authority. Audio was not available for verification of the content of these remarks.

Statement on the Hajj and Eid al-Adha
November 15, 2010

Michelle and I extend our greetings for a happy Eid al-Adha to Muslims worldwide and wish safe travels to those performing Hajj. This year, nearly 3 million pilgrims from more than 160 countries, including the United States, have gathered in Mecca and neighboring sites to perform the Hajj rituals and stand together in prayer.

On Eid, Muslims around the world will commemorate Abraham's willingness to sacrifice his son and distribute food to those less fortunate, a reminder of the shared values and the common roots of three of the world's major religions.

On behalf of the American people, we extend our best wishes during this Hajj season. *Eid Mubarak* and *Hajj Mabroor.*

Statement on Earmark Reform
November 15, 2010

I welcome Senator McConnell's decision to join me and members of both parties who support cracking down on wasteful earmark spending, which we can't afford during these tough economic times. As a Senator, I helped eliminate anonymous earmarks, and as President, I've called for new limitations on earmarks and set new, higher standards of transparency and accountability. But we can't stop with earmarks, as they represent only part of the problem. In the days and weeks to come, I look forward to working with Democrats and Republicans to not only end earmark spending, but to find other ways to bring down our deficits for our children.

Message to the Senate Transmitting the Hungary-United States Taxation Convention
November 15, 2010

To the Senate of the United States:

I transmit herewith, for the advice and consent of the Senate to its ratification, the Convention between the Government of the United States of America and the Government of the Republic of Hungary for the Avoidance of Double Taxation and the Prevention of Fiscal Evasion with Respect to Taxes on Income, signed on February 4, 2010, at Budapest (the "proposed Convention") and a related agreement effected by an exchange of notes on February 4, 2010. I also transmit for the information of the Senate the report of the Department of State, which includes an Overview of the proposed Convention and related agreement.

The proposed Convention and related agreement were negotiated to bring U.S.-Hungary tax treaty relations into closer conformity with current U.S. tax treaty policies. For example, the proposed Convention contains comprehensive provisions designed to address "treaty shopping," which is the inappropriate use of a tax treaty by residents of a third country. The existing Convention with Hungary, signed in 1979, does not contain treaty shopping protections and, as a result, has been abused by third-country investors in recent years. For this reason, concluding the proposed Convention has been a top priority for the Department of the Treasury's tax treaty program.

I recommend that the Senate give early and favorable consideration to the proposed Convention and related agreement and give its advice and consent to their ratification.

BARACK OBAMA

The White House,
November 15, 2010.

Message to the Senate Transmitting the Protocol Amending the Luxembourg-United States Taxation Convention
November 15, 2010

To the Senate of the United States:

I transmit herewith, for the advice and consent of the Senate to its ratification, the Protocol Amending the Convention between the Government of the United States of America and the Government of the Grand Duchy of Luxembourg for the Avoidance of Double Taxation and the Prevention of Fiscal Evasion with Respect to Taxes on Income and Capital, signed on May 20, 2009, at Luxembourg (the "proposed Protocol") and a related agreement effected by the exchange of notes also signed on May 20, 2009. I also transmit for the information of the Senate the report of the Department of State, which includes an Overview of the proposed Protocol and related agreement.

The proposed Protocol and related agreement provide for more robust exchange of information between tax authorities in the two countries to facilitate the administration of each country's tax laws. They generally follow the current U.S. Model Income Tax Convention and the Organization for Economic Cooperation and Development standards for exchange of tax information.

I recommend that the Senate give early and favorable consideration to the proposed Protocol and related agreement and give its advice and consent to their ratification.

BARACK OBAMA

The White House,
November 15, 2010.

Remarks on Presenting the Congressional Medal of Honor to Staff Sergeant Salvatore A. Giunta
November 16, 2010

Good afternoon, everybody. Please be seated. On behalf of Michelle and myself, welcome to the White House. Thank you, Chaplain Carver, for that beautiful invocation.

Of all the privileges that come with serving as President of the United States, I have none greater than serving as Commander in Chief of the finest military that the world has ever known. And of all the military decorations that a President and a nation can bestow, there is none higher than the Medal of Honor.

Now, today is particularly special. Since the end of the Vietnam war, the Medal of Honor has been awarded nine times for conspicuous gallantry in an ongoing or recent conflict. Sadly, our Nation has been unable to present this decoration to the recipients themselves, because each gave his life—his last full measure of devotion—for our country. Indeed, as President, I have presented the Medal of Honor three times, and each time to the families of a fallen hero.

Today, therefore, marks the first time in nearly 40 years that the recipient of the Medal of Honor for an ongoing conflict has been able to come to the White House and accept this recognition in person. It is my privilege to present our Nation's highest military decoration, the Medal of Honor, to a soldier as humble as he is heroic: Staff Sergeant Salvatore A. Giunta.

Now, I'm going to go off script here for a second and just say, I really like this guy. [*Laughter*] I think anybody—we all just get a sense of people and who they are, and when you meet Sal and you meet his family, you are just absolutely convinced that this is what America is all about. And it just makes you proud. And so this is a joyous occasion for me, something that I have been looking forward to.

The Medal of Honor reflects the gratitude of an entire nation. So we are also joined here today by several Members of Congress, including both Senators and several Representatives from Staff Sergeant Giunta's home State of Iowa. We are also joined by leaders from across my administration and the Department of Defense, including the Secretary of Defense, Robert Gates; chairman of the Joint Chiefs of Staff Admiral Mike Mullen—where's Mike?—there he is, right there; Army Secretary John McHugh; and Chief of Staff of the Army General George Casey.

We are especially honored to be joined by Staff Sergeant Giunta's fellow soldiers, his teammates and brothers from Battle Company, 2d of the 503d of the 173d Airborne Brigade, and several members of that rarest of fraternities that now welcomes him into its ranks, the Medal of Honor Society. Please give them a big round of applause.

We also welcome the friends and family who made Staff Sergeant Giunta into the man that he is, including his lovely wife Jenny and his parents Steven and Rosemary, as well as his siblings, who are here. It was his mother, after all, who apparently taught him as a young boy in small-town Iowa how to remove the screen from his bedroom window in case of fire. [*Laughter*] What she didn't know was that by teaching Sal how to jump from his bedroom and sneaking off in the dead of night, she was unleashing a future paratrooper—[*laughter*]—who would one day fight in the rugged mountains of Afghanistan 7,000 miles away.

Now, during the first of his two tours of duty in Afghanistan, Staff Sergeant Giunta was forced early on to come to terms with the loss of comrades and friends. His team leader at the time gave him a piece of advice: "You just try—you just got to try to do everything you can when it's your time to do it." You've just got to try to do everything you can when it's your time to do it.

Salvatore Giunta's time came on October 25, 2007. He was a specialist then, just 22 years old.

Sal and his platoon were several days into a mission in the Korengal Valley, the most dangerous valley in northeast Afghanistan. The Moon was full. The light it cast was enough to travel by without using their night-vision goggles. With heavy gear on their backs and air support overhead, they made their way single file down a rocky ridge crest, along terrain so steep that sliding was sometimes easier than walking.

They hadn't traveled a quarter mile before the silence was shattered. It was an ambush so close that the cracks of the guns and the whiz of the bullets were simultaneous. Tracer fire hammered the ridge at hundreds of rounds per minute, "more," Sal said later, "than the stars in the sky."

The Apache gunships above saw it all, but couldn't engage with the enemy so close to our soldiers. The next platoon heard the shooting, but were too far away to join the fight in time.

And the two lead men were hit by enemy fire and knocked down instantly. When the third was struck in the helmet and fell to the ground, Sal charged headlong into the wall of bullets to pull him to safety behind what little cover there was. As he did, Sal was hit twice, one round slamming into his body armor, the other shattering a weapon slung across his back.

They were pinned down, and two wounded Americans still lay up ahead. So Sal and his comrades regrouped and counterattacked. They threw grenades, using the explosions as cover to run forward, shooting at the muzzle flashes still erupting from the trees. Then they did it again, and again, throwing grenades, charging ahead. Finally, they reached one of their men. He'd been shot twice in the leg, but he had kept returning fire until his gun jammed.

As another soldier tended to his wounds, Sal sprinted ahead, at every step meeting relentless enemy fire with his own. He crested a hill alone, with no cover but the dust kicked up by the storm of bullets still biting into the ground. There, he saw a chilling sight: the silhouettes of two insurgents carrying the other wounded American away, who happened to be one of Sal's best friends. Sal never broke stride. He leapt forward. He took aim. He killed one of the insurgents and wounded the other, who ran off.

Sal found his friend alive, but badly wounded. Sal had saved him from the enemy; now he had to try to save his life. Even as bullets impacted all around him, Sal grabbed his friend by the vest and dragged him to cover. For nearly half an hour, Sal worked to stop the bleeding and help his friend breathe until the medevac arrived to lift the wounded from the ridge. American gunships worked to clear the enemy from the hills. And with the battle over, 1st Platoon picked up their gear and resumed their march through the valley. They continued their mission.

It had been as intense and violent a firefight as any soldier will experience. By the time it was finished, every member of 1st Platoon had shrapnel or a bullet hole in their gear. Five were wounded, and two gave their lives: Sal's friend, Sergeant Joshua C. Brennan, and the platoon medic, Specialist Hugo V. Mendoza.

Now, the parents of Joshua and Hugo are here today. And I know that there are no words that, even 3 years later, can ease the ache in your hearts or repay the debt that America owes to you. But on behalf of a grateful nation, let me express profound thanks to your sons' service and their sacrifice. And could the parents of Joshua and Hugo please stand briefly?

Now, I already mentioned I like this guy Sal. And as I found out myself when I first spoke with him on the phone and when we met in the Oval Office today, he is a low-key guy, a humble guy, and he doesn't seek the limelight. And he'll tell you that he didn't do anything special, that he was just doing his job, that any of his brothers in the unit would do the same thing. In fact,

he just lived up to what his team leader instructed him to do years before: "You do everything you can."

Staff Sergeant Giunta, repeatedly and without hesitation, you charged forward through extreme enemy fire, embodying the warrior ethos that says, "I will never leave a fallen comrade." Your actions disrupted a devastating ambush before it could claim more lives. Your courage prevented the capture of an American soldier and brought that soldier back to his family. You may believe that you don't deserve this honor, but it was your fellow soldiers who recommended you for it. In fact, your commander specifically said in his recommendation that you lived up to the standards of the most decorated American soldier of World War II, Audie Murphy, who famously repelled an overwhelming enemy attack by himself for one simple reason: "They were killing my friends."

That's why Salvatore Giunta risked his life for his fellow soldiers, because they would risk their lives for him. That's what fueled his bravery, not just the urgent impulse to have their backs, but the absolute confidence that they had his. One of them, Sal has said—of these young men that he was with, he said, "They are just as much of me as I am." They are just as much of me as I am.

So I would ask Sal's team, all of Battle Company who were with him that day, to please stand and be recognized as well. Gentlemen, thank you for your service. We're all in your debt. And I'm proud to be your Commander in Chief.

These are the soldiers of our Armed Forces, highly trained, battle-hardened, each with specialized roles and responsibilities, but all with one thing in common: They volunteered. In an era when it's never been more tempting to chase personal ambition or narrow self-interest, they chose the opposite. They felt a tug; they answered a call. They said, "I'll go." And for the better part of a decade, they have endured tour after tour in distant and difficult places, they have protected us from danger, they have given others the opportunity to earn a better and more secure life.

They are the courageous men and women serving in Afghanistan even as we speak. They keep clear focus on their mission: to deny safe haven for terrorists who would attack our country, to break the back of the Taliban insurgency, to build the Afghans' capacity to defend themselves. They possess the steely resolve to see their mission through. They are made of the same strong stuff as the troops in this room, and I am absolutely confident that they will continue to succeed in the missions that we give them, in Afghanistan and beyond.

After all, our brave service men and women and their families have done everything they've been asked to do. They have been everything that we have asked them to be. "If I am a hero," Sal has said, "then every man who stands around me, every woman in the military, every person who defends this country is." And he's right.

This medal today is a testament to his uncommon valor, but also to the parents and the community that raised him, the military that trained him, and all the men and women who served by his side.

All of them deserve our enduring thanks and gratitude. They represent a small fraction of the American population, but they and the families who await their safe return carry far more than their fair share of our burden. They fight halfway around the globe, but they do it in hopes that our children and our grandchildren won't have to.

They are the very best part of us. They are our friends, our family, our neighbors, our classmates, our coworkers. They are why our banner still waves, our founding principles still shine, and our country—the United States of America—still stands as a force for good all over the world.

So please join me in welcoming Staff Sergeant Salvatore A. Giunta for the reading of the citation.

NOTE: The President spoke at 2:07 p.m. in the East Room at the White House. In his remarks, he referred to Maj. Gen. Douglas L. Carver, USA, Chief of Chaplains; Reps. Leonard L. Boswell, Bruce Braley, and Steve King; Mario Giunta, brother, and Katie Giunta, sister, of S. Sgt. Giunta; Michael Brennan, father, and Janice Gates, mother, of Sgt. Joshua C. Brennan, USA; Jesus C. Mendoza, father, and Sara Mendoza, mother, of Spc. Hugo V. Mendoza, USA; and Capt. Daniel P. Kearney, USA, former commander, Company B, 2d Battalion (Airborne), 503d Infantry Regiment, 173d Airborne Brigade Combat Team.

Remarks on Presenting the National Medals of Science and National Medals of Technology and Innovation
November 17, 2010

The President. Thank you so much, everybody. Thank you. Wonderful to see you. Please, everyone sit down, sit down. We've got a lot of work to do here. [*Laughter*] Have a seat.

Welcome to the White House. It is a great honor to be joined by so many leading researchers and innovators. I want to give some special thanks to a few members of my Cabinet, Members of Congress who are here today. Secretary Gary Locke, our Commerce Secretary, is here. Members of Congress: We have Arlen Specter of Pennsylvania and Bart Gordon of Tennessee. Please give them a big round of applause for their great work.

We also have NASA Administrator Bolden, who is here—Charlie. Dr. Subra Suresh, who's the Director of our National Science Foundation, is here. Mr. Dave Kappos, who's the Director of the Patent and Trademark Office, he was here—he may have had some work to do; Dr. Patrick Gallagher, who's the Director of our National Institute of Standards and Technology; and Dr. Larry Strickling, Administrator of the National Telecommunications and Information Administration.

Now, the achievements of the men and women who are onstage today stand as a testament to the ingenuity, to their zeal for discovery, and to the willingness to give of themselves and to sacrifice in order to expand the reach of human understanding.

All of us have benefited from their work. The scientists in this room helped develop the semiconductors and microprocessors that have propelled the information age. They've modeled the inner workings of the human mind and the complex processes that shape the Earth's climate. They've conducted pioneering research, from mathematics to quantum physics, into the sometimes strange and unexpected laws that govern our universe.

Folks here can also claim inventions like the digital camera, which has revolutionized photography—as all these folks back here will testify—[*laughter*]—as well as superglue, which, in addition to fascinating children—[*laughter*]—has actually saved lives as a means of sealing wounds. And the men and women we celebrate today have helped to unlock the secrets of genetics and disease, of nanotechnology and solar energy, of chemistry and biology, breakthroughs that provide so many benefits and hold so much potential, from new sources of electricity to new ways of diagnosing and treating illness.

Along the way, many of these folks have broken down barriers for women and minorities, who've traditionally been underrepresented in scientific fields, but obviously are no less capable of contributing to the scientific enterprise. Just as an example, at the start of her career, decades ago, Esther Cornwell [Conwell]° was hired as an assistant engineer, but soon after, she was told that this position wasn't open to a woman. She had to serve as an engineer's assistant instead. Of course, that didn't stop her from becoming a pioneer in semiconductors and materials science.

It's no exaggeration to say that the scientists and innovators in this room have saved lives, improved our health and well-being, helped unleash whole new industries and millions of jobs, transformed the way we work and learn and communicate. And this incredible contribution serves as proof not only of their incredible cre-

ativity and skill, but of the promise of science itself.

Every day, in research laboratories and on proving grounds, in private labs and university campuses, men and women conduct the difficult, often frustrating work of discovery. It isn't easy. It may take years to prove a hypothesis correct or decades to learn that it isn't correct. Often the competition can be fierce, whether in designing a product or securing a grant. And rarely do those who give their all to this pursuit receive the attention or the acclaim they deserve.

Yet it is in these labs, often late at night, often fueled by a dangerous combination of coffee and obsession—[*laughter*]—that our future is being won. For in a global economy, the key to our prosperity will never be to compete by paying our workers less or building cheaper, lower quality products. That's not our advantage. The key to our success, as it has always been, will be to compete by developing new products, by generating new industries, by maintaining our role as the world's engine of scientific discovery and technological innovation. It's absolutely essential to our future.

And that's why we're here today and why I look forward to events like these. I believe one of the most important jobs that I have as President is to restore science to its rightful place. That means strengthening our commitment to research. It means ensuring that our Government makes decisions based on the best evidence, rather than politics. It means reforming and improving math and science education and encouraging the private sector to inspire young people to pursue careers in science and engineering. And it means fostering a climate of innovation and entrepreneurship, from incentives in clean energy to tax breaks to startups. I'd also point out, that's not just a job for government. Creating this climate depends on all of us, including businesses and universities and nonprofits.

One of the most important ways in which we can restore science to its rightful place is by celebrating the contributions of men and women

---

° White House correction.

like all of you, because that's how we'll excite a new generation to follow in your footsteps. That's how we can spark the imagination of a young person who just might change the world. I was reminded of how important this is just a few weeks ago. We held a science fair here at the White House. Some of you may have heard about it.

We welcome all the time championship sports teams to the White House to celebrate their victories. I thought we ought to do the same thing for the winners of science fairs and robotic contests and math competitions, because those young people often don't get the credit that they deserve. Nobody rushes on the field and dumps Gatorade on them—[*laughter*]—when you win a science award. Maybe they should. [*Laughter*]

So I got to meet these incredibly talented and enthusiastic young men and women. There was a team of high school kids from Tennessee that had designed a self-powered water purification system. We had robots running all over through the State Dining Room. [*Laughter*]

The last young person I spoke to was a young woman from Texas. She was 16 years old. She was studying biology as a freshman, decided she was interested in cancer research, so taught herself chemistry during the summer, then designed a science project to look at new cancer drugs based on some experimental drugs that are activated by light. They could allow a more focused treatment that targets the cancer cells while living, healthy cells remain unharmed.

She goes on to design her own drug, wins the international science competition. And she told me that she and her high school science teacher are being approached by laboratories across the country to collaborate on this potential new cancer treatment. This is a true story: 16 years old, taught herself chemistry, incredibly inspiring.

And at a time of significant challenge in this country, at a moment when people are feeling so much hardship in their lives, this has to give us hope for the future. It ought to remind us of the incredible potential of this country and its people, as long as we unlock it, as long as we put resources into it and we celebrate it and we encourage it, we embrace it.

You know, Carl Sagan once said, "Science is a way of thinking much more than it is a body of knowledge." That way of thinking, that combination of curiosity and skepticism, the sense of wonder and the willingness to test our assumptions, it's what, at root, we are honoring today. It's what has spurred countless advances and conferred untold benefits on our society. And it's an idea that has driven our success for as long as we have been a nation.

And I'm confident that this spirit of discovery and invention will continue to help us succeed in the years and decades to come. And our country owes every one of our laureates with us today a big measure of thanks for nurturing that spirit and expanding the boundaries of human knowledge.

So it is now my privilege to present the National Medals of Science and the National Medals of Technology and Innovation.

[*At this point, Maj. Reginald McClam, USMC, Marine Corps Aide to the President, read the citations, and the President presented the medals.*]

The President. Well, let me make two closing points. Number one, I feel really smart just standing up here with these folks. [*Laughter*] I think it kind of rubbed off on me. [*Laughter*] Number two, I want to congratulate our military aide for being able to read all those things. [*Laughter*] I want to assure you, he practiced a lot. [*Laughter*]

And finally, let me just once again say to all the honorees who are here tonight, you have truly revolutionized the world in ways that are profoundly important to people in their day-to-day lives, but also help to create those steps in human progress that really make us who we are as human beings. And so we could not be prouder of you, could not be more grateful to you for your contributions.

Please give them one last big round of applause.

All right. Everybody, enjoy the party. [*Laughter*]

NOTE: The President spoke at 5:25 p.m. in the East Room at the White House. In his remarks, he referred to White House science fair partici-pant Amy Chyao of Plano, TX, and her chemistry teacher Vashka Desai.

Statement on Senate Action on Paycheck Fairness Legislation
November 17, 2010

I am deeply disappointed that a minority of Senators have prevented the "Paycheck Fairness Act" from finally being brought up for a debate and receiving a vote. This bill passed in the House almost 2 years ago; today it had 58 votes to move forward, the support of the majority of Senate, and the support of the majority of Americans. As we emerge from one of the worst recessions in history, this bill would ensure that American women and their families aren't bringing home smaller paychecks because of discrimination. It also helps businesses that pay equal wages as they struggle to compete against discriminatory competition. But a partisan minority of Senators blocked this commonsense law. Despite today's vote, my administration will continue to fight for a woman's right to equal pay for equal work.

NOTE: The statement referred to S. 3772.

Statement on General Motors Company
November 17, 2010

General Motors' initial public offering (IPO) marks a major milestone in the turnaround of not just an iconic company, but the entire American auto industry. Through the IPO, the Government will cut its stake in GM by nearly half, continuing our disciplined commitment to exit this investment while protecting the American taxpayer. Supporting the American auto industry required tough decisions and shared sacrifices, but it helped save jobs, rescue an industry at the heart of America's manufacturing sector, and make it more competitive for the future.

Remarks Prior to a Meeting on the Strategic Arms Reduction Treaty and an Exchange With Reporters
November 18, 2010

The President. I want to begin by thanking the incredible leaders who are around this table, not only the Vice President and the Secretary of State, but also some of the most able statesmen from both parties that we've had in modern American history, who are sitting around this table.

We are here to discuss the importance of ratifying the START Treaty. And let me be clear: It is in the national security imperative—it is a national security imperative that the United States ratify the new START Treaty this year.

There is no higher national security priority for the lame duck session of Congress. The stakes for American national security are clear, and they are high. The new START Treaty responsibly reduces the number of nuclear weapons and launchers that the United States and Russia deploy, while fully maintaining America's nuclear deterrent.

If we ratify this treaty, we're going to have a verification regime in place to track Russia's strategic nuclear weapons, including U.S. inspectors on the ground. If we don't, then we don't have a verification regime: no inspectors, no insights into Russia's strategic arsenal, no framework for cooperation between the world's two nuclear superpowers. As Ronald Reagan said, we have to trust, but we also have to verify.

In order for us to verify, we've got to have a treaty.

The new START Treaty is also a cornerstone of our relations with Russia. And this goes beyond nuclear security. Russia's been fundamental to our efforts to put strong sanctions in place to put pressure on Iran to deal with its nuclear program. It's been critical in supporting our troops in Afghanistan through the Northern Distribution Network. It's been critical in working with us to secure all vulnerable nuclear materials around the world and to enhance European security.

We cannot afford to gamble on our ability to verify Russia's strategic nuclear arms. And we can't jeopardize the progress that we've made in securing vulnerable nuclear materials or in maintaining a strong sanctions regime against Iran. These are all national interests of the highest order.

Let me also say—and I think the group around the table will confirm—that this new START Treaty is completely in line with a tradition of bipartisan cooperation on this issue. This is not a Democratic concept; this is not a Republican concept. This is a concept of American national security that has been promoted by Ronald Reagan, George H.W. Bush, Bill Clinton, George W. Bush, and now my administration.

We've taken the time to do this right. To ensure that the treaty got a fair hearing, we submitted to the Senate last spring. Because of the leadership of John Kerry and Dick Lugar, there have been 18 hearings on this subject. There have been multiple briefings. It has been fully and carefully vetted and has the full endorsement of our Nation's military leadership. Our vice chairman of the Joint Chiefs of Staff Hoss Cartwright is here and will confirm that this is in our national security interests.

My administration is also prepared to go the extra mile to ensure that our remaining stockpile and nuclear infrastructure is modernized, which I know is a key concern of many around this table and also many on Capitol Hill. We've committed to invest $80 billion on the effort to modernize over the next decade. And based on our consultations with Senator Kyl, we've

agreed to request an additional $4.1 billion over the next 5 years.

So the key point here is, this is not about politics, it's about national security. This is not a matter that can be delayed. Every month that goes by without a treaty means that we are not able to verify what's going on on the ground in Russia. And if we delay indefinitely, American leadership on nonproliferation and America's national security will be weakened.

Now, as Senator Reid said yesterday, there is time on the Senate calendar to get this treaty ratified this year. So I've asked Vice President Biden to focus on this issue day and night until it gets done. It's important to our national security to let this treaty go up for a vote. I'm confident that it's the right thing to do. The people around this table think it's the right thing to do.

I would welcome the press to query the leadership here, people who have been National Security Advisers, Secretaries of State, and key advisers, Defense Secretaries for Democratic and Republican administrations, and they will confirm that this is the right thing to do.

So we've got a lot on our plate during this lame duck session. I recognize that, given the difficulties in the economy, that there may be those—perhaps Democrats and Republicans on the Hill—who think this is not a top priority. I would not be emphasizing this and these folks would not have traveled all this way if we didn't feel that this was absolutely important to get done now.

And so I'm looking forward to strong cooperation between Democrats and Republicans on Capitol Hill, as exemplified by John Kerry and Dick Lugar, to get this done over the course of the next several weeks.

All right? Thank you very much.

Senate Ratification

Q. Do you have the votes in the Senate?

The President. I'm confident that we should be able to get the votes. Keep in mind that every President since Ronald Reagan has presented a arms treaty with Russia and been able to get ratification. And for the most part, these treaties have been debated on the merits; the majority of them have passed overwhelmingly with bipartisan support. There's no reason that we shouldn't be able to get that done this time as well.

All right? Thank you, guys. Thank you.

NOTE: The President spoke at 10:36 a.m. in the Roosevelt Room at the White House. In his remarks, he referred to former Secretaries of State Madeleine K. Albright, James A. Baker III, and Henry A. Kissinger; former Secretaries of Defense William S. Cohen and William J. Perry; former National Security Adviser Brent Scowcroft; and former Sen. Samuel A. Nunn.

Remarks on the United States Auto Industry
November 18, 2010

Hello, everybody. Good afternoon. Today one of the toughest tales of the recession took another big step towards becoming a success story. General Motors relaunched itself as a public company, cutting the Government's stake in the company by nearly half. What's more, American taxpayers are now positioned to recover more than my administration invested in GM. And that's a very good thing.

Last year, we told GM's management and workers that if they made the tough decisions necessary to make themselves more competitive in the 21st century—decisions requiring real leadership, fresh thinking, and also some shared sacrifice—then we would stand by them. And because they did, the American auto industry—an industry that's been the proud symbol of America's manufacturing might for a century, an industry that helped to build our middle class—is once again on the rise.

Our automakers are in the midst of their strongest period of job growth in more than a decade. Since GM and Chrysler emerged from bankruptcy, the industry has created more than 75,000 new jobs. For the first time in 6 years, Ford, GM, and Chrysler are all operating at a profit. In fact, last week, GM announced its best quarter in over 11 years. And most importantly, American workers are back at the assembly line manufacturing the high-quality, fuel-efficient, American-made cars of tomorrow, capable of going toe to toe with any other manufacturer in the world.

Just 2 years ago, this seemed impossible. In fact, there were plenty of doubters and naysayers who said it couldn't be done, who were prepared to throw in the towel and read the American auto industry last rites. Independent esti-mates suggested, however, that had we taken that step, had we given up, we would have lost more than 1 million jobs across all 50 States. It would have also resulted in economic chaos, devastating communities across the country and costing governments tens of billions of dollars in additional social safety net benefits and lost revenue.

That wasn't an acceptable option—to throw up our hands and to quit. That's not what we do. This is a country of optimistic and determined people who don't give up when times are tough. We do what's necessary to move forward.

So these last 2 years haven't been easy on anybody. They haven't been without pain or sacrifice, as the tough restructuring of GM reminds us. And obviously, we've still got a long road ahead and a lot of work to do to rebuild this economy, to put people back to work, to make America more competitive for the future, and to secure the American Dream for our children and our grandchildren.

But we are finally beginning to see some of these tough decisions that we made in the midst of crisis pay off. And I'm absolutely confident that we're going to keep on making progress. I believe we're going to get through this tougher and stronger than we were before. Because just as I had faith in the ability of our autoworkers to persevere and succeed, I have faith in the American people's ability to persevere and succeed. And I have faith that America's best days and America's—and American manufacturing's best days are still ahead of us.

Finally, I just want to embarrass a couple of people. Ron Bloom and Brian Deese are key members of the team that helped to engineer this rescue of GM and Chrysler. So had it not been for these two gentlemen, a whole lot of people might be out of work right now. We are very proud of them, and I figured that I'd go ahead and—you can see they're all looking sheepish—point them out to you.

So thank you very much, everybody.

NOTE: The President spoke at 4:14 p.m. in the James S. Brady Press Briefing Room at the White House. In his remarks, he referred to Ron A. Bloom, Treasury Department Senior Adviser for Auto Issues; and Brian Deese, Special Assistant to the President for Economic Policy.

Statement on Senate Confirmation of Jacob J. "Jack" Lew as Director of the Office of Management and Budget
November 18, 2010

I am pleased that Jack Lew has been confirmed, with wide bipartisan support, to serve as my next Director of the Office of Management and Budget. He brings unparalleled experience and wisdom to this important job at a critical time in our Nation's history. After years of irresponsibility in Washington, we need to make the tough choices to put our country back on a sustainable fiscal path and lay the foundation for long-term job creation and economic growth. We need to cut waste where we find it and create a Government that is efficient, effective, and responsive to the American people. I am confident Jack Lew can lead us in these efforts and look forward to working with him in the days ahead.

Remarks Following a Meeting With President Anibal Antonio Cavaco Silva of Portugal in Lisbon, Portugal
November 19, 2010

President Cavaco Silva. Good afternoon. I would like to start by thanking President Barack Obama for having accepted my invitation for a working meeting during his first visit to Portugal.

Portugal is honored to welcome President Obama. The meeting we just had and the working lunch which followed enabled a fruitful exchange of viewpoints, thus highlighting the excellent political relationship between Portugal and the U.S.A., a solid relationship grounded on a strong identity of viewpoints and sharing of values and principles.

The proximity of our relationship is also due to the role of the Portuguese and Luso descendant community in the U.S., a community which holds on to its roots while, at the same time, is closely linked to its host country, a community which has produced an increasingly number of leading political personalities at the Federal and State levels.

Our cooperation with the U.S.A. is growing stronger and more diversified. However, there is still margin to do more, and that is why the common interest in strengthening dialogue and cooperation have been highlighted, of course, based on the defense and cooperation agreement signed in 1995 and which represents the institutional framework of our relationship.

In the economic sector, there has been an increase in our recent commercial trade, as well as an increase in the Portuguese investment in the United States. However, our exports to the U.S. are still far from what they could be, considering the quality and diversification of our products and the U.S. market I mentioned. Also, the volume of U.S. investments in Portugal is far from what one would expect.

I also had the opportunity to discuss with President Obama the current economic and financial situation in both our countries and at the global level. And I was happy to hear the U.S. authorities reiterate their trust on the Portuguese capability to overcome the challenges it is faced with.

Our meeting also enabled a reflection on NATO summit's agenda. Portugal, a founding member of the alliance and an Atlantic nation, has always defended transatlantic ties. Portugal and the United States want a reinvigorated alliance, which will be capable of responding in an efficient manner to the challenges and threats transatlantic security may be faced with. This is the object of the major reform that will be discussed and, I hope, approved in the Lisbon summit.

Furthermore, considering the recent election of Portugal to the security sector—to the Security Council, we agreed on the need to strengthen the political dialogue on the United Nations agenda.

I would like to once again thank President Obama for his visit to Portugal.

President Obama. Thank you for your warm welcome. And thank you and the people of Lisbon and Portugal for welcoming us to this beautiful and ancient city.

It is very fitting that we are gathering here in Lisbon. It was from here that the great explorers set out to discover new worlds. It was here, a gateway of Europe, through which generations of immigrants and travelers have passed and bound our countries together. And it was here that Europeans came together to sign the landmark treaty that strengthened their union.

Now we've come to Lisbon again to revitalize the NATO alliance for the 21st century and to strengthen the partnership between the United States and the European Union.

Mr. President, I thank you and all the people of Portugal for everything you've done to make these summits a success.

Our meeting was also an opportunity to reaffirm the strong partnership between the United States and Portugal. President Cavaco Silva is commander of Portugal's Armed Forces and will be representing Portugal at the NATO summit. We pledged to continue the excellent cooperation between our militaries, especially Lajes Field in the Azores, which provides critical support to American and NATO forces in Iraq and Afghanistan.

I expressed my gratitude to the Portuguese Armed Forces who are serving alongside us in Afghanistan. And here in Lisbon, I look forward to working with our NATO and our ISAF partners as we move towards a new phase, a transition to Afghan responsibility that begins in 2011, with Afghan forces taking the lead for security across Afghanistan by 2014.

So this summit is an important opportunity for us to align an approach to transition in Afghanistan.

Finally, we discussed ways to expand our bilateral cooperation. On the economic front, we're looking to deepen our partnership in trade and investment, in science and technology. I am very impressed with the outstanding work that Portugal has done in areas like clean energy, and we think that we can collaborate more.

On the security front, Portugal's upcoming seat at the U.N. Security Council will be an opportunity to advance peace and security that both our nations seek around the world.

So, Mr. President, I want to thank you and the Portuguese people for your hospitality. I'm confident that we're going to have two successful summits and that we will continue to deepen an extraordinarily strong partnership between the United States and Portugal, one that's based not just on relations between heads of states, not just on the basis of treaties, but based on an enormous warmth between our two peoples; one that in part is forged by the wonderful contributions that are made by Portuguese Americans each and every day.

So thank you so much, Mr. President.

NOTE: The President spoke at 2:25 p.m. at Belem Palace. President Cavaco Silva spoke in Portuguese, and his remarks were translated by an interpreter.

Remarks Following a Meeting With Prime Minister Jose Socrates Carvalho Pinto de Sousa of Portugal in Lisbon
November 19, 2010

Prime Minister Socrates. Mr. President, it's an honor to welcome you in Portugal on your first visit to my country. And I think this is the right moment to reaffirm in front of you the transatlantic relationship as one of the most important pillars of Portugal's foreign policy.

Portugal and the United States of America share the same values and same vision for the future. This, I think, can explain the excellent bilateral relation between our two countries.

We are very good friends, and we are very good allies. But please, Mr. President, allow me to continue in Portuguese, because I would like to address myself to the Portuguese public opinion.

[*At this point, Prime Minister Socrates spoke in Portuguese, and no translation was provided.*]

Once again, Mr. President Obama, welcome to Portugal, and I give you the floor.

President Obama. Well, thank you very much, Mr. Prime Minister. I want to begin by expressing my gratitude to you and to the people of Portugal for hosting me here today and for hosting the NATO summit. And I have to say that your English is much better than my Portuguese.

These are obviously difficult times—difficult economic times—for the world and for Portugal. But, Mr. Prime Minister, your determination to strengthen the Portuguese economy and to host these summits speaks to your leadership and to Portugal's leadership, not only in Europe, but around the world. So I thank you very much for that.

Portugal and the United States have been partners for more than 200 years and allies for more than 60 years. Immigrants from Portugal, the Azores, and Madeira formed strong Portuguese American communities across our country, including, by the way, in my home State of Hawaii.

And I understand that there's been a fair amount of interest here about how my family has been enriched by Portugal as well, specifically, Bo, our dog. [*Laughter*] He is the most popular member of the White House. [*Laughter*]

As the Prime Minister said, we had some excellent discussions, first over lunch and just now in our meeting. I told the Prime Minister how grateful we are for the service of Portuguese soldiers in our efforts in Afghanistan, where next year we will begin the transition to Afghan responsibility for security.

We discussed NATO's new strategic concept, which will ensure that the alliance can meet the new challenges of the 21st century. And as Portugal prepares to take its seat on the U.N. Security Council, we discussed how we can work together around the world, including our shared goal of promoting development in Africa, where Portugal has historic ties.

But the focus of our meeting was on the highest priority for both our countries, and that is, creating jobs and prosperity for our people. And one of the ways to do that is to increase trade and investment between the United States and Portugal, trade which supports both jobs and innovation in both our countries.

So we discussed how we can work to expand trade and investment and forge new collaborations in science and technology, including through our U.S.-Portugal Bilateral Commission. We agreed that a major opportunity for closer economic cooperation is clean and renewable energy, an area where I want to congratulate the Prime Minister and the Portuguese people for the extraordinary leadership that you've shown in clean energy.

New partnerships between Portuguese and American companies are leading the way in wind power. The Prime Minister's leadership on electric cars will create new opportunities for American companies here in Portugal, as I believe we'll see tomorrow, and this is an example of what Portugal and America can achieve together.

And obviously, Portugal is working through challenges created by some of the financial markets, and I think that it's important to note that the Prime Minister has committed himself to a very vigorous package of economic steps, and we are going to be working with all of Europe, as well as Portugal, in support of these efforts, and we want to say how much we appreciate some of the work that you are doing.

So again, I want to thank not only the Prime Minister, the President, who previously hosted me, but most of all, the Portuguese people for your friendship, your commitment to a strong alliance between our two countries. And I am very much looking forward to spending the next few days in this beautiful city so that we can continue to strengthen a relationship that I think is not only important to both our countries, but important to Europe and the world as well. *Obrigado.*

NOTE: The President spoke at 3:07 p.m. in the Prime Minister's office. In his remarks, he referred to President Anibal Antonio Cavaco Silva of Portugal.

Statement on the Anniversary of the Birth of the Founder of Sikhism
November 19, 2010

On Sunday, many around the world will observe the anniversary of birth of Guru Nanak Dev Ji, the founder of Sikhism. I send my best wishes to all those observing this extraordinary occasion. This is also an opportunity to recognize the many contributions that Sikh Americans have made to our Nation and to reflect on the pluralism that is a hallmark of America. Sikhism's principles of equality, service, interfaith cooperation, and respect are principles shared by all Americans. As Sikhs celebrate the birth of Guru Nanak, people of good will everywhere can identify with his teachings on the equality of all humankind and the need for compassion in our service to others.

Statement on Senate Passage of Legislation Settling Claims Against the Department of Agriculture
November 19, 2010

I applaud the Senate for passing the claims settlement act of 2010, which will at long last provide funding for the agreements reached in the *Pigford II* lawsuit, brought by African American farmers, and the *Cobell* lawsuit, brought by Native Americans over the management of Indian trust accounts and resources. I particularly want to thank Attorney General Holder and Secretaries Salazar and Vilsack for their continued work to achieve this outcome. I urge the House to move forward with this legislation as they did earlier this year, and I look forward to signing it into law.

This bill also includes settlements for four separate water rights suits made by Native American tribes. I support these settlements, and my administration is committed to addressing the water needs of tribal communities. While these legislative achievements reflect important progress, they also serve to remind us that much work remains to be done. That is why my administration also continues to work to resolve claims of past discrimination made by women and Hispanic farmers against the USDA.

NOTE: The statement referred to H.R. 4783.

Remarks at the North Atlantic Treaty Organization Summit in Lisbon
November 19, 2010

Good evening, everybody. I just wanted to take a few minutes to talk about the substantial progress that the United States and our NATO allies have made here today.

We head into tomorrow's meeting with an alliance that is fully aligned in its vision and approach to collective security for the 21st century. After a year of discussions, and sometimes debate, the new strategic concept that we are embracing shows that NATO is fully united about the way forward and committing to addressing the full range of security challenges of this century.

Our article 5 commitment remains the center of our approach, of course. An attack on one NATO member is an attack on all. And just as we will always back up that commitment with the conventional and nuclear strength that is necessary to defend our allies, we are now backing up that commitment with new capabilities as well.

That's why I'm pleased to announce that for the first time we've agreed to develop missile defense capability that is strong enough to cover all NATO European territory and populations, as well as the United States. This important step forward builds on the new phased adaptive approach to missile defense that I announced for the United States last year. It offers a role for all of our allies. It responds to the threats of our times. It shows our determination to protect our citizens from the threat of ballistic missiles. And tomorrow we look forward to working with Russia to build our cooperation with them in this area as well, recognizing that we share many of the same threats.

Under the leadership of Secretary General Rasmussen, I'm also pleased that we're looking at the full range of capabilities that we need to secure our people, from more deployable capabilities, to new measures to deal with new threats like improvised explosives, to the cyber defenses that will be so essential in the years to come.

And just as we have full agreement on our new strategic concept, tomorrow our NATO allies, ISAF partners, and the Afghan Government will work to align our approach on Afghanistan, particularly in two areas: our transition to full Afghan lead between 2011 and 2014, and the long-term partnership that we're building in Afghanistan.

Finally, let me say a few words about the need to ratify the new START Treaty. As I've said, this is a national security imperative for the United States. We need to ratify new START to put in place on-the-ground inspections of Russian nuclear arsenals, to reduce our deployed weapons and launchers, and to build on our cooperation with Russia, which has helped us put pressure on Iran and helped us to equip our mission in Afghanistan.

But just as this is a national security priority for the United States, the message that I've received since I've arrived from my fellow leaders here at NATO could not be clearer: New START will strengthen our alliance, and it will strengthen European security.

Nobody is aware—nobody is more aware of the need for a strong, secure, and democratic Europe than our Eastern and Central European allies. And my friend, the Foreign Minister of Poland, Radoslaw Sikorski, put it well when he said that new START will, and I quote, "bolster our country's security, and that of Europe as a whole."

On the other hand, we know that failure to ratify and move forward with new START will put at risk the substantial progress that has been made in advancing our nuclear security and our partnership with Russia on behalf of global security.

Indeed, tomorrow we will build on the reset of U.S.-Russian relations by resetting relations between NATO and Russia as well through the NATO-Russia Council, which opens the door to cooperation on a range of security interests, cooperation that can lead to a more secure Europe and a more secure world.

So I want to thank all of my fellow leaders for the work that has been done. The progress that we've already made here today gives me great confidence that this will be a landmark summit in Lisbon and that the strong ties between the United States and Europe will continue to grow in the years to come.

Thanks very much, everybody.

NOTE: The President spoke at 7:34 p.m. at the Feria Internacional de Lisboa. In his remarks, he referred to Secretary General Anders Fogh Rasmussen of the North Atlantic Treaty Organization.

The President's Weekly Address
November 20, 2010

Today I'd like to speak with you about an issue that is fundamental to America's national security: the need for the Senate to approve the new START Treaty this year.

This treaty is rooted in a practice that dates back to Ronald Reagan. The idea is simple: As the two nations with over 90 percent of the world's nuclear weapons, the United States and Russia have a responsibility to work together to reduce our arsenals. And to ensure that our national security is protected, the United States has an interest in tracking Russia's nuclear arsenal through a verification effort that puts U.S. inspectors on the ground. As President Reagan said when he signed a nuclear arms treaty with the Soviet Union in 1987, "Trust, but verify."

That is precisely what the new START Treaty does. After nearly a full year of negotiations, we completed an agreement earlier this year that cuts by a third the number of long-range nuclear weapons and delivery vehicles that the United States and Russia can deploy, while ensuring that America retains a strong nuclear deterrent and can put inspectors back on the ground in Russia.

The treaty also helped us reset our relations with Russia, which led to concrete benefits. For instance, Russia has been indispensable to our efforts to enforce strong sanctions on Iran, to secure loose nuclear material from terrorists, and to equip our troops in Afghanistan.

All of this will be put to risk if the Senate does not pass the new START Treaty.

Without ratification this year, the United States will have no inspectors on the ground and no ability to verify Russian nuclear activities. So those who would block this treaty are breaking President Reagan's rule. They want to trust, but not verify.

Without ratification, we put at risk the coalition that we have built to put pressure on Iran and the transit route through Russia that we use to equip our troops in Afghanistan. And without ratification, we risk undoing decades of American leadership on nuclear security and decades of bipartisanship on this issue. Our security and our position in the world are at stake.

Indeed, since the Reagan years, every President has pursued a negotiated, verified, arms reduction treaty. And every time that these treaties have been reviewed by the Senate, they have passed with over 85 votes. Bipartisan support for new START could not be stronger. It has been endorsed by Republicans from the Reagan administration and both Bush administrations, including Colin Powell, George Shultz, Jim Baker, and Henry Kissinger. And it was approved by the Senate Foreign Relations Committee by a strong bipartisan vote of 14 to 4.

Over the last several months, several questions have been asked about new START, and we have answered every single one. Some have asked whether it will limit our missile defense; it will not. Some, including Senator Jon Kyl, have asked that we modernize our nuclear infrastructure for the 21st century. We are doing so and plan to invest at least $85 billion in that effort over the next 10 years, a significant increase from the Bush administration.

Finally, some make no argument against the treaty, they just ask for more time. But remember this: It has already been 11 months since we've had inspectors in Russia, and every day that goes by without ratification is a day that we lose confidence in our understanding of Russia's nuclear weapons. If the Senate doesn't act this year—after 6 months, 18 hearings, and nearly a thousand questions answered—it would have to start over from scratch in January.

The choice is clear: A failure to ratify new START would be a dangerous gamble with America's national security, setting back our understanding of Russia's nuclear weapons, as well as our leadership in the world. That is not what the American people sent us to Washington to do.

There is enough gridlock, enough bickering. If there is one issue that should unite us—as Republicans and Democrats—it should be our national security.

Some things are bigger than politics. As Republican Dick Lugar said the other day, "Every

Senator has an obligation in the national security interest to take a stand, to do his or her duty."

Senator Lugar is right. And if the Senate passes this treaty, it will not be an achievement for Democrats or Republicans, it will be a win for America.

Thanks.

NOTE: The address was recorded at approximately 4:15 p.m. on November 18 in the Blue Room at the White House for broadcast on November 20. In the address, the President referred to former Secretaries of State Colin L. Powell, George P. Shultz, James A. Baker III, and Henry A. Kissinger. The transcript was made available by the Office of the Press Secretary on November 19, but was embargoed for release until 6 a.m., e.s.t., on November 20. The Office of the Press Secretary also released a Spanish language transcript of this address.

The President's News Conference in Lisbon, Portugal
November 20, 2010

The President. Good afternoon, everyone. We have just concluded an extremely productive NATO summit, and I want to thank our hosts, the Government and the people of Portugal, for their hospitality in this beautiful city of Lisbon. And I thank my fellow leaders for the sense of common purpose that they brought to our work here.

For more than 60 years, NATO has proven itself as the most successful alliance in history. It's defended the independence and freedom of its members. It has nurtured young democracies and welcomed them into Europe that is whole and free. It has acted to end ethnic cleansing beyond our borders. And today, we stand united in Afghanistan, so that terrorists who threaten us all have no safe haven and so that the Afghan people can forge a more hopeful future.

At no time during these past six decades was our success guaranteed. Indeed, there have been many times when skeptics have predicted the end of this alliance. But each time NATO has risen to the occasion and adapted to meet the challenges of that time. And now, as we face a new century with very different challenges from the last, we have come together here in Lisbon to take action in four areas that are critical to the future of the alliance.

First, we aligned our approach on the way forward in Afghanistan, particularly on a transition to full Afghan lead that will begin in early 2011 and will conclude in 2014.

It is important for the American people to remember that Afghanistan is not just an American battle. We are joined by a NATO-led coalition made up of 48 nations with over 40,000 troops from allied and partner countries. And we honor the service and sacrifice of every single one.

With the additional resources that we've put in place we're now achieving our objective of breaking the Taliban's momentum and doing the hard work of training Afghan security forces and assisting the Afghan people. And I want to thank our allies who committed additional trainers and mentors to support the vital mission of training Afghan forces. With these commitments I am confident that we can meet our objective.

Here in Lisbon, we agreed that early 2011 will mark the beginning of a transition to Afghan responsibility, and we adopted the goal of Afghan forces taking the lead for security across the country by the end of 2014. This is a goal that President Karzai has put forward.

I've made it clear that even as Americans transition and troop reductions will begin in July, we will also forge a long-term partnership with the Afghan people. And today NATO has done the same. So this leaves no doubt that as Afghans stand up and take the lead they will not be standing alone.

As we look ahead to a new phase in Afghanistan, we also reached agreement in a second area: a new strategic concept for NATO that recognizes the capabilities and partners that the alliance needs to meet the challenges of the 21st century. I want to give special thanks to Secretary General Rasmussen for his outstanding leadership in forging a vision that preserves the enduring strengths of the alliance while adapting it to meet the missions of the future.

As I said yesterday, we have reaffirmed the central premise of NATO: our article 5 commitment that an attack on one is an attack on all. And to ensure this commitment has meaning, we agreed to take action in a third area: to modernize our conventional forces and develop the full range of military capabilities that we need to defend our nations.

We'll invest in technologies so that allied forces can deploy and operate together more effectively. We'll deploy new defenses against threats such as cyber attacks. And we will reform alliance command structures to make them more flexible and more efficient. Most important, we agreed to develop a missile defense capability for NATO territory, which is necessary to defend against the growing threat from ballistic missiles.

The new approach to European missile defense that I announced last year—the phased adaptive approach—will be the United States contribution to this effort and a foundation for greater collaboration. After years of talk about how to meet this objective, we now have a clear plan to protect all of our allies in Europe as well as the United States.

When it comes to nuclear weapons, our strategic concept reflects both today's realities as well as our future aspirations. The alliance will work to create the conditions so that we can reduce nuclear weapons and pursue the vision of a world without them. At the same time, we've made it very clear that so long as these weapons exist, NATO will remain a nuclear alliance and the United States will maintain a safe, secure, and effective nuclear arsenal to defer—deter adversaries and guarantee the defense of all our allies.

Finally, we agreed to keep forging the partnership beyond NATO that helped make our alliance a pillar of global security. We'll continue to enhance NATO's cooperation with the EU, which I will talk about in my summit later this afternoon with EU leaders. After a 2-year break, we are also resuming cooperation between NATO and Russia.

I was very pleased that my friend and partner, President Dmitry Medvedev, joined us today at the NATO-Russia Council Summit. Together, we've worked hard to reset the relations between the United States and Russia, which has led to concrete benefits for both our nations. Now we're also resetting the NATO-Russia relationship. We see Russia as a partner, not an adversary. And we agreed to deepen our cooperation in several critical areas: on Afghanistan, counternarcotics, and a range of 21st-century security challenges. And perhaps most significantly, we agreed to cooperate on missile defense, which turns a source of past tension into a source of potential cooperation against a shared threat.

So overall, this has been an extremely productive 2 days. We came to Lisbon with a clear task, and that was to revitalize our alliance to meet the challenges of our time. That's what we've done here.

Of course, it's work that cannot end here. And so I'm pleased to announce that the United States will host the next NATO summit in 2012, a summit that will allow us to build on the commitments that we've made here today as we transition to full Afghan lead, build new capabilities, expand our partnerships, and ensure that the most successful alliance in history will continue to advance our security and our prosperity well into the future.

And I said to Prime Minister Socrates that considering he has thrown such a successful summit here in Lisbon, I've been taking notes. You set a very high bar of outstanding hospitality, and so I appreciate everything that the people of Portugal have done, and we will try to reciprocate that hospitality when we host in 2012.

So with that, let me take some questions. And I'm going to start with Margaret Warner of PBS. Margaret, why don't you get a microphone.

Europe-U.S. Relations/North Atlantic Treaty Organization Summit/Strategic Arms Reduction Treaty/U.S. Congress

Q. Thank you, Mr. President. What message do you hope this summit sends to Senator Jon Kyl and other Republicans in the Senate who are resisting voting on and ratifying START in the lame duck session?

The President. Well, a couple of messages that I just want to send to the American people. Number one, I think that Americans should be proud that an alliance that began 60 years ago, through the extraordinary sacrifices, in part, of American young men and women, sustained throughout a cold war, has resulted in a Europe that's more unified than it's ever been before, that is an extraordinarily strong ally of the United States, and that continues to be a cornerstone of prosperity not just for the United States and Europe but for the world. This is a direct result of American efforts and American sacrifice. And I think the world appreciates it.

The second message I want to send is that after a period in which relations between the United States and Europe were severely strained, that strain no longer exists. There are occasions where there may be disagreements on certain tactical issues, but in terms of a broad vision of how we achieve transatlantic security that alliance has never been stronger. And that's something that Americans should feel good about.

Number three, I think the Americans should know that American leadership remains absolutely critical to achieving some of these important security objectives. And I think our European partners would be the first to acknowledge that.

What we ratified here today is the direct result of work that we've done over the last 2 years to get to this point. And just to take the example of Afghanistan. I think that if you said even a year ago, or even maybe 6 months ago that we would have a unified approach on the part of our allies to move forward in Afghanistan with a sustained commitment where we actually increased the resources available and closed the training gap in order to be successful, I think a lot of skeptics would have said that's not going to happen. It has happened, in part because we have rebuilt those strong bonds of trust between the United States and our allies.

The fourth thing—and this finally goes to your specific question—unprompted, I have received overwhelming support from our allies

here that START, the new START Treaty, is a critical component to U.S. and European security. And they have urged both privately and publicly that this gets done.

And I think you've seen the comments of a wide range of European partners on this issue, including those who live right next to Russia, who used to live behind the Iron Curtain, who have the most cause for concern with respect to Russian intentions and who have uniformly said that they will feel safer and more secure if this treaty gets ratified—in part, because right now we have no verification mechanism on the ground with respect to Russian arsenals. And Ronald Reagan said, "Trust, but verify." We can't verify right now.

In part because, as a consequence of the reset between the United States and Russia, we have received enormous help from the Russians in instituting sanctions on Iran that are tougher than anything we've seen before. We have transit agreements with Russia that allows us to supply our troops. There are a whole range of security interests in which we are cooperating with Russia, and it would be a profound mistake for us to slip back into mistrust as a consequence of our failure to ratify.

And the third reason is that with the cold war over, it is in everybody's interests to work on reducing our nuclear arsenals, which are hugely expensive and contain the possibilities of great damage, if not in terms of direct nuclear war, then in terms of issues of nuclear proliferation.

So we've got our European allies saying this is important. We've got the U.S. military saying this is important. We've got the National Security Advisers and the Secretaries of Defense and generals from the Reagan administration, the Bush administration—Bush I and Bush II—as well as from the Clinton administration and my administration saying this is important to our national security. We've got the Republican chairman of the Foreign Relations Committee saying this is in our national interest to get done now. This is an issue that traditionally has received strong bipartisan support. We've gone through 18 hearings; we've answered 1,000 questions. We have met the concerns about modernizing our nuclear stockpile with concrete budget numbers.

It's time for us to go ahead and get it done. And my hope is that we will do so.

There's no other reason not to do it than the fact that Washington has become a very partisan place. And this is a classic area where we have to rise above partisanship. Nobody is going to score points in the 2012 election around this issue, but it's something that we should be doing because it helps keep America safe. And my expectation is, is that my Republican friends in the Senate will ultimately conclude that it makes sense for us to do this.

All right, Karen DeYoung [Washington Post]. There's a mike coming, Karen.

President Hamid Karzai of Afghanistan/U.S. Military Operations in Afghanistan

Q. Thank you, Mr. President. I wonder if you could talk to us a bit about your conversation with President Karzai. He has made some complaints recently, part of a long line of complaints. Did he raise those with you and did you address them correctly—directly? Has he stepped back from his call to reduce the military footprint there? Thank you.

The President. Well, Karen, I want to put your question in the context of what's taken place this weekend here in Lisbon. President Karzai is the head of a government of a sovereign nation that has gone through 30 years of war, and understandably, he is eager to reassert full sovereignty, including control of security operations within his country. At the same time, the United States and all of our ISAF allies have every interest in wanting to turn over responsibility—security responsibility—to Afghan forces as soon as is practicable.

So in that sense, our interests align. And the 2014 date that was stated in the document coming out of this summit and was widely agreed to didn't simply come from us; it wasn't an arbitrary date. This is a date that President Karzai identified as a appropriate target for when Afghans could take over full responsibility.

Now, between now and 2014, our constant effort is going to be to train up Afghan security forces so that they can take more and more re-

sponsibility. That's what transition is all about. And during that time, President Karzai, in his eagerness to accelerate that transition, is going to be interested in reducing our footprint, finding ways that Afghans can take more responsibility. And those are things that we welcome. We want him to be assertive as possible in moving towards Afghan responsibility. But in that transition there are also going to be a whole series of judgment calls and adjustments that are necessary to make that effective.

So, for example, President Karzai raised concerns about private security contractors and what he perceived as heavy-handedness on the part of these contractors in Afghanistan. I think that concern is perfectly appropriate. On the other hand, what I've told him in the past and I repeated in our meeting today is I can't send U.S. aid workers or civilians into areas where I can't guarantee their safety. So, theoretically, it would be nice if I could just send them in and they could help build a road or construct a school or engage in an irrigation project without a full battalion around them, but I have to think practically. And so we're going to have to balance the issues of being sensitive to our footprint with the need to get certain objectives done.

Now, I've instituted ongoing conversations with President Karzai. I talk to him by videoconference at least once every 6 weeks or so. Secretary Clinton, Secretary Gates are in constant communications with him. General Petraeus, Karl Eikenberry are in constant communications with him.

And what I've communicated to President Karzai is two things. Number one, we have to make sure that we understand our objectives are aligned, the endpoint that we want to reach is the same. And number two, we have to be in good enough communications with each other that when issues come up that raise sensitivities about Afghan sovereignty, that may alienate Afghan populations, that we should be sensitive to them and we will be listening to him.

At the same time, he's got to be sensitive to our concerns about the security of our personnel; about making sure that taxpayer dollars from the United States or other ISAF countries or other partners aren't being wasted as a consequence of corruption; that sacrifices that are being made by our military to clear out areas are reinforced by good governance practices on the part of the Afghans so that we're not just clearing an area, but unable to hold it because people have no confidence in, for example, the administration of justice in that area through Afghan Government structures.

So that's going to be a constant conversation. I don't think it's going to go away immediately, but what we're trying to do is make sure that our goals are aligned, and then work through these problems in a systematic way.

I will say that for all the noise that has existed in the press, the fact of the matter is over the last year we've made progress. And I expect that we're going to make more progress next year and it will not be without occasional controversies and occasional differences.

Adam Entous, Wall Street Journal. Adam is back there.

U.S. Military Operations in Afghanistan/President Karzai of Afghanistan

Q. To follow up on the last question, Mr. Karzai is the President of the country. If he makes a request, why isn't that good enough and why wouldn't there be a change of course? And on—just to—on—we're getting close to December, excuse me. Do you think the strategy, the surge strategy, is working? And do you think, at this point, that you'll be able to make a substantial troop reduction in July?

The President. Let me take the second question first. When I went through a rigorous and sometimes painful review process, as you remember, last December, our goal was to make sure that we had blunted the Taliban. The whole point of ramping up our troop presence was not because we wanted to maintain a long-term, large presence in Afghanistan, but it was to immediately blunt the momentum that we were seeing from the Taliban and to create the space for the training of effective Afghan security forces.

And on both those fronts I think the objective assessment is, is that we have made progress. You have fewer areas of Afghanistan under

Taliban control. You have the Taliban on the defensive in a number of areas that were their strongholds. We have met or exceeded our targets in terms of recruitment of Afghan security forces. And our assessments are that the performance of Afghan security forces has improved significantly.

So thanks to the hard work of people like Dave Petraeus and Mark Sidwell and others, and obviously the incredible sacrifices of the troops on the ground from the ISAF forces, we are in a better place now than we were a year ago.

As a consequence, I'm confident that we are going to be able to execute our transition starting in July of next year. And General Petraeus is, in fact, in the process now of planning and mapping out where are those areas where we feel there's enough security that we can begin thinning out our troops in those areas, where are areas that need further reinforcements as certain areas get thinned out, so that we can continually consolidate the security gains and then backfill it with the effective civilian improvements that are going to be needed.

So we have made progress. The key is to make sure that we don't stand still but we keep accelerating that progress, that we build on it. And the contributions of our coalition forces around trainers is particularly important. And I've already said this, but when countries like Canada, which had originally said they were going to pull out at the end of next year, say, we are willing to supplement the training forces—a very difficult political decision—when countries like Italy are willing to come in and step up on the trainers, that's a testament to the confidence they have in General Petraeus's plans and the fact that we are much more unified and clear about how we're going to achieve our ultimate end state in Afghanistan.

Now, to go to the point about President Karzai, we are there at their invitation. You are absolutely correct. Afghanistan is a sovereign nation. President Karzai believes that it is very important for us to help him with security and development issues over not just the next couple of years, but over the long term. That partnership is obviously a two-way street. So my message to President Karzai is: We have to be sensitive to his concerns and the concerns of the Afghan people. We can't simply tell them what's good for them. We have to listen and learn and be mindful of the fact that Afghans ultimately make decisions about how they want to structure their governance, how they want to structure their justice system, how they want to approach economic development.

On the other hand, if we're putting in big resources, if we're ponying up billions of dollars, if the expectation is that our troops are going to be there to help secure the countryside and ensure that President Karzai can continue to build and develop his country, then he's got to also pay attention to our concerns as well.

And I don't think that's unreasonable, and I don't think he thinks that's unreasonable. But there is going to have to be a constant conversation to make sure that we're moving in the right direction.

And sometimes, that conversation is very blunt. There are going to be some strong disagreements. And sometimes there are real tensions; for example, the issue of civilian casualties. That's an entirely legitimate issue on the part of President Karzai. He's the President of a country, and you've got foreign forces who, in the heat of battle, despite everything we do to avoid it, may occasionally cause civilian casualties, and that is understandably upsetting. I don't fault President Karzai for raising those issues.

On the other hand, he's got to understand that I've got a bunch of young men and women from small towns and big cities all across America who are in a foreign country being shot at and having to traverse terrain filled with IEDs, and they need to protect themselves. And so if we're setting things up where they're just sitting ducks for the Taliban, that's not an acceptable answer either.

And so we've got to go back and forth on all these issues.

Chuck Todd [NBC News].

Strategic Arms Reduction Treaty/Iran/U.S. Transportation Security Administration's Enhanced Screening Policies

Q. Thank you, Mr. President. I want to follow up on Margaret's question. It sounds like you believe Senator Kyl's opposition on START is purely political or mostly political. Is that what you're telling your fellow world leaders on this stage? And do you think failure to ratify by the end of the year, is that going to undermine your ability on the world stage?

And then, second, do you care to comment on the dustup over TSA pat-downs?

The President. I have spoken to Senator Kyl directly and I believe that Senator Kyl wants a safe and secure America, just like I do, and is well motivated. And so what I said in terms of partisanship is that the climate in Washington is one where it's hard to get parties to cooperate, especially after a big election.

That's understandable. Folks are reorganizing. You've got a lame duck session; there's a limited amount of time. It's been a long year; we've done a lot of stuff. People are thinking about Thanksgiving and then thinking about getting off to Christmas. And I'm sure that the Republican caucus in the Senate is really focused on next year and we're going to have a Republican House and what are the things that we want to get done and what are our priorities.

So Senator Kyl has never said to me that he does not want to see START ratified. He hasn't publicly said that he's opposed to the treaty. What he said is, is that he just felt like there wasn't enough time to get it done in the lame duck. And I take him at his word.

But what I've been trying to communicate is that this is an issue of critical national security interest that has been fully vetted, it has been extensively debated, it has received strong bipartisan support coming out of the Foreign Relations Committee, it has received strong backing from our U.S. military, it has received strong backing from Republican predecessors in the National Security office and the Secretary of Defense's office, Secretary of State. And so in that context, I want to emphasize to everybody that this is important and there is a time element to this.

We don't have any mechanism to verify what's going on right now on the ground in Russia. Six months from now—that's a 6-month gap in which we don't have good information. So even if you—let me take this—let me say it this way: Especially if you mistrust Russian intentions, you should want to get this done right away.

Now, I happen to think that President Medvedev is actually—has made every effort to move Russia in the right direction. And so if you agree with me on that front, then it's also important that we don't leave a partner hanging after having negotiated a agreement like this that's good for both countries.

And there's another element to this. We've instituted Iran sanctions. Thanks to the work of the EU, thanks to the work of Russia, thanks to the work of some of our other partners, these are the strongest sanctions we've ever implemented. But we have to maintain sustained pressure as Iran makes a calculation about whether it should return to negotiations on its nuclear program. This is the wrong time for us to be sending a message that there are divisions between the P–5-plus-1, that there's uncertainty.

So my point here, Chuck, is there are going to be a lot of issues to debate between Democrats and Republicans over the next 2 years. This shouldn't be one of them.

With respect to the TSA, let me, first of all, make a confession. I don't go through security checks to get on planes these days, so I haven't personally experienced some of the procedures that have been put in place by TSA. I will also say that in the aftermath of the Christmas Day bombing, our TSA personnel are, properly, under enormous pressure to make sure that you don't have somebody slipping on a plane with some sort of explosive device on their persons. And since the explosive device that was on Mr. Abdulmutallab was not detected by ordinary metal detectors, it has meant that TSA has had to try to adapt to make sure that passengers on planes are safe.

Now, that's a tough situation. One of the most frustrating aspects of this fight against terrorism is that it has created a whole security apparatus around us that causes huge inconvenience for all of us. And I understand people's frustrations. And what I've said to the TSA is that you have to constantly refine and measure whether what we're doing is the only way to assure the American people's safety. And you also have to think through are there ways of doing it that are less intrusive.

But at this point, TSA, in consultation with our counterterrorism experts, have indicated to me that the procedures that they've been putting in place are the only ones right now that they consider to be effective against the kind of threat that we saw in the Christmas Day bombing.

But I'm going to—every week I meet with my counterterrorism team, and I'm constantly asking them whether—is what we're doing absolutely necessary? Have we thought it through? Are there other ways of accomplishing it that meet the same objectives?

Bill Plante [CBS News].

Afghanistan/Counterterrorism Efforts

Q. Thank you, Mr. President. NATO's commitment to Afghanistan extends through 2014. What about the U.S.? It's possible, given the circumstances, that there may be a need for troops and combat action after 2014. Is the U.S. committed? If it's your decision, will you keep U.S. troops committed in a combat role if necessary?

The President. Well, your last point was "if necessary," and so let me start there. My first and most important job as President of the United States is to keep the American people safe. So I'll always do what's necessary to keep the American people safe. That's true today; that will be true for as long as I'm President of the United States. And maybe that will be the case in 2014.

What NATO has committed to is that we are going to undergo a transition between 2011 and 2014, and the United States is part of NATO, so we are completely aligned in what we're going to be doing. Our goal is that the Afghans have taken the lead in 2014, and in the same way that we have transitioned in Iraq, we will have successfully transitioned so that we are still providing a training and support function.

There may still be extensive cooperation with the Afghan Armed Services to consolidate the security environment in that area. But our every intention is that Afghans are in the lead and we're partnering with them the way we partner with countries all around the world to make sure that both our country and their country is safe.

The other thing that I'm pretty confident we will still be doing after 2014 is maintaining a counterterrorism capability until we have confidence that Al Qaida is no longer operative and is no longer a threat to the American homeland and to American allies and personnel around the world. And so it's going to be important for us to continue to have platforms to be able to execute those counterterrorism operations.

That's true in Iraq as well. And obviously, that's even more true when it comes to core Al Qaida. We don't want—after having made these extraordinary efforts by so many countries, we don't have to—we don't want to have to suddenly find ourselves in a situation where they waited us out and they reconsolidated there.

But my goal is to make sure that by 2014 we have transitioned, Afghans are in the lead, and it is a goal to make sure that we are not still engaged in combat operations of the sort that we're involved with now. Certainly our footprint will have been significantly reduced. But beyond that, it's hard to anticipate exactly what is going to be necessary to keep the American people safe as of 2014. I'll make that determination when I get there.

The last question is Vitor Goncalves [RTP] of Portugal.

Global Economic Stabilization/Group of Twenty (G–20) Summit/President Obama's Visit to Portugal

Q. Good afternoon, Mr. President. Thank you very much for answering my question. First, I'd like to ask you in what ways the recovery of American economy can boost European economies? This is a matter of great concern here in Europe.

And secondly, this is your first trip to Portugal. What are you taking from Lisbon? Thank you very much.

The President. One of the things that we learned over the last several years as we have dealt with this worldwide economic crisis is that every economy is interlinked. We can't separate what happens in the United States from what happens in Portugal, from what happens in Korea, from what happens in Thailand, what happens in South Africa or Brazil. We are all interconnected now in a global economy. And obviously, as the world's largest economy, what happens in the United States is going to have a profound impact on Europe.

The same is true, by the way, in the reverse direction. Our general assessment is, is that the trajectory of U.S. growth was moving at a stronger pace right before the issues of sovereign debt in Greece came up in the spring of this year. And when that happened, not only did that cause a significant dip in our stock market, but a lot of companies contracted in terms of their investment plans because they were uncertain. They understood that what happens in Europe could end up affecting what happens in the United States.

The most important thing that I can do for Europe is the same thing that I need to do for the United States, and that is to promote growth and increased employment in the United States. We have now grown for five consecutive quarters. We have seen private sector job growth for 10 consecutive months. But the pace is too slow. And my main task when I get back to the States and over the coming year is to work with Republicans and Democrats to move that growth process forward and to make sure that we are growing faster and that we are putting people back to work.

It is a difficult task. Historically, what's happened is, is that when you have a financial crisis, the recession that follows is more severe and long lasting than a normal business cycle crisis would be. And we are, I think, digging out of a hole of debt and deleveraging and the severe fall in our housing market. And all those things create a strong headwind when it comes to growth.

But we've taken some important steps already. That's why the economy is now growing instead of contracting. I want to take more steps to encourage business investment, to help small businesses hire. We think that infrastructure development in the United States has the potential of boosting our growth rates at a significant level.

We're going to have to do all this, though, at the same time as we're mindful of a significant public debt that has to be dealt with. And it would be nice if we didn't have the inheritance of big deficits and big debt and we could simply pump up the economy. What we have to do now is to make sure that we're speeding up recovery, but still focusing on reducing our debts in the medium and long term.

But I think every European should have a great interest in making sure that the United States is growing faster.

One thing we talked about at the G–20 was the fact that for all of us to grow faster, we need to rebalance the world economy. Before this crisis you had a situation where the world economic engine was U.S. consumers taking out huge debt—using credit cards, using home equity loans—to finance a lot of imports from other countries, and other countries developing huge surpluses, a lot of money washing around the world financial system, looking for investments with high returns that—all of which contributed to the instability of the system.

And what we said at the G–20, and what we will continue to push for, is countries with big surpluses have to figure how they can expand demand. Countries with significant deficits, we've got to save more and focus not just on consumption, but also on production and on exports.

The currency issue plays into this. And there's going to be an ongoing debate about making sure that surplus countries are not artificially devaluing their currencies in a way that inhibits not only our growth, but a world economic growth.

In terms of Portugal, everybody has been magnificent. I admit that the weather is better today than it was yesterday. Everybody assures me that Lisbon is supposed to be beautiful this time of year. Yesterday was a little sad, but I was indoors all day anyway, so it didn't matter.

But the people of Portugal have been unbelievably kind and generous to us. I want to thank again Prime Minister Socrates and the entire Government for the excellent work that they've done. And I hope that we're going to be able to return the favor next year.

So *obrigado*. Thank you very much.

NOTE: The President's news conference began at 4:47 p.m. at the Feria Internacional de Lisboa. In his remarks, the President referred to Secretary General Anders Fogh Rasmussen of the North Atlantic Treaty Organization; President Dmitry A. Medvedev of Russia; Prime Minister Jose Socrates Carvalho Pinto de Sousa of Portugal; Sen. Richard G. Lugar, in his capacity as ranking member of the Senate Foreign Relations Committee; Gen. David H. Petraeus, USA, commander, NATO International Security Assistance Force, Afghanistan; U.S. Ambassador to Afghanistan Karl W. Eikenberry; Mark Sidwell, Senior Civilian Representative in Afghanistan, North Atlantic Treaty Organization; and Umar Farouk Abdulmutallab, who was charged for the December 25, 2009, explosive device incident on Northwest Airlines Flight 253.

Remarks Following the European Union-United States Summit in Lisbon
November 20, 2010

Well, thank you very much. Good evening, everyone. It is a pleasure to be here with President Barroso and President Van Rompuy.

I am proud to be here. I was proud to meet with the leaders of the 27 European member states during our summit in Prague last year. I was pleased to welcome President Barroso and the EU leadership to the White House last fall. I have been pleased to work with both Herman and Jose at the G–20 context, and today marks our first summit under the EU's Lisbon Treaty. So—it was also wonderful to meet Cathy Ashton, who's doing outstanding work.

This summit was not as exciting as other summits because we basically agree on everything. But nevertheless, I value these meetings for a simple reason: America's relationship with our European allies and partners is the cornerstone of our engagement with the world, and it's a catalyst for global cooperation.

Whether it's creating jobs for our people, sustaining global economic recovery, protecting our citizens, preventing nuclear proliferation, the United States has no closer partner than Europe. And we're not simply united by shared interests. We're united by shared history, by shared democratic values, a shared set of traditions that have endured for generations.

That's why the United States needs and wants a strong and united Europe. That's why our summit today focused on three important areas of mutual interest.

First, we agreed to take a series of steps to increase trade and investment, which already amounts to a $4.4 trillion relationship and supports millions of jobs on both sides of the Atlantic. We directed our Transatlantic Economic Council to focus on streamlining regulations, encouraging innovation, eliminating barriers that hamper trade and investment. And building on the progress of the G–20 summit in Seoul, we reaffirmed the need for currencies that are market driven and for countries with large surpluses to boost domestic demand.

Second, we reviewed our close security cooperation. We saw with the recent security alerts in Europe, as well as the plot that was disrupted to detonate explosives in cargo flights, that we have to work every day to keep our citizens safe. And we will continue to do so.

From our common efforts to address Iran's nuclear program to our work together in Sudan, we're also partners in promoting stability and averting crises around the world. And now that the—that NATO has agreed that the transition to Afghan responsibility will begin early next year, the EU's role as a major donor to Afghanistan and a trainer for police forces will only become more important.

Finally, we're coordinating on a series of global issues. With regard to climate change, we directed our U.S.-EU Energy Council to find ways to bring clean energy technologies to market faster, and we're standing by our Copenhagen commitments to reduce emissions as we work towards Cancun.

And as the world's source of most of—as the source of most of the world's development assistance, we agreed to better coordinate our assistance and ensure a more effective division of labor to avoid duplication and inefficiency, as I've called for in our new development strategy.

So again, I want to thank President Barroso, President Van Rompuy for their strong leadership and their partnership. I am confident that if we continue to deepen the close cooperation between the United States and the EU, we can deliver greater security and greater prosperity for our 800 million citizens on both sides of the Atlantic.

And let me just use this opportunity once again to thank the people of Portugal for the wonderful hospitality. I plan to come back when I have fewer meetings. [*Laughter*]

Thank you very much.

NOTE: The President spoke at 7:45 p.m. at the Portuguese Pavilion. In his remarks, he referred to President Jose Manuel Durao Barroso of the European Commission; President Herman Van Rompuy of the European Council; and High Representative of the European Union for Foreign Affairs and Security Policy Catherine M. Ashton.

Statement on the Death of Margaret T. Burroughs
November 21, 2010

Michelle and I are saddened by the passing of Dr. Margaret Burroughs, who was widely admired for her contributions to American culture as an esteemed artist, historian, educator, and mentor. In 1961, Dr. Burroughs founded the DuSable Museum of African American History on the South Side of Chicago, which served as a beacon of culture and a resource worldwide for African American history. She was also admired for her generosity and commitment to underserved communities through her children's books, art workshops, and community centers that both inspired and educated young people about African American culture.

Our thoughts and prayers go out to Dr. Burroughs's family and loved ones. Her legacy will live on in Chicago and around the world.

Statement on Lebanon's Independence Day
November 22, 2010

On behalf of the American people, I offer my deepest congratulations to President Sleiman, Speaker Berri, Prime Minister Hariri, and all citizens of Lebanon on the occasion of Lebanon's Independence Day. This celebration comes at a particularly opportune time, in light of the challenges Lebanon currently faces. This important day exemplifies Lebanon's sovereignty, independence, and national and cultural identity. The United States is committed to strengthening these characteristics through support of Lebanon's state institutions and voices of peace and moderation.

We are grateful to the Government of Lebanon for its steadfast leadership under difficult circumstances. It has shown vision in its search for peace, stability, and consensus. We continue to support the Special Tribunal for Lebanon, which will end the era of political assassinations with impunity in Lebanon. Lebanon and its children need a future where they can fulfill their dreams free of fear and intimidation.

I am committed to doing everything I can to support Lebanon and ensure it remains free from foreign interference, terrorism, and war. Lebanon deserves peace and prosperity, and those who believe otherwise are no friend to Lebanon. I hope you will carry this message to your friends and family. Lebanon has fought enough fights. The only way ahead is for all Lebanese to work together, not against each other, for a sovereign and independent Lebanon that enjoys both justice and stability.

Lebanon's multiethnic democratic system ensures representation by all of Lebanon's different religious and ethnic backgrounds. This unique facet sets Lebanon apart and has allowed Lebanese citizens to flourish and build their country and the rich tapestry that is Lebanese society. It is much the same in our own country, where Lebanese Americans have for generations contributed deeply to the American community, economy, and culture through their leadership in Congress, the business world, the U.S. military, and even in my Cabinet. We salute Lebanon today for its greatest resource—its people—and wish all of Lebanon a happy independence day.

Remarks at the Chrysler Indiana Transmission Plant II in Kokomo, Indiana
November 23, 2010

Everybody, have a seat. Thank you so much. Thank you, Joe. Thank you, Kokomo. I have to just say, by the way, Joe is not only one of the best Vice Presidents in history, he's also one of the best introducers in history. [*Laughter*] I try to take him wherever I can.

I want to thank your plant manager, Jeremy Keating, for the great tour and the great work that he's doing here. He is proud of the work that's being done at this plant. I want to thank your local UAW president, Richie Boruff, who's here; thank them for showing me around.

A couple other hotshots: U.S. Senator Evan Bayh is here; Congressman Joe Donnelly is in the house; Congressman Andre Carson is here; Congressman Baron Hill is here. By the way, Congressman Baron Hill is in the Indiana Basketball Hall of Fame. Now, that's pretty cool. Being a Congressman's cool; being in the Basketball Hall of Fame in Indiana, that's something.

Mayor of Kokomo, Greg Goodnight, is here, doing outstanding work. The CEO of Chrysler Group, Sergio Marchionne, is here. President of UAW, Bob King, is in the house.

We've got some of the best workers in the United States of America right here at this plant. And I had a chance to meet some of you as we were going around seeing these amazing transmissions that you're building. And I was very happy to hear that after a couple of tough years, this plant is now running at full capacity. And that's why I'm here today. That's why I'm here today.

Now, we all know that one plant by itself doesn't mean that there aren't people in Kokomo who are still hurting. I had lunch with the mayor and some firefighters, and there's still a long way to go. The mayor's got all kinds of great plans, and there are businesses that are looking to start expanding. But the fact is there are millions of people around the country who are still looking for work in the wake of the worst recession in our lifetimes. I don't have to tell you that. Many of you still have friends or neighbors, a husband or a wife who is still struggling.

And I know that before this plant started rehiring, a lot of you were in the same position. So you remember that it is a tough, tough thing when you're out of work, especially when you've taken a lifetime of pride in working and supporting a family and making great products.

But even as we continue to face serious challenges, what's happening here at this plant, the changes we're seeing throughout Kokomo, are signs of hope and confidence in the future, in our future, together. You're showing us the way forward. You're living up to that spirit of optimism and determination, that grit that's always been at the heart of who we are as a people, at the heart of America.

I remember coming to Kokomo a little over 2 years ago. Joe will remember this. Some of you might have been here. What was happening here reflected what was happening all over the country, all over this region. For a decade or more, families had felt a growing sense of economic insecurity. A lot of manufacturing had left the area. And then a recession started taking hold, and folks were seeing job losses and facing new hardships.

That was before anybody knew how devastating the recession was going to be. So by the time I took office, just a few months later, the financial crisis had hit, the auto industry teetered on the brink, and we were losing millions of jobs.

And that left Joe and I with some tough choices. One was to help the auto industry restructure. And that wasn't an easy call. I understood that there were some reservations of those who said that the industry should pay a price for some poor decisions by the part of management. But we also knew that millions of jobs hung in the balance. We also knew that the very survival of places like Kokomo were on the line. And we knew that the collapse of the American auto industry would lead to an even deeper disaster for our economy.

And you know what, we also believed that America, which popularized the automobile, whose middle class was made on the basis of manufacturing, that we couldn't just give up. We couldn't throw in the towel. That was not an option.

There were those who were prepared to give up on Kokomo and our auto industry. There were those who said it was going to be too difficult or that it was bad politics or it was throwing good money after bad. You remember the voices arguing for us to do nothing. They were pretty loud, suggesting we should just step back and watch an entire sector of our economy fall apart.

But we knew that the auto industry was not built, and this country was not built, by doing the easy thing. It wasn't built by doing nothing. It was built by doing what was necessary, even when it's difficult. So we made the decision to stand behind the auto industry if automakers, if CEOs like Sergio, were willing to do what was necessary to make themselves competitive in the 21st century and if they had the cooperation of workers, who were taking pride in the products that they made.

We made the decision to stand with you because we had confidence in the American worker, more than anything. And today, we know that was the right decision. We know that was the right decision.

Today, each of the Big Three automakers has increased their market share—each of them. For the first time in over a decade, Americans are buying a larger share of Chryslers, Fords, and GM cars and a smaller share of their foreign counterparts—for the first time in decades.

We're coming back; we're on the move. All three American companies are profitable, and they are growing. Some of you read last week, GM's stock offering exceeded expectations as investors expressed their confidence in a future that seemed so dim just 18 months ago. And as a result, the Treasury was able to sell half of its GM stock.

So here's the lesson: Don't bet against America. Don't bet against the American auto industry. Don't bet against American ingenuity. Don't bet against the American worker. Don't bet against us. Don't bet against us.

Don't bet against us. This plant is a shining example of why you shouldn't. Two years ago, production here was plummeting. A lot of folks had lost their jobs. Today, this plant is coming back. The company has invested more than $300 million in this factory to retool.

But it gets better. Sergio just told me today, Chrysler is announcing an additional investment of more than $800 million in its Kokomo facilities—$800 million. That's good; that's good news. That's real money, $800 million. See, the mayor's got a big grin on his face. All right, you're pretty happy about that.

Over the next few years, folks here expect to manufacture more transmissions than ever before. And as a result, hundreds of workers are back on the job, and Jeremy said we're going to be hiring more.

This includes—I'm going to name a couple of people just to embarrass them a little bit. Where's Sharon Ybarra? Is Sharon here? Right here. Sharon lost her job of 20 years at a paper mill. She was only able to find work that paid her far less than her old job, until she was hired by Chrysler. And now she is doing a great job right here at Chrysler. We're proud of you.

Jim Faurote is here. Where's Jim? Jim's right next to her. Jim worked for Chrysler for a decade, right? Then he lost his job when the plant he worked at in New Castle shut down. Over the next few years, he could only find intermittent work on and off. It wasn't until after the restructuring that he was able to have a job he could count on. And he is back at work now for more than a year, doing an outstanding job, making great products here at Chrysler. So— [*applause*].

At a plant down the road, workers are manufacturing parts for hybrid vehicles. That's already led to dozens of jobs and will lead to nearly 200 jobs over the next few years. A few miles outside of Kokomo, in Tipton, a clean energy company called Abound is going to be able to hire 900 workers, taking over a plant that had to shut down a few years ago.

So a factory that was empty and dark will come back to life. And when people have a paycheck, as Joe said, they can go to the store, they're able to spend. That helps the economy grow. And so on Main Street in Kokomo, we're seeing a revival with new businesses opening downtown.

So for anybody who says our country's best days are behind us, anybody who would doubt our prospects for the future, anybody who doesn't believe in the Midwest, anybody who doesn't believe in manufacturing, have them come to Kokomo. Have them come to Kokomo. Come here, meet these workers, visit these plants. Come back to this city that's fighting block by block, business by business, job by job.

This is a reminder of what we do as Americans—what we can do as Americans when we come together, when we're not divided. We're not spending all our time bickering, but instead focusing on getting the job done. We don't give up, we don't turn back. We fight for our future.

No, we're not out of the woods yet. It took a lot of years to get us into this mess. It will take longer than anybody would like to get us out. But I want everybody to be absolutely clear: We are moving in the right direction. We learned that the economy—[*applause*]—we learned today that the economy is growing at a faster pace than we previously thought. That's welcome news. But we're going to keep on making it grow faster. We're going to keep on creating more jobs. We need to do everything we can to make that happen.

That's why in the coming days it is so important, the coming months it's so important that Democrats and Republicans work together to speed up our recovery. We've got to put aside our differences. The election's over. We've got to find places where we can agree. We've got to remember the most important contest we face, it's not between Democrats and Republicans, it's between America and our economic competitors. Other nations are already making investments in—[*applause*]. Other nations are making investments in education, energy and infrastructure, technology, because they know that's how they're going to be able to attract the new jobs of the future. And throughout our history, Democrats and Republicans have agreed on making these investments.

If we don't want to cede our economic leadership to nations like China, we've got to do the same today. We've got to make sure our workers have the skills and the training to compete with any workers in the world. We should give our businesses more incentive to invest in research and innovation that leads to new jobs and new products and new industries like the ones we're seeing here in Kokomo. We should make it easier, not harder, for middle class families to get ahead.

I'll give you an example on taxes. Next year, taxes are set to go up for middle class families, unless Congress acts. If we don't act by the end of the year, a typical middle class family will wake up on January 1 to a tax increase of $3,000 per year.

So in the next few weeks, I'm asking Congress to take up this issue. The last thing we can afford to do right now is raise taxes on middle class families. If we allow these taxes to go up, the result would be that a lot of people most likely would spend less, and that means that the economy would grow less. So we ought to resolve this issue in the next couple of weeks so you've got the assurance that your taxes won't go up when the clock strikes midnight.

Now, this is actually an area where Democrats and Republicans agree. The only place where we disagree is whether we can afford to also borrow $700 billion to pay for an extra tax cut for the wealthiest Americans, for millionaires and billionaires. I don't think we can afford it right now, not when we are going to have to make some tough decisions to rein in our deficits. That's going to require sacrifice from all Americans, including those who can most afford it. So I'm eager to sit down with leaders from both parties next week and to hammer this out, but we need to hammer it out.

Long before transmissions were coming off the line at this plant—and by the way, you look at these transmissions today and somebody 20 years ago or 10 years ago might not recognize them; they're amazing. Before Henry Ford built the Model T or Walter Chrysler took up the reins at a startup called Buick, a man by the name of Elwood Haynes decided to do a little experiment right here in Kokomo.

He set up a 1-horsepower boat engine on his kitchen; he bolted it to the ground. His idea was that he might be able to rig the motor to a carriage. So he starts it up, and the engine worked great. In fact, it worked so well that it came loose from the bolts and destroyed the kitchen floor. And after a brief and what I imagine was a difficult conversation with his wife, Elwood decided to continue his tests in his machine shop. And he toiled for months. But when he was finished, he had completed one of the earliest working automobiles ever built in America. And he named it the Pioneer.

So Kokomo has a storied place in our history. This is a city where people came to invent things and to build things, to make things here in America, to work hard in the hopes of producing something of value and something that people could be proud of.

That's the legacy of all of you. You are all heirs to that tradition right here at this plant. That's the legacy that has made this country the envy of the world. And I am absolutely convinced this legacy is one you will continue to uphold for years and decades to come.

Congratulations, Chrysler. Congratulations, Kokomo. Proud of you.

NOTE: The President spoke at 2 p.m. The transcript released by the Office of the Press Secretary also included the remarks of Vice President Joe Biden.

Remarks at the Thanksgiving Turkey Presentation Ceremony
November 24, 2010

The President. Please, everybody, have a seat. Good morning.

Audience members. Good morning.

The President. I have my two trusty assistants here—[*laughter*]—Malia and Sasha, for one of the most important duties that I carry out as President.

Before everybody heads home for Thanksgiving, there is one official duty I am sworn to uphold as the leader of the most powerful nation on Earth. Today I have the awesome responsibility of granting a Presidential pardon to a pair of turkeys. Now, for the record, let me say that it feels pretty good to stop at least one shellacking this November. [*Laughter*]

This year's national turkey goes by the name of Apple, and his feathered understudy is appropriately named Cider. They are being presented today by the chairman of the National Turkey Federation, Yubert Envia—and I want to just point out that Yubert seems very comfortable with that turkey—[*laughter*]—as well as the man who helped raise and handle them since birth, Ira Brister. Where's Ira? There's Ira. Give Ira a big round of applause for raising such outstanding turkeys. I want to thank you both for joining us here at the White House.

Now, Apple and Cider came to us from the Foster Farms Wellsford Ranch, just outside of Modesto, California. Out of about 20,000 turkeys born at Foster Farms this summer, 25 were selected for a final competition that involved strutting their stuff before a panel of judges with an eclectic mix of music playing in the background. [*Laughter*] It's kind of like a turkey version of "Dancing With the Stars"—[*laughter*]—except the stakes for the contestants was much higher. [*Laughter*]

Only one pair would survive and win the big prize: life—[*laughter*]—and an all-expenses-paid trip to Washington, where they've been living it up on corn feed at the W hotel. The W hotel has really been putting them up. [*Laughter*] It's great advertising. [*Laughter*] It makes you want to stay at the W. [*Laughter*] And after today, Apple and Cider will spend their retirement at the same beautiful place our first President spent his: Mount Vernon, Virginia.

So later this afternoon, our family will also deliver two turkeys who didn't quite make the cut to Martha's Table, which is an organization that does extraordinary work helping folks who are struggling here in DC. And I want to thank the good people at Jaindl's Turkey Farm in Orefield, Pennsylvania, who have now donated these turkeys 2 years in a row.

Now, this, of course, is what's truly meant by Thanksgiving, a holiday that asks us to be thankful for what we have and generous to those who have less. It's a time to spend with the ones we love and a chance to show compassion and concern to people we've never met. It's a tradition that's brought us together as a community since before we were a nation, when the ground we're standing on was nothing but wilderness.

Back then, the simple act of survival was often the greatest blessing of all. And later, President Lincoln declared the first National Day of Thanksgiving in the midst of the Civil War. During the depths of the Great Depression, local businesses gave donations and charities opened their doors to families who didn't have a place to celebrate Thanksgiving. In times of war, our military has gone through great lengths to give our men and women on the frontlines a turkey dinner and a taste of home.

So in America, we come together when times are hard. We don't give up, we don't complain, and we don't turn our backs on one another. Instead, we look out for another and we pitch in and we give what we can. And in the process, we reveal to the world what we love so much about this country.

That's who we are. And that's who Thanksgiving reminds us to be. So I hope everyone takes some time during this holiday season to give back and serve their community in some way. And I also want to take a moment to say how grateful I am to the men and women who are serving this country bravely and selflessly in places far away from home right now. You and your families are in our thoughts and in our prayers, and you make me so very proud to be your Commander in Chief.

So on behalf of Michelle, Sasha, Malia, and myself, I want to wish everybody a wonderful and happy and safe Thanksgiving. And now it is my great honor as well to give Apple and Cider a new lease on life. So as President of the United States, you are hereby pardoned from the Thanksgiving dinner table. [*Laughter*] May you have a wonderful and joyful life at Mount Vernon.

God bless you, and God bless the United States of America. All right.

[*At this point, the President and his daughters Sasha and Malia left the podium to approach the turkey. As they approached, the turkey gobbled.*]

The President. You see? He made a little noise to thank me. [*Laughter*] Let's go take a closer look at him.

National Turkey Federation Chairman Yubert Envia. Mr. President, I'd like to introduce Apple.

The President. That's some kind of waddle. All right, you have my blessing. [*Laughter*] You want to touch him on the back of the head? You want to touch him? Not really?

[*The President began to pet the turkey.*]

The President. Yeah, buddy.

Mr. Envia. You keep doing that, he's going to fall asleep.

The President. Now, can somebody explain to me what the whole waddle thing is about?

Mr. Envia. The whole waddle, that's how they dissipate heat.

The President. That's how they dissipate heat?

Mr. Envia. They don't have sweat glands, so all the blood rushes to the waddle, and that's how they dissipate heat in the wild.

The President. Interesting. I guess we're glad we have sweat glands. [*Laughter*] Otherwise, we'd be carrying these around.

This feels pretty good, do you want to try it? No? No.

All right, thank you very much.

Mr. Envia. Thank you very much. Appreciate it. Thank you.

The President. All right. Have a good life, man. [*Laughter*]

NOTE: The President spoke at 10:40 a.m. in the Rose Garden at the White House.

Memorandum on Review of Human Subjects Protection
November 24, 2010

Memorandum for Dr. Amy Gutmann, Chair, Presidential Commission for the Study of Bioethical Issues

Subject: Review of Human Subjects Protection

Recently, we discovered that the U.S. Public Health Service conducted research on sexually transmitted diseases in Guatemala from 1946 to 1948 involving the intentional infection of vulnerable human populations. The research was clearly unethical. In light of this revelation, I want to be assured that current rules for research participants protect people from harm or unethical treatment, domestically as well as internationally.

I ask you, as the Chair of the Presidential Commission for the Study of Bioethical Issues, to convene a panel to conduct, beginning in January 2011, a thorough review of human subjects protection to determine if Federal regulations and international standards adequately guard the health and well-being of participants in scientific studies supported by the Federal Government. I also request that the Commission oversee a thorough fact-finding investigation into the specifics of the U.S. Public Health Service Sexually Transmitted Diseases Inoculation Study.

In fulfilling this charge, the Commission should seek the insights and perspective of international experts, including from Guatemala; consult with its counterparts in the global community; and convene at least one meeting outside the United States. I expect the Commission to complete its work within 9 months and provide me with a report of its findings and recommendations.

While I believe the research community has made tremendous progress in the area of human subjects protection, what took place in Guatemala is a sobering reminder of past abuses. It is especially important for the Commission to use its vast expertise spanning the fields of science, policy, ethics, and religious values to carry out this mission. We owe it to the people of Guatemala and future generations of volunteers who participate in medical research.

BARACK OBAMA

Letter to Congressional Leaders Transmitting the "Strategy to Support the Disarmament of the Lord's Resistance Army"
November 24, 2010

Dear _____:

I am pleased to transmit to the Congress, consistent with section 4 of the Lord's Resistance Army Disarmament and Northern Uganda Recovery Act of 2009 (Public Law 111–172), the enclosed strategic plan entitled, "Strategy to Support the Disarmament of the Lord's Resistance Army."

The strategy guides U.S. support across the region to mitigate and eliminate the threat to civilians and regional stability posed by the Lord's Resistance Army (LRA). It has four objectives that support regional and multilateral efforts: (a) increase protection of civilians; (b) apprehend or remove from the battlefield Joseph Kony and senior commanders; (c) promote the defection, disarmament, demobilization, and reintegration of remaining LRA fighters; and (d) increase humanitarian access and provide continued relief to affected communities.

The strategy identifies priority actions related to protecting civilians and eliminating the threat posed by the LRA. It also provides a framework for the coordination of U.S. efforts and a description of broader efforts in the region. Given the necessity of bringing political, economic, military, and intelligence support to bear in addressing the threat posed by the LRA, the development of the strategy relied on the significant involvement of the Department of State, the Department of Defense, the U.S. Agency for International Development, and the Intelligence Community. All will remain engaged throughout implementation.

My Administration looks forward to working closely with the Congress on this important issue.

Sincerely,

BARACK OBAMA

NOTE: Identical letters were sent to Daniel K. Inouye, chairman, and W. Thad Cochran, vice chairman, Senate Committee on Appropriations; John F. Kerry, chairman, and Richard G. Lugar, ranking member, Senate Committee on

Foreign Relations; David R. Obey, chairman, and Jerry Lewis, ranking member, House Committee on Appropriations; and Howard L. Ber-

man, chairman, and Ileana Ros-Lehtinen, ranking member, House Committee on Foreign Affairs.

The President's Weekly Address
November 25, 2010

Today, like millions of other families across America, Michelle, Malia, Sasha, and I will sit down to share a Thanksgiving filled with family and friends—and a few helpings of food and football too. And just as folks have done in every Thanksgiving since the first, we'll spend some time taking stock of what we're thankful for: the God-given bounty of America and the blessings of one another.

This is also a holiday that captures that distinctly American impulse to give something of ourselves. Even as we speak, there are countless Americans serving at soup kitchens and food pantries, contributing to their communities, and standing guard around the world.

And in a larger sense, that's emblematic of what Americans have always done. We come together and done what's required to make tomorrow better than today. That's who we are.

Consider our journey since that first Thanksgiving. We are among the world's youngest of peoples, but time and again, we have boldly and resiliently led the way forward. Against tough odds, we are a people who endure, who explored and settled a vast and untamed continent, who built a powerful economy and stood against tyranny in all its forms, who marched and fought for equality and connected a globe with our science and imagination.

None of that progress was predestined. None of it came easily. Instead, the blessings for which we give thanks today are the product of choices made by our parents and grandparents and generations before whose determination and sacrifice ensured a better future for us.

This holiday season, we must resolve once more to do the same.

This is not the hardest Thanksgiving America has ever faced. But as long as many members of our American family are hurting, we've got to look out for one another. As long as many of our sons and daughters and husbands and wives are

at war, we've got to support their mission and honor their service. And as long as many of our friends and neighbors are looking for work, we've got to do everything we can to accelerate this recovery and keep our economy moving forward.

And we will. But we won't do it as any one political party. We've got to do it as one people. And in the coming weeks and months, I hope that we can work together, Democrats and Republicans and Independents alike, to make progress on these and other issues.

That's why next week I've invited the leadership of both parties to the White House for a real and honest discussion. Because I believe that if we stop talking at one another and start talking with one another, we can get a lot done.

For what we are called to do again today isn't about Democrats or Republicans. It's not about left or right. It's about us. It's about what we know this country is capable of. It's about what we want America to be in this new century: a vibrant nation that makes sure its children are the best educated in the world; a healthy, growing economy that runs on clean energy and creates the jobs of tomorrow; a responsible government that reduces its deficits; an America where every citizen is able to go as far as he or she desires.

We can do all this, because we've done it before. We're made of the same sturdy stuff as the travelers who first sat down to that Thanksgiving dinner, and all who came after, who worked and sacrificed and invested because they believed that their efforts would make the difference for us.

That's who we are. We shape our own destiny with conviction and compassion and clear and common purpose. We honor our past and press forward with the knowledge that tomorrow will be better than today. We are Americans. That's the vision we won't lose sight of. That's the legacy that falls to our generation. That's the challenge that together, we are going to meet.

To every American, I am thankful for the privilege of being your President. To all our servicemembers stationed around the world, I am honored to be your Commander in Chief. And from the Obama family to yours, have a very happy Thanksgiving. Thanks.

NOTE: The address was recorded at approximately 12:45 p.m. on November 24 in the Diplomatic Reception Room at the White House for broadcast on November 25. The transcript was made available by the Office of the Press Secretary on November 24, but was embargoed for release until 6 a.m. on November 25.

Remarks on Fiscal Responsibility
November 29, 2010

Good morning, everybody. Let me begin by pointing out that although Washington is supposed to be a town of sharp elbows, it's getting a little carried away. For those of you who are worried about my lip, I should be okay. The doctor has given me a clean bill of health, and I will continue to be playing basketball whenever I get a chance. In fact, I played yesterday with Sasha and Malia, and they took it easy on me because they were feeling pity.

I hope everybody had a great Thanksgiving, but now it's time to get back to work. Congress is back in town this week. And I'm looking forward to sitting down with Republican leaders tomorrow to discuss many issues, foremost among them the American people's business that remains to be done this year. My hope is that tomorrow's meeting will mark a first step towards a new and productive working relationship. Because we now have a shared responsibility to deliver for the American people on the issues that define not only these times, but our future, and I hope we can do that in a cooperative and serious way.

Our two most fundamental challenges are keeping the American people safe and growing our economy, and it's in that spirit that I look forward to sitting down tomorrow and talking about urgent matters like the ratification of the new START Treaty, which is so essential to our safety and security, and the status of the Bush-era tax cuts that are set to expire at the end of this year. And this is just one of the many economic issues we've got to tackle together in the months ahead.

As I said a few weeks ago, the most important contest of our time is not the contest between Democrats and Republicans, it's between America and our economic competitors all around the world. And winning that contest means that we've got to ensure our children are the best educated in the world, that our research and development is second to none, and that we lead the globe in renewable energy and technological innovation.

It also means making sure that in the future we're not dragged down by long-term debt. This is a challenge that both parties have a responsibility to address: to get Federal spending under control and bring down the deficits that have been growing for most of the last decade.

Now, there's no doubt that if we want to bring down our deficits, it's critical to keep growing our economy. More importantly, there's still a lot of pain out there, and we can't afford to take any steps that might derail our recovery or our efforts to put Americans back to work and to make Main Street whole again. So we can't put the brakes on too quickly. And I'm going to be interested in hearing ideas from my Republican colleagues, as well as Democrats, about how we continue to grow the economy and how we put people back to work.

But we do have to correct our long-term fiscal course. And that's why earlier this year I created a bipartisan deficit commission that is poised to report back later this week with ideas that I hope will spark a serious and long-overdue conversation in this town. Those of us who have been charged to lead will have to confront some very difficult decisions, cutting spending we don't need in order to invest in the things that we do.

As President, I'm committed to doing my part. From the earliest days of my administration, we've worked to eliminate wasteful spending and streamline Government. I promised to go through the budget line by line to eliminate programs that have outlived their usefulness, and in each of the budgets I've put forward so far, we've proposed approximately $20 billion in savings through shrinking or ending more than 120 of such programs.

I've also set goals for this Government that we're on track to meet: reducing improper payments by $50 billion, saving $40 billion in contracting, and selling off $8 billion of unneeded Federal land and buildings.

I've also proposed a 3-year freeze on all nonsecurity discretionary spending, a step that would bring that spending to its lowest level as a share of the economy in 50 years. And we've brought unprecedented transparency to Federal spending by placing all of it online at USAspending.gov and recovery.gov so Americans can see how their tax dollars are spent.

The hard truth is that getting this deficit under control is going to require some broad sacrifice. And that sacrifice must be shared by the employees of the Federal Government.

After all, small businesses and families are tightening their belts; their Government should too. And that's why, on my first day as President, I froze all pay for my senior staff. This year, I've proposed extending that freeze for senior political appointees throughout the Government and eliminating bonuses for all political appointees.

And today I'm proposing a 2-year pay freeze for all civilian Federal workers. This would save $2 billion over the rest of this fiscal year and $28 billion in cumulative savings over the next 5 years. And I want to be clear: This freeze does not apply to the men and women of our Armed Forces, who along with their families continue to bear enormous burdens with our Nation at war.

I did not reach this decision easily. This is not just a line item on a Federal ledger, these are people's lives. They're doctors and nurses who care for our veterans, scientists who search for better treatments and cures, men and women who care for our national parks and secure our borders and our skies, Americans who see that the Social Security checks get out on time, who make sure that scholarships comes through, who devote themselves to our safety. They're patriots who love their country and often make many sacrifices to serve their country.

In these challenging times, we want the best and brightest to join and make a difference. But these are also times where all of us are called on to make some sacrifices. And I'm asking civil servants to do what they've always done: play their part.

Going forward, we're going to have to make some additional very tough decisions that this town has put off for a very long time. And that's what this upcoming week is really about. My hope is that, starting today, we can begin a bipartisan conversation about our future, because we face challenges that will require the cooperation of Democrats, Republicans, and Independents. Everybody is going to have to cooperate. We can't afford to fall back onto the same old ideologies or the same stale sound bites. We're going to have to budge on some deeply held positions and compromise for the good of the country. We're going to have to set aside the politics of the moment to make progress for the long term.

And as I've often said, we're going to have to think not just about the next election, but about the next generation, because if there's anything the American people said this month, it's that they want their leaders to have one single focus: making sure their work is rewarded so that the American Dream remains within their reach. It would be unwise to assume they prefer one way of thinking over another. That wasn't the lesson that I took when I entered into office, and it's not the lesson today.

So while our ideas may be different, our goals must be the same: growing this economy, putting people back to work, and securing the dream for all who work for it; to summon what's best for each of us to make lives better for all of us. And that's why we are here, and that's why we serve. That's how we've moved this country forward in the past, and I'm absolutely confident that that is how we are going to move this country forward once again.

Thank you very much, everybody.

NOTE: The President spoke at 12:05 p.m. at the Dwight D. Eisenhower Executive Office Building.

Statement on the 35th Anniversary of the Individuals with Disabilities Education Act
November 29, 2010

In America, we believe that every child, regardless of class, color, creed, or ability, deserves access to a world-class education. But as recently as 35 years ago, an American child with a disability might have attended school without the interventions and accommodations necessary for their success or been involuntarily isolated in a State-run institution or even received no education at all.

That was wrong, and America set out to right it. Today, across the United States, nearly 6.6 million students with disabilities rely on the provisions of the landmark Individuals with Disabilities Education Act (IDEA) to ensure that they enjoy the same educational rights as all children.

And as we mark the 35th anniversary of that law, we remember what it was all about: equal opportunity, equal access; not dependence, but independence. We know that our education system must hold children with disabilities to the same high standards as those without disabilities and hold them accountable for their success and their growth. We remember that disability rights are civil rights too and pledge to enforce those rights in order to live up to our founding principles and ensure the promise of opportunity for all our people. And even as we celebrate children with disabilities and their parents, teachers, advocates, and all who still strive to tear down the true barriers to success, even as we celebrate how far we've come, we commit ourselves to the ever-unfinished work of forming that more perfect Union.

Remarks Following a Meeting With Congressional Leaders
November 30, 2010

Hello, everybody. By the way, for those of you who are curious, we're using this room because we've got about a hundred volunteers decorating the White House. So we're spending a little more time in the EEOB.

I just wrapped up a meeting with leaders from both parties. It was our first chance to get together face to face since the election to talk about how we can best work together to move the country forward.

It's no secret that we have had differences that have led us to part ways on many issues in the past. But we are Americans first, and we share a responsibility for the stewardship of our Nation. The American people did not vote for gridlock. They didn't vote for unyielding partisanship. They're demanding cooperation, and they're demanding progress. And they'll hold all of us—and I mean all of us—accountable for it.

And I was very encouraged by the fact that there was broad recognition of that fact in the room.

I just want to say I thought it was a productive meeting. I thought that people came to it with a spirit of trying to work together. And I think it's a good start as we move forward.

I think everybody understands that the American people want us to focus on their jobs, not ours. They want us to come together around strategies to accelerate the recovery and get Americans back to work. They want us to confront the long-term deficits that cloud our future. They want us to focus on their safety and security and not allow matters of urgent importance to become locked up in the politics of Washington.

So today we had the beginning of a new dialogue that I hope—and I'm sure most Americans hope—will help break through the noise and produce real gains. And as we all agreed, that should begin today because there's some things we need to get done in the weeks before Congress leaves town for the holidays.

First, we should work to make sure that taxes will not go up by thousands of dollars on hardworking middle class Americans come January 1, which would be disastrous for those families, but also could be crippling for the economy. There was broad agreement that we need to work to get that resolved before the end of the year.

Now, there's still differences about how to get there. Republican leaders want to permanently extend tax cuts not only to middle class families, but also to some of the wealthiest Americans at the same time. And here we disagree. I believe—and the other Democrats who were in the room believe—that this would add an additional $700 billion to our debt in the next 10 years. And I continue to believe that it would be unwise and unfair, particularly at a time when we're contemplating deep budget cuts that require broad sacrifice.

Having said that, we agreed that there must be some sensible common ground. So I appointed my Treasury Secretary, Tim Geithner, and my Budget Director, Jack Lew, to work with representatives of both parties to break through this logjam. I've asked the leaders to appoint Members to help in this negotiation process. They agreed to do that. That process is beginning right away and we expect to get some answers back over the next couple of days about how we can accomplish our key goal, which is to make sure the economy continues to grow and we are putting people back to work. And we also want to make sure that we're giving the middle class the peace of mind of knowing that their taxes will not be raised come January 1.

I also urged both parties to move quickly to preserve a number of other tax breaks for individuals and businesses that are helping our recovery right now and that are set to expire at the end of the year. This includes a tax credit for college tuition, a tax credit for 95 percent—a tax break for 95 percent of working families that I initiated at the beginning of my Presidency, as

well as a tax cut worth thousands of dollars for businesses that hire unemployed workers.

We discussed a number of other issues as well, including the importance of ratifying the new START Treaty so we can monitor Russia's nuclear arsenal, reduce our nuclear weapons, and strengthen our relationship with Russia. I reminded the room that this treaty has been vetted for 7 months now; it's gone through 18 hearings; it has support from Senators of both parties; it has broad bipartisan support from National Security Advisers and Secretaries of Defense and Secretaries of State from previous administrations, both Democrat and Republican; and that it's absolutely essential to our national security. We need to get it done.

We also talked about the work of the bipartisan deficit reduction commission and the difficult choices that will be required in order to get our fiscal house in order. We discussed working together to keep the Government running this year and running in a fiscally responsible way. And we discussed unemployment insurance, which expires today. I've asked that Congress act to extend this emergency relief without delay to folks who are facing tough times by no fault of their own.

Now, none of this is going to be easy. We have two parties for a reason. There are real philosophical differences, deeply held principles to which each party holds. And although the atmosphere in today's meeting was extremely civil, there's no doubt that those differences are going to remain no matter how many meetings we have. And the truth is, there's always going to be a political incentive against working together, particularly in the current hyperpartisan climate. There are always those who argue that the best strategy is simply to try to defeat your opposition instead of working with them.

And frankly, even the notion of bipartisanship itself has gotten caught up in this mentality. A lot of times, coming out of these meetings, both sides claim they want to work together, but try to paint the opponent as unyielding and unwilling to cooperate. Both sides come to the table, they read their talking points, then they head out to the microphones, trying to win the news cycle instead of solving problems, and it becomes just another move in an old Washington game.

But I think there was recognition today that that's a game that we can't afford, not in these times. And in a private meeting that I had without staff—without betraying any confidences— I was pleased to see several of my friends in the room say, let's try not to duplicate that. Let's not try to work the Washington spin cycle to suggest that somehow the other side is not being cooperative. I think that there was a sincere effort on the part of everybody involved to actually commit to work together to try to deal with these problems.

And they understand that these aren't times for us to be playing games. As I told the leaders at the beginning of the meeting, the next election is 2 years away and there will be plenty of time for campaigning. But right now we're facing some very serious challenges. We share an obligation to meet them. And that will require

choosing the best of our ideas over the worst of our politics.

So that's the spirit in which I invited both parties here today. I'm happy with how the meeting went. And I told all the leadership that I look forward to holding additional meetings, including at Camp David.

Harry Reid mentioned that he's been in Congress for 28 years; he's never been to Camp David. And so I told him, well, we're going to have to get them all up there sometime soon.

And I very much appreciate their presence today. I appreciate the tenor of the conversations. I think it will actually yield results before the end of the year, and I look forward to continuing this dialogue in the months ahead.

Thank you very much, everybody.

NOTE: The President spoke at 12:50 p.m. in Room 430 of the Dwight D. Eisenhower Executive Office Building.

Statement on Senate Passage of Food Safety Modernization Legislation
November 30, 2010

With the Senate's passage of the Food Safety Modernization Act, we are one step closer to having critically important new tools to protect our Nation's food supply and keep consumers safe. This legislation ensures more frequent inspections of food manufacturing facilities and will require these facilities to take preventative actions to reduce the risks of outbreaks and

foodborne illness. I urge the House, which has previously passed legislation demonstrating its strong commitment to making our food supply safer, to act quickly on this critical bill, and I applaud the work that was done to ensure its broad bipartisan passage in the Senate.

NOTE: The statement referred to S. 510.

Statement on House of Representatives Passage of Legislation Settling Claims Against the Department of Agriculture
November 30, 2010

I am pleased that today the House has joined the Senate in passing the claims settlement act of 2010. This important legislation will fund the agreements reached in the *Pigford II* lawsuit, brought by African American farmers, and the *Cobell* lawsuit, brought by Native Americans over the management of Indian trust accounts and resources. I want to thank Attorney General Holder and Secretaries Salazar and Vilsack for all their work to reach this outcome, and I

applaud Congress for acting in a bipartisan fashion to bring this painful chapter in our Nation's history to a close.

This bill also provides funding for settlements reached in four separate water rights suits brought by Native American tribes, and it represents a significant step forward in addressing the water needs of Indian Country. Yet, while today's vote demonstrates important progress, we must remember that much work remains to be done. And my administration will continue our efforts to resolve claims of past discrimination made by women and His-panic farmers and others in a fair and timely manner.

NOTE: The statement referred to H.R. 4783.

Statement on a Department of Defense Report on the "Don't Ask, Don't Tell" Policy
November 30, 2010

As Commander in Chief, I have pledged to repeal the "don't ask, don't tell" law because it weakens our national security, diminishes our military readiness, and violates fundamental American principles of fairness and equality by preventing patriotic Americans who are gay from serving openly in our Armed Forces. At the same time, as Commander in Chief, I am committed to ensuring that we understand the implications of this transition and maintain good order and discipline within our military ranks. That is why I directed the Department of Defense earlier this year to begin preparing for a transition to a new policy.

Today's report confirms that a strong majority of our military men and women and their families—more than two-thirds—are prepared to serve alongside Americans who are openly gay and lesbian. This report also confirms that, by every measure, from unit cohesion to re-cruitment and retention to family readiness, we can transition to a new policy in a responsible manner that ensures our military strength and national security. And for the first time since this law was enacted 17 years ago, today both the Secretary of Defense and the chairman of the Joint Chiefs of Staff have publicly endorsed ending this policy.

With our Nation at war and so many Americans serving on the frontlines, our troops and their families deserve the certainty that can only come when an act of Congress ends this dis-criminatory policy once and for all. The House of Representatives has already passed the nec-essary legislation. Today I call on the Senate to act as soon as possible so I can sign this repeal into law this year and ensure that Americans who are willing to risk their lives for their coun-try are treated fairly and equally. Our troops represent the virtues of selfless sacrifice and love of country that have enabled our freedoms. I am absolutely confident that they will adapt to this change and remain the best led, best trained, best equipped fighting force the world has ever known.

Message to the Congress Transmitting an Alternative Plan for Pay Increases for Civilian Federal Employees
November 30, 2010

To the Congress of the United States:

The law authorizes me to implement an al-ternative pay plan for locality pay increases for civilian Federal employees covered by the Gen-eral Schedule and certain other pay systems in January 2011, if I view the adjustments that would otherwise take effect as inappropriate due to "national emergency or serious economic conditions affecting the general welfare." Our country faces serious economic conditions af-fecting the general welfare. As the economic re-covery continues, the time has come to put our Nation back on a sustainable fiscal course, an effort that requires tough choices and shared sacrifice. Accordingly, I have determined that it is appropriate to exercise my statutory alterna-tive plan authority under 5 U.S.C. 5304a to set alternative January 2011 locality pay rates. This decision will not materially affect our ability to attract and retain a well-qualified Federal work-force.

Under the authority of section 5304a of title 5, United States Code, I have determined that the current locality pay percentages in Schedule 9 of Executive Order 13525 of December 23, 2009, shall not increase from their 2010 levels. Pursuant to the Non-Foreign Area Retirement Equity Assurance Act of 2009 (sections 1911–1919, Public Law 111–84), I am also establishing applicable 2011 locality pay rates for Alaska and Hawaii that are based on 2010 locality pay levels.

The locality pay rates established in 2010, and continued in 2011 under this alternative plan, are shown in the attachment.

BARACK OBAMA

The White House,
November 30, 2010.

Remarks Following a Meeting With Former Secretary of State Colin L. Powell and an Exchange With Reporters
December 1, 2010

The President. I want to thank General Colin Powell for being here with me today. He is not only a great statesman and a great public servant, but also a great friend and a great counselor. And periodically I check in with him, and I know my entire team, including the Vice President, checks in with him, because he continues to have an unparalleled sense of our national security needs and I think really taps into the best impulses of the American people.

The first thing that I want to do is I want to congratulate him and his wife Alma for the extraordinary work that he's been doing with America's Promise, which focuses on how can we finally get serious about education reform, because he understands, Alma understands, and all of us understand that our kids are going to be competing not just against each other here in this country, but they're now competing worldwide.

And America's Promise has been at the forefront on education reform. They just issued a report, "Building a Grad Nation," that notes that we have made some progress over the last several years in reducing the number of dropout factories that we have around the country, that we are seeing a greater emphasis on kids staying in school, but we've still got a lot more work to do. And it's going to require all of us— parents, teachers, administrators, the public and the private sector—to make sure that we continue on this trend of improvement.

So thank you for the work you're doing there, Colin.

Most of the discussion we had was around national security issues. We talked about some of the challenges across the landscape, from North Korea to Iran to Afghanistan. But we spent, in particular, a lot of time talking about the START Treaty. General Powell has been involved with just about every arms control treaty since there were arms control treaties. I hate to——

Former Secretary of State Powell. Not quite that long.

The President. I hate to date him, but from the Reagan administration on, he has helped to shepherd through a variety of these arms control treaties, and the reason is, is because he understands, as so many others understand, that a world without binding U.S.-Russia arms control treaties is a more dangerous world.

And he and I discussed why START is so important. In the absence of START, without the new START Treaty being ratified by the Senate, we do not have a verification mechanism to ensure that we know what the Russians are doing, and they don't know what we're doing, and when you have uncertainty in the area of nuclear weapons, that's a much more dangerous world to live in.

We also discussed the fact that Russia has cooperated with us on critical issues to our national security like Iran sanctions, transit to supply our troops in Afghanistan, working on securing loose nuclear materials.

And the relationships and trust that are built from the new START Treaty spill over into a whole host of other national security issues that are of vital importance to America.

So Colin is one of a number of former National Security Advisers, Secretaries of Defense, Secretaries of State—from both Democratic and Republican administrations—that have emphasized how important it is to get this done. And we discussed the fact that the Senate appropriately has a role in advice and consent, and it ultimately needs to ratify this treaty. That's why we have made sure that we have had 18 separate hearings. We have answered over a thousand questions. We have offered to brief every single Senator—Republican and Democrat—around these issues. But now it's time to get this done.

I'm gratified by the leadership of the ranking Republican on the Senate Foreign Relations Committee, Richard Lugar, as well as the ranking Democrat, the chairman, John Kerry, for their extraordinary cooperation and work on this issue.

It is important for us to make sure that we complete the evaluation process, we finish the debate, and we go ahead and finish this up before the end of the year.

And so I just want to again thank General Powell for his good counsel, his friendship, most importantly his service to our country. And I very much appreciate the fact that he supports an effort that all of us should support in order to make America more safe.

[*At this point, former Secretary of State Powell made brief remarks, concluding as follows.*]

Mr. Powell. And so I'm sorry I missed the meeting the President had with the other Sec-

retaries and National Security Advisers the week before last, but I'm glad I had this opportunity to share my thoughts with the President.

So I hope that the Senate will move quickly and give its advice and consent to the ratification of this treaty.

The President. Thank you so much, everybody.

Meeting With Republican Leaders/Bipartisanship

Q. ——Senate Republicans, what McConnell did today, is that—didn't break the spirit? Didn't break the spirit of yesterday, what Senator McConnell did?

The President. I am absolutely—I am confident that nobody wants to see taxes on middle class families go up starting January 1, and so there's going to be some lingering politics that have to work themselves out in all the caucuses, Democrat and Republican. But at the end of the day, I think that people of good will can come together and recognize that given where the economy is at right now, given the struggles that a lot of families are still going through right now, that we're going to be able to solve this problem. And I think we got off to a good start yesterday. There are going to be ups and downs to this process, but I'm confident that we're going to be able to get it done. All right?

NOTE: The President spoke at 3:34 p.m. in the Oval Office at the White House. In his remarks, he referred to Alma J. Powell, chair, America's Promise Alliance. The transcript released by the Office of the Press Secretary also included the remarks of former Secretary of State Powell.

Statement on the 55th Anniversary of the Bus Boycott in Montgomery, Alabama
December 1, 2010

Fifty-five years ago, Rosa Parks refused to give up her seat on a bus, an act that challenged the moral conscience of an entire nation. The Montgomery bus boycott marked a turning point in American history: the moment where we began the march toward the civil rights

movement and the eventual outlawing of racial segregation and discrimination. Rosa Parks and the many other leaders and foot soldiers in that struggle for justice championed our founding principles of freedom and equality for all, and today, as we commemorate the anniversary of the Montgomery bus boycott, I encourage all Americans to honor their legacy, the legacy of Americans who marched bravely, worked tire- lessly, and devoted their lives to the never-ending task of making our country a more perfect Union.

Remarks Prior to a Meeting With Newly Elected Governors
December 2, 2010

Thank you very much. Please, have a seat, have a seat. Well, congratulations, first of all, to all of you for your victories, and welcome to the Blair House. You are part of a long line of illustrious visitors in this space. Winston Churchill used to hang out here when he was in the midst of working with FDR during World War II. Truman stayed here for 4 years when they were redoing the White House residence. And Abraham Lincoln was a close friend of the Blairs, so he used to visit here almost every night.

And as some of you I'm sure are aware, I read Lincoln a lot and think about Lincoln a lot. And I think one story that comes to mind right now is, at the time that he was President, visitors used to be able to come in, Secret Service weren't there to nag you and frisk you. And somebody demands to see him and insists on waiting. And finally, Lincoln lets him in, and then the guy says, "I'm responsible for you being elected President of the United States." And Lincoln says, "Really?" He says, "Yes, I did all the work. I was one of your hardest workers. And now I expect some help." And Lincoln says, "Well, let me tell you, if you are indeed responsible for helping me get elected, I forgive you." [*Laughter*]

Now, some of you may feel the same way, or at least you will in a month or so. But the truth is that as somebody who served in State government, I'm aware of the fact that State government and local government is where rubber hits the road. A lot of times we have a lot of abstract debates here in Washington, but each day—and every day—you are close to the ground and you are seeing the impacts of the decisions that are made, whether in Washington or in your State capitals, in very intimate ways.

And so I have nothing but respect and regard for the chief executives of all 50 of our States. And I am looking forward to working with each and every one of you. I want to spend most of my time in a dialogue, so I'm not going to give a long speech. I'm just going to remark on a couple of points.

Point number one, we have just had a very vigorously contested election, but the election is over. And now I think it's time for all of us to make sure that we're working together. I am a very proud Democrat, as some of you in the room are, although not as many as I had expected. [*Laughter*] Some of you are very proud Republicans. But we're all prouder to be Americans.

And this country has just gone through a wrenching 2 years: the worst financial crisis since the Great Depression and the toughest economy that most of us have seen in our lifetimes. And so as a consequence, I think it's absolutely critical that whatever our positions, whatever our parties, that wherever we can we can pull together to make sure that we're doing right by the American people. And I know that everybody in this room believes that.

In that spirit, just earlier this week, we had a meeting with both Democratic and Republican leaders here in Washington to start talking about how we can find ways to agree on promoting growth and promoting jobs across all 50 States. And I'm actually optimistic that before the end of the year we are going to have come to some agreements on some critical issues.

Obviously, issue number one is making sure that on January 1, middle class families aren't seeing their taxes go up as a consequence of the expiration of some of the Bush tax cuts that are currently in place and some of the tax cuts that we've put in place over the last 2 years. And so that's going to be an important discussion over the next several days. I believe it will get resolved.

That doesn't mean there may not be some posturing over the next several days. But I'm confident in the end people are going to recognize that it's important for families who are still struggling to have some relief, and it's important for our economy to make sure that money is still out there circulating at a time when we are recovering, but we're not recovering as fast as we need to.

Along those same lines, I'm hopeful that we get the issue of unemployment insurance resolved. Some of you may be aware that as of today, you've got 2 million people who stand to lose their unemployment insurance. Over the course of the year, if we don't do something, 7 million people could lose their unemployment insurance. That's not also—that's not just a potential tragedy for those individual families, it could have a huge impact on your local economies, because every economist of every stripe will tell you that unemployment insurance dollars are probably the ones that are most likely to be spent, most likely to be recirculated, most likely to help to boost small business and services all across your States, and are going to have an effect on your sales revenue.

So our hope and expectation is, is that unemployment insurance—something that traditionally has had bipartisan support—is something that once again will be dealt with as part of a broader package.

Here's the good news: The economy is on the uptick. We've now had 5 consecutive quarters of economic growth, and we've had 10 consecutive months of private sector job growth. But I think we all recognize that it's not moving as quickly as it needs to be. And there are going to be a whole range of issues that we're going to have to focus on together, at the Federal and State levels, to assure not only that we get out of this crisis, but more importantly, that we're laying the foundation for long-term growth in the future.

And although there are going to be some disagreements on how we get there, there are going to be some areas where I think we agree. We all agree that we're going to have to have the best educated workforce in the world because our children are now not just competing against other children in other States in our Union, they're now competing against kids in Beijing and Bangalore and Seoul, South Korea.

And if they don't have what it takes to compete, then America is going to have problems economically over the long term.

That's why I'm so proud, under the guidance of Arne Duncan, that we have initiated some reforms that have garnered strong bipartisan support. And frankly, as a Democrat, I've been willing to go after some long-held dogmas in our party in order to spring loose a smarter conversation about how we're educating our kids.

Our Race to the Top program is something that has allowed States across the country to initiate reforms in a competitive way and make sure that ideas like charter schools get traction, despite previous resistance. And I'm hoping that we can cooperate with all of you to see how we can continue to make progress on the education front.

All of us are going to be interested in innovation and research and development. And there are Governors here or Governors-elect here from both parties who are interested in clean energy, for example, and what can we do to make sure that wind turbines and solar panels and electric cars are made here in the United States, that that doesn't become one more source of imports from other countries. And I'm eager to work with all of you on those issues.

I think it's going to be very important that we work together on issues of spending. And each of you are going to be struggling with some very tough budgets. Washington is going to be in very tough budget circumstances. And many of you were elected on the basis that we've got to get control of spending, because you care about the next generation. And if we continue down the path that we're on, then we're going to have problems. And what that means is, we're going to be interested in hearing from all of you about programs that you think are working, but also programs that you think are not working. Contrary to the mythology, believe it or not, it turns out that I would love to eliminate programs that don't work. And you guys are the ones oftentimes who are implementing them.

If there's redtape or bureaucracy that we can eliminate it, we want to eliminate that. We have no interest in making your life harder. We want to be a partner for all of you in being responsive to your constituencies.

Now, I will confess that there are going to be times where we do believe that having basic national standards are going to be important, that there are certain things that we as a country, we as a people, aspire to, and that we need to maintain some consistency across the States. But for the most part, if there are going to be—if there's going to be experimentation, if States are going to continue to be laboratories for democracy, that's something that we welcome and embrace.

And so if you have ideas around any of the issues that my Cabinet members who are here are responsible for, I guarantee you will get a serious response from them in terms of how we can work together.

So to sum up my initial remarks, I heard—I overheard Joe say that he will always take your call. I promise you, he will be calling you. At a certain point you may say, "Golly, it's Biden again." [*Laughter*] But I think the same is going to be true for Valerie Jarrett, who heads up our intergovernmental affairs. The same is going to be true for our various Cabinet officials. They are going to want to hear from you.

And the one thing that I would urge is, don't wait until you're really mad about something before you call us. We'd prefer not to read about it in the press. [*Laughter*] We'd rather you call us ahead of time and say, you know what, we think this isn't working. We think this is a better way of doing things. And we'll work with you. And if we don't agree with you, we will spell out in great detail why we don't agree with you. And it's not going to be based on ideology, it's not going to be based on partisanship, it will be based upon our best judgment about

how we move forward with the policy objectives that we all share.

And if we end up disagreeing on something, I promise you we will not be disagreeable about it. And we will keep on working until, hopefully, we can figure out a way to solve problems.

In the end, I think that's what this most recent election was all about. People are frustrated, understandably, with an economy that has stalled and is not doing as well as it should for American families. And that was true not just during this crisis, but it was true for the decade before this crisis. And I think what the American people are expecting from all of us is that—not that we suddenly put aside politics, not that we put aside principles, because everybody here is driven oftentimes with some very strongly held principles about what America should be and how we can move forward, but that at a certain point we also concern ourselves with governing and delivering for them.

And I know of no group of people who more consistently steer in that direction than Governors, because ultimately the buck stops with you in your State, just as the buck stops with me at the national level.

And so I look forward to working with you, and I look forward to seeing you again fairly soon. We usually host a Governors' bash early in the year, and that way I'll have a chance to meet all your spouses and you guys will get dressed up and look really good. [*Laughter*]

All right? Okay. With that, we're going to clear the press out of the room so that all these folks can be—tell me what they really think about me. [*Laughter*]

NOTE: The President spoke at 1:04 p.m. in the Blair House. The transcript released by the Office of the Press Secretary also included the remarks of Vice President Joe Biden.

Remarks on Lighting the Hanukkah Menorah
December 2, 2010

The President. Oh, this is a good-looking group right here. [*Laughter*] Good evening, everybody.

Audience members. Good evening.

The President. Welcome to the White House. I want to thank all of you for joining us in celebrating the second night of Hanukkah. Happy Hanukkah, everybody.

We are joined tonight by Ambassador Michael Oren of Israel. Where's Michael? He's way back there. And so I want to begin by offering our deepest condolences to the families and loved ones of all of those who've died as a result of the terrible forest fire in northern Israel.

As rescuers and firefighters continue in their work, the United States is acting to help our Israeli friends respond to the disaster. A short while ago, our Ambassador in Tel Aviv, Jim Cunningham, issued a disaster declaration which has launched an effort across the U.S. Government to identify the firefighting assistance we have available and provide it to Israel as quickly as possible. Of course, that's what friends do for each other.

And, Mr. Ambassador, our thoughts and prayers are with everybody in Israel who is affected by this tragedy and the family and loved ones of those in harm's way.

Tonight it's an honor to welcome so many friends and leaders from the Jewish community and beyond. And I want to start by recognizing my Special Envoy for Middle East Peace, George Mitchell, who is here. Please give him a round of applause, and all the other outstanding members of the diplomatic corps who are here.

One third of the Supreme Court is here. One of my favorites, Justice Ginsburg, is hiding out here in the front. [*Laughter*] She really is here. It's hard to see. [*Laughter*] Justice Breyer is here. And—where's Justice Breyer? There he is right here. And our newest addition and former colleague of mine when we were teaching together, Elena Kagan is in the house.

I want to also acknowledge somebody who I rely on day in, day out, who is not only a great Vice President, but is also—[*laughter*]—one of my dearest friends, Joe Biden is in the house.

And to all the members of the administration and Members of Congress and all the State and local leaders who are with us today, welcome. I want to thank Joshua Redman for gracing us with his talent and helping us with the music. And finally, I want to thank the rabbis and lay leaders who have traveled from all over the country to be here. Yes, you can give yourselves a round of applause.

Now, tonight we gather to celebrate a story as simple as it is timeless. It's a story of ancient Israel, suffering under the yoke of empire, where Jews were forbidden to practice their religion openly and the Holy Temple, including the Holy of Holies, had been desecrated.

It was then that a small band of believers, led by Judah Maccabee, rose up to take back their city and free their people. And when the Maccabees entered the temple, the oil that should have lasted for a single night ended up burning for eight.

That miracle gave hope to all those who had been struggling in despair. And in the 2,000 years since, in every corner of the world, the tiny candles of Hanukkah have reminded us of the importance of faith and perseverance. They have illuminated a path for us when the way forward was shrouded in darkness.

And as we prepare to light another candle on the menorah, let us remember the sacrifices that others have made so that we may all be free. Let us pray for the members of our military who guard that freedom every day and who may be spending this holiday far away from home.

Let us also think of those for whom these candles represent not just a triumph of the past, but also hope for the future: the men, women, and children of all faiths who still suffer under tyranny and oppression.

That's why families everywhere are taught to place the menorah in public view, so the entire world can see its light. Because, as the Talmud teaches us, "So long as a person still has life, they should never abandon faith."

Now, the menorah we're using tonight, and the family who is going to help us light it, both stand as powerful symbols of that faith.

This beautiful menorah has been generously loaned to us by Congregation Beth Israel in New Orleans. Five years ago, when Hurricane Katrina hit, the synagogue was covered in 8 feet of water. Later, as the cleanup crew dug through the rubble, they discovered this menorah caked in dirt and mold. And today it stands as a reminder of the tragedy and a source of inspiration for the future.

And that feeling is shared by Susan Retik. It's a feeling they know all too well. After her husband David was killed on September 11th, Susan could have easily lost herself in feelings of hopelessness and grief. But instead, she turned her personal loss into a humanitarian mission, cofounding Beyond the 11th, a group that reaches out to Afghan widows facing their own struggles.

So on this second night of Hanukkah, let us give thanks to the blessings that all of us enjoy. Let us be mindful of those who need our prayers. And let us draw strength from the words of a great philosopher who said that a miracle is "a confirmation of what is possible."

And now I'd like to turn it over to Susan, who, by the way, has been on this stage before, receiving a Presidential award for her outstanding work. But she happens to be joined by a beautiful family: Donald, Ben, Molly, Dina, and Rebecca. [*Laughter*] Rebecca is down here. So I want to turn—there she is.

Audience members. Aww!

The President. Yes, she is adorable. [*Laughter*] As Michelle said as we were getting on stage, she will be stealing the show. [*Laughter*] So we're going to turn it over to Susan and her family for the blessings.

[*At this point, a blessing was offered, and the menorah was lit. Afterwards, saxophonist Joshua Redman performed a Hanukkah song. Some members of the audience sang along.*]

The President. So happy Hanukkah to all of you. We're going to see most of you downstairs. Be patient in the line. [*Laughter*] And I just want to let everybody know that, yes, they will be able to Photoshop my lip for the picture. [*Laughter*] Happy Hanukkah, everybody.

NOTE: The President spoke at 6:44 p.m. in the East Room at the White House. In his remarks, he referred to Donald Ger, husband of Susan Retik, and their children Benjamin Retik, Molly Retik, Dina Retik, and Rebecca Ger.

Statement on the National Commission on Fiscal Responsibility and Reform Report
December 3, 2010

I want to thank the members of the National Commission on Fiscal Responsibility and Reform for their important work in highlighting the magnitude of the challenge before us and outlining an array of options to confront it. Jobs and growth are our most urgent need. But if we want an America that can compete for the jobs of tomorrow, we simply cannot allow our Nation to be dragged down by our debt. We must correct our fiscal course.

Nothing would be more valuable to addressing this challenge than strong, sustained economic growth. But the Commission's report underscores that to sustain growth in the medium and long term we need to face some difficult choices to curb runaway debt. It will require cutting the spending we don't need in order to invest in what's necessary to grow our economy and our middle class. It will require all of us, Democrats and Republicans, to find common

ground without compromising the fundamental principles we hold dear. Because the undeniable fact is that no one party can successfully tackle this challenge alone.

Chairmen Bowles and Simpson met the charge that I gave them and the Commission: to bring our deficits down in the medium term and to meaningfully improve our long-run fiscal situation so that we can keep commitments made to future generations. The Commission's majority report includes a number of specific proposals that I, along with my economic team, will study closely in the coming weeks as we develop our budget and our priorities for the coming year. This morning, my budget director, Jack Lew, spoke with Chairman Bowles and invited the entire Commission in to meet with him and Secretary Geithner to discuss the Commission's proposals. Overall, my goal is to build on the steps we've already taken to reduce our deficit, like slowing the growth of health care costs, proposing a 3-year freeze in nonsecurity discretionary spending and a 2-year pay freeze for Federal civilian workers, and restoring the rule that we pay for all of our priorities.

I don't doubt our ability to meet this challenge, but our success depends on our willingness to engage in the kind of honest conversation and cooperation that hasn't always happened in Washington. We cannot afford to fall back on old ideologies, and we will all have to budge on long-held positions. So I ask members of both parties to maintain an open mind and a commitment to progress as we work to lift this burden from the shoulders of future generations.

NOTE: The statement referred to Erskine B. Bowles and Alan K. Simpson, Cochairs, National Commission on Fiscal Responsibility and Reform; and Jacob J. "Jack" Lew, Director, Office of Management and Budget.

Statement on the Presidential Election in Cote d'Ivoire
December 3, 2010

I congratulate Alassane Ouattara on his victory in Cote d'Ivoire's November 28 elections. The Independent Electoral Commission, credible and accredited observers, and the United Nations have all confirmed this result and attested to its credibility.

Cote d'Ivoire is now at a crossroads. I urge all parties, including incumbent President Laurent Gbagbo, to acknowledge and respect this result and to allow Cote d'Ivoire to move forward toward a peaceful, democratic future, leaving long years of conflict and missed opportunities in the past. The international community will hold those who act to thwart the democratic process and the will of the electorate accountable for their actions.

Statement on the South Korea-United States Free Trade Agreement
December 3, 2010

I am very pleased that the United States and South Korea have reached agreement on a landmark trade deal that is expected to increase annual exports of American goods by up to $11 billion and support at least 70,000 American jobs. Last month in Seoul, I directed our negotiators to achieve the best deal for American workers and companies, and this agreement meets that test.

American manufacturers of cars and trucks will gain more access to the Korean market and a level playing field to take advantage of that access. We are strengthening our ability to create and defend manufacturing jobs in the United States, increasing exports of agricultural products for American farmers and ranchers, and opening Korea's services market to American companies. High standards for the protection of workers' rights and the environment make this a model for future trade agreements, which must be both free and fair.

Today's agreement is an integral part of my administration's efforts to open foreign markets to U.S. goods and services, create jobs for American workers, farmers, and businesses, and achieve our goal of doubling of U.S. exports over 5 years. It deepens the strong alliance between the United States and the Republic of Korea and reinforces American leadership in the Asia-Pacific. I look forward to working with Congress and leaders in both parties to get this done and to ensure that America competes aggressively for the jobs and markets of the 21st century.

Remarks to United States and Coalition Troops at Bagram Air Base, Afghanistan
December 3, 2010

The President. Hello, everybody! [*Applause*] I'm sorry, Bagram, I can't hear you. [*Applause*] Air Assault! [*Applause*] It is great to be back.

Let me first of all thank the 101st Airborne Division Band. Where's the band? Give them a big round of applause. Thank you to Chief Thomas Hager—and—the commander and conductor. I gather we had a couple of other bands playing: Manifest Destiny and Nuts. I don't know about, you know—I don't know how they sounded. What did you think? Were they pretty good?

Audience members. Hooah!

The President. It is great to be back. And I apologize for keeping you guys up late, coming on such short notice. But I wanted to make sure that I could spend a little time this holiday with the men and women of the finest fighting force that the world has ever known, and that's all of you.

I want to thank General Petraeus, not only for the introduction and the T-shirts, but for General Petraeus's lifetime of service. This is somebody who has helped change the way we fight wars and win wars in the 21st century. And I am very grateful that he agreed to take command of our efforts here in Afghanistan. He has been an extraordinary warrior on behalf of the American people. Thank you, David Petraeus.

I want to thank all your outstanding leaders who welcomed me here, including General John Campbell, Admiral Bill McRaven; from the 455th Air Expeditionary Wing, Colonel Todd Canterbury. I want to salute your great senior enlisted leaders, including Command Sergeant Major Scott Schroeder, Command Sergeant Major Chris Farris, and Command Chief Craig Adams.

I also want to acknowledge the outstanding work that our civilians are doing each and every day, starting with Karl Eikenberry all the way through to your senior civilian representative, Thomas Gibbons, and all the civilians who are here. They are fighting alongside you. They are putting themselves at risk. They are away from

their families. And we are very, very grateful to them as well. So give them a big round of applause.

I think we've got every service here tonight. We've got Army. We've got Navy. We've got Air Force. I think we may have a few Marines around too, and a whole lot of folks from the 101st Airborne Division, the "Screaming Eagles."

Audience members. [*Inaudible*]

The President. Here in Afghanistan, you are all—Coast Guard, is that what I heard? [*Laughter*] Here in Afghanistan, all of you are part of one team, serving together, succeeding together, except maybe in next week's Army-Navy game. As your Commander in Chief, I've got to stay neutral on that. [*Laughter*] We also have some ISAF partners here as well.

You know, when I was here in the spring, we had a coalition of 43 nations. Now we've got a coalition of 49 nations. And this sends a powerful message that the coalition of nations that supports Afghanistan is strong and is growing.

Now, I'm not here to give a long speech. I want to shake as many hands as I can. But let me say that at this time of year, Americans are giving thanks for all the blessings that we have. And as we begin this holiday season, there is no place that I'd rather be than be here with you.

I know it's not easy for all of you to be away from home, especially during the holidays. And I know it's hard on your families. They've got an empty seat at the dinner table. Sometimes during the holiday season, that's when you feel the absence of somebody you love most acutely.

But here's what I want you to know. As President of the United States, I have no greater responsibility than keeping the American people secure. I could not meet that responsibility, we could not protect the American people, we could not enjoy the blessings of our liberty without the extraordinary service that each and every one of you perform each and every day.

So on behalf of me, on behalf of Michelle, on behalf of Malia and Sasha, on behalf of more than 300 million Americans, we are here to say thank you. We are here to say thank you for everything that you do.

Now, I also want to say thank you to your families back home so that when you talk to them, you know that they know. They're serving here with you in mind and spirit, if not in body.

Millions of Americans give thanks this holiday season just as generations have before when they think about our Armed Services. You're part of an unbroken line of Americans who have given up your comfort, your ease, your convenience for America's security.

It was on another cold December more than 200 years ago that a band of patriots helped to found our Nation, defeat an empire. From that icy river to the fields of Europe, from the islands in the Pacific to the hills of Korea, from the jungles of Vietnam to the deserts of Iraq, those who went before you, they also found themselves in this season of peace serving in war. They did it for the same reason that all of you do, because the freedom and the liberty that we treasure, that's not simply a birthright. It has to be earned by the sacrifices of generations, generations of patriots. Men and women who step forward and say: "Send me. I know somebody has got to do it, and I'm willing to serve." Men and women who are willing to risk all, and some who gave all, to keep us safe and to keep us free.

In our time, in this 21st century, when so many other institutions seem to be shirking their responsibilities, you've embraced your responsibilities. You've shown why the United States military remains the most trusted institution in America. And that's the legacy that your generation has forged during this decade of trial in Iraq and here in Afghanistan. That's the legacy that you're carrying forward.

As General Petraeus mentioned, 1 year ago I ordered additional troops to serve in this country that was the staging ground for the 9/11 attacks. All of those troops are now in place. And thanks to your service, we are making important progress. You are protecting your country. You're achieving your objectives. You will succeed in your mission.

We said we were going to break the Taliban's momentum, and that's what you're doing. You're going on the offense, tired of playing defense, targeting their leaders, pushing them out of their strongholds. Today, we can be proud that there are fewer areas under Taliban control and more Afghans have a chance to build a more hopeful future.

We said a year ago that we're going to build the capacity of the Afghan people. And that's what you're doing, meeting our recruitment targets, training Afghan forces, partnering with those Afghans who want to build a stronger and more stable and more prosperous Afghanistan.

Now, I don't need to tell you this is a tough fight. I just came from the medical unit and saw our wounded warriors, pinned some Purple Hearts. I just talked to the platoon that lost six of their buddies in a senseless act of violence.

This is tough business. Progress comes slow. There are going to be difficult days ahead. Progress comes at a high price. So many of you have stood before the solemn battle cross, display of boots, a rifle, a helmet, and said goodbye to a fallen comrade.

This year alone nearly 100 members of the 101st have given their last full measure of devotion. There are few days when I don't sign a letter to a military family expressing our Nation's gratitude and grief at their profound sacrifice. And this holiday season, our thoughts and prayers are with those who've lost a loved one: the father and mother, the son or daughter, the brother or sister or friend who's not coming home. And we know that their memories will never be forgotten and that their life has added to the life of our Nation.

And because of the service of the men and women of the United States military, because of the progress you're making, we look forward to a new phase next year, the beginning of a transition to Afghan responsibility.

As we do, we continue to forge a partnership with the Afghan people for the long term. And we will never let this country serve as a safe haven for terrorists who would attack the United States of America again. That will never happen.

This part of the world is the center of a global effort where we are going to disrupt and dismantle and defeat Al Qaida and its extremist allies. And that's why you're here. That's why your mission matters so much. That's why you must succeed, because this effort is about the safety of our communities back home and the dignity of the Afghan people who don't want to live in tyranny.

Now, even though it is a hallmark of American democracy that we have our arguments back home, we have our debates, we have our elections, I can say without hesitation that there is no division on one thing, no hesitation on one thing, and that is the uniform support of our men and women who are serving in the Armed Services.

Everybody is behind you. Everybody back home is behind you. Everybody, from north to south to east to west, from sea to shining sea, the American people are united in support of you and your families.

And as your Commander in Chief, I also want you to know that we will do whatever it takes to make sure that you have the strategy and the resources and the equipment and the leadership to get this done.

You may have noticed that during these tough budget times, I took the step of freezing pay for our Federal workforce. But because of the service that you rendered, all who wear the uniform of the United States of America are exempt from that action.

And we're going to make—we're going to spare no effort to make sure that your families have the support that they deserve as well. That doesn't just matter to me. It's also a top priority for Michelle to make sure that Americans understand the sacrifices that your families are making. As she likes to say, 100 percent of Americans need to be right there supporting you and your families—100 percent. Only 1 percent are fighting these wars, but 100 percent of us have to be behind you and your families.

Your generation, the generation of Afghanistan and Iraq, has met every mission that you've been given. You've served tour after tour. You've earned not just our admiration; you've earned your place in American history alongside those greatest generations.

And the stories of those who served in these wars are too numerous to tell. But one of my greatest privileges as President is to get to know the stories of those who earn the Medal of Honor.

Two months ago, I presented the Medal to the parents of Staff Sergeant Robert Miller, who gave his life here in Afghanistan as a member of the Green Berets. His valor, charging toward some 150 insurgents, saved the lives of nearly 2 dozen American and Afghan comrades.

Last month, we held another ceremony. For the first time in nearly 40 years, the recipient of the Medal of Honor for an ongoing conflict was actually able to accept it in person. His name is Staff Sergeant Salvatore Giunta. And some of you may have seen his story, but I want to tell it again tonight because of what it says not just about our Armed Forces, but also what it says about the country that we love.

So 3 years ago, Sal and his platoon were in Korengal Valley. When their patrol was ambushed, two Americans lay wounded up ahead. That's when Sal and his men counterattacked, again and again and again. They were being rained down with fire, but they just kept counterattacking because they wanted to get their two buddies.

And when he saw one of his teammates wounded and being carried away by insurgents, Sal rushed in to help his friends, despite the bullets. Despite the danger, he kept on pressing forward. It was an incredibly intense firefight. And by the time it was finished, every single member of that platoon had shrapnel or a bullet hole in their gear. Five were wounded, and two had given their lives.

Now, Sal is a pretty humble guy. And so when he came to the White House, he said, "You know, I didn't do anything special." He said he was just doing his job, that he didn't do anything that his brothers wouldn't have done for him.

"If I'm a hero," he said, "then every man who stands around me, every woman in the military, every person who defends this country is also a hero."

And he's right. Each of you has your own story. Each of you is writing your own chapter in the story of America and the story of American Armed Forces. Each of you have some losses. Each of you have made sacrifices. You come from every conceivable background: from big cities and small towns, from every race and faith and station. You've come together to serve a greater cause, one that matters to the citizens of your country back home and to strangers who live a world away.

So make no mistake, through your service, you demonstrate the content of the American character. Sal is right: Every single one of you is a hero.

Some people ask whether America's best days lie ahead or whether our greatness stretches back behind us in the stories of those who've gone before. And when I look out at all of you, I know the answer to that. You give me hope. You give me inspiration. Your resolve shows that Americans will never succumb to fear. Your selfless service shows who we are, who we always will be—united as one people and united as one Nation—for you embody and stand up for the values that make us what we are as a people.

America is not defined by our borders. We are defined by a common creed. In this holiday season, it's worth remembering that "we hold these truths to be self-evident, that all men are created equal, that we are endowed by our Creator with certain inalienable rights, that among these are the right to life and liberty and the pursuit of happiness."

And that's what you're fighting for here in Afghanistan, and that's what you're protecting back home. And that belief is more powerful than any adversary.

So we may face a tough enemy in Afghanistan, and we're in a period of tough challenges back home, but we did not become the nation that we are because we do what's easy. As Americans we've endured and we've grown stronger and we remain the land of the free only because we are also home of the brave.

And because of you, I know that once more, we will prevail. So thank you. God bless you, and God bless the United States of America.

Thank you, everybody, and happy New Year. Thank you, everybody. God bless you.

NOTE: The President spoke at 10:37 p.m. In his remarks, he referred to Chief Warrant Officer Thomas Hager, USA, commander and conductor, 101st Airborne Division Band; Gen. David H. Petraeus, USA, commander, NATO International Security Assistance Force, Afghanistan; Maj. Gen. John F. Campbell, USA, commanding general, 101st Airborne Division (Air Assault), and regional commander east, NATO International Security Assistance Force, Afghanistan; Vice Adm. William H. McRaven, USN, commander, Joint Special Operations Command; CSM Scott Schroeder, USA, command sergeant major, 101st Airborne Division (Air Assault); Chief Master Sgt. Craig Adams, USAF, command chief, 15th Expeditionary Mobility Task Force; U.S. Ambassador to Afghanistan Karl W. Eikenberry; and Thomas Gibbons, Regional Command East senior civilian representative, NATO International Security Assistance Force, Afghanistan. He also referred to Col. Todd D. Canterbury, USAF, and Command Sgt. Maj. Chris Farris, USA.

Remarks on the South Korea-United States Free Trade Agreement
December 4, 2010

Good afternoon, everybody. Today I want to speak briefly about two issues that matter most to me and matter most to the American people: creating jobs and economic growth on which our country's prosperity depends.

Yesterday's job report showed that despite 11 consecutive months of private sector job growth, despite creating more than 1 million private sector jobs this year, it's not enough. We have to do more to accelerate the economic recovery and create jobs for the millions of Americans who are still looking for work.

And essential to that effort is opening new markets around the world to products that are

"Made in America." Because we don't simply want to be an economy that consumes other countries' goods, we want to be building and exporting the goods that create jobs here in America and that keeps the United States competitive in the 21st century.

That's why today I am very pleased that the United States and South Korea have reached agreement on a landmark trade deal between our two countries. I'm joined this morning by my outstanding U.S. Trade Representative, Ambassador Ron Kirk, as well as Michael Froman, who was one of our lead negotiators. As you'll remember, we did not finalize this agreement on my recent visit to South Korea. And I didn't agree to it then for a very simple reason: The deal wasn't good enough. It wasn't good enough for the American economy, and it wasn't good enough for American workers.

As I said in Seoul, I'm not interested in signing trade agreements for the sake of signing trade agreements, I'm interested in agreements that increase jobs and exports for the American people and that also help our partners grow their economies. So I told Ron and our team to take the time to get this right and get the best deal for America. And that is what they have done. The agreement we're announcing today includes several important improvements and achieves what I believe trade deals must do: It's a win-win for both our countries.

This deal is a win for American workers. For our farmers and ranchers, it will increase exports of American agricultural products. From aerospace to electronics, it will increase our manufacturing exports to Korea, which already support some 200,000 American jobs and many small businesses. In particular, manufacturers of American cars and trucks will have much more access to the Korean market, we'll encourage the development of electric cars and green technology in the United States, and we'll continue to ensure a level playing field for American automakers here at home.

In short, the tariff reductions in this agreement alone are expected to boost annual exports of American goods by up to $11 billion. And all told, this agreement, including the opening of the Korean services market, will support at least 70,000 American jobs. It will contribute significantly to achieving my goal of doubling U.S. exports over the next 5 years. In fact, it's estimated that today's deal alone will increase American economic output by more than our last nine free trade agreements combined.

This deal is also a win for our ally and friend South Korea. They will gain greater access to our markets and make American products more affordable for Korean households and businesses, resulting in more choices for Korean consumers and more jobs for Americans.

I would add that today is also a win for the strong alliance between the United States and South Korea, which for decades has ensured that the security that has maintained stability on the peninsula continues. It's also allowed South Korea its extraordinary rise from poverty to prosperity. At a time in which there are increasing tensions on the Korean Peninsula, following the North's unprovoked attack on the South Korean people, today we are showing that the defense alliance and partnership of the United States and South Korea is stronger than ever.

I'm especially pleased that this agreement includes groundbreaking protections for workers' rights and for the environment. In this sense, it's an example of the kind of fair trade agreement that I will continue to work for as President, in Asia and around the world.

This agreement also shows that the United States of America is determined to lead and compete in our global economy. We're going to stand up for American companies and American workers, who are among the most productive and innovative in the world. And we're going to compete aggressively for the jobs and markets of the 21st century.

Now, reaching this agreement was not easy. But I want to give special thanks to my partner, South Korean President Lee, for his commitment to a successful outcome. And again, I want to thank Ron and Mike for their outstanding work and their entire team for their tireless efforts. They were up late a lot of nights over the last several months.

We're going to continue to work with our Korean partners to fully implement this agreement and build on our progress in other areas, such as ensuring full access for U.S. beef to the Korean market.

And I look forward to working with Congress and leaders in both parties to approve this pact. Because if there's one thing Democrats and Republicans should be able to agree on, it should be creating jobs and opportunity for our people.

Which brings me to the other issue I want to address. Earlier today the Senate voted on two provisions to extend tax cuts for the middle class. And I'll admit, I am very disappointed that the Senate did not pass legislation that had already passed the House of Representatives to make middle class tax cuts permanent. Those provisions should have passed. I continue to believe that it makes no sense to hold tax cuts for the middle class hostage to permanent tax cuts for the wealthiest 2 percent of Americans, especially when those high income tax cuts would cost an additional $700 billion that we don't have and would add to our deficit.

But with so much at stake, today's votes cannot be the end of the discussion. It is absolutely essential to our hard-working middle class families and to our economy to make sure that their taxes don't go up on January 1.

I've spoken with the Democratic leadership in Congress, and I look forward to speaking with the Republican leadership as well. And my message to them is going to be the same: We need to redouble our efforts to resolve this impasse in the next few days to give the American people the peace of mind that their taxes will not go up on January 1. It will require some compromise, but I'm confident that we can get it done. And the American people should expect no less.

As we work our way through this issue, we must not forget that last week some 2 million Americans who have lost their jobs also saw their unemployment insurance expire, right in the middle of the holiday season. And that's not how we should do business here in America. I believe it is simply wrong to even consider giving permanent tax breaks to the wealthiest Americans while denying relief to so many Americans who desperately need it and have lost their jobs through no fault of their own.

So we are going to continue to work on this issue through the weekend, into early next week. And I'm going to be rolling up my sleeves with the leaders of both parties in Congress. We need to get this resolved, and I'm confident we can do it.

Thank you very much, everybody.

NOTE: The President spoke at 12:21 p.m. in Room 430 of the Dwight D. Eisenhower Executive Office Building. In his remarks, he referred to Deputy National Security Adviser for International Economic Affairs Michael B. Froman.

Remarks at the Kennedy Center Honors Reception
December 5, 2010

The President. Everybody, thank you so much. Please have a seat, have a seat. Well, what a good-looking crowd. [*Laughter*] Say we do what we can, huh? [*Laughter*] Happy holidays, everybody. And on behalf of Michelle and myself, I want to welcome all of you to the White House.

And I want to start by giving special thanks to Speaker Nancy Pelosi and all the Members of Congress who are here. Nobody has done more for our country over the last couple of years than Nancy Pelosi.

None of this would be possible without some people who have put great effort into this evening: David Rubenstein, Michael Kaiser, the Kennedy Center trustees, and all the people who have made the Kennedy Center such a wonderful place for Americans of all ages to enjoy the arts.

And on that note, I also want to give special thanks to Caroline Kennedy—where's—is Caroline here tonight? Hey, Caroline—and all the other members of the Kennedy family who are here tonight. It's wonderful to see them.

And finally, I want to recognize the Cochairs of the President's Committee on the Arts and Humanities—my good friend George Stevens.

George and his son Michael are the brains behind the Kennedy Center Honors, and I want to thank them all for their great creativity.

This is a season of celebration and of giving. And that's why it's my greatest privilege as President to honor the five men and women who have given our Nation the extraordinary gift of the arts.

The arts have always had the power to challenge and the power to inspire, to help us celebrate in times of joy and find hope in times of trouble. And although the honorees on this stage each possess a staggering amount of talent, the truth is, they aren't being recognized tonight simply because of their careers as great lyricists or songwriters or dancers or entertainers. Instead, they're being honored for their unique ability to bring us closer together and to capture something larger about who we are, not just as Americans, but as human beings.

That's what Merle Haggard has been doing for more than 40 years. Often called the "poet of the common man," Merle likes to say that he's living proof that things can go wrong in America, but also that things can go right. [*Laughter*]

In a day and age when so many country singers claim to be rambling, gambling outlaws, Merle actually is one. [*Laughter*] He hopped his first freight train at the age of 10 and was locked up some 17 times as a boy, pulling off almost as many escapes.

Later, after becoming a bona fide country star, Merle met Johnny Cash and mentioned that he had seen Cash perform years earlier at San Quentin prison. "That's funny," Cash said, "because I don't remember you being in the show." [*Laughter*] And Merle had to explain to the Man in Black that he hadn't been in the show, he had been in the audience. [*Laughter*]

That performance had inspired Merle to start writing songs, and he's written thousands of them since, about three or four hundred "keepers" in Merle's opinion. Thirty-eight of those songs have been number one on the charts, including "Okie from Muskogee," which he per-

formed for Richard Nixon right here in this room back in 1973.

Through it all, Merle's power has always come from the truth he tells about life and love and everything in between. As he says, "the best songs feel like they've always been there." So tonight we honor a man who feels like he's always been here, Merle Haggard.

Now, growing up in New Jersey, Jerry Herman and his family used to play Broadway tunes in the living room: Jerry on the piano, his mother on the accordion, and his father playing the sax. And he never took a music lesson, but always had the ability to play anything he heard by ear.

Then, when he was 14, Jerry went to see the great Ethel Merman perform in "Annie Get Your Gun." In his words, "I got a load of that great lady and was gone." [*Laughter*] Jerry was determined to be a songwriter, even though he didn't think he could ever make a career out of doing something that was so much fun.

But that's exactly what he's done, penning songs for such iconic musicals as "Hello, Dolly!" and "La Cage aux Folles" and drawing audiences everywhere out of their seats and into the world of his imagination. Those songs earned Jerry a shelf full of Tonys, and he's still the only composer and lyricist to have had three shows on Broadway at the same time.

Today, that same kid from Jersey City is still doing what he loves. As Jerry says, "I never wanted to do anything but make people hum." So thank you, Jerry, for doing just that. Jerry Herman.

If Jerry Herman wanted to make people hum, Bill T. Jones wanted to open their eyes and make them move. The youngest of 12 children, Bill's parents were migrant workers—"poorer than poor"—who made a living picking fruits and vegetables up and down the East Coast. Early on, Bill struggled to find his identity in a segregated world where he often felt like he didn't belong.

Then he began to dance. Bill likes to say that a good dancer has "heart, guts, strength, intelligence, and personality," and he's been blessed with plenty of each. As the cofounder of the Bill T. Jones/Arnie Zane Dance Company, Bill has earned widespread acclaim and artistic success in the hypercompetitive world of modern dance, all while battling poverty and homophobia and racism.

His unique performances have always been provocative, challenging audiences to confront important issues in a way that is at once captivating, agitating, and extremely personal. To date, he's created over 140 works on subjects ranging from terminal illness to Abraham Lincoln, securing his place as one of the most decorated and controversial choreographers of our time.

And through it all, Bill has never compromised his sense of purpose or lost his ability to inspire others to greater heights. "I'm not afraid to stand up," Bill once said. "I'm not afraid to be looked at. Making my art is a way of saying to people—gay people, HIV-positive people—that life is worth it." And for that, we are forever grateful. Bill T. Jones.

Now, there's not a lot that I can tell you about our next honoree that you don't already know. I can tell you he's become something of a regular here at the White House. We decided we would just give him all possible awards this year. [*Laughter*]

So this summer, Paul McCartney was here to accept the Gershwin Prize for Popular Song. It was a thrill of a lifetime to hear him sing "Michelle" to Michelle. Although apparently, Paul joked afterwards that he was worried he might become the "first guy ever to get punched out by the President." [*Laughter*]

I will say he was a little emotive during the song. [*Laughter*] I can't afford another one. [*Laughter*] You have nothing to worry about. I just recovered from my last tussle on the basketball court. [*Laughter*]

And so tonight I am pleased once again to honor a man widely considered to be among the greatest songwriters in history. Paul first picked up a guitar at age 14, and soon it never left his side. Homework went undone, my understanding is. Comics went unread. He would play it in the bathroom.

It wasn't long before he gravitated towards other young musicians who shared his passion, including a young man named John Lennon.

But when Paul and his bandmates played their first set in a hole-in-the-wall jazz club in England, expectations were still low: They thought they'd be pretty big in Liverpool.

That band went on to change the way the world thought about music. Their songs were the soundtrack for an era of immense creativity and change. And when Paul continued his musical journey alone after the Beatles broke up, he would become one of the few performers inducted into the Rock and Roll Hall of Fame twice, as a Beatle and as a solo artist.

Now, Paul admits that the only possible explanation is supernatural. He says, "The most important ingredient to making a song work is magic. You've got a melody, you've got words, but on the most successful songs, there's a sort of magic glow that just makes the songs sort of roll out."

We may not understand it, Paul, but for the last five decades, you've taken millions of fans on a pretty magical ride. And I should point out, that includes a whole new generation. When Malia and Sasha were here—remember, Michelle? We went upstairs, and she said, "That song 'Penny Lane,' that's a really neat song." [*Laughter*] And she started trying to play it on our piano upstairs. And so you continue to inspire, all those years since Liverpool. Thank you, Paul McCartney.

And what can I say about our final honoree? Michelle and I love Oprah Winfrey. [*Laughter*] Personally love this woman. And the more you know Oprah, the more spectacular you realize her character and her soul are and the more you appreciate what a wonderful, gifted person she is.

It's easy to forget sometimes that Oprah was once a girl with a funny name—[*laughter*]—in a little town down South. Back then, nobody would have ever dreamed that she would become someone who moves an entire nation each and every day. But the signs were there.

After 2 days of kindergarten, Oprah wrote a note to her teacher that read: "I don't think I belong here because I know a lot of big words." [*Laughter*] Her teacher agreed, and she moved on to the first grade.

And while she was working as a reporter in Baltimore, Oprah was told she was too engaged and too emotional about her stories, so the station put her on a talk show to run out her contract. That worked well. [*Laughter*] How's payback? [*Laughter*] That planted the seed for what would become the highest rated talk show in American television history.

Oprah's gift—as a host, as a producer, as an Oscar-nominated actress—has always been her ability to relate to her audience, to laugh with us, to cry with us, to draw us in and connect our most fervent hopes and deepest fears to her own. The reason we share ourselves with Oprah is because she shares herself with us: her childhood of abuse, her personal battles, her life as a woman, as an African American, as someone who is determined to confront both great injustices of the world and the private struggles of everyday life.

She has taught us to find strength in overcoming, to take a stand for ourselves and what we know is right. And she has shown millions of people around the world—people she probably will never meet—what it means to believe in "the dream of your own life." Oprah Winfrey.

So Merle Haggard, Jerry Herman, Bill T. Jones, Paul McCart—what's your name again?—[*laughter*]—Paul McCartney, Oprah Winfrey. Their lives and their stories as are——

[*At this point, a cell phone rang.*]

The President. Who's calling? [*Laughter*]

——are as diverse as any you can imagine. Yet in their own way, each of these honorees help us understand the human experience—to illuminate our past, to help us understand our present, and to give us the courage to face our future.

Being here with tonight's honorees, reflecting on their contributions, I'm reminded of a Supreme Court opinion by the great Justice Oliver Wendell Holmes. In a case argued before the Court in 1926, the majority ruled that the State of New York couldn't regulate the price of theater tickets because, in the opinion of the majority, the theater was not a public necessity. They argued, in effect, that the experience of attending the theater was superfluous. And this is what Justice Holmes had to say: "Too many people," he wrote in his dissent, "the"—let me start that over. "To many people, the superfluous—superfluous"—it's this lip that's—[*laughter*]—it's hard to say. [*Laughter*] You try it when you've had 12 stitches. [*Laughter*] "The superfluous"—[*applause*]—thank you. All right. "To many people, the superfluous is necessary."

The theater is necessary. Dance is necessary. Song is necessary. The arts are necessary. They are a necessary part of our lives.

The men and women here tonight embody that idea. Their work has enriched our lives. It's inspired us to greatness. And tonight it is my honor to offer them the appreciation of a grateful nation.

Thank you very much, all five of you. God bless you. Thank you.

NOTE: The President spoke at 5:14 p.m. in the East Room at the White House. In his remarks, he referred to David M. Rubenstein, chairman, and Michael M. Kaiser, president, John F. Kennedy Center for the Performing Arts; Caroline B. Kennedy, daughter of former President John F. Kennedy; George Stevens, Jr., and Margo Lion, Cochairs, President's Committee on the Arts and the Humanities; and Michael Stevens, coproducer with George Stevens, Jr., Kennedy Center Honors Gala.

Remarks at Forsyth Technical Community College in Winston-Salem, North Carolina
December 6, 2010

Thank you, everybody. Thank you so much. Everybody, please, everybody have a seat, have a seat. It is good to be back in North Carolina. Love North Carolina. Although, I have to say, I came down here for slightly warmer weather. [*Laughter*] What's snow doing on the ground in North Carolina? [*Laughter*] Come on, now. Anyway, it is a great honor to be with you here at Forsyth Technical Community College.

There are a few people I want to acknowledge who are just doing outstanding work. First of all, your incredibly impressive college president, Gary Green, is here. Your wonderful Governor, Bev Perdue, is in the house; your Senators, Richard Burr and the better looking one, Kay Hagan; two hard-working Congressmen, Mel Watt and Brad Miller, are here. We've got Secretary of State Elaine Marshall in the house. And Mayor Allen Joines is here.

Well, it's been about a month now since the midterm elections. And in Washington, at least, much of the chatter is still about the political implications of those elections: what the results mean for Democrats, what they mean for Republicans. And already, we're hearing what this means for the next election. And I have to tell you, I came to Winston-Salem because I believe that right now there are bigger issues at stake for our country than politics. And these issues call on us to respond not as partisans, but as Americans.

At this moment, we are still emerging from a once-in-a-lifetime recession that has taken a terrible toll on millions of families, many here in North Carolina who have lost their jobs or their businesses, and their sense of security.

Now, fortunately, we've seen some encouraging signs that a recovery is beginning to take hold. An economy that had been shrinking for nearly a year is now growing. After nearly 2 years of job loss, our economy has added over 1 million private sector jobs in 2010.

Now, I was just talking to Bev, and she was mentioning that here in North Carolina, we've seen 50,000 new jobs here in North Carolina. And after teetering on the brink of liquidation not 2 years ago, our auto industry is posting healthy gains. So we're seeing progress across the country.

But as we also saw in November's jobs report, the recovery is simply not happening fast enough. Plenty of Americans are still without work. Plenty of Americans are still hurting. And our challenge now is to do whatever it takes to accelerate job creation and economic growth.

Now, in the short term, that means preventing the middle class tax increase that's currently scheduled for January 1. Right now Democrats and Republicans in Congress are working through some differences to try to get this done. And there are some serious debates that are still

taking place. Republicans want to make permanent the tax cuts for the wealthiest Americans. I have argued that we can't afford it right now. But what I've also said is we've got to find consensus here, because a middle class tax hike would be very tough not only on working families, it would also be a drag on our economy at this moment.

So I believe we should keep in place tax cuts for workers and small businesses that are set to expire. We've got to make sure that we're coming up with a solution, even if it's not a hundred percent of what I want or what the Republicans want. There's no reason that ordinary Americans should see their taxes go up next year.

We should also extend unemployment insurance for workers who've lost their jobs through no fault of their own. That is a priority. And I should mention that's not only the right thing to do, it's the smart thing to do, because if millions of Americans who aren't getting unemployment benefits stop spending money, that slows down businesses. That slows down hiring. It slows down our recovery.

Now, even if we take these and other steps to boost our recovery in the short term, we're also going to have to make some serious decisions about our economy in the long run. We've got to look ahead, not just to the next year but to the next 10 years, the next 20 years. We've got to ask ourselves, where will the new jobs come from? What will it take to get them? And what will it take to keep the American Dream alive for our children and our grandchildren?

Think about North Carolina. Obviously, this recession had a devastating effect here, like it did everywhere else. But the trends have been going on for quite some time.

I was just visiting with President Green, with some of the students here in the biotech field, wonderful people, from every walk of life. You had folks who had just gotten out of high school, and you had folks who had—were in midlife and had been laid off from a manufacturing job and had come here to retrain. But a bunch of them mentioned, "Well, I was laid off because the textile industry has moved away here in North Carolina." "I was laid off because the furniture industry has moved away here in North Carolina."

Those were long-term trends. And that means we've got to have a long-term vision about where we want to be 10 years from now, 20 years from now, 30 years from now.

Just like past generations did, we must be prepared to answer these questions in our time. And over the next several weeks, I'm going to be meeting with my economic team, with business leaders, and others to develop specific policies and budget recommendations for the coming year. Today I want to outline the broader vision that I believe should guide these policies, and it's a vision that will keep our economy strong and growing and competitive in the 21st century.

And that vision begins with a recognition of how our economy has changed over time. When Forsyth Technical opened 50 years ago, it was known as Forsyth County Industrial Education Center, right? That's a mouthful. [*Laughter*] Machine shops and automotive mechanics were some of the first classes you could take. Of course, back then you didn't even need a degree to earn a decent living. You could get a job at the local tobacco or textile plant and still be able to provide for yourself and your family.

That world has changed. In the last few decades, revolutions in communications, revolutions in technology, have made businesses mobile and has made commerce global. So today, a company can set up shop, hire workers, and sell their products wherever there's an Internet connection. That's a transformation that's touched off a fierce competition among nations for the jobs and industries of the future.

Some of you know I traveled through Asia several weeks ago. You've got a billion people in India who are suddenly plugged into the world economy. You've got over a billion people in China who are suddenly plugged into the global economy. And that means competition is going to be much more fierce, and the winners of this competition will be the countries that have the most educated workers, a serious commitment to research and technology, and access to quality infrastructure like roads and airports and high-speed rail and high-speed Internet. Those

are the seeds of economic growth in the 21st century. Where they are planted, the most jobs and businesses will take root.

Now, in the last century, America was that place where innovation happened and jobs and industry always took root. The business of America was business. Our economic leadership in the world went unmatched. Now it's up to us to make sure that we maintain that leadership in this century. And at this moment, the most important contest we face is not between Democrats and Republicans, it's between America and our economic competitors all around the world. That's the competition we've got to spend time thinking about.

Now, I have no doubt we can win this competition. We are the home of the world's best universities, the best research facilities, the most brilliant scientists, the brightest minds, some of the hardest working, most entrepreneurial people on Earth, right here in America. It's in our DNA. Think about it. People came from all over the world to live here in the United States. That's been our history. And those were the go-getters, the risk takers who came here. The folks who didn't want to take risks, they stayed back home. [*Laughter*] Right? So there's no doubt that we are well equipped to win.

But as it stands right now, the hard truth is this: In the race for the future, America is in danger of falling behind. That's just the truth. And when—if you hear a politician say it's not, they're not paying attention. In a generation, we have fallen from first place to ninth place in the proportion of young people with college degrees. When it comes to high school graduation rates, we're ranked 18th out of 24 industrialized nations—18th. We're 27th in the proportion of science and engineering degrees we hand out. We lag behind other nations in the quality of our math and science education.

When global firms were asked a few years back where they planned on building new research and development facilities, nearly 80 percent said either China or India, because those countries are focused on math and science, and they're focused on training and educating their workforce.

I sat down with President Lee of South Korea, and I asked him, what's the biggest problem you have in education? He said, "You know, these parents, they come to me and they are constantly pressuring me; they want their kids to learn so fast, so much—they're even making me import English-speaking teachers in, because they want first-graders to know English." I asked him about investment in research and development. He says, "We're putting aside 5 percent of our gross domestic product in research and development, 3 percent of it in clean energy."

You go to Shanghai, China, and they've built more high-speed rail in the last year than we've built in the last 30 years. The largest private solar research and development facility in the world has recently opened in China, by an American company. Today, China also has the fastest trains and the fastest supercomputer in the world.

In 1957, just before this college opened, the Soviet Union beat us into space by launching a satellite known as Sputnik. And that was a wake-up call that caused the United States to boost our investment in innovation and education, particularly in math and science. And as a result, once we put our minds to it, once we got focused, once we got unified, not only did we surpass the Soviets, we developed new American technologies, industries, and jobs.

So, 50 years later, our generation's Sputnik moment is back. This is our moment. If the recession has taught us anything, it's that we cannot go back to an economy that's driven by too much spending, too much borrowing, running up credit cards, taking out a lot of home equity loans, paper profits that are built on financial speculation. We've got to rebuild on a new and stronger foundation for economic growth.

We need to do what America has always been known for: building, innovating, educating, making things. We don't want to be a nation that simply buys and consumes products from other countries. We want to create and sell products all over the world that are stamped with three simple words: Made in America. That's our goal.

So I came to Forsyth today because you've shown what this future can look like. Half a century later, you're still giving students the skills and training they need to get good jobs, but of course—but courses in machine shop and car mechanics have now broadened to degrees in mechanical engineering technology and nanotechnology and biotechnology. And meanwhile, your unique partnerships that you're building with advanced manufacturing and biotechnology firms will ensure that the businesses of the future locate here: they come here, they stay here, they hire right here in Winston-Salem.

As a national leader in bioscience and innovation, North Carolina is now the country's third largest employer in biotechnology. And when Caterpillar recently decided to build a plant in this community, they told President Green one of the main reasons was they were convinced that Forsyth Tech had the capability of providing them with the technical workforce that they need.

That's something everybody in this room should be very proud of. And I know that business leaders from throughout the community have worked intensively with President Green and others to help make this happen. And I know that your congressional delegation, as well as your Governor, have worked hard to make this happen.

Now, none of this progress happened by itself. It happened thanks to the hard work of students here at Forsyth, the commitment of local leaders, foresight of local business leaders. Most importantly, it happened because there was a decision made to invest in the collective future of this community. It happened because there was a decision to invest in this college, and there were loans and scholarships that made it affordable to go here.

To invest in the basic research and development that helped jump-start North Carolina's biotech industry, to invest in new buildings and laboratories and research facilities that make your work possible, these are the kinds of investments we need to keep making in communities across America, investments that will grow our economy and help us to stay competitive in the 21st century.

Now, I want to emphasize I say this knowing full well we face a very difficult fiscal situation. I'm looking at the books back in Washington, and folks weren't doing a real good job with their math for the last decade. So now that the threat of a depression has passed and a recovery is beginning to take hold, reducing our long-term deficit has to be a priority. And in the long run, we won't be able to compete with countries like China if we keep borrowing from countries like China. We won't be able to do it.

So we've already started making some tough decisions. And they're unpopular and people get mad, but we've got to make some decisions. I've proposed a 3-year freeze in all spending that doesn't have to do with national security. And I proposed a 2-year freeze in the pay for Federal workers. That's why we're currently studying recommendations of the bipartisan deficit reduction panel that I commissioned. We're going to have to be bold and courageous in eliminating spending and programs that we don't need and we can't afford.

But here's where there's going to be a debate in Washington over the next year and over the next couple of years and maybe over the next 5 years, because I will argue and insist that we cannot cut back on those investments that have the biggest impact on our economic growth. Because I was talking with President Green, and he said much of the equipment here would not be here if it hadn't been for the assistance of the Recovery Act, the assistance of the Department of Labor. All this stuff that we've done over the last couple of years that people were questioning, you can see it translated in the classrooms right here. The work that we're doing on student loans and Pell grants, you can see it in the students who are able to finance their retraining right here.

So we can't stop making those investments. The best antidote to a growing deficit, by the way, is a growing economy. To borrow an analogy, cutting the deficit by cutting investments in areas like education, areas like innovation, that's like trying to reduce the weight of an overloaded aircraft by removing the engine. It's not a good idea. There may be some things you need

to get rid of, but you got to keep the engine. [*Laughter*]

That's why even as we scour the budget for cuts and savings in the months ahead, I will continue to fight for those investments that will help America win the race for the jobs and industries of the future, and that means investments in education and innovation and infrastructure. I will be fighting for that.

In an era where most new jobs will require some kind of higher education, we have to keep investing in the skills and education of our workers. And that's why we are going—we are well on our way to meeting the goal I set when I took office 2 years ago: By 2020, America will once again have the highest proportion of college graduates in the world. That's a commitment that we're making.

So to get there, we're making college more affordable for millions of students. We've made an unprecedented investment in community colleges just like this one. And just like Forsyth, we've launched a nationwide initiative to connect graduates that need a job with businesses that need their skills.

We're reforming K–12 education not from the top down, but from the bottom up. Instead of indiscriminately pouring money into a system that's not working, we're challenging schools and States to compete with each other to see who can come up with reforms that raise standards and recruit and retain good teachers, raise student achievement, especially in math and science. We call it Race to the Top, where you get more funding if you show more results, because part of the argument here is, is that if we're going to have a government that's smart and helping people compete in this new global economy, then we've got to spend our money wisely. And that means we want to invest in things that are working, not in things that aren't working just because that's how things have always been done.

Now, once our students graduate with the skills they need for the jobs of the future, we've also got to make sure those jobs end up right here in America. We've got to make sure that the United States is the best place to do business and the best place to innovate. So it's time, for example, that we have a Tax Code that encourages job creation here in America.

And to boost our recovery, I've already proposed that all American businesses should be allowed to write off all the investments they do in 2011. We want to jump-start, starting next year, plants and equipment investment right here in Winston-Salem and all across North Carolina and all across the United States of America.

To encourage homegrown American innovation we should make it easier to patent a new idea or a new invention. And if you want to know one reason why more companies are choosing to do their research and development in places like China and India, it's because the United States now ranks 24th out of 38 countries in the generosity of the tax incentives we provide for research and development. So that's why I've proposed a bigger, permanent tax credit for companies for all the research and innovation they do right here in America—all of it.

Now, what's also true is a lot of companies don't invest in basic research because it doesn't pay off right away. But that doesn't mean it's not essential to our economic future. Forty years ago, it probably didn't seem useful or profitable for scientists and engineers to figure out how to increase the capacity of integrated circuits. Forty years later, I'm still not sure what that means. [*Laughter*] What I do know is that discoveries in integrated circuits made back then led to the iPod and cell phones and GPS and CT scans, products that have led to new companies and countless new jobs in manufacturing and retail and other sectors. That's why I've set a goal of investing a full 3 percent—not 2 percent, not 2.5 percent—a full 3 percent of our gross domestic product into research and development. That has to be a priority.

If this is truly going to be our Sputnik moment, we need a commitment to innovation that we haven't seen since President Kennedy challenged us to go to the Moon. And we're directing a lot of that research into one of the most promising areas for economic growth and job creation, and that's clean energy technology. I don't want to see new solar panels or electric cars or advanced batteries manufactured in Europe or in Asia. I want to see them made right here in America, by American businesses and American workers.

I also want to make it easier for our businesses and workers to sell their products all over the world. The more we export abroad, the more jobs we support at home. We've got to change the formula. We've got to flip the script, because what's been happening is, is that we've been doing all the buying; somebody else has been doing all the selling. We've got to start selling and have them do some buying. And that's why we've set a goal of doubling U.S. exports in 5 years. And that's why I'm pleased that last week, we came closer to meeting that goal by finalizing a trade agreement with our ally, South Korea. This is a nation that offers one of the fastest growing markets for American goods.

Now, here in North Carolina and all across the country, there are a lot of people that say, trade, we're not sure that that helps us. It seems like maybe it's hurt us in areas like furniture. Look, right now the status quo: South Korea is selling a whole bunch of stuff here, and we're not selling it there. The current deal is not a good one for us.

Think about—there are a lot of Hyundais on the road. [*Laughter*] But there aren't a lot of Fords in Seoul, because the formula has been: Let's sign any trade agreement; let's cut any deal, without thinking ahead about how this is going to impact America. What this deal does is boost our annual exports to South Korea by $11 billion. That means it will support at least 70,000 American jobs—70,000 American jobs.

Now, the final area where greater investment will lead to more jobs and economic growth is in America's infrastructure: our roads, our railways, our runways, our information superhighways. Over the last 2 years, our investment in infrastructure projects—yes, through the Recovery Act—have led to thousands of good private sector jobs and improved infrastructure here in North Carolina and all across the country.

But we've got a long way to go. There is no reason that over 90 percent of the homes in South Korea have broadband Internet access and only 65 percent of American households do. Think about that. There's no reason why China should have nearly 10,000 miles of high-speed rail by 2020 and America has 400. Think about that number. They've got 10,000; we've got 400. They've got trains that operate at speeds of over 200 mph, and I don't know how fast our trains are going. [*Laughter*]

We're the nation that built the transcontinental railroad. We're the nation that took the first airplane into flight. We constructed a massive Interstate Highway System. We introduced the world to the Internet. America has always been built to compete. And if we want to attract the best jobs and businesses to our shores, we've got to be that nation again.

And throughout history, the investments I've talked about—in education and innovation and infrastructure—have historically commanded the support from both Democrats and Republicans. It was Abraham Lincoln who launched the transcontinental railroad and opened the National Academy of Sciences. He did it in the middle of a war, by the way. But he knew this was so important we had to make these investments for future generations. Dwight Eisenhower helped build our highways. Republican Members of Congress worked with FDR to pass the GI bill.

More recently, infrastructure bills have found support on both sides of the congressional aisle. The permanent extension of research and development tax credits was proposed by both Bill Clinton and George W. Bush. Our education reforms have been praised by both Democratic and Republican Governors.

So the point is there should not be any inherent ideological differences that prevent Democrats and Republicans from making our economy more competitive with the rest of the world. If we're willing to put aside short-term politics, if our objective is not simply winning elections but winning the future, then we should be able to get our act together here, because we are all Americans and we are in this race together.

So those of us who work in Washington have a choice to make in the coming weeks and months. We can focus on what's necessary for each party to win the news cycle or the next election. We can do what we've been doing. Or we can do what this moment demands and focus on what's necessary for America to win the future.

For as difficult as the times may be, the good news is that we know what the future could look like for the United States. We can see it in the classrooms that are experimenting with groundbreaking reforms and giving children new math and science skills at an early age. We can see it in the wind farms and solar plants and advanced battery plants that are opening all across America. We can see it here at Forsyth, in your laboratories and your research facilities, and over at the biotechnology firms that are churning out jobs and businesses and lifesaving discoveries.

You see it in the faces of the young people who we just visited to—visited with, Dr. Green and myself—some not-so-young faces, but people who, despite layoffs, despite hardships, felt confident in their future.

Just the other month, I saw part of America's future during a science fair we held at the White House. It was the first science fair we've ever held. And we talked to some of these amazing young people. It was probably as much fun as I've had in several months. Now, that's a low bar, given—[*laughter*]. But there was a team from Tennessee that had designed a self-powered water filtration plant so that homes in Appalachia could have access to clean water. And then there were these young people— these are all high school, some younger than high school—there were young people who had designed a way to make an entire town more energy efficient.

And there were young people who had entered into rocket contests, and they were showing me all the rockets that they had been shooting up, and they had won an international contest, and explained to me the designs of these things—and robots that were running around in the State Dining Room and bumping into things. [*Laughter*]

And then the last person I spoke to was a young woman from Dallas, Texas, and her name was Amy Chyao. She's 16 years old. She's a child of immigrants. Her parents came to the United States from China, but Amy was born here. And when she was a freshman in high school, she got interested in cancer research. She had studied biology and she got interested in cancer research. So she decided—get this— she decided to teach herself chemistry over the summer. And then she designed a device that uses light to kill hard-to-reach cancer cells while leaving the healthy ones untouched. This is her summer science project—[*laughter*]—16 years old.

She goes on to win the international science competition. All these kids from all around the world—she wins the competition. So now she's being approached by laboratories all across the country who want to work with her on developing this potential breakthrough cancer drug that she's designed. Sixteen years old.

And I'm talking to Amy and pretending like I understand what she is explaining. [*Laughter*] And as I'm listening to her, I'm looking at the portrait of Abraham Lincoln that hangs over her head in the State Dining Room. And I remem-

bered all that we've been through and all that we've overcome. And I thought to myself, you know what, the idea of America is alive and well. We are going to be just fine.

We are going to be just fine as long as there are people like Amy and her parents who still want to come to this country and add to our story; as long as there are people like the men and women here at Forsyth Technical, who are keeping us at the top of our game; as long as we are willing to look past the disagreements of the moment and focus on the future that we share. We will be fine.

If we can do that, I have no doubt that this will be remembered as another American century. We will meet that Sputnik moment, but we're going to all have to do it together.

Thank you very much, everybody. God bless you, and God bless America.

NOTE: The President spoke at 12:28 p.m. in the West Campus auditorium.

Remarks on Tax Reform and the Extension of Unemployment Insurance Benefits
December 6, 2010

For the past few weeks, there's been a lot of talk around Washington about taxes, and there's been a lot of political positioning between the two parties. But around kitchen tables, Americans are asking just one question: Are we going to allow their taxes to go up on January 1, or will we meet our responsibilities to resolve our differences and do what's necessary to speed up the recovery and get people back to work?

Now, there's no doubt that the differences between the parties are real and they are profound. Ever since I started running for this office I've said that we should only extend the tax cuts for the middle class. These are the Americans who've taken the biggest hit not only from this recession, but from nearly a decade of costs that have gone up while their paychecks have not. It would be a grave injustice to let taxes increase for these Americans right now, and it would deal a serious blow to our economic recovery.

Now, Republicans have a different view. They believe that we should also make permanent the tax cuts for the wealthiest 2 percent of Americans. I completely disagree with this. A permanent extension of these tax cuts would cost us $700 billion at a time when we need to start focusing on bringing down our deficit. And economists from all across the political spectrum agree that giving tax cuts to millionaires and billionaires does very little to actually grow our economy.

This is where the debate has stood for the last couple of weeks. And what is abundantly clear to everyone in this town is that Republicans will block a permanent tax cut for the middle class unless they also get a permanent tax cut for the wealthiest Americans, regardless of the cost or impact on the deficit.

We saw that in two different votes in the Senate that were taken this weekend. And without a willingness to give on both sides, there's no reason to believe that this stalemate won't continue well into next year. This would be a chilling prospect for the American people whose taxes are currently scheduled to go up on January 1 because of arrangements that were made back in 2001 and 2003 under the Bush tax cuts.

I am not willing to let that happen. I know there's some people in my own party and in the other party who would rather prolong this battle, even if we can't reach a compromise. But I'm not willing to let working families across this country become collateral damage for political warfare here in Washington. And I'm not willing to let our economy slip backwards just as we're pulling ourselves out of this devastating recession.

I'm not willing to see 2 million Americans who's—stand to lose their unemployment insurance at the end of this month be put in a situation where they might lose their home or their car or suffer some additional economic catastrophe.

So, sympathetic as I am to those who prefer a fight over compromise, as much as the political wisdom may dictate fighting over solving problems, it would be the wrong thing to do. The American people didn't send us here to wage symbolic battles or win symbolic victories. They would much rather have the comfort of knowing that when they open their first paycheck on January of 2011, it won't be smaller than it was before, all because Washington decided they preferred to have a fight and failed to act.

Make no mistake: Allowing taxes to go up on all Americans would have raised taxes by $3,000 for a typical American family. And that could cost our economy well over a million jobs.

At the same time, I'm not about to add $700 billion to our deficit by allowing a permanent extension of the tax cuts for the wealthiest Americans. And I won't allow any extension of these tax cuts for the wealthy, even a temporary one, without also extending unemployment insurance for Americans who've lost their jobs or additional tax cuts for working families and small businesses. Because if Republicans truly believe we shouldn't raise taxes on anyone while our economy is still recovering from the recession, then surely we shouldn't cut taxes for wealthy people while letting them rise on parents and students and small businesses.

As a result, we have arrived at a framework for a bipartisan agreement. For the next 2 years, every American family will keep their tax cuts, not just the Bush tax cuts, but those that have been put in place over the last couple of years that are helping parents and students and other folks manage their bills.

In exchange for a temporary extension of the tax cuts for the wealthiest Americans, we will be able to protect key tax cuts for working families: the earned-income tax credit that helps families climb out of poverty, the child tax credit that makes sure families don't see their taxes jump up to $1,000 for every child, and the American opportunity tax credit that ensures over 8 million students and their families don't suddenly see the cost of college shooting up. These are the tax cuts for some of the folks who've been hit hardest by this recession, and it would be simply unacceptable if their taxes went up while everybody else's stayed the same.

Now, under this agreement, unemployment insurance will also be extended for another 13 months, which will be welcome relief for 2 million Americans who are facing the prospect of having this lifeline yanked away from them right in the middle of the holiday season.

This agreement would also mean a 2-percent employee payroll tax cut for workers next year, a tax cut that economists across the political spectrum agree is one of the most powerful things we can do to create jobs and boost economic growth.

And we will prevent—we will provide incentives for businesses to invest and create jobs by allowing them to completely write off their investments next year. This is something identified back in September as a way to help American businesses create jobs. And thanks to this compromise, it's finally going to get done.

In exchange, the Republicans have asked for more generous treatment of the estate tax than I think is wise or warranted. But we have insisted that that will be temporary.

I have no doubt that everyone will find something in this compromise that they don't like. In fact, there are things in here that I don't like, namely the extension of the tax cuts for the wealthiest Americans and the wealthiest estates. But these tax cuts will expire in 2 years. And I'm confident that as we make tough choices about bringing our deficit down, as I engage in a conversation with the American people about the hard choices we're going to have to make to secure our future and our children's future and our grandchildren's future, it will become apparent that we cannot afford to extend those tax cuts any longer.

As for now, I believe this bipartisan plan is the right thing to do. It's the right thing to do for jobs. It's the right thing to do for the middle class. It is the right thing to do for business. And it's the right thing to do for our economy. It offers us an opportunity that we need to seize.

It's not perfect, but this compromise is an essential step on the road to recovery. It will stop middle class taxes from going up. It will spur our private sector to create millions of new jobs and add momentum that our economy badly needs.

Building on that momentum is what I'm focused on. It's what Members of Congress should be focused on. And I'm looking forward to working with members of both parties in the coming days to see to it that we get this done

before everyone leaves town for the holiday season. We cannot allow this moment to pass.

And let me just end with this. There's been a lot of debate in Washington about how this would ultimately get resolved. I just want everybody to remember over the course of the coming days, both Democrats and Republicans, that these are not abstract fights for the families that are impacted. Two million people will lose their unemployment insurance at the end of this month if we don't get this resolved. Millions more of Americans will see their taxes go up at a time when they can least afford it. And my singular focus over the next year is going to be on how do we continue the momentum of the recovery, how do we make sure that we grow this economy and we create more jobs.

We cannot play politics at a time when the American people are looking for us to solve problems. And so I look forward to engaging the House and the Senate, members of both parties, as well as the media in this debate. But I am confident that this needs to get done, and I'm confident ultimately Congress is going to do the right thing.

Thank you very much, everybody.

NOTE: The President spoke at 6:32 p.m. in Room 430 of the Dwight D. Eisenhower Executive Office Building.

The President's News Conference
December 7, 2010

The President. Good afternoon, everybody. Before I answer a few questions, I just wanted to say a few words about the agreement we've reached on tax cuts.

My number-one priority is to do what's right for the American people, for jobs, and for economic growth. I'm focused on making sure that tens of millions of hard-working Americans are not seeing their paychecks shrink on January 1 just because the folks here in Washington are busy trying to score political points.

And because of this agreement, middle class Americans won't see their taxes go up on January 1, which is what I promised, a promise I

made during the campaign, a promise I made as President.

Because of this agreement, 2 million Americans who lost their jobs and are looking for work will be able to pay their rent and put food on their table. And in exchange for a temporary extension of the high-income tax breaks—not a permanent but a temporary extension—a policy that I opposed but that Republicans are unwilling to budge on, this agreement preserves additional tax cuts for the middle class that I fought for and that Republicans opposed 2 years ago.

I'll cite three of them. Number one, if you are a parent trying to raise your child or pay college tuition, you will continue to see tax breaks next year. Second, if you're a small business looking to invest and grow, you'll have a tax cut next year. Third, as a result of this agreement, we will cut payroll taxes in 2011, which will add about $1,000 to the take-home pay of a typical family.

So this isn't an abstract debate. This is real money for real people that will make a real difference in the lives of the folks who sent us here. It will make a real difference in the pace of job creation and economic growth. In other words, it's a good deal for the American people.

Now, I know there are some who would have preferred a protracted political fight, even if it had meant higher taxes for all Americans, even if it had meant an end to unemployment insurance for those who are desperately looking for work.

And I understand the desire for a fight. I'm sympathetic to that. I'm as opposed to the high-end tax cuts today as I've been for years. In the long run, we simply can't afford them. And when they expire in 2 years, I will fight to end them, just as I suspect the Republican Party may fight to end the middle class tax cuts that I've championed and that they've opposed.

So we're going to keep on having this debate. We're going to keep on having this battle. But in the meantime, I'm not here to play games with the American people or the health of our economy. My job is to do whatever I can to get this economy moving. My job is to do whatever I can to spur job creation. My job is to look out for middle class families who are struggling right now to get by and Americans who are out of work through no fault of their own.

A long political fight that carried over into next year might have been good politics, but it would be a bad deal for the economy and it would be a bad deal for the American people. And my responsibility as President is to do what's right for the American people. That's a responsibility I intend to uphold as long as I am in this office.

So with that, let me take a couple of questions.

Ben Feller [Associated Press].

Cooperation With Congress/Taxes/Unemployment Insurance

Q. Thank you, Mr. President. You've been telling the American people all along that you oppose extending the tax cuts for the wealthier Americans. You said that again today. But what you never said was that you oppose the tax cuts, but you'd be willing to go ahead and extend them for a couple years if the politics of the moment demand it.

So what I'm wondering is, when you take a stand like you had, why should the American people believe that you're going to stick with it? Why should the American people believe that you're not going to flip-flop?

The President. Hold on a second, Ben. This isn't the politics of the moment. This has to do with what can we get done right now. So the issue—here's the choice. It's very stark. We can't get my preferred option through the Senate right now. As a consequence, if we don't get my option through the Senate right now, and we do nothing, then on January 1 of this—2011, the average family is going to see their taxes go up about $3,000. Number two, at the end of this month, 2 million people will lose their unemployment insurance.

Now, I have an option, which is to say, you know what, I'm going to keep fighting a political fight, which I can't win in the Senate—and by the way, there are going to be more Republican Senators in the Senate next year sworn in than there are currently. So the likelihood that the dynamic is going to improve for us getting my preferred option through the Senate will be diminished. I've got an option of just holding fast to my position and, as a consequence, 2 million people may not be able to pay their bills and tens of millions of people who are struggling right now are suddenly going to see their paychecks smaller. Or alternatively, what I can do is I can say that I am going to stick to my position that those folks get relief, that people get help for unemployment insurance. And I will continue to fight before the American people to make the point that the Republican position is wrong.

Now, if there was not collateral damage, if this was just a matter of my politics or being able to persuade the American people to my side, then I would just stick to my guns, because the fact of the matter is, the American people already agree with me. There are polls showing right now that the American people for the most part think it's a bad idea to provide tax cuts to the wealthy.

But the issue is not me persuading the American people; they're already there. The issue is, how do I persuade the Republicans in the Senate who are currently blocking that position? I have not been able to budge them. And I don't think there's any suggestion anybody in this room thinks realistically that we can budge them right now.

And in the meantime, there are a whole bunch of people being hurt and the economy would be damaged. And my first job is to make sure that the economy is growing, that we're creating jobs out there, and that people who are struggling are getting some relief. And if I have to choose between having a protracted political battle on the one hand, but those folks being hurt, or helping those folks and continuing to fight this political battle over the next 2 years, I will choose the latter.

Cooperation With Congress/President's Decisionmaking

Q. If I may follow up quickly, sir. You're describing the situation you're in right now. What about the last 2 years when it comes to your preferred option? Was there a failure either on the part of the Democratic leadership on the Hill or here that you couldn't preclude these wealthier cuts from going forward?

The President. Well, let me say that on the Republican side, this is their holy grail, these tax cuts for the wealthy. This is—seems to be their central economic doctrine. And so, unless we had 60 votes in the Senate at any given time, it would be very hard for us to move this forward. I have said that I would have liked to have seen a vote before the election. I thought this was a strong position for us to take into the election, to crystallize the positions of the two parties, because I think the Democrats have better

ideas. I think our proposal to make sure that the middle class is held harmless, but that we don't make these Bush tax cuts permanent for wealthy individuals, because it was going to cost the country at a time when we've got these looming deficits, that that was the better position to take. And the American people were persuaded by that.

But the fact of the matter is, I haven't persuaded the Republican Party. I haven't persuaded Mitch McConnell and I haven't persuaded John Boehner. And if I can't persuade them, then I've got to look at what is the best thing to do, given that reality, for the American people and for jobs.

Julianna [Julianna Goldman, Bloomberg News].

National Economy/Taxes/Unemployment Insurance

Q. Thank you, Mr. President. Back in July, your budget office's midsession review forecast that unemployment would be 7.7 percent in the second—in the fourth quarter of 2012. Will this package deal lower that projected rate? And also, is it going to do more to boost growth and create jobs than your Recovery Act?

The President. This is not as significant a boost to the economy as the Recovery Act was, but we're in a different situation now. I mean, when the Recovery Act passed, we were looking at a potential Great Depression, and we might have seen unemployment go up to 15 percent, 20 percent. We don't know. In combination with the work we did in stabilizing the financial system, the work that the Federal Reserve did, that's behind us now. We don't have the danger of a double-dip recession.

What we have is a situation in which the economy, although growing, although company profits are up, although we are seeing some job growth in the private sector, the economy is not growing fast enough to drive down the unemployment rate given the 8 million jobs that were lost before I came into office and just as I was coming into office.

So what this package does is provide an additional boost that is substantially more significant than I think most economic forecasters had expected. And in fact, you've already seen some, just over the last 24 hours, suggest that we may see faster growth and more job growth as a consequence of this package. I think the payroll tax holiday will have an impact. Unemployment insurance probably has the biggest impact in terms of making sure that the recovery that we have continues and perhaps at a faster pace.

So overall, every economist I've talked to suggests that this will help economic growth and this will help job growth over the next several months. And that is the main criteria by which I made this decision.

Look, this is something that I think everybody has to remember, and I would speak especially to my fellow Democrats, who I think rightly are passionate about middle class families, working families, low-income families who are having the toughest time in this economy: The single most important jobs program we can put in place is a growing economy. The single most important antipoverty program we can put in place is making sure folks have jobs and the economy is growing.

We can do a whole bunch of other stuff, but if the economy is not growing, if the private sector is not hiring faster than it's currently hiring, then we are going to continue to have problems no matter how many programs we put into place.

And that's why, when I look at what our options were, for us to have another 3, 4, 5 months of uncertainty, not only would that have a direct impact on the people who see their paychecks get smaller, not only would that have a direct impact on people who are unemployed and literally depend on unemployment insurance to pay the bills or keep their home or keep their car, but in terms of macroeconomics, the overall health of the economy, that would have been a damaging thing.

Unemployment Rate/National Economy

Q. Just to follow up. The unemployment rate was just north of 8 percent when the last Recovery Act was put in place. It's now 9.8 percent. Are you prepared to say today that the unemployment rate is going to go down as a result of this package?

The President. My expectation is that the unemployment rate is going to be going down because the economy is growing. And even though it's growing more slowly that I'd like, it's still growing.

Now, how fast it's going to go down, how quickly the economy is going to grow, when are private sector businesses going to start making the investments in plant and equipment and actually start hiring people again? There are a lot of economists out there who have been struggling with that question.

So I'm not going to make a prediction. What I can say with confidence is that this package will help strengthen the economy—will help strengthen the recovery. That I'm confident about.

Chuck Todd [NBC News].

Cooperation With Congress/Taxes/Unemployment Insurance

Q. Mr. President, what do you say to Democrats who say you're rewarding Republican obstruction here? You yourself used in your opening statement, they were "unwilling to budge" on this. A lot of progressive Democrats are saying they're unwilling to budge, and you're asking them to get off the fence and budge. Why should they be rewarding Republican obstruction?

The President. Well, let me use a couple of analogies. I've said before that I felt that the middle class tax cuts were being held hostage to the high-end tax cuts. I think it's tempting not to negotiate with hostage takers, unless the hostage gets harmed. Then people will question the wisdom of that strategy. In this case, the hostage was the American people, and I was not willing to see them get harmed.

Again, this not an abstract political fight. This is not isolated here in Washington. There are people right now who, when their unemployment insurance runs out, will not be able to pay the bills. There are folks right now who are just barely making it on the paycheck that they've got, and when that paycheck gets smaller on January 1, they're going to have to scramble to figure out, how am I going to pay all my bills? How am I going to keep on making the payments for my child's college tuition? What am I going to do exactly?

Now, I could have enjoyed the battle with Republicans over the next month or two, because as I said, the American people are on our side. This is not a situation in which I have failed to persuade the American people of the rightness of our position. I know the polls. The polls are on our side on this. We weren't operating from a position of political weakness with respect to public opinion. The problem is that Republicans feel that this is the single most important thing that they have to fight for as a party. And in light of that, it was going to be a protracted battle, and they would have a stronger position next year than they do currently.

So I guess another way of thinking about it is that if—certainly if we had made a determination that the deal was a permanent tax break for high-income individuals in exchange for these short-term things that people need right now, that would have been unacceptable. And the reason is, is because you would be looking at $700 billion that would be added to the deficit with very little on the short term that would help to offset that.

The deal that we've struck here makes the high-end tax cuts temporary, and that gives us the time to have this political battle without having the same casualties for the American people that are my number-one concern.

President's Decisionmaking/Cooperation With Congress

Q. If I may follow, aren't you telegraphing, though, a negotiating strategy of how the Republicans can beat you in negotiations all the way through the next year, because they can just stick to their guns, stay united, be unwilling to budge—to use your words—and force you to capitulate?

The President. I don't think so. And the reason is because this is a very unique circumstance. This is a situation in which tens of millions of people would be directly damaged and immediately damaged, and at a time when the economy is just about to recover.

Now, keep in mind, I've just gone through 2 years, Chuck, where the rap on me was I was too stubborn and wasn't willing to budge on a whole bunch of issues, including, by the way, health care, where everybody here was writing about how, despite public opinion and despite this and despite that, somehow the guy is going to bulldoze his way through this thing.

Q. Tell that to the left. They weren't happy——

The President. Well, but that's my point. My point is I don't make judgments based on what the conventional wisdom is at any given time. I make my judgments based on what I think is right for the country and for the American people right now.

And I will be happy to see the Republicans test whether or not I'm itching for a fight on a whole range of issues. I suspect they will find I am. And I think the American people will be on my side on a whole bunch of these fights. But right now, I want to make sure that the American people aren't hurt because we're having a political fight, and I think that this agreement accomplishes that.

And as I said, there are a whole bunch of things that they are giving up. I mean, the truth of the matter is, from the Republican perspective, the earned-income tax credit, the college tuition tax credit, the child tax credit—all those things that are so important for so many families across the country—those are things they really opposed. And so temporarily, they are willing to go along with that, presumably because they think they can beat me on that over the course of the next 2 years.

And I'm happy to have that battle. I'm happy to have that conversation. I just want to make sure that the American people aren't harmed while we're having that broader argument.

Scott Horsley [National Public Radio].

South Korea-United States Free Trade Agreement/Cooperation With Congress

Q. Thank you, Mr. President. Last week, the—members of your administration were boasting that your willingness to walk away from the Korean negotiations led to a better deal. Can you explain how this is—[*inaudible*].

The President. The difference is that if I didn't get the Korea deal done on January 1, the taxes of middle class America wouldn't go up. It's pretty straightforward. If we didn't get the Korea deal done by January 1, 2 million people weren't suddenly looking at having no way to support their families.

And that's why—this goes to Chuck's question as well about what's going to be different in the future. You've got a situation here that was urgent for millions of people. But as I recall, with the Korea free trade agreement, that was deemed by conventional wisdom as an example of us not getting something done. I remember a story above the fold on that. Then when we got it done with a better deal that has the endorsement of not only the U.S. auto companies, but also of labor, the story was sort of below the fold. So I would just point that out. I think—I am happy to be tested over the next several months about our ability to negotiate with Republicans.

National Economy/Job Growth/Education/Infrastructure/Taxes

Q. Having bought that time now, do you hope to use this 2-year window to push for a broader overhaul of the Tax Code?

The President. Yes. And the answer is yes. Part of what I want to do is to essentially get the American people in a safe place so that we can then get the economy in a stable place. And then we're going to have to have a broad-based discussion across the country about our priorities. And I started doing that yesterday down in North Carolina.

Here's going to be the long-term issue. We've had 2 years of emergency: emergency economic action on the banking industry, the auto industry, on unemployment insurance, on a whole range of issues—on State budgets. The situation has now stabilized, although for those folks who are out of work, it's still an emergency. So we've still got to focus short term on job growth.

But we've got to have a larger debate about how is this country going to win the economic competition of the 21st century? How are we going to make sure that we've got the best trained workers in the world? There was just a study that came out today showing how we've slipped even further when it comes to math education and science education.

So what are we doing to revamp our schools to make sure our kids can compete? What are we doing in terms of research and development to make sure that innovation is still taking place here in the United States of America? What are we doing about our infrastructure so that we have the best airports and the best roads and the best bridges? And how are we going to pay for all that at a time when we've got both short-term deficit problems, medium-term deficit problems, and long-term deficit problems?

Now, that's going to be a big debate. And it's going to involve us sorting out what Government functions are adding to our competitiveness and increasing opportunity and making sure that we're growing the economy, and which aspects of the Government aren't helping.

And then, we've got to figure out how do we pay for that. And that's going to mean looking at the Tax Code and saying, what's fair, what's efficient. And I don't think anybody thinks the Tax Code right now is fair or efficient. But we've got to make sure that we don't just paper over those problems by borrowing from China or Saudi Arabia. And so that's going to be a major conversation.

And in that context, I don't see how the Republicans win that argument. I don't know how they're going to be able to argue that extending permanently these high-end tax cuts is going to be good for our economy when, to offset them, we'd end up having to cut vital services for our kids, for our veterans, for our seniors.

But I'm happy to listen to their arguments. And I think the American people will benefit from that debate. And that's going to be starting next year.

Marc Ambinder [National Journal].

Deficit and National Debt/Federal Budget Negotiations/Cooperation With Congress

Q. Mr. President, thank you. How do these negotiations affect negotiations or talks with Republicans about raising the debt limit? Because it would seem that they have a significant amount of leverage over the White House now, going in. Was there ever any attempt by the White House to include raising the debt limit as a part of this package?

The President. When you say it would seem they'll have a significant amount of leverage over the White House, what do you mean?

Q. Just in the sense that they'll say essentially we're not going to raise the—we're not going to agree to it unless the White House is able to or willing to agree to significant spending cuts across the board that probably go deeper and further than what you're willing to do. I mean, what leverage would you have——

The President. Look, here's my expectation— and I'll take John Boehner at his word—that nobody, Democrat or Republican, is willing to see the full faith and credit of the United States Government collapse, that that would not be a good thing to happen. And so I think that there will be significant discussions about the debt limit vote. That's something that nobody ever likes to vote on. But once John Boehner is sworn in as Speaker, then he's going to have responsibilities to govern. You can't just stand on the sidelines and be a bomb thrower.

And so my expectation is, is that we will have tough negotiations around the budget, but that ultimately we can arrive at a position that is keeping the Government open, keeping Social Security checks going out, keeping veterans services being provided, but at the same time is prudent when it comes to taxpayer dollars.

Jonathan Weisman [Wall Street Journal], last question.

Cooperation With Congress/President's Agenda/President's Decisionmaking

Q. Some on the left have questioned—have looked at this deal and questioned what your core values are, what specifically you will go to the mat on. I'm wondering if you can reassure them with some specific things in saying, all right, this is where I don't budge. And along those lines, what's going to be different in 2012, when all of these tax cuts again are up for expiration?

The President. Well, what's going to be different in 2012 we've just discussed, which is we will have had 2 years to discuss the budget, not

in the abstract, but in concrete terms. Over the last 2 years, the Republicans have had the benefit of watching us take all these emergency actions, having us preside over a $1.3 trillion deficit that we inherited and just pointing fingers and saying, that's their problem.

Well, over the next 2 years, they're going to have to show me what it is that they think they can do. And I think it becomes pretty clear, after you go through the budget line by line, that if in fact they want to pay for $700 billion worth of tax breaks to wealthy individuals, that that's a lot of money and that the cuts—corresponding cuts that would have to be made are very painful. So either they rethink their position, or I don't think they're going to do very well in 2012. So that's on the first point.

With respect to the bottom line in terms of what my core principles are——

Q. Where is your line in the sand?

The President. Well, look, I've got a whole bunch of lines in the sand. Not making the tax cuts for the wealthy permanent—that was a line in the sand. Making sure that the things that most impact middle class families and low-income families, that those were preserved—that was a line in the sand. I would not have agreed to a deal, which, by the way, some in Congress were talking about, of just a 2-year extension on the Bush tax cuts and 1 year of unemployment insurance, but meanwhile all the other provisions, the earned-income tax credit or other important breaks for middle class families like the college tax credit, that those had gone away just because they had Obama's name attached to them instead of Bush's name attached to them.

So this notion that somehow we are willing to compromise too much reminds me of the debate that we had during health care. This is the public option debate all over again. So I pass a signature piece of legislation where we finally get health care for all Americans, something that Democrats had been fighting for, for a hundred years, but because there was a provision in there that they didn't get that would have affected maybe a couple of million people, even though we got health insurance for 30 million people and the potential for lower premiums for a hundred million people, that somehow that was a sign of weakness and compromise.

Now, if that's the standard by which we are measuring success or core principles, then let's face it, we will never get anything done. People will have the satisfaction of having a purist position and no victories for the American people. And we will be able to feel good about ourselves and sanctimonious about how pure our intentions are and how tough we are, and in the meantime, the American people are still seeing themselves not able to get health insurance because of preexisting conditions or not being able to pay their bills cause their unemployment insurance ran out.

That can't be the measure of how we think about our public service. That can't be the measure of what it means to be a Democrat. This is a big, diverse country. Not everybody agrees with us. I know that shocks people. The New York Times editorial page does not permeate across all of America; neither does the Wall Street Journal editorial page. Most Americans, they're just trying to figure out how to go about their lives and how can we make sure that our elected officials are looking out for us. And that means, because it's a big, diverse country and people have a lot of complicated positions, it means that in order to get stuff done, we're going to compromise. This is why FDR, when he started Social Security, it only affected widows and orphans. You did not qualify. And yet now it is something that really helps a lot of people. When Medicare was started, it was a small program. It grew.

Under the criteria that you just set out, each of those were betrayals of some abstract ideal. This country was founded on compromise. I couldn't go through the front door at this country's founding. And if we were really thinking about ideal positions, we wouldn't have a Union.

So my job is to make sure that we have a north star out there. What is helping the American people live out their lives? What is giving them more opportunity? What is growing the economy? What is making us more competitive? And at any given juncture, there are going to be times where my preferred option, what I am absolutely positive is right, I can't get done.

And so then my question is, does it make sense for me to tack a little bit this way or tack a little bit that way, because I'm keeping my eye on the long term and the long fight—not my day-to-day news cycle, but where am I going over the long term?

And I don't think there's a single Democrat out there who, if they looked at where we started when I came into office and look at where we are now, would say that somehow we have not moved in the direction that I promised.

Take a tally. Look at what I promised during the campaign. There's not a single thing that I've said that I would do that I have not either done or tried to do. And if I haven't gotten it done yet, I'm still trying to do it.

And so the—to my Democratic friends, what I'd suggest is, let's make sure that we understand this is a long game. This is not a short game. And to my Republican friends, I would suggest—I think this is a good agreement, because I know that they're swallowing some things that they don't like as well, and I'm looking forward to seeing them on the field of competition over the next 2 years.

Thanks very much everybody.

NOTE: The President's news conference began at 2:25 p.m. in the James S. Brady Press Briefing Room at the White House.

Statement on the Death of Elizabeth A. Edwards
December 7, 2010

Michelle and I were deeply saddened to learn of the passing of Elizabeth Edwards. This afternoon I spoke to Cate Edwards and John Edwards and offered our family's condolences. I came to know and admire Elizabeth over the course of the Presidential campaign. She was a tenacious advocate for fixing our health care system and fighting poverty, and our country has benefited from the voice she gave to the cause of building a society that lifts up all those left behind.

In her life, Elizabeth Edwards knew tragedy and pain. Many others would have turned inward; many others in the face of such adversity would have given up. But through all that she endured, Elizabeth revealed a kind of fortitude and grace that will long remain a source of inspiration. Our thoughts and prayers are with her family and friends.

Remarks Following a Meeting With President Bronislaw Komorowski of Poland and an Exchange With Reporters
December 8, 2010

President Obama. Good morning, everybody. I want to extend the warmest possible greetings to President Komorowski and his delegation. Poland is one of our strongest and closest allies in the world and is a leader in Europe. And so it is fitting that my first visitor from Central and Eastern Europe is, in fact, the Polish President.

Before I mention the substance of our meeting, let me just say something very quickly to the American news crews about something that's on everybody's minds, and that is the current debate about the tax agreement that we've come up with.

We announced this agreement, and over the last couple of days economists throughout the country have looked at what would be the results of getting this agreement through Congress. And I think it's worth noting that the majority of economists have upwardly revised their forecasts for economic growth and noted that as a consequence of this agreement we could expect to see more job growth in 2011 and 2012 than they originally anticipated.

And I just think it's very important for Congress to examine the agreement, look at the facts, have a thorough debate, but get this done. The American people are watching, and they're expecting action on our parts.

I don't think you need to translate that.

Now, having said that, I just want to say that I first spoke to President Komorowski in the wake of a tragedy that broke the hearts not only of the Polish people, but caused the entire world to grieve. The loss of President Kaczynski, the First Lady, the entire planeload full of extraordinary Polish leaders caused extraordinary shock. But I have been so impressed with the steady hand and the leadership that President Komorowski has shown as he stepped in to guide the Polish people forward.

Something that the Polish people and the American people have long shared is not only a love of freedom, but also a deep faith and resilience in the face of hardship. And President Komorowski exhibited all those traits as the leader of Poland during this difficult period.

So given these strong bonds between our two peoples—bonds that I feel very personally given that I'm from Chicago, which has the largest Polish population outside of Poland—this has been a very productive meeting and we discussed a wide range of issues.

We started with the issue that is at the heart of our relationship, and that is our status as allies in NATO. And coming out of the Lisbon summit, we once again reaffirmed the centrality of article 5 as the central tenet of the NATO alliance. And I reiterated my determination and the American people's determination to always stand by Poland in its defense and its security needs.

And that commitment is exemplified by the joint adoption at Lisbon by NATO of a NATO-wide missile defense capacity. It's exemplified by the Air Force detachment that will be placed in Poland as part of our ongoing relationship in the training process. It is indicated by the SM–3s and the interceptors that are going to be located in Poland as part of our phased adoptive approach to missile defense. And most importantly, it's affirmed by the fact that not only are we NATO allies, but strong bilateral allies, and that bond between our two countries is unbreakable.

I know that was a mouthful, I'm sorry. [*Laughter*]

[*At this point, an interpreter translated President Obama's initial remarks into Polish.*]

We also discussed the tremendous sacrifices that the Polish military are making as part of the ISAF alliance in Afghanistan and reaffirmed what all of us agreed to in Lisbon, that next year will be a year in which transition begins so that we can start giving Afghans more responsibility for their security and, over time, make sure that our emphasis is more on training rather than direct combat in that nation.

I also thanked the President for the very strong support that the Polish Government, as well as the governments throughout Eastern Europe and Central Europe have shown towards the new START Treaty. As we embark on a debate of that treaty in the United States Senate, I indicated to him how important it was for U.S. Senators to hear from those who are Russia's neighbors that they feel it is very important to make sure that the new START Treaty is ratified so that we can continue the verification process that is so important in reducing risks throughout that region.

And finally, because our relationship is not restricted to security, we discussed a range of economic issues as well, including Polish leadership on energy independence issues in Central and Eastern Europe. And we also discussed Poland's leadership as a key democracy and how it can help its neighbors to continue down a path of greater freedom and greater openness and transparency.

This year we mark the 30th anniversary of Solidarity. And all those around the world remember how inspired we were by the brave Poles who sought their freedom, including a young—or younger—President Komorowski, who himself was imprisoned. And we continue to draw inspiration from the tremendous strides that Poland has made. We continue to deeply appreciate the strong friendship between our two countries.

And I'm so grateful to President Komorowski for having come here today because it is one more reaffirmation that our alliance is strong and will continue to be strong for decades to come.

President Komorowski. Mr. President, ladies and gentlemen, I would like to express the absolute same perspective on what happened in Lisbon. This goes both for the full acceptance of the arrangements by NATO as to the future of Afghan operation. And first and above all, this is about the reaffirmation of the significance of article 5 Washington treaty.

And we agreed that what happened in Lisbon was the renewal and the reaffirmation of the internal cohesion of the Alliance and also the sense of the existence of NATO as the alliance as going to defend the territorial integrity of its member states.

And this is also connected with the reaffirmation of the necessity to implement the language from the contingency plans in the forms of exercises, also NATO infrastructure in the territory of the member states. And an element of this is also the American activity and presence in the form of the military participation both in Europe and in Poland.

NATO now plays new roles, but it does not reject its old role, which continues as fundamental for its future. I allowed myself to illustrate this to President Obama in a very illustrative way, a very picturesque way. I simply said that if we are to go hunting very far away from our house, we have to be absolutely sure that our house, our women and our children are well guarded. And then you hunt better.

And I also wanted to say that this is needed to renew and reaffirm good Polish-American relations. And the fundament of these relations is both American and Polish love for freedom. And we want also to make sure that this reaffirmation is a visible sign that these relations, instead of some difficulties underway, are getting stronger and not weaker.

And thirdly, I wanted to say also that we talked about something that is very important for creating very good texture for the cooperation between the United States and Poland. Poland is economically successful. We are the only country that has kept positive GDP growth in Europe. We want to see the greatest interest and the activity of the American capital in Poland.

However, on the principles of healthy competition, because I am absolutely convinced that as in other areas of our life, in economy, it also stands true good competition is always good.

And the last thing, but is also very important is the Polish attitude to the current issues, which are very important from the perspective of the security of our world. Poland supports and fully accepts the aspiration for the ratification of the new START because we believe that this is the investment in a better and safer future. And this is also the investment in the real control over the current situation.

If you live just next door with somebody for 1,000 years, it is not possible to reset all the past relations using just one push of the reset button. We are not able to fully reset and delete 1,000 years of uneasy history with Russians. But we do not want to be an obstacle, we want to be a help in the process of resetting the relations between the Western world with Russia. We want to invest in relations with Russia.

Two days ago in Poland, we had a visit of President of the Russian Federation Medvedev. And it is our very open will, our greatest conviction and open heart with which we want to invest in better relations with Russia.

But we also are absolutely sure of this old Russian proverb, "You have to have the confidence, but you also have to verify," because then, perhaps at the end of the process we will also push the reset button after 1,000 years of our history. And this is what we would like to have very much.

President Obama. Thank you so much.

So we've got time for two questions. I think on the American side I'm going to call on Bill Plante [CBS News].

Cooperation With Congress/Taxes/Strategic Arms Reduction Treaty

Q. Mr. President, now that you've negotiated with the Republicans, are you willing to negotiate with the Democrats who think they've—that you've betrayed them on the tax package?

And when you talked to the Republicans, did they give you any assurances that they would take up START and "don't ask" in the lame duck?

President Obama. Well, first of all, Bill, I think it is inaccurate to characterize Democrats writ large as feeling betrayed. I think Democrats are looking at this bill, and you've already had a whole bunch of them who said this makes sense. And I think the more they look at it, the more of them are going to say this makes sense.

As I've indicated, you've just had economists over the last 24, 48 hours examine this and say this is going to boost the economy, it is going to grow the economy, it is going to increase the likelihood that we can drive down the unemployment rate. And it's going to make sure that 2 million people who stand to lose unemployment insurance at the end of this month get it, that folks who count on college tax credits or child tax credits or the earned-income tax credit, that they're getting relief, and that tens of millions of Americans are not going to see their paychecks shrink come January 1.

So this is the right thing to do. I expect everybody to examine it carefully. When they do, I think they're going to feel confident that, in fact, this is the right course, while understanding that for the next 2 years we're going to have a big debate about taxes and we're going to have a big debate about the budget and we're going to have a big debate about deficits. And Republicans are going to have to explain to the American people over the next 2 years how making those tax cuts for the high-end permanent squares with their stated desire to start reducing deficits and debt.

I don't think that formula works. But they'll have the opportunity to make the case. I'll have the opportunity to make the case that we've got to have tax reform, that we've got to simplify the system, that we do have to cut spending where it makes sense. But we're also going to have to make sure that we've got a Tax Code that is fair and that looks after the interest of middle class Americans and continues to grow the economy.

With respect to START, I feel confident that when you've got previous Secretaries of State, Defense, basically the entire national security apparatus of previous Democratic and Republican administrations, our closest allies who are most impacted by relations with Russia, and as President Komorowski indicated, have a thousand years of uneasy relations with Russia, saying that the new START Treaty is important, that we are going to be able to get it through the Senate.

That's not linked to taxes. That's something that on its own merits is close to get done—needs to get done. And I have discussed it with Senate Republican leader McConnell. I am confident that we are going to be able to get the START Treaty on the floor, debated, and completed before we break for the holidays.

U.S. Visa Waiver Program/Poland-U.S. Relations

Q. This is a question for both Presidents. Have you at all discussed the inclusion of Poland into the visa waiver program? And if so, Mr. President, what has your administration done in order to include Poland into this program?

President Obama. I will—why don't I answer that just very quickly. First of all, I want all Poles and Polish Americans to know that President Komorowski raised this issue very robustly with me. I am well aware that this is a source of irritation between two great friends and allies, and we should resolve it.

The challenge I have right now is, is that there is a congressional law that prevents my administration from taking unilateral executive action. So we're going to have to work with Congress to make some modifications potentially on the law.

In the meantime, what I indicated to President Komorowski is that I am going to make this a priority. And I want to solve this issue before very long. My expectation is, is that this problem will be solved during my Presidency.

Q. So it has not been your priority in the past 2 years?

President Obama. I'm sorry, what I said was that it has been a priority and we've been continuing to work on it, but it hasn't gotten solved yet.

President Komorowski. It's nice for me to hear President Obama reaffirm that we have talked about it. I take these declarations with good faith. I feel simply committed to say that Polish public opinion completely does not understand why all the neighbors of Poland, the neighborhood of Poland, can use that visa waiver program and we can't.

So Poles somehow cope, because we are a member of the European Union, and we can travel and we can work in all the member states of the European Union. So I just want to say that I know that it would be quite logical for us to be able also to travel without visas to the United States.

But from the perspective of Poland, we have said everything about it. And we also—I'm completely sure that this issue will be reconsidered and revisited by the American party, also from the perspective of the relations between the citizens of Poland and the United States.

President Obama. Well, Mr. President, thank you so much for the wonderful visit. And I just want to make—as the press leaves, you might want to note that I got this beautiful Christmas tree ornament from the President, and it's already on my tree. We hung it up. And it's the prettiest one on the tree, so you may want to take a look at it.

President Komorowski. I also want to say that I'm absolutely convinced that your numerous neighbors from Chicago make exactly the same decorations. [*Laughter*] And I also have a decoration from the White House, a Christmas tree decoration, and I'm going to put it on my Christmas tree in Warsaw.

President Obama. Merry Christmas. Thank you.

Thank you, everybody.

NOTE: The President spoke at 11:45 a.m. in the Oval Office at the White House. President Komorowski spoke in Polish, and his remarks were translated by an interpreter.

Joint Statement by President Barack Obama and President Bronislaw Komorowski of Poland
December 8, 2010

President Barack Obama and President Bronislaw Komorowski reaffirmed today their commitment to strengthening the U.S.-Polish alliance by expanding strategic and defense cooperation, supporting deeper economic links, and promoting democratic institutions in Europe and around the world. The two leaders resolved to continue to work together to ensure that transatlantic ties remain strong and relevant to the challenges and opportunities of the 21st century.

President Obama conveyed his deepest condolences over the devastating and tragic loss of President Lech Kaczynski and First Lady Maria Kaczynska, along with many of Poland's top civilian and military leaders, in the April 10, 2010 air crash. President Obama reiterated his admiration for the strength of Poland's institutions and the resilience of its people.

President Komorowski expressed his gratitude to the President of the United States and the American people for their solidarity and compassion in those difficult times.

A STRATEGIC PARTNERSHIP FOR THE 21st CENTURY

Both Presidents applauded the outcomes of the Lisbon NATO Summit, including the allied commitment to reaffirm the primacy of our Article 5 obligations to one another's security and to adopt territorial missile defense as a core mission. President Obama confirmed the commitment of the United States to implement the Phased Adaptive Approach to European missile defense, including basing land-based SM–3 interceptors in Poland as part of this program in the 2018 timeframe, and expressed his gratitude for the commitment by the government of Poland to host this system. Poland's commitment is an extremely valuable contribution to the development of a NATO missile defense capability.

The two leaders agreed to enhance bilateral defense ties in the spirit of the 2008 U.S.-Polish Declaration on Strategic Cooperation. This includes increased cooperation between our two Air Forces with the aim of strengthening interoperability as NATO allies through regular joint training exercises and establishment of a U.S. air detachment in Poland to support periodic rotation of U.S. military aircraft.

President Obama expressed appreciation for Poland's contribution to increased worldwide nuclear security, including the removal of highly enriched uranium from the reactor in Poland. President Komorowski expressed Poland's strong support for the prompt ratification of the New START Treaty, as it would bolster Polish and European security and contribute to the Non-Proliferation Treaty's disarmament goals. The United States and Poland also emphasized the continued need for practical actions to prevent the spread of weapons of mass destruction (WMD) and their delivery systems to states of proliferation concern and to terrorist groups. The two countries reaffirmed their commitment to work together under the Proliferation Security Initiative to counter illicit trade in WMD and missiles.

The Presidents appreciated the results of NATO summit in Lisbon regarding Afghanistan and highlighted their support for NATO's efforts there, where U.S. and Polish troops fight side-by-side. They also noted with satisfaction that ISAF and the Government of Afghanistan are entering a new phase of joint effort. The United States will place 800 U.S. troops under Polish tactical command in Ghazni Province, a testament to Poland's military leadership, and will also provide logistical assistance by loaning an additional 20 Mine-Resistant Ambush-Protected (MRAP) vehicles to the Polish military.

SUPPORTING MUTUAL PROSPERITY THROUGH EXPORTS, INVESTMENT, AND TECHNOLOGY

The two leaders discussed their efforts to deepen mutual dialogue on energy security, and to that end they welcomed agreement in principle on a bilateral Memorandum of Understanding to enhance cooperation on scientific, technical and policy aspects of clean and efficient energy technologies. They underlined their respective governments' readiness to cooperate in good faith and in a fair, open and transparent manner on a broad range of energy-related issues, including civilian nuclear power, unconventional gas, energy efficiency, renewable energy and other clean power resources in Poland. They welcomed new and continuing efforts under the Global Shale Gas Initiative.

JOINT EFFORTS TO PROMOTE DEMOCRACY IN EASTERN EUROPE AND AROUND THE WORLD

Pointing to the successful democratic transition of Poland and other Central European states, President Obama cited Poland as a model for other countries striving to build democratic institutions and praised Poland's leadership in the Community of Democracies.

The United States and Poland call for genuinely free and fair presidential elections in Belarus on December 19. President Obama and President Komorowski reiterated their strong support for the EU's Eastern Partnership Initia-

tive, designed to strengthen ties between the EU and Armenia, Azerbaijan, Belarus, Georgia, Moldova and Ukraine, and to spur reform and strengthen democracy in those countries. The two leaders hailed NATO's historic decision in Lisbon to create a strategic and modern partnership with Russia. The United States and Poland are pursuing complementary policies of strengthening ties with Russia.

EXPANDING CITIZEN CONTACTS

The two leaders committed to expanding the Fulbright program; our two governments will also discuss expansion of the Parliamentary Youth Exchange. President Obama and President Komorowski applauded the partnership between the Polish American Freedom Foundation and leading U.S. companies to bring Polish university students and young professionals to the United States for internships in the private sector.

President Komorowski thanked President Obama and the American people for their hospitality, and extended an invitation to President Obama to visit Poland.

NOTE: An original was not available for verification of the content of this joint statement.

Remarks on Signing the Claims Resolution Act of 2010
December 8, 2010

Welcome, everybody. We are thrilled to have you here. And I want to start by acknowledging a few people who have worked so hard to allow us to be here today on this wonderful occasion: our Attorney General, Eric Holder—you can give him a round of applause; two outstanding members of my Cabinet who couldn't have worked harder to make today happen, Secretary of the Interior Ken Salazar and Secretary of Agriculture Tom Vilsack; and four outstanding leaders who made it their business to see this thing through, Senator Max Baucus, Democrat of Montana, Senator Jeff Bingaman, Democrat of New Mexico, Representative Jim Clyburn, Democrat of South Carolina, and Representa-

tive Tom Cole, Republican of Oklahoma. Please give them a big round of applause.

And one last person who doesn't get a lot of notice but put a huge amount of time and actually crossed the t's and dotted the i's to help this thing along, my good friend from law school, even though he now looks younger than me because I've gotten the gray hair and he hasn't— [*laughter*]—and what's the official title? Is it deputy or—it's associate—Associate Attorney General Tom Perrelli.

Obviously, despite the extraordinary leadership on the stage, this also would not have gotten done without the activists, the tribal leaders, and the outstanding Members of Congress, both Democrat and Republican, who have come together and done so much over the years to make this a reality.

Here in America, we believe that all of us are equal and that each of us deserves the chance to pursue our own version of happiness. It's what led us to become a nation. It's at the heart of who we are as a people. And our history is defined by the struggle to fulfill this ideal: to build a more perfect Union, to ensure that all of us, regardless of our race or religion, our color or our creed, are afforded the same rights as Americans and the fair and equal treatment under the law.

I think all of us understand that we haven't always lived up to those ideals. When we've fallen short, it's been up to ordinary citizens to stand up to inequality and unfairness wherever they find it. That's how we've made progress. That's how we've moved forward. And that's why we are here today: to sign a bill into law that closes a long and unfortunate chapter in our history.

First, for many years African American farmers claimed they were discriminated against when they applied for Federal farm loans, making it more difficult for them to stay in business and maintain their farms. In 1999, a process was established to settle these claims. But the settlement was implemented poorly and tens of thousands of African American families who filed paperwork after the deadline were denied their chance to make their case.

And that's why, as Senator, I introduced legislation to provide these farmers the right to have their claims heard. That's why I'm proud that Democrats and Republicans have come together to lay this case to rest. And that's why I'm proud that Secretary Vilsack and everybody at the Department of Agriculture are continuing to address claims of past discrimination by other farmers throughout our country.

The second case we're addressing today has to do with the responsibilities that the Government has to Native Americans. It began when Elouise Cobell, who is here today, charged the Interior Department with failing to account for tens of billions of dollars that they were supposed to collect on behalf of more than 300,000 of her fellow Native Americans.

Elouise's argument was simple: The Government, as a trustee of Indian funds, should be able to account for how it handles that money. And now, after 14 years of litigation, it's finally time to address the way that Native Americans were treated by their Government. It's finally time to make things right.

The bipartisan agreement finalized this month will result in payments to those affected by this case. It creates a scholarship fund to help make higher education a reality for more Native Americans. It helps put more land in the hands of tribes to manage for their members. And it also includes money to settle lawsuits over water rights, giving seven tribes in Arizona, Montana, and New Mexico permanent access to secure water supplies year round.

After years of delay, this bill will provide a small measure of justice to Native Americans whose funds were held in trust by a Government charged with looking out for them. And it represents a major step forward in my administration's efforts to fulfill our responsibilities and strengthen our government-to-government relationship with the tribal nations.

In the end, the work that is represented on this stage and among these Members of Congress, this isn't simply a matter of making amends. It's about reaffirming our values on which this Nation was founded, principles of fairness and equality and opportunity. It's about helping families who suffered through no fault of their own get back on their feet. It's about restoring a sense of trust between the American people and the Government that plays such an important role in their lives.

As long as I have the privilege of serving as your President, I will continue to do everything I can to restore that trust. And that's why I am so extraordinarily proud to sign this bill today.

I want to thank once again all those Members of Congress. We got a lot of members here— the Congressional Black Caucus, who I know worked the *Pigford* issue tirelessly. We've got, as I said, Democrats and Republicans who were supportive of this issue for so long. This is one of those issues where you don't always get political credit, but it's just the right thing to do. And I couldn't be prouder of you.

Thank you very much.

NOTE: The President spoke at 5:34 p.m. in the South Court Auditorium of the Dwight D. Eisen-hower Executive Office Building. In his remarks, he referred to Elouise C. Cobell, executive director, Native American Community Development Corporation. H.R. 4783, approved December 8, was assigned Public Law No. 111–291.

Statement on Signing the Claims Resolution Act of 2010
December 8, 2010

Today I have signed into law H.R. 4783, the "Claims Resolution Act of 2010." This Act, among other things, provides funding and statutory authorities for the settlement agreements reached in the *Cobell* lawsuit, brought by Native Americans; the *Pigford II* lawsuit, brought by African American farmers; and four separate water rights suits, brought by Native American tribes. While I am pleased that this Act reflects important progress, much work remains to be done to address other claims of past discrimination made by women and Hispanic farmers against the Department of Agriculture as well as to address needs of tribal communities.

I am also pleased that the Act includes authorities proposed by my Administration concerning Unemployment Compensation program integrity, to expand the ability of the Federal Government to recover from individual income tax overpayments certain Unemployment Compensation debts that are due to an individual's failure to report earnings. My Administration has been working to protect taxpayer funds through improved recovery of improper Federal payments, and the additional authorities in this Act will assist in that effort. In order to ensure that the intent and effect of these program integrity provisions are realized, my Administration is working with the Congress to correct an inadvertent technical drafting error in section 801(a)(3)(C), so that the provision can be implemented as intended.

BARACK OBAMA

The White House,
December 8, 2010.

NOTE: H.R. 4783, approved December 8, was assigned Public Law No. 111–291.

Statement on Senate Action on Legislation To Limit Cuts in Medicare Payments to Physicians
December 8, 2010

I am pleased Democratic and Republican leaders in the Senate have agreed on legislation that will prevent a significant pay cut for doctors from taking effect and help ensure seniors on Medicare can continue to see the doctor they know and trust. I encourage Congress to act quickly on this proposal. This agreement is an important step forward to stabilize Medicare, but our work is far from finished. For too long, we have confronted this reoccurring problem with temporary fixes and stopgap measures. It's time for a permanent solution that seniors and their doctors can depend on, and I look forward to working with Congress to address this matter once and for all in the coming year.

NOTE: The statement referred to H.R. 4994.

Statement on House of Representatives Passage of Legislation Providing Citizenship Opportunities for Alien Minors
December 8, 2010

I congratulate the House of Representatives, Speaker Pelosi, Congressman Berman, the Congressional Hispanic Caucus, and other congressional leaders for taking the historic step of passing the "DREAM Act" today with a bipartisan vote. This vote is not only the right thing to do for a group of talented young people who seek to serve a country they know as their own by continuing their education or serving in the military, but it is the right thing for the United States of America. We are enriched by their talents, and the success of their efforts will contribute to our Nation's success and security. And as the nonpartisan Congressional Budget Office found, the "DREAM Act" would cut the deficit by $2.2 billion over the next 10 years. I strongly urge the U.S. Senate to also pass the "DREAM Act" so that I can sign it into law as soon as possible.

This vote is a vitally important step to doing what the American people expect their policymakers to do: work together to address the Na-

tion's most pressing problems. The "DREAM Act" corrects one of the most egregious flaws of a badly broken immigration system. A flaw that forces children who have grown up in America, who speak English, who have excelled in our communities as academics, athletes, or volunteers to put their lives and talent on hold at a great cost to themselves and our Nation.

I also congratulate the House for moving past the tired sound bites and false debates that have pushed immigration rhetoric into the extremes for far too long. The "DREAM Act" is not amnesty, it's about accountability and about tapping into a pool of talent we've already invested in. The "DREAM Act" is a piece of a larger debate that is needed to restore responsibility and accountability to our broken immigration system broadly. My administration will continue to do everything we can to move forward on immigration reform; today's House vote is an important step in this vital effort.

Remarks Prior to a Meeting With the President's Export Council
December 9, 2010

Everybody have a seat, have a seat. Well, good morning, everybody. And thank you for once again coming together to help us figure out how we're going to sell a lot of stuff all around the world.

I want to thank Secretary Locke and members of my Cabinet and administration. I want to thank the Members of Congress who are here. And I want to thank Jim and Ursula, the Chair and Vice Chairs of the President's Export Council, and all the other members here today for your extraordinary work.

Now, everyone in this room is committed to promoting a strong and growing economy, one that's creating jobs, fostering a thriving middle class, and extending opportunity for all who are willing to work for it.

And as we meet here, there is an important debate I think most of you are aware of on Cap-

itol Hill that will determine, in part, whether our economy moves forward or backward. The bipartisan framework that we've forged on taxes will not only protect working Americans from seeing a major tax increase on January 1, it will provide businesses incentives to invest, grow, and hire. And every economist that I've talked to or that I've read over the last couple of days acknowledges that this agreement would boost economic growth in the coming years and has the potential to create millions of jobs. The average American family will start 2011 knowing that there will be more money to pay the bills each month, more money to pay for tuition, more money to raise their children.

But if this framework fails, the reverse is true. Americans would see it in smaller paychecks that would have the effect of fewer jobs. So as we meet here today to talk about one important facet of our economic strategy for the future, I urge Members of Congress to move forward on this essential priority.

Now, the top priority of my administration since I took office has been to get the American people back on their feet and back on the job in the aftermath of the most devastating recession in our lifetime. That's job one. But as I said in greater detail on Monday, we've also got to ask ourselves how do we position our economy to be strong, growing, and competitive in the long run.

One strategy that will help us do both—to create good jobs that pay well today and create new markets for jobs tomorrow—is to increase our exports to the rest of the world. That's why, in my State of the Union Address, I set a goal for America: We will double our exports for goods and services over 5 years. And I relaunched this Council because, as business leaders and labor leaders, as Members of Congress, and as members of my administration, I value your advice in terms of how we best achieve that goal.

What we all agree on is that we've got to rebuild our economy on a new and stronger foundation for growth. And part of that means getting back to doing what America has always been known for doing—what our workers and our businesses have always done best—and that's making great products and selling them around the world.

The world wants products made in America. We've got workers ready to make them. And the fact is, exporting is good for our economy. The more our companies export, the more they produce. The more they produce, the more workers they hire. Every $1 billion that we increase in exports supports more than 5,000 jobs, and companies that export often pay better wages.

So at a time when jobs are in short supply, growing our export markets is an imperative. And growing our exports today will create the jobs of tomorrow. Ninety-five percent of the world's customers and the fastest growing markets are beyond our borders. If we want to find new growth streams for our economy, we've got to compete aggressively for those customers,

because other nations are competing aggressively. And as long as I'm President of the United States, we are going to fight for every job, every industry, every market, everywhere, and we intend to win.

That's why I set this goal. We're on track to meet it. Exports are up nearly 18 percent so far over last year. Today I'd like to offer an update on some of the steps we've taken to get there, and steps we're taking based on this Council's recommendations, to keep making progress.

Earlier this year, I launched the National Export Initiative, an effort to marshal the full resources of the Federal Government behind America's businesses, large and small, in order to best help them sell their goods, services, and ideas to the rest of the world.

One of the things I pledged to do as part of this initiative was to move forward on new trade agreements with some of our key partners. And I promised to do it in a way that secures a level playing field for our companies and a fair shake for our workers without compromising our most cherished values.

That's why I am so pleased that the United States and South Korea reached agreement on a landmark trade deal last week. We expect this deal's tariff reductions alone to boost annual exports of American goods by up to $11 billion. And all told, this agreement, including the opening of the Korean services market, will support more than 70,000 American jobs.

I hoped to finalize this agreement—I had hoped to finalize this agreement when I traveled to Korea last month, but I didn't agree to it at that time for one simple reason: It wasn't yet good enough for our workers or our economy. As much as I believe that looking out for American workers requires competing in the global marketplace, I also believe that as we compete in the global marketplace, we've got to look out for American workers. So I said let's take the time to get this right. And we did.

It is now a deal that is good for our workers, good for our businesses, good for our farmers, good for our ranchers, good for aerospace, good for electronics manufacturers. In particular, American car and truck manufacturers will have more access to Korea's markets. And here at home, we'll encourage the development of electric cars and green technologies and continue to ensure a level playing field for our automakers.

It's also good for our friend and ally South Korea. They will grow their economy, gain greater access to our markets, and will also get American products that'll be more affordable for Korean households and businesses. And that means more choices for them and more jobs for us.

And it's good for American leadership. As I've insisted all along, it—the deal that we've struck includes strong protections for workers' rights and environmental standards, and as a consequence, I believe it's a model for future trade agreements that I will pursue.

It's an agreement supported by Members of Congress on both side of the aisle and Americans on all sides of the political spectrum, from the UAW to the Chamber of Commerce. And I look forward to working with Congress and leaders in both parties to approve it, because if there's one thing we should all agree on, it's creating jobs and opportunity for the American people.

Another thing that we said we'd do is to go to bat as a stronger advocate for our businesses abroad. This is an effort that I pledged to lead personally. And that's why, on the same trip where we were working to get the Korea deal done, I visited India to highlight the role American business played there and took the opportunity to sell our exports to one of the fastest growing markets in the world. While I was there, we reached several landmark deals, from Boeing jets and GE engines to medical and mining equipment, deals that are worth nearly $10 billion in exports and will support more than 50,000 American jobs.

I also believe that strong economic partnerships can create prosperity at home and advance it around the world. And that's why we focused on deepening our economic cooperation with Russia on a range of fronts, from aerospace to agriculture, including restarting American poultry exports earlier this year, which was an important victory for many American farmers. I believe that Russia belongs in the WTO and that we should support all efforts to make

that happen. I think President Medvedev is doing important work trying to reform and move Russia forward on a whole host of issues, and I told him that the United States would be a partner with him in that effort. Welcoming Russia to the WTO would be good for them; it would also be good for us and good for the global economy.

Finally, we've also been working to reform our export control system with high-tech companies like some of yours in mind, so that American firms that make products with national security implications can stay competitive even as we better protect our national security interests.

When this Council met in September, some of you asked that we make it easier for businesses to participate in these reform efforts. So today I am pleased to announce that we're publishing a first set of guidelines for what products should be controlled going forward and the licensing policies that will apply to them. As an example, we've applied those policies to one category of products. In that one category, about three-quarters of products previously subjected to stricter controls will be shifted to a more flexible list, and many are expected to fall off the list altogether. And we want input from businesses, from Congress, and from our allies as we complete this reform.

Today we're also unveiling a new export control reform web page as part of the revamped export.gov. This is something that Secretary Locke mentioned in our last meeting. Typically, all businesses that export have to go through a maze of different lists, different formats, from different departments, to make sure they're not selling their products somewhere or to someone that they shouldn't be. As important as that is, the process is repetitive; it's redundant and particularly onerous for small businesses without the means to navigate it all.

So we're changing that. Effective today, businesses can, for the very first time, go to export.gov and download one consolidated list of entities that have special export requirements.

So that's a lot of work that we've been doing to double our exports, to open up new markets and level the playing field for American workers and businesses, all with the overarching purpose of growing and strengthening the American economy.

I'm very much looking forward to the discussion we're going to be having as you guys continue your work. I'm grateful for all of you for being here, because while those around this table may not always agree on every issue, what does bind us together is that we want to see our businesses grow. We want to see our workers get hired. We want our people to succeed. We want America to compete. We want to stay on top in the 21st century. And I'm confident we can do that with your help.

So thank you very much, everybody. And I think you guys are going to strike this podium so I can sit down and listen a little bit. Thank you.

NOTE: The President spoke at 10:19 a.m. in Room 430 of the Dwight D. Eisenhower Executive Office Building. In his remarks, he referred to W. James McNerney, Jr., Chair, and Ursula M. Burns, Vice Chair, President's Export Council.

Remarks on Lighting the National Christmas Tree
December 9, 2010

The President. Merry Christmas, everybody!

Audience members. Merry Christmas!

The President. Happy holidays. We are just thrilled to have all of you here.

Thank you, Secretary Salazar, for the kind introduction and for all that you're doing to protect our national parks and our public lands for the future of generations. I also want to recognize Neil Mulholland and everyone at the National Park Foundation and at the National Park Service who helped put this event together.

I want to thank Pastor Darrell Morton for that wonderful invocation, and of course, thanks to Common and all of tonight's performers for joining us here as we light the National Christmas Tree for the 88th time.

This is a very proud holiday tradition. Snow or shine, in good times and in periods of hardship, folks like you have gathered with Presidents to light our national tree. Now, it hasn't always gone off without a hitch. On one occasion, two sheep left the safety of the nativity scene and wandered into rush-hour traffic. [*Laughter*] That caused some commotion. [*Laughter*]

Often, the ceremony itself has reflected the pain and sacrifice of the times. There were years during the Second World War when no lights were hung in order to save electricity. In the days following Pearl Harbor, Winston Churchill joined President Roosevelt to wish our Nation a happy Christmas even in such perilous days.

But without fail, each year, we have gathered here; each year, we've come together to celebrate a story that has endured for two millennia. It's a story that's dear to Michelle and me as Christians, but it's a message that's universal: A child was born far from home to spread a simple message of love and redemption to every human being around the world.

It's a message that says no matter who we are or where we are from, no matter the pain we endure or the wrongs we face, we are called to love one another as brothers and as sisters.

And so during a time in which we try our hardest to live with a spirit of charity and good will, we remember our brothers and sisters who have lost a job or are struggling to make ends meet. We pray for the men and women in uniform serving in Afghanistan and Iraq and in faraway places who can't be home this holiday season. And we thank their families, who will mark this Christmas with an empty seat at the dinner table.

On behalf of Malia, Sasha, Michelle, Marian—who's our grandmother-in-chief—[*laughter*]—and Bo—don't forget Bo—I wish all of you a merry Christmas and a blessed holiday season.

And now I'm going to invite the entire Obama crew up here to help me light this Christmas tree.

All right, everybody, we're going to count from five: five, four, three, two, one.

NOTE: The President spoke at 5:18 p.m. on the Ellipse at the White House. In his remarks, he referred to Neil J. Mulholland, president and chief executive officer, National Park Foundation; Darrell D. Morton, pastor, Evangelical Lutheran Church in America; and musician Lonnie R. "Common" Lynn, Jr. He also referred to his mother-in-law Marian Robinson.

Statement on Senate Action on Defense Authorization Legislation
December 9, 2010

I am extremely disappointed that yet another filibuster has prevented the Senate from moving forward with the "National Defense Authorization Act." Despite having the bipartisan support of a clear majority of Senators, a minority of Senators are standing in the way of the funding upon which our troops, veterans, and military families depend. This annual bill has been enacted each of the past 48 years, and our Armed Forces deserve nothing less this year.

A minority of Senators were willing to block this important legislation largely because they oppose the repeal of "don't ask, don't tell." As Commander in Chief, I have pledged to repeal this discriminatory law, a step supported by the Secretary of Defense and the chairman of the Joint Chiefs of Staff and informed by a comprehensive study that shows overwhelming majorities of our Armed Forces are prepared to serve with Americans who are openly gay or lesbian. A great majority of the American people agree. This law weakens our national security, diminishes our military readiness, and violates fundamental American principles of fairness, integrity, and equality.

I want to thank Majority Leader Reid, Armed Services Committee Chairman Levin, and Senators Lieberman and Collins for all the work they have done on this bill. While today's vote was disappointing, it must not be the end of our efforts. I urge the Senate to revisit these important issues during the lame duck session.

NOTE: The statement referred to H.R. 5136.

Remarks Following a Meeting With Former President William J. Clinton and an Exchange With Reporters
December 10, 2010

President Obama. I thought it was a slow day, so I'd——

Q. Slow news day, huh?

President Obama. ——bring the other guy in. Obviously, there's a big debate going on about taxes and about the need to grow the economy and to create jobs. And just about every day this week, I've been making an argument as to why the agreement that we've struck to provide billions of dollars in payroll tax cuts that can immediately help rejuvenate the economy, as well as tax cuts for middle class families, unemployment insurance for folks who desperately need it, credits for college, credits for— child tax credits, as well as a range of business investments credits are so important to make sure that we keep this recovery moving.

I just had a terrific meeting with the former President, President Bill Clinton. And we just happened to have this as a topic of conversation. And I thought, given the fact that he presided over as good an economy as we've seen in our lifetimes, that it might be useful for him to share some of his thoughts.

I'm going to let him speak very briefly. And then I've actually got to go over and do some— just one more Christmas party. So he may decide he wants to take some questions, but I want to make sure that you guys heard from him directly.

[*At this point, former President Clinton made remarks, concluding as follows.*]

Former President Clinton. So in my opinion, this is a good bill. And I hope that my fellow Democrats will support it. I thank the Republican leaders for agreeing to include things that were important to the President.

There is never a perfect bipartisan bill in the eyes of a partisan. And we all see this differently. But I really believe this will be a significant net plus for the country. I also think that in general a lot of people are heaving a sigh of relief that there's finally been some agreement on something.

But don't minimize the impact of the unemployment relief for working families, of the payroll tax relief, and of the continuation of the incentives to grow jobs, which will trigger more credit coming out of the banks.

Keep in mind, ultimately the long-term answer here is to get the $2 trillion which banks now have in cash reserves uncommitted to loans out there in the economy again, the $1.8 trillion in corporate treasuries not now being invested out there in the economy again. I think this is a net plus.

And you know how I feel. I think the people that benefit most should pay most. That's always been my position, not for class warfare reasons, for reasons of fairness and rebuilding the middle class in America. But we have the distribution of authority we have now in the Congress and what we're going to have in January, and I think this is a much, much better agreement than would be reached were we to wait until January. And I think it will have a much more positive impact on the economy.

So for whatever it's worth, that's what I think.

President Obama. That's worth a lot.

Former President Clinton. I would like to say one other thing on another subject, just to be recorded on record. They don't need my support on this because we have some good Republican support, including the first President Bush. I think this START agreement is very important to the future of our national security.

And it is not a radical agreement. Boris Yeltsin and I agreed in principle on this same reduction, and there was no way in the wide world he could get it through the Russian Duma that existed at the time in his second term. So we didn't proceed because it couldn't be ratified there. I'm not sure the Senate would have ratified it then, but I think they will now with enough encouragement.

But the cooperation that we will get from the Russians, and the signal that will be sent to the world on nonproliferation, when all these other things are going on which threaten to increase nuclear proliferation, is very important. One of the things you know is that when people fool with these weapons, they're expensive to build, expensive to maintain, and expensive to secure the material that goes into making the weapons.

This is something that is profoundly important. This ought to be way beyond party. They worked very hard. They've worked out, in my opinion, the details. And I hope it will be ratified.

[*Former President Clinton answered a question and then received an additional question as follows.*]

Cooperation With Congress

Q. And then as a follow-up, you mentioned the Republican Congress taking office in January. What was your advice to President Obama today about how to deal with the Congress from the opposition party?

Former President Clinton. I have a general rule, which is that whatever he asked me about my advice and whatever I say should become public only if he decides to make it public. He can say whatever he wants, but we——

Q. What do you think? [*Laughter*]

President Obama. Here's what I'll say, is I've been keeping the First Lady waiting for about half an hour, so I'm going to take off, but——

Former President Clinton. I don't want to make her mad. Please go.

President Obama. You're in good hands, and Gibbs will call last question.

[*President Obama left, and former President Clinton took more questions.*]

NOTE: The President spoke at 4:20 p.m. in the James S. Brady Press Briefing Room at the White House. The transcript released by the Office of the Press Secretary also included former President Clinton's remarks and exchange with reporters.

Statement on the Awarding of the Nobel Peace Prize to Liu Xiaobo
December 10, 2010

One year ago, I was humbled to receive the Nobel Peace Prize, an award that speaks to our highest aspirations and that has been claimed by giants of history and courageous advocates who have sacrificed for freedom and justice. Mr. Liu Xiaobo is far more deserving of this award than I was.

All of us have a responsibility to build a just peace that recognizes the inherent rights and dignity of human beings, a truth upheld within the Universal Declaration of Human Rights. In our own lives, our own countries, and in the world, the pursuit of a just peace remains incomplete, even as we strive for progress. This past year saw the release of Nobel laureate Aung San Suu Kyi, even as the Burmese people continue to be denied the democracy that they deserve. Nobel laureate Jose Ramos-Horta has continued his tireless work to build a free and prosperous East Timor, having made the transition from dissident to President. And this past year saw the retirement of Nobel laureate Desmond Tutu, whose own career demonstrates the universal power of freedom and justice to overcome extraordinary obstacles.

The rights of human beings are universal; they do not belong to one nation, region, or faith. America respects the unique culture and traditions of different countries. We respect China's extraordinary accomplishment in lifting millions out of poverty and believe that human rights include the dignity that comes with freedom from want. But Mr. Liu reminds us that human dignity also depends upon the advance of democracy, open society, and the rule of law. The values he espouses are universal, his struggle is peaceful, and he should be released as soon as possible. I regret that Mr. Liu and his wife were denied the opportunity to attend the ceremony that Michelle and I attended last year. Today, on what is also International Human Rights Day, we should redouble our efforts to advance universal values for all human beings.

NOTE: The statement referred to Liu Xia, wife of Nobel laureate Liu Xiaobo.

Statement on United States Special Representative for Afghanistan and Pakistan Richard C. Holbrooke
December 10, 2010

Earlier today I spoke to Richard Holbrooke's wife Kati and told her that Michelle and I are praying for Richard. Richard Holbrooke is a towering figure in American foreign policy, a critical member of my Afghanistan and Pakistan team, and a tireless public servant who has won the admiration of the American people and people around the world. I know that Secretary Clinton, Admiral Mullen, Tom Donilon, and other members of our team have been with him at George Washington hospital, and we continue to pray for his recovery and support his family in this difficult time.

NOTE: The statement referred to Kati Marton, wife of Ambassador Holbrooke; and National Security Adviser Thomas E. Donilon.

The President's Weekly Address
December 11, 2010

Right now there's a big debate taking place in Washington that'll affect how much you pay in taxes next year. If Congress doesn't act, tax rates will automatically go up for just about everyone in our country. Typical middle class families would end up paying an extra $3,000.

That's unacceptable to me. Not when we know that it's the middle class that was hit the hardest by the recession. And not when we know that taking this money out of the pockets of working people is exactly the wrong thing to do to get our economy growing faster. Economists tell us that this tax hike on working families would actually cost us well over a million jobs.

That's why I've been fighting so hard to cut middle class taxes. And that's why I brought both Democrats and Republicans to the table, to put together a compromise and work through our differences so we could get this done.

Now, the Republicans in Congress strongly favored permanent tax breaks for the wealthiest taxpayers and the wealthiest estates, most of which would go to millionaires and even billionaires. I didn't believe that these tax cuts were worth the cost. They'd add to our deficits without really boosting the economy.

I believed instead that the best way to help the economy and working families was to keep middle class tax rates low and cut taxes for working parents, college students, and small businesses. And I believed that with millions of people looking for jobs, it would be a terrible mistake to end unemployment insurance, not only for people who are out of work, but for our entire economy.

So we hammered out a deal that reflects ideas from both sides. It wasn't easy, and it's by no means perfect. And as with any compromise, everybody had to live with elements they didn't like. But this is a good deal for the American people. The vast majority of the tax cuts in this plan will help the middle class, including a new tax cut in payroll taxes that will save the average family about a thousand dollars. And as this plan is debated in Congress, what I want to make clear is the real difference it will make in people's lives.

It's going to make a difference for a single mom with two kids in Ohio working as a cashier. With this plan, she'd get a new payroll tax cut and a bigger child tax credit together worth more than $2,300.

It's going to make a difference for a couple in Florida earning about $50,000 and trying to put one of their two kids through college. They'd save more than $4,000 because of the middle class tax cuts, including a $2,500 tax credit to go toward college tuition.

And it's going to make an enormous difference for people looking for work. For many of these families, emergency unemployment insurance is the last line of defense between hardship and catastrophe. And I'd point out, if these folks stop spending money, it will also hurt businesses, which will hurt hiring, which will damage our economy.

So this plan is going to help millions of families to make ends meet because of tax cuts and unemployment insurance for people who've lost their jobs by no fault of their own. And we included tax relief for businesses too, making it easier for them to invest and expand. All told, this will not only directly help families and businesses. By putting more money in people's pockets and helping companies grow, we're going to see people being able to spend a little more, we're going to spur hiring, we're going to strengthen our entire economy.

Now, I recognize that many of my friends in my own party are uncomfortable with some of what's in this agreement, in particular the temporary tax cuts for the wealthy. I share their concerns. I don't like those tax cuts either. It's clear that over the long run, if we're serious about balancing the budget, we cannot continue to afford these tax breaks for the wealthiest taxpayers, especially when we know that cutting the deficit is going to demand sacrifice from everyone. That's the reality.

But at the same time, we can't allow the middle class in this country to be caught in the political crossfire of Washington. People want us to find solutions, not score points. And I will not allow middle class families to be treated like pawns on a chessboard.

The opportunity for families to send their kids to college hinges on this debate. The ability of parents to put food on the table while looking for a job depends on this debate. And our recovery will be strengthened or weakened based on the choice that now rests with Congress.

So I strongly urge members of both parties to pass this plan. And I'm confident that they will do the right thing, strengthening the middle class and our economic recovery.

Thanks.

NOTE: The address was recorded at approximately 1:40 p.m. on December 10 in the Map Room at the White House for broadcast on December 11. The transcript was made available by the Office of the Press Secretary on December 10, but was embargoed for release until 6 a.m. on December 11. The Office of the Press Secretary also released a Spanish language transcript of this address.

Remarks at "Christmas in Washington"
December 12, 2010

Thank you, everybody. Please, please have a seat. Merry Christmas and happy holidays, everybody. I want to thank our wonderful host, Ellen DeGeneres, for being here tonight. And of course, a special thanks to all of tonight's extraordinary performers: Mariah Carey, Andrea Bocelli, Miranda Cosgrove, Annie Lennox, Maxwell, Matthew Morrison, the Washington Youth Choir, the American Family Choir, and the United States Army Band Herald Trumpets. Please give them a huge round of applause.

What a wonderful show here at the National Building Museum. And we're grateful that the Children's National Medical Center is the beneficiary of tonight's performance. Day in and day out, the folks there are saving lives and bringing healing and comfort to our children.

This season reminds us that more than 2,000 years ago, a child born in a stable brought our world a redeeming gift of peace and salvation. It's a story with a message that speaks to us to this day—that we are called to love each other as we love ourselves, that we are our brother's keeper and our sister's keeper and our destinies are linked.

It's a message that guides my Christian faith, and it focuses us as we think about all those whose holidays may be a bit tougher this year. We pray for our troops serving far away from the warmth of family and homespun traditions. We remember those who are out of work or struggling just to get by. We hold in our hearts all those who've fallen on hard times this holiday season.

Because, while Christmas is a time to celebrate, a time to sing chorals and exchange gifts, it's also something more. It's a time to rediscover the meaning of words like "charity" and "compassion" and "good will," to do our part for our neighbors, to serve God through serving others. So from our family to yours, happy holidays, everybody. Merry Christmas, and God bless you all, and God bless the United States of America.

Thank you very much.

NOTE: The President spoke at approximately 6 p.m. at the National Building Museum. In his remarks, he referred to comedian and talk show host Ellen DeGeneres. The transcript was released by the Office of the Press Secretary on December 13.

Remarks on Signing the Healthy, Hunger-Free Kids Act of 2010
December 13, 2010

The President. Thank you, everybody. Please, please have a seat. Good morning, everybody.

Audience members. Good morning.

The President. Well, I want to thank all the students and faculty and staff here at Tubman Elementary for hosting us today at your beautiful school. And we want to thank Principal Harry Hughes for doing outstanding work here.

Thank you. Give them all a big round of applause.

We are thrilled to be here with all of you as I sign the healthy, hungry-free kids act, a bill that's vitally important to the health and welfare of our kids and to our country. But before I do this, I just want to acknowledge a few of the folks who are here, as well as a few who are not here but who played a hugely important role in getting this legislation passed.

On the stage, we have Madam Speaker, Nancy Pelosi; two outstanding Senators, Blanche Lincoln and Tom Harkin, who worked so hard to get this done; Members of the House of Representatives Miller, DeLauro, and Platts, who all worked so hard to make this happen—we're grateful to you; and three of my outstanding members of my Cabinet who worked tirelessly on this issue, Secretary of Agriculture Tom Vilsack—it happens to be his birthday today, happy birthday—Secretary Arne Duncan, our great Secretary of Education, and Secretary Kathleen Sebelius of Health and Human Services.

Not—they couldn't be here today, but they played a huge role in making this happen: Senator Harry Reid, the majority leader in the Senate; Senator Mike [Mitch]° McConnell, the ranking Republican who helped facilitate the smooth passage of this bill; Senator Chambliss, who was the lead Republican; Representatives Hoyer, Clyburn, and McCarthy all played important roles, and so we're very grateful to them. Give them a big round of applause.

It is worth noting that this bill passed with bipartisan support in both Houses of Congress. That hasn't happened as often as we'd like over the last couple of years, but I think it says something about our politics. It reminds us that no matter what people may hear about how divided things are in Washington, we can still come together and agree on issues that matter for our children's future and for our future as a nation. And that's really what today is all about.

At a very basic level, this act is about doing what's right for our children. Right now, across the country, too many kids don't have access to school meals. And often, the food that's being offered isn't as healthy or as nutritious as it should be. That's part of the reason why one in three children in America today are either overweight or obese.

And we're seeing this problem in every part of the country in kids from all different backgrounds and all walks of life. As a result, doctors are now starting to see conditions like high blood pressure, high cholesterol, and type 2 diabetes in children. These are things that they only used to see in adults. And this bill is about reversing that trend and giving our kids the healthy futures that they deserve.

And this bill is also about doing what's right for our country, because we feel the strains that treating obesity-related health conditions puts on our economy. We've seen the connection between what our kids eat and how well they perform in school. And we know that the countries that succeed in the 21st century will be the ones that have the best prepared, best educated workforce around.

So we need to make sure our kids have the energy and the capacity to go toe to toe with any of their peers, anywhere in the world. And we need to make sure that they're all reaching their potential. That's precisely what this bill, the healthy, hungry-free kids act, will accomplish.

This legislation will help 115,000 children gain access to school meal programs. And wherever we can, we're doing away with bureaucracy and redtape so that families don't have to fill out mountains of paperwork to get their kids the nutrition they need.

We're improving the quality of those meals by reimbursing schools an additional 6 cents per lunch to help them provide with healthier options, the first real increase, by the way, in over 30 years. Because when our kids walk into the lunchroom, we want to be sure that they're getting balanced, nutritious meals that they need to succeed in the classroom.

We're empowering parents by making information more available about the quality of school meals, helping families understand what their kids are eating during the day. And to support our schools' efforts to serve fresh fruits and vegetables, we're connecting them with local farmers.

We're also improving food safety in schools and boosting the quality of commodities like cheese that schools get from the Department of Agriculture and use in their lunch and breakfast programs.

° White House correction.

It's also important to note that while this bill is fully paid for, it won't add a dime to the deficit, some of the funding comes from rolling back a temporary increase in food stamp benefits—or SNAP as it's now called—starting in the fall of 2013. I know a number of Members of Congress have expressed concerns about this offset being included in the bill, and I'm committed to working with them to restore these funds in the future.

We know that every day across this country, parents are working as hard as they can to make healthy choices for their kids. Schools are doing everything possible to provide the nutritious food they need to thrive. Communities are coming together to help our young people lead healthier lives right from the beginning. And it's time that we made that work a little bit easier. So these folks are fulfilling their responsibilities to our kids. This legislation helps ensure that we fulfill our responsibilities as well.

Shortly after signing the first law establishing school lunches, Harry Truman said that "nothing is more important in our national life than the welfare of our children, and proper nourishment comes first in attaining this welfare."

So today I'm very proud to sign this bill that continues that legacy. Not only am I very proud of the bill, but had I not been able to get this passed, I would be sleeping on the couch. [*Laughter*]

So now I am very proud to introduce somebody who's done so much to shine a light on these critical issues related to childhood nutrition and obesity and exercise: America's First Lady, my First Lady, Michelle Obama.

[*At this point, the First Lady made brief remarks.*]

The President. Let's go sign this bill.
The First Lady. Let's go do it.

NOTE: The President spoke at 10:33 a.m. at Harriet Tubman Elementary School. S. 3307, approved December 13, was assigned Public Law No. 111–296. The transcript released by the Office of the Press Secretary also included the remarks of the First Lady.

Remarks Honoring the 2010 National Basketball Association Champion Los Angeles Lakers
December 13, 2010

The President. Hello, everybody!
Audience members. Hello!
The President. Well, it is great to be here at THEARC with the Boys and Girls Club of Greater Washington.

Give it up for the world champion Los Angeles Lakers. I want to congratulate everybody on the team, everybody who works for the organization, and all the fans who cheer them on year after year.

We've also got, by the way, one of California's great Members of Congress in the house: Grace Napolitano is here. Hello, Grace.

Now, I have to say that there is a longstanding tradition of welcoming championship sports teams to the White House. But here's the thing: These guys have been there so often; they were just there last year because they won the title. And Kobe and Derek have been there so many times now, they could lead tours themselves. The same is true for Coach Jackson.

So I thought we'd change things up a little bit. We teamed up with NBA Cares to come here to THEARC and spend a little time with the unbelievable young people who are here, as well as the terrific staff. And I was just walking around watching these players work with students assembling care packages for our wounded warriors, putting together some toiletry kits for the homeless here in Washington, DC, and trying to keep up with the kids on the "Big Brain Academy" challenge, which I didn't even try because it was moving way too fast for me.

But that's the beauty of service, anybody can do it. The Lakers have a proud tradition of performing community service in the L.A. community, and I'm glad that they took the time to help us during the holiday season here in

Washington, DC. We celebrate that spirit of service off the court, because it's very hard to do what these guys do on the court, but everybody can serve off the court.

Now, on the court, there aren't too many folks who can do what the Los Angeles Lakers do. This year, they won their 2d title in a row and their 16th championship overall. That's one behind the Boston Celtics for the most of all time. The Boston Celtics, of course, they beat in this year's finals.

I want to congratulate Coach Phil Jackson on earning his 11th NBA championship ring. It was his fifth championship with the Lakers, which I should point out, is still one behind the six he won with the Chicago Bulls.

Kobe Bryant. Not for long.

The President. Kobe said, not for long, though. [*Laughter*] We are still grateful for you, Coach, in Chicago. And it has been a long drought since Phil left Chicago, although I have to say they witnessed in person on Friday that my Bulls are showing some signs of life. [*Laughter*]

I want to congratulate Kobe Bryant, the NBA Finals MVP for the second year in a row. Kobe was there when we organized a little pickup game for my 49th birthday. Pau Gasol and some other NBA players participated; Derek was there. Kobe was sidelined because he had just gotten some treatment on his knee. I was not yet sidelined with my busted lip. But nobody was taking it easy on me because Pau was on my team, so I kept on just passing to him. And now I got to see how everybody else on the Lakers gets so many open looks, if you've got Pau Gasol in the middle.

So I just want to congratulate all the L.A. Lakers for being one of the outstanding sports franchises in our country and in our history. I wish all of you guys great luck for the rest of the season.

But especially, I just want to thank you for being so generous with your time with these kids. These young people here are working hard. They're doing well in school. They were really helping me out as I was going through that line packing those care boxes, making sure I didn't screw up. We are incredibly proud of them.

But every once in a while they need a little encouragement and they need to know that no dream is beyond their reach. And so when they see people like the Los Angeles Lakers who are willing to spend time with them, that sends a message to them that they're special. And you guys can't give a better gift than that during the holiday season.

So thank you very much. We're really proud of you. Congratulations.

NOTE: The President spoke at 3:09 p.m. at the Town Hall Education Arts Recreation Campus. In his remarks, he referred to Kobe Bryant, guard, Derek Fisher, guard, and Pau Gasol, forward-center, Los Angeles Lakers.

Remarks on Congressional Action on Legislation To Extend Tax Cuts and Unemployment Insurance Benefits
December 13, 2010

Hello, everybody. I am pleased to announce, at this hour the United States Senate is moving forward on a package of tax cuts that has strong bipartisan support. This proves that both parties can, in fact, work together to grow our economy and look out for the American people.

Once the Senate completes action on this bill, it will move over to the House of Representative for its consideration. I've been talking with several Members of that body. I recognize that folks on both sides of the political spectrum are unhappy with certain parts of the package, and I understand those concerns. I share some of them. But that's the nature of compromise: sacrificing something that each of us cares about to move forward on what matters to all of us. Right now that's growing the economy and creating jobs. And nearly every economist agrees that that is what this package will do.

Taken as a whole, the bill that the Senate will allow to proceed does some very good things for America's economy and the American people.

First and foremost, it is a substantial victory for middle class families across the country who would no longer have to worry about a massive tax hike come January 1. It would offer hope to millions of Americans who have lost their jobs through no fault of their own by making sure that they won't suddenly find themselves out in the cold without the unemployment insurance benefits that they were counting on. And it would offer real tax relief for Americans who are paying for college, parents raising their children, and business owners looking to invest in their businesses and propel our economy forward.

So I urge the House of Representatives to act quickly on this important matter. Because if there's one thing we can agree on, it's the urgent work of protecting middle class families, removing uncertainty for America's businesses, and giving our economy a boost as we head into the new year.

Thanks very much, everybody.

NOTE: The President spoke at 5:31 p.m. in the James S. Brady Press Briefing Room at the White House. In his remarks, he referred to H.R. 4853. The Office of the Press Secretary also released a Spanish language transcript of these remarks.

Remarks at a Reception at the Department of State
December 13, 2010

Thank you. I have to say, just first of all, looking out at the audience, I'm reminded of, Hillary, how hard we've been working because I recognize everybody. [*Laughter*] I've seen all of you here. I've seen you in your home countries. And we are grateful to you.

First of all, thanks not only to Hillary for her gracious introduction, but I think there's a consensus building that this may be one of the best Secretaries of State we've ever had in this country's history—[*inaudible*]. One of my better decisions. [*Laughter*] It is a bipartisan view, by the way. [*Laughter*]. That doesn't happen very often.

Before I say anything else, I want to echo what I know Hillary addressed earlier, just say a few words about our friend and partner, Richard Holbrooke. We're honored to be joined by Richard's wife Kati and their family, David, Anthony, Lizzie, Christopher. I just had a chance to take a few moments with them before we came out to talk about their husband, dad, friend.

Richard Holbrooke has been serving this Nation with distinction for nearly 50 years, from a young Foreign Service officer in Vietnam to the architect of the accords that ended the slaughter in the Balkans, to advancing our regional efforts as our Special Representative to Afghanistan and Pakistan, and countless crises and hot

spots in between. He is simply one of the giants of American foreign policy.

And as anyone who has ever worked with him knows, or had the clear disadvantage of negotiating across the table from him, Richard is relentless. He never stops, he never quits, because he's always believed that if we stay focused, if we act on our mutual interests, that progress is possible. Wars can end; peace can be forged.

This is the conviction that animates his work in Afghanistan and Pakistan and that of his SRAP team, many of whom join us tonight. Where are they? There they are back there. Richard recruited them. He mentored them. And I want you to know that in our meetings he consistently gave you guys unbelievable credit. He was so proud—and is so proud—of the work that you do. And I thank you for all the progress that we're making in that region, which is so vital to our national security.

So tonight we're all praying for Richard's recovery. To Kati and the family, our thoughts are with you. And I know that everyone here joins me when I say that America is more secure and the world is a safer place because of the work of Ambassador Richard Holbrooke. So Michelle and I, to the entire family, just know we are thinking and praying for you and for Richard every single day. And he is a tough son of a gun, so we are confident that, as hard as this is, that he is going to be putting up a tremendous fight.

Now, part of the reason that Hillary Clinton wanted Richard as part of her team is because she too is relentless. She too is tough. She too does not quit. She recently pulled off what one journalist called "a Central Asian hat trick." She went to Kazakhstan, Kyrgyzstan, and Uzbekistan, and then she threw in, as a bonus, Bahrain. [*Laughter*] And because of the time differences, she was able to accomplish this all in one day. [*Laughter*]

Despite the jetlag, she has not lost her sense of humor. She recently cautioned foreign publics against watching too much American TV, because, she said, you'd think that we Americans spend all our time "wrestling and wearing bikinis." [*Laughter*]

So thank you, Secretary Clinton, for your leadership, for your sense of humor, for your incredible dedication to our national security, more broadly, your incredible dedication to a world that's more peaceful and secure and provides opportunity for all.

Now, I wanted to be here tonight, I'm grateful for the invitation, despite the fact that, as I said, I've met most of you. I've had a chance to work with many of you. We recently hosted a reception over at the White House, and we—I've had the opportunity to receive some of you, the newest Ambassadors to the United States, in the Oval Office. But I wanted to be here today for two reasons.

First, I want to thank our extraordinary State Department employees for the tireless work that you do. You are the backbone of American foreign policy, especially those of you who are serving far away from home on—during the holidays.

Day in, day out, you strengthen our alliances. You forge new partnerships. You prevent conflicts and the spread of deadly weapons. You promote global prosperity and global health. You stand up for human rights, and you stand up for universal values. In other words, you show the world the very best of America. And on behalf of the American people, I want to say thank you. You are doing an extraordinary job.

Now, the other reason I wanted to be here was to say how much the United States values the partnerships and friendships of the nations that are represented here. As you know, my administration has pursued a new era of engagement around the world, an engagement that's grounded in mutual interest and mutual respect. It depends on trust. It depends on candor. That's the essence of our diplomacy and the essence of our partnerships.

And our commitment to diplomacy, to building partnerships of mutual interest and mutual respect, is going to remain a fundamental cornerstone of our foreign policy. It will not change, because not only is it right for America, but it's right for the world.

And let me say that our engagement includes building partnerships between our peoples. That's what Michelle and I worked to do during our recent visit to India, for example, which occurred during Diwali. As many of you've seen, during a Diwali celebration with some of the schoolchildren, Michelle joined in the dancing. So did I. The difference was, she was good. [*Laughter*] The headlines were a little bruising to my ego. [*Laughter*] They said, "President Obama Visits India; Michelle Obama Rocks India." [*Laughter*]

It was just one small example, but it spoke to a larger truth, one that's at the heart of this holiday season. When we reach out to one another, when we see beyond the differences that supposedly divide us, when we come together—even if it's for some dance or some song or a shared story, a shared memory—we're reminded that fundamentally we are the same. There's a commonality between us. There is an essential human experience that we all share.

And it gets lost in politics and it gets lost in rivalries. And there are barriers of ethnicity and religion and language. And yet scratch the surface, take the time to get to know somebody else from a different culture, a different race, a different ethnicity, and it turns out that there are hopes and dreams that bind us together.

And our jobs, both as political leaders and as diplomats, is to make sure that those bonds are strengthened and broadened; that they penetrate into our respective nations; that each of us is able to stand in the other person's shoes and see through the other person's eyes; that people are no longer simply "the other," or simply foreigners, but are in fact our brothers and sisters.

And if we're insistent enough about the capacity to understand each other, then that translates concretely into some war that doesn't happen, some village that isn't destroyed, some child that gets something to eat, some disaster that is averted. That's what all of you do. That's your essential task. And you do it very, very well.

And so to Secretary Clinton, to the State Department, thank you for doing so much extraordinary work over the past year, much of it to little notice and little acclaim. I know what you do, and I know how important you are.

And to the diplomats and dignitaries from our friends and partners around the world, let me say to you that we are absolutely confident that in the new year we will have more opportunities to work together and that if we stay focused on our task, then the world is going to be a better place for our children and our grandchildren.

So merry Christmas and happy holidays, everybody. God bless you.

NOTE: The President spoke at 6:04 p.m. In his remarks, he referred to David and Anthony Holbrooke, sons, and Elizabeth and Christopher Jennings, stepchildren, of Ambassador Richard C. Holbrooke.

Statement on the Death of United States Special Representative for Afghanistan and Pakistan Richard C. Holbrooke
December 13, 2010

Michelle and I are deeply saddened by the passing of Richard Holbrooke, a true giant of American foreign policy, who has made America stronger, safer, and more respected. He was a truly unique figure who will be remembered for his tireless diplomacy, love of country, and pursuit of peace.

For nearly 50 years, Richard served the country he loved with honor and distinction. He worked as a young Foreign Service officer during the Vietnam war and then supported the Paris peace talks which ended that war. As a young Assistant Secretary of State for East Asian and Pacific Affairs, he helped normalize relations with China. As U.S. Ambassador to Germany, he helped Europe emerge from a long cold war and encouraged NATO to welcome new members.

As Assistant Secretary of State for European and Canadian Affairs, he was the tireless chief architect of the Dayton Accords that ended the war in Bosnia 15 years ago this week, saving countless lives. As Ambassador to the United Nations, Richard helped break a political impasse and strengthen our Nation's relationship with the U.N. and elevated the cause of AIDS

and Africa on the international agenda. And throughout his life, as a child of refugees, he devoted himself to the plight of people displaced around the world.

When I became President, I was grateful that Richard agreed to serve as Special Representative for Afghanistan and Pakistan. The progress that we have made in Afghanistan and Pakistan is due in no small measure to Richard's relentless focus on America's national interest and pursuit of peace and security. He understood, in his life and his work, that our interests encompassed the values that we hold so dear. And as usual, amidst his extraordinary duties, he also mentored young people who will serve our country for decades to come. One of his friends and admirers once said that "if you're not on the team and you're in his way, God help you." Like so many Presidents before me, I am grateful that Richard Holbrooke was on my team, as are the American people.

Earlier this evening at the State Department, I met with Richard's wife Kati and their family, David, Anthony, Lizzie, Christopher, and Sarah, and I spoke to Kati after Richard's passing. I expressed to them the gratitude of the

American people for his lifetime of service. They are in our thoughts and prayers tonight.

Tonight, there are millions of people around the world whose lives have been saved and enriched by his work. As I said earlier this evening, the United States is safer and the world is more secure because of the half century of patriotic service of Ambassador Richard Holbrooke.

NOTE: The statement referred to Kati Marton, wife, David and Anthony Holbrooke, sons, Elizabeth and Christopher Jennings, stepchildren, and Sarah Holbrooke, daughter-in-law, of Ambassador Holbrooke.

Remarks on Legislation To Extend Tax Cuts and Unemployment Insurance Benefits
December 15, 2010

Good morning, everybody. Today the Senate is poised to pass tax cuts and unemployment insurance, putting the House of Representatives in the position to send me this critical economic package so I can sign it into law.

I am absolutely convinced that this tax cut plan, while not perfect, will help grow our economy and create jobs in the private sector. It'll help lift up middle class families, who will no longer need to worry about a New Year's Day tax hike. It will offer emergency relief to help tide folks over until they find another job. And it includes tax cuts to make college more affordable, help parents provide for their children, and help businesses—large and small—expand and hire.

I know there are different aspects of this plan to which Members of Congress on both sides of the aisle object. That's the nature of compromise. But we worked hard to negotiate an agreement that's a win for middle class families and a win for our economy, and we can't afford to let it fall victim to either delay or defeat. So I urge Members of Congress to pass these tax cuts as swiftly as possible.

Getting that done is an essential ingredient in spurring economic growth over the short run. And spurring economic growth is what I'll talk about later this morning when I meet with some of America's top business leaders. That includes Jim McNerney of Boeing, who also heads up my Export Council, and several members of my Economic Recovery Advisory Board. This is one of many discussions we'll be having in the months ahead to find new ways to spur hiring,

put Americans back to work, and move our economy forward.

As I said when I was running for President and as I've said since, I believe that the primary engine of America's economic success is not government. It's the ingenuity of America's entrepreneurs. It's the dynamism of our markets. And for me, the most important question about an economic idea is not whether it's good shortterm politics or meets somebody's litmus test, it's whether it will help spur businesses, jobs, and growth.

That's why I've set a goal of doubling U.S. exports in the next 5 years to create more jobs selling more products abroad. That's why I'm so pleased that earlier this month, after intensive negotiations, we finalized a trade agreement with our ally South Korea that will boost the annual exports of American goods by $11 billion, a deal that, all told, will support at least 70,000 American jobs. It's an agreement that won support from business and labor because it's good for the economy.

This morning I hope to elicit ideas from these business leaders that will help us not only climb out of recession, but seize the promise of this moment: ideas about tax reform, ideas about a balanced approach to regulation that will promote rather than undermine growth, ideas that will help encourage businesses to invest in America and American jobs at a time when they're holding nearly $2 trillion on their books. I want to discuss our shared mission of building a strong economy for the long run.

We know some of what we need to do to outcompete other countries in the 21st century.

We need to offer our children the best education in the world. We need to spur innovation and new industries like clean energy that will create the jobs of tomorrow. We need to upgrade America's crumbling infrastructure, its roads and bridges, update high-speed rail and high-speed Internet to connect every community. And we need to redouble our commitment to fiscal discipline and address our long-term deficit challenges.

We know the path that will lead to economic success. The only question is whether we will take it, whether we have the political will to do the work. I'm committed to taking that path. I know America's business leaders are as well. And I look forward to talking to them this morning and working with them in the months and years to come to make sure that we're adopting the best ideas for growing our economy and making the 21st century another great American century.

Thank you very much, everybody.

NOTE: The President spoke at 9:23 a.m. in Room 430 of the Dwight D. Eisenhower Executive Office Building.

Statement on the International Criminal Court's Announcement Concerning the 2007–2008 Postelection Violence in Kenya
December 15, 2010

Today, as the International Criminal Court announces the names of six suspects alleged to have participated in the postelection violence that threatened to tear Kenya apart 3 years ago, I encourage all Kenyans take a moment to reflect on the tremendous progress their country has made since those dark days. Together, you have been working to reconcile your communities, to reform your institutions to better serve the public good, and to put your country on a path to lasting peace and prosperity. Kenya is turning a page in its history, moving away from impunity and divisionism toward an era of accountability and equal opportunity. The path ahead is not easy, but I believe that the Kenyan people have the courage and resolve to reject those who would drag the country back into the past and rob Kenyans of the singular opportunity that is before them to realize the country's vast potential.

In pursuit of these goals, I urge all of Kenya's leaders, and the people whom they serve, to co-operate fully with the ICC investigation and remain focused on implementation of the reform agenda and the future of your nation. Those found responsible will be held accountable for their crimes as individuals. No community should be singled out for shame or held collectively responsible. Let the accused carry their own burdens, and let us keep in mind that under the ICC process they are innocent until proven guilty. As you move forward, Kenyans can count on the United States as a friend and partner.

NOTE: The statement referred to Deputy Prime Minister and Minister for Finance Uhuru Kenyatta, Secretary to the Cabinet Francis K. Muthaura, Minister of Higher Education, Science, and Technology William Samoei Ruto, Minister for Industrialization Henry Kiprono Kosgey, and former Commissioner of Police Mohamed Hussein Ali of Kenya; and Joshua arap Sang, radio presenter, Kass FM.

Statement on the Terrorist Attack in Chabahar, Iran
December 15, 2010

I strongly condemn the outrageous terrorist attack on a mosque in Chabahar, Iran. The murder of innocent civilians in their place of worship during Ashura is a despicable offense, and those who carried it out must be held accountable. This is a disgraceful and cowardly act.

This and other similar acts of terrorism recognize no religious, political, or national boundaries.

The United States condemns all acts of terrorism wherever they occur.

The United States stands with the families and loved ones of those killed and injured and with the Iranian people in the face of this injustice.

Together, the people of the world must condemn and oppose all forms of terrorism and support the universal right of human beings to live free from fear and senseless violence.

Statement on Senate Passage of Legislation To Extend Tax Cuts and Unemployment Insurance Benefits
December 15, 2010

Today the Senate passed with strong bipartisan support a bill that's a win for American families, American businesses, and our economic recovery. This vote brings us one step closer to ensuring that middle class families across the country won't have to worry about a massive tax hike at the end of the year. It would offer hope to millions of Americans who are out of work, that they won't suddenly find themselves without the unemployment insurance they need to make ends meet as they fight to find a job. And it would offer additional tax relief to families across the country and encourage businesses to grow and hire.

I know that not every Member of Congress likes every piece of this bill, and it includes some provisions that I oppose. But as a whole, this package will grow our economy, create jobs, and help middle class families across the country. As this bill moves to the House of Representatives, I hope that members from both parties can come together in a spirit of common purpose to protect American families and our economy as a whole by passing this essential economic package.

NOTE: The statement referred to H.R. 4853. The Office of the Press Secretary also released a Spanish language version of this statement.

Statement on House of Representatives Passage of Legislation Repealing the United States Military's "Don't Ask, Don't Tell" Policy
December 15, 2010

I applaud the House for passing, with bipartisan support, the "Don't Ask, Don't Tell Repeal Act of 2010." Legislative repeal is supported by the Secretary of Defense and the chairman of the Joint Chiefs of Staff. The process contained in this legislation allows for a smooth and responsible repeal of "don't ask, don't tell" in a way that maintains good order and discipline in our military ranks. Indeed, all of the service chiefs have said that when this law is changed, they will implement an orderly transition effectively and efficiently. As the comprehensive study by the Department of Defense clearly shows, we can move to a new policy in a responsible manner that ensures our military strength and our national security.

I particularly want to thank Speaker Nancy Pelosi, Majority Leader Steny Hoyer, and Congressman Patrick Murphy for their leadership on this issue. I have consistently called for the repeal of this law. Moving forward with the repeal is not only the right thing to do, it will also give our military the clarity and certainty it deserves. We must ensure that Americans who are willing to risk their lives for their country are treated fairly and equally by their country.

NOTE: The statement referred to H.R. 2965. The Office of the Press Secretary also released a Spanish language version of this statement.

Letter to Congressional Leaders on the Global Deployments of United States Combat-Equipped Armed Forces
December 15, 2010

Dear Madam Speaker: (Dear Mr. President:)

I am providing this supplemental consolidated report, prepared by my Administration and consistent with the War Powers Resolution (Public Law 93–148), as part of my efforts to keep the Congress informed about deployments of U.S. Armed Forces equipped for combat.

MILITARY OPERATIONS AGAINST AL-QA'IDA, THE TALIBAN, AND ASSOCIATED FORCES AND IN SUPPORT OF RELATED U.S. COUNTERTERRORISM OBJECTIVES

Since October 7, 2001, the United States has conducted combat operations in Afghanistan against al-Qa'ida terrorists and their Taliban supporters. In support of these and other overseas operations, the United States has deployed combat-equipped forces to a number of locations in the U.S. Central, Pacific, European, Southern, and Africa Command areas of operation. Previous such operations and deployments have been reported, consistent with Public Law 107–40 and the War Powers Resolution, and operations and deployments remain ongoing. These operations, which the United States has carried out with the assistance of numerous international partners, have been successful in seriously degrading al-Qa'ida's capabilities and brought an end to the Taliban's leadership of Afghanistan.

United States Armed Forces are actively pursuing and engaging remaining al-Qa'ida and Taliban fighters in Afghanistan. The total number of U.S. forces in Afghanistan is approximately 97,500, of which more than 81,500 are assigned to the International Security Assistance Force (ISAF) in Afghanistan. The U.N. Security Council most recently reaffirmed its authorization of ISAF for a 12-month period from October 13, 2010, in U.N. Security Council Resolution 1943 (October 13, 2010). The mission of ISAF, under NATO command and in partnership with the Government of the Islamic Republic of Afghanistan, is to conduct population-centric counterinsurgency operations, enable expanded and effective capabilities of the Afghan National Security Forces, support improved governance and development in order to protect the Afghan people, and promote sustainable security. Presently, 48 partner nations contribute to ISAF, including all 28 NATO Allies. These combat operations are gradually pushing insurgents to the edges of secured population areas in a number of important regions, largely resulting from the increase in U.S. forces over the past year. U.S. and ISAF forces will continue to execute the strategy of clear-shape-hold-build, and transition, until conditions on the ground allow for the full transition of the lead in operations to the Afghan National Security Forces.

The United States continues to detain several hundred al-Qa'ida, Taliban, and associated force fighters who are believed to pose a continuing threat to the United States and its interests. The combat-equipped forces deployed since January 2002 to Naval Base, Guantanamo Bay, Cuba, continue to conduct secure detention operations for the approximately 170 detainees at Guantanamo Bay under Public Law 107–40 and consistent with principles of the law of war.

In furtherance of U.S. efforts against members of al-Qa'ida, the Taliban, and associated forces who pose a continuing and imminent threat to the United States, its friends, its allies, and U.S. forces abroad, the United States continues to work with partners around the globe, with a particular focus on the U.S. Central Command's area of operations. In this context, the United States has deployed U.S. combat-equipped forces to assist in enhancing the counterterrorism capabilities of our friends and allies, including special operations and other forces for sensitive operations in various locations around the world. The United States is committed to thwarting the efforts of al-Qa'ida and its associated forces to carry out future acts of international terrorism, and we have continued to work with our counterterrorism partners to disrupt and degrade the capabilities of al-Qa'ida and its associated forces. As necessary, in response to the terrorist threat, I will direct additional measures against al-Qa'ida, the Taliban, and associated forces to protect U.S. citizens and interests. It is not possible to know at this time the precise scope or the duration of the deployments of U.S. Armed Forces necessary to counter this terrorist threat to the United States. A classified annex to this report provides further information.

MILITARY OPERATIONS IN IRAQ

Since the expiration of the authorization and mandate for the Multinational Force in Iraq in U.N. Security Council Resolution 1790 on December 31, 2008, U.S. forces have continued operations to support Iraq in its efforts to maintain security and stability in Iraq pursuant to the bilateral Agreement Between the United States of America and the Republic of Iraq on the Withdrawal of United States Forces from Iraq and the Organization of Their Activities during Their Temporary Presence in Iraq (Security Agreement), which entered into force on January 1, 2009. These contributions have included, but have not been limited to, assisting in building the capability of the Iraqi security forces, supporting the development of Iraq's political institutions, improving local governance, enhancing ministerial capacity, and providing critical humanitarian and reconstruction assistance to the Iraqis. The United States continues its responsible drawdown, in accordance with commitments in the Security Agreement, to withdraw U.S. forces from Iraq by December 31, 2011. The number of U.S. forces in Iraq at this time is approximately 48,400.

MARITIME INTERCEPTION OPERATIONS

As noted in previous reports, the United States continues to conduct maritime interception operations on the high seas in the areas of responsibility of each of the geographic combatant commands. These maritime operations are aimed at stopping the movement, arming, and financing of certain international terrorist groups.

U.S./NATO OPERATIONS IN KOSOVO

The U.N. Security Council authorized Member States to establish a NATO-led Kosovo Force (KFOR) in Resolution 1244 on June 10, 1999. The original mission of KFOR was to monitor, verify, and, when necessary, enforce compliance with the Military Technical Agreement between NATO and the then Federal Republic of Yugoslavia (now Serbia), while maintaining a safe and secure environment. Today, KFOR deters renewed hostilities and, with local authorities and international institutions, contributes to the maintenance of a safe and secure environment.

Currently, 24 NATO Allies contribute to KFOR. Eight non-NATO countries also participate by providing military and other support personnel. The United States contribution to KFOR is approximately 808 U.S. military personnel, or approximately 9 percent of the total strength of approximately 8,721 personnel. The United States forces participating in KFOR have been assigned to the eastern region of Kosovo, but also have operated in other areas of the country based on mission requirements. The principal military task of U.S. KFOR forces is to help maintain a safe and secure environment and freedom of movement.

I have directed the participation of U.S. Armed Forces in all of these operations pursuant to my constitutional and statutory authority as Commander in Chief (including the authority to carry out Public Law 107–40 and other statutes) and as Chief Executive, as well as my statutory and constitutional authority, to conduct the foreign relations of the United States. Officials of my Administration and I communicate regularly with the leadership and other Members of Congress with regard to these deployments, and we will continue to do so.

Sincerely,

BARACK OBAMA

NOTE: Identical letters were sent to Nancy Pelosi, Speaker of the House of Representatives, and Daniel K. Inouye, President pro tempore of the Senate.

Remarks at the American Indian and Alaska Native Tribal Nations Conference
December 16, 2010

Thank you very much. Everybody please be seated. Thank you. Thank you, Fawn, for that wonderful introduction. Thanks to all of you. It is wonderful to be with you here today.

I see a lot of friends, a lot of familiar faces in the house. I want to thank all the tribal leaders who have traveled here for this conference. And I also want to recognize all the wonderful Members of Congress who are here, as well as members of my Cabinet, including Secretary Salazar, who is doing terrific work here at Interior on behalf of the first Americans and on behalf of all Americans. So thank you very much, everybody.

Yesterday I had the chance to meet with several tribal leaders at the White House, continuing a conversation that began long before I was President. And while I'm glad to have the opportunity to speak with you this morning, I'm also very eager to see the results of today's meeting. I want to hear more from you about how we can strengthen the relationship between our governments, whether in education or health care or in fighting crime or in creating jobs.

And that's why we're here today. That's a promise I've made to you. I remember, more than 2 years ago, in Montana, I visited the Crow Nation, one of the many times I met with tribal leaders on the campaign trail. You may know that on that trip, I became an adopted Crow Indian. My Crow name is "One Who Helps People Throughout the Land." And my wife, when I told her about this, she said, "You should be named 'One Who Isn't Picking Up His Shoes and His Socks.'" [*Laughter*]

Now—but I like the first name better. And I want you to know that I'm working very hard to live up to that name.

What I said then was that as President, I would make sure that you had a voice in the White House. I said that so long as I held this office, never again would Native Americans be forgotten or ignored. And over the past 2 years, my administration, working hand in hand with many of you, has strived to keep that promise. And you've had strong partners in Kim Teehee,

my senior adviser for Native American issues, and Jodi Gillette, in our intergovernmental affairs office. You can give them a big round of applause. They do outstanding work.

Last year, we held the largest gathering of tribal leaders in our history. And at that conference—you remember, most of you were there—I ordered every Cabinet agency to promote more consultation with the tribal nations. Because I don't believe that the solutions to any of our problems can be dictated solely from Washington. Real change depends on all of us doing our part.

So over the past year my administration has worked hard to strengthen the relationship between our nations. And together, we have developed a comprehensive strategy to help meet the challenges facing Native American communities.

Our strategy begins with the number-one concern for all Americans right now, and that's improving the economy and creating jobs. We've heard time and again from tribal leaders that one of the keys to unlocking economic growth on reservations is investments in roads and high-speed rail and high-speed Internet and the infrastructure that will better connect your communities to the broader economy. That's essential for drawing capital and creating jobs on tribal lands. So to help spur the economy, we've boosted investment in roads throughout the Bureau of Indian Affairs and the Indian Reservation Road Program, and we've offered new loans to reach reservations with broadband.

And as part of our plan to revive the economy, we've also put billions of dollars into pressing needs like renovating schools. We're devoting resources to job training, especially for young people in Indian Country, who too often have felt like they don't have a chance to succeed. And we're working with you to increase the size of tribal homelands in order to help you develop your economies.

I also want to note that I support legislation to make clear, in the wake of a recent Supreme Court decision, that the Secretary of Interior can take land into trust for all federally recognized tribes. That's something that I discussed yesterday with tribal leaders.

We're also breaking down bureaucratic barriers that have prevented tribal nations from developing clean energy like wind and solar power. It's essential not just to your prosperity, but to the prosperity of our whole country. And I've proposed increasing lending to tribal businesses by supporting community financial institutions so they can finance more loans. It is essential in order to help businesses expand and hire in areas where it can be hard to find credit.

Another important part of our strategy is health care. We know that Native Americans die of illnesses like diabetes, pneumonia, flu, even tuberculosis, at far higher rates than the rest of the population. Make no mistake: These disparities represent an ongoing tragedy. They're cutting lives short, causing untold pain and hardship for Native American families. And closing these gaps is not just a question of policy; it's a question of our values, it's a test of who we are as a nation.

Now, last year at this conference, tribal leaders talked about the need to improve the health care available to Native Americans and to make quality insurance affordable to all Americans. And just a few months later, I signed health reform legislation into law, which permanently authorizes the Indian Health Care Improvement Act—permanently. It's going to make it possible for Indian tribes and tribal organizations to purchase health care for their employees, while making affordable coverage available to everybody, including those who use the Indian Health Service—that's most American Indians and native—Alaska Natives. So it's going to make a huge difference.

Of course, there are few steps we can take that will make more of a difference for the future of your communities than improving education on tribal lands. We've got to improve the education we provide to our children. That's the cornerstone on which all of our progress will be built. We know that Native Americans are far more likely to drop out of high school and far less likely to go to college. That not only damages the prospects for tribal economies, it's a

heartbreaking waste of human potential. We cannot afford to squander the promise of our young people. Your communities can't afford it, and our country can't afford it. And we are going to start doing something about it.

We're rebuilding schools on tribal lands, while helping to ensure that tribes play a bigger role in determining what their children learn. We're working to empower parents with more and better options for schools for their kids, as well as with support programs that actually work with Indian parents to give them a real voice in improving education in your communities.

We're also working to improve the programs available to students at tribal colleges. Students who study at tribal colleges are much less likely to leave college without a degree, and the vast majority end up in careers serving their tribal nation. And these schools are not only helping to educate Native Americans, they're also helping to preserve rich but often endangered languages and traditions. I'd also like to point out, last year I signed historic reforms that are increasing student aid and making college loans more affordable. That's especially important to Native Americans struggling to pay for a college degree.

Now, all these efforts—improving health care, education, the economy—ultimately, these efforts will not succeed unless all of our communities are safe places to grow up and attend school and open businesses, and where people are not living under the constant threat of violence and crime. And that threat remains real, as crime rates in Indian Country are anywhere from twice to 20 times the national average. That's a sobering statistic—represents a cloud over the future of your communities.

So the Justice Department, under the leadership of Eric Holder, is working with you to reform the way justice is done on Indian reservations. And I was proud to sign the Tribal Law and Order Act into law, which is going to help tribes combat drug and alcohol abuse, to have more access to criminal databases, and to gain greater authority to prosecute and punish criminals in Indian Country. That's important.

We've also resolved a number of longstanding disputes about the ways that our Government has treated, or in some cases mistreated, folks in Indian Country, even in recent years. We've settled cases where there were allegations of discrimination against Native American farmers and ranchers by the Department of Agriculture. And after a 14-year battle over the accounting of tribal resources in the *Cobell* case, we reached a bipartisan agreement, which was part of a law I signed just a week ago. We're very proud of that, and I want to thank all the legislators who helped make that happen.

This will put more land in the hands of tribes to manage or otherwise benefit their members. This law also includes money to settle lawsuits over water rights for seven tribes in Arizona, Montana, and New Mexico, and it creates a scholarship fund so more Native Americans can afford to go to college.

These cases serve as a reminder of the importance of not glossing over the past or ignoring the past, even as we work together to forge a brighter future. That's why, last year, I signed a resolution, passed by both parties in Congress, finally recognizing the sad and painful chapters in our shared history, a history too often marred by broken promises and grave injustices against the first Americans. It's a resolution I fully supported, recognizing that no statement can undo the damage that was done; what it can do is help reaffirm the principles that should guide our future. It's only by heeding the lessons of our history that we can move forward.

And as you know, in April, we announced that we were reviewing our position on the U.N. Declaration on the Rights of Indigenous Peoples. And today I can announce that the United States is lending its support to this declaration.

The aspirations it affirms, including the respect for the institutions and rich cultures of Native peoples, are one we must always seek to fulfill. And we're releasing a more detailed statement about U.S. support for the declaration and our ongoing work in Indian Country. But I want to be clear: What matters far more than words, what matters far more than any resolution or declaration, are actions to match those words. And that's what this conference is about—[*applause*]—that's what this conference is about. That's the standard I expect my administration to be held to.

So we're making progress. We're moving forward. And what I hope is that we are seeing a turning point in the relationship between our nations. The truth is, for a long time, Native Americans were implicitly told that they had a choice to make. By virtue of the longstanding failure to tackle wrenching problems in Indian Country, it seemed as though you had to either abandon your heritage or accept a lesser lot in life; that there was no way to be a successful part of America and a proud Native American.

But we know this is a false choice. To accept it is to believe that we can't and won't do better. And I don't accept that. I know there is not a single person in this room who accepts that either. We know that ultimately this is not just a matter of legislation, not just a matter of policy. It's a matter of whether we're going to live up to our basic values. It's a matter of upholding an ideal that has always defined who we are as Americans: *E pluribus unum*—out of many, one.

That's why we're here. That's what we're called to do. And I'm confident that if we keep up our efforts, that if we continue to work together, that we will live up to this simple motto and we will achieve a brighter future for the first Americans and for all Americans.

So thank you very much. God bless you. Thank you.

NOTE: The President spoke at 9:39 a.m. at the Department of the Interior. In his remarks, he referred to Fawn R. Sharp, president, Quinault Indian Nation; White House Senior Policy Adviser for Native American Affairs Kimberly K. Teehee; and Associate Director of the White House Office of Public Engagement and Deputy Associate Director of the Office of Intergovernmental Affairs Jodi Archambault Gillette. The Office of the Press Secretary also released a Spanish language transcript of these remarks.

Remarks on United States Military and Diplomatic Strategies for Afghanistan and Pakistan
December 16, 2010

Good morning, everybody. When I announced our new strategy for Afghanistan and Pakistan last December, I directed my national security team to regularly assess our efforts and to review our progress after 1 year. That's what we've done consistently over the course of the past 12 months, in weekly updates from the field, in monthly meetings with my national security team, and in my frequent consultations with our Afghan, Pakistani, and coalition partners. And that's what we've done as part of our annual review, which is now complete.

I want to thank Secretary Clinton and Secretary Gates for their leadership. Since Joint Chief of Staff Chairman Admiral Mullen is in Afghanistan, I'm pleased that we're joined by Vice Chairman General Cartwright.

Our efforts also reflect the dedication of Ambassador Richard Holbrooke, whose memory we honor and whose work we'll continue. Indeed, the tributes to Richard that have poured in from around the globe speak to both the enormous impact of his life and to the broad international commitment to our shared efforts in this critical region.

I have spoken with President Karzai of Afghanistan as well as President Zardari of Pakistan and discussed our findings and the way forward together. Today I want to update the American people on our review, our assessment of where we stand and areas where we need to do better. I want to be clear: This continues to be a very difficult endeavor. But I can report that thanks to the extraordinary service of our troops and civilians on the ground, we are on track to achieve our goals.

It's important to remember why we remain in Afghanistan. It was Afghanistan where Al Qaida plotted the 9/11 attacks that murdered 3,000 innocent people. It is the tribal regions along the Afghan-Pakistan border from which terrorists have launched more attacks against our homeland and our allies. And if an even wider insurgency were to engulf Afghanistan, that would give Al Qaida even more space to plan these attacks.

And that's why, from the start, I've been very clear about our core goal. It's not to defeat every last threat to the security of Afghanistan, because ultimately, it is Afghans who must secure their country. And it's not nation-building, because it is Afghans who must build their nation. Rather, we are focused on disrupting, dismantling, and defeating Al Qaida in Afghanistan and Pakistan and preventing its capacity to threaten America and our allies in the future.

In pursuit of our core goal, we are seeing significant progress. Today, Al Qaida's senior leadership in the border region of Afghanistan and Pakistan is under more pressure than at any point since they fled Afghanistan 9 years ago. Senior leaders have been killed. It's harder for them to recruit, it's harder for them to travel, it's harder for them to train, it's harder for them to plot and launch attacks. In short, Al Qaida is hunkered down. It will take time to ultimately defeat Al Qaida, and it remains a ruthless and resilient enemy bent on attacking our country. But make no mistake: We are going to remain relentless in disrupting and dismantling that terrorist organization.

In Afghanistan, we remain focused on the three areas of our strategy: our military effort to break the Taliban's momentum and train Afghan forces so they can take the lead, our civilian effort to promote effective governance and development, and regional cooperation, especially with Pakistan, because our strategy has to succeed on both sides of the border.

Indeed, for the first time in years, we've put in place the strategy and the resources that our efforts in Afghanistan demand. And because we've ended our combat mission in Iraq and brought home nearly 100,000 of our troops from Iraq, we're in a better position to give our forces in Afghanistan the support and equipment they need to achieve their missions. And our drawdown in Iraq also means that today there are tens of thousands fewer Americans deployed in harm's way than when I took office.

With those additional forces in Afghanistan, we are making considerable gains toward our military objectives. The additional military and civilian personnel that I ordered in Afghanistan are now in place, along with additional forces from our coalition, which has grown to 49 nations. Along with our Afghan partners, we've gone on the offensive, targeting the Taliban and its leaders and pushing them out of their strongholds.

As I said when I visited our troops in Afghanistan earlier this month, progress comes slowly and at a very high price in the lives of our men and women in uniform. In many places, the gains we've made are still fragile and reversible. But there is no question we are clearing more areas from Taliban control and more Afghans are reclaiming their communities.

To ensure Afghans can take responsibility, we continue to focus on training. Targets for the growth of Afghan security forces are being met. And because of the contributions of additional trainers from our coalition partners, I'm confident we will continue to meet our goals.

I would add that much of this progress—the speed with which our troops deployed this year, the increase in recruits—in recruiting and training of Afghan forces, and the additional troops and trainers from other nations—much of this is the result of us having sent a clear signal that we will begin the transition of responsibility to Afghans and start reducing American forces next July.

This sense of urgency also helped galvanize the coalition around the goals that we agreed to at the recent NATO summit in Lisbon that we are moving toward a new phase in Afghanistan, a transition to full Afghan lead for security that will begin early next year and will conclude in 2014, even as NATO maintains a long-term commitment to training and advising Afghan forces. Now, our review confirms, however, that for these security gains to be sustained over time, there is an urgent need for political and economic progress in Afghanistan.

Over the past year, we've dramatically increased our civilian presence, with more diplomats and development experts working alongside our troops, risking their lives and partnering with Afghans. Going forward, there must be a continued focus on the delivery of basic services, as well as transparency and accountability. We will also fully support an Afghan political process that includes reconciliation with those Taliban who break ties with Al Qaida, renounce violence and accept the Afghan Constitution. And we will forge a new strategic partnership with Afghanistan next year, so that we make it clear that the United States is committed to the long-term security and development of the Afghan people.

Finally, we will continue to focus on our relationship with Pakistan. Increasingly, the Pakistani Government recognizes that terrorist networks in its border regions are a threat to all our countries, especially Pakistan. We've welcomed major Pakistani offensives in the tribal regions. We will continue to help strengthen Pakistanis' capacity to root out terrorists. Nevertheless, progress has not come fast enough. So we will continue to insist to Pakistani leaders that terrorist safe havens within their borders must be dealt with.

At the same time, we need to support the economic and political development that is critical to Pakistan's future. As part of our strategic dialogue with Pakistan, we will work to deepen trust and cooperation. We'll speed up our investment in civilian institutions and projects that improve the lives of Pakistanis. We'll intensify our efforts to encourage closer cooperation between Pakistan and Afghanistan.

And next year, I look forward to an exchange of visits, including my visit to Pakistan, because the United States is committed to an enduring partnership that helps deliver improved security, development, and justice for the Pakistani people.

Again, none of these challenges that I've outlined will be easy. There are more difficult days ahead. But as a nation, we can draw strength from the service of our fellow Americans.

On my recent visit to Afghanistan, I visited a medical unit and pinned Purple Hearts on some of our wounded warriors. I met with a platoon that had just lost six of their teammates. Despite the tough fight, despite all their sacrifice, they continue to stand up for our security and for our values that we hold so dear.

We're going to have to continue to stand up. We'll continue to give our brave troops and civilians the strategy and resources they need to succeed. We will never waver from our goal of disrupting, dismantling, and ultimately defeating Al Qaida. We will forge enduring partnerships with people who are committed to progress and to peace. And we will continue to do everything in our power to ensure the security and the safety of the American people.

So with that, Vice President Biden and myself will depart, and I'm going to turn it over to Secretaries Clinton, Gates, as well as Vice Chairman Cartwright, and they will be able to answer your questions and give you a more detailed briefing.

Thank you very much.

NOTE: The President spoke at 11:50 a.m. in the James S. Brady Press Briefing Room at the White House.

Remarks and a Question-and-Answer Session at Long Branch Elementary School in Arlington, Virginia
December 17, 2010

[*Prior to his remarks, the President read aloud to the assembled students from two books.*]

The President. Now, let me just say one more thing, and then maybe we can take a picture together. One of the things about Christmas obviously is getting presents and having stockings full and spending time with your family and eating good stuff. But part of the Christmas spirit is also making sure that we're kind to each other and we're thinking about people who aren't as lucky as we are.

And so I hope that all of you, even as you're having a lot of fun during the holidays, whether it's Christmas or Hanukkah, I want to make sure that all of you are also thinking about how can you guys be nicer to each other and think about people who have less than you do, because not everybody is as lucky as we are. There are a lot of kids out there who they may not be able to get a lot of presents for Christmas because their parents don't have a lot of money.

There are a lot of parents right now who are maybe away from their families. Some of them are in our military and they're fighting overseas, and so they can't be home for Christmas or the holidays. So I hope you guys think about them too, all right? And I want you all to remember that the spirit of Christmas is making sure that—not just that you're getting something from somebody, but that you're also giving back to other people. Does that make sense?

Students. Yes.

The President. Who wants to take a picture with me?

[*At this point, the students took a picture with the President.*]

The President. Okay, so—now, is today the last day of school before the holidays?

Students. No!

The President. The teachers are all, like, "No." [*Laughter*] When do you guys get out?

Students. On the 23d.

The President. Not until Wednesday, huh? All right. Well, listen, I hope you guys have so much fun during the holidays. And I'm so proud of you. You guys are all working hard in school and learning all kinds of stuff. It's really exciting to see you guys doing so well.

So—and I want to thank all the teachers and the faculty, the staff who are here, because I know that you guys put your heart and soul into doing this great work.

You guys have a couple questions for me before I go? I thought so.

What's your question?

President's Daughters

Q. I don't have a question, but my name is Malia.

The President. Your name is Malia too? Give me a high five for that. That's a great name. That's a great name.

All right, let's see. What's your name?

White House Holiday Decorations

Q. Sebastian.

The President. Hey, Sebastian.

Q. I don't have a question, but I do know Mrs. Obama gave us these ornaments so we could make them for your Christmas tree.

The President. Excellent. Well, thank you so much. We have all these volunteers come out to decorate the whole White House, and it's pretty spectacular. But one of those ornaments might have been yours. Way to go. Appreciate it.

What's your name?

Signing Autographs

Q. Can I have an autograph?

The President. Here's the thing. If I sign autographs, then I have to sign them for everybody.

Students. Yay! [*Laughter*]

The President. I'd be here a really long time. But here's what I did, though, is I signed my book. So it's in the library. And so that's for the whole school. All right?

How about you?

President's Book, "Of Thee I Sing: A Letter to My Daughters"

Q. How did you get the—since you're so busy, how did you get to write that book since you're so busy?

The President. You know what happened was, I actually wrote it a couple of years ago, before I was sworn in as President, because I had written a couple books for adults, and then they said, well, would you be interested in writing a children's book and then you can give the money to charity? And I said I would, so I wrote the book, but then it takes a really long time be-cause the art is so nice—the artists, they—it's like each page is like a painting. So it takes them a long time to make it. So that's why it's just coming out now. Yes.

All right. What else?

Letters to the President

Q. [*Inaudible*]

The President. I get 10,000 letters every day. That's a lot. That's a lot. Now, I want to be honest, I don't read every single piece of mail I get, because then obviously—well, I just couldn't get through all of it. So I have a whole staff that just reads my mail, and then they give me letters that they think are really especially terrific, and I read those.

All right.

[*The students pointed to a student off camera.*]

The President. Oh, it's Lawrence.

What were you going to say?

Living in the White House

Q. How much fun is it just going around—running around the White House all day?

The President. You know, the truth is, I run around a lot in the White House, but most of the time I'm working. So it's not like I'm just running around having fun. But sometimes it's fun. Because the White House—how many people have visited the White House? So it's a pretty—it's a beautiful building, and there's a big yard in the back called the South Lawn. So a lot of times I walk Bo at night, and that's fun. Sometimes, I run around with Bo, although I have to—sometimes I have to scoop up his poop.

Students. Eww!

The President. Because I don't want to just leave it in the lawn. So if you guys have a dog, you got to walk your dog too and clean up after him a little bit.

All right, guys, I've got to get going. Merry Christmas, everybody! Happy holidays!

Students. Merry Christmas!

The President. Thank you. Thank you.

[*There was a break while the President moved to another classroom.*]

The President. Well, hello, everybody!

Students. Hello!

The President. So I just wanted to come by and wish everybody a wonderful holiday, merry Christmas, happy New Year, happy Hanukkah, happy, happy all, everything.

And now, I thought this was the last day of school. I just found out you guys are actually in until Wednesday.

But I did just want to come by to say how proud I am of all of you. This is just a wonderful school. The staff, the teachers do such a great job. And you guys, the students, are doing a great job. And I just left a children's book that I wrote called "Of Thee I Sing," so I left that as a Christmas present. I had a chance to read "The Night Before Christmas." So—but I suspect everybody here has read it.

Students. We saw you.

The President. Oh, you were watching. Well, that's amazing. Well, then all I want to do is come in here and say, guys, I'm proud of you. I hope you guys have a wonderful holiday. And keep working hard, keep paying attention, because your teachers know more than you do. At least for now. But if they do a really good job, then at some point you'll know more than them. All right?

But we couldn't be prouder. So from Michelle, Malia, Sasha, and from Bo, we want to wish you guys a wonderful holiday. All right? Bye-bye, everybody. Thanks.

NOTE: The President spoke at 11:14 a.m.

Remarks on Signing the Tax Relief, Unemployment Insurance Reauthorization, and Job Creation Act of 2010
December 17, 2010

Thank you, everybody. Please have a seat.

Good afternoon, everybody. Before I get started, I just want to acknowledge some of the extraordinary people who did some extraordinary work in a very short period of time. And I'm going to start with somebody who has been a champion for the middle class, but has also been just an extraordinary partner on every important initiative in this administration, my friend Joe Biden, the Vice President.

I want to acknowledge and thank Senator Mitch McConnell and the rest of the Republican leadership in the Senate, Dave Camp, Republican over in the House, for their willingness, as Joe indicated, to do what was right for the country, even though it caused occasional political discomfort. I especially want to thank the folks who are here—Dick Durbin, Max Baucus, Danny Davis, Allyson Schwartz, Rob Andrews—part of a broader team that worked very diligently both in the House and the Senate on the Democratic side to make this happen.

And we've got a bunch of other Members of Congress who are here, as well as activists and economists and business leaders and people who generally recognize that at this critical juncture, we've got to think about what's best to grow the economy and what's best to put people back to work.

We are here with some good news for the American people this holiday season. By a wide bipartisan margin, both Houses of Congress have now passed a package of tax relief that will protect the middle class, that will grow our economy, and will create jobs for the American people. Not only do I want to thank all the leaders here today, but I want to thank mayors and Governors from across the country who couldn't be here today and all who worked together to get this done.

First and foremost, the legislation I'm about to sign is a substantial victory for middle class families across the country. They're the ones hit hardest by the recession we've endured. They're the ones who need relief right now. And that's what is at the heart of this bill.

This bipartisan effort was prompted by the fact that tax rates for every American were poised to automatically increase on January 1. If that had come to pass, the average middle class family would have had to pay an extra $3,000 in taxes next year. That wouldn't have just been a blow to them, it would have been a blow to our economy, just as we're climbing out of a devastating recession.

I refused to let that happen. And because we acted, it's not going to. In fact, not only will middle class Americans avoid a tax increase, but tens of millions of Americans will start the new year off right by opening their first paycheck to see that it's actually larger than the one they get right now. Over the course of 2011, 155 million workers will receive tax relief from the new payroll tax cut included in this bill, about $1,000 for the average family.

This is real money that's going to make a real difference in people's lives. And I would not have signed this bill if it didn't include other extensions of relief that were also set to expire, relief that's going to help families cover the bills, parents raise their children, students pay for college, and business owners to take the reins of the recovery and propel this economy forward.

As soon as I sign this legislation, 2 million Americans looking for work who lost their jobs through no fault of their own can know with certainty that they won't lose their emergency unemployment insurance at the end of this month. Over the past few weeks, 600,000 Americans have been cut off from that lifeline. But with my signature, States can move quickly to reinstate their benefits. And we expect that in almost all States, they'll get them in time for Christmas.

Eight million college students who otherwise would have faced a tuition hike as soon as next semester will instead continue to have access to a $2,500 tax credit to afford their studies. Twelve million families with 24 million children will benefit from extensions of the earned-income tax credit and the child tax credit. And when combined with the payroll tax cut, 2 million American families who otherwise would have lived in poverty next year will instead be lifted out of it. And millions of entrepreneurs who have been waiting to invest in their businesses will receive new tax incentives to help them expand, buy

new equipment, or make upgrades, freeing up other money to hire new workers.

Putting more money in the pockets of families most likely to spend it, helping businesses invest and grow, that's how we're going to spark demand, spur hiring, and strengthen our economy in the new year.

Now, candidly speaking, there are some elements of this legislation that I don't like. There are some elements that members of my party don't like. There are some elements that Republicans here today don't like. That's the nature of compromise: yielding on something each of us cares about to move forward on what all of us care about. And right now what all of us care about is growing the American economy and creating jobs for the American people. Taken as a whole, that's what this package of tax relief is going to do. It's a good deal for the American people. This is progress, and that's what they sent us here to achieve.

There will be moments, I am certain, over the next couple of years in which the holiday spirit won't be as abundant as it is today. [*Laughter*] Moreover, we've got to make some difficult choices ahead when it comes to tackling the deficit. In some ways, this was easier than some of the tougher choices we're going to have to make next year. There will be times when we won't agree, and we'll have to work through those times together. But the fact is, I don't believe that either party has cornered the market on good ideas. And I want to draw on the best thinking from both sides.

So wherever we can, whenever we can, it makes sense for our country's success and our children's future to work with people in both parties who are willing to come to the table for the hard work of moving our economy and our country forward. What happened with this economic package was a good example of that. A bipartisan group made up of Senators Baucus and Kyl and Representatives Van Hollen and Camp sat down with Secretary Geithner, who is here today, and Director Jack Lew of the Office of Management and Budget to begin negotiations in good faith. Leaders like Nancy Pelosi, John Boehner, Harry Reid, and Mitch, other

Members who are here together worked to bring this bill across the finish line.

And the final product proves when we can put aside the partisanship and the political games, when we can put aside what's good for some of us in favor of what's good for all of us, we can get a lot done. And if we can keep doing it, if we can keep that spirit, I'm hopeful that we won't just reinvigorate this economy and restore the American Dream for all who work for it. I'm also hopeful that we might refresh the American people's faith in the capability of their leaders to govern in challenging times, belief in the capacity of their institutions in this town to deliver in a rapidly changing world, and most of all, confidence that our best days as a nation are still ahead of us.

The President's Weekly Address
December 18, 2010

This week, Congress passed—and I signed into law—an essential economic package that will help grow our economy, spur businesses, and jump-start job creation.

Instead of a New Year's Day tax hike on the vast majority of Americans, 2 million Americans who've lost their jobs through no fault of their own will now know with certainty that they won't lose their emergency unemployment insurance at the end of the month. Eight million college students who'd otherwise face a tuition hike next semester will continue having access to the American opportunity tax credit. Twelve million families with 24 million children will benefit from extensions of the earned-income tax credit and child tax credit. And millions of entrepreneurs who've been waiting to invest in their businesses will receive new tax incentives to help them expand, buy new equipment, or make upgrades, freeing up money to hire new workers.

This package, which is so important for our economy at this pivotal time, was the product of hard negotiations. And like any negotiations, there was give and take on both sides. But I'm heartened by our ability to come together to do what's best for middle class fam-

So to all of you who worked so diligently on this issue, thank you very much. To those on my staff who were working night and day and on the Senate and House staffs in both parties who were working so hard, we're very grateful to you. And with that, let me sign this bill to make sure that people are seeing a bigger paycheck come January.

NOTE: The President spoke at 4 p.m. in the South Court Auditorium of the Dwight D. Eisenhower Executive Office Building. H.R. 4853, approved December 17, was assigned Public Law No. 111–312. The transcript released by the Office of the Press Secretary also included the remarks of Vice President Joe Biden.

ilies across this country and for our economy as a whole.

Before going away for the holiday break, I'm hopeful we can also come together on another urgent national priority, and that is the new START Treaty that will reduce the world's nuclear arsenals and make America more secure. Twenty-five years ago, the Soviet Union and United States each had about 25,000 nuclear weapons. In the decades since, that number has been reduced by over 70 percent, and we've had onsite inspections of Russian nuclear facilities. That progress would not have been possible without strategic arms control treaties.

During the past year, however, our old treaty with Russia expired, and without a new one, we won't be able to verify Russia's nuclear arsenal, which would undercut President Reagan's call to trust, but verify, when it comes to nuclear weapons.

Without a new treaty, we'll risk turning back the progress we've made in our relationship with Russia, which is essential to enforce strong sanctions against Iran, secure vulnerable nuclear materials from terrorists, and resupply our troops in Afghanistan. And we'll risk undermining American leadership not only on nuclear proliferation, but a host of other challenges around the world.

Ratifying a treaty like START isn't about winning a victory for an administration or a political party, it's about the safety and security of the United States of America. That's why this treaty is supported by both Presidents Bill Clinton and George H.W. Bush. That's why it's supported by every living Republican Secretary of State, by our NATO allies, and the leadership of the United States military. Indeed, the vice chairman of the Joint Chiefs of Staff, General Hoss Cartwright, said this week that the military needs this treaty, and they need it badly. And that's why every President since Ronald Reagan has pursued a treaty like START, and every one that has been reviewed by the Senate has passed with strong bipartisan support.

We have taken the time to get this right. The START Treaty has now been under review by the Senate for over 7 months. It's gone through 18 hearings. Nearly 1,000 questions have been asked and answered. Several Republican Senators have come out in support of ratification. Meanwhile, further delay comes at a cost. Every minute we drag our feet is a minute that we have no inspectors on the ground at those Russian nuclear sites.

It's time to get this done. It's time to show the same spirit of common purpose on our security that we showed this week on our economy. It's time to remember the old saying that politics stops at the water's edge. That saying was coined by a Republican Senator, Arthur Vandenberg, who partnered with a Democratic President, Harry Truman, to pass landmark national security measures at the dawn of the cold war. Today, over 60 years later, when we're threatened not only by nuclear weapons, but an array of other dangers, that's a principle we must continue to uphold.

Thanks, and have a nice weekend.

NOTE: The address was recorded at approximately 3:15 p.m. on December 17 in the Diplomatic Reception Room at the White House for broadcast on December 18. The transcript was made available by the Office of the Press Secretary on December 17, but was embargoed for release until 6 a.m. on December 18.

Statement on Senate Action on Legislation Providing Citizenship Opportunities for Alien Minors
December 18, 2010

In an incredibly disappointing vote today, a minority of Senators prevented the Senate from doing what most Americans understand is best for the country. As I said last week, when the House passed the "DREAM Act," it is not only the right thing to do for talented young people who seek to serve a country they know as their own, it is the right thing for the United States of America. Our Nation is enriched by their talents and would benefit from the success of their efforts. The "DREAM Act" is important to our economic competitiveness, military readiness, and law enforcement efforts. And as the nonpartisan Congressional Budget Office reported, the "DREAM Act" would cut the deficit by $2.2 billion over the next 10 years. There was simply no reason not to pass this important legislation.

It is disappointing that common sense did not prevail today. But my administration will not give up on the "DREAM Act" or on the important business of fixing our broken immigration system. The American people deserve a serious debate on immigration, and it's time to take the polarizing rhetoric off our national stage.

I thank Senators Durbin, Reid, and Menendez for their tireless efforts. Moving forward, my administration will continue to do everything we can to fix our Nation's broken immigration system so that we can provide lasting and dedicated resources for our border security, while at the same time, restoring responsibility and accountability to the system at every level.

NOTE: The Office of the Press Secretary also released a Spanish language version of this statement.

Statement on Senate Passage of Legislation Repealing the United States Military's "Don't Ask, Don't Tell" Policy
December 18, 2010

Today the Senate has taken an historic step toward ending a policy that undermines our national security while violating the very ideals that our brave men and women in uniform risk their lives to defend. By ending "don't ask, don't tell," no longer will our Nation be denied the service of thousands of patriotic Americans forced to leave the military, despite years of exemplary performance, because they happen to be gay. And no longer will many thousands more be asked to live a lie in order to serve the country they love.

As Commander in Chief, I am also absolutely convinced that making this change will only underscore the professionalism of our troops as the best led and best trained fighting force the world has ever known. And I join the Secretary of Defense and the chairman of the Joint Chiefs of Staff, as well as the overwhelming majority of servicemembers asked by the Pentagon, in knowing that we can responsibly transition to a new policy, while ensuring our military strength and readiness.

I want to thank Majority Leader Reid, Senators Lieberman and Collins, and the countless others who have worked so hard to get this done. It is time to close this chapter in our history. It is time to recognize that sacrifice, valor, and integrity are no more defined by sexual orientation than they are by race or gender, religion or creed. It is time to allow gay and lesbian Americans to serve their country openly. I urge the Senate to send this bill to my desk so that I can sign it into law.

NOTE: The statement referred to H.R. 2965.

Letter to Senate Leadership on the Strategic Arms Reduction Treaty and Missile Defense
December 18, 2010

Dear Senator:

As the Senate considers the New START Treaty, I want to share with you my views on the issue of missile defense, which has been the subject of much debate in the Senate's review of the treaty.

Pursuant to the National Missile Defense Act of 1999 (Public Law 106–38), it has long been the policy of the United States to deploy as soon as is technologically possible an effective National Missile Defense system capable of defending the territory of the United States against limited ballistic missile attack, whether accidental, unauthorized, or deliberate. Thirty ground-based interceptors based at Fort Greely, Alaska, and Vandenberg Air Force Base, California, are now defending the nation. All United States missile defense programs—including all phases of the European Phased Adaptive Approach to missile defense (EPAA) and programs to defend United States deployed forces, allies, and partners against regional threats—are consistent with this policy.

The New START Treaty places no limitations on the development or deployment of our missile defense programs. As the NATO Summit meeting in Lisbon last month underscored, we are proceeding apace with a missile defense system in Europe designed to provide full coverage for NATO members on the continent, as well as deployed U.S. forces, against the growing threat posed by the proliferation of ballistic missiles. The final phase of the system will also augment our current defenses against intercontinental ballistic missiles from Iran targeted against the United States.

All NATO allies agreed in Lisbon that the growing threat of missile proliferation, and our Article 5 commitment of collective defense, requires that the Alliance develop a territorial missile defense capability. The Alliance further agreed that the EPAA, which I announced in September 2009, will be a crucial contribution to this capability. Starting in 2011, we will begin deploying the first phase of the EPAA, to protect large parts of southern Europe from short- and medium-range ballistic missile threats. In subsequent phases, we will deploy longer-range and more effective land-based Standard Missile–3 (SM–3) interceptors in Romania and Poland to protect Europe against medium- and intermediate-range ballistic missiles. In the final phase, planned for the end of the decade, further upgrades of the SM–3 interceptor will provide an ascent-phase intercept capability to augment our defense of NATO European territory, as well as that of the United States, against future threats of ICBMs launched from Iran.

The Lisbon decisions represent an historic achievement, making clear that all NATO allies believe we need an effective territorial missile defense to defend against the threats we face now and in the future. The EPAA represents the right response. At Lisbon, the Alliance also invited the Russian Federation to cooperate on missile defense, which could lead to adding Russian capabilities to those deployed by NATO to enhance our common security against common threats. The Lisbon Summit thus demonstrated that the Alliance's missile defenses can be strengthened by improving NATO-Russian relations.

This comes even as we have made clear that the system we intend to pursue with Russia will not be a joint system, and it will not in any way limit United States' or NATO's missile defense capabilities. Effective cooperation with Russia could enhance the overall effectiveness and efficiency of our combined territorial missile defenses, and at the same time provide Russia with greater security. Irrespective of how cooperation with Russia develops, the Alliance alone bears responsibility for defending NATO's members, consistent with our Treaty obligations for collective defense. The EPAA and NATO's territorial missile defense capability will allow us to do that.

In signing the New START Treaty, the Russian Federation issued a statement that ex-

pressed its view that the extraordinary events referred to in Article XIV of the Treaty include a "build-up in the missile defense capabilities of the United States of America such that it would give rise to a threat to the strategic nuclear potential of the Russian Federation." Article XIV(3), as you know, gives each Party the right to withdraw from the Treaty if it believes its supreme interests are jeopardized.

The United States did not and does not agree with the Russian statement. We believe that the continued development and deployment of U.S. missile defense systems, including qualitative and quantitative improvements to such systems, do not and will not threaten the strategic balance with the Russian Federation, and have provided policy and technical explanations to Russia on why we believe that to be the case. Although the United States cannot circumscribe Russia's sovereign rights under Article XIV(3), we believe that the continued improvement and deployment of U.S. missile defense systems do not constitute a basis for questioning the effectiveness and viability of the New START Treaty, and therefore would not give rise to circumstances justifying Russia's withdrawal from the Treaty.

Regardless of Russia's actions in this regard, as long as I am President, and as long as the Congress provides the necessary funding, the United States will continue to develop and deploy effective missile defenses to protect the United States, our deployed forces, and our allies and partners. My Administration plans to deploy all four phases of the EPAA. While advances of technology or future changes in the threat could modify the details or timing of the later phases of the EPAA—one reason this approach is called "adaptive"—I will take every action available to me to support the deployment of all four phases.

Sincerely,

BARACK OBAMA

NOTE: Identical letters were sent to Sens. Harry M. Reid and A. Mitchell McConnell.

Statement on the Formation of Iraq's Government
December 21, 2010

Today's vote in the Council of Representatives is a significant moment in Iraq's history and a major step forward in advancing national unity. I congratulate Iraq's political leaders, the Members of the Council of Representatives, and the Iraqi people on the formation of a new Government of national partnership.

Yet again, the Iraqi people and their elected representatives have demonstrated their commitment to working through a democratic process to resolve their differences and shape Iraq's future. Their decision to form an inclusive partnership Government is a clear rejection of the efforts by extremists to spur sectarian division.

Iraq faces important challenges, but the Iraqi people can also seize a future of opportunity. The United States will continue to strengthen our long-term partnership with Iraq's people and leaders as they build a prosperous and peaceful nation that is fully integrated into the region and international community.

Statement on the Federal Communications Commission's Vote on Internet Neutrality
December 21, 2010

Today's decision will help preserve the free and open nature of the Internet while encouraging innovation, protecting consumer choice, and defending free speech. Throughout this process, parties on all sides of this issue—from consumer groups to technology companies to broadband providers—came together to make their voices heard. This decision is an important component of our overall strategy to advance American innovation, economic growth, and job creation.

As a candidate for President, I pledged to preserve the freedom and openness that have allowed the Internet to become a transformative and powerful platform for speech and expression. That's a pledge I'll continue to keep as President. As technology and the market continue to evolve at a rapid pace, my administration will remain vigilant and see to it that innovation is allowed to flourish, that consumers are protected from abuse, and that the democratic spirit of the Internet remains intact.

I congratulate the FCC, its chairman, Julius Genachowski, and Congressman Henry Waxman for their work achieving this important goal today.

Remarks on Signing the Don't Ask, Don't Tell Repeal Act of 2010
December 22, 2010

The President. Thank you, thank you, thank you. You know, I am just overwhelmed. This is a very good day. And I want to thank all of you, especially the people on this stage, but each and every one of you who have been working so hard on this, members of my staff who worked so hard on this. I couldn't be prouder.

Sixty-six years ago, in the dense, snow-covered forests of Western Europe, Allied Forces were beating back a massive assault in what would become known as the Battle of the Bulge. And in the final days of fighting, a regiment in the 80th Division of Patton's Third Army came under fire. The men were traveling along a narrow trail. They were exposed, and they were vulnerable. Hundreds of soldiers were cut down by the enemy.

And during the firefight, a private named Lloyd Corwin tumbled 40 feet down the deep side of a ravine. And dazed and trapped, he was as good as dead. But one soldier, a friend, turned back. And with shells landing around him, amid smoke and chaos and the screams of wounded men, this soldier, this friend, scaled down the icy slope, risking his own life to bring Private Corwin to safer ground.

For the rest of his years, Lloyd credited this soldier, this friend, named Andy Lee, with saving his life, knowing he would never have made it out alone. It was a full four decades after the war, when the two friends reunited in their golden years, that Lloyd learned that the man who saved his life, his friend Andy, was gay. He had no idea, and he didn't much care. Lloyd knew what mattered. He knew what had kept him alive, what made it possible for him to come home and start a family and live the rest of his life. It was his friend.

And Lloyd's son is with us today. And he knew that valor and sacrifice are no more limited by sexual orientation than they are by race or by gender or by religion or by creed; that what made it possible for him to survive the battlefields of Europe is the reason that we are here today. That's the reason we are here today.

So this morning I am proud to sign a law that will bring an end to "don't ask, don't tell." It is a law—[*applause*]—this law I'm about to sign will strengthen our national security and uphold the ideals that our fighting men and women risk their lives to defend.

No longer will our country be denied the service of thousands of patriotic Americans who were forced to leave the military—regardless of their skills, no matter their bravery or their zeal, no matter their years of exemplary performance—because they happen to be gay. No longer will tens of thousands of Americans in uniform be asked to live a lie or look over their shoulder in order to serve the country that they love.

As Admiral Mike Mullen has said: "Our people sacrifice a lot for their country, including their lives. None of them should have to sacrifice their integrity as well." That's why I believe this is the right thing to do for our military. That's why I believe it is the right thing to do, period.

Now, many fought long and hard to reach this day. I want to thank the Democrats and Republicans who put conviction ahead of politics to get this done together. I want to recognize Nancy Pelosi, Steny Hoyer, and Harry Reid.

Today we're marking an historic milestone, but also the culmination of two of the most productive years in the history of Congress, in no small part because of their leadership. And so we are very grateful to them.

I want to thank Joe Lieberman and Susan Collins. And I think Carl Levin's still working—[*laughter*]—but I want to add Carl Levin. They held their shoulders to the wheel in the Senate. I am so proud of Susan Davis, who's on the stage, and a guy you might know, Barney Frank. They kept up the fight in the House. And I've got to acknowledge Patrick Murphy, a veteran himself, who helped lead the way in Congress.

I also want to commend our military leadership. Ending "don't ask, don't tell" was a topic in my first meeting with Secretary Gates, Admiral Mullen, and the Joint Chiefs. We talked about how to end this policy. We talked about how success in both passing and implementing this change depended on working closely with the Pentagon. And that's what we did.

And 2 years later, I am confident that history will remember well the courage and the vision of Secretary Gates, of Admiral Mike Mullen, who spoke from the heart and said what he believed was right, of General James Cartwright, the vice chairman of the Joint Chiefs, and Deputy Secretary William Lynn, who is here. Also, the authors of the Pentagon's review, Jeh Johnson and General Carter Ham, who did outstanding and meticulous work; and all those who laid the groundwork for this transition.

And finally, I want to express my gratitude to the men and women in this room who have worn the uniform of the United States Armed Services. I want to thank all the patriots who are here today, all of them who were forced to hang up their uniforms as a result of "don't ask, don't tell," but who never stopped fighting for this country, and who rallied and who marched and who fought for change. I want to thank everyone here who stood with them in that fight.

Because of these efforts, in the coming days we will begin the process laid out by this law. Now, the old policy remains in effect until Secretary Gates, Admiral Mullen, and I certify the military's readiness to implement the repeal. And it's especially important for servicemembers to remember that. But I have spoken to every one of the service chiefs, and they are all committed to implementing this change swiftly and efficiently. We are not going to be dragging our feet to get this done.

Now, with any change, there's some apprehension. That's natural. But as Commander in Chief, I am certain that we can effect this transition in a way that only strengthens our military readiness; that people will look back on this moment and wonder why it was ever a source of controversy in the first place.

I have every confidence in the professionalism and patriotism of our servicemembers. Just as they have adapted and grown stronger with each of the other changes, I know they will do so again. I know that Secretary Gates, Admiral Mullen, as well as the vast majority of servicemembers themselves, share this view. And they share it based on their own experiences, including the experience of serving with dedicated, duty-bound servicemembers who were also gay.

As one special operations warfighter said during the Pentagon's review—this was one of my favorites—it echoes the experience of Lloyd Corwin decades earlier: "We have a gay guy in the unit. He's big, he's mean, he kills lots of bad guys." [*Laughter*] "No one cared that he was gay." [*Laughter*] And I think that sums up perfectly the situation.

Finally, I want to speak directly to the gay men and women currently serving in our military. For a long time your service has demanded a particular kind of sacrifice. You've been asked to carry the added burden of secrecy and isolation. And all the while, you've put your lives on the line for the freedoms and privileges of citizenship that are not fully granted to you.

You're not the first to have carried this burden, for while today marks the end of a particular struggle that has lasted almost two decades, this is a moment more than two centuries in the making.

There will never be a full accounting of the heroism demonstrated by gay Americans in service to this country; their service has been obscured in history. It's been lost to prejudices that have waned in our own lifetimes. But at every turn, at every crossroads in our past, we

know gay Americans fought just as hard, gave just as much to protect this Nation and the ideals for which it stands.

There can be little doubt there were gay soldiers who fought for American independence, who consecrated the ground at Gettysburg, who manned the trenches along the western front, who stormed the beaches of Iwo Jima. Their names are etched into the walls of our memorials. Their headstones dot the grounds at Arlington.

And so, as the first generation to serve openly in our Armed Forces, you will stand for all those who came before you, and you will serve as role models to all who come after. And I know that you will fulfill this responsibility with integrity and honor, just as you have every other mission with which you've been charged.

And you need to look no further than the service men and women in this room: distinguished officers like former Navy Commander Zoe Dunning; marines like Eric Alva, one of the first Americans to be injured in Iraq; leaders like Captain Jonathan Hopkins, who led a platoon into northern Iraq during the initial invasion, quelling an ethnic riot, earning a Bronze Star with valor. He was discharged, only to receive e-mails and letters from his soldiers saying they had known he was gay all along—[*laughter*]—and thought that he was the best commander they ever had.

There are a lot of stories like these, stories that only underscore the importance of enlisting the service of all who are willing to fight for this country. That's why I hope those soldiers, sailors, airmen, marines, and coastguardsmen who have been discharged under this discriminatory policy will seek to reenlist once the repeal is implemented.

That is why I say to all Americans, gay or straight, who want nothing more than to defend this country in uniform: Your country needs you, your country wants you, and we will be honored to welcome you into the ranks of the finest military the world has ever known.

Some of you remembered I visited Afghanistan just a few weeks ago. And while I was walking along the rope line—it was a big crowd, about 3,000—a young woman in uniform was shaking my hand and other people were grabbing and taking pictures. And she pulled me into a hug and she whispered in my ear, "Get 'don't ask, don't tell' done." [*Laughter*] And I said to her, "I promise you I will."

For we are not a nation that says, "Don't ask, don't tell." We are a nation that says, "Out of many, we are one." We are a nation that welcomes the service of every patriot. We are a nation that believes that all men and women are created equal. Those are the ideals that generations have fought for. Those are the ideals that we uphold today. And now it is my honor to sign this bill into law.

[*At this point, the President signed the bill.*]

The President. This is done.

NOTE: The President spoke at 9:10 a.m. at the Department of the Interior. In his remarks, he referred to Miles Corwin, son of World War II veteran Lloyd Corwin. H.R. 2965, approved December 22, was assigned Public Law No. 111–321. The transcript released by the Office of the Press Secretary also included the remarks of Vice President Joe Biden.

The President's News Conference
December 22, 2010

The President. Good afternoon. I know everybody is itching to get out of here and spend some time with their families. I am too. I noticed some of your colleagues have been reporting from Hawaii over the last week. But I just wanted to say a few words about the progress that we've made on some important issues over these last few weeks.

A lot of folks in this town predicted that after the midterm elections, Washington would be headed for more partisanship and more gridlock. And instead, this has been a season of progress for the American people. That progress is reflecting—is a reflection of the message that voters sent in November, a message that said it's time to find common ground on challenges facing our country. That's a message that I will take to heart in the new year, and I hope my Democratic and Republican friends will do the same.

First of all, I am glad that Democrats and Republicans came together to approve my top national security priority for this session of Congress: the new START Treaty. This is the most significant arms control agreement in nearly two decades, and it will make us safer and reduce our nuclear arsenals along with Russia. With this treaty, our inspectors will also be back on the ground at Russian nuclear bases. So we will be able to trust, but verify.

We'll continue to advance our relationship with Russia, which is essential to making progress on a host of challenges, from enforcing strong sanctions on Iran to preventing nuclear weapons from falling into the hands of terrorists. And this treaty will enhance our leadership to stop the spread of nuclear weapons and seek the peace of a world without them.

The strong, bipartisan vote in the Senate sends a powerful signal to the world that Republicans and Democrats stand together on behalf of our security. And I especially want to thank the outstanding work done by Vice President Joe Biden; the chairman of the Foreign Relations Committee, Senator John Kerry; and the ranking Republican, Senator Richard Lugar, for their extraordinary efforts.

In fact, I just got off the phone with Dick Lugar, and reminded him the first trip I ever took as Senator—foreign trip—was with Dick Lugar to Russia to look at nuclear facilities there. And I told him how much I appreciated the work he had done and that there was a direct line between that trip that we took together when I was a first-year Senator and the results of the vote today on the floor.

This all speaks to a tradition of bipartisan support for strong American leadership around the world, and that's a tradition that was reinforced by the fact that the new START Treaty won the backing of our military and our allies abroad.

In the last few weeks, we also came together across party lines to pass a package of tax cuts and unemployment insurance that will spur jobs, businesses, and growth. This package includes a payroll tax cut that means nearly every American family will get an average tax cut next year of about a thousand dollars delivered in their paychecks. It will make a difference for millions of students and parents and workers and people still looking for work. It's led economists across the political spectrum to predict that the economy will grow faster than they originally thought next year.

In our ongoing struggle to perfect our Union, we also overturned a 17-year-old law and a longstanding injustice by finally ending "don't ask, don't tell." As I said earlier today, this is the right thing to do for our security; it's the right thing to do, period.

In addition, we came together across party lines to pass a food safety bill, the biggest upgrade of America's food safety laws since the Great Depression. And I hope the House will soon join the Senate in passing a 9/11 health bill that will help cover the health care costs of police officers, firefighters, rescue workers, and residents who inhaled toxic air near the World Trade Center on that terrible morning and the days that followed.

So I think it's fair to say that this has been the most productive postelection period we've had in decades, and it comes on the heels of the most productive 2 years that we've had in generations.

That doesn't mean that our business is finished. I am very disappointed Congress wasn't able to pass the "DREAM Act" so we can stop punishing kids for the actions of their parents and allow them to serve in the military or earn an education and contribute their talents to the country where they grew up.

I'm also disappointed we weren't able to come together around a budget to fund our Government over the long term. I expect we'll have a robust debate about this when we return from the holidays, a debate that will have to answer an increasingly urgent question, and that

is, how do we cut spending that we don't need while making investments that we do need, investments in education, research and development, innovation, and the things that are essential to grow our economy over the long run, create jobs, and compete with every other nation in the world? I look forward to hearing from folks on both sides of the aisle about how we can accomplish that goal.

If there's any lesson to draw from these past few weeks, it's that we are not doomed to endless gridlock. We've shown, in the wake of the November elections, that we have the capacity not only to make progress, but to make progress together.

And I'm not naive. I know there will be tough fights in the months ahead. But my hope heading into the new year is that we can continue to heed the message of the American people and hold to a spirit of common purpose in 2011 and beyond. And if we do that, I'm convinced that we will lift up our middle class, we will rebuild our economy, and we will make our contribution to America's greatness.

Finally, before I take questions, I want to send a message to all those Americans who are spending Christmas serving our Nation in harm's way. As I said in Afghanistan earlier this month, the American people stand united in our support and admiration for you. And in this holiday season, I'd ask the American people to keep our troops in your prayers and lend a hand to those military families who have an empty seat at the table.

So with that, I'm going to take some questions. And I'm going to start with Caren Bohan [Reuters].

Bipartisanship

Q. Thank you, Mr. President. You racked up a lot of wins in the last few weeks that a lot of people thought would be difficult to come by. Are you ready to call yourself the comeback kid? And also, as you look ahead to 2011, are you worried that bipartisan agreement will be a lot harder to reach on issues like deficit reduction and maybe even tax reform?

The President. Well, look, as I said right after the midterm elections, we took a shellacking.

And I take responsibility for that. But I think what's happened over the last several weeks is not a victory for me, it's a victory for the American people. And the lesson I hope that everybody takes from this is that it's possible for Democrats and Republicans to have principled disagreements, to have some lengthy arguments, but to ultimately find common ground to move the country forward.

That's what we did with taxes. Those arguments have not gone away. I still believe that it doesn't make sense for us to provide tax cuts to people like myself who don't need them when our deficit and debts are growing. That's a debate that's going to continue into 2011, and I know the Republicans feel just as strongly on the other side of that.

I think that we're still going to have disagreements in terms of spending priorities. It's vital for us to make investments in education and research and development—all those things that create an innovative economy—while at the same time cutting those programs that just aren't working. And there are going to be debates between the parties on those issues.

But what we've shown is that we don't have to agree on a hundred percent to get things done that enhance the lives of families all across America. And if we can sustain that spirit, then regardless of how the politics play out in 2012, the American people will be better for it. And that's my ultimate goal.

Jake Tapper [ABC News].

U.S. Military's "Don't Ask, Don't Tell" Policy/Same-Sex Marriage

Q. Thanks, Mr. President. Merry Christmas.
The President. Merry Christmas.
Q. I have a couple questions about "don't ask, don't tell." First of all, congratulations. What was your conversation like with Marine Commandant Amos when he expressed to you his concerns and yet he said that he would abide by whatever the ruling was? Can you understand why he had the position he did? And then on the other hand, is it intellectually consistent to say that gay and lesbians should be able to fight and die for this country but they should not be able to marry the people they love?

The President. You know, I don't want to go into detail about conversations in the Oval Office with my service chiefs. Jim Amos expressed the same concerns to me privately that he expressed publicly during his testimony. He said that there could be disruptions as a consequence of this. And what I said to him was that I was confident, looking at the history of the military with respect to racial integration, with respect to the inclusion of women in our Armed Forces, that that could be managed. And that was confirmed by the attitudinal studies that was done prior to this vote.

And what he assured me of, and what all the service chiefs have assured me of, is that regardless of their concerns about disruptions, they were confident that they could implement this policy without it affecting our military cohesion and good discipline and readiness. And I take them at their word. And I've spoken to them since the vote took place and they have all said that we are going to implement this smartly and swiftly, and they are confident that it will not have an effect on our military effectiveness.

So I'm very heartened by that. And I want to again give Bob Gates and Admiral Mullen enormous credit for having guided this process through in a way that preserves our primary responsibility to keep America safe and at the same time allows us to live up to our values.

With respect to the issue of whether gays and lesbians should be able to get married, I've spoken about this recently. As I've said, my feelings about this are constantly evolving. I struggle with this. I have friends, I have people who work for me, who are in powerful, strong, long-lasting gay or lesbian unions. And they are extraordinary people, and this is something that means a lot to them and they care deeply about.

At this point, what I've said is, is that my baseline is a strong civil union that provides them the protections and the legal rights that married couples have. And I think that's the right thing to do. But I recognize that from their perspective it is not enough, and I think this is something that we're going to continue to debate and I personally am going to continue to wrestle with going forward.

1943

Q. But the military does not recognize civil unions, right?

The President. I understand. And as I said, this is going to be an issue that is not unique to the military; this is an issue that extends to all of our society, and I think we're all going to have to have a conversation about it.

Dan Lothian [CNN].

President's Agenda/Bipartisanship

Q. Thank you, Mr. President, and happy holidays.

The President. Happy holidays.

Q. Can you give us an update on that car that you talk about so much about being in the ditch? Can you give us an update as to where it is today? What kind of highway do you think it will be driving on in 2011? Who will really be behind the wheel, given the new makeup in Congress? And what do you think Republicans will be sipping and saying next year? [*Laughter*]

The President. Dan, you gave some thought to that question, didn't you?

Q. I did. [*Laughter*]

The President. Well, I do think that the car is on level ground. I mean, the car is the economy. And I think we are past the crisis point in the economy, but we now have to pivot and focus on jobs and growth. And my singular focus over the next 2 years is not rescuing the economy from potential disaster, but rather jumpstarting the economy so that we actually start making a dent in the unemployment rate and we are equipping ourselves so that we can compete in the 21st century.

And that means we've got to focus on education, that means we have to focus on research and development, we have to focus on innovation. We have to make sure that in every sector, from manufacturing to clean energy to high-tech to biotech, that we recognize the private sector is going to be the driving force. And what the Government can do is to make sure that we are a good partner with them, that we're a facilitator, that in some cases we're a catalyst when it's a fledgling industry.

And that means that we've got to look at some of our old dogmas—both Democrats and Republicans, conservatives and liberals—to think about what works. If there are regulations that are in place that are impeding innovation, let's get rid of those regulations. Let's make sure that we're also protecting consumers and we're protecting the environment and protecting workers in the process. But let's find ways to do business that helps business.

People were doubtful about the approach that we took to the auto industry, but that was an example of there may be occasions, certainly during crisis, where a timely intervention that's limited and restricted can end up making a difference.

And so I think Democrats, Republicans, House, Senate, the White House, all of us have to be in a conversation with the private sector about what's going to ensure that we can export and sell our products instead of just buying exports from someplace else. How do we make sure that the green technologies of the future are made here in America?

And how do we get all these profits that companies have been making since the economy recovered into productive investment and hiring? That's a conversation that I had with the 20 CEOs who came here, and that's a conversation I expect to continue in the months ahead.

But the answer about who drives: The American people are driving the car. They're the ones who are going to be making an assessment as to whether we're putting in place policies that are working for them. And both parties are going to be held accountable and I'm going to be held accountable if we take a wrong turn on that front.

Q. And what will the Republicans be sipping? [*Laughter*]

The President. You know, my sense is the Republicans recognize that with greater power is going to come greater responsibility. And some of the progress that I think we saw in the lame duck was a recognition on their part that people are going to be paying attention to what they're doing as well as what I'm doing and what the Democrats in Congress are doing.

Mark Knoller [CBS Radio].

Tax Reform/Federal Budget

Q. Yes, sir. Mr. President, can you explain the anger and even outrage many Democrats felt when the tax cut bill extended tax cuts not just for the middle class, but also for the wealthy? And is that a divide that you may be contributing to when you and the Vice President talk about morally inappropriate tax cuts for the wealthy?

The President. Look, the frustration that people felt about that was frustration I share. I've said that before, and I'll probably say it again. I don't think that over the long run we can afford a series of tax breaks for people who are doing very well and don't need it; were doing well when Bill Clinton was in office. They were still rich then, and they will still be rich if those tax cuts went away.

And so this is going to be a debate that we're going to be having over the next couple of years. Because I guarantee you, as soon as the new Congress is sworn in, we're going to have to have a conversation about how do we start balancing our budget, or at least getting to a point that's sustainable when it comes to our deficit and our debt.

And that's going to require us cutting programs that don't work, but it also requires us to be honest about paying for the things that we think are important. If we think it's important to make sure that our veterans are getting care that they need when they come back home from fighting in Afghanistan or Iraq, we can't just salute and wish them well and have a Veterans Day parade. We got to make sure that there are doctors and nurses and facilities for post-traumatic stress disorder, and that costs money.

If we say that education is going to be the single most important determinant for our children's success and this country's success in the 21st century, we can't have schools that are laying off so many teachers that they start going to 4 days a week, as they've done in Hawaii, for example.

We've got to make sure that young people can afford to go to college. If we want to keep our competitive edge in innovation, well, we've got to invest in basic research; the same basic research that resulted in the Internet, the same basic research that invited—that resulted in GPS. All those things originated in research funded by the Government.

So we are going to have to compare the option of maintaining the tax cuts for the wealthy permanently versus spending on these things that we think are important. And that's a debate that I welcome. But I completely understand why not just Democrats but some Republicans might think that that part of the tax package we could have done without.

Having said that, I want to repeat: Compromise, by definition, means taking some things you don't like. And the overall package was the right one to ensure that this economy has the best possible chance to grow and create jobs. And there is no better antipoverty program than an economy that's growing. There is no better deficit-reduction program than an economy that is growing. And if the economy started contracting, as it might have had we not gotten this tax agreement, then the choices that we would have to make would be even tougher.

Distribution of Wealth/Economic Opportunity

Q. Sir, is there a divide between middle class and wealthy Americans?

The President. I think middle class folks would confirm what the statistics say, which is that they have not seen a real increase in their incomes in a decade, while their costs have skyrocketed. That's just a fact.

What is also a fact is that people in the top 1 percent, people in the top one-tenth of 1 percent or one one-hundredth of 1 percent have a larger share of income and wealth than any time since the 1920s. Those are just facts. That's not a feeling on the part of Democrats. Those are facts.

And something that's always been the greatest strength of America is a thriving, booming middle class, where everybody has got a shot at the American Dream. And that should be our goal. That should be what we're focused on. How are we creating opportunity for everybody? So that we celebrate wealth. We celebrate somebody like a Steve Jobs, who has created two or three different revolutionary products. We expect that person to be rich, and that's a good thing. We want that incentive. That's part of the free market.

But we also want to make sure that those of us who have been extraordinarily fortunate, that we're contributing to the larger American community so that a whole bunch of other kids coming up are doing well. And that means schools that work and infrastructure like roads and airports that function, and it means colleges and universities that teach and aren't restricted to just people who can afford it, but are open to anybody with talent and a willingness to work. And that's going to be, I think, part of the conversation that we've got to have over the next couple years.

Juan Carlos Lopez [CNN En Espanol].

"Development, Relief, and Education for Alien Minors (DREAM) Act"/Border Security

Q. Gracias, Presidente. Feliz Navidad.
The President. Feliz Navidad.
Q. Mr. President, you've been able to fulfill many of your promises. Immigration reform isn't one of them. Just this last weekend, the "DREAM Act" failed cloture by five votes. And five Democrats didn't support it; three Republicans did. How are you going to be able to keep your promise when the Republicans control the House when you haven't been able to do so with Democrats controlling both the Senate and the House, and when Republicans say they want to focus on border security before they do anything on immigration?

The President. Well, let me say, there are a number of things that I wanted to get accomplished that we did not get accomplished. For example, collective bargaining for firefighters and public safety workers—that was something that I thought was important. We didn't get it done. I'm disappointed in that. I think we're still going to have to figure out how we work on energy, and that's an area that I want to immediately engage with Republicans to figure out.

But I will tell you, maybe my biggest disappointment was this "DREAM Act" vote. You know, I get letters from kids all across the country—came here when they were 5, came here when they were 8; their parents were undocumented. The kids didn't know—kids are going to school like any other American kid, they're growing up, they're playing football, they're going to class, they're dreaming about college. And suddenly they come to 18, 19 years old, and they realize, even though I feel American, I am an American, the law doesn't recognize me as an American. I'm willing to serve my country, I'm willing to fight for this country, I want to go to college and better myself, and I'm at risk of deportation.

And it is heartbreaking. That can't be who we are, to have kids—our kids, classmates of our children—who are suddenly under this shadow of fear through no fault of their own. They didn't break a law; they were kids.

So my hope and expectation is that, first of all, everybody understands I am determined and this administration is determined to get immigration reform done. It is the right thing to do. I think it involves securing our borders, and my administration has done more on border security than any administration in recent years. We have more of everything: ICE, Border Patrol, surveillance, you name it.

So we take border security seriously. And we take going after employers who are exploiting and using undocumented workers, we take that seriously. But we need to reform this immigration system so we are a nation of laws and we are a nation of immigrants. And at minimum, we should be able to get the "DREAM Act" done.

And so I'm going to go back at it, and I'm going to engage in Republicans who I think some of them, in their heart of hearts, know it's the right thing to do, but they think the politics is tough for them.

Well, that may mean that we've got to change the politics. And I've got to spend some time talking to the American people and others have to spend time talking to the American people, because I think that if the American people knew any of these kids—they probably do, they just may not know their status—they'd say, of course we want you. That's who we are. That's the better angels of our nature.

And so one thing I hope people have seen during this lame duck: I am persistent. I am persistent. If I believe in something strongly, I stay on it. And I believe strongly in this.

And I am happy to engage with the Republicans about—if they've got ideas about more on border security, I'm happy to have that conversation. And I think that it is absolutely appropriate for the American people to expect that we don't have porous borders and anybody can come in here any time. That is entirely legitimate.

But I also think about those kids. And I want to do right by them, and I think the country is going to want to do right by them as well.

Mike Emanuel [FOX News].

Guantanamo Bay Detention Center/Trials for Terrorist Suspects

Q. Thank you, Mr. President. Merry Christmas.

The President. Merry Christmas.

Q. Guantanamo, sir. I understand a draft of an Executive order is being prepared for you, and I don't expect you to comment then on that——

The President. Right.

Q. It hasn't gotten to you yet.

The President. Yes.

Q. But it makes me wonder where you are, sir, at about the 2-year mark on Guantanamo, when closing it was one of your initial priorities, sir?

The President. Obviously, we haven't gotten it closed. And let me just step back and explain that the reason for wanting to close Guantanamo was because my number-one priority is keeping the American people safe. One of the most powerful tools we have to keep the American people safe is not providing Al Qaida and jihadists recruiting tools for fledgling terrorists.

And Guantanamo is probably the number-one recruitment tool that is used by these jihadist organizations. And we see it in the web sites that they put up. We see it in the messages that they're delivering.

And so my belief is that we can keep the American people safe, go after those who would engage in terrorism. And my administration has been as aggressive in going after Al Qaida as any

administration out there. And we've seen progress, as I noted during the Afghan review.

Every intelligence report that we're seeing shows that Al Qaida is more hunkered down than they have been since the original invasion of Afghanistan in 2001, that they have reduced financing capacity, reduced operational capacity. It is much more difficult for their top folks to communicate, and a lot of those top folks can't communicate because they're underground now.

But it is important for us, even as we're going aggressively after the bad guys, to make sure that we're also living up to our values and our ideals and our principles. And that's what closing Guantanamo is about, not because I think that the people who are running Guantanamo are doing a bad job, but rather because it's become a symbol. And I think we can do just as good of a job housing them somewhere else.

Now, to the issue you had about the review. You're right, I won't comment right now on a review that I have not received yet. I can tell you that over the last 2 years, despite not having closed Guantanamo, we've been trying to put our battle against terrorists within a legal structure that is consistent with our history of rule of law. And we've succeeded on a number of fronts.

One of the toughest problems is what to do with people that we know are dangerous, that we know are—have engaged in terrorist activity, are proclaimed enemies of the United States, but because of the manner in which they were originally captured, the circumstances right after 9/11 in which they are interrogated, it becomes difficult to try them, whether in a Article III court or in a military commission.

Releasing them at this stage could potentially create greater danger for the American people. And so how do we manage that? And that's what this team has been looking at. Are there ways for us to make sure these folks have lawyers, to make sure that these folks have the opportunity to challenge their detention, but at the same time, making sure that we are not simply releasing folks who could do us grievous harm and have shown a capacity and willingness to engage in brutal attacks in the past?

And so when I get that report, I'm sure that I'll have more comments on it. The bottom line is, is that striking this balance between our security and making sure that we are consistent with our values and our Constitution is not an easy task, but ultimately that's what's required for practical reasons.

Because the more people are reminded of what makes America special—the fact that we stand for something beyond just our economic power or our military might, but we have these core ideals that we observe even when it's hard—that's one of our most powerful weapons.

And I want to make sure that we don't lose that weapon in what is a serious struggle.

So with that, everybody, I want to wish you all a merry Christmas. Happy holidays. Happy New Year. See you in 2011.

NOTE: The President's news conference began at 4:16 p.m. in the South Court Auditorium of the Dwight D. Eisenhower Executive Office Building. In his remarks, the President referred to U.S. Marine Corps Commandant Gen. James F. Amos, USMC; and Steven P. Jobs, chief executive officer, Apple Inc.

Statement on the Inauguration of Alpha Conde as President of Guinea
December 22, 2010

On behalf of the American people, I congratulate the people of Guinea as they witness the inauguration of their first democratically elected President since becoming an independent state in 1958. Just over a year ago, the world's attention was drawn to Guinea by horrifying atrocities and dangerous instability. Today, people all over the world are coming together to congratulate Guinea and to express genuine admiration for the voters who steadfastly acted to support peace and democracy. They have set their country on a path for a more prosperous and stable future.

As the country begins its new democratic era, I extend congratulations to President Alpha Conde on his inauguration. I also express my appreciation for the way in which Cellou Dalein Diallo gracefully accepted the outcome of the election and spoke of the importance of a unified

Guinea in moving forward. While the road ahead may be challenging, the United States looks forward to working with the incoming administration as it pursues an inclusive government that represents the people of Guinea irrespective or ethnicity, religion, and gender; establishes a platform of economic development for all to realize the dividends of democracy; and works to enact critical reforms in the security sector.

The past year will remain a powerful example of how a country at such a pivotal moment can make a choice for a better future, and the responsibility of those in positions of authority to put the country first. As such, I also recognize and honor the leadership of interim President General Sekouba Konate, who provided the necessary vision and support for Guinea's historic transition.

The President's Weekly Address
December 25, 2010

The President. Merry Christmas, everybody. Michelle and I just wanted to take a moment today to send greetings from our family to yours.

The First Lady. This is one of our favorite times of year. And we're so fortunate to be able to celebrate it together in this wonderful home.

This is the people's house. So Barack and I try to open it to as many people as we can, especially during the holiday season.

This month, more than 100,000 Americans have passed through these halls. And the idea behind this year's theme, "Simple Gifts," is that the greatest blessings of all are the ones that don't cost a thing: the comfort of spending time with loved ones, the freedoms we enjoy as Americans, and the joy we feel upon giving something of ourselves.

So in this time of family and friends and good cheer, let's also be sure to look out for those who are less fortunate, who've hit a run of bad luck, or who are hungry and alone this holiday season.

The President. Because this is the season when we celebrate the simplest yet most profound gift of all: the birth of a child who devoted his life to a message of peace, love, and redemption. A message that says no matter who we are, we are called to love one another; we are our brother's keeper, we are our sister's keeper, our separate stories in this big and busy world are really one.

Today we're also thinking of those who can't be home for the holidays, especially all our courageous countrymen serving overseas.

That's the message I delivered when I visited our troops in Afghanistan a few weeks ago, that while you may be serving far from home, every American supports you and your families. We are with you. And I have no greater honor than serving as your Commander in Chief.

Today's soldiers, sailors, airmen, marines, and coastguardsmen make up the finest fighting force in the history of the world. Just like their predecessors, they do extraordinary things in service to their country. What makes that all the more remarkable is that today's military is an all-volunteer force, a force of mothers and fathers, sons and daughters, husbands and wives.

The First Lady. That's right. And as First Lady, I've had the honor to meet members of our military and their families on bases and in communities all across the country. I've gotten to know husbands and wives doing the parenting of two while their spouse is on another deployment, children trying their best in school but always wondering when mom or dad is coming home, patriots putting their lives on hold to help with a loved one's recovery or carry on the memory of a fallen hero.

When our men and women in uniform answer the call to serve, their families serve too. And they're proud and glad to do it. But as long

as that service keeps the rest of us safe, their sacrifice should also be our own. Even heroes can use a hand, especially during the holidays.

The President. So we're encouraging Americans to ask what you can do to support our troops and their families in this holiday season. For some ideas on how to get started, just visit serve.gov.

The First Lady. You'll see that you don't need to be an expert in military life to give back to those who give so much to us. There are countless ways to contribute by harnessing your unique talents.

If you live near a base, you can reach out through your local school or your church. If you don't, you can volunteer with organizations that support military families. And anybody can send a care package or prepaid calling card to the frontlines or give what's sometimes the most important gift of all: simply saying thank you.

The President. America's brave service men and women represent a small fraction of our population. But they and the families who await their safe return carry far more than their fair share of the burden. They've done everything they've been asked to do. They've been everything we've asked them to be. And even as we speak, many are fighting halfway around the globe, in hopes that someday our children and grandchildren won't have to.

So let's all remind them this holiday season that we're thinking of them and that America will forever be here for them, just as they've been there for us.

And on behalf of Michelle, Malia, Sasha——

The First Lady. ——and Bo.

The President. ——and Bo, have a very merry Christmas.

The First Lady. ——and an even happier New Year.

NOTE: The address was recorded at approximately 3:30 p.m. on December 17 in the Diplomatic Reception Room at the White House for broadcast on December 25. The transcript was made available by the Office of the Press Secretary on December 24, but was embargoed for release until 6 a.m. on December 25.

Statement on the Terrorist Attack in Khar, Pakistan
December 25, 2010

I strongly condemn the outrageous terrorist attack in Khar, Pakistan. Killing innocent civilians outside a World Food Programme distribution point is an affront to the people of Pakistan and to all humanity. The United States stands with the people of Pakistan in this difficult time and will strongly support Pakistan's efforts to ensure greater peace, security, and justice for its people.

Statement on the Observance of Kwanzaa
December 26, 2010

Michelle and I extend our warmest thoughts and wishes to all those who are celebrating Kwanzaa this holiday season. Today is the first of a joyful 7-day celebration of African American culture and heritage. The seven principles of Kwanzaa—unity, self-determination, collective work and responsibility, cooperative economics, purpose, creativity, and faith—are some of the very values that make us Americans.

As families across America and around the world light the *kinara* today in the spirit of *umoja*, or unity, our family sends our well wishes and blessings for a happy and healthy new year.

NOTE: This statement was released by the Office of the Press Secretary as a statement by the President and the First Lady.

Statement on the First Anniversary of the Terrorist Attack on Central Intelligence Agency Personnel in Afghanistan
December 30, 2010

One year ago today, at a remote outpost at Khost, Afghanistan, seven American patriots showed us the true meaning of honor, integrity, and selfless sacrifice. For their colleagues and friends at the CIA, it was a heartbreaking loss of experienced veterans and young officers who served on the frontlines in the fight to keep our Nation safe. For Americans to whom the work of our intelligence community is largely unknown, it was a rare glimpse into the risks that our intelligence professionals accept in defense of the security and freedoms that we cherish. And for those of us who gathered at Langley last February to pay tribute to these seven heroes and to comfort their families, it was an occasion to rededicate ourselves to their work and to the ideals for which they died.

In the year since, that is what we have done. As President, I rely on our intelligence, military, and civilian personnel every day, and I know that our country is more secure and the American people are safer because of their extraordinary service. Today, Al Qaida's senior leadership is under more pressure than ever before and is hunkered down in the border region of Afghanistan and Pakistan. We are relentlessly pursuing our mission to disrupt, dismantle, and ultimately defeat that terrorist organization. In the United States and around the world, plots have been thwarted, attacks have been disrupted, and the lives of Americans have been saved.

This is the legacy of the courageous Americans who gave their lives 1 year ago and whose stars now grace the Memorial Wall at Langley, just as it is the legacy of our troops who have given their lives in Afghanistan and Iraq. As we mark the first anniversary of their sacrifice at Khost, this is the work to which we recommit ourselves today. We will ensure that our dedicated intelligence professionals have the training and tools they need to meet the missions we ask of them. We will do everything in our power to ensure the safety and security of the American people. And like our seven patriots at Khost, we will never waver in defense of the security and liberties that keep America strong and free.

Statement on the Removal of Highly Enriched Uranium From Ukraine
December 31, 2010

I congratulate President Yanukovych on the recent shipment of highly enriched uranium from Ukraine for secure disposal in Russia, which advances a top priority for my administration and for global security. This action brings us all one step closer to securing all vulnerable nuclear materials, as President Yanukovych and I and 45 other world leaders pledged to do this April at the Nuclear Security Summit. The low-enriched uranium and nuclear safety equipment provided to Ukraine in connection with this shipment will support Ukraine's development of safe and secure nuclear energy. These actions represent continued Ukrainian leadership in making sure that nuclear weapons never fall into the hands of a terrorist and working toward a world without nuclear weapons.

Appendix A—Digest of Other White House Announcements

The following list includes the President's pub-
lic schedule and other items of general interest
announced by the Office of the Press Secretary
and not included elsewhere in this book.

July 1

In the morning, in the Oval Office, the President had an intelligence briefing. Then, also in the Oval Office, he met with Secretary of the Treasury Timothy F. Geithner.

In the afternoon, in the Old Family Dining Room, the President had lunch with business leaders. Later, in the Oval Office, he and Vice President Joe Biden met with Senate Majority Leader Harry M. Reid. Then, in the Situation Room, they were briefed on the oil spill in the Gulf of Mexico.

Later in the afternoon, in the Oval Office, the President met with Vice President Biden.

The President announced his intention to nominate Alexander A. Arvizu to be Ambassador to Albania.

The President announced his intention to nominate Nisha D. Biswal to be Assistant Administrator for Asia at the U.S. Agency for International Development.

The President announced his intention to nominate Michele T. Bond to be Ambassador to Lesotho.

The President announced his intention to nominate Paul W. Jones to be Ambassador to Malaysia.

The President announced his intention to nominate George A. Krol to be Ambassador to Uzbekistan.

The President announced his intention to nominate Francis J. Ricciardone to be Ambassador to Turkey.

The President announced his intention to nominate Timothy C. Scheve to be a member of the Internal Revenue Service Oversight Board.

The President announced his intention to nominate Duane E. Woerth to the rank of Ambassador during his tenure of service as U.S.

Representative on the Council of the International Civil Aviation Organization.

The President announced his intention to appoint James M. Kesteloot as a member of the Committee for Purchase From People Who Are Blind or Severely Disabled.

The President announced his intention to appoint Wayne Newell, Stacy Phelps, and Patricia Whitefoot as members of the National Advisory Council on Indian Education.

The President declared a major disaster in Maine and ordered Federal aid to supplement State and local recovery efforts in the area struck by severe storms and flooding from March 12 through April 1.

July 2

In the morning, the President and Vice President Joe Biden traveled to Charleston, WV.

In the afternoon, the President traveled to Camp David, MD.

The President declared a major disaster in Minnesota and ordered Federal aid to supplement State and local recovery efforts in the area struck by severe storms, tornadoes, and flooding from June 17 through 26.

July 3

In the evening, the President and Mrs. Obama returned to Washington, DC.

July 4

In the evening, on the South Lawn, the President and Mrs. Obama hosted a barbecue and concert for military personnel and their families. Later, they watched the Independence Day fireworks display on the National Mall from the roof of the White House.

July 5

In the morning, the President had an intelligence briefing.

In the afternoon, the President had a conference call with U.S. Ambassador to Afghanistan Karl W. Eikenberry and Gen. David H.

Petraeus, USA, commander, NATO International Security Assistance Force, Afghanistan.

During the day, the President had a telephone conversation with Acting President and President-elect Bronislaw Komorowski of Poland to congratulate him on his July 4 election victory, to discuss Poland-U.S. relations and Poland's military contribution to the NATO mission in Afghanistan, and to offer his condolences for Polish military personnel killed in Afghanistan.

July 6

In the morning, in the Oval Office, the President had an intelligence briefing followed by an economic briefing.

In the afternoon, in the Cabinet Room, the President and Vice President Joe Biden had a working lunch with Prime Minister Benjamin Netanyahu of Israel. Later, in the Oval Office, they met with Secretary of Defense Robert M. Gates.

July 7

In the morning, in the Oval Office, the President and Vice President Joe Biden had an intelligence briefing. Then, also in the Oval Office, he met with his senior advisers. Later, in the Roosevelt Room, he met with members of the President's Export Council.

In the afternoon, in the Oval Office, the President and Vice President Biden had a briefing on the oil spill in the Gulf of Mexico. Then, in the Private Dining Room, they had lunch. Later, in the Oval Office, they met with Secretary of the Treasury Timothy F. Geithner.

Later in the afternoon, in the Oval Office, the President and Vice President Biden met with Secretary of State Hillary Rodham Clinton.

The President announced the designation of the following individuals as members of a Presidential delegation to Bosnia and Herzegovina to attend the ceremony commemorating the 15th anniversary of the Srebrenica genocide on July 11: Charles L. English (head of delegation); Stephen J. Rapp; and Samantha Power.

The President announced that he has appointed the following individuals as members of the President's Export Council:

Mary Vermeer Andringa;
Stephanie A. Burns;
Scott Davis;
Richard L. Friedman;
Gene Hale;
C. Robert Henrikson;
William Hite;
Robert A. Iger;
Charles R. Kaye;
Jeffrey Kindler;
Andrew N. Liveris;
Robert A. Mandell;
Alan Mulally;
Raul Pedraza;
Ivan Seidenberg;
Glenn Tilton;
James S. Turley; and
Patricia A. Woertz.

The President announced his recess appointment of Donald M. Berwick as Administrator of the Centers for Medicare and Medicaid Services at the Department of Health and Human Services.

The President announced his recess appointment of Philip E. Coyle III as Associate Director for National Security and International Affairs at the Office of Science and Technology Policy.

The President announced his recess appointment of Joshua Gotbaum as Director of the Pension Benefit Guaranty Corporation.

July 8

In the morning, in the Oval Office, the President had an intelligence briefing. Later, he traveled to Kansas City, MO.

In the afternoon, the President toured Smith Electric Vehicles. Later, he traveled to Las Vegas, NV.

In the evening, at the Aria Resort and Casino, the President attended a dinner fundraiser for Senate Majority Leader Harry M. Reid.

The President announced his intention to appoint the following individuals as members of the Council of the Administrative Conference of the U.S.:

Ronald A. Cass;
Mariano-Florentino Cuellar;
Julius M. Genachowski;
Theodore B. Olson;
Thomas Perez;
Jane C. Sherburne; and
Patricia McGowan Wald.

The President announced that he has appointed Preeta D. Bansal as Vice Chair of the Council of the Administrative Conference of the U.S.

The President announced that he has appointed Thomasina Rogers and Michael Fitzpatrick as members of the Council of the Administrative Conference of the U.S.

July 9

In the morning, the President had an intelligence briefing. Later, he returned to Washington, DC, arriving in the afternoon.

During the day, the President had a telephone conversation with President Mahmoud Abbas of the Palestinian Authority to discuss Middle East peace efforts and the situation in Gaza and the West Bank.

The White House announced that the President will host President Leonel Fernandez Reyna of the Dominican Republic at the White House on July 12 for a working meeting.

The President announced his intention to nominate Pamela E. Bridgewater to be Ambassador to Jamaica.

The President announced his intention to nominate Sean P. "Jack" Buckley to be Commissioner of Education Statistics at the National Center for Education Statistics at the Department of Education.

The President announced his intention to nominate Robert P. Mikulak for the rank of Ambassador during his tenure as U.S. Representative to the Organisation for the Prohibition of Chemical Weapons.

The President announced his intention to nominate Phyllis M. Powers to be Ambassador to Panama.

July 10

The President declared a major disaster in Montana and ordered Federal aid to supplement State and local recovery efforts in the area struck by severe storms and flooding beginning on June 15 and continuing.

July 12

In the morning, in the Oval Office, the President and Vice President Joe Biden had an intelligence briefing followed by an economic briefing. Later, he had a telephone conversation with President Yoweri Kaguta Museveni of Uganda to express his condolences for those killed in the July 11 terrorist bombings in Kampala and offered U.S. assistance.

In the afternoon, in the Oval Office, the President met with his senior advisers. Later, also in the Oval Office, he met with Boy Scouts of America participants and executive leadership.

July 13

In the morning, in the Oval Office, the President and Vice President Joe Biden had an intelligence briefing. Then, also in the Oval Office, he met with his senior advisers. Later, in the Roosevelt Room, he and Vice President Biden met with Senate Democratic leaders to discuss legislative priorities before the August recess.

In the afternoon, in the Private Dining Room, the President and Vice President Bidenhad lunch. Later, in the Oval Office, they met with Secretary of Defense Robert M. Gates.

The President announced his intention to nominate Jacob J. "Jack" Lew to be Director of the Office of Management and Budget.

July 14

In the morning, in the Oval Office, the President and Vice President Joe Biden had an intelligence briefing followed by an economic briefing. Later, also in the Oval Office, he met with his senior advisers. He then met with Warren E. Buffett, chief executive officer and chairman, Berkshire Hathaway Inc.

In the afternoon, in the Roosevelt Room, the President and Vice President Biden had lunch with Sens. Amy J. Klobuchar, Sheldon Whitehouse, Sherrod Brown, Robert P. Casey, Jr., and Claire McCaskill. Later, at the Dwight D. Eisenhower Executive Office Building, he attended a meeting on the administration's progress in increasing and improving cybersecurity. Then, in the Roosevelt Room, he and Vice President Biden hosted a meeting with former President William J. Clinton and business leaders.

Later in the afternoon, the President had a conference call with Secretary of Energy Steven Chu, Secretary of Homeland Security Janet A. Napolitano, Secretary of the Interior Kenneth L. Salazar, Environmental Protection Agency Administrator Lisa P. Jackson, Adm. Thad W. Allen, USCG (Ret.), in his capacity as national incident commander for the Deepwater Horizon oil spill, and Assistant to the President for Energy and Climate Change Carol M. Browner to discuss oil spill response efforts in the Gulf of Mexico and BP p.l.c.'s efforts to cap the Deepwater Horizon oil well. Later, in the Oval Office, he and Vice President Biden met with Secretary of State Hillary Rodham Clinton. Then, also in the Oval Office, they met with House Democratic leaders to discuss legislative priorities before the August recess.

The President announced that he has nominated Mark F. Green to be U.S. attorney for the Eastern District of Oklahoma.

The President announced that he has nominated Joseph H. Hogsett to be U.S. attorney for the Southern District of Indiana.

The President announced that he has nominated Marco A. Hernandez to be a judge on the U.S. District Court for the District of Oregon.

The President announced that he has nominated Beryl A. Howell to be a judge on the U.S. District Court for the District of Columbia.

The President announced that he has nominated Steve C. Jones to be a judge on the U.S. District Court for the Northern District of Georgia.

The President announced that he has nominated Diana Saldana to be a judge on the U.S.

District Court for the Southern District of Texas.

The President announced that he has nominated Michael H. Simon to be a judge on the U.S. District Court for the District of Oregon.

The President announced that he has nominated Victoria F. Nourse to be a judge on the U.S. Court of Appeals for the Seventh Circuit.

The President announced that he has nominated Conrad E. Candelaria to be U.S. marshal for the District of New Mexico.

The President announced that he has nominated James E. Clark to be U.S. marshal for the Western District of Kentucky.

The President announced that he has nominated Joseph A. Papili to be U.S. marshal for the District of Delaware.

The President announced that he has nominated James A. Thompson to be U.S. marshal for the District of Utah.

The President declared a major disaster in Wyoming and ordered Federal aid to supplement State and local recovery efforts in the area struck by flooding from June 4 through 18.

July 15

In the morning, in the Oval Office, the President had an intelligence briefing. Then, also in the Oval Office, he met with his senior advisers. Later, he traveled to Grand Rapids, MI, arriving in the afternoon.

Later in the afternoon, at Gerald R. Ford International Airport, the President participated in an interview with Chuck Todd of NBC News. He then returned to Washington, DC.

During the day, the President had a telephone conversation with President Ali Abdallah Salih of Yemen.

The President announced his intention to nominate Kristie A. Kenney to be Ambassador to Thailand.

The President announced his intention to nominate Jo Ellen Powell to be Ambassador to Mauritania.

The President declared a major disaster in Nebraska and ordered Federal aid to supplement State and local recovery efforts in the area struck by severe storms, flooding, and tornadoes beginning on June 1 and continuing.

July 16

In the morning, the President, Mrs. Obama, and their daughters Sasha and Malia traveled to Bar Harbor, ME, arriving in the afternoon.

Later in the afternoon, the President, Mrs. Obama, and their daughters visited Acadia National Park. Later, they toured Frenchman Bay. They then returned to Bar Harbor.

July 17

In the morning, the President had an intelligence briefing.

In the afternoon, the President, Mrs. Obama, and their daughters Sasha and Malia visited Acadia National Park. Later, they returned to Bar Harbor, ME.

July 18

In the morning, the President, Mrs. Obama, and their daughters Sasha and Malia returned to Washington, DC, arriving in the afternoon.

July 19

In the morning, in the Oval Office, the President had an intelligence briefing followed by an economic briefing.

In the afternoon, in the Oval Office, the President met with his senior advisers. Later, also in the Oval Office, he met with former Senator and astronaut John H. Glenn, Jr., to discuss the future of the space program.

July 20

In the morning, in the Oval Office, the President had an intelligence briefing. Then, also in the Oval Office, he met with his senior advisers. Later, also in the Oval Office, he met with Prime Minister David Cameron of the United Kingdom.

In the afternoon, in the State Dining Room, the President and Vice President Joe Biden hosted a working lunch with Prime Minister Cameron.

During the day, the President was briefed on the situation surrounding the firing of Shirley Sherrod, former Georgia State Director for Rural Development at the U.S. Department of Agriculture.

The President announced his intention to nominate Mark M. Boulware to be Ambassador to Chad.

The President announced his intention to nominate Christopher J. McMullen to be Ambassador to Angola.

The President announced his intention to nominate Joseph A. Mussomeli to be Ambassador to Slovenia.

The President announced his intention to nominate Wanda L. Nesbitt to be Ambassador to Namibia.

The President announced his intention to nominate Karen Brevard Stewart to be Ambassador to Laos.

The President announced his intention to appoint Helen Hurcombe, Kathleen Martinez, and Pamela C. Schwenke as members of the Committee for Purchase From People Who Are Blind or Severely Disabled.

July 21

In the morning, in the Oval Office, the President had an intelligence briefing followed by an economic briefing. Later, also in the Oval Office, he met with Vice President Joe Biden.

In the afternoon, in the Roosevelt Room, the President and Vice President Biden had lunch with Members of the House of Representatives. Later, in the Oval Office, he met with his senior advisers. Then, in the Situation Room, he was briefed on the oil spill in the Gulf of Mexico.

During the day, the President was briefed on the situation surrounding the firing of Shirley Sherrod, former Georgia State Director for Rural Development at the U.S. Department of Agriculture.

In the evening, the President had a telephone conversation with Secretary of Agriculture Thomas J. Vilsack.

The President announced that he has nominated Charles B. Day to be a judge on the U.S. District Court for the District of Maryland.

The President announced that he has nominated Kathleen M. Williams to be a judge on the U.S. District Court for the Southern District of Florida.

The President announced that he has nominated Albert Najera to be U.S. marshal for the Eastern District of California.

The President announced that he has nominated William C. Sibert to be U.S. marshal for the Eastern District of Missouri.

The President announced that he has nominated Myron M. Sutton to be U.S. marshal for the Northern District of Indiana.

July 22

In the morning, in the Oval Office, the President had an intelligence briefing followed by an economic briefing. Then, also in the Oval Office, he met with his senior advisers.

In the afternoon, the President had a telephone conversation with Shirley Sherrod, former Georgia State Director for Rural Development at the U.S. Department of Agriculture. Later, in the Oval Office, he met with Gen. Raymond T. Odierno, USA, commanding general, U.S. Forces—Iraq, and U.S. Ambassador to Iraq Christopher R. Hill. Then, also in the Oval Office, he met with Secretary of the Treasury Timothy F. Geithner.

The President announced his intention to appoint Howard L. Gottlieb as a member of the President's Committee on the Arts and the Humanities.

The President announced his intention to appoint Elaine Wynn as a member of the Board of Trustees of the John F. Kennedy Center for the Performing Arts.

July 23

In the morning, in the Oval Office, the President had an intelligence briefing. Then, also in the Oval Office, he met with his senior advisers.

During the day, in the Situation Room, the President was briefed by Rear Adm. Peter V. Neffenger, USCG, in his capacity as deputy national incident commander for the Deepwater Horizon oil spill, Federal Emergency Management Agency Administrator W. Craig Fugate, and Federal Emergency Management Agency Deputy Administrator Richard Serino on the response to the oil spill in the Gulf of Mexico and the potential impact of Tropical Storm Bonnie on cleanup efforts.

The President declared a major disaster in Kentucky and ordered Federal aid to supplement Commonwealth and local recovery efforts in the area struck by severe storms, flooding, and mudslides beginning on July 17 and continuing.

July 26

In the afternoon, in the Oval Office, the President met with Space Shuttle *Atlantis* and International Space Station crewmembers. Later, also in the Oval Office, he had an intelligence briefing. He then met with his senior advisers.

Later in the afternoon, in the Oval Office, he had an economic briefing, followed by a meeting with Secretary of State Hillary Rodham Clinton. Later, also in the Oval Office, he met with Reps. Steny H. Hoyer, James R. Langevin, and Frank J. Sensenbrenner, Jr., and Sen. Thomas R. Harkin.

During the day, the President had a telephone conversation with Carl-Henric Svanberg, chairman of the board of BP p.l.c., to discuss the company's change in leadership.

The President announced his intention to appoint David Grubb, William R. Hambrecht, and Charlene Harvey as members of the Board of Directors of the Presidio Trust.

The President announced that he has appointed Daphne Kwok as Chair of the President's Advisory Commission on Asian Americans and Pacific Islanders.

The President declared a major disaster in Oklahoma and ordered Federal aid to supplement State and local recovery efforts in the area struck by severe storms, tornadoes, straightline winds, and flooding from June 13 through 15.

July 27

In the morning, in the Oval Office, the President had an intelligence briefing followed by an economic briefing.

In the afternoon, in the Roosevelt Room, the President had lunch with Members of the House of Representatives. Later, in the East Room, he met with the Warner Robins, GA, softball team to congratulate them on winning the 2009 Little League Softball World Series.

Then, in the Oval Office, he met with Secretary of the Treasury Timothy F. Geithner.

Later in the afternoon, in the Oval Office, the President met with Secretary of Defense Robert M. Gates.

In the evening, at the Mandarin Oriental, Washington, DC, hotel, the President attended a Democratic National Committee fundraising dinner.

The President declared a major disaster in Idaho and ordered Federal aid to supplement State and local recovery efforts in the area struck by severe storms and flooding from June 2 through 10.

July 28

In the morning, in the Oval Office, the President had an intelligence briefing. Then, also in the Oval Office, he met with his senior advisers. Later, also in the Oval Office, he met with Sen. John F. Kerry.

In the afternoon, the President traveled to Edison, NJ, where, at the Tastee Sub Shop, he met with small-business owners to discuss the economy and small-business legislation. Later, he traveled to New York City, where, at ABC Studios, he participated in an interview for "The View" program.

Later in the afternoon, at the Four Seasons Hotel New York, the President attended a Democratic National Committee fundraiser.

In the evening, at a private residence, the President attended a Democratic National Committee fundraiser. Later, he returned to Washington, DC.

The President announced the designation of the following individuals as members of a Presidential delegation to Colombia to attend the inauguration of Juan Manuel Santos Calderon on August 7: James L. Jones, Jr. (head of delegation); and William R. Brownfield.

The President announced that he has nominated Ripley E. Rand to be U.S. attorney for the Middle District of North Carolina.

The President announced that he has nominated M. Scott Bowen to be U.S. attorney for the Western District of Michigan.

The President announced that he has nominated Marina Garcia Marmolejo to be a judge

on the U.S. District Court for the Southern District of Texas.

The President announced that he has nominated Maria E. Raffinan to be an associate judge on the Superior Court of the District of Columbia.

The President announced that he has nominated Beverly J. Harvard to be U.S. marshal for the Northern District of Georgia.

The President announced that he has nominated David M. Singer to be U.S. marshal for the Central District of California.

July 29

In the morning, in the Situation Room, the President and Vice President Joe Biden met with their national security team to discuss the situation in Afghanistan and Pakistan.

In the afternoon, in the Private Dining Room, the President had lunch with Vice President Biden. Later, in the Oval Office, he had an intelligence briefing.

During the day, in the Roosevelt Room, the President dropped by a meeting between National Security Adviser James L. Jones, Jr., Secretary of Veterans Affairs Eric K. Shinseki, and representatives of veterans service organizations.

In the evening, at a private residence, the President attended a Democratic National Committee fundraiser.

The President declared a major disaster in South Dakota and ordered Federal aid to supplement State and local recovery efforts in the area struck by severe storms, tornadoes, and flooding from June 16 through 24.

The President declared a major disaster in Iowa and ordered Federal aid to supplement State and local recovery efforts in the area struck by severe storms, flooding, and tornadoes beginning on June 1 and continuing.

July 30

In the morning, the President traveled to Detroit, MI, where he toured the Chrysler Jefferson North Assembly Plant.

In the afternoon, the President traveled to Hamtramck, MI, where he toured the General Motors Detroit-Hamtramck Assembly Center. Later, he participated in an interview with

Harry Smith of CBS News. He then returned to Washington, DC.

August 1

In the afternoon, at the Verizon Center, the President and his daughter Sasha attended a basketball game between the Women's National Basketball Association's Washington Mystics and Tulsa Shock.

August 2

In the morning, the President traveled to Atlanta, GA.

In the afternoon, the President returned to Washington, DC. Then, in the Oval Office, he met with his senior advisers.

August 3

In the morning, in the Oval Office, the President had an intelligence briefing followed by an economic briefing.

In the afternoon, at the Dwight D. Eisenhower Executive Office Building, the President met with African Growth and Opportunity Act Trade and Economic Cooperation Forum participants. Later, in the Oval Office, he met with Secretary of Defense Robert M. Gates.

During the day, on the South Lawn, the President met with children attending a "Let's Move!" initiative tennis clinic.

In the evening, the President was briefed on the Gulf of Mexico oil spill by Assistant to the President for Energy and Climate Change Carol M. Browner. He then had a telephone conversation with Secretary of Energy Steven Chu and Thomas O. Hunter, former President and Director, Sandia National Laboratories, to discuss BP p.l.c.'s static kill procedure.

The President declared a major disaster in Texas and ordered Federal aid to supplement State and local recovery efforts in the area struck by Hurricane Alex beginning on June 30 and continuing.

August 4

In the morning, in the Oval Office, the President had an intelligence briefing. Then, also in the Oval Office, he met with his senior advisers and was briefed on the Gulf of Mexico oil spill. Later, he met with Adm. Thad W. Allen, USCG (Ret.), in his capacity as national incident commander for the Deepwater Horizon oil spill.

Later in the morning, the President had a telephone conversation with Mrs. Obama and their daughter Sasha, who both wished him a happy birthday. Then, he had a telephone conversation with his daughter Malia, who also wished him a happy birthday.

In the afternoon, in the Roosevelt Room, the President had lunch with Senators. Later, in the Oval Office, he met with Senate Minority Leader A. Mitchell McConnell.

Later in the afternoon, the President traveled to Chicago, IL. Upon arrival, he traveled to the Obama residence in Hyde Park.

The President announced his intention to nominate Scott C. Doney to be Chief Scientist at the National Oceanic and Atmospheric Administration at the Department of Commerce.

The President announced his intention to nominate Nancy E. Lindborg to be Assistant Administrator of the Democracy, Conflict, and Humanitarian Assistance Bureau at the U.S. Agency for International Development.

The President announced his intention to nominate Kevin G. Nealer to be a member of the Board of Directors of the Overseas Private Investment Corporation.

The President announced his intention to nominate Chase T. Rogers and Wilfredo Martinez to be members of the State Justice Institute.

The President announced his intention to appoint Warren M. Stern to be Director of the Domestic Nuclear Detection Office at the Department of Homeland Security.

The President announced that he has nominated Jeffrey T. Holt to be U.S. marshal for the Western District of Tennessee.

The President announced that he has nominated Steven C. Stafford to be U.S. marshal for the Southern District of California.

The President announced that he has nominated Paul C. Thielen to be U.S. marshal for the District of South Dakota.

August 5

In the morning, the President toured a Ford Motor Company assembly plant.

In the evening, at a private residence, the President attended a Democratic National Committee fundraiser. Later, he returned to Washington, DC.

The President announced his intention to nominate Allison Blakely to be a member of the National Council on the Humanities.

The President announced his intention to nominate David B. Buckley to be Inspector General of the Central Intelligence Agency.

The President announced his intention to nominate Cora B. Marrett to be Deputy Director of the National Science Foundation.

The President announced his intention to nominate Donald K. Steinberg to be Deputy Administrator of the U.S. Agency for International Development.

The President announced his intention to nominate Juan F. Vasquez to be a judge on the U.S. Tax Court.

August 6

In the morning, the President had a telephone conversation with Prime Minister David Cameron of the United Kingdom. Later, in the Oval Office, he had an intelligence briefing followed by an economic briefing. Later, he toured Gelberg Signs.

In the afternoon, in the Oval Office, the President met with Secretary of State Hillary Rodham Clinton.

August 8

In the afternoon, at Fort McNair, the President played a basketball game with college and professional basketball players for wounded military personnel and participants in the White House Mentorship Program.

In the evening, on the South Lawn, the President, Mrs. Obama, and their daughter Sasha attended a barbecue to celebrate his birthday.

August 9

In the morning, the President traveled to Austin, TX.

In the afternoon, the President traveled to Dallas, TX. Later, he returned to Washington, DC, arriving in the evening.

August 10

In the morning, in the Oval Office, the President had an intelligence briefing, during which he was briefed on the flooding in Pakistan. Then, also in the Oval Office, he had an economic briefing.

In the afternoon, in the Oval Office, the President met with his senior advisers. Later, also in the Oval Office, he participated in a credentialing ceremony for newly appointed Ambassadors. Then, also in the Oval Office, he met with Secretary of Defense Robert M. Gates.

In the evening, the President had a telephone conversation with Sen. Michael F. Bennet to congratulate him on his Colorado primary election victory.

The President declared a major disaster in Kansas and ordered Federal aid to supplement State and local recovery efforts in the area struck by severe storms, flooding, and tornadoes from June 7 through July 21.

August 11

In the morning, in the Oval Office, the President had an intelligence briefing, during which he was briefed on the flooding in Pakistan. Then, also in the Oval Office, he met with his senior advisers. Later, in the Situation Room, he and Vice President Joe Biden met with the President's national security team to discuss the drawdown of U.S. military forces in Iraq, the upcoming end of U.S. combat operations in Iraq, and Iraq's efforts to form a new Government after the March 7 parliamentary elections.

In the afternoon, in the Private Dining Room, the President had lunch with Vice President Biden. Later, in the Oval Office, he met with Secretary of the Navy Raymond E. Mabus, Jr. Then, also in the Oval Office, he met with Secretary of State Hillary Rodham Clinton.

The President declared a major disaster in Wisconsin and ordered Federal aid to supplement State and local recovery efforts in the area struck by severe storms, tornadoes, and flooding from July 20 through 24.

August 12

In the morning, in the Oval Office, the President had an intelligence briefing, during which he was briefed on the flooding in Pakistan. Then, also in the Oval Office, he had an economic briefing followed by a meeting with his senior advisers.

During the day, in the Rose Garden, the President participated in a photograph with the White House summer interns. He also had a telephone conversation with President Dmitry A. Medvedev of Russia to express his condolences for the country's losses during the recent wildfires and to inform him that the U.S. Agency for International Development, the Department of Defense, the U.S. Forest Service, and the State of California are mobilizing firefighting and airlift equipment in response to Russia's request for technical assistance in combating the wildfires.

August 13

In the morning, in the Oval Office, the President had an intelligence briefing, during which he was briefed on the flooding in Pakistan. Then, also in the Oval Office, he met with his senior advisers.

During the day, in the Oval Office, the President participated in the departure ceremony of Lt. Col. David Kalinske, USMC, Marine Corps Aide to the President. He also had a video teleconference with President Hamid Karzai of Afghanistan, U.S. Ambassador to Afghanistan Karl W. Eikenberry, and Gen. David H. Petraeus, USA, commander, NATO International Security Assistance Force, Afghanistan.

August 14

In the morning, the President, Mrs. Obama, and their daughter Sasha traveled to Panama City Beach, FL. He and Mrs. Obama then traveled to U.S. Coast Guard Station Panama City.

In the afternoon, the President and Mrs. Obama traveled to the Bay Point Marriott Golf Resort & Spa, where they met Sasha. Later, he and Sasha swam at Alligator Point.

August 15

In the morning, the President, Mrs. Obama, and their daughter Sasha toured St. Andrews Bay, FL.

In the afternoon, the President, Mrs. Obama, and Sasha returned to Washington, DC.

August 16

In the morning, the President traveled to Menomonee Falls, WI, where he toured the ZBB Energy Corporation manufacturing facility. He then met with 103-year-old World War II veteran and Milwaukee resident James Edwards.

In the afternoon, the President traveled to Milwaukee, WI. Later, he traveled to Los Angeles, CA. Upon arrival, he traveled to the Beverly Hilton hotel.

In the evening, the President traveled to a private residence. Later, he returned to the Beverly Hilton hotel.

August 17

In the morning, the President had an intelligence briefing, during which he was briefed on the terrorist attack in Baghdad, Iraq. He then traveled to Seattle, WA.

In the afternoon, the President traveled to Columbus, OH, arriving in the evening. He then traveled to the Westin Columbus Hotel.

The White House announced that the President will participate in the North Atlantic Treaty Organization Summit on November 19 and 20 in Lisbon, Portugal.

The White House announced that the President will participate in a summit with European Union leaders, European Council President Herman Van Rompuy, and European Commission President Jose Manuel Durao Barroso on November 20 in Lisbon, Portugal.

The President declared a major disaster in Missouri and ordered Federal aid to supplement State and local recovery efforts in the area struck by severe storms, flooding, and tornadoes from June 12 through July 31.

August 18

In the morning, the President traveled to the home of Rhonda and Joe Weithman, where he met with them and their children Rachel and Josh.

In the afternoon, the President traveled to Miami, FL.

In the evening, at Jerry's Famous Deli, the President had dinner with Rep. Kendrick B. Meek, participated in a photograph with deli staff members, and met with patrons. He then returned to Washington, DC.

August 19

In the afternoon, the President traveled to Martha's Vineyard, MA.

The President announced his intention to recess appoint Maria del Carmen Aponte as U.S. Ambassador El Salvador.

The President announced his intention to recess appoint Elisabeth A. Hagen as Under Secretary for Food Safety at the Department of Agriculture.

The President announced his intention to recess appoint Winslow L. Sargeant as Chief Counsel for Advocacy at the Small Business Administration.

The President announced his intention to recess appoint Richard Sorian as Assistant Secretary for Public Affairs at the Department of Health and Human Services.

The President declared a major disaster in Illinois and ordered Federal aid to supplement State and local recovery efforts in the area struck by severe storms and flooding from July 22 through August 7.

August 21

In the morning, the President had an intelligence briefing.

August 23

In the morning, the President had an intelligence briefing.

August 24

In the morning, the President had an intelligence briefing. Later, he had an economic briefing.

August 25

In the morning, the President had an intelligence briefing. Later, he had a conference call with Secretary of the Treasury Timothy F. Geithner, Council of Economic Advisers Chair Christina D. Romer, and National Economic Council Director Lawrence H. Summers to discuss the economic situation, global financial markets situation, and efforts to strengthen the economy.

During the day, the President had a telephone conversation with Prime Minister David Cameron of the United Kingdom to congratulate him and his wife Samantha on the birth of their daughter Florence Rose Endellion and to discuss Middle East peace efforts.

August 26

In the morning, the President had an intelligence briefing.

August 27

In the morning, the President had an intelligence briefing.

August 28

In the morning, the President had an intelligence briefing.

August 29

In the morning, the President, Mrs. Obama, and their daughters Sasha and Malia traveled to New Orleans, LA.

In the afternoon, at Parkway Bakery & Tavern, the President, Mrs. Obama, and their daughters had lunch and met with staff members and patrons. Then, at Xavier University, he met with community leaders. Later, at the Columbia Parc at the Bayou District housing development, he participated in an interview with Brian Williams of "NBC Nightly News."

Later in the afternoon, the President and Mrs. Obama toured the Columbia Parc housing development with Secretary of Housing and Urban Development Shaun L.S. Donovan and Mayor Mitchell J. Landrieu of New Orleans, LA. They then met with Columbia Parc resident Maude Smith and her grandchildren ShaLynde Smith and David Robichaux, Jr.

Later, they returned to Washington, DC, arriving in the evening.

August 30

In the morning, in the Oval Office, the President met with his senior advisers. Then, also in the Oval Office, he had an intelligence briefing.

In the afternoon, in the Oval Office, the President had an economic briefing. Later, at Walter Reed Army Medical Center, he met with U.S. military personnel wounded in Afghanistan and Iraq and awarded 14 Purple Heart medals.

August 31

In the morning, the President had an intelligence briefing, during which he was briefed on the arrest of two U.S. residents by Dutch authorities upon their arrival in Amsterdam, the Netherlands, on suspicion of conspiracy to commit a terrorist attack. He then traveled to Fort Bliss, TX. While en route aboard Air Force One, he had a telephone conversation with former President George W. Bush to discuss the end of combat operations and drawdown of U.S. military forces in Iraq.

Later in the morning, upon arrival at Biggs Army Airfield, the President met with U.S. military personnel and Gold Star families. Then, at the Fort Bliss mess hall, he met with U.S. military personnel. Later, he returned to Washington, DC, arriving in the afternoon.

During the day, the President had a telephone conversation with King Abdallah bin Abd al-Aziz Al Saud of Saudi Arabia to discuss regional issues, Middle East peace efforts, and the end of U.S. combat operations in Iraq.

September 1

In the morning, the President had a telephone conversation with Federal Emergency Management Agency Administrator W. Craig Fugate, who briefed him on the disaster preparedness efforts being made on the East Coast in advance of Hurricane Earl and the impact of Hurricane Earl on Puerto Rico and the U.S. Virgin Islands.

In the afternoon, in the Oval Office, the President met with President Mahmoud Abbas of the Palestinian Authority. Later, also in the Oval Office, he met with King Abdullah II of Jordan to discuss Middle East peace efforts, regional issues, and Jordan-U.S. relations. Then, also in the Oval Office, he met with President Mohamed Hosni Mubarak of Egypt to discuss Middle East peace efforts, Egypt-U.S. relations, and democracy and civil and human rights efforts in Egypt.

In the evening, in the Old Family Dining Room, the President hosted a working dinner with Prime Minister Benjamin Netanyahu, President Abbas, King Abdullah II, and President Mubarak.

The President declared an emergency in North Carolina and ordered Federal aid to supplement State and local response efforts due to the emergency conditions resulting from Hurricane Earl beginning on September 1 and continuing.

September 2

In the morning, in the Situation Room, the President met with his national security team, during which Homeland Security and Counterterrorism Adviser John O. Brennan briefed him on the Vermilion 380 platform fire in the Gulf of Mexico and the subsequent Federal response efforts.

In the afternoon, in the Oval Office, the President had an economic briefing. He then had a telephone conversation with Federal Emergency Management Agency Administrator W. Craig Fugate to discuss the disaster preparedness efforts being made in advance of Hurricane Earl.

During the day, the President had a telephone conversation with President Nicolas Sarkozy of France to thank him for his support of efforts to reach a comprehensive Middle East peace agreement and to discuss the next steps in encouraging further direct talks between Israel and the Palestinian Authority.

The President declared an emergency in Massachusetts and ordered Federal aid to supplement Commonwealth and local response efforts in the area struck by Hurricane Earl beginning on September 1 and continuing.

September 3

In the afternoon, the President traveled to Camp David, MD.

The White House announced that the President will welcome Secretary General Anders Fogh Rasmussen of the North Atlantic Treaty Organization to the White House on September 7.

The White House announced that the President will host a meeting with leaders of the Association of Southeast Asian Nations (ASEAN) in New York City on September 24.

September 4

In the morning, the President had an intelligence briefing.

September 5

In the afternoon, the President returned to Washington, DC.

September 6

In the afternoon, the President traveled to Milwaukee, WI. Later, he returned to Washington, DC.

September 7

In the morning, in the Oval Office, the President and Vice President Joe Biden had an intelligence briefing followed by an economic briefing. Then, also in the Oval Office, they met with Secretary of State Hillary Rodham Clinton. Later, also in the Oval Office, he met with Secretary General Anders Fogh Rasmussen of the North Atlantic Treaty Organization.

In the afternoon, in the Private Dining Room, the President had lunch with Vice President Biden. Then, in the Oval Office, he met with his senior advisers. Later, also in the Oval Office, he and Vice President Biden met with Secretary of Defense Robert M. Gates.

During the day, the President had separate telephone conversations with Prime Minister David Cameron of the United Kingdom and Prime Minister Julia E. Gillard of Australia. He also met with Harvard Law School Leo Gottlieb Professor of Law Elizabeth Warren to discuss the creation of the Consumer Financial Protection Bureau.

September 8

In the morning, in the Oval Office, the President and Vice President Joe Biden had an intelligence briefing.

In the afternoon, the President traveled to Parma, OH. Later, at Cuyahoga Community College Western Campus, he participated in an interview with George Stephanopoulos of ABC's "Good Morning America" program. He then returned to Washington, DC.

Later in the afternoon, in the Oval Office, the President met with his senior advisers.

September 9

In the morning, in the Oval Office, the President and Vice President Joe Biden had an intelligence briefing. Then, also in the Oval Office, he met with his senior advisers. Later, he participated in a telephone interview with Tom Joyner of "The Tom Joyner Morning Show" for later broadcast and an interview with Antonieta Cadiz of La Opinion newspaper.

In the afternoon, the President met with Secretary of the Treasury Timothy F. Geithner.

During the day, the President had a telephone conversation with S. Sgt. Salvatore A. Giunta, USA, to inform him that he will be awarded the Congressional Medal of Honor for acts of gallantry at the risk of his life that went above and beyond the call of duty while serving as a rifle team leader with Company B, 2d Battalion (Airborne), 503d Infantry Regiment, 173d Airborne Brigade during combat operations in the Korengal Valley, Afghanistan, on October 25, 2007.

September 10

In the morning, in the Oval Office, the President had an intelligence briefing.

In the afternoon, in the Oval Office, the President met with his senior advisers.

The President announced the designation of the following individuals as members of a Presidential delegation to Mexico City to attend the bicentennial of the independence of Mexico on September 14:

Hilda L. Solis (head of delegation);
Carlos Pascual;

Maria Otero; and
Julian Castro.

The President announced his intention to nominate Cameron Munter to be Ambassador to Pakistan.

The President announced his intention to nominate Pamela A. White to be Ambassador to the Gambia.

The President announced his intention to nominate Samuel E. Angel to be a Commissioner of the Mississippi River Commission.

The President announced his intention to nominate Marsha Ternus to be a member of the Board of Directors of the State Justice Institute.

The President announced his intention to nominate Thomas M. Beck to be a member of the National Mediation Board.

The President announced his intention to appoint Karen L. Braitmayer and Howard A. Rosenblum as members of the Architectural and Transportation Barriers Compliance Board (U.S. Access Board).

The President announced his intention to appoint the following individuals as members of the President's Board of Advisers on Historically Black Colleges and Universities:

Demetria Henderson;
Helen T. McAlpine;
Alma J. Powell;
E. John Rice, Jr.; and
Dianne Boardley Suber.

The President announced that he has designated Austan D. Goolsbee as Chair of the Council of Economic Advisers.

September 11

In the morning, at 8:46 a.m., in the Diplomatic Reception Room, the President participated in a moment of silence to commemorate the ninth anniversary of the September 11, 2001, terrorist attacks. Later, he traveled to Arlington, VA.

Later in the morning, the President returned to Washington, DC. Then, at Ronald H. Brown Middle School of Technology, he participated in a service project with Armed Services YMCA volunteers for Operation Kid Comfort in honor of the National Day of Service and Remembrance.

During the day, the President had a telephone conversation with Gov. Arnold A. Schwarzenegger of California to express his condolences for the loss of life and his concern for those recovering from injuries due to the September 9 gas line explosion in San Bruno and offered Federal assistance.

September 12

In the evening, the President had a telephone conversation with Prime Minister Recep Tayyip Erdogan of Turkey at the start of the 2010 FIBA World Championship game between the Turkey and U.S. basketball teams to congratulate him on the country's successful hosting of the tournament and to discuss democracy efforts in the country after its vote on the Turkish constitutional referendum.

September 13

In the morning, in the Oval Office, the President had an intelligence briefing. Later, in the Situation Room, he met with his national security team to discuss the situation in Afghanistan and Pakistan.

In the afternoon, the President traveled to Fairfax, VA, where, at the residence of John Nicholas and Nicole Armstrong, he met with them and their children Trevor and Olivia. Later, he returned to Washington, DC. Then, in the Oval Office, he met with his senior advisers.

Later in the afternoon, the President met with Secretary of Defense Robert M. Gates.

The President announced the designation of the following individuals as members of a Presidential delegation to Santiago, Chile, to attend the bicentennial of the Republic of Chile on September 18: Arturo Valenzuela (head of delegation); and Alejandro D. Wolff.

The President declared a major disaster in New Mexico and ordered Federal aid to supplement State and local recovery efforts in the area struck by severe storms and flooding from July 25 through August 9.

September 14

In the morning, in the Oval Office, the President and Vice President Joe Biden had an intelligence briefing followed by an economic briefing. Then, also in the Oval Office, he met with his senior advisers. Later, he traveled to Philadelphia, PA, arriving in the afternoon.

Later in the afternoon, the President returned to Washington, DC.

In the evening, he had separate telephone conversations with several congressional candidates to discuss the primary election results.

September 15

In the morning, in the Oval Office, the President had an intelligence briefing. Then, also in the Oval Office, he met with his senior advisers. Later, also in the Oval Office, he and Vice President Joe Biden met with Gen. Raymond T. Odierno, USA, incoming commander, U.S. Joint Forces Command, to thank him for his leadership of U.S. Forces—Iraq, his over 4 years of service in Iraq, and his role in supervising the drawdown of U.S. military forces in Iraq.

In the afternoon, in the Cabinet Room, the President held a Cabinet meeting. Later, in the Oval Office, he met with Secretary of Education Arne Duncan and Rep. George Miller.

The President announced his intention to nominate Carol Fulp, C. Jeanne Shaheen, and Roger F. Wicker to be U.S. Representatives to the 65th Session of the United Nations General Assembly.

The President announced his intention to nominate Gregory J. Nickels to be U.S. Alternate Representative to the 65th Session of the United Nations General Assembly.

The President announced his intention to appoint Marcelite J. Harris and Arlen D. Jameson as members of the Board of Visitors to the U.S. Air Force Academy.

The President announced his intention to appoint the following individuals as members of the Advisory Committee for Trade Policy and Negotiations:

Jill Appell;
Pamela G. Bailey;

C. Fred Bergsten;
Bobbi Brown;
Michael E. Campbell;
Lisa Carty;
Christopher J. Christie;
Michael L. Ducker;
John "Buddy" Dyer;
John B. Emerson;
Bill Frenzel;
Dean C. Garfield;
Leo W. Gerard;
Joseph T. Hansen;
James P. Hoffa;
Robert Holleyman;
Sandra Kennedy;
Jim Kolbe;
Fred Krupp;
David Lane;
Kase Lawal;
Robert A. McDonald;
Harold T. McGraw III;
Wade Randlett;
Robert W. Roche;
Matthew Rubel;
David H. Segura;
Bob Stallman;
John P. Surma; and
Luis A. Ubinas.

The President declared a major disaster in Tennessee and ordered Federal aid to supplement State and local recovery efforts in the area struck by severe storms and flooding from August 17 through 21.

September 16

In the morning, the President and Vice President Joe Biden received a report on the National Export Initiative. Later, in the Oval Office, they had an economic briefing followed by an intelligence briefing. Then, also in the Oval Office, he met with his senior advisers.

In the afternoon, in the Private Dining Room, the President had lunch with Vice President Biden. Then, in the Oval Office, he participated in a credentialing ceremony for newly appointed Ambassadors. Later, also in the Oval Office, he met with Sen. Robert Menendez and Reps. Nydia M. Velazquez and Luis V. Gutierrez to discuss immigration reform.

Later in the afternoon, the President traveled to Stamford, CT.

During the day, the President met with Sen. Sheldon Whitehouse.

In the evening, at a private residence, the President attended a Democratic National Committee fundraiser. Later, he returned to Washington, DC.

The President announced his intention to appoint the following individuals as members of the President's Advisory Commission on Asian Americans and Pacific Islanders:

Sefa Aina;
Debra T. Cabrera;
Kamuela J.N. Enos;
Frances Eneski Francis;
Farooq Kathwari;
Hyeok Kim;
Ramey Ko;
Rozita Villanueva Lee;
Sunil Puri;
Amardeep Singh;
Unmi Song;
Dilawar A. Syed;
Khampha Thephavong;
Doua Thor;
Hector L. Vargas, Jr.; and
Hines Ward.

The President announced his intention to appoint John B. Nathman and Frank E. Petersen as members of the Board of Visitors to the U.S. Naval Academy.

The President announced that he has nominated Charles M. Oberly III to be U.S. attorney for the District of Delaware.

September 17

In the morning, in the Oval Office, the President and Vice President Joe Biden had an intelligence briefing.

The President announced his intention to nominate Rebecca F. Dye and Mario Cordero to be Commissioners of the Federal Maritime Commission.

The President announced his intention to nominate Stacia A. Hylton to be Director of the U.S. Marshals Service.

The President announced his intention to appoint the following individuals as members of the President's Committee on the National Medal of Science:

Carlos Castillo-Chavez;
Joseph S. Francisco;
Inez Fung; and
Margaret Murnane.

The President announced that he has appointed Elizabeth Warren as Assistant to the President and Special Adviser to the Secretary of the Treasury on the Consumer Financial Protection Bureau.

September 20

In the morning, in the Oval Office, the President had an intelligence briefing. Then, also in the Oval Officer, he met with his senior advisers.

In the afternoon, the President traveled to Philadelphia, PA. Later, he visited the Reading Terminal Market.

In the evening, the President returned to Washington, DC.

September 21

In the morning, in the Oval Office, the President had an intelligence briefing. Then, also in the Oval Office, he met with his senior advisers.

In the afternoon, in the Private Dining Room, the President had lunch with Vice President Joe Biden. Later, in the Oval Office, they met with Secretary of Defense Robert M. Gates.

Later in the afternoon, in the Map Room, the President participated in an interview with Jose Diaz-Balart of Telemundo's "Enfoque" program. Then, on the Rose Garden Patio, he participated in an interview with Mario "Don Francisco" Kreutzberger of Univision's "Sabado Gigante" program.

During the day, the President had a telephone conversation with members of the Seattle Storm to congratulate them on winning the

WNBA Finals for the second time and for their success during the regular season and playoffs.

The President announced the designation of the following individuals as members of a Presidential delegation to South Korea to attend the Seoul liberation commemoration ceremonies on September 27 and 28:

Eric K. Shinseki (head of delegation);
Kathleen Stephens;
John M. McHugh; and
Andrew J. Shapiro.

September 22

In the morning, in the Oval Office, the President had an intelligence briefing. Then, also in the Oval Office, he met with his senior advisers. Later, at the Dwight D. Eisenhower Executive Office Building, he dropped by a meeting between Secretary of Health and Human Services Kathleen Sebelius and Secretary of Labor Hilda L. Solis and State insurance commissioners.

Later in the morning, the President traveled to Falls Church, VA.

In the afternoon, the President returned to Washington, DC. Later, he traveled to New York City.

In the evening, the President traveled to the Waldorf-Astoria Hotel.

The President announced his intention to nominate William R. Brownfield to be Assistant Secretary for International Narcotics and Law Enforcement Affairs at the Department of State.

The President announced his intention to nominate Eugene L. Dodaro to be Comptroller General of the U.S.

The President announced his intention to nominate Matthew M.T. Kennedy to be a member of the Board of Directors of the Overseas Private Investment Corporation.

The President announced his intention to nominate Kurt W. Tong for the rank of Ambassador during his tenure of service as U.S. Senior Coordinator for the Asia-Pacific Economic Cooperation (APEC) Forum.

The President announced his intention to appoint Tom A. Bernstein as Chairman of the U.S. Holocaust Memorial Council.

The President announced his intention to appoint Joshua B. Bolten as Vice Chairman of the U.S. Holocaust Memorial Council.

The President announced his intention to appoint the following individuals as members of the U.S. Holocaust Memorial Council:

Matthew L. Adler;
Katharine D. Dukakis;
Karen Chaya Friedman;
Mark D. Goodman;
Ronald A. Ratner;
Menachem Z. Rosensaft; and
Kirk A. Rudy.

September 23

In the morning, the President had an intelligence briefing. He then traveled to United Nations Headquarters. Later, he returned to the Waldorf-Astoria Hotel.

In the afternoon, the President returned to U.N. Headquarters, where he attended a luncheon hosted by Secretary-General Ban Ki-moon of the United Nations. He then traveled to the Sheraton New York Hotel & Towers, where he was joined by Mrs. Obama. Later, they returned to the Waldorf-Astoria.

In the evening, the President and Mrs. Obama traveled to the American Museum of Natural History, where they hosted a reception in honor of the heads of delegations attending the U.N. General Assembly. Later, they returned to the Waldorf-Astoria.

The President announced his intention to nominate Paige E. Alexander to be Assistant Administrator for Europe and Eurasia at the U.S. Agency for International Development.

The President announced his intention to appoint the following individuals as general trustees of the Board of Trustees of the John F. Kennedy Center for the Performing Arts:

Gordon J. Davis;
Fred Eychaner;
Charles B. Ortner; and
Penny S. Pritzker.

The President declared a major disaster in South Dakota and ordered Federal aid to supplement State and local recovery efforts in the area struck by severe storms and flooding from July 21 through 30.

September 24

In the morning, the President met with President Ilham Aliyev of Azerbaijan. He then had a telephone conversation with Chancellor Angela Merkel of Germany to discuss Middle East peace efforts, the situation in Afghanistan, and Germany-U.S. relations.

In the afternoon, the President participated in a photograph with Association of Southeast Asian Nations (ASEAN) leaders. He then traveled to United Nations Headquarters. Later, he returned to the Waldorf-Astoria Hotel, where he met with President and Prime Minister Roza Otunbaeva of Krygyzstan.

Later in the afternoon, the President returned to Washington, DC, arriving in the evening.

September 27

In the morning, in the Green Room, the President participated in an interview with Matt Lauer of NBC's "Today" program. Later, in the Oval Office, he had an intelligence briefing. Then, also in the Oval Office, he met with his senior advisers.

In the afternoon, the President traveled to Albuquerque, NM, arriving in the evening.

The President announced the designation of the following individuals as members of a Presidential delegation to Nigeria to attend the 50th anniversary independence celebration on October 1:

Rajiv Shah (head of delegation);
Johnnie Carson;
James P. McAnulty; and
Walter C. Jones.

September 28

In the morning, the President met with Andrew D. and Etta Cavalier at their home. Later, he visited the Barelas Coffee House, where he met with staff members and patrons.

In the afternoon, the President traveled to Madison, WI. While en route aboard Air Force One, he had a telephone conversation with former President Jimmy Carter to wish him well after a recent illness and hospitalization. Later, he visited Robert M. La Follette High School, where he met with students and faculty.

Later in the afternoon, at the Madison Concourse Hotel and Governor's Club, the President attended a Democratic National Committee finance reception.

In the evening, the President participated in a radio interview with Warren Ballentine of "The Warren Ballentine Show." He then participated in a radio interview with Russ Parr of "The Russ Parr Morning Show" for later broadcast. Later, he traveled to Des Moines, IA, where he visited Baby Boomer's Cafe.

The President announced the designation of the following individuals as members of a Presidential delegation to Bremen, Germany, to attend the 20th anniversary of German unity on October 3: James L. Jones, Jr. (head of delegation); Philip D. Murphy; and Robert Hormats.

The President declared a major disaster in the U.S. Virgin Islands and ordered Federal aid to supplement Territory recovery efforts in the area struck by Hurricane Earl from August 29 through 31.

September 29

In the morning, at the residence of Jeff Clubb and Sandy Hatfield Clubb, the President met with them and their children Tristan and Skyelar.

In the afternoon, the President traveled to Richmond, VA. Later, at the Southampton Recreation Association, he met with Matthew and Stephanie Perry and their children Matthew and Lucy. Later, he returned to Washington, DC.

During the day, the President had a telephone conversation with Gov. Arnold A. Schwarzenegger of California.

The President announced his intention to nominate Mark F. Green and Alan J. Patricof to be members of the Board of Directors of the Millennium Challenge Corporation.

The President announced his intention to nominate Paula Barker Duffy and Martha Wagner Weinberg to be members of the National Council on the Humanities.

The President announced his intention to nominate Isabel Framer to be a member of the Board of Directors of the State Justice Institute.

The President announced his intention to nominate Susan H. Hildreth to be Director of the Institute of Museum and Library Services.

The President announced his intention to nominate Thomas R. Nides to be Deputy Secretary for Management and Resources at the Department of State.

The President announced his intention to nominate Jo Ann Rooney to be Principal Deputy Under Secretary for Personnel and Readiness at the Department of Defense.

The President announced his intention to nominate Michael Vickers to be Under Secretary for Intelligence at the Department of Defense.

The President announced that he has nominated Caitlin J. Halligan to be a judge on the U.S. Court of Appeals for the District of Columbia Circuit.

The President announced that he has nominated Jimmie V. Reyna to be a judge on the U.S. Court of Appeals for the Federal Circuit.

The President announced that he has nominated Mae A. D'Agostino to be a judge on the U.S. District Court for the Northern District of New York.

The President announced that he has nominated R. Brooke Jackson to be a judge on the U.S. District Court for the District of Colorado.

The President announced that he has nominated William C. Eldridge to be U.S. attorney for the Western District of Arkansas.

The President announced that he has nominated Kenneth F. Bohac to be U.S. marshal for the Central District of Illinois.

September 30

In the morning, in the Oval Office, the President and Vice President Joe Biden had an economic briefing. Then, also in the Oval Office, he had an intelligence briefing. Later, also in the Oval Office, he met with Secretary of the Treasury Timothy F. Geithner.

In the afternoon, in the Oval Office, the President met with Democratic congressional leaders. Later, also in the Oval Office, he met with his senior advisers.

During the day, the President had a telephone conversation with Prime Minister David Cameron of the United Kingdom to inform him that the U.S. Senate provided its advice and consent to the U.S.-United Kingdom Defense Trade Cooperation Treaty on the evening of September 29 and to discuss counterterrorism cooperation efforts and Middle East peace efforts.

October 1

In the morning, in the Oval Office, the President had an intelligence briefing. Then, he had a telephone conversation with President Dmitry A. Medvedev of Russia to discuss Russia's progress towards entry into the World Trade Organization, the prospects of their legislatures approving the new Strategic Arms Reduction Treaty, Iran's compliance with its international obligations, and the upcoming independence referendum in Southern Sudan. Later, also in the Oval Office, he met with Secretary of State Hillary Rodham Clinton.

In the afternoon, at the Supreme Court, the President attended Associate Justice Elena Kagan's investiture ceremony. Later, in the Oval Office, he had an economic briefing. Then, also in the Oval Office, he met with Secretary of Defense Robert M. Gates.

Also in the afternoon, the President had a telephone conversation with President Alvaro Colom Caballeros of Guatemala to express his deepest regrets regarding a U.S. Public Heath Service study on sexually transmitted diseases in the 1940s that infected Guatemalan citizens without their knowledge or consent, and to reassure him of the United States commitment to ethical medical practices.

October 2

In the morning, the President, Mrs. Obama, and their daughters Sasha and Malia traveled to Camp David, MD.

October 3

In the afternoon, the President, Mrs. Obama, and their daughters Sasha and Malia returned to Washington, DC.

October 4

In the morning, in the Oval Office, the President had an intelligence briefing. Later, in the Situation Room, he had a video teleconference with President Hamid Karzai of Afghanistan to discuss Afghanistan-U.S. relations, recent Afghan parliamentary elections, and regional elections. Then, in the Oval Office, he had a meeting with his senior advisers.

The President announced his intention to appoint James Q. Crowe as Chairman of the President's National Security Telecommunications Advisory Committee.

The President announced his intention to appoint Maggie Wilderotter as Vice Chairman of the President's National Security Telecommunications Advisory Committee.

The President announced his attention to appoint Donna A. James as Chairperson of the National Women's Business Council.

The President declared a major disaster in Arizona and ordered Federal aid to supplement State and local recovery efforts in the area struck by severe storms and flooding from July 20 through August 7.

October 5

In the morning, in the Oval Office, the President had an intelligence briefing followed by an economic briefing. Then, also in the Oval Office, he met with his senior advisers. Later, also in the Oval Office, he participated in a bill signing ceremony for S. 1055, awarding the Congressional Gold Medal to the Army's 100th Infantry Battalion and the 442d Regimental Combat Team.

October 6

In the morning, in the Oval Office, the President had an intelligence briefing followed by an economic briefing.

In the afternoon, in the Private Dining Room, the President had lunch with Vice President Joe Biden. Later, in the Oval Office, he met with his senior advisers. He then traveled to Cresskill, NJ.

During the day, the President had a telephone conversation with President Rafael Correa Delgado of Ecuador to discuss U.S. support for Ecuador's democratic institutions.

In the evening, the President returned to Washington, DC.

October 7

In the morning, in the Oval Office, the President had an intelligence briefing followed by a meeting with his senior advisers.

In the afternoon, in the Oval Office, the President participated in bill signing ceremonies for H.R. 553, the Reducing Over-Classification Act, and H.R. 2701, the Intelligence Authorization Act for Fiscal Year 2010. Later, also in the Oval Office, he met with Secretary of the Treasury Timothy F. Geithner.

Later in the afternoon, the President traveled to Bowie, MD. Later, he traveled to Chicago, IL.

In the evening, at a private residence, the President attended a dinner for senatorial candidate Alexi Giannoulias. He then returned to Washington, DC.

October 8

In the morning, the President had a telephone conversation with Prime Minister Fredrick Reinfeldt of Sweden to congratulate him on his reelection. Then, also in the Oval Office, he had an intelligence briefing. Later, he traveled to Bladensburg, MD, where he toured Ernest Maier Inc.

In the afternoon, the President returned to Washington, DC. Then, in the Oval Office, he met with his senior advisers.

October 9

In the morning, the President had an intelligence briefing.

October 10

In the afternoon, the President traveled to Philadelphia, PA.

In the evening, the President returned to Washington, DC.

October 11

In the morning, in the Oval Office, the President had an intelligence briefing. Later, in the State Dining Room, he met with Cabinet members, former Secretaries of Transportation, Governors, and mayors to discuss infrastructure investment. Then, in the Oval Office, he met with his senior advisers.

In the afternoon, in the Oval Office, the President met with the students profiled in the "Waiting for 'Superman' " documentary. Later, he traveled to Miami, FL.

In the evening, the President visited El Mago De Las Fritas restaurant. Later, he returned to Washington, DC.

During the day, at the Dwight D. Eisenhower Executive Office Building, the President and White House Senior Adviser Valerie B. Jarrett dropped by a meeting of African American journalists and bloggers. He also had a telephone conversation with Prime Minster David Cameron of the United Kingdom to express his condolences on the death of British aid worker Linda Norgrove, who was kidnapped in Afghanistan on September 26, and was killed during a rescue attempt by U.S. and Afghan special forces.

October 12

In the morning, in the Oval Office, the President had an intelligence briefing followed by an economic briefing. Later, also in the Oval Office, he met with his senior advisers.

In the afternoon, in the Oval Office, the President met with the Network for Teaching Entrepreneurship's National Youth Entrepreneurship Challenge finalists. Later, he met with actor and activist George Clooney.

During the day, in the Oval Office, the President attended a briefing by Secretary of the Department of Homeland Security Janet A. Napolitano and Administrator of the Transportation Security Administration John S. Pistole on transportation security. He also had a telephone conversation with Prime Minister Valdis Dombrovskis of Latvia to congratulate him on his reelection.

The President announced his intention to appoint John W. Rogers, Jr., as Chair of the President's Advisory Council on Financial Capability.

The President announced his intention to appoint Lorraine Cole as Vice Chair of the President's Advisory Council on Financial Capability.

The President announced his intention to appoint the following individuals as members of the President's Advisory Council on Financial Capability:

Roland A. Arteaga;
Theodore Beck;
John Hope Bryant;
Samuel T. Jackson;
Richard Ketchum;
Beth Kobliner;
A. Barry Rand;
Amy Rosen;
Carrie Schwab-Pomerantz; and
Kenneth Wade.

October 13

In the morning, in the Oval Office, the President had an intelligence briefing followed by an economic briefing. Then, also in the Oval Office, he met with his senior advisers.

The President declared a major disaster in Minnesota and ordered Federal aid to supplement State and local recovery efforts in the area struck by severe storms and flooding beginning on September 22 and continuing.

October 14

In the morning, in the Oval Office, the President and Vice President Joe Biden had an intelligence briefing. Then, also in the Oval Office, he met with his senior advisers.

In the afternoon, in the Private Dining Room, the President and Vice President Biden had lunch. Later, in the Oval Office, he met with Secretary of the Treasury Timothy F. Geithner.

During the day, the President had a telephone conversation with President Sebastian Pinera Echenique of Chile to congratulate him on the rescue of 33 miners trapped in the San Jose mine in Copiapo, Chile, since August 5.

The President declared a major disaster in New York and ordered Federal aid to supplement State and local recovery efforts in the area struck by severe storms, tornadoes, and straight-line winds on September 16.

The President declared a major disaster in North Carolina and ordered Federal aid to supplement State and local recovery efforts in the area struck by severe storms, flooding, and straight-line winds associated with Tropical Storm Nicole from September 27 through October 1.

October 15

In the morning, in the Oval Office, the President had an intelligence briefing. Later, he traveled to Wilmington, DE, arriving in the afternoon.

In the afternoon, the President returned to Washington, DC. Later, in the Oval Office, he met with former Secretary of State Condoleezza Rice.

October 16

In the afternoon, the President traveled to Boston, MA.

In the evening, the President returned to Washington, DC.

October 17

In the afternoon, the President and Mrs. Obama traveled to Cleveland, OH.

In the evening, the President and Mrs. Obama traveled to Columbus, OH, where, at Ohio State University, they attended a private fundraiser for the Democratic National Committee. Later, they returned to Washington, DC.

October 18

In the morning, in the Oval Office, the President had an intelligence briefing followed by a meeting with his senior advisers. Later, in the State Dining Room, he viewed projects exhibited at the White House science fair.

In the afternoon, the President had a telephone conversation with Prime Minister David Cameron of the United Kingdom to discuss global security and ongoing counterterrorism cooperation.

October 19

In the morning, in the Oval Office, the President had an intelligence briefing. Later, also in the Oval Office, he met with Secretary of the Treasury Timothy F. Geithner.

In the afternoon, in the Oval Office, the President had a meeting with his senior advisers. Later, also in the Oval Office, he met with Secretary of Defense Robert M. Gates.

October 20

In the morning, in the Oval Office, the President had an intelligence briefing. Then, also in the Oval Office, he met with Secretary of State Hillary Rodham Clinton. Later, in the Situation Room, he met with his national security team to discuss the ongoing situation in Afghanistan and Pakistan.

In the afternoon, in the Diplomatic Reception Room, the President taped an antibullying message for the It Gets Better Project. He then met with the Pakistani delegation to the U.S.-Pakistan Strategic Dialogue. He then traveled to Portland, OR, where, at the Oregon Convention Center, he attended a private fundraiser for gubernatorial candidate John A. Kitzhaber.

In the evening, the President traveled to Seattle, WA.

October 21

In the afternoon, the President traveled to San Francisco, CA.

In the evening, the President traveled to Atherton, CA, where, at a private residence, he attended a fundraiser for District Attorney Kamala D. Harris.

October 22

In the morning, the President traveled to Los Angeles, CA.

In the afternoon, at Piolin Productions Studios in Glendale, CA, the President participated in an interview with Eddie "Piolin" Sotelo of Univision's "Piolin por la Manana" program. Later, he traveled to Las Vegas, NV.

In the evening, at a private residence, the President attended a fundraiser for Sen. Harry M. Reid.

The President announced his intention to appoint Denis R. McDonough as Deputy National Security Adviser.

October 23

In the morning, the President traveled to Minneapolis, MN, arriving in the afternoon.

In the afternoon, at a Democratic Congressional Campaign Committee dinner, the President was joined by Speaker of the House of Representatives Nancy Pelosi. Later, he and Speaker Pelosi traveled to Minneapolis-St. Paul International Airport, where they met with Richard and Gloria Cauley, parents of Specialist George W. Cauley, USA, of Walker, MN, who was killed in Afghanistan on October 10.

In the evening, the President and Speaker Pelosi returned to Washington, DC.

October 25

In the morning, in the Oval Office, the President had an intelligence briefing followed by a meeting with his senior advisers. Later, also in the Oval Office, he met with Secretary of State Hillary Rodham Clinton.

Later, in the Oval Office, the President participated in separate phone interviews for the radio programs of Tom Joyner, Rickey Smiley, and Yolanda Adams.

In the afternoon, the President traveled to Warwick, RI. He then traveled to Woonsocket, RI, where he toured American Cord & Webbing Co., Inc.

In the evening, the President traveled to Providence, RI. Later in the evening, he returned to Washington, DC.

October 26

In the morning, in the Oval Office, the President had an intelligence briefing followed by an economic briefing. Later, also in the Oval Office, the President met with his senior advisers. He then had a telephone conversation with President Asif Ali Zardari of Pakistan to discuss the progress made during the recent U.S.-Pakistan Strategic Dialogue and to reinforce the U.S. commitment to partner with Pakistan on economic, development, and governance priorities.

In the afternoon, in the Oval Office, the President participated in separate phone interviews for the radio programs of Rev. Alfred C. Sharpton, Jr., Steve Harvey, and April Ryan. Later, in the Oval Office, he met with Secretary of Defense Robert M. Gates.

The President declared a major disaster in Puerto Rico and ordered Federal aid to supplement Commonwealth and local recovery efforts in the area struck by severe storms, flooding, mudslides, and landslides from October 4 through 8.

October 27

In the morning, in the Oval Office, the President had an intelligence briefing followed by an economic briefing. Later, in the Oval Office, he participated in an interview with radio host Michael Smerconish.

In the afternoon, in the Roosevelt Room, the President participated in a blogger roundtable discussion.

In the evening, at the Harman Center for the Arts, the President participated in an interview with Jon Stewart of Comedy Central's "The Daily Show."

October 28

In the morning, in the Oval Office, the President had an intelligence briefing. Later, he met with his senior advisers.

In the afternoon, in the Oval Office, the President met with American rescue workers involved with freeing 33 trapped miners in San Jose, Chile. Later, in the Roosevelt Room, the President had an economic briefing.

In the evening, the President participated in a telephone conference call with Young Democrats of America and College Democrats of America. He then made telephone remarks to separate telephone town hall meetings hosted by Sens. Barbara Boxer, Harry M. Reid, and Michael F. Bennet.

Later in the evening, the President was informed by Homeland Security and Counterterrorism Adviser John O. Brennan of potential terrorist threats originating from Yemen. In response, he directed U.S. intelligence and law enforcement agencies and the Department of Homeland Security to take necessary security measures. He received additional updates throughout the evening.

October 29

In the morning, in the Oval Office, the President had an intelligence briefing. Later, he traveled to Beltsville, MD, where he toured Stromberg Metal Works, Inc.

In the afternoon, the President returned to Washington, DC. Later, he had a telephone conversation with former President Thabo Mbeki of South Africa to discuss the situation in Sudan.

During the day, in the Situation Room, the President met with his national security team to discuss the discovery of explosive devices aboard U.S.-bound flights.

In the evening, the President traveled to Joint Base Andrews, MD. He then traveled to Charlottesville, VA. Later, he returned to Washington, DC.

October 30

In the morning, the President had separate telephone conversations with Prime Minister David Cameron of the United Kingdom and King Abdallah bin Abd al-Aziz Al Saud of Saudi Arabia to discuss the explosive devices found aboard airplanes bound for the U.S. and ongoing counterterrorism efforts. Later, he traveled to Philadelphia, PA.

In the afternoon, at the Famous 4th Street Delicatessen, the President had lunch and visited with patrons. He then traveled to Bridgeport, CT. Later, he traveled to Chicago, IL, arriving in the evening.

October 31

In the morning, at Valois restaurant, the President had breakfast with Gov. Patrick J. Quinn III of Illinois and Illinois senatorial candidate Alexi Giannoulias and visited with patrons. He then traveled to Cleveland, OH.

In the afternoon, the President returned to Washington, DC.

In the evening, on the North Portico, the President and Mrs. Obama greeted trick-or-treaters. Later, they hosted a Halloween reception for military families and local students.

November 1

In the morning, in the Oval Office, the President had an intelligence briefing followed by a meeting with his senior advisers. He then participated in separate telephone interviews with radio hosts Patty Jackson of WDAS in Philadelphia, PA, Faith Daniels of WMOJ in Cincinnati, OH, and Bailey Coleman of WKKV in Milwaukee, WI.

In the afternoon, the President had a telephone conversation with President-elect Dilma Rousseff of Brazil to congratulate her on her election victory and discuss Brazil-U.S. relations. Later, he participated in separate telephone interviews for the radio programs of Michael Baisden, Ryan Seacrest, Russ Parr, and Steve Harvey. He also participated in separate telephone interviews with radio hosts Michael Perry and Larry Price of KSSK in Honolulu, HI, and Lorenzo "Ice Tea" Thomas of WEDR in Miami, FL.

In the evening, the President had separate telephone conversations with Democratic volunteers and activists in Florida, New Hampshire, New Mexico, and Hawaii. Later, he had a telephone conversation with President Lee Myung-bak of South Korea to discuss the upcoming Group of Twenty (G–20) nations summit and the South Korea-U.S. free trade agreement.

The President announced the designation of the following individuals as members of a Presidential delegation to Bridgetown, Barbados, to attend the funeral of Prime Minister David Thompson on November 30: Gil Kerlikowske (head of delegation); D. Brent Hardt; and Eugene Gray.

November 2

In the morning, the President had an intelligence briefing, followed by an economic briefing. He then had a telephone conversation with President Ali Abdallah Salih of Yemen to discuss ongoing counterterrorism efforts and Yemen-U.S. relations. Later, in the Oval Office, he had an intelligence briefing followed by an economic briefing. Then, also in the Oval Office, he participated in separate telephone interviews with radio hosts Kurt "Big Boy" Alexander of KPWR in Los Angeles, CA, and Loni Swain of WGCI in Chicago, IL.

In the afternoon, in the Oval Office, the President participated in separate telephone interviews with radio hosts JoJo of WSOL in Jacksonville, FL, and J Noise and Krayzie Kat of KVEG in Las Vegas, NV. Later, also in the Oval Office, he met with Secretary of Defense Robert M. Gates. Later, also in the Oval Office, the President participated in separate telephone interviews with Doug Banks of "The Doug Banks Radio Show" and radio host Cliff Kelley of WVON in Chicago, IL.

During the day, the President had a telephone conversation with members of the San Francisco Giants to congratulate the team on winning the World Series.

In the evening, the President had separate telephone conversations with Reps. Nancy Pelosi, John A. Boehner, and Steny H. Hoyer and Sen. A. Mitchell McConnell.

The President declared a major disaster in South Dakota and ordered Federal aid to supplement State, local, and tribal recovery efforts in the area struck by severe storms and flooding on September 22 and 23.

November 3

In the morning, in the Oval Office, the President had an intelligence briefing.

In the afternoon, the President had a telephone conversation with Prime Minister Mark Rutte of the Netherlands to congratulate him on the formation of his Cabinet and discuss Netherlands-U.S. relations. Later, in the Oval Office, he met with his senior advisers.

November 4

In the morning, the President had an intelligence briefing.

In the afternoon, in the Private Dining Room, the President had lunch with Vice President Joe Biden.

November 5

In the morning, the President and Mrs. Obama traveled to Mumbai, India, arriving the following afternoon.

During the day, the President had a telephone conversation with President Cristina Fernandez de Kirchner of Argentina to offer his condolences on the death of her husband, former President Nestor C. Kirchner of Argentina.

The President announced the appointment of Mimi A. Drew, Dave Stewart, and Garret Graves as State representatives of the Gulf Coast Ecosystem Restoration Task Force.

The President declared a major disaster in the U.S. Virgin Islands and ordered Federal aid to supplement Territory efforts in the area struck by severe storms, flooding, mudslides, and landslides associated with Tropical Storm Otto from October 1 through 8.

November 6

In the afternoon, upon arrival in Mumbai, India, the President and Mrs. Obama traveled to the Taj Mahal Palace hotel. While en route, he met with President's Export Council Chair W. James McNerney, Jr. Later, at the Taj Mahal Palace hotel, the President and Mrs. Obama toured a memorial to victims of the November 26, 2008, terrorist attacks and signed the guest book. They then visited the Mani Bhavan Gandhi Sangrahalaya museum.

Later in the afternoon, the President traveled to the Trident Nariman Point hotel. Later, he returned to the Taj Mahal Palace hotel.

During the day, the President had a telephone conversation with President Felipe de Jesus Calderon Hinojosa of Mexico to discuss counternarcotics efforts and Mexico-U.S. relations.

November 7

In the morning, the President and Mrs. Obama traveled to Holy Name High School, where they visited students and attended a Diwali lamp-lighting ceremony and performance.

In the afternoon, the President and Mrs. Obama traveled to New Delhi, India. Later, at the U.S. Embassy, they met with U.S. Embassy staff. Then, they toured Emperor Humayun's tomb.

In the evening, at the Prime Minister's residence, the President met with Prime Minister Manmohan Singh of India. Later, also at the Prime Minister's residence, he and Mrs. Obama attended a dinner hosted by Prime

Minister Singh and his wife Gursharan Kaur. They then traveled to the ITC Maurya hotel.

November 8

In the morning, the President and Mrs. Obama traveled to the Raj Ghat, where they participated in a wreath-laying ceremony. Then, at Hyderabad House, he met with Prime Minister Manmohan Singh of India.

In the afternoon, at the Hyderabad House, the President stopped by a meeting of business leaders. Later, at ITC Maurya hotel, he met separately with Vice President Mohammad Hamid Ansari of India, Leader of the Opposition (lower House) Sushma Swaraj, and Member of Parliament (lower House) Sonia Gandhi, president of the Indian National Congress Party and chairperson of the ruling United Progressive Alliance parliamentary coalition. He then traveled to Parliament House.

In the evening, at Rashtrapati Bhavan, the President and Mrs. Obama met with President Pratibha Devisingh Patil of India. They then traveled to the ITC Maurya hotel.

November 9

In the morning, the President and Mrs. Obama traveled to Jakarta, Indonesia, arriving in the afternoon. They then traveled to the Istana Merdeka, where they participated in an arrival ceremony with President Susilo Bambang Yudhoyono of Indonesia and his wife Kristiani Herrawati and signed the visitor's book.

In the evening, the President and Mrs. Obama traveled to the Shangri-La Hotel. They then traveled to the Istana Negara. Later, they returned to the Shangri-La Hotel.

The President announced his intention to nominate Sue K. Brown to be Ambassador to Montenegro.

The President announced his intention to nominate David L. Carden to be U.S. Representative to the Association of Southeast Asian Nations, with the rank of Ambassador.

The President announced that he has appointed Stephen E. Condrey as Chairman of the Federal Salary Council.

The President announced that he has appointed the following individuals as members of the Federal Salary Council:

Lou Cannon;
Jeffery D. Cox;
Rex L. Facer;
Bill Fenaughty;
Colleen Kelley; and
Jacqueline Simon.

November 10

In the morning, at the Shangri-La Hotel, the President and Mrs. Obama met with U.S. Embassy staff. They then toured the Istiqlal Mosque.

Later in the morning, the President traveled to the University of Indonesia. He then traveled to Seoul, South Korea, arriving in the evening.

In the evening, the President traveled to the Grand Hyatt Seoul hotel.

November 11

In the morning, the President had an intelligence briefing. He then traveled to U.S. Army Garrison—Yongsan, where he participated in a Veterans Day wreath-laying ceremony.

In the afternoon, at the Blue House, the President had a working lunch with President Lee Myung-bak of South Korea. Later, he traveled to the Grand Hyatt Hotel.

During the day, the President had a telephone conversation with former Prime Minister Ayad Allawi of Iraq to discuss the formation of Iraq's coalition Government. He also received a briefing from U.S. Ambassador to Iraq James F. Jeffrey on the formation of Iraq's coalition Government.

In the evening, at the National Museum of Korea, the President attended a Group of Twenty (G–20) nations summit welcome reception and working dinner. He then traveled to the Grand Hyatt Seoul hotel.

The President announced his intention to nominate Eric G. Postel to be Assistant Administrator for Economic Growth, Agriculture, and Trade at the U.S. Agency for International Development.

The President announced his intention to nominate Frances M.D. Gulland to be a member of the Marine Mammal Commission.

The President announced his intention to nominate Roberto R. Herencia and James A. Torrey to be members of the Board of Directors of the Overseas Private Investment Corporation.

November 12

In the morning, the President traveled to the Coex Center, where he participated in two plenary sessions at the Group of Twenty (G–20) summit. Later, he participated in a photograph with G–20 leaders. He then participated in a third plenary session at the G–20 summit.

In the afternoon, at the Coex Center, the President attended a Group of Twenty (G–20) summit working lunch. He then participated in two plenary sessions at the G–20 summit.

In the evening, the President traveled to Yokohama, Japan. While en route aboard Air Force One, he had separate telephone conversations with Prime Minister Nuri al-Maliki of Iraq and President Masoud Barzani of the Iraqi Kurdistan Regional Government to congratulate them on steps taken to form a coalition Government. Upon arrival in Yokohama, Japan, he traveled to the InterContinental Yokohama Grand hotel.

The President announced his intention to nominate Joseph A. Smith, Jr., to be Director of the Federal Housing Finance Agency.

November 13

In the morning, the President traveled to the Yokohama Royal Park Hotel. He then returned to the InterContinental Yokohama Grand hotel.

In the afternoon, at the InterContinental Yokohama Grand hotel, the President participated in a working lunch and leaders' retreat with the Asia-Pacific Economic Cooperation (APEC). Later, he traveled to the Pacifico Yokohama Conference Center, where he attended a meeting with the APEC Business Advisory Council. He then returned to the InterContinental Yokohama Grand hotel.

In the evening, the President traveled to the Pacifico Yokohama Conference Center, where he viewed technology exhibits and cultural performances and participated in a photo opportunity with APEC leaders. Later, he met briefly with Prime Minister Stephen Harper of Canada. He then attended a dinner reception for APEC leaders.

Later in the evening, the President returned to the InterContinental Yokohama Grand hotel.

November 14

In the morning, at the InterContinental Yokohama Grand hotel, the President attended the Asia-Pacific Economic Cooperation (APEC) closing retreat. He then participated in a meeting and photo opportunity with Trans-Pacific Partnership leaders.

In the afternoon, at the InterContinental Yokohama Grand hotel, the President attended the APEC declaration ceremony followed by the APEC closing lunch.

Later in the afternoon, the President traveled to Kamakura, Japan, where he toured the Kotoku-in temple and visited the Great Buddha of Kamakura statue. Later, he traveled to Washington, DC, crossing the international date line and arriving in the afternoon.

November 15

In the morning, in the Roosevelt Room, the President met with his senior advisers and Vice President Joe Biden to discuss tax cuts and the economy.

During the day, the President had a telephone conversation with Speaker of the House of Representatives Nancy Pelosi and Senate Majority Leader Harry M. Reid to discuss tax cut extensions for the middle class.

The President announced his intention to nominate Daniel L. Shields III to be Ambassador to Brunei.

The President announced his intention to nominate Joseph M. Torsella to be U.S. Representative to the United Nations for U.N. Management and Reform with the rank of Ambassador.

The President announced his intention to nominate Andrew Traver to be Director of the

Bureau of Alcohol, Tobacco, Firearms, and Explosives at the Department of Justice.

The President announced his intention to appoint Barbaralee Diamonstein-Spielvogel as a member of the American Battle Monuments Commission.

November 16

In the morning, in the Oval Office, the President and Vice President Joe Biden had an intelligence briefing, followed by a meeting with his senior advisers to assess progress in Iraq. Then, in the Roosevelt Room, he had an economic briefing.

In the afternoon, in the Oval Office, the President and Mrs. Obama greeted Medal of Honor recipient Staff Sgt. Salvatore Giunta, USA, and his family. Later, he met with Sen. Robert Menendez and Reps. Luis V. Gutierrez and Nydia M. Velazquez of the Congressional Hispanic Caucus to discuss options for immigration reform. Then, also in the Oval Office, he met with Secretary of Defense Robert M. Gates.

The President announced his intention to appoint Mark C. Alexander, Mark Brzezinski, Lisa M. Caputo, and Shelby F. Lewis as members of the J. William Fulbright Foreign Scholarship Board.

November 17

In the morning, in the Oval Office, the President had an intelligence briefing followed by a meeting with his senior advisers. Later, in the Situation Room, he and Vice President Joe Biden met with the President's national security team to discuss the situation in Afghanistan and Pakistan.

In the afternoon, in the Private Dining Room, the President had lunch with Vice President Biden, during which he wished Vice President Biden an early happy birthday. Then, the President dropped by a meeting between White House Senior Adviser Valerie B. Jarrett and leading women's rights advocates to express his appreciation for their work and to reaffirm his commitment to eliminate wage disparity.

Later in the afternoon, in the Oval Office, the President and Vice President Biden met with Secretary of State Hillary Rodham Clinton.

The President announced the designation of the following individuals as members of a Presidential delegation to the Holy See to attend a ceremony elevating Vatican Chief Justice Archbishop Raymond Burke and Archbishop Donald W. Wuerl to the College of Cardinals from November 20 through 21: Miguel H. Diaz (head of delegation); and Daniel M. Rooney.

The President announced his intention to nominate Ryan C. Crocker and Sim Farar to be members of the U.S. Advisory Commission on Public Diplomacy.

The President announced his intention to appoint Benjamin L. Cardin and John Cornyn as members of the Board of Trustees of the James Madison Memorial Fellowship Foundation.

The President announced his intention to appoint Elizabeth Young McNally as a member of the Board of Visitors to the U.S. Military Academy.

The President announced that he has nominated Cathy Bissoon to be a judge on the U.S. District Court for the Western District of Pennsylvania.

The President announced that he has nominated Vincent L. Briccetti to be a judge on the U.S. District Court for the Southern District of New York.

The President announced that he has nominated Roy B. Dalton, Jr., to be a judge on the U.S. District Court for the Middle District of Florida.

The President announced that he has nominated Sara L. Darrow to be a judge on the U.S. District Court for the Central District of Illinois.

The President announced that he has nominated John A. Kronstadt to be a judge on the U.S. District Court for the Central District of California.

The President announced that he has nominated Kevin H. Sharp to be a judge on the U.S. District Court for the Middle District of Tennessee.

The President announced that he has nominated Charles E. Andrews to be U.S. marshal for the Southern District of Alabama.

The President announced that he has nominated Darrell J. Bell to be U.S. marshal for the District of Montana.

The President announced that he has nominated William B. Berger, Sr., to be U.S. marshal for the Middle District of Florida.

The President announced that he has nominated Russel E. Burger to be U.S. marshal for the District of Oregon.

The President announced that he has nominated Joseph C. Moore to be U.S. marshal for the District of Wyoming.

The President announced that he has nominated Edwin D. Sloane and Esteban Soto III to be U.S. marshals for the District of Columbia.

The President announced that he has nominated S. Amanda Marshall to be U.S. attorney for the District of Oregon.

November 18

In the morning, in the Oval Office, the President had an intelligence briefing. Then, in the Roosevelt Room, he dropped by a meeting hosted by Vice President Joe Biden to discuss U.S. national security interests in the new START Treaty. Later, in the Oval Office, he and Vice President Biden met with Speaker of the House of Representatives Nancy Pelosi and Senate Majority Leader Harry M. Reid.

Later in the morning, the President met with his senior advisers.

In the afternoon, in the Oval Office, the President and Vice President Biden met with Secretary of the Treasury Timothy F. Geithner.

In the evening, the President traveled to Lisbon, Portugal, arriving the following morning.

November 19

In the morning, upon arrival at the Lisbon International Airport, the President traveled to the Lisbon Marriott Hotel, where he met with U.S. Embassy staff.

In the afternoon, the President traveled to Belem National Palace in Lisbon, where he attended an arrival ceremony with President Anibal Antonio Cavaco Silva of Portugal and signed the Palace guest book. Then, he and President Cavaco Silva participated in a working lunch. Later, he traveled to Feria Internacional de Lisboa to attend an arrival reception for North Atlantic Treaty Organization (NATO) leaders followed by NATO Advisory Council opening and working sessions.

During the day, the President met with President Abdullah Gul of Turkey to discuss new NATO capabilities to respond to 21st-century challenges.

In the evening, also at the Feria Internacional de Lisboa, the President participated in a photo opportunity with NATO leaders. He then met with President Mikheil Saakashvili of Georgia to discuss strengthening bilateral relations and increasing cooperation between the two countries. Later, he attended the NATO Advisory Council working dinner.

November 20

In the morning, the President traveled to the Feria Internacional de Lisboa, where he attended the opening and working sessions of the North Atlantic Treaty Organization (NATO) meeting on Afghanistan. Later, in an adjoining convention hall, he visited a display of the Opel Ampera, an electric vehicle made by General Motors Co.

In the afternoon, at the Feria Internacional de Lisboa, the President attended a North Atlantic Council working session. Later, he participated in the opening and working sessions of the NATO-Russia Council. He then met separately with President Dmitry A. Medvedev of Russia to discuss the President's November 19 meeting with President Mikheil Saakashvili of Georgia and the new Strategic Arms Reduction Treaty (START) negotiations.

Later in the afternoon, at the Feria Internacional de Lisboa, the President met with President Hamid Karzai of Afghanistan. He then traveled to the Portuguese Pavilion, where he participated in the official photograph for the European Union-United States summit and attended the summit meeting.

In the evening, the President returned to Washington, DC.

The White House announced that the President will welcome President Bronislaw Komorowski of Poland to the White House on December 8.

November 23

In the morning, in the Oval Office, the President had an intelligence briefing. Later, he traveled to Kokomo, IN.

In the afternoon, at a Kokomo Fire Department station, the President and Vice President Joe Biden had lunch and visited local firefighters. Then, at Sycamore Elementary School, they met with students and faculty. Later, at the Chrysler Indiana Transmission Plant II, they toured the facility and met with employees.

Later in the afternoon, at the Gingerbread House Bakery, the President and Vice President Biden visited with patrons. Later, he returned to Washington, DC.

During the day, the President had a telephone conversation with King Abdallah bin Abd al-Aziz Al Saud of Saudi Arabia to discuss Saudi Arabia-U.S. relations and the King's medical treatment in the U.S.

In the evening, the President met with his national security team to discuss the situation on the Korean Peninsula. He then had a telephone conversation with President Lee Myung-bak of South Korea to discuss South Korea-U.S. relations and the North Korean artillery attack on Yeonpyeoung Island.

November 24

In the morning, in the Oval Office, the President had an intelligence briefing. Later, also in the Oval Office, he met with Secretary of Defense Robert M. Gates.

In the afternoon, at Martha's Table, Inc., the President, Mrs. Obama, and their daughters Sasha and Malia handed out Thanksgiving groceries to families.

The President declared a major disaster in the U.S. Virgin Islands and ordered Federal aid to supplement Territory recovery efforts in the area struck by sever storms, flooding, rock-

slides, and mudslides associated with Tropical Storm Tomas from November 8 through 12.

November 25

In the morning, the President had Thanksgiving holiday telephone conversations with 10 U.S. servicemembers serving in Afghanistan and Iraq.

November 29

In the morning, in the Oval Office, the President had an intelligence briefing followed by an economic briefing. Then, also in the Oval Office, he met with his senior advisers.

In the afternoon, in the Oval Office, the President met with Wal-Mart Stores, Inc., Chief Executive Officer Michael T. Duke. Later, also in the Oval Office, he met with the Joint Chiefs of Staff.

November 30

In the morning, in the Oval Office, the President and Vice President Joe Biden had an intelligence briefing. Later, in the Private Dining Room, they met with bipartisan congressional leaders.

In the afternoon, in the Oval Office, the President met with Nobel laureates. Later, also in the Oval Office, he and Vice President Biden met with Secretary of Defense Robert M. Gates.

December 1

In the morning, in the Oval Office, the President and Vice President Joe Biden had an economic briefing followed by an intelligence briefing. Later, also in the Oval Office, he met with his senior advisers.

In the afternoon, in the Private Dining Room, the President had lunch with Mayor-elect Vincent C. Gray of the District of Columbia.

The President announced his intention to nominate Janice Lehrer-Stein to be a member of the National Council on Disability.

The President announced his intention to appoint Richard J. Danzig and Daniel Meltzer as members of the President's Intelligence Advisory Board.

The President announced that he has nominated Arenda L. Wright Allen to be a judge on the U.S. District Court for the Eastern District of Virginia.

The President announced that he has nominated Claire C. Cecchi and Esther Salas to be judges on the U.S. District Court for the District of New Jersey.

The President announced that he has nominated Mark R. Hornak to be a judge on the U.S. District Court for the Western District of Pennsylvania.

The President announced that he has nominated Robert D. Mariani to be a judge on the U.S. District Court for the Middle District of Pennsylvania.

The President announced that he has nominated John A. Ross to be a judge on the U.S. District Court for the Eastern District of Missouri.

The President announced that he has nominated Michael F. Urbanski to be a judge on the U.S. District Court for the Western District of Virginia.

The President announced that he has nominated Bernice B. Donald to be a judge on the U.S. Court of Appeals for the Sixth Circuit.

The President announced that he has nominated Christopher R. Thyer to be U.S. attorney for the Eastern District of Arkansas.

December 2

In the morning, in the Oval Office, the President and Vice President Joe Biden had an intelligence briefing. Then, also in the Oval Office, he met with Gov. Theodore Strickland of Ohio. Later, in the Oval Office, he met with his senior advisers.

In the afternoon, in the Private Dining Room, the President and Vice President Biden had lunch. Later, in the Oval Office, they met with Secretary of the Treasury Timothy F. Geithner. Then, he met with his national security team.

In the evening, the President traveled to Bagram Air Base, Afghanistan, arriving the following evening.

The President announced his intention to nominate Kathryn D. Sullivan to be Assistant Secretary for Observation and Prediction at the Department of Commerce.

The President announced his intention to nominate Leon Rodriguez to be Administrator of the Wage and Hour Division at the Department of Labor.

The President announced his intention to appoint David Chavern as a member of the Advisory Committee for Trade Policy and Negotiations.

December 3

In the morning, while en route to Bagram Air Base, Afghanistan, aboard Air Force One, the President met with his national security team.

In the evening, upon arrival at Bagram Air Base, the President traveled to 101st Airborne Division Headquarters, where he had a telephone conversation with President Hamid Karzai of Afghanistan. Then, he met with Gen. David H. Petraeus, USA, commander, NATO International Security Assistance Force, Afghanistan, U.S. Ambassador to Afghanistan Karl W. Eikenberry, National Security Adviser Thomas E. Donilon, and Deputy National Security Adviser for Iraq and Afghanistan Douglas E. Lute.

Later in the evening, at Staff Sgt. Heathe N. Craig Joint Theater Hospital at Bagram Air Base, the President met with wounded U.S. military personnel and civilian contractors and presented Purple Hearts to five servicemembers. He then met with members of Bravo Troop, 1st Squadron, 61st Calvary Regiment, 4th Brigade Combat Team, 101st Airborne Division, which saw six soldiers killed during a training mission on November 29 in Nangarhar Province, Afghanistan. Later, he met with U.S. Special Forces personnel.

In the late evening, the President returned to Washington, DC, arriving the following morning. While en route aboard Air Force One, he had a telephone conversation with Prime Minister Benjamin Netanyahu of Israel to express condolences on the loss of life resulting from wildfires in northern Israel and to offer U.S. assistance.

The President announced his intention to nominate Kelvin K. Droegemeier to be a member of the National Science Board.

The President announced his intention to nominate Maurice B. Foley to be a judge on the U.S. Tax Court.

The President announced his intention to nominate Daniel M. Ashe to be Director of the Fish and Wildlife Service at the Department of the Interior.

December 5

In the evening, at the John F. Kennedy Center for the Performing Arts, the President and Mrs. Obama attended the Kennedy Center Honors Gala.

Later in the evening, in the Oval Office, the President had a telephone conversation with President Hu Jintao of China to discuss North Korea, China-U.S. relations, and Iran.

December 6

In the morning, in the Oval Office, the President had an intelligence briefing. Then, he traveled to Winston-Salem, NC. Later, at Forsyth Technical Community College, he toured classroom facilities and met with faculty and students.

In the afternoon, the President returned to Washington, DC. Later, in the Oval Office, he met with his senior advisers.

December 7

In the morning, in the Oval Office, the President and Vice President Joe Biden had an intelligence briefing.

In the afternoon, in the Oval Office, the President participated in a credentialing ceremony for newly appointed Ambassadors to the U.S. Later, also in the Oval Office, he had an economic briefing and met with his senior advisers.

The President announced his intention to nominate the following individuals to be members of the National Council on the Humanities: Albert J. Beveridge; Constance M. Carroll; and Cathy N. Davidson.

December 8

In the morning, in the Oval Office, the President and Vice President Joe Biden had an intelligence briefing.

In the afternoon, in the Oval Office, the President and Vice President Biden met with Secretary of State Hillary Rodham Clinton. Then, in the Cabinet Room, he held a Cabinet meeting. Later, in the Oval Office, he met with his senior advisers.

The President announced his intention to nominate Aaron Dworkin to be a member of the National Council on the Arts.

The President announced his intention to nominate Clyde E. Terry to be a member of the National Council on Disability.

The President announced his intention to appoint the following individuals as members of the President's National Security Telecommunications Advisory Committee:

Linda Gooden;
Mark T. Greenquist;
Dan Hesse;
Mark McLaughlin;
Paul Sagan; and
Gary Smith.

December 9

In the morning, in the Oval Office, the President and Vice President Joe Biden had an intelligence briefing. Later, also in the Oval Office, he met with his senior advisers.

In the afternoon, in the Private Dining Room, the President and Vice President Biden had lunch. Later, in the Oval Office, they had an economic briefing. Then, also in the Oval Office, he met with Adm. Michael G. Mullen, USN, Chairman, Joint Chiefs of Staff.

The President announced his intention to nominate Peter B. Lyons to be Assistant Secretary for Nuclear Energy at the Department of Energy.

The President announced his intention to nominate Denise E. O'Donnell to be Director of Justice Assistance at the Department of Justice.

The President announced his intention to nominate Stephanie O'Sullivan to be Principal

Deputy National Intelligence Director at the Office of the Director of National Intelligence.

The President announced his intention to nominate David B. Shear to be Ambassador to Vietnam.

The President announced his intention to appoint Harvey S. Wineberg as a member of the President's Advisory Council on Financial Capability.

December 10

In the afternoon, in the Oval Office, the President met with former President William J. Clinton.

December 11

In the morning, the President had separate telephone conversations with Prime Minister Recep Tayyip Erdogan of Turkey to discuss Turkey-U.S. relations and President Felipe de Jesus Calderon Hinojosa of Mexico to discuss the United Nations Climate Change Conference held in Cancun, Mexico, and Mexico-U.S. relations.

December 13

In the morning, in the Oval Office, the President and Vice President Joe Biden had an intelligence briefing. Then, also in the Oval Office, he met with his senior advisers.

In the afternoon, in the Map Room, the President participated in separate television interviews with Emily Riemer of WSYX in Columbus, OH, Kevin Cooney of KCCI in Des Moines, IA, Adam Schrager of KUSA in Denver, CO, and Keith Cate of WFLA in St. Petersburg, FL. Later, in the South Court Auditorium at the Dwight D. Eisenhower Executive Building, he greeted recipients of the 2009 Presidential Early Career Award for Scientists and Engineers.

Later in the afternoon, at the Town Hall Education Arts Recreation Campus (THEARC), the President participated in a service project with the National Basketball Association Los Angeles Lakers and members of the Boys and Girls Club of Greater Washington. Later, in the Cabinet Room, he dropped by a meeting of United Nations Security Council permanent representatives. Then, in the Oval Office, he

and Vice President Biden met with Secretary of Defense Robert M. Gates.

December 14

In the morning, in the Oval Office, the President and Vice President Joe Biden had an intelligence briefing. Then, also in the Oval Office, he met with William H. and Melinda Gates and Warren E. Buffett to discuss their philanthropic project, "The Giving Pledge." Later, in the Situation Room, the President and Vice President Biden met with the President's national security team to discuss Afghanistan and Pakistan.

In the afternoon, in the Private Dining Room, the President and Vice President Biden had lunch. Later, in the Roosevelt Room, the President dropped by a meeting of the National Policy Alliance hosted by White House Senior Adviser Valerie B. Jarrett to discuss the bipartisan tax agreement.

The President announced his intention to appoint Patty Stonesifer as Chair of the White House Council for Community Solutions.

The President announced his intention to appoint the following individuals as members of the White House Council for Community Solutions:

Byron Auguste;
Diana Aviv;
Paula Boggs;
Jon Bon Jovi;
John Bridgeland;
James Canales;
Scott Cowen;
John Donahoe;
Michael Fleming;
David Friedman;
Jim Gibbons;
Michele Jolin;
Michael Kempner;
Steven Lerner;
Maruice Lim Miller;
Laurene Powell Jobs;
Norman Rice;
Kristin Richmond;
Judith Rodin;
Nancy H. Rubin;

Paul Schmitz;
Jill Schumann;
Bobbi Silten; and
Bill Strickland.

December 15

In the morning, at the Blair House, the President met with business leaders to discuss the national economy.

In the afternoon, in the Oval Office, the President met with Secretary of State Hillary Rodham Clinton.

In the evening, the President had a telephone conversation with President Hamid Karzai of Afghanistan.

During the day, the President met with American Indian tribal leaders.

The President announced his intention to nominate Carolyn N. Lerner to be Special Counsel, Office of Special Counsel.

The President announced his intention to appoint Timothy Broas as a member of the Board of Trustees of the Woodrow Wilson International Center for Scholars.

December 16

In the morning, in the Oval Office, the President and Vice President Joe Biden had an intelligence briefing.

In the afternoon, in the South Court Auditorium of the Dwight D. Eisenhower Executive Building, the President greeted recipients of the 2009 Presidential Award for Excellence in Mathematics and Science Teaching.

In the evening, in the Map Room, the President met with Organizing for America volunteers.

The President announced his intention to nominate Elisebeth Collins Cook and James X. Dempsey to be a members of the Privacy and Civil Liberties Oversight Board.

The President announced his intention to appoint Kevin J. Kennedy as a member of the President's National Security Telecommunications Advisory Committee.

December 17

In the morning, in the Oval Office, the President met with his senior advisers. Later, also

in the Oval Office, he met with Secretary of the Treasury Timothy F. Geithner.

In the afternoon, in the Roosevelt Room, the President met with labor organization leaders to discuss the national economy.

December 18

During the day, the President had telephone conversations with Members of Congress to discuss legislation to repeal the U.S. military's "don't ask, don't tell" policy.

December 20

In the morning, in the Oval Office, the President had an intelligence briefing followed by a meeting with his senior advisers.

In the afternoon, in the Oval Office, the President participated in a bill signing ceremony for S. 3817, the CAPTA Reauthorization Act of 2010.

The President announced his intention to nominate Judy Ansley and John A. Lancaster to be members of the Board of Directors of the U.S. Institute of Peace.

The President announced his intention to nominate Ann Begeman to be a member of the Surface Transportation Board.

The President announced his intention to nominate Nils M.P. Daulaire to be Representative of the U.S. on the Executive Board of the World Health Organization.

The President announced his intention to nominate Terry Lewis to be a member of the Board of Directors of the Overseas Private Investment Corporation.

December 21

In the morning, in the Oval Office, the President and Vice President Joe Biden had an intelligence briefing. Later, also in the Oval Office, he met members of the Congressional Hispanic Caucus to discuss immigration reform.

During the day, the President had a telephone conversation with Prime Minister David Cameron of the United Kingdom to discuss military operations and diplomatic efforts in Afghanistan, ongoing counterterrorism efforts, and United Kingdom-U.S. relations. He also had a telephone conversation with Prime Minister Nuri al-Maliki of Iraq on the formation of Iraq's coalition Government and Iraq-U.S. relations.

The President announced his intention to appoint Jerry Patterson and Alice T. Perry as State representatives of the Gulf Coast Ecosystem Restoration Task Force.

The President declared a major disaster in Arizona and ordered Federal aid to supplement State, tribal, and local recovery efforts in the area struck by severe storms and flooding from October 3 through 6.

December 22

In the morning, in the Oval Office, the President met with Secretary of the Treasury Timothy F. Geithner.

In the afternoon, the President had separate telephone conversations with President Goodluck Jonathan of Nigeria to discuss the situation in Cote d'Ivoire and First Vice President Salva Kiir Mayardit of Sudan to discuss the situation in Sudan.

In the evening, the President traveled to Honolulu, HI. Later, he traveled to Kailua, HI.

The White House announced that the President will welcome President Hu Jintao of China to the White House on January 19.

The President announced the designation of the following individuals as members of a Presidential delegation to Brasilia, Brazil, to attend the inauguration of Dilma Rousseff as President of Brazil on January 1, 2011: Hillary Rodham Clinton (head of delegation); Thomas A. Shannon; and Daniel A. Restrepo.

The President announced his intention to nominate Agnes Gund to be a member of the National Council on the Arts.

The President announced his intention to appoint John Casteen as a member of the Board of Trustees of the Woodrow Wilson International Center for Scholars.

The President declared a major disaster in Vermont and ordered Federal aid to supplement State and local recovery efforts in the area struck by severe storms from December 1 through 5.

December 23

In the morning, the President had an intelligence briefing.

During the day, the President had a telephone conversation with President Dmitry A. Medvedev of Russia to discuss the new START Treaty and Russia-U.S. relations.

December 24

In the morning, the President had an intelligence briefing.

December 25

In the morning, the President had an intelligence briefing.

In the afternoon, the President and Mrs. Obama traveled to Marine Corps Base Hawaii, Kaneohe Bay, where, in the mess hall, they met with marines and their families. Later, they returned to Kailua, HI.

December 26

In the morning, the President met with members of his national security team to discuss ongoing counterterrorism efforts and the deaths of eight American citizens in a traffic accident in Aswan, Egypt. Later, he had a telephone conversation with King Abdallah bin Abd al-Aziz Al Saud of Saudi Arabia, who congratulated him on the passage of the new START Treaty. They also discussed the King's recovery from medical treatment in the U.S. and Saudi Arabia-U.S. relations.

December 27

In the morning, the President had an intelligence briefing.

December 28

In the morning, the President had an intelligence briefing.

December 29

In the morning, the President had an intelligence briefing.

The President announced his intention to recess appoint William J. Boarman as Public Printer of the U.S.

The President announced his intention to recess appoint Matthew J. Bryza as Ambassador to Azerbaijan.

The President announced his intention to recess appoint James M. Cole as Deputy Attorney General at the Department of Justice.

The President announced his intention to recess appoint Norman J. Eisen as Ambassador to the Czech Republic.

The President announced his intention to recess appoint Robert S. Ford as Ambassador to Syria.

The President announced his intention to recess appoint Francis J. Ricciardone, Jr., as Ambassador to Turkey.

December 30

In the morning, the President had an intelligence briefing.

December 31

In the morning, the President had an intelligence briefing.

Appendix B—Nominations Submitted to the Senate

The following list does not include promotions of members of the Uniformed Services, nominations to the Service Academies, or nominations of Foreign Service Officers.

Submitted July 12

Alexander A. Arvizu,
of Virginia, a career member of the Senior Foreign Service, class of Minister-Counselor, to be Ambassador Extraordinary and Plenipotentiary of the United States of America to the Republic of Albania.

Pamela E. Bridgewater Awkard,
of Virginia, a career member of the Senior Foreign Service, class of Career Minister, to be Ambassador Extraordinary and Plenipotentiary of the United States of America to Jamaica.

Nisha Desai Biswal,
of the District of Columbia, to be an Assistant Administrator of the U.S. Agency for International Development, vice James R. Kunder, resigned.

Michele Thoren Bond,
of the District of Columbia, a career member of the Senior Foreign Service, class of Minister-Counselor, to be Ambassador Extraordinary and Plenipotentiary of the United States of America to the Kingdom of Lesotho.

Sean P. Buckley,
of New York, to be Commissioner of Education Statistics for a term expiring June 21, 2015, vice Mark S. Schneider, resigned.

Paul W. Jones,
of New York, a career member of the Senior Foreign Service, class of Minister-Counselor, to be Ambassador Extraordinary and Plenipotentiary of the United States of America to Malaysia.

Robert P. Mikulak,
of Virginia, for the rank of Ambassador during his tenure of service as U.S. Representative to the Organization for the Prohibition of Chemical Weapons.

Phyllis Marie Powers,
of Virginia, a career member of the Senior Foreign Service, class of Minister-Counselor, to be Ambassador Extraordinary and Plenipotentiary of the United States of America to the Republic of Panama.

Francis Joseph Ricciardone, Jr.,
of Massachusetts, a career member of the Senior Foreign Service, class of Career Minister, to be Ambassador Extraordinary and Plenipotentiary of the United States of America to the Republic of Turkey.

Duane E. Woerth,
of Nebraska, for the rank of Ambassador during his tenure of service as Representative of the United States of America on the Council of the International Civil Aviation Organization.

Submitted July 14

Conrad Ernest Candelaria,
of New Mexico, to be U.S. Marshal for the District of New Mexico for the term of 4 years, vice Gorden Edward Eden, Jr., term expired.

James Edward Clark,
of Kentucky, to be U.S. Marshal for the Western District of Kentucky for the term of 4 years, vice Ronald Richard McCubbin, Jr., term expired.

Mark F. Green,
of Oklahoma, to be U.S. Attorney for the Eastern District of Oklahoma for the term of 4 years, vice Sheldon J. Sperling, term expired.

Joseph H. Hogsett,
of Indiana, to be U.S. Attorney for the Southern District of Indiana for the term of 4 years, vice Susan W. Brooks, resigned.

Marco A. Hernandez,
of Oregon, to be U.S. District Judge for the District of Oregon, vice Garr M. King, retired.

Beryl Alaine Howell,
of the District of Columbia, to be U.S. District Judge for the District of Columbia, vice Paul L. Friedman, retired.

Steve C. Jones,
of Georgia, to be U.S. District Judge for the Northern District of Georgia, vice Orinda D. Evans, retired.

Sue E. Myerscough,
of Illinois, to be U.S. District Judge for the Central District of Illinois, vice Jeanne E. Scott, resigned.

Victoria Frances Nourse,
of Wisconsin, to be U.S. Circuit Judge for the Seventh Circuit, vice Terence T. Evans, retired.

Joseph Anthony Papili,
of Delaware, to be U.S. Marshal for the District of Delaware for the term of 4 years, vice David William Thomas, term expired.

Diana Saldana,
of Texas, to be U.S. District Judge for the Southern District of Texas, vice George P. Kazen, retired.

Michael H. Simon,
of Oregon, to be U.S. District Judge for the District of Oregon, vice Ancer L. Haggerty, retired.

James Alfred Thompson,
of Utah, to be U.S. Marshal for the District of Utah for the term of 4 years, vice Randall Dean Anderson, term expired.

Withdrawn July 14

Sue E. Myerscough,
of Illinois, to be U.S. District Judge for the Central District of Illinois, vice Joe B. McDade, retired, which was sent to the Senate on June 17, 2010.

Submitted July 19

Donald M. Berwick,
of Massachusetts, to be Administrator of the Centers for Medicare and Medicaid Services, vice Mark B. McClellan, to which position he was appointed during the last recess of the Senate.

Philip E. Coyle III,
of California, to be an Associate Director of the Office of Science and Technology Policy, vice Rosina M. Bierbaum, to which position he was appointed during the last recess of the Senate.

Joshua Gotbaum,
of the District of Columbia, to be Director of the Pension Benefit Guaranty Corporation, vice Charles E. F. Millard, to which position he was appointed during the last recess of the Senate.

Kristie Anne Kenney,
of Virginia, a career member of the Senior Foreign Service, class of Career Minister, to be Ambassador Extraordinary and Plenipotentiary of the United States of America to the Kingdom of Thailand.

Jo Ellen Powell,
of Maryland, a career member of the Senior Foreign Service, class of Minister-Counselor, to be Ambassador Extraordinary and Plenipotentiary of the United States of America to the Islamic Republic of Mauritania.

Submitted July 21

Mark M. Boulware,
of Texas, a career member of the Senior Foreign Service, class of Minister-Counselor, to be Ambassador Extraordinary and Plenipotentiary

of the United States of America to the Republic of Chad.

Christopher J. McMullen,
of Virginia, a career member of the Senior Foreign Service, class of Minister-Counselor, to be Ambassador Extraordinary and Plenipotentiary of the United States of America to the Republic of Angola.

Joseph A. Mussomeli,
of Virginia, a career member of the Senior Foreign Service, class of Minister-Counselor, to be Ambassador Extraordinary and Plenipotentiary of the United States of America to the Republic of Slovenia.

Wanda L. Nesbitt,
of Pennsylvania, a career member of the Senior Foreign Service, class of Minister-Counselor, to be Ambassador Extraordinary and Plenipotentiary of the United States of America to the Republic of Namibia.

Karen Brevard Stewart,
of Florida, a career member of the Senior Foreign Service, class of Minister-Counselor, to be Ambassador Extraordinary and Plenipotentiary of the United States of America to the Lao People's Democratic Republic.

Charles Bernard Day,
of Maryland, to be U.S. District Judge for the District of Maryland, vice Peter J. Messitte, retired.

Albert Najera,
of California, to be U.S. Marshal for the Eastern District of California for the term of 4 years, vice Antonio Candia Amador, term expired.

William Claud Sibert,
of Missouri, to be U.S. Marshal for the Eastern District of Missouri for the term of 4 years, vice Ronald Henderson, term expired.

Myron Martin Sutton,
of Indiana, to be U.S. Marshal for the Northern District of Indiana for the term of 4 years, vice David Reid Murtaugh.

Kathleen M. Williams,
of Florida, to be U.S. District Judge for the Southern District of Florida, vice Daniel T.K. Hurley, retired.

Submitted August 3

Timothy Charles Scheve,
of Pennsylvania, to be a member of the Internal Revenue Service Oversight Board for a term expiring September 14, 2010, vice Nancy Killefer, term expired.

Timothy Charles Scheve,
of Pennsylvania, to be a member of the Internal Revenue Service Oversight Board for a term expiring September 14, 2015 (reappointment).

Submitted August 4

Jeffrey Thomas Holt,
of Tennessee, to be U.S. Marshal for the Western District of Tennessee for the term of 4 years, vice David Glenn Jolley, term expired.

Steven Clayton Stafford,
of California, to be U.S. Marshal for the Southern District of California for the term of 4 years, vice George W. Venables.

Paul Charles Thielen,
of South Dakota, to be U.S. Marshal for the District of South Dakota for the term of 4 years, vice Warren Douglas Anderson, term expired.

Submitted August 5

Allison Blakely,
of Massachusetts, to be a member of the National Council on the Humanities for a term expiring January 26, 2016, vice Craig Haffner, term expired.

David B. Buckley,
of Virginia, to be Inspector General, Central Intelligence Agency, vice John Leonard Helgerson.

Scott C. Doney,
of Massachusetts, to be Chief Scientist of the National Oceanic and Atmospheric Administration, vice Kathryn D. Sullivan.

Jacob J. Lew,
of New York, to be Director of the Office of Management and Budget, vice Peter R. Orszag, resigned.

Nancy E. Lindborg,
of the District of Columbia, to be an Assistant Administrator of the U.S. Agency for International Development, vice Michael E. Hess, resigned.

Cora B. Marrett,
of Wisconsin, to be Deputy Director of the National Science Foundation, vice Kathie L. Olsen.

Wilfredo Martinez,
of Florida, to be a member of the Board of Directors of the State Justice Institute for a term expiring September 17, 2010, vice Tommy Edward Jewell III, term expired.

Wilfredo Martinez,
of Florida, to be a member of the Board of Directors of the State Justice Institute for a term expiring September 17, 2013 (reappointment).

Kevin Glenn Nealer,
of Maryland, to be a member of the Board of Directors of the Overseas Private Investment Corporation for a term expiring December 17, 2011, vice Sanford Gottesman, term expired.

Chase Theodora Rogers,
of Connecticut, to be a member of the Board of Directors of the State Justice Institute for a term expiring September 17, 2012, vice Arthur A. McGiverin, term expired.

Donald Kenneth Steinberg,
of California, to be Deputy Administrator of the U.S. Agency for International Development, vice Frederick W. Schieck, resigned.

Juan F. Vasquez,
of Texas, to be a Judge of the U.S. Tax Court for a term of 15 years (reappointment).

Withdrawn August 5

John J. Sullivan,
of Maryland, to be a member of the Federal Election Commission for a term expiring April 30, 2013, vice Ellen L. Weintraub, term expired, which was sent to the Senate on May 4, 2009.

Submitted September 13

Samuel Epstein Angel,
of Arkansas, to be a member of the Mississippi River Commission for a term of 9 years (reappointment).

Mari Carmen Aponte,
of the District of Columbia, to be Ambassador Extraordinary and Plenipotentiary of the United States of America to the Republic of El Salvador, to which position she was appointed during the last recess of the Senate.

Thomas M. Beck,
of Virginia, to be a member of the National Mediation Board for a term expiring July 1, 2013, vice Elizabeth Dougherty, term expired.

Alan D. Bersin,
of California, to be Commissioner of Customs, Department of Homeland Security, vice W. Ralph Basham.

Donald M. Berwick,
of Massachusetts, to be Administrator of the Centers for Medicare and Medicaid Services, vice Mark B. McClellan.

Peter A. Diamond,
of Massachusetts, to be a member of the Board of Governors of the Federal Reserve System for the unexpired term of 14 years from February 1, 2000, vice Frederic S. Mishkin.

Jeffrey Alan Goldstein,
of New York, to be an Under Secretary of the Treasury, vice Robert K. Steel, resigned.

Elisabeth Ann Hagen,
of Virginia, to be Under Secretary of Agriculture for Food Safety, vice Richard A. Raymond, resigned, to which position she was appointed during the last recess of the Senate.

Cameron Munter,
of California, a career member of the Senior Foreign Service, class of Counselor, to be Ambassador Extraordinary and Plenipotentiary of the United States of America to the Islamic Republic of Pakistan.

Winslow Lorenzo Sargeant,
of Wisconsin, to be Chief Counsel for Advocacy, Small Business Administration, vice Thomas M. Sullivan, to which position he was appointed during the last recess of the Senate.

Richard Sorian,
of New York, to be an Assistant Secretary of Health and Human Services, vice Christina H. Pearson, resigned, to which position he was appointed during the last recess of the Senate.

Marsha Ternus,
of Iowa, to be a member of the Board of Directors of the State Justice Institute for a term expiring September 17, 2012, vice Robert A. Miller, term expired.

Pamela Ann White,
of Maine, a career member of the Senior Foreign Service, class of Career Minister, to be Ambassador Extraordinary and Plenipotentiary of the United States of America to the Republic of The Gambia.

Louis B. Butler, Jr.,
of Wisconsin, to be U.S. District Judge for the Western District of Wisconsin, vice John C. Shabaz, retired.

Robert Neil Chatigny,
of Connecticut, to be U.S. Circuit Judge for the Second Circuit, vice Guido Calabresi, retired.

Edward Milton Chen,
of California, to be U.S. District Judge for the Northern District of California, vice Martin J. Jenkins, resigned.

Goodwin Liu,
of California, to be U.S. Circuit Judge for the Ninth Circuit, vice a new position created by Public Law 110–177, approved January 7, 2008.

John J. McConnell, Jr.,
of Rhode Island, to be U.S. District Judge for the District of Rhode Island, vice Ernest C. Torres, retired.

Submitted September 15

Carol Fulp,
of Massachusetts, to be a Representative of the United States of America to the Sixty-fifth Session of the General Assembly of the United Nations.

Gregory J. Nickels,
of Washington, to be an Alternate Representative of the United States of America to the Sixty-fifth Session of the General Assembly of the United Nations.

Jeanne Shaheen,
of New Hampshire, to be a Representative of the United States of America to the Sixty-fifth Session of the General Assembly of the United Nations.

Roger F. Wicker,
of Mississippi, to be a Representative of the United States of America to the Sixty-fifth Session of the General Assembly of the United Nations.

Submitted September 16

George Albert Krol,
of New Jersey, a career member of the Senior Foreign Service, class of Minister-Counselor, to be Ambassador Extraordinary and Plenipotentiary of the United States of America to the Republic of Uzbekistan.

Charles M. Oberly III,
of Delaware, to be U.S. Attorney for the District of Delaware for the term of 4 years, vice Colm F. Connolly, resigned.

Submitted September 20

Mario Cordero,
of California, to be a Federal Maritime Commissioner for the term expiring June 30, 2014, vice Harold J. Creel, Jr., resigned.

Rebecca F. Dye,
of North Carolina, to be a Federal Maritime Commissioner for the term expiring June 30, 2015 (reappointment).

Stacia A. Hylton,
of Virginia, to be Director of the U.S. Marshals Service, vice John F. Clark, resigned.

Submitted September 23

William R. Brownfield,
of Texas, a career member of the Senior Foreign Service, class of Career Minister, to be an Assistant Secretary of State (International Narcotics and Law Enforcement Affairs), vice David T. Johnson, resigned.

Eugene Louis Dodaro,
of Virginia, to be Comptroller General of the U.S. for a term of 15 years, vice David M. Walker, resigned.

Matthew Maxwell Taylor Kennedy,
of California, to be a member of the Board of Directors of the Overseas Private Investment Corporation for a term expiring December 17, 2012, vice Samuel E. Ebbesen, term expired.

Kurt Walter Tong,
of Maryland, a career member of the Senior Foreign Service, class of Counselor, for the rank of Ambassador during his tenure of service as U.S. Senior Official for the Asia-Pacific Economic Corporation (APEC) Forum.

Submitted September 27

Paige Eve Alexander,
of Georgia, to be an Assistant Administrator of the U.S. Agency for International Development, vice Douglas Menarchik, resigned.

Submitted September 29

Kenneth F. Bohac,
of Illinois, to be U.S. Marshal for the Central District of Illinois for the term of 4 years, vice Steven D. Deatherage, term expired.

Mae A. D'Agostino,
of New York, to be U.S. District Judge for the Northern District of New York, vice Frederick J. Scullin, Jr., retired.

William Conner Eldridge,
of Arkansas, to be U.S. Attorney for the Western District of Arkansas for the term of 4 years, vice Robert Cramer Balfe III, resigned.

Caitlin Joan Halligan,
of New York, to be U.S. Circuit Judge for the District of Columbia Circuit, vice John G. Roberts, Jr., elevated.

Richard Brooke Jackson,
of Colorado, to be U.S. District Judge for the District of Colorado, vice Phillip S. Figa, deceased.

Jimmie V. Reyna,
of Maryland, to be U.S. Circuit Judge for the Federal Circuit, vice Haldane Robert Mayer, retired.

Paula Barker Duffy,
of Illinois, to be a member of the National Council on the Humanities for a term expiring January 26, 2016, vice Harvey Klehr, term expired.

Isabel Framer,
of Ohio, to be a member of the Board of Directors of the State Justice Institute for a term expiring September 17, 2012, vice Carlos R. Garza, term expired.

Mark Green,
of Wisconsin, to be a member of the Board of Directors of the Millennium Challenge Corporation for a term of 3 years, vice William H. Frist, term expiring.

Susan H. Hildreth,
of Washington, to be Director of the Institute of Museum and Library Services, vice Anne-Imelda Radice.

Thomas R. Nides,
of the District of Columbia, to be Deputy Secretary of State for Management and Resources, vice Jacob J. Lew.

Alan J. Patricof,
of New York, to be a member of the Board of Directors of the Millennium Challenge Corporation for a term of 2 years (reappointment).

Jo Ann Rooney,
of Massachusetts, to be Principal Deputy Under Secretary of Defense for Personnel and Readiness, vice Michael L. Dominguez.

Michael Vickers,
of Virginia, to be Under Secretary of Defense for Intelligence, vice James R. Clapper, Jr.

Martha Wagner Weinberg,
of Massachusetts, to be a member of the National Council on the Humanities for a term expiring January 26, 2016, vice Herman Belz, term expired.

Withdrawn September 29

Teresa Takai,
of California, to be an Assistant Secretary of Defense, vice John G. Grimes, which was sent to the Senate on April 12, 2010.

Submitted November 15

Sue Kathrine Brown,
of Texas, a career member of the Senior Foreign Service, class of Minister-Counselor, to be Ambassador Extraordinary and Plenipotentiary of the United States of America to Montenegro.

David Lee Carden,
of New York, to be Representative of the United States of America to the Association of Southeast Asian Nations, with the rank of Ambassador Extraordinary and Plenipotentiary.

Timothy J. Feighery,
of New York, to be Chairman of the Foreign Claims Settlement Commission of the U.S. for a term expiring September 30, 2012, vice Mauricio J. Tamargo, term expired.

Frances M.D. Gulland,
of California, to be a member of the Marine Mammal Commission for a term expiring May 13, 2012, vice Vera Alexander, term expired.

Roberto R. Herencia,
of Illinois, to be a member of the Board of Directors of the Overseas Private Investment Corporation for a term expiring December 17, 2012, vice Patrick J. Durkin, term expired.

Eric G. Postel,
of Wisconsin, to be an Assistant Administrator of the U.S. Agency for International Development, vice Jacqueline Ellen Schafer, resigned.

Joseph A. Smith, Jr.,
of North Carolina, to be Director of the Federal Housing Finance Agency for a term of 5 years (new position).

Pamela L. Spratlen,
of California, a career member of the Senior Foreign Service, class of Counselor, to be Ambassador Extraordinary and Plenipotentiary of the United States of America to the Kyrgyz Republic.

James A. Torrey,
of Connecticut, to be a member of the Board of Directors of the Overseas Private Investment Corporation for a term expiring December 17, 2010, vice Dianne I. Moss, term expired.

James A. Torrey,
of Connecticut, to be a member of the Board of Directors of the Overseas Private Investment

Corporation for a term expiring December 17, 2013 (reappointment).

Submitted November 17

Daniel L. Shields III,
of Pennsylvania, a career member of the Senior Foreign Service, class of Counselor, to be Ambassador Extraordinary and Plenipotentiary of the United States of America to Brunei Darussalam.

Joseph M. Torsella,
of Pennsylvania, to be Representative of the United States of America to the United Nations for U.N. Management and Reform, with the rank of Ambassador.

Joseph M. Torsella,
of Pennsylvania, to be Alternate Representative of the United States of America to the Sessions of the General Assembly of the United Nations, during his tenure of service as Representative of the United States of America to the United Nations for U.N. Management and Reform.

Andrew L. Traver,
of Illinois, to be Director, Bureau of Alcohol, Tobacco, Firearms, and Explosives (new position).

Charles Edward Andrews,
of Alabama, to be U.S. Marshal for the Southern District of Alabama for the term of 4 years, vice William Smith Taylor, term expired.

Darrell James Bell,
of Montana, to be U.S. Marshal for the District of Montana for the term of 4 years, vice Dwight MacKay, term expired.

William Benedict Berger, Sr.,
of Florida, to be U.S. Marshal for the Middle District of Florida for the term of 4 years, vice Thomas Dyson Hurlburt, Jr., term expired.

Cathy Bissoon,
of Pennsylvania, to be U.S. District Judge for the Western District of Pennsylvania, vice Thomas M. Hardiman, elevated.

Vincent L. Briccetti,
of New York, to be U.S. District Judge for the Southern District of New York, vice Kimba M. Wood, retired.

Russel Edwin Burger,
of Oregon, to be U.S. Marshal for the District of Oregon for the term of 4 years, vice Dennis Cluff Merrill, term expired.

Roy Bale Dalton, Jr.,
of Florida, to be U.S. District Judge for the Middle District of Florida, vice Henry Lee Adams, Jr., retired.

Sara Lynn Darrow,
of Illinois, to be U.S. District Judge for the Central District of Illinois, vice Joe B. McDade, retired.

John A. Kronstadt,
of California, to be U.S. District Judge for the Central District of California, vice Florence-Marie Cooper, deceased.

S. Amanda Marshall,
of Oregon, to be U.S. Attorney for the District of Oregon for the term of 4 years, vice Karin J. Immergut, term expired.

Joseph Campbell Moore,
of Wyoming, to be U.S. Marshal for the District of Wyoming for the term of 4 years, vice James Anthony Rose, term expired.

Kevin Hunter Sharp,
of Tennessee, to be U.S. District Judge for the Middle District of Tennessee, vice Robert L. Echols, retired.

Edwin Donovan Sloane,
of Maryland, to be U.S. Marshal for the District of Columbia for the term of 4 years, vice George Breffni Walsh, term expired.

Esteban Soto III,
of Maryland, to be U.S. Marshal for the Superior Court of the District of Columbia for the term of 4 years, vice Stephen Thomas Conboy, resigned.

Withdrawn November 17

Marsha Ternus,
of Iowa, to be a member of the Board of Directors of the State Justice Institute for a term expiring September 17, 2012, vice Robert A. Miller, term expired, which was sent to the Senate on September 13, 2010.

Submitted December 1

Arenda L. Wright Allen,
of Virginia, to be U.S. District Judge for the Eastern District of Virginia, vice Jerome B. Friedman, retired.

Claire C. Cecchi,
of New Jersey, to be U.S. District Judge for the District of New Jersey, vice Joseph A. Greenaway, elevated.

Bernice Bouie Donald,
of Tennessee, to be U.S. Circuit Judge for the Sixth Circuit, vice Ronald Lee Gilman, retired.

Mark Raymond Hornak,
of Pennsylvania, to be U.S. District Judge for the Western District of Pennsylvania, vice Donetta W. Ambrose, retired.

Robert David Mariani,
of Pennsylvania, to be U.S. District Judge for the Middle District of Pennsylvania, vice James M. Munley, retired.

John Andrew Ross,
of Missouri, to be U.S. District Judge for the Eastern District of Missouri, vice Charles A. Shaw, retired.

Esther Salas,
of New Jersey, to be U.S. District Judge for the District of New Jersey, vice Katharine Sweeney Hayden, retired.

Christopher R. Thyer,
of Arkansas, to be U.S. Attorney for the Eastern District of Arkansas for the term of 4 years, vice Harry E. Cummins III, resigned.

Michael Francis Urbanski,
of Virginia, to be U.S. District Judge for the Western District of Virginia, vice Norman K. Moon, retired.

Submitted December 3

Janice Lehrer-Stein,
of California, to be a member of the National Council on Disability for a term expiring September 17, 2013, vice Victoria Ray Carlson, term expired.

Leon Rodriguez,
of Maryland, to be Administrator of the Wage and Hour Division, Department of Labor, vice Paul DeCamp.

Kathryn D. Sullivan,
of Ohio, to be an Assistant Secretary of Commerce, vice Phillip A. Singerman.

Submitted December 6

Daniel M. Ashe,
of Maryland, to be Director of the U.S. Fish and Wildlife Service, vice Samuel D. Hamilton.

Kelvin K. Droegemeier,
of Oklahoma, to be a member of the National Science Board, National Science Foundation for a term expiring May 10, 2016 (reappointment).

Maurice B. Foley,
of Maryland, to be a Judge of the U.S. Tax Court for a term of 15 years (reappointment).

Submitted December 8

Albert J. Beveridge III,
of the District of Columbia, to be a member of the National Council on the Humanities for a term expiring January 26, 2016, vice James Davison Hunter, term expired.

Constance M. Carroll,
of California, to be a member of the National Council on the Humanities for a term expiring January 26, 2016, vice Tamar Jacoby, term expired.

Cathy M. Davidson,
of North Carolina, to be a member of the National Council on the Humanities for a term expiring January 26, 2016, vice Marvin Bailey Scott, term expired.

Submitted December 9

Aaron Paul Dworkin,
of Michigan, to be a member of the National Council on the Arts for a term expiring September 3, 2014, vice Karen Lias Wolff, term expired.

Submitted December 13

Peter Bruce Lyons,
of New Mexico, to be an Assistant Secretary of Energy (Nuclear Energy), vice Warren F. Miller, Jr., resigned.

Denise Ellen O'Donnell,
of New York, to be Director of the Bureau of Justice Assistance, vice Domingo S. Herraiz, resigned.

Stephanie O'Sullivan,
of Virginia, to be Principal Deputy Director of National Intelligence, vice David C. Gompert, resigned.

David Bruce Shear,
of New York, a career member of the Senior Foreign Service, class of Minister-Counselor, to be Ambassador Extraordinary and Plenipotentiary of the United States of America to the Socialist Republic of Vietnam.

Submitted December 15

Clyde E. Terry,
of New Hampshire, to be a member of the National Council on Disability for a term expiring September 17, 2013, vice John R. Vaughn, resigned.

Submitted December 17

Elisebeth Collins Cook,
of Illinois, to be a member of the Privacy and Civil Liberties Oversight Board for a term expiring January 29, 2014 (new position).

James Xavier Dempsey,
of California, to be a member of the Privacy and Civil Liberties Oversight Board for a term expiring January 29, 2016 (new position).

Carolyn N. Lerner,
of Maryland, to be Special Counsel, Office of Special Counsel, for the term of 5 years, vice Scott J. Bloch, resigned.

Submitted December 20

Judith A. Ansley,
of Massachusetts, to be a member of the Board of Directors of the U.S. Institute of Peace for the remainder of the term expiring September 19, 2011, vice Ron Silver.

Judith A. Ansley,
of Massachusetts, to be a member of the Board of Directors of the U.S. Institute of Peace for a term of 4 years (reappointment).

Ann D. Begeman,
of Virginia, to be a member of the Surface Transportation Board for a term expiring December 31, 2015, vice Charles D. Nottingham, term expiring.

Nils Maarten Parin Daulaire,
of Virginia, to be Representative of the U.S. on the Executive Board of the World Health Organization, vice Joxel Garcia.

John A. Lancaster,
of New York, to be a member of the Board of Directors of the U.S. Institute of Peace for the remainder of the term expiring September 19, 2011, vice Kathleen Martinez.

John A. Lancaster,
of New York, to be a member of the Board of Directors of the U.S. Institute of Peace for a term of 4 years (reappointment).

Terry Lewis,
of Michigan, to be a member of the Board of Directors of the Overseas Private Investment Corporation for a term expiring December 17, 2011, vice C. William Swank, term expired.

Withdrawn December 20

Beatrice A. Hanson,
of New York, to be Director of the Office for Victims of Crime, vice John W. Gillis, which was sent to the Senate on December 23, 2009.

Submitted December 22

Agnes Gund,
of New York, to be a member of the National Council on the Arts for a term expiring September 3, 2016 (new position).

Appendix C—Checklist of White House Press Releases

The following list contains releases of the Office of the Press Secretary that are neither printed items nor covered by entries in the Digest of Other White House Announcements.

Released July 1

Transcript of a press briefing by Press Secretary Robert L. Gibbs and Deepwater Horizon Oil Spill Incident Commander Adm. Thad W. Allen, USCG

Statement by the Press Secretary on House of Representatives passage of legislation extending unemployment insurance benefits

Statement by the Press Secretary on disaster assistance to Maine

Advance text of the President's remarks on signing the Comprehensive Iran Sanctions, Accountability, and Divestment Act of 2010

Released July 2

Transcript of a teleconference press briefing by Deputy National Security Adviser for Strategic Communications Benjamin J. Rhodes and National Security Council Senior Director for the Middle East and North Africa Daniel B. Shapiro on the upcoming visit of Prime Minister Benjamin Netanyahu of Israel

Statement by the Press Secretary: Background on the President's Recovery Act Announcement Tomorrow (dated July 1)

Statement by the Press Secretary announcing that the President signed H.R. 5569, H.R. 5611, and H.R. 5623

Statement by the Press Secretary on disaster assistance to Minnesota

Fact sheet: Executive Order on Optimizing the Security of Biological Select Agents and Toxins in the United States

Text: Statement by Council of Economic Advisers Chair Christina D. Romer on the employment situation in June

Released July 3

Fact sheet: President's Recovery Act Announcement

Released July 4

Text: Statement by National Security Council Spokesman Michael A. Hammer on Syrian convictions of human rights activists

Released July 6

Statement by the Press Secretary: Administration Officials Continue Travel Across the Country for "Recovery Summer" Events, Project Site Visits

Released July 7

Transcript of a press briefing by Press Secretary Robert L. Gibbs

Statement by the Press Secretary: President Obama Provides Progress Report on National Export Initiative, Announces Members of the President's Export Council

Statement by the Press Secretary announcing that the President has signed S. 1660, S. 2865, and S.J. Res. 32

Advance text of the President's opening remarks announcing the creation of the President's Export Council

Released July 8

Transcript of a press gaggle by Deputy Press Secretary William Burton

Statement by the Press Secretary: White House To Unveil National HIV/AIDS Strategy

Advance text of the President's remarks at Smith Electric Vehicles in Kansas City, MO

Released July 9

Statement by the Press Secretary on the visit of President Leonel Fernandez Reyna of the Dominican Republic

Text: Statement by National Security Council Spokesman Michael A. Hammer on the U.N. Security Council Presidential Statement on the *Cheonan*

Advance text of the President's remarks at the University of Nevada, Las Vegas, in Las Vegas, NV

Released July 10

Statement by the Press Secretary on disaster assistance to Montana

Released July 12

Transcript of a press briefing by Press Secretary Robert L. Gibbs

Statement by the Press Secretary: White House To Unveil National HIV/AIDS Strategy

Released July 13

Transcript of a press briefing by Press Secretary Robert L. Gibbs

Statement by the Press Secretary: First Lady Michelle Obama, Dr. Jill Biden, HHS Secretary Sebelius To Discuss New Preventive Health Benefits

Statement by the Press Secretary: White House Announces National HIV/AIDS Strategy

Statement by the Press Secretary announcing that the President has signed S. 3104

Text: Statement by National Security Council Spokesman Michael A. Hammer on the International Criminal Court appeals court ruling

Text: Statement by Deputy National Security Council Spokesman Benjamin Chang on meetings between National Security Adviser James L. Jones, Jr., and NATO Secretary General Rasmussen, senior French officials, and other allies in Paris and Brussels

Announcement: President Obama To Honor WNBA Champion Phoenix Mercury at the White House

Released July 14

Transcript of a teleconference press briefing by senior administration officials on the Al Shabaab terrorist group (dated July 13; released July 14)

Transcript of a press briefing by Press Secretary Robert L. Gibbs

Statement by the Press Secretary: Vice President Biden, CEA Chair Romer Release New Analysis on Job and Economic Impact of the Recovery Act

Statement by the Press Secretary: Department of Energy Releases New Report on Economic Impact of Recovery Act Advanced Vehicle Investments

Statement by the Press Secretary on disaster assistance to Wyoming

Released July 15

Transcript of a press gaggle by Press Secretary Robert L. Gibbs

Statement by the Press Secretary on disaster assistance to Nebraska

Advance text of the President's remarks at Compact Power, Inc., in Holland, MI

Text: Statement by National Security Council Spokesman Michael A. Hammer on the Council of Inspectors General on Integrity and Efficiency Evaluation of the IG's Operations in Afghanistan

Text: Statement by Deputy National Security Council Spokesman Benjamin Chang on National Security Adviser James L. Jones, Jr.'s visit to New Delhi, India

Released July 16

Text: Statement by Deputy National Security Council Spokesman Benjamin Chang on National Security Adviser James L. Jones, Jr.'s visit to Afghanistan

Released July 19

Transcript of a press briefing by Press Secretary Robert L. Gibbs

Statement by the Press Secretary: President Obama Calls on Republicans To End Obstruction of Unemployment Benefits, Urges Congress To Pass Critical Aid for Millions of Americans

Statement by the Press Secretary: President Obama To Sign Wall Street Reform Bill

Advance text of the President's remarks on legislation extending unemployment insurance benefits

Released July 20

Statement by the Press Secretary: President Obama Expands Greenhouse Gas Reduction Target for Federal Operations

Released July 21

Transcript of a press briefing by Press Secretary Robert L. Gibbs

Statement by the Press Secretary on the continued Senate delay of extending unemployment insurance legislation

Statement by the Press Secretary on the President's forum with young African leaders

Advance text of the President's remarks on signing the Dodd-Frank Wall Street Reform and Consumer Protection Act

Released July 22

Transcript of a press briefing by Press Secretary Robert L. Gibbs

Statement by the Press Secretary: President Obama To Sign Improper Payments Elimination and Recovery Act

Statement by the Press Secretary: First Family To Travel to Florida's Gulf Coast

Statement by the Press Secretary announcing that the President has signed H.R. 4213

Fact sheet: The Improper Payment Elimination and Recovery Act and the Administration's Efforts To Cut Wasteful Improper Payments

Released July 23

Statement by the Press Secretary: President Obama To Deliver Speech on Education Reform at the National Urban League Convention

Statement by the Press Secretary: President Obama To Visit Auto Plants in Michigan, Illinois

Statement by the Press Secretary: President Obama To Discuss the Economy in New Jersey

Statement by the Press Secretary on transparency in the energy sector

Statement by the Press Secretary on disaster assistance to Kentucky

Released July 25

Text: Statement of National Security Adviser James L. Jones, Jr., on the WikiLeaks web site posting documents concerning military operations in Afghanistan

Released July 26

Transcript of a press briefing by Press Secretary Robert L. Gibbs

Statement by the Press Secretary: President Obama To Discuss the Economy in New Jersey

Statement by the Press Secretary on disaster assistance to Oklahoma

Released July 27

Transcript of a press briefing by Press Secretary Robert L. Gibbs

Statement by the Press Secretary: President Obama To Meet With Small Business Owners, Urge Congress To Act To Support Small Businesses and Create Jobs

Statement by the Press Secretary: President Obama To Visit Two Auto Plants in Michigan

Statement by the Press Secretary announcing that the President has signed H.R. 689, H.R. 3360, H.R. 4840, H.R. 5502, and H.J. Res. 83

Statement by the Press Secretary on disaster assistance to Idaho

Fact sheet: President Obama Urges Congress To Act To Support Small Businesses Seeking To Invest, Grow and Hire

Released July 28

Transcript of a press gaggle by Deputy Press Secretary William Burton

Statement by the Press Secretary: Super Bowl Champion New Orleans Saints To Visit White House

Released July 29

Transcript of a press briefing by Press Secretary Robert L. Gibbs, Treasury Department Senior Adviser for Auto Issues Ron Bloom, and Director of Recovery for Auto Communities and Workers Edward B. Montgomery

Statement by the Press Secretary on BP's contribution to support unemployed oil rig workers

Statement by the Press Secretary: President Obama To Speak at Disabled American Veterans National Convention in Atlanta, GA

Statement by the Press Secretary announcing that the President has signed H.R. 4899 and H.R. 5610

Statement by the Press Secretary on disaster assistance to Iowa

Statement by the Press Secretary on disaster assistance to South Dakota

Text: Statement by Treasury Department Senior Adviser for Auto Issues Ron Bloom and Director of Recovery for Auto Communities and Workers Edward B. Montgomery on rebuilding the American auto industry

Text: Report: Rebuilding the American Auto Industry

Released July 30

Transcript of a press gaggle by Press Secretary Robert L. Gibbs and Special Assistant to the President for Economic Policy Brian Deese

Statement by the Press Secretary announcing that the President has signed H.R. 5849 and S. 3372

Fact sheet: Recovery Act in Michigan

Text: Statement by Council of Economic Advisers Chair Christina D. Romer on the second quarter and GDP revisions for the 2010 advance GDP estimate

Released August 1

Statement by the Press Secretary announcing that the President has signed H.R. 5900

Released August 2

Transcript of a press gaggle by Deputy Press Secretary William Burton

Statement by the Press Secretary: President Obama To Present the 2010 Citizens Medal

Advance text of the President's remarks at the national convention of Disabled American Veterans in Atlanta, GA

Text: Facts and Figures on Drawdown in Iraq

Released August 3

Transcript of a press briefing by Press Secretary Robert L. Gibbs

Statement by the Press Secretary announcing that the President has signed H.R. 4861, H.R. 5051, H.R. 5099, and S. 1789

Statement by the Press Secretary on disaster assistance to Texas

Fact sheet: The President's Engagement in Africa

Text: Statement by National Security Council Spokesman Michael A. Hammer on human rights issues in Russia

Text: Op-ed piece by Secretary of the Treasury Timothy F. Geithner for the New York Times: Welcome to the Recovery

Released August 4

Transcript of a press briefing by Press Secretary Robert L. Gibbs, Deepwater Horizon Oil Spill Incident Commander Adm. Thad W. Allen, USCG, Assistant to the President for Energy and Climate Change Carol M. Browner, and National Oceanic and Atmospheric Administration Administrator Jane Lubchenco

Transcript of remarks by Press Secretary Robert L. Gibbs to the travel pool

Statement by the Press Secretary: Agriculture Secretary Vilsack Announces Over 120 Recovery Act Broadband Projects To Bring Jobs, Economic Opportunity to Rural Communities

Statement by the Press Secretary: President Obama Honors Winners of the 2010 Citizens Medals

Released August 5

Statement by the Press Secretary: Dr. Christina Romer, Chair of the Council of Economic Advisers, To Return to the University of California, Berkeley

Released August 6

Statement by the Press Secretary announcing that the President has signed H.R. 4684 and S. 1053

Text: Statement by Council of Economic Advisers Chair Christina D. Romer on the employment situation in July

Released August 9

Transcript of a press gaggle by Deputy Press Secretary William Burton

Text: Statement by National Security Adviser James L. Jones, Jr., on the U.S. Response to Flooding in Pakistan

Advance text of the President's remarks at the University of Texas at Austin in Austin, TX

Released August 10

Transcript of a press briefing by Deputy Press Secretary William Burton

Statements by the Press Secretary announcing that the President signed H.R. 1586, H.R. 2765, H.R. 5874, and S. 1749

Statement by the Press Secretary on disaster assistance to Kansas

Released August 11

Transcript of a press briefing by Press Secretary Robert L. Gibbs

Statement by the Press Secretary announcing that the President signed H.R. 5872 and H.R. 5981

Statement by the Press Secretary on disaster assistance to Wisconsin

Released August 12

Statement by the Press Secretary: President Obama To Travel to Wisconsin Monday

Fact sheet: President's Strategic and Integrated Southwest Border Security Strategy

Released August 13

Transcript of a press briefing by Press Secretary Robert L. Gibbs and Secretary of Homeland Security Janet A. Napolitano

Statement by the Press Secretary: President Obama To Honor NCAA Champion Student Athletes at the White House

Statement by the Press Secretary announcing that the President signed H.R. 6080

Announcement: Expected Attendees at the White House Iftar Dinner

Text: Statement by National Security Council Spokesman Michael A. Hammer on national elections in Rwanda

Advance text of the President's remarks at an iftar dinner

Released August 14

Advance text of the President's remarks in Panama City Beach, FL

Released August 16

Transcript of a press gaggle by Deputy Press Secretary William Burton

Statement by the Press Secretary: President Obama To Visit Ohio

Statement by the Press Secretary: President Obama To Visit Miami, Florida

Advance text of the President's remarks at ZBB Energy Corporation in Menomonee Falls, WI

Released August 17

Transcript of a press gaggle by Deputy Press Secretary William Burton

Statement by the Press Secretary: President Obama's Participation in Summit With European Union

Statement by the Press Secretary: President Obama To Participate in NATO Summit in Lisbon on November 19–20

Statement by the Press Secretary on disaster assistance to Missouri

Released August 18

Transcript of a press gaggle by Deputy Press Secretary William Burton

Statement by the Press Secretary: Vice President Biden Announces Recovery Act Investments in

Broadband Projects To Bring Jobs, Economic Opportunity to Communities Nationwide

Released August 19

Transcript of a press gaggle by Deputy Press Secretary William Burton

Statement by the Press Secretary on disaster assistance to Illinois

Released August 20

Transcript of a press briefing by Deputy Press Secretary William Burton and Assistant to the President for Homeland Security and Counterterrorism John O. Brennan

Released August 24

Transcript of a press briefing by Deputy Press Secretary William Burton and Assistant to the President for Homeland Security and Counterterrorism John O. Brennan

Released August 25

Statement by the Press Secretary: President Obama and Administration Officials To Mark 5th Anniversary of Hurricane Katrina With Travel to Gulf Coast, Project Site Visits

Statement by the Press Secretary: President Obama To Travel to Fort Bliss, Texas and Address the Nation on the Iraq War

Statement by the Press Secretary: President Obama To Deliver Back-to-School Speech on September 14

Released August 26

Statement by the Press Secretary: President Obama, First Lady Travel to New Orleans, LA

Released August 28

Statement by the Press Secretary: President Obama Travel to Fort Bliss, Texas

Released August 29

Advance text of the President's remarks at Xavier University in New Orleans, LA

Released August 30

Transcript of a press briefing by Press Secretary Robert L. Gibbs

Statement by the Press Secretary: President Obama Lays the Foundation for a New Export Control System To Strengthen National Security and the Competeveness of Key U.S. Manufacturing and Technology Sectors

Statement by the Press Secretary: President Obama To Speak at the Milwaukee Laborfest

Released August 31

Transcript of a press gaggle by Deputy Press Secretary William Burton and Deputy National Security Adviser for Strategic Communications Benjamin J. Rhodes

Transcript of a press briefing by U.S. Special Envoy for Middle East Peace George J. Mitchell on upcoming Middle East peace talks

Statement by the Press Secretary on the terrorist attack in the southern West Bank

Excerpts of the President's national address on the end of combat operations in Iraq

Advance text of the President's national address on the end of combat operations in Iraq

Released September 1

Statement by the Press Secretary on disaster assistance to North Carolina

Released September 2

Transcript of a press briefing by Press Secretary Robert L. Gibbs

Statement by the Press Secretary: New Details: President Obama To Speak at Milwaukee Laborfest

Statement by the Press Secretary: President Obama To Hold Events on Economy in Wisconsin and Ohio, Press Conference at End of the Week

Statement by the Press Secretary on disaster assistance to Massachusetts

Released September 3

Statement by the Press Secretary: President Obama To Host Second U.S.-ASEAN Leaders Meeting

Statement by the Press Secretary: President Obama To Award Medal of Honor

Statement by the Press Secretary on disaster assistance to New Mexico

Text: Memorandum from Chief Performance Officer Jeffrey D. Zients for the Senior Executive Service reviewing the Accountable Government Initiative

Released September 15

Transcript of a press briefing by Press Secretary Robert L. Gibbs

Statement by the Press Secretary: In New Video, President Obama Encourages Troops and Veterans To Claim "Stop Loss" Pay

Statement by the Press Secretary: Increasing America's Competitiveness in the Global Economy

Statement by the Press Secretary on disaster assistance to Tennessee

Advance text of the President's remarks at the Congressional Hispanic Caucus Institute Annual Awards Gala

Released September 16

Transcript of a press briefing by senior administration officials on the parliamentary elections in Afghanistan

Statement by the Press Secretary: White House Releases Report to the President on the National Export Initiative (dated September 15; embargoed until September 16)

Statement by the Press Secretary: President Obama To Announce Major Expansion of "Educate To Innovate" Campaign To Improve Science, Technology, Engineering and Math (STEM) Education (dated September 15; embargoed until September 16)

Released September 17

Transcript of a press briefing by Press Secretary Robert L. Gibbs

Statement by the Press Secretary: President Obama To Award Medal of Honor

Statement by the Press Secretary: President Obama To Travel to Philadelphia

Released September 18

Advance text of the President's remarks at the Congressional Black Caucus Foundation Phoenix Awards Dinner

Released September 20

Transcript of a teleconference press briefing by Deputy National Security Adviser for Strategic Communications Benjamin J. Rhodes, Permanent Representative to the U.N. Susan E. Rice, and Senior Director of Multilateral Affairs Samantha Power

Statement by the Press Secretary: President Obama Travel to New York City

Statement by the Press Secretary: Advancing U.S. Interests at the United Nations

Released September 21

Transcript of a press briefing by Press Secretary Robert L. Gibbs

Statement by the Press Secretary: Dr. Lawrence H. Summers, Director of the National Economic Council, To Return to Harvard University at the End of the Year

Released September 22

Transcript of a press gaggle by Press Secretary Robert L. Gibbs

Transcript of a teleconference press briefing by Deputy National Security Adviser for International Economics Michael B. Froman and Senior Director for International Development Gayle Smith previewing the President's speech at the United Nations Millennium Development Goals Summit

Fact sheet: The Six Month Anniversary of the Affordable Care Act (dated September 21; embargoed until September 22)

Fact sheet: U.S. Global Development Policy

Fact sheet: President Obama's Development Policy and the Global Climate Change Initiative

Fact sheet: President Obama's Global Development Policy and Global Food Security

Fact sheet: President Obama's Global Development Policy and the Global Health Initiative

Advance text of the President's remarks at the United Nations Millennium Development Goals Summit in New York City

Released September 23

Transcript of a press briefing by Press Secretary Robert L. Gibbs, National Security Council Senior Director for Asian Affairs Jeffery A. Bader, and Deputy National Security Adviser for Strategic Communications Benjamin J. Rhodes

Statement by the Press Secretary on the Justice Department filing in *Log Cabin Republicans* v. *United States of America*

Statement by the Press Secretary on disaster assistance to South Dakota

Fact sheet: U.S. Commitment to Civil Society

Fact sheet: U.S. Support for Open Government

Fact sheet: Advancing Democracy and Human Rights

Excerpts of the President's remarks to the United Nations General Assembly (dated September 22; embargoed until September 23)

Advance text of the President's remarks to the United Nations General Assembly

Released September 24

Transcript of a briefing by National Security Council Chief of Staff Denis R. McDonough on the United Nations Ministerial Meeting on Sudan

Transcript of a background briefing by a senior administration official on the President's interview with BBC Persian

Statement by the Press Secretary: President Obama To Visit Des Moines, Iowa

Statement by the Press Secretary: President Obama To Visit Albuquerque, New Mexico

Fact sheet: U.S. Assistance to Kyrgyzstan

Excerpt from the President's interview with BBC Persian

Released September 27

Statement by the Press Secretary: President Obama Announces Goal of Recruiting 10,000 STEM Teachers Over the Next Two Years

Statement by the Press Secretary: President Obama To Visit Richmond, VA

Statement by the Press Secretary announcing that the President signed H.R. 6102 and S. 3656

Released September 28

Transcript of a press gaggle by Deputy Press Secretary William Burton

Statement by the Press Secretary: President Obama To Address 2010 *Fortune* Most Powerful Women Summit on October 5th in Washington, DC

Statement by the Press Secretary on a stem cell research court decision

Statement by the Press Secretary on disaster assistance to the U.S. Virgin Islands

Released September 29

Transcript of a press gaggle by Deputy Press Secretary William Burton

Statement by the Press Secretary on the new Executive order designating Iranian officials responsible for or complicit in serious human rights abuses

Released September 30

Transcript of a press briefing by Press Secretary Robert L. Gibbs

Statement by the Press Secretary announcing that the President signed H.R. 3081

Statement by the Press Secretary announcing that the President signed H.R. 1445, H.R. 3562, H.R. 3940, H.R. 3978, H.R. 4505, H.R. 4667, H.R. 5682, H.R. 6190, S. 3814, and S. 3839

Text: Statement by National Security Council Spokesman Michael A. Hammer on Senate Approval of the Hague Convention on the International Recovery of Child Support and Other Forms of Family Maintenance

Text: Statement by National Security Council Spokesman Michael A. Hammer on the Freedom of Assembly and Association Resolution at the U.N. Human Rights Council

Released October 1

Transcript of a press briefing by Press Secretary Robert L. Gibbs

Statement by the Press Secretary: President Obama To Award Medal of Honor

Text: Statement by National Security Council Spokesman Michael A. Hammer on the Resolution on Elimination of Discrimination Against Women at the U.N. Human Rights Council

Released October 2

Fact sheet: President's Clean Energy Radio Address

Released October 4

Transcript of a press briefing by Press Secretary Robert L. Gibbs

Statement by the Press Secretary: President Obama To Announce Launch of *Skills for America's Future*

Statement by the Press Secretary: President Obama Travel to Chicago

Statement by the Press Secretary: President Obama Travel to New Jersey

Statement by the Press Secretary on disaster assistance to Arizona

Released October 5

Statement by the Press Secretary announcing that the President has signed H.R. 1517, S. 846, S. 1055, S. 1674, S. 2781, and S. 3717

Fact sheet: Building American Skills by Strengthening Community Colleges

Advance text of the President's remarks at the Fortune Most Powerful Women Summit in Washington, DC

Advance text of National Security Adviser James L. Jones, Jr., at the Sochi Security Council Gathering in Sochi, Russia

Released October 7

Transcript of a press briefing by Press Secretary Robert L. Gibbs

Statement by the Press Secretary: President Obama Travel to Philadephia

Statement by the Press Secretary announcing that the President signed H.R. 553

Released October 8

Statement by the Press Secretary: President Obama Travel to Miami

Statement by the Press Secretary announcing that the President signed H.R. 714, H.R. 1177, S. 2868, S. 3751, S. 3828, and S. 3847

Text: Statement by Council of Economic Advisers Chairman Austan D. Goolsbee

Released October 11

Statement by the Press Secretary: President Obama Holds Meeting on Infrastructure Investment, New Report Shows Positive Economic Impact on States and Communities

Statement by the Press Secretary announcing that the President signed S. 3729

Released October 12

Transcript of a press briefing by Press Secretary Robert L. Gibbs

Statement by the Press Secretary: President Obama Travel to Delaware

Statement by the Press Secretary announcing that the President signed H.R. 2923, H.R. 3553, H.R. 3689, H.R. 3980, S. 1132, and S. 3397

Released October 13

Statement by the Press Secretary: President Obama To Highlight the American Opportunity Tax Credit; Treasury Report Highlights Impact on College Students and Families (dated October 12; embargoed until October 13)

Statement by the Press Secretary: President and First Lady Travel to Ohio

Statement by the Press Secretary announcing that the President signed H.R. 946, H.R. 3219, H.R. 4543, H.R. 5341, H.R. 5390, H.R. 5450, and H.R. 6200

Statement by the Press Secretary on disaster assistance to Minnesota

Released October 14

Transcript of a press briefing by Press Secretary Robert L. Gibbs

Transcript of a press gaggle by Press Secretary Robert L. Gibbs

Statement by the Press Secretary: President Obama Travel to Boston

Statement by the Press Secretary on disaster assistance to New York

Statement by the Press Secretary on disaster assistance to North Carolina

Released October 15

Transcript of a press gaggle by Deputy Press Secretary William Burton

Statement by the Press Secretary: President Obama Honors Nation's Top Scientists and Innovators

Statement by the Press Secretary: President Obama To Host White House Science Fair

Statement by the Press Secretary on the Social Security Administration's decision not to provide a cost of living adjustment and economic recovery payments

Statement by the Press Secretary announcing that the President signed S. 1510 and S. 3196

Released October 18

Statement by the Press Secretary: President Obama To Host White House Science Fair (dated October 17; embargoed until October 18)

Statement by the Press Secretary: President Obama To Visit Seattle, Washington

Statement by the Press Secretary: President Obama To Award Medal of Honor

Statement by the Press Secretary announcing that the President signed S. 3802

Released October 19

Transcript of a press briefing by Press Secretary Robert L. Gibbs

Statement by the Press Secretary: President Obama Signs Executive Order Renewing the White House Initiative on Educational Excellence for Hispanics

Fact sheet: Improving Educational Opportunities and Outcomes for Latino Students

Released October 20

Transcript of a press gaggle by Press Secretary Robert L. Gibbs

Fact sheet: Environmental Liabilities Settlement With GM

Released October 21

Transcript of a press gaggle by Press Secretary Robert L. Gibbs

Statement by the Press Secretary: President Obama To Visit Rhode Island

Statement by the Press Secretary on the National Economic Council's report on jobs and economic security for America's women (dated October 20; embargoed until October 21)

Statement by the Press Secretary on disaster assistance to Nebraska

Statement by the Press Secretary on disaster assistance to Wisconsin

Text: Report: Jobs and Economic Security for America's Women (dated October 20; embargoed until October 21)

Released October 25

Transcript of a press gaggle by Deputy Press Secretary William Burton

Fact sheet: How Small Businesses Can Benefit From the Small Business Jobs Act (dated October 24; embargoed until October 25)

Advance text of remarks by Special Assistant to the President and Senior Director for the Central Region Dennis B. Ross at the American Israel Public Affairs Committee national summit

Released October 26

Transcript of a press briefing by Press Secretary Robert L. Gibbs

Statement by the Press Secretary: President Obama To Visit Charlottesville, VA

Statement by the Press Secretary on disaster assistance to Puerto Rico

Released October 27

Transcript of a press gaggle by Press Secretary Robert L. Gibbs, Under Secretary of State for

Political Affairs William Burns, Deputy National Security Adviser for International Economics Michael B. Froman, and Deputy National Security Adviser for Strategic Communications Benjamin J. Rhodes

Fact sheet: Obama Administration Highlights Unprecedented Coordination Across Federal Government To Combat Violence Against Women

Released October 28

Transcript of a press briefing by Press Secretary Robert L. Gibbs

Transcript of a press briefing by Deputy Press Secretary Joshua R. Earnest, National Security Council Senior Director for Asian Affairs Jeffery A. Bader, and Deputy National Security Adviser for Strategic Communications Benjamin J. Rhodes on the President's visit to Asia

Released October 29

Transcript of press briefing by Press Secretary Robert L. Gibbs and Assistant to the President for Homeland Security and Counterterrorism John O. Brennan

Statement by the Press Secretary: Obama Administration Releases Report Outlining Benefits of Expensing Proposal in Encouraging Business Expansion, Hiring Now

Statement by the Press Secretary on explosive devices found aboard flights bound for the U.S.

Text: Statement by Assistant to the President for Homeland Security and Counterterrorism John O. Brennan on Saudi Arabia's assistance in detecting and interdicting explosive devices aboard flights bound for the U.S.

Text: Statement by Council of Economic Advisers Chairman Austan D. Goolsbee on the advance estimate of GDP for the third quarter of 2010

Released November 1

Transcript of a press gaggle by Press Secretary Robert L. Gibbs, Deputy National Security Adviser for International Economic Affairs Michael B. Froman, Deputy National Security Adviser for Strategic Communications Benjamin J.

Rhodes, and Treasury Department Under Secretary for International Affairs Lael Brainard on the President's visit to Asia

Statement by the Press Secretary on the hostage situation at a church in Baghdad, Iraq

Released November 2

Statement by the Press Secretary on the planned execution of Sakineh Mohammadi Ashtiani in Iran

Statement by the Press Secretary on disaster assistance to South Dakota

Released November 4

Transcript of a press briefing by Press Secretary Robert L. Gibbs

Released November 5

Statement by the Press Secretary on disaster assistance to the U.S. Virgin Islands

Released November 6

Transcript of a press briefing by Press Secretary Robert L. Gibbs, National Security Adviser Thomas E. Donilon, Deputy National Security Adviser for International Economic Affairs Michael B. Froman, Deputy National Security Adviser for Strategic Communications Benjamin J. Rhodes, and Under Secretary of State for Political Affairs William Burns on the President's visit to India (dated November 5; released November 6)

Fact sheet: Background on United States-India Economic Relationship

Fact sheet: The National Export Initiative: U.S.-India Transactions

Fact sheet: Expo on Agriculture and Food Security

Fact sheet: Expo on Democracy and Open Government

Fact sheet: U.S.-India Economic and Trade Relationship: Indian Investment in the U.S.

Released November 8

Fact sheet: U.S. & India: The Indispensable Partnership

Fact sheet: U.S.-India Cooperation in Agriculture—Partnership For An Evergreen Revolution

Fact sheet: U.S.-India Strengthening Cooperation on Cybersecurity

Fact sheet: Nuclear Security

Fact sheet: Supporting Afghanistan's Development

Fact sheet: Enhancing U.S.-India Cooperation on Education

Fact sheet: U.S.-India Space Cooperation

Fact sheet: U.S.-India Counterterrorism Cooperation

Fact sheet: U.S.-India Economic and Financial Partnership

Fact sheet: U.S.-India Trade and Economic Cooperation

Fact sheet: Deepening U.S.-India Strategic Ties

Fact sheet: Securing the Air, Sea, and Space Domains

Fact sheet: The U.S.-India CEO Forum

Fact sheet: U.S.-India Partnership on Clean Energy, Energy Security, and Climate Change

Fact sheet: U.S.-India Partnership on Export Controls and Non-Proliferation

Fact sheet: U.S.-India Defense Cooperation

Fact sheet: United States and India Announce Partnership on Open Government

Released November 9

Transcript of a press gaggle by National Security Council Senior Director for Asian Affairs Jeffrey A. Bader and Deputy National Security Adviser for Strategic Communications Benjamin J. Rhodes

Fact sheet: The United States and Indonesia—Building a 21st Century Partnership

Fact sheet: Higher Education Partnership With Indonesia

Fact sheet: The IKAT-U.S. Partnership—Civil Societies Innovating Together

Fact sheet: Indonesia and the Millennium Challenge Corporation

Fact sheet: Expanding the U.S.-Indonesia Partnership on Climate Change and Clean Energy

Fact sheet: Economic and Trade Cooperation with Indonesia

Fact sheet: U.S. Response to Natural Disasters in Indonesia

Fact sheet: Expanding U.S.-Indonesia Collaboration on Science & Technology

Released November 10

Statement by the Deputy Press Secretary on the initial proposal by the Bipartisan National Commission on Fiscal Responsibility and Reform

Text: Statement by National Security Council Spokesman Michael A. Hammer on the terrorist attacks in Iraq

Fact sheet: Indonesia: Follow-up to the President's Cairo Speech (released November 9; embargoed until November 10)

Advance text: President's remarks in Jakarta, Indonesia (released November 9; embargoed until November 10)

Released November 11

Advance text: President's remarks at a Veterans' Day ceremony at the U.S. Army Garrison—Yongsan in Seoul, South Korea (released November 10; embargoed until November 11)

Released November 12

Fact sheet: G–20/Seoul: $528 Million Announced for a New Global Framework To Fund Innovative SME Finance Models

Fact sheet: G–20/Seoul: Sustainable External Imbalances and Orderly Global Adjustment

Fact sheet: G–20/Seoul: IMF Reform

Fact sheet: G–20/Seoul: U.S. Financial Reform and the G–20 Leaders' Agenda

Fact sheet: G–20/Seoul: Shared Commitment to Fighting Corruption

Fact sheet: G–20/Seoul: U.S. Global Development Policy and the G–20 Development Framework

Fact sheet: G–20/Seoul: Energy Issues

Released November 13

Fact sheet: New initiatives from the Asia-Pacific Economic Cooperation summit

Fact sheet: U.S.-Japan Cooperation on Reducing Nuclear Risks

Released November 14

Text: Trans-Pacific Partnership: Progress Towards a Regional Agreement

Text: The 18th APEC Economic Leaders' Meeting: The Yokohama Vision—Bogor and Beyond

Text: The APEC Leaders' Growth Strategy

Text: Leaders' Statement on the 2010 Bogor Goals Assessment

Text: Pathways to a Free Trade Area of the Asia-Pacific (FTAAP)

Released November 15

Statement by the Press Secretary: President Obama Announces 2010 White House Tribal Nations Conference

Statement by the Press Secretary on voter registration in Sudan

Released November 16

Transcript of a teleconference press briefing by U.S. Ambassador to NATO Ivo H. Daalder, Deputy National Security Adviser for Iraq and Afghanistan Lt. Gen. Douglas E. Lute, Senior Director for European Affairs Elizabeth Sherwood-Randall, and Deputy National Security Adviser for Strategic Communications Benjamin J. Rhodes on the NATO and EU summits in Lisbon, Portugal

Statement by the Press Secretary on the rescheduling of a bipartisan meeting with congressional leaders

Text: Statement from the Vice President on the new START Treaty

Released November 17

Transcript of a press gaggle by Press Secretary Robert L. Gibbs

Statement by the Press Secretary: President Obama Signs Executive Order To Implement Reform Recommendations of the President's Advisory Council on Faith-Based and Neighborhood Partnerships

Statement by the Press Secretary: President Obama Names Presidential Medal of Freedom Recipients

Fact sheet: An Enduring Commitment to the U.S. Nuclear Deterrent

Released November 18

Statement by the Press Secretary: President Obama, Vice President Biden To Visit Kokomo, IN

Statement by the Press Secretary: CEA Releases New Quarterly Analysis on Job and Economic Impact of the Recovery Act

Text: Statement by National Security Council Spokesman Michael A. Hammer on the passage of a U.N. Resolution on Iran's human rights violations

Released November 19

Transcript of a press briefing by U.S. Ambassador to the North Atlantic Treaty Organization Ivo H. Daalder and Deputy National Security Adviser for Strategic Communications Benjamin J. Rhodes

Text: Op-ed piece by President Obama for the International Herald Tribune: Europe and America, Aligned for the Future

Released November 20

Statement by the Press Secretary on the visit of President Bronislaw Komorowski of Poland

Fact sheet: President Obama's Participation in the NATO Summit Meetings in Lisbon

Fact sheet: United States' Relationship With the European Union: An Enduring Partnership

Text: Statement by National Security Council Spokesman Michael A. Hammer on Ukraine's Holodomor Remembrance Day

Text: Transcript of statements by European Foreign Ministers in support of the new START Treaty

Released November 22

Transcript of a press briefing by Press Secretary Robert L. Gibbs

Released November 23

Transcript of a press gaggle by Deputy Press Secretary William Burton

Statement by the Press Secretary: President Obama Welcomes New HIV Prevention Research Results

Statement by the Press Secretary on the North Korean artillery shelling of the South Korean island of Yeonpyeong

Released November 24

Statement by the Press Secretary announcing that the President signed S. 3774

Statement by the Press Secretary on disaster assistance to the U.S. Virgin Islands

Released November 28

Statement by the Press Secretary on the WikiLeaks web site posting Department of State documents concerning diplomatic relations with foreign governments

Released November 29

Transcript of a press briefing by Press Secretary Robert L. Gibbs

Transcript of a press briefing by White House Communications Director H. Daniel Pfieffer and Chief Performance Officer and Office of Management and Budget Deputy Director for Management Jeffrey D. Zients on Federal employee issues

Statement by the Press Secretary on Medicare payments to doctors

Fact sheet: Cutting the Deficit by Freezing Federal Employee Pay

Released November 30

Transcript of a press briefing by Press Secretary Robert L. Gibbs

Statement by the Press Secretary announcing that the President signed H.R. 5712, S. 1376, S. 3567, and S.J. Res. 40

Text: Statement by National Security Council Spokesman Michael A. Hammer on the elections in Egypt

Released December 1

Transcript of a press briefing by Press Secretary Robert L. Gibbs

Fact sheet: U.S. Government Mitigation Efforts in Light of the Recent Unlawful Disclosure of Classified Information

Released December 2

Statement by the Press Secretary: New CEA Report Underscores Urgent Need To Extend Unemployment Benefits

Statement by the Press Secretary on middle class tax cuts

Text: Statement by National Security Council Spokesman Michael A. Hammer on the elections in Cote d'Ivoire

Released December 3

Transcript of a press briefing by Press Secretary Robert L. Gibbs and Deputy National Security Adviser for Strategic Communications Benjamin J. Rhodes

Transcript of a press briefing by Deputy National Security Adviser for Iraq and Afghanistan Douglas E. Lute and Deputy National Security Adviser for Strategic Communications Benjamin J. Rhodes on the President's visit to Afghanistan

Statement by the Press Secretary: President Obama Grants Nine Pardons

Text: Statements of Support for the U.S.-Korea Trade Agreement

Text: Statement by Council of Economic Advisers Chairman Austan D. Goolsbee on the employment situation in November

Fact sheet: The U.S.-Korea Free Trade Agreement: More American Jobs, Faster Economic Recovery Through Exports

Fact sheet: Economic Value of the US-Korea Free Trade Agreement: More American Exports, More American Jobs

Fact sheet: Increasing U.S. Auto Exports and Growing U.S. Auto Jobs Through the U.S.-Korea Trade Agreement

Released December 4

Statement by the Press Secretary announcing that the President signed H.J. Res. 101

Transcript of a weekly address by Vice President Joe Biden (released December 3; embargoed until December 4)

Text: Statements by Members of Congress, trade groups, and corporations in support of the U.S.-Korea free trade agreement

Released December 6

Transcript of a press gaggle by Deputy Press Secretary William Burton

Text: Statement by Deputy National Security Council Spokesman Benjamin Chang on the meeting between National Security Adviser Thomas E. Donilon, Foreign Minister Seiji Maehara of Japan, and Foreign Minister Kim Sung-hwan of South Korea

Released December 7

Text: Statements by economists, advocacy groups, pundits, and editorial boards in support of the framework agreement for middle class tax cuts and unemployment insurance

Released December 8

Transcript of a press gaggle by Press Secretary Robert L. Gibbs, National Economic Council Director Lawrence H. Summers, and White House Senior Adviser David M. Axelrod

Text: Interested Parties Memo on the Impact of the Tax Agreement on Economic Expansion and Job Growth

Released December 9

Transcript of a press briefing by Press Secretary Robert L. Gibbs

Statement by the Press Secretary: President Obama Announces First Steps Toward Implementation of New U.S. Export Control System

Statement by the Press Secretary: New Biden Email Features Goolsbee "White Board" Video

on Middle Class Tax Cuts, Unemployment Insurance and Jobs

Statement by the Press Secretary on Senate action on the "Development Relief and Education for Alien Minors (DREAM) Act"

Statement by the Press Secretary announcing that the President signed H.R. 1722, H.R. 5283, H.R. 5566, and S. 3689

Text: More Economic Reviews on the Middle Class Tax Cuts Framework's Impact on Jobs and Growth

Released December 10

Statement by the Press Secretary: The Tax Relief, Unemployment Insurance Reauthorization, and Job Creation Act of 2010: Win for Women, Mothers and Working Families

Statement by the Press Secretary on the reauthorization of the Child Abuse Prevention and Treatment Act and the Family Violence Prevention and Services Act

Text: Statement by National Economic Council Deputy Director Jason Furman: Victories For Working Families and Jobs in the Agreement on Tax Cuts and Unemployment Insurance

Released December 13

Transcript of a press briefing by Press Secretary Robert L. Gibbs

Released December 14

Transcript of a press briefing by Press Secretary Robert L. Gibbs

Statement by the Press Secretary: President Obama Announces Members of the White House Council for Community Solutions

Statement by the Press Secretary announcing that the President signed H.R. 4387, H.R. 5651, H.R. 5706, H.R. 5773, H.R. 5758, H.R. 6162, H.R. 6166, H.R. 6237, H.R. 6387, S. 1338, S. 1421, and S. 3250

Text: Op-ed piece by Attorney General Eric H. Holder, Jr., and Secretary of Health and Human Services Kathleen Sebelius for the Washington Post: Health Reform Will Survive Its Legal Fight

Released December 15

Statement by the Press Secretary on the new START Treaty

Statement by the Press Secretary announcing that the President signed H.R. 6118, H.R. 4994, and S. 2847

Released December 16

Transcript of a press briefing by Press Secretary Robert L. Gibbs, Secretary of State Hillary Rodham Clinton, Secretary of Defense Robert M. Gates, and Gen. James E. Cartwright, USMC, Vice Chairman, Joint Chiefs of Staff

Statement by the Press Secretary on House of Representatives passage of the "Post-9/11 Veterans Educational Assistance Improvements Act of 2010"

Statement by the Press Secretary announcing that Brooke Anderson will serve as chief of staff and counselor for the national security team

Text: Statement by National Security Council Spokesman Michael A. Hammer on an attack on the village of Khor Abeche in southern Darfur

Text: Overview of the Afghanistan and Pakistan Annual Review

Released December 17

Statement by the Press Secretary on U.S.-EU Transatlantic Economic Council meetings

Text: U.S.-EU Transatlantic Economic Council Joint Statement

Text: Scientific Integrity: Fueling Innovation, Building Public Trust

Released December 18

Statement by the Press Secretary on Senate passage of legislation repealing the U.S. military's "don't ask, don't tell" policy

Statements by the Press Secretary announcing that the President signed H.R. 2480, H.R. 3237, H.R. 6184, H.R. 6399, H.J. Res. 105, S. 3789, and S. 3987

Released December 20

Transcript of a press briefing by Press Secretary Robert L. Gibbs

Statement by the Press Secretary on Belarusian elections and political violence

Statement by the Press Secretary announcing that the President signed S. 3817

Released December 21

Transcript of a press briefing by Press Secretary Robert L. Gibbs

Statement by the Press Secretary on the adoption of the U.S.-sponsored amendment to ensure that sexual orientation remains covered by the U.N. resolution on extrajudicial, summary, and arbitrary execution

Statement by the Press Secretary on disaster assistance to Arizona

Released December 22

Transcript of a press briefing by Press Secretary Robert L. Gibbs and Assistant to the President for Homeland Security and Counterterrorism John O. Brennan

Statement by the Press Secretary on the visit of President Hu Jintao of China

Statements by the Press Secretary announcing that the President signed H.R. 1061, H.R. 2941, H.R. 3082, H.R. 4337, H.R. 5591, H.R. 6198, H.R. 6278, H.R. 6473, H.R. 6516, S. 30, S. 1275, S. 1405, S. 1448, S. 1609, S. 1774, S. 2906, S. 3199, S. 3794, S. 3860, S. 3984, S. 3998, S. 4005, and S. 4010

Statement by the Press Secretary on disaster assistance to Vermont

Fact sheet: Security Enhancements

Text: Statement by Assistant to the President for Homeland Security and Counterterrorism John O. Brennan on security enhancements during the holiday season

Released December 27

Statement by the Press Secretary on a Russian court decision to convict businessmen Mikhail Khodorkovsky and Platon Lebedev

Released December 29

Statement by the Press Secretary announcing that the President signed H.R. 6398, H.R. 6517, S. 3386, and S. 4058

Appendix D—Presidential Documents Published in the *Federal Register*

This appendix lists Presidential documents released by the Office of the Press Secretary and published in the Federal Register. The texts of the documents are printed in the Federal Register (F.R.) at the citations listed below. The documents are also printed in title 3 of the Code of Federal Regulations and in the Compilation of Presidential Documents.

PROCLAMATIONS

PROCLAMATIONS (Continued)

PROCLAMATIONS (Continued)

EXECUTIVE ORDERS

EXECUTIVE ORDERS (Continued)

OTHER PRESIDENTIAL DOCUMENTS

OTHER PRESIDENTIAL DOCUMENTS (Continued)

OTHER PRESIDENTIAL DOCUMENTS (Continued)

Subject Index

Administration of Barack Obama, 2010

Housing—Continued
  Housing market
    Decline—1045, 1051, 1069, 1143, 1174, 1231,
      1286, 1311, 1314, 1318, 1322, 1356, 1369, 1446,
      1510–1511, 1513, 1569, 1600, 1631, 1664, 1670,
      1686, 1705
    Improvement—1467
    Stabilization efforts—1231, 1369, 1446, 1512
  Mortgage refinancing regulations—1515
Housing and Urban Development, Department of
  Secretary—1099, 1250, 1252–1253, 1691, 1963
  Sustainable Communities Initiative—1636
Housing Finance Agency, Federal—1979
Humanities, National Council on the—1961, 1971,
  1984
Hungary, Taxation Convention, Hungary-U.S.—1824
Hurricanes. See Disaster assistance; Natural disasters;
  specific Federal agency or State

Idaho, disaster assistance—1959
Illinois
  Chicago
    Ford Motor Company Chicago Assembly
      Plant—1150, 1961
    Mayor, retirement—1282
    Valois restaurant—1976
    WGCI—1977
    WVON—1977
    Democratic Party events—1154, 1159, 1536, 1708,
      1961, 1972
    Disaster assistance—1963
    Governor—1154, 1541, 1976
    President's visits—1150, 1154, 1158–1159, 1536,
      1708, 1960–1961, 1972, 1976
Immigration and naturalization
  See also Defense and national security; specific
    country or region
  American "melting pot"—1002
  Citizenship—1004–1005, 1433, 1445, 1585, 1905
  Illegal immigration—1003–1005, 1445, 1583, 1587
  Reform—1001, 1003–1005, 1190, 1321, 1331–
    1334, 1433, 1445, 1491, 1583, 1585, 1905, 1935,
    1942, 1946, 1968, 1980, 1986
  Visa policy, U.S.—1002, 1900
Improper Payments Elimination and Recovery Act of
  2010—1090, 1092
Independence Day—1011, 1013, 1016, 1018, 1044,
  1053, 1953
India
  Afghanistan, role—1754, 1758, 1764, 1772
  Agriculture Exposition and Open Government and
    Technology Exposition in Mumbai—1745
  Agriculture, food security initiative with U.S.—1747,
    1754, 1758, 1768, 1771

India—Continued
  Business leaders, meeting with President
    Obama—1978
  Counterterrorism efforts, cooperation with U.S.—1737,
    1746, 1756, 1758, 1764, 1772
  Economic growth and development—1738–1744,
    1746–1747, 1749–1753, 1761–1762, 1767, 1769–
    1771, 1774
  Emperor Humayun's tomb in New Delhi—1977
  Energy
    Alternative and renewable sources and technolo-
      gies—1747, 1766, 1771
    Cooperation with U.S.—1758, 1766, 1770–1771
  Governmental accountability and transparency,
    strengthening efforts—1747, 1750
  Independence Day—1191
  Indian National Congress Party president—1978
  Jammu and Kashmir, status dispute with Paki-
    stan—1759
  Leader of the Opposition (Lower House)—1978
  Minister of Commerce and Industry—1739–1740
  Mumbai
    Agriculture Exposition and Open Government
      and Technology Exposition—1745
    Holy Name High School—1977
    Mani Bhavan Gandhi Sangrahalaya—1977
    November 26, 2008, terrorist attacks—1736,
      1746, 1754, 1764, 1772, 1977
    Rajghat, wreath-laying ceremony—1978
  Poverty and economic instability—1747, 1749
  President—1756, 1768, 1775, 1978
  President Obama's visit—1191, 1412, 1733–1736, 1738,
    1741, 1745–1746, 1749, 1752, 1756, 1760, 1768–1769,
    1775, 1789, 1813–1814, 1822, 1907, 1977
  Prime Minister—1737, 1746–1747, 1751, 1756,
    1763, 1769, 1771, 1775, 1808, 1814, 1977–1978
  Relations with Pakistan—1753, 1759, 1772
  Relations with U.S.—1191, 1736–1737, 1740–1741,
    1743–1748, 1750–1751, 1756–1757, 1759–1760,
    1763, 1768–1772, 1774–1775
  Research and technology cooperation with
    U.S.—1758, 1766–1768, 1771
  Science and technology—1747
  Security cooperation with U.S.—1764
  Speaker of Lok Sabha—1769
  Strategic Dialogue, India-U.S.—1758, 1768
  Student and teacher exchanges with U.S.—1758,
    1768, 1772
  Trade with U.S.—1738–1744, 1746, 1758, 1762,
    1765–1767, 1771, 1813–1814
  U.N. Security Council, membership bid—1758,
    1760, 1763, 1771–1772
  U.S. Embassy staff, meeting with President
    Obama—1977

A–18

Name Index

Document Categories List